CW00671445

SWINDON TOWN

1879 - 2009

A HISTORY IN FACTS AND FIGURES
THE COMBINED VOLUME

By Paul Plowman

A FOOTPRINT PUBLICATION

Published in Great Britain by Footprint Publications
P O Box 145, SWINDON SN3 4YZ

First Published in 2009

Previous volumes by this author :
Swindon Town - First in Wiltshire 1894-1920 (Published 1981)
Swindon Town - In the Third South 1920-1958 (1982)
Swindon Town - To Wembley and Beyond 1958-1985 (1985)
Swindon Town - A Champion Season 1985-86 (1986)
All titles now out of print

 Maps on pages 7/8 reproduced from Ordnance Survey 1886 and 1900.

Printed and bound by CPI Antony Rowe Limited, Chippenham

ISBN 978-0-9562819-0-6

INTRODUCTION

This volume brings my account of Swindon Town into the 21st century for the first time. The club has seen another generation of supporters since the appearance of my last work 'A Champion Season', back in 1986.

As all my earlier works have long since been out of circulation, this book has given me the opportunity to not only place every season easily to hand under one cover, but also to expand on those early Southern League years and to correct many of the errors and omissions that further years of research have brought to light.

Whilst the majority of the statistics included in those previous volumes have been included here, some have unfortunately fallen victim to space constraints. The penultimate section of this book shows a comprehensive 'A-Z' of every man listed in the preceding pages - almost 1,100 players - for whom a detailed biography will appear in a forthcoming volume, now at a well advanced stage of preparation.

THE STORY SO FAR

During the 27 years since Volume One first appeared, those newspaper archives not converted to micro-fiche have continued to gather dust on the shelves until occasionally disturbed by a researcher such as myself. This book expands on the 'bare bones' of that primitive first volume, now with full team line-ups and final League tables for the pre-First War era. Also listed for the first time are the various mid-week fixtures completed by the club - in the Western and United Leagues - between 1897 and 1906 and later for the Southern Charity Cup.

The mapping of Town's Football League history between 1920 and 1985 remains largely unchanged from that which appeared in Volumes Two and Three, one major addition being the inclusion of attendance figures for the period between the wars and the early post-War era. Clubs were enforced to publish these from 1925 - earlier figures are estimates only, generally taken from newspapers or supplied by fellow club historians.

The appearance of Volume Two in 1982, with its match by match line-ups, seemed to set a benchmark for club histories. A now well-known publishing house in Derby very quickly latched on to this format, producing its first book just two years later.

This Combined Volume takes that popular formula one stage further, with home and away fixtures now split into separate columns, so that results sequences can be more easily highlighted. Half-time scores and days of the week have also been included for the first time, as have goal times for the last fifty years - since the abolition of the regionalised Third Divisions. Finally the identification of those substitutes who were named, but not called upon during the game, are also listed - thus presenting a depth of content not found in any other book or annual.

Perhaps Swindon Town will once again lead the country in print - if not always on the field !

Paul Plowman
Swindon, July 2009

ABOUT THE AUTHOR

Born in Upper Stratton in 1949, Paul has now devoted over thirty years to researching the history of Swindon Town and in the early 1990's was one of the pioneers in the discovery of the club's true formation date.

A former computer programmer and IT consultant for British Rail, Paul's club programme collection dates back to before the First War. A founding member of the away supporters' organisation SAS Travel, in 1989, Paul attended every away first team game in an unbroken period of 35 years, from 1970 to 2005 and was also the first manager of the County Ground Superstore.

NOTES

In the 'season-by-season' and League tables sections which follow, club names appear as they did at the time, i.e. in 1894/95, Gillingham, Millwall and Southampton are listed as New Brompton, Millwall Athletic and Southampton St Marys respectively.

For continuity, all sponsors' names have been omitted. Thus, the Football League Cup - won by the club in 1969 - is referred to as such throughout, as is the Associate Members Cup introduced in 1983. This was superseded by the Football League Trophy in 1992, although it has carried a sponsors name every season.

From 1925/26, attendance figures shown were as submitted to the Football League. However, some home gate figures, particularly in the period between 1970 and 1985, have been adjusted to reflect the number of actual paying customers and do not always agree with those previously published. Hence, 'official' records show the Town's record gates for League and F.A.Cup games as 29,106 and 32,000 respectively, but these included complimentary tickets. The only exceptions were for some Sunday fixtures for which trading laws at the time dictated a 'free' turnstile.

Players are shown only by initials, their first or 'popular' names being listed in the 'A to Z' section of this volume. Until 1938/39 no shirt numbers were actually worn by the players, but numbers have been allocated here for clarity. Almost throughout this period, team formation was of two full-backs (shown as 2 and 3), three half-backs (4-6) and five forwards (7-11).

Players shown in the 'A-Z' in *italics* are those who were signed on loan or as a guest in War time. 'Previous' and subsequent clubs shown in this section do not necessarily indicate a direct transfer between those clubs, as the player may have been unattached following release from a contract. Those signed as amateurs - an 'A' shown in the column following appearance totals - may have played for other clubs at the same time as Swindon Town. Finally, players who progressed through the club's junior, apprentice or trainee schemes may have made senior appearances before the date shown as 'signed'. The date shown is generally that when the player signed a professional contract.

FRONT COVER - Nine of the all-time top goalscorers :
1: Sam Parkin (73)
2: Harry Morris (229)
3: Dave Moss (82)
4: Harold Fleming (206)
5: Maurice Owen (165)
6: Steve White (111)
7: Archie Bown (142)
8: Andy Rowland (98)
9: Don Rogers (180)

BACK - The top nine appearance makers :
1: John Trollope (889)
2: Billy Tout (436)
3: Sam Burton (509)
4: 'Garth' Hudson (427)
5: Fraser Digby (505)
6: Maurice Owen (601)
7: Jimmy Allan (436)
8: Don Rogers (490)
9: Joe Butler (428)

contents

AN INDEX TO ILLUSTRATIONS can be found in the right-hand column of the A-Z section, starting page 275

acknowledgements

Many thanks to my fellow historian Alan Harding who helped to fill many of those annoying little gaps; to Peter Holme at the Football League Museum and Nick Jones at the Football League for assistance in checking names and transfer dates; to Brian Tabner, who supplied missing attendance figures; to Mike Davage, who helped with tracking career paths of players for the index section; to Roger Trayhurn and colleagues at Swindon Reference Library; to the staff at the British Museum Newspaper Library; to the Swindon Advertiser for the use of many pictures - with special thanks to Melissa Turk in the library and photographer Dave Evans; to Andy Crook, Ray Marsh, Chris Scott and Ken Mackenzie and to Chris Adams and Chris Tanner at Swindon Town F C for more recent ones; and to anyone whose picture has been used but the author could not be established - with apologies if this inadvertently infringes the copyright; to Ian Stonham for his expertise with the cover; and finally to Richard Banyard of www.swindon-town-fc.co.uk for much appreciated help in promoting the book.

from spartan beginnings

"So gentlemen, are we in agreement that our grand new entity be known as the Swindon Association Football Club ?", asked Prebendary Pitt of his gathering of young railway workers at the King William Street School. "Because that name was rather a mouthful to shout out, we decided to change the name to the Spartans", the Reverend Pitt told a supporters meeting at the County Ground over thirty years later.

The first recorded match played by SAFC was on Saturday November 29 1879 - the match report for which was published in the Swindon Advertiser - albeit two weeks later ! Wiltshire was then still in the grip of rugby and there seemed to be little interest in the 'round ball' game.

The game was played on a field not too far from the club's current headquarters, close to the Wilts and Berks Canal which passed through what is now known as the 'magic roundabout'. Owned by Thomas Hooper Deacon, an auctioneer based in Newport Street, it was known as The Wharf, and was located close to where the Fire Station now stands. The embryonic club fell to a 0-4 defeat, possibly due to being a man short. The Advertiser printed only ten names in the team - although it was not uncommon for the newspapers of the day to 'lose' a name somewhere along the way !

William Baker Pitt *(pictured opposite holding the ball)* was then 23 and the curate of Swindon Christ Church. He lodged in nearby Belle Vue Road with the family of Frederick Osman, a grocer. But in 1881, the Reverend Pitt was appointed rector of Liddington and, with no cars or public transport in those days, moved out of Swindon thus severing his connection with the football club.

From The Wharf, the Spartans moved up the hill to Old Swindon. Their first stop was on land owned by James Vickery, proprietor of the Duke of Wellington Inn on Eastcott Hill. This site later became known as the Globe Field, which has now disappeared under Brunswick Street and Lansdown Road. A field in what is now the Avenue Road area was also used briefly. James Bradford, a High Street solicitor, was the provider this time, but might well have been called upon in his professional capacity when a boy fell through railings into an adjacent quarry one match day !

In 1883/84, the club adopted the name 'Swindon Town', which was quite innovative as there would still be two distinct boroughs of Old and New Swindon until 1900. The first skipper under the new guise was goalkeeper Billy Rose, who made three of his five appearances for England during that season.

The club's final port of call in Old Town was at The Croft in Devizes Road, where they took up residence in 1884 and remained until moving to the County Ground in 1895. Swindon Rugby Club also used The Croft, but there were still no dressing room facilities available. For this luxury the teams had to walk along Devizes Road to and from the Fountain Inn ! The entire fixture list consisted of friendlies every season, but in 1886/87 a competitive edge was added in the form of the Wiltshire Cup and the F.A.Cup. Town proved they were without doubt the strongest side in the county when they lifted the Wilts Cup in every one of the first six seasons and from 1892/93, the reserves were asked to contest the trophy.

But it was a different story in the national competition. After an initial victory in 1886/87, Town were hammered 7-1 by Slough-based Swifts, whose England forward Charlie Bambridge scored a hat-trick. Sadly, that would be generally indicative of the clubs efforts in the F.A.Cup for the next twenty years.

If Swindon Town was to progress, it clearly needed to face stronger opposition on a regular basis and the formation of the Football League in 1888 - by clubs from the Midlands and the north - provided the catalyst for the introduction of a similar competition in the south. Several meetings took place between 1890 and 1894 before the Southern League finally got under way with just nine member clubs in its First Division (which included Swindon Town) and seven in the Second.

And so it all began at The Croft on a very wet Saturday afternoon, on September 22 1894…………….

WILTSHIRE CUP					Home	Away
1886/87						
SF	S	Feb	12	St Marks YMFS	W6-0	
Final	S	Mar	19	Trowbridge Town		W3-1
1887/88						
1	F	Oct	14	Bradford	walkover	
2	S	Dec	10	Devizes	W9-0	
SF	S	Mar	3	St Marks YMFS	W1-0	
Final	Th		29	Swindon Temperance	W5-0	
1888/89						
2	S	Dec	15	Chippenham Town	W9-0	
SF	S	Feb	16	Trowbridge Town	W1-0	
Final	S	Apr	6	Swindon Temperance	W7-0	
1889/90						
Final	S	Mar	29	Trowbridge Town	W7-1	
1890/91						
Final	Th	Mar	26	Swindon Town Reserves	W2-0	
1891/92						
Final	S	Mar	12	Swindon Town 'B'	W13-0	

SPARTANS F C : 1879

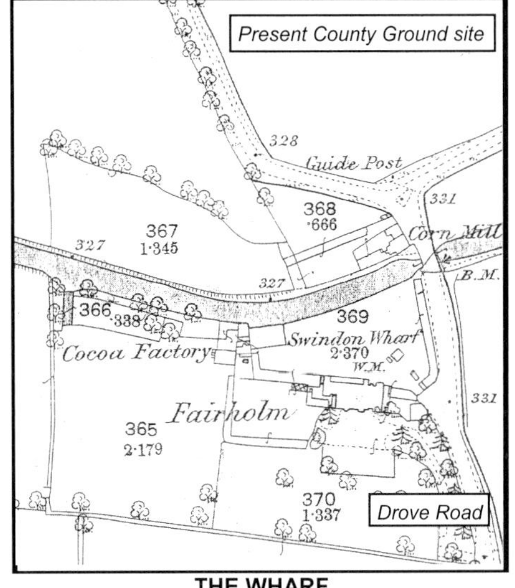

THE WHARF

SEASON 1887/88

				Home	Away
S	Oct	1	Swindon & District	W6-0	
S		15	Marlow	L2-3	
S		29	Maidenhead		D0-0
S	Nov	12	Oxford United College Servants	W5-1	
S	Dec	3	South Reading		W2-0
S		17	Trowbridge Town		W6-0
W		21	Somerset Rovers	D3-3	
W		28	Warmley		L0-1
S	Jan	7	Trowbridge Town	W6-0	
S		21	Marlow		L1-2
S	Feb	11	C Lacy-Sweet's XI	W3-1	
S	Mar	10	South Reading	W3-2	
S		17	London Caledonians	W2-1	
S		31	C Lacy-Sweet's XI	W3-1	
M	Apr	2	West London	L1-3	

N.B. Reports of games played prior to 1887/88 were very sporadic and thus results have not been included here.

SEASON 1888/89

				Home	Away
S	Sep	29	Reading Albions	D1-1	
S	Oct	6	Clevedon	D2-2	
S		13	Great Marlow		L0-1
S	Nov	10	Bristol Eastville Rovers		W7-0
S	Dec	1	Bristol St George	W3-1	
M		24	Oxford United College Servants	W3-2	
S	Jan	5	Clifton	W5-0	
S		12	Trowbridge Town		W7-4
S		19	Oxford United College Servants		D0-0
S		26	Clevedon		W4-3
S	Feb	2	Great Marlow	D5-5	
S		9	Trowbridge Town	W4-0	
S		23	Clifton		L1-2
S	Mar	2	Bristol St George		W3-0
S		9	Maidenhead	W2-0	
S		23	South Reading		W7-1
S	Apr	13	C Lacy-Sweet's XI	W3-1	
S		20	Wiltshire XI	W5-1	
M		22	West London	W1-0	

SEASON 1889/90

				Home	Away
S	Sep	21	C Mooney's XI	D1-1	
S		28	C Lacy-Sweet's XI	L0-1	
S	Oct	12	Reading Albions		W4-1
S		19	Clifton		W4-1
S	Nov	9	Bristol St George		W5-0
S		16	Gloucester	W10-0	
S		23	Trowbridge Town		W4-0
S	Dec	21	Oxford United College Servants	W4-1	
S	Jan	4	Trowbridge Town		W4-0
S		11	Kildare	W4-1	
S		18	Grove House (West London)	W3-1	
S		25	Oxford United College Servants		W4-1
S	Feb	8	Reading Albions	W3-1	
S	Mar	1	Tottenham Hotspur	W2-1	
S		8	Bristol St George	W3-1	
S		15	Bath	W3-2	
S		22	Clifton	L1-2	
S	Apr	5	West London	L2-3	
Tu		8	Bristol & District		W5-1

SEASON 1890/91

				Home	Away
S	Sep	20	South Reading	W13-0	
S		27	Reading	D3-3	
S	Oct	11	Reading Albions	W6-0	
S		18	Newbury		L0-3
S	Nov	1	Trowbridge Town	W5-1	
S		8	Southampton St Marys		W3-2
S		22	Bristol St George	W5-2	
S	Dec	6	Windsor Pheonix	D2-2	
S		13	Clapton		W2-1
W		24	Oxford United College Servants	W9-0	
S	Jan	31	Reading Albions		W4-1
S	Feb	7	Chatham		L1-3
S		14	London Welsh	W6-1	
S		21	93rd Highland Regiment	L1-5	
Tu	Mar	31	Clifton	W8-0	
S	Apr	4	Tottenham Hotspur	W8-2	
S		11	Clapton	L2-5	
S		18	Casuals	W3-0	

Early Friendly Fixtures Played

SEASON 1891/92

				Home	Away
S	Sep	5	C Mooney's XI	W13-1	
S		12	Warmley	W5-1	
S		19	Clifton	W7-1	
S		26	London Casuals	W9-1	
S	Oct	17	Cameronians	W5-0	
S		24	Clapton		W4-3
S		31	Southampton St Marys	W5-1	
S	Nov	7	Bedminster	W13-0	
S		14	Millwall Athletic		L1-2
S		21	Old St Marks	D1-1	
S		28	Reading Albions		L1-2
S	Dec	5	Canadians	L2-3	
S	Jan	2	1st Lincolnshire Regiment	L0-6	
S		9	Southampton St Marys		L1-3
S		23	2nd Scots Guards	W1-0	
S		30	London Hospital	W9-2	
S	Feb	6	Clifton	W1-0 *	
S		13	Reading Albions	D2-2	
S		27	Newbury	W6-2	
S	Mar	26	Casuals	W5-0	
S	Apr	2	City Ramblers	W3-1	
S		9	Wolverhampton Wanderers	W6-4	
S		16	Sheffield FC	W4-2	
S		23	Windsor Phoenix	W3-0	
S		30	Clapton	W4-1	

SEASON 1893/94

				Home	Away
S	Sep	9	Old St Stephens	W5-1 *	
S		16	Uxbridge	W4-1	
S		23	Wolverton Town	W5-1	
S		30	Chatham		W5-4
S	Oct	7	Marlow		L2-3
S		21	71st Highland Regiment	W3-2	
S		28	1st Royal Lancaster Regiment	W5-3	
S	Nov	11	Accrington	W1-0	
S		18	1st Lincolnshire Regiment	W4-1	
S	Dec	9	Worcestershire Regiment	W8-2	
S		23	Clapton		W4-1
S	Jan	13	Freemantle	W4-1	
S		20	2nd Scots Guards	W5-1	
S		27	Ilford	W4-3	
S	Feb	10	New Brompton		L1-2
S		17	Freemantle		L0-3
S		24	2nd Scots Guards		L1-2
S	Mar	3	15th Royal Artillery	W1-0	
S		17	Mansfield Greenhalghs	L0-3	
S		24	Uxbridge		L0-1
M		26	Sheffield FC	D3-3	
S		31	New Brompton	W2-0	
S	Apr	7	Marlow	W2-1	
W		11	Sheffield United	D1-1	
S		14	Chatham	D2-2	
S		21	Clapton	W6-3	
S		28	London Welsh	W4-1	

F.A. AMATEUR CUP

Town entered the Amateur Cup on just one occasion - in 1893/94 - when the Second Round draw handed them a trip to Colchester based Sherwood Foresters.

The game took place on Saturday February 3, when Town were trailing by two goals at half-time.

DICK JONES pulled a goal back after the break, but the visitors were unable to find an equaliser.

Town : Williams C, Allen TG, Richardson W, Parker JM, Wainwright EG, Spackman HJ, Jones RL, Reynolds R, Davies R, Hayward HJ, Andrews A.

SEASON 1892/93

				Home	Away
S	Sep	3	Casuals	L2-3	
S		17	71st Highland Regiment	L2-5	
S		24	Clifton	W13-0	
S	Oct	1	City Ramblers		W4-1
S		8	London Welsh	W4-0	
S		22	2nd Scots Guards	W3-1	
S	Nov	5	Southampton St Marys		W5-0
S		12	Sheffield United	L0-6	
S	Dec	3	Newbury	W3-1	
S	Jan	14	Millwall Athletic	D2-2	
S		21	Clapton		D2-2
S	Feb	4	1st Royal Lancaster Regiment	L1-2	
S		11	71st Highland Regiment	W3-1	
S		18	North Staffordshire Regiment	W8-0	
S	Mar	4	Newbury		W2-1
S		11	Millwall Athletic		L1-4
S	Apr	1	Sheffield FC	L1-2	
S		8	Sherwood Foresters	L1-3	
S		15	City Ramblers	W4-0	
S		22	Clapton	W3-0	

* Played at the County Ground (all other home games played at The Croft)

GLOBE (VICKERY'S) FIELD

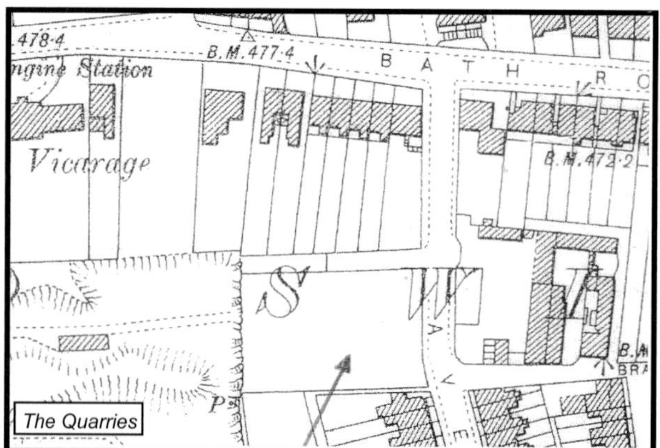

BRADFORD'S FIELD

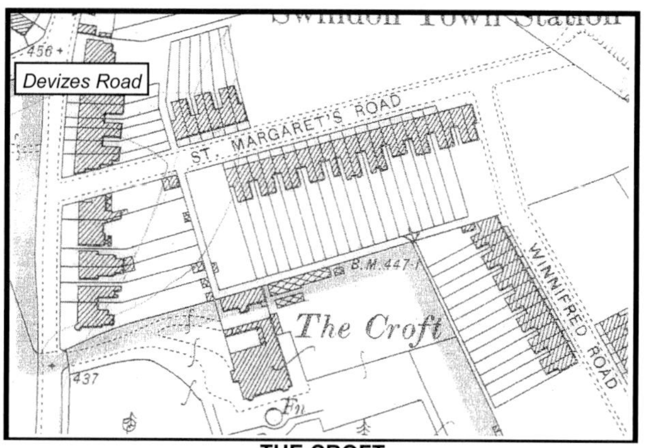

THE CROFT

Early F.A.Cup Record

Figure in first column denotes Round (Q = Qualifying Round)

SEASON 1886/87

Rd					Home	Away	H-T	Goalscorers
1	S	Oct	23	Watford Rovers		W1-0	(0-0)	Jones R
2	S	Nov	20	Swifts		L1-7	(1-6)	Thomas J

SEASON 1887/88

Rd					Home	Away	H-T	Goalscorers
1	S	Oct	8	Old Brightonians		L0-1	(0-1)	

SEASON 1888/89

Rd					Home	Away	H-T	Goalscorers
2Q	S	Oct	27	Great Marlow	L2-5		(2-1)	Bennett,(scrimmage)

SEASON 1889/90

Rd					Home	Away	H-T	Goalscorers
1Q	S	Oct	5	Watford Rovers		L3-5	(2-2)	Jones R,Owen,Bennett

	Bennett T	Crossley F	Everitt G J	Gibbs F	Horsington R T	Jones R L	Jones S	Lewis E	MacLeod W	Offer T H	Owen M L	Pearce L N	Povey W	Reynolds R	Thomas H O	Thomas J	Thomas S J	White T	Williams W H	
1886/87	9		4	6	7	10		11					1		3	8	5	2		1
	9		6	4	7	10		8					1		3	11	5	2		2
	2		2	2	2	2		2					2		2	2	2	2		Apps
						1										1				Goals
1887/88	9	1	4	3	7	10			5	2					11	8	6			1
1888/89	9	1	4	3	7	10			5	2		8			11		6			2Q
1889/90	10	1	3			8	7				9			11	2	5	4		6	1Q

SEASON 1890/91

Rd					Home	Away	H-T	Goalscorers
1Q	S	Oct	4	Maidenhead	W9-0		(5-0)	Reynolds 3,Skinner 2,Jones 2,Thomas J,Everitt F
2Q	S		25	Great Marlow	W2-0		(1-0)	Reynolds,Jones
3Q	S	Nov	15	93rd Highland Regiment		L0-6	(0-3)	

SEASON 1891/92

Rd					Home	Away	H-T	Goalscorers
1Q	S	Oct	3	Luton Town		L3-4	(2-0)	Jones,Offer,Reynolds

SEASON 1892/93

Rd					Home	Away	H-T	Goalscorers
1Q	S	Oct	15	Cowes		+ W2-1	(0-1)	Price,Offer
2Q	S		29	Warmley	W8-1		(6-1)	Jones 4,Reynolds 2,Andrews,Wainwright
3Q	S	Nov	19	Reading	W2-1		(1-0)	Wainwright,Andrews
4Q	S	Dec	10	Marlow		L0-1	(0-1)	

+ After Extra Time

SEASON 1893/94

Rd					Home	Away	H-T	Goalscorers
1Q	S	Oct	14	Maidenhead		* W4-0	(2-0)	Jones 2,Richardson,Andrews
2Q	S	Nov	4	Marlow	W1-0		(1-0)	Reynolds
3Q	S		25	Weymouth		W4-0	(1-0)	Allen,Jones,Davies 2
4Q	S	Dec	16	Reading	L0-2		(0-1)	

* Played at The Croft

	Allen T G	Andrews A	Butterworth G M	Crossley F	Davies R	Everitt F T	Everitt G J	Fulton R W	Hayward H J	Jones R L	Lewis H	McLeod W	Mantell W J	Offer T H	Parker J M	Plimley G	Price W E	Reynolds R	Richardson W	Skinner A E	Spackman H J	Thomas J	Thomas S J	Wainwright E G	Williams C	
1890/91				1		8	4			10	6	5				2		7	3	11		9				1Q
				1		8	4			10	6	5				2		7	3	11		9				2Q
				1		8	4			10	6	5				2		7	3	11		9				3Q
				3		3	3			3	3	3				3		3	3	3		3				Apps
						1				3								4		2		1				Goals
1891/92				1	9				7	8	6			10		2		11	3				4	5		1Q
1892/93		11	1		9			3			4			10	6		8	7	2					5		1Q
		11	1		9			3		10	4			8	6			7	2					5		2Q
		11	1		9			3		10	4				6		8	7	2					5		3Q
		11	1		9			3		10	4			8	6			7	2					5		4Q
		4	4		4			4		3	4			3	4		2	4	4					4		Apps
		2								4				1			1	2						2		Goals
1893/94	8	11			9			2		10			6		4			7	3					5	1	1Q
	8	11			9			2		10			6		4			7	3					5	1	2Q
	8	11			9			2		10			6		4			7	3					5	1	3Q
	8	11			9			2		10					4			7	3		6			5	1	4Q
	4	4			4			4		4			3		4			4	4		1			4	4	Apps
	1	1			2					3								1	1							Goals

No numbers actually worn on shirts

ROLL CALL : 1886/87 to 1893/94

All Players Amateurs

Surname	Initials	Known As	Pos	Born	Died	Seasons at STFC	Apps	Gls.
Allen	T G	Tommy	IF/FB	1865	1911	1893/94,1894/95	5	1
Andrews	A	Alf	WF	1873	1951	1892/93-1894/95	9	3
Bennett	T	Tom	CF	1868		1886/87-1889/90	5	2
Butterworth	G M	George	G	1858		1892/93	4	0
Crossley	F	Frank	G	1863	1947	1887/88-1891/92	7	0
Davies	R	Bobby	CF			1891/92-1893/94	10	2
Everitt	F T	Frank	IF	1870	1932	1890/91	3	1
Everitt	G J	George	WH	1864	1933	1886/87-1890/91	8	0
Fulton	R W	Bob	FB	1872	1952	1892/93-1895/96,1901/02	8	0
Gibbs	F	Fred	WH/FB	1868	1897	1886/87-1888/89	4	0
Hayward	H J	Jimmy	WF	1872		1891/92-1895/96	2	0
Horsington	R T	Dick	WF	1866	1928	1886/87-1888/89	4	0
Jones	R L	Dick	F	1867	1951	1886/87-1896/97	17	14
Jones	S		WF			1889/90	1	0
Lewis	E	Teddy	F	1862		1883/84-1886/87	2	0
Lewis	H	Howell	WH	1871	1900	1890/91-1892/93	8	0
McLeod	W	Bill	CH	1866	1933	1887/88-1890/91	5	0
Mantell	W J	Will	WH	1873	1949	1893/94,1894/95	3	0
Offer	T H	Harry	IF/FB	1869	1947	1887/88-1892/93	6	1
Owen	M L	Morris	CF	1868	1937	1889/90	1	1
Parker	J M	Jack	WH	1871	1960	1892/93,1893/94	9	0
Pearce	L N	Lemuel	F	1867	1950	1888/89	1	0
Plimley	G	George	FB	1866	1919	1890/91,1891/92	4	0
Povey	W	Will	G	1854	1891	1884/85-1886/87	2	0
Price	W E	Wally	IF	1874		1892/93-1894/95	2	1
Reynolds	R	Robbie	WF	1871	1954	1889/90-1895/96	14	8
Richardson	W	Wally	FB	1869	1911	1890/91-1896/97	13	1
Skinner	A E	Bert	WF	1867	1921	1890/91	3	2
Spackman	H J	Harry	WH	1872	1935	1893/94,1894/95	2	0
Thomas	H O	Harry	FB/WF	1865	1913	1884/85-1889/90	5	0
Thomas	J	Jack	F	1862		1886/87-1890/91	7	2
Thomas	S J	Steve	HB	1861		1884/85-1891/92	6	0
Wainwright	E G	Teddy	CH	1869	1943	1891/92-1893/94	10	2
White	T	Tom	FB	1861	1942	1881/82-1886/87	2	0
Williams	C	Charlie	G		1940	1893/94-1895/96,1901/02	5	0
Williams	W H	Billy	WH	1867	1909	1889/90	1	0

ALF ANDREWS

DICK JONES

CHARLIE WILLIAMS

Only appearences in the F A Cup and F A Amateur Cup have been included

In the following section, Gillingham were known as New Brompton until 1912 and West Ham United were known as Thames Ironworks during Season 1899-1900. >> >>

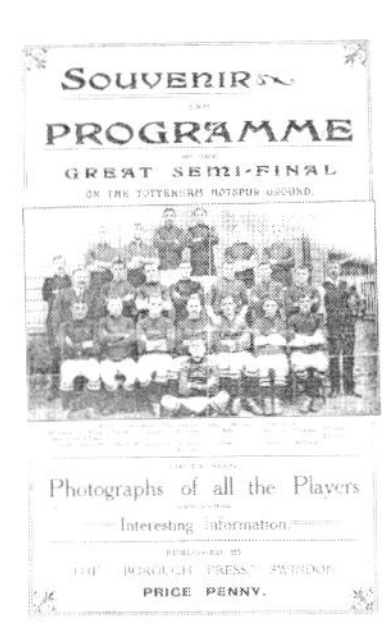

Left to right : Cigarette card from 1907 : Souvenir programme for F.A.Cup sem-final 1910 : Fixture card 1910/11: Charity Cup Programme 1911

moonrakers and shunters

NON-LEAGUE DAYS

Harold Fleming (right) meets Jock Maconnachie of Everton in the F.A.Cup 4th Round in 1912. The Scot signed for Town in 1920.

After rarely straying out of the county during their formative years, participation in the new Southern League was to prove something of a culture shock to the hardy amateurs who the club had come to rely on. Many were sadly out of their depth - if they were lucky enough to get time off work to play in the first place ! The club soon adopted professionalism and offers of employment at the Great Western Railway Works to bolster their income enticed a number of more experienced players south.

But the latter obviously had to be paid and Town struggled financially, coming close to extinction around the turn of the 20th century - much like events of 100 years later ! That all changed in 1907 when Harold Fleming - discovered playing for a local church side - arrived on the scene and the club became one of the strongest outside the Football League. They won the Southern League (effectively the Third Division) twice and reached the F.A.Cup semi-finals twice - all within the space of four years. Had the Great War not intervened, Swindon Town might well have gone on to win the coveted trophy. The high profile of the local railway industry earned the club the 'Shunters' tag, which became as regularly used as that based on the Wiltshire legend of the 'Moonrakers'.

Left to right : The 'town' end of the original North Stand : a supporters' pin badge from 1911 : Bob Jefferson scores against Plymouth in 1910

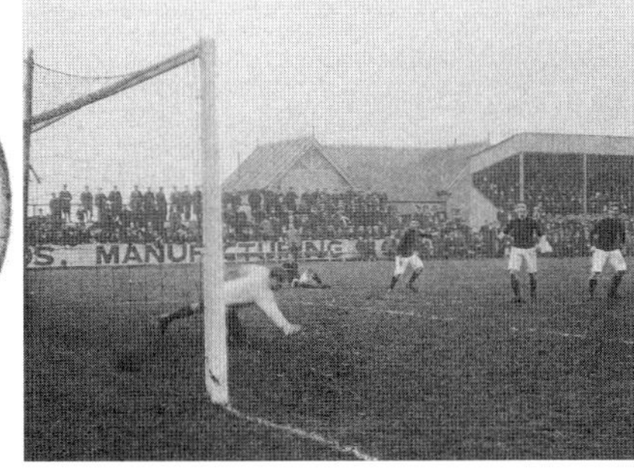

SEASON 1894/95

Southern League Division One
Final League Position : 9th (Last)
Home Ground : The Croft
Colours : Red and Black Quarters

No	Day	Month	Date	Opponents	Home	Away	H-T	Goalscorers
1	S	Sep	22	Reading	L3-4		(0-1)	Reynolds 2,Andrews
2	S		29	Millwall Athletic		L0-9	(0-6)	
3	S	Oct	6	Ilford		L0-1	(0-1)	
4	S	Nov	10	Reading		W3-0	(3-0)	Mantell,Andrews,Hamlin C
5	S	Dec	22	Chatham	L0-2		(0-1)	
6	S		29	Royal Ordnance Factories	W3-1		(1-1)	Reynolds 2,Walman
7	S	Jan	26	Clapton		L0-3	(0-1)	
8	S	Feb	9	Millwall Athletic	L1-5		(0-3)	Shaw
9	S		23	Southampton St Marys	L2-3		(1-1)	Walman,Shaw
10	S	Mar	2	Ilford	W7-3		(2-1)	Reynolds 2,Jones R 3,Richardson pen.,Kemp
11	S		9	Luton Town		L0-2	(0-0)	
12	S		23	Royal Ordnance Factories		D0-0		
13	S		30	Southampton St Marys		L1-7	(1-4)	Jeffrey o.g.
14	S	Apr	6	Luton Town	L0-3		(0-0)	
15	S		13	Chatham		L2-4	(0-3)	Humphrey o.g.,Andrews
16	S		20	Clapton	W2-1		(0-0)	Andrews,Hayward

*Test Match **

Day	Month	Date	Opponents		Result	H-T	Goalscorers
S	Apr	27	New Brompton	*	L1-5	(0-2)	Lawless

* Relegation decider - played at Caversham Cricket Ground (Reading)

F A Cup

Rd	Day	Month	Date	Opponents	Home	Away	H-T	Goalscorers
1Q	S	Oct	13	Bristol St George	W4-2		(3-0)	Jones R 2,Andrews,Reynolds
2Q	S	Nov	3	Marlow		L2-4	(1-2)	Richardson,Reynolds

SEASON 1895/96

Southern League Division One
Final League Position : 7th
Home Ground : County Ground
Colours : Red and Black Quarters

No	Day	Month	Date	Opponents	Home	Away	H-T	Goalscorers
1	S	Sep	21	Royal Ordnance Factories		W2-1	(1-0)	Munro 2
2	S	Oct	5	Ilford	W2-0		(2-0)	Edmunds,Sutherland
3	S		19	Millwall Athletic	D2-2		(1-1)	Hayward,Hames
4	S	Nov	9	Clapton		W4-3	(3-2)	Sutherland 3,Jones R
5	S		30	Luton Town	L0-2		(0-2)	
6	S	Dec	7	Southampton St Marys		L2-4	(1-2)	Edwards,Munro
7	S		21	New Brompton	W4-0		(2-0)	Calderwood,Jones R,Sutherland,Edwards
8	S	Jan	11	Reading		L1-2	(1-2)	Hayward
9	S	Feb	8	Chatham	L2-5		(2-0)	Moore,Davies
10	S		15	Southampton St Marys	L0-2		(0-0)	
11	S		22	Luton Town		L1-7	(0-5)	Sutherland
12	S	Mar	14	Ilford		W10-0	(3-0)	Jones R,Hopewell,Boggie 5,Hayward,Sutherland,Munro
13	S		21	Reading	L1-2		(0-1)	Turner
14	S		28	Royal Ordnance Factories	D0-0			
15	S	Apr	4	Chatham		W5-1	(1-1)	Hopewell,Boggie,Jones M 2,Richardson G
16	M		6	New Brompton		D1-1	(1-0)	Boggie
17	S		18	Clapton	D0-0			
18	S		25	Millwall Athletic		L1-9	(1-2)	Sutherland

F A Cup

Rd	Day	Month	Date	Opponents	Home	Away	H-T	Goalscorers	Gate
1Q	S	Oct	12	Trowbridge Town		W3-1	(1-1)	Sutherland,Hames 2	2,500
2Q	S	Nov	2	Warmley	W2-1		(1-1)	Reeves o.g.,Sutherland	1,200
3Q	S		23	Uxbridge		L0-5	(0-0)		1,200

For Final League Tables - see overleaf >>

Allen T G	Andrews A	Dibsdall A G	Done C	Fulton R W	Hamlin C	Hamlin S	Hayward H J	Hobson A T	Jerrom H J	Jones A	Jones R L	Kemp G C	Lawless C H J	Mantell W J	Mills A R P	Noble W	Price W E	Reynolds R	Richardson W	Ross J	Selwood C	Shaw H	Southall H R	Spackman H J	Walman H	Webb G H	Webb W	Williams C		
2	9	5									8				11			7	3		6			4	10			1		**1**
2	9										8				11			7	3		6		1	4	10	5				**2**
		5							7		8			4	11		9		3		6		1		10				*2 = Pope W E*	**3**
	9			2	8	4	11							5				7	3		6		1		10					**4**
	9	5	4	2			11				8							7			6				10			1	*3 = Vowles V H*	**5**
	5		4				11				8		6			2		7	3						10			1	*9 = Dodd A*	**6**
	5		4	6	9		11				8					2		7	3						10			1		**7**
			4	6			11			5	8					2			3			7			10			1	*9 = Griffin W E*	**8**
	5						11	4			9		6			2		7	3			8			10			1		**9**
	5						11	4			8	10				2		7	3	6		9						1		**10**
	5						11	4			8	10				2		7	3	6		9						1		**11**
	5		9				11	4								2		7	3	6		10						1	*8 = Rogers*	**12**
	9						11	4					5			2		7	3	6		8			10			1		**13**
	9	5					11		7		10		4			2			3	6					8			1		**14**
	9	2					11		10				5						3	6					8		7	1		**15**
	9	2	4				11				10		5						3	6							8	1	*7 = Painter F*	**16**
2	14	6	6	4	2	1	13	5	3	1	12	2	6	2	3	9	1	11	15	7	5	6	3	2	12	1	2	13		Apps
	4				1		1				3	1		1				6	1			2			2					Goals
	6	2	4				11				10		5			9		7	3			8						1		
	9	5		2							10			4			7	8	3		6		1		11					**1Q**
	9	5		2	4		11				8							7	3		6		1		10					**2Q**
	2	2		2	1		1				2			1			1	2	2		2		2		2					Apps
	1										2							2	1											Goals

Boggie A	Calderwood J	Davies J W	Dibsdall A G	Edmunds J T	Edwards A J	Fulton R W	Hames A	Hayward H J	Hopewell R	Jones M	Jones R L	Lawless C H J	Leighfield W J	Moore I	Munro J	Potter J W J	Reynolds R	Richardson G	Richardson W	Sutherland M N	Taylor W H	Turner	Williams C	Wright W J	
		6	2				7	11	4		10				5				3	9			1	8	**1**
		6	2	8				11	4		10				5				3	9			1	7	**2**
		6	2				7	11	4		10		1		5				3	9				8	**3**
		6	2				7	11	4		10				5				3	9			1	8	**4**
		6	2				7	11	4		10				5				3	9			1	8	**5**
		6	2		10		7	11	4			5			8				3	9			1		**6**
	9	6	2		10			11	4		7				5				3	8			1		**7**
	9	6	2					11	4		7			8	5				3	10			1		**8**
		6	2		10			11	4		7			8	5				3	9			1		**9**
	1	6	2		10			11	4		7			8	5					9	3				**10**
	1	5	2		10			11	4			6		8	9					7	3				**11**
9	1		2					11	4		7			6	5				3	10		8			**12**
9	1		2					11	4		7			6	5				3	10		8			**13**
9	1		2					11	4		7			6	5				3	10		8			**14**
9	1		2			4		11	8	10				6	5			7	3						**15**
9	1		2			4		11	8	10				6	5			7	3						**16**
9	1					4		11	8	10				6	5			7	3	2					**17**
9	1					2		11	4					6	5	7		8	3	10					**18**
7	11	11	16	1	5	4	5	18	18	3	12	2	1	11	18	1	0	4	16	16	2	3	8	5	Apps
7	1	1		1	2		1	3	2	2	3			1	4			1		8		1			Goals
		6	2				8	11	4		10				5				3	9			1	7	**1Q**
		6	2				7	11	4		10				5				3	9			1	8	**2Q**
		6	2				7	11	4		10				3		8			9			1	5	**3Q**
		3	3				3	3	3		3				3		1		2	3			3	3	Apps
							2													2					Goals

No numbers actually worn on shirts

Opponents 1 goal

SEASON 1896/97

Southern League Division One
Final League Position : 6th
Secretary : Len Dodson
Colours : Red and Black Quarters

					Home	Away	H-T	Goalscorers
1	S	Sep	19	Wolverton L & N W Railway	W4-0		(3-0)	Skea 2,Munro,Richardson G
2	S		26	Millwall Athletic		L1-2	(1-1)	Munro
3	S	Oct	3	New Brompton		L1-3	(1-2)	Skea
4	S		17	Reading	W4-1		(2-1)	Cox,Skea 2,Murray
5	S		24	Chatham	L2-6		(2-3)	Cox,Jones M
6	S	Nov	7	Millwall Athletic	L2-5		(1-2)	Hallam 2
7	S		14	Tottenham Hotspur		L1-3	(0-1)	Cox
8	S	Dec	5	Southampton St Marys	L0-2		(0-1)	
9	S		19	Northfleet	D2-2		(0-0)	Cox,Hallam
10	S		26	Chatham		L2-6	(1-4)	Munro,Murray
11	S	Jan	9	Tottenham Hotspur	W1-0		(1-0)	Murray
12	S		16	Reading		D0-0		
13	S		30	Gravesend United	D1-1		(1-0)	Richardson G
14	S	Feb	6	Northfleet		W4-0	(3-0)	Munro pen.,Morris,King o.g.,Daniels
15	S		13	New Brompton	W2-1		(0-1)	Jones R,Morris
16	S		27	Southampton St Marys		L0-2	(0-0)	
17	S	Mar	13	Wolverton L & N W Railway		W1-0	(0-0)	Hallam
18	Tu		23	Sheppey United		W1-0	(1-0)	Murray
19	S		27	Sheppey United	W2-0		(0-0)	Palmer,Jones M
20	M	Apr	19	Gravesend United		L2-3	(2-2)	Richardson G,Munro

F A Cup

					Home	Away	H-T	Goalscorers	Gate
3Q	S	Nov	21	Uxbridge	W3-2		(3-1)	Jones M,Cox 2	3,000
4Q	S	Dec	12	Royal Artillery	W4-1		(0-0)	Richardson G 2,Hallam,Murray	
5Q	S	Jan	2	Southampton St Marys		L2-8	(2-4)	Meston o.g.,Munro	5,000

SEASON 1894/95

ROBBIE REYNOLDS
top scorer

	P	W	D	L	F	A	W	D	L	F	A	Pts	G/A
1 Millwall Athletic	16	7	1	0	42	10	5	3	0	26	9	28	3.58
2 Luton Town	16	6	1	1	22	9	3	3	2	14	13	22	1.64
3 Southampton St Marys	16	5	1	2	23	10	4	1	3	11	15	20	1.36
4 Ilford	16	4	1	3	13	16	2	2	4	13	24	15	0.65
5 Reading	16	2	2	3	13	14	4	0	4	20	24	14	0.87
6 Chatham	16	2	4	2	14	13	2	1	5	8	12	13	0.88
7 Royal Ordnance Factories	16	3	3	2	11	7	0	3	5	9	23	12	0.67
8 Clapton	16	2	1	5	12	16	3	0	5	10	22	11	0.58
9 SWINDON TOWN	16	3	0	5	18	22	1	1	6	6	26	9	0.50

SEASON 1895/96

MALCOLM SUTHERLAND
top scorer

	P	W	D	L	F	A	W	D	L	F	A	Pts	G/A
1 Millwall Athletic	18	9	0	0	52	6	7	1	1	23	10	33	4.69
2 Luton Town	18	8	0	1	49	8	5	1	3	19	6	27	4.86
3 Southampton St Marys	18	9	0	0	33	3	3	0	6	11	20	24	1.91
4 Reading	18	7	0	2	27	16	4	1	4	18	22	23	1.18
5 Chatham	18	5	1	3	23	16	4	1	4	20	29	20	0.96
6 New Brompton	18	4	3	2	23	7	3	1	5	7	30	18	0.81
7 SWINDON TOWN	18	3	2	4	15	16	3	2	4	23	25	16	0.93
8 Clapton	18	3	2	4	17	23	1	0	8	13	44	10	0.45
9 Royal Ordnance Factories	18	2	1	6	16	20	1	2	6	7	24	9	0.52
10 Ilford	18	0	0	9	2	34	0	0	9	8	47	0	0.12

Almond J	Andrews A	Boggie A	Calderwood J	Clark F	Cook J	Cox R	Daniels A G	Dibsdall A G	Edwards A J	Edwards J H	Elkins E J	Fulton R W	Fulton J W	Hallam J	Hopewell R	Jones M	Jones R L	Leighfield W J	Morris A G	Munro J	Murray J J	Palmer G	Richardson G	Richardson W	Shutt H	Skea D F	Taylor W H	Uzzell W L	
		6	1	2		7								8	4					5	10		11			9		3	**1**
		6	1	2		7								8	4					5	10		11			9		3	**2**
	5	6	1			7						2		8	4					3	10		11			9			**3**
	5	6	1	2		8								7	4	11				3	10					9			**4**
	5	6	1	2		8								7	4	11				3	10					9			**5**
	10	6	1	2										7	4	11				5	8			3		9			**6**
		6	1	2		9			11				3	7	4		10			5	8								**7**
	5	6	1						11					8	4					3	10	9	7		2				**8**
	5	6	1			8								9	4	11				3	10		7		2				**9**
		6						4						8		11		1		5	10	9	7		2		3		**10**
	5	6			1				11					8	4					3	10	9	7		2				**11**
	5	6			1				11					8	4					3	10	9	7		2				**12**
3	5	6			1		9		11											4	10	8	7		2				**13**
6		4			1		8		11				3						9	5	10		7		2				**14**
6	5	4			1		8										11		9	3	10		7		2				**15**
6	5	4			1		8		11					7					9	3	10				2				**16**
6	5	4			1		9							8			11			3	10		7		2				**17**
4	5	9			1		8								6	11				3	10		7		2				**18**
6		4			1								2		8	11				5	10	9	7		3				**19**
6	5	4			1				11	2									9	8	10		7		3				**20**
8	14	20	9	6	10	7	6	1	8	1	0	1	3	14	13	7	3	1	4	20	20	6	15	1	13	6	1	2	Apps
						4	1							4		2	1		2	5	4	1	3			5			Goals

Opponents 1 goal

Almond J	Andrews A	Boggie A	Calderwood J	Clark F	Cook J	Cox R	Daniels A G	Dibsdall A G	Edwards A J	Edwards J H	Elkins E J	Fulton R W	Fulton J W	Hallam J	Hopewell R	Jones M	Jones R L	Leighfield W J	Morris A G	Munro J	Murray J J	Palmer G	Richardson G	Richardson W	Shutt H	Skea D F	Taylor W H	Uzzell W L	
	9	6	1			8					5		2		4	11				3	10		7						**3Q**
	5	6	1			8							2	9	4	11				3	10		7						**4Q**
		6		2										7	4	11		1		5	9	10	8		3				**5Q**
	2	3	2	1		2					1		2	2	3	3		1		3	3	1	3		1				Apps
						2								1		1				1	1		2						Goals

No numbers actually worn on shirts

Opponents 1 goal

		P	W	D	L	F - A		W	D	L	F - A		Pts	G/A
1	Southampton St Marys	20	8	2	0	44	11	7	3	0	19	7	35	3.50
2	Millwall Athletic	20	6	3	1	32	9	7	2	1	31	15	31	2.63
3	Chatham	20	7	1	2	35	15	6	0	4	19	14	27	1.86
4	Tottenham Hotspur	20	7	2	1	28	13	2	2	6	15	16	22	1.48
5	Gravesend United	20	6	1	3	22	13	3	3	4	13	21	22	1.03
6	SWINDON TOWN	20	5	2	3	20	18	3	1	6	13	19	19	0.89
7	Reading	20	7	1	2	19	16	1	2	7	12	33	19	0.63
8	New Brompton	20	5	0	5	15	14	2	2	6	17	28	16	0.76
9	Northfleet	20	3	4	3	17	17	2	0	8	7	29	14	0.52
10	Sheppey United	20	3	1	6	22	16	2	0	8	12	31	11	0.72
11	Wolverton L & N W Railway	20	2	0	8	11	22	0	0	10	6	52	4	0.23
12	Royal Ordnance Factories *	7	0	0	3	3	16	0	0	4	5	30	0	

* Withdrew in November

JIMMY MUNRO

and fellow Scot Richie Cox scored just six goals apiece, but this meagre tally was enough to make them joint leading scorers. Jimmy was the club skipper and influential in many of his fellow countrymen heading south to assist Town. Prior to his arrival, he had five years Football League experience with Bolton Wanderers and Burton Swifts. Although he stood little more than 5'6", he could play almost anywhere in the line-up, becoming one of the first true utility players. But his career came to a tragic end in early January 1899. Over exuberant celebrations following a pre-hogmanay victory against Spurs resulted in Jimmy suffering spinal meningitis after allegedly falling from a lamppost. Still only 28, he died just four days later leaving a widow of just five months.

SEASON 1897/98

Southern League Division One
Final League Position : 10th
Secretary : Len Dodson
Colours : Green and White

No	Day	Month	Date	Opponent	Home	Away	H-T	Goalscorers
1	S	Sep	11	Reading		L0-1	(0-1)	
2	S		18	New Brompton	L0-3		(0-3)	
3	S	Oct	2	Chatham		L0-4	(0-0)	
4	S		23	Millwall Athletic	L0-5		(0-2)	
5	S	Nov	6	Southampton		L1-4	(0-1)	Cox
6	S		13	Wolverton L & N W Railway		L1-2	(0-2)	Wilson
7	S	Dec	4	Reading	W2-1		(1-1)	Morris 2
8	S		18	Bristol City	D2-2		(0-1)	Bell,Morris
9	M		27	Gravesend United		D2-2	(2-0)	Bell,Wilson
10	S	Jan	1	Wolverton L & N W Railway	W4-0		(0-0)	Wilson,Wain o.g.,Munro,Richardson G
11	S		8	Northfleet		W2-1	(2-1)	Bell,Anthony
12	S		15	Millwall Athletic		L2-4	(0-1)	Anthony,Morris
13	S		22	Sheppey United	W4-1		(2-1)	Richardson W 2,Walker o.g.,Morris
14	S		29	Northfleet	W7-2		(1-1)	Morris 3,Anthony,Bell,Munro pen.,Murray
15	S	Feb	5	Tottenham Hotspur	W3-0		(3-0)	Morris 2,Almond
16	S		12	New Brompton		W2-1	(0-1)	Morris 2
17	S		19	Bristol City		L1-4	(1-2)	Richardson W
18	S	Mar	5	Southampton	L0-2		(0-1)	
19	S		19	Gravesend United	L1-2		(0-0)	Wilson
20	S		26	Chatham	L1-2		(1-0)	Almond
21	S	Apr	2	Sheppey United		L1-3	(1-2)	Wilson
22	M		11	Tottenham Hotspur		L0-2	(0-0)	

Western League Division One
Final League Position : 2nd

No	Day	Month	Date	Opponent	Home	Away	H-T	Goalscorers
1	W	Sep	15	Bristol Eastville Rovers		W1-0	(1-0)	Richardson G
2	W	Oct	6	Bristol City		D3-3	(2-3)	Bell,Morris 2
3	W		13	Trowbridge Town	W3-0		(2-0)	Morris,Slugg o.g.,George o.g.
4	W		20	Eastleigh Athletic		L0-2	(0-1)	
5	W	Nov	17	Bristol St George	W4-0		(1-0)	Richardson G 2,Wilson,Morris
6	W	Feb	16	Eastleigh Athletic	W7-1		(1-0)	Munro,Morris 4,Bell,Richardson G
7	S		26	Warmley	W2-1		(1-1)	Morris 2
8	M		28	Bristol St George		L1-3	(1-2)	Boggie
9	S	Mar	12	Trowbridge Town		W1-0	(1-0)	Morris
10	W		30	Bristol Eastville Rovers	W3-0		(3-0)	Richardson W,Morris 2
11	Tu	Apr	12	Warmley		L1-4	(0-4)	Morris
12	W		13	Bristol City	W1-0		(0-0)	Richardson W
13	S		16	Reading		L0-1	(0-1)	
14	S		23	Reading	W5-1		(3-0)	Henderson o.g.,Richardson W,Morris 2,Munro pen.

F A Cup

Rd	Day	Month	Date	Opponent	Home	Away	H-T	Goalscorers	Gate
3Q	S	Oct	30	Reading		D0-0			8,000
Rp	W	Nov	3	Reading	W3-2		(2-2)	Cox,Morris,Wilson	2,000
4Q	S		20	Southampton	L1-3		(0-3)	Bell	5,000

GRENVILLE MORRIS
was just 19 when he arrived from Aberystwyth Town in February 1897. With 29 goals in 34 games in 1897/98, it was no surprise that scouts soon flocked to the County Ground to see the young Welshman. Nottingham Forest offered £200 for him - a big sum in 1898 - and to this day he remains the highest ever goalscorer in that club's history.

Western League

	P	W	D	L	F	A	Pts
1 Bristol City	14	11	1	2	51	16	23
2 SWINDON TOWN	14	9	1	4	32	16	19
3 Reading	14	7	2	5	28	25	16
4 Bristol St George	14	6	3	5	26	28	15
5 Bristol Eastville Rovers	14	6	2	6	32	26	14
6 Warmley	14	5	3	6	36	27	13
7 Eastleigh Athletic	14	3	2	9	23	54	8
8 Trowbridge Town	14	2	0	12	15	58	4

Almond J	Anthony S T	Bell J	Boggie A	Calderwood J	Clarke J	Cook J	Cox R	McElhaney R	Mellars W	Morris A G	Mountain G	Munro J	Murray J J	Richardson G	Richardson W	Shutt H	Taylor W H	Wallis C J	Wilson T C	Wylie T	
6		8			4	1		7	3	9		5	10			2			11		1
6		10			4	1		8	3	9		5		7		2			11		2
		10	6		5	1	8			9	4	3		7		2			11		3
6		10			4	1			3	9		5	8	7		2			11		4
6		10				1	8	4	3	9		5		7		2			11		5
6		10			4	1	8		3	9		5		7		2			11		6
6	7	9	4			1			3	10		5		8		2			11		7
6		9	4			1	8		3	10		5		7		2			11		8
6	8	9	5		4	1			3			2	10	7					11		9
6	8	9	4			1			3			5	10	7		2			11		10
6	8	9	4			1			3	10		5		7		2			11		11
6	8	9	4			1			3	10		5		7		2			11		12
6	7	9	4			1			3	10		5			8	2			11		13
6	7	9	5		4	1				10		3	11		8	2					14
6	7	9	4			1			3	10		5	8			2			11		15
6	7	9	4			1			3	10		5	11		8	2					16
6	7	9	4			1			3	10		5	11		8	2					17
6	8	9	5		4	1				10				7		2	3		11		18
6	8	10	4			1			3			5		7		2		9	11		19
6		8	4			1	7			10		5			9	2	3		11		20
6		8	4			1	7		3	10		5			9	2			11		21
6		10	4			1	8		3			5		7	9	2			11		22
21	12	22	17	0	8	22	7	3	18	18	1	21	8	14	7	21	2	1	19	0	Apps
2	3	4					1			12		2	1	1	3				5		Goals

Opponents 2 goals

Almond J	Anthony S T	Bell J	Boggie A	Calderwood J	Clarke J	Cook J	Cox R	McElhaney R	Mellars W	Morris A G	Mountain G	Munro J	Murray J J	Richardson G	Richardson W	Shutt H	Taylor W H	Wallis C J	Wilson T C	Wylie T	
6		9			4	1		8	3			5	10	7		2			11		1
6		10	5		4	1	8			9		3		7		2			11		2
5		10	6		4	1	8			9		3		7		2			11		3
11		10	6		4	1	8			9		3		7		2				5	4
		10	6		4	1		8	3	9		5		7		2			11		5
6		9	4			1			3	10		5	11	7	8	2					6
6			5		4	1	8		3	10				7	9	2			11		7
6		9	5	1	4				3	10				7	8		2		11		8
6	8	9	5		4	1			3	10				7		2			11		9
6		8	4			1	7		3	10		5			9	2			11		10
6		8				1	7		3	10		5		4	9	2			11		11
6		8				1	7		3	10		5		4	9	2			11		12
6		8	4			1	7		3	10		5			9	2			11		13
6		8				1	7		3	10		5		4	9	2			11		14
13	1	13	10	1	8	13	9	2	11	13	0	11	2	12	8	13	1	0	12	1	Apps
		2	1							16		2		4	3				1		Goals

Opponents 3 goals

Almond J	Anthony S T	Bell J	Boggie A	Calderwood J	Clarke J	Cook J	Cox R	McElhaney R	Mellars W	Morris A G	Mountain G	Munro J	Murray J J	Richardson G	Richardson W	Shutt H	Taylor W H	Wallis C J	Wilson T C	Wylie T	
6		10	4			1	8		3	9		5		7		2			11		3Q
6		10	4			1	8		3	9		5		7		2			11		Rp
6		10	4			1	8		3	9		5		7		2			11		4Q
3		3	3			3	3		3	3		3		3		3			3		Apps
		1					1			1									1		Goals

No numbers actually worn on shirts

Southern League

		P	W	D	L	F	A	W	D	L	F	A	Pts	G/A
1	Southampton	22	10	0	1	34	7	8	1	2	19	11	37	2.94
2	Bristol City	22	9	2	0	44	15	4	5	2	23	18	33	2.03
3	Tottenham Hotspur	22	9	2	0	36	6	3	2	6	16	25	28	1.68
4	Chatham	22	7	4	0	37	14	5	0	6	13	20	28	1.47
5	Reading	22	7	3	1	26	11	1	4	6	13	20	23	1.26
6	New Brompton	22	6	1	4	18	13	3	3	5	19	24	22	1.00
7	Sheppey United	22	9	1	1	30	9	1	0	10	10	40	21	0.82
8	Gravesend United	22	4	5	2	15	12	3	1	7	13	27	20	0.72
9	Millwall Athletic	22	5	1	5	33	20	3	1	7	15	25	18	1.07
10	SWINDON TOWN	22	5	1	5	24	20	2	1	8	12	29	16	0.73
11	Northfleet	22	4	1	6	19	22	0	2	9	10	38	11	0.48
12	Wolverton L & N W Railway	22	3	0	8	17	25	0	1	10	11	57	7	0.34

SEASON 1898/99

Southern League Division One
Final League Position : 9th
Secretary : Len Dodson
Colours : Green and White

No	Day	Month	Date	Opponents	Home	Away	H-T	Goalscorer
1	S	Sep	3	Royal Artillery	W3-2		(2-2)	Coupar 2,Morris
2	S		17	Reading	W6-1		(5-0)	Coupar,Kirton,Munro,Henderson,Little,Morris
3	S		24	Millwall Athletic		L1-2	(1-1)	Sharples
4	S	Oct	8	New Brompton		L1-5	(0-3)	Morris
5	S		15	Gravesend United	W4-1		(2-0)	Coupar,Morris,Kirton,Munro pen.
6	S		22	Southampton	D1-1		(0-0)	Sharples
7	S	Nov	5	Bristol City		L2-4	(1-3)	Morris 2
8	S		12	Brighton United	W3-1		(1-1)	Bullimer o.g.,Richardson W,Morris
9	S	Dec	17	Millwall Athletic	L2-4		(1-1)	Sharples,Henderson
10	S		24	Southampton		L1-4	(0-2)	Kirton
11	S		31	Tottenham Hotspur	W4-3		(1-2)	Sharples 2,Coupar,Kirton
12	S	Jan	14	Bedminster	W4-3		(0-3)	Richardson W,Kelso o.g.,Richardson G,Coupar
13	S		28	Brighton United		L0-2	(0-2)	
14	S	Feb	4	Bristol City	D2-2		(1-1)	Kirton,Henderson
15	S		11	Sheppey United		W2-1	(2-1)	Kirton,Little
16	S		18	Chatham	D2-2		(2-1)	Henderson,Sharples
17	S		25	Chatham		L0-2	(0-0)	
18	S	Mar	4	Sheppey United	D1-1		(1-1)	Smith
19	S		11	Royal Artillery		L0-1	(0-1)	
20	S		18	Reading		L0-1	(0-1)	
21	S	Apr	1	Bedminster		W1-0	(0-0)	Richardson W.
22	M		3	Tottenham Hotspur		D1-1	(1-0)	Logan
23	S		8	New Brompton	W1-0		(1-0)	Coupar
24	S		15	Gravesend United		L1-5	(1-1)	Kirton

Western League Division One
Final League Position : Champions

No	Day	Month	Date	Opponents	Home	Away	H-T	Goalscorer
1	W	Sep	7	Bristol Eastville Rovers	L1-3		(0-2)	Morris
2	S	Oct	1	Southampton	W3-0		(1-0)	Sharples,Morris 2
3	W		5	Bristol Eastville Rovers		W2-1	(1-1)	Hallam,Little
4	W	Nov	30	Bristol St George	W2-1		(1-1)	Coupar,Sharples
5	Tu	Jan	23	Bristol St George		W3-1	(2-0)	Sharples 2,Kirton
6	M	Mar	6	Bedminster		D0-0		
7	F		31	Southampton		L2-3	(1-2)	Sharples,Anthony
8	S	Apr	22	Bedminster	W3-1		(0-0)	Sharples 2,Little

*Expunged Games ** *(Appearances/Goals not included in totals)*

Comp	Day	Month	Date	Opponents	Home	Away	H-T	Goalscorer
S/Lge	S	Sep	10	Warmley	W5-0		(3-0)	Munro pen.,Morris 2,Sharples,Henderson
W/Lge	W	Oct	19	Trowbridge Town		W4-0	(2-0)	Little 2,Morris,Coupar
S/Lge	S	Nov	26	Warmley		W4-2	(3-0)	Sharples,Richardson W 2,Little
W/Lge	W	Dec	28	Warmley		W2-1	(1-1)	Henderson,Kirton

F A Cup

Rd	Day	Month	Date	Opponents	Home	Away	H-T	Gate
3Q	S	Oct	29	Warmley		L0-1	(0-1)	1,607

JACK KIRTON
had two spells at the County Ground, in 1898/99 and 1900/01. A Mancunian, he arrived from Small Heath (later Birmingham City), left for Sunderland - where he spent an entire season in the reserves - then came back, only to move on again to Millwall in the summer of 1901 ! While with Town, Jack was a railway labourer in the GWR engine shops.

Western League

	P	W	D	L	F	A	Pts
1 SWINDON TOWN	8	5	1	2	16	10	11
2 Bristol St George	8	4	1	3	18	15	9
3 Southampton	8	4	0	4	18	15	8
4 Bristol Eastville Rovers	8	2	2	4	14	18	6
5 Bedminster	8	2	2	4	9	16	6
6 Warmley *	5	2	0	3	6	15	4
7 Trowbridge Town *	5	0	0	5	4	18	0

* Clubs disbanded mid-season

Anthony S T	Boulton T	Coupar J	Hallam J	Henderson G	Kirton J W	Little T	Logan N	Menham R W	Mills A	Morris A G	Munro J	Richardson G	Richardson W	Sharples J	Shutt H	Smith A	Taylor W H	
		8		4	11	9	5	1	3	10	2			7		6		**1**
	1	8		4	11	9	5		3	10	2			7		6		**2**
	1	8		4	11	9	5		3	10				7	2	6		**3**
		8		4	11	9	5	1	3	10				7	2	6		**4**
	1	8		4	11	9			3	10	5			7	2	6		**5**
	1	8		4	11	9	5		3	10				7	2	6		**6**
	1	8		4	11	9			3	10	5			7	2	6		**7**
	1			4	11	10	5		3	8			9	7	2	6		**8**
		8		4	11	10		1	3		5		9	7	2	6		**9**
		8		4	11		5	1	3		10	2	9	7		6		**10**
		8		4	11	9	5	1	3		10			7	2	6		**11**
		8		4	11	10	5	1				3	9	7	2	6		**12**
		8		4	11	10	5	1	3				9	7	2	6		**13**
		8		4	11	10	5	1	3				9	7	2	6		**14**
		10		4	9	11	5	1	3			8		7	2	6		**15**
		10		4	9	11	5	1	3			8		7	2	6		**16**
		10		4	9	11	5	1	3				8	7	2	6		**17**
		10		4	9	11	5	1	3				8	7	2	6		**18**
7		10				11	5	1				4	9	8	2	6	3	**19**
7		10		6		11	5	1	3			4	9	8	2			**20**
8		10		6		11	5	1	3			4	9	7	2			**21**
8		11				10	9	1	3			4	5	7	2	6		**22**
7		8		5	11	10	9	1	3			4			2	6		**23**
8		10		5	11		9	1	3			4		7	2	6		**24**
6	6	23	0	22	20	22	21	18	22	8	7	10	12	23	21	22	1	Apps
		7		4	7	2	1			7	2	1	3	6		1		Goals

Opponents 2 goals

NEIL LOGAN

Anthony S T	Boulton T	Coupar J	Hallam J	Henderson G	Kirton J W	Little T	Logan N	Menham R W	Mills A	Morris A G	Munro J	Richardson G	Richardson W	Sharples J	Shutt H	Smith A	Taylor W H	
		8	7	4	11		5	1	3	10	2			9		6		**1**
8	1			4	11	9	5		3	10				7	2	6		**2**
10		8	7	6	11	9		1	3		5	4			2			**3**
		8		4	11	10	5	1	3				9	7	2	6		**4**
		8		4	11	10	5	1	3				9	7	2	6		**5**
7		10		4	11	9	5	1	3					8	2	6		**6**
8		10		5		11	9	1	3			4		7	2	6		**7**
8		10		5	11	9	3	1				4		7	2	6		**8**
5	1	7	2	8	7	7	7	7	7	2	2	3	2	7	7	7	0	Apps
1		1	1		1	2				3				7				Goals

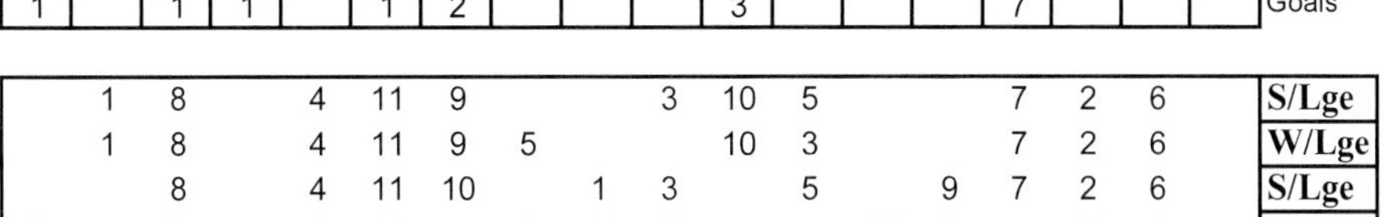

Anthony S T	Boulton T	Coupar J	Hallam J	Henderson G	Kirton J W	Little T	Logan N	Menham R W	Mills A	Morris A G	Munro J	Richardson G	Richardson W	Sharples J	Shutt H	Smith A	Taylor W H	
	1	8		4	11	9			3	10	5			7	2	6		**S/Lge**
	1	8		4	11	9	5			10	3			7	2	6		**W/Lge**
		8		4	11	10		1	3		5		9	7	2	6		**S/Lge**
7		8		4	11		5	1	3			10	9		2	6		**W/Lge**

ALEC SMITH

Anthony S T	Boulton T	Coupar J	Hallam J	Henderson G	Kirton J W	Little T	Logan N	Menham R W	Mills A	Morris A G	Munro J	Richardson G	Richardson W	Sharples J	Shutt H	Smith A	Taylor W H	
10	1	8		4	11	9	5				3			7	2	6		**3Q**

No numbers actually worn on shirts

Southern League

		P	W	D	L	F	A	W	D	L	F	A	Pts	G/A
1	Southampton	24	9	2	1	34	9	6	3	3	20	15	35	2.25
2	Bristol City	24	11	0	1	39	16	4	3	5	16	17	33	1.67
3	Millwall Athletic	24	7	2	3	34	17	5	4	3	25	18	30	1.69
4	Chatham	24	6	4	2	19	8	4	4	4	13	15	28	1.39
5	Reading	24	9	2	1	24	4	0	6	6	7	20	26	1.29
6	New Brompton	24	7	3	2	24	9	3	2	7	14	21	25	1.27
7	Tottenham Hotspur	24	8	2	2	24	11	2	2	8	16	25	24	1.11
8	Bedminster	24	7	1	4	19	13	3	3	6	16	26	24	0.90
9	SWINDON TOWN	24	7	4	1	33	21	2	1	9	10	28	23	0.88
10	Brighton United	24	6	2	4	23	13	3	0	9	14	35	20	0.77
11	Gravesend United	24	6	3	3	31	20	1	2	9	11	32	19	0.81
12	Sheppey United	24	5	2	5	16	19	0	1	11	7	35	13	0.43
13	Royal Artillery	24	3	4	5	11	16	1	0	11	6	44	12	0.28
14	Warmley *	17	1	0	6	10	21	1	2	7	15	37	6	

SEASON 1899/1900

Southern League Division One
Final League Position : 5th
Secretary : Len Dodson
Colours : Green and White

No.	Day	Month	Date	Opponents	Home	Away	H-T	Goalscorers
1	S	Sep	2	Bristol City		L2-3	(1-3)	Sharples,Wilson T
2	S		16	Southampton		W1-0	(0-0)	Wilson T
3	S		23	Millwall	W2-1		(0-1)	Sharples,Logan
4	S	Oct	7	Chatham	W2-0		(2-0)	Chapman 2
5	S		14	Reading		D1-1	(0-1)	Sharples
6	S	Nov	4	Bedminster	W2-1		(1-1)	Henderson pen.,Sharples
7	S		11	Bristol Rovers		L2-7	(2-4)	Coupar,Henderson
8	S		18	Sheppey United	W4-0		(3-0)	Henderson,Smith W,Sharples 2
9	S		25	Thames Ironworks		L0-1	(0-0)	
10	S	Dec	2	Tottenham Hotspur	L0-2		(0-1)	
11	S		9	New Brompton		L2-4	(1-1)	Wilson T 2
12	S		16	Gravesend United	W2-1		(1-1)	Turner,Sharples
13	S		30	Bristol City	W2-1		(2-0)	Coupar,Sharples
14	S	Jan	13	Southampton	* W2-1		(2-0)	Smith W,Turner
15	S		20	Millwall		L1-2	(0-1)	Smith W
16	S	Feb	10	Chatham		L0-1	(0-1)	
17	S		17	Reading	W2-1		(2-1)	Smith W,Anthony
18	S		24	Sheppey United		W4-1	(1-1)	Sharples,Henderson,Wilson T,Smith W
19	S	Mar	10	Bedminster		L1-2	(0-1)	Sharples
20	S		17	Bristol Rovers	W1-0		(1-0)	Green
21	S		24	Portsmouth		L0-1	(0-1)	
22	S		31	Thames Ironworks	W3-1		(0-0)	Smith W 2,Anthony
23	S	Apr	7	Tottenham Hotspur		L0-3	(0-1)	
24	S		14	New Brompton	D1-1		(1-0)	Smith W
25	M		16	Queens Park Rangers		W5-3	(1-3)	Henderson 2 (1 pen.),Logan,Coupar,Wilson T
26	W		18	Queens Park Rangers	W4-0		(2-0)	Smith W 2,Coupar,Anthony
27	S		21	Gravesend United		L1-2	(0-1)	Anthony
28	M		30	Portsmouth	W3-1		(3-1)	Sharples 2,Smith W

* Played at Elm Park Reading (County Ground under suspension)

Western League Division One
Final League Position : 3rd

No.	Day	Month	Date	Opponents	Home	Away	H-T	Goalscorers
1	W	Sep	20	Bristol City	W1-0		(1-0)	Wilson T
2	W	Nov	15	Bedminster		W2-1	(0-0)	Logan,Smith W
3	W	Dec	13	Bristol City		L1-3	(0-2)	Logan
4	M		25	Bristol Rovers		L1-2	(1-1)	Sharples
5	W	Jan	17	Bedminster	L0-1		(0-0)	
6	S		27	Bristol Rovers	W2-0		(0-0)	Sharples 2

Expunged Games *(Appearances/Goals not included in totals)*

Comp	Day	Month	Date	Opponents	Home	Away	H-T	Goalscorers
S/Lge	S	Sep	9	Cowes	W3-1		(2-1)	Sharples,Smith W,Turner
S/Lge	W	Feb	7	Brighton United		D2-2	(1-0)	Wilson T,Smith W
S/Lge	S	Mar	3	Brighton United	W4-0		(2-0)	Henderson pen.,Coupar,Green,Sharples

F A Cup

Round	Day	Month	Date	Opponents	Home	Away	H-T	Goalscorers	Gate
3Q	S	Oct	28	Portsmouth		L1-2	(1-0)	Coupar	10,000

JIMMY SHARPLES
was Town's top goalscorer for the second season running - following his 13 goals in 1898/99 with 15 this term. And he was also denied two more on each occasion, when he netted against clubs who failed to fulfil their fixtures. In 1900, he left to get a better pay deal at Millwall - joining other Town players George Henderson and Jack Shutt, with whom he shared 'digs' in Poplar. Jimmy died from throat cancer in 1920, aged 47.

Western League

	P	W	D	L	F	A	Pts
1 Bristol Rovers	6	3	1	2	8	6	7
2 Bedminster	6	3	1	2	10	12	7
3 SWINDON TOWN	6	3	0	3	7	7	6
4 Bristol City	6	2	0	4	12	12	4

Anthony S T	Chapman H	Coupar J	Cutts G W	Fulton J W	Green A W	Henderson G	Logan N	Menham R W	Richardson G	Sharples J	Shutt H	Smith A	Smith W	Smithson C E	Turner P	Wilson J	Wilson T C	
	8	10				5		1	4	7	2	6	9			3	11	**1**
		8				5	9	1	4	7	2	6	10			3	11	**2**
		8				5	9	1	4	7	2	6	10			3	11	**3**
	8					5	9	1	4	7	2	6	10			3	11	**4**
	8					5	9	1	4	7	2	6	10			3	11	**5**
		8				6	5	1	4	7	2		10		9	3	11	**6**
		8				5	9	1	4	7	2	6	10			3	11	**7**
		8				5	9	1	4	7	2	6	10			3	11	**8**
		8				5	9	1	4	7	2	6	10			3	11	**9**
		8				5	9	1	4	7	2	6	10			3	11	**10**
		8				5	9	1	4	7	2	6	10			3	11	**11**
		11		2		10	5	1	4	7	3	6	9		8			**12**
8		10				6	5	1	4	7	2		9	11		3		**13**
		10				6	5	1	4	7	2		9		8	3	11	**14**
8		10				6	5	1	4	7		2	9			3	11	**15**
8		10				6	5	1	4	7	2	3				9	11	**16**
8		9				6	5	1	4	7	2	3	10				11	**17**
		11				8	5	1	4	7	2	6	9			3	10	**18**
		8			9	6	5	1	4	7	2	3	10				11	**19**
8		11			9	6	5	1	4	7	2	3	10					**20**
		10			8	6	5	1	4	7	2	3	9				11	**21**
8		10				6	5	1	4	7	2	3	9				11	**22**
8		10				6	5	1	4	7	2	3	9				11	**23**
		10				6	5	1		7	2	4	9		8	3	11	**24**
		10				6	5	1		7	2	4	9		8	3	11	**25**
8		10				6	5	1	4	7	2	3	9				11	**26**
8		10				6	5	1	4	7	2	3	9				11	**27**
8		10				6	5	1	4	7	2	3	9				11	**28**
10	3	26	0	1	3	28	27	28	26	28	27	25	27	1	5	18	25	Apps
4	2	4			1	6	2			12			11		2		6	Goals

TOMMY ANTHONY

Anthony S T	Chapman H	Coupar J	Cutts G W	Fulton J W	Green A W	Henderson G	Logan N	Menham R W	Richardson G	Sharples J	Shutt H	Smith A	Smith W	Smithson C E	Turner P	Wilson J	Wilson T C	
7		8				5	9	1	4	3	2	6	10				11	**1**
		8				5	9	1	4	7	2	6	10			3	11	**2**
		8	1	2		5	9		4	7		6	10			3	11	**3**
8		11				5	9	1	4	7	2	6	10			3		**4**
						8	5	1	4	7	2	6	9		10	3	11	**5**
8		10				6	5	1	4	7	2	3	9				11	**6**
3	0	5	1	1	0	6	6	5	6	6	5	6	6	0	1	4	5	Apps
							2			3			1				1	Goals

Anthony S T	Chapman H	Coupar J	Cutts G W	Fulton J W	Green A W	Henderson G	Logan N	Menham R W	Richardson G	Sharples J	Shutt H	Smith A	Smith W	Smithson C E	Turner P	Wilson J	Wilson T C	
		8				5		1	4	7	2	6	9		10	3	11	**S/Lge**
7						6	5	1	4	8	2	3	9		11		10	**S/Lge**
		8			9	6	5	1	4	7		3	10			2	11	**S/Lge**

BOB MENHAM

Anthony S T	Chapman H	Coupar J	Cutts G W	Fulton J W	Green A W	Henderson G	Logan N	Menham R W	Richardson G	Sharples J	Shutt H	Smith A	Smith W	Smithson C E	Turner P	Wilson J	Wilson T C	
		8				5	9	1	4	7	2	6	10			3	11	**3Q**

No numbers actually worn on shirts

Southern League

For Final Table - see overleaf >>

SEASON 1899/1900

Southern League

		P	W	D	L	F	A	W	D	L	F	A	Pts	G/A
1	Tottenham Hotspur	28	13	1	0	42	8	7	3	4	25	18	44	2.58
2	Portsmouth	28	14	0	0	39	5	6	1	7	28	21	41	2.58
3	Southampton	28	11	0	3	52	14	6	1	7	18	19	35	2.12
4	Reading	28	10	2	2	25	6	5	0	9	16	22	32	1.46
5	SWINDON TOWN	28	12	1	1	30	11	3	1	10	20	31	32	1.19
6	Bedminster	28	9	1	4	27	18	4	1	9	17	17	28	1.26
7	Millwall	28	9	0	5	25	17	3	3	8	11	20	27	0.97
8	Queens Park Rangers	28	8	2	4	28	19	4	0	10	21	38	26	0.86
9	Bristol City	28	9	0	5	33	23	0	7	7	10	24	25	0.91
10	Bristol Rovers	28	9	2	3	31	16	2	1	11	15	39	25	0.84
11	New Brompton	28	7	3	4	26	17	2	3	9	13	32	24	0.80
12	Gravesend United	28	7	4	3	28	25	3	0	11	10	33	24	0.66
13	Chatham	28	9	1	4	26	16	1	2	11	12	42	23	0.66
14	Thames Ironworks	28	6	4	4	19	13	2	1	11	11	32	21	0.67
15	Sheppey United	28	1	5	8	10	25	2	2	10	14	41	13	0.36
16	Brighton United *	26	2	3	8	13	23	1	1	11	12	40	10	
17	Cowes *	13	2	0	5	9	26	1	1	4	8	17	7	

* Withdrew before end of season - Cowes in December, Brighton United in March

SEASON 1900/01

Western League

		P	W	D	L	F	A	Pts
1	Portsmouth	16	11	2	3	36	23	24
2	Millwall	16	9	5	2	33	14	23
3	Tottenham Hotspur	16	8	5	3	37	19	21
4	Queens Park Rangers	16	7	4	5	39	24	18
5	Bristol City	16	6	4	6	27	24	16
6	Reading	16	5	5	6	23	31	15
7	Southampton	16	5	2	9	19	29	12
8	Bristol Rovers	16	4	1	11	18	42	9
9	SWINDON TOWN	16	2	2	12	9	35	6

Southern League

		P	W	D	L	F	A	W	D	L	F	A	Pts	G/A
1	Southampton	28	13	1	0	44	12	5	4	5	14	14	41	2.23
2	Bristol City	28	12	2	0	40	6	5	3	6	14	21	39	2.00
3	Portsmouth	28	12	2	0	33	6	5	2	7	23	26	38	1.75
=4	Millwall	28	11	1	2	36	10	6	1	7	19	22	36	1.72
=4	Tottenham Hotspur	28	12	1	1	35	8	5	1	8	20	24	36	1.72
6	West Ham United	28	10	2	2	28	10	4	3	7	12	18	33	1.43
7	Bristol Rovers	28	10	3	1	29	8	4	1	9	17	27	32	1.31
8	Queens Park Rangers	28	9	1	4	29	21	2	3	9	14	27	26	0.90
9	Reading	28	7	2	5	16	10	1	6	7	8	15	24	0.96
10	Luton Town	28	9	1	4	32	20	2	1	11	11	29	24	0.88
11	Kettering Town	28	7	4	3	21	12	0	5	9	12	34	23	0.72
12	New Brompton	28	5	4	5	20	19	2	1	11	14	32	19	0.67
13	Gravesend United	28	5	5	4	23	27	1	2	11	9	58	19	0.38
14	Watford	28	6	3	5	17	16	0	1	13	7	36	16	0.46
15	SWINDON TOWN	28	3	6	5	15	18	0	2	12	4	29	14	0.40
16	Chatham *	10	1	1	1	4	5	0	1	6	2	27	4	

* Withdrew in December

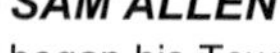

SAM ALLEN

began his Town career in 1895 when he joined the club's committee. Listed in the 1891 census as a 'railway engine shunter', he came to the Great Western Railway Works to take up a clerical position in 1893 - and remained in that employment until 1926. Considering this full-time job, his achievements as both club secretary and team manager from 1902 were remarkable. Two of Town's most influential figures - Harold Fleming and Harry Morris - were among hundreds who were signed by Sam.

He campaigned vigorously to get Southern League clubs Football League status long before this eventually happened in 1920. Sam then became a well respected member of the Third South Executive Committee and pursued other causes, typically to increase the number of clubs promoted from just one. Sadly he did not live to see this adopted. Following Town's last place finish in 1933, Sam reverted to secretary and Ted Vizard *(see page 88)* took over team affairs.

Sam was still in that post when he died on New Years Day 1946, just a day before his 78th birthday.

SEASON 1901/02

Western League

	P	W	D	L	F	A	Pts
1 Portsmouth	16	13	1	2	53	16	27
2 Tottenham Hotspur	16	11	3	2	42	17	25
3 Reading	16	7	3	6	29	22	17
4 Millwall	16	8	1	7	25	29	17
5 Bristol Rovers	16	8	0	8	25	31	16
6 Southampton	16	7	1	8	30	28	15
7 West Ham United	16	6	2	8	30	20	14
8 Queens Park Rangers	16	5	1	10	17	43	11
9 SWINDON TOWN	16	0	2	14	8	53	2

Southern League

	P	W	D	L	F	A	W	D	L	F	A	Pts	G/A
1 Portsmouth	30	11	4	0	35	5	9	3	3	32	19	47	2.79
2 Tottenham Hotspur	30	11	2	2	42	11	7	4	4	19	11	42	2.77
3 Southampton	30	12	2	1	54	10	6	4	5	17	18	42	2.54
4 West Ham United	30	10	2	3	27	13	7	4	4	18	15	40	1.61
5 Reading	30	10	4	1	38	9	6	3	6	19	15	39	2.38
6 Millwall	30	9	3	3	33	13	4	3	8	15	18	32	1.55
7 Luton Town	30	8	5	2	16	10	3	5	7	15	25	32	0.89
8 Kettering Town	30	9	4	2	31	12	3	1	11	13	27	29	1.13
9 Bristol Rovers	30	11	1	3	37	10	1	4	10	6	29	29	1.10
10 New Brompton	30	10	2	3	27	8	0	5	10	12	30	27	1.03
11 Northampton Town	30	7	3	5	40	30	4	2	9	13	34	27	0.83
12 Queens Park Rangers	30	6	5	4	21	16	2	2	11	12	39	23	0.60
13 Watford	30	7	2	6	21	19	2	2	11	15	41	22	0.60
14 Wellingborough	30	8	2	5	23	18	1	2	12	11	54	22	0.47
15 Brentford	30	7	2	6	23	21	0	4	11	11	40	20	0.56
16 SWINDON TOWN	30	2	3	10	13	27	0	0	10	4	66	7	0.18

SEASON 1905/06

United League

	P	W	D	L	F	A	Pts
1 Watford	18	13	4	1	49	15	30
2 Crystal Palace	18	13	1	4	51	21	27
3 Leyton	18	8	4	6	33	31	20
4 Luton Town	18	7	4	7	47	27	18
5 Clapton Orient	18	5	8	5	24	27	18
6 SWINDON TOWN	18	7	3	8	33	29	17
7 Brighton & Hove Albion	18	6	4	8	28	28	16
8 New Brompton	18	7	2	9	26	27	16
9 Grays United	18	4	2	12	21	64	10
10 Southern United	18	3	2	13	21	64	8

Southern League

	P	W	D	L	F	A	W	D	L	F	A	Pts	G/A
1 Fulham	34	10	7	0	22	6	9	5	3	22	9	50	2.93
2 Southampton	34	13	2	2	32	11	6	5	6	26	28	45	1.49
3 Portsmouth	34	13	3	1	39	11	4	6	7	22	24	43	1.74
4 Luton Town	34	12	3	2	43	13	5	4	8	21	27	41	1.60
5 Tottenham Hotspur	34	13	2	2	36	11	3	5	9	10	18	39	1.59
6 Plymouth Argyle	34	11	3	3	32	13	5	4	8	20	20	39	1.58
7 Norwich City	34	9	8	0	31	11	4	2	11	15	27	36	1.21
8 Bristol Rovers	34	11	1	5	37	23	4	4	9	19	33	35	1.00
9 Brentford	34	11	3	3	28	19	3	4	10	15	33	35	0.83
10 Reading	34	9	7	1	34	15	3	2	12	19	31	33	1.15
11 West Ham United	34	12	2	3	30	9	2	3	12	12	30	33	1.08
12 Millwall	34	9	4	4	26	16	2	7	8	12	25	33	0.93
13 Queens Park Rangers	34	9	3	5	39	14	3	4	10	19	30	31	1.32
14 Watford	34	7	6	4	28	20	1	4	12	10	37	26	0.67
15 SWINDON TOWN	34	6	4	7	21	23	2	5	10	10	29	25	0.60
16 Brighton & Hove Albion	34	8	5	4	24	24	1	2	14	6	31	25	0.55
17 New Brompton	34	5	5	7	10	20	2	3	12	10	42	22	0.32
18 Northampton Town	34	5	4	8	17	22	3	1	13	15	57	21	0.41

SEASON 1900/1901

Southern League Division One
Final League Position : 15th
Secretary : Len Dodson
Colours : Green and White

No.	Day	Month	Date	Opponents	Home	Away	H-T	Goalscorers
1	S	Sep	1	Bristol City	L0-1		(0-0)	
2	S		8	Queens Park Rangers		L1-7	(1-5)	Smith
3	S		15	Watford		D1-1	(0-1)	Gardner
4	S		22	Luton Town	W2-1		(2-0)	Gardner,Smith
5	S		29	Tottenham Hotspur		L0-2	(0-1)	
6	S	Oct	6	West Ham United	L0-1		(0-1)	
7	S		13	Portsmouth		L0-2	(0-1)	
8	S		20	New Brompton	L2-3		(1-1)	Anthony 2
9	S		27	Bristol Rovers		L0-1	(0-0)	
10	S	Nov	10	Kettering Town		D0-0		
11	S		24	Millwall		L0-4	(0-2)	
12	S	Dec	1	Southampton	W2-1		(0-0)	McEleny,Gardner
13	S		15	Bristol City		L0-2	(0-1)	
14	S		22	Queens Park Rangers	W4-2		(3-0)	Kirton 2,Oakley,Brown
15	S		29	Watford	D1-1		(0-1)	Smith
16	S	Jan	5	Gravesend United	D0-0			
17	S		12	Tottenham Hotspur	D1-1		(1-0)	Oakley
18	S		19	West Ham United		L1-3	(1-1)	Downie
19	S		26	Luton Town		L1-2	(1-1)	Kirton
20	S	Feb	9	New Brompton		L0-1	(0-0)	
21	S		16	Bristol Rovers	L0-1		(0-0)	
22	S		23	Portsmouth	L0-3		(0-2)	
23	S	Mar	2	Kettering Town	D2-2		(1-0)	Davies,Kirton
24	S		9	Gravesend United		L0-2	(0-1)	
25	S		16	Millwall	D1-1		(0-0)	Davies
26	S		23	Southampton		L0-1	(0-0)	
27	F	Apr	5	Reading		L0-1	(0-0)	
28	M		15	Reading	D0-0			

*Test Match **

Day	Month	Date	Opponents	Home	Away
M	Apr	29	Brentford		D0-0

* Relegation decider - played at Elm Park, Reading (bad light halted play during extra-time)

Western League Division One
Final League Position : 9th (Last)

No.	Day	Month	Date	Opponents	Home	Away	H-T	Goalscorers
1	W	Nov	28	Portsmouth	L0-1		(0-0)	
2	W	Dec	5	Tottenham Hotspur	L0-1		(0-1)	
3	Tu		25	Southampton		L0-3	(0-2)	
4	W		26	Reading		D0-0		
5	W	Jan	2	Queens Park Rangers		L1-3	(1-2)	Davies
6	W		9	Millwall	D1-1		(1-1)	Downie
7	W	Feb	13	Reading	L0-1		(0-1)	
8	W		27	Tottenham Hotspur		L0-5	(0-1)	
9	M	Mar	4	Millwall		L0-6	(0-3)	
10	W		13	Queens Park Rangers	W3-2		(0-1)	Anthony,Kirton,Menham pen.
11	S		30	Bristol City		L0-4	(0-3)	
12	W	Apr	10	Portsmouth		L0-1	(0-0)	
13	S		13	Southampton	W3-1		(0-0)	Kirton,Pettican,Smith
14	S		20	Bristol Rovers	L0-1		(0-0)	
15	W		24	Bristol City	L0-1		(0-1)	
16	S		27	Bristol Rovers		L1-4	(1-1)	Oakley

F A Cup

Rd	Day	Month	Date	Opponents	Home	Away	H-T	Goalscorers	Gate
3Q	S	Nov	3	Bristol East		* D1-1	(1-1)	Richardson	
Rp	M		12	Bristol East	W5-0		(2-0)	Davies,Brown,Smith 2 (1 pen.),Gardner	
4Q	S		17	Staple Hill		* D2-2	(1-1)	Davies,Smith	
Rp	W		21	Staple Hill	W6-0		(2-0)	Davies,Smith,McEleny,Kirton,Gardner,Menham pen.	
5Q	S	Dec	8	Bristol Rovers		L1-5	(0-2)	Oakley	5,000

* Played at County Ground (by arrangement)

For Final League Tables - see previous page <<

Anthony S T	Boulton T	Brown R	Cutts G W	Davies T O	Day W G	Downie A L B	Edwards A J	Fagan M W	Gardner A	Kirton J	Logan N	Lloyd A E	McEleny C	Menham R W	Oakley G	Pettican J	Richardson G	Ritchie A	Selby W R	Smith W	Smithson C	Stephenson J W	
		7				10			8	11	5		6	1			4	2		9		3	**1**
		7				10			8	11	5		6	1			4	2		9		3	**2**
8		7							10	11	5		6	1			4	2		9		3	**3**
						4	11		10	9	5		6	1			7	2		8		3	**4**
		7				8	11		10		5		6	1			4	2		9		3	**5**
8		7				4	11		10		5		6	1				2		9		3	**6**
		7				9			8	11	5		6	1			4	2		10		3	**7**
8		7				10			11		5		6	1			4	2		9		3	**8**
		7				4			11		5		6	1	10		8	2		9		3	**9**
		7		8					10	11	5		6	1			4	2		9		3	**10**
		7		8		6			11	9			5	1			4	2		10		3	**11**
		7		8		5			11				6	1	10		4	2		9		3	**12**
		7		8		5			11	9			6	1			4	2		10		3	**13**
		7		8		5				9			6	1	11		4	2		10		3	**14**
11		7		8		5				9			6	1			4	2		10		3	**15**
		7		8	10	5				9			6	1	11		4	2				3	**16**
		7		8		5					9		6	1	11		4	2		10		3	**17**
		7		8		5				9			6	1	11		4	2		10		3	**18**
		7		8		5				9	10		6	1	11		4	2				3	**19**
10		7		8		5				9			6	1	11		4	2				3	**20**
10		7		8		4				9	5		6	1	11			2				3	**21**
		7		8		4				9	5		6	1	11	10		2				3	**22**
	1	7		8		5				11	9		6				4	2		10		3	**23**
7				8		5				9			6	1	11		4	2		10		3	**24**
7				8		5		2		11	9		6	1			4			10		3	**25**
7				8		5		2		11	9		6	1			4			10		3	**26**
7				8		5		3		11	9		6	1			4	2		10			**27**
7				8		5				11			6	1		9	4	2		10		3	**28**
11	1	22	0	19	1	26	3	3	13	22	18	0	28	27	11	2	25	26	0	23	0	27	Apps
2		1		2		1			3	4			1		2					3			Goals

Anthony S T	Boulton T	Brown R	Cutts G W	Davies T O	Day W G	Downie A L B	Edwards A J	Fagan M W	Gardner A	Kirton J	Logan N	Lloyd A E	McEleny C	Menham R W	Oakley G	Pettican J	Richardson G	Ritchie A	Selby W R	Smith W	Smithson C	Stephenson J W
7				8		5				9	2		6	1	11	10	4					3

Anthony S T	Boulton T	Brown R	Cutts G W	Davies T O	Day W G	Downie A L B	Edwards A J	Fagan M W	Gardner A	Kirton J	Logan N	Lloyd A E	McEleny C	Menham R W	Oakley G	Pettican J	Richardson G	Ritchie A	Selby W R	Smith W	Smithson C	Stephenson J W	
8		7				5			11				6	1	10		4	2		9		3	**1**
8		7				4			11		5	6		1	10			2		9		3	**2**
8	1	7				5				9			6		11		4	2		10		3	**3**
		7		8		5		2		9			6	1	11		4			10		3	**4**
10		7		8		5		2		11	9		6	1			4					3	**5**
		7		8		5				9			6	1	11		4	2		10		3	**6**
10		7		8		5					9		6	1	11		4	2				3	**7**
		7		8		5				10	9		6	1			4	2			11	3	**8**
	1	7		8		5				9	6				11		4	2		10		3	**9**
7				8		5				11	9		6	1			4	2		10		3	**10**
7				8		5				11	9		6	1			4	2		10		3	**11**
		7		8		5		2					6	1	11	9	4			10		3	**12**
7				8		5				11			6	1		9	4	2		10		3	**13**
7				8		5				11	2		6	1		9	4			10		3	**14**
		7				5				11	2		6	1		9	4		8	10		3	**15**
		7	1			5				9	2		6		11	8	4			10		3	**16**
9	2	12	1	11	0	16	0	3	2	12	10	1	14	13	9	5	15	10	1	13	1	16	Apps
1				1		1				2				1	1	1				1			Goals

Anthony S T	Boulton T	Brown R	Cutts G W	Davies T O	Day W G	Downie A L B	Edwards A J	Fagan M W	Gardner A	Kirton J	Logan N	Lloyd A E	McEleny C	Menham R W	Oakley G	Pettican J	Richardson G	Ritchie A	Selby W R	Smith W	Smithson C	Stephenson J W	
		7		8					9	11	5		6	1			4	2		10		3	**3Q**
		7		8					11	9	5		6	1			4	2		10		3	**Rp**
		7		8					11	9	5		6	1			4	2		10		3	**4Q**
		7		8					11	9	5		6	1			4	2		10		3	**Rp**
		7		8					11		5		6	1	10		4	2		9		3	**5Q**
		5		5					5	4	5		5	5	1		5	5		5		5	Apps
		1		3					2	1			1	1	1		1			4			Goals

No numbers actually worn on shirts

ALEC DOWNIE

GEORGIE RICHARDSON

SEASON 1901/02

Southern League Division One
Final League Position : 16th (Last)
Secretary : Len Dodson
Colours : Maroon and White

No.	Day	Month	Date	Opponents	Home	Away	H-T	Goalscorers
1	S	Sep	7	Brentford	D0-0			
2	S		14	Kettering Town	L1-2		(1-1)	Edwards
3	S		21	Luton Town		L0-3	(0-2)	
4	S		28	Millwall	W2-1		(2-0)	Becton,Bradshaw
5	S	Oct	5	Queens Park Rangers		L0-4	(0-3)	
6	S		12	Reading	L0-4		(0-3)	
7	S		19	Southampton		L1-6	(0-3)	Oakden
8	S		26	Bristol Rovers	L0-1		(0-1)	
9	S	Nov	9	Northampton Town	L1-3		(0-0)	Edwards
10	S		23	Tottenham Hotspur	L1-3		(1-2)	Edwards
11	S	Dec	7	Portsmouth	L1-2		(1-2)	Downie
12	S		14	West Ham United		L1-2	(1-1)	Becton
13	S		21	Brentford		L0-2	(0-2)	
14	S		28	Kettering Town		L1-10	(1-6)	Draper o.g.
15	S	Jan	4	Luton Town	L1-2		(0-0)	Becton
16	S		11	Millwall		L0-3	(0-1)	
17	S		18	Queens Park Rangers	L0-3		(0-1)	
18	S		25	Watford		L0-3	(0-0)	
19	S	Feb	1	Southampton	D0-0			
20	S		15	New Brompton	D1-1		(1-1)	Haydon
21	S		22	Northampton Town		L0-8	(0-5)	
22	S	Mar	1	Watford	L1-3		(0-2)	McKendrick
23	M		3	Wellingborough		L0-4	(0-3)	
24	S		8	Tottenham Hotspur		L1-7	(0-3)	Becton
25	S		15	Wellingborough	W4-1		(2-1)	Edwards,McKendrick,Becton 2
26	S		22	Portsmouth		L0-4	(0-1)	
27	S		29	West Ham United	L0-1		(0-1)	
28	Tu	Apr	1	Bristol Rovers		L0-1	(0-0)	
29	S		5	Reading		L0-3	(0-2)	
30	S		12	New Brompton		L0-5	(0-3)	

Test Match *

Day	Month	Date	Opponents	Home	Away	H-T	Goalscorers
W	Apr	30	Fulham		W3-1	(2-0)	Becton 2,Cowan

* Relegation decider - played at Elm Park, Reading

Western League Division One
Final League Position : 9th (Last)

No.	Day	Month	Date	Opponents	Home	Away	H-T	Goalscorers
1	M	Sep	2	Reading	L0-2		(0-1)	
2	W		11	Reading		L0-4	(0-4)	
3	W		18	Bristol Rovers	L0-2		(0-2)	
4	W		25	Queens Park Rangers	D1-1		(1-0)	Oakden
5	W	Oct	23	Southampton	L0-3		(0-0)	
6	M		28	Millwall		L1-3	(1-2)	Edwards
7	M	Nov	11	Tottenham Hotspur		L0-6	(0-4)	
8	W	Dec	18	Southampton		L0-4	(0-0)	
9	Th		26	Portsmouth		L1-5	(-)	Davies
10	W	Jan	15	West Ham United	L0-4		(0-2)	
11	M	Feb	10	West Ham United		L0-6	(0-5)	
12	M	Mar	10	Queens Park Rangers		L2-4	(1-3)	McKendrick,Becton
13	W		19	Millwall	D2-2		(1-0)	McKendrick,Cowan
14	M	Apr	7	Bristol Rovers		L1-4	(0-2)	Edwards
15	W		9	Tottenham Hotspur	L0-1		(0-1)	
16	W		23	Portsmouth	L0-2		(0-2)	

F A Cup

Rd	Day	Month	Date	Opponents	Home	Away	H-T	Goalscorers	Gate
3Q	S	Nov	2	Yeovil Casuals	W4-0		(3-0)	Davies,Edwards,Oakley,Becton	2,000
4Q	S		16	Weymouth	W2-1		(0-0)	Becton 2	1,000
5Q	S		30	Bristol Rovers	L0-1		(0-0)		4,000

Anthony S T	Becton F	Bevan F	Bradshaw T D	Codling R	Cowan D	Davenport W	Davies T O	Day W G	Dibsdall G J	Downie A L B	Edwards A J	Fagan M W	Goddard G W	Hall G	Haydon W	Keogh P J	Logan N	McKendrick D	Major W H	Menham R W	Oakden H	Oakley G	Pettican J	Pollard W J	Richardson G	Vernon C J	Williams C	
7	10		9	6	8	2				5			11				3			1					4			1
7	10		9	6		2	8			5	11								3	1					4			2
	10		8	6	7					2							5			1		11	9		4	3		3
	9		10	6			8		2	3							5			1	7	11			4			4
	9		10	6	7		8		2	3							5			1		11			4			5
	9		10	6			8			3		2					5			1	7	11			4			6
8	9			6						3		2					5			1	7	11	10		4			7
8	10		9	4						6	11	2					5		3	1	7							8
	9			4			8			6	11	2					5		3		7	10		1				9
7	9						8	4	2	6	11						5		3	1		10						10
	9			6	7		8	4	3	10	11	2					5			1								11
	9			6	7		8	4	3	10	11	2					5			1								12
	9			6	7		8	4	3	10	11	2					5			1								13
7	9						8		2	3	11	1						4			6	10		*5 = Morris A W*				14
7	9			*4 = Fulton R W*			8	6	2	10	11					1	5		3									15
7	9						8	6		2	11						5	10	3	1	4							16
	8							6	2	4	11				9		5	10	3	1	7							17
	9						8	6		4	11	2					5	10	3	1	7							18
	9				7		8			6	11						5	10	3	1	4			*2 = Rose G F*				19
	8				7				2		11			6	9		5	10	3	1	4							20
7	8								2	6	11				9		5	10	3	1	4							21
7	9						8		2	4	11			6		1	5	10	3									22
	9				7		8		3	4	11	2		6		1	5	10										23
7	9						8	4	2	6	11					1	5	10	3									24
	9				8		7		2	6	11					1	5	10	3		4							25
	9				8		7		2	6	11						5	10	3	1	4							26
8	9	10					7			6	11						5		3	1	4			*2 = Fulton R W*				27
	9				8		7			6	11	2					5		3	1	4	10						28
	9				8		7			6	11	2					5		3	1	4	10						29
8	9	4					7		2	3	11						5	10		1	6							30
13	30	2	7	12	13	2	23	9	17	29	24	12	1	3	3	5	28	13	18	23	18	10	2	1	7	1	0	Apps
	6		1							1	4				1			2			1							Goals

Opponents 1 goal

Anthony S T	Becton F	Bevan F	Bradshaw T D	Codling R	Cowan D	Davenport W	Davies T O	Day W G	Dibsdall G J	Downie A L B	Edwards A J	Fagan M W	Goddard G W	Hall G	Haydon W	Keogh P J	Logan N	McKendrick D	Major W H	Menham R W	Oakden H	Oakley G	Pettican J	Pollard W J	Richardson G	Vernon C J	Williams C
	9				8		7		3	6	11	2					5	10		1	4						

For Final League Tables - see page 23

Match 9 : only 10 players used

Anthony S T	Becton F	Bevan F	Bradshaw T D	Codling R	Cowan D	Davenport W	Davies T O	Day W G	Dibsdall G J	Downie A L B	Edwards A J	Fagan M W	Goddard G W	Hall G	Haydon W	Keogh P J	Logan N	McKendrick D	Major W H	Menham R W	Oakden H	Oakley G	Pettican J	Pollard W J	Richardson G	Vernon C J	Williams C	
	10		9	6	7	2	8			5			11				3			1					4			1
7	10		9	4	8	2				5			11				3			1			*6 = Jeacock A E*					2
7	10		9	6		2	8			5	11						3							1	4			3
	10		9	6	8				2	3							5			1	7	11			4			4
8	9			6						3	11	2					5			1	7	10			4			5
	10		9	4			8	6		3	11	2					5			1	7							6
	9			4			8			6	11	2					5		3		7	10		1				7
				6	7		8	4	2		11	3			9		5			1		10						8
7	9			6			8					2				1	5	3			4	10						9
7	9							6		2	11					8	5	10	3	1	4							10
	8			*1 = Lewis T P*			7		3	6	11				9		5	10			4		*2 = Bown A J W*					11
	9				7		8		2	4	11	6					5	10					*3 = Bown A J W*				1	12
	9				8		7		2	6	11						5	10	3		4						1	13
	9				8		7		3	6	11	2					5	10		1	4							14
	9				8		7		3	6	11	2					5	10		1	4							15
	9				8		7		3	6	11	2					5	10		1	4							16
5	15	0	5	9	9	3	12	3	8	14	12	9	2	0	2	2	16	8	3	10	11	5	0	2	4	0	2	Apps
	1				1		1				2							2			1							Goals

Anthony S T	Becton F	Bevan F	Bradshaw T D	Codling R	Cowan D	Davenport W	Davies T O	Day W G	Dibsdall G J	Downie A L B	Edwards A J	Fagan M W	Goddard G W	Hall G	Haydon W	Keogh P J	Logan N	McKendrick D	Major W H	Menham R W	Oakden H	Oakley G	Pettican J	Pollard W J	Richardson G	Vernon C J	Williams C	
	9			4			8			6	11	2					5		3	1	7	10						3Q
	9			4			8		2	6	11						5		3	1	7	10						4Q
	9	8						4	2	6	11						5		3	1	7	10						5Q
	3	1		2			2	1	2	3	3	1					3		3	3	3	3						Apps
	3						1				1											1						Goals

No numbers actually worn on shirts

SEASON 1902/03

Southern League Division One
Final League Position : 12th
Secretary/Manager : Sam Allen
Colours : Red and White

No.	Day	Month	Date	Opponents	Home	Away	H-T	Goalscorers
1	S	Sep	6	Millwall	W3-2		(2-1)	Poppitt,Neyland,Kirby
2	S		13	Kettering Town		L0-2	(0-1)	
3	S		20	Luton Town	W2-1		(1-1)	Kirby,Pugh
4	S		27	Reading		L1-6	(0-5)	Davies
5	S	Oct	4	Queens Park Rangers	W2-0		(0-0)	Edwards 2
6	S		11	Southampton		L0-1	(0-0)	
7	S		25	Bristol Rovers		W3-2	(2-0)	Cartlidge o.g.,Pugh,Davies
8	S	Nov	8	Watford		L3-5	(0-5)	Bannister,Neyland,Poppitt
9	S		22	Tottenham Hotspur		L0-2	(0-2)	
10	S	Dec	6	Portsmouth		L2-3	(2-2)	Poppitt,Kirby
11	S		20	Millwall		W2-1	(0-0)	Poppitt,Edwards
12	F		26	New Brompton		L1-2	(1-0)	Davies
13	S		27	Kettering Town	D1-1		(0-0)	Bannister pen.
14	S	Jan	3	Luton Town		D0-0		
15	S		10	Reading	D1-1		(0-0)	Poppitt
16	S		17	Queens Park Rangers		L0-2	(0-1)	
17	S		24	Southampton	D1-1		(0-0)	Poppitt
18	S		31	Wellingborough		L1-4	(0-3)	Edwards
19	S	Feb	7	Bristol Rovers	W2-1		(0-1)	Poppitt,Kirby
20	S		14	Northampton Town		L0-1	(0-1)	
21	S		21	Watford	W3-0		(2-0)	Becton 2 (1 pen.),Bannister
22	S		28	Brentford		L0-1	(0-0)	
23	S	Mar	14	West Ham United		D1-1	(1-1)	Pugh
24	S		21	Portsmouth	W2-1		(0-0)	Pugh,Bannister
25	S		28	New Brompton	D1-1		(1-0)	Kirby
26	S	Apr	4	West Ham United	D1-1		(0-1)	Poppitt
27	S		11	Northampton Town	L0-2		(0-1)	
28	S		18	Brentford	W3-0		(2-0)	Reid,Cowley,Kirby
29	W		22	Tottenham Hotspur	W2-0		(1-0)	Poppitt,Becton
30	S		25	Wellingborough	L0-1		(0-1)	

F A Cup

Rd	Day	Month	Date	Opponents	Home	Away	H-T	Goalscorers	Gate
2Q	S	Oct	18	Chippenham Town		* W5-0	(3-0)	Poppitt 2,Edwards,Davies,Pugh	
3Q	S	Nov	1	Yeovil Casuals		W4-0	(3-0)	Kirby 3,Davies	1,200
4Q	S		15	Poole	W7-1		(2-1)	Neyland 2,Kirby pen.,Pugh 3,Oakden	
5Q	S		29	Whitehead Torpedo Works		W9-0	(5-0)	Poppitt,Cowley,Bannister,Pugh 3,Davies,Neyland,Kirby	
IM	S	Dec	13	Barnsley		L0-4	(0-3)		4,000

* Played at County Ground (by arrangement)

JIMMY POPPITT

like Billy Kirby *(opposite)* was one of many who joined Town twice during their career. Born in Shropshire, at Lilleshall, he arrived from Wolves in 1902 and was top scorer at the County Ground in his first season. Jimmy moved to Reading for the 1903/04 season, re-joining Town a year later.

He became the licensee of the Whale Inn in Medgbury Road in 1923, but he died just seven years later - at the age of 55. Jimmy's son Granville was also a Town forward, but he did not progress beyond the reserve side.

Bannister C	Becton F	Bullock A E	Cowley J B	Davies T O	Day W G	Edwards A J	Hartley E C R	Hemmings F G	Holmes W	Howell H A	Jones A T	Kirby W	Lewis T P	Major W H	Menham R W	Neyland M	O'Brien J	O'Brien P	Oakden H	Poppitt J	Pugh J	Reid Rev. E	
5			6	7					3			9			1	11	2		4	8	10		**1**
5			6	7					3			9			1	11	2		4	8	10		**2**
5			6	7					3			9			1	11	2		4	8	10		**3**
			6	7	5				3			9			1	11	2		4	8	10		**4**
5			6	7		11			3			9			1	8	2		4		10		**5**
5			6	7		11					3	9			1		2		4	8	10		**6**
5			6	7							3	11			1	10	2		4	8	9		**7**
5		4	6	7							3	11			1	10	2			8	9		**8**
5			6	7							3	11			1	10	2		4	8	9		**9**
5			6	7							3	9			1	11	2		4	8	10		**10**
5		4	6	7		11		1			3	9					2			8	10		**11**
5		4	6	7		11		1			3	9					2			8	10		**12**
5			6	7		11		1			3	9					2	10	4	8			**13**
5		10	6	7		11		1			3					9	2		4	8			**14**
5			6	7			9	1			3	11					2		4	8	10		**15**
5			6	7				1			3	9				11	2		4	8	10		**16**
5			6	7		11		1			3	9					2		4	8	10		**17**
5			6	7		11		1			3					9	2		4	8	10		**18**
5	9		6	7				1	3		2	11							4	8	10		**19**
5	9		6					1	3	7		11				8	2		4		10		**20**
5	9		6	7				1			3	11					2		4	8	10		**21**
5	9		6	7				1			3	11					2		4	8	10		**22**
5	9		6	7				1			3	11					2		4	8	10		**23**
5	9		6	7				1			3	11					2		4	8	10		**24**
5	9		6	7		11		1			3	10					2		4	8			**25**
5	9		6	7				1			3	11					2		4	8	10		**26**
5	9		6	7				1			3	11					2		4	8	10		**27**
		5	6	7				1	3			11					2		4	8	10	9	**28**
	10	4	5	7				1			3	11				6	2			8		9	**29**
	10	7	5					1				11		3		6	2		4	8		9	**30**
26	11	7	30	28	1	9	1	20	8	1	22	28	0	1	10	15	29	1	26	28	25	3	Apps
4	3		1	3		4						6				2				9	4	1	Goals

Opponents 1 goal

Bannister C	Becton F	Bullock A E	Cowley J B	Davies T O	Day W G	Edwards A J	Hartley E C R	Hemmings F G	Holmes W	Howell H A	Jones A T	Kirby W	Lewis T P	Major W H	Menham R W	Neyland M	O'Brien J	O'Brien P	Oakden H	Poppitt J	Pugh J	Reid Rev. E	
5			6	7		11					3	9			1		2		4	8	10		**2Q**
5		4	6	7							3	9			1	11	2			8	10		**3Q**
5			6	7							3	11			1	10	2		4	8	9		**4Q**
5			6	7							3	9			1	11	2		4	8	10		**5Q**
5			6	7							3	9	1			11	2		4	8	10		**IM**
5		1	5	5		1					5	5	1		4	4	5		4	5	5		Apps
1			1	3		1						5				3			1	3	7		Goals

No numbers actually worn on shirts

BILLY KIRBY

		P	W	D	L	F - A		W	D	L	F - A		Pts	G/A
1	Southampton	30	12	2	1	53	7	8	6	1	30	13	48	4.15
2	Reading	30	12	2	1	47	14	7	5	3	25	16	45	2.40
3	Portsmouth	30	11	2	2	36	13	6	5	4	33	19	41	2.16
4	Tottenham Hotspur	30	10	5	0	34	9	4	2	9	13	22	35	1.52
5	Bristol Rovers	30	9	5	1	33	12	4	3	8	13	22	34	1.35
6	New Brompton	30	9	4	2	24	9	2	7	6	13	26	33	1.06
7	Millwall	30	9	2	4	33	16	5	1	9	19	21	31	1.41
8	Northampton Town	30	7	3	5	23	19	5	3	7	16	29	30	0.81
9	Queens Park Rangers	30	8	3	4	25	16	3	3	9	9	26	28	0.81
10	West Ham United	30	8	5	2	25	14	1	5	9	10	35	28	0.71
11	Luton Town	30	8	3	4	28	14	2	4	9	15	30	27	0.98
12	SWINDON TOWN	30	8	5	2	24	13	2	2	11	14	33	27	0.826
13	Kettering Town	30	5	8	2	19	12	3	3	9	14	28	27	0.825
14	Wellingborough	30	9	2	4	27	15	2	1	12	9	41	25	0.64
15	Watford	30	5	1	9	22	33	1	3	11	13	54	16	0.40
16	Brentford	30	2	1	12	10	36	0	0	15	17	67	5	0.26

SEASON 1903/04

Southern League Division One
Final League Position : 10th
Secretary/Manager : Sam Allen

No.	Day	Month	Date	Opponents	Home	Away	H-T	Goalscorers
1	S	Sep	5	Bristol Rovers		L0-2	(0-1)	
2	M		7	Brentford		L1-2	(1-2)	Green
3	S		12	Kettering Town	D0-0			
4	S		19	Brighton and Hove Albion		W1-0	(1-0)	Oakden
5	S		26	Southampton	D1-1		(0-0)	Cowley
6	S	Oct	3	Portsmouth		L0-1	(0-1)	
7	S		10	Fulham	D2-2		(1-0)	Pugh 2
8	S		17	Northampton Town		D1-1	(1-1)	Lean
9	S		24	Millwall	L0-4		(0-1)	
10	S	Nov	7	Queens Park Rangers	D1-1		(1-0)	Green
11	S		21	Plymouth Argyle	W2-0		(0-0)	Milligan,Reid
12	S	Dec	5	Reading	W2-1		(1-1)	Pugh,Hogan
13	S		12	Luton Town		L0-3	(0-1)	
14	S		19	Wellingborough		L2-6	(2-3)	Hogan,Cowley pen.
15	S		26	New Brompton	W3-0		(1-0)	Hogan,Bannister,Pugh
16	M		28	New Brompton		L1-3	(1-0)	Beadsworth
17	S	Jan	2	Bristol Rovers	L0-2		(0-1)	
18	S		9	Kettering Town		D1-1	(0-0)	Cowley pen.
19	S		16	Brighton and Hove Albion	D1-1		(0-1)	Beadsworth
20	S		23	Southampton		L0-2	(0-1)	
21	S		30	Portsmouth	L0-1		(0-1)	
22	S	Feb	6	Luton Town	W1-0		(0-0)	Hogan
23	S		20	Millwall		L1-3	(0-2)	Hogan
24	M		22	Tottenham Hotspur		L0-1	(0-0)	
25	S		27	Brentford	D1-1		(0-1)	Lean
26	S	Mar	5	Queens Park Rangers		L0-1	(0-0)	
27	S		12	West Ham United	W1-0		(1-0)	Beadsworth
28	S		19	Plymouth Argyle		D0-0		
29	S		26	Tottenham Hotspur	D0-0			
30	S	Apr	2	Reading		D1-1	(0-1)	Lean
31	Tu		5	Fulham		W2-1	(2-1)	Pugh 2
32	S		16	Wellingborough	W1-0		(1-0)	Lean
33	S		23	Northampton Town	W2-0		(1-0)	Pugh,Lean
34	S		30	West Ham United		W1-0	(0-0)	Toombs

F A Cup

Rd	Day	Month	Date	Opponents	Home	Away	H-T	Goalscorers	Gate
3Q	S	Oct	31	Poole	W9-0		(4-0)	Pugh 3,Green 2,Bullock 3,Cowley	
4Q	S	Nov	14	Staple Hill	*	W5-0	(2-0)	Atterbury 2,Oakden,Cowley,Pugh	2,000
5Q	S		28	Plymouth Argyle		L0-2	(0-2)		4,862

* Played at County Ground (by arrangement)

JIMMY PUGH
originated from the Wirral, but had previous Southern League experience with Gravesend United - where he was leading scorer in 1900/01 - and Wellingborough. He signed for Town in September 1902 and was top goalscorer in 1903/04. A former professional cricketer, he played for both Cumberland and Wiltshire. He died in Swindon in 1950.

Archer H T	Atterbury S	Bannister C	Beadsworth A	Bown A J W	Bullock A E	Colvin R	Cowley J B	Davies J C	Green T A	Hemmings F G	Hogan C	Howell H A	Lean W L F	Logan N	Milligan A A	Oakden H	Peers S A	Pugh J	Reid Rev.E	Ricketts L	Sanderson T	Toombs E R	Wolfe G	
	3	5				7	6	11	9	1			8		2	4		10						1
	3	5				7	6		9	1			8		2			10		11			4	2
	3	5				7	6		9	1			8		2	4		10		11				3
	3	5					11			1			9		2	4		10	7			8	6	4
	3	5					11		8	1			9		2	4		10	7				6	5
	3	5					11		9	1			8		2	4		10	7				6	6
	3	5					11		9	1			8		2	4		10	7				6	7
	3	5					11		9	1			8		2	4		10	7				6	8
	3	5				11	6		9	1			8		2	4		10	7					9
	3	4			8		11		9	1				6	2			10	7				5	10
	3	5	8				6		7	1	9				2	4		10	11					11
	3	5	8				6		7	1	9				2	4		10	11					12
	3	5	8				6		7	1	9				2	4		10	11					13
	3	5	8				6		7	1	9					4		10	11				2	14
	3	5	8				6			1	9				2	4	11	10	7					15
	3	5	8				6			1	9	7			2	4	11	10						16
	3	5	10				6			1	9			8	2	4	11		7					17
	3	5	10				6			1	8			9	2	4	11		7					18
	3	5	10				6			1				9	2	4	11	8	7					19
	3	5	8				6		7	1				9	2	4		10	11					20
	3	5	8				11		7	1	9			6		4		10					2	21
3	2	5	7				11			1	9		8	6		4		10						22
3	2	5	7				11			1	9		8	6		4		10						23
3	2	5	7				11			1	9		8	6		4		10						24
	3	5	7	10			11			1			8	6	2	4		9						25
	3	5	10				11		7	1	9		8	6	2								4	26
	3	5	10				11		7	1			9	6	2	4		8						27
	3	5	10				11		7	1			9	6	2		8						4	28
	3	5	10				11		7	1			9	6	2			8					4	29
	3	5	10				11		7	1			9	6	2			8					4	30
	3	5	10				11		7	1			9	6	2			8					4	31
	3	5	10				6		7	1			9		2			8				11	4	32
	3	5	10				6		7	1			9		2			8				11	4	33
	3	5	10				6		7	1			9		2						8	11	4	34
3	34	34	24	1	1	4	34	1	24	34	13	1	22	16	29	24	6	29	16	2	1	4	17	Apps
		1	3				3		2		5		5		1	1		7	1			1		Goals

LOUIS LEAN

Archer H T	Atterbury S	Bannister C	Beadsworth A	Bown A J W	Bullock A E	Colvin R	Cowley J B	Davies J C	Green T A	Hemmings F G	Hogan C	Howell H A	Lean W L F	Logan N	Milligan A A	Oakden H	Peers S A	Pugh J	Reid Rev.E	Ricketts L	Sanderson T	Toombs E R	Wolfe G	
	3	4			8		11		9	1				6	2			10	7				5	3Q
	4	5					11		9	1				6	2	8		10	7				3	4Q
	3	5			8		6		7	1				9	2	4		10	11					5Q
	3	3			2		3		3	3				3	3	2		3	3				2	Apps
	2				3		2		2							1		4						Goals

No numbers actually worn on shirts

	P	W	D	L	F	A	W	D	L	F	A	Pts	G/A
1 Southampton	34	12	3	2	42	15	10	3	4	37	15	50	2.63
2 Tottenham Hotspur	34	10	5	2	34	19	6	6	5	20	18	43	1.46
3 Bristol Rovers	34	11	4	2	38	12	6	4	7	28	30	42	1.57
4 Portsmouth	34	11	4	2	24	11	6	4	7	17	27	42	1.08
5 Queens Park Rangers	34	13	3	1	34	12	2	8	7	19	25	41	1.43
6 Reading	34	8	6	3	27	15	6	7	4	21	20	41	1.37
7 Millwall	34	10	2	5	41	20	6	6	5	23	22	40	1.52
8 Luton Town	34	12	4	1	23	9	2	8	7	15	24	40	1.15
9 Plymouth Argyle	34	8	5	4	27	16	5	5	7	17	18	36	1.29
10 SWINDON TOWN	34	7	7	3	18	14	3	4	10	12	28	31	0.71
11 Fulham	34	7	6	4	23	14	2	6	9	10	20	30	0.97
12 West Ham United	34	8	4	5	26	14	2	3	12	12	29	27	0.88
13 Brentford	34	8	4	5	25	18	1	5	11	9	30	27	0.71
14 Wellingborough	34	7	4	6	34	25	4	1	12	10	38	27	0.70
15 Northampton Town	34	8	4	5	22	20	2	3	12	14	49	27	0.52
16 New Brompton	34	4	10	3	18	15	2	3	12	8	28	25	0.60
17 Brighton & Hove Albion	34	5	6	6	27	29	1	6	10	18	50	24	0.57
18 Kettering Town	34	6	4	7	23	23	0	3	14	7	55	19	0.38

Extract from wages book

SEASON 1904/05

Southern League Division One
Final League Position : 16th
Secretary/Manager : Sam Allen

No.	Day	Month	Date	Opponents	Home	Away	H-T	Goalscorers
1	Th	Sep	1	Luton Town	W1-0		(1-0)	Poppitt
2	S		3	Wellingborough	W2-0		(2-0)	Poppitt,Beadsworth
3	S		10	Southampton		L3-4	(2-3)	Lean 2,Chalmers pen.
4	S		17	Fulham	W2-1		(0-1)	Lean,Chalmers
5	S		24	Watford		L0-1	(0-0)	
6	S	Oct	1	Plymouth Argyle	W4-0		(1-0)	Toombs,Chalmers,Kirby,Lean
7	S		8	West Ham United		L0-2	(0-2)	
8	S		15	Reading	L1-2		(0-0)	Chalmers
9	S		22	Bristol Rovers		L0-3	(0-3)	
10	S	Nov	5	Portsmouth		L0-2	(0-1)	
11	S		12	Brentford	L1-3		(0-1)	Reid
12	S		19	Queens Park Rangers		L1-4	(1-1)	Beadsworth
13	S	Dec	3	Tottenham Hotspur		L3-6	(1-2)	Chalmers pen.,Beadsworth,Kirby
14	S		17	Brighton and Hove Albion	W1-0		(0-0)	Chalmers
15	S		24	New Brompton		D0-0		
16	M		26	New Brompton	L1-2		(1-1)	Lean
17	S		31	Wellingborough		W1-0	(1-0)	Lean
18	S	Jan	7	Southampton	L0-2		(0-1)	
19	S		14	Luton Town		L1-4	(1-2)	Bowell
20	S		21	Watford	W2-0		(2-0)	Chalmers pen.,Main o.g.
21	S		28	Plymouth Argyle		L0-3	(0-2)	
22	S	Feb	4	West Ham United	D3-3		(2-1)	Wheatcroft,Chalmers 2
23	S		11	Reading		L1-2	(1-1)	Wheatcroft
24	S		18	Bristol Rovers	W2-1		(2-0)	Poppitt,Wheatcroft
25	S		25	Northampton Town		L0-5	(0-4)	
26	S	Mar	4	Portsmouth	W3-1		(2-0)	Wheatcroft 2,Beadsworth
27	S		11	Brentford		D1-1	(1-0)	Poppitt
28	S		18	Queens Park Rangers	D0-0			
29	S		25	Millwall		D0-0		
30	S	Apr	1	Tottenham Hotspur	W2-1		(2-0)	Bowell,Chalmers
31	M		3	Fulham		L0-3	(0-1)	
32	W		12	Millwall	W2-1		(1-0)	Beadsworth 2
33	S		15	Brighton and Hove Albion		L0-2	(0-1)	
34	S		29	Northampton Town	W3-0		(2-0)	Chalmers,Beadsworth 2

F A Cup

Round	Day	Month	Date	Opponents	Home	Away	H-T	Goalscorers	Gate
3Q	S	Oct	29	Whitehead Torpedo Works	*	W7-0	(2-0)	Atterbury,Pugh 2,Lean 2,Kirby,Poppitt	
4Q	S	Nov	12	Longfleet St Mary's	W8-0		(3-0)	Sanderson,Pugh 3,Wheatcroft 3,Toombs	
5Q	S		26	Green Waves		L1-2	(1-2)	Kirby	5,000

* Played at County Ground (by arrangement)

JIM CHALMERS
was a Scottish winger with plenty of experience, having started his League career with Morton in 1896. His previous highest goal tally for a season was just five, but he doubled that with Town in 1904/05 - albeit with the aid of penalties. He continued playing until 1913. Jimmy served with the Black Watch during the First War and was sadly one of the many thousands killed at the Somme in 1916.

Archer H T	Atterbury S	Beadsworth A	Bowell O C	Chalmers J	Cowley J B	Dixon J	Erentz H B	Hemmings F G	Jones A E J	Kirby W	Lean W L F	Logan N	Major W H	Milligan A A	Oakden H	Oakley G	Parkes F	Poppitt J	Pugh J	Reid Rev.E	Sanderson T	Stringfellow H	Toombs E R	Wheatcroft F G	Wolfe G	
	3	10		11	6			1		7	9			2				8				5			4	**1**
3		10		11	6			1		7	9			2				8				5			4	**2**
	3	10		11	6			1		7	9			2				8				5			4	**3**
	3	10		11	6			1		7	9			2				8				5			4	**4**
	3	10		11	6			1		7	9			2				8				5			4	**5**
	3	10		11	6			1		7	9			2								4	8		5	**6**
	3	10		11	6			1		7	9			2								4	8		5	**7**
	3	10		11				1		7	9	6		2				8				4			5	**8**
3	2	10						1	5	7	9				4			8					11		6	**9**
	3	7		11				1			9			2	4			8	10			6			5	**10**
	3	10						1		7	9			2	4			8		11		6			5	**11**
	3	10		11				1		7		5		2	4			8	9			6				**12**
	3	10		11		1				7	9	6		2				8				5			4	**13**
	3	10		11			2	1			9	6						8				5	7		4	**14**
	3	10		11			2	1		8	9	6										5	7		4	**15**
	3	10		11			2	1		8	9	6										5	7		4	**16**
	3	10	7				2	1		11	9	6						8				5			4	**17**
	3	10		11			2	1		7	9	6						8				5			4	**18**
	3	10	7	11		1	2				9	6						8				5			4	**19**
	3		7	11			2	1		9	8	6			4							5		10		**20**
	3		7	11			2	1		9	8	6			4							5		10		**21**
	3		7	11			2	1		9	8	6			4							5		10		**22**
	3	10	7	11			2	1			8	6						4				5		9		**23**
		10	7	11		1	2				5	6						8				4		9	3	**24**
		10	7	11		1	2				5	6						8				4		9	3	**25**
	3	10	7	11			2	1				6			4			8						9	5	**26**
	3	10	7	11			2	1			4	6						8						9	5	**27**
	3	10	7	11			2	1			4	6						8						9	5	**28**
	3		7	11			2	1			10	6						8				4		9	5	**29**
	3	10	7	11				1			2	6						8				4		9	5	**30**
	3	10	7	11				1			2	6						8				4		9	5	**31**
	3	10	7	11				1			2	6						8				4		9	5	**32**
	3	10	7	11				1	2			6						8				4		9	5	**33**
	3	10	7	11				1	2		9	6						8				4			5	**34**
2	31	30	17	31	7	4	16	30	3	19	31	24	0	12	8	0	0	27	2	1	0	30	6	14	29	Apps
		8	2	11						2	6							4					1	5		Goals

Opponents 1 goal

Archer H T	Atterbury S	Beadsworth A	Bowell O C	Chalmers J	Cowley J B	Dixon J	Erentz H B	Hemmings F G	Jones A E J	Kirby W	Lean W L F	Logan N	Major W H	Milligan A A	Oakden H	Oakley G	Parkes F	Poppitt J	Pugh J	Reid Rev.E	Sanderson T	Stringfellow H	Toombs E R	Wheatcroft F G	Wolfe G	
	3			11				1		7	9			2	4			8	10			6			5	**3Q**
3						1			5			6	2			11	4		10		7		8	9		**4Q**
3				11		1				9	10	6		2				8			7	4			5	**5Q**
2	1			2		2		1	1	2	2	2	1	2	1	1	1	2	2		2	2	1	1	2	Apps
	1									2	2							1	5		1		1	3		Goals

No numbers actually worn on shirts

	P	W	D	L	F - A		W	D	L	F - A		Pts	G/A
1 Bristol Rovers	34	13	4	0	51	11	7	4	6	23	25	48	2.06
2 Reading	34	13	3	1	36	12	5	4	8	21	26	43	1.50
3 Southampton	34	9	4	4	29	21	9	3	5	25	19	43	1.35
4 Plymouth Argyle	34	14	3	0	38	11	4	2	11	19	28	41	1.46
5 Tottenham Hotspur	34	10	3	4	34	15	5	5	7	19	19	38	1.56
6 Fulham	34	10	5	2	32	9	4	5	8	14	25	38	1.35
7 Queens Park Rangers	34	10	2	5	36	12	4	6	7	26	27	36	1.59
8 Portsmouth	34	12	1	4	39	19	4	3	10	22	37	36	1.09
9 New Brompton	34	8	7	2	25	13	3	4	10	15	28	33	0.98
10 West Ham United	34	9	3	5	30	15	3	5	9	18	27	32	1.14
11 Brighton & Hove Albion	34	9	2	6	25	15	4	4	9	19	30	32	0.98
12 Northampton Town	34	8	4	5	26	17	4	4	9	17	37	32	0.80
13 Watford	34	12	0	5	30	19	2	3	12	11	25	31	0.93
14 Brentford	34	5	7	5	17	14	5	2	10	16	26	29	0.83
15 Millwall	34	7	6	4	26	15	4	1	12	12	32	29	0.81
16 SWINDON TOWN	34	11	2	4	30	17	1	3	13	11	42	29	0.69
17 Luton Town	34	11	1	5	35	18	1	2	14	10	36	27	0.83
18 Wellingborough	34	4	3	10	16	37	1	0	16	9	67	13	0.24

SEASON 1905/06

Southern League Division One
Final League Position : 15th
Secretary/Manager : Sam Allen

No.	Day	Month	Date	Opponent	Home	Away	H-T	Goalscorers
1	S	Sep	2	West Ham United		L0-1	(0-0)	
2	S		9	Fulham	L1-4		(0-1)	Abbott
3	S		16	Queens Park Rangers		L0-3	(0-1)	
4	S		23	Bristol Rovers	L1-2		(0-1)	Dean pen.
5	S		30	New Brompton		D0-0		
6	S	Oct	7	Portsmouth	W2-1		(1-0)	Atterbury,Abbott
7	S		14	Northampton Town	L1-2		(1-1)	Wheatcroft
8	S		21	Millwall		D0-0		
9	S		28	Luton Town	D1-1		(0-0)	Dean pen.
10	S	Nov	4	Tottenham Hotspur		L1-2	(1-1)	Dean
11	S		11	Brentford	D1-1		(0-1)	Logan
12	S		25	Plymouth Argyle	W2-1		(2-0)	Wheatcroft,Capes
13	S	Dec	2	Southampton		L0-2	(0-1)	
14	S		16	Watford		W2-1	(2-0)	Wheatcroft,Dean
15	S		23	Brighton and Hove Albion	W2-0		(1-0)	Lyon 2
16	M		25	Norwich City		L0-1	(0-0)	
17	S		30	West Ham United	L2-3		(1-1)	Dean,Capes
18	S	Jan	6	Fulham		D1-1	(1-0)	Dean pen.
19	S		20	Queens Park Rangers	L1-2		(1-1)	Dean
20	S		27	Bristol Rovers		L1-2	(1-1)	Wheatcroft
21	S	Feb	10	Portsmouth		W2-1	(1-1)	Chalmers,Lyon
22	S		17	Northampton Town		L0-3	(0-2)	
23	S		24	Millwall	D0-0			
24	S	Mar	3	Luton Town		L0-4	(0-1)	
25	S		10	Tottenham Hotspur	W2-0		(1-0)	Capes,Tait o.g.
26	S		17	Brentford		L1-3	(0-3)	Capes
27	M		19	New Brompton	W2-0		(1-0)	Monks,Chalmers
28	S		24	Norwich City	L1-3		(1-0)	Dean
29	S		31	Plymouth Argyle		L0-3	(0-2)	
30	S	Apr	7	Southampton	L0-3		(0-1)	
31	S		14	Reading		D1-1	(0-1)	Dean pen.
32	S		21	Watford	D0-0			
33	W		25	Reading	W2-0		(2-0)	Capes,Lyon
34	S		28	Brighton and Hove Albion		D1-1	(1-0)	Lyon

United League Division One
Final League Position : 6th

No.	Day	Month	Date	Opponent	Home	Away	H-T	Goalscorers
1	M	Sep	4	New Brompton		L0-1	(0-1)	
2	W		13	Leyton	W2-0		(1-0)	Wheatcroft 2
3	W		20	Brighton and Hove Albion	W3-0		(0-0)	Clare o.g.,Lyon,Tout
4	W		27	Clapton Orient	D1-1		(1-1)	Oakden
5	M	Oct	9	Luton Town		L2-4	(2-1)	Dean pen.,Chalmers
6	W		18	Watford	L1-3		(1-1)	Monks
7	W		25	Grays United	L0-1		(0-0)	
8	W	Nov	1	Crystal Palace	L1-6		(1-3)	Chalmers pen.
9	W	Jan	24	Luton Town	W3-2		(1-1)	Lyon 2,Capes
10	W		31	Grays United		W1-0	(1-0)	Cowley
11	S	Feb	3	Leyton		L2-3	(1-1)	Capes,Tout
12	Th		8	Southern United		W2-1	(0-1)	Lyon, Chalmers pen.
13	F		16	Clapton Orient		L1-3	(0-0)	Capes
14	W	Mar	7	Crystal Palace		D1-1	(0-1)	Monks
15	W		21	Watford		D0-0		
16	F	Apr	13	Brighton and Hove Albion		L0-1	(0-0)	
17	M		16	New Brompton	W3-2		(1-1)	Dean pen.,Capes,Abbott
18	M		30	Southern United	W10-0		(5-0)	Capes 2,Lyon 3,Dean 2,Tout 2,Bowell

F A Cup

Rd	Day	Month	Date	Opponent	Home	Away	H-T	Goalscorers	Gate
5Q	S	Dec	9	West Hampstead	W4-0		(1-0)	Capes,Wheatcroft,Lyon 2	3,000
1	S	Jan	13	Brighton and Hove Albion		L0-3	(0-2)		6,500

For Final League Tables - see page 23

Abbott H	Atterbury S	Beaumont W E	Bowell O C	Capes A J	Chalmers J	Coates R J	Cowley J B	Dean A	Edwards A J	Gill J E	Hemmings F G	Hemmins B R P	Hindle W	Holyhead J	Jones A E J	Ling A S	Logan N	Lyon H H S B C	Monks A	Muir	O'Brien J	Oakden H	Potter J M	Tout W E B	Warman H	Wheatcroft F G	
	3				11			7					4	5		1	6	10	8		2					9	**1**
10	3				11			7						5		1	6	4	8		2					9	**2**
					11			7		3			4	5		1	6	10	8		2					9	**3**
	3				11			7					4	6		1	5	10	8		2					9	**4**
8	3				11			7					4	6		1		9	10		2	5					**5**
8	3				11			7			1		4	6				9	10		2	5					**6**
	3				11			7					4	6		1		9	10		2	5				8	**7**
10	5				11			7		3			4			1		9			2		6			8	**8**
	3				11			7		2			4			1		9	10			5	6			8	**9**
	3				11			7		2			4			1		9	10			5	6			8	**10**
	3				11			7		2			4			1	6	9	10			5				8	**11**
9	3			10	11			7		2			4			1		6				5				8	**12**
	3			10	11			7		2			4			1		6	9			5				8	**13**
				10	11		6	7		2			4			1	5	9			3					8	**14**
				10	11		6	7		2			4			1	5	9			3					8	**15**
8				10	11		6	7		2			4			1	5	9			3						**16**
	3			10	11			7		2			4			1	5	9						6		8	**17**
	3			10	11			7		2			4			1		9				5		6		8	**18**
	3			5	11		6	7					4			1		9			2			10		8	**19**
	3			10	11			7								1	5	9			2	4		6		8	**20**
				10	11			7		2			4			1	5	9			3			6		8	**21**
8		6	7	10	11					2						1	5	9			3			4			**22**
		5		10	11			7		2			4			1		9			3			6		8	**23**
8		5		10	11			7		2			4			1		9			3			6			**24**
8		5		10	11			7		2			4			1		9			3			6			**25**
8		5		10	11			7		2			4			1		9			3			6			**26**
8					11			7		2			4			1	5	9	10		3			6			**27**
8		6		10	11			7		2			4			1		9			3			5			**28**
8		4	7	5			11	2		3						1		9	10					6			**29**
8	3			5			6	7		2			4			1		9	10					11			**30**
8	3	5		10	11			7		2			4			1		9						6			**31**
8	3	5		10	11			7		2			4			1		9						6			**32**
8	3	5		10				7		2			4			1		9	11					6			**33**
8	3	5		10	11		6	7		2			4			1		9									**34**
18	21	11	2	22	31	0	7	33	0	26	1	0	30	7	0	33	13	34	15	0	21	10	3	17	0	19	Apps
2	1			5	2			9									1	5	1							4	Goals

Opponents 1 goal

Abbott H	Atterbury S	Beaumont W E	Bowell O C	Capes A J	Chalmers J	Coates R J	Cowley J B	Dean A	Edwards A J	Gill J E	Hemmings F G	Hemmins B R P	Hindle W	Holyhead J	Jones A E J	Ling A S	Logan N	Lyon H H S B C	Monks A	Muir	O'Brien J	Oakden H	Potter J M	Tout W E B	Warman H	Wheatcroft F G	
10	3				11								4	5		1	6	9	8		2			7			**1**
8	3				11			7		2			4	5		1	6	10								9	**2**
8	3				11			7					4	6		1	5	9			2			10			**3**
8					11		6	7							5	1		9	10		2	4			3		**4**
	3				11		6	7		2	1		4	5				9	10					8			**5**
	3						6	7			1	10	4	5				9	8		2			11			**6**
8			7		11					3				4		1		9		5	2		6	10			**7**
	3		7		11		6							4		1		9	10	5	2			8			**8**
			7	10	11					2			*4 = Parkes F*			1	5	9	8					6	3		**9**
	4		7	10			11			2						1	5	9	8		3			6			**10**
	3			10			11	7					4			1	5	9	8		2			6			**11**
	4		7	10	11					2						1	5	9	8		3			6			**12**
8		4	7	10	11					2						1	5	9			3			6			**13**
8		4		5	11			7		2						1		9	10		3			6			**14**
	2		7		11	9	6						*8 = Richardson*			1	5		10			4			3		**15**
		4		9				7	11							1	5	8	10		2			6	3		**16**
10		5	8	9				7	11	2			4			1					3			6			**17**
		5	8	10			6	7		2						1	4	9			3			11			**18**
8	10	5	9	9	12	1	8	10	2	10	2	1	7	7	1	16	11	16	12	2	14	2	1	15	4	1	Apps
1			1	6	3		1	4										7	2			1		4		2	Goals

Opponents 1 goal

Abbott H	Atterbury S	Beaumont W E	Bowell O C	Capes A J	Chalmers J	Coates R J	Cowley J B	Dean A	Edwards A J	Gill J E	Hemmings F G	Hemmins B R P	Hindle W	Holyhead J	Jones A E J	Ling A S	Logan N	Lyon H H S B C	Monks A	Muir	O'Brien J	Oakden H	Potter J M	Tout W E B	Warman H	Wheatcroft F G	
				10	11		6	7		2	1		4					9			3	5				8	**5Q**
	6			10	11			7		2			4			1		9			3	5				8	**1**
	1			2	2		1	2		2	1		2			1		2			2	2				2	Apps
				1														2								1	Goals

No numbers actually worn on shirts

SEASON 1906/07

Southern League Division One
Final League Position : 17th
Secretary/Manager : Sam Allen

No	Day	Month	Date	Opponents	Home	Away	H-T	Goalscorers
1	S	Sep	1	Southampton	W1-0		(0-0)	Birtles
2	S		8	West Ham United		L0-2	(0-0)	
3	S		15	Tottenham Hotspur	D0-0			
4	W		19	Queens Park Rangers	D0-0			
5	S		22	Bristol Rovers		L0-2	(0-1)	
6	S		29	Norwich City		D1-1	(1-0)	Murphy
7	W	Oct	3	Fulham	D2-2		(2-0)	Smith,Wardrope
8	S		6	Luton Town	W4-0		(2-0)	Coates,Birtles 2,Murphy
9	S		13	Crystal Palace		L2-3	(0-2)	Wardrope pen.,Kidd
10	S		20	Brentford	W2-0		(1-0)	Birtles,Coates
11	S		27	Millwall		L1-2	(0-1)	Wardrope pen.
12	S	Nov	3	Leyton	W2-1		(2-0)	Reynolds 2
13	S		10	Portsmouth		L0-1	(0-0)	
14	S		17	New Brompton	W2-0		(1-0)	Murphy 2
15	S		24	Plymouth Argyle		D2-2	(2-1)	Kidd 2
16	S	Dec	1	Brighton and Hove Albion	D0-0			
17	S		15	Watford	D0-0			
18	S		22	Northampton Town		L1-2	(1-1)	Birtles
19	W		26	Brighton and Hove Albion		L0-1	(0-0)	
20	S		29	Southampton		D1-1	(1-1)	Birtles
21	S	Jan	5	West Ham United	W2-0		(2-0)	Wardrope,Kidd
22	S		19	Tottenham Hotspur		L0-3	(0-1)	
23	S		26	Bristol Rovers	W1-0		(0-0)	Birtles
24	S	Feb	9	Luton Town		L2-6	(1-1)	Smith 2
25	S		16	Crystal Palace	W2-1		(0-1)	Wardrope pen.,Smith
26	S		23	Norwich City	W3-1		(1-1)	Smith,Kidd,Birtles
27	S	Mar	2	Millwall	L0-2		(0-1)	
28	S		9	Leyton		L1-2	(1-1)	Smith
29	W		13	Reading		L0-1	(0-1)	
30	S		16	Portsmouth	D0-0			
31	S		23	New Brompton		L1-2	(1-1)	Smith
32	F		29	Fulham		L0-4	(0-3)	
33	S		30	Plymouth Argyle	D1-1		(0-1)	Wardrope
34	M	Apr	1	Queens Park Rangers		L1-6	(0-3)	Wardrope
35	M		8	Brentford		L2-5	(1-4)	Smith 2
36	S		13	Reading	W1-0		(1-0)	Wardrope
37	S		20	Watford		D0-0		
38	S		27	Northampton Town	W5-0		(4-0)	Kidd,Murphy 2,Smith 2

F A Cup

Rd	Day	Month	Date	Opponents	Home	Away	H-T	Goalscorers	Gate
5Q	S	Dec	8	Burslem Port Vale	L1-2		(0-1)	Wardrope pen.	7,000

ANDY SMITH

was born in Stirlingshire in 1877 and spent three years with both West Bromwich Albion and Bristol Rovers - and a couple of months at Millwall - before coming to the County Ground. Joint leading scorer with Billy Wardrope prior to the last game of the season, Andy hit a brace as Swindon thumped bottom-of-the-table Northampton - who had just appointed former Town inside-forward Herbert Chapman as manager. Andy moved on to Southern League rivals Leyton in May 1907.

Atterbury S	Bannister C	Beaumont W E	Birtles T J D	Bown A J W	Coates R J	Dibsdall G J	Gill J E	Hemmings F G	Innes R	Kidd J	Lean W L F	Ling A S	Murphy E	Reynolds W	Smith A	Tout W E B	Wardrope W	Warman H	
3	5	4	7				2				8	1	11		9	6	10		**1**
3	5	4	7				2				9	1	11		8	6	10		**2**
3	5	4	7				2				9	1	11		10	6	8		**3**
2	5	6	7						4	8		1	11		10		9	3	**4**
3	5	4	7							8		1	11		9	6	10	2	**5**
3	5	4	7				2			8		1	11		9	6	10		**6**
3	5	4	7							8	2	1	11		9	6	10		**7**
3	5	4	7		9		2			8		1	11			6	10		**8**
3		5	7				2		4	8		1	11		9	6	10		**9**
3	5	4	7		9		2			8		1	11			6	10		**10**
3	5	4	7				2			8		1	11		9	6	10		**11**
3	5	6	7				2		4	8		1	11	10			9		**12**
3	5	6	7				2		4	8		1	11	10			9		**13**
3	5	6	7				2		4	8		1	11		9		10		**14**
3	5	6	7				2		4	8		1	11		9		10		**15**
3	5	6	7				2		4	8		1	11		9		10		**16**
3	5	4	7				2			8	9	1	11			6	10		**17**
3		4	7		9		2			8	5	1	11			6	10		**18**
	5	4	7				2		3	8	9	1		11		6	10		**19**
	5	4	7	9			2			8	3	1	11			6	10		**20**
	5	4	7	9			2			8	3	1	11			6	10		**21**
	5	4	7	9			2			8	3	1	11			6	10		**22**
	5	4	7			2				8	3	1	11		9	6	10		**23**
	5	4	7				2	1		8	3		11		9	6	10		**24**
3	5	4	7				2			8		1	11		9	6	10		**25**
3		4	7						5	8	2	1	11		9	6	10		**26**
		4	7				2		5	8	3	1	11		9	6	10		**27**
3		5	7				2		4	8		1		11	9	6	10		**28**
3		5	7				2		4	8		1	11		9	6	10		**29**
3		5	7				2		4	8		1	11		9	6	10		**30**
3		5	7				2		4	8		1	11		9	6	10		**31**
3	5	6	7				2		4	8		1	11		9		10		**32**
3	5	6	7				2		4		9	1	11		8		10		**33**
3		5	7				2		4		9	1	11		8	6	10		**34**
3	5	6	7		8		2		4			1	11		9		10		**35**
3	5	6	7						4	8	2	1	11		9		10		**36**
3		6	7				2		4	8		1	11		9	5	10		**37**
		6	7			3	2		4	8		1	11		9	5	10		**38**
30	27	38	38	3	4	2	32	1	21	32	17	37	36	4	28	28	38	2	Apps
			8		2					6			6	2	11		8		Goals

3	5	6	7				2		4	8		1	11		9		10		**5Q**

No numbers actually worn on shirts

TOMMY BIRTLES

		P	W	D	L	F - A		W	D	L	F - A		Pts	G/A
1	Fulham	38	13	5	1	34	12	7	8	4	24	20	53	1.81
2	Portsmouth	38	15	3	1	45	11	7	4	8	19	25	51	1.78
3	Brighton & Hove Albion	38	10	4	5	33	16	8	5	6	20	27	45	1.23
4	Luton Town	38	12	4	3	38	22	6	5	8	14	30	45	1.00
5	West Ham United	38	12	5	2	39	12	3	9	7	21	29	44	1.46
6	Tottenham Hotspur	38	13	4	2	46	12	4	5	10	17	33	43	1.40
7	Millwall	38	14	3	2	53	11	4	3	12	18	39	42	1.42
8	Norwich City	38	9	6	4	34	21	6	6	7	23	27	42	1.19
9	Watford	38	9	7	3	31	18	4	9	6	15	25	42	1.07
10	Brentford	38	14	3	2	39	16	3	5	11	18	40	42	1.02
11	Southampton	38	9	6	4	31	18	4	3	12	18	38	35	0.88
12	Reading	38	12	3	4	42	11	2	3	14	15	36	34	1.21
13	Leyton	38	9	6	4	26	23	2	6	11	12	37	34	0.63
14	Bristol Rovers	38	10	4	5	41	20	2	5	12	14	34	33	1.02
15	Plymouth Argyle	38	7	9	3	26	14	3	4	12	17	36	33	0.86
16	New Brompton	38	9	4	6	30	21	3	5	11	17	38	33	0.797
17	SWINDON TOWN	38	11	7	1	28	8	0	4	15	15	46	33	0.796
=18	Queens Park Rangers	38	9	5	5	32	16	2	5	12	15	39	32	0.85
=18	Crystal Palace	38	7	4	8	29	28	4	6	9	18	27	32	0.85
20	Northampton Town	38	5	8	6	22	24	0	1	18	7	64	19	0.33

SEASON 1907/08

Southern League Division One
Final League Position : 5th
Secretary/Manager : Sam Allen

					Home	Away	H-T	Goalscorers
1	M	Sep	2	West Ham United		W2-1	(1-0)	Warburton 2
2	S		7	Plymouth Argyle		L0-2	(0-1)	
3	S		14	West Ham United	D1-1		(1-1)	Warburton pen.
4	S		21	Queens Park Rangers		L1-2	(1-1)	Fenton
5	S		28	Tottenham Hotspur	W1-0		(1-0)	Fenton
6	S	Oct	5	New Brompton	W1-0		(0-0)	Rushton
7	S		12	Crystal Palace		L1-4	(0-2)	Rushton
8	S		19	Luton Town	W4-0		(3-0)	Warburton,Kidd,Rushton,Fleming
9	S		26	Brighton and Hove Albion		D2-2	(0-1)	Fenton,Tout
10	S	Nov	2	Portsmouth	D0-0			
11	S		9	Bradford Park Avenue		D2-2	(0-1)	Fenton,Bown
12	S		16	Millwall	W2-0		(2-0)	Bown,Fleming
13	S		23	Brentford		L0-2	(0-2)	
14	S		30	Bristol Rovers	W4-1		(4-0)	Fleming 2,Johnston,Rushton
15	S	Dec	7	Leyton		W2-1	(0-1)	Fleming,Bown
16	S		14	Reading	W2-0		(1-0)	Johnston,Fleming
17	S		21	Watford		D0-0		
18	W		25	Southampton	L0-2		(0-1)	
19	Th		26	Northampton Town		L0-1	(0-0)	
20	S		28	Norwich City	D1-1		(0-1)	Fleming
21	S	Jan	4	Plymouth Argyle	W1-0		(1-0)	Fleming
22	S		25	Tottenham Hotspur		L0-1	(0-1)	
23	S	Feb	8	Crystal Palace	D0-0			
24	S		15	Luton Town		L0-1	(0-0)	
25	S		29	Portsmouth		L0-2	(0-0)	
26	S	Mar	7	Bradford Park Avenue	W4-0		(2-0)	Lyon,Bannister,Fleming 2
27	S		14	Millwall		L0-2	(0-2)	
28	S		21	Brentford	D0-0			
29	S		28	Bristol Rovers		L0-1	(0-1)	
30	W	Apr	1	New Brompton		W1-0	(1-0)	Fleming
31	S		4	Leyton	D2-2		(1-0)	Warburton,Moles o.g.
32	W		8	Brighton and Hove Albion	W5-1		(3-1)	Fleming 3,Johnston,Bown
33	S		11	Reading		W1-0	(0-0)	Rushton
34	F		17	Northampton Town	W3-1		(1-0)	Bown 2,Rushton
35	S		18	Watford	W2-0		(1-0)	Bown,Johnston
36	M		20	Southampton		D1-1	(0-1)	Fleming
37	S		25	Norwich City		L1-3	(1-0)	Bown
38	Th		30	Queens Park Rangers	W8-3		(2-0)	Warburton 4,Fleming 2,Fenton 2

F A Cup

					Home	Away	H-T	Goalscorers	Gate
1	S	Jan	11	Sheffield United	D0-0				11,289
1R	Th		16	Sheffield United	+	W3-2	(1-0)	Warburton,Tout,Johnston	19,566
2	S	Feb	1	Queens Park Rangers	W2-1		(1-1)	Johnston,Warburton	9,771
3	S		22	Wolverhampton Wanderers		L0-2	(0-0)		26,856

+ After Extra Time

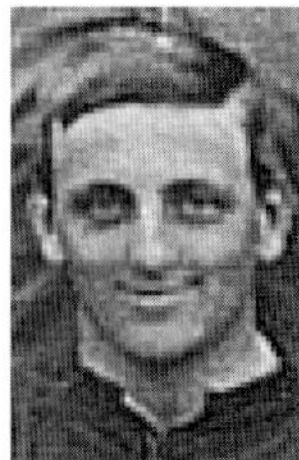

HAROLD FLEMING
was discovered playing for local church side St Marks and given a trial in the Town's reserve side against Salisbury on October 12 1907. He scored twice in a 4-0 win, was quickly promoted to first team duty a week later and within 18 months was called up for the full England side. And with Harold scoring freely, Town went from mediocrity to one of the best sides outside the Football League's two divisions within two years. An inside-forward with excellent ball skills, Harold was almost 'untouchable' on his day, only foul play stopping him. Top scorer for Town in three of his first four seasons at the County Ground, the Great War robbed him of four years of his career, which went on until 1924. He died from cancer in 1955 aged 68.

Aitken D	Bannister C	Bown A J W	Chambers P	Dibsdall G J	Fenton F	Fleming H J	Gill J E	Hemmings F G	Heppinstall F	Innes R	Johnston J	Jones W J	Kidd J	Ling A S	Lyon H H S B C	Rushton G	Tout W E B	Walker J	Warburton F	
	5		6		11		2				7		8	1		9	4	3	10	**1**
	5		6		11		2				7		8	1		9	4	3	10	**2**
	5		6		11		2				7		8	1		9	4	3	10	**3**
			6		11		2			4	7	5		1	8	9		3	10	**4**
			6		11		2			5			8	1	9	7	4	3	10	**5**
			6		11		2			5	7			1	8	9	4	3	10	**6**
2			6		11					5	7			1	8	9	4	3	10	**7**
			6		11	7	2			4			8	1		9	5	3	10	**8**
			6		11	7	2			4			8	1		9	5	3	10	**9**
	5		6		11	7	2						8	1		9	4	3	10	**10**
	5	10	6		11	8	2				7			1		9	4	3		**11**
	5	10	6		11	8	2				7			1		9	4	3		**12**
	5	10	6		11	8	2				7			1		9	4	3		**13**
	5	10	6		11	8	2				7			1		9	4	3		**14**
	5	10	6		11	8	2				7			1	9		4	3		**15**
	5	10	6		11	8	2				7			1		9	4	3		**16**
	5	10	6		11	8	2				7			1	4	9		3		**17**
	5		6		11		2				7		8	1		9	4	3	10	**18**
	5				11	8	2			6	7			1	10	9	4	3		**19**
	5	10	6		11	8	2				7			1		9	4	3		**20**
	5		6		11	8	2				7			1	10	9	4	3		**21**
	5		6	2		11					7			1	8	9	4	3	10	**22**
		10			11	8	2			5	7			1		9	4	3	6	**23**
	5					8	2				7	6		1	10	9	4	3	11	**24**
	5	10				8	2				7	6		1	9		4	3	11	**25**
	5				11	8	2				7	6		1	9		4	3	10	**26**
	5					8	2		11		7	6		1	9		4	3	10	**27**
	5		6			8	2		11		7			1	9		4	3	10	**28**
	5		6			10	2		11		7		8	1			4	3	9	**29**
			6			10	2		11		7	5	8	1			4	3	9	**30**
			6			10	2	1	11		7	5	8				4	3	9	**31**
	5	10	6			8	2	1	11		7						4	3	9	**32**
	5	10	6				2	1	11		7					9	4	3	8	**33**
	5	10	6				2	1	11		7		8			9	4	3		**34**
	5	10	6	2		8		1	11		7					9	4	3		**35**
	5	10	6	2	11	8		1			7					9	4	3		**36**
		10	6		11	8	2	1			7	5					4	3	9	**37**
	5	10	6	2	11	8		1			7						4	3	9	**38**
1	28	17	32	4	26	28	33	8	9	8	34	8	12	30	14	27	36	38	25	Apps
	1	8			6	17					4		1		1	6	1		9	Goals

Opponents 1 goal

FRANK WARBURTON

Aitken D	Bannister C	Bown A J W	Chambers P	Dibsdall G J	Fenton F	Fleming H J	Gill J E	Hemmings F G	Heppinstall F	Innes R	Johnston J	Jones W J	Kidd J	Ling A S	Lyon H H S B C	Rushton G	Tout W E B	Walker J	Warburton F	
	5		6		11	8	2				7			1	10	9	4	3		**1**
	5		6			11	2				7		8	1	9		4	3	10	**1R**
	5		6		11	8	2				7			1		9	4	3	10	**2**
	5		6			11	2				7			1	8	9	4	3	10	**3**
	4		4		2	4	4				4		1	4	3	3	4	4	3	Apps
											2						1		2	Goals

No numbers actually worn on shirts

For Final League Table - see page 44

JOCK WALKER
was one of many Scots who came south to improve their career prospects. A tough and fearless full-back, Jock was signed from Cowdenbeath for less than £100. By the time he left for Middlesbrough in April 1913, he had nine Scotland caps. Jock missed few games in his six years at the County Ground, assisting Town to two F.A.Cup semi-finals and the Southern League championship in 1911. His move to 'Boro, at £1,126 plus Allan McRobbie - valued at £250 - almost set a British transfer record fee. Jock came back to 'guest' for Town during the War, making about forty appearances between 1915 and 1917. In 1921, he signed for Reading where he made another 60 appearances.

SEASON 1908/09

Southern League Division One
Final League Position : 2nd
Secretary/Manager : Sam Allen

					Home	Away	H-T	Goalscorers
1	W	Sep	2	Watford		L0-1	(0-1)	
2	S		5	Norwich City	W10-2		(6-1)	Bown 2,Hogan 4,Fleming 3,Heppinstall
3	W		9	New Brompton	W6-1		(3-0)	Hogan 3,Fleming 2,Bown
4	S		12	Reading		L1-2	(1-2)	Fleming
5	S		19	Southampton	L0-2		(0-2)	
6	S		26	Leyton		W2-1	(0-0)	Tout pen.,Bown
7	S	Oct	3	West Ham United	W3-0		(2-0)	Jefferson,Fleming,Hogan
8	W		7	Exeter City	W2-1		(0-1)	Jefferson,Tout
9	S		10	Brighton and Hove Albion		L0-3	(0-1)	
10	S		17	Crystal Palace	W4-0		(2-0)	Fleming 2,Bown,Hogan
11	S		24	Brentford		L0-1	(0-1)	
12	S		31	Luton Town	W4-1		(1-1)	Heppinstall,Bown,Lavery,Fleming
13	S	Nov	7	Plymouth Argyle		D1-1	(0-1)	Jefferson
14	S		14	Portsmouth		L1-3	(1-1)	Lavery
15	S		21	Queens Park Rangers	W3-1		(2-1)	Mitchell o.g.,Lavery 2
16	S		28	Northampton Town		D1-1	(0-0)	Tout pen.
17	S	Dec	12	Millwall		L1-4	(0-2)	Bown
18	S		19	Southend United	W4-2		(3-1)	Bown,Lavery,Fleming 2
19	F		25	Coventry City		D1-1	(0-1)	Lavery
20	S		26	Bristol Rovers	L0-1		(0-1)	
21	M		28	Watford	W4-1		(1-0)	Rushton,Fleming,Lavery 2
22	S	Jan	2	Norwich City		D0-0		
23	S		9	Reading	W5-1		(3-1)	Fleming 3,Fenton,Lavery
24	S		23	Southampton		W6-0	(2-0)	Fleming 2,Heppinstall,Bown 2,Rushton
25	S		30	Leyton	W3-0		(0-0)	Rushton 2,Fleming
26	S	Feb	13	Brighton and Hove Albion	W2-0		(0-0)	Bannister,Bown
27	S		20	Crystal Palace		D1-1	(1-0)	Fleming
28	S		27	Brentford	W2-1		(2-1)	Lavery 2
29	M	Mar	8	West Ham United		L2-4	(2-2)	Fleming,Tout pen.
30	S		13	Plymouth Argyle	W5-0		(3-0)	Rushton,Jefferson 2,Bown 2
31	W		17	Exeter City		W4-1	(1-0)	Rushton 2,Fleming,Jefferson
32	S		20	Portsmouth	W5-0		(4-0)	Jefferson,Bown,Fleming 2,Tout pen.
33	S		27	Queens Park Rangers		L1-5	(0-4)	Fenton
34	S	Apr	3	Northampton Town	W1-0		(0-0)	Lavery
35	F		9	Bristol Rovers		W3-1	(0-1)	Jefferson,Tout,Bown
36	S		10	New Brompton		L1-3	(1-1)	Mavin o.g.
37	M		12	Coventry City	W2-1		(2-0)	Lavery,Fleming
38	S		17	Millwall	W3-0		(1-0)	Fleming 2,Bown
39	W		21	Luton Town		L0-1	(0-1)	
40	S		24	Southend United		L2-6	(1-3)	Fleming 2

F A Cup

					Away	H-T	Gate
1	S	Jan	16	Plymouth Argyle	L0-1	(0-1)	21,388

ARCHIE BOWN

scored almost 150 goals at a rate of almost one every other game for Town. But he started as an amateur full-back in the Swindon & District League while working as an apprentice engine fitter. He made his debut for the club in February 1902, but did not sign professional forms until November 1907. Archie was top goalscorer for Town in 1911/12, 1912/13 and 1914/15 and leading scorer on the club's South American tour in 1912 - with eleven goals in eight games. Then, in a 6-0 victory against champions-elect Watford in April 1915, Archie scored all six ! He moved to Bristol City in December 1919 but his final League appearance was not until five months before his 40th birthday in 1922. Archie was to continue playing for Weymouth for another seven years until finally retiring in 1929.

Bannister C	Bown A J W	Chambers P	Fenton F	Fleming H J	Heppinstall F	Hogan J	Innes R	Jefferson R W	Kay H	Lavery J	Ling A S	Lockhead M	Lowe J	Marshall W	Rushton G	Saunders A W	Skillen J	Tout W E B	Walker J	
5	10	6		8	11	9		7	2		1							4	3	**1**
5	10	6		9	11	8		7			1			2				4	3	**2**
5	10	6		9	11	8		7			1			2				4	3	**3**
5	10	6		9	11	8		7			1			2				4	3	**4**
5	10	6		9	11	8		7			1			2				4	3	**5**
	10				11	8		7	2		1	5			9	6		4	3	**6**
5	9			10	11	8		7	2		1	6						4	3	**7**
5	10			8	11			7	2		1	6		3	9			4		**8**
5	10			8	11			7	2		1	6			9			4	3	**9**
5	9	6		10	11	8		7	2		1							4	3	**10**
5	9	6		10	11	8		7	2		1							4	3	**11**
5	9	6		8	11			7	2	10	1							4	3	**12**
5	9	6		8	11			7	2	10	1							4	3	**13**
5	9	6		8	11			7	2	10	1							4	3	**14**
5	9	6		8	11			7	2	10	1							4	3	**15**
5	9	6	11	8				7	2	10	1							4	3	**16**
5	9	6	11	8				7	2	10	1							4	3	**17**
5	9	6	11	8				7	2	10	1							4	3	**18**
5	10	6			11		4	7		8	1			2	9				3	**19**
5	9	6		8	11		4	7		10	1			2					3	**20**
	9		11	8			4	7		10	1	5		2	6				3	**21**
			11	8				7		10	1	5		2	6		9	4	3	**22**
5		6	11	8				7		10	1			2	9			4	3	**23**
5	10	6		8	11			7			1			2	9			4	3	**24**
5	10	6		8	11			7			1			2	9			4	3	**25**
5	10	6			11			7		8	1			2			9	4	3	**26**
5	10	6		8	11			7		9	1			2				4	3	**27**
5	10	6		8	11			7		9	1			2				4	3	**28**
5	10	6		8	11			7			1			2	9			4	3	**29**
5	10	6	11	8				7			1			2	9			4	3	**30**
		6	11	8				7		10	1	5		2	9			4	3	**31**
5	10	6	11	8				7			1			2	9			4	3	**32**
5	10	6	11	8				7			1			2	9			4	3	**33**
5	10	6			11			7		8	1			2	9			4	3	**34**
5	10	6	11					7		8	1			2	9			4	3	**35**
5	10	6	11					7		8	1			2	9			4	3	**36**
5	10		11	8				7		9	1	6		2				4	3	**37**
5	10	6	11	8				7			1			2	9			4	3	**38**
5	10	6	11	8				7			1			2	9			4	3	**39**
	10	6		8				11			1	5	7	2	9			4	3	**40**
35	37	33	15	34	24	9	3	40	14	20	40	9	1	27	20	1	2	37	39	Apps
1	16		2	29	3	9		8		13					7			6		Goals

Opponents 2 goals

Bannister C	Bown A J W	Chambers P	Fenton F	Fleming H J	Heppinstall F	Hogan J	Innes R	Jefferson R W	Kay H	Lavery J	Ling A S	Lockhead M	Lowe J	Marshall W	Rushton G	Saunders A W	Skillen J	Tout W E B	Walker J	
5		6	11	8				7		10	1			2	9			4	3	**1**

No numbers actually worn on shirts

JACK LAVERY

For Final League Table - see page 44

DUBONNET CUP ***THURSDAY MAY 5 1910*** **>>**

Town played in an exhibition match at the Velodrome du Parc des Princes in Paris at the end of the 1909/10 season. Losing semi-finalists in the F.A.Cup, they met Barnsley, who were the losing finalists.

Swindon Town : Skiller, Kay, Walker, Tout, Bannister, Silto, Jefferson, Fleming, Burkinshaw, Bown, Lamb.

Town made two changes from their regular line-up with reserve Sammy Lamb coming in at outside-left and new centre-forward Jack Burkinshaw - only signed three days earlier - replacing Freddy Wheatcroft, who was working as a schoolteacher. Burkinshaw set up both goals for Harold Fleming in a 2-1 victory in front of a modest 7,000 crowd.

The team returned to Swindon with a massive bronze trophy which weighed about 50 kg !

SEASON 1909/10

Southern League Division One
Final League Position : 2nd
Secretary/Manager : Sam Allen

No.	Day	Month	Date	Opponent	Home	Away	H-T	Goalscorers
1	W	Sep	1	Coventry City	W2-1		(2-0)	Fleming 2
2	S		4	Watford		W1-0	(1-0)	Jefferson
3	W		8	Brentford	W4-0		(2-0)	Bannister,Jefferson 2,Bown
4	S		11	Reading	W9-1		(6-1)	Wheatcroft 4,Bannister,McCulloch 2,Tout,Jefferson
5	S		18	Southend United		D1-1	(0-1)	Wheatcroft
6	S		25	Leyton	L0-1		(0-0)	
7	M		27	Brentford		D1-1	(0-1)	Wheatcroft
8	S	Oct	2	Plymouth Argyle		D0-0		
9	M		4	Luton Town		D1-1	(1-1)	Fleming
10	S		9	Southampton	D1-1		(0-1)	Fleming
11	S		16	Croydon Common		W3-0	(1-0)	Fleming,Wheatcroft 2
12	S		23	Millwall	W4-0		(2-0)	Fleming,McCulloch,Jefferson,Bolland
13	S		30	New Brompton		L2-3	(1-0)	Wheatcroft,Fleming
14	S	Nov	6	Northampton Town	L1-4		(0-3)	Jefferson
15	S		13	Queens Park Rangers		W3-0	(1-0)	Lavery,Fleming,Jefferson
16	S		20	Reading		W4-1	(1-1)	Wheatcroft 3,Bown
17	S		27	Exeter City	W3-1		(1-0)	Wheatcroft,Jones o.g.,Fleming
18	S	Dec	4	Crystal Palace		L0-2	(0-0)	
19	S		11	Brighton and Hove Albion	W1-0		(1-0)	Fleming
20	S		18	West Ham United		D2-2	(1-0)	Fleming,Lavery
21	S		25	Portsmouth	W3-1		(1-1)	Jefferson,Bown 2
22	M		27	Portsmouth		L1-3	(1-1)	Wheatcroft
23	Tu		28	Norwich City	W7-1		(3-0)	Fleming 3,Jefferson 2,Tout pen.,Bown
24	S	Jan	1	Coventry City		W2-0	(2-0)	Fleming,Wheatcroft
25	S		8	Watford	D3-3		(2-2)	Bown 2,Wheatcroft
26	S		29	Southend United	W6-1		(2-1)	Bown 2,Wheatcroft,Silto,Tout,Fleming
27	S	Feb	12	Plymouth Argyle	W4-1		(3-0)	Bannister,Wheatcroft,Jefferson 2
28	S		26	Croydon Common	L1-2		(1-2)	Chambers
29	S	Mar	12	New Brompton	W4-1		(2-1)	Lavery,Wheatcroft,Bown,Fleming
30	S		19	Northampton Town		L0-3	(0-1)	
31	F		25	Bristol Rovers		D0-0		
32	M		28	Bristol Rovers	W2-0		(1-0)	Fleming,Bown
33	Tu		29	Norwich City		W3-1	(2-0)	Bolland,Bown,Druce o.g.
34	S	Apr	2	Luton Town	D0-0			
35	M		4	Southampton		D1-1	(0-0)	Wheatcroft
36	S		9	Exeter City		W1-0	(0-0)	Jefferson
37	M		11	Millwall		L0-1	(0-0)	
38	S		16	Crystal Palace	W2-1		(1-0)	Wheatcroft,Bown
39	M		18	Leyton		L2-3	(2-3)	Bown,Fenton
40	S		23	Brighton and Hove Albion		L1-3	(1-2)	Fenton
41	W		27	Queens Park Rangers	W1-0		(1-0)	Tout pen.
42	S		30	West Ham United	W5-0		(3-0)	Silto,Bown 2,Fleming,Wheatcroft

F A Cup

Rd	Day	Month	Date	Opponent	Home	Away	H-T	Goalscorers	Gate
1	S	Jan	15	Crystal Palace		W3-1	(1-1)	Tout,Fleming,Bown	15,000
2	S	Feb	5	Burnley	W2-0		(1-0)	Bown,Fleming	11,000
3	S		19	Tottenham Hotspur	W3-2		(1-1)	Fleming 3	11,818
4	S	Mar	5	Manchester City	W2-0		(0-0)	Jefferson,Bown	14,429
SF	S		26	Newcastle United	*	L0-2	(0-0)		33,000

* Played at White Hart Lane

Southern Charity Cup

Rd	Day	Month	Date	Opponent	Home	Away	H-T	Goalscorers	Gate
1	W	Sep	22	Bristol Rovers	W4-1		(1-0)	McCulloch 2,Bown 2	2,000
2	W	Oct	27	Exeter City	W4-0		(2-0)	Bown, Fleming, Jefferson, Lavery	900
SF	M	Feb	21	Brighton & Hove Albion	*	L0-3	(0-1)		7,000

* Played at Stamford Bridge

For Final League Table - see overleaf >>

Bannister C	Boland W	Bolland W T	Bown A J W	Chambers P	Fenton F	Fleming H J	Hemmings F G	Hornby E J	Jefferson R W	Kay H	Lavery J	McCulloch A	Marshall W	Rushton G	Saunders A W	Silto W A	Skiller L F	Tout W E B	Walker J	Wheatcroft F G	Woolford F O K	
5		11		6		8			7	2	10	9					1	4	3			**1**
5		11		6		8			7			9				4	1	2	3	10		**2**
5		11	10	6		8			7			9				4	1	2	3			**3**
5		11		6		8			7			9				4	1	2	3	10		**4**
5		11		6		8			7			9				4	1	2	3	10		**5**
5		11		6		8			7			9				4	1	2	3	10		**6**
5						8			7	2	11	10				6	1	4	3	9		**7**
5					11	8			7	2		9				6	1	4	3	10		**8**
			10	6	11	8			7	2	9					5	1	4	3			**9**
5					11	10			7		8		2			6	1	4	3	9		**10**
5		11				8			7			9	2			6	1	4	3	10		**11**
5		11				8			7			9	2			6	1	4	3	10		**12**
5		11				8			7	2	9					6	1	4	3	10		**13**
5		11				8			7	2	9					6	1	4	3	10		**14**
5			10			8			7	2	11					6	1	4	3	9		**15**
5			10			8			7	2	11					6	1	4	3	9		**16**
5			10			8			7	2	11					6	1	4	3	9		**17**
5			10			8			7	2	11					6	1	4	3	9		**18**
5			10			8			7	2	11	9				6	1	4	3			**19**
5			10			8			7	2	11					6	1	4	3	9		**20**
5			10	6					7	2	11	9					1	4	3	8		**21**
5			10			8			7	2	11					6	1	4	3	9		**22**
			10	6		8			7	2	11					5	1	4	3	9		**23**
5		11	10			8			7	2						6	1	4	3	9		**24**
5		11	10			8			7	2						6	1	4	3	9		**25**
5			10			8			7	2	11					6	1	4	3	9		**26**
5			10						7	2	11	8				6	1	4	3	9		**27**
5			10	6	11				7	2		8					1	4	3	9		**28**
		7	10	6		8				2	11					5	1	4	3	9		**29**
5		7	10		11					2		8				6	1	4	3	9		**30**
	10	7		6	11		1	5				8	3	9	4						2	**31**
5		7	10	6	11	8				2							1	4	3	9		**32**
		7	10	6	11					2		8	3	9		5	1	4				**33**
5		7	10	6	11					2		8		9			1	4	3			**34**
		11	10						7			8	2	5		6	1	4	3	9		**35**
5		11	10			8			7	2						6	1	4	3	9		**36**
5			10		11						7	8	2	9		6	1	4	3			**37**
			10		11	8			7				2	5		6	1	4	3	9		**38**
5			10		11	8			7	2						6	1	4	3	9		**39**
5			10		11	8				2		7				6	1	4	3	9		**40**
5			10	6	11	8				2				9		4	1	7	3			**41**
5			10		11	8				2	7					6	1	4	3	9		**42**
35	1	20	29	16	15	33	1	1	32	30	20	21	8	7	1	36	41	41	40	33	1	Apps
3		2	16	1	2	19			13		3	3				2		4		22		Goals

Opponents 2 goals

Bannister C	Boland W	Bolland W T	Bown A J W	Chambers P	Fenton F	Fleming H J	Hemmings F G	Hornby E J	Jefferson R W	Kay H	Lavery J	McCulloch A	Marshall W	Rushton G	Saunders A W	Silto W A	Skiller L F	Tout W E B	Walker J	Wheatcroft F G	Woolford F O K	
5			10			8			7	2	11					6	1	4	3	9		**1**
5			10			8			7	2	11					6	1	4	3	9		**2**
5			10			8			7	2	11					6	1	4	3	9		**3**
5			10			8			7	2	11					6	1	4	3	9		**4**
5			10			8			7	2	11					6	1	4	3	9		**SF**
5			5			5			5	5	5					5	5	5	5	5		Apps
			3			5			1									1				Goals

Bannister C	Boland W	Bolland W T	Bown A J W	Chambers P	Fenton F	Fleming H J	Hemmings F G	Hornby E J	Jefferson R W	Kay H	Lavery J	McCulloch A	Marshall W	Rushton G	Saunders A W	Silto W A	Skiller L F	Tout W E B	Walker J	Wheatcroft F G	Woolford F O K	
5		11	10	6		8			7			9				4	1	2	3			**1**
		11	10	6		8			7		9		2			5	1	4	3			**2**
		11	10	6		8			7	2		9				5	1	4	3			**SF**
1		3	3	3		3			3	1	1	2	1			3	3	3	3			Apps
			3			1			1		1	2										Goals

FREDDY WHEATCROFT
(see Page 60)

SEASON 1907/08

	P	W	D	L	F	A	W	D	L	F	A	Pts	G/A
1 Queens Park Rangers	38	12	4	3	46	26	9	5	5	36	31	51	1.44
2 Plymouth Argyle	38	13	5	1	33	13	6	6	7	17	19	49	1.56
3 Millwall	38	10	5	4	24	10	9	3	7	25	22	46	1.53
4 Crystal Palace	38	10	4	5	35	28	7	6	6	19	23	44	1.06
5 SWINDON TOWN	38	12	6	1	41	12	4	4	11	14	28	42	1.38
6 Bristol Rovers	38	11	5	3	36	19	5	5	9	23	37	42	1.05
7 Tottenham Hotpsur	38	11	2	6	33	18	6	5	8	26	30	41	1.23
8 Northampton Town	38	9	5	5	30	17	6	6	7	20	24	41	1.22
9 Portsmouth	38	14	1	4	43	19	3	5	14	20	33	40	1.21
10 West Ham United	38	9	6	4	27	16	6	4	9	20	32	40	0.98
11 Southampton	38	11	5	3	32	21	5	1	13	19	39	38	0.85
12 Reading	38	12	1	6	38	18	3	5	11	17	18	36	1.53
13 Bradford Park Avenue	38	6	7	6	30	27	6	5	8	23	27	36	0.98
14 Watford	38	9	4	6	31	22	3	6	10	16	37	34	0.80
15 Brentford	38	13	3	3	38	15	1	2	16	11	37	33	0.942
16 Norwich City	38	10	4	5	31	16	2	5	12	15	33	33	0.939
17 Brighton & Hove Albion	38	9	6	4	29	19	3	2	14	17	40	32	0.78
18 Luton Town	38	9	4	6	21	17	3	2	14	12	39	30	0.59
19 Leyton	38	6	6	7	30	31	2	5	12	21	42	27	0.70
20 New Brompton	38	7	3	9	24	29	2	4	13	20	46	25	0.59

SEASON 1908/09

	P	W	D	L	F	A	W	D	L	F	A	Pts	G/A
1 Northampton Town	40	15	3	2	51	14	10	2	8	39	31	55	2.00
2 SWINDON TOWN	40	18	0	2	68	15	4	5	11	28	40	49	1.75
3 Southampton	40	13	4	3	44	26	6	6	8	23	32	48	1.16
4 Portsmouth	40	13	5	2	42	17	5	5	10	26	43	46	1.13
5 Bristol Rovers	40	13	5	2	39	20	4	4	12	21	43	43	0.95
6 Exeter City	40	13	2	5	37	28	5	4	11	19	37	42	0.86
7 New Brompton	40	12	2	6	30	22	5	5	10	18	37	41	0.81
8 Reading	40	7	9	4	33	19	4	9	7	27	38	40	1.05
9 Luton Town	40	16	1	3	45	14	1	5	14	14	46	40	0.983
10 Plymouth Argyle	40	9	6	5	28	16	6	4	10	18	31	40	0.979
11 Millwall	40	14	3	3	37	18	2	3	15	22	43	38	0.97
12 Southend United	40	12	6	2	33	14	2	4	14	19	40	38	0.96
13 Leyton	40	13	3	4	35	12	2	5	13	17	43	38	0.95
14 Watford	40	12	6	2	37	16	2	3	15	14	48	37	0.80
15 Queens Park Rangers	40	10	6	4	41	24	2	6	12	11	26	36	1.04
16 Crystal Palace	40	10	4	6	42	23	2	8	10	20	39	36	1.00
17 West Ham United	40	16	1	3	43	13	0	3	17	13	47	36	0.93
18 Brighton & Hove Albion	40	11	4	5	46	20	3	3	14	14	41	35	0.98
19 Norwich City	40	10	8	2	42	21	2	3	15	17	54	35	0.79
20 Coventry City	40	9	4	7	44	37	6	0	14	20	54	34	0.70
21 Brentford	40	10	5	5	40	26	3	2	15	19	48	33	0.80

SEASON 1909/10

	P	W	D	L	F	A	W	D	L	F	A	Pts	G/A
1 Brighton & Hove Albion	42	18	2	1	50	11	5	11	5	39	16	59	3.30
2 SWINDON TOWN	42	15	3	3	63	20	7	7	7	29	26	54	2.00
3 Queens Park Rangers	42	12	5	4	41	28	7	8	6	15	19	51	1.19
4 Northampton Town	42	16	3	2	66	11	6	1	14	24	33	48	2.05
5 Southampton	42	11	7	3	39	25	5	9	7	25	30	48	1.16
6 Portsmouth	42	13	5	3	43	18	7	2	12	27	45	47	1.11
7 Crystal Palace	42	14	2	5	48	19	6	4	11	21	31	46	1.38
8 Coventry City	42	11	6	4	50	24	8	2	11	21	36	46	1.18
9 West Ham United	42	10	7	4	43	23	5	8	8	26	33	45	1.23
10 Leyton	42	11	4	6	45	22	5	7	9	15	24	43	1.30
11 Plymouth Argyle	42	14	5	2	40	8	2	6	13	21	46	43	1.13
12 New Brompton	42	16	2	3	52	21	3	3	15	24	53	43	1.03
13 Bristol Rovers	42	13	5	3	25	8	3	5	13	12	40	42	0.77
14 Brentford	42	13	5	3	33	13	3	4	14	17	45	41	0.86
15 Luton Town	42	10	6	5	45	34	5	5	11	27	58	41	0.78
16 Millwall	42	9	6	6	24	17	6	1	14	21	42	37	0.76
17 Norwich City	42	11	5	5	42	26	2	4	15	17	52	35	0.76
18 Exeter City	42	12	4	5	45	21	2	2	17	15	48	34	0.87
19 Watford	42	8	8	5	32	24	2	5	14	19	52	33	0.67
20 Southend United	42	10	4	7	26	17	2	5	14	25	73	33	0.57
21 Croydon Common	42	8	2	11	29	38	5	3	13	23	54	31	0.57
22 Reading	42	7	6	8	27	25	0	4	17	11	48	24	0.52

SEASON 1910/11

		P	W	D	L	F	A	W	D	L	F	A	Pts	G/A
1	SWINDON TOWN	38	16	2	1	54	9	8	3	8	26	22	53	2.58
2	Northampton Town	38	14	3	2	39	7	4	9	6	15	20	48	2.00
3	Brighton & Hove Albion	38	15	2	2	41	12	5	6	8	17	23	48	1.66
4	Crystal Palace	38	11	5	3	35	23	6	8	5	20	25	47	1.15
5	West Ham United	38	12	6	1	44	17	5	5	9	19	29	45	1.37
6	Queens Park Rangers	38	11	6	2	37	16	2	8	9	15	25	40	1.27
7	Leyton	38	13	3	3	37	15	3	5	11	20	37	40	1.10
8	Plymouth Argyle	38	10	6	3	37	14	5	3	11	17	41	39	0.98
9	Luton Town	38	13	4	2	42	18	2	4	13	25	45	38	1.06
10	Norwich City	38	12	5	2	31	13	3	3	13	15	35	38	0.958
11	Coventry City	38	12	4	3	47	21	4	2	13	18	47	38	0.956
12	Brentford	38	12	5	2	32	13	2	4	13	9	29	37	0.98
13	Exeter City	38	8	5	6	32	29	6	4	9	19	24	37	0.96
14	Watford	38	10	5	4	32	23	3	4	12	17	42	35	0.75
15	Millwall	38	8	3	8	21	20	3	6	10	21	34	31	0.78
16	Bristol Rovers	38	6	6	7	24	23	4	4	11	18	32	30	0.76
17	Southampton	38	8	3	8	25	28	3	5	11	17	39	30	0.63
18	New Brompton	38	10	5	4	19	15	1	3	15	15	50	30	0.52
19	Southend United	38	7	4	8	28	26	3	5	11	19	38	29	0.73
20	Portsmouth	38	6	10	3	21	15	2	1	16	13	38	27	0.64

SEASON 1911/12

		P	W	D	L	F	A	W	D	L	F	A	Pts	G/A
1	Queens Park Rangers	38	12	5	2	36	14	9	6	4	23	21	53	1.69
2	Plymouth Argyle	38	16	2	1	42	7	7	4	8	21	24	52	2.03
3	Northampton Town	38	16	2	1	57	15	6	5	8	25	26	51	2.00
4	SWINDON TOWN	38	14	3	2	52	19	7	3	9	30	31	48	1.64
5	Brighton & Hove Albion	38	15	2	2	54	12	4	7	8	19	23	47	2.09
6	Coventry City	38	14	3	2	47	13	3	5	11	19	41	42	1.22
7	Crystal Palace	38	11	5	3	43	14	4	5	10	27	32	40	1.52
8	Millwall	38	11	6	2	43	19	4	4	11	17	38	40	1.05
9	Watford	38	10	5	4	35	20	3	5	11	21	48	36	0.82
10	Stoke	38	10	3	6	35	26	3	7	9	14	37	36	0.78
11	Reading	38	10	7	2	35	14	1	7	11	8	55	36	0.62
12	Norwich City	38	7	11	1	27	18	3	3	13	13	42	34	0.67
13	West Ham United	38	10	3	6	40	27	3	4	12	24	42	33	0.93
14	Brentford	38	10	5	4	43	18	2	4	13	17	47	33	0.92
15	Exeter City	38	8	6	5	30	22	3	5	11	18	40	33	0.77
16	Southampton	38	9	3	7	29	27	1	8	10	17	36	31	0.73
17	Bristol Rovers	38	7	8	4	24	18	2	5	12	17	44	31	0.66
18	New Brompton	38	7	6	6	23	23	4	3	12	12	49	31	0.49
19	Luton Town	38	7	5	7	32	28	2	5	12	17	33	28	0.80
20	Leyton	38	6	8	5	15	19	1	3	15	12	43	25	0.44

SEASON 1912/13

		P	W	D	L	F	A	W	D	L	F	A	Pts	G/A
1	Plymouth Argyle	38	15	2	2	47	9	7	4	8	30	25	50	2.26
2	SWINDON TOWN	38	13	5	1	44	16	7	3	9	22	25	48	1.61
3	West Ham United	38	11	6	2	39	15	7	6	6	27	31	48	1.43
4	Queens Park Rangers	38	14	4	1	33	10	4	6	9	13	25	46	1.31
5	Crystal Palace	38	13	3	3	38	13	4	8	7	17	23	45	1.53
6	Millwall	38	14	0	5	36	17	5	7	7	26	26	45	1.44
7	Exeter City	38	13	3	3	29	16	5	5	9	19	28	44	1.09
8	Reading	38	12	3	4	34	20	5	5	9	25	35	42	1.07
9	Brighton & Hove Albion	38	12	5	2	39	19	1	7	11	9	28	38	1.02
10	Northampton Town	38	11	4	4	42	17	1	8	10	19	31	36	1.27
11	Portsmouth	38	11	5	3	28	15	3	3	13	13	34	36	0.84
12	Merthyr Town	38	8	9	2	27	18	4	3	12	15	42	36	0.70
13	Coventry City	38	9	4	6	42	27	4	4	11	11	32	34	0.90
14	Watford	38	8	4	7	28	24	4	6	9	15	26	34	0.86
15	Gillingham	38	7	7	5	19	21	5	3	11	17	32	34	0.68
16	Bristol Rovers	38	9	6	4	37	23	3	3	13	18	41	33	0.86
17	Southampton	38	7	7	5	28	25	3	4	12	12	47	31	0.56
18	Norwich City	38	8	7	4	26	17	2	2	15	13	33	29	0.78
19	Brentford	38	10	3	6	27	17	1	2	16	15	38	27	0.76
20	Stoke	38	8	3	8	21	17	2	1	16	18	58	24	0.52

SEASON 1910/11

Southern League Division One
Final League Position : Champions
Secretary/Manager : Sam Allen

No	Day	Month	Date	Opponent	Home	Away	H-T	Goalscorers
1	S	Sep	3	Crystal Palace	D0-0			
2	S		10	Brentford		D1-1	(0-0)	Fleming
3	S		17	Leyton	W2-0		(2-0)	Fleming,Jefferson
4	S		24	Watford		W3-1	(0-0)	Lamb,Wheatcroft 2
5	S	Oct	1	Plymouth Argyle	W4-0		(1-0)	Bown 3,Lamb
6	S		8	Southampton		W4-0	(2-0)	Fleming 2,Wheatcroft,Jefferson
7	S		15	Southend United	W4-0		(0-0)	Fleming,Bown 2,Wheatcroft
8	S		22	Coventry City		D2-2	(1-2)	Wheatcroft 2
9	S		29	New Brompton	W5-0		(2-0)	Fleming 2,Bown,Tout pen.,Bolland
10	S	Nov	5	Millwall		L0-2	(0-2)	
11	S		12	Queens Park Rangers	W2-1		(0-1)	Fleming,Tout
12	S		19	West Ham United		L0-1	(0-0)	
13	S		26	Luton Town	W4-1		(2-0)	Jefferson,Burkinshaw,Rushton,Bown
14	S	Dec	3	Portsmouth		W2-1	(0-0)	Warner o.g.,Burkinshaw
15	S		10	Northampton Town	W2-1		(0-0)	Burkinshaw,Wheatcroft
16	S		17	Brighton and Hove Albion		W1-0	(0-0)	Burkinshaw
17	S		24	Exeter City	L0-1		(0-1)	
18	M		26	Norwich City		W2-1	(2-1)	Jefferson,Tout pen.
19	Tu		27	Norwich City	W5-1		(3-1)	Fleming 3,Wheatcroft,Bown
20	S		31	Crystal Palace		W5-2	(3-2)	Wheatcroft 2,Fleming,Jefferson,Silto
21	S	Jan	7	Brentford	W3-0		(2-0)	Fleming,Wheatcroft,Bown
22	S		21	Leyton		L1-3	(1-3)	Fleming
23	S		28	Watford	W5-1		(3-0)	Burkinshaw 2,Fleming,Bown,Tout pen.
24	S	Feb	11	Southampton	W5-1		(1-0)	Bown,Burkinshaw 2,Jefferson,Wheatcroft
25	S		18	Southend United		W1-0	(1-0)	Bown
26	S	Mar	4	New Brompton		L0-1	(0-1)	
27	S		18	Queens Park Rangers		L0-1	(0-0)	
28	S		25	West Ham United	W4-1		(1-1)	Tout pen.,Wheatcroft 2,Fleming
29	W		29	Plymouth Argyle		D1-1	(1-0)	Fleming
30	S	Apr	1	Luton Town		L1-2	(0-1)	Tout pen.
31	W		5	Millwall	W1-0		(1-0)	Tout pen.
32	S		8	Portsmouth	W2-1		(2-0)	Bown,Jefferson
33	F		14	Bristol Rovers		L0-1	(0-0)	
34	S		15	Northampton Town		W1-0	(1-0)	Fleming
35	M		17	Bristol Rovers	D0-0			
36	S		22	Brighton and Hove Albion	W3-0		(2-0)	Tout pen.,Wheatcroft,Fleming
37	W		26	Coventry City	W3-0		(0-0)	Rushton,Bown 2
38	S		29	Exeter City		L1-2	(1-2)	Wheatcroft

F A Cup

No	Day	Month	Date	Opponent	Home	Away	H-T	Goalscorers	Gate
1	S	Jan	14	Notts County	W3-1		(2-0)	Bown 2,Fleming	12,332
2	S	Feb	4	Woolwich Arsenal	W1-0		(0-0)	Jefferson	14,861
3	S		25	Darlington		W3-0	(2-0)	Bolland,Fleming,Jefferson	9,000
4	S	Mar	11	Chelsea		L1-3	(0-2)	Bown	77,952

Southern Charity Cup

No	Day	Month	Date	Opponent	Home	Away	H-T	Goalscorers	Gate
1	W	Sep	7	Plymouth Argyle		W2-1	(0-1)	Jefferson,Tout	4,500
2	W	Oct	26	Bristol Rovers	W6-2		(3-1)	Bown 2,Tout pen.,Burkinshaw 3	600
SF	M	Nov	28	Queens Park Rangers	^	D1-1	(1-0)	Burkinshaw	4,000
Rp	M	Dec	12	Queens Park Rangers	*	D1-1	(1-0)	Tout	2,000
Rp	Tu	Apr	4	Queens Park Rangers	*	D0-0			4,000
Rp	Tu		18	Queens Park Rangers	**	W3-2	(0-2)	Lamb,Mabberley 2	5,414
F	M		24	Brighton and Hove Albion	*	D0-0			3,000
Rp	Th		27	Brighton and Hove Albion	*	W1-0	(1-0)	Bown	1,500

^ Played at Stamford Bridge
* Played at Craven Cottage
** Played at White Hart Lane

Bannister C	Boland W	Bolland W T	Bown A J W	Burkinshaw J D L	Chambers P	Fleming H J	Hemmings F G	Hicks F	Jefferson R W	Kay H	Lamb S	Langley A E	Mabberley I	Marshall W	Morrison J	Rushton G	Silto W A	Skiller L F	Tout W E B	Walker J	Wheatcroft F G	Woolford F O K	
5			10			8			7	2	11						6	1	4	3	9		**1**
5			10			8			7	2	11						6	1	4	3	9		**2**
5			10			8			7	2	11						6	1	4	3	9		**3**
5			10			8			7	2	11						6	1	4	3	9		**4**
5			10			8			7	2	11						6	1	4	3	9		**5**
5			10			8			7	2	11						6	1	4	3	9		**6**
5		11	10			8			7	2							6	1	4	3	9		**7**
5			10			8			7	2	11						6	1	4	3	9		**8**
5		11	10			8			7	2							6	1	4	3	9		**9**
5		11	10			8			7	2							6	1	4	3	9		**10**
5		11	10	9		8			7	2							6	1	4	3			**11**
5		11	10			8			7	2							6	1	4	3	9		**12**
5		11	10	9					7	2						8	6	1	4	3			**13**
5		11		9		8			7	2							6	1	4	3	10		**14**
5		11		9		8			7	2							6	1	4	3	10		**15**
5				9		8			7	2	11						6	1	4	3	10		**16**
5						8			7	2	11					9	6	1	4	3	10		**17**
5		11	10			8			7	2							6	1	4	3	9		**18**
5		11	10			8			7	2							6	1	4	3	9		**19**
5			10			8			7	2	11						6	1	4	3	9		**20**
5		11	10			8			7	2							6	1	4	3	9		**21**
5		11	10			8	1		7	2							6		4	3	9		**22**
5		11	10	9		8	1		7	2							6		4	3			**23**
5		11	10	8	6		1		7	2									4	3	9		**24**
		11	10	8					7	2					6	5		1	4	3	9		**25**
5		11	10	8						2						7	6	1	4	3	9		**26**
5		11	10	8					7	2							6	1	4		9	3	**27**
5		11	10			8			7	2							6	1	4	3	9		**28**
5		11	10	9		8			7	2							6	1	4	3			**29**
5			10			8			7	2	11						6	1	4		9	3	**30**
5			10	9		8			7	2	11				6			1	4	3			**31**
5			10			8			7	2	11				6			1	4	3	9		**32**
5			10	8					7	2	11						6	1	4	3	9		**33**
5			10			8			7	2	11						6	1	4	3	9		**34**
5			10			8			7	2	11						6	1	4	3	9		**35**
5			10			8			7	2	11						6	1	4	3	9		**36**
5			10							2	11		7			9	6	1	4	8		3	**37**
5			10		6					2	11		7			8		1	4	3	9		**38**
37	0	19	34	13	2	30	3	0	35	38	19	0	2	0	3	6	33	35	38	36	32	3	Apps
		1	15	8		19			7		2					2	1		8		16		Goals

Opponents 1 goal

Bannister C	Boland W	Bolland W T	Bown A J W	Burkinshaw J D L	Chambers P	Fleming H J	Hemmings F G	Hicks F	Jefferson R W	Kay H	Lamb S	Langley A E	Mabberley I	Marshall W	Morrison J	Rushton G	Silto W A	Skiller L F	Tout W E B	Walker J	Wheatcroft F G	Woolford F O K	
5		11	10			8			7	2							6	1	4	3	9		**1**
5		11	10	9		8	1		7	2							6		4	3			**2**
5		11	10			8			7	2							6	1	4	3	9		**3**
5		11	10			8			7	2							6	1	4	3	9		**4**
4		4	4	1		4	1		4	4							4	3	4	4	3		Apps
		1	3			2			2														Goals

Bannister C	Boland W	Bolland W T	Bown A J W	Burkinshaw J D L	Chambers P	Fleming H J	Hemmings F G	Hicks F	Jefferson R W	Kay H	Lamb S	Langley A E	Mabberley I	Marshall W	Morrison J	Rushton G	Silto W A	Skiller L F	Tout W E B	Walker J	Wheatcroft F G	Woolford F O K	
5			10	9		8			7	2	11						6	1	4	3			**1**
5		11	10	9					7	2						8	6	1	4	3			**2**
		11	10	9					7					2	5	8	6	1	4	3			**SF**
		11	10	9	6				7						5	8		1	4	3		2	**Rp**
	10	11			6		1					8	7	2	5	4					9	3	**Rp**
		7	10		6			4			11		9	2	5	8		1				3	**Rp**
		11	10	9		8			7	2					5	4	6	1		3			**F**
5			10							2	11		7			8	6	1	4	3	9		**Rp**
3	1	6	7	5	3	2	1	1	5	4	3	1	3	3	5	7	5	7	5	6	2	3	Apps
			3	4					1		1		2						3				Goals

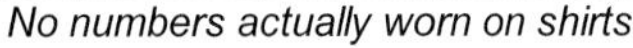

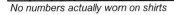

No numbers actually worn on shirts

HARRY KAY

BILLY TOUT

For Final League Table - see previous page <<

SEASON 1911/12

Southern League Division One
Final League Position : 4th
Secretary/Manager : Sam Allen

No	Day	Month	Date	Opponents	Home	Away	H-T	Goalscorers
1	S	Sep	2	Leyton		W3-0	(1-0)	Bown,Fleming,Jefferson
2	S		9	Norwich City	W5-3		(3-1)	Tout pen.,Wheatcroft,Jefferson,Bown,Fleming
3	S		16	Crystal Palace		D2-2	(1-0)	Bown 2
4	S		23	Southampton	W2-1		(0-0)	Wheatcroft,Bown
5	S		30	Plymouth Argyle		D1-1	(1-1)	Bown
6	S	Oct	7	Reading	W3-0		(2-0)	Fleming,Bown,Jefferson
7	S		14	Watford		L0-2	(0-2)	
8	S		21	New Brompton	W5-0		(2-0)	Tout,Fleming 2,Bown,Wheatcroft
9	S		28	Exeter City		W4-1	(3-1)	Fleming 2,Lamb,Wheatcroft
10	S	Nov	4	Brentford	W2-0		(0-0)	Tout pen.,Jefferson
11	S		11	Queens Park Rangers		W3-1	(1-0)	Bown,Fleming,Lamb
12	S		18	Millwall	W4-1		(2-0)	Fleming 2,Bown,Wheatcroft
13	S		25	West Ham United		W2-0	(1-0)	Tout pen.,Bown
14	S	Dec	2	Bristol Rovers	W2-0		(1-0)	Jefferson,Fleming
15	S		9	Luton Town	W4-2		(0-1)	Lamb,Fleming.Bown,Wheatcroft
16	S		16	Northampton Town		L0-4	(0-2)	
17	S		23	Brighton and Hove Albion	L1-3		(0-1)	Jefferson
18	M		25	Stoke	W3-0		(3-0)	Jefferson 2,Tout
19	Tu		26	Stoke		W4-1	(1-0)	Fleming,Bown 2,Jefferson
20	W		27	Plymouth Argyle	W2-0		(1-0)	Wheatcroft,Bown
21	S		30	Leyton	W6-2		(4-1)	McCulloch 2,Jefferson 2,Bown,Fleming
22	S	Jan	6	Norwich City		L3-4	(2-1)	Fleming,Bown,Tout pen.
23	S		20	Crystal Palace	W2-1		(0-1)	Lamb,Fleming
24	S		27	Southampton		W3-1	(2-0)	Wheatcroft 2,Bown
25	S	Feb	10	Reading		L0-2	(0-1)	
26	S		17	Watford	W4-0		(2-0)	Burkinshaw,Tout pen.,Lamb,Bown
27	S	Mar	2	Exeter City	L0-1		(0-0)	
28	S		16	Queens Park Rangers	D1-1		(1-0)	Bown
29	S		23	Millwall		L0-1	(0-1)	
30	F	Apr	5	Coventry City	D2-2		(0-1)	Jefferson 2
31	S		6	Bristol Rovers		L0-3	(0-0)	
32	M		8	Coventry City		D1-1	(0-0)	Wheatcroft
33	S		13	Luton Town		W3-0	(1-0)	Lamb 2,Bown
34	W		17	New Brompton		L1-3	(0-2)	Bown
35	S		20	Northampton Town	D1-1		(1-1)	Silto pen.
36	M		22	West Ham United	W3-1		(1-1)	McCulloch 2,Bown
37	W		24	Brentford		L0-2	(0-0)	
38	S		27	Brighton and Hove Albion		L0-2	(0-0)	

F A Cup

Rd	Day	Month	Date	Opponents	Home	Away	H-T	Goalscorers	Gate
1	S	Jan	13	Sutton Junction	W5-0		(3-0)	Fleming 4,Bown	12,000
2	S	Feb	3	Notts County	W2-0		(1-0)	Jefferson,Wheatcroft	13,780
3	S		24	West Ham United		D1-1	(1-1)	Fleming	18,000
3R	W		28	West Ham United	W4-0		(2-0)	Glover 2 o.g.,Jefferson,Wheatcroft	13,328
4	S	Mar	9	Everton	W2-1		(2-0)	Jefferson,Bown	13,989
SF	S		30	Barnsley	+	D0-0			48,057
Rp	W	Apr	3	Barnsley	*	L0-1	(0-0)		18,000

\+ Played at Stamford Bridge (after extra time)
* Played at Meadow Lane

F A Charity Shield

Rd	Day	Month	Date	Opponents	Result	H-T	Goalscorers	Gate
F	M	Sep	25	Manchester United	L4-8	(3-4)	Fleming,Wheatcroft,Tout pen.,Jefferson	12,000

Played at Stamford Bridge

Southern Charity Cup

Rd	Day	Month	Date	Opponents	Result	H-T	Goalscorers	Gate
1	W	Sep	20	Exeter City	L0-2	(0-0)		1,700

Bannister C	Bolland W T	Bown A J W	Burkinshaw J D L	Chambers P	Fleming H J	Handley F B	Hemmings F G	Hicks F	Hill A V W P	Jefferson R W	Kay H	Lamb S	Lochhead M	McCulloch A	Rushton G	Silto W A	Skiller L F	Tout W E B	Walker J	Wheatcroft F G	
		10			8	6				7	2	11				5	1	4	3	9	**1**
		10			8	6				7	2	11				5	1	4	3	9	**2**
5		10			8	4				7	2	11				6	1	3		9	**3**
5	11	10			8	4				7	2					6	1	3		9	**4**
5	7	10				4					2	11		8		6	1	3		9	**5**
		10			8	4				7	2	11			5	6	1	3		9	**6**
5		10			8					7	2	11				6	1	4	3	9	**7**
5		10			8					7	2	11				6	1	4	3	9	**8**
5		10			8					7	2	11				6	1	4	3	9	**9**
5		10			8					7	2	11				6	1	4	3	9	**10**
5		10			8					7	2	11				6	1	4	3	9	**11**
5		10			8					7	2	11				6	1	4	3	9	**12**
		10			8	5				7	2	11				6	1	4	3	9	**13**
		10			8	5				7	2	11				6	1	4	3	9	**14**
5	7	10			8						2	11				6	1	4	3	9	**15**
	7	10				5				8	2	11				6	1	4	3	9	**16**
		10			8	5				7	2	11				6	1	4	3	9	**17**
		10				6				7	2	11		8		5	1	4	3	9	**18**
		10			11	6				7	2			8		5	1	4	3	9	**19**
		10			11	6				7	2			8		5	1	4	3	9	**20**
		10			8	6				7	2	11		9		5	1	4	3		**21**
		10			8	6			2	7		11				5	1	4	3	9	**22**
		10			8	6				7	2	11		9		5	1	4	3		**23**
5		10								7	2	11		8		6	1	4	3	9	**24**
		10				6				7	2	11		8		5	1	4	3	9	**25**
		10	8			6				7	2	11				5	1	4	3	9	**26**
	11	10	8			6			3	7	2					5	1	4		9	**27**
5		10	8			6			3	7	2	11					1	4		9	**28**
	7	10	8			6		4	3		2	11	5				1			9	**29**
		10	9	6				4	2	7		11	5	8			1		3		**30**
	11	10	9			6		4	2	7			5	8			1		3		**31**
		10				4			2	7		11	6	8		5	1		3	9	**32**
		10	8	6						7	2	11	4			5	1		3	9	**33**
		10	9					4		7	2	11	6	8		5	1		3		**34**
		10	8	6			1			7	2	11	4			5			3	9	**35**
	7	10	9	6			1				2	11	4	8		5			3		**36**
		10	9					4		7	2	11	6	8		5	1		3		**37**
		10	8	6					3	7	2	11		4			1		5	9	**38**
12	8	38	12	5	20	23	2	5	8	34	34	33	9	15	1	33	36	28	31	31	Apps
		23	1		16					13		7		4		1		7		10	Goals

BOB
JEFFERSON

Bannister C	Bolland W T	Bown A J W	Burkinshaw J D L	Chambers P	Fleming H J	Handley F B	Hemmings F G	Hicks F	Hill A V W P	Jefferson R W	Kay H	Lamb S	Lochhead M	McCulloch A	Rushton G	Silto W A	Skiller L F	Tout W E B	Walker J	Wheatcroft F G	
		10			8	6				7	2	11				5	1	4	3	9	**1**
		10			8	6				7	2	11				5	1	4	3	9	**2**
		10			8	6				7	2	11				5	1	4	3	9	**3**
	11	10			8	6				7	2					5	1	4	3	9	**3R**
		10			8	6				7	2	11				5	1	4	3	9	**4**
		10		6	8	4				7	2	11				5	1		3	9	**SF**
		10	8	6		4				7	2	11				5	1		3	9	**Rp**
	1	7	1	2	6	7				7	7	6				7	7	5	7	7	Apps
		2			5					3										2	Goals

Opponents 2 goals

SAMMY
LAMB

Bannister C	Bolland W T	Bown A J W	Burkinshaw J D L	Chambers P	Fleming H J	Handley F B	Hemmings F G	Hicks F	Hill A V W P	Jefferson R W	Kay H	Lamb S	Lochhead M	McCulloch A	Rushton G	Silto W A	Skiller L F	Tout W E B	Walker J	Wheatcroft F G	
5		10			8	4				7	2	11				6	1	3		9	**F**

Bannister C	Bolland W T	Bown A J W	Burkinshaw J D L	Chambers P	Fleming H J	Handley F B	Hemmings F G	Hicks F	Hill A V W P	Jefferson R W	Kay H	Lamb S	Lochhead M	McCulloch A	Rushton G	Silto W A	Skiller L F	Tout W E B	Walker J	Wheatcroft F G	
5	11	10	9		8	4				7	2					6	1	3			**1**

No numbers actually worn on shirts

For Final League Table - see page 45

SEASON 1912/13

Southern League Division One
Final League Position : 2nd
Secretary/Manager : Sam Allen

					Home	Away	H-T	Goalscorers
1	Th	Sep	5	Coventry City		L1-2	(1-2)	Bown
2	S		7	Crystal Palace	W1-0		(1-0)	Tout pen.
3	W		11	Coventry City	W1-0		(1-0)	Bown
4	S		14	Plymouth Argyle		L1-3	(1-2)	Tout pen.
5	S		21	Southampton	W5-0		(1-0)	Burkinshaw 2,Wheatcroft,Bown 2
6	S		28	Reading		W1-0	(0-0)	Bolland
7	S	Oct	5	Norwich City	W3-0		(1-0)	Bown 2,Burkinshaw
8	S		12	Gillingham		D0-0		
9	S		19	Northampton Town	W2-1		(2-0)	Jefferson,Burkinshaw
10	S		26	Queens Park Rangers		L0-2	(0-1)	
11	S	Nov	2	Brentford	W2-0		(0-0)	Bown,Wheatcroft
12	S		9	Millwall		W1-0	(0-0)	Batty
13	S		16	Bristol Rovers	D2-2		(0-1)	Tout pen.,Batty
14	S		23	Stoke		D1-1	(0-1)	Batty
15	S		30	Portsmouth		W2-1	(0-1)	Batty,Burkinshaw
16	S	Dec	7	Exeter City	D2-2		(1-2)	Burkinshaw,Tout pen.
17	S		14	West Ham United		L1-4	(1-2)	Wheatcroft
18	S		21	Brighton and Hove Albion	W4-0		(2-0)	Jefferson 2,Tout,Lamb
19	W		25	Watford	L1-2		(0-2)	Tout pen.
20	Th		26	Watford		L1-3	(0-0)	Wheatcroft
21	S		28	Crystal Palace		L0-1	(0-1)	
22	S	Jan	4	Plymouth Argyle	D2-2		(1-1)	Bown 2
23	S		18	Southampton		L0-2	(0-1)	
24	S		25	Reading	D1-1		(1-1)	Lamb
25	S	Feb	8	Norwich City		W2-0	(1-0)	Fleming,Wheatcroft
26	S		15	Gillingham	W2-1		(2-0)	Batty,Wheatcroft
27	S	Mar	1	Queens Park Rangers	W4-1		(3-0)	Wheatcroft,Fleming,Tout pen.,Bown
28	S		8	Brentford		W3-0	(2-0)	Fleming,Lamb,Bown
29	S		15	Millwall	W2-1		(2-0)	Wheatcroft,Jefferson
30	F		21	Merthyr Town	W3-0		(2-0)	Lamb,Bown,Tout pen.
31	S		22	Bristol Rovers		W4-1	(2-1)	Fleming 3,Bown
32	M		24	Merthyr Town		L0-1	(0-1)	
33	S		29	Stoke	W3-2		(2-0)	Fleming 2,Milne o.g.
34	S	Apr	5	Portsmouth	W3-0		(2-0)	Jefferson,Wheatcroft,Tout
35	S		12	Exeter City		W3-1	(3-1)	Bown,Wheatcroft 2
36	Th		17	Northampton Town		D1-1	(1-0)	Tout pen.
37	S		19	West Ham United	D1-1		(1-1)	Fleming
38	S		26	Brighton and Hove Albion		L0-2	(0-2)	

F A Cup

					Home	Away	H-T	Goalscorers	Gate
1	S	Jan	11	Rochdale		W2-0	(0-0)	Bown,Jefferson	8,801
2	S	Feb	1	Huddersfield Town		W2-1	(1-0)	Wheatcroft,Bown	17,585
3	S		22	Sunderland		L2-4	(0-3)	Fleming,Wheatcroft	24,865

Southern Charity Cup

					Home	Away	H-T	Goalscorers	Gate
1	W	Nov	27	Bristol Rovers	W3-2		(3-1)	Tout pen.,Jefferson 2	
2	W	Feb	12	Exeter City		L0-2	(0-1)		2,500

LEN SKILLER
was a Cornishman, whose mother came from the Scilly Isles and his father from Alabama in the United States. Len learned his trade in the east end of London, but joined Town in July 1909 afer a year at Aston Villa. He missed few games between then and 1915 and consequently was involved in the club's many achievements during that time - twice Southern League champions, twice runners-up, two F.A.Cup semi-finals and a quarter-final. Town only took the second of those championships - in 1914 - on goal average, and had Len not made an outstanding save in the dying minutes of the final game at Cardiff, Palace would have pipped them to the title. He retired in 1922.

Batty W	Bolland W T	Bown A J W	Burkinshaw J D L	Cousin D P	Davies A S	Fleming H J	Giles C	Handley F B	Hasell A A	Hicks F	Jefferson R W	Kay H	Kennedy J J	Lamb S	Lee J L	Lochhead M	McCulloch A	Maunders G C	Silto W A	Skiller L F	Tout W E B	Walker J	Ward A	Wheatcroft F G	Woolford F O K	
		10	9								7	2	5	11			8		6	1	4	3				**1**
		10									7	2	5	11			8		6	1	4	3		9		**2**
	11	10	9								7	2	5				8		6	1	4	3				**3**
	11	10						6			7	2					8		5	1	4	3		9		**4**
	11	10	9					6			7	2							5	1	4	3		8		**5**
	11	10	9					6			7	2							5	1	4	3		8		**6**
	11	10	9					6			7	2							5	1	4	3		8		**7**
	11	10	9					6			7	2							5	1	4	3		8		**8**
	11	10	9					6			7	2							5	1	4	3		8		**9**
		10	9					6			7	2		11					5	1	4	3		8		**10**
		10	9								7	2		11		6			5	1	4	3		8		**11**
8		10									7	2	5	11					6	1	4	3		9		**12**
8			9								7	2	5	11					6	1	4	3		10		**13**
10	7		9					6				2	5	11	8					1	4	3				**14**
10	11		9					6			7	2	5							1	4	3		8		**15**
10			9					6			7	2		11					5	1	4			8	3	**16**
10			9					6			7	2		11					5	1	4	3		8		**17**
8		10									7	2	5	11					6	1	4	3		9		**18**
		10	8					6			7	2	5	11						1	4	3		9		**19**
		10	8					6			7	2	5	11						1	4	3		9		**20**
	11		9				2				7		5		8			10	6	1	4	3				**21**
		10	9				2				7		5	11	8				6	1	4	3				**22**
		10	8					6			7	2		11		5				1	4	3		9		**23**
		10				8		4			7	2		11		5			6	1		3		9		**24**
		10				8	2	6			7			11					5	1	4	3		9		**25**
10				2		8		6			7			11					5	1	4	3		9		**26**
		10				8		6			7	2		11					5	1	4	3		9		**27**
		10				8		6			7	2		11					5	1	4	3		9		**28**
8		10						6			7	2		11		3			5	1	4			9		**29**
8		10						6			7	2	5	11		3				1	4			9		**30**
	11	10				8		6			7	2							5	1	4	3		9		**31**
		10				8		6			7	2		11					5	1	4	3		9		**32**
		10				8	2	6			7		5	11						1	4	3		9		**33**
10			8				2	6			7			11		3			5	1	4			9		**34**
		10				8	2	6			7			11		3			5	1	4			9		**35**
	11	10				8	2	6			7					3			5	1	4			9		**36**
	11	10				8	2	6	1		7					3			5		4			9		**37**
	11	10				8	2	6			7					3			5	1	4			9		**38**
11	14	30	20	1	0	12	9	29	1	0	37	28	14	25	3	10	4	1	31	37	37	30	0	33	1	Apps
5	1	14	6			9					5			4							10			11		Goals

Opponents 1 goal

Batty W	Bolland W T	Bown A J W	Burkinshaw J D L	Cousin D P	Davies A S	Fleming H J	Giles C	Handley F B	Hasell A A	Hicks F	Jefferson R W	Kay H	Kennedy J J	Lamb S	Lee J L	Lochhead M	McCulloch A	Maunders G C	Silto W A	Skiller L F	Tout W E B	Walker J	Ward A	Wheatcroft F G	Woolford F O K	
		10	8								7	2		11		5			6	1	4	3		9		**1**
		10				8		6			7	2		11					5	1	4	3		9		**2**
		10				8		6			7	2		11					5	1	4	3		9		**3**
		3	1			2		2			3	3		3		1			3	3	3	3		3		Apps
		2				1					1													2		Goals

Batty W	Bolland W T	Bown A J W	Burkinshaw J D L	Cousin D P	Davies A S	Fleming H J	Giles C	Handley F B	Hasell A A	Hicks F	Jefferson R W	Kay H	Kennedy J J	Lamb S	Lee J L	Lochhead M	McCulloch A	Maunders G C	Silto W A	Skiller L F	Tout W E B	Walker J	Ward A	Wheatcroft F G	Woolford F O K	
10	11		9					6			7				8	5				1	4	3			2	**1**
10	7		8		11		2			4			5			6				1			9		3	**2**
2	2		2		1		1	1		1	1		1		1	2				2	1	1	1		2	Apps
											2										1					Goals

No numbers actually worn on shirts

For Final League Table - see page 45

SEASON 1913/14

Southern League Division One
Final League Position : Champions
Secretary/Manager : Sam Allen

No	Day	Month	Date	Opponents	Home	Away	H-T	Goalscorers
1	M	Sep	1	Queens Park Rangers	W3-0		(1-0)	Jefferson 2,Fleming
2	S		6	West Ham United		W3-2	(1-2)	Wheatcroft,Tout pen.,Fleming
3	S		13	Plymouth Argyle	W4-1		(4-0)	Bown 2,Fleming,Bolland
4	S		20	Southampton		W2-1	(2-1)	Bown,Wheatcroft
5	S		27	Reading	W3-0		(0-0)	Fleming 3
6	S	Oct	4	Crystal Palace		W1-0	(0-0)	Wheatcroft
7	S		11	Coventry City	W6-1		(1-1)	Batty,Tout pen.,Bown,Wheatcroft,Long 2
8	S		18	Watford		W2-1	(1-0)	Batty 2
9	S		25	Norwich City	W2-0		(2-0)	Jefferson,Bown
10	S	Nov	1	Gillingham		W3-2	(1-2)	Batty 3
11	S		8	Northampton Town	D1-1		(1-0)	Batty
12	S		15	Southend United		L0-2	(0-0)	
13	S		22	Brighton and Hove Albion	D1-1		(0-0)	Jefferson
14	S		29	Portsmouth		D1-1	(1-0)	Jefferson
15	S	Dec	6	Millwall	W2-0		(0-0)	Bown,Tout pen.
16	S		13	Exeter City		W2-0	(1-0)	Fleming,Bown
17	S		20	Cardiff City	L1-2		(1-1)	Fleming
18	Th		25	Bristol Rovers		L2-5	(1-4)	Wheatcroft,Bown
19	F		26	Bristol Rovers	W5-0		(3-0)	Bown,Bolland,Fleming,Wheatcroft,Jefferson
20	S		27	West Ham United	W4-1		(1-0)	Fleming 2,Wheatcroft,Tout
21	S	Jan	3	Plymouth Argyle		L1-3	(1-1)	Bolland
22	S		17	Southampton	W3-0		(2-0)	Fleming 2,Jefferson
23	S		24	Reading		L0-2	(0-2)	
24	S	Feb	7	Crystal Palace	L0-2		(0-0)	
25	S		14	Coventry City		D1-1	(1-0)	Bown
26	S		21	Watford	W3-0		(0-0)	Bown 2,Tout pen.
27	S		28	Norwich City		W2-1	(0-1)	Fleming,Tout
28	S	Mar	7	Gillingham	W5-1		(2-1)	Tout pen.,Bown 2,Wheatcroft,Batty
29	Th		12	Queens Park Rangers		L2-4	(0-2)	Bolland,Jefferson
30	S		14	Northampton Town		L0-1	(0-0)	
31	S		21	Southend United	W5-0		(1-0)	Wheatcroft,Bown 3,Fleming
32	S		28	Brighton and Hove Albion		L0-2	(0-2)	
33	S	Apr	4	Portsmouth	W5-0		(3-0)	Rogers 4,Tout pen.
34	F		10	Merthyr Town		D1-1	(1-0)	Bown
35	S		11	Millwall		D1-1	(0-0)	Batty
36	M		13	Merthyr Town	W3-0		(1-0)	Fleming 3
37	S		18	Exeter City	D1-1		(0-1)	Batty
38	S		25	Cardiff City		D0-0		

F A Cup

No	Day	Month	Date	Opponents	Home	Away	H-T	Goalscorers	Gate
1	S	Jan	10	Manchester United	W1-0		(0-0)	Fleming	18,107
2	S		31	Bolton Wanderers		L2-4	(1-1)	Batty 2	50,453

Southern Charity Cup

No	Day	Month	Date	Opponents	Home	Away	H-T	Goalscorers	Gate
1	M	Nov	23	Coventry City		L0-2	(0-1)		1,000

DAVE ROGERS
was born in Cheadle and was stationed at Bulford Camp with the Royal Field Artillery when he signed amateur forms for Town in March 1914. He made a sensational start to his career at the County Ground, firing a hat-trick on his debut for the reserves - and then repeated the feat in the first half-hour of his League debut ! He returned from the Great War to finish the 1919/20 season as the club's top scorer. Despite being five goals behind George Travers at Easter, Dave hit six in the last four games. This alerted the England selectors, who invited him to join a tour to South Africa in the summer. Although he bagged five goals, Dave waited in vain for a further call-up. He remained with Town until 1926, but spent the latter years at wing-half. After retiring in 1928, Dave became a steward at the High Street Club in Old Town.

Batty W	Bolland W T	Bown A J W	Brewer W A	Davies A S	Fellows H A J	Fleming H J	Giles C	Handley F B	Hasell A A	Hayward R	Jefferson R W	Kay H	Lee J L	Lochhead M	Long E J	McRobbie A S	Rogers D	Silto W A	Simms S	Skiller L F	Stanners J G	Tout W E B	Weston A M	Wheatcroft F G	
	11	10				8		6			7	2		5		3			9	1		4			**1**
	11	10				8		6			7	2		5		3				1		4		9	**2**
	11	10				8		6			7	2				3		5		1		4		9	**3**
	11	10				8		6			7	2				3		5		1		4		9	**4**
	11	10				8		6			7	2				3		5		1		4		9	**5**
8	11	10						6			7	2		3				5		1		4		9	**6**
8	7	10					3		1			2		6	11			5				4		9	**7**
8	11	10					3				7	2		6				5		1		4		9	**8**
8	11	10					3				7	2		6				5		1		4		9	**9**
8	11	10					3				7	2		6				5		1		4		9	**10**
8		10				11	3				7	2		6				5		1		4		9	**11**
	11	10				8	3				7	2		6				5		1		4		9	**12**
10	11					8	3				7	2		6				5		1		4		9	**13**
	11	10				8	3				7	2		6				5		1		4		9	**14**
	11	10				8	3	6			7	2						5		1		4		9	**15**
	11	10				8	3	6			7	2						5		1		4		9	**16**
	11	10	9			8	3	6			7					2		5		1		4			**17**
	11	10					3	6			7			5		2			8	1		4		9	**18**
	11	10				8	3	6			7	2						5		1		4		9	**19**
	11	10				8	3	6			7	2						5		1		4		9	**20**
	11	10					3				7		8	5		2			9	1	6	4			**21**
	11	10				8	3	6			7	2						5		1		4		9	**22**
8	11	10					3	6			7	2		5						1		4		9	**23**
10	11					8	3	6			7	2		5						1		4		9	**24**
9	11	10				8	3	6			7	2						5		1		4			**25**
	11	10				8	3	6			7	2						5		1		4		9	**26**
9	11	10				8	3	6			7	2						5		1		4			**27**
8	7	10						6				2			11	3		5		1		4		9	**28**
9	11	10				8	3	6			7	2						5		1		4			**29**
8	11	10				7	3	6								2		5		1		4		9	**30**
8	11	10				7	3	6								2		5		1		4		9	**31**
8	11	10				7		6				2				3		5		1		4		9	**32**
	11	10					3	6			7	2					9	5		1		4		8	**33**
	11	10					3	6			7	2					9	5		1		4		8	**34**
8	11	10					3	6			7	2					9	5		1		4			**35**
	11	10				8	3	6			7	2						5		1		4		9	**36**
8	11	10					3	6			7	2					9	5		1		4			**37**
8	11	10					3	6			7	2						5		1		4		9	**38**
19	37	36	1	0	0	24	30	29	1	0	33	33	1	15	2	12	4	32	3	37	1	38	0	30	Apps
10	4	18				18					8				2		4					8		9	Goals

Batty W	Bolland W T	Bown A J W	Brewer W A	Davies A S	Fellows H A J	Fleming H J	Giles C	Handley F B	Hasell A A	Hayward R	Jefferson R W	Kay H	Lee J L	Lochhead M	Long E J	McRobbie A S	Rogers D	Silto W A	Simms S	Skiller L F	Stanners J G	Tout W E B	Weston A M	Wheatcroft F G	
	11	10				8	3	6			7	2						5		1		4		9	**1**
8	11	10					3	6			7					2		5		1		4		9	**2**
1	2	2				1	2	2			2	1				1		2		2		2		2	Apps
2						1																			Goals

Batty W	Bolland W T	Bown A J W	Brewer W A	Davies A S	Fellows H A J	Fleming H J	Giles C	Handley F B	Hasell A A	Hayward R	Jefferson R W	Kay H	Lee J L	Lochhead M	Long E J	McRobbie A S	Rogers D	Silto W A	Simms S	Skiller L F	Stanners J G	Tout W E B	Weston A M	Wheatcroft F G	
		10		11	2					4			8	5	7				9	1	6		3		**1**

No numbers actually worn on shirts

For Final League Table - see page 57

SEASON 1914/15

Southern League Division One
Final League Position : 9th
Secretary/Manager : Sam Allen

No.	Day	Month	Date	Opponents	Home	Away	H-T	Goalscorers
1	W	Sep	2	Croydon Common		D0-0		
2	S		5	Northampton Town	D2-2		(1-1)	Wheatcroft,Fleming
3	S		12	Watford		L0-3	(0-2)	
4	W		16	Bristol Rovers	W4-1		(3-0)	Batty,Jefferson,Bolland,Denyer
5	S		19	Plymouth Argyle	W3-2		(1-2)	Denyer 2,Batty
6	S		26	West Ham United		D1-1	(0-0)	Fleming
7	S	Oct	3	Norwich City	W4-0		(2-0)	Fleming 3,Handley pen.
8	S		10	Gillingham		L0-4	(0-2)	
9	S		17	Brighton and Hove Albion	W2-1		(1-0)	Fleming 2
10	S		24	Cardiff City		L0-3	(0-0)	
11	S		31	Exeter City	W4-0		(2-0)	Tout,Jefferson,Denyer,Bown
12	S	Nov	7	Luton Town		D2-2	(1-1)	Denyer,Bolland
13	S		14	Portsmouth	L1-3		(0-2)	Tout pen.
14	S		21	Crystal Palace		L1-3	(1-1)	Wheatcroft
15	W	Dec	2	Southend United		L1-2	(0-0)	Jefferson
16	S		5	Queens Park Rangers	L1-2		(0-2)	Handley
17	S		12	Millwall		W2-1	(2-0)	Bown,Wheatcroft
18	F		25	Reading		D2-2	(1-1)	Wheatcroft 2
19	S		26	Reading	D1-1		(0-1)	Denyer
20	M		28	Croydon Common	W7-1		(3-1)	Bown,Bolland,Wheatcroft,Denyer 3,Jefferson
21	S	Jan	2	Northampton Town		W3-2	(2-0)	Tout,Wheatcroft,Batty
22	S		23	Plymouth Argyle		L1-3	(1-1)	Wheatcroft
23	S		30	West Ham United	D1-1		(0-0)	Jefferson
24	S	Feb	6	Norwich City		D1-1	(0-1)	Fleming
25	S		13	Gillingham	W5-1		(2-0)	Bown 3,Fleming 2
26	S		20	Brighton and Hove Albion		W3-1	(1-1)	Jefferson 2,Fleming
27	S		27	Cardiff City	D0-0			
28	S	Mar	6	Exeter City		W1-0	(0-0)	Bown
29	S		13	Luton Town	D2-2		(1-2)	Fleming,Wheatcroft
30	S		20	Portsmouth		D1-1	(1-1)	Tout pen.
31	S		27	Crystal Palace	W5-2		(2-0)	Tout pen.,Scanlan,Batty,Bown 2
32	F	Apr	2	Southampton	W2-0		(1-0)	Batty,Scanlan
33	S		3	Southend United	W4-0		(2-0)	Batty 2,Jefferson 2
34	M		5	Southampton		L1-4	(0-3)	Tout pen.
35	Tu		6	Watford	W6-0		(4-0)	Bown 6
36	S		10	Queens Park Rangers		L2-4	(1-1)	Silto,Batty
37	S		17	Millwall	L1-2		(0-2)	Batty
38	S		24	Bristol Rovers		L0-1	(0-1)	

F A Cup

No.	Day	Month	Date	Opponents	Home	Away	H-T	Goalscorers	Gate
1	S	Jan	9	Chelsea	* D1-1		(1-1)	Denyer	22,944
1R	S		16	Chelsea		L2-5	(1-1)	Wheatcroft,Jefferson	18,610

* Played at Stamford Bridge (by arrangement)

Southern Charity Cup

No.	Day	Month	Date	Opponents	Home	Away	H-T	Goalscorers	Gate
1	W	Nov	11	Southampton		W2-1	(0-0)	Jefferson,Denyer	2,000
2	W	Feb	3	Reading		L1-3	(1-2)	Bown	2,000

BERTIE DENYER
was brought up in the east end of London and was signed from West Ham in April 1914. Known as 'Twinkle Toes' he stood little more than 5'6", but spent his early career as a centre-forward. The Great War came close to ending his career, Bertie being shipped home with severe internal injuries which left him unable to play throughout the 1919-20 season. But he confounded the medical experts who had 'written him off' and returned to action as a winger, clocking up a further 350 first team appearances for Town ! He died on March 15 1969, on the day of one of Town's greatest triumphs. His son, Bertie junior, had a brief spell at the County Ground just after the Second War.

Batty W	Bolland W T	Bown A J W	Denyer A E C	Fleming H J	Handley F B	Hasell A A	Ing A A	Jefferson R W	Kay H	Milton A	Piggin L	Scanlan E	Silto W A	Skiller L F	Thomson M	Tout W E B	Weston A M	Wheatcroft F G	
	11	10		8				7	2	3			5	1	6	4		9	1
	11	10		8				7	2	3			5	1	6	4		9	2
10	11			8	6			7	2	3			5	1		4		9	3
10	11		9	8	6			7	2	3			5	1		4			4
10	11		9	8	6			7	2	3			5	1		4			5
10	11		9	8	6			7	2	3			5	1		4			6
10	11			9	6			7	2	3		8	5	1	4				7
10	11		9	8	6			7	2	3				1	4			5	8
8	11			9	6			7	2	3			5	1	4			10	9
10					6		11	7	2	3		8	5	1		4		9	10
	11	10	9	8	6			7	2	3			5	1		4			11
8	11	10	9		6			7	2	3			5	1		4			12
	11	10	9	8	6			7		3	2		5	1		4			13
8	11	10			6	1		7	2	3			5			4		9	14
	11	10	9		6	1		7	2	3		8	5			4			15
	11		9	7	6				2	3		8	5	1		4		10	16
	11	10	8		6			7	2	3			5	1		4		9	17
	11	10	8		6			7	2				5	1		4	3	9	18
9	11	10	8		6			7		3			5	1		4	2		19
	11	10	8					7		3			5	1	6	4	2	9	20
10	11		8		6	1		7		3					5	4	2	9	21
	11		8	10	6			7		3			5	1		4	2	9	22
	11		8	10	6			7	2				5	1		4	3	9	23
	11	10	7	8	6				2	3			5	1		4		9	24
	11	10		8	6			7	2	3			5	1		4		9	25
	11	10		8	6			7	2	3			5	1		4		9	26
	11	10		8	6			7	2	3			5	1		4		9	27
	11	10		8	6			7	2	3			5	1		4		9	28
	11	10		8	6			7	2	3			5	1		4		9	29
	11	10		8	6			7	2					1	5	4	3	9	30
9	11	10			6	1		7				8	5		4	2	3		31
9	11	10			6			7	2			8	5	1		4	3		32
9	11	10		8	6			7	2				5	1		4	3		33
	11	10		8	6			7	2					1	5	4	3	9	34
9	11	10			6			7	2			8	5	1		4	3		35
9	11	10			6	1		7	2			8	5			4	3		36
8	11	10			6			7	2				5	1		4	3	9	37
7	11	10			6				2			8	5	1		4	3	9	38
19	37	26	17	23	35	5	1	35	32	27	1	9	34	33	10	35	15	24	Apps
9	3	15	9	12	2			9				2	1			6		9	Goals

TOMMY BOLLAND

Batty W	Bolland W T	Bown A J W	Denyer A E C	Fleming H J	Handley F B	Hasell A A	Ing A A	Jefferson R W	Kay H	Milton A	Piggin L	Scanlan E	Silto W A	Skiller L F	Thomson M	Tout W E B	Weston A M	Wheatcroft F G	
	11		8	10	6			7		3			5	1		4	2	9	1
	11		8	10	6			7		3			5	1		4	2	9	1R
	2		2	2	2			2		2			2	2		2	2	2	Apps
			1					1										1	Goals

Batty W	Bolland W T	Bown A J W	Denyer A E C	Fleming H J	Handley F B	Hasell A A	Ing A A	Jefferson R W	Kay H	Milton A	Piggin L	Scanlan E	Silto W A	Skiller L F	Thomson M	Tout W E B	Weston A M	Wheatcroft F G	
8	11	10	9					7	2	3			5	1	6	4			1
9	11	10	8		6				2			7		1	5	4	3		2
2	2	2	2		1			1	2	1		1	1	2	2	2	1		Apps
		1	1					1											Goals

No numbers actually worn on shirts

For Final League Table - see overleaf >>

SOUTH AMERICAN TOUR 1912

Swindon Town played eight games during a close season tour of Argentina and Uruguay during June and July 1912. Sixteen players travelled from Liverpool Docks aboard RMS Ortiga on May 16. They were Tommy Bolland, Archie Bown, Jack Burkinshaw, Harold Fleming, Bob Jefferson, Harry Kay, Sammy Lamb, Matty Lochhead, Alex McCulloch, Billy Silto, Len Skiller, Billy Tout, Jock Walker and 'Corby' Woolford from the squad that had come so close to reaching the F.A.Cup Final, plus new signings Jim Kennedy from Tottenham and Billy Batty from Lincoln City.

There must have been a little trepidation in the minds of one or two aboard, considering that just five weeks earlier the Titanic had gone down with such a mammoth loss of life.

Although Fleming travelled, he did not take part in any of the games as he was recovering from a serious injury sustained in a bruising F.A.Cup semi-final replay with Barnsley. The only notable absentees were Charlie Bannister and Freddy Wheatcroft. Charlie had announced his retirement and was travelling in the opposite direction - to Perth in Western Australia. Freddy, *(pictured page 43)* although now a professional, was working as a schoolteacher. While his colleagues were away, he married Jessie Jobson - also a teacher - on July 20 1912.

After numerous stops en route, the Town party arrived in Montevideo on Saturday June 8 and, with a week to recover from their ordeal, were treated to various sightseeing trips - each member of the party being given £20 in expenses ! They were also wined and dined after every game and secretary Sam Allen reported that a number of the players had put on weight. Although the Town were undefeated throughout the tour, Sam was still disappointed that they did not win their opening fixture against what he deemed to be a poor side.

Archie Bown, who had suffered quite badly with sea sickness on the trip, soon recovered and helped himself to eleven goals in total. He, with Len Skiller and Jock Walker - appointed captain in Fleming's absence - were the only players to feature in all eight games.

The party returned on the SS Vandyke, arriving back at Southampton Docks on August 2.

TOWN ON TOUR
Some of the Town squad on the 1912 Tour :

(left to right) Jim Kennedy, 'Corby' Woolford, Jack Burkinshaw, Alex McCulloch, Tommy Bolland, Harry Kay, Len Skiller, Jock Walker, Archie Bown, Billy Silto and Bob Jefferson.

					H-T	Goalscorers	Batty W	Bolland W T	Bown A J W	Burkinshaw J D L	Jefferson R W	Kay H	Kennedy J J	Lamb S	Lochhead M	McCulloch A	Silto W A	Skiller L F	Tout W E B	Walker J	Woolford F O K	
1	Su	Jun	16 North Argentina	D2-2	(0-0)	Bown,Jefferson	8		10		7	2		11	6	9	5	1	4	3		1
2	S		22 San Isidro	W4-1	(2-0)	Bown 2,Burkinshaw,McCulloch		7	10	9		2	5	11		8	6	1	4	3		2
3	Su		23 South Argentina	W2-0	(1-0)	Bown 2		11	10	9	7	2	5		4	8	6	1		3		3
4	S		29 Rosario	W3-1	(1-1)	Bown 2,Batty	8	7	10			2	5	11	6	9		1	4	3		4
5	Su		30 Liga Argentina	D2-2	(2-1)	Burkinshaw,Lamb			10	9	7		5	11	6	8		1	4	3	2	5
6	Th	Jul	4 Atletico Estudiantes	W4-0	(3-0)	Bown 2,Burkinshaw,Lamb	8	11	10	9	7	2			5	6		1	4	3		6
7	Su		7 Liga Uruguaya	W3-0	(1-0)	Lamb,Bown 2			10	9	7	2	5	11	6	8		1	4	3		7
8	Tu		9 Argentinos	W1-0	(1-0)	Jefferson			10	9	7	2		11	5	8	6	1	4	3		8
							3	4	8	6	6	7	5	6	7	8	4	8	7	8	1	Apps
							1		11	3	2			3		1						Goals

SEASON 1913/14

	P	W	D	L	F	A	W	D	L	F	A	Pts	G/A
1 SWINDON TOWN	38	14	3	2	57	11	7	5	7	24	30	50	1.98
2 Crystal Palace	38	12	5	2	41	13	5	11	3	19	19	50	1.88
3 Northampton Town	38	11	8	0	31	9	3	11	5	19	28	47	1.35
4 Reading	38	14	4	1	32	11	3	6	10	11	25	44	1.19
5 Plymouth Argyle	38	11	6	2	25	12	4	7	8	21	30	43	1.10
6 West Ham United	38	9	7	3	39	22	6	5	8	22	38	42	1.02
7 Brighton & Hove Albion	38	12	5	2	31	16	3	7	9	12	29	42	0.96
8 Queens Park Rangers	38	10	6	3	27	14	6	3	10	18	29	41	1.05
9 Portsmouth	38	10	7	2	31	13	4	5	10	26	35	40	1.19
10 Cardiff City	38	10	6	3	27	11	3	6	10	19	31	38	1.10
11 Southampton	38	11	2	6	35	22	4	5	10	20	32	37	1.02
12 Exeter City	38	7	8	4	21	11	3	8	8	18	27	36	1.03
13 Gillingham	38	10	6	3	36	15	3	3	13	12	34	35	0.98
14 Norwich City	38	7	10	2	34	19	2	7	10	15	32	35	0.96
15 Millwall	38	10	6	3	34	20	1	6	12	17	36	34	0.91
16 Southend United	38	7	7	5	29	28	3	5	11	12	38	32	0.62
17 Bristol Rovers	38	10	5	4	32	25	0	6	13	14	42	31	0.69
18 Watford	38	9	4	6	37	20	1	5	13	13	36	29	0.89
19 Merthyr Town	38	7	7	5	23	18	2	3	14	15	43	28	0.62
20 Coventry City	38	4	8	7	28	28	2	6	11	15	40	26	0.63

SEASON 1914/15

	P	W	D	L	F	A	W	D	L	F	A	Pts	G/A
1 Watford	38	11	4	4	37	15	11	4	4	31	31	52	1.48
2 Reading	38	12	4	3	37	16	9	3	7	31	27	49	1.58
3 Cardiff City	38	16	1	2	51	12	6	3	10	21	26	48	1.89
4 West Ham United	38	14	4	1	42	18	4	5	10	16	29	45	1.23
5 Northampton Town	38	11	5	3	37	23	5	6	8	19	28	43	1.10
6 Southampton	38	14	3	2	56	28	5	2	12	22	46	43	1.05
7 Portsmouth	38	10	5	4	26	14	6	5	8	28	28	42	1.29
8 Millwall	38	9	4	6	28	23	7	6	6	22	28	42	0.98
9 SWINDON TOWN	38	11	5	3	55	21	4	6	9	22	38	41	1.31
10 Brighton & Hove Albion	38	11	5	3	29	16	5	2	12	17	31	39	0.98
11 Exeter City	38	10	3	6	32	16	5	5	9	18	25	38	1.22
12 Queens Park Rangers	38	8	4	7	30	28	5	8	6	25	26	38	1.02
13 Norwich City	38	10	6	3	33	16	1	8	10	20	40	36	0.95
14 Luton Town	38	6	3	10	27	34	7	5	7	34	39	34	0.84
15 Crystal Palace	38	8	4	7	24	25	5	4	10	23	36	34	0.77
16 Bristol Rovers	38	12	2	5	42	28	2	1	16	11	47	31	0.71
17 Plymouth Argyle	38	8	7	4	34	25	0	7	12	17	36	30	0.84
18 Southend United	38	8	5	6	27	20	2	3	14	17	44	28	0.69
19 Croydon Common	38	7	6	6	28	18	2	3	14	19	45	27	0.75
20 Gillingham	38	6	6	7	32	29	0	2	17	11	53	20	0.52

SEASON 1915/16

South Western Combination League
Final League Position : 6th

					Home	Away	Goalscorers
1	S	Jan	8	Cardiff City	L0-2		
2	S		15	Cardiff City		L0-1	
3	S	Feb	12	Bristol City		L0-1	
4	S	Mar	4	Bristol Rovers		D0-0	
5	S		18	Southampton	W3-1		Bolland,Henderson,Jefferson
6	S		25	Southampton		L3-5	Maunders,Lee 2
7	S	Apr	1	Portsmouth	L1-2		Tout
8	S		8	Newport County	W1-0		Critchley
9	S		15	Bristol City	L1-2		Critchley
10	S		22	Bristol Rovers	D2-2		Davies 2
11	S		29	Portsmouth		L1-6	Lee

Newport County (away) : *Fixture not played*

	P	W	D	L	F	A	Pts
1 Portsmouth	12	9	0	3	29	11	18
2 Southampton	12	8	1	3	38	19	17
3 Cardiff City	12	7	0	5	21	18	14
4 Bristol Rovers	12	5	3	4	17	20	13
5 Bristol City	12	5	1	6	13	16	11
6 SWINDON TOWN	11	2	2	7	12	22	6
7 Newport County	11	1	1	9	8	32	3

SEASON 1919/20

Southern League Division One
Final League Position : 13th
Secretary/Manager : Sam Allen

				Home	Away	H-T	Goalscorers
1	S	Aug	30 Plymouth Argyle		L0-3	(0-0)	
2	Tu	Sep	1 Merthyr Town	W1-0		(1-0)	Jefferson
3	S		6 Bristol Rovers	W4-1		(2-0)	Davies,Tout pen.,Bolland,Jefferson
4	M		8 Merthyr Town		D0-0		
5	S		13 Reading		D1-1	(0-0)	Covey
6	S		20 Southampton	L1-2		(0-1)	Travers
7	S		27 Luton Town		L1-3	(0-0)	Davies
8	S	Oct	4 Gillingham	W5-2		(2-1)	Davies 2,Tout pen.,Jefferson,Fleming
9	S		11 Swansea Town		L0-1	(0-1)	
10	W		15 Crystal Palace		W2-1	(1-0)	Rogers,Davies
11	S		18 Exeter City	D1-1		(1-0)	Rogers
12	S		25 Cardiff City		D3-3	(1-1)	Fleming,Rogers,Lockhead
13	S	Nov	1 Queens Park Rangers	W5-2		(1-1)	Travers,Davies,Rogers 2,Pullen o.g.
14	S		8 Watford	L1-2		(1-1)	Travers
15	S		15 Millwall		W2-0	(0-0)	Travers,Fleming
16	S		22 Brighton and Hove Albion	W2-1		(1-0)	Jefferson,Rogers
17	S		29 Newport County		L0-2	(0-1)	
18	S	Dec	6 Portsmouth	L0-3		(0-0)	
19	S		13 Northampton Town		W3-2	(2-1)	Travers 2,Batty
20	S		20 Crystal Palace	D2-2		(1-1)	Travers 2
21	Th		25 Norwich City	L0-1		(0-0)	
22	S		27 Southend United		W1-0	(1-0)	Travers
23	S	Jan	3 Plymouth Argyle	W2-1		(2-1)	Ing,Warren
24	S		17 Bristol Rovers		L1-2	(0-0)	Tout pen.
25	S		24 Reading	D0-0			
26	S	Feb	7 Luton Town	W1-0		(1-0)	Bolland
27	S		14 Gillingham		L1-3	(1-2)	Jefferson
28	S		21 Swansea Town	W3-1		(1-0)	Travers,Rogers,Davies
29	S		28 Exeter City		L1-3	(1-2)	Travers
30	S	Mar	6 Cardiff City	D2-2		(2-1)	Davies,Rogers
31	M		8 Southampton		L0-1	(0-1)	
32	S		13 Queens Park Rangers		L1-2	(1-1)	Fleming
33	S		20 Watford		L1-3	(0-2)	Travers
34	Th		25 Norwich City		L1-4	(1-1)	Rogers
35	S		27 Millwall	W1-0		(0-0)	Bolland
36	F	Apr	2 Brentford		L0-2	(0-1)	
37	S		3 Brighton and Hove Albion		L0-2	(0-2)	
38	M		5 Brentford	W3-1		(1-1)	Fleming 2,Batty
39	S		10 Newport County	W3-0		(1-0)	Rogers,Fleming,Davies
40	S		17 Portsmouth		L1-4	(1-1)	Rogers
41	S		24 Northampton Town	W5-2		(3-1)	Rogers 3,Fleming 2
42	S	May	1 Southend United	W3-2		(2-0)	Fleming,Simms pen.,Rogers

F A Cup

					H-T	Goalscorers	Gate
1	S	Jan	10 Fulham	W2-1	(2-1)	Travers 2	30,000
2	S		31 Chelsea	L0-4	(0-0)		67,054

GEORGE TRAVERS
was the son of music hall entertainers Hyram Travers and Emily Picton and at times seemed to lead as colourful a life as his parents. He began his career at Birmingham in 1907 and was an F.A.Cup winner with Barnsley in 1912. By the time George arrived at the County Ground in June 1919, he could command a top wage - earning £1 per week more than Harold Fleming ! But George struggled with his finances and found himself in court on a number of occasions. He ended his days working as a labourer on the railways in New Zealand - where he died in 1943.

Alford F J	Arman B J	Batty W	Beasant E A W	Bolland W T	Clayton P	Covey A S	Davies A S	Fleming H J	Hinton W F W	Ing A A	Jefferson R W	Kay H	Lochhead M	Nash E M	Pocock J H	Rogers D	Silto W A	Simms S	Smith G A	Taylor W H	Tout W E B	Travers G E	Warren J G	Weston A M	
				11			10	8	1		7	2					6	5			4	9		3	**1**
				11			10		1		7	2	6			8		5			4	9		3	**2**
				11			10		1	6	7	2				8		5			4	9		3	**3**
				11			10		1	6	7	2	5			8			9		4			3	**4**
				11		9	10		1		7	2				5				6	4	8		3	**5**
				11			10	8	1		7	2				5				6	4	9		3	**6**
	3			11			10	8	1		7	2				5				6	4	9			**7**
	3			11			10	8	1		7	2	6			9		5			4				**8**
				11			10		1		7	2	6			9		5			4	8		3	**9**
				11			10		1		7	2	6			9		5			4	8		3	**10**
				11			10		1		7	2	6			9		5			4	8		3	**11**
					2		10	11	1		7		6			9		5			4	8		3	**12**
					6		10	11	1		7	2				9		5			4	8		3	**13**
				11	6		10		1		7	2				9		5			4	8		3	**14**
					6		10	11	1		7	2				9		5			4	8		3	**15**
					6		10	11	1		7	2				9		5			4	8		3	**16**
11					6		10		1		7	2				9		5			4	8		3	**17**
				11	6		10		1		7	2				9		5			4	8		3	**18**
		10			6		11		1		7	2				9		5			4	8		3	**19**
		10			6		11		1		7	2				9		5			4	8		3	**20**
		9		11	6		10		1		7	2						5			4	8		3	**21**
		10		7	6		11		1	4		2									5	8	9	3	**22**
				11	6		10		1	7		2						5			4	8	9	3	**23**
		10		7	3		11		1			2	6					5			4	8	9		**24**
		10			3		11	8	1	4	7	2	6								5	9			**25**
		10		7	2		11	8	1							6		5			4	9		3	**26**
		10		11	2				1	6	7					9		5			4	8		3	**27**
		10			6		11	7	1			2				9		5			4	8		3	**28**
		10			6		11	7	1			2				9		5			4	8		3	**29**
				7	4		11	10	1			2				9	6	5				8		3	**30**
		10		7	6		11		1			2				9	5				4	8		3	**31**
				7	4		11	10	1			2				9	6	5				8		3	**32**
				7	4		11	10	1			2				9	6	5				8		3	**33**
		10		7			11		1	4		2	6			9		5				8		3	**34**
		10	3	7			11	8		4			6	1		9		5						2	**35**
		10		7	2		11		1				6			9		5			4	8		3	**36**
		10		7	2		11		1				6			9		5			4	8		3	**37**
		10	3				11	8	1		7	2	6			9		5			4				**38**
		10					11	8	1		7	2	6			9		5			4			3	**39**
		10				8	11		1		7	2	6			9		5			4			3	**40**
		10	3				11	8			7			1	6	9		5			4			2	**41**
		10					11	8		4	7			1	6	9		5			2			3	**42**
1	2	20	3	27	24	2	41	20	39	9	28	34	16	3	2	36	5	35	1	3	37	34	3	37	Apps
		2		3		1	9	10		1	5		1			15		1			3	12	1		Goals

Opponents 1 goal

Alford F J	Arman B J	Batty W	Beasant E A W	Bolland W T	Clayton P	Covey A S	Davies A S	Fleming H J	Hinton W F W	Ing A A	Jefferson R W	Kay H	Lochhead M	Nash E M	Pocock J H	Rogers D	Silto W A	Simms S	Smith G A	Taylor W H	Tout W E B	Travers G E	Warren J G	Weston A M	
		10		7	3		11	8	1			2	6					5			4	9			**1**
		10			2		11	8	1		7		6					5			4	9		3	**2**
		2		1	2		2	2	2		1	1	2					2			2	2		1	Apps
																						2			Goals

No numbers actually worn on shirts

For Final League Table - see overleaf >>

in memoriam : ww1

In all, six players with Town connections were lost during the bloody battles of the Great War. Two - ALBERT MILTON and FREDDY WHEATCROFT - were still on the club's payroll at the time.

Albert cost a sizeable £500 fee from Sunderland in May 1914, but was soon called up for service with the Royal Field Artillery. He died in Belgium in October 1917.

Freddy Wheatcroft *(pictured page 43)* first joined Town as an amateur in 1904/05, hitting a hat-trick on his debut in the F.A.Cup. A schoolteacher, he continued to combine his two occupations throughout his career. Freddy joined Fulham in 1906 but returned to the County Ground in 1909 and grabbed 22 goals in his first season back. A lieutenant with the East Surreys, he died in Bourlon, France in November 1917.

ARTHUR BEADSWORTH spent two years with the club, from 1903 to 1905, during which time he played alongside JIM CHALMERS *(see page 32)* and BILLY KIRBY *(pictured page 29)*.

The last was Sgt WILLIAM BREWER, from Langley Burrell, who had made just one League appearance for the Town in 1913/14, but who perished just a few months into the War.

ARTHUR BEADSWORTH

ALBERT MILTON

SEASON 1919/20

		P	W	D	L	F	A	W	D	L	F	A	Pts	G/A
1	Portsmouth	42	13	6	2	48	14	10	6	5	25	13	58	2.70
2	Watford	42	15	3	3	39	12	11	3	7	30	30	58	1.64
3	Crystal Palace	42	15	5	1	44	15	7	7	7	25	28	56	1.60
4	Cardiff City	42	15	3	3	44	14	3	14	4	26	29	53	1.63
5	Plymouth Argyle	42	13	5	3	36	8	7	5	9	21	21	50	1.97
6	Queens Park Rangers	42	12	7	2	34	13	6	3	12	28	37	46	1.24
7	Reading	42	11	5	5	30	14	5	8	8	21	29	45	1.19
8	Southampton	42	13	4	4	51	22	5	4	12	21	41	44	1.14
9	Swansea Town	42	11	4	6	28	14	5	7	9	25	31	43	1.18
10	Exeter City	42	14	3	4	44	22	3	6	12	13	29	43	1.12
11	Southend United	42	10	8	3	32	18	3	9	9	14	30	43	0.96
12	Norwich City	42	13	6	2	46	18	2	5	14	18	39	41	1.12
13	SWINDON TOWN	42	13	4	4	45	26	4	3	14	20	42	41	0.96
14	Millwall	42	10	7	4	32	21	4	5	12	20	34	40	0.95
15	Brentford	42	11	5	5	35	21	4	5	12	17	38	40	0.88
16	Brighton & Hove Albion	42	11	5	5	43	28	3	3	15	17	44	36	0.83
17	Bristol Rovers	42	10	7	4	43	29	1	6	14	18	49	35	0.78
18	Newport County	42	10	6	5	30	18	3	1	17	15	52	33	0.64
19	Northampton Town	42	8	4	9	35	40	4	5	12	29	63	33	0.62
20	Luton Town	42	7	7	7	29	28	3	3	15	22	48	30	0.67
21	Merthyr Town	42	7	6	8	30	31	2	5	14	17	47	29	0.60
22	Gillingham	42	7	5	9	24	23	3	2	16	10	51	27	0.46

at the gates

COUNTY GROUND PROGRESSIVE ATTENDANCE RECORDS

							Receipts
1908	Jan	11	11,289	v	Sheffield United	F.A.Cup First Round	£535
1910	Feb	19	11,818	v	Tottenham Hotspur	F.A.Cup Third Round	£756
	Mar	5	14,429	v	Manchester City	F.A.Cup Fourth Round	£912
1911	Feb	4	14,861	v	Woolwich Arsenal	F.A.Cup Second Round	£950
1914	Jan	10	18,107	v	Manchester United	F.A.Cup First Round	£1,183
1921	Jan	8	18,685	v	Sheffield United	F.A.Cup First Round	£1,846
	Jan	29	21,261	v	Chelsea	F.A.Cup Second Round	£2,158
1924	Feb	2	22,884	v	Oldham Athletic	F.A.Cup Second Round	£1,488
1929	Jan	30	24,730	v	Burnley	F.A.Cup Fourth Round	£1,615
1946	Oct	5	25,007	v	Bristol City	F/Lge Third Division South	£1,910
1947	Nov	15	26,401	v	Bristol City	F/Lge Third Division South	£1,980
1948	Jan	24	27,130	v	Notts County	F.A.Cup Fourth Round	£2,396
1952	Feb	2	28,140	v	Stoke City	F.A.Cup Fourth Round	£2,657
1963	Sep	10	28,173	v	Manchester City	F/League Second Division	£4,252
1964	Feb	15	28,582	v	West Ham United	F.A.Cup Fifth Round	£5,472
1969	Mar	29	28,898	v	Watford	F/Lge Third Division	£6,273
1972	Jan	15	31,668	v	Arsenal	F.A.Cup Third Round	£12,594

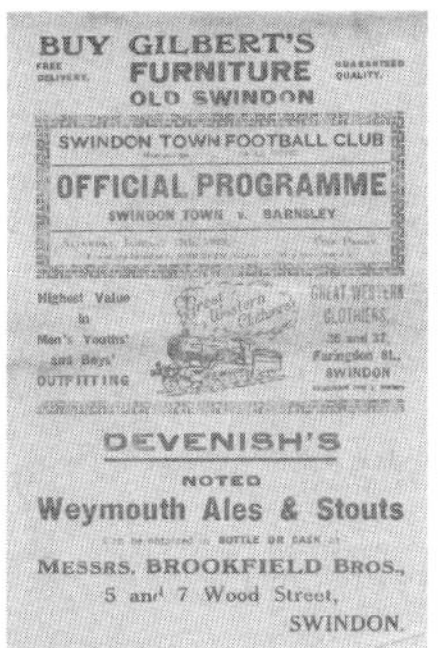

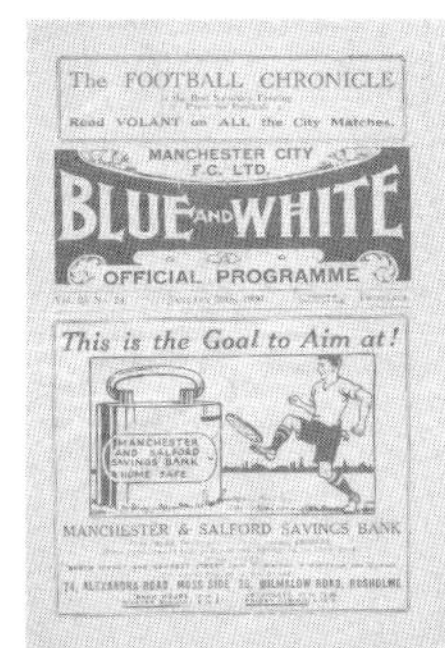

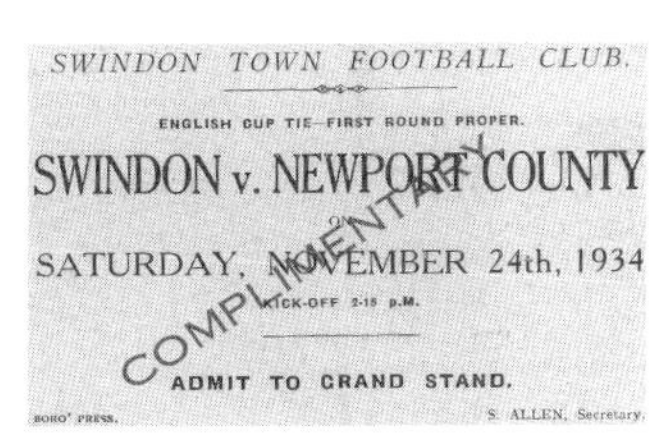
SWINDON TOWN FOOTBALL CLUB.

ENGLISH CUP TIE—FIRST ROUND PROPER.

SWINDON v. NEWPORT COUNTY

SATURDAY, NOVEMBER 24th, 1934

KICK-OFF 2-15 P.M.

COMPLIMENTARY

ADMIT TO GRAND STAND.

S. ALLEN, Secretary.

Left to right : Programme from 1923 : and from the record F.A.Cup defeat in 1930 : Match ticket from 1934 : Programme from FA.Cup tie in 1938

harry's heyday

AND THE INTER-WAR YEARS

1920 - 1939

After just one season following the resumption of peace-time football in 1919, the Southern League was taken under the umbrella of the Football League as its new Third Division - and a young centre-forward was plucked from the playing fields of Hackney Marshes to join Fulham. Harry Morris signed for Town in 1926 and soon took advantage of a recent change in the offside law, leading to numerous club scoring records falling during the next seven years.

Town failed to win any honours in that time, but the crowds were entertained and several First Division 'giants' were given a rough ride in the F.A.Cup.

Following Harry's departure in 1933, Town soon found another goalscoring hero in little Alan Fowler. They were as different as chalk and cheese - Harry the big bustling type, Alan a nimble fellow who tipped the scales at not much more than nine stones. Sadly, the Second War claimed Alan's life, while Harry escaped to neutral Sweden to take up coaching.

Left to right : Town at Swindon station en route to Newport 1927 : Arthur Briggs : Alan Fowler nurses a broken ankle : Ben Morton in training

SEASON 1920/21

Football League Division Three
Final League Position : 4th
Secretary/Manager : Sam Allen

					Home	Away	H-T	Goalscorers	Gate
1	S	Aug	28	Luton Town	W9-1		(5-1)	Batty 2,Davies,Fleming 4,Jefferson,Mathieson o.g.	10,000
2	M		30	Southampton		L0-4	(0-4)		11,500
3	S	Sep	4	Luton Town		L0-2	(0-0)		9,000
4	M		6	Southampton	W3-2		(2-1)	Stokoe 2,Denyer	9,000
5	S		11	Southend United		W3-1	(2-0)	Stokoe 2,Jefferson	8,000
6	S		18	Southend United	W3-0		(1-0)	Stokoe 2,Fleming	9,500
7	S		25	Merthyr Town	W3-0		(2-0)	Fleming 2,Stokoe	11,000
8	S	Oct	2	Merthyr Town		D2-2	(1-1)	Rogers 2	13,000
9	S		9	Plymouth Argyle		D0-0			19,050
10	S		16	Plymouth Argyle	D1-1		(0-0)	Fleming	11,974
11	Th		21	Newport County		W1-0	(0-0)	Denyer	10,000
12	S		23	Exeter City		L0-1	(0-1)		9,000
13	S		30	Exeter City	D1-1		(1-1)	Batty	10,000
14	S	Nov	6	Millwall		L0-5	(0-3)		10,000
15	S		13	Millwall	W4-1		(1-0)	Fleming,Batty,Jefferson 2	10,000
16	S		27	Newport County	W5-0		(1-0)	Simms pen.,Batty 3,Fleming	7,000
17	S	Dec	11	Gillingham	D1-1		(0-1)	Batty	9,000
18	S		18	Portsmouth		D1-1	(0-0)	Rogers	11,111
19	S		25	Reading		W3-2	(1-0)	Wareing,Batty 2	11,000
20	M		27	Reading	W2-0		(1-0)	Fleming 2	15,395
21	S	Jan	1	Portsmouth	W5-2		(4-1)	Davies 2,Denyer 2,Batty	8,000
22	S		15	Bristol Rovers	W2-1		(1-1)	Denyer 2	9,000
23	S		22	Bristol Rovers		L1-3	(0-2)	Davies	12,000
24	S	Feb	5	Watford		W1-0	(0-0)	Davies	7,000
25	S		12	Brentford	W1-0		(1-0)	Batty	6,200
26	S		19	Brentford		W1-0	(0-0)	Wareing	10,000
27	S		26	Norwich City	W4-2		(2-2)	Wareing,Simms 2,Fleming	12,000
28	S	Mar	5	Norwich City		L2-3	(0-2)	Fleming,Jefferson	10,000
29	S		12	Crystal Palace	L1-3		(0-0)	Denyer	12,000
30	S		19	Crystal Palace		L0-1	(0-1)		17,000
31	S		26	Brighton and Hove Albion		W3-0	(2-0)	Jefferson pen.,Denyer,Fleming	7,000
32	M		28	Northampton Town	W2-1		(2-0)	Hawley,Fleming	9,700
33	Tu		29	Northampton Town		W2-1	(2-0)	Rogers 2	10,000
34	S	Apr	2	Brighton and Hove Albion	W2-0		(1-0)	Metcalf,Weston pen.	8,000
35	S		9	Grimsby Town		L0-3	(0-2)		10,000
36	W		13	Gillingham		D1-1	(0-1)	Metcalf	8,000
37	S		16	Grimsby Town	D0-0				6,000
38	W		20	Watford	W2-0		(1-0)	Metcalf 2	6,000
39	S		23	Queens Park Rangers		L0-1	(0-1)		12,000
40	S		30	Queens Park Rangers	L0-1		(0-1)		7,000
41	M	May	2	Swansea Town		D1-1	(0-0)	Metcalf	7,000
42	S		7	Swansea Town	D0-0				6,000

Approx. Average Home Attendance : **9,200**
Approx. Average Away Attendance : **10,500**

F A Cup

					Home/Away	H-T	Goalscorers	Gate
1	S	Jan	8	Sheffield United	W1-0	(1-0)	Fleming	18,685
2	S		29	Chelsea	L0-2	(0-1)		21,261

BILLY BATTY
had the honour of scoring Town's first ever Football League goal, just six minutes into an emphatic victory over the Hatters on the opening day. Billy joined the club from Lincoln in May 1912 - a month before they set sail for their South American tour - and stayed at the County Ground for ten years before taking over as player-coach at Barnsley in June 1922.

Archer A A E	Batty W	Bolland W T	Covey A S	Davies A S	Denyer A E C	Fleming H J	Hawley F	Ing A A	Jefferson R W	Kay H	Langford T S	Maconnachie J S J	Metcalf A	Nash E M	Pocock J H	Rogers D	Simms S	Skiller L F	Stokoe J	Tout W E B	Wareing W	Weston A M	
	10			11		8	5		7	2	4	3		1		9					6		**1**
	10			11		8	5		7		4	3				9		1			6	2	**2**
				11	10		5		7	2	4	3		1		9			8		6		**3**
			10	11	9		5	4	7	2				1	6				8	3			**4**
				11		10	5		7	2	4	3		1		9			8		6		**5**
				11		10	5		7	2	4	3		1		9			8		6		**6**
				11		10			7	2	4	3				9	5	1	8		6		**7**
	10			11					7	2	4	3				9	5	1	8		6		**8**
				11		10	5		7	2	4					9		1	8	3	6		**9**
				11		10	5	4	7	2		3				9		1	8		6		**10**
				11	10		5		7	2		3				9	4	1	8		6		**11**
	10			11			5		7	2		3				9		1	8	4	6		**12**
	10			11	9		5		7	2	4	3						1	8		6		**13**
	10			11	9	8	5		7	2		3						1		4	6		**14**
	10			11	9	8	5		7	2							4	1			6	3	**15**
	10			11	9	8	5		7	2		3					4	1			6		**16**
	10			11	9	8	5		7	2		3					4	1			6		**17**
	10			11		8	5		7	2	4					9		1			6	3	**18**
	10			11	9		5		7	2	4		8					1			6	3	**19**
	10			11	9	8	5		7		4	3						1			6	2	**20**
	10			11	9	8	5		7		4	3						1			6	2	**21**
	10			11	9		5		7	2	4							1	8		6	3	**22**
				11	9				7		4	3	10		6		5	1	8			2	**23**
	10			11	9		5		7	2	4		8					1			6	3	**24**
	10			11	9		5		7	2	4		8					1			6	3	**25**
	10	11			8		5		7	2	4						9	1			6	3	**26**
	10			11		8	5		7	2	4						9	1			6	3	**27**
	10			11		8	5		7	2	4						9	1			6	3	**28**
	10			11	9	8	5		7	2	4							1			6	3	**29**
	10	11				8	5		7		4	3					9	1			6	2	**30**
	10				8	11	5		7		4	3				9		1			6	2	**31**
	10				8	11	5		7		4	3				9		1			6	2	**32**
5		11							7		4	3	10			9		1	8		6	2	**33**
4	10					11	5					3	8			9		1	7		6	2	**34**
4	10			11		8	5		7			3				9		1			6	2	**35**
				11	8		5		7		4	3	10			9		1			6	2	**36**
				11	7	8	5				4	3	10			9		1			6	2	**37**
				11		8	5		7			3	10		4	9		1			6	2	**38**
		11			8		5		7			3	10		4	9		1			6	2	**39**
		11			8		5		7		4	3	9		10			1			6	2	**40**
					8	11	5		7		4	3	10			9		1			6	2	**41**
		11				8	5		7			3	9		10	4		1			6	2	**42**
3	25	6	1	32	24	26	38	2	40	25	29	30	13	5	6	23	11	37	15	4	40	27	Apps
	12			5	8	16	1		6				5			5	3		7		3	1	Goals

Opponents 1 goal

Archer A A E	Batty W	Bolland W T	Covey A S	Davies A S	Denyer A E C	Fleming H J	Hawley F	Ing A A	Jefferson R W	Kay H	Langford T S	Maconnachie J S J	Metcalf A	Nash E M	Pocock J H	Rogers D	Simms S	Skiller L F	Stokoe J	Tout W E B	Wareing W	Weston A M	
	10			11		8	5		7	2	4					9		1			6	3	**1**
	10			11	9		5		7	2	4							1	8		6	3	**2**
	2			2	1	1	2		2	2	2					1		2	1		2	2	Apps
						1																	Goals

No numbers actually worn on shirts

BILLY WAREING

For Final League Table - see page 100

SEASON 1921/22

Football League Division Three South
Final League Position : 6th
Secretary/Manager : Sam Allen

					Home	Away	H-T	Goalscorers	Gate
1	S	Aug	27	Queens Park Rangers		D0-0			18,000
2	M		29	Northampton Town	W4-2		(2-0)	Phillipson,Metcalf,Fleming,Maconnachie	9,700
3	S	Sep	3	Queens Park Rangers	W2-0		(1-0)	Phillipson 2	10,000
4	M		5	Northampton Town		L1-2	(0-1)	Davies	7,000
5	S		10	Southampton		L1-3	(1-0)	Jefferson	12,000
6	S		17	Southampton	L2-3		(0-1)	Fleming 2	9,000
7	S		24	Swansea Town		W3-1	(3-1)	Phillipson 2,Batty	14,000
8	S	Oct	1	Swansea Town	W1-0		(0-0)	Fleming	9,000
9	S		8	Newport County	W3-2		(1-0)	Batty,Phillipson,Weston pen.	9,000
10	S		15	Newport County		L0-4	(0-2)		10,000
11	S		22	Exeter City	D1-1		(1-0)	Batty	7,000
12	S		29	Exeter City		W4-1	(1-0)	Batty 2,Cooke,Fleming	6,550
13	S	Nov	5	Plymouth Argyle	L1-2		(1-2)	Batty	10,000
14	S		12	Plymouth Argyle		L0-1	(0-1)		20,000
15	S		19	Millwall		D0-0			15,000
16	S		26	Millwall	D1-1		(1-1)	Metcalf	8,000
17	S	Dec	10	Merthyr Town	W3-0		(1-0)	Davies,Maconnachie pen.,Rogers	7,000
18	M		12	Merthyr Town		L1-4	(0-1)	Rogers	6,000
19	S		24	Gillingham		D2-2	(1-1)	Rogers,Fleming	8,000
20	M		26	Luton Town	D1-1		(1-0)	Turner	12,134
21	Tu		27	Luton Town		L1-2	(1-1)	Davies	15,671
22	S		31	Portsmouth	D0-0				10,000
23	S	Jan	14	Portsmouth		W3-1	(1-1)	Denyer 2,Weston pen.	9,461
24	S		21	Norwich City		W2-1	(2-0)	Johnson 2	3,500
25	S	Feb	4	Reading		D1-1	(0-1)	Johnson	8,000
26	S		11	Reading	W4-0		(1-0)	Denyer 2,Phillipson,Johnson	7,327
27	S		18	Bristol Rovers		D1-1	(0-0)	Johnson	16,000
28	S		25	Bristol Rovers	L0-1		(0-1)		10,000
29	S	Mar	4	Brentford		L0-3	(0-1)		5,000
30	S		11	Brentford	W2-1		(2-1)	Cooke,Fleming	6,900
31	S		18	Aberdare Athletic	D2-2		(1-1)	Maconnachie pen.,Johnson	7,000
32	M		20	Gillingham	D0-0				2,000
33	S		25	Aberdare Athletic		L2-3	(0-1)	Cooke 2	9,000
34	S	Apr	1	Brighton and Hove Albion	W1-0		(1-0)	Fleming	4,500
35	S		8	Brighton and Hove Albion		L1-2	(0-1)	Weston pen.	7,500
36	F		14	Southend United		W2-1	(2-1)	Cooke,Johnson	8,000
37	S		15	Watford	L0-3		(0-0)		5,100
38	M		17	Southend United	W6-1		(2-0)	Fleming 2,Cooke 2,Phillipson,Archer	5,000
39	S		22	Watford		D2-2	(1-1)	Fleming,Cooke	4,000
40	S		29	Charlton Athletic	D0-0				5,000
41	M	May	1	Norwich City	W6-1		(3-1)	Johnson 3,Cooke,Denyer,Wareing pen.	3,000
42	S		6	Charlton Athletic		W5-4	(1-2)	Cooke,Johnson,Phillipson 2,Denyer	8,000

Approx. Average Home Attendance : **7,450**
Approx. Average Away Attendance : **10,050**

F A Cup

					Home	Away	H-T	Goalscorers	Gate
1	S	Jan	7	Leeds United	W2-1		(1-1)	Fleming 2	16,000
2	S		28	Blackburn Rovers	L0-1		(0-0)		19,143

BOB COOKE
finished the season just one goal behind Harold Fleming, despite finding the net just twice in his first eight games. In the final ten games, he grabbed eight. Born in Nottinghamshire, Bob arrived from Sunderland in May 1921. After two seasons at the County Ground, Accrington Stanley paid £40 for his services. Bob later became a licensed victualler in north Wales.

Archer A A E	Batty W	Colebourne J	Cooke F R	Davies A S	Dawe E R	Denyer A E C	Fleming H J	Hawley F	Ing A A	Jefferson R W	Johnson J H	Kay H	Langford T S	Maconnachie J S J	Metcalf A	Nash E M	Phillipson T W	Pocock J H	Rogers D	Skiller L F	Stokoe J	Turner O C	Wareing W	Weston A M	
				11				5		7			4	3	10		9			1	8		6	2	**1**
				11			8	5		7			4	3	10		9			1			6	2	**2**
				11			8	5		7			4	3	10		9		6	1				2	**3**
			10	11				5		7		2	4	3			9		6	1	8				**4**
		2		11			8	5		7				3	10		9		4	1			6		**5**
		4		11		7	8	5						3	10		9	6		1				2	**6**
	10			11		7	8	5				2	4				9			1			6	3	**7**
	10			11		7	8	5				2	4				9			1			6	3	**8**
	10			11	6	7	8	5	4			2					9			1				3	**9**
	10			11	6	7	8	5	4			2					9			1				3	**10**
	10	2					11	5		7							9	4		1	8		6	3	**11**
5	10		9				11			7				3			8	4		1			6	2	**12**
	10		9	11				5		7				3			8	4		1			6	2	**13**
	10		9	11				5		7				3			8		4	1			6	2	**14**
	10		8				11	5		7				3			9		4	1			6	2	**15**
	10						11	5		7				3	8		9		4	1			6	2	**16**
	10	2		11	4		8	5						3		1	7		9				6		**17**
	10	2		11	4	7		5						3		1	8		9				6		**18**
	10			11	6		8	5					4	3			7		9	1				2	**19**
	8					7		5			10		4	3					9	1		11	6	2	**20**
5				8	6	7			4		10			3	9					1		11		2	**21**
	8	2		11		7		5			10		4	3					9	1			6		**22**
5		2		11		7					10		4		8				9	1			6	3	**23**
5		2				8					10		4		9		7			1		11	6	3	**24**
		2		11		8		5			10		4		9		7			1			6	3	**25**
5				11		8					10		4	3	9	1	7						6	2	**26**
5		2		11		8					10		4		9	1	7						6	3	**27**
5		2		11		8					10				9	1	7		4				6	3	**28**
5		2		11		7	8				10			3			9		4	1			6		**29**
	10		9				8	5						3			7		4	1		11	6	2	**30**
			9				8	5			10			3			7		4	1		11	6	2	**31**
		2	9			7	8	5	6		10			3					4	1		11			**32**
		2	9				11	5	6	7	10				8				4	1				3	**33**
			9				11	5		7	10			3	8				4	1			6	2	**34**
		2	9			8	11	5		7					10				4	1			6	3	**35**
		2	9					5			10				8		7		4	1		11	6	3	**36**
		2	9					5			10				8		7		4	1		11	6	3	**37**
5		2	9				8				10			3			7		4	1		11	6		**38**
		2	9				8	5			10			3		1	7		4			11	6		**39**
		2	9				8	5			10			3		1	7		4			11	6		**40**
5		2	9			8					10					1	7		4			11	6	3	**41**
		2	9			8		5			10					1	7		4			11	6	3	**42**
10	16	22	18	23	6	20	24	32	5	14	21	5	14	26	18	9	34	4	27	33	3	13	33	32	Apps
1	6		10	3		6	11			1	11			3	2		10		3			1	1	3	Goals

Archer A A E	Batty W	Colebourne J	Cooke F R	Davies A S	Dawe E R	Denyer A E C	Fleming H J	Hawley F	Ing A A	Jefferson R W	Johnson J H	Kay H	Langford T S	Maconnachie J S J	Metcalf A	Nash E M	Phillipson T W	Pocock J H	Rogers D	Skiller L F	Stokoe J	Turner O C	Wareing W	Weston A M	
		2		11			8	5			10		4	3			7		9	1			6		**1**
				11			8	5			10		4	3			7		9	1			6	2	**2**
		1		2			2	2			2		2	2			2		2	2			2	1	Apps
							2																		Goals

No numbers actually worn on shirts

For Final League Table - see page 100

SEASON 1922/23

Football League Division Three South
Final League Position : 9th
Secretary/Manager : Sam Allen

					Home	Away	H-T	Goalscorers	Gate
1	S	Aug	26	Northampton Town	W2-0		(2-0)	Johnson,Cooke	9,002
2	M		28	Merthyr Town		D1-1	(1-0)	Johnson	8,000
3	S	Sep	2	Northampton Town		W2-1	(1-0)	Johnson 2 (1 pen.)	12,000
4	M		4	Merthyr Town	W4-0		(3-0)	Cooke,Davies,Johnson 2	6,732
5	S		9	Millwall		D1-1	(1-0)	Denyer	25,000
6	S		16	Millwall	D0-0				9,579
7	S		23	Luton Town		L2-3	(2-1)	Johnson,Wareing	8,000
8	S		30	Luton Town	D1-1		(0-1)	Norton	7,000
9	M	Oct	2	Swansea Town		L0-5	(0-2)		11,000
10	S		7	Queens Park Rangers		W2-0	(1-0)	Phillipson,John o.g.	12,000
11	S		14	Queens Park Rangers	W1-0		(0-0)	Cooke	7,610
12	S		21	Norwich City	L1-2		(0-2)	Cooke	9,000
13	S		28	Norwich City		D0-0			9,504
14	S	Nov	4	Gillingham		D0-0			6,000
15	S		11	Gillingham	L0-1		(0-1)		6,000
16	S		18	Brighton and Hove Albion	W3-0		(1-0)	Hawley,Phillipson,Johnson pen.	6,000
17	S		25	Brighton and Hove Albion		D1-1	(0-0)	Phillipson	9,000
18	S	Dec	9	Swansea Town	W2-1		(1-1)	Phillipson 2	5,530
19	S		23	Aberdare Athletic	W5-4		(3-2)	Denyer 2,Johnson 2,Hawley	4,000
20	Tu		26	Bristol City		L1-3	(1-3)	Dawe	28,500
21	W		27	Bristol City	L0-1		(0-1)		7,309
22	S		30	Newport County	D2-2		(1-1)	Daniel,Weston pen.	4,000
23	S	Jan	6	Newport County		D2-2	(2-1)	Phillipson,Daniel	10,000
24	S		20	Exeter City		L1-2	(0-0)	Hawley	5,000
25	S		27	Exeter City	W2-1		(2-0)	Johnson,Norton	5,000
26	S	Feb	3	Brentford	W3-0		(2-0)	Fleming,Hunter o.g.,Johnson	9,000
27	S		10	Brentford		L0-3	(0-1)		4,000
28	S		17	Watford	D1-1		(1-1)	Fleming	4,306
29	S		24	Watford		W3-0	(1-0)	Fleming,Denyer,Phillipson	4,000
30	Th	Mar	1	Aberdare Athletic		D3-3	(2-1)	Johnson 3	6,000
31	S		3	Charlton Athletic	W2-1		(1-0)	Wareing,Rogers	8,000
32	S		17	Plymouth Argyle		L0-2	(0-1)		10,000
33	S		24	Plymouth Argyle	W2-1		(1-0)	Denyer,Wareing	7,000
34	F		30	Portsmouth		L1-4	(0-4)	Denyer	13,401
35	S		31	Bristol Rovers		L0-2	(0-1)		10,000
36	M	Apr	2	Portsmouth	W3-0		(2-0)	Wareing,Johnson pen.,Fleming	7,000
37	S		7	Bristol Rovers	W1-0		(1-0)	Phillipson	5,595
38	S		14	Reading		L0-1	(0-1)		7,000
39	S		21	Reading	W3-1		(1-1)	Phillipson,Johnson 2 (1 pen.)	5,000
40	S		28	Southend United		L0-2	(0-1)		6,000
41	Th	May	3	Charlton Athletic		L1-3	(1-2)	Johnson	2,000
42	S		5	Southend United	W3-0		(2-0)	Phillipson 2,Johnson	3,000

Approx. Average Home Attendance : **6,450**
Approx. Average Away Attendance : **9,800**

F A Cup

					Home	Away	H-T	Goalscorers	Gate
1	S	Jan	13	Barnsley	D0-0				20,261
1R	Th		18	Barnsley		L0-2	(0-1)		22,951

TED NASH
made his Town debut as a 15-year old in 1917, but he would have learned little from the many friendlies he took part in during the Great War, with a 15-0 win followed a fortnight later by a 14-3 defeat being a typical scenario. Fellow Swindonian Freddy Hinton was preferred when peace-time football returned in 1919 and Ted had to wait until August 1920 to make his League debut. He then went on to serve the Town for ten years, clocking up over 250 first team appearances. In 1929 Ted married Florence Bryant, goalkeeper for Swindon Ladies !

Archer A A E	Bentley H	Colebourne J	Cooke F R	Cooper R	Daniel C H	Davies A S	Dawe E R	Denyer A E C	Fleming H J	Hawley F	Johnson J H	Lees A A	Maconnachie J S J	Nash E M	Norton J	Phillipson T W	Rogers D	Turner O C	Wareing W	Weston A M	
5		2	9			11		8			10	4		1	7				6	3	**1**
5		2	9	4		11	6	8			10			1	7					3	**2**
5		2	9			11		8			10			1	7		4		6	3	**3**
5		2	9			8		7			10			1			4	11	6	3	**4**
5	2	3	9			11		8			10			1		7	4		6		**5**
5		2	9			8		7			10			1	11		4		6	3	**6**
5		2	9			8		7			10			1	11		4		6	3	**7**
5		2	9			8					10			1	7		4	11	6	3	**8**
5		2	9			8					10			1	7		4	11	6	3	**9**
		2	9			11				5	10			1	7	8	4		6	3	**10**
		2	9			11				5	10			1	7	8	4		6	3	**11**
		2	9			11				5	10			1	7	8	4		6	3	**12**
		2	9			11				5	10			1	7	8	4		6	3	**13**
		2	9			11				5	10			1	7	8	4		6	3	**14**
		2	9			11			8	5	10			1	7		4		6	3	**15**
		2					4	7	8	5	10			1	11	9			6	3	**16**
		2					4	7	8	5	10			1	11	9		6		3	**17**
		2				11	4	8		5	10			1	7	9			6	3	**18**
	4	2				11		8		5	10			1	7	9			6	3	**19**
		2				11	4	8		5	10			1	7	9			6	3	**20**
		2			10	11	4	8		5				1	7	9	6			3	**21**
		2			10	11	4	8		5				1	7	9	6			3	**22**
		2			10	11	4	8		5				1	7	9	6			3	**23**
		2		4	10	11		8		5			3	1	7	9			6		**24**
		2				11	4		8	5	10			1	7	9			6	3	**25**
		2				11	4		8	5	10			1	7	9			6	3	**26**
		2				11		8		5	10			1	7	9	4		6	3	**27**
		2				11		7	8	5	10			1		9	4		6	3	**28**
		2				11	5	7	8		10			1		9	4		6	3	**29**
5		2		4		11	6	7			10			1		9	8			3	**30**
		2		4		11		7		5	10			1		9	8		6	3	**31**
		2				11	5	7	8		10			1		9	4		6	3	**32**
		2				11	5	7	8		10			1		9	4		6	3	**33**
		2		4		11	5	7			10			1		9	8		6	3	**34**
5		2				11	6	8			10			1	7	9	4			3	**35**
	2					11	5	7	8		10			1		9	4		6	3	**36**
	2					11	5	7	8		10			1		9	4		6	3	**37**
	2					11	5	7	8		10			1		9	4		6	3	**38**
	2					11	5	7	8		10			1		9	4		6	3	**39**
	2				9	11	6	7			10			1		8	4		5	3	**40**
	2				9	11	6	7			10			1		8	4		5	3	**41**
	2					11	6	7	8		10			1		9	4		5	3	**42**
11	9	35	15	5	6	40	23	32	14	20	38	1	1	42	26	33	32	4	35	40	Apps
			4		2	1	1	6	4	3	20				2	11	1		4	1	Goals

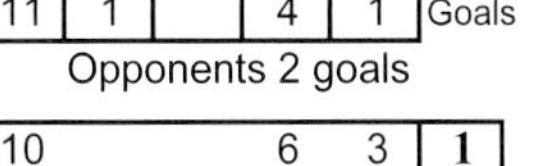

Opponents 2 goals

Archer A A E	Bentley H	Colebourne J	Cooke F R	Cooper R	Daniel C H	Davies A S	Dawe E R	Denyer A E C	Fleming H J	Hawley F	Johnson J H	Lees A A	Maconnachie J S J	Nash E M	Norton J	Phillipson T W	Rogers D	Turner O C	Wareing W	Weston A M	
		2	9			11	4	8		5				1	7	10			6	3	**1**
		2	9			11	4	7	8	5				1		10			6	3	**1R**
		2	2			2	2	2	1	2				2	1	2			2	2	Apps
																					Goals

No numbers actually worn on shirts

TOM PHILLIPSON

For Final League Table - see page 100

SEASON 1923/24

Football League Division Three South
Final League Position : 6th
Secretary/Manager : Sam Allen

					Home	Away	H-T	Goalscorers	Gate
1	S	Aug	25	Bournemouth & Boscombe Athletic	W3-1		(1-0)	Johnson 3	9,445
2	M		27	Millwall		L0-1	(0-1)		12,000
3	S	Sep	1	Bournemouth & Boscombe Athletic		D0-0			6,614
4	M		3	Millwall	W1-0		(1-0)	Daniel	7,666
5	S		8	Queens Park Rangers	D0-0				9,217
6	S		15	Queens Park Rangers		D2-2	(0-1)	Phillipson,Johnson	6,000
7	S		22	Plymouth Argyle	L0-1		(0-1)		8,961
8	S		29	Plymouth Argyle		W3-1	(2-0)	Daniel 2,Phillipson	12,000
9	S	Oct	6	Merthyr Town	W3-0		(1-0)	Rogers,Daniel 2	6,614
10	S		13	Merthyr Town		L0-2	(0-1)		6,000
11	S		20	Reading	W1-0		(1-0)	Johnson pen.	7,000
12	S		27	Reading		L0-1	(0-1)		8,752
13	S	Nov	3	Charlton Athletic		L1-3	(1-2)	Crossley	5,000
14	S		10	Charlton Athletic	D1-1		(1-0)	Denyer	5,312
15	S		17	Norwich City		L0-2	(0-2)		7,000
16	S		24	Norwich City	W4-2		(0-1)	Crossley 2,Phillipson,Denyer	4,784
17	S	Dec	1	Newport County		L0-3	(0-2)		8,000
18	S		8	Newport County	W3-0		(1-0)	Denyer,Johnson 2 (1 pen.)	4,626
19	S		15	Watford	D0-0				5,250
20	S		22	Watford		D0-0			4,500
21	W		26	Northampton Town	W2-0		(0-0)	Daniel,Watson o.g.	10,000
22	Th		27	Northampton Town		D1-1	(0-1)	Crossley	9,000
23	S		29	Swansea Town		D1-1	(1-0)	Johnson	16,000
24	S	Jan	5	Swansea Town	W1-0		(0-0)	Daniel	8,200
25	S		19	Aberdare Athletic	W3-1		(2-1)	Fleming,Johnson 2	5,208
26	S		26	Aberdare Athletic		D2-2	(1-2)	Daniel,Ruddlesdin	7,000
27	S	Feb	9	Southend United		W2-0	(0-0)	Crossley 2	4,000
28	S		16	Exeter City	L0-1		(0-0)		5,797
29	S	Mar	1	Portsmouth	D0-0				5,500
30	S		15	Brentford		D2-2	(2-1)	Ruddlesdin,Johnson	6,000
31	W		19	Exeter City		L1-3	(0-2)	Daniel	4,000
32	S		22	Brentford	W2-1		(2-0)	Fleming,Crossley	6,000
33	S		29	Bristol Rovers		W1-0	(0-0)	Ruddlesdin	10,000
34	W	Apr	2	Southend United	W3-0		(2-0)	Daniel,Crossley,Bew	3,100
35	S		5	Bristol Rovers	D0-0				5,060
36	S		12	Brighton and Hove Albion		D1-1	(0-1)	Davies	5,000
37	F		18	Gillingham		L0-1	(0-1)		9,000
38	S		19	Brighton and Hove Albion	W4-0		(3-0)	Ruddlesdin 2,Fleming,Davies	5,500
39	M		21	Gillingham	W4-1		(2-0)	Johnson pen.,Davies,Broadhead 2	5,000
40	S		26	Luton Town		L2-3	(1-1)	Johnson,Dawe	7,000
41	W		30	Portsmouth		L1-4	(1-3)	Daniel	18,000
42	S	May	3	Luton Town	W3-2		(1-0)	Daniel,Rogers,Anderson o.g.	4,716

Approx. Average Home Attendance : **6,350**
Approx. Average Away Attendance : **8,150**

F A Cup

					Home	Away	H-T	Goalscorers	Gate
1	S	Jan	12	Bradford Park Avenue	W4-0		(3-0)	Wareing,Crossley,Denyer,Johnson	15,227
2	S	Feb	2	Oldham Athletic	W2-0		(0-0)	Denyer,Crossley	22,884
3	S		23	Crystal Palace		W2-1	(1-1)	Wareing,Fleming	20,000
4	S	Mar	8	Burnley	D1-1		(0-1)	Fleming	22,310
4R	W		12	Burnley		L1-3	(0-1)	Johnson	34,089

BERTIE DAVIES

made maximum appearances for Town this season. He was originally taken on as an amateur in 1912 and then signed a professional contract at ten shillings (50p !) a week. But in 1914, he could not agree terms and went to Middlesbrough. The Great War brought him back to Wiltshire and after assisting the Town during 1915/16, he re-signed for the 1919/20 season - and remained a regular until 1926. After the last War, he held the posts of assistant trainer, assistant manager and assistant secretary at the County Ground until he finally retired in 1963.

Archer A A E	Bentley H	Bew D C	Broadhead A	Cooper R	Crossley C A	Daniel C H	Davies A S	Dawe E R	Denyer A E C	Dickenson W	Fleming H J	Greaves E	Ing A A	Johnson J H	Mason G	Nash E M	O'Neill H	Phillipson T W	Randall O J H	Rogers D	Ruddlesdin A	Thompson C	Wareing W	Weston A M	
		5			8		11		7	2				10		1		9		4			6	3	**1**
		5			8		11		7	2				10		1		9		4			6	3	**2**
		5			8		11		7	2				10		1		9		4			6	3	**3**
		5				9	11		7	2				10		1		8		4			6	3	**4**
		5				9	11		7	2				10		1		8		4			6	3	**5**
		5				9	11			2				10		1		7		4	8		6	3	**6**
		5				9	10			2						1		8		4	7	11	6	3	**7**
		5				9	11		7	2				10		1		8		4			6	3	**8**
		5				9	11		7	2				10		1		8		4			6	3	**9**
		5				9	11		7	2				10		1		8		4			6	3	**10**
		5				9	11		7	2				10		1		8		4			6	3	**11**
		5			8		11			2				10	7	1		9		4			6	3	**12**
		5			10	9	11		7	2						1		8		4			6	3	**13**
		5			10	9	11		7	2						1		8		4			6	3	**14**
		5			8		11		7	2				10				9	1	4			6	3	**15**
		5			8		11		7	2				10				9	1	4			6	3	**16**
		5			8		11		7	2				10				9	1	4			6	3	**17**
		5			8		11		7	2				10				9	1	4			6	3	**18**
		5		4	8		11		7	2				10				9	1				6	3	**19**
		5		4	8		11		7	2				10			3	9	1				6		**20**
		5		4	8	9	11		7	2				10					1				6	3	**21**
		5		4	8		11			2	9		7	10					1				6	3	**22**
		5		4	8		9			2			7	10			3		1			11	6		**23**
		5		4	8	9	11	6	7	2				10					1					3	**24**
		5		4		8	11		7	2	9			10					1				6	3	**25**
		5		4		9	11		7	2				10					1		8		6	3	**26**
		5		4	8	9	11		7	2				10					1				6	3	**27**
		5		4	8	9	11		7	2				10					1				6	3	**28**
		5		4	8	9	11		7	2				10					1				6	3	**29**
		5		4	8		11	6	7	2				10			3		1		9				**30**
5						10	11	4	7			6					2		1	8	9			3	**31**
		5		4	8		11		7		9			10			2		1				6	3	**32**
		5		4	8	10	11		7								2		1	6	9			3	**33**
	2	5		4	8	10	11		7										1	6	9			3	**34**
	2	5		4	8	10	11		7		9								1	6				3	**35**
		5		4	8	10	11		7	2									1	6	9			3	**36**
		5		4	8	10	11		7	2									1	6	9			3	**37**
		5		4			11		7	2	9			10					1	6	8			3	**38**
		5	8	4		9	11		7	2				10					1	6				3	**39**
		5		4		9	11	6	7	2				10					1	8				3	**40**
		5		4		9	11		7	2				10					1	6	8			3	**41**
		5		4		9	11		7	2				10					1	6	8			3	**42**
1	2	41	1	23	26	27	42	4	37	37	5	1	2	33	1	14	6	20	28	29	12	2	29	39	Apps
		1	2		8	12	3	1	3		3			13				3		2	5				Goals

Opponents 2 goals

Archer A A E	Bentley H	Bew D C	Broadhead A	Cooper R	Crossley C A	Daniel C H	Davies A S	Dawe E R	Denyer A E C	Dickenson W	Fleming H J	Greaves E	Ing A A	Johnson J H	Mason G	Nash E M	O'Neill H	Phillipson T W	Randall O J H	Rogers D	Ruddlesdin A	Thompson C	Wareing W	Weston A M	
		5		4	8		11		7	2	9			10					1				6	3	**1**
		5		4	8		11		7	2	9			10					1				6	3	**2**
		5		4	8		11		7	2	9			10					1				6	3	**3**
		5		4	8		11		7	2	9			10					1				6	3	**4**
		5		4	8		11		7	2	9			10					1				6	3	**4R**
		5		5	5		5		5	5	5			5					5				5	5	Apps
					2				2		2			2									2		Goals

No numbers actually worn on shirts

For Final League Table - see page 101

SEASON 1924/25

Football League Division Three South
Final League Position : 4th
Secretary/Manager : Sam Allen

				Home	Away	H-T	Goalscorers	Gate
1	S	Aug	30 Swansea Town		L0-2	(0-0)		20,000
2	M	Sep	1 Plymouth Argyle	W1-0		(1-0)	Crossley	9,749
3	S		6 Aberdare Athletic	W2-0		(1-0)	Johnson 2 (1 pen.)	7,000
4	M		8 Plymouth Argyle		L0-2	(0-1)		10,000
5	S		13 Norwich City		L0-4	(0-1)		8,000
6	W		17 Bristol City		D0-0			7,000
7	S		20 Brentford	W2-0		(0-0)	Johnson,Bew	3,755
8	W		24 Southend United	W3-0		(1-0)	Johnson 2 pens.,Crossley	3,809
9	S		27 Millwall		W2-1	(0-1)	Richardson,Johnson	23,000
10	S	Oct	4 Luton Town	W4-1		(1-0)	Denyer,Richardson,Ruddlesdin,Davies	7,886
11	S		11 Gillingham		D1-1	(0-1)	Richardson	7,000
12	S		18 Bournemouth & Boscombe Athletic	W4-0		(3-0)	Davies 2,Johnson,Ruddlesdin	7,313
13	S		25 Exeter City		L0-1	(0-0)		8,000
14	S	Nov	1 Bristol Rovers	W3-0		(1-0)	Richardson,Johnson,Davies	6,016
15	S		8 Newport County		L1-3	(1-2)	Ruddlesdin	10,000
16	S		15 Queens Park Rangers	W5-3		(2-0)	Ruddlesdin 3,Davies,Richardson	6,923
17	S		22 Watford		L0-1	(0-0)		7,000
18	S		29 Northampton Town	W5-0		(2-0)	Richardson 3,Johnson,Ruddlesdin	8,674
19	S	Dec	6 Charlton Athletic		L0-1	(0-0)		10,000
20	S		20 Merthyr Town		W5-1	(2-0)	Johnson 2,Richardson 3	4,000
21	Th		25 Reading	W2-1		(1-1)	Johnson,Daniel	9,400
22	F		26 Reading		D1-1	(0-0)	Crossley	18,764
23	S		27 Swansea Town	L0-2		(0-1)		9,000
24	S	Jan	17 Norwich City	W1-0		(0-0)	Richardson	6,000
25	S		24 Brentford		D0-0			7,000
26	S		31 Millwall	W1-0		(1-0)	Fort o.g.	6,000
27	S	Feb	7 Luton Town		D2-2	(1-0)	Denyer,Johnson	5,000
28	S		14 Gillingham	W2-0		(0-0)	Daniel,Purcell	5,000
29	S		21 Bournemouth & Boscombe Athletic		D0-0			5,000
30	S		28 Exeter City	W1-0		(1-0)	Richardson	8,000
31	S	Mar	7 Bristol Rovers		W1-0	(0-0)	Daniel	10,000
32	S		14 Newport County	D2-2		(2-2)	Purcell,Richardson	8,028
33	S		21 Southend United		D0-0			11,000
34	S		28 Watford	L0-1		(0-0)		6,173
35	S	Apr	4 Northampton Town		D0-0			8,000
36	F		10 Brighton and Hove Albion		L1-3	(0-0)	Crossley	11,781
37	S		11 Charlton Athletic	D2-2		(1-0)	Johnson,Daniel	7,000
38	M		13 Brighton and Hove Albion	W3-0		(2-0)	Richardson,Daniel,Bew	10,000
39	S		18 Queens Park Rangers		L0-1	(0-1)		9,000
40	Th		23 Aberdare Athletic		D1-1	(1-1)	Daniel	5,000
41	S		25 Merthyr Town	W5-1		(4-0)	Johnson 2,Daniel 2,Bew	5,000
42	S	May	2 Bristol City	W3-0		(2-0)	Johnson,Daniel,Weston	8,361

Approx. Average Home Attendance : **7,100**
Approx. Average Away Attendance : **9,750**

F A Cup

				Home	Away	H-T	Goalscorers	Gate
1	S	Jan	10 Fulham	L1-2		(1-1)	Johnson	20,301

JACK JOHNSON
was top scorer for Town for the third season in succession. A Bristolian, he was discovered playing for his local chocolate factory side and signed amateur forms for Town in March 1921. His partnership with new signing Frank Richardson yielded 33 goals this season, but Jack's hat-trick in the 10-1 thrashing of Cup minnows Farnham United Breweries in November 1925 were his last senior goals for the club. He signed for Queens Park Rangers in 1927, but later returned west and at the age of 38 was still playing for Swindon Corporation. Jack died in Uffington in 1974.

Archer A A E	Bew D C	Cooper R	Crossley C A	Daniel C H	Davies A S	Denyer A E C	Dickenson W	Furniss S	Johnson J H	Nash E M	O'Neill H	Price J W	Purcell G W	Randall O J H	Richardson F	Rogers D	Ruddlesdin A	Rutherford J B	Waite R A	Wareing W	Weston A M	
	5		8		11	7	2	4	10					1				9		6	3	**1**
	5		8		11	7	2	4	10					1				9		6	3	**2**
	5		8		11	7	2	4	10		3			1				9		6		**3**
	5	6	8		11	7	2	4			3			1	10			9				**4**
	5	6	8		11	7	2	4			3			1	10			9				**5**
	5	4	8	10	11	7	2				3			1	10		9			6		**6**
	5	4	8		11	7	2		10					1	9					6	3	**7**
	5	4	8		11	7	2		10					1	9					6	3	**8**
	5	6			11	7	2	4	10					1	9		8				3	**9**
	5	6			11	7	2	4	10					1	9		8				3	**10**
5		4			11	7	2		10					1	9		8			6	3	**11**
5		4			11	7	2		10					1	9		8			6	3	**12**
		4			11	7	2	5	10					1	9		8			6	3	**13**
		4			11	7	2	5	10					1	9		8			6	3	**14**
		4			11	7	2	5	10					1	9		8			6	3	**15**
		4			11	7	2	5	10					1	9		8			6	3	**16**
	5	4			11	7	2		10					1	9		8			6	3	**17**
	5	4			11	7			10			2		1	9		8			6	3	**18**
	5	4			11	7	2		10					1	9		8			6	3	**19**
	5		8		11	7	2		10					1	9	4				6	3	**20**
	5			11		7	2		10					1	9	4				6	3	**21**
	5	6	8	11		7	2		10					1	9	4					3	**22**
	5	6		11		7	2		10					1	9	4	8				3	**23**
		6			11	7	2		10		3			1	9	4	8		5			**24**
		4			11	7	2		10		3		8	1	9	5				6		**25**
	5	4			11	7	2		10				8	1	9	6					3	**26**
	5	4			11	7	2		10				8	1	9	6					3	**27**
	5	4		9	11	7	2		10				8	1		6					3	**28**
	5	4		9	11	7	2		10				8	1		6					3	**29**
	5	4			11	7	2		10				8	1	9	6					3	**30**
	5	4		10		7	2		11				8	1	9	6					3	**31**
	5	4			11	7	2		10				8	1	9	6					3	**32**
	5	4			11	7	2		10				8	1	9	6					3	**33**
	5	4			11	7	2		10				8	1	9	6					3	**34**
	5	4		10	11	7	2							1	9	6	8				3	**35**
	5	4	8	10	11	7	2							1	9	6					3	**36**
4	5			9	11	7			10			2		1		6	8				3	**37**
4	5			9	11	7			6	1	2		8		10						3	**38**
	5			9	11	7			6		2		8	1	10	4					3	**39**
	5			9	11	7	2		10				8	1		4				6	3	**40**
	5	4		9	11		2		10				7	1	8	6					3	**41**
6	5	4		9	11		2		10				7	1	8						3	**42**
5	34	33	11	15	38	40	38	11	37	1	8	2	15	41	34	21	16	5	1	19	36	Apps
	3		4	9	5	2			17				2		15		7				1	Goals

Opponents 1 goal

Archer A A E	Bew D C	Cooper R	Crossley C A	Daniel C H	Davies A S	Denyer A E C	Dickenson W	Furniss S	Johnson J H	Nash E M	O'Neill H	Price J W	Purcell G W	Randall O J H	Richardson F	Rogers D	Ruddlesdin A	Rutherford J B	Waite R A	Wareing W	Weston A M	
	5	4	8		11	7	2		10					1	9					6	3	**1**

No numbers actually worn on shirts

CYRIL DANIEL

For Final League Table - see page 101

SEASON 1925/26

Football League Division Three South
Final League Position : 6th
Secretary/Manager : Sam Allen

No.	Day	Month	Date	Opponents	Home	Away	H-T	Goalscorers	Gate
1	S	Aug	29	Bournemouth & Boscombe Athletic		L0-2	(0-0)		9,006
2	M		31	Bristol City	L1-3		(1-0)	Richardson	11,960
3	S	Sep	5	Charlton Athletic	W3-0		(1-0)	Richardson,Wall 2	6,076
4	W		9	Bristol City		L1-5	(0-0)	Richardson	12,362
5	S		12	Gillingham		W1-0	(1-0)	Richardson	7,312
6	W		16	Bristol Rovers	W4-2		(2-0)	Wall,Richardson 2,Denyer	6,469
7	S		19	Merthyr Town	L0-2		(0-1)		2,954
8	W		23	Millwall	D1-1		(0-0)	Furniss	5,888
9	S		26	Newport County		W4-0	(2-0)	Johnson,Denyer 2,Wall	8,144
10	S	Oct	3	Luton Town	W2-0		(1-0)	Wall 2	7,848
11	S		10	Queens Park Rangers		D1-1	(1-1)	Clark	9,877
12	S		17	Crystal Palace	W3-1		(1-0)	Weston pen.,Clark 2	7,564
13	S		24	Brentford		L1-3	(1-0)	Clark	8,282
14	S		31	Southend United	W2-0		(1-0)	Richardson,Johnson	6,658
15	S	Nov	7	Plymouth Argyle		D1-1	(1-1)	Davies	14,580
16	S		14	Aberdare Athletic	W2-1		(2-1)	Denyer,Wall	7,608
17	S		21	Northampton Town		L0-2	(0-1)		8,782
18	S	Dec	5	Norwich City		D2-2	(1-1)	Richardson 2	5,405
19	S		19	Brighton and Hove Albion		L1-3	(0-1)	Richardson	6,098
20	F		25	Reading		L0-2	(0-1)		12,058
21	S		26	Reading	D1-1		(0-0)	Richardson	17,295
22	M		28	Bristol Rovers		W2-1	(2-1)	O'Neill pen.,Daniel	6,396
23	S	Jan	2	Bournemouth & Boscombe Athletic	W8-2		(4-2)	Richardson 4,Daniel 2,Thompson,Petrie	5,625
24	S		16	Charlton Athletic		L0-2	(0-1)		3,823
25	S		23	Gillingham	W1-0		(1-0)	Richardson	3,368
26	S	Feb	6	Newport County	W2-1		(1-1)	Wall,Daniel	5,687
27	S		13	Luton Town		L1-4	(0-1)	Daniel	8,588
28	S		20	Queens Park Rangers	W2-0		(1-0)	Richardson 2	6,063
29	M		22	Merthyr Town		L1-2	(0-0)	Weston pen.	3,687
30	S		27	Crystal Palace		L0-1	(0-1)		11,534
31	S	Mar	6	Brentford	W2-1		(1-0)	Petrie 2	4,932
32	S		13	Southend United		L0-3	(0-0)		6,796
33	S		20	Plymouth Argyle	W2-0		(0-0)	Clark,Wall	8,814
34	S		27	Aberdare Athletic		D1-1	(0-0)	Bew	5,087
35	F	Apr	2	Exeter City	W2-1		(1-0)	Davies,Denyer	7,389
36	S		3	Northampton Town	L1-2		(0-0)	Clark	6,192
37	M		5	Exeter City		W2-1	(1-0)	Rowley 2	10,031
38	S		10	Millwall		L0-3	(0-0)		18,098
39	S		17	Norwich City	W3-1		(1-1)	Petrie 2,Wall	3,930
40	W		21	Watford	W5-3		(4-0)	Wall,Dickenson pen.,Clark,Davies,Denyer	2,668
41	S		24	Watford		L2-3	(1-0)	Petrie,Wall	4,823
42	S	May	1	Brighton and Hove Albion	W1-0		(0-0)	Wall	4,616

Average Home Attendance : **6,648**
Average Away Attendance : **8,608**

F A Cup

No.	Day	Month	Date	Opponents	Home	Away	H-T	Goalscorers	Gate
1	S	Nov	28	Farnham United Breweries		W10-1	(7-0)	Johnson 3,Richardson 4,Denyer 2,Wall	3,261
2	S	Dec	12	Sittingbourne	W7-0		(5-0)	Davies 2,Richardson 4,Denyer	10,030
3	S	Jan	9	Clapton		* W3-2	(0-0)	Richardson 2,Moore o.g.	27,100
4	S		30	Nottingham Forest		L0-2	(0-1)		14,000

* Played at Boleyn Ground (Upton Park)

FRANK RICHARDSON
arrived from West Ham in June 1924, but was only at the County Ground for 20 months before joining Reading - although he returned to the club for the 1930/31 season. His goalscoring feats in 1925/26 were remarkable. After hitting 28 in just 23 games for Town, he netted another dozen in only 13 games following his £1,100 move to Elm Park in February 1926 - four on the final day of the season in a 7-1 win clinching the Third South title for the Biscuitmen. He rejoined Town in June 1930 at the age of 33.

Adey T W	Archer A A E	Bew D C	Clark J R	Cooper R	Daniel C H	Davies A S	Denyer A E C	Dickenson W	Furniss S	Johnson J H	Nash E M	O'Neill H	Petrie C	Purcell G W	Randall O J H	Richardson F	Rogers D	Rowley R W M	Ruddlesdin A	Thompson J	Waite R A	Wall A	Weston A M	
		5		4	9	11		2		10				7	1	8	6						3	**1**
	5			4	9	11		2		10				7	1	8	6						3	**2**
		5	10	4		11		2			1			7		9	6					8	3	**3**
6		5	10			11	7	2	4		1					9						8	3	**4**
6		5				11	7	2	4	10	1					9						8	3	**5**
6		5				11	7	2	4	10	1					9						8	3	**6**
		5		6		11	7	2	4		1		10						9			8	3	**7**
	6	5	9			11	7	2	4	10	1											8	3	**8**
	6	5	9			11	7	2	4	10	1											8	3	**9**
	6	5	9			11	7	2	4	10	1											8	3	**10**
	6	5	9			11	7	2	4	10	1											8	3	**11**
	6	5	9			11	7	2	4	10	1											8	3	**12**
		5	11			6	7	2	4	10	1					9						8	3	**13**
6		5				11	7	2	4	10	1					9						8	3	**14**
6		5				11	7	2	4	10	1					9						8	3	**15**
6		5				11	7	2	4	10	1					9						8	3	**16**
6	4	5				11	7	2		10	1					9						8	3	**17**
6	4	5				11	7	2		10	1					9						8	3	**18**
6	4	5				11	7	2		10	1					9						8	3	**19**
6	4	5				11	7	2		10	1					9						8	3	**20**
6	4	5				11	7	2		10	1					9						8	3	**21**
6	4	5			8		7	2			1	3	10			9				11				**22**
	4	5			8		7				1	2	10			9	6			11			3	**23**
6	4		9				7	2		11	1		10								5	8	3	**24**
6		5					7	2	4	10	1					9				11		8	3	**25**
6		5			9		7	2			1		10				4			11		8	3	**26**
6	4	5			9		7	2			1		10							11		8	3	**27**
6	4				10		7	2			1					9				11	5	8	3	**28**
6	4	5	9		10		7	2			1									11		8	3	**29**
6	4				9	11	7	2			1	3	10								5	8		**30**
6	4	5			9	11	7	2			1		10						8				3	**31**
6	4	5	9			11	7	2			1		10									8	3	**32**
6	4	5	9			11	7	2			1		10									8	3	**33**
6	4	5	9			11	7	2			1		10									8	3	**34**
6		5	9	4		11	7	2			1		10									8	3	**35**
6		5	9	4		11	7	2			1		10									8	3	**36**
	6	5		4	10	11	7	2			1							9				8	3	**37**
	6	5	10	4	9	11	7	2			1											8	3	**38**
	6	5	9	4		11	7	2			1		10									8	3	**39**
	6	5	9	4		11	7	2			1		10									8	3	**40**
	6	5		4		11	7	2			1		10					9				8	3	**41**
	6	5		4	9	11	7	2		10	1											8	3	**42**
25	28	38	18	12	13	34	39	41	14	21	40	3	16	3	2	19	5	2	2	7	3	37	40	Apps
		1	7		5	3	6	1	1	2		1	6			18		2		1		13	2	Goals

Adey T W	Archer A A E	Bew D C	Clark J R	Cooper R	Daniel C H	Davies A S	Denyer A E C	Dickenson W	Furniss S	Johnson J H	Nash E M	O'Neill H	Petrie C	Purcell G W	Randall O J H	Richardson F	Rogers D	Rowley R W M	Ruddlesdin A	Thompson J	Waite R A	Wall A	Weston A M	
6	4	5				11	7	2		10	1					9						8	3	**1**
6	4	5				11	7	2		10	1					9						8	3	**2**
6	4	5			10		7	2			1					9				11		8	3	**3**
6		5					7	2		10	1					9	4			11		8	3	**4**
4	3	4			1	2	4	4		3	4					4	1			2		4	4	Apps
						2	3			3						10						1		Goals

No numbers actually worn on shirts

Opponents 1 goal

For Final League Table - see page 101

SEASON 1926/27

Football League Division Three South
Final League Position : 5th
Secretary/Manager : Sam Allen

					Home	Away	H-T	Goalscorers	Gate
1	S	Aug	28	Southend United	W5-1		(2-1)	Morris 3 (1 pen.),Thom,Denyer	8,943
2	M		30	Exeter City	W4-2		(2-1)	Thom,Morris 3	8,364
3	S	Sep	4	Luton Town		D1-1	(1-0)	Morris	11,386
4	S		11	Norwich City	W3-2		(2-1)	Thom,Morris 2	8,042
5	M		13	Bournemouth & Boscombe Athletic	W2-0		(1-0)	Eddleston,Petrie	7,578
6	S		18	Brighton and Hove Albion		L3-9	(3-5)	Eddleston 2,Petrie	10,303
7	W		22	Bournemouth & Boscombe Athletic		W2-1	(1-0)	Wall,Thom	5,647
8	S		25	Northampton Town	W3-1		(2-0)	Wall,Morris,Eddleston	8,298
9	S	Oct	2	Brentford		D2-2	(2-0)	Wall,Morris pen.	15,404
10	S		9	Millwall	W3-0		(0-0)	Thom,Morris,Denyer	8,676
11	S		16	Charlton Athletic		D2-2	(2-1)	Morris 2	7,863
12	S		23	Bristol City	D2-2		(2-0)	Hughes o.g.,Wall	20,057
13	S		30	Plymouth Argyle		L1-3	(1-1)	Morris	15,102
14	S	Nov	6	Newport County	W3-1		(1-0)	Petrie,Dickenson pen.,Morris	4,870
15	S		20	Gillingham	W1-0		(1-0)	Morris	5,493
16	S	Dec	4	Crystal Palace	W6-1		(2-1)	Dickenson pen.,Morris 4,Wall	6,190
17	S		11	Aberdare Athletic		W4-1	(1-1)	Morris,Eddleston 2,Wall	2,699
18	S		18	Queens Park Rangers	W6-2		(3-1)	Wall,Morris 5	6,706
19	S		25	Merthyr Town	W3-2		(2-1)	Thom,Morris,Dickenson pen.	9,330
20	M		27	Merthyr Town		W2-1	(0-1)	Eddleston,Morris	8,662
21	Tu		28	Coventry City		W3-1	(2-0)	Petrie,Morris 2	17,551
22	S	Jan	1	Exeter City		L1-3	(0-1)	Morris	6,516
23	S		8	Watford		D2-2	(1-1)	Morris,Thom	6,438
24	S		15	Southend United		D2-2	(2-0)	Eddleston 2	7,118
25	S		22	Luton Town	W2-0		(0-0)	Morris,Thom	7,567
26	S		29	Norwich City		L1-2	(0-1)	Denyer	6,423
27	S	Feb	5	Brighton and Hove Albion	D2-2		(1-2)	Petrie,Archer pen.	15,317
28	S		12	Northampton Town		L0-1	(0-0)		5,267
29	S		26	Millwall		L1-4	(0-3)	Morris	18,779
30	S	Mar	5	Charlton Athletic	W2-0		(2-0)	Flood,Morris	6,300
31	W		9	Brentford	W4-2		(1-1)	Denyer,Eddleston,Flood 2	4,659
32	S		12	Bristol City		L0-2	(0-1)		31,417
33	S		19	Plymouth Argyle	L1-2		(0-1)	Morris	13,631
34	S		26	Newport County		L3-5	(2-2)	Morris 3	4,751
35	S	Apr	2	Aberdare Athletic	W3-2		(1-1)	Denyer,Jefferies 2	4,629
36	S		9	Gillingham		D4-4	(3-0)	Bailey,Eddleston,Weston pen.,Morris	3,724
37	F		15	Bristol Rovers	L3-5		(2-2)	Jefferies 2,Brown	8,988
38	S		16	Watford	W4-2		(4-0)	Daniel,Johnson S,Morris 2	5,274
39	M		18	Bristol Rovers		L1-3	(0-0)	Morris	9,779
40	S		23	Crystal Palace		L0-5	(0-1)		10,670
41	S		30	Coventry City	D2-2		(0-2)	Morris 2	4,839
42	S	May	7	Queens Park Rangers		W1-0	(0-0)	Morris	10,158

Average Home Attendance : **8,274**
Average Away Attendance : **10,269**

F A Cup

					Home	Away	H-T	Goalscorers	Gate
1	S	Nov	27	Bournemouth & Boscombe Athletic		D1-1	(0-1)	Morris	9,417
1R	M		29	Bournemouth & Boscombe Athletic	L3-4		(3-1)	Thom,Wall 2	7,120

HARRY MORRIS
virtually rewrote Town's record book during his seven year stay at the County Ground - and was the club's top goalscorer in all seven seasons. Born into a Jewish community in London's east end, Harry was discovered playing on Hackney Marshes by a Fulham scout. Plucked from Swansea Town's reserve side for a mere £110 - just a tenth of the fee received for Frank Richardson only four months earlier - it was a typically astute piece of business by boss Sam Allen. Harry hit hat-tricks in his first two games for Town and never looked back. Between the end of October and January he found the net in eleven successive League games - notching 19 goals. His 48 goals for the season and his feat of twice scoring five League goals in a game (once away) are club records that have survived to the present day - 80 years on.

Archer A A E	Bailey G S J	Bew D C	Bourne J T	Brooke P	Brown A	Cooper R	Daniel C H	Davies A S	Denyer A E C	Dickenson W	Eddleston J	Flood C W	Furniss S	Hicks L A G	Jefferies C E	Johnson J H	Johnson S	Morris D H	Nash E M	O'Neill H	Petrie C	Thom A	Wall A	Weston A M	Wylie T	
		5							7	2	10		4				6	9	1			11	8	3		**1**
		5							7	2	10		4				6	9	1			11	8	3		**2**
6		5			4					2	7							9	1		10	11	8	3		**3**
6		5			4						7							9	1	2	10	11	8	3		**4**
6		5			4						7							9	1	2	10	11	8	3		**5**
6		5	1		4				7		9									2	10	11	8	3		**6**
6		5	1	2		4			7		10							9				11	8	3		**7**
6		5	1			4			7	2	10							9				11	8	3		**8**
6		5	1			4			7	2	10							9				11	8	3		**9**
6		5	1			4			7	2	10							9				11	8	3		**10**
6		5	1			4			7	2	10							9				11	8	3		**11**
6		5			4				7	2	10							9	1			11	8	3		**12**
6		5	1		4				7	2	10							9				11	8	3		**13**
6		5	1		4					2	7							9			10	11	8	3		**14**
6		5	1		4				7	2	10							9				11	8	3		**15**
6		5	1			4			7	2	10							9				11	8	3		**16**
6		5	1			4			7	2	10							9				11	8	3		**17**
6		5	1			4			7	2	10							9				11	8	3		**18**
6		5	1			4			7	2	10							9				11	8	3		**19**
		5	1			4		7		2	10						6	9			8	11		3		**20**
5			1		4			7		2	10						6	9			8	11		3		**21**
6		5	1		4			7		2	10							9			8	11		3		**22**
6		5	1			4		7		2	8							9			10	11		3		**23**
6		5				4			7	2	8							9	1		10	11		3		**24**
		5	1						7	2	8		4				6	9			10	11		3		**25**
		5	1						7		8		4				6	9		2	10	11			3	**26**
6		5	1			4		8	7									9			10	11		3	2	**27**
6		5	1			4	8	11	7	2								9			10				3	**28**
6		5	1			4			7	2	10	8				11		9						3		**29**
5	11		1						7		10	8	4				6	9						3	2	**30**
5	11		1						7		10	8	4				6	9						3	2	**31**
6		5	1					11	7		10	8	4					9						3	2	**32**
6		5	1						7		10	8	4				11	9						3	2	**33**
6		5	1						7		10		4		8		11	9						3	2	**34**
6	11	5	1	2					7		10		4		8			9						3		**35**
6	11	5	1	2					7		10		4		8			9						3		**36**
6	11	5	1		4				7		10				8			9						3	2	**37**
6		5	1		4		8		7		10			2			11	9		3						**38**
5	11		1		4		8		7		10						6	9		2				3		**39**
6		5			4		8		7	2	10						11	9	1	3						**40**
6	11	5				4			7		10							9	1	2	8			3		**41**
6		5	1			4		11	7	2	10							9			8			3		**42**
37	7	38	33	3	14	17	4	8	34	25	40	5	11	1	4	1	13	41	9	8	16	27	19	38	9	Apps
1	1				1		1		5	3	11	3			4		1	47			5	8	7	1		Goals

Opponents 1 goal

Archer A A E	Bailey G S J	Bew D C	Bourne J T	Brooke P	Brown A	Cooper R	Daniel C H	Davies A S	Denyer A E C	Dickenson W	Eddleston J	Flood C W	Furniss S	Hicks L A G	Jefferies C E	Johnson J H	Johnson S	Morris D H	Nash E M	O'Neill H	Petrie C	Thom A	Wall A	Weston A M	Wylie T	
6		5	1			4			7	2	10							9				11	8	3		**1**
6		5	1			4			7	2	10							9				11	8	3		**1R**
2		2	2			2			2	2	2							2				2	2	2		Apps
																		1				1	2			Goals

No numbers actually worn on shirts

For Final League Table - see page 102

SEASON 1927/28

Football League Division Three South
Final League Position : 6th
Secretary/Manager : Sam Allen

					Home	Away	H-T	Goalscorers	Gate
1	S	Aug	27	Bournemouth & Boscombe Athletic		L0-2	(0-0)		10,208
2	M		29	Coventry City	W6-0		(1-0)	Morris 4,Eddleston 2	8,846
3	S	Sep	3	Queens Park Rangers	L0-2		(0-1)		9,659
4	M		5	Coventry City		L0-4	(0-0)		9,553
5	S		10	Watford		W5-2	(4-1)	Dickenson 2 pens.,Thom,Morris 2	10,483
6	S		17	Charlton Athletic	D2-2		(1-0)	Dickenson pen.,Morris	8,077
7	S	Oct	1	Plymouth Argyle	D2-2		(1-1)	Morris 2	6,792
8	S		8	Merthyr Town		L2-8	(1-5)	Morris,Roberts	5,418
9	S		15	Walsall	W5-0		(2-0)	Morris 3,Eddleston,Roberts	6,938
10	S		22	Millwall		D3-3	(3-1)	Morris 2,Roberts	8,338
11	S		29	Luton Town	W4-2		(2-0)	Roberts,Morris,Thom,Dickenson pen.	7,580
12	S	Nov	5	Brentford		W4-1	(1-0)	Eddleston 2,Thom,Morris	9,527
13	S		12	Crystal Palace	D3-3		(2-3)	Morris 2,Thom	7,608
14	S		19	Exeter City		D0-0			6,310
15	S	Dec	3	Norwich City		W3-1	(1-0)	Roberts 2,Low	7,479
16	S		24	Brighton and Hove Albion	W4-3		(1-1)	Dickenson pen.,Morris,Thom 2	7,455
17	M		26	Newport County		W3-1	(0-1)	Morris,Thom,Eddleston	3,610
18	Tu		27	Newport County	W4-1		(3-0)	Dickenson pen.,Roberts,Morris 2	9,715
19	S	Jan	7	Queens Park Rangers		W1-0	(0-0)	Denyer	9,981
20	S		21	Watford	W4-0		(2-0)	Roberts,Archer,Morris 2	6,356
21	S	Feb	4	Bristol Rovers	W2-1		(0-1)	Dickenson pen.,Morris	5,593
22	S		11	Plymouth Argyle		L0-3	(0-0)		13,052
23	S		18	Merthyr Town	L1-2		(1-2)	Eddleston	6,464
24	S		25	Walsall		W2-1	(2-0)	Roberts,Morris	7,591
25	S	Mar	3	Millwall	W3-0		(0-0)	Morris 2,Roberts	11,716
26	S		10	Luton Town		L1-2	(0-1)	Morris	6,973
27	W		14	Southend United		D1-1	(0-0)	Thom	3,159
28	S		17	Brentford	D1-1		(1-0)	Walker	6,300
29	W		21	Bournemouth & Boscombe Athletic	W3-2		(1-2)	Morris,Denyer,Roberts	2,685
30	S		24	Crystal Palace		L0-1	(0-0)		8,373
31	S		31	Exeter City	W3-0		(0-0)	Morris,Eddleston,Denyer	2,999
32	F	Apr	6	Gillingham		W1-0	(1-0)	Roberts	7,930
33	S		7	Northampton Town		L0-3	(0-1)		14,174
34	M		9	Gillingham	W6-1		(2-1)	Morris,Eddleston 2 (1 pen.),Denyer,Walker,Roberts	7,901
35	S		14	Norwich City	D1-1		(0-1)	Morris	4,980
36	W		18	Bristol Rovers		L0-1	(0-1)		5,445
37	S		21	Torquay United		L1-2	(1-1)	Thom	2,808
38	W		23	Northampton Town	W4-0		(2-0)	Morris,Roberts,Denyer,Eddleston	5,289
39	S		28	Southend United	L0-1		(0-0)		4,899
40	M		30	Charlton Athletic		L1-3	(0-2)	Daniel	2,900
41	W	May	2	Torquay United	D2-2		(0-1)	Morris,Eddleston	2,528
42	S		5	Brighton and Hove Albion		L2-4	(1-3)	Morris 2	5,757

Average Home Attendance : **6,685**
Average Away Attendance : **7,575**

F A Cup

					Home	Away	H-T	Goalscorers	Gate
1	S	Nov	26	Newport County		W1-0	(1-0)	Morris	9,600
2	S	Dec	10	Crystal Palace	D0-0				16,360
2R	W		14	Crystal Palace		W2-1	(1-0)	Morris 2	8,500
3	S	Jan	14	Clapton Orient	W2-1		(1-0)	Morris 2	19,079
4	S		28	Sheffield Wednesday	L1-2		(1-0)	Morris	17,494

LES ROBERTS

stayed at the County Ground for three years - twice as long as any of his stints at 14 other League clubs he served during a twenty year career. A tall, deep-lying inside forward, Les filled the void left by the talented Alec Wall - whose career was ended by a broken leg on Christmas Day 1926. In the modern game, Les would be classed as an attacking midfielder - and his 34 goals in little more than a hundred League appearances for the Town proved his worth. Signed from Bolton, he moved on to Brentford in May 1930.

Archer A A E	Bew D C	Bourne J T	Chivers W A	Cooper R	Daniel C H	Denyer A E C	Dickenson W	Eddleston J	Flood C W	Humphreys B	Jefferies C E	Johnson S	Low D	Morris D H	Nash E M	O'Neill H	Roberts C L	Thom A	Thompson F	Walker J	Weale R H	Weston A M	Wylie T	
6	5	1				7	2	8					4	9			10	11	3					**1**
6	5	1				7	2	8					4	9			10		3	11				**2**
6	5	1				7		8					4	9			10	11				3	2	**3**
3		1	4			7		9	8	5		6					10			11			2	**4**
6	5	1				7	2	10	8				4	9				11					3	**5**
6	5	1					2	10	8				4	9				11			7		3	**6**
	5	1					2	10				6	4	9			8	11			7	3		**7**
4	5	1				7	2	10				6		9			8	11				3		**8**
6						7	2	10		5			4	9	1		8	11				3		**9**
6						7	2	10		5			4	9	1		8	11				3		**10**
6						7	2	10		5			4	9	1		8	11				3		**11**
6						7	2	10		5			4	9	1		8	11				3		**12**
6						7	2	10		5			4	9	1		8	11				3		**13**
6						7	2	10		5			4	9	1		8	11				3		**14**
6						7	2	10		5			4	9	1		8	11				3		**15**
6						7	2	10		5			4	9	1		8	11					3	**16**
6						7	2	10		5			4	9	1		8	11					3	**17**
6						7	2	10		5			4	9	1		8	11					3	**18**
6						7	2	10		5			4	9	1		8	11					3	**19**
6						7	2	10		5			4	9	1		8	11					3	**20**
6						7	2	10		5			4	9	1		8	11					3	**21**
6						7	2	10		5			4	9	1		8	11					3	**22**
6						7	2	10		5			4	9	1		8			11			3	**23**
6						7	2	10		5			4	9	1		8			11			3	**24**
6						7	2	10		5			4	9	1		8			11			3	**25**
6						7	2	10		5			4	9	1		8			11			3	**26**
6						7	2	10		5			4	9	1			11		8			3	**27**
6						7	2	10		5			4		1		8	11		9			3	**28**
6	5					7	2	10					4	9	1		8	11					3	**29**
6	5				9	7	2	10					4		1		8	11					3	**30**
6	5					7	2	10					4	9	1		8	11					3	**31**
	5					7	2	10				6	4	9	1		8	11					3	**32**
	5					7	2	10				6	4	9	1		8	11					3	**33**
6	5					7	2	10					4	9	1		8			11			3	**34**
6	5					7		10					4	9	1	2	8			11			3	**35**
6	5					7		10			11	3	4	9	1		8		2					**36**
5					9	7		10				6	4		1		8	11	2			3		**37**
6	5					7		10					4	9	1		8		2		11		3	**38**
6	5					7		10				3	4	9	1		8		2		11			**39**
	5			6	9	7		10				3	4		1				2	8	11			**40**
6	5					7	2	10				3	4	9	1					11	8			**41**
	5			4			2	10				6		9	1		8	11			7	3		**42**
37	20	8	1	2	3	39	34	42	3	21	1	11	39	37	34	1	37	29	7	12	7	12	25	Apps
1					1	5	7	12					1	38			14	9		2				Goals

Archer A A E	Bew D C	Bourne J T	Chivers W A	Cooper R	Daniel C H	Denyer A E C	Dickenson W	Eddleston J	Flood C W	Humphreys B	Jefferies C E	Johnson S	Low D	Morris D H	Nash E M	O'Neill H	Roberts C L	Thom A	Thompson F	Walker J	Weale R H	Weston A M	Wylie T	
6						7	2	10		5			4	9	1		8			11		3		**1**
6						7	2	10		5			4	9	1		8	11				3		**2**
6						7	2	10		5			4	9	1		8	11					3	**2R**
6						7	2	10		5			4	9	1		8	11					3	**3**
6						7	2	10		5			4	9	1		8	11					3	**4**
5						5	5	5		5			5	5	5		5	4		1		2	3	Apps
														6										Goals

No numbers actually worn on shirts

For Final League Table - see page 102

SEASON 1928/29

Football League Division Three South
Final League Position : 10th
Secretary/Manager : Sam Allen

					Home	Away	H-T	Goalscorers	Gate
1	S	Aug	25	Bristol Rovers	W2-1		(1-1)	Eddleston pen.,Roberts	9,315
2	W		29	Plymouth Argyle		L0-3	(0-0)		11,557
3	S	Sep	1	Watford		L2-3	(1-1)	Morris 2	10,959
4	W		5	Plymouth Argyle	D0-0				7,711
5	S		8	Walsall	W5-1		(2-1)	Eddleston 2,Morris 3	6,693
6	M		10	Brentford		L0-2	(0-2)		7,231
7	S		15	Newport County		W1-0	(0-0)	Culley	7,737
8	S		22	Crystal Palace	W3-2		(3-1)	Roberts,Morris 2	7,999
9	S		29	Brighton and Hove Albion		D2-2	(2-2)	Weale 2	9,338
10	S	Oct	6	Torquay United		W4-2	(3-1)	Viggars,Morris,Weale 2	5,823
11	S		13	Gillingham	W2-1		(2-1)	Morris,Dickenson pen.	6,751
12	S		20	Norwich City	L1-2		(0-1)	Roberts	6,403
13	S		27	Charlton Athletic		L1-4	(0-3)	Weale	9,309
14	S	Nov	3	Northampton Town	L0-1		(0-1)		7,099
15	S		10	Coventry City		L1-4	(1-3)	Weale	16,706
16	S		17	Luton Town	W4-2		(2-0)	Eddleston,Roberts,Morris,Thom	6,992
17	S	Dec	1	Bournemouth & Boscombe Athletic	D3-3		(0-2)	Morris,Thom,Weale	6,031
18	S		15	Southend United	W3-1		(1-0)	Morris 2,Eddleston	2,879
19	S		22	Exeter City		D1-1	(1-1)	Roberts	5,208
20	Tu		25	Queens Park Rangers		L2-4		Morris,Roberts	14,962
21	W		26	Queens Park Rangers	W2-1		(0-1)	Eddleston,Roberts	9,392
22	S		29	Bristol Rovers		W4-1	(2-1)	Morris 3,Dickenson	5,593
23	S	Jan	5	Watford	W5-0		(2-0)	Denyer 2,Morris 3	4,417
24	S		19	Walsall		D1-1	(1-1)	Roberts	7,405
25	S	Feb	2	Crystal Palace		L1-6	(1-1)	Walker	10,364
26	S		9	Brighton and Hove Albion	D2-2		(1-2)	Walker,Dickenson pen.	3,092
27	S		23	Gillingham		D0-0			3,618
28	S	Mar	2	Norwich City		D1-1	(0-0)	Archer	6,363
29	S		9	Charlton Athletic	D1-1		(0-1)	Eddleston	6,886
30	S		16	Northampton Town		D1-1	(1-1)	Dickenson pen.	10,070
31	S		23	Coventry City	L1-2		(0-1)	Morris	4,518
32	F		29	Fulham		L0-2	(0-1)		26,868
33	S		30	Luton Town		L3-5	(1-4)	Eddleston 2,Morris	9,772
34	M	Apr	1	Fulham	L1-2		(1-0)	Thom	6,540
35	S		6	Brentford	W3-1		(1-0)	Roberts,Denyer,Dickenson pen.	3,107
36	S		13	Bournemouth & Boscombe Athletic		L1-2	(0-1)	Roberts	5,176
37	M		15	Merthyr Town		D0-0			2,720
38	S		20	Merthyr Town	W2-1		(2-0)	Thom,Morris	2,741
39	W		24	Torquay United	D1-1		(1-1)	Thom	1,757
40	S		27	Southend United		D1-1	(0-0)	Morris	5,312
41	W	May	1	Newport County	W5-2		(3-2)	Morris 2,Denyer,Thom,Eddleston	1,542
42	S		4	Exeter City	W2-0		(1-0)	Eddleston 2	2,697

Average Home Attendance : **5,455**
Average Away Attendance : **9,147**

F A Cup

					Home	Away	H-T	Goalscorers	Gate
3	S	Jan	12	Newcastle United	W2-0		(1-0)	Morris 2	17,689
4	S		26	Burnley		D3-3	(3-1)	Morris 2,Denyer	30,689
4R	W		30	Burnley	W3-2		(1-2)	Dickenson pen.,Eddleston,Morris	24,730
5	S	Feb	16	Arsenal	D0-0				16,692
5R	W		20	Arsenal		L0-1	(0-1)		49,382

JOE EDDLESTON
stood just 5'5", but he had been top scorer for Third Division North club Nelson for five successive seasons before coming to the County Ground in August 1926. He proved to be an ideal foil for his new strike partner - the burly Harry Morris - and Joe continued to score consistently, achieving double figures in five of his six seasons with Town.
He was granted a free transfer in July 1932, by which time he was 35, signing for Accrington Stanley.

Archer A A E	Bew D C	Culley W N	Daniel C H	Denyer A E C	Devlin T	Dickenson W	Eddleston J	Humphreys B	Johnson S	Low D	Morris D H	Nash E M	Powell A E E	Roberts C L	Thom A	Viggars R W	Walker J	Weale R H	Weston A M	Wylie T	
6				7		2	10	5		4	9	1		8	11					3	**1**
				7		2	10	5	6	4	9	1		8	11					3	**2**
				7		2	10	5	6	4	9	1		8	11					3	**3**
				7		2	10	5	6	4	9	1		8	11					3	**4**
						2	10	5	6	4	9	1		8	11			7		3	**5**
						2	10	5	6	4	9	1		8	11			7		3	**6**
		9				2	10	5		4		1		8		6	11	7		3	**7**
						2	10	5	3	4	9	1		8		6	11	7			**8**
						2	10	5	3	4	9	1		8	11	6		7			**9**
						2	10	5	3	4	9	1		8	11	6		7			**10**
						2	10	5		4	9	1		8	11	6		7		3	**11**
						2	10	5		4	9	1		8	11	6		7	3		**12**
						2	10	5		4	9	1		8	11	6		7	3		**13**
6	5					2	10		3	4	9	1		8	11			7			**14**
6	5	8			10	2					9	1			11	4		7		3	**15**
6	5					2	8			4	9	1		10	11			7		3	**16**
6	5					2	8		3	4	9	1		10	11			7			**17**
6	5			7		2	8			4	9	1		10	11					3	**18**
6	5			7		2	8			4	9	1		10	11					3	**19**
6	5			7		2	8			4	9	1		10	11					3	**20**
6	5			7		2	8			4	9	1		10			11			3	**21**
6	5					2	8			4	9	1	7	10			11			3	**22**
6	5	8		7		2				4	9	1		10	11					3	**23**
6	5			7		2	8			4	9	1		10	11					3	**24**
6				7		2	8			4		1		10	11	5	9		3		**25**
6				7		2	8		3	4		1		10	11	5	9				**26**
6	5		9	7		2	8			4		1		10	11					3	**27**
6	5					2	8			4	9	1	7	10	11				3		**28**
6	5					2	8			4	9	1	7	10	11					3	**29**
6	5					2	8			4	9	1		10	11		7			3	**30**
6	5		8	7		2				4	9	1		10	11					3	**31**
6	5			7		2	8			4	9	1		10	11					3	**32**
	5			7		2	8			4	9	1		10	11	6				3	**33**
6	5			7		2	8			4	9	1		10	11					3	**34**
6	5			7		2	8			4	9	1		10	11				3		**35**
6	5			7		2	8			4	9	1		10	11					3	**36**
6	5					2	7			4	9	1		10		8	11		3		**37**
6	5			7		2	8			4	9	1		10	11					3	**38**
6	5			7		2	8			4	9	1		10	11					3	**39**
6	5			7		2	8			4	9	1		10	11					3	**40**
6	5			7		2	8			4	9	1		10	11					3	**41**
	5			7		2	8			4	9	1		10	11	6				3	**42**
28	27	3	2	24	1	42	39	13	11	41	38	42	3	41	37	13	8	13	6	30	Apps
1		1		4		5	12				26			10	6	1	2	7			Goals

WALLY DICKENSON

Archer A A E	Bew D C	Culley W N	Daniel C H	Denyer A E C	Devlin T	Dickenson W	Eddleston J	Humphreys B	Johnson S	Low D	Morris D H	Nash E M	Powell A E E	Roberts C L	Thom A	Viggars R W	Walker J	Weale R H	Weston A M	Wylie T	
6	5			7		2	8			4	9	1		10	11					3	**3**
6	5			7		2	8			4	9	1		10	11					3	**4**
6				7		2	8			4	9	1		10	11	5				3	**4R**
6	5			7		2	8			4	9	1		10	11					3	**5**
6	5			7		2	8			4	9	1		10	11					3	**5R**
5	4			5		5	5			5	5	5		5	5	1				5	Apps
				1		1	1				5										Goals

No numbers actually worn on shirts

For Final League Table - see page 102

SEASON 1929/30

Football League Division Three South
Final League Position : 14th
Secretary/Manager : Sam Allen

					Home	Away	H-T	Goalscorers	Gate
1	S	Aug	31	Brentford		L2-3	(1-1)	Morris,Dickenson pen.	11,084
2	Th	Sep	5	Newport County		L1-2	(1-2)	Dickenson pen.	4,860
3	S		7	Bristol Rovers	D2-2		(0-1)	Morris,Dickenson pen.	7,020
4	M		9	Newport County	W5-1		(2-0)	Morris 3,Thom,Eddleston	4,952
5	S		14	Brighton and Hove Albion		L0-3	(0-2)		9,641
6	M		16	Coventry City	D1-1		(0-1)	Eddleston	5,592
7	S		21	Crystal Palace	W3-1		(1-1)	Morris,Eddleston,McCartney	6,606
8	M		23	Walsall		L0-4	(0-3)		4,314
9	S		28	Plymouth Argyle	L1-2		(0-2)	Dent	8,663
10	S	Oct	5	Merthyr Town	W6-3		(1-0)	Eddleston 3,Denyer 2,Dent	3,507
11	S		12	Torquay United	W2-1		(0-1)	Eddleston,Morris	6,058
12	S		19	Gillingham		D0-0			5,597
13	S		26	Northampton Town	W2-0		(0-0)	Morris,Brett o.g.	7,695
14	S	Nov	2	Exeter City		L1-5	(0-3)	Morris	6,356
15	S		9	Southend United	W5-1		(3-0)	McCartney 2,Morris 2,Dent	6,638
16	S		16	Luton Town		D1-1	(1-1)	Eddleston	2,547
17	S		23	Bournemouth & Boscombe Athletic	D1-1		(1-1)	Morris	6,007
18	S		30	Crystal Palace		L0-1	(0-1)		11,128
19	S	Dec	7	Queens Park Rangers	D2-2		(0-1)	Morris,Humphreys	3,954
20	S		21	Norwich City	W2-1		(0-0)	Roberts,Dent	4,524
21	W		25	Clapton Orient		L1-2	(1-1)	Dent	10,123
22	Th		26	Clapton Orient	D0-0				10,818
23	S		28	Brentford	L0-2		(0-0)		4,317
24	W	Jan	1	Fulham		L1-4	(0-2)	Roberts	5,542
25	S		4	Bristol Rovers		L2-3	(1-0)	Denyer,Roberts	8,997
26	S		18	Brighton and Hove Albion	L0-1		(0-0)		6,617
27	S	Feb	8	Merthyr Town		D3-3	(1-1)	Eddleston,Roberts,Morris	1,554
28	S		15	Torquay United		D1-1	(1-0)	Eddleston	3,473
29	S		22	Gillingham	W3-0		(0-0)	Morris 2,Humphreys	3,170
30	S	Mar	1	Northampton Town		D3-3	(2-3)	Dowdall,Roberts 2	9,254
31	S		8	Exeter City	W1-0		(0-0)	Denyer	3,928
32	S		15	Southend United		L1-3	(0-0)	Morris	6,106
33	S		22	Luton Town	D1-1		(0-0)	McCartney	3,710
34	W		26	Plymouth Argyle		L0-5	(0-1)		14,931
35	S		29	Bournemouth & Boscombe Athletic		W3-1	(1-0)	Morris 2,Roberts	4,753
36	S	Apr	5	Walsall	W3-1		(1-0)	Dent,Roberts,Morris	3,208
37	S		12	Queens Park Rangers		L3-8	(1-3)	Morris 2,Dickenson pen.	7,534
38	F		18	Watford	L1-3		(0-2)	Dowdall	4,656
39	S		19	Fulham	D1-1		(0-0)	Morris	2,306
40	M		21	Watford		L1-4	(0-0)	Weale	9,292
41	S		26	Norwich City		W5-1	(2-0)	Morris 5	7,591
42	S	May	3	Coventry City		W2-1	(1-1)	Roberts 2	10,014

Average Home Attendance : **5,426**
Average Away Attendance : **7,366**

F A Cup

					Home	Away	H-T	Goalscorers	Gate
3	S	Jan	11	Manchester United		W2-0	(1-0)	Eddleston,Roberts	33,226
4	S		25	Manchester City	D1-1		(1-1)	McCloy o.g.	23,697
4R	W		29	Manchester City		L1-10	(0-4)	Morris	46,082

HERBIE WEBSTER
was the unfortunate 'keeper on the receiving end of Town's record 10-1 thrashing at Maine Road in January 1930.
The 19 year old was forced into action when Teddy Nash was ruled out with a thigh strain and he was given little protection from City's Bobby Marshall who helped himself to five goals on the day. Herbie made just seven League appearances for Town before being released in the summer of 1931.

Archer A A E	Bew D C	Braithwaite E	Crook M S	Dent F	Denyer A E C	Dickenson W	Dowdall C	Eddleston J	Girvan H MacD	Humphreys B	Johnson R	Low D	McCartney J	Morris D H	Nash E M	Penn T	Roberts C L	Thom A	Viggars R W	Weale T J	Webster H	Wylie T	
6	5				7	2		8				4		9	1		10	11				3	**1**
6	5				7	2		8				4		9	1		10	11				3	**2**
6	5				7	2		8				4		9	1		10	11				3	**3**
6		10			7	2		8			5	4		9	1			11				3	**4**
6		10			7	2		8			5	4		9	1			11				3	**5**
		6		10	7	2		8			5	4	11	9	1							3	**6**
		6		10	7	2		8			5	4	11	9	1							3	**7**
		6	7	10		2		8			5	4	11	9	1							3	**8**
		6		10	7	2		8			5	4	11	9							1	3	**9**
		6		9	7	2		8			5	4	11		1		10					3	**10**
		6		10	7			8	3		5	4	11	9	1	2							**11**
	5	6		10	7			8	3		4		11	9	1	2							**12**
6				10	7			8	3		5	4	11	9	1	2							**13**
6				10	7			8	3		5	4	11	9	1	2							**14**
		6		10	7			8	3	5		4	11	9	1	2							**15**
		6		10	7			8	3	5		4	11	9	1	2							**16**
		6		10	7			8	3	5		4	11	9	1	2							**17**
		6		10	7				3	5		4	11	9	1	2	8						**18**
		6			7			8	3	5		4	11	9	1	2	10						**19**
6				8	7			9	3	5		4	11		1	2	10						**20**
6				8	7			9	3	5		4	11		1	2	10						**21**
6		8		9	7				3	5		4	11		1	2	10						**22**
6	5	8						7	3			4	11	9	1	2	10						**23**
6								8	3	5		4	11	9	1	2	10			7			**24**
		6			7			8	3	5		4	11	9	1	2	10						**25**
6					7			8	3	5		4	11	9	1	2	10						**26**
6					7			8	3	5		4	11	9		2	10				1		**27**
		6			7	3		8		5		4	11	9	1	2	10						**28**
		6			7	3		8		5		4	11	9	1	2	10						**29**
	5	6			7		8		3			4	11	9	1	2	10						**30**
	5	6			7		8		3			4	11	9	1	2	10						**31**
	5	6			7		8		3			4	11	9	1	2	10						**32**
	5	6			7		8		3			4	11	9	1	2	10						**33**
6	5	4		10	7		8						11	9	1	2						3	**34**
6	5	4		8				7					11	9	1	2	10					3	**35**
6		4		8	7					5			11	9	1	2	10					3	**36**
6		4			7	2	8		3	5				9	1		10	11					**37**
		6			7		8	4	3	5				9	1		10	11				2	**38**
		6			7			8	3	5			11	9			10		4		1	2	**39**
		6					8		3	5			11	9			10		4	7	1	2	**40**
		6		8				7	3	5		4	11	9			10				1	2	**41**
		6		8				7	3	5		4	11	9			10				1	2	**42**
18	11	32	1	21	35	13	8	32	27	21	11	34	35	38	36	26	28	7	2	2	6	18	Apps
				6	4	4	2	10		2			4	28			10	1		1			Goals

Opponents 1 goal

Archer A A E	Bew D C	Braithwaite E	Crook M S	Dent F	Denyer A E C	Dickenson W	Dowdall C	Eddleston J	Girvan H MacD	Humphreys B	Johnson R	Low D	McCartney J	Morris D H	Nash E M	Penn T	Roberts C L	Thom A	Viggars R W	Weale T J	Webster H	Wylie T	
6					7			8	3	5		4	11	9	1	2	10						**3**
6					7			8	3	5		4	11	9	1	2	10						**4**
6					7			8	3	5		4	11	9		2	10				1		**4R**
3					3			3	3	3		3	3	3	2	3	3				1		Apps
								1						1			1						Goals

No numbers actually worn on shirts

Opponents 1 goal

For Final League Table - see page 103

SEASON 1930/31

Football League Division Three South
Final League Position : 12th
Secretary/Manager : Sam Allen

					Home	Away	H-T	Goalscorers	Gate
1	S	Aug	30	Bournemouth & Boscombe Athletic	W4-1		(4-0)	Morris 2,Brown o.g.,Whipp	6,903
2	W	Sep	3	Walsall	W4-3		(2-0)	Cruickshank,Morris 2,Whipp	7,370
3	S		6	Watford		L0-3	(0-1)		8,516
4	M		8	Coventry City		L0-4	(0-2)		13,081
5	S		13	Notts County	L1-2		(0-0)	Cruickshank	6,797
6	W		17	Coventry City	W4-0		(2-0)	Morris 2,Eddleston,Batty	3,330
7	S		20	Clapton Orient		W3-2	(2-1)	Eddleston 2,Richardson	5,263
8	S		27	Thames	W3-0		(1-0)	Eddleston,Morris, Igoe o.g.	6,281
9	S	Oct	4	Norwich City		L0-2	(0-0)		8,714
10	W		8	Brighton and Hove Albion		L0-1	(0-1)		3,716
11	S		11	Queens Park Rangers	W4-1		(2-1)	Richardson,Whipp,Munnings,Jones	6,151
12	S		18	Southend United		L3-5	(3-2)	Whipp,Robinson o.g.,Kirby	7,532
13	S		25	Luton Town	D0-0				4,671
14	S	Nov	1	Bristol Rovers		L1-4	(1-1)	Cockburn	7,762
15	S		8	Newport County	D4-4		(2-4)	Eddleston 3,Morris	4,808
16	S		15	Gillingham		W1-0	(0-0)	Munnings	5,909
17	S		22	Exeter City	W2-1		(2-0)	Kirby pen.,Morris	3,148
18	S	Dec	6	Torquay United	W4-0		(0-0)	Eddleston,Richardson,Morris 2	3,658
19	S		13	Northampton Town		L0-3	(0-3)		7,625
20	S		20	Brentford	W3-2		(3-1)	Morris 2,Richardson	4,728
21	Th		25	Fulham	W4-1		(2-0)	Kirby pen.,Morris 2,Richardson	4,670
22	F		26	Fulham		L1-6	(0-3)	Gibbons o.g.	7,246
23	S		27	Bournemouth & Boscombe Athletic		L1-4	(0-2)	Eddleston	6,284
24	S	Jan	3	Watford	W2-1		(1-0)	Woodward o.g.,Richardson	3,958
25	S		17	Notts County		L0-2	(0-1)		11,448
26	S		24	Clapton Orient	W5-1		(2-0)	Eddleston,Morris 3,Richardson	4,646
27	S		31	Thames		L2-3	(0-0)	Cruickshank,Morris	1,149
28	S	Feb	7	Norwich City	W5-2		(2-0)	Richardson 2,Morris 2,Hannah o.g.	4,543
29	S		14	Queens Park Rangers		W2-1	(2-1)	Morris,Eddleston	7,914
30	S		21	Southend United	D1-1		(0-1)	Dixon o.g.	4,994
31	S		28	Luton Town		L0-4	(0-2)		5,057
32	S	Mar	7	Bristol Rovers	W3-1		(2-1)	Morris,Kirby pen.,Munnings	4,066
33	S		14	Newport County		L1-3	(0-2)	Kirby	2,872
34	S		21	Gillingham	W5-2		(2-1)	Morris 4,Eddleston	4,112
35	S		28	Exeter City		L1-3	(0-3)	Morris	4,121
36	F	Apr	3	Crystal Palace		L1-3	(0-2)	Eddleston	12,283
37	S		4	Brighton and Hove Albion	D1-1		(0-1)	Morris	6,123
38	M		6	Crystal Palace	D4-4		(3-2)	Whipp,Morris 2,Kirby	4,842
39	S		11	Torquay United		L0-5	(0-3)		3,814
40	S		18	Northampton Town	W5-1		(2-1)	Richardson,Cruickshank,Morris 3	3,330
41	S		25	Brentford		L2-5	(2-3)	Richardson,Morris	4,327
42	S	May	2	Walsall		D2-2	(1-0)	Richardson,Stansfield pen.	3,061

Average Home Attendance : **4,911**
Average Away Attendance : **6,557**

F A Cup

					Home	Away	H-T	Goalscorers	Gate
1	S	Nov	29	Norwich City		L0-2	(0-1)		11,856

NORMAN KIRBY
played in England, Scotland and Ireland during a near twenty year career. He made his League debut as a triallist for Stockport before picking up a losers medal in the 1928 F.A.Amateur Cup Final with his home village club Cockfield. Further trials took him to Manchester United and Newcastle, amongst others, prior to signing for Bury. He arrived at the County Ground in June 1930 and made maximum appearances in his first season, laying on a plentiful supply of crosses for the goal-hungry Harry Morris. Norman joined the Distillery club of Belfast in August 1932, representng the Irish League twice before spending the remaining pre-War years with Dundee.

Archer A A E	Batty W	Braithwaite E	Cockburn W O	Cope H	Cruickshank A	Eddleston J	Girvan H MacD	Guyan G W	Jones G B	Kirby N R	Low D	McCartney J	Morris D H	Munnings C E	Murray D	Penn T	Richardson F	Rushton R	Stansfield H F	Webster H	Whipp P L	
	2	6	5	1	7		3			11			9				10	4			8	**1**
	2	6	5	1	7		3			11			9				10	4			8	**2**
	2	6	5	1	7		3			11	4		9				10				8	**3**
	2	6	5	1	7		3			11	4		9				10				8	**4**
	2	6	5	1	7	10	3			11	4		9								8	**5**
	2	6	5	1	7	8	3			11	4		9				10					**6**
	2	6	5	1	7	8	3			11	4		9				10					**7**
	2	6	5	1	7	8	3			11	4		9				10					**8**
	2	6	5	1	7	8	3			11	4		9				10					**9**
	2	6	5	1	7		3			11			9				10	4			8	**10**
	2	6	5	1			3		9	11				7			10	4			8	**11**
	2	6	5	1			3			11			9	7			10	4			8	**12**
	2	6	5	1		8	3			11			9	7			10	4				**13**
	2	6	5	1		8	3		10	11			9	7				4				**14**
6		4	5	1		8	3		10	11			9	7		2						**15**
6		4	5	1		8	3			11			9	7			10		2			**16**
5		6		1		8	3			11	4		9	7			10		2			**17**
5		6		1	7	8	3			11	4		9				10		2			**18**
5		6		1	7	8	3			11	4		9				10		2			**19**
6		4	5	1	7	8	3			11			9				10		2			**20**
6		4	5	1	7	8	3			11			9				10		2			**21**
6		4	5	1	7	8	3			11			9				10		2			**22**
		6	5	1	7	8	3		9	11	4						10		2			**23**
		6	5	1	7	8	3			11	4		9				10		2			**24**
6		4	5	1	7	8	3			11			9				10		2			**25**
6		4	5	1	7	8	3			11			9				10		2			**26**
6		4	5	1	7	8	3			11			9				10		2			**27**
	6	4	5		7	8	3			11			9				10		2	1		**28**
	6	4	5	1	7	8	3			11			9				10		2			**29**
	6	4	5	1	7	8	3			11			9				10		2			**30**
	6	4	5	1		8	3			11			9	7			10		2			**31**
		6	5	1			3	8		11	4		9	7			10		2			**32**
		6	5	1			3	8		11	4		9	7			10		2			**33**
		6	5	1		8	3			11	4		9	7			10		2			**34**
		6	5	1		8	3			11	4		9	7			10		2			**35**
		6	5	1		8	3			11	4		9	7			10		2			**36**
		6	5	1		8	3			11	4		9	7			10		2			**37**
		6	5	1		7	3			11	4	10	9						2		8	**38**
		6	5	1		7	3			11	4	10	9				8		2			**39**
		6		1	7	8	3			11	4		9		5		10		2			**40**
		6	5	1	7	8	3			11	4		9				10		2			**41**
		6	5	1	7	8	3			11	4		9				10		2			**42**
11	18	42	38	41	26	33	42	2	4	42	23	2	40	14	1	1	38	7	27	1	9	Apps
	1		1		4	13			1	6			35	3			12		1		5	Goals

Opponents 7 goals

Archer A A E	Batty W	Braithwaite E	Cockburn W O	Cope H	Cruickshank A	Eddleston J	Girvan H MacD	Guyan G W	Jones G B	Kirby N R	Low D	McCartney J	Morris D H	Munnings C E	Murray D	Penn T	Richardson F	Rushton R	Stansfield H F	Webster H	Whipp P L	
5		6		1	7	8	3			11	4		9				10		2			**1**

No numbers actually worn on shirts

HECTOR GIRVAN

For Final League Table - see page 103

SEASON 1931/32

Football League Division Three South
Final League Position : 17th
Secretary/Manager : Sam Allen

No.	Day	Month	Date	Opponents	Home	Away	H-T	Goalscorers	Gate
1	S	Aug	29	Mansfield Town		L2-3	(2-3)	Morris,Lawley	12,232
2	W	Sep	2	Watford	W4-1		(2-1)	Starsmore 2,Morris,Laycock	5,534
3	S		5	Brighton and Hove Albion	L1-2		(1-0)	Brett o.g.	5,643
4	Th		10	Queens Park Rangers		W2-1	(1-0)	Morris 2	7,646
5	S		12	Norwich City		L2-4	(1-2)	Kirby,Keeling	9,754
6	W		16	Queens Park Rangers	L1-2		(1-2)	Morris	5,065
7	S		19	Reading	L0-2		(0-1)		9,368
8	S		26	Clapton Orient	L2-3		(1-1)	Starsmore,Eddleston	4,685
9	S	Oct	3	Torquay United		L1-2	(1-1)	Morris	4,483
10	S		10	Bristol Rovers	W2-1		(1-1)	Morris 2	5,650
11	S		17	Southend United		L0-3	(0-1)		10,430
12	S		24	Fulham	D2-2		(2-0)	Starsmore,Morris	4,994
13	S		31	Thames		D1-1	(1-0)	Morris	2,300
14	S	Nov	7	Brentford	L1-3		(1-2)	Dransfield pen.	6,415
15	S		14	Exeter City		D1-1	(0-1)	Braithwaite	3,565
16	S		21	Coventry City	D2-2		(1-1)	Kirby,Greenwell	5,124
17	S	Dec	5	Luton Town	W3-2		(1-1)	Morris 3	2,532
18	S		19	Northampton Town	W3-0		(0-0)	Burgess,Starsmore,Eddleston	3,919
19	F		25	Crystal Palace		D0-0			17,713
20	S		26	Crystal Palace	W3-2		(1-2)	Braithwaite,Eddleston,Morris	9,995
21	S	Jan	2	Mansfield Town	W5-2		(2-1)	Morris 3,Starsmore,Keeling	4,481
22	S		9	Gillingham		L1-2	(0-1)	Eddleston	6,287
23	S		16	Brighton and Hove Albion		L0-1	(0-1)		6,388
24	S		23	Norwich City	W2-0		(0-0)	Keeling,Nickalls	5,079
25	S		30	Reading		L2-5	(1-1)	Eddleston,Braithwaite	11,041
26	S	Feb	6	Clapton Orient		L2-4	(1-1)	Morris,Timbrell	6,457
27	S		13	Torquay United	W3-0		(0-0)	Starsmore,Morris 2	3,457
28	S		20	Bristol Rovers		W2-0	(1-0)	Kirby,Keeling	5,460
29	S		27	Southend United	L1-2		(1-1)	Starsmore	4,480
30	S	Mar	5	Fulham		D2-2	(0-0)	Lawley 2	17,555
31	S		12	Thames	W2-0		(1-0)	Dransfield pen.,Eddleston	3,764
32	S		19	Brentford		L0-2	(0-0)		10,179
33	F		25	Bournemouth & Boscombe Athletic	W3-0		(1-0)	Morris,Keeling,Lawley	5,631
34	S		26	Exeter City	W2-1		(1-0)	Keeling,Morris	3,328
35	M		28	Bournemouth & Boscombe Athletic		L1-2	(1-1)	Kirby	6,245
36	S	Apr	2	Coventry City		L2-3	(0-2)	Morris 2	11,167
37	S		9	Gillingham	W4-0		(1-0)	Morris 3,Laycock	2,775
38	W		13	Cardiff City		L0-3	(0-1)		4,018
39	S		16	Luton Town		L0-6	(0-3)		3,982
40	S		23	Cardiff City	L1-4		(1-3)	Morris	3,728
41	S		30	Northampton Town		L1-4	(1-2)	Keeling	5,058
42	S	May	7	Watford		L1-4	(0-3)	Morris	4,645

Average Home Attendance : **5,031**
Average Away Attendance : **7,934**

F A Cup

No.	Day	Month	Date	Opponents	Home	Away	H-T	Goalscorers	Gate
1	S	Nov	28	Luton Town	L0-5		(0-2)		9,266

JACK STARSMORE
joined Swindon in May 1931 from Kettering Town - where he had no less than four spells during his career. After scoring nearly forty goals for the Poppies in 1930/31, Jack was hoping to make the most of a second chance in League football, having previously spent two years with Coventry. An 'ever-present' in his first term at the County Ground, he led the attack whenever Harry Morris was unavailable, but Jack failed to reach a double figure goal tally in either of his two seasons with the club. He signed for Third Division North Barrow in August 1933.

Braithwaite E	Burgess R	Cope H	Dransfield E	Eddleston J	Giles S	Girvan H MacD	Godfrey T	Greenwell J W	Hammond N	Keeling H	Kirby N R	Lambie A	Lawley G H	Laycock F W	Low D	Morris D H	Nickalls J S	Stansfield H F	Starsmore J G	Timbrell H J	
6		1				3	4	5					11	10		9	7	2	8		1
6		1				3	4	5					11	10		9	7	2	8		2
6		1				3	4	5					11	10		9	7	2	8		3
6		1				3	4	5					11	10		9	7	2	8		4
		1	3	8			4	5	6	10	11						7	2	9		5
6		1				3	4	5					11	10		9	7	2	8		6
6		1				3		5		10	11		7		4	9		2	8		7
6		1	3	10			4	5			11		7			9		2	8		8
6		1				3	4		5				11	10		9	7	2	8		9
6		1				3	4	5					11	10		9	7	2	8		10
6		1				3	4	5					11	10		9	7	2	8		11
6		1	2			3	4	5			11			10		9	7		8		12
6		1	2			3	4	5			11			10		9	7		8		13
6		1	2			3	4	5					11	10		9	7		8		14
6			2	8	1	3	4	5			11		7	10					9		15
6			2		1	3	4	5			11		7	10		9			8		16
6			2	7	1	3	4			10		5		11		9			8		17
6	11	1	2	7		3	4			10		5				9			8		18
6	11	1	2	7		3	4			10		5				9			8		19
6	11	1	2	7		3	5			10					4	9			8		20
6	11	1	2	7		3	4			10		5				9			8		21
6	11	1	2	7		3	4			10		5				9			8		22
6	11	1	2	7		3	4			10		5				9			8		23
6		1	2			3	4			10		5	11			9	7		8		24
6	11	1	2	7		3	4					5		10		9			8		25
6		1	2	7		3	4				11	5				9			8	10	26
6		1	2	7		3	4				11	5				9			8	10	27
6		1	2			3	4			10	11	5	7			9			8		28
6		1	2	8		3	4			10	11	5	7						9		29
6		1	2	8		3	4			10	11	5	7						9		30
6			2	7	1	3	4			10	11	5				9			8		31
6			2		1	3	4			10	11	5	7			9			8		32
6			2		1	3	4			10	11	5	7			9			8		33
			2		1	3	4			10	11	5	7		6	9			8		34
			2		1	3	4			10	11	5	7		6	9			8		35
			2		1	3	4			10	11	5	7		6	9			8		36
			2		1	3	4				11	5	7	10	6	9			8		37
			2		1	3	4			10	11	5	7		6	9			8		38
			2		1	3	4			10	11	5	7		6	9			8		39
			2		1	3	4			10	11	5	7		6	9			8		40
			2	7	1	3	4			10	11	5			6	9			8		41
			2		1	3	4			10	11	5	7		6	9			8		42
32	7	27	33	17	15	40	41	15	2	24	24	25	27	16	11	38	13	11	42	2	Apps
3	1		2	6				1		7	4		4	2		29	1		8	1	Goals

Opponents 1 goal

Braithwaite E	Burgess R	Cope H	Dransfield E	Eddleston J	Giles S	Girvan H MacD	Godfrey T	Greenwell J W	Hammond N	Keeling H	Kirby N R	Lambie A	Lawley G H	Laycock F W	Low D	Morris D H	Nickalls J S	Stansfield H F	Starsmore J G	Timbrell H J	
6			2		1	3	4				11		7	10		9		5	8		1

No numbers actually worn on shirts

HARRY KEELING

For Final League Table - see page 103

SEASON 1932/33

Football League Division Three South
Final League Position : 22nd (Last)
Secretary/Manager : Sam Allen

No	Day	Month	Date	Opponents	Home	Away	H-T	Goalscorers	Gate
1	S	Aug	27	Bournemouth & Boscombe Athletic		L1-5	(0-2)	Morris	6,364
2	W		31	Newport County	W2-0		(1-0)	Scott W H, Morris	5,074
3	S	Sep	3	Reading	L0-1		(0-1)		9,688
4	M		5	Newport County		W2-1	(1-0)	Morris,Scott W H	3,674
5	S		10	Clapton Orient	D3-3		(0-1)	Starsmore,Scott W H,Munnings	5,962
6	S		17	Northampton Town		L0-6	(0-2)		7,955
7	S		24	Bristol City	L1-4		(0-2)	Munnings	7,507
8	S	Oct	1	Coventry City		L1-2	(0-1)	Scott W H	8,076
9	S		8	Brentford	D0-0				6,659
10	S		15	Torquay United		L3-4	(3-2)	Young 2,Morris	4,273
11	S		22	Norwich City		L2-5	(1-2)	Starsmore 2	9,292
12	W	Nov	2	Brighton and Hove Albion	W5-1		(3-0)	Morris 2,Brookes,Munnings 2	2,689
13	S		5	Bristol Rovers		L0-1	(0-0)		10,560
14	S		12	Aldershot	W3-2		(2-1)	Starsmore,Scott W H,Morris	5,119
15	S		19	Queens Park Rangers		L2-4	(2-3)	Starsmore,Munnings	5,802
16	S	Dec	3	Crystal Palace		L3-4	(2-1)	Quinn 2,Morris	8,936
17	S		17	Watford		D2-2	(2-2)	Lambie,Morris	6,794
18	S		24	Cardiff City	W6-2		(1-1)	Munnings 3,Braithwaite,Dransfield pen.,Brookes	6,145
19	M		26	Exeter City	D2-2		(0-1)	Brookes,Munnings	10,733
20	Tu		27	Exeter City		L0-5	(0-1)		12,628
21	S		31	Bournemouth & Boscombe Athletic	W2-0		(0-0)	Starsmore,Morris	4,512
22	S	Jan	7	Reading		L1-7	(1-4)	Morris	9,181
23	S		21	Clapton Orient		L1-7	(0-2)	Wilkins	5,386
24	S		28	Northampton Town	W2-1		(1-1)	Scott A,Wilkins	2,937
25	S	Feb	4	Bristol City		L1-5	(1-1)	Wilkins	4,353
26	S		11	Coventry City	L1-2		(0-2)	Wilkins	3,477
27	S		18	Brentford		L0-1	(0-0)		11,559
28	S		25	Torquay United	D0-0				1,528
29	W	Mar	1	Southend United	D2-2		(1-1)	Brookes,Morris	2,201
30	S		4	Norwich City	L2-4		(2-1)	Quinn,Brookes	5,144
31	S		11	Brighton and Hove Albion		L1-5	(1-2)	Hayes	5,813
32	S		18	Bristol Rovers	D1-1		(1-0)	Munnings	4,276
33	S		25	Aldershot		W1-0	(1-0)	Wilkins	4,068
34	S	Apr	1	Queens Park Rangers	D0-0				3,848
35	S		8	Southend United		D0-0			5,383
36	F		14	Luton Town		L2-6	(1-4)	Brookes,Wilkins	5,535
37	S		15	Crystal Palace	W1-0		(1-0)	Scott A	4,642
38	M		17	Luton Town	D1-1		(0-0)	Wilkins	4,693
39	S		22	Gillingham		L1-3	(0-2)	Wilkins	6,272
40	W		26	Gillingham	D1-1		(1-1)	Scott A	2,954
41	S		29	Watford	L1-2		(1-1)	Braithwaite	2,955
42	S	May	6	Cardiff City		L0-3	(0-2)		7,871

Average Home Attendance : **4,893**
Average Away Attendance : **7,132**

F A Cup

No	Day	Month	Date	Opponents	Home	Away	H-T	Goalscorers	Gate
1	S	Nov	26	Dulwich Hamlet	W4-1		(4-0)	Starsmore,Quinn 2,Brookes	10,047
2	S	Dec	10	Southport		W2-1	(1-0)	Little o.g.,Morris	7,900
3	S	Jan	14	Burnley	L1-2		(1-2)	Munnings	16,543

EDDIE MUNNINGS
rejoined Town from Hull in June 1932, having previously spent the 1930/31 season at the County Ground. His four goals over the festive period in 1932 - which included a hat-trick on Christmas Eve - helped him to finish as second top scorer, just two goals behind goal machine Harry Morris. But Town's miserable League form in the New Year, starting with two successive 7-1 defeats, culminated in a bottom of the table finish and most of the squad being released in the summer of 1933. Eddie was amongst them. Lincolnshire-born, he ended his career there, playing in local football in Scunthorpe.

Berry G L	Braithwaite E	Briggs A L	Brookes S	Brown S	Cousins H	Dransfield E	Giles S	Girvan H MacD	Godfrey T	Hayes G E	Lambie A	Morris D H	Munnings C E	Quinn C	Scott A	Scott W H	Seabrook E	Stansfield H F	Starsmore J G	Thomson N S	Thorne F L C	Wilkins L	Young H	
1			6		4	2		3			5	9		7	10	8							11	**1**
1			6		4	2		3			5	9		7	8	10							11	**2**
1	4		6					3			5	9	11	7	8	10		2						**3**
1	4		6					3			5	9	11	7	8	10					2			**4**
1	4		6			2		3			5		11	7	8	10			9					**5**
1	6					2		3	4		5		7	11	9	8						10		**6**
1	6				4			3			5	9	7		8			2				10	11	**7**
1	6					2		3			5		7		9	10			8			4	11	**8**
1	6				4	2		3			5	9	7			10			8				11	**9**
1	6				4	2		3			5	9	7			10			8				11	**10**
1	6				4	2		3			5	9	7			10			8				11	**11**
1	6		10		4	2		3			5	9	7						8				11	**12**
1	6				4	2		3	5			9	7			10			8				11	**13**
1	6			3	4	2					5	9	7			10			8				11	**14**
1	6			3	4	2					5	9	7			10			8				11	**15**
1	6		10		4	2		3			5	9	7	11		8								**16**
1	6		10		4	2		3			5	9	7	11					8					**17**
1	6		10		4	2		3			5	9	7	11					8					**18**
1	6		10			2		3	4		5	9	7	11					8					**19**
1	6		10			2		3	4		5	9	7	11					8					**20**
1	6		10			2		3			5	9				7			8			4	11	**21**
1	6		10			2		3				9	7				5		8			4	11	**22**
	6		10		4	2	1	3			5	9				7			8			11		**23**
	6				4		1	3			5			7	9			2		8		10	11	**24**
	6				4		1	3			5		7	11	9			2		8		10		**25**
					4		1	3			5	9	7	11		6		2		8		10		**26**
			10		4	2	1	3			5	9	7	11					8			6		**27**
	6	1	10		4	2		3			5	9	7	11					8					**28**
	6	1	10		4	2		3			5	9	7	11					8					**29**
	6	1	10		4	2		3		9	5		7	11								8		**30**
		1	10		4	2		3		9	5		7	11		8						6		**31**
	6	1	10		4	2		3		9	5		7	11								8		**32**
	6	1	10		4			3		9	5		7	11				2				8		**33**
	6	1	10		4			3		9	5		7	11				2				8		**34**
	6	1	10		4	2		3			5		7	11	8				9					**35**
	6	1	10		4			3	5					11	8			2	9			7		**36**
	6	1	10		4			3	5					11	8			2	9			7		**37**
	6	1	10		4				5					11	8		3	2	9			7		**38**
		1	10		4	2		3	5			9		11	8		6					7		**39**
	6	1	10		4	2		3			5	9	7	11	8									**40**
	6	1	10		4	2		3			5	9		11	8							7		**41**
	6	1	10		4	2		3			5	9		11	8				7					**42**
22	36	15	30	2	33	31	5	39	8	5	36	28	31	30	18	18	3	10	24	3	1	20	14	Apps
	2		6			1				1	1	12	10	3	3	5			6			8	2	Goals

Berry G L	Braithwaite E	Briggs A L	Brookes S	Brown S	Cousins H	Dransfield E	Giles S	Girvan H MacD	Godfrey T	Hayes G E	Lambie A	Morris D H	Munnings C E	Quinn C	Scott A	Scott W H	Seabrook E	Stansfield H F	Starsmore J G	Thomson N S	Thorne F L C	Wilkins L	Young H	
1	6		10		4	2		3			5		7	11		8			9					**1**
1	6		10		4	2		3			5	9	7	11					8					**2**
1	6		10		4	2		3			5	9	7	11					8					**3**
3	3		3		3	3		3			3	2	3	3		1			3					Apps
			1									1	1	2					1					Goals

No numbers actually worn on shirts

Opponents 1 goal

For Final League Table - see page 104

SEASON 1933/34

Football League Division Three South
Final League Position : 8th
Manager : Ted Vizard

					Home	Away	H-T	Goalscorers	Gate
1	S	Aug	26	Newport County		W2-1	(1-1)	Armstrong,Peters	8,871
2	W		30	Queens Park Rangers	W3-1		(0-1)	Armstrong pen.,Barrie o.g.,Blakemore pen.	9,342
3	S	Sep	2	Norwich City	D0-0				11,837
4	Th		7	Queens Park Rangers		L0-1	(0-1)		5,956
5	S		9	Bristol City		D2-2	(0-1)	Armstrong 2	9,863
6	S		16	Clapton Orient	W3-0		(0-0)	Armstrong,Peters 2	12,963
7	S		23	Coventry City		L1-5	(0-3)	Peters	12,388
8	S		30	Brighton and Hove Albion		L0-3	(0-2)		6,609
9	S	Oct	7	Aldershot	W1-0		(0-0)	Armstrong	11,457
10	S		14	Luton Town		W3-2	(0-1)	Peters,Armstrong,Fisher	7,756
11	S		21	Southend United	L1-4		(1-2)	Peters	10,943
12	S		28	Bristol Rovers		L0-3	(0-2)		11,523
13	S	Nov	4	Crystal Palace	W3-2		(2-0)	Peters 2,Fisher	8,908
14	S		11	Gillingham		D3-3	(0-2)	Timbrell,Armstrong 2	6,068
15	S		18	Exeter City	D1-1		(0-0)	Timbrell	8,986
16	S	Dec	2	Bournemouth & Boscombe Athletic	W3-2		(2-0)	Peters 2,Farrow o.g.	7,019
17	S		16	Watford	W1-0		(0-0)	Blakemore	6,603
18	S		23	Reading		L0-2	(0-0)		12,179
19	M		25	Torquay United		L0-2	(0-1)		4,082
20	Tu		26	Torquay United	W2-0		(1-0)	Fisher,Blakemore	10,953
21	S		30	Newport County	D1-1		(1-0)	Blakemore	7,809
22	S	Jan	6	Norwich City		L2-3	(1-0)	Fisher 2	9,339
23	W		17	Cardiff City		W1-0	(1-0)	Peters	2,859
24	S		20	Bristol City	W4-2		(2-1)	Peters 3,Blakemore	8,697
25	S		27	Clapton Orient		L0-1	(0-0)		8,272
26	S	Feb	3	Coventry City	L0-1		(0-1)		7,926
27	S		10	Brighton and Hove Albion	D1-1		(1-0)	Armstrong	8,288
28	S		17	Aldershot		W2-1	(1-0)	Flanagan 2	3,382
29	S		24	Luton Town	W3-1		(2-0)	Armstrong,Fisher 2	7,689
30	S	Mar	3	Southend United		L1-4	(1-0)	Armstrong	5,869
31	S		10	Bristol Rovers	W1-0		(0-0)	Armstrong	9,872
32	S		17	Crystal Palace		D0-0			8,327
33	S		24	Gillingham	W3-1		(2-1)	Armstrong 2 (1 pen.),Peters	6,168
34	F		30	Northampton Town	D1-1		(0-1)	Fisher	10,858
35	S		31	Exeter City		D2-2	(0-1)	Blakemore,Fisher	5,214
36	M	Apr	2	Northampton Town		D2-2	(1-2)	Blakemore,Armstrong	7,059
37	S		7	Cardiff City	W6-3		(4-2)	Armstrong 2,Fisher 3,Blakemore	7,163
38	S		14	Bournemouth & Boscombe Athletic		D1-1	(0-1)	Fisher	3,596
39	S		21	Charlton Athletic	L1-3		(0-1)	Armstrong pen.	9,102
40	S		28	Watford		L0-4	(0-2)		3,179
41	W	May	2	Charlton Athletic		L0-1	(0-1)		4,236
42	S		5	Reading	W3-1		(1-0)	Armstrong 2,Peters	8,868

Average Home Attendance : **9,117**
Average Away Attendance : **6,982**

F A Cup

					Home	Away	H-T	Goalscorers	Gate
1	S	Nov	25	Ilford		W4-2	(2-1)	Armstrong,Fisher,Timbrell,Flanagan	7,100
2	S	Dec	9	Dartford	W1-0		(1-0)	Armstrong pen.	10,543
3	S	Jan	13	Brighton and Hove Albion		L1-3	(0-1)	Helsby	13,650

Third Division South Cup

					Home	Away	H-T	Goalscorers	Gate
1	Th	Jan	25	Newport County		L2-7	(0-2)	Manuel,Fisher	2,000

TED VIZARD

was a former Welsh international winger with 22 caps. He had a 20-year career with Bolton, where he made over 500 appearances and helped them to win the first Wembley Cup Final in 1923. His first task after taking over from Sam Allen - who reverted to club secretary - was to offload most of the players who had failed to get Town off the foot of the table in 1932/33, only three being retained. Town secured a top ten finish in three of Ted's six seasons at the club. He left in May 1939 when Queens Park Rangers offered him a reported £1,000 a year salary.

Armstrong T H	Blakemore C	Bowl T H	Briggs A L	Cousins H	Duckworth T C	Fisher F	Flanagan W J A	Frater D T	Haddleton A	Harris B I	Helsby T	Herod E R B	Hicks G W	Kirkwood D	Lambie A	Manuel P E	Merrick C	Nixon T	Peters F	Timbrell H J	Turner R F	
9	10		1	4						2	8	3			5		6		7		11	**1**
9	10		1	4						2	8	3			5		6		7		11	**2**
9	10		1	4						2	8	3			5		6		7		11	**3**
9	10		1	4						2	8	3			5		6		7		11	**4**
9	10		1	4						2	8	3	11				6	5	7			**5**
9			1	4					10	2	8	3	11		5		6		7			**6**
9			1	4					10	2	8	3					6	5	7	11		**7**
9	10		1	4							8	3	11		5		6	2	7			**8**
9	10		1	4		8				2		3	11		5		6		7			**9**
9	10		1	4		8	11			2		3					6	5	7			**10**
9	10		1	4		8	11			2		3					6	5	7			**11**
9			1	4		8	11			2	10	3					6	5	7			**12**
			1	4		10	7			2	8	3					6	5	9	11		**13**
9			1	4		10	7			2	8	3					6	5		11		**14**
9			1	4		10	7			2	8	3			5		6			11		**15**
9			1	6		10	11			2	4	3		8	5				7			**16**
	9		1	6		10	11			2		3		8	5			4	7			**17**
	9		1	6		10	11			2		3		8	5			4	7			**18**
	9		1	6			11		10	2		3		8	5			4	7			**19**
	7		1	6		10	11			2	4	3		8				5	9			**20**
	7		1	6		10	11			2		3		8	5			4	9			**21**
	10		1	6		9	11			2	4	3		8				5	7			**22**
	10		1	6		9	11		8		4	3			5			2	7			**23**
	10		1	6		9	11		8		4	3			5			2	7			**24**
	10		1	6		9	11		8		4	3			5			2	7			**25**
			1	6	2	9		10	8		4	3			5				7	11		**26**
9			1	4	2	10	11				8	3			5		6		7			**27**
9			1	4	2	10	11				8	3					6	5	7			**28**
9			1	4	2	10	11				8	3					6	5	7			**29**
9			1	4	2	10	11				8	3					6	5	7			**30**
9			1	4	2	10	11				8	3					6	5	7			**31**
9	10		1	4	2	8	11					3					6	5	7			**32**
9			1	4	2	10	11				8	3					6	5	7			**33**
9	10		1		2	8	11				4	3			5		6		7			**34**
9	7		1	4	2	10	11			6	8	3			5							**35**
9	7		1	4	2	10	11			6	8	3			5							**36**
9	7		1	4	2	10	11			6	8	3			5							**37**
9	7		1	4	2	10	11			6	8	3						5				**38**
9	7		1	4	2	10	11				8	3					6	5				**39**
9	10		1	4	2		11				8	3					6	5	7			**40**
9		10	1	4	2		11				8	3					6	5	7			**41**
9		10	1	4	2		11				8	3					6	5	7			**42**
31	26	2	42	41	17	30	32	1	7	25	34	42	4	7	22	0	27	28	35	5	4	Apps
21	8					13	2												16	2		Goals

Opponents 2 goals

Armstrong T H	Blakemore C	Bowl T H	Briggs A L	Cousins H	Duckworth T C	Fisher F	Flanagan W J A	Frater D T	Haddleton A	Harris B I	Helsby T	Herod E R B	Hicks G W	Kirkwood D	Lambie A	Manuel P E	Merrick C	Nixon T	Peters F	Timbrell H J	Turner R F	
9			1	6		10	7			2	4	3			5				8	11		**1**
9			1	6		10	11			2	4	3		8	5				7			**2**
	10		1	6		9	11			2	8	3			5			4	7			**3**
2	1		3	3		3	3			3	3	3		1	3			1	3	1		Apps
2						1	1				1									1		Goals

Armstrong T H	Blakemore C	Bowl T H	Briggs A L	Cousins H	Duckworth T C	Fisher F	Flanagan W J A	Frater D T	Haddleton A	Harris B I	Helsby T	Herod E R B	Hicks G W	Kirkwood D	Lambie A	Manuel P E	Merrick C	Nixon T	Peters F	Timbrell H J	Turner R F	
			1	10		9			8	2	4	3				11	6	5	7			**1**

No numbers actually worn on shirts

FRED FISHER

For Final League Table - see page 104

TOMMY ARMSTRONG

was brought in by Ted Vizard to fill the centre-forward berth vacated by Harry Morris - a tough act to follow for the 5'6" Glaswegian. Tommy had only Scottish League experience on his CV, but he adapted to the English game well and thrived on good support from his much taller strike partner Cecil Blakemore and winger Frank Peters. Tommy spent more time at inside-right following the arrival of Alan Fowler in 1934, but again the partnership produced a healthy return of goals.

SEASON 1934/35

Football League Division Three South
Final League Position : 16th
Manager : Ted Vizard

					Home	Away	H-T	Goalscorers	Gate
1	S	Aug	25	Queens Park Rangers	W3-1		(3-0)	Fowler,Peters 2	12,176
2	W		29	Bristol Rovers		D2-2	(1-1)	Gunson,Armstrong T	12,675
3	S	Sep	1	Torquay United		L1-2	(1-2)	Fisher	4,333
4	W		4	Bristol Rovers	W1-0		(1-0)	Peters	10,908
5	S		8	Reading	D1-1		(0-0)	Peters	14,854
6	S		15	Aldershot	W3-2		(2-1)	Peters 2,Gunson	9,004
7	S		22	Cardiff City		W3-1	(1-0)	Peters,Jack,Bowl	7,111
8	S		29	Brighton and Hove Albion	D4-4		(1-2)	Fowler,Peters,Gunson 2	7,369
9	S	Oct	6	Luton Town		L0-2	(0-1)		7,801
10	S		13	Southend United	W5-0		(2-0)	Fowler 3,Peters,Gunson	9,122
11	S		20	Northampton Town		L2-4	(1-2)	Bowl,Peters	7,033
12	S		27	Bournemouth & Boscombe Athletic	L0-2		(0-1)		7,645
13	S	Nov	3	Clapton Orient		L0-2	(0-1)		10,021
14	S		10	Gillingham	W3-0		(1-0)	Fowler 2,Peters	5,289
15	S		17	Exeter City		D3-3	(2-0)	Peters,Bowl 2	4,844
16	S	Dec	1	Millwall		L0-1	(0-1)		9,436
17	S		15	Watford		L4-7	(2-3)	Bowl,Fowler 3	3,990
18	S		22	Newport County	D0-0				6,122
19	Tu		25	Charlton Athletic		L0-6	(0-3)		15,817
20	W		26	Charlton Athletic	D2-2		(1-2)	Armstrong T,Fisher	12,883
21	S		29	Queens Park Rangers		D1-1	(0-0)	Fowler	6,150
22	S	Jan	5	Torquay United	W5-0		(2-0)	Fowler 2,Peters,Dickenson o.g.,Gunson	8,401
23	S		19	Reading		L1-2	(0-1)	Fowler	11,210
24	W		30	Aldershot		L0-3	(0-1)		1,852
25	S	Feb	2	Cardiff City	W2-1		(2-1)	Fowler,Armstrong T pen.	6,043
26	S		9	Brighton and Hove Albion		D2-2	(1-2)	Bowl,Gunson	5,831
27	S		16	Luton Town	L0-1		(0-1)		5,428
28	S		23	Southend United		L0-2	(0-1)		5,756
29	S	Mar	2	Northampton Town	W5-3		(1-2)	Peters,Armstrong T 2 (1 pen.),Fowler,Newberry	5,661
30	S		9	Bournemouth & Boscombe Athletic		D1-1	(1-0)	Gunson	3,493
31	S		16	Clapton Orient	D1-1		(1-0)	Fowler	5,714
32	S		23	Gillingham		L0-2	(0-1)		3,796
33	S		30	Exeter City	W6-1		(3-1)	Peters 3,Fowler 2,Armstrong T	5,122
34	S	Apr	6	Bristol City		L0-2	(0-1)		5,900
35	W		10	Bristol City	W1-0		(1-0)	Armstrong T	3,458
36	S		13	Millwall	L0-1		(0-0)		5,897
37	F		19	Crystal Palace		L0-7	(0-5)		13,510
38	S		20	Coventry City		L0-3	(0-1)		7,769
39	M		22	Crystal Palace	D1-1		(0-1)	Armstrong T	5,660
40	S		27	Watford	W2-1		(1-1)	Armstrong T,Horrocks	3,396
41	W	May	1	Coventry City	D0-0				3,234
42	S		4	Newport County		W2-1	(1-1)	Fisher,Jack	2,110

Average Home Attendance : **7,304**
Average Away Attendance : **7,164**

F A Cup

1	S	Nov	24	Newport County	W4-0	(0-0)	Fowler 3,Gunson	12,776
2	S	Dec	8	Lincoln City	W4-3	(2-2)	Fowler 2,Bowl,Gunson	14,931
3	S	Jan	12	Chesterfield	W2-1	(1-0)	Bowl,Fowler	19,165
4	S		26	Preston North End	L0-2	(0-1)		24,480

Third Division South Cup

1	W	Sep	26	Bournemouth & Boscombe Athletic	L0-3	(0-2)	2,202

ALAN FOWLER

looked set to become a top division marksman after scoring in four successive games for Leeds in October 1933. But Ted Vizard managed to secure his signature in May 1934 and he went on to hit 100 goals for Town. Alan was only 5'6" and weighed under ten stones, but he still finished as the club's top scorer in three of his six seasons at the County Ground. In September 1935 he scored one of the quickest ever hat-tricks, in the first six minutes of a Third South Cup tie against Luton. Like many players of that era, his career was halted by the Second War, but the little Yorkshireman paid the ultimate price. A sergeant with the 4th Dorsets, Alan lost his life in the battle to reclaim Caen in July 1944. He was 32.

Armstrong T H	Armstrong W	Bowl T H	Briggs A L	Cousins H	Duckworth T C	Fisher F	Flanagan W J A	Fowler A	Gunson J G	Herod E R B	Horrocks S	Houldsworth F C	Jack R R	McDonald R	Merrick C	Newberry F O	Nixon T	Peters F	Wallace R	Wright R	
9			1	4	2	10		8	11	3					6		5	7			1
9			1	4	2	10		8	11	3					6		5	7			2
9			1	4	2	10		8	11	3					6		5	7			3
9				4	2	10		8	11	3		1			6		5	7			4
9				4	2	10		8	11	3		1			6		5	7			5
9	4				2	10		8	11	3		1			6		5	7			6
	4	10			2			8	11	3		1	9		6		5	7			7
	4	10			2			8	11	3		1	9		6		5	7			8
		10			2			8	11	3	4	1	9		6		5	7			9
		10			2			9	11	3	4	1	8		6		5	7			10
		10			2			9	11	3	4	1	8		6		5	7			11
		10		6	2			9	11		4	1	8		3		5	7			12
		10		6	2	8		9	11	3	4	1					5	7			13
8	4	10			2			9	11	3	6	1					5	7			14
8	4	10			2			9	11	3	6	1					5	7			15
8	5	10		4	2			9	11	3		1			6			7			16
8	5	10			2			9	11	3	4	1	7		6						17
	4	10			2	9	7		11	3	6	1	8				5				18
	5	10		4		9	7		11	3	6	1	8				2				19
8	5	10		4		9	11			3		1	7		6		2				20
8	5	10		4			11	9		3		1	7		6		2				21
8	5	10		4				9	11	3		1			6			7	2		22
8	5	10		4	2			9	11	3		1			6			7			23
8	5	10		4				9	11	3		1					6	7	2		24
8	5	10		4				9	11	3		1	7		6				2		25
8	5	10		4				9	11	3		1	7				6		2		26
8	5	10		4				9	11	3		1					6	7	2		27
10				4	2	11		9		3		1	8			6	5	7			28
8	5			4	2			9		3	6	1				11		7		10	29
8	5			4				9	11	3	6	1	7						2	10	30
8	5	7		4				9	11	3	6	1							2	10	31
8	5	7		4				9	11	3	6	1							2	10	32
8	5			4	2		11	9		3		1				6		7		10	33
8	5	10	1	4	2		11	9		3	6					6		7			34
8	5		1	4	2			9	11	3	6							7		10	35
8	5		1	4	2	10		9	11	3	6							7			36
8	5		1	4	2			9	11	3	6							7		10	37
8	5		1	4	2	9	11			3	6		7							10	38
8	5		1	4		9	11			3	6		7						2	10	39
9	5		1	4		11				3	6		8					7	2	10	40
9	5		1	4			11				6		8				2	7	3	10	41
9	5		1	4		10					6		8			11	2	7	3		42
33	31	24	12	32	27	16	9	34	31	39	22	30	20	0	19	5	25	30	12	11	Apps
9		6				3		19	8		1		2			1		17			Goals

Opponents 1 goal

Armstrong T H	Armstrong W	Bowl T H	Briggs A L	Cousins H	Duckworth T C	Fisher F	Flanagan W J A	Fowler A	Gunson J G	Herod E R B	Horrocks S	Houldsworth F C	Jack R R	McDonald R	Merrick C	Newberry F O	Nixon T	Peters F	Wallace R	Wright R	
8	5	10		4	2			9	11	3		1			6			7			1
8	5	10		4	2		7	9	11	3		1			6						2
8	5	10		4	2			9	11	3		1			6			7			3
8	5	10		4				9	11	3		1					6	7	2		4
4	4	4		4	3		1	4	4	4		4			3		1	3	1		Apps
		2						6	2												Goals

Armstrong T H	Armstrong W	Bowl T H	Briggs A L	Cousins H	Duckworth T C	Fisher F	Flanagan W J A	Fowler A	Gunson J G	Herod E R B	Horrocks S	Houldsworth F C	Jack R R	McDonald R	Merrick C	Newberry F O	Nixon T	Peters F	Wallace R	Wright R	
	4	10			2	9		8	11			1		3		6	5	7			1

No numbers actually worn on shirts

FRANK PETERS

For Final League Table - see page 104

SEASON 1935/36

Football League Division Three South
Final League Position : 19th
Manager : Ted Vizard

No.	Day	Month	Date	Opponent	Home	Away	H-T	Goalscorers	Gate
1	S	Aug	31	Newport County		D2-2	(0-1)	Peters,Fowler	11,408
2	W	Sep	4	Torquay United	W4-1		(0-0)	Fowler 3,Peters	9,953
3	S		7	Exeter City	D1-1		(0-0)	Peters pen.	12,114
4	W		11	Torquay United		L1-2	(0-0)	Hunt o.g.	4,447
5	S		14	Brighton and Hove Albion		W2-0	(1-0)	Lowry 2	8,463
6	W		18	Aldershot		W3-1	(2-0)	Fowler,Peters,Cochrane	3,543
7	S		21	Queens Park Rangers	D2-2		(1-0)	Lowry,Fowler	11,628
8	S		28	Watford		L1-2	(0-1)	Fowler	8,846
9	S	Oct	5	Bristol City	D1-1		(0-1)	Lowry	11,945
10	S		12	Millwall		L0-1	(0-1)		12,136
11	S		19	Reading		L0-2	(0-0)		13,775
12	S		26	Cardiff City	W2-1		(1-1)	Parmley 2 (1 pen.)	8,224
13	S	Nov	2	Gillingham		L1-3	(1-3)	Peters	5,058
14	S		9	Northampton Town	W3-1		(1-0)	Parmley 2,Peters	7,670
15	S		16	Luton Town		L1-2	(1-1)	Lowry	12,213
16	S		23	Notts County	W2-1		(1-1)	Lowry,Peters	8,233
17	S	Dec	7	Clapton Orient	D2-2		(1-1)	Bowl,Fowler	5,504
18	S		21	Bournemouth & Boscombe Athletic	L2-3		(1-1)	Fowler,Parmley	3,733
19	W		25	Crystal Palace	L0-2		(0-0)		5,450
20	Th		26	Crystal Palace		L1-5	(0-0)	Peters	15,867
21	S		28	Newport County	D1-1		(1-0)	Wells	5,629
22	S	Jan	4	Exeter City		W3-0	(1-0)	Lowry,Fowler,Wilcockson	4,594
23	W		15	Bristol Rovers		L1-2	(0-0)	Lowry	2,418
24	S		18	Brighton and Hove Albion	L1-2		(0-0)	Lowry	4,720
25	S		25	Queens Park Rangers		L1-5	(0-3)	Lowry	10,797
26	S	Feb	1	Watford	L1-6		(0-3)	Lowry	5,341
27	S		8	Bristol City		L0-5	(0-2)		8,304
28	S		15	Millwall	W3-1		(3-1)	Peters 2,Fowler	4,645
29	S		22	Reading	W4-1		(3-0)	Fowler,Wells 3	6,331
30	S		29	Northampton Town		D0-0			4,226
31	S	Mar	7	Southend United	L1-3		(0-1)	Peters pen.	5,721
32	S		14	Cardiff City		L1-2	(0-1)	Lowry	8,637
33	S		21	Luton Town	W3-0		(1-0)	Lowry,Peters,McPhail	7,839
34	S		28	Notts County		D0-0			4,798
35	S	Apr	4	Bristol Rovers	W3-0		(0-0)	Wells,Bowl,Parmley	4,516
36	S		11	Clapton Orient		W2-1	(0-1)	Shanks,Parmley	6,169
37	M		13	Coventry City	L1-2		(0-0)	Parmley	9,710
38	Tu		14	Coventry City		L1-2	(0-0)	Parmley	25,898
39	S		18	Gillingham	W3-0		(1-0)	Wells 2,Storey	5,502
40	S		25	Bournemouth & Boscombe Athletic		L0-1	(0-0)		3,951
41	W		29	Southend United		L0-1	(0-0)		3,072
42	S	May	2	Aldershot	W3-2		(2-1)	Jones,McPhail,Lowry	4,713

Average Home Attendance : **7,101**
Average Away Attendance : **8,506**

F A Cup

Rd	Day	Month	Date	Opponent	Home	Away	H-T	Goalscorers	Gate
1	S	Nov	30	Southall		L1-3	(0-1)	Bowl	7,100

Third Division South Cup

Rd	Day	Month	Date	Opponent	Home	Away	H-T	Goalscorers	Gate
1	W	Sep	25	Luton Town	W5-3		(3-1)	Fowler 4,Brae	3,057
2	W	Oct	23	Notts County	W4-3		(4-1)	Peters 3,Fowler	1,814
3	W	Nov	13	Brighton and Hove Albion	W2-1		(0-0)	Peters 2	1,761
SF	W	Feb	26	Northampton Town	W1-0		(0-0)	Fowler	2,605
F/1	W	Mar	25	Coventry City	L0-2		(0-2)		3,610
F/2	Th	Apr	2	Coventry City		L2-3	(0-1)	Peters,McPhail	2,077

For Final League Table - see page 105

Armstrong W	Bailey H	Beecham E C	Bowl T H	Brae W	Cochrane A F	Cousins H	Duckworth T C	Edmonds F H A	Finnigan R P	Fowler A	Horrocks S	Jones R W	Lowry S H	McCarthy T T	McPhail D D	Newberry F O	Parkhouse R M	Parmley J S	Peters F	Rutherford J	Shanks R	Smith A J	Storey W C	Wells T C	Wilcockson E S	
5					8		2			9	4		10						7	1		3		11	6	**1**
5					8	4	2			9			10						7	1		3		11	6	**2**
5			10		8	4	2			9									7	1		3		11	6	**3**
5					8	4	2						10					9	7	1		3		11	6	**4**
5					8	4	2			9			10						7	1		3		11	6	**5**
5					8	4	2			9			10						7	1		3		11	6	**6**
5					8	4	2			9			10						7	1		3		11	6	**7**
5					8	4	2			9			10						7	1		3		11	6	**8**
5				10	8	4	2			9			11						7	1		3			6	**9**
5				10			2			8			9				4		7	1		3		11	6	**10**
5					8	4	2			9			10			6			7	1		3		11		**11**
5						4	2			8			10			6		9	7	1		3		11		**12**
5					8	4	2			9			10			6			7	1		3		11		**13**
5						4	2			8			10			6		9	7	1		3		11		**14**
5			8	10		4	2						9			6			7	1		3		11		**15**
5			8	10		4	2						9			6			7	1		3		11		**16**
5			8	10		4	2			9									7	1		3		11	6	**17**
5			10			4	2			8								9	7	1		3		11	6	**18**
5			10			4	2			8								9	7	1		3		11	6	**19**
5		1	10		8	4	2						9						7			3		11	6	**20**
5		1	10			4				8			9						7		2	3		11	6	**21**
5		1	8			4	2			7			9								6	3		11	10	**22**
5		1	8			4	2						9						7		6	3		11	10	**23**
5		1	10			4	2			8			9						7			3		11	6	**24**
5		1	10			4	2			8			11					9	7			3			6	**25**
5		1		10	8	4	2			7			9					11				3			6	**26**
4	3	1	8				2			9								11	7		5	6			10	**27**
			10			4	2			9									7	1	5	3	8	11	6	**28**
						4	2			9			10						7	1	5	3	8	11	6	**29**
			10			4	2			9						6			7	1	5	3	8	11		**30**
			10			4	2			9									7	1	5	3	8	11	6	**31**
						4	2			9			10						7	1	5	3	8	11	6	**32**
						4	2			9			10		11				7	1	5	3	8		6	**33**
						4	2			9					11			10	7	1	5	3	8		6	**34**
			10			4	2								7			9		1	5	3	8	11	6	**35**
			10			4	2								7			9		1	5	3	8	11	6	**36**
						4	2						10		7			9		1	5	3	8	11	6	**37**
4							2			8			10					9	7	1	5	3		11	6	**38**
						4	2	1		10					7			9			5	3	8	11	6	**39**
						4	2	1		10			9		7						5	3	8	11	6	**40**
						4	2	1		10			9		11				7		5	3	8		6	**41**
						4	2	1		8		9	10		11				7		5	3			6	**42**
28	1	8	18	6	13	38	41	4	0	34	1	1	30	0	9	7	1	14	35	30	19	42	13	34	35	Apps
			2		1					12		1	14		2			9	12		1		1	7	1	Goals

Opponents 1 goal

Armstrong W	Bailey H	Beecham E C	Bowl T H	Brae W	Cochrane A F	Cousins H	Duckworth T C	Edmonds F H A	Finnigan R P	Fowler A	Horrocks S	Jones R W	Lowry S H	McCarthy T T	McPhail D D	Newberry F O	Parkhouse R M	Parmley J S	Peters F	Rutherford J	Shanks R	Smith A J	Storey W C	Wells T C	Wilcockson E S	
5			8	10		4	2						9			6			7	1		3		11		**1**

Armstrong W	Bailey H	Beecham E C	Bowl T H	Brae W	Cochrane A F	Cousins H	Duckworth T C	Edmonds F H A	Finnigan R P	Fowler A	Horrocks S	Jones R W	Lowry S H	McCarthy T T	McPhail D D	Newberry F O	Parkhouse R M	Parmley J S	Peters F	Rutherford J	Shanks R	Smith A J	Storey W C	Wells T C	Wilcockson E S	
5				10	8	4				9			11	2		6		7		1		3				**1**
5						4	2		1	8			10			6		9	7			3		11		**2**
5					10	4	2			8			9			6			7	1		3		11		**3**
						4	2			9			10						7	1	5	3	8	11	6	**SF**
						4	2			9			10		11				7	1	5	3	8		6	**F/1**
						4	2			9					11			10	7	1	5	3	8		6	**F/2**
3				1	2	6	5		1	6			5	1	2	3		3	5	5	3	6	3	3	3	Apps
				1						6					1				6							Goals

No numbers actually worn on shirts

SEASON 1936/37

Football League Division Three South
Final League Position : 13th
Manager : Ted Vizard

No	Day	Month	Date	Opponents	Home	Away	H-T	Goalscorers	Gate
1	S	Aug	29	Northampton Town	W2-0		(1-0)	Cookson,Fowler	11,150
2	W	Sep	2	Bristol Rovers		L1-2	(1-2)	Chandler	13,920
3	S		5	Bournemouth & Boscombe Athletic		L2-5	(2-2)	Chandler,Hetherington	9,913
4	S		12	Brighton and Hove Albion	L1-2		(0-2)	Cookson	9,060
5	W		16	Aldershot	W5-1		(3-1)	Chandler,Fowler,Storey,Hetherington,McPhail	5,914
6	S		19	Watford		D2-2	(0-2)	Chandler pen.,Fowler	9,665
7	W		23	Bristol Rovers	W4-1		(1-0)	Cookson 3,Fowler	8,551
8	S		26	Southend United	W4-0		(2-0)	Chandler 2 (1 pen.),Cookson,Morrall	9,701
9	S	Oct	3	Newport County		D1-1	(0-0)	Fowler	6,084
10	S		10	Gillingham	W3-0		(2-0)	Fowler,Cookson 2	8,748
11	S		17	Queens Park Rangers		D1-1	(1-0)	Cookson	12,405
12	S		24	Bristol City	L0-1		(0-1)		13,121
13	S		31	Torquay United		L0-2	(0-1)		3,857
14	S	Nov	7	Notts County	D2-2		(2-1)	Hetherington,Cookson	10,410
15	S		14	Clapton Orient		D1-1	(0-1)	Hetherington	7,495
16	S		21	Walsall	W3-0		(1-0)	Jones 2,Cookson	8,381
17	S	Dec	5	Cardiff City	W4-2		(4-1)	Cookson 2,Jones 2	10,724
18	S		19	Exeter City	W3-1		(1-0)	Cookson 3	7,057
19	F		25	Reading		D2-2	(0-1)	Cookson 2	12,692
20	S		26	Northampton Town		L0-4	(0-3)		16,177
21	M		28	Reading	L1-2		(0-2)	Hetherington	8,800
22	F	Jan	1	Bournemouth & Boscombe Athletic	W3-1		(2-1)	Hetherington,Chandler,Morrall	7,408
23	S		9	Brighton and Hove Albion		L0-2	(0-1)		10,864
24	S		16	Crystal Palace		L0-2	(0-1)		7,648
25	S		23	Watford	D1-1		(1-1)	Cookson pen.	5,277
26	S		30	Southend United		L0-2	(0-1)		4,793
27	S	Feb	6	Newport County	L1-2		(1-0)	McPhail	7,872
28	S		13	Gillingham		L1-4	(1-4)	Musgrave	6,442
29	S		20	Queens Park Rangers	D1-1		(0-1)	Morrall	6,741
30	S	Mar	6	Torquay United	W4-2		(1-0)	Cousins,Fowler,Bradley,Hetherington	5,265
31	S		13	Notts County		L2-3	(1-2)	Cookson,Fowler	16,531
32	S		20	Clapton Orient	L1-3		(0-1)	Morrall	5,864
33	F		26	Millwall		D1-1	(1-0)	Hetherington	30,907
34	S		27	Walsall		L2-5	(1-1)	Cookson,Fowler	4,842
35	M		29	Millwall	W3-0		(1-0)	Cookson,Hetherington,Jones	10,959
36	S	Apr	3	Luton Town		D2-2	(1-1)	Hetherington 2	10,432
37	S		10	Cardiff City		W2-1	(1-1)	Cookson,Musgrave	9,066
38	S		17	Crystal Palace	W4-0		(3-0)	Cookson 2 (1 pen.),Jones,Fowler	6,306
39	W		21	Luton Town		L1-5	(0-3)	Fowler	11,668
40	S		24	Exeter City		D1-1	(1-0)	Fowler	4,200
41	W		28	Bristol City		W2-1	(0-0)	Fowler 2	3,537
42	S	May	1	Aldershot		L1-2	(0-2)	Jones	1,892

Average Home Attendance : **7,967**
Average Away Attendance : **10,240**

F A Cup

No	Day	Month	Date	Opponents	Home	Away	H-T	Goalscorers	Gate
1	S	Nov	28	Dulwich Hamlet	W6-0		(1-0)	Hetherington,Bradley 2,Cookson,Jones,Fowler	12,622
2	S	Dec	12	Cardiff City		L1-2	(1-0)	Cookson	18,833

Third Division South Cup

No	Day	Month	Date	Opponents	Home	Away	H-T	Goalscorers	Gate
1	W	Sep	30	Bristol Rovers	L0-3		(0-2)		1,823

JIM COOKSON
came to the County Ground with an excellent scoring pedigree, having netted 200 League goals. After failing to register a first team appearance for Manchester City - where his brother Sam was a full-back - Jim joined Chesterfield in 1925 and grabbed 86 goals in just 75 games. West Bromwich Albion signed him in 1927, when he scored in four of his first five games and then hit six in his sixth ! His partnership at Swindon with Alan Fowler yielded over forty goals in 1936/37 but Jim's second term with Town was blighted by injury, forcing him to retire from the full-time game. But Jim still turned out in local football until 1952.

Bailey H	Bradley J	Brock J G G	Chandler F E J	Cookson J	Cousins H	Duckworth T C	Edmonds F H A	Fowler A	Hetherington J A	Jones E M	McPhail D D	Morrall G R	Musgrave J	Shanks R	Smith A J	Storey W C	Ware E A G	Wilcockson E S	Wildman F R	Wise K K	
			10	9	4	2		8	11		7	5			3		6		1		**1**
			8		4	2		9	11	7		5			3	10	6		1		**2**
			8		4	2		9	11	7		5			3	10	6		1		**3**
			10	9	4	2		8	11		7	5			3			6	1		**4**
			9		4	2		8	11		7	5			3	10		6	1		**5**
			10	9	4	2		8	11		7	5			3			6	1		**6**
			10	9	4	2		8	11	7		5			3			6	1		**7**
			10	9	4	2		8	11	7		5			3			6	1		**8**
			10	9	4	2		8	11	7				5	3			6	1		**9**
			10	9	4	2		8	11	7				5	3			6	1		**10**
			10	9	4	2		8	11	7		5			3			6	1		**11**
			10		4	2		8	11	7		5			3			6	1	9	**12**
			10	9	4	2		8	11		7	5			3			6	1		**13**
				9	4	2		8	11	7		5			3	10		6	1		**14**
	10			9	4	2		8	11	7		5			3			6	1		**15**
	10			9	4	2		8	11	7		5			3			6	1		**16**
	10			9	4	2		8	11	7		5			3			6	1		**17**
	10			9	4	2	1	8	11	7		5			3			6			**18**
	10			9	4	2	1	8	11	7		5			3			6			**19**
	10		9		4	2	1	8	11	7		5			3			6			**20**
	10		9		4	2	1	8	11	7		5			3			6			**21**
	10	1	11		4	2		8	9		7	5			3			6			**22**
	10	1	11		4	2		8	9		7			5	3			6			**23**
	10	1		9	4	2		8	11		7			5	3			6			**24**
		1	11	9	4	2		8	10		7	5			3			6			**25**
		1		9	4	2		8	11	7			10	5	3			6			**26**
				9	4	2		8	11		7		10	5	3			6	1		**27**
	10				4	2		8	11	7		5	9		3			6	1		**28**
2	10			9	4			8	11	7		5	6		3				1		**29**
2	10		8	9	4			7	11			5	6		3				1		**30**
2	10		8	9	4			7	11			5	6		3				1		**31**
	10		8	9	4	2		7	11			5	6		3				1		**32**
				9	4	2		8	11	7		5	10		3		6		1		**33**
				9	4	2		8	11	7			10		3		6	5	1		**34**
				9	4	2		8	11	7		5	10		3			6	1		**35**
				9	4	2		8	11	7		5	10		3			6	1		**36**
				9	4	2		8	11	7		5	10		3			6	1		**37**
				9	4	2		8	11	7		5	10		3			6	1		**38**
				9	4	2		8	11	7		5	10		3			6	1		**39**
				9	4	2		8	11	7		5	10		3			6	1		**40**
				9	4	2		8	11	7		5	6		3			10	1		**41**
				9	4	2		8	11	7		5	6		3			10	1		**42**
3	15	5	21	33	42	39	4	42	42	29	10	35	17	6	42	4	5	34	33	1	Apps
	1		7	25	1			14	11	7	2	4	2			1					Goals

ARTHUR HETHERINGTON

Bailey H	Bradley J	Brock J G G	Chandler F E J	Cookson J	Cousins H	Duckworth T C	Edmonds F H A	Fowler A	Hetherington J A	Jones E M	McPhail D D	Morrall G R	Musgrave J	Shanks R	Smith A J	Storey W C	Ware E A G	Wilcockson E S	Wildman F R	Wise K K	
	10			9	4	2		8	11	7		5			3			6	1		**1**
	10			9	4	2		8	11	7		5			3			6	1		**2**
	2			2	2	2		2	2	2		2			2			2	2		Apps
	2			2				1	1	1											Goals

Bailey H	Bradley J	Brock J G G	Chandler F E J	Cookson J	Cousins H	Duckworth T C	Edmonds F H A	Fowler A	Hetherington J A	Jones E M	McPhail D D	Morrall G R	Musgrave J	Shanks R	Smith A J	Storey W C	Ware E A G	Wilcockson E S	Wildman F R	Wise K K
3	11		6	9	4	2				7	10					8		5	1	

No numbers actually worn on shirts

For Final League Table - see page 105

SEASON 1937/38

Football League Division Three South
Final League Position : 8th
Manager : Ted Vizard

					Home	Away	H-T	Goalscorers	Gate
1	S	Aug	28	Notts County		L0-3	(0-0)		17,313
2	W	Sep	1	Crystal Palace	W4-0		(1-0)	Lucas,Fowler,Cookson 2	8,776
3	S		4	Newport County	W3-2		(2-2)	Cookson,Jones,Lucas	10,958
4	W		8	Crystal Palace		W1-0	(0-0)	Fowler	8,879
5	S		11	Bristol City		D1-1	(0-0)	Hetherington	15,969
6	W		15	Aldershot	W2-0		(2-0)	Fowler,Hetherington	7,686
7	S		18	Watford	L0-2		(0-0)		12,169
8	S		25	Gillingham		D0-0			5,792
9	S	Oct	2	Exeter City	W3-0		(1-0)	Fowler 2,Lucas	9,987
10	S		9	Clapton Orient		L0-1	(0-1)		8,848
11	S		16	Torquay United	W1-0		(0-0)	Musgrave	9,219
12	S		23	Mansfield Town		L0-2	(0-1)		5,264
13	S		30	Bristol Rovers	W2-1		(1-0)	Fowler 2	11,421
14	S	Nov	6	Northampton Town		L0-1	(0-1)		7,806
15	S		13	Walsall	D1-1		(0-1)	Morrall	9,710
16	S		20	Cardiff City		D2-2	(0-1)	Bradley 2	15,404
17	S	Dec	4	Brighton and Hove Albion		L1-3	(0-2)	Bradley	6,824
18	S		18	Southend United		D0-0			6,785
19	S		25	Reading		L1-2	(1-2)	Fowler	10,992
20	M		27	Reading	D0-0				18,760
21	Tu		28	Queens Park Rangers	L1-3		(1-1)	Fowler	7,255
22	S	Jan	1	Notts County	W1-0		(0-0)	Bradley pen.	9,897
23	S		15	Newport County		L0-2	(0-1)		4,340
24	W		26	Bournemouth & Boscombe Athletic	W1-0		(0-0)	Jones pen.	2,332
25	S		29	Watford		L0-4	(0-3)		11,343
26	S	Feb	5	Gillingham	W3-0		(0-0)	Cookson,Armstrong o.g.,Fowler	8,543
27	S		12	Exeter City		D0-0			5,397
28	S		19	Clapton Orient	W1-0		(1-0)	Fowler	6,603
29	S		26	Torquay United		L0-1	(0-1)		2,102
30	S	Mar	5	Mansfield Town	D3-3		(3-1)	Wise,Fowler,Jones pen.	7,728
31	S		12	Bristol Rovers		W2-1	(0-1)	Morton,Jones pen.	7,019
32	S		19	Northampton Town	W1-0		(0-0)	Lucas	7,678
33	S		26	Walsall		W3-2	(2-1)	Lucas 2,Morton	3,261
34	S	Apr	2	Cardiff City	W2-0		(0-0)	Morton,Lucas	8,797
35	S		9	Bournemouth & Boscombe Athletic		W2-1	(1-0)	Fowler 2	5,843
36	F		15	Millwall		W2-0	(1-0)	Chiverton o.g.,Fowler	38,501
37	S		16	Brighton and Hove Albion	L0-1		(0-0)		13,954
38	M		18	Millwall	L1-2		(1-1)	Morton	15,399
39	S		23	Queens Park Rangers		L0-3	(0-0)		15,482
40	S		30	Southend United	D1-1		(0-0)	Bradley	5,028
41	S	May	4	Bristol City	L2-3		(1-2)	Cookson,Morton	10,532
42	Tu		7	Aldershot		D1-1	(0-0)	Cookson	3,598

Average Home Attendance : **9,640**
Average Away Attendance : **9,846**

F A Cup

					Home	Away	H-T	Goalscorers	Gate
1	S	Nov	27	Gillingham		W4-3	(1-2)	Bradley 3 (2 pens.),Jones	5,000
2	S	Dec	11	Queens Park Rangers	W2-1		(2-0)	Jones 2	17,536
3	S	Jan	8	Grimsby Town		D1-1	(1-0)	Jones	14,000
3R	W		12	Grimsby Town	W2-1		(0-1)	Morton,Fowler	23,101
4	S		22	Luton Town		L1-2	(0-1)	Morton	25,746

Third Division South Cup

					Home	Away	H-T	Goalscorers	Gate
2	W	Nov	17	Exeter City	W2-0		(2-0)	Lucas,Emery pen.	1,000
3	W	Feb	16	Millwall	L1-2		(1-1)	Moreland	922

For Final League Table - see page 105

Bailey H	Bradley J	Bryan W	Chambers J	Cookson J	Cousins H	Emery D K J	Fowler A	France J	Hetherington J A	Jones E M	Lucas W H	Moreland A G	Morrall G R	Morton B W	Musgrave J	Richardson W	Smith A J	Swinden S A	Tonner A E McS	Wilcockson E S	Wildman F R	Wise K K	Woods C	
				9	4		8		11	7	10		5				3	2		6	1			1
				9	4		8		11	7	10		5				3	2		6	1			2
				9	4		8		11	7	10		5				3	2		6	1			3
				9	4		8		11	7	10		5				3	2		6	1			4
				9	4		8		11	7	10		5				3	2		6	1			5
				9	4		8		11	7	10		5		6		3	2			1			6
					4		8		11	7	10		5				3	2		6	1		9	7
					4		8		11	7	10		5				3	2		6	1		9	8
					4		8		11	7	10		5				3	2		6	1		9	9
					4		8		11	7	10		5				3	2		6	1		9	10
					4		8		11	7	10		5		9		3	2		6	1			11
				9	4		8		11	7	10		5				3	2		6	1			12
					4		8		11	7	10		5	9			3	2		6	1			13
					4		8		11	7	10		5	9			3	2		6	1			14
	10				4		8	6	11	7			5	9			3	2			1			15
	10						8		11	7			5	9		4	3		2	6	1			16
	10	1					9		11	7	8		5			4	3		2	6				17
	10	1					8		11	7			5	9		4	3		2	6				18
	10						8		11	7			5	9		4	3		2	6	1			19
	10						8		11	7			5	9		4	3		2	6	1			20
				9			8			7			5	10	11	4	3		2	6	1			21
	11	1		10			8			7			5	9		4	3		2	6				22
		1			4		8			7	10			9	6	5	3		2			11		23
		1			4		8		11	7	10		5	9	6		3		2					24
		1			4		8		11	7	10		5	9	6		3		2					25
		1		9	4		8			7			5	10			3		2	6		11		26
		1		9	4		8			7			5	10			3		2	6		11		27
		1		9	4		8		11	7			5	10			3		2	6				28
		1		9	4		8			7	11		5	10			3		2	6				29
		1			4		8			7	10		5	9			3		2	6		11		30
					4		8			7	10		5	9				2	3	6	1	11		31
					4		8			7	10		5	9				3	2	6	1	11		32
					4		8			7	10		5	9				3	2	6	1	11		33
					4		8			7	10		5	9				3	2	6	1	11		34
					4		8			7	10		5	9				3	2	6	1	11		35
					4		8			7	10		5	9				3	2	6	1	11		36
					4		8			7	10		5	9				3	2	6	1	11		37
3	10			9	4					7	8			11		5		2		6	1			38
			5	9	4		8			7	10			11				3	2	6	1			39
	11				4		8			7	10		5	9				3	2	6	1			40
	11			8	4		7				10		5	9				3	2	6	1			41
				8	4	11	7				10		5	9				3	2	6	1			42
1	10	11	1	17	35	1	41	1	23	40	32	0	39	29	6	9	30	27	26	37	31	11	4	Apps
	5			6			15		2	4	7		1	5	1							1		Goals

Opponents 2 goals

Bailey H	Bradley J	Bryan W	Chambers J	Cookson J	Cousins H	Emery D K J	Fowler A	France J	Hetherington J A	Jones E M	Lucas W H	Moreland A G	Morrall G R	Morton B W	Musgrave J	Richardson W	Smith A J	Swinden S A	Tonner A E McS	Wilcockson E S	Wildman F R	Wise K K	Woods C	
	10	1					9		11	7	8		5			4	3		2	6				1
	10	1					8		11	7			5	9		4	3		2	6				2
	10	1			4		8		11	7			5	9			3		2	6				3
	10	1			4		8		11	7			5	9			3		2	6				3R
		1			4		8		11	7	10		5	9	6		3		2					4
	4	5			3		5		5	5	2		5	4	1	2	5		5	4				Apps
	3						1			4				2										Goals

Bailey H	Bradley J	Bryan W	Chambers J	Cookson J	Cousins H	Emery D K J	Fowler A	France J	Hetherington J A	Jones E M	Lucas W H	Moreland A G	Morrall G R	Morton B W	Musgrave J	Richardson W	Smith A J	Swinden S A	Tonner A E McS	Wilcockson E S	Wildman F R	Wise K K	Woods C	
	10					9			11	7	8		5			4	3	2		6	1			2
3		1	5		4		7		8		10	9							2	6		11		3
1	1	1	1		1	1	1		2	1	2	1	1			1	1	1	1	2	1	1		Apps
						1					1	1												Goals

No numbers actually worn on shirts

SEASON 1938/39

Football League Division Three South
Final League Position : 9th
Manager : Ted Vizard

					Home	Away	H-T	Goalscorers	Gate
1	S	Aug	27	Notts County	W4-1		(2-0)	Morton 2,Lucas,Fowler	13,370
2	W		31	Clapton Orient	W2-0		(0-0)	Morton,Francis	10,364
3	S	Sep	3	Aldershot		L0-1	(0-0)		6,790
4	W		7	Torquay United		W3-1	(1-0)	Lucas,Francis,Morton	3,214
5	S		10	Bristol City	W1-0		(1-0)	Morton	17,763
6	S		17	Crystal Palace		D1-1	(0-0)	Wilcockson	20,100
7	S		24	Watford	W3-0		(1-0)	Francis pen.,Morton 2	12,941
8	S	Oct	1	Port Vale		L0-2	(0-0)		10,082
9	S		8	Queens Park Rangers	D2-2		(1-0)	Fowler,Morton	12,268
10	S		15	Southend United		W3-2	(2-1)	Jones E,Lucas,Fowler	7,619
11	S		22	Mansfield Town	L1-2		(1-1)	Morton	11,853
12	S		29	Cardiff City		L1-2	(1-1)	Morton	14,313
13	S	Nov	5	Ipswich Town	D1-1		(1-1)	Francis pen.	10,437
14	S		12	Reading		L0-3	(0-2)		13,455
15	S		19	Bristol Rovers	W2-1		(1-0)	Lucas,Emery	9,423
16	S	Dec	3	Bournemouth & Boscombe Athletic	W4-2		(2-0)	Morton 3,Wilcockson	8,704
17	S		17	Exeter City	W2-1		(0-1)	Morton,Barraclough	6,819
18	S		24	Notts County		L0-2	(0-0)		9,998
19	M		26	Newport County	W8-0		(4-0)	Barraclough,Morton 3,Lucas,Jones E,Francis 2	9,023
20	Tu		27	Newport County		L4-6	(1-4)	Barraclough 2,Jones E,Francis pen.	20,586
21	S		31	Aldershot	W2-1		(1-1)	Morton 2	11,156
22	S	Jan	7	Brighton and Hove Albion		L0-4	(0-3)		5,224
23	S		14	Bristol City		D1-1	(1-1)	Francis	10,111
24	S		21	Crystal Palace	D2-2		(2-0)	Lucas 2	11,823
25	S		28	Watford		L1-4	(1-1)	Francis	7,450
26	S	Feb	4	Port Vale	D1-1		(0-1)	Wilcockson	8,823
27	S		11	Queens Park Rangers		L1-2	(0-1)	Francis pen.	11,635
28	S		18	Southend United	W2-1		(1-0)	Francis,Fowler	8,270
29	S		25	Mansfield Town		D1-1	(0-1)	Morton	4,111
30	S	Mar	4	Cardiff City	W4-1		(2-1)	Morton 2,Francis,Barraclough	8,861
31	S		11	Ipswich Town		L1-3	(0-1)	Francis	11,727
32	S		18	Reading	W4-2		(2-2)	Wilcockson,Barraclough,Morton,Jones E	12,441
33	S		25	Bristol Rovers		L0-5	(0-3)		6,695
34	S	Apr	1	Brighton and Hove Albion	W3-2		(0-2)	Francis,Morton 2	9,111
35	F		7	Northampton Town	W1-0		(1-0)	Francis	14,910
36	S		8	Bournemouth & Boscombe Athletic		L0-2	(0-0)		7,325
37	M		10	Northampton Town		W2-0	(1-0)	Fowler,Morton	9,203
38	S		15	Walsall	L1-4		(0-2)	Francis	6,716
39	S		22	Exeter City		D0-0			4,622
40	M		24	Walsall		L0-5	(0-2)		5,703
41	S		29	Clapton Orient		L0-5	(0-1)		5,790
42	S	May	6	Torquay United	W3-1		(3-0)	Morton 2,Lucas	5,657

Average Home Attendance : **10,511**
Average Away Attendance : **9,322**

F A Cup

					Home	Away	H-T	Goalscorers	Gate
1	S	Nov	26	Lowestoft Town	W6-0		(5-0)	Jones E,Lucas 2,Morton 3	10,816
2	S	Dec	10	Southport		L0-2	(0-1)		10,993

Third Division South Cup

					Home	Away	H-T	Goalscorers	Gate
1	W	Sep	14	Exeter City		D1-1	(1-1)	Fowler	1,500
1R	W	Oct	19	Exeter City	L2-3		(1-0)	Fowler,Morton	1,381

BEN MORTON
became the first ever £1,000 signing by Town. Ted Vizard saw the Torquay and former Manchester United reserve centre-forward as a ready made replacement for the injury prone Jim Cookson. Six-footer Ben had netted 33 goals in only 49 League games for the Gulls before his arrival at the County Ground in October 1937. He had to wait until his tenth game to hit his first goal for the club, but when it finally came, it could hardly have been better timed. Town had secured a creditable draw at Grimsby in the F.A.Cup Third Round and Ben's strike saw them go on to secure another top flight scalp in the replay. When the War interrupted play in 1940, Ben joined home town club Stourbridge and finished his playing days there as a centre-half.

Barraclough A	Bryan W	Butcher F	Chambers J	Cousins H	Emery D K J	Ephgrave G A	Fowler A	Francis C T	Hedley F	Jones D G	Jones E M	Lucas W H	Morrall G R	Morton B W	Murphy J P	Olney J F	Parkhouse R McD	Swinden S A	Tonner A E McS	Wilcockson E S	Wildman F R	Wise K K	Woolhouse R	
11				4			8				7	10	5	9				3	2	6	1			1
11				4				10			7	8	5	9				3	2	6	1			2
11				4				10			7	8	5	9				3	2	6	1			3
				4			8	11				10	5	9				3	2	6	1		7	4
		3	5	4			8	11				10		9					2	6	1		7	5
		3		4			8	11			7	10	5	9					2	6	1			6
		3		4			8	11			7	10	5	9					2	6	1			7
		3		4			8	11			7	10	5	9					2	6	1			8
		3		4			8	11			7	10	5	9					2	6	1			9
		3		4			8	11			7	10	5	9					2	6	1			10
		3		4			8	11				10	5	9					2	6	1		7	11
		3	5	4			8	11				10		9				2		6	1		7	12
		3	5	4			8	11			7	10		9				2		6	1			13
				4	10		8	11			7			9			5	3	2	6	1			14
		3		4	8			11		5	7	10		9					2	6	1			15
11		3		4				8			7	10	5	9					2	6	1			16
11		3		4				8			7	10	5	9		6	2				1			17
11		3		4				8			7	10	5	9		6	2				1			18
11		3		4				8			7	10	5	9		6	2				1			19
11		3		4				8			7	10	5	9		6	2				1			20
11		3		4				8			7	10	5	9		6	2				1			21
11		3		4	6			8			7	10	5	9			2				1			22
11		3		4				8			7	10	5	9		6	2				1			23
		3		4			11	8			7	10	5	9		6	2				1			24
11	1	3		4				8			7	10	5	9				2		6				25
11		3		4			9	8			7	10	5				2			6	1			26
		3		4			9	8		5	7	10				6	2				1	11		27
11		3		4			10	8		5	7			9		6	2				1			28
11		3		4			10	8		5	7			9			2			6	1			29
11		3		4				8		5	7	10		9			2			6	1			30
11		3		4				8		5	7	10		9			2			6	1			31
11	1	3		4				8			7	10	5	9			2			6				32
11	1	3		4				8			7	10	5	9			2			6				33
11	1	3		4				8		5	7	10		9	6		2							34
11	1	3		4				8		5	7	10		9	6		2							35
	1	3		4			7	8		5		10		9	6		2			11				36
	1	3		4	11		7	8		5		10		9			2			6				37
	1	3		4	11		7	8		5		10		9	6		2							38
	1	3		4	11			8		5	7	10		9			2			6				39
	1	3		4	11			8		5	7	10		9				2		6				40
		3		4	11	1		8		5	7	10		9			2			6				41
	1			4			7	8	11	5		10		9		6	2		3					42
21	11	36	3	42	8	1	21	41	1	15	34	39	23	40	4	10	25	9	15	28	30	1	4	Apps
6					1		5	16			4	8		28						4				Goals

Barraclough A	Bryan W	Butcher F	Chambers J	Cousins H	Emery D K J	Ephgrave G A	Fowler A	Francis C T	Hedley F	Jones D G	Jones E M	Lucas W H	Morrall G R	Morton B W	Murphy J P	Olney J F	Parkhouse R McD	Swinden S A	Tonner A E McS	Wilcockson E S	Wildman F R	Wise K K	Woolhouse R	
		3		4	8			11			7	10	5	9					2	6	1			1
11		3		4	8						7	10	5	9					2	6	1			2
1		2		2	2			1			2	2	2	2					2	2	2			Apps
											1	2		3										Goals

Barraclough A	Bryan W	Butcher F	Chambers J	Cousins H	Emery D K J	Ephgrave G A	Fowler A	Francis C T	Hedley F	Jones D G	Jones E M	Lucas W H	Morrall G R	Morton B W	Murphy J P	Olney J F	Parkhouse R McD	Swinden S A	Tonner A E McS	Wilcockson E S	Wildman F R	Wise K K	Woolhouse R	
		3	5		4		8	11				10		9					2	6	1		7	1
	1	3	5	4	6		8	11			7	10		9			2							1R
	1	2	2	1	2		2	2			1	2		2			1		1	1	1		1	Apps
							2							1										Goals

For Final League Table - see page 106

SEASON 1920/21

Div.3

	P	W	D	L	F	A	W	D	L	F	A	Pts	G/A	*Avge. Home Gate
1 Crystal Palace	42	15	4	2	45	17	9	7	5	25	17	59	2.06	13,300
2 Southampton	42	14	5	2	46	10	5	11	5	18	18	54	2.29	12,450
3 Queens Park Rangers	42	14	4	3	38	11	8	5	8	23	21	53	1.91	14,600
4 SWINDON TOWN	42	14	5	2	51	17	7	5	9	22	32	52	1.49	9,000
5 Swansea Town	42	9	10	2	32	19	9	5	7	24	26	51	1.24	13,550
6 Watford	42	14	4	3	40	15	6	4	11	19	29	48	1.34	7,350
7 Millwall	42	11	5	5	25	8	7	6	8	17	22	47	1.40	18,950
8 Merthyr Town	42	13	5	3	46	20	2	10	9	14	29	45	1.22	12,600
9 Luton Town	42	14	6	1	51	15	2	6	13	10	41	44	1.09	9,100
10 Bristol Rovers	42	15	3	3	51	22	3	4	14	17	35	43	1.19	12,750
11 Plymouth Argyle	42	10	7	4	25	13	1	14	6	10	21	43	1.03	13,800
12 Portsmouth	42	10	8	3	28	14	2	7	12	18	34	39	0.96	15,500
13 Grimsby Town	42	12	5	4	32	16	3	4	14	17	43	39	0.83	9,750
14 Northampton Town	42	11	4	6	32	23	4	4	13	27	52	38	0.79	7,500
15 Newport County	42	8	5	8	20	23	6	4	11	23	41	37	0.67	8,900
16 Norwich City	42	9	10	2	31	14	1	6	14	13	39	36	0.83	8,500
17 Southend United	42	13	2	6	32	20	1	6	14	12	41	36	0.72	7,300
18 Brighton & Hove Albion	42	11	6	4	28	20	3	2	16	14	41	36	0.69	8,950
19 Exeter City	42	9	7	5	27	15	1	8	12	12	39	35	0.72	7,750
20 Reading	42	8	4	9	26	22	4	3	14	16	37	31	0.71	7,150
21 Brentford	42	7	9	5	27	23	2	3	16	15	44	30	0.63	8,650
22 Gillingham	42	6	9	6	19	24	2	3	16	15	50	28	0.46	8,250

SEASON 1921/22

Div.3S

	P	W	D	L	F	A	W	D	L	F	A	Pts	G/A	*Avge. Home Gate
1 Southampton	42	14	7	0	50	8	9	8	4	18	13	61	3.24	12,200
2 Plymouth Argyle	42	17	4	0	43	4	8	7	6	20	20	61	2.63	14,800
3 Portsmouth	42	13	5	3	38	18	5	12	4	24	21	53	1.59	13,650
4 Luton Town	42	16	2	3	47	9	6	6	9	17	26	52	1.83	8,650
5 Queens Park Rangers	42	13	7	1	36	12	5	6	10	17	32	49	1.20	12,250
6 SWINDON TOWN	42	10	7	4	40	21	6	6	9	32	39	45	1.20	7,450
7 Watford	42	9	9	3	34	21	4	9	8	20	27	44	1.13	6,100
8 Aberdare Athletic	42	11	6	4	38	18	6	4	11	19	33	44	1.12	9,500
9 Brentford	42	15	2	4	41	17	1	9	11	11	26	43	1.21	9,000
10 Swansea Town	42	11	8	2	40	19	2	7	12	10	28	41	1.06	11,700
11 Merthyr Town	42	14	2	5	33	15	3	4	14	12	41	40	0.80	8,500
12 Millwall	42	6	13	2	22	10	4	5	12	16	32	38	0.90	16,500
13 Reading	42	10	5	6	28	15	4	5	12	12	32	38	0.85	8,500
14 Bristol Rovers	42	8	8	5	32	24	6	2	13	20	43	38	0.78	12,000
15 Norwich City	42	8	10	3	29	17	4	3	14	21	45	37	0.81	7,750
16 Charlton Athletic	42	10	6	5	28	19	3	5	13	15	37	37	0.77	10,100
17 Northampton Town	42	13	3	5	30	17	0	8	13	17	54	37	0.66	6,700
18 Gillingham	42	11	4	6	36	20	3	4	14	11	40	36	0.78	8,800
19 Brighton & Hove Albion	42	9	6	6	33	19	4	3	14	12	32	35	0.88	8,000
20 Newport County	42	8	7	6	22	18	3	5	13	22	43	34	0.72	7,500
21 Exeter City	42	7	5	9	22	29	4	7	10	16	30	34	0.64	6,200
22 Southend United	42	7	5	9	23	23	1	6	14	11	51	27	0.46	6,400

SEASON 1922/23

Div.3S

	P	W	D	L	F	A	W	D	L	F	A	Pts	G/A	*Avge. Home Gate
1 Bristol City	42	16	4	1	43	13	8	7	6	23	27	59	1.65	17,150
2 Plymouth Argyle	42	18	3	0	47	6	5	4	12	14	23	53	2.10	11,200
3 Swansea Town	42	13	6	2	46	14	9	3	9	32	31	53	1.73	14,600
4 Brighton & Hove Albion	42	15	3	3	39	13	5	8	8	13	21	51	1.53	8,700
5 Luton Town	42	14	4	3	47	18	7	3	11	21	31	49	1.39	8,550
6 Millwall	42	9	10	2	27	13	5	8	8	18	27	46	1.13	16,050
7 Portsmouth	42	10	5	6	34	20	9	3	9	24	32	46	1.12	12,000
8 Northampton Town	42	13	6	2	40	17	4	5	12	14	27	45	1.23	8,600
9 SWINDON TOWN	42	14	4	3	41	17	3	7	11	21	39	45	1.11	6,450
10 Watford	42	10	6	5	35	23	7	4	10	22	31	44	1.06	7,550
11 Queens Park Rangers	42	10	4	7	34	24	6	6	9	20	25	42	1.10	10,350
12 Charlton Athletic	42	11	6	4	33	14	3	8	10	22	37	42	1.08	7,350
13 Bristol Rovers	42	7	9	5	25	19	6	7	8	10	17	42	0.97	10,550
14 Brentford	42	9	4	8	27	23	4	8	9	14	28	38	0.80	8,250
15 Southend United	42	10	6	5	35	18	2	7	12	14	36	37	0.91	7,500
16 Gillingham	42	13	4	4	38	18	2	3	16	13	41	37	0.86	6,300
17 Merthyr Town	42	10	4	7	27	17	1	10	10	12	31	36	0.81	5,550
18 Norwich City	42	8	7	6	29	26	5	3	13	22	45	36	0.72	8,400
19 Reading	42	9	8	4	24	15	1	6	14	12	40	34	0.65	6,950
20 Exeter City	42	10	4	7	27	18	3	3	15	20	66	33	0.56	6,150
21 Aberdare Athletic	42	6	8	7	25	23	3	3	15	17	47	29	0.60	7,550
22 Newport County	42	8	6	7	28	21	0	5	16	12	49	27	0.57	7,850

* Attendance figures are approximate and shown only for comparison purposes

SEASON 1923/24

Div.3S

	P	W	D	L	F	A	W	D	L	F	A	Pts	G/A	*Avge. Home Gate
1 Portsmouth	42	15	3	3	57	11	9	8	4	30	19	59	2.90	12,850
2 Plymouth Argyle	42	13	6	2	46	15	10	3	8	24	19	55	2.06	10,350
3 Millwall	42	17	3	1	45	11	5	7	9	19	27	54	1.68	16,650
4 Swansea Town	42	18	2	1	39	10	4	6	11	21	38	52	1.25	15,300
5 Brighton & Hove Albion	42	16	4	1	56	12	5	5	11	12	25	51	1.84	7,650
6 SWINDON TOWN	42	14	5	2	38	11	3	8	10	20	33	47	1.32	6,350
7 Luton Town	42	11	7	3	35	19	5	7	9	15	25	46	1.14	7,800
8 Northampton Town	42	14	3	4	40	15	3	8	10	24	32	45	1.36	9,200
9 Bristol Rovers	42	11	7	3	34	15	4	6	11	18	31	43	1.13	9,300
10 Newport County	42	15	4	2	39	15	2	5	14	17	49	43	0.88	8,050
11 Norwich City	42	13	5	3	45	18	3	3	15	15	41	40	1.02	8,150
12 Aberdare Athletic	42	9	9	3	35	18	3	5	13	10	40	38	0.78	6,150
13 Merthyr Town	42	11	8	2	33	19	0	8	13	12	46	38	0.69	6,900
14 Charlton Athletic	42	8	7	6	26	20	3	8	10	12	25	37	0.84	5,550
15 Gillingham	42	11	6	4	27	15	1	7	13	16	43	37	0.74	6,100
16 Exeter City	42	14	3	4	33	17	1	4	16	4	35	37	0.71	5,600
17 Brentford	42	9	8	4	33	21	5	0	16	21	50	36	0.76	6,750
18 Reading	42	12	2	7	35	20	1	7	13	16	37	35	0.89	6,600
19 Southend United	42	11	7	3	35	19	1	3	17	18	65	34	0.63	6,650
20 Watford	42	8	8	5	35	18	1	7	13	10	36	33	0.83	6,200
21 Bournemouth & Boscombe Athletic	42	6	8	7	19	19	5	3	13	21	46	33	0.62	5,250
22 Queens Park Rangers	42	9	6	6	28	26	2	3	16	9	51	31	0.48	8,850

SEASON 1924/25

Div.3S

	P	W	D	L	F	A	W	D	L	F	A	Pts	G/A	*Avge. Home Gate
1 Swansea Town	42	17	4	0	51	12	6	7	8	17	23	57	1.94	15,450
2 Plymouth Argyle	42	17	3	1	55	12	6	7	8	22	26	56	2.03	12,700
3 Bristol City	42	14	5	2	40	10	8	4	9	20	31	53	1.46	10,900
4 SWINDON TOWN	42	17	2	2	51	13	3	9	9	15	25	51	1.74	7,100
5 Millwall	42	12	5	4	35	14	6	8	7	23	24	49	1.53	15,300
6 Newport County	42	13	6	2	35	12	7	3	11	27	30	49	1.48	8,450
7 Exeter City	42	13	4	4	37	19	6	5	10	22	29	47	1.23	6,550
8 Brighton & Hove Albion	42	14	3	4	43	17	5	5	11	16	28	46	1.31	7,900
9 Northampton Town	42	12	3	6	34	18	8	3	10	17	26	46	1.16	6,950
10 Southend United	42	14	1	6	34	18	5	4	12	17	43	43	0.84	7,900
11 Watford	42	12	3	6	22	20	5	6	10	16	27	43	0.81	6,200
12 Norwich City	42	10	8	3	39	18	4	5	12	14	33	41	1.04	7,500
13 Gillingham	42	11	8	2	25	11	2	6	13	10	33	40	0.80	5,200
14 Reading	42	9	6	6	28	15	5	4	12	9	23	38	0.97	7,800
15 Charlton Athletic	42	12	6	3	31	13	1	6	14	15	35	38	0.96	7,400
16 Luton Town	42	9	10	2	34	15	1	7	13	15	42	37	0.86	6,650
17 Bristol Rovers	42	10	5	6	26	13	2	8	11	16	36	37	0.857	9,650
18 Aberdare Athletic	42	13	4	4	40	21	1	5	15	14	46	37	0.81	5,600
19 Queens Park Rangers	42	10	6	5	28	19	4	2	15	14	44	36	0.67	8,900
20 Bournemouth & Boscombe Athletic	42	8	6	7	20	17	5	2	14	20	41	34	0.69	5,550
21 Brentford	42	8	7	6	28	26	1	0	20	10	65	25	0.42	7,150
22 Merthyr Town	42	8	3	10	24	27	0	2	19	11	50	21	0.45	4,700

SEASON 1925/26

Div.3S

	P	W	D	L	F	A	W	D	L	F	A	Pts	G/A	Avge. Home Gate
1 Reading	42	16	5	0	49	16	7	6	8	28	36	57	1.48	12,765
2 Plymouth Argyle	42	16	2	3	71	33	8	6	7	36	34	56	1.60	13,728
3 Millwall	42	14	6	1	52	12	7	5	9	21	27	53	1.87	14,952
4 Bristol City	42	14	3	4	42	15	7	6	8	30	36	51	1.41	11,962
5 Brighton & Hove Albion	42	12	4	5	47	33	7	5	9	37	40	47	1.15	8,109
6 SWINDON TOWN	42	16	2	3	48	22	4	4	13	21	42	46	1.08	6,648
7 Luton Town	42	16	4	1	60	25	2	3	16	20	50	43	1.07	7,515
8 Bournemouth & Boscombe Athletic	42	10	5	6	44	30	7	4	10	31	61	43	0.82	5,388
9 Aberdare Athletic	42	11	6	4	50	24	6	2	13	24	42	42	1.12	4,815
10 Gillingham	42	11	4	6	36	19	6	4	11	17	30	42	1.08	6,293
11 Southend United	42	13	2	6	50	20	6	2	13	28	53	42	1.07	7,427
12 Northampton Town	42	13	3	5	47	26	4	4	13	35	54	41	1.03	6,978
13 Crystal Palace	42	16	1	4	50	21	3	2	16	25	58	41	0.95	12,767
14 Merthyr Town	42	13	3	5	51	25	1	8	12	18	50	39	0.92	5,910
15 Watford	42	12	5	4	47	26	3	4	14	26	63	39	0.82	6,808
16 Norwich City	42	11	5	5	35	26	4	4	13	23	47	39	0.79	7,036
17 Newport County	42	11	5	5	39	27	3	5	13	25	47	38	0.86	5,977
18 Brentford	42	12	4	5	44	32	4	2	15	25	62	38	0.73	9,146
19 Bristol Rovers	42	9	4	8	44	28	6	2	13	22	41	36	0.96	8,612
20 Exeter City	42	13	2	6	54	25	2	3	16	18	45	35	1.03	6,334
21 Charlton Athletic	42	9	7	5	32	23	2	6	13	16	45	35	0.71	7,403
22 Queens Park Rangers	42	5	7	9	23	32	1	2	18	14	52	21	0.44	7,545

* Attendance figures are approximate and shown only for comparison purposes

SEASON 1926/27

Div.3S		P	W	D	L	F	A	W	D	L	F	A	Pts	G/A	Avge. Home Gate
1	Bristol City	42	19	1	1	71	24	8	7	6	33	30	62	1.93	16,360
2	Plymouth Argyle	42	17	4	0	52	14	8	6	7	43	47	60	1.56	10,849
3	Millwall	42	16	2	3	55	19	7	8	6	34	32	56	1.75	14,173
4	Brighton & Hove Albion	42	15	4	2	61	24	6	7	8	18	26	53	1.58	9,551
5	SWINDON TOWN	42	16	3	2	64	31	5	6	10	36	54	51	1.18	8,274
6	Crystal Palace	42	12	6	3	57	33	6	3	12	27	48	45	1.04	11,645
7	Bournemouth & Boscombe Athletic	42	13	2	6	49	24	5	6	10	29	42	44	1.18	5,453
8	Luton Town	42	12	9	0	48	19	3	5	13	20	47	44	1.03	7,817
9	Newport County	42	15	4	2	40	20	4	2	15	17	51	44	0.80	5,193
10	Bristol Rovers	42	12	4	5	46	28	4	5	12	32	52	41	0.98	8,145
11	Brentford	42	10	9	2	46	20	3	5	13	24	41	40	1.15	9,713
12	Exeter City	42	14	4	3	46	18	1	6	14	30	55	40	1.04	7,201
13	Charlton Athletic	42	13	5	3	44	22	3	3	15	16	39	40	0.98	6,951
14	Queens Park Rangers	42	9	8	4	41	27	6	1	14	24	44	39	0.92	9,076
15	Coventry City	42	11	4	6	44	33	4	3	14	27	53	37	0.83	10,274
16	Norwich City	42	10	5	6	41	25	2	6	13	18	46	35	0.83	7,458
17	Merthyr Town	42	11	5	5	42	25	2	4	15	21	55	35	0.79	3,170
18	Northampton Town	42	13	4	4	36	23	2	1	18	23	64	35	0.68	6,053
19	Southend United	42	12	3	6	44	25	2	3	16	20	52	34	0.83	7,109
20	Gillingham	42	10	5	6	36	26	1	5	15	18	46	32	0.75	4,974
21	Watford	42	9	6	6	36	27	3	2	16	21	60	32	0.66	6,894
22	Aberdare Athletic	42	8	2	11	38	48	1	5	15	24	53	25	0.61	2,500

SEASON 1927/28

Div.3S		P	W	D	L	F	A	W	D	L	F	A	Pts	G/A	Avge. Home Gate
1	Millwall	42	19	2	0	87	15	11	3	7	40	35	65	2.54	17,677
2	Northampton Town	42	17	3	1	67	23	6	6	9	35	41	55	1.59	10,095
3	Plymouth Argyle	42	17	2	2	60	19	6	5	10	25	35	53	1.57	9,994
4	Brighton & Hove Albion	42	14	4	3	51	24	5	6	10	30	45	48	1.17	7,630
5	Crystal Palace	42	15	3	3	46	23	3	9	9	33	49	48	1.10	10,946
6	SWINDON TOWN	42	12	6	3	60	26	7	3	11	30	43	47	1.30	6,685
7	Southend United	42	14	2	5	48	19	6	4	11	32	45	46	1.25	6,128
8	Exeter City	42	11	6	4	49	27	6	6	9	21	33	46	1.17	6,876
9	Newport County	42	12	5	4	52	38	6	4	11	29	46	45	0.96	4,533
10	Queens Park Rangers	42	8	5	8	37	35	9	4	8	35	36	43	1.01	10,407
11	Charlton Athletic	42	12	5	4	34	27	3	8	10	26	43	43	0.86	8,734
12	Brentford	42	12	4	5	49	30	4	4	13	27	44	40	1.03	7,331
13	Luton Town	42	13	5	3	56	27	3	2	16	38	60	39	1.08	7,530
14	Bournemouth & Boscombe Athletic	42	12	6	3	44	24	1	6	14	28	55	38	0.91	5,290
15	Watford	42	10	5	6	42	34	4	5	12	26	44	38	0.87	7,193
16	Gillingham	42	10	3	8	33	26	3	8	10	29	55	37	0.77	4,881
17	Norwich City	42	9	8	4	41	26	1	8	12	25	44	36	0.94	8,233
18	Walsall	42	9	6	6	52	35	3	3	15	23	66	33	0.74	6,580
19	Bristol Rovers	42	11	3	7	41	36	3	1	17	26	57	32	0.72	6,843
20	Coventry City	42	5	8	8	40	36	6	1	14	27	60	31	0.70	9,388
21	Merthyr Town	42	7	6	8	38	40	2	7	12	15	51	31	0.58	2,745
22	Torquay United	42	4	10	7	27	36	4	4	13	26	67	30	0.51	4,175

SEASON 1928/29

Div.3S		P	W	D	L	F	A	W	D	L	F	A	Pts	G/A	Avge. Home Gate
1	Charlton Athletic	42	14	5	2	51	22	9	3	9	35	38	54	1.43	11,478
2	Crystal Palace	42	14	2	5	40	25	9	6	6	41	42	54	1.21	15,584
3	Northampton Town	42	14	6	1	68	23	6	6	9	28	34	52	1.68	10,131
4	Plymouth Argyle	42	14	6	1	51	13	6	6	9	32	38	52	1.63	10,658
5	Fulham	42	14	3	4	60	31	7	7	7	41	40	52	1.42	18,250
6	Queens Park Rangers	42	13	7	1	50	22	6	7	8	32	39	52	1.34	13,487
7	Luton Town	42	16	3	2	64	28	3	8	10	25	45	49	1.22	10,090
8	Watford	42	15	3	3	55	31	4	7	10	24	43	48	1.07	9,712
9	Bournemouth & Boscombe Athletic	42	14	4	3	54	31	5	5	11	30	46	47	1.09	5,554
10	SWINDON TOWN	42	12	5	4	48	27	3	8	10	27	45	43	1.04	5,455
11	Coventry City	42	9	6	6	35	23	5	8	8	27	34	42	1.09	14,353
12	Southend United	42	10	7	4	44	27	5	4	12	36	48	41	1.07	5,960
13	Brentford	42	11	4	6	34	21	3	6	12	22	39	38	0.93	8,159
14	Walsall	42	11	7	3	47	25	2	5	14	26	54	38	0.92	6,527
15	Brighton & Hove Albion	42	14	2	5	39	28	2	4	15	19	48	38	0.76	6,871
16	Newport County	42	8	6	7	37	28	5	3	13	32	58	35	0.80	4,029
17	Norwich City	42	12	3	6	49	29	2	3	16	20	52	34	0.85	7,245
18	Torquay United	42	10	3	8	46	36	4	3	14	20	48	34	0.79	4,919
19	Bristol Rovers	42	9	6	6	39	28	4	1	16	21	51	33	0.76	7,549
20	Merthyr Town	42	11	6	4	42	28	0	2	19	13	75	30	0.53	3,154
21	Exeter City	42	7	6	8	49	40	2	5	14	18	48	29	0.76	5,743
22	Gillingham	42	7	8	6	22	24	3	1	17	21	59	29	0.52	4,610

SEASON 1929/30

Div.3S

	P	W	D	L	F	A	W	D	L	F	A	Pts	G/A	Avge. Home Gate
1 Plymouth Argyle	42	18	3	0	63	12	12	5	4	35	26	68	2.58	15,233
2 Brentford	42	21	0	0	66	12	7	5	9	28	32	61	2.14	12,123
3 Queens Park Rangers	42	13	5	3	46	26	8	4	9	34	42	51	1.18	10,960
4 Northampton Town	42	14	6	1	53	20	7	2	12	29	38	50	1.41	8,833
5 Brighton & Hove Albion	42	16	2	3	54	20	5	6	10	33	43	50	1.38	8,477
6 Coventry City	42	14	3	4	54	25	5	6	10	34	48	47	1.21	12,985
7 Fulham	42	12	6	3	54	33	6	5	10	33	50	47	1.05	15,489
8 Norwich City	42	14	4	3	55	28	4	6	11	33	49	46	1.14	9,904
9 Crystal Palace	42	14	5	2	56	26	3	7	11	25	48	46	1.09	13,455
10 Bournemouth & Boscombe Athletic	42	11	6	4	47	24	4	7	10	25	37	43	1.18	6,271
11 Southend United	42	11	6	4	41	19	4	7	10	28	40	43	1.17	6,821
12 Clapton Orient	42	10	8	3	38	21	4	5	12	17	41	41	0.89	9,967
13 Luton Town	42	13	4	4	42	25	1	8	12	22	53	40	0.82	7,612
14 SWINDON TOWN	42	10	7	4	42	25	3	5	13	31	58	38	0.88	5,426
15 Watford	42	10	4	7	37	30	5	4	12	23	43	38	0.82	8,227
16 Exeter City	42	10	6	5	45	29	2	5	14	22	44	35	0.92	6,592
17 Walsall	42	10	4	7	45	24	3	4	14	26	54	34	0.91	5,607
18 Newport County	42	9	9	3	48	29	3	1	17	26	56	34	0.87	3,918
19 Torquay United	42	9	6	6	50	38	1	5	15	14	56	31	0.68	4,271
20 Bristol Rovers	42	11	3	7	45	31	0	5	16	22	62	30	0.72	7,169
21 Gillingham	42	9	5	7	38	28	2	3	16	13	52	30	0.64	5,049
22 Merthyr Town	42	5	6	10	39	49	1	3	17	21	86	21	0.44	2,503

SEASON 1930/31

Div.3S

	P	W	D	L	F	A	W	D	L	F	A	Pts	G/A	Avge. Home Gate
1 Notts County	42	16	4	1	58	13	8	7	6	39	33	59	2.11	12,257
2 Crystal Palace	42	17	2	2	71	20	5	5	11	36	51	51	1.51	13,181
3 Brentford	42	14	3	4	62	30	8	3	10	28	34	50	1.41	8,236
4 Brighton & Hove Albion	42	13	5	3	45	20	4	10	7	23	33	49	1.28	7,119
5 Southend United	42	16	0	5	53	26	6	5	10	23	34	49	1.27	5,804
6 Northampton Town	42	10	6	5	37	20	8	6	7	40	39	48	1.31	7,846
7 Luton Town	42	15	3	3	61	17	4	5	12	15	34	46	1.49	6,718
8 Queens Park Rangers	42	15	0	6	57	23	5	3	13	25	52	43	1.09	8,785
9 Fulham	42	15	3	3	49	21	3	4	14	28	54	43	1.03	10,825
10 Bournemouth & Boscombe Athletic	42	11	7	3	39	22	4	6	11	33	51	43	0.99	5,375
11 Torquay United	42	13	5	3	56	26	4	4	13	24	58	43	0.95	4,373
12 SWINDON TOWN	42	15	5	1	68	29	3	1	17	21	65	42	0.95	4,911
13 Exeter City	42	12	6	3	55	35	5	2	14	29	55	42	0.93	4,950
14 Coventry City	42	11	4	6	55	28	5	5	11	20	37	41	1.15	10,327
15 Bristol Rovers	42	12	3	6	49	36	4	5	12	26	56	40	0.82	6,607
16 Gillingham	42	10	6	5	40	29	4	4	13	21	47	38	0.80	5,030
17 Walsall	42	9	5	7	44	38	5	4	12	34	57	37	0.82	5,091
18 Watford	42	9	4	8	41	29	5	3	13	31	46	35	0.96	6,447
19 Clapton Orient	42	12	3	6	47	33	2	4	15	16	58	35	0.69	5,471
20 Thames	42	12	5	4	34	20	1	3	17	20	73	34	0.58	2,315
21 Newport County	42	10	5	6	45	31	1	1	19	24	80	28	0.622	2,840
22 Norwich City	42	10	7	4	37	20	0	1	20	10	56	28	0.618	8,337

SEASON 1931/32

Div.3S

	P	W	D	L	F	A	W	D	L	F	A	Pts	G/A	Avge. Home Gate
1 Fulham	42	15	3	3	72	27	9	6	6	39	35	57	1.79	17,647
2 Reading	42	19	1	1	65	21	4	8	9	32	46	55	1.45	9,629
3 Southend United	42	12	5	4	41	18	9	6	6	36	35	53	1.45	7,986
4 Crystal Palace	42	14	7	0	48	12	6	4	11	26	51	51	1.17	15,132
5 Brentford	42	11	6	4	40	22	8	4	9	28	30	48	1.31	11,347
6 Luton Town	42	16	1	4	62	25	4	6	11	33	45	47	1.36	7,027
7 Exeter City	42	16	3	2	53	16	4	4	13	24	46	47	1.24	6,257
8 Brighton & Hove Albion	42	12	4	5	42	21	5	8	8	31	37	46	1.26	8,120
9 Cardiff City	42	14	2	5	62	29	5	6	10	25	44	46	1.19	7,684
10 Norwich City	42	12	7	2	51	22	5	5	11	25	45	46	1.13	10,892
11 Watford	42	14	4	3	49	27	5	4	12	32	52	46	1.03	8,372
12 Coventry City	42	17	2	2	74	28	1	6	14	34	69	44	1.11	12,235
13 Queens Park Rangers	42	11	6	4	50	30	4	6	11	29	43	42	1.08	13,303
14 Northampton Town	42	12	3	6	48	26	4	4	13	21	43	39	1.00	6,535
15 Bournemouth & Boscombe Athletic	42	8	8	5	42	32	5	4	12	28	46	38	0.90	5,747
16 Clapton Orient	42	7	8	6	41	35	5	3	13	36	55	35	0.86	7,593
17 SWINDON TOWN	42	12	2	7	47	31	2	4	15	23	53	34	0.83	5,031
18 Bristol Rovers	42	11	6	4	46	30	2	2	17	19	62	34	0.71	7,279
19 Torquay United	42	9	6	6	49	39	3	3	15	23	67	33	0.68	3,718
20 Mansfield Town	42	11	5	5	54	45	0	5	16	21	63	32	0.69	7,330
21 Gillingham	42	8	6	7	26	26	2	2	17	14	56	28	0.49	5,357
22 Thames	42	6	7	8	35	35	1	2	18	18	74	23	0.49	2,623

SEASON 1932/33

Div.3S		P	W	D	L	F	A	W	D	L	F	A	Pts	G/A	Avge. Home Gate
1	Brentford	42	15	4	2	45	19	11	6	4	45	30	62	1.84	13,300
2	Exeter City	42	17	2	2	57	13	7	8	6	31	35	58	1.83	7,665
3	Norwich City	42	16	3	2	49	17	6	10	5	39	38	57	1.60	10,930
4	Reading	42	14	5	2	68	30	5	8	8	35	41	51	1.45	9,840
5	Crystal Palace	42	14	4	3	51	21	5	4	12	27	43	46	1.22	10,877
6	Coventry City	42	16	1	4	75	24	3	5	13	31	53	44	1.38	12,479
7	Gillingham	42	14	4	3	54	24	4	4	13	18	37	44	1.18	6,597
8	Northampton Town	42	16	5	0	54	11	2	3	16	22	55	44	1.15	6,056
9	Bristol Rovers	42	13	5	3	38	22	2	9	10	23	34	44	1.09	9,984
10	Torquay United	42	12	7	2	51	26	4	5	12	21	41	44	1.07	3,991
11	Watford	42	11	8	2	37	22	5	4	12	29	41	44	1.05	7,297
12	Brighton & Hove Albion	42	13	3	5	42	20	4	5	12	24	45	42	1.02	6,361
13	Southend United	42	11	5	5	39	27	4	6	11	26	55	41	0.79	6,083
14	Luton Town	42	12	8	1	60	32	1	5	15	18	46	39	1.00	5,824
15	Bristol City	42	11	5	5	59	37	1	8	12	24	53	37	0.92	8,636
16	Queens Park Rangers	42	9	8	4	48	32	4	3	14	24	55	37	0.83	7,707
17	Aldershot	42	11	6	4	37	21	2	4	15	24	51	36	0.85	5,140
18	Bournemouth & Boscombe Athletic	42	10	7	4	44	27	2	5	14	16	54	36	0.74	4,822
19	Cardiff City	42	12	4	5	48	30	0	3	18	21	69	31	0.70	7,008
20	Clapton Orient	42	7	8	6	39	35	1	5	15	20	58	29	0.63	6,064
21	Newport County	42	9	4	8	42	42	2	3	16	19	63	29	0.58	4,401
22	SWINDON TOWN	42	7	9	5	36	29	2	2	17	24	76	29	0.57	4,893

SEASON 1933/34

Div.3S		P	W	D	L	F	A	W	D	L	F	A	Pts	G/A	Avge. Home Gate
1	Norwich City	42	16	4	1	55	19	9	7	5	33	30	61	1.80	13,586
2	Coventry City	42	16	3	2	70	22	5	9	7	30	32	54	1.85	14,093
3	Reading	42	17	4	0	60	13	4	8	9	22	37	54	1.64	9,912
4	Queens Park Rangers	42	17	2	2	42	12	7	4	10	28	39	54	1.37	10,022
5	Charlton Athletic	42	14	5	2	53	27	8	3	10	30	29	52	1.48	10,574
6	Luton Town	42	14	3	4	55	28	7	7	7	28	33	52	1.36	7,941
7	Bristol Rovers	42	14	4	3	49	21	6	7	8	28	26	51	1.64	11,358
8	SWINDON TOWN	42	13	5	3	42	25	4	6	11	22	43	45	0.94	9,117
9	Exeter City	42	12	5	4	43	19	4	6	11	25	38	43	1.19	5,916
10	Brighton & Hove Albion	42	12	7	2	47	18	3	6	12	21	42	43	1.13	6,338
11	Clapton Orient	42	14	4	3	60	25	2	6	13	15	44	42	1.09	9,119
12	Crystal Palace	42	11	6	4	40	25	5	3	13	31	42	41	1.06	10,996
13	Northampton Town	42	10	6	5	45	32	4	6	11	26	46	40	0.91	6,271
14	Aldershot	42	8	6	7	28	27	5	6	10	24	44	38	0.73	4,542
15	Watford	42	12	4	5	43	16	3	3	15	28	47	37	1.13	6,602
16	Southend United	42	9	6	6	32	27	3	4	14	19	47	34	0.69	5,866
17	Gillingham	42	8	8	5	49	41	3	3	15	26	55	33	0.78	5,896
18	Newport County	42	6	9	6	25	23	2	8	11	24	47	33	0.70	6,066
19	Bristol City	42	7	8	6	33	22	3	5	13	25	63	33	0.68	9,147
20	Torquay United	42	10	4	7	32	28	3	3	15	21	65	33	0.57	3,352
21	Bournemouth & Boscombe Athletic	42	7	7	7	41	37	2	2	17	19	65	27	0.59	5,305
22	Cardiff City	42	6	4	11	32	43	3	2	16	25	62	24	0.54	7,959

SEASON 1934/35

Div.3S		P	W	D	L	F	A	W	D	L	F	A	Pts	G/A	Avge. Home Gate
1	Charlton Athletic	42	17	2	2	62	20	10	5	6	41	32	61	1.98	15,713
2	Reading	42	16	5	0	59	23	5	6	10	30	42	53	1.37	9,345
3	Coventry City	42	14	5	2	56	14	7	4	10	30	36	51	1.72	15,060
4	Luton Town	42	12	7	2	60	23	7	5	9	32	37	50	1.53	8,685
5	Crystal Palace	42	15	3	3	51	14	4	7	10	35	50	48	1.34	13,357
6	Watford	42	14	2	5	53	19	5	7	9	23	30	47	1.55	7,734
7	Northampton Town	42	14	4	3	40	21	5	4	12	25	46	46	0.97	6,420
8	Bristol Rovers	42	14	6	1	54	27	3	4	14	19	50	44	0.95	9,302
9	Brighton & Hove Albion	42	15	4	2	51	16	2	5	14	18	46	43	1.11	6,570
10	Torquay United	42	15	2	4	60	22	3	4	14	21	53	42	1.08	3,442
11	Exeter City	42	11	5	5	48	29	5	4	12	22	46	41	0.93	5,009
12	Millwall	42	11	4	6	33	26	6	3	12	24	36	41	0.92	11,021
13	Queens Park Rangers	42	14	6	1	49	22	2	3	16	14	50	41	0.88	7,344
14	Clapton Orient	42	13	3	5	47	21	2	7	12	18	44	40	1.00	8,652
15	Bristol City	42	14	3	4	37	18	1	6	14	15	50	39	0.76	8,870
16	SWINDON TOWN	42	11	7	3	45	22	2	5	14	22	56	38	0.86	7,304
17	Bournemouth & Boscombe Athletic	42	10	5	6	36	26	5	2	14	18	45	37	0.76	5,375
18	Aldershot	42	12	6	3	35	20	1	4	16	15	55	36	0.67	4,105
19	Cardiff City	42	11	6	4	42	27	2	3	16	20	55	35	0.76	9,908
20	Gillingham	42	10	7	4	36	25	1	6	14	19	50	35	0.73	5,289
21	Southend United	42	10	4	7	40	29	1	5	15	25	49	31	0.83	6,729
22	Newport County	42	7	4	10	36	40	3	1	17	18	72	25	0.48	5,186

SEASON 1935/36

Div.3S

	Team	P	W	D	L	F	A	W	D	L	F	A	Pts	G/A	Avge. Home Gate
1	Coventry City	42	19	1	1	75	12	5	8	8	27	33	57	2.27	19,232
2	Luton Town	42	13	6	2	56	20	9	6	6	25	25	56	1.80	12,995
3	Reading	42	18	0	3	52	20	8	2	11	35	42	54	1.40	9,811
4	Queens Park Rangers	42	14	4	3	55	19	8	5	8	29	34	53	1.58	11,113
5	Watford	42	12	3	6	47	29	8	6	7	33	25	49	1.48	8,338
6	Crystal Palace	42	15	4	2	64	20	7	1	13	32	54	49	1.30	12,613
7	Brighton & Hove Albion	42	13	4	4	48	25	5	4	12	22	38	44	1.11	7,659
8	Bournemouth & Boscombe Athletic	42	9	6	6	36	26	7	5	9	24	30	43	1.07	7,232
9	Notts County	42	10	5	6	40	25	5	7	9	20	32	42	1.05	7,320
10	Torquay United	42	14	4	3	41	27	2	5	14	21	35	41	1.00	4,048
11	Aldershot	42	9	6	6	29	21	5	6	10	24	40	40	0.87	4,487
12	Millwall	42	9	8	4	33	21	5	4	12	25	50	40	0.82	10,565
13	Bristol City	42	11	5	5	32	21	4	5	12	16	38	40	0.81	9,671
14	Clapton Orient	42	13	2	6	34	15	3	4	14	21	46	38	0.90	7,586
15	Northampton Town	42	12	5	4	38	24	3	3	15	24	66	38	0.69	7,050
16	Gillingham	42	9	5	7	34	25	5	4	12	32	52	37	0.86	6,009
17	Bristol Rovers	42	11	6	4	48	31	3	3	15	21	64	37	0.73	8,322
18	Southend United	42	8	7	6	38	21	5	3	13	23	41	36	0.98	7,283
19	SWINDON TOWN	42	10	5	6	43	33	4	3	14	21	40	36	0.88	7,101
20	Cardiff City	42	11	5	5	37	23	2	5	14	23	50	36	0.82	9,528
21	Newport County	42	8	4	9	36	44	3	5	13	24	67	31	0.54	5,892
22	Exeter City	42	7	5	9	38	41	1	6	14	21	52	27	0.63	5,200

SEASON 1936/37

Div.3S

	Team	P	W	D	L	F	A	W	D	L	F	A	Pts	G/A	Avge. Home Gate
1	Luton Town	42	19	1	1	69	16	8	3	10	34	37	58	1.94	15,315
2	Notts County	42	15	3	3	44	23	8	7	6	30	29	56	1.42	14,129
3	Brighton & Hove Albion	42	15	5	1	49	16	9	0	12	25	27	53	1.72	10,667
4	Watford	42	14	4	3	53	21	5	7	9	32	39	49	1.42	9,237
5	Reading	42	14	5	2	53	23	5	6	10	23	37	49	1.27	9,086
6	Bournemouth & Boscombe Athletic	42	17	3	1	45	20	3	6	12	20	39	49	1.10	8,036
7	Northampton Town	42	15	4	2	56	22	5	2	14	29	46	46	1.25	9,960
8	Millwall	42	12	4	5	43	24	6	6	9	21	30	46	1.19	19,009
9	Queens Park Rangers	42	12	2	7	51	24	6	7	8	22	28	45	1.40	10,293
10	Southend United	42	10	8	3	49	23	7	3	11	29	44	45	1.16	8,049
11	Gillingham	42	14	5	2	36	18	4	3	14	16	48	44	0.79	7,004
12	Clapton Orient	42	10	8	3	29	17	4	7	10	23	35	43	1.00	8,027
13	SWINDON TOWN	42	12	4	5	52	24	2	7	12	23	49	39	1.03	7,967
14	Crystal Palace	42	11	7	3	45	20	2	5	14	17	41	38	1.02	10,870
15	Bristol Rovers	42	14	3	4	49	20	2	1	18	22	60	36	0.89	10,579
16	Bristol City	42	13	3	5	42	20	2	3	16	16	50	36	0.83	9,686
17	Walsall	42	11	3	7	38	34	2	7	12	25	51	36	0.74	5,672
18	Cardiff City	42	10	5	6	35	24	4	2	15	19	63	35	0.62	15,644
19	Newport County	42	7	7	7	37	28	5	3	13	30	70	34	0.68	8,781
20	Torquay United	42	9	5	7	42	32	2	5	14	15	48	32	0.71	3,754
21	Exeter City	42	9	5	7	36	37	1	7	13	23	51	32	0.67	5,423
22	Aldershot	42	5	6	10	29	29	2	3	16	21	60	23	0.56	4,018

SEASON 1937/38

Div.3S

	Team	P	W	D	L	F	A	W	D	L	F	A	Pts	G/A	Avge. Home Gate
1	Millwall	42	15	3	3	53	15	8	7	6	30	22	56	2.24	22,758
2	Bristol City	42	14	6	1	37	13	7	7	7	31	27	55	1.70	16,917
3	Queens Park Rangers	42	15	3	3	44	17	7	6	8	36	30	53	1.702	13,799
4	Watford	42	14	4	3	50	15	7	7	7	23	28	53	1.698	10,529
5	Brighton & Hove Albion	42	15	3	3	40	16	6	6	9	24	28	51	1.45	10,164
6	Reading	42	17	2	2	44	21	3	9	9	27	42	51	1.13	8,960
7	Crystal Palace	42	14	4	3	45	17	4	8	9	22	30	48	1.43	13,501
8	SWINDON TOWN	42	12	4	5	33	19	5	6	10	16	30	44	1.00	9,640
9	Northampton Town	42	12	4	5	30	19	5	5	11	21	38	43	0.89	7,416
10	Cardiff City	42	13	7	1	57	22	2	5	14	10	32	42	1.24	20,009
11	Notts County	42	10	6	5	29	17	6	3	12	21	33	41	1.00	12,354
12	Southend United	42	12	5	4	43	23	3	5	13	27	45	40	1.03	7,279
13	Bournemouth & Boscombe Athletic	42	8	10	3	36	20	6	2	13	20	37	40	0.98	7,119
14	Mansfield Town	42	12	5	4	46	26	3	4	14	16	41	39	0.93	7,241
15	Bristol Rovers	42	10	7	4	28	20	3	6	12	18	41	39	0.75	8,359
16	Newport County	42	9	10	2	31	15	2	6	13	12	37	38	0.83	9,249
17	Exeter City	42	10	4	7	37	32	3	8	10	20	38	38	0.81	6,245
18	Aldershot	42	11	4	6	23	14	4	1	16	16	45	35	0.66	5,298
19	Clapton Orient	42	10	7	4	27	19	3	0	18	15	42	33	0.69	7,835
20	Torquay United	42	7	5	9	22	28	2	7	12	16	45	30	0.52	3,877
21	Walsall	42	10	4	7	34	37	1	3	17	18	51	29	0.59	4,564
22	Gillingham	42	9	5	7	25	25	1	1	19	11	52	26	0.47	5,465

Div.3S		P	W	D	L	F - A		W	D	L	F - A		Pts	G/A	Avge. Home Gate
1	Newport County	42	15	4	2	37	16	7	7	7	21	29	55	1.29	11,448
2	Crystal Palace	42	15	4	2	49	18	5	8	8	22	34	52	1.37	14,799
3	Brighton & Hove Albion	42	14	5	2	43	14	5	6	10	25	35	49	1.39	8,392
4	Watford	42	14	6	1	44	15	3	6	12	18	36	46	1.22	7,539
5	Reading	42	12	6	3	46	23	4	8	9	23	36	46	1.17	8,375
6	Queens Park Rangers	42	10	8	3	44	15	5	6	10	24	34	44	1.39	10,669
7	Ipswich Town	42	14	3	4	46	21	2	9	10	16	31	44	1.19	11,975
8	Bristol City	42	14	5	2	42	19	2	7	12	19	44	44	0.97	10,430
9	SWINDON TOWN	42	15	4	2	53	25	3	4	14	19	52	44	0.94	10,511
10	Aldershot	42	13	6	2	31	15	3	6	12	22	51	44	0.80	6,138
11	Notts County	42	12	6	3	36	16	5	3	13	23	38	43	1.09	10,410
12	Southend United	42	14	5	2	38	13	2	4	15	23	51	41	0.95	5,910
13	Cardiff City	42	12	1	8	40	28	3	10	8	21	37	41	0.94	14,217
14	Exeter City	42	9	9	3	40	32	4	5	12	25	50	40	0.79	6,055
15	Bournemouth & Boscombe Athletic	42	10	8	3	38	22	3	5	13	14	36	39	0.90	5,936
16	Mansfield Town	42	10	8	3	33	19	2	7	12	11	43	39	0.71	4,770
17	Northampton Town	42	13	5	3	41	20	2	3	16	10	38	38	0.88	8,001
18	Port Vale	42	10	5	6	36	23	4	4	13	16	35	37	0.90	7,587
19	Torquay United	42	7	5	9	27	28	7	4	10	27	42	37	0.77	3,926
20	Clapton Orient	42	10	9	2	40	16	1	4	16	13	39	35	0.96	7,943
21	Walsall	42	9	6	6	47	23	2	5	14	21	46	33	0.99	7,364
22	Bristol Rovers	42	8	8	5	30	17	2	5	14	25	44	33	0.90	7,999

SEASON 1938/39

For 1939/40 Final League Table - see page 109

LEAGUE JUBILEE

To mark the 50th anniversary of the inauguration of the Football League, a Jubilee Benevolent Fund was set up. Launched on May 30 1938, the Management Committee aimed to raise £100,000 to 'assist needy players'.

Local 'derby' games were arranged and played as pre-season fixtures in 1938/39 and 1939/40.

Aug 20 1938 — Att : 5,341

Newport County 3
SWINDON TOWN 3 (Morton,Lucas,Barraclough)

Wildman; Tonner, Swinden; Cousins, Morrall, Wilcockson;
Jones, Fowler, Morton, Lucas, Barraclough.

ARTHUR BARRACLOUGH

Aug 19 1939 — Att : 6,000

SWINDON TOWN 2 (Morton 2)
Newport County 1

Wildman; Lawrence, Lowe; Cousins, Olney, Ryan;
Jones, Francis, Morton, Lucas, Hedley.

JIM OLNEY
(see Page 112)

The Management Committee also decided to officially recognise regulated watering of pitches up to the end of October and again from March 1.

A motion to make the numbering of players' shirts compulsory for all Football League fixtures was carried by 24 votes to 20, but another proposal put forward to allow the promotion and relegation between divisions to be increased to four clubs was defeated by 28 votes to 21. Thus, in the Third Division South - where Swindon Town remained from 1920 to 1958 - only the champions were promoted each season.

ROLL CALL : 1939-40 and 1945/46

Surname	Initials	Known As	Pos	Intl	Born	Died	Parent Club	Signed	Apps	Gls.
Barlow	R	Ray	WH	E	1926		West Bromwich Albion	Oct 1945	1	2
Bicknell	R	Roy	CH		1926	2005	Wolverhampton Wanderers	Feb 1946	1	0
Blanchflower	R D	Danny	WH	NI	1926	1993	Glentoran	Feb 1946	1	0
Brinton	J V	Jack	W		1916	1997	Derby County	Oct 1945	1	0
Carr	L L	Lance	W		1910	1983	Newport County	May 1940	1	0
Catterall	G	George	FB		1918	1987	Bolton Wanderers	Apr 1940	1	0
Collins	J H	Jimmy	CF		1911	1983	Cardiff City	Mar 1940	2	0
Cox	F J A	Freddie	W		1920	1973	Tottenham Hotspur	Dec 1939	1	1
Curran	F	Frank	CF		1917	1998	Bristol City	May 1940	1	0
Egan	H	Harry	CF		1912	1979	Cardiff City	Nov 1939	2	0
Emmanuel	T	Tom	FB		1915	1997	Southampton	Oct 1939	12	1
Forde	S	Steve	FB		1914	1992	West Ham United	Dec 1939	1	0
Geldard	A	Albert	F	E	1914	1989	Bolton Wanderers	Mar 1940	1	0
Hall	F W	Fred	CH		1917	1989	Blackburn Rovers	Nov 1945	4	0
Hampson	H	Harry	F		1918	1942	Sheffield United	Mar 1940	2	0
Hanford	H	Harry	CH	W	1907	1995	Sheffield Wednesday	Feb 1940	4	0
Harris	R	Nobby	WH				South Marston	Aug 1945	1	0
Harris	N	Neil (Jnr)	CF		1920		Swansea Town	May 1940	1	2
Harris **	N	Neil (Snr)	F	S	1894	1941	**	Jun 1939	1	0
Hinton	E G A	Ted	G	NI	1922	1988	Belfast Distillery	Feb 1946	1	0
Holland	E D	Ted	W		1927	1997	Arsenal	Oct 1945	5	1
Howe	D	Donny	IF		1917	1978	Bolton Wanderers	Mar 1940	4	4
Hurst	J	Jack	CH		1914	2002	Bolton Wanderers	Mar 1940	2	0
Jackman	H J W	Harry	W		1924	2003	Wolverhampton Wanderers	Sep 1945	11	2
Kelso	J	Jimmy	FB		1910	1987	Cardiff City	May 1940	1	0
			Returned from				Ebbw Vale *	Nov 1945	17	0
Lawrance	R S	Ray	CH		1911	1987	Newport County	Nov 1939	11	0
Low	N H	Norman	CH		1914	1994	Newport County	Oct 1945	1	0
McDonald	P	Paddy	FB		1922		Glasgow Celtic	Sep 1945	22	0
McGibbon	D	Doug	F		1919	2002	Southampton	Aug 1945	5	3
Maggs	P	Percy	G		1906	1985	Torquay United	May 1940	1	0
Manning	G	George	FB		1919	1988	Troedyrhiew	Mar 1946	1	0
Martin **	H	Harry	G	E	1891	1974	**	Aug 1936	1	0
Mathers	J		WH				St Johnstone	Sep 1945	6	0
Morgan	A S	Stan	IF		1920	1971	Arsenal	Sep 1945	2	1
Pritchard	R T	Roy	FB		1925	1993	Wolverhampton Wanderers	Feb 1946	1	0
Reilly	L H	Len	CH		1917	1998	Norwich City	Aug 1945	1	0
Rosenthal	A W	Abe	IF		1921	1986	Tranmere Rovers	Sep 1945	12	5
Skinner	G E H	George	IF		1917	2002	Tottenham Hotspur	Oct 1945	1	0
Sturgess *	M D	Merv	G		1922	2001	*	Aug 1945	1	0
Thomas	D S L	Dai	CF		1920	1993	Swansea Town	Dec 1945	6	3
Thompson	J V	Val	FB		1918		Bolton Wanderers	Mar 1940	3	0
Tovey	S G	Sid	HB		1919	1994	Ipswich Town	Sep 1945	2	0
Tudor	W	Bill	CH		1918	1965	West Bromwich Albion	Jan 1946	7	0
Webb	J A	Jack	FB		1908	1984	Newport County	May 1940	1	0
Williams	C E	Cyril	IF		1921	1980	Bristol City	May 1940	1	0
Winter	D T	Danny	FB		1918	2004	Bolton Wanderers	Feb 1940	1	0
Woodman *	D W M	Doug	FB		1922	1999	*	Aug 1945	21	0
Woodward	T	Tom	IF		1917	1994	Bolton Wanderers	Sep 1945	1	0

TOM EMMANUEL

DONNY HOWE

RAY LAWRANCE

DOUG WOODMAN

No fixtures played from August 1940 to May 1945 due to County Ground being commissioned by the War Department

*All Guest Players except * (Swindon Town contract players) and ** (STFC coaching and management staff)*

SEASON 1939/40

Football League Division Three South
Final League Position : 20th
Manager : Neil Harris
(Competition abandoned on September 3)

					Home	Away	H-T	Goalscorers	Gate
1	S	Aug	26	Northampton Town		L0-1	(0-1)		8,315
2	W		30	Cardiff City	L0-1		(0-1)		9,672
3	S	Sep	2	Aldershot	D2-2		(2-1)	Fowler 2	7,722

South-West Regional League
Final League Position : 5th

					Home	Away	H-T	Goalscorers	Gate
1	S	Oct	21	Newport County		W2-0	(0-0)	Fowler 2	1,824
2	S		28	Torquay United	W2-0		(0-0)	Bowl,Fowler	2,260
3	S	Nov	4	Bristol City		W6-2	(1-1)	Bowl,Francis 2,Jones E,Lawrence pen.,Fowler	3,168
4	S		11	Cardiff City	D2-2		(1-0)	Fowler,Lucas pen.	4,161
5	S		18	Plymouth Argyle		L1-2	(0-0)	Fowler	2,415
6	S		25	Swansea Town		W3-1	(2-0)	Fowler,Lucas,Hedley	1,500
7	S	Dec	2	Bristol Rovers	D3-3		(1-0)	Cox,Bowl,Lucas pen.	3,512
8	S		9	Newport County	W2-1		(0-0)	Bowl,Lucas pen.	3,145
9	S		16	Torquay United		L1-5	(1-1)	Bowl	800
10	S		23	Bristol City	W7-2		(2-1)	Bowl 3,Hedley,Fowler 2,Jones E	2,027
11	M		25	Bristol Rovers		W4-3	(0-1)	Fowler,Hedley,Lucas pen.,Jones E	2,494
12	Tu		26	Bristol Rovers	D1-1		(0-0)	Bowl	5,673
13	S		30	Cardiff City		D1-1	(0-0)	Bowl	2,000
14	S	Jan	6	Plymouth Argyle	W2-0		(1-0)	Hedley,Emery pen.	3,801
15	S		13	Swansea Town	W4-1		(2-0)	Emery,Fowler 2,Hedley	3,307
16	S		20	Bristol Rovers		L2-5	(0-3)	Day,Smith o.g.	600
17	S	Feb	10	Bristol City		L1-5	(0-2)	Emmanuel T	1,500
18	S		24	Plymouth Argyle		L2-4	(1-2)	Fowler,Emery	3,912
19	S	Mar	2	Swansea Town		L1-2	(0-1)	Fowler	3,000
20	S		16	Newport County	D3-3		(2-0)	Howe,Hedley,Fowler	3,182
21	S		23	Torquay United		L3-4	(2-3)	Fowler,Howe 2 (1 pen.)	1,230
22	S		30	Bristol City	L1-3		(1-1)	Howe pen.	3,006
23	S	Apr	6	Cardiff City		D1-1	(0-1)	Hedley	3,000
24	S		20	Cardiff City	D2-2		(1-1)	Bowl,Painter	1,665
25	S	May	4	Torquay United	L1-3		(0-0)	Jones E	
26	S		11	Plymouth Argyle	D2-2		(1-2)	Harris jnr 2	1,947
27	S		18	Newport County		L2-5	(1-2)	Painter 2	600
28	S		25	Swansea Town	W4-0		(2-0)	Jones E,Fowler 2,Williams	

Approx.Average Home Attendance : **2,000**
Approx.Average Away Attendance : **1,400**

NB : Some line-ups shown here differ from those reported in the press. Those printed opposite were taken from the official team sheets submitted to the Football League by the Swindon Town F C Secretary Sam Allen.

War League Cup

					Home	Away	H-T	Goalscorers	Gate
Pr	S	Apr	13	Torquay United	D1-1		(1-1)	Fowler	4,643
Pr	W		17	Torquay United		L0-5	(0-2)		1,281

NEIL HARRIS
was appointed to the County Ground hot seat in June 1939, having previously spent five years in charge at Swansea Town. A former Scottish international forward, his career took him to Partick Thistle, Newcastle, Notts County, Oldham and Third Lanark, before he became player-manager at Burton in 1931. Neil's future plans for Town were almost immediately thwarted when the League programme was suspended after just three games. A hurriedly formed Regional League saw results fluctuate as wildly as the availability of players - and in January, at the age of 45, Neil was forced into playing. Sadly he was not given the chance to prove himself under peace-time conditions as he died in December 1941.

Cousins H	Day A	Fowler A	Francis C T	Hedley F	Imrie W N	Jones E M	Lawrence S W	Lowe H	Lucas W H	Mackenzie J A	Morton B W	Olney J F	Parkhouse R M	Ryan T	Wildman F R	
4			8	11		7	2	3	10		9	5		6	1	**1**
			8	11	4	7		3	10		9	5	2	6	1	**2**
	6	7	8	11	4			3	10	9		5	2		1	**3**
1	1	1	3	3	2	2	1	3	3	1	2	3	2	2	3	Apps
		2														Goals

Bailey H	Bowl T H	Collins J H	Cousins H	Cox F J A	Day A	Egan H	Emery D K J	Emmanuel T	Fowler A	Francis C T	Geldard A	Hampson H	Hanford H	Harris N jnr.	Harris N snr.	Hedley F	Howe D	Hurst J	Jones D G	Jones E M	Lawrance R S	Lawrence S W	Lucas W H	Painter E G	Parkhouse R M	Thompson J V	Webb J A	Wildman F R	Williams C E	
	9		4		6			3	11	8										7		2	10		5			1		**1**
	9		4		6			3	11	8										7		2	10		5			1		**2**
	9		4		6			3	11	8										7		2	10		5			1		**3**
	9		4		6			3	8							11				7	5		10		2			1		**4**
			4		6	9		3	8							11				7	5		10		2			1		**5**
			4		6	9		3	8							11				7	5	2	10					1		**6**
	9		4	11	6			3	8											7	5		10		2			1		**7**
	9		4		6		3		8							11				7	5		10		2			1		**8**
	9		4		6		3		8							11				7	5		10		2			1		**9**
	9		4		6		3		8			*10=Lloyd W L*				11			5	7					2			1		**10**
	9		4		6		3		8							11				7	5		10		2			1		**11**
	9		4		6		3		8							11				7	5			10	2			1		**12**
	9		4		6			3	8							11				7	5		10		2			1		**13**
	9		4		6		10	3	8							11				7	5				2			1		**14**
	9		4		6		10	3	8							11				7		2			5			1		**15**
	10		4		6		3		8						9	11				7	5				2			1		**16**
	9		4				10	3	8				5			11			6	7					2			1		**17**
	9		4		6		10		8				5			11				7	*2=Winter D T*				3			1		**18**
		9	4		6		10	3	8		7		5			11						2						1		**19**
			4		6				9			8	5			11	10			7					3	2		1		**20**
	9		4		6				8							11	10	5		7					2	3		1		**21**
			4		6				8			9				11	10	5		7					2	3		1		**22**
	9		4		6				8		*3=Catterall G*					11	10			7		2			5			1		**23**
3	9		5		6		4		8		*2=Butcher F*					11				7				10				1		**24**
3			4		6		2		8		*9=Curran F*					11				7				10	5			1		**25**
3			4		6				8					9		11	*1=Maggs P*			7				10	5		2			**26**
3		9	4		6				8		*11=Carr L L*									7		2		10	5			1		**27**
			4		6	*1=Martin H*			9		*3=Kelso J*					11				7		2		8	5				10	**28**
4	19	2	28	1	27	2	13	12	28	3	1	2	4	1	1	23	4	2	2	27	11	9	11	6	25	3	1	26	1	Apps
	11			1	1		3	1	18	2				2		7	4			5		1	5	3					1	Goals

Opponents 1 goal

Bailey H	Bowl T H	Butcher F	Cousins H	Day A	Emery D K J	Fowler A	Hedley F	Howe D	Jones E M	Lawrence S W	Morton B W	Parkhouse R M	Ryan T	Wildman F R	
		3	4	6		8	11	10	7	2	9	5		1	**Pr**
3	9		4	6	10	8	11		7	2			5	1	**Pr**
1	1	1	2	2	1	2	2	1	2	2	1	1	1	2	Apps
						1									Goals

South-West Regional League

	P	W	D	L	F	A	Pts
1 Plymouth Argyle	28	16	4	8	72	41	36
2 Torquay United	28	14	6	8	73	62	34
3 Bristol Rovers	28	9	10	9	62	55	28
4 Newport County	28	12	4	12	70	63	28
5 SWINDON TOWN	28	10	8	10	66	63	28
6 Swansea Town	28	10	6	12	54	60	26
7 Cardiff City	28	6	13	9	45	63	25
8 Bristol City	28	7	5	16	15	58	19

SEASON 1945/46

Division Three South (Southern Section)
Final League Position : 6th
Manager : Louis Page

					Home	Away	H-T	Goalscorers	Gate
1	S	Aug	25	Exeter City	L1-4		(1-1)	McGibbon	11,824
2	S	Sep	1	Exeter City		D1-1	(1-0)	Jackman	6,301
3	W		12	Brighton and Hove Albion	W3-2		(2-2)	McGibbon 2,Morgan	5,262
4	S		22	Torquay United		W1-0	(1-0)	Godwin	4,000
5	S		29	Torquay United	D1-1		(0-1)	Godwin	10,942
6	S	Oct	6	Reading	W3-0		(2-0)	Lucas pen.,Godwin,Rosenthal	13,786
7	S		13	Reading		W2-1	(0-0)	Jackman,Lucas	8,858
8	S		20	Bristol Rovers		L0-2	(0-1)		11,500
9	W		24	Bournemouth & Boscombe Athletic		W4-2	(1-2)	Barlow 2,Derrick,Rosenthal	2,630
10	S		27	Bristol Rovers	L2-3		(0-2)	Holland,Rosenthal	11,869
11	S	Nov	3	Crystal Palace	L1-3		(0-2)	Rosenthal	13,280
12	W		7	Bournemouth & Boscombe Athletic	W2-1		(0-1)	Emery,Denyer	4,612
13	S		10	Crystal Palace		L1-10	(0-2)	Emery pen.	10,000
14	S	Dec	1	Cardiff City	L1-2		(0-1)	Williams	11,876
15	S		8	Cardiff City		L0-3	(0-1)		6,000
16	S		22	Aldershot	W2-0		(1-0)	Emery,Thomas	11,000
17	Tu		25	Bristol City	W4-3		(3-1)	Emery,Williams,Thomas,Jones	9,470
18	W		26	Bristol City		L1-4	(0-4)	Jones	14,369
19	S		29	Brighton and Hove Albion		L3-4	(1-1)	Thomas,Williams 2	6,183
20	W	Apr	10	Aldershot		D1-1	(1-1)	Jones	1,110

Approx.Average Home Attendance : **10,400**
Approx.Average Away Attendance : **7,100**

F A Cup

					Home	Away	H-T	Goalscorers	Gate
1/1	S	Nov	17	Bristol Rovers	W1-0		(1-0)	Emery	11,181
1/2	S		24	Bristol Rovers		L1-4	(0-4)	Francis	11,500

Division Three South Cup
(Southern Section Qualifying Competition)
Final Position : 9th
** South and North Cup fixture*

					Home	Away	H-T	Goalscorers	Gate
1	S	Jan	12	Bristol City	D1-1		(1-0)	Painter	10,353
2	S		19	Bristol City		L1-2	(1-1)	Rosenthal	8,791
3	S		26	Reading	W3-2		(1-0)	Lucas,Jones,Williams	9,000
4	S	Feb	2	Reading		L0-5	(0-3)		8,040
5	S		9	Bournemouth & Boscombe Athletic	D0-0				9,149
6	S		16	Bournemouth & Boscombe Athletic		L1-6	(1-1)	Williams	7,169
7	S		23	Northampton Town *	L1-4		(0-2)	Williams	8,815
8	S	Mar	2	Northampton Town *		L1-5	(1-2)	Derrick	4,000
9	S		9	Aldershot		W3-1	(1-0)	Williams,Derrick,Painter	3,217
10	S		16	Aldershot	W4-0		(1-0)	Jones 2 (1 pen.),Derrick,Lucas	8,073
11	S		23	Cardiff City	W3-2		(1-1)	Williams,Painter,Derrick	11,779
12	S		30	Cardiff City		L0-2	(0-1)		19,500
13	S	Apr	6	Bristol Rovers		D0-0			9,029
14	S		13	Bristol Rovers	W2-1		(2-0)	Derrick,Williams	10,330
15	S		20	Torquay United		L1-4	(0-3)	Williams	5,381
16	M		22	Torquay United	D0-0				11,165

Approx.Average Home Attendance : **9,800**
Approx.Average Away Attendance : **8,300**

LOUIS PAGE
had been an outstanding sportsman in his playing days. Apart from gaining seven soccer caps for England, he was eight times a baseball international. During the War Louis was manager of Liverpool Combination club Carlton, while working as a dock labourer. He arrived at the County Ground in July 1945 and set about building from scratch, as the club had been shut down since 1940. Louis also took on the secretary's duties when Sam Allen died early in 1946. But two fourth place finishes in three seasons were testament to his organisational nous. This, however, became increasingly eroded by the directors and, with little financial backing, his Town days became numbered. Louis moved to Chester in June 1953.

Barlow R J	Burton S	Cousins H	Denyer A F T	Derrick A E	Emery D K J	Francis C T	Godwin R G	Hall F W	Holland E D	Jackman H J W	Jones E M	Kelso J	Lloyd W L	Lovesey W S	Lucas W H	McDonald P	McGibbon D	Mather J	Morgan A S	Onslow L G	Painter E G	Parkhouse R McD	Rosenthal A W	Skinner G E H	Thomas D S L	Tovey S G	Wildman F R	Williams G G	Woodman D W M	
	1	4				8			11=Hedley F			9=Morton B W					7		6= Ryan T			2		5=Reilly L H				10	3	**1**
	1	4				6=Harris R				7						3	9		10		8					5		11	2	**2**
	1	4			8=Woodward T					7					10	3	9		11							5		6	2	**3**
		4	7				9			8						3	11	6		5	10						1		2	**4**
			7				9			8					10	3	11	6		5			4				1		2	**5**
		4					9		11	7					10	3		6		5			8				1		2	**6**
		4	11=Brinton J V				9			7					10	3		6		5			8				1		2	**7**
		4					9		11	7						3		6		5	8			10			1		2	**8**
10		4	7	9					11		5=Low N H			6		3							8				1		2	**9**
		4	7				9		11					3	8			6		5			10				1		2	**10**
		4			9			5	11	7		3		6	10	2							8				1			**11**
		4	7		9	8		5				3	6			2							10				1	11		**12**
		4	7		9	8						3		6		2				5			10				1	11		**13**
		4	7			8		5				3		6			2=Forde S				10				9		1	11		**14**
		4	8					5		7		3	6								10				9		1	11	2	**15**
		5			8						7	3	4	6									10		9		1	11	2	**16**
		5			10	8					7	3	4	6											9		1	11	2	**17**
		5			10					7	8	3	4	6											9		1	11	2	**18**
		5			10					7	8	3	4	6											9		1	11	2	**19**
	1	5		9							7		4	6	8					2	10							11		**20**
1	4	19	8	2	7	5	6	4	5	11	5	9	7	10	7	11	5	6	2	8	6	1	9	1	6	2	16	12	15	Apps
2			1	1	4		3		1	2	3				2		3		1				4		3			4		Goals

Barlow R J	Burton S	Cousins H	Denyer A F T	Derrick A E	Emery D K J	Francis C T	Godwin R G	Hall F W	Holland E D	Jackman H J W	Jones E M	Kelso J	Lloyd W L	Lovesey W S	Lucas W H	McDonald P	McGibbon D	Mather J	Morgan A S	Onslow L G	Painter E G	Parkhouse R McD	Rosenthal A W	Skinner G E H	Thomas D S L	Tovey S G	Wildman F R	Williams G G	Woodman D W M	
	1	5	7		9	8						3	4	6							10							11	2	**1/1**
		5	7		9	8						3	4	6	10												1	11	2	**1/2**
	1	2	2		2	2						2	2	2	1						1						1	2	2	Apps
					1	1																								Goals

Bicknell R	Bingham W P	Blanchflower R D	Burton S	Cousins H	Denyer A F T	Derrick A E	Francis C T	Hinton E G A	Jones E M	Kelso J	Lloyd W L	Lovesey W S	Lucas W H	McDonald P	Manning G	Painter E G	Preece J C	Pritchard R T	Rosenthal A W	Saunders R A	Sturgess M D	Tudor W	Wildman F R	Williams G G	Woodman D W M	Young A E	
				5			9		7	3	4	6				8			10				1	11	2		**1**
				4		9			7	3	6		8						10			5	1	11	2		**2**
				4		9			7	3	6		8						10			5	1	11	2		**3**
		8		4		9		1	7	3	6		10									5		11	2		**4**
			1	4		9			7		10	6	8	3								5		11	2		**5**
5					8	9			7		4	6	10	3				2					1	11			**6**
				4		9	8		7		6		10	3								5	1	11	2		**7**
				2		8			7	3	4	6	10							9	1	5		11			**8**
			1	5		9			7		4	6	8	3		10						2		11			**9**
			1	5		9			7		4	6	8	3		10								11		2	**10**
			1	5		9			7		4	6	8	3		10	2							11			**11**
			1	5		9			7		4	6	8	10	3		2							11			**12**
			1	5		9			7		4	6	8	3		10	2							11			**13**
			1	5		9			7	3	4	6	8	2		10								11			**14**
			1	5		9			7	3	4	6	8	2		10								11			**15**
	5		1	4		9			7	3	6		8	2		10								11			**16**
1	1	1	9	15	1	15	2	1	16	8	16	11	15	11	1	8	3	1	3	1	1	7	5	16	6	1	Apps
						5			3				2			3			1					7			Goals

For Final League Tables - see overleaf >>

SEASON 1945/46

Division Three South (Southern Section)

		P	W	D	L	F	A	W	D	L	F	A	Pts
1	Crystal Palace	20	7	2	1	32	7	6	1	3	23	24	29
2	Cardiff City	20	8	1	1	40	12	5	1	4	29	19	28
3	Bristol City	20	7	2	1	32	13	4	0	6	19	27	24
4	Brighton & Hove Albion	20	8	0	2	35	22	2	1	7	14	28	21
5	Bristol Rovers	20	3	4	3	21	21	4	2	4	23	23	20
6	SWINDON TOWN	20	5	1	4	20	19	3	2	5	15	28	19
7	Bournemouth & Boscombe Athletic	20	6	0	4	33	20	1	3	6	19	30	17
8	Aldershot	20	3	3	4	20	27	3	2	5	18	29	17
9	Exeter City	20	4	2	4	16	18	2	2	6	17	23	16
10	Reading	20	4	2	4	26	21	1	3	6	17	28	15
11	Torquay United	20	3	2	5	13	23	2	2	6	9	29	14

Division Three South Cup (Southern Section Qualifying Competition)

		P	W	D	L	F	A	W	D	L	F	A	Pts
1	Bournemouth & Boscombe Athletic	16	6	2	0	27	9	2	2	4	10	11	20
2	Bristol Rovers	16	5	2	1	17	7	3	1	4	10	12	19
3	Reading	16	6	1	1	26	7	2	1	5	20	22	18
4	Crystal Palace	16	4	2	2	24	11	3	2	3	13	19	18
5	Cardiff City	16	7	0	1	24	7	1	1	6	15	15	17
6	Bristol City	16	6	1	1	19	8	1	2	5	11	19	17
7	Torquay United	16	6	1	1	15	7	0	3	5	4	23	16
8	Exeter City	16	4	2	2	12	7	1	2	5	10	21	14
9	SWINDON TOWN	16	4	3	1	14	10	1	1	6	7	25	14
10	Aldershot	16	2	3	3	14	21	1	1	6	9	27	10
11	Brighton & Hove Albion	16	1	3	4	17	21	0	3	5	6	24	8

This competition was a complex affair, as indicated by the table above showing that not all clubs played each other twice. Town in fact did not play three of the clubs - Crystal Palace, Exeter City or Brighton - either at home or away. But with those fixtures excluded, this would leave a total of 14 games played. The remaining two, which included Town's only home defeat, were against Northampton Town - members of the Northern Section of the competition !

HARRY COUSINS
signed for Town in July 1932 and remained with the club for 43 years ! A tough tackling wing-half, Harry made nearly 300 appearances before 'War stopped play' and could possibly have doubled that total had the County Ground not been shut down for five years. When the peace-time Football League programme resumed in August 1946, Harry was not far short of his 39th birthday, but he was soon taken on as a member of the back-room staff and continued in active service until May 1975, by which time he was 67. He died in 1981.

in memoriam : ww2

In addition to the tragic loss of 1930's goalscoring hero ALAN FOWLER *(see page 90)*, three other players with Town connections were victims of the Second World War.

JIM OLNEY, a 6'2" half-back *(pictured page 106)* who arrived from Birmingham in December 1938 served with the Coldstream Guards in Belgium and lost his life near Antwerp. He was just 30.

Goalkeeper BILL BRYAN joined Town in July 1937 and played in the F.A.Cup victory over First Division Grimsby in the following January. He joined Wrexham in 1939 and married a Swindon girl - Gwen Walters - soon afterwards. Bill was killed in France, serving with the Dorsets, in August 1944. He was 31.

Welsh winger ALBERT POWELL, who was with Town for just five months during 1928/29, was a gunner with the 34th Signal Training Regiment stationed at Dover Castle. He died in the underground Military Hospital there in October 1940. He was 32.

BILL IMRIE has been cited as having been 'killed in action' during the conflict in Europe. The centre-half, capped twice for Scotland, was brought to Swindon by Neil Harris just two months before War was declared. Bill attained the rank of corporal in the RAF but was discharged when he was found to be suffering from stomach cancer, from which he died at his home in Fife on Boxing Day 1944.

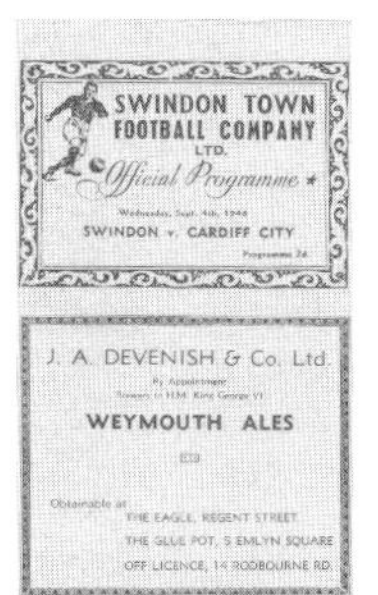

Left to right : Programme from 1946 : and from a Festival of Britain game in 1951 : the County Ground around 1952 : Programme from 1955

boom and gloom

THE POST-WAR YEARS

1946 - 1958

Starved of League football for seven long years, the crowds flocked back in considerable numbers in 1946/47. And from mid-way through that season, those at the County Ground found a new hero - a 22 year old former car works apprentice from Abingdon - Maurice Owen. Manager Louis Page soon found himself fighting off the 'big boys' who began tempting the centre-forward to move to more illustrious surroundings. But he chose to stay with Town, who sadly could not elevate themselves any higher than the Third Division South - and twice came close to losing that status with re-election pleas in successive years. Managerless for a period, Bert Head's appointment late in 1956 began to bear fruit when Town narrowly missed out on promotion in 1958.

Left to right : Action from the Public Practice match in 1951 : George Hudson : Keeper Sam Burton watches as Peter Hilton takes control

SEASON 1946/47

Football League Division Three South
Final League Position : 4th
Manager : Louis Page

				Opponents	Home	Away	H-T	Goalscorers	Gate
1	S	Aug	31	Northampton Town		L1-4	(0-1)	Williams	12,013
2	W	Sep	4	Cardiff City	W3-2		(1-1)	Stephens J W 2,Williams	14,354
3	S		7	Aldershot	W7-0		(2-0)	Williams 2,Stephens J W 4 (1 pen.),Lucas	16,622
4	Th		12	Norwich City		W5-1	(1-0)	Williams,Robinson o.g.,Stephens J W 2,Denyer	15,488
5	S		14	Brighton and Hove Albion		W4-1	(1-1)	Stephens J W,Edwards,Lucas,Stephens A	8,801
6	S		21	Exeter City	W2-0		(2-0)	Stephens J W,Stephens A	20,855
7	M		23	Cardiff City		L0-5	(0-1)		19,172
8	S		28	Port Vale		D1-1	(0-1)	Lloyd	12,900
9	S	Oct	5	Bristol City	D1-1		(0-1)	Williams	25,031
10	S		12	Southend United		L0-2	(0-2)		11,275
11	S		19	Bristol Rovers	W1-0		(1-0)	Stephens J W	16,019
12	S		26	Mansfield Town		D1-1	(1-1)	Williams	7,583
13	S	Nov	2	Torquay United	L2-4		(1-3)	Williams,Jones	16,151
14	S		9	Crystal Palace		L1-4	(0-3)	Lucas	15,741
15	S		16	Reading	D2-2		(1-2)	Paterson,Ithell	18,534
16	S		23	Walsall		W1-0	(1-0)	Lucas	14,291
17	S	Dec	7	Ipswich Town		L1-3	(0-1)	Stephens J W	9,941
18	S		21	Queens Park Rangers		L0-7	(0-2)		9,576
19	W		25	Notts County		D0-0			18,439
20	Th		26	Notts County	W4-2		(2-1)	Stephens J W 2,Williams,Jones	17,894
21	S		28	Northampton Town	W3-1		(0-0)	Lucas 2,Stephens J W	15,456
22	S	Jan	4	Aldershot		L0-2	(0-2)		4,796
23	S		11	Watford	W5-0		(2-0)	Williams 2,Owen 3	13,981
24	S		18	Brighton and Hove Albion	D2-2		(2-0)	Paterson,Lucas	17,638
25	S		25	Exeter City		D1-1	(0-0)	Paterson	8,697
26	S	Feb	1	Port Vale	W2-1		(1-1)	Stephens J W,Owen	9,935
27	S		8	Bristol City		L1-3	(0-0)	Owen	13,205
28	S		22	Bristol Rovers		L0-3	(0-2)		8,052
29	S	Mar	1	Mansfield Town	W6-1		(3-1)	Owen 4,Paterson,Lucas	12,257
30	S		8	Torquay United		W5-1	(3-0)	Lucas,Stephens J W 3,Owen	6,385
31	S		15	Crystal Palace	W1-0		(0-0)	Stephens J W pen.	13,711
32	S		22	Reading		D3-3	(2-0)	Lucas,Emery,Paterson	16,610
33	S		29	Walsall	W4-1		(1-0)	Stephens J W 2,Emery,Williams	14,544
34	F	Apr	4	Bournemouth & Boscombe Athletic		L2-5	(1-2)	Stephens J W,Lucas	14,056
35	S		5	Watford		D1-1	(0-1)	Lucas	9,992
36	M		7	Bournemouth & Boscombe Athletic	L1-3		(0-2)	Lloyd	20,051
37	S		12	Ipswich Town	W2-1		(1-0)	Lucas,Owen	13,209
38	S		19	Leyton Orient		D0-0			9,804
39	S		26	Queens Park Rangers	W3-2		(1-2)	Owen,Stephens J W,Lucas	20,884
40	S	May	3	Norwich City	D1-1		(1-0)	Owen	13,570
41	S		10	Southend United	W2-1		(2-1)	Stephens J W,Owen	13,498
42	S		17	Leyton Orient	W2-0		(0-0)	Owen 2	12,064

Average Home Attendance : **16,012**
Average Away Attendance : **11,753**

F A Cup

				Opponents	Home	Away	H-T	Goalscorers	Gate
1	S	Nov	30	Cambridge Town	W4-1		(3-0)	Lucas 2,Stephens J W 2 (1 pen.)	16,161
2	S	Dec	14	Notts County		L1-2	(0-1)	Paterson	18,522

BILL STEPHENS
and his brother Alf became the first twins to appear in the same Town side since Cliff and Sid Hamlin back in November 1894. But the Stephens' became the first pair to score in the same game - which they achieved twice in successive League fixtures in September 1946. They had both joined Leeds United in 1938 from East Cramlington Brick Works in their native Northumberland, before moving south to the County Ground. Bill soon hit the goal trail as Town scored 22 in their opening six games. In the New Year, he found a new partner in young Maurice Owen, the two collecting 26 goals in the remaining 20 games. Bill was snapped up by West Ham in December 1947, but he suffered a broken leg twice which effectively ended his career. Alf joined Southern League Dartford.

Bingham W P	Boulton F P	Burton S	Cousins H	Denyer A F T	Derrick A E	Edwards D S	Emery D K J	Ithell W J	Jones E M	Leslie M H	Lloyd W L	Lovesey W S	Lucas W H	Onslow L G	Owen M	Painter E G	Parkhouse R M	Paterson G L	Shanks R	Stephens A	Stephens J W	Trim R F	Williams G G	Young A E	
6	1							5	7		4		8							10	9	3	11	2	1
6	1							5	7		4		8							10	9	3	11	2	2
6	1			7				5			4		8							10	9	3	11	2	3
6	1			7				5			4		8							10	9	3	11	2	4
6	1			7		11		5			4		8							10	9	3		2	5
6	1			7		11		5			4		8							10	9	3		2	6
6	1			7		11		5			4		8							10	9	3		2	7
6	1		4					5	7		10		8								9	3	11	2	8
6	1		4					5	7		10		8								9	3	11	2	9
5	1		4						7		6		8			10					9	3	11	2	10
	1		4					5	7		10	6	8								9	3	11	2	11
6	1		5						7		4		8					10			9	3	11	2	12
6	1		5						7		4		8					10			9	3	11	2	13
6	1							5	7		4		8					10			9	3	11	2	14
6		1			7		2	5			4		8					10			9	3	11		15
6		1	4				3	5			2		8					10		7	9		11		16
6		1					3	5	7		4		8					10			9		11	2	17
		1					3	5	7		4		8					6		10	9		11	2	18
5		1	4				3	6	7		2		8					10			9		11		19
5		1					3	6	7		2		8	4				10			9		11		20
5		1					3	6	7		2		8	4				10			9		11		21
	1		4				3	5	7		2		8			6		10			9		11		22
	1							5	7		4		8		9	6	2	10					11	3	23
	1						3	5	7		4		8		9	6		10					11	2	24
	1							5			2	4	8		9	6		10			7		11	3	25
	1							5			2	4	8		9	6		10			7		11	3	26
	1						11	5			2	4	8		9	6		10			7			3	27
	1							5			2		8		9	6		10	4		7		11	3	28
	1						3	5			4		8		9	6		10			7		11	2	29
	1						3	5			4		8		9	6		10			7		11	2	30
	1						3	5			4		8		9	6		10			7		11	2	31
	1						3	5			4		8		9	6		10			7		11	2	32
	1			7			3	5			4		8			6		10			9		11	2	33
	1			7			3	5			4		8			6		10			9		11	2	34
	1						3	5	7		4		8			6		10			9		11	2	35
	1						3	5	11		4		8		9	6		10			7			2	36
		1					3	5			4		8		9	6				10	7		11	2	37
		1					3	5			4		8		9	6				10	7		11	2	38
		1					3	5			4		8		9	6				10	7		11	2	39
		1					3	5			4		8		9	6				10	7		11	2	40
		1					3	5	7		4		8		9	6					10		11	2	41
	1							5	7	3	4		8		9	6					10		11	2	42
19	30	12	9	7	1	3	23	39	21	1	42	4	42	2	17	22	1	25	1	13	40	15	37	36	Apps
				1		1	2	1	2		2		14		16			5		2	26		12		Goals

Opponents 1 goal

Bingham W P	Boulton F P	Burton S	Cousins H	Denyer A F T	Derrick A E	Edwards D S	Emery D K J	Ithell W J	Jones E M	Leslie M H	Lloyd W L	Lovesey W S	Lucas W H	Onslow L G	Owen M	Painter E G	Parkhouse R M	Paterson G L	Shanks R	Stephens A	Stephens J W	Trim R F	Williams G G	Young A E	
6		1	4				3	5			2		8					10		7	9		11		1
		1	4				3	5	7		6		8					10			9		11	2	2
1		2	2				2	2	1		2		2					2		1	2		2	1	Apps
													2					1			2				Goals

For Final League Table - see page 138

OFF THEIR TROLLEY !

The team had an eventful trip to the away fixture at Queens Park Rangers four days before Christmas 1946. After their train had become fogbound at Hanwell, they had to complete the journey by trolleybus. But the day did not get any better for Town at Loftus Road, where they conceded five second-half goals to end up 0-7 losers.

SEASON 1947/48

Football League Division Three South
Final League Position : 16th
Manager : Louis Page

				Opponents	Home	Away	H-T	Goalscorers	Gate
1	S	Aug	23	Northampton Town	D0-0				18,138
2	M		25	Bristol Rovers		L1-3	(1-2)	Owen	19,304
3	S		30	Aldershot		D2-2	(2-1)	Maguire,Bain	7,033
4	W	Sep	3	Bristol Rovers	D1-1		(1-1)	Williams	17,674
5	S		6	Crystal Palace	D0-0				17,619
6	W		10	Brighton and Hove Albion	D1-1		(1-1)	Maguire	15,216
7	S		13	Torquay United		D1-1	(0-1)	Owen	7,174
8	W		17	Brighton and Hove Albion		L0-1	(0-0)		5,741
9	S		20	Newport County	L1-2		(0-2)	Lucas	18,642
10	S		27	Port Vale	W1-0		(0-0)	Lucas	16,828
11	S	Oct	4	Queens Park Rangers		W2-0	(1-0)	Owen 2	25,092
12	S		11	Southend United		L0-1	(0-0)		11,605
13	S		18	Notts County	D1-1		(1-0)	Maguire	18,198
14	S		25	Swansea Town		L0-1	(0-0)		20,948
15	S	Nov	1	Bournemouth & Boscombe Athletic	L0-1		(0-0)		17,386
16	S		8	Ipswich Town		W1-0	(0-0)	Dryden	14,787
17	S		15	Bristol City	D2-2		(1-1)	Dryden,Owen	26,401
18	S		22	Reading		W3-2	(1-1)	Owen 2,Jones	20,838
19	S	Dec	6	Leyton Orient		W3-0	(2-0)	Jones 2,Dryden	6,298
20	F		26	Norwich City	W3-2		(1-1)	Lucas,Owen,Jones	19,021
21	S		27	Norwich City		D2-2	(1-0)	Owen 2	19,855
22	S	Jan	3	Aldershot	W1-0		(0-0)	Paterson	13,893
23	S		17	Crystal Palace		D1-1	(0-0)	Kaye	11,881
24	S		31	Torquay United	D2-2		(1-1)	Jones,Owen	15,392
25	S	Feb	14	Port Vale		L0-1	(0-0)		14,263
26	S		21	Queens Park Rangers	D0-0				14,683
27	S		28	Southend United	D0-0				14,858
28	S	Mar	6	Notts County		L1-2	(0-2)	Jones	27,767
29	S		13	Swansea Town	W1-0		(0-0)	Jones	14,557
30	Th		18	Northampton Town		D0-0			6,241
31	S		20	Bournemouth & Boscombe Athletic		L0-1	(0-1)		17,267
32	F		26	Watford	W3-0		(2-0)	Jones,Bain,Owen	15,000
33	S		27	Ipswich Town	L0-1		(0-1)		14,440
34	M		29	Watford		L0-1	(0-1)		13,825
35	S	Apr	3	Bristol City		D2-2	(1-1)	Owen 2	16,859
36	Th		8	Newport County		L0-2	(0-0)		7,421
37	S		10	Reading	D1-1		(0-0)	Owen	15,876
38	W		14	Exeter City	W3-2		(3-1)	Jones 2,Maguire	10,154
39	S		17	Walsall		L0-1	(0-0)		10,094
40	S		24	Leyton Orient	L0-1		(0-1)		10,075
41	W		28	Walsall	L0-3		(0-2)		8,362
42	S	May	1	Exeter City		L1-2	(1-2)	Owen	6,934

Average Home Attendance : **15,829**
Average Away Attendance : **13,868**

F A Cup

				Opponents	Home	Away	H-T	Goalscorers	Gate
1	S	Nov	29	Ipswich Town	W4-2		(3-1)	Jones 2,Bell o.g.,Lucas	20,382
2	S	Dec	13	Aldershot	+	D0-0			12,108
2R	S		20	Aldershot	W2-0		(1-0)	Jones 2	19,700
3	S	Jan	10	Burnley		W2-0	(2-0)	Dryden,Owen	34,229
4	S		24	Notts County	W1-0		(0-0)	Lucas	27,130
5	S	Feb	7	Southampton		L0-3	(0-1)		29,134

+ After Extra Time

MAURICE OWEN

signed on as a part-time professional for Town in December 1946. Eight goals in three Combination games quickly earned Maurice a place in the first team and he wasted little time, hitting a hat-trick on his League debut in a 5-0 win over Watford. He finished his first term with 16 goals from just 17 games. Maurice turned down several offers to sign for a higher division club, instead continuing to fire in the goals for Town. He was top scorer in five of the six seasons between 1950 and 1956, after which he began to play a deeper role, eventually finishing up at centre-half. His last League appearance came in May 1963, just ten days before Town clinched a promotion place for the first time in the club's hstory. Maurice continued as trainer, reserve team manager, scout and groundsman before finally retiring in 1984. He died in 2000, four days after his 76th birthday.

Bain J A	Bingham W P	Boulton F P	Burton S	Dryden J G	Emery D K J	Ferguson A S B	Ithell W J	Jones W M	Kaye G H	Lloyd W L	Lucas W H	Maguire J E	Nunn W	Onslow L G	Onslow R E	Owen M	Painter E G	Paterson G L	Preece J C	Saunders R A	Stephens A	Stephens J W	Williams G G	Young A E	
11		1		8			5		4	3	10	7	6			9								2	**1**
11		1					5		4	3	8	7	6			9						10		2	**2**
11			1		3		5		4		8	7				9	6	10						2	**3**
11			1		3		5		4		8	7				9	6						10	2	**4**
11			1		3		5		4		8	7				9	6						10	2	**5**
11			1		3		5		4	2	8	7				9	6				10				**6**
					3	1	5		4	2	8	7				9	6				10		11		**7**
					3	1	5		4	2	8	7				9	6				10		11		**8**
11				10	3	1	5		4	2	8	7				9	6								**9**
11					10	1	5		4	3	8					9	6					7		2	**10**
11					10	1	5		4	3	8					9	6					7		2	**11**
11					10	1	5		4	3	8					9	6					7		2	**12**
11		1			10		5		4	3	8	7					6					9		2	**13**
11		1		7	10		5		4	3	8						6					9		2	**14**
11		1		7			5		4	3	8						6	10				9		2	**15**
11		1		7	3		5		4		8				9		6	10	2						**16**
11				7	3	1			4		8		5			9	6	10	2						**17**
11		1		7	3			10	4		8		5			9	6							2	**18**
11		1		7	3		5	10	4		8					9	6							2	**19**
11		1		7	3		5	10	4		8					9	6							2	**20**
		1		7	3		5	10	4		8	11				9	6							2	**21**
		1		7	3		5	9	4		8	11					6	10						2	**22**
		1		7	3		5	10	4		8	11				9	6		2						**23**
		1		7	3		5	10	4			11				9	6	8						2	**24**
		1		7	3		5	10		4	8	11				9	6							2	**25**
11		1		7	3		5	10		4	8					9							6	2	**26**
11		1			3		5	10			8	7				9	4						6	2	**27**
11		1			3		5	9			8	7					4	10					6	2	**28**
11		1			3		5	9			8	7					4	10					6	2	**29**
11		1			3		5	10				7				9	4	8					6	2	**30**
11		1			3		5	10				7				9	4	8					6	2	**31**
11		1		7	3		5	10		4						9	6	8						2	**32**
11		1		7	3		5	10		4						9	6	8						2	**33**
11		1			3			10		4		7				9	6	8		5				2	**34**
11		1			3		5	10		4		7				9	6	8						2	**35**
11		1			3		5	10				7				9	4	8					6	2	**36**
11		1			3		5	10				7				9	4	8					6	2	**37**
11		1			3		5	10		2		7				9	4	8					6		**38**
11		1		8			5	10		3		7				9	4		2				6		**39**
11			1	8			5	10		3		7		4		9	6		2						**40**
	5	1		8	3		6	10	4			7				9			2				11		**41**
		1		7	3		5	10		4						9	6	8	2				11		**42**
33	1	30	5	21	37	7	39	25	25	22	28	28	4	1	1	35	38	18	7	1	3	7	16	30	Apps
2				3				10	1		3	4				16		1					1		Goals

Bain J A	Bingham W P	Boulton F P	Burton S	Dryden J G	Emery D K J	Ferguson A S B	Ithell W J	Jones W M	Kaye G H	Lloyd W L	Lucas W H	Maguire J E	Nunn W	Onslow L G	Onslow R E	Owen M	Painter E G	Paterson G L	Preece J C	Saunders R A	Stephens A	Stephens J W	Williams G G	Young A E	
11		1		7	3		5	10	4		8					9	6							2	**1**
11		1		7	3		5	10	4		8					9	6							2	**2**
11		1		7	3		5	10	4		8					9	6							2	**2R**
		1		7	3		5	10	4		8	11				9	6							2	**3**
		1		7	3		5	10	4		8	11				9	6							2	**4**
		1		7	3		5	10	4		8	11				9	6							2	**5**
3		6		6	6		6	6	6		6	3				6	6							6	Apps
				1				4			2					1									Goals

Opponents 1 goal

For Final League Table - see page 138

KEEPER OF THE RECORD

When keeper ALEX FERGUSON turned out for Town against his old club Bristol City for his last League appearance, he was 44 years and 102 days, five years and a day older than the previous record holder Harry Cousins. Alex's League debut was in 1924 - two years before colleague Sam Burton was born !

SEASON 1948/49

Football League Division Three South
Final League Position : 4th
Manager : Louis Page

No.	Day	Month	Date	Opponents	Home	Away	H-T	Goalscorers	Gate
1	S	Aug	21	Brighton and Hove Albion		D1-1	(0-1)	Owen	21,593
2	W		25	Aldershot	W3-1		(1-0)	Dawson,Jones,Williams	18,365
3	S		28	Southend United	W2-1		(1-1)	Dawson,Jones	19,863
4	W	Sep	1	Aldershot		W2-1	(1-1)	Jones 2	5,995
5	S		4	Northampton Town		W1-0	(0-0)	Owen	9,410
6	M		6	Port Vale		L0-2	(0-1)		17,581
7	S		11	Norwich City	D3-3		(1-1)	Jones 2,Owen	18,222
8	W		15	Port Vale	L0-2		(0-2)		16,894
9	S		18	Exeter City		L1-3	(0-1)	Owen	11,596
10	Th		23	Notts County		W2-1	(1-1)	Jones pen.,Baynham	19,527
11	S		25	Bristol City	W2-1		(2-1)	Jones 2	22,932
12	Th		30	Swansea Town		L0-4	(0-3)		25,107
13	S	Oct	2	Newport County		L1-4	(0-3)	Lunn	11,657
14	S		9	Bristol Rovers	D1-1		(0-0)	Bain	20,720
15	S		16	Torquay United		L1-3	(1-1)	Owen	7,727
16	S		23	Watford	W1-0		(1-0)	Harris o.g.	14,663
17	S		30	Crystal Palace		D1-1	(1-1)	Jones	12,290
18	S	Nov	6	Ipswich Town	W4-0		(0-0)	Owen,Jones pen.,Dawson 2	15,916
19	S		13	Bournemouth & Boscombe Athletic		L0-3	(0-1)		19,495
20	S		20	Walsall	W2-1		(1-0)	Cowie,Bain	15,034
21	S	Dec	4	Newport County	W5-2		(2-0)	Jones 2,Dawson,Owen,Bain	14,893
22	S		18	Brighton and Hove Albion	D0-0				15,825
23	S		25	Millwall		L1-3	(0-1)	Owen	20,546
24	M		27	Millwall	W2-0		(1-0)	Jones 2	20,008
25	S	Jan	1	Southend United		W4-3	(3-3)	Owen 2,Jones,Bain	6,763
26	S		15	Northampton Town	D2-2		(1-0)	Owen,Dawson	14,306
27	S		22	Norwich City		D0-0			28,154
28	S	Feb	5	Exeter City	D1-1		(0-0)	Jones	13,444
29	S		19	Bristol City		W3-1	(0-0)	Owen 2,Bain	15,728
30	S	Mar	5	Bristol Rovers		D1-1	(1-1)	Owen	13,366
31	S		12	Torquay United	D1-1		(1-0)	Jones	11,673
32	S		19	Watford		W3-0	(1-0)	Jones 2 (1 pen.),Young	8,830
33	S		26	Crystal Palace	W1-0		(0-0)	Jones	11,678
34	S	Apr	2	Ipswich Town		L2-4	(0-2)	Dawson,Jones	12,908
35	W		6	Reading	D1-1		(1-0)	Jones	16,590
36	S		9	Bournemouth & Boscombe Athletic	D2-2		(0-2)	Bain,Jones	14,154
37	F		15	Leyton Orient		D1-1	(0-0)	Cowie	12,304
38	S		16	Walsall		W1-0	(1-0)	Dawson	9,831
39	M		18	Leyton Orient	D1-1		(1-0)	Owen	14,969
40	S		23	Notts County	W3-0		(1-0)	Owen,Jones,Hudson	17,761
41	S		30	Reading		D0-0			18,936
42	S	May	7	Swansea Town	W1-0		(0-0)	Owen	21,390

Average Home Attendance : **16,633**
Average Away Attendance : **14,731**

F A Cup

Rd	Day	Month	Date	Opponents	Home	Away	H-T	Goalscorers	Gate
3	S	Jan	8	Stoke City	L1-3		(0-2)	Owen	26,335

MORRIS JONES
was signed in November 1947 for a sizeable £2,500 fee from Port Vale, but Town still made a profit on him when he moved to Crystal Palace two-and-a-half years later - despite Morris having then passed his 30th birthday. Like many of his age, he lost valuable years of his career to the War, although Morris did manage to get some games under his belt while spending from 1940 until 1943 with Glasgow Celtic. A rampaging forward - in the mould of Harry Morris 20 years earlier - Morris top scored for Town in both his full seasons with the club, his partnership with Maurice Owen during his stay producing no less than 98 goals.

Bain J A	Baynham J	Boulton F P	Burton S	Cowie A D	Dawson T	Foxton J D	Hudson G W	Hunt R G A	Ithell W J	Jackson W P	Jones W M	Kaye G H	Lloyd W L	Lunn H	Onslow L G	Onslow R E	Owen M	Painter E G	Paterson G L	White A	Williams G G	Young A E	
		1		4	8				5		10	6		7			9			2	11	3	1
		1		4	8				5		10	6		7			9			2	11	3	2
		1		4	8				5		10	6		7			9			2	11	3	3
		1		4	8				5		10	6		7			9			2	11	3	4
		1		4	8				5		10	6		7			9			2	11	3	5
		1		4							10	6		7	5		9		8	2	11	3	6
11		1		4					5		10			7			9	6	8	2		3	7
11		1		4					5		10	6		7		8	9			2		3	8
11		1		4				2	5		10	6		7			9		8			3	9
11	8	1		4					5		10	6		7			9			2		3	10
11	8	1		4				2	5		10	6		7			9					3	11
11		1		4	8	6		2	5		10			7			9					3	12
11		1		4	8	6		2	5		10			7			9					3	13
11	8	1		4	6		5	2			10			7			9					3	14
11		1		4	8		5	2			10			7			9	6				3	15
11			1	4	8				5		10		3	7			9	6		2			16
11			1	4	8				5		10		3	7			9	6		2			17
11			1	4	8	6			5		10		3	7			9			2			18
11			1	4	8	6			5		10		3	7			9			2			19
11			1	4	8	6			5		10		3	7			9			2			20
11			1	4	8	6			5		10		3	7			9			2			21
11			1	4	8	6			5		10		3	7			9			2			22
11			1	4	8	6			5		10			7			9			2		3	23
11	8		1		4	6			5		10			7			9			2		3	24
11			1	4	8	6			5		10			7			9			2		3	25
11			1	4	8	6			5		10			7			9			2		3	26
11			1	4	8	6	5				10			7			9			2		3	27
11			1	4	8	6	5				10			7			9			2		3	28
11			1		8	6	5				10	4		7			9			2		3	29
11			1		8	6	5				10	4		7			9			2		3	30
11			1		8		5			6	10	4		7			9			2		3	31
11			1		8	6	5				10	4		7			9			2		3	32
11			1		8	6	5				10	4		7			9			2		3	33
11			1		8	6	5				10	4		7			9			2		3	34
11			1	4	8	6	5				10			7			9			2		3	35
11			1	4	8	6	5				10		2	7			9					3	36
11		1		4	8		5				10	6	2	7			9					3	37
11		1		4	8		5				10	6	2	7			9					3	38
11		1		4	8		5				10	6	2	7			9					3	39
11		1		2	8	6	5				10	4		7			9					3	40
11		1		2	8	6	5				10	4		7			9					3	41
11		1		2	8	6	5				10	4	3	7			9						42
36	4	21	21	35	36	23	18	6	23	1	42	22	12	42	1	1	42	4	3	29	6	34	Apps
6	1			2	8		1				25			1			17				1	1	Goals

Opponents 1 goal

Bain J A	Baynham J	Boulton F P	Burton S	Cowie A D	Dawson T	Foxton J D	Hudson G W	Hunt R G A	Ithell W J	Jackson W P	Jones W M	Kaye G H	Lloyd W L	Lunn H	Onslow L G	Onslow R E	Owen M	Painter E G	Paterson G L	White A	Williams G G	Young A E	
11			1	4	8	6			5		10			7			9			2		3	3

TOMMY DAWSON

For Final League Table - see page 138

TOWN AGAIN DEFEATED BY FOG

Some 13,300 turned up at the County Ground for a friendly with Charlton Athletic on January 29 1949. Maurice Owen is said to have scored almost directly from the kick-off, although few saw it in the dense fog ! The match was eventually abandoned on the hour with Swindon leading 3-2.

SEASON 1949/50

Football League Division Three South
Final League Position : 14th
Manager : Louis Page

No.	Day	Month	Date	Opponents	Home	Away	H-T	Goalscorers	Gate
1	S	Aug	20	Reading	W2-0		(1-0)	Dawson,Owen	25,038
2	W		24	Millwall	D1-1		(0-0)	Jones	18,080
3	S		27	Torquay United		L0-1	(0-1)		10,863
4	M		29	Millwall		L0-1	(0-0)		23,390
5	S	Sep	3	Aldershot	W2-1		(1-0)	Jones 2	15,599
6	S		10	Nottingham Forest		L1-2	(0-0)	Jones pen.	24,709
7	Tu		13	Bristol City		L0-1	(0-1)		27,255
8	S		17	Northampton Town	W6-1		(2-0)	Lunn,Jones 2,Bain,Owen,Dawson	15,219
9	S		24	Norwich City		L0-4	(0-1)		27,448
10	S	Oct	1	Newport County	D1-1		(1-0)	Lunn	15,284
11	S		8	Watford	L0-1		(0-1)		14,298
12	S		15	Crystal Palace		D2-2	(2-1)	Simner,Jones pen.	15,954
13	S		22	Bournemouth & Boscombe Athletic	W3-1		(2-0)	Simner 2,Owen	15,084
14	S		29	Bristol Rovers		L0-2	(0-1)		17,523
15	S	Nov	5	Southend United	D2-2		(1-1)	Bain,Owen	11,992
16	S		12	Notts County		L0-3	(0-1)		37,220
17	S		19	Port Vale	D0-0				9,039
18	S	Dec	3	Exeter City	W7-1		(4-0)	Simner,Owen 2,Bain 2,Lunn 2	10,885
19	S		17	Reading		L3-4	(2-0)	Simner 2,Jones	16,078
20	S		24	Torquay United	L1-2		(0-1)	Jones pen.	13,751
21	M		26	Brighton and Hove Albion		W1-0	(1-0)	Dawson	14,306
22	Tu		27	Brighton and Hove Albion	W4-2		(2-2)	Simner 2,Dawson,Lunn	18,872
23	S		31	Aldershot		D0-0			6,506
24	S	Jan	14	Nottingham Forest	L0-5		(0-4)		15,604
25	S		21	Northampton Town		W1-0	(1-0)	Owen	14,633
26	S		28	Ipswich Town		L1-3	(0-1)	Owen	9,160
27	S	Feb	4	Norwich City	D1-1		(0-1)	Bain	13,238
28	S		11	Leyton Orient		W3-1	(1-0)	Jones 2,Owen	9,955
29	S		18	Newport County		W2-1	(0-0)	Onslow,Bain	10,622
30	S		25	Watford		W2-1	(1-1)	Owen,Dawson	11,214
31	S	Mar	4	Crystal Palace	W4-2		(3-1)	Onslow,Dawson,Jones 2	15,067
32	S		11	Bournemouth & Boscombe Athletic		D1-1	(1-0)	Dawson	11,216
33	S		18	Bristol Rovers	W1-0		(0-0)	Kaye	11,955
34	S		25	Southend United		L0-2	(0-1)		9,276
35	S	Apr	1	Notts County	D1-1		(1-1)	Peart	19,876
36	F		7	Walsall		D0-0			8,305
37	S		8	Port Vale		W1-0	(0-0)	Peart	9,607
38	M		10	Walsall	W4-3		(3-1)	Wheeler,Cowie 2,Jackson	10,218
39	S		15	Ipswich Town	L0-3		(0-2)		10,438
40	S		22	Exeter City		L0-3	(0-2)		8,744
41	S		29	Leyton Orient	L0-1		(0-1)		5,617
42	S	May	6	Bristol City	D1-1		(1-0)	Simner	10,401

Average Home Attendance : **14,074**
Average Away Attendance : **15,428**

F A Cup

No.	Day	Month	Date	Opponents	Home	Away	H-T	Goalscorers	Gate
1	S	Nov	26	Bristol Rovers	W1-0		(1-0)	Owen	19,640
2	S	Dec	10	Carlisle United		L0-2	(0-2)		18,604

HARRY KAYE
was born and bred in Liverpool and had been at Anfield six years prior to signing for Town in May 1947. The popular wing-half also spent six seasons at the County Ground - and that might have been more had it not been for injury. Harry had played in every game in 1947/48, helping Town to an F.A.Cup Fifth Round encounter with Southampton. But he broke his left ankle just eight minutes into the tie at The Dell and - with no substitutes then - Town's interest in the competition was soon on the wane. Harry made a full recovery and was still urging them on as they made it to the same stage in 1951/52. An unfortunate second break to the same ankle in a reserve game ended Harry's career.

Bain J A	Boulton F P	Burton S	Cowie A D	Dawson T	Foxton J D	Hudson G W	Hunt R G A	Ithell W J	Jackson W P	Jones W M	Kaye G H	Lloyd W L	Lunn H	Onslow R E	Owen M	Painter E G	Paterson G L	Peart R C	Simmer J	Uprichard W N McC	Wheeler A J	White A	Whiteside C W	Williams G G	Young A E	
11	1		2	8	6	5				10	4		7		9										3	**1**
11	1		2	8	6	5				10	4		7		9										3	**2**
11	1		2		6	5				10	4		7		9						8				3	**3**
11	1		2	8	6	5				10	4		7		9										3	**4**
11	1		2		6	5				8	4		7		9				10						3	**5**
11	1		2		6	5				8	4		7		9				10						3	**6**
11	1		2	8	6	5				10	4		7		9										3	**7**
11	1		2	8	6	5				10	4		7		9										3	**8**
11	1		2	8	6	5				10	4		7		9										3	**9**
11	1		2	8	6	5				10	4		7		9										3	**10**
11	1		2			5				10	4		7		9	6							8		3	**11**
	1		2			5				10	4		8		9	6			11		7				3	**12**
	1		2			5				10	4		8		9	6			11		7				3	**13**
	1		2			5				10	4		8		9	6			11		7				3	**14**
11	1		4	8	6			5					7		9				10			2			3	**15**
11	1		4	8	6			5					7		9				10			2			3	**16**
11		1	4	8	6			5					7		9				10			2			3	**17**
11		1	4	8				5			6		7		9				10			2			3	**18**
		1		8				5		10	6		7		9	4			11			2			3	**19**
				8		5				10	6		7	9		4			11	1		2			3	**20**
11				8		5	2				4					6	10		9	1	7				3	**21**
				8		5	2				6		7			4	10		9	1	11				3	**22**
11				8		5	2				4					6	10		9	1	7				3	**23**
				8		5	2	3			4		7		9	6	10		11	1						**24**
		1	4	8		5	2				6	3			9		10				7			11		**25**
11		1		8	6	5	2				4	3		7	9		10									**26**
11		1	4	8		5	2				6	3		7	9		10									**27**
11		1	4	8		5	2			10	6	3		7	9											**28**
11		1	4	8		5	2			10	6	3		7	9											**29**
11		1	4	8		5	2			10	6	3		7	9											**30**
11		1	4	8		5	2			10	6	3		7	9											**31**
11		1	4	8		5	2			10	6	3		7	9											**32**
11		1	4	8	2	5				10	6	3		7				9								**33**
11		1	4	8	2	5				10	6	3		7	9											**34**
11		1	4	8	2	5					6	3		7				9	10							**35**
11		1	4	8	2	5					6	3		7				9	10							**36**
11		1	8		2	5			10		6	3		7				9			4					**37**
11		1	8		2	5			10		6	3		7				9			4					**38**
11		1	8		2	5				10	6	3		7				9			4					**39**
11		1	8		2	5				10	6	3		7					9		4					**40**
11		1	4		2	5			10	8	6	3							9		7					**41**
11		1	4		2	5				10	6	3		9					8		7					**42**
34	16	21	35	29	24	37	12	6	3	27	39	18	22	17	29	10	7	6	20	5	14	6	1	1	23	Apps
6			2	7					1	13	1		5	2	10			2	9		1					Goals

Bain J A	Boulton F P	Burton S	Cowie A D	Dawson T	Foxton J D	Hudson G W	Hunt R G A	Ithell W J	Jackson W P	Jones W M	Kaye G H	Lloyd W L	Lunn H	Onslow R E	Owen M	Painter E G	Paterson G L	Peart R C	Simmer J	Uprichard W N McC	Wheeler A J	White A	Whiteside C W	Williams G G	Young A E	
11		1	4	8				5			6		7		9				10			2			3	**1**
11		1	4	8				5			6		7		9				10			2			3	**2**
2		2	2	2				2			2		2		2				2			2			2	Apps
															1											Goals

For Final League Table - see page 139

SEASON 1950/51

Football League Division Three South
Final League Position : 17th
Manager : Louis Page

					Home	Away	H-T	Goalscorers	Gate
1	S	Aug	19	Bristol Rovers		L0-1	(0-0)		18,795
2	W		23	Colchester United	D1-1		(1-1)	Millar	15,717
3	S		26	Crystal Palace	W2-0		(1-0)	Peebles,Hudson	13,699
4	Th		31	Colchester United		L1-4	(0-4)	Hudson	12,579
5	S	Sep	2	Brighton and Hove Albion		L0-1	(0-0)		14,204
6	W		6	Exeter City	W1-0		(0-0)	Court	9,467
7	S		9	Newport County	W2-0		(1-0)	Bain,Simner	14,021
8	W		13	Exeter City		L0-1	(0-1)		9,866
9	S		16	Norwich City		L0-2	(0-1)		23,289
10	S		23	Northampton Town	W1-0		(1-0)	Owen	13,708
11	S		30	Port Vale		L1-2	(1-2)	Court	9,517
12	S	Oct	7	Southend United	W4-1		(1-0)	Williams,Bain,Simner,Owen	12,623
13	S		14	Reading		L1-3	(1-1)	Owen	24,256
14	S		21	Plymouth Argyle	L1-2		(1-0)	Owen	16,763
15	S		28	Ipswich Town		L1-4	(0-2)	Bain	12,945
16	S	Nov	4	Leyton Orient	W2-0		(1-0)	Thomas,Onslow	9,277
17	S		11	Walsall		L0-1	(0-1)		7,795
18	S		18	Watford	W3-2		(3-1)	Wheeler 2,Bain	8,177
19	S	Dec	2	Bristol City	W1-0		(1-0)	Simner	13,079
20	S		16	Bristol Rovers	L1-2		(1-1)	Onslow	7,033
21	S		23	Crystal Palace		L0-2	(0-1)		7,267
22	M		25	Torquay United	W2-1		(0-0)	Owen,Thomas	7,039
23	Tu		26	Torquay United		L0-1	(0-1)		9,459
24	S		30	Brighton and Hove Albion	D0-0				7,743
25	S	Jan	6	Bournemouth & Boscombe Athletic	W2-1		(0-1)	Millar,Bain	6,971
26	S		13	Newport County		L1-2	(1-1)	Lunn	12,485
27	S		20	Norwich City	W1-0		(1-0)	Bain	13,140
28	S		27	Bournemouth & Boscombe Athletic		L1-2	(0-1)	Lunn	10,034
29	S	Feb	3	Northampton Town		W2-1	(2-0)	Owen,Millar	7,195
30	S		10	Millwall		L0-1	(0-0)		20,988
31	S		17	Port Vale	W2-1		(1-1)	Peart,Millar	7,889
32	S		24	Southend United		L2-8	(2-5)	Onslow,Owen	8,037
33	S	Mar	3	Reading	D1-1		(1-1)	Lunn	21,485
34	S		10	Plymouth Argyle		L1-5	(1-1)	Hudson pen.	12,019
35	S		17	Ipswich Town	W2-0		(0-0)	Bain,Hudson	7,442
36	F		23	Aldershot		W1-0	(0-0)	Hudson	8,951
37	S		24	Leyton Orient		L1-2	(0-1)	Onslow	10,029
38	M		26	Aldershot	W4-0		(0-0)	Bain,Owen,Hudson pen.,Millar	10,249
39	S		31	Walsall	D1-1		(1-1)	Lunn	7,413
40	S	Apr	7	Watford		W2-1	(0-1)	Owen,Onslow	3,658
41	S		14	Millwall	L0-1		(0-0)		8,819
42	W		18	Nottingham Forest		L1-2	(1-1)	Onslow	27,644
43	S		21	Bristol City		L0-2	(0-2)		16,129
44	S		28	Gillingham	W2-0		(1-0)	Peart 2	3,915
45	W	May	2	Gillingham		L1-2	(1-0)	Thomas	8,295
46	S		5	Nottingham Forest	L2-3		(1-1)	Wheeler,Kaye	10,707

Average Home Attendance : **10,712**
Average Away Attendance : **12,845**

F A Cup

					Away	H-T	Goalscorers	Gate
1	W	Nov	29	Southend United	W3-0	(0-0)	Bain,Simner,Onslow	9,000
2	S	Dec	9	Exeter City	L0-3	(0-1)		14,764

JIMMY BAIN

supplied countless crosses for the likes of Maurice Owen and Morris Jones between 1947 and 1953. And he chipped in with a fair number of goals himself, finishing the 1950/51 season as joint leading scorer. The Scottish left-winger arrived at the County Ground from Stamford Bridge - where he had played in the 3-3 draw with Moscow Dynamo in 1945 - and he hit more than forty goals for Town before moving to Southern League Headington in July 1954. Jimmy emigrated to Canada, where he worked for the same manufacturing company for thirty years and died there in December 2002.

Bain J A	Batchelor E	Burton S	Court H J	Cowie A D	Farr B S	Foxton J D	Hill C J	Hudson G W	Hunt R G A	Kaye G H	Lloyd W L	Lunn H	May H	Millar W	Onslow R E	Owen M	Page R M	Painter E G	Peart R C	Peebles R W	Simner J	Thomas J W	Uprichard W N McC	Wheeler A J	Williams G G	
11		1	8	4				5	2	6			3	7		9				10						**1**
11	5	1	8	4				9	2	6			3	7						10						**2**
11	5	1	8	4				9	2	6			3	7						10						**3**
11	5	1	8	4				9	2	6			3	7						10						**4**
11	5	1	8	4				9	2	6			3	7						10						**5**
11		1	8	4				5	2	6			3	7						10	9					**6**
11		1	8	4				5	2	6			3	7						10	9					**7**
11		1	8	4				5	2				3	7				6		10	9					**8**
11		1	8	4				5	2				3							10	9	7		6		**9**
11		1	10	4				5	2	6			3			9				8		7				**10**
11		1	10	4				5	2	6			3			9				8		7				**11**
11		1		4				5	2	6			3			9					8	7			10	**12**
11		1		4				5	2	6			3			9					8	7			10	**13**
11		1		4				5	2	6			3			9					8	7			10	**14**
11		1	10	4				5	2	6			3		9							7		8		**15**
11		1	10	4				5	2	6			3		9							7		8		**16**
11		1	10	4		3		5	2	6				7	9									8		**17**
11		1	10	4				5	2	6		7	3		9									8		**18**
11	6	1						5	2	4		7	3		9						10			8		**19**
11	6	1						5	2	4		7	3		9						10			8		**20**
11	6	1					10	5	2	4			3		8	9						7				**21**
11	6	1					10	5	2	4			3		8	9						7				**22**
	6		10					5	2	4			3	11	8	9						7	1			**23**
10	6							5	2	4			3	11	8	9						7	1			**24**
10	6							5	2	4		7	3	11	8	9							1			**25**
11	6							5	2	4		7	3	10	8	9							1			**26**
11	6							5	2	4		7	3	10	8	9							1			**27**
11	6							5	2	4		7	3	10	8	9							1			**28**
11	6							5		4	2	7	3	10	8	9							1			**29**
11	6							5		4	2	7	3	10	8	9							1			**30**
11	6							5		4	2	7	3	10	8				9				1			**31**
11	6							5		4	2	7	3	10	8	9							1			**32**
11	6							5		4	2	7	3	10	8	9							1			**33**
11	6					2		5		4		7	3	10	8	9							1			**34**
11	6	1						5		4	2	7	3	10	8	9										**35**
11	6	1						5		4	2	7	3	10	8	9										**36**
11	6	1		2				5		4		7	3	10	8	9										**37**
11	6	1						5		4	2	7	3	10	8	9										**38**
11	6	1						5		4	2	7	3	10	8	9										**39**
11	6	1						5		4	2	7	3	10	8	9										**40**
11	6	1						5		4	2	7	3	10	8	9										**41**
11		1					6	5		4	2	7	3		8	9			10							**42**
11		1					6	5		4	2	7	3	10	8	9										**43**
		1			4			5				7	3		8		2	6	9	10		11				**44**
		1			4			5				7	3		9		2	6			10	11		8		**45**
		1			4			5		6		7	3	10	9		2					11		8		**46**
42	27	34	16	19	3	2	4	46	28	42	13	25	45	30	32	28	3	3	3	12	10	15	12	9	3	Apps
8			2					6		1		4		5	6	9			3	1	3	3		3	1	Goals

Bain J A	Batchelor E	Burton S	Court H J	Cowie A D	Farr B S	Foxton J D	Hill C J	Hudson G W	Hunt R G A	Kaye G H	Lloyd W L	Lunn H	May H	Millar W	Onslow R E	Owen M	Page R M	Painter E G	Peart R C	Peebles R W	Simner J	Thomas J W	Uprichard W N McC	Wheeler A J	Williams G G	
11	6	1						5	2	4		7	3		9						10			8		**1**
11	6	1						5	2	4		7	3		9						10			8		**2**
2	2	2						2	2	2		2	2		2						2			2		Apps
1															1						1					Goals

For Final League Table - see page 139

FESTIVAL OF BRITAIN MATCHES

May 14 1951 SWINDON TOWN 2 (o.g.,Onslow) B V BORUSSIA DORTMUND 1

Burton, Page, May, Farr, Hudson, Kaye, Lunn, Wheeler, Onslow, Williams, Bain.

May 19 1951 SWINDON TOWN 1 (Onslow) HAMBORN '07 0

Burton, Page, May, Farr, Hudson, Kaye, Lunn, Wheeler, Onslow, Williams, Bain.

ROY ONSLOW

SEASON 1951/52

Football League Division Three South
Final League Position : 16th
Manager : Louis Page

No	Day	Month	Date	Opponents	Home	Away	H-T	Goalscorers	Gate
1	S	Aug	18	Norwich City	D1-1		(1-0)	Lunn	14,617
2	M		20	Bristol Rovers		L0-1	(0-0)		24,275
3	S		25	Exeter City		W2-1	(0-1)	Onslow,Bain	9,005
4	W		29	Bristol Rovers	D0-0				12,425
5	S	Sep	1	Colchester United	W2-1		(2-1)	Owen,Onslow	10,717
6	Th		6	Watford		W7-1	(3-0)	Lunn 2,Owen 3,Betteridge,Onslow	9,808
7	S		8	Crystal Palace		W1-0	(1-0)	Onslow	14,204
8	W		12	Watford	L0-1		(0-1)		11,878
9	S		15	Bournemouth & Boscombe Athletic		L1-4	(0-2)	Onslow	9,622
10	S		22	Leyton Orient	W2-0		(1-0)	Millar,Betteridge	10,520
11	S		29	Walsall		D0-0			8,004
12	S	Oct	6	Brighton & Hove Albion	L0-2		(0-0)		11,825
13	S		13	Gillingham		L0-4	(0-4)		15,704
14	S		20	Torquay United	W2-1		(0-0)	Bain,Betteridge	8,106
15	S		27	Ipswich Town		W5-1	(1-1)	Betteridge 2,Rees o.g.,Owen 2	11,606
16	S	Nov	3	Bristol City	D0-0				16,296
17	S		10	Port Vale		D2-2	(0-1)		9,142
18	S		17	Northampton Town	D1-1		(0-0)	Betteridge	11,226
19	S	Dec	1	Newport County	D1-1		(0-0)	Lunn	12,007
20	S		8	Southend United		D2-2	(2-0)	Owen,Millar	6,791
21	S		22	Exeter City	W3-1		(1-1)	May,Bain,Owen	8,614
22	Tu		25	Millwall	D2-2		(1-1)	Owen,Millar	9,060
23	W		26	Millwall		D0-0			20,090
24	S		29	Colchester United		L0-2	(0-0)		7,407
25	S	Jan	5	Crystal Palace	L0-2		(0-1)		10,663
26	S		19	Bournemouth & Boscombe Athletic	W2-0		(1-0)	Owen,Hudson	16,503
27	Th		24	Shrewsbury Town		W1-0	(1-0)	Bain	4,025
28	S		26	Leyton Orient		L0-1	(0-1)		11,725
29	S	Feb	9	Walsall	D1-1		(0-0)	Owen	10,270
30	W		13	Plymouth Argyle		L0-3	(0-1)		13,194
31	S		16	Brighton & Hove Albion		L0-4	(0-3)		18,526
32	W		27	Plymouth Argyle	D2-2		(1-0)	Owen,Kaye	7,024
33	S	Mar	1	Gillingham	W2-1		(2-0)	Betteridge,Owen	9,769
34	S		8	Torquay United		L0-9	(0-3)		7,084
35	S		15	Ipswich Town	L1-2		(0-1)	Owen	7,733
36	S		22	Bristol City		L1-2	(1-0)	Onslow	14,823
37	S	Apr	5	Northampton Town		L0-1	(0-1)		7,419
38	F		11	Aldershot		L0-4	(0-2)		8,028
39	S		12	Reading	W2-0		(0-0)	Millar,Owen	17,984
40	M		14	Aldershot	D1-1		(0-0)	Millar	8,664
41	S		19	Newport County		D0-0			9,217
42	W		23	Reading		L0-2	(0-0)		11,406
43	S		26	Southend United	W1-0		(0-0)	Kaye	7,469
44	M		28	Port Vale	W2-0		(2-0)	Owen,Bain	4,835
45	W		30	Shrewsbury Town	L1-2		(0-1)	Bain	4,772
46	S	May	3	Norwich City		L0-2	(0-1)		13,988

Average Home Attendance : **10,564**
Average Away Attendance : **11,526**

F A Cup

Rd	Day	Month	Date	Opponents	Home	Away	H-T	Goalscorers	Gate
1	S	Nov	24	Bedford Town	W2-0		(1-0)	Betteridge,Owen	15,899
2	S	Dec	15	Torquay United	D3-3		(2-3)	Owen 2,Millar	15,259
2R	W		19	Torquay United		+ D1-1	(0-0)	Betteridge	7,435
Rp	W	Jan	2	Torquay United	*	W3-1	(2-1)	Onslow,Bain,Owen	12,241
3	S		12	Cardiff City		D1-1	(0-1)	Owen	36,000
3R	W		16	Cardiff City	+ W1-0		(0-0)	Owen	24,207
4	S	Feb	2	Stoke City	D1-1		(1-0)	Bain	28,140
4R	M		4	Stoke City		W1-0	(1-0)	Millar	29,332
5	S		23	Luton Town		L1-3	(1-1)	Betteridge	27,553

* Played at Ashton Gate + After Extra Time

Bain J A	Batchelor E	Betteridge R M	Bines H M	Burton S	Farr B S	Godwin R G	Gray G J P	Gulliver J	Hindmarsh J W	Hudson G W	Hunt R G A	Kaye G H	Lunn H	May H	Millar W	Nagy M	Onslow R E	Owen M	Page R M	Peart R C	Thomas J W	Uprichard W N McC	
11		10		1			6		2	5		4	7	3			8	9					1
11		10		1			6		2	5		4	7	3			8	9					2
11		10		1	4				2	5		6	7				8	9	3				3
11		10			4				2	5		6	7				8	9	3			1	4
11	6	10			4				2	5			7	3			8	9				1	5
11	6	10			4				2	5			7	3			8	9				1	6
11	6	10			4				2	5			7	3			8	9				1	7
11	6	10			4				2	5			7	3			8	9				1	8
11	6	10			4				2	5			7	3			8	9				1	9
11	6	10					4	3	2	5					7		8	9				1	10
11	6	10					4	3	2	5					7		8	9				1	11
11	6	10		1		8	4	3		5	2				7			9					12
	6						4	3		5	2					8	7	9		10	11	1	13
11	6	10						3		5	2	4	7			8		9				1	14
11	6	10						3		5	2	4	7				8	9				1	15
11	6	10						3		5	2	4	7				8	9				1	16
11	6	10						3		5	2	4	7				8	9				1	17
11	6	10						3		5	2	4	7				8	9				1	18
11	6	10						3		5	2	4	7				8	9				1	19
11	6	10						3		5	2	4	7		8			9				1	20
11		10					6			5	2	4	7	3	8			9				1	21
11		10					6			5	2	4	7	3	8			9				1	22
11		10					6			5	2	4	7	3	8		9					1	23
11		10					6			5	2	4	7	3	8					9		1	24
11		10					6			5	2	4	7	3			8	9				1	25
11		10					6			5	2	4	7	3			8	9				1	26
11						8	6			5	2	4	7	3	10			9				1	27
11		10			4		6			5	2		7	3	8					9		1	28
11		10					6			5	2	4	7	3	8			9				1	29
11							6			5	2	4	7	3	10		8	9				1	30
11		10					6			5	2	4	7	3	8			9				1	31
		10					6			5	2	4	7	3	8			9			11	1	32
11		10					6			5	2	4	7	3	8			9				1	33
11		10					6			5	2	4	7	3	8			9				1	34
11		10					6			5	2	4	7	3	8			9				1	35
11		10					6			5	2	4	7	3			8	9				1	36
11		10					6			5	2	4	7	3			8	9				1	37
11		10					6			5	2		7	3		4	8	9				1	38
11		10					6			5	2	4		3	7		8	9				1	39
11		10					6			5	2	4		3	7		8	9				1	40
11		10					6			5	2	4		3	7		8	9				1	41
11		10					6			5	2	4	7	3	8			9				1	42
11	6	10								5	2	4		3	7		8	9				1	43
11	6	10								5	2	4		3	7		8	9				1	44
11	6	10								5	2	4		3	7		8			9		1	45
11		10	6							5	2	4	8	3	7		9					1	46
44	19	43	1	4	8	2	28	11	11	46	35	35	36	33	25	3	31	41	2	4	2	42	Apps
6		7								1		2	4	1	5		6	18					Goals

Opponents 1 goal

Bain J A	Batchelor E	Betteridge R M	Bines H M	Burton S	Farr B S	Godwin R G	Gray G J P	Gulliver J	Hindmarsh J W	Hudson G W	Hunt R G A	Kaye G H	Lunn H	May H	Millar W	Nagy M	Onslow R E	Owen M	Page R M	Peart R C	Thomas J W	Uprichard W N McC	
11	6	10						3		5	2	4	7				8	9				1	1
11		10					6	3		5	2	4	7		8			9				1	2
11		10					6			5	2	4	7	3	8			9				1	2R
11		10					6			5	2	4	7	3			8	9				1	Rp
11		10					6			5	2	4	7	3			8	9				1	3
11		10					6			5	2	4	7	3			8	9				1	3R
11		10					6			5	2	4	7	3			8	9				1	4
11		10					6			5	2	4	7	3	8			9				1	4R
11		10					6			5	2	4	7	3	8			9				1	5
9	1	9					8	2		9	9	9	9	7	4		5	9				9	Apps
2		3													2		1	6					Goals

NORMAN UPRICHARD

For Final League Table - see page 139

SEASON 1952/53

Football League Division Three South
Final League Position : 18th
Manager : Louis Page

					Home	Away	H-T	Goalscorers	Gate
1	S	Aug	23	Coventry City		W2-1	(0-1)	Owen,Ryder	18,330
2	W		27	Southend United	L1-3		(1-1)	Ryder pen.	14,276
3	S		30	Norwich City	W2-1		(1-0)	Ryder 2	14,699
4	Tu	Sep	2	Southend United		L0-3	(0-2)		9,323
5	S		6	Colchester United		L1-3	(1-1)	Betteridge	9,062
6	W		10	Gillingham	D0-0				8,291
7	S		13	Aldershot	W3-2		(0-0)	Owen,Millar,Ryder	10,410
8	W		17	Gillingham		D0-0			10,788
9	S		20	Bournemouth & Boscombe Athletic	L1-2		(1-1)	Owen	11,220
10	Th		25	Northampton Town		L1-3	(1-1)	Ryder	8,746
11	S		27	Queens Park Rangers		D1-1	(1-0)	Johnson	10,762
12	W	Oct	1	Walsall	L1-2		(1-0)	Betteridge	4,279
13	S		4	Shrewsbury Town	D2-2		(1-2)	Betteridge 2	8,143
14	S		11	Watford		L1-2	(1-1)	Bain	16,541
15	S		18	Brighton and Hove Albion	W3-0		(0-0)	Bain,Johnson,Ryder pen.	10,278
16	S		25	Newport County		L0-3	(0-1)		7,971
17	S	Nov	1	Crystal Palace	L3-6		(2-1)	Owen 2,Bain	9,080
18	S		8	Bristol City		L2-4	(1-3)	Owen 2	21,266
19	S		15	Torquay United	W2-0		(0-0)	Ryder pen.,Owen	5,502
20	S	Dec	13	Reading	W2-0		(1-0)	Lunn,Ryder	9,496
21	S		20	Coventry City	L2-3		(2-0)	Millar,Betteridge	7,368
22	F		26	Exeter City		W2-1	(0-1)	Bain,Ryder	13,620
23	S		27	Exeter City	W5-2		(1-1)	Millar,Ryder,Betteridge,Bain 2	10,580
24	S	Jan	3	Norwich City		D1-1	(0-0)	Ryder	18,124
25	W		14	Millwall	L1-2		(0-1)	Owen	3,526
26	S		17	Colchester United	L0-1		(0-0)		8,545
27	S		24	Aldershot		D2-2	(0-1)	Rogers o.g.,Bain	5,780
28	S		31	Millwall		L0-3	(0-1)		18,430
29	S	Feb	7	Bournemouth & Boscombe Athletic		D1-1	(0-1)	Owen	8,799
30	S		14	Queens Park Rangers	L1-3		(1-1)	Lunn	7,387
31	S		21	Shrewsbury Town		L1-2	(1-1)	Ryder pen.	8,556
32	S		28	Watford	D0-0				8,081
33	S	Mar	7	Brighton and Hove Albion		W2-1	(2-1)	Owen,Betteridge	12,824
34	S		14	Newport County	W2-0		(2-0)	Lunn,Betteridge	7,445
35	W		18	Leyton Orient	D1-1		(0-1)	Owen	2,980
36	S		21	Crystal Palace		L0-3	(0-1)		10,462
37	S		28	Bristol City	D0-0				10,026
38	F	Apr	3	Bristol Rovers	L1-3		(1-1)	Lunn	24,459
39	S		4	Torquay United		L1-3	(1-2)	Millar	6,334
40	M		6	Bristol Rovers		W2-1	(1-1)	Bain,Lunn	24,406
41	S		11	Northampton Town	W3-0		(2-0)	Millar,Bain pen.,Owen	9,564
42	W		15	Ipswich Town		D1-1	(1-0)	Millar	5,378
43	S		18	Leyton Orient		D2-2	(1-1)	Betteridge,Owen	11,133
44	Th		23	Walsall		W2-1	(1-1)	Owen,Betteridge	5,304
45	S		25	Ipswich Town	W2-0		(1-0)	Owen,Millar	8,518
46	F	May	1	Reading		L1-4	(0-2)	Millar	7,188

Average Home Attendance : **9,311**
Average Away Attendance : **11,701**

F A Cup

					Home	Away	H-T	Goalscorers	Gate
1	S	Nov	22	Newport I O W	W5-0		(3-0)	Lunn,Owen 3,Millar	10,157
2	S	Dec	6	Northampton Town	W2-0		(1-0)	Owen,Millar	12,936
3	S	Jan	10	Manchester City		L0-7	(0-4)		28,953

For Final League Table - see page 140

TERRY RYDER
stood just 5'4", but his speed and skill more than compensated for his lack of inches. Starting his League career with home town club Norwich City, just after the War, he was the son of a former Canaries reserve centre-forward - also named Terry. He came to the County Ground in July 1952 in a £2,000 deal from Portsmouth. But after just one season with Town, Terry returned to Norfolk to take the player-manager's job at Kings Lynn.

Bain J A	Batchelor E	Betteridge R M	Bines H M	Brandon K A	Burton S	Cryle G	Elwell T T	Gray G J P	Hudson G W	Hunt R G A	Johnson R	Johnston J C	Kaye G H	Lunn H	Millar W	Owen M	Parker W	Prouton R O	Radford A	Ryder T R	Uprichard W N McC	Williams G G	
11		8					3	6	5	2			4	7		9				10	1		**1**
11		8					3	6	5	2			4	7		9				10	1		**2**
11		8					3	6	5	2			4	7		9				10	1		**3**
11		8				4		6	5	2				7		9			3	10	1		**4**
		8						6	5	2			4	7	11	9			3	10	1		**5**
		8				6			5	2			4	7	11	9			3	10	1		**6**
11		8				4		6	5	2					10	9			3	7	1		**7**
11		8				4		6	5	2					10	9			3	7	1		**8**
11		8				4		6	5	2					10	9			3	7	1		**9**
		10				4		6	5	2	9					8			3	7	1	11	**10**
		10					3	6	5	2	9		4			8				7	1	11	**11**
		10			1	4	3	6	5	2	9					8				7		11	**12**
11	6	10			1	4	3		5	2				8		9				7			**13**
11	6	10			1	4	3		5	2				8		9				7			**14**
11	6	10				4	3		5	2	9			8						7	1		**15**
11	6	10				4	3		5	2	9			8						7	1		**16**
11	6	4					3		5	2	10			8		9				7	1		**17**
11		4			1		3		5	2				7	8	9		6		10			**18**
11		4			1				5	2				7	8	9		6	3	10			**19**
11	5	4			1					2	9			8	10			6	3	7			**20**
11	5	4			1					2	9			8	10			6	3	7			**21**
11		4			1				5	2				8	10	9		6	3	7			**22**
11		4			1				5	2	9			8	10			6	3	7			**23**
11		4			1				5	2	9			8	10			6	3	7			**24**
11		10			1	4			5	2				8		9		6	3	7			**25**
		4		11	1				5	2	9			8		10		6	3	7			**26**
11	5	4			1		3	6		2				8		9				7		10	**27**
11	5	4			1		3	6		2				8		9				7		10	**28**
11	5	4	6		1		3							7		9	10		2			8	**29**
11	5	4	6		1		3			2				8		9	10			7			**30**
	5	4		11	1		3			2				8		9	10	6		7			**31**
	5	4		11	1		3			2				8		9	10	6		7			**32**
	5	8		11	1		3	4		2				7		9	10	6					**33**
	5	8		11	1		3	4		2				7		9	10	6					**34**
11	5	8			1		3	4		2		6		7		9	10						**35**
11	5	8	6		1		3	4		2				7		9	10						**36**
11	5	4	6		1		3			2				8		9	10			7			**37**
11	5	4			1		3			2		6		8		9	10			7			**38**
11	5	8	6		1		3			2		4		7	10	9							**39**
11	5	8			1		3			2		4		7	10	9						6	**40**
11	5	8			1		3			2		4		7	10	9						6	**41**
11		8			1		3		5	2		4		7	10	9						6	**42**
11		8			1		3		5	2		4		7	10	9						6	**43**
11		8			1		3		5	2		4		7	10	9						6	**44**
11		8			1		3		5	2		4		7	10	9						6	**45**
11		8			1		3		5	2		4		7	10	9						6	**46**
36	22	46	5	5	32	12	31	17	29	45	11	10	6	40	20	40	10	13	16	33	14	13	Apps
9		9									2			5	8	17				13			Goals

Opponents 1 goal

Bain J A	Batchelor E	Betteridge R M	Bines H M	Brandon K A	Burton S	Cryle G	Elwell T T	Gray G J P	Hudson G W	Hunt R G A	Johnson R	Johnston J C	Kaye G H	Lunn H	Millar W	Owen M	Parker W	Prouton R O	Radford A	Ryder T R	Uprichard W N McC	Williams G G	
11		4			1				5	2				7	8	9		6	3	10			**1**
11		4			1				5	2				7	8	9		6	3	10			**2**
11		4			1				5	2				8	10	9		6	3	7			**3**
3		3			3				3	3				3	3	3		3	3	3			Apps
														1	2	4							Goals

MICK BETTERIDGE

TITUS OKERE

claimed his own piece of Town history by becoming the first black player to earn a professional contract with the club. Dubbed 'Golden Boy', he toured Britain with the Nigerian national side in 1949. Born in Okpuala in 1928, Titus was appointed captain of his country in 1951 and arrived at the County Ground in January 1953. But he was released at the end of the season, after struggling to adapt to both the British weather and playing in football boots !

SEASON 1953/54

Football League Division Three South
Final League Position : 19th
Manager : Maurice Lindley

				Home	Away	H-T	Goalscorers	Gate
1	W	Aug	19 Bournemouth & Boscombe Athletic	W2-1		(0-1)	Lunn 2	14,751
2	S		22 Newport County	W7-1		(2-1)	Betteridge,Owen 3,Lambert,Bull,Lunn	13,444
3	W		26 Aldershot	W3-1		(0-0)	Betteridge,Owen 2	14,964
4	S		29 Norwich City		D2-2	(1-1)	Bull 2	15,474
5	W	Sep	2 Aldershot		L0-1	(0-1)		7,338
6	S		5 Queens Park Rangers	L0-1		(0-0)		15,157
7	Th		10 Walsall		W1-0	(1-0)	Bain	7,784
8	S		12 Southampton		L1-3	(1-0)	Lunn	19,296
9	W		16 Walsall	W3-0		(1-0)	Lunn,Betteridge,Bain	8,832
10	S		19 Colchester United	W3-0		(1-0)	Betteridge 2,Lewis o.g.	12,284
11	W		23 Exeter City		L1-3	(1-2)	Bull	8,140
12	S		26 Crystal Palace		L2-3	(1-2)	Lambert,Cross	18,766
13	W		30 Exeter City	L2-4		(0-2)	Betteridge 2	7,727
14	S	Oct	3 Bristol City	W5-0		(2-0)	Owen,Bull,Cross,Lambert,Lunn	15,481
15	S		10 Leyton Orient	W2-1		(0-0)	Bull,Lambert	12,617
16	S		17 Millwall		L1-6	(1-3)	Bull	9,654
17	S		24 Ipswich Town	L1-2		(0-1)	Lunn	13,147
18	S		31 Bournemouth & Boscombe Athletic		L0-4	(0-1)		7,625
19	S	Nov	7 Coventry City	D1-1		(0-0)	Bain pen.	10,666
20	S		14 Gillingham		L0-1	(0-0)		11,682
21	S		28 Torquay United		L1-2	(1-0)	Onslow	6,440
22	S	Dec	5 Watford	D2-2		(2-1)	Owen,Sampson	8,769
23	S		19 Newport County		L0-2	(0-1)		9,296
24	F		25 Shrewsbury Town	W2-1		(1-0)	Bull,Lunn	6,611
25	S		26 Shrewsbury Town		L0-1	(0-0)		10,665
26	S	Jan	2 Norwich City	D0-0				7,990
27	S		9 Southend United	W3-0		(2-0)	Lunn,Onslow,Anderson o.g.	8,217
28	S		16 Queens Park Rangers		W2-0	(2-0)	Owen,Bull	9,122
29	S		23 Southampton	L0-1		(0-0)		12,942
30	S		30 Southend United		L1-3	(1-0)	Sampson	3,333
31	S	Feb	6 Colchester United		D2-2	(2-1)	Owen,Sampson	6,824
32	S		13 Crystal Palace	D1-1		(0-1)	Lunn	8,907
33	S		20 Bristol City		L1-5	(1-3)	Onslow	23,749
34	S		27 Leyton Orient		D1-1	(1-1)	Lambert	12,242
35	S	Mar	6 Millwall	W2-1		(0-0)	Bull,Johnson	8,903
36	S		13 Northampton Town		L0-2	(0-1)		6,821
37	S		20 Torquay United	W6-1		(2-1)	Bull,Hudson pen.,Owen,Thomas R o.g.,Sampson,Onslow	8,493
38	S		27 Coventry City		D0-0			7,523
39	S	Apr	3 Gillingham	W2-1		(0-0)	Bull,Sampson	7,150
40	W		7 Brighton and Hove Albion		D1-1	(0-0)	Onslow	19,440
41	S		10 Watford		L1-2	(0-1)	Sampson	11,634
42	F		16 Reading	W1-0		(0-0)	Johnson	12,743
43	S		17 Brighton and Hove Albion	L0-1		(0-1)		12,319
44	M		19 Reading		L1-3	(1-1)	Beards	12,011
45	S		24 Ipswich Town		L0-2	(0-1)		17,801
46	W		28 Northampton Town	D0-0				5,195

Average Home Attendance : **10,753**
Average Away Attendance : **11,420**

F A Cup

				Home	Away	H-T	Goalscorers	Gate
1	S	Nov	21 Newport I O W	W2-1		(0-1)	Batchelor 2	12,176
2	S	Dec	12 Hastings United		L1-4	(0-3)	Sampson	9,917

For Final League Table - see page 140

MAURICE LINDLEY
took over first team coaching duties at the County Ground when Harry Martin reached 60 and two years later, in 1953, succeeded Louis Page as team manager. A former physical training instructor in the Royal Air Force, Maurice originated from Keighley and joined Everton from his hometown club in 1936. His managerial reign at Swindon was not a happy one, with two bottom six finishes and an ignominious Cup exit at Southern League Hastings. Hampered by financial constraints, Maurice took something of a gamble in October 1954, spending over £2,000 on Portsmouth's reserve forward Matt Gemmell, who made just nine senior appearances for Town, scoring twice. Mr Lindley's contract was not renewed in May 1955.

Bain J A	Batchelor E	Beards A	Betteridge R M	Bull M F	Burton S	Churchill T	Cross J K	Elwell T T	Hilton P B	Hudson G W	Hunt R G A	Johnson R	Johnston J C	Lambert K	Lunn H	Onslow R E	Owen M	Page R M	Sampson R V	Tilley D S	Williams G G	Williamson S H	
	5		10	11	1		4	3			2		6	8	7		9						1
	5		10	11	1		4	3			2		6	8	7		9						2
	5		10	11	1		4	3			2		6	8	7		9						3
	5		10	11		1	4	3			2		6	8	7		9						4
	5		10	11		1	4	3			2		6	8	7		9						5
	5		10	11		1	4	3			2	9	6	8	7								6
10	5			11		1	4	3			2		6	8	7		9						7
11	5		8		1		4	3			2		6	10	7		9						8
11	5		8			1	4	3			2		6	10	7		9						9
11	5		8			1	4	3			2		6	10	7		9						10
11	5			7	1		4	3			2		6	10	8		9						11
11	5		8			1	4	3			2		6	10	7		9						12
	5		8	11		1	4	3			2		6	10	7		9						13
			8	11	1		4		3	5	2		6	10	7		9						14
			8	11	1		4		3	5	2		6	10	7		9						15
			8	11	1		4		3	5	2		6	10	7	9							16
8			9	11		1	4		3	5	2		6	10	7								17
8			9	11		1	4	3		5	2		6	10	7								18
8	9			11		1	4	3		5	2		6	10	7								19
			8	11	1		4	3		5	2		10		7		9				6		20
	5			7	1		4	3			2	9	6	10		8			11				21
	5		8	7	1		4	3			2		6	10			9		11				22
				11	1		4	3		5	2	9	6	10	7	8							23
				11	1		4	3		5	2	9	6	10	7	8			10				24
7			8	11	1		4		3	5	2	9	6			10							25
				11	1		4	3		5	2	9	6		7	8			10				26
				11	1		4	3		5	2	9	6		7	8			10				27
				11	1		4	3		5	2		6		7	8	9		10				28
				11	1		4	3		5	2		6		7	8	9		10				29
				11	1		4	3		5	2		6		7	8	9		10				30
				11	1		4	3		5	2		6		7	8	9		10				31
				11	1		4	3		5	2		6		7	8	9		10				32
				11	1		4	3		5	2		6	10	7	8	9						33
				11	1		4	3		5	2		6	7		10	9		8				34
				11	1		4		3	5	2	9	6	7		8			10				35
		11			1		4		3	5	2	9	6	7		8			10				36
		11		7	1		4		3	5	2		6			8	9		10				37
		11		7	1		4		3	5	2		6			8	9		10				38
				11	1				3	5	2		6		7	8	9		10			4	39
		11		7	1					5	2		4			8	9	3	10			6	40
		11		7	1					5	2		4			8	9	3	10			6	41
		11		7	1		4			5	2	9	6			8		3	10				42
		11		7	1		4			5	2	9	6			8		3	10				43
		11		7	1		4			5	2	9	6			8		3	10				44
	5			7	1		4	3	2			10	6			8	9		11				45
	5			7	1		4		3			9	6	10		8		2	11				46
10	18	8	19	41	35	11	43	30	12	29	44	14	46	27	31	26	29	6	23		1	3	Apps
3		1	7	12			2			1		2		5	10	5	10		6				Goals

Opponents 3 goals

Bain J A	Batchelor E	Beards A	Betteridge R M	Bull M F	Burton S	Churchill T	Cross J K	Elwell T T	Hilton P B	Hudson G W	Hunt R G A	Johnson R	Johnston J C	Lambert K	Lunn H	Onslow R E	Owen M	Page R M	Sampson R V	Tilley D S	Williams G G	Williamson S H	
	9		10	11	1		4	3		5	2		6	8	7								1
	5			7	1		4	3			2		6		10	8			11	9			2
	2		1	2	2		2	2		1	2		2	1	2	1			1	1			Apps
	2																		1				Goals

JIMMY JOHNSTON

MICKEY BULL

took over from Scottish winger Jimmy Bain - who was now almost 34 - and his dozen goals were enough to make him Town's top scorer ahead of his fellow wide man Harry Lunn and Maurice Owen. Mickey had been with Brentford for five years, but had managed only a handful of first team outings at Griffin Park. Equally at home on either flank, Mickey was less effective in his second term at the County Ground and joined Hastings United in July 1955.

SEASON 1954/55

Football League Division Three South
Final League Position : 21st
Manager : Maurice Lindley

No.	Day	Month	Date	Opponents	Home	Away	H-T	Goalscorers	Gate
1	S	Aug	21	Colchester United		D0-0			9,767
2	Tu		24	Watford		L0-3	(0-1)		10,841
3	S		28	Norwich City	W1-0		(0-0)	Onslow	13,599
4	W	Sep	1	Watford	W6-1		(3-0)	Onslow,Owen 2,Williams H 3	10,279
5	S		4	Southend United		L1-4	(1-1)	Owen	9,648
6	W		8	Bournemouth & Boscombe Athletic		D1-1	(1-0)	Owen	11,454
7	S		11	Aldershot	W1-0		(1-0)	Hunter	9,949
8	W		15	Bournemouth & Boscombe Athletic	L0-2		(0-1)		7,996
9	S		18	Gillingham		L1-2	(1-1)	Onslow	12,125
10	W		22	Queens Park Rangers	W2-0		(1-0)	Owen 2	6,423
11	S		25	Crystal Palace		D0-0			16,483
12	M		27	Queens Park Rangers		L1-3	(1-1)	Bull	8,241
13	S	Oct	2	Northampton Town	L0-1		(0-0)		8,899
14	S		9	Shrewsbury Town	W2-1		(2-0)	Hunter,Onslow	8,953
15	S		16	Walsall		W2-1	(2-0)	Owen,Onslow	9,010
16	S		23	Bristol City	D2-2		(2-0)	Owen,Hunter	19,880
17	S		30	Leyton Orient		L0-1	(0-0)		15,020
18	S	Nov	6	Brighton and Hove Albion	L0-2		(0-1)		8,846
19	S		13	Brentford		L2-4	(0-2)	Owen,Gemmell	10,634
20	S		27	Southampton		D1-1	(1-0)	Cross	12,001
21	S	Dec	4	Millwall	D1-1		(1-0)	Beards pen.	6,715
22	S		11	Northampton Town		L0-1	(0-0)		6,609
23	S		18	Colchester United	D1-1		(1-0)	McClelland	5,254
24	S		25	Exeter City		L1-2	(0-1)	Gemmell	6,527
25	M		27	Exeter City	W2-0		(2-0)	Beards,Cross	9,530
26	S	Jan	1	Norwich City		L1-2	(1-1)	Beards pen.	11,307
27	S		22	Aldershot		D0-0			4,326
28	S		29	Reading		L1-2	(1-0)	Bull	7,891
29	S	Feb	5	Gillingham	W2-1		(2-1)	Sampson 2 (1 pen.)	6,477
30	S		12	Crystal Palace	D0-0				4,715
31	S	Mar	5	Walsall	D2-2		(1-1)	Gibson,Williams H	5,148
32	S		12	Bristol City		L0-3	(0-1)		24,390
33	S		19	Leyton Orient	D0-0				8,624
34	S		26	Brighton and Hove Albion		L1-3	(0-1)	Owen	8,761
35	S	Apr	2	Brentford	D1-1		(1-0)	Owen	5,924
36	W		6	Torquay United		D1-1	(1-1)	Owen	4,285
37	F		8	Newport County		D2-2	(1-1)	Sampson 2	8,595
38	S		9	Coventry City		L0-1	(0-1)		9,427
39	M		11	Newport County	L1-3		(1-1)	Bull	7,957
40	S		16	Southampton	W1-0		(0-0)	Hope	12,924
41	W		20	Southend United	L0-1		(0-0)		4,230
42	S		23	Millwall		L0-1	(0-0)		6,304
43	W		27	Coventry City	W3-0		(2-0)	Williams H 2,Riseborough	4,293
44	S		30	Torquay United	D0-0				6,011
45	W	May	4	Reading	W2-0		(1-0)	Williams H,Reeves o.g.	5,147
46	F		6	Shrewsbury Town		L0-7	(0-3)		5,305

Average Home Attendance : **8,164**
Average Away Attendance : **9,954**

F A Cup

No.	Day	Month	Date	Opponents	Home	Away	H-T	Goalscorers	Gate
1	S	Nov	20	Crystal Palace	L0-2		(0-2)		11,359

SAM BURTON
was one of Town's first post-War signings in July 1945. He was on a part-time contract while working in the South Wales mines as a 'Bevin boy', before going full-time in 1948. Along with centre-half 'Garth' Hudson, he recorded maximum appearances this season and in 1957/58. Sam went on to complete 17 years service at the County Ground, amassing a then club record 509 first team appearances.

Batchelor E	Beards A	Brennan J	Bull M F	Burton S	Cross J K	Gemmell M	Gibson D J	Hilton P B	Hope A J H	Hudson G W	Hunt R G A	Hunter R R	Jackson R L	Johnson R	Johnston J C	Lambert K	McClelland W J	Onslow R E	Owen M	Page R M	Riseborough C	Sampson R V	Thompson F N	Williams G G	Williams H G	Williamson S H	
	11		7	1	4					5	2				6			8	9	3					10		1
			7	1	4				11	5	2				6			8	9	3					10		2
			11	1	4					5	2	7			6			8	9	3					10		3
			11	1	4					5	2	7			6			8	9	3					10		4
			11	1	4					5	2	7			6			8	9	3					10		5
			11	1	4					5	2	7			6			8	9	3					10		6
			11	1	4					5	2	7			6	10			9	3					8		7
	11		7	1	4					5	2				6	10			9	3					8		8
			11	1	4					5	2	7			6	10		8	9	3							9
				1	4			3	11	5	2	7			6			8	9			10					10
				1	4			3	11	5	2	7			6		8		9			10					11
			7	1	4			3	11	5	2				6		8		9			10					12
		2	11	1	4			3		5		7			6		8		9			10					13
	11			1		10		3		5	2	7			4			8	9					6			14
			11	1		10		3		5	2	7			4			8	9					6			15
			11	1		10		3		5	2	7			4			8	9					6			16
			7	1		10		3	11	5	2				4			8	9					6			17
			7	1		10		3	11	5	2				4		8		9					6			18
			11	1		10	7			5	2				4			8	9	3				6			19
	11			1	4		7			5	2							8	9	3		10				6	20
	11			1	4		7			5	2							8	9	3		10				6	21
	11			1	4		7			5	2						8		9	3		10				6	22
	11			1	4		7			5	2						8		9	3		10				6	23
	11			1	4	10	7			5	2						8			3		9				6	24
	11			1	4		7			5	2	9					8			3		10				6	25
	11			1	4		7			5	2	9					8			3		10				6	26
	11			1	4					5	2	7					8		9	3		10				6	27
	11		7	1	4					5	2	9					8			3		10				6	28
			7	1	4			3		5	2			9			8					10		11		6	29
			7	1				3		5	2		4	9			8					10		11		6	30
				1	4		7	3		5	2								9			8		11	10	6	31
	11			1	4		7	3		5	2								9			8		6	10		32
			11	1	4			3		5	2							8	9		7	10		6			33
			11	1	4			3		5	2							8	9		7	10		6			34
			11	1	4			3		5	2						8		9		7	10		6			35
			11	1			7	3		5	2		4					8	9			10		6			36
			11	1	4		7	3		5	2							8	9			10		6			37
			11	1	4		7	3		5	2							8	9			10		6			38
			11	1	4		7	3		5	2							8	9			10		6			39
				1	4	10	7	3	11	5	2							8						6		9	40
				1	4		7		11	5	2							8		3		10		6		9	41
4				1					11	5	2							9		3	7	8		6	10		42
4				1				3	11	5	2							9			7	8		6	10		43
4				1				3	11	5	2							9			7	8		6	10		44
4			11	1				3		5	2							9			7	8		6	10		45
4			11	1			7	3		5	2							9				8	6	10			46
5	13	1	28	46	33	8	17	25	11	46	45	16	2	2	19	3	14	28	33	21	7	30	1	24	14	14	Apps
	3		3		2	2	1		1			3					1	5	12		1	4			7		Goals

Opponents 1 goal

Batchelor E	Beards A	Brennan J	Bull M F	Burton S	Cross J K	Gemmell M	Gibson D J	Hilton P B	Hope A J H	Hudson G W	Hunt R G A	Hunter R R	Jackson R L	Johnson R	Johnston J C	Lambert K	McClelland W J	Onslow R E	Owen M	Page R M	Riseborough C	Sampson R V	Thompson F N	Williams G G	Williams H G	Williamson S H	
			11	1		10				5	2	7			4			8	9	3				6			1

For Final League Table - see page 140

SEASON 1955/56

Football League Division Three South
Final League Position : 24th (Last)
Manager : None
(Player-Coach Geoff Fox from Oct.1)

No	Day	Month	Date	Opponents	Home	Away	H-T	Goalscorers	Gate
1	S	Aug	20	Southampton		L1-2	(1-1)	Edwards	17,773
2	W		24	Northampton Town	L0-1		(0-1)		8,552
3	S		27	Shrewsbury Town	W2-1		(2-1)	Owen,Edwards	6,671
4	Th	Sep	1	Northampton Town		L1-2	(1-1)	Edwards	11,102
5	S		3	Ipswich Town		L2-6	(0-1)	Edwards,Owen	13,238
6	W		7	Brighton and Hove Albion	D0-0				6,090
7	S		10	Walsall	L1-2		(0-0)	Gibson	7,576
8	W		14	Brighton and Hove Albion		L0-2	(0-1)		10,694
9	S		17	Torquay United		L0-4	(0-3)		7,547
10	W		21	Aldershot	D1-1		(0-1)	Owen	4,293
11	S		24	Newport County	L1-2		(1-1)	Micklewright	7,870
12	M		26	Queens Park Rangers		L0-1	(0-0)		5,181
13	S	Oct	1	Coventry City		L0-6	(0-1)		17,202
14	S		8	Exeter City	L0-1		(0-0)		6,788
15	S		15	Leyton Orient		L0-4	(0-3)		14,744
16	S		22	Colchester United	W3-1		(0-0)	Micklewright 2,Owen	6,373
17	S		29	Norwich City		L1-4	(0-2)	Cross	12,885
18	S	Nov	5	Bournemouth & Boscombe Athletic	D2-2		(2-1)	Owen 2	7,664
19	S		12	Gillingham		L0-4	(0-3)		9,412
20	S		26	Reading		W1-0	(0-0)	Edwards	8,241
21	S	Dec	3	Watford	D0-0				7,268
22	S		17	Southampton	D1-1		(1-0)	Parker o.g.	7,046
23	S		24	Shrewsbury Town		D1-1	(0-1)	Brennan	6,375
24	M		26	Crystal Palace	D0-0				9,082
25	Tu		27	Crystal Palace		W2-0	(2-0)	Edwards,Micklewright	10,710
26	S		31	Ipswich Town	L0-1		(0-0)		10,909
27	S	Jan	14	Walsall		L0-4	(0-1)		10,961
28	S		21	Torquay United	W2-1		(1-1)	Edwards,Gibson	7,148
29	S	Feb	11	Coventry City	D1-1		(1-0)	Edwards pen.	6,414
30	S		18	Exeter City		W2-1	(0-1)	Owen 2	4,937
31	S		25	Leyton Orient	L1-2		(0-2)	Edwards	9,829
32	W		29	Millwall	W1-0		(1-0)	Owen	6,864
33	S	Mar	3	Colchester United		L0-5	(0-3)		6,836
34	S		10	Norwich City	D1-1		(0-1)	Owen	9,716
35	M		12	Brentford		W2-1	(1-0)	Edwards,Owen	7,249
36	S		17	Bournemouth & Boscombe Athletic		L0-4	(0-4)		6,648
37	S		24	Gillingham	L0-1		(0-0)		7,035
38	F		30	Southend United		D0-0			10,774
39	S		31	Millwall		D1-1	(0-0)	Gibson	7,420
40	M	Apr	2	Southend United	D1-1		(1-0)	Owen	8,728
41	S		7	Reading	D0-0				7,397
42	Th		12	Newport County		L0-1	(0-0)		2,346
43	S		14	Watford		L1-2	(0-0)	Edwards	3,505
44	S		21	Brentford	L0-1		(0-0)		5,790
45	W		25	Queens Park Rangers	L0-1		(0-0)		4,617
46	S		28	Aldershot		D1-1	(0-1)	Owen	3,972

Average Home Attendance : **7,379**
Average Away Attendance : **9,120**

F A Cup

Rd	Day	Month	Date	Opponents	Home	Away	H-T	Goalscorers	Gate
1	S	Nov	19	Hereford United	W4-0		(2-0)	Micklewright 2,Gibson,Owen	13,364
2	S	Dec	10	Peterborough United	D1-1		(0-1)	Owen	23,983
2R	Th		15	Peterborough United	+	W2-1	(1-0)	Micklewright,Cross	16,672
3	S	Jan	7	Worksop Town	W1-0		(0-0)	Edwards	16,060
4	S		28	Charlton Athletic		L1-2	(0-1)	Edwards	28,042

\+ After Extra Time

Following the departure of Maurice Lindley in the summer of 1955, the board of directors took over team affairs. At the beginning of October ***GEOFF FOX*** - previously at Bristol Rovers for eight years, but still only 30 - was appointed as player-coach. It was a tough task, with the club already bottom of the table with just four points from twelve games. And there was little improvement after Christmas, with no wins and only four goals in the final eleven, giving Town no chance of avoiding the division's 'wooden spoon'. A month after Bert Head's arrival, Geoff quit full-time football and returned to Bristol.

Agar F R	Baillie D R D C	Brennan J	Burton S	Cross J K	Edds E F	Edwards R H	Fox G R	Gibson D J	Gill C J P	Hilton P B	Hudson G W	Hunt R G A	Johnson R	McShane A	Micklewright A A J	Moss T J	Onslow R E	Owen M	Richards J B	Riseborough C	Sampson R V	Thompson F N	Williams G G	
			1		11	10				3	5	2		4			8	9		7			6	**1**
			1		11	10				3	5	2		4				9		7	8		6	**2**
			1		11	10		8		3	5	2		4				9		7			6	**3**
			1	4		10		7		3	5	2		6			8	9			11			**4**
			1	4		10		8		3	5	2		6				9		7	11			**5**
			1	4		10		8		3	5	2		6				9		7	11			**6**
			1	4		10		8			5	2		6				9		7	11		3	**7**
			1			10		7		3	5	2	8	4				9			11		6	**8**
			1			10		8		3	5	2		4				9		7	11	6		**9**
			1	4		10		8		3	5	2		6				9		7	11			**10**
			1	4		10				3	5	2			8			9		7	11		6	**11**
		3	1	4		10		7			5	2			8			9				6	11	**12**
		3	1	4		11		8			5	2			9					7	10	6		**13**
			1			11	3	8			5	2		4	10		9			7			6	**14**
			1			11	3	7			5	2		4	10		8	9					6	**15**
			1	4		10	3	7			5	2		6	8			9					11	**16**
			1	4		10	3	7		2	5			6	8			9					11	**17**
			1	4		10	3	7			5	2		6	8			9					11	**18**
				4		10	3	7	1		5	2		6	8			9					11	**19**
			1	4		10	3	7			5	2	11	6	8			9						**20**
			1	4		10	3	7			5	2	11	6	8			9						**21**
			1	4		10	3	7			5	2	11	6	8			9						**22**
		11	1	4		10	3	7			5	2		6	8			9						**23**
		11	1	4		10	3	7			5	2		6	8			9						**24**
		11	1	4		10	3	7			5	2		6	8			9						**25**
		11	1	4		10	3	7			5	2		6	8			9						**26**
		11	1	4		10		7		3	5	2		6	8			9						**27**
		11	1	4		10	3	7			5	2		6	8			9						**28**
		11	1	4		10	3	7			5	2		6	8			9						**29**
		11	1	4		10	3	7			5	2		6	8			9						**30**
		11	1	4		10	3	7			5	2		6	8			9						**31**
		11	1	4		10	3	7			5	2		6	8			9						**32**
		11	1	4		10	3	7			5	2		6	8			9						**33**
		11	1	4		10	3	7			5	2		6	8			9						**34**
			1	4		10	3	7			5	2		6	8	11		9						**35**
			1	4		10	3	7			5	2		6	8	11		9						**36**
10			1	4		6	3	7			5	2			8	11		9						**37**
8			1	4		10	3	7			5	2				11		9					6	**38**
8			1			10	3	7			5	2			4	11		9					6	**39**
8			1			10	3	7			5	2			4	11		9					6	**40**
8			1	4		10	3	7			5	2			11			9					6	**41**
8			1	4		10	3	7			5	2			11			9					6	**42**
8	9		1	4		11	3	7			5	2						10					6	**43**
8			1	4		11	3	7			5	2						9	10				6	**44**
8			1	4		11	3	7			5	2						9	10				6	**45**
		2	1	4		10				3	5				8	11		9		7			6	**46**
9	1	15	45	37	3	46	31	42	1	13	46	44	4	33	32	7	4	44	2	12	10	3	22	Apps
		1		1		11		3							4			13						Goals

Opponents 1 goal

Agar F R	Baillie D R D C	Brennan J	Burton S	Cross J K	Edds E F	Edwards R H	Fox G R	Gibson D J	Gill C J P	Hilton P B	Hudson G W	Hunt R G A	Johnson R	McShane A	Micklewright A A J	Moss T J	Onslow R E	Owen M	Richards J B	Riseborough C	Sampson R V	Thompson F N	Williams G G	
			1	4		10	3	7			5	2	11	6	8			9						**1**
			1	4		10	3	7			5	2	11	6	8			9						**2**
			1	4		10	3	7			5	2	11	6	8			9						**2R**
		11	1	4		10	3	7			5	2		6	8			9						**3**
		11	1	4		10	3	7			5	2		6	8			9						**4**
		2	5	5		5	5	5			5	5	3	5	5			5						Apps
				1		2		1							3			2						Goals

For Final League Table - see page 166

SEASON 1956/57

Football League Third Division South
Final League Position : 23rd
Manager : Bert Head (from Oct.3)

No.	Day	Month	Date	Opponents	Home	Away	H-T	Goalscorers	Gate
1	S	Aug	18	Aldershot	L1-2		(1-0)	Edwards pen.	10,966
2	Tu		21	Brentford		L1-4	(0-1)	Micklewright	13,510
3	S		25	Watford		W4-3	(1-1)	Richards,Gibbs 2,Edwards	10,944
4	W		29	Brentford	L1-3		(0-0)	Gibbs	11,995
5	S	Sep	1	Shrewsbury Town	L1-2		(1-2)	Richards	9,196
6	W		5	Gillingham		L0-3	(0-2)		6,783
7	S		8	Walsall		W2-1	(1-1)	Owen,Edwards	12,763
8	W		12	Gillingham	L2-3		(0-2)	Gibbs,Owen	6,082
9	S		15	Ipswich Town	W3-1		(1-0)	Owen,Edwards 2	8,409
10	W		19	Queens Park Rangers	W1-0		(0-0)	Edwards	8,705
11	S		22	Bournemouth & Boscombe Athletic		L0-7	(0-3)		10,638
12	M		24	Queens Park Rangers		L0-3	(0-1)		9,526
13	S		29	Torquay United	L1-2		(0-0)	Richards	8,260
14	S	Oct	6	Southend United	W3-2		(1-1)	Pembery,Richards,Gibson	7,572
15	S		13	Crystal Palace		D0-0			13,459
16	S		20	Exeter City	L3-5		(3-5)	Owen,Edwards 2	8,441
17	S		27	Southampton		L1-2	(1-1)	Edwards	16,739
18	S	Nov	3	Coventry City	D2-2		(2-1)	Gibson,Edwards	11,160
19	S		10	Norwich City		W4-2	(3-0)	Richards,Edwards 2 (1 pen.),Darcy	11,025
20	S		24	Newport County		L1-2	(0-1)	Darcy	9,570
21	S	Dec	1	Reading	W3-2		(2-2)	Edwards 2,Gibbs	10,257
22	S		15	Aldershot		D2-2	(1-1)	Edwards 2	3,044
23	S		22	Watford	W2-0		(1-0)	Edwards,Richards	6,312
24	W		26	Millwall		L1-2	(1-1)	Darcy	3,255
25	S		29	Shrewsbury Town		L3-7	(0-4)	Edwards 2,Pembery	8,229
26	S	Jan	5	Brighton and Hove Albion		L0-2	(0-2)		6,370
27	S		12	Walsall	L1-2		(1-1)	Edwards	8,948
28	S		19	Ipswich Town		L1-4	(1-2)	Richards	13,375
29	S		26	Brighton and Hove Albion	W3-0		(2-0)	Owen 2,Darcy	8,003
30	S	Feb	2	Bournemouth & Boscombe Athletic	W2-1		(2-0)	Fountain,Edwards pen.	11,388
31	S		9	Torquay United		L0-7	(0-2)		7,028
32	S		16	Southend United		L0-1	(0-1)		8,397
33	S		23	Crystal Palace	W3-1		(2-0)	Fountain,Edwards 2 (1 pen.)	6,499
34	S	Mar	2	Exeter City		L2-3	(1-2)	Richards,Edwards	5,244
35	S		9	Plymouth Argyle	L0-3		(0-2)		8,864
36	S		16	Coventry City		L0-3	(0-0)		8,819
37	S		23	Norwich City	D1-1		(0-1)	Micklewright	7,763
38	S		30	Colchester United		D1-1	(1-1)	Richards	9,275
39	S	Apr	6	Newport County	W1-0		(1-0)	Edwards	7,889
40	W		10	Millwall	W1-0		(1-0)	Owen	6,619
41	S		13	Reading		L0-1	(0-1)		5,925
42	S		20	Southampton	D0-0				10,515
43	M		22	Northampton Town	W4-0		(2-0)	O'Mahoney 2,Edwards,Micklewright	7,573
44	Tu		23	Northampton Town		L0-2	(0-1)		4,950
45	S		27	Colchester United	W4-1		(3-0)	Micklewright 2,O'Mahoney 2	9,600
46	M		29	Plymouth Argyle		L0-1	(0-0)		9,052

Average Home Attendance : **8,740**
Average Away Attendance : **9,040**

F A Cup

No.	Day	Month	Date	Opponents	Home	Away	H-T	Goalscorers	Gate
1	S	Nov	17	Coventry City		W2-1	(0-0)	Edwards,Richards	17,097
2	S	Dec	8	Bournemouth & Boscombe Athletic		L0-1	(0-0)		17,410

BERT HEAD
was a defender for Torquay for 15 years either side of the War and then, at the age of 35, joined Bury. He began his coaching career at Gigg Lane and was assistant-manager there before taking over at the County Ground in October 1956. After picking up the pieces following Town's sixteen 'managerless' months, Bert gradually gave the club a major overhaul. Implementing a youth policy that was to produce many stars of the future, the fruits of his labour brought the first ever promotion in 1963. But one by one, those assets were sold and after only two seasons Town were back in the Third. Bert was relieved of his duties and briefly went back to Bury before moving to Crystal Palace.

Agar F R	Burton S	Cameron D G B	Chandler R E J	Cross J K	Darcy A J	Dear G A	Earl S J W	Edwards R H	Fountain J	Fox G R	Gibbs A M	Gibson D J	Hogg A	Hudson G W	Hunt R G A	Jack V	Lee J	McShane A	Micklewright A A J	Miller J Mc	O'Mahoney F K	Owen M	Pembery G D	Richards J B	Riseborough C	Thompson F N	Whyte F	Williams G G	
	1							10		3	8	7		5	2			4		11			6	9					1
	1							10		3	8			5	2			4	9	11			6	7					2
	1							8		3	9			5	2			4		11			10	7				6	3
	1							8		3	9			5	2			4		11			10	7				6	4
8	1									3				5	2			4		11		9	10	7				6	5
	1			4				10			9		3	5	2				8	11		7	6						6
	1			4				10		3	8				2					11		7	6	9			5		7
	1			4				10		3	8				2					11		9	6		7		5		8
	1			4				11		3	8			5	2							9	6	10	7				9
	1			4				10		3	8			5	2					11		9	6		7				10
	1									3	8			5	2			4		11		9	6	7		10			11
10			1							3	8				2							9	6	7	11		5	4	12
10			1	4						3		8			2					11		9	6	7			5		13
			1	4				10		3		8			2					11		9	6	7			5		14
			1	4						3		8			2			10				9	6	7			5	11	15
			1	4				10		3		8			2							9	6	7			5	11	16
			1	4				10		3		7			2	5			8			9	6	11					17
			1	4	11			10		3		7			2	5			8			9	6						18
			1	4	11		3	10				7			2	5						9	6	8					19
			1	4	11		3	10				7			2	5						9	6	8					20
			1	4	11		3	10			8				2	5						9	6	7					21
			1	4	11		3	10			8				2	5						9	6		7				22
			1	4	11		3	10			8				2	5						9	6	7					23
			1	4	11	3		10			8				2	5						9	6	7					24
			1	4	11	3		10			8					5	2					9	6	7					25
			1	4	11			10				7				5	2	6				9	3	8					26
			1	2	11		3	10	4			7				5						9	6	8					27
	1			4	11		3	10	6						2	5						9	8	7					28
	1			4	11		3	10	6						2	5			9			7	8						29
	1			4	11		3	10	6						2	5			9			7	8						30
	1			4	11		3	10	6						2	5			9			7	8						31
	1			2	11		3	10	4							5			9			7	6	8					32
	1			2	11		3	10	4							5			9			7	6	8					33
	1			2	11		3	10	4							5			9			7	6	8					34
	1			2	11	5		10	4						3				9			7	6	8					35
	1	7		4	11	5	3	10	6						2							8		9					36
	1			4	11		3	10	6						2	5			9			8		7					37
	1			4	11		3	10	6					5	2				9			8		7					38
	1			4	11		3	10	6					5	2				9			8		7					39
	1			4	11		3	10	6					5	2				9			8		7					40
	1				11		3	10	6					5	2	4			9				8	7					41
	1			4	11		3	10	6					5	2				9				8	7					42
	1			4	11		3	10	6					5	2				8		9				7				43
	1			4	11		3	10	6					5	2				8		9				7				44
	1			4	11			10	6					5	2		3		8		9			7					45
	1			4	11			10	6					5	2		3		9			8		7					46
3	30	1	16	38	29	4	22	41	20	17	16	11	1	18	40	20	4	8	21	12	3	37	37	36	7	1	7	6	Apps
					4			26	2		5	2							5		4	7	2	9					Goals

Agar F R	Burton S	Cameron D G B	Chandler R E J	Cross J K	Darcy A J	Dear G A	Earl S J W	Edwards R H	Fountain J	Fox G R	Gibbs A M	Gibson D J	Hogg A	Hudson G W	Hunt R G A	Jack V	Lee J	McShane A	Micklewright A A J	Miller J Mc	O'Mahoney F K	Owen M	Pembery G D	Richards J B	Riseborough C	Thompson F N	Whyte F	Williams G G	
			1	4	11		3	10				7			2	5						9	6	8					1
			1	4	11		3	10			8				2	5						9	6	7					2
			2	2	2		2	2			1	1			2	2						2	2	2					Apps
								1																1					Goals

For Final League Table - see page 166

BOB EDWARDS

grabbed 14 goals in the last twelve games of 1956 to put him firmly on course to end the season as Town's top marksman. But a leaky defence - with only one 'clean sheet' during that time - ensured that the club had to apply for re-election for a second successive year. The six-foot striker arrived from Chelsea in July 1955 and was leading scorer again in 1958/59. He joined Norwich in December 1959 in a double transfer deal with John Richards, valued at £6,000.

SEASON 1957/58

Football League Third Division South
Final League Position : 4th
Manager : Bert Head

					Home	Away	H-T	Goalscorers	Gate
1	S	Aug	24	Newport County	W4-0		(4-0)	Edwards 2,Owen 2	14,394
2	Tu		27	Watford		D0-0			12,109
3	S		31	Port Vale		L1-3	(0-3)	Richards	16,503
4	W	Sep	4	Watford	D0-0				10,519
5	S		7	Plymouth Argyle	W1-0		(1-0)	O'Mahoney	11,305
6	W		11	Queens Park Rangers	D1-1		(0-0)	Darcy	10,630
7	S		14	Aldershot		L1-2	(1-1)	Micklewright	5,164
8	M		16	Queens Park Rangers		L1-2	(1-1)	Owen	8,413
9	S		21	Northampton Town	W5-1		(1-1)	Edwards 2,Richards 2,Skull	9,934
10	W		25	Southend United		W3-2	(2-1)	Duffy o.g.,Micklewright,Skull	8,716
11	S		28	Millwall	W3-0		(1-0)	Clayton,Richards 2	11,218
12	W	Oct	2	Southend United	W2-1		(1-1)	Richards 2	8,001
13	S		5	Gillingham		L1-2	(0-0)	Skull	8,544
14	W		9	Southampton		W3-1	(3-0)	Micklewright,Edwards 2	8,829
15	S		12	Crystal Palace		L1-4	(0-4)	Micklewright	14,953
16	S		19	Torquay United	W3-1		(2-0)	Neal pen.,Richards,Micklewright	13,079
17	S		26	Brentford		D0-0			13,676
18	S	Nov	2	Colchester United	W4-0		(2-0)	Micklewright,Edwards,Skull,Richards	14,198
19	S		9	Norwich City		D1-1	(0-0)	Richards	22,578
20	S		23	Walsall		D1-1	(1-1)	Edwards	6,549
21	S		30	Coventry City	W2-1		(1-0)	Edwards,Griffiths o.g.	12,236
22	S	Dec	7	Shrewsbury Town		W3-1	(1-1)	Roost 3	7,140
23	S		14	Reading	D1-1		(1-0)	Richards	14,418
24	S		21	Newport County		L1-4	(0-1)	Skull	7,815
25	W		25	Brighton and Hove Albion	D2-2		(0-2)	Edwards pen.,Darcy	12,269
26	Th		26	Brighton and Hove Albion		L0-1	(0-1)		21,635
27	S		28	Port Vale	D0-0				14,997
28	S	Jan	4	Exeter City	W5-1		(4-1)	Moore 2,Richards,Thompson,Micklewright	11,292
29	S		11	Plymouth Argyle		D2-2	(1-2)	Micklewright 2	16,589
30	S		18	Aldershot	W3-0		(1-0)	Darcy,Richards,Micklewright	11,612
31	S		25	Bournemouth & Boscombe Athletic	W1-0		(1-0)	Richards	12,434
32	S	Feb	1	Northampton Town		L0-3	(0-2)		9,845
33	S		8	Millwall		D1-1	(0-1)	Skull	12,514
34	S		15	Gillingham	D1-1		(1-0)	Edwards	13,128
35	S		22	Crystal Palace	D0-0				10,303
36	S	Mar	1	Torquay United		D2-2	(2-1)	Darcy,Edwards	7,266
37	S		8	Brentford	W4-1		(1-1)	Kelly 3,Skull	12,742
38	S		15	Colchester United		W3-1	(1-0)	Edwards,Richards,Kelly	9,241
39	S		22	Walsall	L2-3		(2-1)	Richards,Edwards	11,202
40	S		29	Reading		W4-0	(4-0)	Micklewright 2,Skull,Kelly	16,988
41	S	Apr	5	Norwich City	L1-2		(0-1)	McCrohan o.g.	10,132
42	M		7	Southampton	W1-0		(1-0)	Darcy	15,170
43	S		12	Coventry City		W1-0	(0-0)	Micklewright	11,986
44	S		19	Shrewsbury Town	W1-0		(1-0)	Darcy	11,728
45	W		23	Exeter City		W1-0	(1-0)	Micklewright	5,255
46	S		26	Bournemouth & Boscombe Athletic		D1-1	(0-0)	Hudson	12,930

Average Home Attendance : **12,041**
Average Away Attendance : **11,532**

F A Cup

					Home	Away	H-T	Goalscorers	Gate
1	S	Nov	16	Reading		L0-1	(0-0)		21,368

JOHN RICHARDS
graduated from Bristol University with a BA in economics and played in the English Universities representative side. He signed amateur forms for Town in November 1955, while serving with the Army Pay Corps in Devizes and made his League debut in the following April. His 16 goals in 1957/58 helped the club secure a top four finish for the first time in nine years. Ably assisted by Bob Edwards and Andy Micklewright, John took Town to within a point of finishing second and only three points behind champions Brighton. He reverted to part-time status with Aldershot in 1961.

Bingley W	Burton S	Cameron D G B	Chamberlain P M	Clayton L	Cross J K	Darcy A J	Donaldson B L	Earl S J W	Edwards R H	Fountain J	Hudson G W	Hunt R G A	Kelly J	Lee J	McDonald G	Micklewright A A J	Moore A	Neal J	O'Mahoney F K	Owen M	Richards J B	Roost W C	Skull J	Thompson F N	
	1			4		11			10	6	5			3			7	2		8		9			1
	1			4		11			10	6	5			3			7	2		8		9			2
	1		10	4		11				6	5			3				2	9	8	7				3
	1		10	4		11				6	5			3		8		2	9		7				4
	1	7	10	4		11				6	5	2				8		3	9						5
	1		10	4	6	11					5	2					7	3	9		8				6
	1			4	6	11			10		5	2				9	7	3		8					7
	1			4	6				10		5	2				9	11	3		8	7				8
	1			4		11			10		5			3	6	9		2			8		7		9
	1		11	4					10		5			3	6	9		2			8		7		10
	1		11	4					10		5			3	6	9		2			8		7		11
	1		11	4			7		10		5	2		3	6				9		8				12
	1			4		11			10		5			3	6			2		9	8		7		13
	1			4		11			10		5			3	6	9		2		8			7		14
	1			4		11			10		5			3	6	9		2		8			7		15
	1			4		11			10		5			3		9		2		6	8		7		16
	1			4		11			10		5			3		9		2		6	8		7		17
	1			4		11			10		5			3	6	9		2			8		7		18
	1			4		11			10		5			3	6	9		2			8		7		19
	1			4		11			10		5			3	6	9		2			8		7		20
	1			4		11			10		5			3				2		6	8	9	7		21
	1			4		11			10		5			3				2		6	8	9	7		22
	1			4		11			10		5			3				2		6	8	9	7		23
	1			4		11			10		5			3			8	2		6		9	7		24
	1			4		11			10		5			3				2		6	8	9	7		25
	1		6			11			10		5			3				2		4	8	9	7		26
	1		6			11		3	10		5							2		4	8	9	7		27
3	1					11			10		5					9	7	2		4	8			6	28
3	1					11			10		5					9	7	2		4	8			6	29
3	1					11			10		5					9	7	2		4	8			6	30
3	1					11			10		5					9	7	2		4	8			6	31
3	1					11			10		5					9	7	2		4	8			6	32
3	1					11			10		5					9		2		4	8		7	6	33
3	1					11			10		5					9		2		4	8		7	6	34
3	1					11			10		5					9		2		4	8		7	6	35
3	1					11			10	6	5		9					2		4	8		7		36
3	1					11			10	6	5		9					2		4	8		7		37
3	1					11			10	6	5		9					2		4	8		7		38
3	1					11			10	6	5		9					2		4	8		7		39
3	1					11			10	6	5		9			8		2		4			7		40
3	1					11			10	6	5		9			8		2		4			7		41
3	1			4		11			10	6	5		9			8		2			7				42
3	1			4		11			10	6	5		9			8		2			7				43
3	1			4		11			10		5		9			8		2		6	7				44
3	1			4		11			10		5		9			8		2		6		7			45
3	1			4		11			10	6	5		9			8		2				7			46
19	46	1	9	30	3	42	1	1	42	14	46	5	11	22	10	29	11	45	5	33	35	11	27	8	Apps
				1		6			14		1		5			14	2	1	1	3	16	3	8	1	Goals

Opponents 3 goals

Bingley W	Burton S	Cameron D G B	Chamberlain P M	Clayton L	Cross J K	Darcy A J	Donaldson B L	Earl S J W	Edwards R H	Fountain J	Hudson G W	Hunt R G A	Kelly J	Lee J	McDonald G	Micklewright A A J	Moore A	Neal J	O'Mahoney F K	Owen M	Richards J B	Roost W C	Skull J	Thompson F N	
	1			4		11			10		5			3	6	9		2			8		7		1

For Final League Table - see page 166

SEASON 1946/47

Div.3S		P	W	D	L	F	A	W	D	L	F	A	Pts	G/A	Avge. Home Gate
1	Cardiff City	42	18	3	0	60	11	12	3	6	33	19	66	3.10	28,604
2	Queens Park Rangers	42	15	2	4	42	15	8	9	4	32	25	57	1.85	16,519
3	Bristol City	42	13	4	4	56	20	7	7	7	38	36	51	1.68	18,849
4	SWINDON TOWN	42	15	4	2	56	25	4	7	10	28	48	49	1.15	16,012
5	Walsall	42	11	6	4	42	25	6	6	9	32	34	46	1.25	11,173
6	Ipswich Town	42	11	5	5	33	21	5	9	7	28	32	46	1.15	13,114
7	Bournemouth & Boscombe Athletic	42	12	4	5	43	20	6	4	11	29	34	44	1.33	10,440
8	Southend United	42	9	7	5	38	22	8	3	10	33	38	44	1.18	9,690
9	Reading	42	11	6	4	53	30	5	5	11	30	44	43	1.12	12,032
10	Port Vale	42	14	4	3	51	28	3	5	13	17	35	43	1.08	10,582
11	Torquay United	42	11	5	5	33	23	4	7	10	19	38	42	0.85	6,286
12	Notts County	42	11	4	6	35	19	4	6	11	28	44	40	1.00	15,376
13	Northampton Town	42	11	5	5	46	33	4	5	12	26	42	40	0.96	7,951
14	Bristol Rovers	42	9	6	6	34	26	7	2	12	25	43	40	0.86	12,527
15	Exeter City	42	11	6	4	37	27	4	3	14	23	42	39	0.87	8,888
16	Watford	42	11	4	6	39	27	6	1	14	22	49	39	0.80	8,343
17	Brighton & Hove Albion	42	8	7	6	31	35	5	5	11	23	37	38	0.75	8,227
18	Crystal Palace	42	9	7	5	29	19	4	4	13	20	43	37	0.79	14,082
19	Leyton Orient	42	10	5	6	40	28	2	3	16	14	47	32	0.72	10,048
20	Aldershot	42	6	7	8	25	26	4	5	12	23	52	32	0.62	4,677
21	Norwich City	42	6	3	12	38	48	4	5	12	26	52	28	0.64	17,138
22	Mansfield Town	42	8	5	8	31	38	1	5	15	17	58	28	0.50	7,029

SEASON 1947/48

Div.3S		P	W	D	L	F	A	W	D	L	F	A	Pts	G/A	Avge. Home Gate
1	Queens Park Rangers	42	16	3	2	44	17	10	6	5	30	20	61	2.00	22,273
2	Bournemouth & Boscombe Athletic	42	13	5	3	42	13	11	4	6	34	22	57	2.17	16,854
3	Walsall	42	13	5	3	37	12	8	4	9	33	28	51	1.75	15,711
4	Ipswich Town	42	16	1	4	42	18	7	2	12	25	43	49	1.10	13,234
5	Swansea Town	42	14	6	1	48	14	4	6	11	22	38	48	1.35	17,858
6	Notts County	42	12	4	5	44	27	7	4	10	24	32	46	1.15	25,380
7	Bristol City	42	11	4	6	47	26	7	3	11	30	39	43	1.18	20,951
8	Port Vale	42	14	4	3	48	18	2	7	12	15	36	43	1.17	13,569
9	Southend United	42	11	8	2	32	16	4	5	12	19	42	43	0.88	10,129
10	Reading	42	10	5	6	37	28	5	6	10	19	30	41	0.97	13,610
11	Exeter City	42	11	6	4	34	22	4	5	12	21	41	41	0.87	9,900
12	Newport County	42	9	8	4	38	28	5	5	11	23	45	41	0.84	11,240
13	Crystal Palace	42	12	5	4	32	14	1	8	12	17	35	39	1.00	14,937
14	Northampton Town	42	10	5	6	35	28	4	6	11	23	44	39	0.81	8,571
15	Watford	42	6	6	9	31	37	8	4	9	26	42	38	0.72	11,506
16	SWINDON TOWN	42	6	10	5	21	20	4	6	11	20	26	36	0.89	15,829
17	Leyton Orient	42	8	5	8	31	32	5	5	11	20	41	36	0.70	13,345
18	Torquay United	42	7	6	8	40	29	4	7	10	23	33	35	1.02	7,186
19	Aldershot	42	5	10	6	22	26	5	5	11	23	41	35	0.67	6,729
20	Bristol Rovers	42	7	3	11	39	34	6	5	10	32	41	34	0.95	15,036
21	Norwich City	42	8	3	10	33	34	5	5	11	28	42	34	0.80	21,444
22	Brighton & Hove Albion	42	8	4	9	26	31	3	8	10	17	42	34	0.59	11,486

SEASON 1948/49

Div.3S		P	W	D	L	F	A	W	D	L	F	A	Pts	G/A	Avge. Home Gate
1	Swansea Town	42	20	1	0	60	11	7	7	7	27	23	62	2.56	22,535
2	Reading	42	17	1	3	48	18	8	4	9	29	32	55	1.54	15,588
3	Bournemouth & Boscombe Athletic	42	15	2	4	42	17	7	6	8	27	31	52	1.44	15,975
4	SWINDON TOWN	42	11	9	1	38	20	7	6	8	26	36	51	1.14	16,633
5	Bristol Rovers	42	13	5	3	42	23	6	5	10	19	28	48	1.20	17,539
6	Brighton & Hove Albion	42	11	5	5	32	26	4	13	4	23	29	48	1.00	17,729
7	Ipswich Town	42	14	3	4	53	30	4	6	11	25	47	45	1.01	13,399
8	Millwall	42	12	7	2	42	23	5	4	12	21	41	45	0.98	24,629
9	Torquay United	42	12	5	4	45	26	5	6	10	20	44	45	0.93	7,939
10	Norwich City	42	11	6	4	32	10	5	6	10	35	39	44	1.37	24,325
11	Notts County	42	15	3	3	68	19	4	2	15	34	49	43	1.50	30,002
12	Exeter City	42	12	5	4	45	26	3	5	13	18	50	40	0.83	10,143
13	Port Vale	42	11	3	7	32	21	3	8	10	19	33	39	0.94	12,069
14	Walsall	42	9	5	7	34	28	6	3	12	22	36	38	0.88	10,772
15	Newport County	42	8	6	7	41	35	6	3	12	27	57	37	0.74	11,878
16	Bristol City	42	8	9	4	28	24	3	5	13	16	38	36	0.71	16,523
17	Watford	42	6	9	6	24	21	4	6	11	17	33	35	0.76	11,161
18	Southend United	42	5	10	6	18	18	4	6	11	23	28	34	0.89	10,500
19	Leyton Orient	42	9	6	6	36	29	2	6	13	22	51	34	0.73	12,444
20	Northampton Town	42	9	6	6	33	20	3	3	15	18	42	33	0.82	9,211
21	Aldershot	42	6	5	10	26	29	5	6	10	22	30	33	0.81	7,351
22	Crystal Palace	42	7	8	6	27	27	1	3	17	11	49	27	0.50	14,870

SEASON 1949/50

Div.3S

		P	W	D	L	F - A		W	D	L	F - A		Pts	G/A	Avge. Home Gate
1	Notts County	42	17	3	1	60	12	8	5	8	35	38	58	1.90	35,176
2	Northampton Town	42	12	6	3	43	21	8	5	8	29	29	51	1.44	12,791
3	Southend United	42	15	4	2	43	15	4	9	8	23	33	51	1.38	12,089
4	Nottingham Forest	42	13	0	8	37	15	7	9	5	30	24	49	1.72	22,148
5	Torquay United	42	13	6	2	40	23	6	4	11	26	40	48	1.05	8,779
6	Watford	42	10	6	5	26	13	6	7	8	19	22	45	1.29	12,161
7	Crystal Palace	42	12	5	4	35	21	3	9	9	20	33	44	1.02	16,874
8	Brighton & Hove Albion	42	9	8	4	32	24	7	4	10	25	45	44	0.83	14,120
9	Bristol Rovers	42	12	5	4	34	18	7	0	14	17	33	43	1.00	16,105
10	Reading	42	15	2	4	48	21	2	6	13	22	43	42	1.09	15,427
11	Norwich City	42	11	5	5	44	21	5	5	11	21	42	42	1.03	23,264
12	Bournemouth & Boscombe Athletic	42	11	6	4	38	19	5	4	12	19	37	42	1.02	14,559
13	Port Vale	42	12	6	3	33	13	3	5	13	14	29	41	1.12	12,983
14	SWINDON TOWN	42	9	7	5	41	30	6	4	11	18	32	41	0.95	14,074
15	Bristol City	42	12	4	5	38	19	3	6	12	22	42	40	0.98	21,449
16	Exeter City	42	9	8	4	37	27	5	3	13	26	48	39	0.84	10,117
17	Ipswich Town	42	9	6	6	36	36	3	5	13	21	50	35	0.66	13,320
18	Leyton Orient	42	10	6	5	33	30	2	5	14	20	55	35	0.62	12,585
19	Walsall	42	8	8	5	37	25	1	8	12	24	37	34	0.98	10,099
20	Aldershot	42	10	5	6	30	16	3	3	15	18	44	34	0.80	7,098
21	Newport County	42	11	5	5	50	34	2	3	16	17	64	34	0.68	11,535
22	Millwall	42	11	1	9	39	29	3	3	15	16	34	32	0.87	20,753

SEASON 1950/51

Div.3S

		P	W	D	L	F - A		W	D	L	F - A		Pts	G/A	Avge. Home Gate
1	Nottingham Forest	46	16	6	1	57	17	14	4	5	53	23	70	2.75	22,636
2	Norwich City	46	16	6	1	42	14	9	8	6	40	31	64	1.82	24,503
3	Reading	46	15	6	2	57	17	6	9	8	31	36	57	1.66	15,973
4	Plymouth Argyle	46	16	5	2	54	19	8	4	11	31	36	57	1.55	16,542
5	Millwall	46	15	6	2	52	23	8	4	11	28	34	56	1.40	20,161
6	Bristol Rovers	46	15	7	1	46	18	5	8	10	18	24	55	1.52	17,763
7	Southend United	46	15	4	4	64	27	6	6	11	28	42	52	1.33	10,362
8	Ipswich Town	46	15	4	4	48	24	8	2	13	21	34	52	1.19	13,130
9	Bournemouth & Boscombe Athletic	46	17	5	1	49	16	5	2	16	16	41	51	1.14	12,730
10	Bristol City	46	15	4	4	41	25	5	7	11	23	34	51	1.08	18,457
11	Newport County	46	13	4	6	48	25	6	5	12	29	45	47	1.10	11,506
12	Port Vale	46	13	6	4	35	24	3	7	13	25	41	45	0.92	10,832
13	Brighton & Hove Albion	46	11	8	4	51	31	2	9	12	20	48	43	0.90	11,163
14	Exeter City	46	11	4	8	33	30	7	2	14	29	55	42	0.73	9,771
15	Walsall	46	12	4	7	32	20	3	6	14	20	42	40	0.84	8,788
16	Colchester United	46	12	5	6	43	25	2	7	14	20	51	40	0.83	10,573
17	SWINDON TOWN	46	15	4	4	38	17	3	0	20	17	50	40	0.82	10,712
18	Aldershot	46	11	8	4	37	20	4	2	17	19	68	40	0.64	7,349
19	Leyton Orient	46	13	2	8	36	28	2	6	15	17	47	38	0.71	11,194
20	Torquay United	46	13	2	8	47	39	1	7	15	17	42	37	0.79	7,805
21	Northampton Town	46	8	9	6	39	30	2	7	14	16	37	36	0.82	10,308
22	Gillingham	46	10	7	6	41	30	3	2	18	28	71	35	0.68	12,256
23	Watford	46	8	5	10	29	28	1	6	16	25	60	29	0.61	9,615
24	Crystal Palace	46	6	5	12	18	39	2	6	15	15	45	27	0.39	13,828

SEASON 1951/52

Div.3S

		P	W	D	L	F - A		W	D	L	F - A		Pts	G/A	Avge. Home Gate
1	Plymouth Argyle	46	19	3	1	70	19	10	5	8	37	34	66	2.02	19,236
2	Reading	46	19	2	2	73	23	10	1	12	39	37	61	1.87	15,455
3	Norwich City	46	18	1	4	55	15	8	8	7	34	35	61	1.78	21,835
4	Millwall	46	16	5	2	46	21	7	7	9	28	32	58	1.40	19,375
5	Brighton & Hove Albion	46	15	4	4	57	24	9	6	8	30	39	58	1.38	17,831
6	Newport County	46	13	7	3	45	26	8	5	10	32	50	54	1.01	9,912
7	Bristol Rovers	46	14	5	4	60	20	6	7	10	29	33	52	1.68	17,369
8	Northampton Town	46	17	1	5	65	31	5	4	14	28	43	49	1.26	11,767
9	Southend United	46	16	6	1	56	17	3	4	16	19	49	48	1.14	8,963
10	Colchester United	46	12	7	4	32	22	5	5	13	24	55	46	0.73	9,414
11	Torquay United	46	10	3	10	53	42	7	7	9	33	56	44	0.878	7,565
12	Aldershot	46	11	4	8	40	27	7	4	12	38	62	44	0.876	7,493
13	Port Vale	46	11	11	1	33	16	3	4	16	17	50	43	0.76	11,272
14	Bournemouth & Boscombe Athletic	46	11	4	8	42	30	5	6	12	27	45	42	0.92	10,872
15	Bristol City	46	13	6	4	44	26	2	6	15	14	43	42	0.84	17,780
16	SWINDON TOWN	46	9	9	5	29	22	5	5	13	22	46	42	0.75	10,564
17	Ipswich Town	46	12	4	7	45	31	4	5	14	18	43	41	0.85	11,377
18	Leyton Orient	46	12	5	6	39	26	4	4	15	16	42	41	0.81	11,487
19	Crystal Palace	46	9	7	7	32	28	6	2	15	29	52	39	0.76	14,873
20	Shrewsbury Town	46	11	3	9	35	29	2	7	14	27	57	36	0.72	9,799
21	Watford	46	7	7	9	34	37	6	3	14	23	44	36	0.70	9,609
22	Gillingham	46	10	7	6	47	31	1	6	16	24	50	35	0.88	12,576
23	Exeter City	46	10	4	9	40	36	3	5	15	25	50	35	0.76	8,321
24	Walsall	46	11	3	9	38	31	2	2	19	17	63	31	0.59	7,084

SEASON 1952/53

Div.3S		P	W	D	L	F	A	W	D	L	F	A	Pts	G/A	Avge. Home Gate
1	Bristol Rovers	46	17	4	2	55	19	9	8	6	37	27	64	2.00	23,411
2	Millwall	46	14	7	2	46	16	10	7	6	36	28	62	1.86	19,289
3	Northampton Town	46	18	4	1	75	30	8	6	9	34	40	62	1.56	12,484
4	Norwich City	46	16	6	1	56	17	9	4	10	43	38	60	1.80	21,121
5	Bristol City	46	13	8	2	62	28	9	7	7	33	33	59	1.56	18,763
6	Coventry City	46	15	5	3	52	22	4	7	12	25	40	50	1.24	13,430
7	Brighton & Hove Albion	46	12	6	5	48	30	7	6	10	33	45	50	1.08	16,161
8	Southend United	46	15	5	3	41	21	3	8	12	28	53	49	0.93	8,697
9	Bournemouth & Boscombe Athletic	46	15	3	5	49	23	4	6	13	25	46	47	1.07	10,768
10	Watford	46	12	8	3	39	21	3	9	11	23	42	47	0.98	13,957
11	Reading	46	17	3	3	53	18	2	5	16	16	46	46	1.08	12,401
12	Torquay United	46	15	4	4	61	28	3	5	15	26	60	45	0.99	6,980
13	Crystal Palace	46	12	7	4	40	26	3	6	14	26	56	43	0.80	12,415
14	Leyton Orient	46	12	7	4	52	28	4	3	16	16	45	42	0.93	10,562
15	Newport County	46	12	4	7	43	34	4	6	13	27	48	42	0.85	8,868
16	Ipswich Town	46	10	7	6	34	28	3	8	12	26	41	41	0.87	9,434
17	Exeter City	46	11	8	4	40	24	2	6	15	21	47	40	0.86	10,339
18	SWINDON TOWN	46	9	5	9	38	33	5	7	11	26	46	40	0.81	9,311
19	Aldershot	46	8	8	7	36	29	4	7	12	25	48	39	0.79	6,553
20	Queens Park Rangers	46	9	9	5	37	34	3	6	14	24	48	39	0.744	12,190
21	Gillingham	46	10	7	6	30	26	2	8	13	25	48	39	0.743	11,558
22	Colchester United	46	9	9	5	40	29	3	5	15	19	47	38	0.78	8,046
23	Shrewsbury Town	46	11	5	7	38	35	1	7	15	30	56	36	0.75	8,540
24	Walsall	46	5	9	9	35	46	2	1	20	21	72	24	0.47	5,991

SEASON 1953/54

Div.3S		P	W	D	L	F	A	W	D	L	F	A	Pts	G/A	Avge. Home Gate
1	Ipswich Town	46	15	5	3	47	19	12	5	6	35	32	64	1.61	15,917
2	Brighton & Hove Albion	46	17	3	3	57	31	9	6	8	29	30	61	1.41	18,880
3	Bristol City	46	18	3	2	59	18	7	3	13	29	48	56	1.33	17,596
4	Watford	46	16	3	4	52	23	5	7	11	33	46	52	1.23	11,856
5	Northampton Town	46	18	4	1	63	18	2	7	14	19	37	51	1.49	10,289
6	Southampton	46	17	5	1	51	22	5	2	16	25	41	51	1.21	14,885
7	Norwich City	46	13	5	5	43	28	7	6	10	30	38	51	1.11	18,580
8	Reading	46	14	3	6	57	33	6	6	11	29	40	49	1.18	11,566
9	Exeter City	46	12	2	9	39	22	8	6	9	29	36	48	1.17	9,344
10	Gillingham	46	14	3	6	37	22	5	7	11	24	44	48	0.92	10,333
11	Leyton Orient	46	14	5	4	48	26	4	6	13	31	47	47	1.08	11,218
12	Millwall	46	15	3	5	44	24	4	6	13	30	53	47	0.96	13,502
13	Torquay United	46	10	10	3	48	33	7	2	14	33	55	46	0.92	7,111
14	Coventry City	46	14	5	4	36	15	4	4	15	25	41	45	1.09	10,505
15	Newport County	46	14	4	5	42	28	5	2	16	19	53	44	0.75	8,922
16	Southend United	46	15	2	6	46	22	3	5	15	23	49	43	0.97	7,372
17	Aldershot	46	11	5	7	45	31	6	4	13	29	55	43	0.86	6,645
18	Queens Park Rangers	46	10	5	8	32	25	6	5	12	28	43	42	0.88	10,983
= 19	Bournemouth & Boscombe Athletic	46	12	5	6	47	27	4	3	16	20	43	40	0.96	9,727
= 19	SWINDON TOWN	46	13	5	5	48	21	2	5	16	19	49	40	0.96	10,753
21	Shrewsbury Town	46	12	8	3	48	34	2	4	17	17	42	40	0.86	9,188
22	Crystal Palace	46	11	7	5	41	30	3	5	15	19	56	40	0.70	12,296
23	Colchester United	46	7	7	9	35	29	3	3	17	15	49	30	0.64	7,712
24	Walsall	46	8	5	10	22	27	1	3	19	18	60	26	0.46	9,279

SEASON 1954/55

Div.3S		P	W	D	L	F	A	W	D	L	F	A	Pts	G/A	Avge. Home Gate
1	Bristol City	46	17	4	2	62	22	13	6	4	39	25	70	2.15	22,219
2	Leyton Orient	46	16	2	5	48	20	10	7	6	41	27	61	1.89	15,216
3	Southampton	46	16	6	1	49	19	8	5	10	26	32	59	1.47	14,724
4	Gillingham	46	12	8	3	41	28	8	7	8	36	38	55	1.17	10,385
5	Millwall	46	14	6	3	44	25	6	5	12	28	43	51	1.06	13,724
6	Brighton & Hove Albion	46	14	4	5	47	27	6	6	11	29	36	50	1.21	12,835
7	Watford	46	11	9	3	45	26	7	5	11	26	36	50	1.15	10,798
8	Torquay United	46	12	6	5	51	39	6	6	11	31	43	48	1.00	6,604
9	Coventry City	46	15	5	3	50	26	3	6	14	17	33	47	1.14	14,202
10	Southend United	46	13	5	5	48	28	4	7	12	35	52	46	1.04	7,815
= 11	Brentford	46	11	6	6	44	36	5	8	10	38	46	46	1.00	11,077
= 11	Norwich City	46	13	5	5	40	23	5	5	13	20	37	46	1.00	15,621
13	Northampton Town	46	13	5	5	47	27	6	3	14	26	54	46	0.90	7,852
14	Aldershot	46	12	6	5	44	23	4	7	12	31	48	45	1.06	6,123
15	Queens Park Rangers	46	13	7	3	46	25	2	7	14	23	50	44	0.92	11,283
16	Shrewsbury Town	46	14	5	4	49	24	2	5	16	21	54	42	0.90	7,796
17	Bournemouth & Boscombe Athletic	46	7	8	8	32	29	5	10	8	25	36	42	0.88	9,810
18	Reading	46	7	10	6	32	26	6	5	12	33	47	41	0.89	8,799
19	Newport County	46	8	8	7	32	29	3	8	12	28	44	38	0.82	8,374
20	Crystal Palace	46	9	11	3	32	24	2	5	16	20	56	38	0.65	10,731
21	SWINDON TOWN	46	10	8	5	30	19	1	7	15	16	45	37	0.72	8,164
22	Exeter City	46	9	7	7	30	31	2	8	13	17	42	37	0.64	8,045
23	Walsall	46	9	6	8	49	36	1	8	14	26	50	34	0.87	11,201
24	Colchester United	46	7	6	10	33	40	2	7	14	20	51	31	0.58	7,400

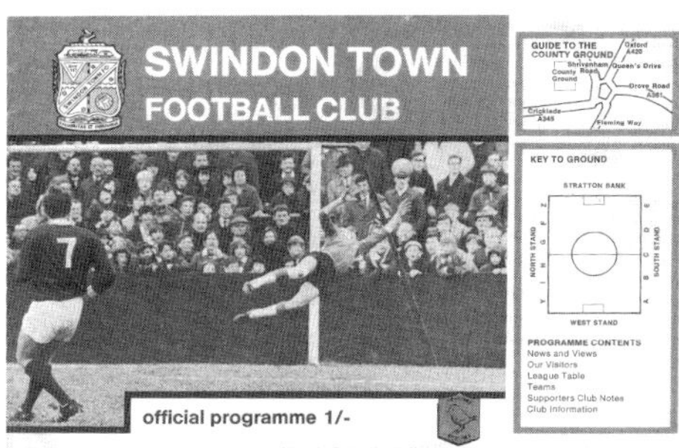

Left and right : Programme covers from the promotion seasons of 1962/63 and 1968/69 Centre : for 1963 to 1965

bert's babes to danny's dynamos

1958 - 1969

The birth of a new national Third Division also saw a resurgent Town finally come out of the re-election doldrums. Bert Head began to lay a solid foundation for the future and by the end of 1960/61 there were no less than nine teenagers in the first team squad. Two seasons later, promotion came for the first time in the club's history.

But, following the sale of many of those young stars, Town found themselves back in the third tier after just two seasons and it was left to a genial Yorkshireman - Danny Williams - to inject new life into the club. With some astute purchases he built a team that, just four years later, not only repeated the feat of promotion but produced one of the outstanding performances of the decade - the lifting of the Football League Cup at Wembley.

*The term **BERTS BABES** was first used in Volume 3 'To Wembley and Beyond' back in 1985*

Left to right : The former Aldershot Tattoo Stand being built on the Shrivenham Road in 1958 : Young meets not so young - Maurice Owen (38) and Terry Wollen (19) : Mike Summerbee - future England star : Stan Harland with the League Cup at Wembley

SEASON 1958/59

Football League Third Division
Final League Position : 15th
Manager : Bert Head

No	Day	Month	Date	Opponent	Home	Away	H-T	Goalscorers	Gate
1	S	Aug	23	Wrexham	W1-0		(0-0)	Darcy 60	15,299
2	W		27	Hull City	W2-0		(0-0)	Micklewright 70,Edwards 78	14,355
3	S		30	Southampton		D1-1	(1-1)	Edwards 30	19,988
4	M	Sep	1	Hull City		D0-0			12,035
5	S		6	Accrington Stanley	L1-2		(0-1)	Darcy 69	13,880
6	W		10	Rochdale		D1-1	(1-1)	Darcy 10	6,617
7	S		13	Halifax Town		L0-1	(0-0)		7,998
8	W		17	Rochdale	W2-1		(0-0)	Chamberlain 87,Moore 90	9,555
9	S		20	Newport County	W2-1		(2-0)	Neal 25,Kelly 40	12,522
10	W		24	Bradford City	D2-2		(0-1)	Clayton 87,Jackson 90	9,488
11	S		27	Chesterfield		W3-1	(3-1)	Kelly 18,33,34	10,535
12	W	Oct	1	Bradford City		W2-1	(1-1)	Kelly 1,58	8,279
13	S		4	Notts County	W3-1		(2-0)	Edwards 9,46,Micklewright 44	13,478
14	S		11	Plymouth Argyle		L2-3	(1-2)	Micklewright 25,Edwards 69	26,051
15	S		18	Tranmere Rovers	L1-2		(0-0)	Micklewright 72	13,765
16	S		25	Stockport County		L0-2	(0-1)		10,544
17	S	Nov	1	Reading	W2-0		(1-0)	Kelly 25,Corbett 87	19,837
18	S		8	Colchester United		L0-1	(0-1)		8,001
19	S		22	Bury		D0-0			8,056
20	S		29	Southend United	W2-1		(0-0)	Kelly 50,Hudson 88 pen.	10,141
21	S	Dec	13	Queens Park Rangers	W2-0		(1-0)	Owen 22,Kelly 50	8,039
22	S		20	Wrexham		L0-1	(0-0)		8,010
23	Th		25	Brentford		D2-2	(1-2)	Edwards 18,56	12,504
24	F		26	Brentford	D1-1		(0-0)	Micklewright 57	12,692
25	S	Jan	3	Southampton	W3-1		(2-1)	Micklewright 20,36,Chamberlain 56	12,070
26	S		10	Bournemouth & Boscombe Athletic	L0-1		(0-1)		10,780
27	S		31	Halifax Town	L0-2		(0-2)		9,568
28	S	Feb	7	Newport County		L0-3	(0-2)		4,346
29	S		14	Chesterfield	L1-2		(0-1)	Owen 70	8,451
30	W		18	Accrington Stanley		D0-0			5,564
31	S		21	Notts County		L0-1	(0-0)		10,575
32	S		28	Plymouth Argyle	L3-4		(1-3)	Marshall 27,88,Anderson o.g.75	13,090
33	S	Mar	7	Tranmere Rovers		L1-3	(1-2)	Skull 41	8,330
34	S		14	Stockport County	W3-0		(0-0)	Richards 47,80,Marshall 63	8,558
35	S		21	Reading		L1-3	(1-2)	Skull 20	10,950
36	F		27	Doncaster Rovers		L0-2	(0-2)		6,435
37	S		28	Colchester United	W2-0		(0-0)	Marshall 70,Darcy 88	8,876
38	M		30	Doncaster Rovers	D0-0				9,504
39	S	Apr	4	Bournemouth & Boscombe Athletic		D3-3	(2-2)	Edwards 23,41,Woollard o.g.46	9,546
40	W		8	Norwich City		D1-1	(0-0)	Marshall 65	29,146
41	S		11	Bury	D0-0				8,602
42	M		13	Mansfield Town		D0-0			5,719
43	S		18	Southend United		W2-0	(1-0)	Richards 30,70	7,353
44	W		22	Mansfield Town	W2-1		(1-1)	Marshall 35,Stephens 69	7,305
45	S		25	Norwich City	W4-3		(2-1)	Butler o.g.10,Darcy 25,Marshall 63,Richards 85	11,225
46	M		27	Queens Park Rangers		L1-2	(1-1)	Micklewright 12	7,628

Average Home Attendance : **11,351**
Average Away Attendance : **10,618**

F A Cup

No	Day	Month	Date	Opponent	Home	Away	H-T	Goalscorers	Gate
1	S	Nov	15	Aldershot	W5-0		(2-0)	Edwards 2,Darcy 3,51,60,Kelly 88	12,316
2	S	Dec	6	Norwich City	D1-1		(1-1)	Richards 20	14,755
2R	Th		11	Norwich City		L0-1	(0-0)		12,235

JIMMY KELLY
assisted Midland League Peterborough in their quest for Football League status, before being signed by Preston in 1955. Jimmy came to the County Ground at the end of February 1958 - for an initial fee of £1,300 - and his five goals in 11 games, including a hat-trick on his home debut, helped Town secure a fourth place finish. Although moving on to Walsall in the first week of February 1959, Jimmy still finished the season as joint top scorer with Bob Edwards.

Bingley W	Burton S	Chamberlain P M	Chandler R E J	Clayton L	Corbett D F	Darcy A J	Edwards R H	Fountain J	Hudson G W	Jack V	Jackson C	Kelly J	Lee J	Marshall W F	Micklewright A A J	Middleton R R	Moore A	Morgan K	Moyse A R	Neal J	Owen M	Richards J B	Roost W C	Sampson R V	Skull J	Stephens W J	Tilley H R	Woodruff R W	
3	1					11	10		5			9			8					2	6					7	4		1
3	1					11	10		5						8		7		9	2	6						4		2
3	1					11	10		5						8		7		9	2	6						4		3
3	1					11	10		5						8		7		9	2	6						4		4
3	1					11	10		5						8		7		9	2	6						4		5
3			1	4		11	10		5						8		7			2	6		9						6
3			1	4		11	10		5						8		7			2	6		9						7
3	1	10		4	7				5			9					11			2	6		8						8
3	1	10		4	7				5			9					11			2	6		8						9
3	1	10		4	7				5		11	9								2	6		8						10
3	1	11			7		10			5		9			8			4		2	6								11
3	1	11			7		10			5		9			8			4		2	6								12
3	1	11			7		10			5		9			8			4		2	6								13
3	1	11			7		10			5		9			8			4		2	6								14
3	1	11			7		10			5		9			8			4		2	6								15
3	1	11			7		10			5		9			8			4		2	6								16
3	1				7	11	10		5			9			8			4		2	6								17
3	1				7	11	10		5			9			8			4		2	6								18
3	1	8			7	11	10		5			9						4		2	6								19
3	1				7	11	10		5			9						4		2	6	8							20
	1				7	11	10	4	5			9	3		8					2	6								21
	1				7	11	10	4	5			9	3		8					2	6								22
	1				7	11	10	4	5			9	3		8					2	6								23
	1				7	11		4	5			9	3		8					2	6			10					24
	1	11			7			4	5				3		10	9				2	6	8							25
	1	11			7			4	5				3		10	9				2	6	8							26
	1				7			4	5		11	9	3		10	8				2	6								27
	1				7	11	10	4	5				3		9	8				2	6								28
	1				7	11	10	4	5				3			8				2	6							9	29
3			1		7	11	10	4	5						8					2	6		9						30
3			1		7	11	10	4	5						8					2	6		9						31
3			1		7	11	10	4	5					9	8					2	6								32
3			1			11	10	4	5					9	8					2	6				7				33
3			1			11		4	5					9	10					2	6	8			7				34
3			1			11		4	5					9	10					2	6	8			7				35
3		5	1			11		4						9						2	6	8			7			10	36
3		5	1			11	10	4						9						2		8			7		6		37
3		5	1			11	10	4						9						2		8			7		6		38
3		5	1			11	10	4						9						2		8				7	6		39
3			1			11	10	4	5					9						2		8				7	6		40
3			1			11	10	4	5					9						2		8				7	6		41
3			1			11	10	4	5					9	8					2						7	6		42
3			1			11	10	4	5					9						2		8				7	6		43
3			1			11		4	5					9	10					2		8				7	6		44
3			1			11		4	5					9	10					2		8				7	6		45
3			1			11		4	5						10					2		8				7	6	9	46
37	27	16	19	5	25	34	33	26	36	6	2	19	9	14	33	5	8	10	4	46	36	15	7	1	6	9	15	3	Apps
		2		1	1	5	9		1		1	9		7	8		1			1	2	5			2	1			Goals

Opponents 3 goals

Bingley W	Burton S	Chamberlain P M	Chandler R E J	Clayton L	Corbett D F	Darcy A J	Edwards R H	Fountain J	Hudson G W	Jack V	Jackson C	Kelly J	Lee J	Marshall W F	Micklewright A A J	Middleton R R	Moore A	Morgan K	Moyse A R	Neal J	Owen M	Richards J B	Roost W C	Sampson R V	Skull J	Stephens W J	Tilley H R	Woodruff R W	
3	1				7	11	10		5			9			8			4		2	6								1
3	1				7	11	10		5			9						4		2	6	8							2
	1				7	11	10	6	5				3					4		2	9	8							2R
2	3				3	3	3	1	3			2	1		1			3		3	3	2							Apps
						3	1					1										1							Goals

For Final League Table - see page 167

SEASON 1959/60

Football League Third Division
Final League Position : 16th
Manager : Bert Head

					Home	Away	H-T	Goalscorers	Gate
1	S	Aug	22	Queens Park Rangers		L0-2	(0-1)		12,206
2	W		26	Barnsley	D1-1		(0-1)	Stephens 75	14,144
3	S		29	Bradford City	W5-3		(1-0)	Richards 38,47,60,Gauld 46,78	12,268
4	W	Sep	2	Barnsley		W3-0	(1-0)	Richards 43,Morgan 80,Layne 83	7,088
5	S		5	Coventry City		L1-3	(1-0)	Layne 40 pen.	16,366
6	W		9	Grimsby Town	W3-2		(2-2)	Layne 6,16 pen.,Woodruff 89	12,678
7	S		12	York City	D1-1		(0-0)	Layne 54	12,908
8	Tu		15	Grimsby Town		L0-3	(0-1)		11,840
9	S		19	Bury	W1-0		(1-0)	Edwards 31	11,241
10	W		23	Wrexham	W4-1		(3-0)	Richards 5,Gauld 16,Hoskins 31,Darcy 78	10,233
11	S		26	Chesterfield		W3-1	(1-0)	Darcy 2,Edwards 52,Hoskins 87	7,376
12	W		30	Wrexham		W2-1	(1-0)	Gauld 1,Edwards 72	15,911
13	S	Oct	3	Newport County	W1-0		(1-0)	Layne 39 pen.	14,493
14	W		7	Accrington Stanley	L0-1		(0-0)		7,884
15	S		10	Southampton		L1-5	(0-2)	Gauld 81	15,467
16	M		12	Accrington Stanley		L1-3	(0-2)	Gauld 85	2,343
17	S		17	Reading	L0-4		(0-1)		14,706
18	S		24	Shrewsbury Town		L0-3	(0-1)		8,552
19	S		31	Halifax Town	D1-1		(0-0)	Edwards 49	11,312
20	S	Nov	7	Norwich City		L2-3	(1-2)	Woodruff 43,Richards 62	22,494
21	S		21	Colchester United		D0-0			6,537
22	S		28	Southend United	W2-0		(0-0)	Edwards 53,Hoskins 57	8,822
23	S	Dec	12	Port Vale	L2-3		(1-2)	Layne 15,Marshall 59	7,716
24	S		19	Queens Park Rangers	W2-1		(2-0)	Layne 11,37	5,789
25	S		26	Bournemouth & Boscombe Athletic		L1-3	(0-1)	Gauld 69	10,969
26	M		28	Bournemouth & Boscombe Athletic	W2-0		(0-0)	Marshall 72,Darcy 79	10,335
27	S	Jan	2	Bradford City		L0-1	(0-0)		10,516
28	S		9	Brentford	D0-0				8,633
29	S		23	York City		L0-1	(0-0)		6,031
30	S	Feb	6	Bury		W3-0	(2-0)	Layne 31,47,Marshall 32	9,072
31	S		13	Chesterfield	D1-1		(1-0)	Layne 1	5,929
32	S		20	Newport County		W3-1	(1-0)	Marshall 27,78,Gauld 86	4,974
33	S		27	Southampton	L0-3		(0-1)		16,645
34	S	Mar	5	Reading		L0-3	(0-0)		11,690
35	S		12	Shrewsbury Town	W4-2		(1-2)	Layne 15,47,61,Hunt 59	7,595
36	S		19	Southend United		W3-1	(1-1)	Layne 18,50,79	8,451
37	S		26	Norwich City	L0-1		(0-1)		9,784
38	M		28	Mansfield Town		W2-1	(0-0)	Layne 55,76	6,407
39	S	Apr	2	Brentford		L1-2	(0-0)	Hunt 73	8,595
40	S		9	Colchester United	W4-3		(3-1)	Morgan 16,Summerbee 22,Gauld 37,58	7,342
41	F		15	Tranmere Rovers		D2-2	(2-1)	Mellor 13,Hunt 34	10,438
42	S		16	Halifax Town		L1-3	(0-1)	Mellor 55	6,524
43	M		18	Tranmere Rovers	D1-1		(0-1)	Gauld 73	10,524
44	S		23	Mansfield Town	W2-1		(2-0)	Chamberlain 9,Mellor 43	7,963
45	S		30	Port Vale		L1-6	(0-4)	Gauld 87	5,514
46	W	May	4	Coventry City	W2-0		(0-0)	Gauld 53,55	6,415

Average Home Attendance : **10,233**
Average Away Attendance : **9,798**

F A Cup

					Home	Away	H-T	Goalscorers	Gate
1	S	Nov	14	Walsall	L2-3		(0-3)	Edwards 61,Darcy 62	13,368

'BRONCO' LAYNE

was still only 19 when he signed for Town in June 1959 and he was at the County Ground only eighteen months. But his scoring record in that time has been matched by few - with 35 goals coming in just 46 appearances. The club then quickly cashed in on their free transfer signing, with Bradford City handing over a cheque for £6,000. And 'Bronco' - real name David - continued to terrorise defences with a further 99 goals in 147 games before his career was suddenly halted in 1964. His former strike partner at Swindon in 1959/60, Jimmy Gauld, implicated him in the infamous 'Bribes Scandal' case and David was handed a four-month jail sentence and a 'life ban' from the game - although that was lifted in 1972.

Atkins W M	Bingley W	Burton S	Chamberlain P M	Corbett D F	Darcy A J	Edwards R H	Fountain J	Gauld J	Higgins J W	Hoskins J F	Hudson G W	Hunt R P	Layne D R	Lyons M C	Marshall W F	Medlock O W	Mellor K E	Morgan K	Richards J B	Stephens W J	Summerbee M G	Thompson F N	Tilley H R	Woodruff R W	Woolford M E G	
8	3	1			11		4	10	2				9				5			7			6			1
	3	1			11		4	10					9				5		8	7		2	6			2
	3	1			11		4	10					9				5		8	7		2	6			3
	3	1			11			10					9				5	4	8	7		2	6			4
	3	1			11			10					9				5	4	8	7		2	6			5
	3	1		7	11			10					9				5	4	8			2		6		6
	3	1		7	11			10					9				5	4	8			2		6		7
	3	1	2		7			10		11		8	9				5	4						6		8
	3	1	2		7	8		10		11			9				5	4						6		9
	3	1	2		7	8		10		11							5	4	9					6		10
	3	1	2		7	8		10		11							5	4	9					6		11
	3	1	2		7	8		10		11							5	4	9					6		12
	3	1	2		7	8		10					11				5	4	9					6		13
	3	1	2		7	8		10					11				5	4	9					6		14
	3	1	2	7	11			10					9				5	4	8					6		15
	3	1	2		11			10				8			9		5	4		7				6		16
	3	1	2		11			10					9				5	4	8	7				6		17
	3		2		11	8	4	9		10	5					1				7				6		18
	3				7	10	4	9		11	5	8		2		1								6		19
			3		7	10	4	9		11	5			2		1			8					6		20
	3	1			7	10	4	9	2	11	5								8					6		21
	3	1			7	10	4	9	2	11							5		8					6		22
	3	1			11		4	10	2				9		8		5			7				6		23
	3	1		7	11		4	10	2				9		8		5							6		24
	3	1	5	7	11		4	10	2				9		8									6		25
	3	1	5	7	11		4		2						8						9			6	10	26
	3	1	5	7	11		6		2						8			4			9				10	27
	3	1	5		11		4	7	2						8						9			6	10	28
	3	1	5		11		4	10	2			7	9		8			6								29
	3	1	5	7	11		4	10	2				9		8			6								30
	3	1	5	7	11		4		2				9		8		10	6								31
	3	1	5	7	11		4	10	2				9		8			6								32
	3	1	5	7	11		4	10	2				9		8			6								33
	3	1	5	7	11		4	10	2				9		8			6								34
	3	1	5		11		4		2			8	9		10			6			7					35
	3	1	5		11				2			8	9		10			4			7		6			36
	3	1	5		11				2			8	9		10			4			7		6			37
	3	1	5		11			10	2			8	9					4			7		6			38
	3	1	5		11			10	2			8	9					4			7		6			39
	3	1	5		11			10	2			8					9	4			7		6			40
	3	1	5		11			10	2			8					9	4			7		6			41
	3	1	5		11			10	2			8					9	4			7		6			42
	3	1	5		11			10	2			8					9	4			7		6			43
	3	1	5		11			10	2			8					9	4			7		6			44
	3	1	5		11			10	2			8					9	4			7		6			45
	3	1	5		11			10	2			8					9	4			7		6			46
1	45	43	34	12	46	11	21	40	27	10	4	16	27	2	16	3	28	33	16	9	15	6	16	22	3	Apps
			1		3	5		14		3		3	20		5		3	2	6	1	1			2		Goals

			3		7	10	4	9	2	11	5	8				1							6		

For Final League Table - see page 167

SEASON 1960/61

Football League Third Division
Final League Position : 16th
Manager : Bert Head

No.	Day	Month	Date	Opponents	Home	Away	H-T	Goalscorers	Gate
1	S	Aug	20	Halifax Town	D1-1		(0-1)	Hunt 54 pen.	13,109
2	M		22	Tranmere Rovers		D2-2	(0-2)	Chamberlain 47,79	11,105
3	S		27	Shrewsbury Town		D1-1	(1-0)	Mellor 37	7,330
4	W		31	Tranmere Rovers	W1-0		(0-0)	Jackson 60	10,781
5	S	Sep	3	Walsall	W1-0		(0-0)	Jackson 69	13,472
6	Tu		6	Bristol City		D1-1	(1-0)	Hunt 2	16,550
7	S		10	Bury		L0-3	(0-1)		6,749
8	S		17	Chesterfield	W2-0		(1-0)	Layne 45,Jackson 53	12,239
9	Tu		20	Watford		L0-1	(0-0)		14,480
10	S		24	Southend United		W2-0	(1-0)	Jackson 12,67	9,280
11	W		28	Watford	L1-2		(0-0)	Layne 90	15,811
12	S	Oct	1	Port Vale	W6-0		(2-0)	Woodruff 7,24,70,Hunt 49,Corbett 53,Summerbee 85	11,960
13	W		5	Torquay United		D1-1	(1-0)	Woodruff 29	5,091
14	S		8	Notts County		L0-1	(0-1)		11,483
15	S		15	Bournemouth & Boscombe Athletic	L0-1		(0-1)		12,295
16	W		19	Bristol City	W3-1		(1-0)	Layne 20,86,89	16,618
17	S		22	Bradford City		L1-2	(0-1)	Jackson 84	6,602
18	S	Nov	12	Colchester United	L0-2		(0-0)		11,782
19	M		28	Grimsby Town		L2-3	(1-1)	Layne 26,68	9,895
20	S	Dec	3	Reading		D1-1	(0-1)	Summerbee 53	9,555
21	S		10	Coventry City	L1-2		(1-1)	Layne 31	8,703
22	S		17	Halifax Town		D1-1	(1-1)	Bell 44	4,512
23	F		23	Brentford		L1-2	(0-0)	Jackson 71	4,410
24	S		31	Shrewsbury Town	D2-2		(1-2)	Woodruff 23,60	9,670
25	S	Jan	7	Brentford	D1-1		(1-0)	Hunt 15	8,663
26	S		21	Bury	W4-0		(2-0)	Jackson 35,57,Summerbee 43,71	9,803
27	S		28	Newport County		L0-2	(0-1)		3,350
28	S	Feb	4	Chesterfield		D1-1	(0-0)	Summerbee 80	3,099
29	S		11	Southend United	D1-1		(0-0)	Hunt 73 pen.	8,746
30	S		18	Port Vale		L1-4	(0-1)	Jackson 47	9,673
31	S		25	Reading	D1-1		(1-0)	Hunt 26	9,703
32	S	Mar	4	Bournemouth & Boscombe Athletic		L1-2	(1-2)	Summerbee 11	7,862
33	S		11	Bradford City	W4-0		(1-0)	Summerbee 28,Hunt 67 pen.,77,Woodruff 80	9,678
34	S		18	Barnsley		L1-2	(0-2)	Hunt 47	7,628
35	Tu		21	Walsall		L1-2	(0-1)	Woodruff 65	12,102
36	S		25	Newport County	W2-0		(0-0)	Hunt 71,Darcy 82	7,904
37	F		31	Queens Park Rangers		L1-3	(1-2)	Woodruff 7	14,436
38	S	Apr	1	Colchester United		L1-3	(1-1)	Woodruff 2	3,189
39	M		3	Queens Park Rangers	W1-0		(0-0)	Summerbee 85	11,568
40	S		8	Grimsby Town	W3-0		(1-0)	Woodruff 22,Jobling o.g.53,Hunt 86	10,170
41	W		12	Hull City	D1-1		(0-0)	Hunt 80 pen.	10,875
42	S		15	Hull City		D0-0			5,514
43	W		19	Barnsley	W1-0		(0-0)	Hunt 50	9,776
44	S		22	Notts County	W1-0		(1-0)	Jones F.29	8,904
45	W		26	Torquay United	W3-1		(1-1)	Woodruff 44,70,Bell 60	11,815
46	F		28	Coventry City		D1-1	(1-1)	Hunt 21	7,977

Average Home Attendance : **11,045**
Average Away Attendance : **8,342**

Football League Cup

Rd	Day	Month	Date	Opponents	Home	Away	H-T	Goalscorers	Gate
1	W	Oct	12	Shrewsbury Town	D1-1		(1-0)	Jackson 38	10,350
1R	M		24	Shrewsbury Town		+ D2-2	(1-1)	Layne 10,75	5,343
Rp	W		26	Shrewsbury Town	+ L0-2		(0-0)		6,785

+ After Extra Time

F A Cup

Rd	Day	Month	Date	Opponents	Home	Away	H-T	Goalscorers	Gate
1	S	Nov	5	Bath City	D2-2		(0-2)	Hunt 54,Layne 80	19,369
1R	Th		10	Bath City		W6-4	(2-1)	Layne 11,42,67,82,Hunt 48,58	12,818
2	S		26	Shrewsbury Town	L0-1		(0-0)		11,910

For Final League Table - see page 167

Bell J A	Burton S	Chamberlain P M	Corbett D F	Crook G F	Darcy A J	Higgins J W	Hunt R P	Jackson C	Jones F G	Jones K B	Layne D R	Marshall W F	Mellor K E	Morgan K	Owen M	Summerbee M G	Teague W E	Thompson F N	Trollope N J	Wollen T L	Woodruff R W	
	1				11		8	10					9	4	5	7			3	2	6	1
	1	11					8	10					9	4	5	7			3	2	6	2
	1	11					8	10					9	4	5	7			3	2	6	3
	1	11					8	10					9	4	5	7			3	2	6	4
	1				11		8	10			9			4	5	7			3	2	6	5
	1				11		8	10			9			4	5	7			3	2	6	6
	1	5			11		8	10			9			4		7			3	2	6	7
	1				11		8	10			9			4	5	7			3	2	6	8
	1	5			11		8	10			9			4		7			3	2	6	9
	1	5			11		8	10			9			4		7			3	2	6	10
	1				11		8	10			9			4	5	7			3	2	6	11
6	1		11				8	10						4	5	7			3	2	9	12
6	1		11			2	8	10						4	5	7			3		9	13
6	1		11				8	10						4	5	7			3	2	9	14
	1		7		11		8	10						4	5	9			3	2	6	15
	1				11		8	10			9			4	5	7			3	2	6	16
	1				11		8	10			9			4	5	7			3	2	6	17
	1				11		8	10			9			4	5	7			3	2	6	18
	1		11				8	10			9			4	5	7			3	2	6	19
	1		11				8	10			9			4	5	7			3	2	6	20
	1		11				8	10			9			4	5	7			3	2	6	21
6	1		11				8				9			4	5	7			3	2	10	22
6	1		11				8	10						4	5	7			3	2	9	23
6	1						8	10	11					4	5	7			3	2	9	24
6	1						8	10	11					4	5	7			3	2	9	25
	1				7		8	10	11					4	5	9			3	2	6	26
	1				7		8	10	11					4	5	9			3	2	6	27
	1				7		8	10	11					4	5	9			3	2	6	28
	1				7		8	10	11					4	5	9			3	2	6	29
6	1				7		8	10	11					4	5				3	2	9	30
	1				7		8	10	11					4	5	9			3	2	6	31
6	1	5			7		8	10	11					4		9			3	2		32
6	1		7		11		8			2				4	5	9			3		10	33
6	1		7		10		8		11	2				4	5	9			3			34
6	1		7		11		8			2				4	5	9			3		10	35
6	1		7		11		8			2				4	5	9			3		10	36
6	1		7		11		8			2				4	5	9		3			10	37
6			7		11		8			2				4	5	9	1	3			10	38
6	1				7		8		11	2				4	5	9			3		10	39
6	1		7				8		11	2				4	5	9			3		10	40
6	1	5	7				8		11	2				4		9			3		10	41
6	1	5	7				8		11	2				4		9			3		10	42
6	1		7				8		11	2				4	5	9			3		10	43
6	1		7				8		11	2				4	5	9			3		10	44
6	1		7				8		11	2				4	5	9			3		10	45
6	1		7				8		11	2				4	5	9			3		10	46
23	45	9	22	0	26	1	46	31	18	14	14		4	46	40	45	1	2	44	31	44	Apps
2		2	1		1		14	10	1		8		1			8					13	Goals

Opponents 1 goal

Bell J A	Burton S	Chamberlain P M	Corbett D F	Crook G F	Darcy A J	Higgins J W	Hunt R P	Jackson C	Jones F G	Jones K B	Layne D R	Marshall W F	Mellor K E	Morgan K	Owen M	Summerbee M G	Teague W E	Thompson F N	Trollope N J	Wollen T L	Woodruff R W	
	1		11				8	10				9		4	5	7			3	2	6	1
	1				11		8	10			9			4	5	7			3	2	6	1R
	1				11		8	10			9			4	5	7			3	2	6	Rp
	3		1		2		3	3			2	1		3	3	3			3	3	3	Apps
								1			2											Goals

Bell J A	Burton S	Chamberlain P M	Corbett D F	Crook G F	Darcy A J	Higgins J W	Hunt R P	Jackson C	Jones F G	Jones K B	Layne D R	Marshall W F	Mellor K E	Morgan K	Owen M	Summerbee M G	Teague W E	Thompson F N	Trollope N J	Wollen T L	Woodruff R W	
	1				11		8	10			9			4	5	7			3	2	6	1
				1	11		8	10			9			4	5	7			3	2	6	1R
	1		11				8	10			9			4	5	7			3	2	6	2
	2		1	1	2		3	3			3			3	3	3			3	3	3	Apps
							3				5											Goals

BOBBY WOODRUFF

SEASON 1961/62

Football League Third Division
Final League Position : 9th
Manager : Bert Head

				Home	Away	H-T	Goalscorers	Gate
1	S	Aug	19 Portsmouth	L1-3		(0-2)	Brown o.g.67	16,153
2	M		21 Coventry City		L1-2	(1-1)	Hunt R R 43	13,761
3	S		26 Crystal Palace		L1-3	(0-1)	Trollope 78	24,184
4	Tu		29 Coventry City	D3-3		(0-1)	Summerbee 46,Corbett 52,Hunt R R 54	10,563
5	S	Sep	2 Bournemouth & Boscombe Athletic	D1-1		(0-0)	Hunt R R 59	9,815
6	M		4 Queens Park Rangers		L1-6	(0-2)	Rutter o.g.52	10,255
7	S		9 Watford		L0-2	(0-1)		10,339
8	S		16 Hull City	D1-1		(1-1)	Hunt R R 41	9,252
9	Tu		19 Barnsley	D1-1		(1-0)	Hunt R R 45	9,858
10	S		23 Northampton Town		W2-1	(0-0)	Hunt R P 46,Hunt R R 80	9,263
11	W		27 Barnsley		L2-6	(1-4)	Hunt R R 14,49	3,551
12	S		30 Lincoln City	W4-0		(2-0)	Jackson 4,Hunt R P 22,46,Hunt R R 83	9,593
13	Tu	Oct	3 Grimsby Town	D0-0				11,303
14	S		7 Brentford		L0-1	(0-0)		7,540
15	Tu		10 Grimsby Town		W1-0	(0-0)	Hunt R R 85	9,158
16	F		13 Reading	W4-1		(1-0)	Hunt R R 1,Hunt R P 54,Darcy 55,63	17,301
17	Tu		17 Queens Park Rangers	D0-0				11,314
18	S		21 Bristol City		L3-5	(2-3)	Hunt R P 16 pen.,82,McPherson 21	13,158
19	S		28 Bradford Park Avenue	W3-2		(1-2)	Hunt R R 43,49,McPherson 82	9,400
20	S	Nov	11 Shrewsbury Town	L1-2		(0-1)	Smith 81	7,025
21	S		18 Peterborough United		L2-3	(2-1)	Chamberlain 27,Hunt R P 33 pen.	12,059
22	S	Dec	2 Newport County		D2-2	(1-1)	Jackson 40,Atkins 54	4,506
23	S		9 Southend United	D0-0				6,634
24	S		16 Portsmouth		D2-2	(0-1)	Hunt R P 66,Atkins 71	13,990
25	S		23 Crystal Palace	W5-0		(2-0)	Smith 29,51,Atkins 43,52,Hunt R P 55	7,707
26	S	Jan	13 Bournemouth & Boscombe Athletic		D0-0			9,113
27	S		20 Watford	W3-1		(0-1)	Smith 53,57,Weaver 89	7,688
28	S	Feb	3 Hull City		W1-0	(1-0)	Smith 12	3,729
29	S		10 Northampton Town	D2-2		(0-1)	Smith 65,Atkins 77	8,985
30	F		16 Lincoln City		D2-2	(1-2)	Hunt R P 34,Atkins 75	5,622
31	F		23 Brentford	W5-2		(4-1)	Smith 9,76,Hunt R P 13,23,Atkins 43	7,089
32	F	Mar	2 Reading		D1-1	(1-1)	Hunt R P 5	14,155
33	S		10 Bristol City	L0-4		(0-1)		12,936
34	S		17 Bradford Park Avenue		D2-2	(1-0)	Smith 5,Darcy 80	8,184
35	M		19 Halifax Town		L0-2	(0-1)		4,255
36	F		23 Notts County	W1-0		(1-0)	Summerbee 34	7,477
37	F		30 Shrewsbury Town		W3-1	(1-0)	Atkins 27,62,Smith 72	6,330
38	S	Apr	7 Peterborough United	W3-2		(2-0)	Summerbee 5,Atkins 17,Hunt R P 79	8,835
39	Th		12 Notts County		W1-0	(1-0)	Hunt R P 2	5,369
40	S		14 Port Vale		D1-1	(0-0)	Atkins 60	4,770
41	M		16 Halifax Town	W6-0		(5-0)	Woodruff 7,Smith 10,Darcy 11,44,Hunt R P 38,71	6,973
42	F		20 Torquay United	L0-1		(0-1)		11,795
43	S		21 Newport County	W3-0		(2-0)	Hunt R P 7,Smith 11,Summerbee 68	7,881
44	M		23 Torquay United		L0-3	(0-2)		4,591
45	S		28 Southend United		W2-0	(1-0)	Jackson 37,47	5,713
46	M		30 Port Vale	W1-0		(1-0)	Jackson 39	7,331

Average Home Attendance : **9,692**
Average Away Attendance : **8,852**

Football League Cup

				Home	Away	H-T	Goalscorers	Gate
1	W	Sep	13 Birmingham City		D1-1	(1-0)	Smith 24	11,584
1R	Th		25 Birmingham City	W2-0		(1-0)	Morgan 26,Hunt R R 47	13,063
2	Th	Oct	5 Preston North End		L1-3	(0-1)	Smith 47	8,136

F A Cup

				Home	Away	H-T	Goalscorers	Gate
1	S	Nov	4 Kettering Town	D2-2		(1-0)	McPherson 11,Hunt R R 60	12,577
2	W		8 Kettering Town		L0-3	(0-0)		8,400

For Final League Table - see page 168

Atkins W M	Bell J A	Burton S	Chamberlain P M	Corbett D F	Darcy A J	Hunt R R A	Hunt R P	Jackson C	Jones K B	McPherson K	Morgan K	O'Hara M J	Owen M	Smart R W	Smith J	Summerbee M G	Teague W E	Trollope N J	Turner M G E	Weaver E	Wollen T L	Woodruff R W	
		1			11	10	8		2	9	4		5			7		3				6	**1**
	6	1			11	10	8		2	9	4		5			7		3					**2**
	6	1		7	11	10	8		2		4		5			9		3					**3**
	6	1		11		10			2		4		5		9	7		3				8	**4**
	6			11		10			2		4		5		9	7	1	3				8	**5**
	6					10		11	2	9	4		5			7	1	3				8	**6**
		1		7		10		11	2		4		5		9	8		3				6	**7**
		1		7		10		11	2		4		5		9	8		3				6	**8**
		1				10	8	11	2		4		5		9	7		3				6	**9**
		1				10	8	11	2		4		5		9	7		3				6	**10**
		1		7		10	8	11	2		4		5		9			3				6	**11**
		1		7		10	8	11	2		4		5		9			3				6	**12**
		1		7		10	8	11	2		4		5		9			3				6	**13**
		1			11	10	8		2		4		5		9	7		3				6	**14**
		1			11	10	8		2	9	4		5			7		3				6	**15**
		1			11	10	8		2	9	4		5			7		3				6	**16**
		1			11	10	8		2	9	4		5			7		3				6	**17**
		1			11	10	8		2	9	4		5			7		3				6	**18**
		1				10	8	11	2	9	4		5			7		3				6	**19**
						9	8	11	2		4	1	5		10	7		3				6	**20**
			6	11		9	8				4	1	5		10	7		3			2		**21**
10			6				8	11			4	1	5		9	7		3			2		**22**
10			6				8				4	1	5		9	7		3		11	2		**23**
10			6				8				4	1	5		9	7		3		11	2		**24**
10			6				8				4	1	5		9	7		3		11	2		**25**
10	5		6				8				4	1			9	7		3		11	2		**26**
10			6				8		2		4	1	5		9	7		3		11			**27**
10			6				8				4	1	5		9	7		3			2	11	**28**
10			6				8				4	1	5		9	7		3		11	2		**29**
10			6				8				4	1	5		9	7		3		11	2		**30**
10							8				4	1	5		9	7		3		11	2	6	**31**
10			5				8	11				1		4	9	7		3			2	6	**32**
10							8					1	5	4	9	7		3		11	2	6	**33**
10					11		8				4	1	5		9	7		3			2	6	**34**
10					11		8				4	1	5		9	7		3			2	6	**35**
10							8				4	1	5		9	7		3		11	2	6	**36**
10							8				4	1	5	11	9	7		3			2	6	**37**
10					11		8				4	1	5		9	7		3			2	6	**38**
10					11		8				4	1	5		9	7		3			2	6	**39**
10					11		8				4		5		9	7		3	1		2	6	**40**
10					11		8				4		5		9	7		3	1		2	6	**41**
10					11		8				4		5		9	7		3	1		2	6	**42**
10							8	11			4		5		9	7		3	1		2	6	**43**
							8	11			4		5	10	9	7		3	1		2	6	**44**
10							8	11			4		5		9	7		3	1		2	6	**45**
10							8	11			4		5		9	7		3	1		2	6	**46**
24	6	17	11	9	15	21	41	16	21	8	44	20	44	4	37	43	2	46	7	10	25	35	Apps
11			1	1	5	13	18	5		2					13	4		1		1		1	Goals

Opponents 2 goals

Atkins W M	Bell J A	Burton S	Chamberlain P M	Corbett D F	Darcy A J	Hunt R R A	Hunt R P	Jackson C	Jones K B	McPherson K	Morgan K	O'Hara M J	Owen M	Smart R W	Smith J	Summerbee M G	Teague W E	Trollope N J	Turner M G E	Weaver E	Wollen T L	Woodruff R W	
		1		7		10		11	2		4		5		9	8		3				6	**1**
		1				10	8	11	2		4		5		9	7		3				6	**1R**
		1	5	7			8	11	2		4				9	10		3				6	**2**
		3	1	2		2	2	3	3		3		2		3	3		3				3	Apps
						1					1				2								Goals

Atkins W M	Bell J A	Burton S	Chamberlain P M	Corbett D F	Darcy A J	Hunt R R A	Hunt R P	Jackson C	Jones K B	McPherson K	Morgan K	O'Hara M J	Owen M	Smart R W	Smith J	Summerbee M G	Teague W E	Trollope N J	Turner M G E	Weaver E	Wollen T L	Woodruff R W	
		1				10	8	11	2	9	4		5			7		3				6	**1**
		1				10	8	11	2	9	4		5			7		3				6	**2**
		2				2	2	2	2	2	2		2			2		2				2	Apps
						1				1													Goals

SEASON 1962/63

Football League Third Division
Final League Position : 2nd
Manager : Bert Head

				Home	Away	H-T	Goalscorers	Gate
1	S	Aug	18 Barnsley		D1-1	(0-0)	Jackson 53	7,083
2	Tu		21 Coventry City	W4-1		(3-1)	Darcy 8,13,Smith 23,Curtis o.g.83	14,410
3	S		25 Northampton Town	L2-3		(1-0)	Jackson 10,Darcy 72	12,962
4	Tu		28 Coventry City		L0-2	(0-2)		15,413
5	S	Sep	1 Queens Park Rangers		D2-2	(2-2)	Smart 10,Smith 44	12,573
6	Tu		4 Brighton and Hove Albion		D1-1	(1-1)	Hunt 32	14,438
7	S		8 Hull City	W2-0		(1-0)	Trollope 35,Hunt 75	10,015
8	Tu		11 Brighton and Hove Albion	W5-1		(3-0)	Jackson 12,Hunt 20,46,79 pen.,Smith 31	11,420
9	S		15 Crystal Palace		D0-0			16,376
10	Tu		18 Carlisle United		D0-0			6,602
11	S		22 Wrexham	W3-0		(1-0)	Smart 35,Hunt 51,83	11,771
12	S		29 Halifax Town		L3-4	(2-0)	Jackson 9,Hunt 20 pen.,Smith 55	3,354
13	Tu	Oct	2 Bristol Rovers	W3-0		(2-0)	Jackson 24,Woodruff 44,Smith 83	15,028
14	S		6 Watford	W3-1		(0-1)	Darcy 73,Smith 79,85	13,988
15	Tu		9 Bristol Rovers		L0-2	(0-2)		17,690
16	S		13 Bristol City		D2-2	(2-0)	Jackson 7,Hunt 38 pen.	21,864
17	S		20 Reading	D1-1		(0-0)	Hunt 57	16,345
18	S		27 Port Vale		L1-2	(0-1)	Jackson 90	5,825
19	S	Nov	10 Millwall		W4-3	(1-2)	Jackson 11,52,72,Smith 81	10,103
20	S		17 Southend United	W4-1		(2-0)	Smith 6,10,Summerbee 63,Jackson 88	10,296
21	S	Dec	1 Notts County	W3-1		(1-0)	Jackson 39,57,Rogers 75	11,808
22	S		8 Bournemouth & Boscombe Athletic		D0-0			9,295
23	S		15 Barnsley	W2-1		(1-0)	Summerbee 27,Smith 63	10,217
24	W		26 Bradford Park Avenue		L0-2	(0-1)		6,691
25	S	Jan	12 Queens Park Rangers	W5-0		(1-0)	Smith 39,87,90,Rogers 62,Woodruff 81	7,450
26	S	Feb	2 Crystal Palace	W1-0		(1-0)	Darcy 44	9,712
27	S		23 Watford		D3-3	(1-2)	Hunt 23,75,Summerbee 71	11,338
28	W		27 Wrexham		D0-0			8,616
29	S	Mar	2 Bristol City	W3-2		(0-1)	Hunt 54 pen.,Summerbee 65,Smith 81	16,778
30	F		8 Reading		W2-1	(0-1)	Hunt 66 pen.,76	16,126
31	S		16 Port Vale	L2-3		(1-1)	Smith 12,60	11,938
32	S		23 Shrewsbury Town		W2-1	(0-1)	Jackson 49,Summerbee 86	5,718
33	Tu		26 Northampton Town		D1-1	(1-1)	Smith 14	16,812
34	S		30 Millwall	W1-0		(0-0)	Hunt 51 pen.	11,938
35	Tu	Apr	2 Bradford Park Avenue	W2-1		(0-0)	Smith 60,Stevens 73	14,568
36	S		6 Southend United		D1-1	(1-0)	Stevens 39	11,704
37	F		12 Peterborough United	L2-3		(1-2)	Hunt 1,52	23,239
38	S		13 Colchester United	W6-1		(2-1)	Summerbee 8,Stevens 44,46,50,Hunt 66,85	12,159
39	M		15 Peterborough United		L1-3	(1-2)	Weaver 25	14,972
40	S		20 Notts County		L0-2	(0-0)		5,609
41	S		27 Bournemouth & Boscombe Athletic	W2-1		(1-1)	Stevens 24,Hunt 48 pen.	16,508
42	Tu		30 Carlisle United	W2-0		(1-0)	Stevens 35,Hunt 49	14,221
43	S	May	4 Halifax Town	D1-1		(0-0)	Hunt 82 pen.	14,157
44	M		6 Colchester United		W2-0	(1-0)	Smart 26,50	6,876
45	Tu		14 Shrewsbury Town	W1-0		(0-0)	Smart 88	20,273
46	S		18 Hull City		D1-1	(1-0)	Hunt 23	4,361

Average Home Attendance : **13,530**
Average Away Attendance : **10,845**

Football League Cup

				Home	Away	H-T	Goalscorers	Gate
2	Tu	Sep	25 Darlington	W4-0		(2-0)	Smith 4,73,89,Jackson 26	9,696
3	W	Oct	17 Notts County		L0-5	(0-1)		7,012

F A Cup

				Home	Away	H-T	Goalscorers	Gate
1	S	Nov	3 Reading	W4-2		(0-0)	Smith 47,Hunt 58,76,Spiers o.g.59	17,632
2	S		24 Yeovil Town		W2-0	(1-0)	Hunt 34,Jackson 70	12,292
3	S	Jan	26 Luton Town		W2-0	(2-0)	Jackson 6,25	10,840
4	Tu		29 Everton	L1-5		(0-4)	Smith 72	26,215

For Final League Table - see page 168

Atkins W M	Chamberlain P M	Darcy A J	Dawson O J	Harber W H	Hunt R P	Huxford C J	Jackson C	McPherson K	Morgan K	O'Hara M J	Owen M	Rogers D E	Smart R W	Smith J	Stevens J M	Summerbee M G	Trollope N J	Turner M G E	Weaver E	Wollen T L	Woodruff R W	
10					8		11		4		5			9		7	3	1		2	6	**1**
10		7			8		11		4	1	5			9			3			2	6	**2**
10		7			8		11		4	1	5			9			3			2	6	**3**
	10	7			8		11		4	1	5			9			3			2	6	**4**
		7			8		11		4		5		10	9			3	1		2	6	**5**
		7			8		11		4		5		10	9			3	1		2	6	**6**
		7			8		11		4		5		10	9			3	1		2	6	**7**
		7			8		11		4		5		10	9			3	1		2	6	**8**
		7			8		11		4		5		10	9			3	1		2	6	**9**
		7			8		11		4		5		10	9			3	1		2	6	**10**
					8		11		4		5		10	9		7	3	1		2	6	**11**
		11			8		10		4		5			9		7	3	1		2	6	**12**
		11			8		10		4		5			9		7	3	1		2	6	**13**
		11			8		10		4		5			9		7	3	1		2	6	**14**
		11			8		10		4		5			9		7	3	1		2	6	**15**
		11			8		10		4		5			9		7	3	1		2	6	**16**
		11			8		10	5	4					9		7	3	1		2	6	**17**
		11					10	5	4					8	9	7	3	1		2	6	**18**
		11			8		10	5	4					9		7	3	1		2	6	**19**
					8		10	5	4			11		9		7	3	1		2	6	**20**
					8		10	5	4			11		9		7	3	1		2	6	**21**
					8		10	5	4		2	11		9		7	3	1			6	**22**
					8		10	5	4		2	11		9		7	3	1			6	**23**
10					8			5	4	1	2	11		9		7	3				6	**24**
					8		10	5	4		2	11		9		7	3	1			6	**25**
		11			8		10	5	4	1	2			9		7	3				6	**26**
		11	2		8		10	5	4	1				9		7	3				6	**27**
		11	2		8		10	5	4	1				9		7	3				6	**28**
		11	2		8		10	5	4	1				9		7	3				6	**29**
		11	2		8		10	5	4	1				9		7	3				6	**30**
		11	2		8		10	5	4	1				9		7	3				6	**31**
8		11	2				10	5	4					9		7	3	1			6	**32**
8			2				11	5	4					10	9	7	3	1			6	**33**
			2		8		11	5	4					10	9	7	3	1			6	**34**
			2		8		11	5	4					10	9	7	3	1			6	**35**
			2		8		11	5	4					10	9	7	3	1			6	**36**
					8	2	11	5	4					10	9	7	3	1			6	**37**
				6	8			5	4		2			10	9	7	3	1	11			**38**
				6	8			5	4		2			10	9	7	3	1	11			**39**
					8		10	5	4		2			9		7	3	1	11		6	**40**
					8		10	5	4		2	11			9	7	3	1			6	**41**
		11			8		10	5	4		2				9	7	3	1			6	**42**
10		11			8			5	4		2				9	7	3	1			6	**43**
			2		8		11	5	4				10		9	7	3	1			6	**44**
			2		8		11	5	4				10		9	7	3	1			6	**45**
			2		8		11	5	4				10		9	7	3	1			6	**46**
7	1	26	13	2	43	1	42	30	46	10	27	7	10	40	14	37	46	36	3	21	44	Apps
		5			24		14					2	5	19	7	6	1		1		2	Goals

Opponents 1 goal

Atkins W M	Chamberlain P M	Darcy A J	Dawson O J	Harber W H	Hunt R P	Huxford C J	Jackson C	McPherson K	Morgan K	O'Hara M J	Owen M	Rogers D E	Smart R W	Smith J	Stevens J M	Summerbee M G	Trollope N J	Turner M G E	Weaver E	Wollen T L	Woodruff R W	
		11			8		10		4		5			9		7	3	1		2	6	**2**
		11			8		10		4		5			9		7	3	1		2	6	**3**
		2			2		2		2		2			2		2	2	2		2	2	Apps
							1							3								Goals

Atkins W M	Chamberlain P M	Darcy A J	Dawson O J	Harber W H	Hunt R P	Huxford C J	Jackson C	McPherson K	Morgan K	O'Hara M J	Owen M	Rogers D E	Smart R W	Smith J	Stevens J M	Summerbee M G	Trollope N J	Turner M G E	Weaver E	Wollen T L	Woodruff R W	
		11			8		10	5	4					9		7	3	1		2	6	**1**
					8		10	5	4			11		9		7	3	1		2	6	**2**
					8		10	5	4		2	11		9		7	3	1			6	**3**
					8		10	5	4		2	11		9		7	3	1			6	**4**
		1			4		4	4	4		2	3		4		4	4	4		2	4	Apps
					3		3							2								Goals

JACK SMITH

SEASON 1963/64

Football League Second Division
Final League Position : 14th
Manager : Bert Head

					Home	Away	H-T	Goalscorers	Gate
1	S	Aug	24	Scunthorpe United	W3-0		(1-0)	Hunt 16,66,Stevens 89	18,451
2	W		28	Grimsby Town		W2-1	(0-1)	Smart 74,Hunt 76	15,085
3	S		31	Portsmouth		W4-1	(1-0)	Atkins 36,Summerbee 47,Snowdon o.g.51,Smart 67	21,975
4	Tu	Sep	3	Grimsby Town	W2-1		(1-0)	Atkins 20,Rogers 50	21,866
5	S		7	Rotherham United	W3-1		(2-1)	Smith 25,Smart 35,Summerbee 68	19,448
6	Tu		10	Manchester City	W3-0		(2-0)	Summerbee 3,Smith 37,Hunt 67	28,173
7	S		14	Leeds United		D0-0			33,301
8	W		18	Manchester City		D0-0			23,103
9	S		21	Sunderland	W1-0		(1-0)	Smith 33	26,049
10	S		28	Northampton Town		L0-4	(0-2)		18,177
11	Tu	Oct	1	Charlton Athletic	D2-2		(1-0)	Rogers 45,Summerbee 68	19,132
12	S		5	Bury	W2-1		(1-0)	Smith 14,Morgan 84	17,811
13	S		12	Preston North End		L0-1	(0-1)		21,263
14	S		19	Leyton Orient	W5-0		(1-0)	Hunt 41,86,Summerbee 51,Rogers 52,Morgan 55	18,862
15	S		26	Plymouth Argyle		W4-2	(1-2)	Hunt 19,62,Rogers 84,Woodruff 89	19,471
16	S	Nov	2	Southampton	L1-2		(1-0)	Smith 8	21,787
17	S		9	Middlesbrough		D1-1	(0-1)	Hunt 77	26,476
18	S		16	Newcastle United	D0-0				20,699
19	S		23	Huddersfield Town		L0-2	(0-1)		7,718
20	S		30	Derby County	D0-0				15,843
21	S	Dec	7	Swansea Town		L0-3	(0-2)		8,892
22	S		14	Scunthorpe United		L0-3	(0-1)		5,113
23	S		21	Portsmouth	W2-0		(0-0)	Hunt 55,Stevens 72	13,530
24	Th		26	Norwich City		L2-3	(2-0)	Stevens 12,Atkins 27	20,879
25	S		28	Norwich City	D2-2		(1-1)	Atkins 5,Summerbee 87	17,508
26	S	Jan	11	Rotherham United		D0-0			9,369
27	S		18	Leeds United	D2-2		(2-1)	Atkins 12,14	19,015
28	S	Feb	1	Sunderland		L0-6	(0-2)		41,334
29	S		8	Northampton Town	L2-3		(0-0)	McPherson 65,Rogers 89 pen.	16,833
30	Tu		18	Bury		L0-1	(0-1)		4,058
31	S		22	Preston North End	L1-4		(0-2)	Summerbee 65	14,781
32	S		29	Newcastle United		L1-4	(0-1)	Woodruff 80	23,565
33	S	Mar	7	Plymouth Argyle	W2-1		(0-0)	Large 60,85	13,743
34	S		14	Charlton Athletic		D2-2	(2-2)	Large 26,Atkins 40	12,396
35	S		21	Middlesbrough	W2-0		(1-0)	Atkins 34,Rogers 56	13,577
36	F		27	Cardiff City	L1-2		(1-0)	Large 33	22,096
37	S		28	Leyton Orient		L1-2	(1-1)	Hunt 5	7,210
38	M		30	Cardiff City		L0-1	(0-1)		14,033
39	S	Apr	4	Huddersfield Town	L1-2		(1-0)	Atkins 6	10,824
40	S		11	Derby County		L0-3	(0-2)		9,791
41	S		18	Swansea Town	W2-1		(2-0)	Atkins 21,Rogers 25	13,792
42	S		25	Southampton		L1-5	(0-2)	Hunt 65	16,651

Average Home Attendance : **18,277**
Average Away Attendance : **17,136**

Football League Cup

					Home	Away	H-T	Goalscorers	Gate
2	W	Sep	25	Chelsea	W3-0		(0-0)	Smart 60,Smith 70,75	17,916
3	W	Oct	16	Southend United	W3-0		(2-0)	Rogers 12,Atkins 22,Summerbee 67	12,046
4	Tu	Nov	19	West Ham United	D3-3		(2-2)	Rogers 36,Smith 39,McPherson 83	12,050
4R	M		25	West Ham United		L1-4	(0-1)	Rogers 60	15,778

F A Cup

					Home	Away	H-T	Goalscorers	Gate
3	S	Jan	4	Manchester City	W2-1		(1-0)	Smart 5,75	18,065
4	S		25	Aldershot		W2-1	(0-0)	Rogers 51,Atkins 71	16,000
5	S	Feb	15	West Ham United	L1-3		(1-1)	McPherson 34	28,582

'ERNIE' HUNT
made his League debut in September 1959, aged just 16 years and 182 days - Town's youngest ever debutant until Paul Rideout 21 years later. Real name Roger Patrick, he was nicknamed 'Ernie' after his father. Top scorer for the club for four successive seasons from 1960/61, Ernie had all the attributes - the physique to be a ball-winner and the guile and skill to make the best use of it. Had he not broken two bones in his right foot in March 1965, Ernie might have prolonged his stay at the County Ground. He played in only one of Town's final seven games - their only victory. Relegation came on the final evening of the season and Ernie quickly followed his pal Mike Summerbee to pastures new, signing for Wolves in a £40,000 deal in September 1965.

Atkins W M	Darcy A J	Dawson O J	French G E	Hallett T R	Hicks A J	Hunt R P	Large F	Leggett P R	McPherson K	Morgan K	Oakley N	Rogers D E	Shergold W F	Smart R W	Smith J	Sproates A	Stevens J M	Summerbee M G	Trollope N J	Turner M G E	Wollen T L	Woodruff R W	
		2				8			5	4		11		10			9	7	3	1		6	**1**
		2				8			5	4		11		10	9			7	3	1		6	**2**
8		2							5	4		11		10	9			7	3	1		6	**3**
8		2							5	4		11		10	9			7	3	1		6	**4**
		2				8			5	4		11		10	9			7	3	1		6	**5**
		2				8			5	4		11		10	9			7	3	1		6	**6**
		2				8			5	4		11		10	9			7	3	1		6	**7**
		2				8			5	4		11		10	9			7	3	1		6	**8**
		2				8			5	4		11		10	9			7	3	1		6	**9**
		2				8			5	4		11		10	9			7	3	1		6	**10**
		2				8			5	4		11		10	9			7	3	1		6	**11**
		2				8			5	4		11		10	9			7	3	1		6	**12**
		2				8			5	4		11		10	9			7	3	1		6	**13**
		2				8			5	4		11		10	9			7	3	1		6	**14**
		2				8			5	4		11		10	9			7	3	1		6	**15**
		2				8			5	4		11		10	9			7	3	1		6	**16**
		2				8			5	4		11	10		9			7	3	1		6	**17**
		2				8			5	4		11	10		9			7	3	1		6	**18**
		2	7			8			5	4		11			9			10	3	1		6	**19**
						8			5	4		11	10		9			7	3	1	2	6	**20**
8									5	4		11	10		9			7	3	1	2	6	**21**
10						8			5	4		11					9	7	3	1	2	6	**22**
10		2				8			5	4		11					9	7	3	1		6	**23**
10		2				8			5	4		11					9	7	3	1		6	**24**
10		2				8			5	4		11					9	7	3	1		6	**25**
10		2							5	4		11		8			9	7	3	1		6	**26**
10		2				8			5	4		11		9				7	3	1		6	**27**
10						8			5	4		11		9				7	3	1	2	6	**28**
10				2					5	4		11		9		6		7	3	1		6	**29**
8	10								5	4		11					9	7	3	1	2	6	**30**
8	10	2						7	5	4		11						9	3	1		6	**31**
10	11	2		5						4				8			9	7	3	1		6	**32**
		2		5		8	9	7		4	1	11		6				10	3				**33**
10		2		5		8	9			4	1	11		6				7	3				**34**
10		2		5		8	9			4	1	11		6				7	3				**35**
10		2	11	5		8	9			4	1			6				7	3				**36**
10	7	2	11	5		8	9			4	1			6					3				**37**
10		2	11	5		8	9			4	1			6				7	3				**38**
10		2	11	5		8	9	7		4	1			6					3				**39**
10		2				8	9	7	5	4	1	11		6					3				**40**
10		2				8	9	7	5	4	1	11		6					3				**41**
	11	2				8	9	7	5	4	1		10	6					3				**42**
22	5	36	5	9	0	34	10	6	34	42	10	36	5	31	20	1	8	37	42	32	5	32	Apps
10						12	4		1	2		7		3	5		3	7				2	Goals

Opponents 1 goal

Atkins W M	Darcy A J	Dawson O J	French G E	Hallett T R	Hicks A J	Hunt R P	Large F	Leggett P R	McPherson K	Morgan K	Oakley N	Rogers D E	Shergold W F	Smart R W	Smith J	Sproates A	Stevens J M	Summerbee M G	Trollope N J	Turner M G E	Wollen T L	Woodruff R W	
		2				8			5	4		11		10	9			7	3	1		6	**2**
10		2			1	8		7	5	4		11						9	3			6	**3**
		2	7			8			5	4		11			9			10	3	1		6	**4**
			7	5						2		11		10	9	4		8	3	1		6	**4R**
1		3	2	1	1	3		1	3	4		4		2	3	1		4	4	3		4	Apps
1									1			3		1	3			1					Goals

Atkins W M	Darcy A J	Dawson O J	French G E	Hallett T R	Hicks A J	Hunt R P	Large F	Leggett P R	McPherson K	Morgan K	Oakley N	Rogers D E	Shergold W F	Smart R W	Smith J	Sproates A	Stevens J M	Summerbee M G	Trollope N J	Turner M G E	Wollen T L	Woodruff R W	
10		2							5	4		11		8			9	7	3	1		6	**3**
10						8			5	4		11		9				7	3	1	2	6	**4**
8	10								5	4		11					9	7	3	1	2	6	**5**
3	1	1				1			3	3		3		2			2	3	3	3	2	3	Apps
1									1			1		2									Goals

For Final League Table - see page 168

SEASON 1964/65

Football League Second Division
Final League Position : 21st
Manager : Bert Head

					Home	Away	H-T	Goalscorers	Gate
1	S	Aug	22	Bury		L1-6	(1-4)	Atkins 1	7,106
2	Tu		25	Crystal Palace	W2-0		(1-0)	Hunt 7,46	17,446
3	S		29	Leyton Orient	W1-0		(1-0)	Rogers 21	15,118
4	W	Sep	2	Crystal Palace		L1-3	(0-1)	Summerbee 59	18,517
5	S		5	Charlton Athletic		L2-3	(1-0)	Atkins 40,77	15,809
6	Tu		8	Swansea Town	W3-0		(0-0)	Atkins 51,57,Hunt 78	15,745
7	S		12	Manchester City	L0-1		(0-0)		17,135
8	Tu		15	Swansea Town		L0-4	(0-2)		8,201
9	S		19	Portsmouth		L0-5	(0-5)		12,497
10	S		26	Huddersfield Town	W4-1		(2-0)	Summerbee 25,Smart 28,Hunt 59,Rogers 86	12,545
11	S	Oct	3	Derby County	W4-2		(3-1)	Hunt 21 pen.,40,54,Dawson 43	15,030
12	S		10	Coventry City		L2-3	(2-2)	Skeen 26,Hunt 37 pen.	25,253
13	Tu		13	Southampton	W2-1		(1-1)	Skeen 35,Morgan 85	19,311
14	S		17	Cardiff City	D3-3		(2-0)	Skeen 17,Summerbee 36,Leggett 64	15,737
15	S		24	Preston North End		L1-2	(0-1)	Summerbee 82	13,907
16	S		31	Ipswich Town	W3-1		(2-0)	Atkins 25,McNeil o.g.27,Summerbee 60	14,101
17	S	Nov	7	Plymouth Argyle		L1-2	(1-1)	Atkins 44	16,398
18	S		14	Bolton Wanderers	L1-3		(0-1)	Trollope 58 pen.	14,245
19	S		21	Middlesbrough		L1-4	(1-1)	East 35	14,948
20	S		28	Newcastle United	L1-6		(1-4)	Trollope 26 pen.	15,866
21	S	Dec	5	Northampton Town		L1-2	(0-0)	Brown 62	9,486
22	S		12	Bury	W2-0		(1-0)	Rogers 2,East 79	10,978
23	S		19	Leyton Orient		W3-0	(2-0)	Brown 4,36,52	5,083
24	S		26	Norwich City	L0-1		(0-0)		17,904
25	S	Jan	2	Charlton Athletic	W2-0		(0-0)	Summerbee 75,Rogers 80	12,826
26	S		16	Manchester City		W2-1	(1-0)	Brown 20,Summerbee 62	8,015
27	S		23	Portsmouth	D0-0				14,083
28	S		30	Norwich City		L1-3	(1-1)	Rogers 42	15,459
29	S	Feb	6	Huddersfield Town		L1-2	(0-2)	Brown 83	9,064
30	S		13	Derby County		L1-4	(0-2)	Summerbee 73	10,264
31	S		20	Coventry City	W4-1		(3-0)	Rogers 8,44,Summerbee 39,Dawson 52	14,053
32	S		27	Cardiff City		L0-2	(0-0)		9,197
33	S	Mar	13	Ipswich Town		D0-0			12,454
34	S		20	Plymouth Argyle	L2-3		(1-2)	Smart 34,Summerbee 50	12,175
35	Tu		23	Northampton Town	W4-2		(0-2)	Hunt 49,59,Summerbee 50,Rogers 85	17,686
36	F		26	Bolton Wanderers		D1-1	(0-0)	Brown 81	20,731
37	S	Apr	3	Middlesbrough	L0-1		(0-1)		13,672
38	S		10	Newcastle United		L0-1	(0-1)		32,503
39	F		16	Rotherham United	W3-2		(2-1)	Hunt 5,Smart 27,Summerbee 75	17,280
40	S		17	Preston North End	D2-2		(0-0)	Rogers 59,Summerbee 71	13,946
41	M		19	Rotherham United		L0-1	(0-1)		5,552
42	S		24	Southampton		L1-2	(1-1)	Brown 31	17,331

Average Home Attendance : **15,090**
Average Away Attendance : **13,704**

Football League Cup

					Home	Away	H-T	Goalscorers	Gate
2	W	Sep	23	Swansea Town		L1-3	(0-2)	Skeen 70	6,503

F A Cup

					Home	Away	H-T	Goalscorers	Gate
3	S	Jan	9	Ipswich Town	L1-2		(0-0)	Brown 89	14,802

MIKE SUMMERBEE

was born into a footballing family - his father George having been a pre-War Aldershot and Preston player while his uncle Gordon also played for Shots. Predictably nicknamed 'Buzzer', young Mike made his Town debut in a Wilts Premier League fixture in April 1959 and by Christmas had progressed to the Third Division side. He signed professional forms in March 1960 and soon became a regular on the right wing, or leading the attack. Top scorer in 1964/65, he became unsettled and asked for a move following the club's relegation. And on the eve of the following season he moved to Manchester City - where he was to earn six England caps. Mike eventually clocked up over 700 League appearances.

Atherton F G	Atkins W M	Brown D J	Dawson O J	East K M G	Haffey F	Hallett T R	Hicks A J	Howarth J	Hunt R P	Large F	Leggett P R	McPherson K	Morgan K	Oakley N	Peapell F D	Rogers D E	Shergold W F	Skeen K A	Smart R W	Sproates A	Summerbee M G	Trollope N J	Weaver E	Wollen T L	
	10		2						8	9		5	4	1		11			6		7	3			**1**
	10		2				1		8	9		5	4			11			6		7	3			**2**
	10						1		8	9		5	4			11			6		7	3		2	**3**
	10						1		8			5	4			11		9	6		7	3		2	**4**
	10		2				1		8	9		5	4			11			6		7	3			**5**
	10		2				1		8	9		5	4			11			6		7	3			**6**
	10		2				1		8	9		5	4			11			6		7	3			**7**
			2			6	1		8	9		5	4			11			10		7	3			**8**
			2			6	1		8			5	4		9	11			10		7	3			**9**
			2						8		7	5	4	1		11		10	6		9	3			**10**
			2						8		7	5	4	1		11		10	6		9	3			**11**
			2						8		7	5	4	1		11		10	6		9	3			**12**
			2						8		7	5	4	1		11		10	6		9	3			**13**
			2						8		7	5	4	1		11		10	6		9	3			**14**
	8		2		1	5					7		4			11		10	6		9	3			**15**
	8		2		1	5					7		4			11		10	6		9	3			**16**
	8		2		1	5					7		4			11		10	6		9	3			**17**
	8		2		1	5					7		4			11		10	6		9	3			**18**
	10	8	2	9		5							4	1		11			6		7	3			**19**
	10	8	2	9		5							4	1		11			6		7	3			**20**
		10	2	9		5	1						4			11	8			6	7	3			**21**
		7	2	10			1		8			5	4			11				6	9	3			**22**
6		10	2				1		8			5	4			11	7				9	3			**23**
6		10	2				1	9	8			5	4			11					7	3			**24**
6		10	2				1		8			5	4			11	7				9	3			**25**
6		10	2				1		8			5	4			11	7				9	3			**26**
6		10	2				1		8			5	4			11	7				9	3			**27**
6		10	2				1		8			5	4			11	9				7	3			**28**
6		10	2				1	9	8			5	4			11					7	3			**29**
6	10	9	2				1		8			5				11			4		7	3			**30**
6	10	9	2				1		8			5				11			4		7	3			**31**
6	10	9	2				1		8			5				11			4		7	3			**32**
6	10	9	2				1		8			5				11			4		7	3			**33**
6	10	9	2				1		8			5				11			4		7	3			**34**
6	10	9	2						8			5		1		11			4		7	3			**35**
6		9	2									5	8	1	7	11	4		10			3			**36**
6	10	9	2									5	8	1		11			4		7	3			**37**
6		9	2				1					5	8			11	4		10		7	3			**38**
6		9	2				1		8			5	4			11			10		7	3			**39**
6	8	9	2				1					5	4			11			10		7	3			**40**
6		10	2				1					5	8			11	4				9	3	7		**41**
6		9	2				1					5	4			11	8		10		7	3			**42**
20	21	24	40	4	4	9	27	2	29	7	9	35	36	11	2	42	10	10	32	2	41	42	1	2	Apps
	7	8	2	2					11		1		1			9		3	3		13	2			Goals

Opponents 1 goal

Atherton F G	Atkins W M	Brown D J	Dawson O J	East K M G	Haffey F	Hallett T R	Hicks A J	Howarth J	Hunt R P	Large F	Leggett P R	McPherson K	Morgan K	Oakley N	Peapell F D	Rogers D E	Shergold W F	Skeen K A	Smart R W	Sproates A	Summerbee M G	Trollope N J	Weaver E	Wollen T L	
			2						8		7	5	4	1		11		10	6		9	3			**2**

Atherton F G	Atkins W M	Brown D J	Dawson O J	East K M G	Haffey F	Hallett T R	Hicks A J	Howarth J	Hunt R P	Large F	Leggett P R	McPherson K	Morgan K	Oakley N	Peapell F D	Rogers D E	Shergold W F	Skeen K A	Smart R W	Sproates A	Summerbee M G	Trollope N J	Weaver E	Wollen T L	
6		10	2				1		8			5	4			11	7				9	3			**3**

For Final League Table - see page 169

SEASON 1965/66

Football League Third Division
Final League Position : 7th
Manager : Danny Williams

Substitutes :
s denotes substitute **not** used
* player substituted by *12

No	Day	Month	Date	Opponents	Home	Away	H-T	Goalscorers	Gate
1	S	Aug	21	Oxford United	D0-0				20,409
2	M		23	York City		W2-0	(1-0)	Brown 35,Rogers 60	9,003
3	S		28	Swansea Town		D1-1	(1-0)	Brown 41	10,060
4	W	Sep	1	Hull City		L0-1	(0-1)		23,163
5	S		4	Walsall	D0-0				13,734
6	Tu		7	Bristol Rovers		W1-0	(0-0)	Rogers 85	15,855
7	S		11	Workington		W3-0	(1-0)	Rogers 38,Brown 51,East 67	3,512
8	S		18	Bournemouth & Boscombe Athletic	D0-0				13,933
9	F		24	Southend United		L2-4	(1-3)	Skeen 36,Rogers 68	9,552
10	S	Oct	2	Watford		L0-2	(0-0)		11,432
11	Tu		5	Bristol Rovers	W4-3		(2-2)	Weaver 29,Smart 41,62,Brown 59	18,065
12	S		9	Gillingham	L0-1		(0-1)		13,133
13	S		16	Millwall		L0-1	(0-0)		13,907
14	Tu		19	York City	W6-0		(1-0)	Brown 40,Lawton 53,Trollope 75 pen.,Rogers 83,87,88	12,296
15	S		23	Peterborough United	W3-0		(1-0)	Rogers 9,Brown 58,Smart 68	12,628
16	S		30	Exeter City		D1-1	(0-1)	Lawton 81	6,722
17	S	Nov	6	Reading	W5-0		(1-0)	Lawton 1,Rogers 49,60,70,Brown 88	15,627
18	S		20	Mansfield Town	W6-2		(2-1)	East 12,35,71,74,87,Rogers 49	12,001
19	S		27	Queens Park Rangers		L2-3	(0-2)	East 77,Sanderson o.g.85	6,872
20	S	Dec	11	Scunthorpe United		L1-2	(0-0)	Brown 89	4,303
21	M		27	Grimsby Town		D2-2	(1-2)	East 26,Brown 75	13,284
22	S	Jan	1	Gillingham		L0-1	(0-1)		7,513
23	S		8	Hull City	W3-1		(2-0)	East 5,Smart 26,Henderson 70	15,682
24	S		15	Peterborough United		W3-2	(1-1)	East 19,60,Brown 81	5,065
25	S		29	Oxford United		W3-0	(2-0)	Henderson 11,Brown 44,Nurse 88	16,074
26	S	Feb	5	Swansea Town	D2-2		(0-1)	East 63,67	13,635
27	S		12	Brentford	W2-1		(1-1)	East 37,Trollope 84 pen.	12,376
28	S		19	Walsall		L0-5	(0-3)		9,367
29	S	Mar	5	Brentford		W1-0	(0-0)	Smart 75	9,913
30	S		12	Bournemouth & Boscombe Athletic		L0-1	(0-1)		7,699
31	Tu		15	Millwall	W1-0		(0-0)	Henderson 49	16,628
32	S		19	Southend United	W4-0		(3-0)	Rogers 10,14,Brown 39,East 88	12,352
33	S		26	Watford	L0-1		(0-1)		10,584
34	F	Apr	1	Reading		W2-0	(0-0)	Rogers 54,64	13,758
35	S		9	Brighton & Hove Albion	W3-2		(3-2)	Nurse 5,Brown 20,Weaver 44	13,367
36	M		11	Oldham Athletic	L0-1		(0-0)		12,593
37	Tu		12	Oldham Athletic		D1-1	(0-0)	East 73	10,344
38	S		16	Mansfield Town		W5-1	(2-1)	Brown 37,East 41,Rogers 82,Trollope 88,Dawson 89	3,764
39	S		23	Queens Park Rangers	W2-1		(1-0)	East 26,Rogers 56	13,620
40	Tu		26	Shrewsbury Town	D0-0				11,190
41	S		30	Brighton & Hove Albion		L0-1	(0-0)		10,733
42	Tu	May	3	Workington	L0-1		(0-1)		9,627
43	S		7	Scunthorpe United	D0-0				9,077
44	Tu		10	Grimsby Town	D0-0				8,044
45	W		18	Shrewsbury Town		D1-1	(0-0)	Morgan 72	2,719
46	S		28	Exeter City	D2-2		(1-2)	East 35,Brown 46	6,959

Average Home Attendance : **12,937**
Average Away Attendance : **9,766**

Football League Cup

Rd	Day	Month	Date	Opponents	Home	Away	H-T	Goalscorers	Gate
2	W	Sep	22	Darlington		L1-2	(1-0)	Rogers 22	5,430

F A Cup

Rd	Day	Month	Date	Opponents	Home	Away	H-T	Goalscorers	Gate
1	S	Nov	13	Merthyr Tydfil	W5-1		(1-0)	East 3,53,63,66,Smart 86	15,962
2	S	Dec	4	Grantham		W6-1	(0-0)	Weaver 53,Nurse 60,Brown 66,Smart 67,70,East 73	6,500
3	S	Jan	22	Coventry City	L1-2		(0-1)	Brown 68	20,200

DANNY WILLIAMS
made 500 appearances at wing-half for Rotherham, having joined the club during the War, before he took over at the County Ground in June 1965. By making a number of shrewd signings, Danny built the team that lifted the League Cup and won promotion four years later. Danny then went back to Yorkshire to the hot seat at Hillsborough, but he returned to Swindon in March 1974. By then, lack of investment in the team had resulted in inevitable relegation. He moved 'upstairs' in May 1978 to make way for Bob Smith.

Atherton F G	Brown D J	Butler J W	Dawson O J	Downsborough P	East K M G	Giles J A	Hallett T R	Henderson T W	Hicks A J	Hunt R P	Keyworth K	Lawton J M	Morgan K	Nurse M T G	Richardson B W	Rogers D E	Shergold W F	Skeen K A	Smart R W	Sproates A	Thomas R J	Trollope N J	Walker B A	Weaver E	
6	10		2	1			5			8	9		4			11			s			3		7	**1**
6	10		2	1			5			8	9		4			11			s			3		7	**2**
6	10		2	1			5			8	9		4			11			s			3		7	**3**
6	10		2	1						8	9		4	5		11			s			3		7	**4**
6	10		2	1						8	9		4	5		11			s			3		7	**5**
6	10	2		1	9								4	5		11	s		8			3		7	**6**
6	10	2		1	9								4	5		11	s		8			3		7	**7**
6	10	2	s	1	9								4	5		11			8			3		7	**8**
6	10	2	*12	1								9	4	5		11		*7	8			3			**9**
6	10	2	s	1								9	4	5		11			8			3		7	**10**
6	10	*12	*2	1								9	4	5		11			8			3		7	**11**
		2	s	1							10	9	4	5		11	6		8			3		7	**12**
	10		2	1	9							s	4	5		11	6		8			3		7	**13**
	10	s	2	1								9	4	5		11	6		8			3		7	**14**
	10	s	2	1								9	4	5		11	6		8			3		7	**15**
	10	s	2	1								9	4	5		11	6		8			3		7	**16**
	8		2	1			s					9	4	5		11	6		10			3		7	**17**
	8	s	2	1	9								4	5		11	6		10			3		7	**18**
s	8		2	1	9								4	5		11	6		10			3		7	**19**
	8	*12	2	1	9								4	5		11	6		10			3		*7	**20**
	10	s	2	1	9								4	5		7	6		8			3	11		**21**
	10		2	1	9		s						4	5		7	6		8			3	11		**22**
	8	s	2		9			7	1				4	5	6	11			10			3			**23**
	10	s	2		9			7	1				4	5	6	11			8			3			**24**
	10		2	1	9			7					4	5	6	11			8			3		s	**25**
	10	2		1	9			7					4	5	6	11	s		8			3			**26**
	10		2	1	9		s	7					4	5	6	11			8			3			**27**
			2	1	9			7					4	5	6	10	s		8			3		11	**28**
	10		2	1	9			s					4	5		11	6		8			3		7	**29**
	10		2	1	9								4	5	s	11	6		8			3		7	**30**
	10		2	1	9			7					4	5	6	11	s		8			3			**31**
	10		2	1	9			7					4	5	6	11			8			3		s	**32**
	10		2	1	9		s	7					4	5	6	11			8			3			**33**
	10		2	1	9							s	4	5		11	6		8			3		7	**34**
	10		2	1	9							s	4	5		11	6		8			3		7	**35**
	10		2	1	*12							9	4	5		11	6		*8			3		7	**36**
		3	2		9		4	7	1			s		5	6	11	8					10			**37**
	8		2	1	9		4							5	6	11	10				s	3		7	**38**
	10		2	1	9		4						s	5		11	6		8			3		7	**39**
	10		2	1	9		4						s	5		11	6		8			3		7	**40**
	10		2	1	9		4						6	5		11	s		8			3		7	**41**
	10		2	1	9		s						4	5		11	6		8			3		7	**42**
	s		2	1	9			7					4	5		11	6		8		3	10			**43**
	8		2	1	9	5		s					4			11			6		3	10		7	**44**
	8	10	2	1	9	s							4	5		11			6			3		7	**45**
	8	10	2		9		s		1				4	5		11			6			3		7	**46**
11	42	10	39	42	32	1	8	11	4	5	6	9	42	42	11	46	22	1	39	0	2	46	2	33	Apps
		2	1		1																				Subs
	15		1		19			3				3	1	2		18		1	5			3		2	Goals

Opponents 1 goal

Atherton F G	Brown D J	Butler J W	Dawson O J	Downsborough P	East K M G	Giles J A	Hallett T R	Henderson T W	Hicks A J	Hunt R P	Keyworth K	Lawton J M	Morgan K	Nurse M T G	Richardson B W	Rogers D E	Shergold W F	Skeen K A	Smart R W	Sproates A	Thomas R J	Trollope N J	Walker B A	Weaver E	
	10	s	2	1							9			5		11	4	7	8	6		3			**2**

Atherton F G	Brown D J	Butler J W	Dawson O J	Downsborough P	East K M G	Giles J A	Hallett T R	Henderson T W	Hicks A J	Hunt R P	Keyworth K	Lawton J M	Morgan K	Nurse M T G	Richardson B W	Rogers D E	Shergold W F	Skeen K A	Smart R W	Sproates A	Thomas R J	Trollope N J	Walker B A	Weaver E	
	8	s	2	1	9								4	5		11	6		10			3		7	**1**
	8	s	2	1	9								4	5		11	6		10			3		7	**2**
	10	s	2	1	9			7					4	5	6	11			8			3			**3**
	3		3	3	3			1					3	3	1	3	2		3			3		2	Apps
																									Subs
	2				5									1					3					1	Goals

For Final League Table - see page 169

SEASON 1966/67

Football League Third Division
Final League Position : 8th
Manager : Danny Williams

Substitutes :
s denotes substitute **not** used
* player substituted by *12

				Home	Away	H-T	Goalscorers	Gate
1	S	Aug	20 Brighton & Hove Albion		D2-2	(1-0)	Weaver 3,Brown 66	10,102
2	S		27 Darlington	W4-0		(2-0)	Butler 10,Jacques o.g.15,Weaver 79,Rogers 84 pen.	10,855
3	S	Sep	3 Queens Park Rangers		L1-3	(1-1)	Brown 3	7,900
4	Tu		6 Colchester United	D1-1		(1-1)	Rogers 16	11,600
5	S		10 Watford	L1-2		(1-0)	Brown 7	9,999
6	S		17 Bristol Rovers		L0-3	(0-1)		10,907
7	S		24 Reading		L1-2	(1-0)	Brown 43	9,064
8	M		26 Colchester United		L1-2	(1-0)	Penman 45	7,874
9	S	Oct	1 Doncaster Rovers	L0-1		(0-0)		7,780
10	S		8 Shrewsbury Town	D2-2		(1-0)	Penman 27,66	7,985
11	S		15 Middlesbrough		L0-4	(0-3)		8,126
12	Tu		18 Walsall		D1-1	(0-0)	Rogers 76	9,027
13	S		22 Swansea Town	W4-0		(3-0)	Rogers 9,Nurse 33,Brown 36,Walker 72	8,638
14	S		29 Bournemouth & Boscombe Athletic		W4-1	(2-0)	Brown 5,28,46,57	6,333
15	S	Nov	5 Orient	W5-1		(4-1)	Walker 6,Brown 8,Penman 38,Trollope 40,Rogers 60	8,996
16	S		12 Gillingham		L0-1	(0-1)		7,320
17	S		19 Workington	W3-0		(1-0)	Brown 26,67,Penman 47	9,497
18	S	Dec	3 Oldham Athletic	W6-3		(2-1)	Brown 18,66,Rogers 25,50,87,Walker 69	10,347
19	S		10 Oxford United		D0-0			10,037
20	S		17 Brighton & Hove Albion	D1-1		(1-0)	Rogers 42	9,900
21	F		23 Peterborough United		W2-1	(2-1)	Rogers 21,Nurse 43	5,393
22	M		26 Peterborough United	W4-1		(1-0)	Rogers 32,56,Penman 70,72	14,619
23	S		31 Darlington		L1-2	(0-2)	Nurse 86	5,060
24	S	Jan	14 Watford		L0-2	(0-2)		16,942
25	S		21 Bristol Rovers	L0-1		(0-1)		15,473
26	S	Feb	4 Reading	L0-1		(0-1)		16,964
27	S		11 Doncaster Rovers		L0-1	(0-0)		7,935
28	S		25 Shrewsbury Town		L1-3	(0-2)	Rogers 81 pen.	5,057
29	Tu		28 Grimsby Town	W3-1		(1-1)	Trollope 18,Terry 48,Rogers 74	11,458
30	S	Mar	4 Middlesbrough	W4-1		(1-0)	Gates o.g.42,Rogers 49 pen.,56,72	14,200
31	S		18 Swansea Town		D2-2	(0-2)	Butler 66,Smart 85	5,816
32	S		25 Bournemouth & Boscombe Athletic	W1-0		(0-0)	Rogers 64 pen.	14,099
33	M		27 Torquay United		L0-1	(0-0)		9,711
34	Tu		28 Torquay United	D0-0				14,327
35	S	Apr	1 Orient		D0-0			7,298
36	W		5 Grimsby Town		W4-3	(0-2)	Smart 65,Nurse 79,Rogers 80,Terry 89	4,743
37	S		8 Gillingham	W2-0		(1-0)	Penman 25,Walker 79	10,375
38	Tu		11 Mansfield Town	W3-1		(1-0)	Smart 14,Rogers 58,Terry 67	13,280
39	S		15 Workington		W3-1	(1-1)	Smart 11,Penman 57,Terry 90	1,611
40	Tu		18 Walsall	W3-2		(3-0)	Rogers 23,44 pen.,Terry 29	14,459
41	S		22 Scunthorpe United	W2-1		(0-1)	Smart 49,Penman 58	12,786
42	M		24 Mansfield Town		W3-1	(3-1)	Nurse 16,Morris o.g.20,Terry 38	7,837
43	F		28 Oldham Athletic		L0-1	(0-0)		5,605
44	Tu	May	2 Queens Park Rangers	D1-1		(0-0)	Rogers 65	21,210
45	S		6 Oxford United	W3-0		(1-0)	Terry 28,Smart 74,Rogers 88	13,981
46	F		12 Scunthorpe United		W2-1	(1-0)	Smart 12,Nurse 46	3,544

Average Home Attendance : **12,297**
Average Away Attendance : **7,532**

Football League Cup

				Home	Away	H-T	Goalscorers	Gate
1	W	Aug	24 Bournemouth & Boscombe Athletic	W2-1		(2-1)	Trollope 15,Butler 42	7,769
2	Tu	Sep	13 Portsmouth	W4-1		(2-0)	Brown 22,East 26,67,Rogers 56	7,784
3	Tu	Oct	4 Doncaster Rovers		D1-1	(0-1)	Butler 86	9,190
3R	Tu		11 Doncaster Rovers	+ W4-2		(1-0)	Smart 21,105,Morgan 52,Lawton 100	8,147
4	W		25 West Bromwich Albion	L0-2		(0-0)		16,254

\+ After Extra Time

F A Cup

				Home	Away	H-T	Goalscorers	Gate
1	S	Nov	26 Horsham		W3-0	(1-0)	Rogers 26,Nurse 70,Brown 86	8,000
2	Tu	Jan	10 Ashford Town	W5-0		(1-0)	Brown 38,Rogers 53 pen.,60,Walker 67,Penman 75	12,079
3	S		28 West Ham United		D3-3	(1-2)	Rogers 26,71,Brown 60	37,440
3R	Tu		31 West Ham United	W3-1		(1-0)	Penman 18,Rogers 84,Skeen 89	25,789
4	S	Feb	18 Bury	W2-1		(1-0)	Morgan 18,Rogers 47	24,452
5	S	Mar	11 Nottingham Forest		D0-0			45,898
5R	Tu		14 Nottingham Forest	+ D1-1		(0-1)	Walker 90	28,008
Rp	M		20 Nottingham Forest	* L0-3		(0-0)		52,956

* Played at Villa Park

For Final League Table - see page 169

Brown D J	Butler J W	Dawson O J	Desmeules R L	Downsborough P	East K M G	Giles J A	Harland S C	Hicks A J	Jones R S	Lawton J M	Morgan K	Nurse M T G	Penman W S T	Rogers D E	Skeen K A	Smart R W	Terry P A	Thomas R J	Trollope N J	Walker B A	Weaver E	
8	10	2			s		6	1			4	5		11		9			3		7	1
8	10	2			s		6	1			4	5		11		9			3		7	2
8	10	2					6	1			s	5	9	11		4			3		7	3
8		2		1	9		6				4	5	10	11				s	3		7	4
8	s	2		1			6				4	5	10	11		9			3		7	5
8	2	7		1	9	5	6					*12		11		*4		10	3			6
7	6	2		1	8		9				4	5	10	11				s	3			7
8	10	2		1	9		6				4	5	7	11				s	3			8
*8	2	*12			9	5	6	1			4		7	11				10	3			9
8	s	2					6	1		9	4	5	7	11		10			3			10
8	2				s		6	1		9	4	5	7	11		10			3			11
8				1	9	*12	6						*10	7		4		3	2	11		12
8	10				9		6	1			s	5		7		4		2	3	11		13
8	10			1	s		6					5	9	7		4		2	3	11		14
8	10			1			6				s	5	9	7		4		2	3	11		15
8	10			1		s	6					5	9	7		4		2	3	11		16
8	10			1			6				s	5	9	7		4		2	3	11		17
8	10			1	s		6					5	9	7		4		2	3	11		18
8	10			1		s	6					5	9	7		4		2	3	11		19
8	10						6	1			s	5	9	7		4		2	3	11		20
8	10						6	1				5	9	7	s	4		2	3	11		21
8	10						6	1				5	9	7	s	4		2	3	11		22
8	10						6	1				5	9	7	s	4		2	3	11		23
8	10						6	1				5	9	7		4		2	3	s	11	24
8	s						6	1				5	9	7	10	4		2	3	11		25
7	s						6	1			4	5	8	11	9	10		2	3			26
	s						6	1	7		4	5	8	11	9	10		2	3			27
	10						6	1	11		4	5	9	7	s	8		2	3			28
						s	6	1	11		4	5	8	7		10	9	2	3			29
							6	1	11		4	5	8	7		10	9	2	3		s	30
	8	s				5	6	1	10					11		4	9	2	3		7	31
	s						6	1	11		4	5	8	7		10	9	2	3			32
	s			1			6		11		4	5	8	7		10	9	2	3			33
	s			1			6		11		4	5	8	7		10	9	2	3			34
	8			1			6		*11		4	5	*12	7		10	9	2	3			35
				1			6		s		4	5	8	7		10	9	2	3	11		36
				1			6		s		4	5	8	7		10	9	2	3	11		37
		2		1			6		s		4	5	8	7		10	9		3	11		38
	s			1			6				4	5	8	7		10	9	2	3	11		39
		s		1			6				4	5	8	7		10	9	2	3	11		40
				1			6		s		4	5	8	7		10	9	2	3	11		41
				1			6				4	5	8	7		10	9	2	3	11	s	42
	s	2		1			6				4	5	8	7		10	9		3	11		43
		2		1			6		11		s	5	8	7		10	9	4	3			44
		2		1			6					5	8	7	s	10	9	4	3	11		45
			4	1			6		10			5	s	11		8	9	2	3		7	46
26	23	13	1	26	7	3	46	20	11	2	26	43	39	46	3	42	18	35	46	22	8	Apps
		1				1						1	1									Subs
14	2											6	10	24		7	7		2	4	2	Goals

Opponents 3 goals

Brown D J	Butler J W	Dawson O J	Desmeules R L	Downsborough P	East K M G	Giles J A	Harland S C	Hicks A J	Jones R S	Lawton J M	Morgan K	Nurse M T G	Penman W S T	Rogers D E	Skeen K A	Smart R W	Terry P A	Thomas R J	Trollope N J	Walker B A	Weaver E	
8	10	2			s		6	1			4	5		11		9			3		7	1
8	2	*12		1	9	5	6							11		4		10	3		*7	2
8	10	2				5	6	1		9	s		7	11		4			3			3
8	s	2				5	6	1		9	4		7	11		10			3			3R
8	10				9		6	1			s	5		7		4		2	3	11		4
5	4	3		1	2	3	5	4		2	2	2	2	5		5		2	5	1	2	Apps
		1																				Subs
1	2				2					1	1			1		2			1			Goals

Brown D J	Butler J W	Dawson O J	Desmeules R L	Downsborough P	East K M G	Giles J A	Harland S C	Hicks A J	Jones R S	Lawton J M	Morgan K	Nurse M T G	Penman W S T	Rogers D E	Skeen K A	Smart R W	Terry P A	Thomas R J	Trollope N J	Walker B A	Weaver E	
8	10			1			6					5	9	7	s	4		2	3	11		1
8	10						6	1			s	5	9	7		4		2	3	11		2
7		s					6	1			4	5	8	11	9	10		2	3			3
7		s					6	1			4	5	8	11	9	10		2	3			3R
	s						6	1			4	5	10	7	9	8		2	3	11		4
	s						6	1			4	5	8	7	9	10		2	3	11		5
	s						6	1			4	5	8	7	9	10		2	3	11		5R
		s					6	1			4	5	8	7	9	10		2	3	11		Rp
4	2	0		1			8	7			6	8	8	8	6	8		8	8	6		Apps
																						Subs
3											1	1	2	7	1					2		Goals

DENNIS BROWN

SEASON 1967/68

Football League Third Division
Final League Position : 10th
Manager : Danny Williams

Substitutes :
s denotes substitute **not** used
* player substituted by *12

					Home	Away	H-T	Goalscorers	Gate
1	S	Aug	19	Brighton & Hove Albion	W2-1		(0-1)	Terry 60,Rogers 70	15,790
2	F		25	Stockport County		L0-2	(0-0)		9,103
3	S	Sep	2	Tranmere Rovers	W3-1		(1-0)	Penman 1,82,Rogers 53	12,152
4	M		4	Barrow		D1-1	(0-0)	Terry 90	7,352
5	S		9	Orient		D0-0			4,722
6	S		16	Northampton Town	W4-0		(2-0)	Rogers 14,57,Terry 25,Flowers o.g.77	13,280
7	S		23	Walsall		L2-3	(0-2)	Harland 49,Rogers 63	9,132
8	Tu		26	Barrow	L0-1		(0-1)		13,567
9	S		30	Gillingham	D2-2		(0-1)	Bailey o.g.58,Rogers 83	12,808
10	W	Oct	4	Reading		L1-2	(0-1)	Rogers 52	17,867
11	S		7	Bury		D1-1	(1-1)	Smart 8	8,222
12	S		14	Bournemouth & Boscombe Athletic	W4-0		(3-0)	Terry 2,9,10,Rogers 65	11,135
13	S		21	Colchester United		L1-2	(1-0)	Penman 43	4,907
14	Tu		24	Reading	W5-1		(3-1)	Penman 10,36,Terry 21,48,Harland 76	17,240
15	S		28	Peterborough United	D0-0				12,227
16	S	Nov	4	Mansfield Town		D2-2	(0-2)	Terry 66,Dawson 75	4,619
17	S		11	Watford	W2-0		(2-0)	Terry 20,Rogers 41	13,147
18	M		13	Tranmere Rovers		L2-3	(2-2)	Smart 35,Rogers 36	6,590
19	S		18	Southport		D1-1	(0-0)	Walker 57	5,008
20	S		25	Scunthorpe United	W2-0		(0-0)	Terry 56,Rogers 59	11,769
21	S	Dec	2	Oldham Athletic		W2-0	(2-0)	Rogers 20,Terry 40	6,968
22	S		16	Brighton & Hove Albion		D0-0			9,142
23	Tu		19	Stockport County	W2-0		(0-0)	Butler 59,Rogers 63	12,856
24	Tu		26	Torquay United		D1-1	(1-1)	Butler 31	12,910
25	S		30	Torquay United	W1-0		(1-0)	Rogers 27	18,161
26	S	Jan	20	Northampton Town		L0-2	(0-2)		10,339
27	S	Feb	3	Walsall	W3-0		(2-0)	Rogers 6,Nurse 45,Penman 79	17,111
28	S		10	Gillingham		L1-3	(0-1)	Smart 85	5,116
29	S		24	Bury	L2-3		(0-2)	Noble 55,63	14,464
30	Tu		27	Grimsby Town	W5-0		(3-0)	Rogers 20,26,Terry 44,56,Taylor o.g.70	12,791
31	S	Mar	2	Bournemouth & Boscombe Athletic		L1-2	(0-0)	Terry 88	7,469
32	S		9	Shrewsbury Town		W1-0	(0-0)	Harland 47	7,810
33	Tu		12	Orient	W4-0		(2-0)	Rogers 25,Trollope 32,Harland 68,Taylor o.g.86	14,184
34	S		16	Colchester United	D1-1		(1-1)	Rogers 34	13,515
35	Tu		19	Shrewsbury Town	D0-0				14,541
36	S		23	Peterborough United		D1-1	(0-0)	Trollope 52	4,667
37	S		30	Mansfield Town	D1-1		(1-0)	Butler 43	10,248
38	S	Apr	6	Watford		L0-2	(0-1)		7,569
39	F		12	Oxford United		D0-0			17,751
40	S		13	Southport	D3-3		(1-1)	Rogers 12,90,Smart 48	10,929
41	Tu		16	Oxford United	D1-1		(0-0)	Rogers 78	16,418
42	F		19	Scunthorpe United		L1-3	(1-1)	Nurse 76	2,617
43	Tu		23	Bristol Rovers	W4-1		(1-0)	Terry 35,Rogers 53,Smart 83,90	11,438
44	S		27	Oldham Athletic	D0-0				9,717
45	S	May	4	Bristol Rovers		W2-1	(1-1)	Smart 27,Rogers 77	8,928
46	S		11	Grimsby Town		L2-3	(1-2)	Rogers 25,Harland 70	4,593

Average Home Attendance : **13,456**
Average Away Attendance : **7,974**

Football League Cup

					Home	Away	H-T	Goalscorers	Gate
1/1	Tu	Aug	22	Newport County	D1-1		(0-1)	Rogers 53 pen.	10,870
1/2	Tu		29	Newport County		L0-2	(0-2)		6,537

F A Cup

					Home	Away	H-T	Goalscorers	Gate
1	Tu	Dec	12	Salisbury	W4-0		(0-0)	Penman 46,Terry 67,75,82	12,193
2	S	Jan	6	Luton Town	W3-2		(2-0)	Rogers 18 pen.,40,Heath 83	18,203
3	S		27	Blackburn Rovers	W1-0		(1-0)	Nurse 11	20,830
4	S	Feb	17	Sheffield Wednesday		L1-2	(1-0)	Smart 34	37,457

For Final League Table - see page 170

Bailey J S	Blick M R	Butler J W	Dawson O J	Desmeules R L	Downsborough P	Giles J A	Harland S C	Harper D	Heath D	Jones R J	Lowes B T	Noble P	Nurse M T G	Penman W S T	Rogers D E	Smart R W	Terry P A	Thomas R J	Trollope N J	Walker B A	
					1		6	4			*7		5	8	11	10	9	2	3	*12	**1**
		8	s	4	1		6						5		7	10	9	2	3	11	**2**
		s	7		1		6	4					5	8	11	10	9	2	3		**3**
		*12	7		*1		6	4					5	8	11	10	9	2	3		**4**
		7					6	4		1			5	8	11	10	9	2	3	s	**5**
		4					6	s	7	1			5	8	11	10	9	2	3		**6**
		4	s				6		7	1			5	8	11	10	9	2	3		**7**
		4	s			5	6		7	1				8	11	10	9	2	3		**8**
		4	s		1	5	6		7					8	11	10	9	2	3		**9**
		4	*12		1		6		*7				5	8	11	10	9	2	3		**10**
		4	*12		1		6		7				5	8	11	10	9	*2	3		**11**
		4	s		1		6		7				5	8	11	10	9	2	3		**12**
		4			1	s	6		7				5	8	11	10	9	2	3		**13**
		4	7		1		6						5	8	11	10	9	2	3	s	**14**
		4	7		1	s	6						5	8	11	10	9	2	3		**15**
		4	2		1	5	6		s					8	7	10	9		3	11	**16**
		4	2		1		6		7				5	*8	11	10	9		3	*12	**17**
		4	2		1		6		7				5	8	11	10	9		3	s	**18**
		4	2		1		6		*7				5	8	11	10	9		3	*12	**19**
		4	2		1		6		7				5	8	11	10	9	s	3		**20**
		4	8		1		6		*7				5	*12	11	10	9	2	3		**21**
		4	*12		1		6		7				5	8	11	10	9	2	*3		**22**
		4	s		1		6		7				5	8	11	10	9	2	3		**23**
		4	s		1		6		7				5	8	11	10	9	2	3		**24**
		4	s		1		6		7				5	8	11	10	9	2	3		**25**
		4	*8		1		6		7				5	*12	11	10	9	2	3		**26**
		4			1		6		*7			*12	5	8	11	10	9	2	3		**27**
		4			1		6		7			*12	5	*8	11	10	9	2	3		**28**
		4			1		6				*7	*12	5	8	11	10	9	2	3		**29**
		4			1		6		s			8	5	7	11	10	9	2	3		**30**
		4			1		6		*12			8	5	*7	11	10	9	2	3		**31**
		4	8				6		7	1		*12	5		11	*10	9	2	3		**32**
		10	4				6		7	1		8	5	s	11		9	2	3		**33**
		10	4				6		7	1		8	5	*12	11		*9	2	3		**34**
		10	4			9	6		7	1		8	5	s	11			2	3		**35**
		4	10				6		s	1		8	5	7	11		9	2	3		**36**
		4					6		7	1		s	5	8	11	10	9	2	3		**37**
		4	8				6			1		7	5	*12	11	10	*9	2	3		**38**
		4	5			*9	6		7	1				8	11	10	*12	2	3		**39**
*12		4	5				6		7	1				*8	11	10	9	2	3		**40**
*12		4	5				6			1		*7		8	11	10	9	2	3		**41**
		4	s				6		7	1			5	8	11	10	9	2	3		**42**
s		4	7				6		8	1			5		11	10	9	2	3		**43**
		4	7			5	6		8	1			s		11	10	9	2	3		**44**
	5	s		4		6	9		7	1		10			11	8		2	3		**45**
	5		*12	*4		6	9		7	1		10			11	8		2	3		**46**
0	2	41	22	3	27	8	46	4	32	19	2	10	37	34	46	42	42	41	46	2	Apps
2		1	4						1			4		4			1			3	Subs
		3	1				5					2	2	6	25	7	16		2	1	Goals

Opponents 4 goals

Bailey J S	Blick M R	Butler J W	Dawson O J	Desmeules R L	Downsborough P	Giles J A	Harland S C	Harper D	Heath D	Jones R J	Lowes B T	Noble P	Nurse M T G	Penman W S T	Rogers D E	Smart R W	Terry P A	Thomas R J	Trollope N J	Walker B A	
		8	*12		1		6	*4					5		7	10	9	2	3	11	**1/1**
		10	s		1		6						5	8	7	4	9	2	3	11	**1/2**
		2	0		2		2	1					2	1	2	2	2	2	2	2	Apps
			1																		Subs
															1						Goals

Bailey J S	Blick M R	Butler J W	Dawson O J	Desmeules R L	Downsborough P	Giles J A	Harland S C	Harper D	Heath D	Jones R J	Lowes B T	Noble P	Nurse M T G	Penman W S T	Rogers D E	Smart R W	Terry P A	Thomas R J	Trollope N J	Walker B A	
		4	*8		1		6		7				5	*12		10	9	2	3	11	**1**
		4	2		1	*12	6		7				5	*8	11	10	9		3		**2**
		4	s		1		6		7				5	8	11	10	9	2	3		**3**
		4			1		6		7			*12	5	8	11	10	*9	2	3		**4**
		4	2		4	0	4		4			0	4	3	3	4	4	3	4	1	Apps
						1						1		1							Subs
									1				1	1	2	1	3				Goals

PAT
TERRY

SEASON 1968/69

Football League Third Division
Final League Position : 2nd
Manager : Danny Williams

Substitutes :
s denotes substitute **not** used
* player substituted by *12

				Opponents	Home	Away	H-T	Goalscorers	Gate
1	S	Aug	17	Stockport County	W1-0		(0-0)	Noble 80	13,350
2	S		24	Hartlepool		D0-0			5,732
3	Tu		27	Reading	D0-0				16,765
4	S		31	Plymouth Argyle	W3-0		(1-0)	Rogers 10,57,Smart 64	12,302
5	S	Sep	7	Watford		D0-0			8,668
6	S		14	Walsall	W1-0		(1-0)	Noble 9	10,594
7	W		18	Bournemouth & Boscombe Athletic		L0-2	(0-1)		12,217
8	S		21	Bristol Rovers		L1-2	(0-0)	Taylor o.g.83	10,364
9	S		28	Shrewsbury Town	W3-0		(2-0)	Noble 3,30,Rogers 79	12,092
10	S	Oct	5	Orient	W1-0		(0-0)	Howe o.g.46	12,455
11	W		9	Reading		W1-0	(1-0)	Smart 19	17,451
12	S		12	Brighton & Hove Albion		W3-1	(1-0)	Smith 32,Rogers 55,Butler 87	7,355
13	S		19	Torquay United	W2-1		(1-0)	Rogers 45,Noble 70	15,159
14	S		26	Oldham Athletic		W3-2	(1-1)	Heath 31,Rogers 68,Smart 85	4,238
15	S	Nov	2	Southport	W5-1		(2-0)	Rogers 22,32,78 pen.,89,Smith 48	18,913
16	S		9	Luton Town		L0-2	(0-0)		17,250
17	S		23	Mansfield Town		L0-2	(0-1)		5,471
18	Tu		26	Northampton Town		W6-2	(2-1)	Smith 28,Rogers 40,82,Smart 55,Heath 56,Noble 75	6,827
19	S	Dec	14	Brighton & Hove Albion	W1-0		(0-0)	Rogers 89	10,914
20	S		21	Torquay United		W1-0	(0-0)	Smith 65	8,327
21	Th		26	Orient		L0-1	(0-1)		7,101
22	S	Jan	11	Southport		D1-1	(0-0)	Rogers 74	5,232
23	S		18	Luton Town	D0-0				18,909
24	F		24	Tranmere Rovers		W5-3	(3-1)	Jones 33,38,Rogers 45,Smart 73,Noble 78	8,353
25	Tu		28	Oldham Athletic	W5-1		(3-0)	Burrows 2,Jones 4,43,85,Smart 78	21,316
26	S	Feb	1	Barnsley		D1-1	(1-1)	Trollope 8	13,983
27	Tu		4	Hartlepool	D1-1		(0-0)	Noble 53	18,921
28	S		15	Barrow		W3-0	(0-0)	Smart 54,Noble 79,Jones 88	3,470
29	Tu		18	Tranmere Rovers	W1-0		(0-0)	Noble 86	19,714
30	S		22	Rotherham United	W1-0		(0-0)	Noble 55	23,515
31	Tu		25	Gillingham	W1-0		(0-0)	Noble 90	17,489
32	S	Mar	1	Northampton Town	W1-0		(0-0)	Rogers 62	17,081
33	W		5	Gillingham		L0-2	(0-1)		6,104
34	S		8	Stockport County		L1-2	(1-1)	Noble 45	6,647
35	S		22	Plymouth Argyle		L1-2	(0-1)	Smart 65	20,776
36	Tu		25	Barnsley	W2-0		(0-0)	Noble 50,86	17,198
37	S		29	Watford	L0-1		(0-0)		28,898
38	F	Apr	4	Crewe Alexandra		W2-1	(0-0)	Noble 51,Smith 71	9,053
39	S		5	Shrewsbury Town		D1-1	(1-0)	Harland 17	7,387
40	Tu		8	Bournemouth & Boscombe Athletic	W3-0		(1-0)	Smart 36,Rogers 57,Smith 77	22,464
41	S		12	Bristol Rovers	D2-2		(1-1)	Rogers 1 pen.,64	20,401
42	Tu		15	Crewe Alexandra	W1-0		(0-0)	Penman 74	19,897
43	S		19	Walsall		W2-0	(2-0)	Rogers 18,43	10,654
44	Tu		22	Mansfield Town	W1-0		(1-0)	Ledger o.g.3	21,045
45	F	May	2	Rotherham United		D1-1	(0-0)	Jones 89	9,584
46	M		5	Barrow	W2-0		(1-0)	Smith 37,Rogers 58	21,289

Average Home Attendance : **17,856**
Average Away Attendance : **9,228**

F A Cup

				Opponents	Home	Away	H-T	Goalscorers	Gate
1	S	Nov	16	Canterbury City		W1-0	(0-0)	Rogers 89 pen.	14,367
2	S	Dec	7	Grantham		W2-0	(0-0)	Jones 84,Smith 85	3,922
3	S	Jan	4	Southend United	L0-2		(0-1)		18,828

Football League Cup

See overleaf >>

Blick M R	Burrows F	Butler J W	Dangerfield D J	Dawson O J	Desmeules R L	Downsborough P	Giles J A	Harland S C	Heath D	Jones C M N	Noble P	Penman W S T	Rogers D E	Smart R W	Smith J	Thomas R J	Trollope N J	
	5	s				1		6	7	9	8		11	4	10	2	3	**1**
	5	10				1		6	7	9	8	*12		4	11	2	*3	**2**
	5	3		s		1		6	7	9	8		11	4	10	2		**3**
	5	4		2		1		6	7		10	s	11	8	9	3		**4**
	5	4		2		1	s	6	7		10		11	8	9	3		**5**
	5	4		2		1		6	7	s	10		11	8	9	3		**6**
	5	4		2		1		6	7	s	10		11	8	9	3		**7**
5		4		2		1		6	7	*12	10		11	*8	9	3		**8**
	5	4		2		1		6	7	9	8		11	s	10	3		**9**
	5	4		2		1		6	7	9	8		11	s	10	3		**10**
	5	4		2		1		6	*7	*12	10		11	8	9	3		**11**
	5	4		2		1		6		*9	10	*12	7	8	11	3		**12**
	5	4		*2		1		6	7		10	*12	11	8	9	3		**13**
	5	3				1		6	7	s	10	4	11	8	9	2		**14**
	5			2		1		6	7	*12	10	*4	11	8	9	3		**15**
	5	4		2		1		6	7	s	10		11	8	9	3		**16**
	5	4		2		1		6	7		10	s	11	8	9	3		**17**
5		4		2		1		6	7		10	s	11	8	9	3		**18**
	5			2		1		6	7	*12	*10	4	11	8	9	3		**19**
	5	4		2		1		6	*12		*10	7	11	8	9	3		**20**
	5	4		2		1		6	*12		10	*7	11	8	9	3		**21**
	5	*4		2		1		6	7		10	8	11	*12	9	3		**22**
	5			2		1		6	7	9	8	*10	11	4		3	*12	**23**
	5	4		2		1		6	7	9	10	s	11	8		3		**24**
	5	4		*2		1		6	7	9	10		11	8	*12	3		**25**
	5	4				1		6	s	7	10		11	8	9	2	3	**26**
	5	4				1		6	*12	9	10		7	8	*11	2	3	**27**
	5	4			s	1		6	7	9	10		11	8		2	3	**28**
	5	4	*12			1		6	*7	9	10		11	8		2	3	**29**
	5	4				1		6	s	9	10		11	8	7	2	3	**30**
	5	4				1		6	*12	9	10		11	8	*7	2	3	**31**
	5	4				1		6	7	9	10	s	11	8		2	3	**32**
	5	4				1		6	7	*9	10	*12	11	8		2	3	**33**
	5	4				1		6	7	s	10	9	11	8		2	3	**34**
	5	4				1		6	*7		10	*12	11	8	9	2	3	**35**
	5	4		2	s	1		6			10	7	11	8	9		3	**36**
	5	4		*7		1		6			10	*12	11	8	9	2	3	**37**
	5	4		s		1		6	7		10		11	8	9	2	3	**38**
	5	4		8		1		6	7	s	10		11		9	2	3	**39**
	5	4				1		6	7		10	s	11	8	9	2	3	**40**
	5	4				1		6	7		10	s	11	8	9	2	3	**41**
	5	4		2		1		6	*7		10	*12	11	8	9	3		**42**
	5	4		2		1		6	s		10	7	11	8	9	3		**43**
	5	4		2		1		6	s		10	7	11	8	9	3		**44**
	5	4		2		1		6	*7	*12	10	8	11		9	3		**45**
	5	4		2		1		6	s	9	10	8	11		7		3	**46**
2	44	42	0	29	0	46	0	46	34	18	46	13	45	40	38	44	19	Apps
			1						4	5		7		1	1		1	Subs
	1	1						1	2	7	16	1	22	9	7		1	Goals

Opponents 3 goals

WILLIE PENMAN

Blick M R	Burrows F	Butler J W	Dangerfield D J	Dawson O J	Desmeules R L	Downsborough P	Giles J A	Harland S C	Heath D	Jones C M N	Noble P	Penman W S T	Rogers D E	Smart R W	Smith J	Thomas R J	Trollope N J	
	5	4		2		1		6	7	s	10		11	8	9	3		**1**
	5	4		2		1		6	s	9		10	7	8	11	3		**2**
	5			2		1		6	7		9	*12	11	8	10	3	*4	**3**
	3	2		3		3		3	2	1	2	1	3	3	3	3	1	Apps
												1						Subs
										1			1		1			Goals

For Final League Table - see page 170

SEASON 1968/69

Football League Cup Winners

						Home	Away	H-T	Goalscorers	Gate
1	Tu	Aug	13	Torquay United		W2-1		(0-1)	Smart 60,Noble 70	14,702
2	W	Sep	4	Bradford City			D1-1	(1-0)	Smart 44	7,806
2R	Tu		10	Bradford City		W4-3		(2-2)	Smith 32,Rogers 36 pen.,Smart 68,Noble 74	12,214
3	Tu		24	Blackburn Rovers		W1-0		(1-0)	Rogers 20	15,402
4	W	Oct	16	Coventry City			D2-2	(1-0)	Rogers 42,Smart 71	23,588
4R	M		21	Coventry City		W3-0		(3-0)	Rogers 11,Smart 16,Penman 23	23,828
5	W		30	Derby County			D0-0			35,014
5R	Tu	Nov	5	Derby County		W1-0		(1-0)	Rogers 27	26,973
SF	W		20	Burnley			W2-1	(1-0)	Harland 44,Noble 65	26,231
SF	W	Dec	4	Burnley		L1-2		(0-0)	Smith 57	28,000
Rp.	W		18	Burnley	(at The Hawthorns)		W3-2	(1-0)	Smith 7,Bellamy o.g.104,Noble 108	20,000
F	S	Mar	15	Arsenal	(at Wembley)		W3-1	(1-0)	Smart 34,Rogers 104,119	98,189

ROD THOMAS

Born : Glyncorrwg, Glamorgan January 11 1947

A lean and lanky full-back who became Town's most capped international, Rod was signed from Gloucester City for £500 by Bert Head in July 1964. He gained his first Welsh cap after just thirty Third Division appearances and missed only three Town games between December 1967 and January 1972 - all due to international calls. Curiously, the majority of the 30 Welsh caps he earned while with Swindon were at left-back - not the familiar right-back berth he normally occupied for his club. In November 1973, Rod was former Town manager Dave Mackay's first signing for Derby - at £100,000. He made his 50th and final appearance for Wales two weeks after signing for Cardiff in 1977.

JOHN TROLLOPE

Born : Wroughton, Wilts. June 14 1943

A former schoolboy striker who became a record-breaking full-back, Norman John Trollope MBE - or simply 'Jim' to his team mates - was loyalty personified. He clocked up 367 successive League and Cup appearances - a run only halted by a broken arm at Hartlepool in August 1968. John had made his League debut at just 17 years and 68 days and stormed past Maurice Owen's 555 total during 1973/74. He was within ten games of the all-time one-club record when his contract was terminated in January 1980. But, following a disastrous start to 1980/81, John was recalled and made a record 765th appearance on October 18. On November 12 he took over as manager. *(See page 320)*

JOE BUTLER

Born : Newcastle-on-Tyne February 7 1943

A tough tackling competitor and midfield schemer with a trusty left foot, Joe joined Town as a full-back just after the start of the 1965/66 season. He had previously spent five years with Newcastle, but had made only three League appearances in that time. With few chances in the back line at Swindon, Joe was slotted into the middle, wearing the familiar number four shirt for the first time in a 4-0 win over Northampton in September 1967. Rarely absent between then and March 1975, Joe actually wore every number except one and nine at some time during his Town career - and was handed the number 11 vacated by Don Rogers late in 1972. Joe joined Aldershot in August 1976.

FRANK BURROWS

Born : Larkhall, Lanarks. January 30 1944

A tall, uncompromising centre-back whose aerial strength saved many a day for Town, Frank began as a part-time professional with Raith Rovers while taking an engineering apprenticeship. It was Scunthorpe United who brought Frank south of the border in June 1965 and he spent three years at the Old Show Ground before becoming a £13,000 signing for Town in July 1968. A near automatic choice for the number five jersey, Frank made over 300 appearances for Town over eight seasons. By the time he was superseded by Steve Aizlewood in 1976, Frank had a full F.A. Coaching badge - which led him into a long career in management with Portsmouth in May 1979.

STAN HARLAND

Born : Liverpool June 19 1940 Died : Tintinhull, Somerset August 30 2001

The Wembley skipper, Stan was a Liverpool schoolboy winger and after a spell across the Mersey with New Brighton signed for Everton in December 1959. His League debut came while with Bradford City, where he hit 20 goals in a three-year stay and where he began to appear in the more familiar left-half role. Stan moved to Carlisle in the summer of 1964 and signed for Town in July 1966. He took over the captaincy on the departure of Mel Nurse and was ever-present for three seasons. Prior to being dropped by new manager Dave Mackay in November 1971, Stan missed just one game - and that was due to injury. He soon moved on to Birmingham and was later player-manager at Yeovil.

Blick M R	Burrows F	Butler J W	Dawson O J	Downsborough P	Harland S C	Heath D	Jones C M N	Noble P	Penman W S T	Rogers D E	Smart R W	Smith J	Thomas R J	Trollope N J	
	5	s		1	6	7	9	8		11	4	10	2	3	1
	5	4	2	1	6	7		10	s	11	8	9	3		2
	*5	4	2	1	6	7	*12	10		11	8	9	3		2R
5		4	2	1	6	7	9	8		11	s	10	3		3
	5	4	2	1	6	7		10	s	11	8	9	3		4
	5	2		1	6	7	s	10	4	11	8	9	3		4R
	5	*2	*12	1	6	7		10	4	11	8	9	3		5
	5	4	2	1	6	7	s	10		11	8	9	3		5R
	5	4	2	1	6	7		10	s	11	8	9	3		SF
	5	4	2	1	6	7		10	s	11	8	9	3		SF
	5	4	2	1	6	*7		10	*12	11	8	9	3		Rp.
	5	4		1	6	7		10	*12	11	8	*9	2	3	F
1	11	11	8	12	12	12	2	12	2	12	11	12	12	2	Apps
			1				1		2						Subs
					1			4	1	7	6	3			Goals

Opponents 1 goal

PETER DOWNSBOROUGH

Born : Halifax, Yorks. September 13, 1943

Peter became a goalkeeper only by chance and was a fly-half for his school rugby team before switching to soccer. He made his League debut for his home town club on the final day of 1959/60 and came to Swindon just two days before the start of 1965/66 - in a part-exchange deal involving Bill Atkins. Injury kept Peter out of most of the 1966/67 F.A.Cup run, but he was 'ever-present' in 109 League and Cup games in 1968/69 and 1969/70 - and did not concede a League goal in the opening 568 minutes of the promotion campaign. After eight years at Swindon, Peter failed to agree terms and joined Bradford City - where he ended his career in 1979, having played over 700 League and Cup games.

DON HEATH

Born : Stockton-on-Tees, Co.Durham September 28 1944

A skilful and nippy winger, Don was an apprentice with his local club Middlesbrough before going to Norwich in July 1964. He came to Swindon when Barry Lowes was forced to quit through injury after just two games. Don was a maker - rather than taker - of goals, finding the net only three times for Town in 100 appearances and only one came in front of the County Ground fans. He joined Oldham in the summer of 1970 and on to Peterborough two years later, before moving back to the north-east with Hartlepool - where he made his final League appearance in October 1974.

ROGER SMART

Born : Swindon March 25 1943

An old-fashioned grafter, Roger chased all manner of seemingly lost causes, often harassing opponents into making errors. He rose through the Town's junior ranks, making his third team debut in September 1959 and then scored twice on his reserve team debut seven months later. Roger signed professional forms in May 1960, but had to wait almost two years for his League debut. He popped up to score some timely goals, with the one that clinched promotion in 1963 and the opener at Wembley. Roger seemed to thrive in the glamour of the Cup, with goals in each of his first five outings on the way to that Final. He joined Charlton in May 1973.

JOHN SMITH

Born : Shoreditch, London January 4, 1939 — Died : Harlesden, London February 19 1988

In the semi-final replay John was referred to as a 'remarkable all-purpose player, chunky almost to the point of rotundity', the writer having just witnessed the power behind a shot that had given Town an early lead. A midfield general, John's contribution to the success that season was priceless - and he was snapped up from Torquay for just £7,000 ! He brought vast experience with him, having played for West Ham, Tottenham, Coventry and Orient and had gained an England under-23 cap in 1960. In 1971, he joined Walsall, where he later took over as manager. Following a boardroom squabble John then went to Dundalk in Ireland. He died at just 49.

PETER NOBLE

Born : Sunderland August 19 1944

A striker with springs in his heels, Peter stood just 5'8", but his sparsely covered cranium rose to great heights in search of goals for Town. Newcastle boss Joe Harvey signed him from Consett in November 1964 and Peter scored seven goals in just 15 First Division games in 1966/67. But Danny Williams signed him in January 1968 and he opened his Swindon account with a brace on his fourth appearance as a substitute. Peter contributed 20 goals to the successes of 1968/69, including the winning strikes at both The Hawthorns and Turf Moor - where his career was to take him next in May 1973. And he helped Burnley to finish sixth in the First Division, despite playing at full-back !

DON ROGERS

Born : Old Mills, Somerset October 25 1945

Silky skills and an electrifying turn of speed, combined with the ability to beat a defender with a subtle swing of the hip or dip of the shoulder, Don's name has been synonymous with Swindon Town in recent history. He signed for the club on New Years Eve in 1960 and helped them reach the F.A.Youth Cup Final in 1964. He had two outings with the England under-23's and hit a remarkable 90 goals between August 1966 and May 1969 - a total that no other winger could equal. Bert Head signed Don again, for Crystal Palace in 1972, and he scored seven goals in his first eight games in the top flight. He briefly returned in 1976, but injury soon brought a sad end to the wing maestro's career.

SEASON 1955/56

Div.3S

		P	W	D	L	F	A	W	D	L	F	A	Pts	G/A	Avge. Home Gate
1	Leyton Orient	46	18	3	2	76	20	11	5	7	30	29	66	2.16	16,061
2	Brighton & Hove Albion	46	20	2	1	73	16	9	5	9	39	34	65	2.24	15,323
3	Ipswich Town	46	16	6	1	59	28	9	8	6	47	32	64	1.77	15,489
4	Southend United	46	16	4	3	58	25	5	7	11	30	55	53	1.10	10,028
5	Torquay United	46	11	10	2	48	21	9	2	12	38	42	52	1.37	6,989
6	Brentford	46	11	8	4	40	30	8	6	9	29	36	52	1.05	10,302
7	Norwich City	46	15	4	4	56	31	4	9	10	30	51	51	1.05	15,595
8	Coventry City	46	16	4	3	54	20	4	5	14	19	40	49	1.22	17,658
9	Bournemouth & Boscombe Athletic	46	13	6	4	39	14	6	4	13	24	37	48	1.24	8,035
10	Gillingham	46	12	3	8	38	28	7	7	9	31	43	48	0.97	8,420
11	Northampton Town	46	14	3	6	44	27	6	4	13	23	44	47	0.944	10,476
12	Colchester United	46	14	4	5	56	37	4	7	12	20	44	47	0.938	7,641
13	Shrewsbury Town	46	12	9	2	47	21	5	3	15	22	45	46	1.05	8,471
14	Southampton	46	13	6	4	60	30	5	2	16	31	51	44	1.12	11,612
15	Aldershot	46	9	9	5	36	33	3	7	13	34	57	40	0.78	5,606
16	Exeter City	46	10	6	7	39	30	5	4	14	19	47	40	0.75	8,168
17	Reading	46	10	2	11	40	37	5	7	11	30	42	39	0.89	8,108
18	Queens Park Rangers	46	10	7	6	44	32	4	4	15	20	54	39	0.74	8,455
19	Newport County	46	12	2	9	32	26	3	7	13	26	53	39	0.73	6,545
20	Walsall	46	13	5	5	43	28	2	3	18	25	56	38	0.81	12,644
21	Watford	46	8	5	10	31	39	5	6	12	21	46	37	0.61	8,108
22	Millwall	46	13	4	6	56	31	2	2	19	27	69	36	0.83	9,271
23	Crystal Palace	46	7	3	13	27	32	5	7	11	27	51	34	0.65	11,062
24	SWINDON TOWN	46	4	10	9	18	22	4	4	15	16	56	30	0.44	7,379

SEASON 1956/57

Div.3S

		P	W	D	L	F	A	W	D	L	F	A	Pts	G/A	Avge. Home Gate
1	Ipswich Town	46	18	3	2	72	20	7	6	10	29	34	59	1.87	14,372
2	Torquay United	46	19	4	0	71	18	5	7	11	18	46	59	1.39	8,014
3	Colchester United	46	15	8	0	49	19	7	6	10	35	37	58	1.50	9,267
4	Southampton	46	15	4	4	48	20	7	6	10	28	32	54	1.46	14,784
5	Bournemouth & Boscombe Athletic	46	15	7	1	57	20	4	7	12	31	42	52	1.42	10,968
6	Brighton & Hove Albion	46	15	6	2	59	26	4	8	11	27	39	52	1.32	11,606
7	Southend United	46	14	3	6	42	20	4	9	10	31	45	48	1.12	8,796
8	Brentford	46	12	9	2	55	29	4	7	12	23	47	48	1.03	11,482
9	Shrewsbury Town	46	11	9	3	45	24	4	9	10	27	55	48	0.91	7,550
10	Queens Park Rangers	46	12	7	4	42	21	6	4	13	19	39	47	1.02	9,239
11	Watford	46	11	6	6	44	32	7	4	12	28	43	46	0.96	9,219
12	Newport County	46	15	6	2	51	18	1	7	15	14	44	45	1.05	9,261
13	Reading	46	13	4	6	44	30	5	5	13	36	51	45	0.99	8,832
14	Northampton Town	46	15	5	3	49	22	3	4	16	17	51	45	0.90	8,158
15	Walsall	46	11	7	5	49	25	5	5	13	31	49	44	1.08	11,347
16	Coventry City	46	12	5	6	52	36	4	7	12	22	48	44	0.88	13,686
17	Millwall	46	13	7	3	46	29	3	5	15	18	55	44	0.76	11,545
18	Plymouth Argyle	46	10	8	5	38	31	6	3	14	30	42	43	0.93	12,713
19	Aldershot	46	11	5	7	43	35	4	7	12	36	57	42	0.86	5,098
20	Crystal Palace	46	7	10	6	31	28	4	8	11	31	47	40	0.83	12,081
21	Exeter City	46	8	8	7	37	29	4	5	14	24	50	37	0.77	6,765
22	Gillingham	46	7	8	8	29	29	5	5	13	25	56	37	0.64	7,037
23	SWINDON TOWN	46	12	3	8	43	33	3	3	17	23	63	36	0.69	8,740
24	Norwich City	46	7	5	11	33	37	1	10	12	28	57	31	0.65	12,856

SEASON 1957/58

Div.3S

		P	W	D	L	F	A	W	D	L	F	A	Pts	G/A	Avge. Home Gate
1	Brighton & Hove Albion	46	13	6	4	52	30	11	6	6	36	34	60	1.38	16,420
2	Brentford	46	15	5	3	52	24	9	5	9	30	32	58	1.46	13,084
3	Plymouth Argyle	46	17	4	2	43	17	8	4	11	24	31	58	1.40	19,662
4	SWINDON TOWN	46	14	7	2	47	16	7	8	8	32	34	57	1.58	12,041
5	Reading	46	14	5	4	52	23	7	8	8	27	28	55	1.55	12,806
6	Southampton	46	16	3	4	78	31	6	7	10	34	41	54	1.56	14,851
7	Southend United	46	14	5	4	56	26	7	7	9	34	32	54	1.55	11,190
8	Norwich City	46	11	9	3	41	28	8	6	9	34	42	53	1.07	20,290
9	Bournemouth & Boscombe Athletic	46	16	5	2	54	24	5	4	14	27	50	51	1.09	12,624
10	Queens Park Rangers	46	15	6	2	40	14	3	8	12	24	51	50	0.98	9,386
11	Newport County	46	12	6	5	40	24	5	8	10	33	43	48	1.09	7,174
12	Colchester United	46	13	5	5	45	27	4	8	11	32	52	47	0.97	8,564
13	Northampton Town	46	13	1	9	60	33	6	5	12	27	46	44	1.10	8,127
14	Crystal Palace	46	12	5	6	46	30	3	8	12	24	42	43	0.97	13,229
15	Port Vale	46	12	6	5	49	24	4	4	15	18	34	42	1.16	10,457
16	Watford	46	9	8	6	34	27	4	8	11	25	50	42	0.77	8,284
17	Shrewsbury Town	46	10	6	7	29	25	5	4	14	20	46	40	0.69	7,142
18	Aldershot	46	7	9	7	31	34	5	7	11	28	55	40	0.66	4,999
19	Coventry City	46	10	9	4	41	24	3	4	16	20	57	39	0.75	11,907
20	Walsall	46	10	7	6	37	24	4	2	17	24	51	37	0.81	8,802
21	Torquay United	46	9	7	7	33	34	2	6	15	16	40	35	0.66	7,112
22	Gillingham	46	12	5	6	33	24	1	4	18	19	57	35	0.64	7,030
23	Millwall	46	6	6	11	37	36	5	3	15	26	55	31	0.69	12,112
24	Exeter City	46	10	4	9	37	35	1	5	17	20	64	31	0.58	7,784

SEASON 1958/59

Div.3

		P	W	D	L	F	A	W	D	L	F	A	Pts	G/A	Avge. Home Gate
1	Plymouth Argyle	46	14	7	2	55	27	9	9	5	34	32	62	1.51	22,926
2	Hull City	46	19	3	1	65	21	7	6	10	25	34	61	1.64	14,380
3	Brentford	46	15	5	3	49	22	6	10	7	27	27	57	1.55	13,924
4	Norwich City	46	13	6	4	51	29	9	7	7	38	33	57	1.44	21,098
5	Colchester United	46	15	2	6	46	31	6	8	9	25	36	52	1.06	7,756
6	Reading	46	16	4	3	51	21	5	4	14	27	42	50	1.24	12,674
7	Tranmere Rovers	46	15	3	5	53	22	6	5	12	29	45	50	1.22	11,811
8	Southend United	46	14	6	3	52	26	7	2	14	33	54	50	1.06	11,229
9	Halifax Town	46	14	5	4	48	25	7	3	13	32	52	50	1.04	6,663
10	Bury	46	12	9	2	51	24	5	5	13	18	34	48	1.19	9,441
11	Bradford City	46	13	4	6	47	25	5	7	11	37	51	47	1.11	11,090
12	Bournemouth & Boscombe Athletic	46	12	9	2	40	18	5	3	15	29	51	46	1.00	10,680
13	Queens Park Rangers	46	14	6	3	49	28	5	2	16	25	49	46	0.96	9,155
14	Southampton	46	12	7	4	57	33	5	4	14	31	47	45	1.10	13,717
15	SWINDON TOWN	46	13	4	6	39	25	3	9	11	20	32	45	1.04	11,351
16	Chesterfield	46	12	5	6	40	26	5	5	13	27	38	44	1.05	9,028
17	Newport County	46	15	2	6	43	24	2	7	14	26	44	43	1.01	6,606
18	Wrexham	46	12	6	5	40	30	2	8	13	23	47	42	0.818	10,338
19	Accrington Stanley	46	10	8	5	42	31	5	4	14	29	56	42	0.816	6,267
20	Mansfield Town	46	11	5	7	38	42	3	8	12	35	56	41	0.74	8,467
21	Stockport County	46	9	7	7	33	23	4	3	16	32	55	36	0.83	9,255
22	Doncaster Rovers	46	13	2	8	40	32	1	3	19	10	58	33	0.56	6,664
23	Notts County	46	5	9	9	33	39	3	4	16	22	57	29	0.57	9,529
24	Rochdale	46	8	7	8	21	26	0	5	18	16	53	28	0.47	4,810

SEASON 1959/60

Div.3

		P	W	D	L	F	A	W	D	L	F	A	Pts	G/A	Avge. Home Gate
1	Southampton	46	19	3	1	68	30	7	6	10	38	45	61	1.41	18,052
2	Norwich City	46	16	4	3	53	24	8	7	8	29	30	59	1.52	26,402
3	Shrewsbury Town	46	12	7	4	58	34	6	9	8	39	41	52	1.29	8,999
4	Grimsby Town	46	12	7	4	48	27	6	9	8	39	43	52	1.243	10,543
5	Coventry City	46	14	6	3	44	22	7	4	12	34	41	52	1.238	16,348
6	Brentford	46	13	6	4	46	24	8	3	12	32	37	51	1.28	11,912
7	Bury	46	13	4	6	36	23	8	5	10	28	28	51	1.25	10,628
8	Queens Park Rangers	46	14	7	2	45	16	4	6	13	28	38	49	1.35	10,285
9	Colchester United	46	15	6	2	51	22	3	5	15	32	52	47	1.12	7,812
10	Bournemouth & Boscombe Athletic	46	12	8	3	47	27	5	5	13	25	45	47	1.00	10,403
11	Reading	46	13	3	7	49	34	5	7	11	35	43	46	1.09	11,464
12	Southend United	46	15	3	5	49	28	4	5	14	27	46	46	1.03	10,322
= 13	Newport County	46	15	2	6	59	36	5	4	14	21	43	46	1.01	6,241
= 13	Port Vale	46	16	4	3	51	19	3	4	16	29	60	46	1.01	10,733
15	Halifax Town	46	13	3	7	42	27	5	7	11	28	45	46	0.97	6,768
16	SWINDON TOWN	46	12	6	5	39	30	7	2	14	30	48	46	0.88	10,233
17	Barnsley	46	13	6	4	45	25	2	8	13	20	41	44	0.98	6,315
18	Chesterfield	46	13	3	7	41	31	5	4	14	30	53	43	0.85	6,578
19	Bradford City	46	10	7	6	39	28	5	5	13	27	46	42	0.89	10,163
20	Tranmere Rovers	46	11	8	4	50	29	3	5	15	22	46	41	0.96	9,965
21	York City	46	11	5	7	38	26	2	7	14	19	47	38	0.78	7,507
22	Mansfield Town	46	11	4	8	55	48	4	2	17	26	64	36	0.72	7,183
23	Wrexham	46	12	5	6	39	30	2	3	18	29	71	36	0.67	9,495
24	Accrington Stanley	46	4	5	14	31	53	7	0	16	26	70	27	0.46	4,131

SEASON 1960/61

Div.3

		P	W	D	L	F	A	W	D	L	F	A	Pts	G/A	Avge. Home Gate
1	Bury	46	18	3	2	62	17	12	5	6	46	28	68	2.40	10,207
2	Walsall	46	19	4	0	62	20	9	2	12	36	40	62	1.63	10,657
3	Queens Park Rangers	46	18	4	1	58	23	7	6	10	35	37	60	1.55	9,958
4	Watford	46	12	7	4	52	27	8	5	10	33	45	52	1.18	12,599
5	Notts County	46	16	3	4	52	24	5	6	12	30	53	51	1.06	11,974
6	Grimsby Town	46	14	4	5	48	32	6	6	11	29	37	50	1.12	9,295
7	Port Vale	46	15	3	5	63	30	2	12	9	33	49	49	1.22	9,702
8	Barnsley	46	15	5	3	56	30	6	2	15	27	50	49	1.04	6,489
9	Halifax Town	46	14	7	2	42	22	2	10	11	29	56	49	0.91	5,548
10	Shrewsbury Town	46	13	7	3	54	26	2	9	12	29	49	46	1.11	8,025
11	Hull City	46	13	6	4	51	28	4	6	13	22	45	46	1.00	8,434
12	Torquay United	46	8	12	3	37	26	6	5	12	38	57	45	0.904	6,153
13	Newport County	46	12	7	4	51	30	5	4	14	30	60	45	0.900	5,439
14	Bristol City	46	15	4	4	50	19	2	6	15	20	49	44	1.03	11,488
15	Coventry City	46	14	6	3	54	25	2	6	15	26	58	44	0.96	11,996
16	SWINDON TOWN	46	13	6	4	41	16	1	9	13	21	39	43	1.13	11,045
17	Brentford	46	10	9	4	41	28	3	8	12	15	42	43	0.80	7,392
18	Reading	46	13	5	5	48	29	1	7	15	24	54	40	0.87	7,692
19	Bournemouth & Boscombe Athletic	46	8	7	8	34	39	7	3	13	24	37	40	0.76	7,808
20	Southend United	46	10	8	5	38	26	4	3	16	22	50	39	0.79	8,100
21	Tranmere Rovers	46	11	5	7	53	50	4	3	16	26	65	38	0.69	9,457
22	Bradford City	46	8	8	7	37	36	3	6	14	28	51	36	0.75	7,447
23	Colchester United	46	8	5	10	40	44	3	6	14	28	57	33	0.67	4,962
24	Chesterfield	46	9	6	8	42	29	1	6	16	25	58	32	0.77	5,180

SEASON 1961/62

Div.3

	P	W	D	L	F	A	W	D	L	F	A	Pts	G/A	Avge. Home Gate
1 Portsmouth	46	15	6	2	48	23	12	5	6	39	24	65	1.85	16,652
2 Grimsby Town	46	18	3	2	49	18	10	3	10	31	38	62	1.43	9,469
3 Bournemouth & Boscombe Athletic	46	14	8	1	42	18	7	9	7	27	27	59	1.53	11,622
4 Queens Park Rangers	46	15	3	5	65	31	9	8	6	46	42	59	1.52	11,121
5 Peterborough United	46	16	0	7	60	38	10	6	7	47	44	58	1.30	12,392
6 Bristol City	46	15	3	5	56	27	8	5	10	38	45	54	1.31	12,447
7 Reading	46	14	5	4	46	24	8	4	11	31	42	53	1.17	11,242
8 Northampton Town	46	12	6	5	52	24	8	5	10	33	33	51	1.49	10,899
9 SWINDON TOWN	46	11	8	4	48	26	6	7	10	30	45	49	1.10	9,692
10 Hull City	46	15	2	6	43	20	5	6	12	24	34	48	1.24	6,887
11 Bradford Park Avenue	46	13	5	5	47	27	7	2	14	33	51	47	1.03	8,871
12 Port Vale	46	12	4	7	41	23	5	7	11	24	35	45	1.12	9,010
13 Notts County	46	14	5	4	44	23	3	4	16	23	51	43	0.91	8,252
14 Coventry City	46	11	6	6	38	26	5	5	13	26	45	43	0.90	10,256
15 Crystal Palace	46	8	8	7	50	41	6	6	11	33	39	42	1.04	17,481
16 Southend United	46	10	7	6	31	26	3	9	11	26	43	42	0.83	7,922
17 Watford	46	10	9	4	37	26	4	4	15	26	48	41	0.85	10,609
18 Halifax Town	46	9	5	9	34	35	6	5	12	28	49	40	0.74	4,670
19 Shrewsbury Town	46	8	7	8	46	37	5	5	13	27	47	38	0.87	6,591
20 Barnsley	46	9	6	8	45	41	4	6	13	26	54	38	0.75	6,100
21 Torquay United	46	9	4	10	48	44	6	2	15	28	56	36	0.76	4,982
22 Lincoln City	46	4	10	9	31	43	5	7	11	26	44	35	0.66	5,868
23 Brentford	46	11	3	9	34	29	2	5	16	19	64	34	0.57	8,483
24 Newport County	46	6	5	12	29	38	1	3	19	17	64	22	0.45	5,023

SEASON 1962/63

Div.3

	P	W	D	L	F	A	W	D	L	F	A	Pts	G/A	Avge. Home Gate
1 Northampton Town	46	16	6	1	64	19	10	4	9	45	41	62	1.82	13,424
2 SWINDON TOWN	46	18	2	3	60	22	4	12	7	27	34	58	1.55	13,530
3 Port Vale	46	16	4	3	47	25	7	4	12	25	33	54	1.24	8,130
4 Coventry City	46	14	6	3	54	28	4	11	8	29	41	53	1.20	17,098
5 Bournemouth & Boscombe Athletic	46	11	12	0	39	16	7	4	12	24	30	52	1.37	9,763
6 Peterborough United	46	11	5	7	48	33	9	6	8	45	42	51	1.24	12,016
7 Notts County	46	15	3	5	46	29	4	10	9	27	45	51	0.99	6,860
8 Southend United	46	11	7	5	38	24	8	5	10	37	53	50	0.97	9,978
9 Wrexham	46	14	6	3	54	27	6	3	14	30	56	49	1.01	10,137
10 Hull City	46	12	6	5	40	22	7	4	12	34	47	48	1.07	7,350
11 Crystal Palace	46	10	7	6	38	22	7	6	10	30	36	47	1.17	14,854
12 Colchester United	46	11	6	6	41	35	7	5	11	32	58	47	0.78	5,309
13 Queens Park Rangers	46	9	6	8	44	36	8	5	10	41	40	45	1.12	10,041
14 Bristol City	46	10	9	4	54	38	6	4	13	46	54	45	1.09	11,121
15 Shrewsbury Town	46	13	4	6	57	41	3	8	12	26	40	44	1.02	5,897
16 Millwall	46	11	6	6	50	32	4	7	12	32	55	43	0.94	13,225
17 Watford	46	12	3	8	55	40	5	5	13	27	45	42	0.96	9,756
18 Barnsley	46	12	6	5	39	28	3	5	15	24	46	41	0.85	7,021
19 Bristol Rovers	46	11	8	4	45	29	4	3	16	25	59	41	0.80	9,831
20 Reading	46	13	4	6	51	30	3	4	16	23	48	40	0.95	8,077
21 Bradford Park Avenue	46	10	9	4	43	36	4	3	16	36	61	40	0.81	7,409
22 Brighton & Hove Albion	46	7	6	10	28	38	5	6	12	30	46	36	0.69	9,961
23 Carlisle United	46	12	4	7	41	37	1	5	17	20	52	35	0.69	5,699
24 Halifax Town	46	8	3	12	41	51	1	9	13	23	55	30	0.60	3,561

SEASON 1963/64

Div.2

	P	W	D	L	F	A	W	D	L	F	A	Pts	G/A	Avge. Home Gate
1 Leeds United	42	12	9	0	35	16	12	6	3	36	18	63	2.09	29,938
2 Sunderland	42	16	3	2	47	13	9	8	4	34	24	61	2.19	41,262
3 Preston North End	42	13	7	1	37	14	10	3	8	42	40	56	1.46	18,821
4 Charlton Athletic	42	11	4	6	44	30	8	6	7	32	40	48	1.09	18,282
5 Southampton	42	13	3	5	69	32	6	6	9	31	41	47	1.37	17,217
6 Manchester City	42	12	4	5	50	27	6	6	9	34	39	46	1.27	18,201
7 Rotherham United	42	14	3	4	52	26	5	4	12	38	52	45	1.15	9,959
8 Newcastle United	42	14	2	5	49	26	6	3	12	25	43	45	1.07	29,426
9 Portsmouth	42	9	7	5	46	34	7	4	10	33	36	43	1.13	14,681
10 Middlesbrough	42	14	4	3	47	16	1	7	13	20	36	41	1.29	18,786
11 Northampton Town	42	10	2	9	35	31	6	7	8	23	29	41	0.97	12,705
12 Huddersfield Town	42	11	4	6	31	25	4	6	11	26	39	40	0.89	12,120
13 Derby County	42	10	6	5	34	27	4	5	12	22	40	39	0.84	11,979
14 SWINDON TOWN	42	11	5	5	39	24	3	5	13	18	45	38	0.83	18,277
15 Cardiff City	42	10	7	4	31	27	4	3	14	25	54	38	0.69	13,782
16 Leyton Orient	42	8	6	7	32	32	5	4	12	22	40	36	0.75	10,359
17 Norwich City	42	9	7	5	43	30	2	6	13	21	50	35	0.80	16,294
18 Bury	42	8	5	8	35	36	5	4	12	22	37	35	0.78	8,169
19 Swansea Town	42	11	4	6	44	26	1	5	15	19	48	33	0.85	10,911
20 Plymouth Argyle	42	6	8	7	26	32	2	8	11	19	35	32	0.67	13,001
21 Grimsby Town	42	6	7	8	28	34	3	7	11	19	41	32	0.63	9,515
22 Scunthorpe United	42	8	8	5	30	25	2	2	17	22	57	30	0.63	7,353

SEASON 1964/65 — Div.2

		P	W	D	L	F	A	W	D	L	F	A	Pts	G/A	Avge. Home Gate
1	Newcastle United	42	16	4	1	50	16	8	5	8	31	29	57	1.80	35,659
2	Northampton Town	42	14	7	0	37	16	6	9	6	29	34	56	1.32	15,366
3	Bolton Wanderers	42	13	6	2	46	17	7	4	10	34	41	50	1.38	14,650
4	Southampton	42	12	6	3	49	25	5	8	8	34	38	48	1.32	17,123
5	Ipswich Town	42	11	7	3	48	30	4	10	7	26	37	47	1.10	13,428
6	Norwich City	42	15	4	2	47	21	5	3	13	14	36	47	1.07	18,207
7	Crystal Palace	42	11	6	4	37	24	5	7	9	18	27	45	1.08	18,232
8	Huddersfield Town	42	12	4	5	28	15	5	6	10	25	36	44	1.04	9,644
9	Derby County	42	11	5	5	48	35	5	6	10	36	44	43	1.06	13,820
10	Coventry City	42	10	5	6	41	29	7	4	10	31	41	43	1.03	26,621
11	Manchester City	42	12	3	6	40	24	4	6	11	23	38	41	1.02	14,753
12	Preston North End	42	11	8	2	46	29	3	5	13	30	52	41	0.94	15,645
13	Cardiff City	42	10	7	4	43	25	3	7	11	21	32	40	1.12	10,588
14	Rotherham United	42	10	7	4	39	25	4	5	12	31	44	40	1.01	9,753
15	Plymouth Argyle	42	10	7	4	36	28	6	1	14	27	51	40	0.80	14,881
16	Bury	42	9	4	8	36	30	5	6	10	24	36	38	0.91	7,784
17	Middlesbrough	42	8	5	8	40	31	5	4	12	30	45	35	0.92	15,692
18	Charlton Athletic	42	8	5	8	35	34	5	4	12	29	41	35	0.85	13,065
19	Leyton Orient	42	10	4	7	36	34	2	7	12	14	38	35	0.69	8,920
20	Portsmouth	42	11	4	6	36	22	1	6	14	20	55	34	0.73	13,063
21	SWINDON TOWN	42	12	3	6	43	30	2	2	17	20	51	33	0.78	15,090
22	Swansea Town	42	9	7	5	40	29	2	3	16	22	55	32	0.74	10,467

SEASON 1965/66 — Div.3

		P	W	D	L	F	A	W	D	L	F	A	Pts	G/A	Avge. Home Gate
1	Hull City	46	19	2	2	64	24	12	5	6	45	38	69	1.76	22,828
2	Millwall	46	19	4	0	47	13	8	7	8	29	30	65	1.77	13,978
3	Queens Park Rangers	46	16	3	4	62	29	8	6	9	33	36	57	1.46	8,263
4	Scunthorpe United	46	9	8	6	44	34	12	3	8	36	33	53	1.19	5,181
5	Workington	46	13	6	4	38	18	6	8	9	29	39	52	1.18	3,263
6	Gillingham	46	14	4	5	33	19	8	4	11	29	35	52	1.15	7,492
7	SWINDON TOWN	46	11	8	4	43	18	8	5	10	31	30	51	1.54	12,937
8	Reading	46	13	5	5	36	19	6	8	9	34	44	51	1.11	8,857
9	Walsall	46	13	7	3	48	21	7	3	13	29	43	50	1.20	9,297
10	Shrewsbury Town	46	13	7	3	48	22	6	4	13	25	42	49	1.14	5,118
11	Grimsby Town	46	15	6	2	47	25	2	7	14	21	37	47	1.10	7,239
12	Watford	46	12	4	7	33	19	5	9	9	22	32	47	1.08	7,695
13	Peterborough United	46	13	6	4	50	26	4	6	13	30	40	46	1.21	7,238
14	Oxford United	46	11	3	9	38	33	8	5	10	32	41	46	0.95	9,301
15	Brighton & Hove Albion	46	13	4	6	48	28	3	7	13	19	37	43	1.03	12,799
16	Bristol Rovers	46	11	10	2	38	15	3	4	16	26	49	42	1.00	9,007
17	Swansea Town	46	14	4	5	61	37	1	7	15	20	59	41	0.84	7,694
18	Bournemouth & Boscombe Athletic	46	9	8	6	24	19	4	4	15	14	37	38	0.68	6,329
19	Mansfield Town	46	10	5	8	31	36	5	3	15	28	53	38	0.66	6,087
20	Oldham Athletic	46	8	7	8	34	33	4	6	13	21	48	37	0.68	8,943
21	Southend United	46	15	1	7	43	28	1	3	19	11	55	36	0.65	7,536
22	Exeter City	46	9	6	8	36	28	3	5	15	17	51	35	0.67	5,590
23	Brentford	46	9	4	10	34	30	1	8	14	14	39	32	0.70	8,416
24	York City	46	5	7	11	30	44	4	2	17	23	62	27	0.50	5,921

SEASON 1966/67 — Div.3

		P	W	D	L	F	A	W	D	L	F	A	Pts	G/A	Avge. Home Gate
1	Queens Park Rangers	46	18	4	1	66	15	8	11	4	37	23	67	2.71	13,157
2	Middlesbrough	46	16	3	4	51	20	7	6	10	36	44	55	1.36	17,586
3	Watford	46	15	5	3	39	17	5	9	9	22	29	54	1.33	9,385
4	Reading	46	13	7	3	45	20	9	2	12	31	37	53	1.33	7,119
5	Bristol Rovers	46	13	8	2	47	28	7	5	11	29	39	53	1.13	10,253
6	Shrewsbury Town	46	15	5	3	48	24	5	7	11	29	38	52	1.24	4,936
7	Torquay United	46	17	3	3	57	20	4	6	13	16	34	51	1.35	7,040
8	SWINDON TOWN	46	14	5	4	53	21	6	5	12	28	38	50	1.37	12,297
9	Mansfield Town	46	12	4	7	48	37	8	5	10	36	42	49	1.06	7,800
10	Oldham Athletic	46	15	4	4	51	16	4	6	13	29	47	48	1.27	9,940
11	Gillingham	46	11	9	3	36	18	4	7	12	22	44	46	0.94	6,548
12	Walsall	46	12	8	3	37	16	6	2	15	28	56	46	0.90	8,594
13	Colchester United	46	14	3	6	52	30	3	7	13	24	43	44	1.04	5,567
14	Orient	46	10	9	4	36	27	3	9	11	22	41	44	0.85	5,981
15	Peterborough United	46	12	4	7	40	31	2	11	10	26	40	43	0.93	6,466
16	Oxford United	46	10	8	5	41	29	5	5	13	20	37	43	0.92	7,405
17	Grimsby Town	46	13	5	5	46	23	4	4	15	15	45	43	0.90	5,937
18	Scunthorpe United	46	13	4	6	39	26	4	4	15	19	47	42	0.79	5,239
19	Brighton & Hove Albion	46	10	8	5	37	27	3	7	13	24	44	41	0.86	11,785
20	Bournemouth & Boscombe Athletic	46	8	10	5	24	24	4	7	12	15	33	41	0.68	5,332
21	Swansea Town	46	9	9	5	50	30	3	6	14	35	59	39	0.96	6,347
22	Darlington	46	8	7	8	26	28	5	4	14	21	53	37	0.58	6,591
23	Doncaster Rovers	46	11	6	6	40	40	1	2	20	18	77	32	0.50	7,906
24	Workington	46	9	3	11	35	35	3	4	16	20	54	31	0.62	2,664

SEASON 1967/68

Div.3

	P	W	D	L	F	A	W	D	L	F	A	Pts	G/A	Avge. Home Gate
1 Oxford United	46	18	3	2	49	20	4	10	9	20	27	57	1.47	8,325
2 Bury	46	19	3	1	64	24	5	5	13	27	42	56	1.38	8,281
3 Shrewsbury Town	46	14	6	3	42	17	6	9	8	19	32	55	1.24	6,675
4 Torquay United	46	15	6	2	40	17	6	5	12	20	39	53	1.07	9,096
5 Reading	46	15	5	3	43	17	6	4	13	27	43	51	1.17	8,127
6 Watford	46	15	3	5	59	20	6	5	12	15	30	50	1.48	8,913
7 Walsall	46	12	7	4	47	22	7	5	11	27	39	50	1.21	9,119
8 Barrow	46	14	6	3	43	13	7	2	14	22	41	50	1.20	6,062
9 Peterborough United *	46	14	4	5	46	23	6	6	11	33	44	50	1.18	6,889
10 SWINDON TOWN	46	13	8	2	51	16	3	9	11	23	35	49	1.45	13,456
11 Brighton & Hove Albion	46	11	8	4	31	14	5	8	10	26	41	48	1.04	10,492
12 Gillingham	46	13	6	4	35	19	5	6	12	24	44	48	0.94	5,770
13 Bournemouth & Boscombe Athletic	46	13	7	3	39	17	3	8	12	17	34	47	1.10	5,983
14 Stockport County	46	16	5	2	49	22	3	4	16	21	53	47	0.93	8,237
15 Southport	46	13	6	4	35	22	4	6	13	30	43	46	1.00	5,903
16 Bristol Rovers	46	14	3	6	42	25	3	6	14	30	53	43	0.92	8,105
17 Oldham Athletic	46	11	3	9	37	32	7	4	12	23	33	43	0.92	5,745
18 Northampton Town	46	10	8	5	40	25	4	5	14	18	47	41	0.81	8,937
19 Orient	46	10	6	7	27	24	2	11	10	19	38	41	0.74	4,715
20 Tranmere Rovers	46	10	7	6	39	28	4	5	14	23	46	40	0.84	7,403
21 Mansfield Town	46	8	7	8	32	31	4	6	13	19	36	37	0.76	5,948
22 Grimsby Town	46	10	7	6	33	21	4	2	17	19	48	37	0.75	4,301
23 Colchester United	46	6	8	9	29	40	3	7	13	21	47	33	0.57	3,992
24 Scunthorpe United	46	8	9	6	36	34	2	3	18	20	53	32	0.64	3,845

* Demoted to Fourth Division for 1968/69 season

SEASON 1968/69

Div.3

	P	W	D	L	F	A	W	D	L	F	A	Pts	G/A	Avge. Home Gate
1 Watford	46	16	5	2	35	7	11	5	7	39	27	64	2.18	13,576
2 SWINDON TOWN	46	18	4	1	38	7	9	6	8	33	28	64	2.03	17,856
3 Luton Town	46	20	3	0	57	14	5	8	10	17	24	61	1.95	14,896
4 Bournemouth & Boscombe Athletic	46	16	2	5	41	17	5	7	11	19	28	51	1.33	7,564
5 Plymouth Argyle	46	10	8	5	34	25	7	7	9	19	24	49	1.08	10,599
6 Torquay United	46	13	4	6	35	18	5	8	10	19	28	48	1.17	8,285
7 Tranmere Rovers	46	12	3	8	36	31	7	7	9	34	37	48	1.03	6,040
8 Southport	46	14	8	1	52	20	3	5	15	19	44	47	1.11	4,188
9 Stockport County	46	14	5	4	49	25	2	9	12	18	43	46	0.99	7,173
10 Barnsley	46	13	6	4	37	21	3	8	12	21	42	46	0.92	9,459
11 Rotherham United	46	12	6	5	40	21	4	7	12	16	29	45	1.12	9,077
12 Brighton & Hove Albion	46	12	7	4	49	21	4	6	13	23	44	45	1.11	10,840
13 Walsall	46	10	9	4	34	18	4	7	12	16	31	44	1.02	5,867
14 Reading	46	13	3	7	41	25	2	10	11	26	41	43	1.02	6,552
15 Mansfield Town	46	14	5	4	37	18	2	6	15	21	44	43	0.94	7,049
16 Bristol Rovers	46	12	6	5	41	27	4	5	14	22	44	43	0.89	7,118
17 Shrewsbury Town	46	11	8	4	28	17	5	3	15	23	50	43	0.76	5,516
18 Orient	46	10	8	5	31	19	4	6	13	20	39	42	0.88	5,658
19 Barrow	46	11	6	6	30	23	6	2	15	26	52	42	0.75	4,676
20 Gillingham	46	10	10	3	35	20	3	5	15	19	43	41	0.86	5,387
21 Northampton Town	46	9	8	6	37	30	5	4	14	17	31	40	0.89	6,790
22 Hartlepool	46	6	12	5	25	29	4	7	12	15	41	39	0.57	4,200
23 Crewe Alexandra	46	11	4	8	40	31	2	5	16	12	45	35	0.68	4,804
24 Oldham Athletic	46	9	6	8	33	27	4	3	16	17	56	35	0.60	3,862

SEASON 1969/70

Div.2

	P	W	D	L	F	A	W	D	L	F	A	Pts	G/A	Avge. Home Gate
1 Huddersfield Town	42	14	6	1	36	10	10	6	5	32	27	60	1.84	17,526
2 Blackpool	42	10	9	2	25	16	10	4	7	31	29	53	1.24	15,695
3 Leicester City	42	12	6	3	37	22	7	7	7	27	28	51	1.28	25,104
4 Middlesbrough	42	15	4	2	36	14	5	6	10	19	31	50	1.22	19,856
5 SWINDON TOWN	42	13	7	1	35	17	4	9	8	22	30	50	1.21	19,838
6 Sheffield United	42	16	2	3	50	10	6	3	12	23	28	49	1.92	17,840
7 Cardiff City	42	12	7	2	38	14	6	6	9	23	27	49	1.49	21,502
8 Blackburn Rovers	42	15	2	4	42	19	5	5	11	12	31	47	1.08	12,523
9 Queens Park Rangers	42	13	5	3	47	24	4	6	11	19	33	45	1.16	17,525
10 Millwall	42	14	4	3	38	18	1	10	10	18	38	44	1.00	11,688
11 Norwich City	42	13	5	3	37	14	3	6	12	12	32	43	1.07	13,215
12 Carlisle United	42	10	6	5	39	28	4	7	10	19	28	41	1.04	9,388
13 Hull City	42	11	6	4	43	28	4	5	12	29	42	41	1.03	11,230
14 Bristol City	42	11	7	3	37	13	2	6	13	17	37	39	1.08	16,274
15 Oxford United	42	9	9	3	23	13	3	6	12	12	29	39	0.83	10,812
16 Bolton Wanderers	42	9	6	6	31	23	3	6	12	23	38	36	0.89	10,041
17 Portsmouth	42	8	4	9	39	35	5	5	11	27	45	35	0.83	14,928
18 Birmingham City	42	9	7	5	33	22	2	4	15	18	56	33	0.65	25,004
19 Watford	42	6	8	7	26	21	3	5	13	18	36	31	0.77	17,223
20 Charlton Athletic	42	7	8	6	23	28	0	9	12	12	48	31	0.46	12,693
21 Aston Villa	42	7	8	6	23	21	1	5	15	13	41	29	0.58	27,345
22 Preston North End	42	7	6	8	31	28	1	6	14	12	35	28	0.68	13,548

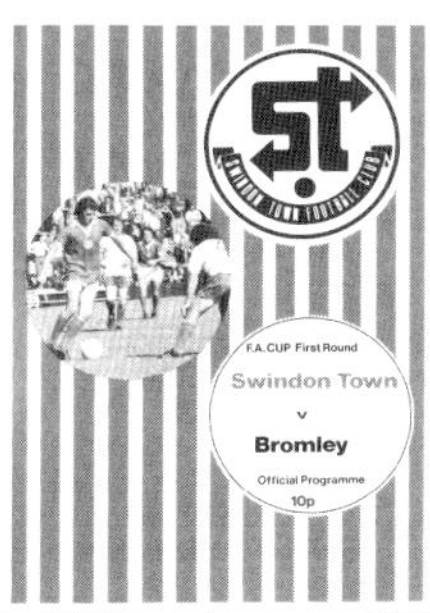

Left to right : Programme covers from the Anglo-Italian Cup Winners Cup in 1969 - and seasons 1971/72, 1976/77 and 1979/80

ford popular but few triumphs !

1969 - 1982

Manager Fred Ford - who succeeded Danny Williams just eleven weeks after Town clinched promotion in 1969 - was much liked and respected by those in the game. He led the team to three Anglo-Italian trophies in two years, but was then ousted in favour of player-manager Dave Mackay.

There was little to celebrate at the County Ground following Fred's departure, with Town hitting rock bottom in the Second Division in 1974. Hopes were raised briefly in 1974/75 when Danny returned but, apart from a League Cup semi-final early in 1980, there were few oases in a desert of mediocrity. Little more than two years later, Town fell through the trapdoor to the Fourth Division for the first time.

DAVE MOSS

the Witney-born winger who first signed for Town in July 1969, hit 80 goals before a £110,000 move to Luton in 1978. He returned on a free transfer in June 1985, but injuries prevented him from making more than a handful of appearances and he was released in the following summer.

Left to right : The new North Stand rises above the old in 1971 : Arthur Horsfield in goalscoring mood : Peter Eastoe on his debut : Andy Rowland celebrates Billy Tucker's late goal at Highbury in December 1979

SEASON 1969/70

Football League Second Division
Final League Position : 5th
Manager : Fred Ford

Substitutes :
s denotes substitute **not** used
* player substituted by *12

					Home	Away	H-T	Goalscorers	Gate
1	S	Aug	9	Blackburn Rovers		L0-2	(0-0)		12,953
2	W		13	Cardiff City		D2-2	(2-2)	Noble 28,Horsfield 34	27,971
3	S		16	Carlisle United	D2-2		(0-1)	Horsfield 74,81	17,055
4	Tu		19	Cardiff City	W2-1		(1-0)	Jones C 11,69	21,562
5	S		23	Aston Villa		W2-0	(2-0)	Horsfield 15,Thomas 41	29,767
6	S		30	Charlton Athletic	W5-0		(0-0)	Smith 46,Noble 59,77,82,Burkett o.g.70	20,229
7	S	Sep	6	Blackpool		L2-3	(1-1)	Rogers 36 pen.,59 pen.	17,201
8	S		13	Oxford United	D0-0				21,903
9	Tu		16	Middlesbrough		D0-0			15,632
10	S		20	Queens Park Rangers		L0-2	(0-2)		22,799
11	S		27	Leicester City	D1-1		(0-0)	Noble 50	22,352
12	Tu		30	Millwall	W2-1		(0-1)	Horsfield 69,90	17,268
13	S	Oct	4	Bolton Wanderers		W1-0	(1-0)	Horsfield 33	9,064
14	Tu		7	Carlisle United		D2-2	(0-0)	Ternent o.g.72,Horsfield 73	9,723
15	S		11	Sheffield United	W2-1		(1-0)	Noble 20,Rogers 70	21,770
16	S		18	Hull City	W1-0		(0-0)	Burrows 90	18,791
17	S		25	Portsmouth		L1-3	(0-1)	Smart 82	18,623
18	S	Nov	1	Norwich City	W2-0		(0-0)	Noble 47,Jones C 88	17,736
19	S		8	Birmingham City		L0-2	(0-2)		28,167
20	S		15	Watford		D0-0			15,404
21	S		22	Huddersfield Town	W2-1		(0-0)	Noble 56,Jones C 88	19,279
22	S		29	Preston North End		L1-3	(1-1)	Smart 35	9,250
23	S	Dec	6	Bristol City	D1-1		(0-1)	Horsfield 72	23,289
24	S		13	Oxford United		D0-0			11,930
25	F		26	Aston Villa	D1-1		(1-0)	Noble 35	22,984
26	S		27	Charlton Athletic		D1-1	(0-1)	Smith 68	14,918
27	S	Jan	10	Queens Park Rangers	D0-0				18,219
28	S		17	Leicester City		W2-0	(1-0)	Horsfield 8,67	24,378
29	S		31	Bolton Wanderers	W3-2		(2-0)	Horsfield 28,Rogers 30,48	18,339
30	M	Feb	9	Sheffield United		W2-1	(1-0)	Trollope 37,Horsfield 57	22,711
31	S		28	Hull City		D1-1	(1-1)	Rogers 20	10,855
32	Tu	Mar	3	Portsmouth	W3-1		(1-1)	Noble 10,82,Jones C 53	19,497
33	S		14	Preston North End	W1-0		(0-0)	Noble 52	17,443
34	S		21	Bristol City		D3-3	(1-0)	Horsfield 8,57,Wimshurst 84 o.g.	24,905
35	Tu		24	Huddersfield Town		D1-1	(1-1)	Burrows 32	24,854
36	S		28	Watford	W1-0		(1-0)	Trollope 34	22,597
37	M		30	Norwich City		L0-1	(0-1)		17,214
38	Tu		31	Birmingham City	W4-1		(2-1)	Butler 11,Rogers 27 pen.,75,Horsfield 62	20,835
39	S	Apr	4	Millwall		L1-3	(0-2)	Rogers 50	13,497
40	Tu		7	Blackpool	D1-1		(1-1)	Horsfield 4	28,520
41	Tu		14	Middlesbrough	L0-3		(0-1)		16,443
42	M		20	Blackburn Rovers	W1-0		(0-0)	Horsfield 46	10,491

Average Home Attendance : **19,838**
Average Away Attendance : **18,182**

Football League Cup

					Home	Away	H-T	Goalscorers	Gate
2	Tu	Sep	2	Swansea Town		W3-1	(1-1)	Noble 45,58,63	11,645
3	W		24	Oxford United		L0-1	(0-0)		18,193

F A Cup

					Home	Away	H-T	Goalscorers	Gate
3	S	Jan	3	Blackburn Rovers		W4-0	(3-0)	Smith 26,Horsfield 32,Rogers 39,Butler 76	11,538
4	S		24	Chester	W4-2		(2-1)	Horsfield 15,49,Jones C 44,Smart 75	21,937
5	S	Feb	7	Scunthorpe United	W3-1		(1-1)	Noble 38,Horsfield 64,Trollope 80	24,612
6	S		21	Leeds United	L0-2		(0-2)		27,500

For Final League Table - see previous page <<   For Anglo-Italian games - see page 204

Blick M R	Burrows F	Butler J W	Dangerfield D A	Dawson O J	Down D F	Downsborough P	Harland S C	Heath D	Horsfield A	Jones C M N	Noble P	Penman W S T	Rogers D E	Smart R W	Smith J	Thomas R J	Trollope N J	
	5	4				1	6		8	s	10		11	9	7	2	3	**1**
	5	4				1	6		8	s	10		11	9	7	2	3	**2**
	5	4				1	6		8	*12	*10		11	9	7	2	3	**3**
	5	4				1	6	s	8	10			11	9	7	2	3	**4**
	5	4				1	6		8	s	10		11	9	7	2	3	**5**
	5	4				1	6		8	s	10		11	9	7	2	3	**6**
	5	4				1	6	s		8	10		11	9	7	2	3	**7**
5		4				1	6	s	8		10		11	9	7	2	3	**8**
	5	4				1	6	s	8		10		11	9	7	2	3	**9**
	5	4				1	6		*8	*12	10		11	9	7	2	3	**10**
	5	4				1	6	7	8	*12	*10		11	9		2	3	**11**
	5	4			*12	1	6	*7	8	10			11	9		2	3	**12**
	5	4				1	6	7	8	s	10		11	9		2	3	**13**
	5	4				1	6	7	8	s	10		11	9		2	3	**14**
	5	4				1	6	*7	8	*12	10		11	9		2	3	**15**
	5	4				1	6	7	8	*12	10		*11	9		2	3	**16**
	5	4				1	6	7	9	11	10			8	s	2	3	**17**
	5	4				1	6	11	9	7	10			8	s	2	3	**18**
	5	4				1	6	11	*9	*12	10			8	7	2	3	**19**
	5	4				1	6	7	9	11		10		8	s	2	3	**20**
	5	4				1	6	*7	9	11	10			8	*12	2	3	**21**
	5	4		s		1	6	7	9	11	10			8		2	3	**22**
	5	4				1	6	7	9	s	10		11	8		2	3	**23**
	5	4				1	6	7	9		10		11	8	s	2	3	**24**
	5	4				1	6	7	9		10		11	8	s	2	3	**25**
	5	4		s		1	6		9		10		11	8	7	2	3	**26**
	5	4				1	6		9	s	10		11	8	7	2	3	**27**
	5	4				1	6	*12	9		*10		11	8	7	2	3	**28**
	5	4				1	6		9	s	10		11	8	7	2	3	**29**
	5	4				1	6		9	s	10		11	8	7	2	3	**30**
	5	4				1	6		9	s	10		11	8	7	2	3	**31**
	5	4				1	*6		9	*12	10		11	8	7	2	3	**32**
	5	6		s		1		7		9	10		11	8	4	2	3	**33**
	5	4				1	6		9	s	10		11	8	7	2	3	**34**
	*5	4				1	6		9	*12	10		11	8	7	2	3	**35**
		4		5		1	6		9	s	10		11	8	7	2	3	**36**
		*4		5		1	6		9	*12	10		11	8	7	2	3	**37**
		4	s	5		1	6		9		10		11	8	7	2	3	**38**
	5	4		s		1	6		9		10		11	8	7	2	3	**39**
	5	4		s		1	6		9		10		11	8	7	2	3	**40**
	5	4	*7			1	6		9		10		11	8	*12	2	3	**41**
	5	4		2	s	1	6		9		10		11	8	7		3	**42**
1	38	42	1	4	0	42	41	16	40	9	39	1	36	42	27	41	42	Apps
					1			1		9					2			Subs
	2	1							18	5	12		9	2	2	1	2	Goals

Blick M R	Burrows F	Butler J W	Dangerfield D A	Dawson O J	Down D F	Downsborough P	Harland S C	Heath D	Horsfield A	Jones C M N	Noble P	Penman W S T	Rogers D E	Smart R W	Smith J	Thomas R J	Trollope N J	
	5	4				1	6		8	s	10		11	9	7	2	3	**2**
	5	4				1	6		8		10	*12	11	9	*7	2	3	**3**
	2	2				2	2		2		2	0	2	2	2	2	2	Apps
												1						Subs
											3							Goals

Blick M R	Burrows F	Butler J W	Dangerfield D A	Dawson O J	Down D F	Downsborough P	Harland S C	Heath D	Horsfield A	Jones C M N	Noble P	Penman W S T	Rogers D E	Smart R W	Smith J	Thomas R J	Trollope N J	
	5	4				1	6		9	s	10		11	8	7	2	3	**3**
	5	4				1	6	s	9	10			11	8	7	2	3	**4**
	5	4				1	6		9	s	10		11	8	7	2	3	**5**
	5	4				1	6		*9	*12	10		11	8	7	2	3	**6**
	4	4				4	4		4	1	3		4	4	4	4	4	Apps
										1								Subs
		1							4	1	1		1	1	1		1	Goals

CHRIS JONES

SEASON 1970/71

Football League Second Division
Final League Position : 12th
Manager : Fred Ford

Substitutes :
s denotes substitute **not** used
* player substituted by *12

					Home	Away	H-T	Goalscorers	Gate
1	S	Aug	15	Hull City	D1-1		(1-0)	Noble 31	16,227
2	S		22	Sheffield United		L1-2	(0-0)	Noble 72	18,718
3	S		29	Sunderland	W2-0		(2-0)	Horsfield 13,Gough 39	17,060
4	Tu	Sep	1	Watford	D1-1		(1-0)	Horsfield 31	16,176
5	S		5	Blackburn Rovers		L0-1	(0-0)		6,330
6	S		12	Portsmouth	W2-1		(2-0)	Noble 19,Horsfield 32	14,682
7	S		19	Carlisle United		L1-2	(0-0)	Rogers 51	10,070
8	S		26	Luton Town	D0-0				18,698
9	Tu		29	Millwall	W3-0		(1-0)	Horsfield 12,Rogers 57 pen.,85	14,389
10	S	Oct	3	Charlton Athletic		L1-2	(1-1)	Noble 40	10,034
11	S		10	Queens Park Rangers	W1-0		(0-0)	Horsfield 73	17,465
12	F		16	Hull City		L0-2	(0-2)		20,958
13	W		21	Norwich City		L0-1	(0-1)		11,357
14	S		24	Middlesbrough	W3-0		(3-0)	Rogers 2,Horsfield 4,13	15,219
15	S		31	Birmingham City		L1-2	(0-0)	Noble 70	18,502
16	S	Nov	7	Bristol City	W2-1		(0-0)	Horsfield 72,Noble 90	16,453
17	S		14	Leicester City		L1-3	(1-1)	Noble 5	26,063
18	S		21	Oxford United		D0-0			15,369
19	S		28	Sheffield Wednesday	W3-0		(2-0)	Rogers 6 pen.,61,Thomas 35	15,412
20	S	Dec	5	Bolton Wanderers		W3-0	(1-0)	Rogers 30,85,Porter 75	7,531
21	S		12	Orient	D1-1		(0-0)	Porter 68	13,863
22	S		19	Sheffield United	W3-0		(1-0)	Reece o.g.4,Rogers 68 pen.,Horsfield 87	14,505
23	S		26	Cardiff City		D1-1	(1-0)	Rogers 36	24,812
24	S	Jan	9	Millwall		D2-2	(0-0)	Rogers 46,Horsfield 58	10,140
25	S		16	Norwich City	W3-2		(1-0)	Burrows 8,Rogers 49,Noble 85	14,977
26	S		30	Sheffield Wednesday		D2-2	(2-1)	Rogers 20 pen.,31	12,964
27	S	Feb	6	Bolton Wanderers	W3-1		(2-0)	Noble 31,43,75	15,106
28	S		13	Orient		L0-1	(0-0)		7,797
29	S		20	Oxford United	W3-0		(2-0)	Noble 10,Porter 29,Rogers 61 pen.	17,744
30	S		27	Birmingham City	L1-2		(0-1)	Porter 46	19,860
31	S	Mar	6	Middlesbrough		L0-3	(0-2)		20,813
32	S		13	Leicester City	L0-1		(0-0)		17,979
33	S		20	Bristol City		L1-2	(0-0)	Horsfield 63	17,127
34	S		27	Blackburn Rovers	W3-0		(1-0)	Butler 18,Gough 70,Jones C 71	11,299
35	S	Apr	3	Sunderland		L2-5	(1-5)	Butler 43,Rogers 87	8,596
36	S		10	Cardiff City	D2-2		(1-2)	Peplow 5,Smart 64	21,158
37	M		12	Portsmouth		W2-0	(1-0)	Peplow 12,80	10,987
38	Tu		13	Charlton Athletic	D1-1		(1-1)	Jones C 36	11,953
39	S		17	Queens Park Rangers		L2-4	(1-3)	Noble 13,56	11,571
40	S		24	Carlisle United	D0-0				11,561
41	W		28	Watford		W2-1	(1-1)	Peplow 26,Horsfield 79	10,793
42	S	May	1	Luton Town		D1-1	(0-1)	Jones C 59	10,205

Average Home Attendance : **15,799**
Average Away Attendance : **13,845**

Football League Cup

					Home	Away	H-T	Goalscorers	Gate
2	Tu	Sep	8	Watford	W4-2		(2-2)	Rogers 7 pen.,89,Horsfield 9,54	13,271
3	Tu	Oct	6	Liverpool	W2-0		(0-0)	Rogers 65,68	23,992
4	Tu		27	Fulham		L0-1	(0-1)		22,576

F A Cup

					Home	Away	H-T	Goalscorers	Gate
3	S	Jan	2	Queens Park Rangers		W2-1	(0-0)	Horsfield 61,Noble 78	14,840
4	S		23	Leeds United		L0-4	(0-2)		36,985

FRED FORD
played for three London clubs in Arsenal, Charlton and Millwall, before a knee injury curtailed his playing career while at Carlisle - where he first took up coaching. During the 50's Fred was trainer to both the England 'B' team and the under-23's until he was appointed manager at Bristol City in 1960. He spent six months as a coach at the County Ground in 1967 before returning to Bristol to take charge at Rovers. Fred succeeded Danny Williams in July 1969, leading Town to within four points of a top flight place nine months later - and to an Anglo-Italian 'double'. With Dave Mackay waiting in the wings, Fred departed in November 1971, following a run of just four wins in 15 games.

Blick M R	Burrows F	Butler J W	Dangerfield D A	Dawson O J	Down D F	Downsborough P	Gough A M	Harland S C	Horsfield A	Hubbard T J	Jones C M N	Jones R J	Noble P	Peplow S T	Porter C J	Potter R C	Rogers D E	Smart R W	Smith J	Thomas R J	Trollope N J	
	5	4				1		6	9		s		10				11	8	7	2	3	1
	5	4				1		6	9				10		s		11	8	7	2	3	2
	5	4				1	8	6	9		7		10				11	s		2	3	3
	5	4				1	8	6	9		7		10	s			11			2	3	4
	5	4					8	6	9		*7	1	10				11	*12		2	3	5
	5	4		*12		1	8	6	9				*10				11		7	2	3	6
	5	4				1	8	6	9		s		10				11		7	2	3	7
	5	4	s			1	8	6	9				10				11		7	2	3	8
	5	4				1	8	6	9		s		10				11		7	2	3	9
	5	4					*8	6	9		*12	1	10				11		7	2	3	10
	5	3	8				4	6	9	*12		1	*10				11		7	2		11
	5	3	8	*12			4	6			*9	1	10				11		7	2		12
	5	3	8		9		4	6				1	10		7		11		s	2		13
	5	4					s	6	9			1	10				11	8	7	2	3	14
	*5	4					*12	6	9			1	10				11	8	7	2	3	15
5		4						6	9			1	10		s		11	8	7	2	3	16
	5	4					s	6	9			1	10				11	8	7	2	3	17
	5	4				1	8	6	9				10		7		11	s		2	3	18
	5	4				1	8	6	9		s		10		7		11			2	3	19
	5	4				1	8	6	9				10		7		11	s		2	3	20
	5	4				1	8	6	9		s		10		7		11			2	3	21
	5	4				1	*8	6	9				10		7		11	*12		2	3	22
		4				1	8	6	9				10		7	5	11	s		2	3	23
		4				1	8	6	9				10		s	5	11		7	2	3	24
	5	4				1	8	6	9				10		7		11		s	2	3	25
	5	4				1	s	6	9				10		7		11	8		2	3	26
	5	4				1	s	6	9				10		7		11	8		2	3	27
	5	4				1		6	9				10		*7		11	8	*12	2	3	28
	5	4				1	s	6	9				10		7		11	8		2	3	29
	5	4						6	9		s	1	10		7		11	8		2	3	30
	5	4					8	6	9			1	10		*7		11	*12		2	3	31
	5	4				1	8	6	9		s		10	7			11			2	3	32
	5	4				1	8	6	9		s		10	7			11			2	3	33
	5	4				1	8	6	*9		*12		10	7			11			2	3	34
	5	4				1	*8	6			9		10	7			11		*12	2	3	35
	5	4				1		6	s		9		10	7			11	8		2	3	36
	5	4				1		6	s		9		10	7	11			8		2	3	37
	5	4				1		6	s		9		10	7	11			8		2	3	38
	5	4				1		6	*12		9		10	7	*11			8		2	3	39
	*5	4				1		6			9		10	7	*12		11	8		2	3	40
		4				1		6	9		*12		*10	7		5	11	8		2	3	41
		4	s			1		6	9		10			7		5	11	8		2	3	42
1	37	42	3	0	1	31	24	42	34	0	11	11	41	11	17	4	39	18	14	42	39	Apps
				2			1		1	1	3				1			3	2			Subs
	1	2					2		12		3		14	4	4		16	1		1		Goals

Opponents 1 goal

Blick M R	Burrows F	Butler J W	Dangerfield D A	Dawson O J	Down D F	Downsborough P	Gough A M	Harland S C	Horsfield A	Hubbard T J	Jones C M N	Jones R J	Noble P	Peplow S T	Porter C J	Potter R C	Rogers D E	Smart R W	Smith J	Thomas R J	Trollope N J	
	5	4				1	*12	6	9				10				11	*8	7	2	3	2
	5	4	*12				8	6	9			1	10				11		7	2	*3	3
	5	4					*12	6	9			1	*10				11	8	7	2	3	4
	3	3	0			1	1	3	3			2	3				3	2	3	3	3	Apps
			1				2															Subs
									2								4					Goals

Blick M R	Burrows F	Butler J W	Dangerfield D A	Dawson O J	Down D F	Downsborough P	Gough A M	Harland S C	Horsfield A	Hubbard T J	Jones C M N	Jones R J	Noble P	Peplow S T	Porter C J	Potter R C	Rogers D E	Smart R W	Smith J	Thomas R J	Trollope N J	
		4				1	8	6	9		s		10			5	11		7	2	3	3
	5	4				1	8	6	9				10		7		11		s	2	3	4
	1	2				2	2	2	2		0		2		1	1	2		1	2	2	Apps
																						Subs
									1				1									Goals

TONY GOUGH

For Final League Table - see page 200 For Anglo-Italian games - see page 204

SEASON 1971/72

Football League Second Division
Final League Position : 11th
Manager : Fred Ford
Dave Mackay (from Nov.1)

Substitutes :
s denotes substitute **not** used
* player substituted by *12

					Home	Away	H-T	Goalscorers	Gate
1	S	Aug	14	Blackpool		L1-4	(0-2)	Rogers 63	13,004
2	S		21	Charlton Athletic	W2-1		(0-0)	Horsfield 74,Butler 90	15,249
3	S		28	Carlisle United		D0-0			9,936
4	W	Sep	1	Watford		D0-0			10,580
5	S		4	Queens Park Rangers	D0-0				15,918
6	S		11	Sunderland		L0-1	(0-0)		12,811
7	S		18	Fulham	W4-0		(2-0)	Noble 22,Rogers 35,Jones C 59,Butler 76	12,967
8	S		25	Cardiff City		W1-0	(0-0)	Jones C 78	16,292
9	W		29	Hull City		L0-2	(0-1)		10,700
10	S	Oct	2	Bristol City	L0-1		(0-0)		21,351
11	S		9	Luton Town		D0-0			13,423
12	S		16	Blackpool	W1-0		(0-0)	Thomas 66	10,360
13	Tu		19	Birmingham City	D1-1		(1-0)	Horsfield 28	14,027
14	S		23	Sheffield Wednesday		L0-1	(0-0)		19,993
15	S		30	Middlesbrough	L0-1		(0-1)		13,544
16	S	Nov	6	Oxford United		D1-1	(0-1)	Butler 50	12,382
17	S		13	Millwall	L0-2		(0-0)		14,852
18	S		20	Preston North End	D1-1		(0-0)	Bird o.g.50	10,833
19	S		27	Burnley		W2-1	(2-0)	Jones C 41,Noble 44	12,224
20	S	Dec	4	Norwich City	L0-1		(0-1)		14,167
21	S		11	Orient		W1-0	(0-0)	Horsfield 89	6,120
22	S		18	Queens Park Rangers		L0-3	(0-3)		13,517
23	M		27	Portsmouth	W3-1		(1-0)	Hall o.g.8,Rogers 46,64	20,494
24	S	Jan	1	Fulham		W4-2	(2-2)	Horsfield 12,44,Rogers 52,70	7,406
25	S		8	Carlisle United	D0-0				13,089
26	S		22	Hull City	W2-1		(1-1)	Noble 12,Horsfield 88	11,563
27	S		29	Birmingham City		L1-4	(0-3)	Horsfield 85	27,824
28	S	Feb	12	Sheffield Wednesday	W1-0		(1-0)	Burrows 29	11,589
29	S		19	Middlesbrough		L0-2	(0-2)		18,205
30	S		26	Oxford United	W4-0		(1-0)	Horsfield 11,66,81,Trollope 83	14,743
31	S	Mar	4	Millwall		D2-2	(1-2)	Mackay 14,Noble 89	16,036
32	S		18	Charlton Athletic		L1-3	(1-0)	Noble 44	7,433
33	S		25	Sunderland	D1-1		(1-1)	Noble 36	12,102
34	F		31	Bristol City		L0-1	(0-0)		21,496
35	S	Apr	1	Portsmouth		W2-1	(0-0)	Noble 73,88	12,157
36	Tu		4	Cardiff City	W3-1		(1-1)	Bunkell 17,Murray o.g.70,Noble 84	15,393
37	S		15	Burnley	L0-1		(0-0)		11,574
38	Tu		18	Luton Town	W2-1		(0-1)	Rogers 60,Horsfield 84	8,960
39	S		22	Norwich City		L0-1	(0-1)		31,736
40	Tu		25	Watford	W2-0		(1-0)	Noble 44,56	8,768
41	S		29	Orient	D2-2		(1-2)	Horsfield 29,Noble 68	8,564
42	M	May	1	Preston North End		D2-2	(0-0)	Noble 65,72	9,566

Average Home Attendance : **13,338**
Average Away Attendance : **14,421**

Football League Cup

					Home	Away	H-T	Goalscorers	Gate
2	W	Sep	8	Colchester United		L1-4	(1-1)	Horsfield 13	7,437

F A Cup

					Home	Away	H-T	Goalscorers	Gate
3	S	Jan	15	Arsenal	L0-2		(0-1)		31,668

DAVE MACKAY
had enjoyed an outstanding playing career prior to his arrival at Swindon, which included a ten-year spell at Spurs - where he was a member of the double-winning side of 1960/61. The role of player-manager looked the likely scenario when he joined Town in May 1971, but with Fred Ford still 'in situ', the Scot refused to assume that title. He soon took over, however, when Mr Ford was dismissed 11 weeks into the season. But Dave's tenure was not a particularly happy or successful one and exactly a year to the day after he took charge, he resigned - following a run of three wins in 16 games. The sale of Don Rogers days earlier was not the most popular decision made by the club that season.

Allan J	Bunkell R K	Burrows F	Butler J W	Dangerfield D A	Dawson O J	Downsborough P	Harland S C	Horsfield A	Hubbard T J	Jones C M N	Jones R J	Legg R D	Mackay D C	Moss D J	Noble P	Peplow S T	Peterson P W	Porter C J	Potter R C	Rogers D E	Smart R W	Stroud K A	Thomas R J	Trollope N J	
		5	4				8	9			1		6		10	7				11	s		2	3	**1**
		5	4			1	8	9					6		10			7		11	s		2	3	**2**
		5	4			1	8	9					6		10	s		7		11			2	3	**3**
	4	5				1	8	s		9			6		10			7		11			2	3	**4**
1		5	4				6	9							10			*7		11	*12	8	2	3	**5**
		5	4			1	6	*9		*12					10			7		11	8		2	3	**6**
		5	4			1	8			9			6		10	s		7		11			2	3	**7**
		5	4			1	8			9			6		10			7		11	s		2	3	**8**
		5	4		s	1	8			9			6		10			7		11			2	3	**9**
	*12	5	4			1	8			9			*6		10	7				11			2	3	**10**
	7	*5	4			1	8	9		*12			6		10					11			2	3	**11**
	7		4			1	5	8		9			6			s				11	10		2	3	**12**
	7		4				5	8		9	1		6			s				11	10		2	3	**13**
	7	5	4				10	8		9	1		6							11	s		2	3	**14**
		5	4				8	*7			1		6		9	*12				11	10		2	3	**15**
	4	5	7	s		1		9					6		10					11	8		2	3	**16**
	4	5	6	7		1		*9				*12			10					11	8		2	3	**17**
		5	4	7		1			s	9			6		8					11	10		2	3	**18**
	8	5	4	7		1	6			9		s			10					11			2	3	**19**
	6	5	4	7		1				9				s	10					11	8		2	3	**20**
	10	5	4	7		1		9					6		8					11	s		2	3	**21**
1	8	5	4	7				9					6		10					11	s		2	3	**22**
1	8	5	4	7				9					6		10	s				11			2	3	**23**
1	8	5	4	7				9	s				6		10					11			2	3	**24**
	8	5	4	7		1		9	s				6		10					11			2	3	**25**
	4	5		*7		1		9	8					*12	10					11	6		2	3	**26**
	4	5	6			1		9	7				s		10		2			11	8			3	**27**
	4	5	2			1		9	7				6		10	s				11	8			3	**28**
		5	2	4		1		*9	7				6	*12	10					11	8			3	**29**
	4	5	2	s		1		9	7				6		10					11	8			3	**30**
	4	5	2	*12		1		9	7				*6		10					11	8			3	**31**
	4	5	2	11		1		9	7				*6	*12	10						8			3	**32**
	4	5	6			1		9	7						10				s	11	8		2	3	**33**
	4	5	6			1		9	7				s		10					11	8		2	3	**34**
	*4	5	6			1		9	7				*12		10					11	8		2	3	**35**
	4	5	6			1		9	7						10	s				11	8		2	3	**36**
	*4	5	6			1		9	7						10	*12				11	8		2	3	**37**
	4	5	6			1		9	7						10	s				11	8		2	3	**38**
	4	5	6			1		9	*7						10					11	8	*12	2	3	**39**
1	4	5	6						8			9		7	10					11	s		2	3	**40**
1	4		6	*12				9	*8					7	10				5	11			2	3	**41**
1	*12		6					9							10	*7			5	11	8	4	2	3	**42**
7	29	38	40	12	0	31	16	33	16	11	4	1	25	2	39	3	1	8	2	41	23	2	36	42	Apps
	2			2						2		1	1	3		2					1	1			Subs
	2	1	3					12		3			1		14					7			1	1	Goals

Opponents 2 goals

Allan J	Bunkell R K	Burrows F	Butler J W	Dangerfield D A	Dawson O J	Downsborough P	Harland S C	Horsfield A	Hubbard T J	Jones C M N	Jones R J	Legg R D	Mackay D C	Moss D J	Noble P	Peplow S T	Peterson P W	Porter C J	Potter R C	Rogers D E	Smart R W	Stroud K A	Thomas R J	Trollope N J	
		5	4			1	6	9		s					10			7		11	8		2	3	**2**

Allan J	Bunkell R K	Burrows F	Butler J W	Dangerfield D A	Dawson O J	Downsborough P	Harland S C	Horsfield A	Hubbard T J	Jones C M N	Jones R J	Legg R D	Mackay D C	Moss D J	Noble P	Peplow S T	Peterson P W	Porter C J	Potter R C	Rogers D E	Smart R W	Stroud K A	Thomas R J	Trollope N J	
	8	5	*4	7		1		9					6		10					11	*12		2	3	**3**

For Final League Table - see page 200

ARTHUR HORSFIELD
arrived in May 1969 for a then club record £17,500. He was signed by Danny Williams before he departed to Hillsborough and was the only major addition to the League Cup winning side. A former Middlesbrough apprentice, Arthur had netted 22 goals as they gained promotion in 1967. Not the speediest of strikers to grace the County Ground, he was however a lethal finisher in and around the 'box' and was Town's top scorer in 1969/70 with 27 in 52 games. Arthur joined Charlton in June 1972 and was top scorer at The Valley in his first two seasons there, netting 44 goals.

SEASON 1972/73

Football League Second Division
Final League Position : 16th
Manager : Dave Mackay
Les Allen (from Nov.10)

Substitutes :
s denotes substitute **not** used
* player substituted by *12

No	Day	Month	Date	Opponents	Home	Away	H-T	Goalscorers	Gate
1	S	Aug	12	Queens Park Rangers	D2-2		(1-1)	Rogers 45,Peplow 57	14,169
2	W		16	Sheffield Wednesday		L1-2	(0-0)	Moss 75	20,841
3	S		19	Carlisle United		L0-3	(0-0)		7,747
4	S		26	Bristol City	W2-1		(1-1)	Peplow 23,81	15,304
5	Tu		29	Sheffield Wednesday	W1-0		(0-0)	Treacy 82	11,376
6	S	Sep	2	Sunderland		L2-3	(0-0)	Treacy 51,Rogers 84	11,674
7	S		9	Blackpool	D0-0				10,069
8	S		16	Aston Villa		L1-2	(1-0)	Rogers 36	30,775
9	Tu		19	Huddersfield Town		D1-1	(0-1)	Peplow 59	7,992
10	S		23	Portsmouth	D1-1		(0-1)	Rogers 75	9,431
11	Tu		26	Luton Town	L0-2		(0-0)		8,466
12	S		30	Hull City		L2-3	(1-1)	Howell 5,Noble 56	9,131
13	S	Oct	7	Burnley		L1-2	(0-1)	Rogers 68 pen.	11,415
14	S		14	Preston North End	W3-2		(0-1)	Treacy 72,Rogers 83,90	8,198
15	S		21	Nottingham Forest		D2-2	(1-0)	Peplow 33,Treacy 83	8,683
16	S		28	Brighton & Hove Albion	D2-2		(1-2)	Treacy 25,Moss 66	10,286
17	S	Nov	4	Luton Town		W1-0	(0-0)	Treacy 56	10,596
18	S		11	Huddersfield Town	D1-1		(0-0)	Treacy 61 pen.	9,673
19	S		18	Orient	W3-1		(1-1)	Noble 13,Peplow 63,70	7,951
20	S		25	Middlesbrough		W2-0	(0-0)	Smart 55,Trollope 61	11,408
21	S	Dec	9	Millwall		D1-1	(1-1)	Butler 32	9,015
22	S		16	Oxford United		L0-1	(0-0)		9,159
23	S		23	Fulham	D2-2		(1-1)	Treacy 32,Thomas 75	9,797
24	Tu		26	Portsmouth		D1-1	(0-0)	Noble 55	7,941
25	S	Jan	6	Bristol City		L0-3	(0-2)		12,481
26	S		20	Sunderland	D1-1		(1-0)	Butler 27	7,010
27	S		27	Blackpool		L0-2	(0-0)		8,277
28	S	Feb	10	Aston Villa	L1-3		(0-1)	Moss 61	13,615
29	S		17	Queens Park Rangers		L0-5	(0-2)		13,472
30	S		24	Oxford United	L1-3		(0-1)	McGovern 64	11,712
31	Tu		27	Cardiff City	W3-0		(3-0)	Thomas 7,Powell o.g.21,Treacy 41	9,770
32	F	Mar	2	Burnley	L0-1		(0-1)		12,483
33	S		10	Preston North End		D1-1	(1-0)	Treacy 22	6,468
34	M		12	Carlisle United	W2-0		(2-0)	Noble 20,Moss 24	7,871
35	S		17	Nottingham Forest	D0-0				9,842
36	S		24	Brighton & Hove Albion		L1-3	(1-2)	Treacy 11 pen.	10,276
37	S		31	Middlesbrough	W1-0		(0-0)	Treacy 90	7,060
38	S	Apr	7	Cardiff City		D1-1	(0-1)	Treacy 75	9,438
39	S		14	Millwall	D0-0				8,459
40	F		20	Fulham		D0-0			8,519
41	S		21	Orient		L0-1	(0-0)		6,386
42	Tu		24	Hull City	W2-1		(1-1)	Legg 16,Bunkell 74	8,191

Average Home Attendance : **10,035**
Average Away Attendance : **11,033**

Football League Cup

Rd	Day	Month	Date	Opponents	Home	Away	H-T	Goalscorers	Gate
2	Tu	Sep	5	Derby County	L0-1		(0-1)		15,730

F A Cup

Rd	Day	Month	Date	Opponents	Home	Away	H-T	Goalscorers	Gate
3	S	Jan	13	Birmingham City	W2-0		(0-0)	Butler 52,Treacy 78 pen.	17,581
4	S	Feb	3	West Bromwich Albion		L0-2	(0-2)		20,795

For Final League Table - see page 200

LES ALLEN
was another member of Tottenham's double-winning squad and, after six years as player and manager at Queens Park Rangers, joined Town as a scout. He was promoted to manager following Dave Mackay's resignation in November 1972. But, given little cash to inject into an ailing side, Les saw Town rapidly slide down the table and he was sacked at the end of February 1974. Six other members of his family all played League football.

Allan J	Bunkell R K	Burrows F	Butler J W	Dangerfield D A	Downsborough P	Howell R R	Hubbard T J	Jenkins T E	Legg R D	McGovern M J	Moss D J	Noble P	Peplow S T	Porter C J	Potter R C	Rogers D E	Smart R W	Stroud K A	Thomas R J	Treacy R C P	Trollope N J	Walker P G	
	8	5	4		1		7		*12			*10	9		6	11			2		3		**1**
	8	5	4		1		10				7		9		6	11	s		2		3		**2**
	*8	5	4		1		10						7		6	11	*12		2	9	3		**3**
	*8	5	4		1	*12	10						7		6	11			2	9	3		**4**
	8	5	4		1	s	10						7		6	11			2	9	3		**5**
	8	5	4		1	*12	*10						7		6	11			2	9	3		**6**
	s	5	4		1		8					10	7		6	11			2	9	3		**7**
	*12	5	*4		1		8					10	7		6	11			2	9	3		**8**
1			6			4	8					10	7		5	11		s	2	9	3		**9**
1			6			4	*8				*12	10	7		5	11			2	9	3		**10**
			6		1	4	8				*12	10	*7		5	11			2	9	3		**11**
		5	s		1	8						10	7		6	11	4		2	9	3		**12**
			6		1	8						10	7		5	11	4	s	2	9	3		**13**
			6		1	*8					*12	10	7		5	11	4		2	9	3		**14**
		5	s		1	8						10	7		6	11	4		2	9	3		**15**
		5			1	*8					*12	10	7		6	11	4		2	9	3		**16**
		5	11		1	8	s					10	7		6		4		2	9	3		**17**
		5	*12		1	8		*11				10	7		6		4		2	9	3		**18**
1		5	11			8						10	7	s	6		4		2	9	3		**19**
1	s	5	11			8						10	7		6		4		2	9	3		**20**
1		5	11			8					s	10	7		6		4		2	9	3		**21**
1		5	11	*12		8						10	7		6		*4		2	9	3		**22**
1	4	5	11			8		*12				10	*7		6				2	9	3		**23**
1	4	5	11			8		7			s	10			6				2	9	3		**24**
1	4	5	11			*8		7				10	*12		6				2	9	3		**25**
1	4	*5	11					7			8	10		*12	6				2	9	3		**26**
1	4		6					7			11	10		s	5		8		2	9	3		**27**
1	4		6			s		7			11	10			5		8		2	9	3		**28**
1		5	4			*12				8	7	10		*11	6				2	9	3		**29**
		5	4		1			*11		8	7	10			6		*12		2	9	3		**30**
		5			1					11	7	10		s	6		8	4	2	9	3		**31**
		5			1					11	7	10			6		8	*4	2	9	3	*12	**32**
	4	5	2		1					11	7	10			6		*8			9	3	*12	**33**
	4	5	3		1					11	*7	10			6		8		2	9		*12	**34**
	4	5	3		1			*12		*11	7	10			6		8		2	9			**35**
	4	5	2		1			11				10			6			s	9	7	3	8	**36**
	4	5	3		1	7		11		*12		*10			6			8	2	9			**37**
	8	5	3		1	7		11	*12			10			6			4	2	9			**38**
	4	5	3		1	*7		11	*12			10			6				2	9		8	**39**
	4	5	3		1	7	8	11	s			10			6				2	9			**40**
	4	5	3		1	7	8	11	s			10		6					2	9			**41**
	4		3		1			11	8	*7	*12	10		5				6	2	9			**42**
13	22	34	36	0	29	22	13	14	1	8	11	37	23	3	40	16	18	5	41	40	34	2	Apps
	1		1	1		3		2	3	1	5		1	1			2					3	Subs
	1		2			1			1	1	4	4	7			7	1		2	13	1		Goals

Opponents 1 goal

Allan J	Bunkell R K	Burrows F	Butler J W	Dangerfield D A	Downsborough P	Howell R R	Hubbard T J	Jenkins T E	Legg R D	McGovern M J	Moss D J	Noble P	Peplow S T	Porter C J	Potter R C	Rogers D E	Smart R W	Stroud K A	Thomas R J	Treacy R C P	Trollope N J	Walker P G	
	8	5	4		1		10				*12		7		*6	11			2	9	3		**2**

Allan J	Bunkell R K	Burrows F	Butler J W	Dangerfield D A	Downsborough P	Howell R R	Hubbard T J	Jenkins T E	Legg R D	McGovern M J	Moss D J	Noble P	Peplow S T	Porter C J	Potter R C	Rogers D E	Smart R W	Stroud K A	Thomas R J	Treacy R C P	Trollope N J	Walker P G	
1	4	5	11			s		7			8	10			6				2	9	3		**3**
1	4		6					7			11	10		s	5		8		2	9	3		**4**
2	2	1	2			0		2			2	2		0	2		1		2	2	2		Apps
																							Subs
			1																	1			Goals

JOHN TROLLOPE

Made his 600th appearance for Town in March

RAY TREACY

arrived from Charlton in a £35,000 deal that saw Arthur Horsfield move to The Valley. The Dubliner was first capped by the Republic in 1966 and went on to play in 42 internationals. He scored in five successive games mid-season on his way to becoming top scorer in 1972/73. But Ray found himself one of very few players with any experience in the squad for the following season - and after just four goals in 17 games, he moved on to Preston.

SEASON 1973/74

Football League Second Division
Final League Position : 22nd (Last)
Manager : Les Allen
Danny Williams (from Mar.6)

Substitutes :
s denotes substitute **not** used
* player substituted by *12

					Home	Away	H-T	Goalscorers	Gate
1	S	Aug	25	Sheffield Wednesday	W3-1		(2-1)	Moss 26,Treacy 31,McGovern 86	8,267
2	S	Sep	1	Preston North End		D1-1	(0-1)	Treacy 87	12,034
3	S		8	West Bromwich Albion	W1-0		(1-0)	Shaw o.g.34	11,583
4	Tu		11	Bristol City	L0-1		(0-1)		13,991
5	S		15	Notts County		L0-2	(0-0)		9,264
6	Tu		18	Nottingham Forest		L0-2	(0-1)		11,031
7	S		22	Millwall	L1-3		(1-1)	Legg 13	7,756
8	S		29	Orient		D0-0			7,799
9	Tu	Oct	2	Nottingham Forest	D0-0				6,353
10	S		6	Middlesbrough	L0-1		(0-0)		6,787
11	S		13	Luton Town		L1-2	(1-2)	Jenkins 22	10,732
12	S		20	Oxford United	W1-0		(1-0)	Legg 4	7,537
13	Tu		23	Bristol City		L0-1	(0-1)		14,474
14	S		27	Portsmouth		L1-3	(0-3)	Treacy 69	11,819
15	S	Nov	3	Carlisle United	D2-2		(1-2)	Eastoe 8,46	6,480
16	S		10	Sunderland		L1-4	(1-1)	Jenkins 28	24,636
17	S		17	Blackpool		L0-2	(0-1)		7,404
18	S		24	Aston Villa	W1-0		(0-0)	Moss 90	8,476
19	S	Dec	1	Crystal Palace		L2-4	(1-1)	Eastoe 37,Syrett 87	17,881
20	S		8	Fulham	D1-1		(0-1)	Eastoe 53	5,568
21	S		15	Bolton Wanderers		L0-2	(0-1)		8,846
22	S		22	Orient	D2-2		(1-1)	Syrett 28,Moss 86	5,718
23	W		26	Cardiff City		L1-2	(0-2)	Syrett 51	10,071
24	S		29	West Bromwich Albion		L0-2	(0-1)		14,555
25	Tu	Jan	1	Preston North End	W3-1		(1-1)	Eastoe 21,Butler 70,Moss 89	8,299
26	S		19	Sheffield Wednesday		L1-2	(1-1)	Eastoe 21	11,944
27	S		26	Hull City	D1-1		(0-0)	Eastoe 51	4,389
28	Su	Feb	3	Bolton Wanderers	D2-2		(2-0)	Clarke 11,Hubbard 45	8,864
29	S		16	Millwall		L0-3	(0-1)		6,725
30	Tu		19	Notts County	L1-4		(1-2)	Moss 28	3,284
31	S		23	Middlesbrough		L1-2	(0-1)	Compton 81	25,194
32	Tu		26	Luton Town	L0-2		(0-2)		2,600
33	S	Mar	2	Cardiff City	D1-1		(0-1)	Compton 65	5,126
34	S		9	Portsmouth	L1-2		(0-2)	McLaughlin 84	5,364
35	Su		17	Oxford United		D1-1	(0-0)	Moss 76	9,554
36	S		23	Sunderland	L0-2		(0-2)		6,178
37	S		30	Carlisle United		L1-5	(0-2)	Syrett 88	6,544
38	S	Apr	6	Aston Villa		D1-1	(0-0)	Eastoe 65	20,709
39	S		13	Blackpool	W1-0		(1-0)	Jenkins 45	4,655
40	M		15	Hull City		W1-0	(0-0)	Clarke 50	5,348
41	S		20	Fulham		L1-4	(1-1)	Moore o.g.25	7,808
42	S		27	Crystal Palace	L0-1		(0-0)		11,961

Average Home Attendance : **7,106**
Average Away Attendance : **12,113**

Football League Cup

					Home	Away	H-T	Goalscorers	Gate
1	Tu	Aug	28	Newport County	D3-3		(2-0)	Treacy 19,Moss 23,Legg 47	6,873
1R	Tu	Sep	4	Newport County		W2-1	(2-0)	McGovern 10,Legg 17	6,007
2	W	Oct	10	Chesterfield		L0-1	(0-1)		4,639

F A Cup

					Home	Away	H-T	Goalscorers	Gate
3	S	Jan	5	Portsmouth		D3-3	(3-1)	Jenkins 2,Moss 23,Trollope 44	16,682
3R	W		9	Portsmouth	L0-1		(0-0)		10,031

For Final League Table - see page 201

Allan J	Bunkell R K	Burrows F	Butler J W	Clarke R C	Collins M A	Compton R	Dixon W E	Eastoe P R	Fiocca P	Gabriel J	Hubbard T J	Jenkins T E	Legg R D	McGovern M J	McLaughlin J	Moss D J	Munks D	Porter C J	Potter R C	Sperti F	Spratley A S	Stroud K A	Syrett D K	Thomas R J	Treacy R C P	Trollope N J	
1		5	6								4	11	10	8		7							s	2	9	3	1
1		5	6								4	11	10	8		7							*12	*2	9	3	2
1		5	2								*4	11	10	8		7						6	*12		9	3	3
1	*12	5	6									11	10	*8		7						4		2	9	3	4
1		5	4		*12							11	10	8		*7						6		2	9	3	5
1		5	4									11	*8			7		*12				6	10	2	9	3	6
1		5	4									11	10	8		7			6				*12	2	*9	3	7
1		5	4									11	10	s		7		8	6					2	9	3	8
1		5	4		10							11	*12			*7		8	6					2	9	3	9
1	8	5	4		10							11				7			*6				*12	2	9	3	10
1		5	4									11	10	8		7						6	s	2	9	3	11
1		5	4		*12							11	10	8		7						6		2	9	*3	12
1		5	3		*12		*4					11	10	8		7						6		2	9		13
1		5	3							4		11	s	8		7			6				10	2	9		14
1		5	3	*12				*9		4		11		8		7						6	10	2			15
1		5	3	*12			2			4		11		*8					6			7	10		9		16
1		5	3							4		11		8		7		10	6	2		s	9				17
1		5	2	9						*4	8	11		*12		7			6				10			3	18
1		5	2	s				10		8	4	11				7			6				9			3	19
1		5	2					10			4	11		8		7		s	6				9			3	20
1		5	2					10			4	11		*8		7		6	*12				9			3	21
1		5	10					9			7	*11			2	*12	4		6				8			3	22
1		5	10					9			8	11			2	7	4		*6				*12			3	23
1		5	6					10			8	7			2		4	*11				*12	9			3	24
1		5	8				2	9				11			s	7	4					6	10			3	25
1		5	10				2	9			8	11			s	7	4					6				3	26
1			10				2	9			8	*11				7	4		5			6	*12			3	27
		5	11	10			2	9			8					7	4		6		1		s			3	28
1			11	9			s				8				2	7	4		5			6	10			3	29
1		5		9	*12		10				*8	11			2	7			6			4				3	30
			6	*12		9	10					11			2	7			5		1	*4	8			3	31
		5	4	10		9	8					11	s		2	7	6				1					3	32
			4			9					8	11	*12		2	7	6		5		1		*10			3	33
			4			*9	8					11	*12		2	7	6		5		1		10			3	34
			10				2	9			*8	11			4	7	6		5		1		*12			3	35
			10	8			2	9				11			4	7	6		5		1		s			3	36
1			10	*11			2	9						*12	4	7			5			6	8			3	37
1			10				s	9			4	11			2	7	6		5				8			3	38
1							8	9			4	11		s	2	7	6		5							3	39
1							8	9			4			11	2	7	6		5			s				3	40
1							2	9	11		4			*12		7	6		5				10			*3	41
1		5					3	9			4			11	2	7	6			s			10				42
35	1	30	37	11	2	4	17	19	1	6	22	36	11	17	16	39	18	5	26	1	7	16	20	14	15	36	Apps
	1			3	4								3	3		1		1	1			1	7				Subs
			1	2		2		8			1	3	2	1	1	6							4		3		Goals

Opponents 2 goals

Allan J	Bunkell R K	Burrows F	Butler J W	Clarke R C	Collins M A	Compton R	Dixon W E	Eastoe P R	Fiocca P	Gabriel J	Hubbard T J	Jenkins T E	Legg R D	McGovern M J	McLaughlin J	Moss D J	Munks D	Porter C J	Potter R C	Sperti F	Spratley A S	Stroud K A	Syrett D K	Thomas R J	Treacy R C P	Trollope N J	
1		5	6								4	11	10	8		7						*12		2	9	3	1
1	s	5	2								4	11	10	8		7						6			9	3	1R
1	*8	5	4		9							11	10	7								6		2	*12	3	2
3	1	3	3		1						2	3	3	3		2						2		2	2	3	Apps
																						1			1		Subs
													2	1		1									1		Goals

Allan J	Bunkell R K	Burrows F	Butler J W	Clarke R C	Collins M A	Compton R	Dixon W E	Eastoe P R	Fiocca P	Gabriel J	Hubbard T J	Jenkins T E	Legg R D	McGovern M J	McLaughlin J	Moss D J	Munks D	Porter C J	Potter R C	Sperti F	Spratley A S	Stroud K A	Syrett D K	Thomas R J	Treacy R C P	Trollope N J	
1		5	10				2	9			8	11				7	4		s			6				3	3
1		5	10				2	9			8	11				7	4		s			6				3	3R
2		2	2				2	2			2	2				2	2		0			2				2	Apps
																											Subs
												1				1										1	Goals

SEASON 1974/75

Football League Third Division
Final League Position : 4th
Manager : Danny Williams

Substitutes :
s denotes substitute **not** used
* player substituted by *12

					Home	Away	H-T	Goalscorers	Gate
1	S	Aug	17	Bury	L0-2		(0-1)		6,441
2	S		24	Port Vale		D2-2	(2-1)	MacLean 15,Moss 17	3,446
3	S		31	Blackburn Rovers	W2-0		(2-0)	Dixon 37,Eastoe 41	4,951
4	Tu	Sep	3	Tranmere Rovers	D0-0				5,511
5	S		7	Crystal Palace		L2-6	(0-5)	Eastoe 61,83	13,964
6	S		14	Plymouth Argyle	W2-0		(0-0)	Hubbard 54,Eastoe 64	5,495
7	Tu		17	Aldershot	W3-2		(2-1)	Moss 27 pen.,Eastoe 40,Jenkins 59	5,733
8	S		21	Charlton Athletic		D3-3	(2-0)	Eastoe 4,82,Syrett 32	4,516
9	Tu		24	Walsall		L0-2	(0-1)		3,595
10	S		28	Watford	D2-2		(1-1)	Burrows 45,Trollope 60 pen.	6,326
11	W	Oct	2	Chesterfield		W2-0	(0-0)	Eastoe 53,84	3,573
12	S		5	Southend United	W2-0		(0-0)	Eastoe 54,62	6,690
13	S		12	Halifax Town		D0-0			1,730
14	S		19	Wrexham	W2-1		(0-1)	Butler 55,Moss 71	6,731
15	M		21	Tranmere Rovers		L0-3	(0-1)		2,404
16	S		26	Huddersfield Town		D2-2	(0-0)	Syrett 46,Eastoe 55	5,792
17	S	Nov	2	Grimsby Town	W3-2		(2-2)	McLaughlin 23,Wiggington o.g.34,Syrett 89	7,198
18	Tu		5	Chesterfield	W1-0		(1-0)	Anderson 44	8,277
19	S		9	Brighton & Hove Albion		D1-1	(1-1)	Burrows 34	8,761
20	S		16	Gillingham	W1-0		(0-0)	Eastoe 62	8,847
21	S		30	Colchester United	W4-1		(2-1)	Moss 20 pen.,52,85 pen.,Eastoe 22	10,072
22	S	Dec	7	Hereford United		L1-2	(1-1)	Eastoe 42	8,635
23	S		21	Peterborough United	L0-1		(0-1)		9,023
24	Th		26	Plymouth Argyle		L3-4	(2-1)	Moss 22,31,McLaughlin 49	18,027
25	S		28	AFC Bournemouth	W2-1		(1-0)	Moss 45 pen.,Eastoe 89	9,929
26	S	Jan	11	Hereford United	W1-0		(0-0)	Butler 54	11,781
27	Tu	Feb	4	Brighton & Hove Albion	W1-0		(0-0)	Moss 84 pen.	9,552
28	S		8	Grimsby Town		L0-2	(0-2)		5,121
29	W		12	Aldershot		W1-0	(1-0)	Eastoe 35	4,538
30	S		15	Preston North End	W1-0		(1-0)	Eastoe 27	11,892
31	Tu		18	Preston North End		L0-2	(0-2)		11,139
32	S		22	Gillingham		L1-3	(1-1)	Trollope 8 pen.	9,172
33	S	Mar	1	Blackburn Rovers		L0-2	(0-1)		13,621
34	Tu		4	Colchester United		L0-2	(0-1)		4,041
35	S		8	Walsall	W3-0		(1-0)	McLaughlin 4,Prophett 58,Moss 80	8,964
36	S		15	Watford		L0-1	(0-1)		5,523
37	Tu		18	Bury		D0-0			3,615
38	S		22	Crystal Palace	D1-1		(0-1)	Eastoe 75	11,542
39	S		29	Peterborough United		D0-0			7,364
40	M		31	AFC Bournemouth		D1-1	(1-1)	Eastoe 29	6,216
41	Tu	Apr	1	Charlton Athletic	W2-0		(1-0)	Prophett 28,Moss 85	9,819
42	S		5	Huddersfield Town	W4-1		(3-1)	Eastoe 15,20,41,Moss 74	7,099
43	F		11	Southend United		L0-2	(0-1)		4,499
44	S		19	Halifax Town	W3-1		(1-0)	Stroud 45,Dixon 52,Eastoe 72	6,615
45	Tu		22	Port Vale	W3-2		(3-0)	Prophett 32,Moss 34 pen.,Anderson 37	7,447
46	S		26	Wrexham		W2-1	(1-0)	Eastoe 39,59	2,928

Average Home Attendance : **8,084**
Average Away Attendance : **6,618**

Football League Cup

					Home	Away	H-T	Goalscorers	Gate
1	Tu	Aug	20	Portsmouth	L0-1		(0-0)		4,779

F A Cup

					Home	Away	H-T	Goalscorers	Gate
1	S	Nov	23	Reading	W4-0		(1-0)	Anderson 33,Eastoe 61,Lenarduzzi o.g.66,Moss 74	13,365
2	S	Dec	14	Maidstone United	W3-1		(1-0)	Prophett 5,Eastoe 65,83	10,016
3	S	Jan	4	Lincoln City	W2-0		(1-0)	Eastoe 45,Moss 48	11,791
4	S		25	West Ham United		D1-1	(0-0)	Eastoe 83	35,679
4R	Tu		28	West Ham United	L1-2		(1-0)	Anderson 29	26,749

For Final League Table - see page 201

Allan J	Anderson T	Barron J	Burrows F	Butler J W	Dillon M L	Dixon W E	Eastoe P R	Hubbard T J	Jenkins T E	MacLean H	McGovern M J	McLaughlin J	Moss D J	Munks D	Potter R C	Prophett C G	Stroud K A	Syrett D K	Trollope N J	
		1				*12	9	4	*11	10		2	7	6	5			8	3	**1**
		1	*12			8	9	4	11	10		2	7	*6	5				3	**2**
		1		6		8	9	4	11	10		2	7		5			s	3	**3**
		1		6		*8	9	4	11	10		2	7		5	*12			3	**4**
		1	*12	10			9	4		11		2	7		5	6		*8	3	**5**
		1		10		s	9	4	11			2	7		5	6		8	3	**6**
		1	5	10		*12	9	4	11			2	7			6		*8	3	**7**
		1	5	10			9	4	11	*12		*2	7			6		8	3	**8**
		1	5	10		2	9	4	*7	11					*12	6		8	3	**9**
		1	6			2	9	4	11	10			*12		5	7		*8	3	**10**
		1		*12		2	9	4	11	10			7		5	6		*8	3	**11**
		1		8		2	9	4	11	10			s		5	6		7	3	**12**
		1	5	8		2	9	4		*10		*12	11			6		7	3	**13**
		1	5	8		11	9	*4		10		2	7			6		*12	3	**14**
1			*12	11		*8	9	4		10		2	7		5	6			3	**15**
1				10		2	9	4		11		*12	*7	6	5			8	3	**16**
		1				2	9	4		11		10	7	s	5	6		8	3	**17**
	11	1	5			2	9	4		*12		10	7			6		*8	3	**18**
	10	1	5			2	9	4		11		8	7			6		s	3	**19**
	11	1	5			2	9	4		10		8	7			6		s	3	**20**
	11	1	5	10		2	9	4	s			8	7			6			3	**21**
	*11	1	5	10		2	9	4				8	7			6		*12	3	**22**
	11	1	5	*10		2	9	4	*12			8	7			6			3	**23**
	11	1	5	s		2	9	4	10			8	7			6			3	**24**
	*12	1	5	10		2	9		11				7			6	4	*8	3	**25**
	11	1	5	10		2	9		s			8	7			6	4		3	**26**
	11	1	5	10		2	9		4			8	7			6	s		3	**27**
	11	1	5	10		2	9		*4			8	7			6	*12		3	**28**
	11	1	5	10		2	9					8	7			6	4	s	3	**29**
	11	1	*5	10		2	9		*12			8	7			6	4		3	**30**
	11	1		10		2	9		7		s	4				6	5	8	3	**31**
	11	1		10		2	9			s	4	8				6	5	7	3	**32**
	11	1	5	10		2	9		7		s	8				6	4		3	**33**
	11	1		10		2	9		4			8	7			6	5	s	3	**34**
	11	1	5	*8		2	9		4			10	7			6	*12		3	**35**
		1	5		*12	2	9		4	*11		10	7			6	8		3	**36**
	11	1	5		4	2	9		8			10	7			6	s		3	**37**
		1	5		*12	2	9		8			*10	7			6	4	11	3	**38**
		1	5		4	2	9		8			10	7			6	s	11	3	**39**
		1	5		4	2	9		8			10	*7			6	*12	11	3	**40**
	11	1	5		4	s	9		8			2	7			6	10		3	**41**
	11	1	5		10	s	9		8			2	7			6	4		3	**42**
1	11		5		10	s	9		8			2	7			6	4		3	**43**
1	11		5		s	2	9		10			8	7			6	4		3	**44**
1	11		5		10	2	9					8	7			6	4	s	3	**45**
1	11		5			2	9		10			8	7			6	4	s	3	**46**
6	24	40	32	26	7	38	46	24	29	17	1	39	40	3	12	41	16	19	46	Apps
	1		3	1	2	2			2	2		2	1		1	1	3	2		Subs
	2		2	2		2	26	1	1	1		3	14			3	1	3	2	Goals

Opponents 1 goal

Allan J	Anderson T	Barron J	Burrows F	Butler J W	Dillon M L	Dixon W E	Eastoe P R	Hubbard T J	Jenkins T E	MacLean H	McGovern M J	McLaughlin J	Moss D J	Munks D	Potter R C	Prophett C G	Stroud K A	Syrett D K	Trollope N J	
		1	*12			8	9	4	11	10		*2	7	6	5				3	**1**

Allan J	Anderson T	Barron J	Burrows F	Butler J W	Dillon M L	Dixon W E	Eastoe P R	Hubbard T J	Jenkins T E	MacLean H	McGovern M J	McLaughlin J	Moss D J	Munks D	Potter R C	Prophett C G	Stroud K A	Syrett D K	Trollope N J	
	11	1	5	10		2	9	4	s			8	7			6			3	**1**
	11	1	5	10		2	9	4	s			8	7			6			3	**2**
	11	1	5	10		2	9	*4	*12			8	7			6			3	**3**
	11	1	5	10		2	9		4			8	7			6		s	3	**4**
	11	1	5	10		2	9		4			8	7			6		s	3	**4R**
	5	5	5	5		5	5	3	2			5	5			5		0	5	Apps
									1											Subs
	2						5						2			1				Goals

PETER EASTOE

SEASON 1975/76

Football League Third Division
Final League Position : 19th
Manager : Danny Williams

Substitutes :
s denotes substitute **not** used
* player substituted by *12

				Home	Away	H-T	Goalscorers	Gate
1	S	Aug	16 Chesterfield	L0-1		(0-0)		7,675
2	S		23 Walsall		D1-1	(1-1)	Eastoe 36	5,146
3	S		30 Gillingham	D2-2		(1-1)	Moss 36 pen.,Eastoe 84	6,786
4	S	Sep	6 Shrewsbury Town		L0-3	(0-1)		4,062
5	S		13 Sheffield Wednesday	W2-1		(0-1)	Anderson 50,Eastoe 83	6,925
6	S		20 Port Vale		L0-3	(0-1)		3,720
7	W		24 Hereford United		L0-1	(0-1)		6,423
8	S		27 Colchester United	L0-1		(0-0)		5,750
9	S	Oct	4 Rotherham United		W2-0	(2-0)	Anderson 21,Moss 35 pen.	4,731
10	S		11 Halifax Town	W3-1		(1-0)	Anderson 26,53,Stroud 50	6,216
11	S		18 Wrexham		L0-2	(0-0)		2,893
12	Tu		21 Bury		L0-5	(0-4)		5,737
13	S		25 Grimsby Town	W3-0		(1-0)	Eastoe 41,62,Anderson 55	5,877
14	F		31 Southend United		L0-3	(0-2)		4,258
15	Tu	Nov	4 Crystal Palace	L1-2		(1-0)	Moss 2	10,599
16	S		8 Preston North End	L1-3		(0-3)	Trollope 81	6,313
17	S		15 Peterborough United		L1-3	(1-1)	Eastoe 31	7,287
18	S		29 Brighton & Hove Albion	W3-2		(0-1)	Syrett 47,Dixon 53,Eastoe 79	6,799
19	S	Dec	6 Mansfield Town		L1-3	(0-1)	Eastoe 51	5,487
20	S		20 Chester		L1-2	(0-0)	Anderson 46	3,674
21	F		26 Cardiff City	W4-0		(2-0)	Anderson 26,Eastoe 44,Burrows 70,Dixon 79	10,005
22	S		27 Millwall		D0-0			7,022
23	S	Jan	10 Gillingham		L2-3	(0-1)	Anderson 55,Burrows 72	6,459
24	S		17 Port Vale	W2-1		(0-0)	McLaughlin 75,Syrett 89	5,546
25	S		24 Sheffield Wednesday		W2-0	(1-0)	Dixon 31,Syrett 49	8,342
26	S		31 Bury	W2-1		(1-1)	Stroud 23,Rudd o.g.74	5,408
27	S	Feb	7 Crystal Palace		D3-3	(1-2)	Stroud 18,Syrett 74,76	15,844
28	Tu		10 Aldershot	W6-3		(5-0)	Syrett 1,Dixon 25,Anderson 30 pen.,41 pen.,Stroud 35,Moss 84	7,335
29	S		14 Preston North End		L2-4	(2-3)	Dixon 22,Butler 32	5,868
30	S		21 Peterborough United	L0-3		(0-2)		7,476
31	Tu		24 Hereford United	L0-1		(0-1)		10,830
32	S		28 Grimsby Town		L0-1	(0-1)		5,218
33	S	Mar	6 Southend United	D0-0				5,587
34	Tu		9 Rotherham United	D1-1		(1-1)	Rogers 29	9,877
35	S		13 Halifax Town		W2-0	(1-0)	Syrett 25,55	1,846
36	S		20 Brighton & Hove Albion		L0-2	(0-0)		18,208
37	S		27 Mansfield Town	L0-2		(0-2)		6,805
38	Tu		30 Chester	W2-1		(2-1)	Moss 1,Syrett 24	5,176
39	S	Apr	3 Chesterfield		L0-4	(0-2)		3,646
40	Tu		6 Colchester United		W2-1	(2-1)	Anderson 19 pen.,Syrett 26	2,694
41	S		10 Shrewsbury Town	W3-0		(1-0)	Syrett 2,Anderson 46,Stroud 56	5,879
42	W		14 Aldershot		W1-0	(1-0)	Dixon 35	4,226
43	S		17 Cardiff City		D0-0			23,428
44	Tu		20 Millwall	L0-2		(0-0)		13,756
45	S		24 Walsall	W5-1		(2-1)	Anderson 27 pen.,33 pen.,54 pen.,Moss 75,Syrett 76	7,491
46	Th		29 Wrexham	D2-2		(1-1)	Syrett 21,71	9,011

Average Home Attendance : **7,527**
Average Away Attendance : **6,792**

Football League Cup

				Home	Away	H-T	Goalscorers	Gate
1/1	Tu	Aug	19 Millwall	W2-1		(1-1)	Stroud 24,Trollope 88 pen.	6,149
1/2	M		25 Millwall		W1-0	(0-0)	Moss 66 pen.	5,935
2/1	Tu	Sep	9 Wolverhampton Wanderers	D2-2		(2-0)	McAlle o.g.10,Trollope 38	12,246
2/2	Tu		16 Wolverhampton Wanderers		L2-3	(1-0)	Moss 18,Eastoe 74	14,072

F A Cup

				Home	Away	H-T	Goalscorers	Gate
1	S	Nov	22 Newport County		D2-2	(0-1)	Moss 74,Syrett 90	5,182
1R	Tu		25 Newport County	W3-0		(0-0)	Love o.g.48,Trollope 50,Dixon 53	7,539
2	S	Dec	13 Hendon		W1-0	(0-0)	Moss 76 pen.	3,349
3	S	Jan	3 Tooting & Mitcham United	D2-2		(2-0)	Eastoe 5,Dixon 6	9,442
3R	Tu		6 Tooting & Mitcham United		L1-2	(0-1)	Green o.g.52	8,000

For Final League Table - see page 201

Aizlewood S	Allan J	Anderson T	Barron J	Burrows F	Butler J W	Chalklin G	Dixon W E	Eastoe P R	Emanuel W J	Farr I S	Gilligan A A	Gilligan J	Hubbard T J	Jenkins T E	McLaughlin J	Moss D J	O'Brien G	Prophett C G	Rogers D E	Stroud K A	Syrett D K	Taylor G W	Trollope N J	
		11	1	5	s			9					4	10	2	7		6		8			3	1
		11	1	5	6		2	9					4	*12	7					8	*10		3	2
	1	11			*10		2	9					4	*12	8	7		6		5			3	3
	1	11		*12	10		2	9					*4		8	7		6		5			3	4
		11	*1	5			2	9						*12	8	7		6		4	10		3	5
	1	11		5	*10		2	9					4	7	8					6	*12		3	6
	1	11		5	10		2	9					*4	*12	8	7				6			3	7
	1	11		5	10		2	9					*4	*12	8	7				6			3	8
	1	11		5	10		2	9					s	4	8	7				6			3	9
	1	11		5	10		2	9						4	8	7		s		6			3	10
	1	11		5	10		2	9					s	4	8	7				6			3	11
	1	11		5	10		2	9					*7	4	8	*12				6			3	12
	1	11		5			2	9				s		4	8	7				10		6	3	13
		11	1	5			2	9				*12		*4	8	7				10		6	3	14
		11	1	5	*4		2	9				*12			8	7					10	6	3	15
		*11	1	5			2	9	10	*12		7			8					4		6	3	16
		11	1	5			*12	9	10			*6			8	7				4		2	3	17
		11	1	5			8	9	4					s		7				6	10	2	3	18
		11	1	5			4	9	6			*12		*8		7					10	2	3	19
		11	1	5	*12		8	9	*4							7				6	10	2	3	20
		11	1	5	10		8	9	6					s	6	7				4		2	3	21
		11	1	5			8	9						*12	7					4	10	*2	3	22
		11	1	5		10	8							s	6	7				4	9	2	3	23
		11	1	5		10	8							s	6	7				4	9	2	3	24
		11	1			*5	8							*12	10	7		6		4	9	2	3	25
		11	1	5			8							s	10	7		6		4	9	2	3	26
		11	1	5			8							s	10	7		6		4	9	2	3	27
		11	1	5			8							s	10	7		6		4	9	2	3	28
		11	1	5	*12		8								10	*7		6		4	9	2	3	29
		11	1		5		8	9					s	7	10			6		4		2	3	30
		11	1	5	s		8	9							10			6		4	7	2	3	31
		11	1	5	2		8	9							10	7		6		*4	*12		3	32
		*11	1	5	2		8	9							10	7		6		4	*12		3	33
		11	1	5	*2		10								4	7		6	8	*12	9		3	34
5		11	1				s								2	7	10	6	8	4	9		3	35
5		11	1				*12								2	7	10	6	*8	4	9		3	36
5		11	1				*12								2	7	10	6	*8	4	9		3	37
5		11	1				8								2	7	10	6	s	4	9		3	38
*5		11	1				8								2	7	10	6	*12	4	9		3	39
		11	1	5			8				s				2	7	10	6	4		9		3	40
		11	1	5			8								2	7	10	6	4	*12	*9		3	41
		*11	1	5			8								2	7	10	6	4	*12	9		3	42
		11	1	5			7								2	*12	10	6	*8	4	9		3	43
		11	1	5	s		8								2	7	10	6	4		9		3	44
		11	1	5			8								2	7	10	6	s	4	9		3	45
		11	1	5			8								2	7	10	6	s	4	9		3	46
5	10	46	36	37	16	3	41	26	6	0	0	2	8	10	44	38	12	26	9	39	28	19	46	Apps
				1	2		3			1		3		7		2			1	3	3			Subs
		15		2	1		6	9							1	6			1	5	14		1	Goals

Opponents 1 goal

Aizlewood S	Allan J	Anderson T	Barron J	Burrows F	Butler J W	Chalklin G	Dixon W E	Eastoe P R	Emanuel W J	Farr I S	Gilligan A A	Gilligan J	Hubbard T J	Jenkins T E	McLaughlin J	Moss D J	O'Brien G	Prophett C G	Rogers D E	Stroud K A	Syrett D K	Taylor G W	Trollope N J	
		11	1	5	*12			9					4	*10	2	7		6		8			3	1/1
		11	1		10		2	9					4	s	8	7		6		5			3	1/2
		11	1	5	10		2	9						s	8	7		6		4			3	2/1
	1	11		5			2	9					10	*12	8	*7		6		4			3	2/2
	1	4	3	3	2		3	4					3	1	4	4		4		4			4	Apps
					1									1										Subs
								1								2				1			2	Goals

Opponents 1 goal

Aizlewood S	Allan J	Anderson T	Barron J	Burrows F	Butler J W	Chalklin G	Dixon W E	Eastoe P R	Emanuel W J	Farr I S	Gilligan A A	Gilligan J	Hubbard T J	Jenkins T E	McLaughlin J	Moss D J	O'Brien G	Prophett C G	Rogers D E	Stroud K A	Syrett D K	Taylor G W	Trollope N J	
		11	1	5			8	9	4				*10			7				6	*12	2	3	1
		11	1	5			*12	9	4				*8			7				6	10	2	3	1R
		11	1	5	s		8	9	4							7				6	10	2	3	2
		11	1	5	*10		8	9	6					*12	2	7				4			3	3
		11	1	5		s	8	9							6	7				4	10	2	3	3R
		5	5	5	1	0	4	5	4				2	0	2	5				5	3	4	5	Apps
							1							1							1			Subs
							2	1								2					1		1	Goals

SEASON 1976/77

Football League Third Division
Final League Position : 11th
Manager : Danny Williams

Substitutes :
s denotes substitute **not** used
* player substituted by *12

					Home	Away	H-T	Goalscorers	Gate
1	S	Aug	21	Port Vale	W1-0		(0-0)	Syrett 47	6,146
2	Tu		24	Portsmouth		L1-2	(0-2)	Anderson 64	7,898
3	S		28	Wrexham	W3-2		(0-0)	Moss 62,90,Prophett 86	6,208
4	S	Sep	4	Chesterfield		W1-0	(0-0)	Rogers 81	4,148
5	S		11	Sheffield Wednesday	W5-2		(1-1)	Moss 16,Syrett 62,84,Anderson 65,Aizlewood 75	8,699
6	S		18	Lincoln City		D0-0			7,379
7	S		25	Gillingham	D2-2		(1-1)	Stroud 13,Aizlewood 53	8,712
8	W		29	Peterborough United		L0-1	(0-1)		5,783
9	S	Oct	2	Reading		L1-4	(0-3)	Moss 81	11,670
10	S		9	Shrewsbury Town	W1-0		(0-0)	Prophett 90	9,026
11	S		16	Walsall		L0-2	(0-1)		5,529
12	S		23	Northampton Town	W5-1		(2-0)	Anderson 21 pen.,87 pen.,Moss 43,McLaughlin 79,Syrett 89	7,288
13	Tu		26	Bury		W1-0	(0-0)	Dixon 79	6,405
14	S		30	Tranmere Rovers	D1-1		(1-1)	Anderson 6 pen.	7,778
15	Tu	Nov	2	Crystal Palace	D1-1		(1-1)	Syrett 28	11,323
16	S		6	Brighton & Hove Albion		L0-4	(0-3)		18,761
17	S		13	Rotherham United	L2-4		(1-2)	Anderson 30 pen.,Stroud 52	7,611
18	S		27	Mansfield Town		D1-1	(0-0)	Anderson 68	6,663
19	S	Dec	18	Chester		L1-2	(1-0)	Moss 45	3,399
20	M		27	Oxford United	W1-0		(0-0)	Prophett 73	13,503
21	S	Jan	22	Port Vale		D2-2	(2-1)	McHale 12,Syrett 16	4,446
22	S	Feb	5	Wrexham		D2-2	(2-1)	McHale 4,Aizlewood 23	7,287
23	Tu		8	Preston North End		L0-2	(0-1)		9,409
24	S		12	Chesterfield	W3-0		(1-0)	Aizlewood 27,Anderson 50,McHale 69 pen.	7,901
25	S		19	Sheffield Wednesday		L1-3	(1-1)	Prophett 26	11,265
26	M		21	Tranmere Rovers		W1-0	(1-0)	Anderson 12	2,648
27	S		26	Lincoln City	D2-2		(1-1)	Stroud 33,Moss 74	8,649
28	S	Mar	5	Gillingham		D2-2	(0-1)	Moss 65,McHale 83	4,994
29	Tu		8	Grimsby Town	W4-1		(1-0)	Gray o.g.35,Prophett 52,Syrett 69,Anderson 88	6,984
30	F		11	Reading	D2-2		(1-2)	Anderson 17,Moss 70	9,892
31	S		19	Shrewsbury Town		D2-2	(1-2)	Anderson 8,Trollope 58	2,702
32	S		26	Walsall	D2-2		(0-1)	McHale 68,Anderson 89	7,535
33	Tu		29	York City	W5-1		(2-1)	Moss 25,79,Syrett 33,McLaughlin 52,McHale 77 pen.	5,874
34	F	Apr	1	Northampton Town		D1-1	(0-0)	Prophett 83	5,609
35	F		8	Oxford United		D0-0			8,821
36	S		9	Peterborough United	L0-4		(0-1)		7,399
37	Tu		12	Crystal Palace		L0-5	(0-1)		18,501
38	S		16	Bury	L0-1		(0-1)		5,230
39	Tu		19	York City		L2-4	(1-2)	Moss 36,McHale 60 pen.	1,848
40	S		23	Rotherham United		D1-1	(0-0)	Anderson 82	5,631
41	S		30	Mansfield Town	L0-1		(0-0)		5,792
42	Tu	May	3	Preston North End	L0-1		(0-0)		4,144
43	S		7	Grimsby Town		L0-2	(0-2)		3,027
44	Tu		10	Brighton & Hove Albion	W2-1		(1-1)	Moss 43,McHale 88	8,535
45	S		14	Chester	W2-1		(1-1)	Moss 45,Stroud 76	4,526
46	Tu		17	Portsmouth	W4-3		(3-0)	Stroud 15,McHale 22,French 43,Aizlewood 81	6,754

Average Home Attendance : **7,631**
Average Away Attendance : **7,123**

Football League Cup

					Home	Away	H-T	Goalscorers	Gate
1/1	S	Aug	14	Northampton Town	W3-2		(1-0)	Stroud 24,Goddard 75,Syrett 85	6,267
1/2	W		18	Northampton Town		L0-2	(0-0)		7,037

F A Cup

					Home	Away	H-T	Goalscorers	Gate
1	S	Nov	20	Bromley	W7-0		(1-0)	McHale 25,Syrett 63,77,Moss 66,89,Anderson 72,87	6,497
2	S	Dec	11	Hitchin Town		D1-1	(1-0)	Dixon 37	4,827
2R	Tu		21	Hitchin Town	W3-1 +		(0-0)	Syrett 68,Moss 114,118	6,064
3	S	Jan	8	Fulham		D3-3	(3-1)	Anderson 5,Moss 40,McHale 44	16,460
3R	Tu		11	Fulham	W5-0		(2-0)	Anderson 43,Syrett 45,57,Moss 73,85	23,883
4	S		29	Everton	D2-2		(1-1)	Syrett 31,Stroud 63	24,347
4R	Tu	Feb	1	Everton		L1-2	(0-0)	Anderson 76	38,063

\+ After Extra Time

For Final League Table - see page 202

Aizlewood S	Allan J	Anderson T	Barron J	Burrows F	Dixon W E	French M J	Gilligan J	Goddard H J	Harris P J	Hooper W	Lewis R	McHale R	McLaughlin J	Moss D J	O'Brien G	Prophett C G	Rogers D E	Stroud K A	Syrett D K	Taylor A	Trollope N J	
5	1	11			s			10					2	7	8	6		4	9	3		**1**
*5	1	11			8			10	*12				2	7		6		4	9	3		**2**
	1	11		5	8			10	s				2	7		6		4	9	3		**3**
	1	11		5	8		s	10					2			6	7	4	9	3		**4**
5	1	11			8			10				s	2	7		6		4	9	3		**5**
5	1	11			8			10				4	2	7	s	6			9	3		**6**
*5	1	11			8			*12				10	2	7		6		4	9	3		**7**
5	1	11			*8							10	2	7	*12	6		4	9	3		**8**
*5	1	11						*12				10	2	7	8	6		4	9	3		**9**
	1			5	s			11				10	2	7	8	6		4	9	3		**10**
	1	11			5							8	2	7	10	6		4	9	3	s	**11**
5	1	11			2							10	8	7	s	6		4	9		3	**12**
5	1	11			2							10		7	8	6	s	4	9		3	**13**
5	1	11			2			*12				*10		7	8	6		4	9		3	**14**
5	1	11			2							10		7	8	6	s	4	9		3	**15**
5	1	11			2							10		*12	8	6		4	9	*7	3	**16**
5	1	11			2		*12	9				*10		7	8	6		4			3	**17**
5	1	11			2							10	8	7	s	6		4	9		3	**18**
5	1	11			2							10	8	7		6		4	9	s	3	**19**
5	1	*11			*12							10	2	7		6	8	4	9		3	**20**
5	1	11			*2							10	8	7		*12		4	9	6	3	**21**
5	1				2					*11		10	8	7		6		4	9	*12	3	**22**
5	1				2					11		10	8	7		6		*4	9	*12	3	**23**
5	1	11			2							10	8	7	4	6	s		9		3	**24**
5	*1	11			2							10	8	7	*12	6		4	9		3	**25**
5	1	11			2							10	8	7	*12	6		*4	9		3	**26**
5	1	11			2	*12						10	8	7		6		4	*9		3	**27**
5	1	*11			8	*12						10	2	7	4	6			9		3	**28**
5		11	1		2					s		10	8	7		6		4	9		3	**29**
5		11	1		2	s						10	8	7		6		4	9		3	**30**
*5		11	1		2	*12						10	8	7		6		4	9		3	**31**
5	1	11			2							10	8	7		6		4	9	s	3	**32**
5	1	11			2	s						10	8	7		6		4	9		3	**33**
5	1	11			2							10	8	7		6		4	9	s	3	**34**
5	1	*11			2	9						10	8	7		6		4		*12	3	**35**
5	1	11			2	*9				*12		10	8	7		6		4			3	**36**
5	1				2					11		*10	*12	7	8	6			9	4	3	**37**
*5	1	11			2	*12						10		7		6		4	9	8	3	**38**
	1	11			2						5	10	s	7		6		4	9	8	3	**39**
5	1	11			s							10	8	7		6		4	9	2	3	**40**
	1	11								*12	5	*10	8	7		6		4	9	2	3	**41**
	1	s						11			5	10	8	7		6		4	9	2	3	**42**
	1	*12						*11			5	10	8	7		6		4	9	2	3	**43**
5	1	11			2							10	8	*7		6		4	9	*12	3	**44**
5	1	11			2							10	8	*7		6		4	9	*12	3	**45**
5	1	11			*2	8				7		10				6		4	9	*12	3	**46**
38	43	40	3	3	38	3	0	10	0	4	4	41	37	43	12	45	2	42	43	20	35	Apps
		1			1	4	1	3	1	2			1	1	3	1				6		Subs
5		14			2	1						9	2	14		6	1	5	8		1	Goals

Opponents 1 goal

Aizlewood S	Allan J	Anderson T	Barron J	Burrows F	Dixon W E	French M J	Gilligan J	Goddard H J	Harris P J	Hooper W	Lewis R	McHale R	McLaughlin J	Moss D J	O'Brien G	Prophett C G	Rogers D E	Stroud K A	Syrett D K	Taylor A	Trollope N J	
5	1	11			8			9					2		10	6	*7	4	*12	3		**1/1**
5	1	11			8			9					2		10	6	7	*4	*12	3		**1/2**
2	2	2			2			2					2		2	2	2	2	0	2		Apps
																			2			Subs
								1										1	1			Goals

Aizlewood S	Allan J	Anderson T	Barron J	Burrows F	Dixon W E	French M J	Gilligan J	Goddard H J	Harris P J	Hooper W	Lewis R	McHale R	McLaughlin J	Moss D J	O'Brien G	Prophett C G	Rogers D E	Stroud K A	Syrett D K	Taylor A	Trollope N J	
5	1	11			2							10	8	7		6	s	4	9		3	**1**
5	1	11			2							10	8	7		6		4	9	s	3	**2**
	1	11		5	2							*10	8	7		6	*12	4	9		3	**2R**
5	1	11			2							10	8	7		*6	*12	4	9		3	**3**
5	1	11			2							10	8	7			s	4	9	6	3	**3R**
5	1	11			2							10	8	7		6		4	9	s	3	**4**
5	1	11			2							10	8	7		6		4	9	s	3	**4R**
6	7	7		1	7							7	7	7		6	0	7	7	1	7	Apps
																	2					Subs
		5			1							2		7				1	6			Goals

TREVOR ANDERSON

SEASON 1977/78

Football League Third Division
Final League Position : 10th
Manager : Danny Williams

Substitutes :
s denotes substitute **not** used
* player substituted by *12

					Home	Away	H-T	Goalscorers	Gate
1	S	Aug	20	Sheffield Wednesday		D1-1	(1-0)	Kamara 15	12,095
2	Tu		23	Peterborough United	W2-0		(2-0)	Guthrie 21,McHale 41	7,124
3	S		27	Portsmouth	W3-1		(1-1)	Kamara 9,McHale 70,Moss 86	9,406
4	S	Sep	3	Walsall		L0-2	(0-1)		4,717
5	S		10	Chesterfield	W2-1		(0-0)	Guthrie 49,Ford 78	6,851
6	Tu		13	Preston North End		D1-1	(1-0)	Anderson 4	6,014
7	F		16	Bury	D1-1		(1-0)	Guthrie 18	8,149
8	S		24	Wrexham		L1-2	(0-1)	Moss 74	8,002
9	Tu		27	Cambridge United		L2-5	(1-2)	Moss 40,McHale 88 pen.	4,423
10	F		30	Shrewsbury Town	W5-0		(1-0)	Kamara 24,Aizlewood 58,Moss 66,Guthrie 76,Trollope 88	6,810
11	Tu	Oct	4	Bradford City	L0-1		(0-0)		7,575
12	S		8	Lincoln City		L1-3	(1-1)	Guthrie 16	4,852
13	S		15	Port Vale	D1-1		(1-1)	Aizlewood 37	6,134
14	S		22	Chester		L0-1	(0-0)		3,292
15	S		29	Exeter City	W4-0		(2-0)	Anderson 18,85,Moss 31,McHale 79	7,028
16	S	Nov	5	Gillingham	W3-2		(0-0)	Moss 67,Aizlewood 70,Anderson 75	7,086
17	F		11	Colchester United		L0-2	(0-1)		4,788
18	S		19	Rotherham United	W2-0		(0-0)	Guthrie 57,McHale 68	6,015
19	S	Dec	3	Hereford United		D1-1	(0-0)	McHale 76 pen.	4,541
20	S		10	Carlisle United	D2-2		(1-1)	Moss 19,Stroud 57	5,899
21	M		26	Oxford United		D3-3	(0-3)	Kamara 51,69,Guthrie 76	8,746
22	Tu		27	Plymouth Argyle	W3-1		(1-1)	Moss 12,Guthrie 82,Kamara 86	9,732
23	S		31	Gillingham		D2-2	(1-1)	Kamara 24,Moss 75	8,012
24	M	Jan	2	Tranmere Rovers	W1-0		(1-0)	McHale 41 pen.	11,063
25	S		14	Sheffield Wednesday	D2-2		(1-0)	McHale 20 pen.,54 pen.	7,619
26	F		20	Portsmouth		W2-1	(0-1)	Moss 49,Kamara 58	11,647
27	S	Feb	25	Shrewsbury Town		W3-2	(1-0)	Stroud 32,Kamara 82,Keay o.g.83	3,112
28	Tu		28	Bury		D0-0			4,423
29	S	Mar	4	Lincoln City	W1-0		(0-0)	Bates 49	6,945
30	Tu		7	Preston North End	L0-2		(0-1)		10,213
31	S		11	Port Vale		L0-1	(0-0)		3,723
32	Tu		14	Wrexham	L1-2		(0-2)	Moss 64	7,702
33	F		17	Chester	D1-1		(1-0)	Kamara 8	4,278
34	W		22	Exeter City		D0-0			4,449
35	S		25	Plymouth Argyle		W2-0	(1-0)	Cunningham 11,Guthrie 76	9,184
36	M		27	Oxford United	W3-2		(1-0)	Moss 34,51,65	9,523
37	F		31	Tranmere Rovers		D1-1	(0-0)	Guthrie 56	2,812
38	Tu	Apr	4	Cambridge United	D0-0				6,783
39	S		8	Colchester United	D0-0				4,599
40	Tu		11	Walsall	L2-3		(1-0)	Stroud 35,Moss 85	3,929
41	S		15	Rotherham United		W3-1	(0-0)	Guthrie 56,Moss 75,Cunningham 86	3,824
42	Tu		18	Peterborough United		L0-2	(0-1)		6,843
43	S		22	Hereford United	W1-0		(0-0)	Cunningham 53	4,272
44	W		26	Bradford City		L1-2	(0-2)	Carter 72	3,448
45	S		29	Carlisle United		D2-2	(1-1)	Guthrie 2,Carter 49	4,351
46	W	May	3	Chesterfield		L1-3	(1-1)	Prophett 28	3,428

Average Home Attendance : **7,162**
Average Away Attendance : **5,684**

Football League Cup

					Home	Away	H-T	Goalscorers	Gate
1/1	S	Aug	13	Swansea City		W3-1	(3-0)	Anderson 25,Trollope 28,Guthrie 35	5,878
1/2	Tu		16	Swansea City	W2-1		(1-0)	Moss 39,Anderson 72	5,424
2	Tu		30	Cardiff City	W5-1		(1-0)	Guthrie 34,Anderson 61,66,Moss 88,McHale 90	8,931
3	Tu	Oct	25	Portsmouth		D1-1	(0-1)	Middleton o.g.84	14,955
3R	Tu	Nov	1	Portsmouth	W4-3		(2-1)	Kamara 6,Anderson 17,Moss 46,McHale 76 pen.	9,383
4	W	Dec	7	Wrexham		L0-2	(0-0)		10,015

F A Cup

					Home	Away	H-T	Goalscorers	Gate
1	S	Nov	26	Boreham Wood		D0-0			2,242
2	Tu		29	Boreham Wood	W2-0		(1-0)	Moss 37,McHale 85	7,021
3	S	Dec	17	Brentford	W2-1		(0-0)	Prophett 77,McHale 88	8,459
4	S	Jan	7	Nottingham Forest		L1-4	(0-1)	Moss 85	28,953

For Final League Table - see page 202

Aizlewood S	Allan J	Anderson T	Bates P D	Carter R W	Cunningham D	Ford A C	French M J	Gilligan A A	Guthrie C W	Kamara C	Lewis R	McHale R	McLaughlin J	Moss D J	Prophett C G	Roberts K J	Stroud K A	Trollope N J	
5	1	11				*12	9			8		10	2	*7	6		4	3	**1**
5	1	*11			*12				9	8		10	2	7	6		4	3	**2**
5	1	11			s				9	8		10	2	7	6		4	3	**3**
5	1	11				*12			9	*8		10	2	7	6		4	3	**4**
5	1	11			s	4			9	8		10	2	7	6			3	**5**
5	1	11				8			9	s		10	2	7	6		4	3	**6**
5	1	11				8			9	s		10	2	7	6		4	3	**7**
5	1	11				*8			9	*12		10	2	7	6		4	3	**8**
5	1	11				*12			*9	8		10	2	7	6		4	3	**9**
5	1	11				s			9	8		10	2	7	6		4	3	**10**
5	1	11				s			9	8		10	2	7	6		4	3	**11**
5	1				11	*12		7	9	*8		10	2		6		4	3	**12**
5	1	*12						11	*9	8		10	2	7	6		4	3	**13**
5	1	*11				2	9			10		*12	4	7	6		8	3	**14**
5		11				2	*12			*9		10	4	7	6	1	8	3	**15**
5	1	11				2	s			9		10	4	7	6		8	3	**16**
5	1	11				*2			*12	9		10	4	7	6		8	3	**17**
5	1	11				2			9	*12		10	4	*7	6		8	3	**18**
5	1	11				*12			9	4		10	2	7	6		*8	3	**19**
	1	*11		*12					9	4	5	10	2	7	6		8	3	**20**
*5	1			*12	11				9	4		10	2	7	6		8	3	**21**
	1			s	11	5			9	4		10	2	7	6		8	3	**22**
	1			5	11	s			9	4		10	2	7	6		8	3	**23**
	1			5	*11	*12			9	4		10	2	7	6		8	3	**24**
	1			5	*11	4		*12		9		10	2	7	6		8	3	**25**
	1			5	11	2			*9	4	*12	10		7	6		8	3	**26**
5	1		8	*11					9	*12		10	2	7	6		4	3	**27**
5	1		8	*12		*11			9	4		10	2	7	6			3	**28**
5	1		11	s					9	8		10	2	7	6		4	3	**29**
*5	1		11	*12					9	8		10	2	7	6		4	3	**30**
5	1		11	4	s	3			9	8		10	2	7	6				**31**
	1		11	5	s	3			9	8		10	2	7	6		4		**32**
	1		11	5	*12	3			9	8		10	2	7	6		*4		**33**
	1		10	5	s	3			9	8			2	7	6		4	11	**34**
	1		*12	5	*11	3			9	8		10	2	7	6			4	**35**
	1		s	5	11	3			9	8		10	2	7	6			4	**36**
	1		s	5	11	3			9	8		10	2	7	6			4	**37**
	1		s	5	11	3			9	8		10	2	7	6			4	**38**
	1		9	5	11	3				8		*10	2	7	6		*12	4	**39**
	1		9	s	11	3				8		10	2	7	6		5	4	**40**
	1			8	11	3			9	s		10	2	7	6		5	4	**41**
	1		*12	8	11	*3			9			10	2	7	6		5	4	**42**
5	1		s	8	11	3			9			10	2	7	6		4		**43**
5	1			8	11	3		*10	9			*12	2	7	6		4		**44**
5	1		11	8	*12	*3			9	4		10	2	7	6				**45**
5	1		11	8	*12				9	4		10	2	7	*6			3	**46**
29	45	18	12	20	17	28	2	3	38	37	1	43	45	45	46	1	36	40	Apps
		1	2	4	4	6	1	1	1	3	1	2					1		Subs
3		4	1	2	3	1			12	10		9		16	1		3	1	Goals

Opponents 1 goal

Aizlewood S	Allan J	Anderson T	Bates P D	Carter R W	Cunningham D	Ford A C	French M J	Gilligan A A	Guthrie C W	Kamara C	Lewis R	McHale R	McLaughlin J	Moss D J	Prophett C G	Roberts K J	Stroud K A	Trollope N J	
5	1	11				s			9	8		10	2	7	6		4	3	**1/1**
*5	1	11				*12			9	8		10	2	7	6		4	3	**1/2**
5	1	11			s				9	8		10	2	7	6		4	3	**2**
*5	1	11				8	9			*12		10	2	7	6		4	3	**3**
5		11				2	s			9	6	10	4	7		1	8	3	**3R**
5	1	*11			*12	2			9	4		10		7	6		8	3	**4**
6	5	6			0	3	1		4	5	1	6	5	6	5	1	6	6	Apps
					1	1				1									Subs
		5							2	1		2		3				1	Goals

Opponents 1 goal

Aizlewood S	Allan J	Anderson T	Bates P D	Carter R W	Cunningham D	Ford A C	French M J	Gilligan A A	Guthrie C W	Kamara C	Lewis R	McHale R	McLaughlin J	Moss D J	Prophett C G	Roberts K J	Stroud K A	Trollope N J	
5	1	11				2			*9	*12		10	4	7	6		8	3	**1**
5	1	11				s			9	4		10	2	7	6		8	3	**2**
*5	1				11	*12			9	4		10	2	7	6		8	3	**3**
	1				11	4			*9	5	*12	10	2	7	6		8	3	**4**
3	4	2			2	2			4	3	0	4	4	4	4		4	4	Apps
						1				1	1								Subs
												2		2	1				Goals

CHRIS GUTHRIE

RAY McHALE

SEASON 1978/79

Football League Third Division
Final League Position : 5th
Manager : Bob Smith

Substitutes :
s denotes substitute **not** used
* player substituted by *12

				Home	Away	H-T	Goalscorers	Gate
1	S	Aug	19 Bury	W2-1		(2-0)	Bates 18,Miller 40	5,430
2	M		21 Tranmere Rovers		D1-1	(0-1)	Carter 60	2,150
3	S		26 Shrewsbury Town		D0-0			2,672
4	S	Sep	2 Mansfield Town	W1-0		(0-0)	Bates 88	6,200
5	S		9 Walsall		L1-4	(0-2)	Williams 81	5,024
6	Tu		12 Brentford	W2-0		(0-0)	McHale 63,Bates 86	6,690
7	S		16 Plymouth Argyle		L0-2	(0-1)		6,099
8	S		23 Blackpool	L0-1		(0-0)		6,607
9	W		27 Chester		L0-2	(0-1)		3,556
10	S		30 Sheffield Wednesday	W3-0		(1-0)	Bates 36,Rowland 64,Gilchrist 67	5,860
11	F	Oct	6 Colchester United		L2-3	(2-0)	Gilchrist 14,Bates 43	3,324
12	S		14 Rotherham United	W1-0		(0-0)	Bates 54	4,482
13	Tu		17 Peterborough United	W3-1		(1-1)	Bates 7,85,Carter 61	4,356
14	S		21 Lincoln City		W3-0	(1-0)	McLaughlin 35,Williams 60,McHale 67	2,982
15	S		28 Carlisle United		L0-2	(0-1)		5,141
16	S	Nov	4 Southend United	W1-0		(0-0)	Gilchrist 68	5,656
17	S		11 Mansfield Town		W1-0	(1-0)	Bates 2	4,721
18	S		18 Shrewsbury Town	W2-1		(0-1)	Gilchrist 50,Aizlewood 86	7,321
19	S	Dec	9 Hull City	W2-0		(0-0)	Miller 52,Carter 55	5,651
20	Tu		26 Swansea City		W2-1	(1-0)	Bates 44,Gilchrist 51	16,159
21	S		30 Watford		L0-2	(0-0)		15,292
22	Tu	Jan	16 Walsall	W4-1		(1-0)	Kamara 25,Bates 52,87,Gilchrist 90	7,282
23	S		20 Plymouth Argyle	L1-3		(1-0)	Carter 16	7,792
24	S	Feb	3 Chester	W2-0		(1-0)	McHale 19,Carter 82	6,041
25	S		24 Rotherham United		W3-1	(1-0)	Mayes 45,64,66	5,128
26	W		28 Chesterfield		D1-1	(1-0)	Kamara 32	4,112
27	S	Mar	3 Lincoln City	W6-0		(4-0)	Rowland 2,33,Mayes 17,McHale 31,Bates 76,Miller 86	6,655
28	S		10 Carlisle United	D0-0				8,390
29	F		16 Southend United		L3-5	(0-3)	McHale 47,Mayes 59,Cawston o.g.74	4,303
30	Tu		20 Colchester United	L1-2		(0-0)	Rowland 57	6,770
31	S		24 Tranmere Rovers	W4-1		(2-1)	Rowland 5,50,Mayes 45,McHale 77	5,678
32	Tu		27 Bury		W1-0	(0-0)	Rowland 60	3,557
33	S		31 Gillingham		D2-2	(2-2)	Mayes 27,Carter 35	9,460
34	Tu	Apr	3 Exeter City	D1-1		(0-0)	Rowland 46	7,937
35	S		7 Chesterfield	W1-0		(0-0)	Carter 58	6,177
36	W		11 Exeter City		W2-1	(2-0)	Bates 25,Rowland 29	5,548
37	S		14 Swansea City	L0-1		(0-1)		16,987
38	M		16 Oxford United		W1-0	(0-0)	Carter 74 pen.	9,076
39	S		21 Watford	W2-0		(1-0)	Jenkins o.g.35,Rowland 79	16,414
40	Tu		24 Peterborough United		L1-2	(0-1)	Hamilton 57	4,121
41	S		28 Hull City		D1-1	(1-0)	Rowland 31	4,980
42	W	May	2 Oxford United	W2-0		(1-0)	Bates 24,Carter 66	8,975
43	S		5 Gillingham	W3-1		(0-0)	Rowland 48,Mayes 51,64	15,125
44	Tu		8 Brentford		W2-1	(1-1)	Miller 11,Mayes 66	13,320
45	F		11 Sheffield Wednesday		L1-2	(0-1)	Mayes 88	9,057
46	Tu		15 Blackpool		L2-5	(1-2)	Aizlewood 35,Carter 89	4,191

Average Home Attendance : **7,760**
Average Away Attendance : **6,260**

Football League Cup

				Home	Away	H-T	Goalscorers	Gate
1/1	S	Aug	12 Portsmouth		D0-0			9,261
1/2	Tu		15 Portsmouth	W4-2		(0-0)	Aizlewood 51,Williams 75,Miller 82,Guthrie 84	7,175
2	W		30 West Ham United		W2-1	(0-0)	Miller 57,Guthrie 59	19,672
3	Tu	Oct	3 Peterborough United		D1-1	(0-0)	Aizlewood 47	6,132
3R	Tu		10 Peterborough United	L0-2		(0-0)		7,674

F A Cup

				Home	Away	H-T	Goalscorers	Gate
1	S	Nov	25 March Town United	W2-0		(2-0)	Gilchrist 21,Bates 25	5,633
2	S	Dec	16 Enfield	W3-0		(0-0)	Bates 61,Carter 77,Gilchrist 80	5,681
3	Tu	Jan	9 Cardiff City	W3-0		(2-0)	McHale 12,Kamara 41,47	9,992
4	Tu		30 Aldershot		L1-2	(0-2)	Rowland 80	10,913

For Final League Table - see page 202

Aizlewood S	Allan J	Bates P D	Carter R W	Cunningham D	Dornan P	Ford A C	Gilchrist P A	Guthrie C W	Hamilton B	Kamara C	Lewis R	McHale R	McLaughlin J	Mayes A K	Miller I	Ogden C J	Roberts K J	Rowland A A	Stroud K A	Trollope N J	Williams B	
5		10	*8			3		9			*12	4	2		7	1			6		11	**1**
5		10	8			3				9	*12	4	2		*7	1			6		11	**2**
5		10	8			3		*9		*12		4	2		7	1			6		11	**3**
5		10	8			3		*9		*12		4	2		7	1			6		11	**4**
*5		10	8			3		9		*12		4	2		7	1			6		11	**5**
*5		10	8			3		9		*12		4	2		7	1			6		11	**6**
5		10	8			3	*12	9		11		4	2		*7	1			6			**7**
5		10	8			3				s		4	2		7	1		9	6		11	**8**
5		*10	8			3				*12		4			7	1		9	6	2	11	**9**
		*10	8	*12		3	7			11	5	4				1		9	6	2		**10**
*12		10	8			3	7			11	5	4				1		*9	6	2		**11**
5		10	8			3	*12			11		4	2		7	1		*9	6			**12**
5		10	8			3	*12			11		4	2		7	1			6		*9	**13**
5		10	*8			3	*12			11		4	2		7	1			6		9	**14**
5	1	9	8	11		3	*12			*10		4	2		7				6			**15**
5		10	8			3	9			11	s	4	2		7	1			6			**16**
5		10	8			3	9			11	*12	*4	2		7	1			6			**17**
5		10	8			3	*9			11		4	2		7	1			6		*12	**18**
5		10	8			3	9			*11		4	2		7	1			6		*12	**19**
5		10	8			3	9			*11		4	2		7	1			6		*12	**20**
5		10	8			3	*9			11		4	2		7	1			6		*12	**21**
5		10	8			3	9		2	11	6	4			*7	1					*12	**22**
5		10	8			3	9		2	11	*6	4			7	1					*12	**23**
5	1	10	8			3	s		2			4			7			9	6		11	**24**
5	1	*12	8			3			2			4		10	7			9	6		*11	**25**
5	1	*12	8			3			2	11		4		10	*7			9	6			**26**
5	1	*12	8			3			2	*11		4		10	7			9	6			**27**
5	1	*12	8			3			2	11		4		10	*7			9	6			**28**
5	1		8			3			2	11		4		10	*7			9	6		*12	**29**
5	1	*12	8			3			2			4		10	*7			9	6		11	**30**
5	1	*12	8			3			2			4		10	7			9	6		*11	**31**
5	1		8			3			2			4		*10	7			9	6	*12	11	**32**
5	1		8			3			*2	11		4		10	7			9	6	*12		**33**
5	1	s	8			3				11		4		10	7			9	6	2		**34**
5	1	*12	8			3						4		*10	7			9	6	2	11	**35**
5	1	*10	8			3	*12		11			4			7			9	6	2		**36**
5	1	*12	8			*3			11			4		10	7			9	6	2		**37**
*5	1	11	8			3			*12			4		10	7			9	6	2		**38**
	1	11	5			3	s		8			4		10	7			9	6	2		**39**
	1	11	5		*12	3			8			4		*10	7			9	6	2		**40**
	1	11	5			3			8		*12	4		*10	7			9	6	2		**41**
5	1	11	*8			3						4		10	7			9	6	2	*12	**42**
*5	1	11	8			3			*12			4		10	7			9	6	2		**43**
	1	11	8			3			*12		*5	4		10	7			9	6	2		**44**
	1	11	5			3			8	*12		4		10	*7			9	6	2		**45**
5	1	11	8			3						4		10	*7			9	6	2	*12	**46**
39	24	34	46	1	0	46	10	6	18	22	5	46	18	21	44	22	0	28	44	16	16	Apps
1		8		1	1		6		3	6	4									2	9	Subs
2		14	10				6		1	2		6	1	11	4			12			2	Goals

Opponents 2 goals

Aizlewood S	Allan J	Bates P D	Carter R W	Cunningham D	Dornan P	Ford A C	Gilchrist P A	Guthrie C W	Hamilton B	Kamara C	Lewis R	McHale R	McLaughlin J	Mayes A K	Miller I	Ogden C J	Roberts K J	Rowland A A	Stroud K A	Trollope N J	Williams B	
5		10	*12			3		9		8		4	2		*7		1		6		11	**1/1**
5		10	s			3		9		8		4	2		7	1			6		11	**1/2**
5		10	8			3		*9		*12		4	2		7	1			6		11	**2**
9		10	8	11		3				7	5	4	s			1			6	2		**3**
9		10	8	11		3				7	*5	4			*12	1			6	2		**3R**
5		5	3	2		5		3		4	2	5	3		3	4	1		5	2	3	Apps
			1							1					1							Subs
2								2							2						1	Goals

Aizlewood S	Allan J	Bates P D	Carter R W	Cunningham D	Dornan P	Ford A C	Gilchrist P A	Guthrie C W	Hamilton B	Kamara C	Lewis R	McHale R	McLaughlin J	Mayes A K	Miller I	Ogden C J	Roberts K J	Rowland A A	Stroud K A	Trollope N J	Williams B	
5		10	8			3	9			11		4	2		7	1			6		s	**1**
5		10	8			3	9			11		4	2		7	1			6		s	**2**
5		10	8			3	9			11	6	4	2		7	1					s	**3**
5	1	10	8			3	*9		2			4			7			*12	6		11	**4**
4	1	4	4			4	4		1	3	1	4	3		4	3		0	3		1	Apps
																		1				Subs
		2	1				2			2		1						1				Goals

'CHIC' BATES

SEASON 1979/80

Football League Third Division
Final League Position : 10th
Manager : Bob Smith

Substitutes :
s denotes substitute **not** used
* player substituted by *12

				Home	Away	H-T	Goalscorers	Gate
1	S	Aug	18 Sheffield United		L1-2	(1-0)	Mayes 21	11,923
2	Tu		21 Reading	D0-0				9,571
3	S		25 Brentford	W4-0		(1-0)	Mayes 40,68,Lewis 48,Rowland 75	6,982
4	F		31 Colchester United		W3-2	(2-1)	Mayes 26,Rowland 42,90	2,794
5	S	Sep	8 Rotherham United		L0-3	(0-3)		4,672
6	S		15 Chesterfield	W2-1		(1-1)	Rowland 32,Kamara 86	6,178
7	Tu		18 Chester	W3-1		(0-0)	Mayes 72,Rowland 77,Miller 88	6,108
8	S		22 Sheffield Wednesday		L2-4	(1-2)	McHale 44 pen.,Mayes 88	11,636
9	S		29 Grimsby Town	W3-0		(1-0)	McHale 28 pen.,Carter 58,Mayes 61	6,827
10	S	Oct	6 Hull City	D0-0				7,459
11	W		10 Reading		L1-2	(1-1)	Rowland 5	9,639
12	S		13 Wimbledon		L0-2	(0-1)		4,206
13	S		20 Southend United	W1-0		(0-0)	Mayes 87	6,212
14	Tu		23 Plymouth Argyle	W2-1		(2-0)	Mayes 8,Rowland 26	6,518
15	S		27 Blackpool		W1-0	(0-0)	Mayes 85	5,741
16	S	Nov	3 Sheffield United	W3-2		(2-0)	Rowland 19,67,Tucker 27	11,839
17	Tu		6 Plymouth Argyle		L0-2	(0-1)		4,157
18	S		10 Mansfield Town		D1-1	(0-0)	Williams 80	4,425
19	S		17 Blackburn Rovers	W2-0		(0-0)	Kamara 56,Miller 75	7,086
20	S	Dec	1 Gillingham		D0-0			8,029
21	S		8 Bury	W8-0		(4-0)	McHale 10,68 pen.,Kamara 23,Mayes 35,85,Rowland 42,56,Tucker 50	7,687
22	W		26 Exeter City	L2-3		(2-1)	Williams 15,Tucker 19	11,612
23	S		29 Brentford		W3-1	(2-1)	Kamara 35,Rowland 44,Mayes 85	12,120
24	S	Jan	12 Barnsley		W2-1	(0-0)	Mayes 51,Rowland 80	10,420
25	W	Feb	6 Oxford United		D2-2	(2-2)	Mayes 12,Carter 29	7,558
26	S		9 Sheffield Wednesday	L1-2		(0-1)	McHale 55 pen.	16,417
27	S		16 Grimsby Town		L0-2	(0-0)		12,675
28	S		23 Wimbledon	W2-1		(0-0)	Stroud 50,McHale 78	10,744
29	F		29 Southend United		L0-1	(0-1)		5,282
30	Tu	Mar	4 Millwall		L2-6	(1-4)	Rowland 32,Sitton o.g.72	6,472
31	S		8 Blackpool	W2-1		(0-0)	McHale 64,Lewis 78	9,517
32	Tu		11 Carlisle United	D0-0				9,755
33	F		14 Hull City		L0-1	(0-0)		5,346
34	W		19 Chester		L0-1	(0-1)		2,611
35	S		22 Mansfield Town	W2-1		(1-0)	Mayes 44,58	7,990
36	Tu		25 Chesterfield		L1-2	(1-0)	Tartt o.g.32	8,101
37	S		29 Blackburn Rovers		L0-2	(0-1)		11,571
38	S	Apr	5 Exeter City		L1-4	(1-3)	Kamara 44	5,442
39	M		7 Oxford United	D1-1		(1-0)	Rowland 19	10,327
40	S		12 Carlisle United		L1-2	(1-2)	Tucker 13	3,472
41	Tu		15 Rotherham United	W6-2		(2-1)	Rowland 26,47,49,65,Carter 36,Mayes 84	7,441
42	S		19 Gillingham	W3-0		(2-0)	Williams 3,Lewis 29,Cockerill 66	9,155
43	Tu		22 Colchester United	L2-3		(1-3)	McHale 24,Mayes 57	7,987
44	S		26 Bury		D0-0			3,164
45	Tu		29 Millwall	W1-0		(0-0)	Rowland 62	8,022
46	S	May	3 Barnsley	L0-1		(0-1)		8,288

Average Home Attendance : **8,684**
Average Away Attendance : **7,020**

F A Cup

				Home	Away	H-T	Goalscorers	Gate
1	S	Nov	24 Brentford	W4-1		(4-0)	Miller 5,39,Kamara 20,Carter 26	9,474
2	Tu	Dec	18 Torquay United		D3-3	(1-1)	Mayes 12,Tucker 69,Rowland 84	5,900
2R	S		22 Torquay United	W3-2		(1-0)	Rowland 17,Mayes 49,69	8,253
3	S	Jan	5 Luton Town		W2-0	(1-0)	Rowland 28,Williams 81	12,458
4	S		26 Tottenham Hotspur	D0-0				25,673
4R	W		30 Tottenham Hotspur		L1-2	(0-0)	McHale 55 pen.	46,707

Football League Cup

See overleaf >>

Abbley S G	Allan J	Bates P D	Carter R W	Cockerill G	Ford A C	Gilchrist P A	Greenwood R T	Hamilton B	Kamara C	Lewis R	McHale R	Mayes A K	Miller I	Ogden C J	Peach D S	Rowland A A	Stroud K A	Templeman J H	Tucker W J	Williams B	
	1		8		3	*12			*11		4	10	7			9	6	2	5		**1**
	1		8		3	s				5	4	10	7			9	6	2		11	**2**
	1		8		3					5	4	10	7			9	6	2	s	11	**3**
	1		8		*3					*12	4	10	7			9	6	2	5	11	**4**
	1		8						*12	*3	4	10	7			9	6	2	5	11	**5**
			8						*12	3	4	*10	7	1		9	6	2	5	11	**6**
			8						*12	3	*4	10	7	1		9	6	2	5	11	**7**
	1		2						8	s	4	10	7			9	6	3	5	11	**8**
	1	s	8							2	4	10	7			9	6	3	5	11	**9**
	1	s	8							3	4	10	7			9	6	2	5	11	**10**
	1		8						s	3	4	10	7			9	6	2	5	11	**11**
	1		8						*12	3	4	10	*7			9	6	2	5	11	**12**
	1		8						s	3	4	10	7			9	6	2	5	11	**13**
	1		8					s		3	4	10	7			9	6	2	5	11	**14**
	1	7	8							3	4	10	s			9	6	2	5	11	**15**
	1	*12	8							3	4	*10	7			9	6	2	5	11	**16**
	1	7	8							3	4	*10	*12			9	6	2	5	11	**17**
	1				3			*12	8	2	4	10	*7			9	6		5	11	**18**
	1		*12		3				8	2	4	10	7			9	6		*5	11	**19**
	1		5		3				8	2	4	10	7			9	6	s		11	**20**
	1		*12		3				*8	2	4	10	7			9	6		5	11	**21**
	1		s		3				8	2	4	10	7			9	6		5	11	**22**
	1		6					s	8	2	4	10	7			9	3		5	11	**23**
	1	*12	6						8	2	4	*10	7			9	3		5	11	**24**
	1	s	6						8	2	4	10	7			9	3		5	11	**25**
	1	s	6						8	2	4	10	7			9	3		5	11	**26**
	1	10	6	s					8	2	4		7			9	3		5	11	**27**
	1	s	6						8	2	4	10	7			9	3		5	11	**28**
	1	*12			3				8	2	4	10	*7			9	6		5	11	**29**
	1	7	*12						8	2	4	10			3	9	6		*5	11	**30**
	1			s					8	2	4	10	7		3	9	6		5	11	**31**
	1		s						8	2	4	10	7		3	9	6		5	11	**32**
	1		9	11				s	8	2	4	10	7		3		6		5		**33**
	1		9	*12					8	2	4	*10	7		3		6		5	11	**34**
	1		11						8	2	4	10	*7		3	9	6		5	*12	**35**
	1		7	*12					8	*2	4	10			3	9	6		5	11	**36**
*12	1		*6	11					8	5	4	10			3	9	2			7	**37**
7	1		6	4					8	5		10	*12		3	9	2			*11	**38**
	1		6	s	3				8		4	10	7			9	2		5	11	**39**
*12	1		11	8	2		10			*6	4		7		3	9			5		**40**
	1		5		3		*12		8	2	4	10	7			9	6			*11	**41**
7	1		5	4	3		*12		8	2		10				*9	6			11	**42**
	1		5		3		s		8	2	4	10	7			9	6			11	**43**
	1		5	4	3		7		8	2	s	10				9	6			11	**44**
s	1		6	4	3				8	5		10	7			9		2		11	**45**
*7	1		6	4	3				8	5		10	*12			9		2		11	**46**
3	44	4	38	8	18	0	2	0	30	42	41	44	37	2	10	44	43	19	35	42	Apps
2		3	3	2		1	2	1	4	1			3							1	Subs
			3	1					5	3	8	19	2			20	1		4	3	Goals

opponents 2 goals

Abbley S G	Allan J	Bates P D	Carter R W	Cockerill G	Ford A C	Gilchrist P A	Greenwood R T	Hamilton B	Kamara C	Lewis R	McHale R	Mayes A K	Miller I	Ogden C J	Peach D S	Rowland A A	Stroud K A	Templeman J H	Tucker W J	Williams B	
	1		5		3				8	2	4	10	7			9	6	s		11	**1**
	1		s		3				8	2	4	10	7			9	6		5	11	**2**
	1		s		3				8	2	4	10	7			9	6		5	11	**2R**
s	1		6						8	2	4	10	7			9	3		5	11	**3**
	1		6					s	8	2	4	10	7			9	3		5	11	**4**
	1		6					*12	8	2	4	10	*7			9	3		5	11	**4R**
	6		4		3			0	6	6	6	6	6			6	6		5	6	Apps
								1													Subs
			1						1		1	3	2			3			1	1	Goals

BILLY TUCKER

SEASON 1979/80

Football League Cup

					Home	Away	H-T	Goalscorers	Gate
1/1	S	Aug	11	Portsmouth		D1-1	(1-1)	Rowland 31	9,978
1/2	Tu		14	Portsmouth	W2-0		(0-0)	Mellor o.g.75,Carter 77	9,105
2/1	Tu		28	Chester	W1-0		(1-0)	Mayes 19	6,969
2/2	W	Sep	5	Chester		D1-1	(0-0)	Mayes 86	3,930
3	W		26	Stoke City		D2-2	(1-2)	Mayes 42,Rowland 87	15,255
3R	Tu	Oct	2	Stoke City	W2-1		(1-0)	McHale 32,Mayes 53	15,826
4	Tu		30	Wimbledon		W2-1	(0-0)	Rowland 53,Bates 85	7,478
5	Tu	Dec	4	Arsenal		D1-1	(0-1)	Tucker 84	38,024
5R	Tu		11	Arsenal	W4-3 +		(2-0)	Walford o.g.10,Mayes 20,Hollins o.g.64,Rowland 116	21,805
SF	Tu	Jan	22	Wolverhampton Wanderers	W2-1		(1-1)	Rowland 13,Mayes 86	25,650
SF	Tu	Feb	12	Wolverhampton Wanderers		L1-3	(0-0)	McHale 61 pen.	41,031

+ After Extra Time

TOASTING SUCCESS following victory over Arsenal

(*Back left to right*)
Russell Lewis
Andy Ford
Ray McHale
Kenny Stroud
Roy Carter
(*Front*)
Chris Kamara
Jimmy Allan
Alan Mayes
Billy Tucker
Andy Rowland
(*Kneeling*)
Ian Miller
Brian Williams

ALAN MAYES** and **ANDY ROWLAND

were as good a striking partnership as any outside the top division. They shared 56 Town goals in 1979/80 and both found the net in no less than 12 games ! Alan arrived from Watford in February 1979 and quickly declared his intent with a hat-trick on his debut - away from home. He joined Chelsea in December 1980 for £175,000, but came back in 1983 on a 'free'. Andy came from Bob Smith's former club Bury in September 1978 and played alongside a number of striker partners after Alan, including a very young Paul Rideout. When Ken Beamish took over in 1983, Andy began to play as a central defender. Following Town's Fourth Division championship season, he joined the coaching staff at the County Ground, initially in charge of the reserves. Andy was dismissed in October 1996, when Mike Walsh arrived at the club.

BOB SMITH

arrived at Swindon following Danny Williams' second spell in charge, in May 1978. Still only 34, Bobby had already been in management almost five years, with Bury and Port Vale. By the 1979/80 season he had built virtually his own side - one which excelled in knockout competitions but failed to last the course in the League. Unfortunately, the failure of some costly acquistions hastened his downfall and not long after five defeats had opened the 1980/81 season, Bob was shown the door.

JIMMY ALLAN

was still seventeen when he made his League debut in September 1971, but two years later he was first choice for the number one slot when long-serving Peter Downsborough could not agree terms. In January 1974, Jimmy became the first professional to exercise his right not to turn out on a Sunday - although later in his career he agreed to play. He lost his place to Jim Barron in the August but was the preferred keeper once again for 1976/77. After missing just four games in four seasons, Jimmy's career came to a shuddering end in October 1983 - a month before his 30th birthday. In a collision with a Rochdale striker, he suffered a badly broken left arm.

Allan J	Bates P D	Carter R W	Ford A C	Gilchrist P A	Hamilton B	Kamara C	Lewis R	McHale R	Mayes A K	Miller I	Rowland A A	Stroud K A	Templeman J H	Tucker W J	Williams B	
1		8	3	*10		*12		4		7	9	6	2	5	11	**1/1**
1		8	3			*12		4	*10	7	9	6	2	5	11	**1/2**
1		8	3		s			4	10	7	9	6	2	5	11	**2/1**
1		8	*3				*12	4	10	7	9	6	2	5	11	**2/2**
1		8				s	2	4	10	7	9	6	3	5	11	**3**
1		8			*12		2	4	10	*7	9	6	3	5	11	**3R**
1	*12	8					3	4	10	*7	9	6	2	5	11	**4**
1		5	3			8	2	4	10	7	9	6		*12	*11	**5**
1		5	3			8	2	4	*10	7	9	6		*12	11	**5R**
1	s	6				8	2	4	10	7	9	3		5	11	**SF**
1		6	s			8	2	4	10	7	9	3		5	11	**SF**
11	0	11	6	1	0	4	7	11	10	11	11	11	7	9	11	Apps
	1				1	2	1							2		Subs
	1	1						2	6		5			1		Goals

opponents 3 goals

	P	W	D	L	F - A		W	D	L	F - A		Pts	G/D	Avge. Home Gate
1 Grimsby Town	46	18	2	3	46	16	8	8	7	27	26	62	+31	10,618
2 Blackburn Rovers	46	13	5	5	34	17	12	4	7	24	19	59	+22	10,311
3 Sheffield Wednesday	46	12	6	5	44	20	9	10	4	37	27	58	+34	18,288
4 Chesterfield	46	16	5	2	46	16	7	6	10	25	30	57	+25	7,760
5 Colchester United	46	10	10	3	39	20	10	2	11	25	36	52	+8	3,816
6 Carlisle United	46	13	6	4	45	26	5	6	12	21	30	48	+10	4,406
7 Reading	46	14	6	3	43	19	2	10	11	23	46	48	+1	6,713
8 Exeter City	46	14	5	4	38	22	5	5	13	22	46	48	-8	4,574
9 Chester	46	14	6	3	29	18	3	7	13	20	39	47	-8	3,726
10 SWINDON TOWN	46	15	4	4	50	20	4	4	15	21	43	46	+8	8,684
11 Barnsley	46	10	7	6	29	20	6	7	10	24	36	46	-3	11,890
12 Sheffield United	46	13	5	5	35	21	5	5	13	25	45	46	-6	16,584
13 Rotherham United	46	13	4	6	38	24	5	6	12	20	42	46	-8	5,993
14 Millwall	46	14	6	3	49	23	2	7	14	16	36	45	+6	5,918
15 Plymouth Argyle	46	13	7	3	39	17	3	5	15	20	38	44	+4	5,776
16 Gillingham	46	8	9	6	26	18	6	5	12	23	33	42	-2	6,131
17 Oxford United	46	10	4	9	34	24	4	9	10	23	38	41	-5	4,832
18 Blackpool	46	10	7	6	39	34	5	4	14	23	40	41	-12	5,818
19 Brentford	46	10	6	7	33	26	5	5	13	26	47	41	-14	7,818
20 Hull City	46	11	7	5	29	21	1	9	13	22	48	40	-18	5,986
21 Bury	46	10	4	9	30	23	6	3	14	15	36	39	-14	4,239
22 Southend United	46	11	6	6	33	23	3	4	16	14	35	38	-11	4,758
22 Mansfield Town	46	9	9	5	31	24	1	7	15	16	34	36	-11	5,467
22 Wimbledon	46	6	8	9	34	38	4	6	13	18	43	34	-29	3,426

abandoned !

RWR = Result when replayed

Season				H	A	Mins	Reason	Goalscorers	Gate	RWR
1899/1900	S	Oct	21 Sheppey United	2-2		65	Fog	Logan,Chapman		W4-0
1900/01	M	Apr	29 Brentford		0-0	E-T	Bad light			*
1903/04	S	Feb	13 Northampton Town	1-0		45	Waterlogged	Hogan		W2-0
1907/08	S	Jan	18 Queens Park Rangers	0-0		75	Fog			W8-3
1910/11	Tu	Apr	4 Queens Park Rangers		0-0	105	Bad light			W3-2
1914/15	S	Nov	28 Southend United		0-1	60	Waterlogged			L1-2
1958/59	S	Jan	17 Accrington Stanley		0-1	37	Frost		5,000	D0-0
1960/61	S	Nov	19 Grimsby Town		0-0	40	Waterlogged		8,000	L2-3
	S	Jan	14 Walsall		0-3	82	Fog		10,159	L1-2
1962/63	S	Jan	19 Hull City		0-0	45	Snow		4,000	D1-1
1974/75	S	Jan	18 Colchester United		0-3	56	Waterlogged		4,415	L0-2
1976/77	Tu	Dec	14 Hitchin Town	1-0		66	Fog	Syrett	7,261	W3-1
	S	Jan	1 Brighton & Hove Albion	4-0		67	Waterlogged	Stroud,Syrett,McHale 2	12,369	W2-1
1987/88	S	Jan	16 Bradford City	3-0		72	Fog	Quinn,King,Calderwood	9,155	D2-2
1990/91	M	Jan	14 Leyton Orient	1-1		54	Frost	Bodin	8,579	W1-0
1992/93	S	Dec	13 Tranmere Rovers	1-2		51	Floodlight failure	Ling	8,757	W2-0
1996/97	S	Dec	28 Grimsby Town	1-0		31	Frost	Watson	8,760	D3-3

* Test Match (played at Elm Park Reading) - abandoned during extra time. No record of any replay taking place

SEASON 1980/81

Football League Third Division
Final League Position : 17th
Manager : Bob Smith
John Trollope (from Nov.12)

Substitutes :
s denotes substitute **not** used
* player substituted by *12

No.	Day	Month	Date	Opponent	Home	Away	H-T	Goalscorers	Gate
1	S	Aug	16	Blackpool	L1-2		(0-1)	Rowland 69	7,043
2	Tu		19	Portsmouth		L0-1	(0-0)		15,810
3	S		23	Fulham	L3-4		(2-1)	Rollings 13,Peach 16 pen.,Mayes 74	6,479
4	S		30	Reading		L1-4	(0-1)	Mayes 89	6,405
5	S	Sep	6	Sheffield United		L0-3	(0-1)		12,089
6	S		13	Rotherham United	W2-1		(0-1)	Greenwood 64,Rowland 68	5,499
7	Tu		16	Oxford United	W1-0		(0-0)	Miller 49	7,714
8	S		20	Barnsley		L0-2	(0-0)		9,747
9	S		27	Huddersfield Town	W1-0		(0-0)	Rowland 69	5,859
10	W	Oct	1	Oxford United		D0-0			6,071
11	S		4	Chester	L1-2		(0-0)	Mayes 89	5,574
12	Tu		7	Gillingham		D0-0			4,066
13	S		11	Millwall		L1-3	(0-0)	Mayes 85	3,571
14	S		18	Carlisle United	D1-1		(0-0)	Mayes 73	5,791
15	Tu		21	Charlton Athletic	L0-3		(0-1)		5,676
16	S		25	Exeter City		W4-3	(2-1)	Mayes 26,Rowland 44,66,Miller 53	4,688
17	S	Nov	1	Burnley	L0-3		(0-1)		6,192
18	Tu		4	Gillingham	D0-0				4,722
19	S		8	Colchester United		L0-1	(0-0)		2,153
20	Tu		11	Portsmouth	L0-2		(0-0)		8,167
21	S		15	Blackpool		D1-1	(0-1)	Mayes 66	3,758
22	S		29	Hull City	W3-1		(1-1)	Stroud 2,Lewis 78,Rideout 88	5,279
23	S	Dec	6	Brentford		D1-1	(0-1)	Peach 79	5,727
24	F		19	Walsall	W3-1		(1-0)	Carter 44,Mayes 68,Greenwood 79	4,525
25	F		26	Newport County		W2-0	(1-0)	Kamara 18,Lewis 60	7,086
26	S		27	Plymouth Argyle	W3-0		(0-0)	Carter 59,Greenwood 68,Rowland 76	9,713
27	S	Jan	10	Chesterfield	L0-1		(0-0)		6,717
28	S		24	Reading	W3-1		(1-0)	Greenwood 45,Carter 70,Rowland 77	8,109
29	S		31	Fulham		L0-2	(0-0)		4,785
30	S	Feb	7	Rotherham United		L0-1	(0-0)		7,162
31	S		14	Sheffield United	W5-2		(3-0)	Miller 22,Rowland 25,54,68,Williams 44 pen.	6,308
32	S		21	Huddersfield Town		W2-0	(2-0)	Kamara 37,40	10,655
33	S		28	Barnsley	W2-0		(1-0)	Hughes 8,Williams 51 pen.	7,827
34	S	Mar	7	Chester		L0-1	(0-1)		1,810
35	S		14	Millwall	D0-0				6,968
36	Tu		17	Carlisle United		L1-2	(1-2)	Carter 39	4,104
37	S		21	Charlton Athletic		D0-0			6,495
38	S		28	Exeter City	D2-2		(1-1)	Rideout 37,Rowland 67	6,511
39	S	Apr	4	Burnley		D0-0			4,726
40	Tu		7	Chesterfield		D2-2	(1-0)	Kamara 11,Carter 83	5,222
41	S		11	Colchester United	W3-0		(1-0)	Rideout 34,76,Rowland 74	6,122
42	Tu		14	Hull City		D0-0			2,789
43	S		18	Plymouth Argyle		D0-0			6,369
44	M		20	Newport County	D1-1		(0-0)	Williams 79 pen.	8,437
45	S		25	Walsall		L1-2	(0-0)	Miller 78	3,429
46	S	May	2	Brentford	D0-0				8,733

Average Home Attendance : **6,694**
Average Away Attendance : **6,031**

Football League Cup

Rd	Day	Month	Date	Opponent	Home	Away	H-T	Goalscorers	Gate
1/1	S	Aug	9	AFC Bournemouth		D1-1	(0-1)	Rowland 67	5,121
1/2	Tu		12	AFC Bournemouth	W2-0 +		(0-0)	McGrath o.g.97,Mayes 118	5,824
2/1	W		27	Lincoln City		D1-1	(0-0)	Rollings 48	4,940
2/2	Tu	Sep	2	Lincoln City	W2-0		(0-0)	Henry 51,Mayes 88	4,911
3	Tu		23	Liverpool		L0-5	(0-2)		16,566

+ After Extra Time

F A Cup

Rd	Day	Month	Date	Opponent	Home	Away	H-T	Goalscorers	Gate
1	S	Nov	22	Weymouth	W3-2		(1-1)	Mayes 26,Lewis 67,Kamara 85	5,477
2	S	Dec	13	Wimbledon		L0-2	(0-2)		3,470

For Final League Table - see page 203

Abbley S G	Allan J	Barrett C	Carter R W	Cockerill G	Greenwood R T	Hamilton B	Henry C A	Hughes B D	Kamara C	Lewis R	McAlister T G	Mayes A K	Miller I	Peach D S	Rideout P D	Rollings A N	Round D L	Rowland A A	Stroud K A	Templeman J H	Trollope N J	Turner C J	Walsh R	Williams B	
	1	2	11	8	s				4			10	7	3		5		9					6		**1**
	1	2	*11	8		*12			4			10	7	3		5		9					6		**2**
	1	2	6	8	11				4			10	7	3		5		*9		*12					**3**
	1		11		9		*12	*8	4	2		10	7	3		5							6		**4**
	1		6		11	8	*12		4	2		10	7	3		5		*9							**5**
	1		6	8	11		2	s	4	5		10	7					9			3				**6**
	1		6	8	11	s	2		4	5		10	7					9			3				**7**
	1		6	8	11		2	s	4	5		10	7					9			3				**8**
	1		6	8	11		2		4	5		10	7				s	9			3				**9**
	1		6	8	11		2		4	5		10	*7					9			3	*12			**10**
	1		6	*8	11		2	7	4	5		10						9			3	*12			**11**
	1		6		11		2	7	4	5		10						9			3	s		8	**12**
	1		6		7		2	*8	4	5		10	*12					9			3			11	**13**
	1		6	8	7				4	5		10						9		2	3	s		11	**14**
	1		6	*11				8	4	5		10	7	3				9			2	*12			**15**
	1		6	8					4	5		10	7	3	s			9			2			11	**16**
	1		6	8					*4	5		10	7	3		*12		9			2			11	**17**
	1		8						4	5		10	7	3		s		9	6		2			11	**18**
	1		8				s		4	5		10	7	3				9	6		2			11	**19**
	1		8						4	2		10	7	3	s	5		9	6					11	**20**
	1		8		s		2		4	5		10	7	3				9	6					11	**21**
	1		8		s				4	5		10	7	3	9				6				2	11	**22**
	1		8		*12				4	5		10	7	3	*9				6				2	11	**23**
	1		8		9		2		4	5		10	7	3	s				6					11	**24**
	*1		8		10		2	*12	4	5			7	3				9	6					11	**25**
			8		10		2	*11	4	5	1		7	3	*12			9	6						**26**
*12	1		8		10		2		4	5			7					9	6				*3	11	**27**
	1		*8		10		2		4	5			7		*12			9	6				3	11	**28**
*12	1		8		10		2		4	5			*7	3				9	6					11	**29**
	1			*8	10		2		4				7	3	*12	5		9	6					11	**30**
	1				s		2	8	4				7	3	10	5		9	6					11	**31**
	1				10		2	8	4				7	3		5		9	6				s	11	**32**
	1			s	10		2	8	4				7	3		5		9	6					11	**33**
	1			*12	10		2	8	*4				7	3		5		9	6					11	**34**
11	1		5	4	*10		2	8	*12				7	3				9	6						**35**
	1		11	s	10		2	8	4	5			7	3				9	6						**36**
	1		4		*10		2	8		5			7	3	*12			9	6					11	**37**
	1		3		s		2	8	4	5			7		10			9	6					11	**38**
	1		3				2	8	4	5			7		10			9	6				s	11	**39**
	1		3				2	*8	4	5			7	*12	10			9	6					11	**40**
	1		8				2	s	4	5			7	3	10			9	6					11	**41**
	1		8				2	s	4	5			7	3	10			9	6					11	**42**
	1		8		s		2		4	5			7	3	10			9	6					11	**43**
	1		8		s		2		4	5			7	3	10			9	6					11	**44**
	1		2		s			8	4	5			7	3	10			9	6					11	**45**
	1		2		s			8	4	5			7	3	10			9	6					11	**46**
1	45	3	41	15	25	1	30	18	44	37	1	24	42	32	12	11	0	42	29	1	14	0	7	31	Apps
2				1	1	1	2	1	1				1	1	4	1				1		3			Subs
			5		4			1	4	2		8	4	2	4	1		12	1					3	Goals

Abbley S G	Allan J	Barrett C	Carter R W	Cockerill G	Greenwood R T	Hamilton B	Henry C A	Hughes B D	Kamara C	Lewis R	McAlister T G	Mayes A K	Miller I	Peach D S	Rideout P D	Rollings A N	Round D L	Rowland A A	Stroud K A	Templeman J H	Trollope N J	Turner C J	Walsh R	Williams B	
	1	2	11	8					4			10	7	3		5		9		s			6		**1/1**
	1	2	11	8	s				4			10	7	3		5		9					6		**1/2**
	1		10		11		s	8	4	2		9	7	3		5							6		**2/1**
	1		6		11		9	8	4	2		10	7	3	s	5									**2/2**
	1		6	8	11		2	s	4	5		10	7					9			3				**3**
	5	2	5	3	3		2	2	5	3		5	5	4	0	4		3		0	1		3		Apps
																									Subs
							1					2				1		1							Goals

Opponent 1 goal

Abbley S G	Allan J	Barrett C	Carter R W	Cockerill G	Greenwood R T	Hamilton B	Henry C A	Hughes B D	Kamara C	Lewis R	McAlister T G	Mayes A K	Miller I	Peach D S	Rideout P D	Rollings A N	Round D L	Rowland A A	Stroud K A	Templeman J H	Trollope N J	Turner C J	Walsh R	Williams B	
	1		8	s			2		4	5		10	7	3				9	6					11	**1**
	1		8		9			*12	4	5		10	7	3					6				*2	11	**2**
	2		2	0	1		1	0	2	2		2	2	2				1	2				1	2	Apps
								1																	Subs
									1	1		1													Goals

SEASON 1981/82

Football League Third Division
Final League Position : 22nd
Manager : John Trollope

Substitutes :
s denotes substitute **not** used
* player substituted by *12

				Home	Away	H-T	Goalscorers	Gate
1	S	Aug	29 Wimbledon	W4-1		(1-0)	Carter R 11,Graham 56,Hughes 65,Greenwood 78	5,643
2	S	Sep	5 Chester		D0-0			1,798
3	S		12 Preston North End	W4-0		(2-0)	Rowland 11,57,Carter R 41,73	5,701
4	S		19 Exeter City		W2-1	(1-0)	Williams 6,Carter R 51	4,372
5	M		21 Southend United		D0-0			4,578
6	S		26 Reading	L0-2		(0-1)		9,321
7	Tu		29 Chesterfield	L1-2		(1-1)	Hughes 26	5,369
8	S	Oct	3 Burnley		W2-0	(2-0)	Rowland 17,Greenwood 37	3,359
9	S		10 Carlisle United	W2-1		(0-1)	Rideout 55,Hughes 72	5,268
10	S		17 Bristol Rovers		W4-1	(2-0)	Rowland 19,38,Henry 53,Rideout 57	8,779
11	Tu		20 Walsall		L0-5	(0-2)		6,010
12	S		24 Doncaster Rovers	D2-2		(1-0)	Carter R 45,Williams 67	6,754
13	S		31 Gillingham		L0-1	(0-0)		8,410
14	Tu	Nov	3 Brentford	L0-3		(0-2)		6,372
15	S		7 Millwall	L1-2		(1-1)	Rowland 6	5,720
16	S		14 Huddersfield Town		L0-3	(0-1)		7,802
17	S		28 Lincoln City		L0-2	(0-0)		3,132
18	S	Dec	5 Bristol City	D0-0				6,953
19	S		26 Plymouth Argyle		L1-2	(0-2)	Rowland 90	8,185
20	W		30 Fulham	L1-4		(0-2)	Rideout 89	5,641
21	S	Jan	23 Wimbledon		D1-1	(0-1)	Rideout 85	2,084
22	Su		31 Exeter City	W3-2		(1-1)	Rideout 41,Carter R 71,Baddeley 90	5,654
23	S	Feb	6 Preston North End		D0-0			5,606
24	Tu		9 Southend United	D0-0				4,474
25	S		13 Burnley	L1-2		(1-2)	Henry 39	5,042
26	S		20 Reading		D1-1	(0-0)	Court o.g.58	4,130
27	Tu		23 Portsmouth	W2-0		(1-0)	Carter R 44 pen.,Williams 67	4,864
28	S		27 Carlisle United		D1-1	(1-1)	Rideout 45	4,633
29	S	Mar	6 Bristol Rovers	W5-2		(1-1)	Parkin o.g.31,Rideout 55,69,Carter R 61 pen.,Henry 89	6,689
30	Tu		9 Walsall	D2-2		(1-1)	Greenwood 43,Lewis 86	4,446
31	F		12 Doncaster Rovers		D0-0			3,532
32	S		20 Gillingham	L0-1		(0-1)		4,910
33	Su		28 Millwall		D0-0			4,381
34	S	Apr	3 Huddersfield Town	L1-5		(1-1)	Rideout 44	3,872
35	W		7 Oxford United		L0-5	(0-2)		7,354
36	S		10 Plymouth Argyle	L0-2		(0-0)		4,056
37	Tu		13 Fulham		L0-2	(0-2)		6,665
38	S		17 Bristol City		W3-0	(1-0)	Pritchard 25,Emmanuel 48,62	6,524
39	M		19 Brentford		L2-4	(0-2)	Carter R 58 pen.,90 pen.	5,374
40	S		24 Lincoln City	W1-0		(0-0)	Rowland 55	3,982
41	Tu		27 Chester	W3-0		(1-0)	Rideout 42,69,88	3,849
42	S	May	1 Chesterfield		L1-2	(0-2)	Carter R 87	2,028
43	Tu		4 Oxford United	W3-2		(0-0)	Rideout 46,87,Carter R 61	7,887
44	S		8 Newport County	D1-1		(1-1)	Carter R 12 pen.	5,679
45	S		15 Portsmouth		L0-3	(0-2)		6,372
46	Tu		18 Newport County		L0-1	(0-0)		5,906

Average Home Attendance : **5,572**
Average Away Attendance : **5,261**

Football League Cup

				Home	Away	H-T	Goalscorers	Gate
1/1	Tu	Sep	1 Wrexham		L2-3	(0-2)	Davis o.g.54,Carter 63 pen.	2,068
1/2	Tu		15 Wrexham	L0-2		(0-0)		6,781

F A Cup

				Home	Away	H-T	Goalscorers	Gate
1	S	Nov	21 Taunton Town		* W2-1	(1-1)	Pritchard 44,90	4,494
2	Tu	Dec	15 Sutton United	W2-1		(1-1)	Carter 41,Pritchard 90	2,895
3	S	Jan	2 Luton Town		L1-2	(0-1)	Emmanuel 73	9,488

* Played at the County Ground

For Final League Table - see page 203

Abbley S G	Allan J	Baddeley K S	Bailie C J	Beamish K G	Carter M	Carter R W	Emmanuel J G	Graham M A	Greenwood R T	Henry C A	Hughes B D	Lewis R	Moores J C	Peach D S	Pritchard H K	Quinn J M	Rideout P D	Rowland A A	Stroud K A	Williams G	
	1					7	8	6	10	2	4	5	11				s	9		3	**1**
7	1	s				11	8	6		2	4	5					10	9		3	**2**
7	1					11	8	6		2	4	5	s				10	9		3	**3**
	1	3				11	8	6	10	2	4	5			s			9		7	**4**
	1	3				7	8	6	10	2	4	5			s			9		11	**5**
11	1	3				7	8	6	10	2	s	5						9		4	**6**
11	1	*3				7		6	10	2	4	5			*12			9		8	**7**
s	1					7	8	6	10	2	4	5		3				9		11	**8**
	1					7	8	6	*10	2	4	5		3			*12	9		11	**9**
	1					7	8	6		2	4	5		3	s		10	9		11	**10**
	1					7	8	6		2	4	5		3			10	9	s	11	**11**
	1					7	8	6		2	4	5	*12	*3			10	9		11	**12**
*12	1					7	8	*6		2	4	5		3			10	9		11	**13**
*12	1					7	8	6		2	4	5		3			*10	9		11	**14**
7	1			s		10	8	6		2	4	5		3				9	11		**15**
7	1					8		6	10	2	4	5		3	*12			9	*11		**16**
	1					8	7	s	10	2	4	5		3	11			9	6		**17**
	1	2				8	7	6	s		4	5			11		10	9		3	**18**
	1	2				8	7	6	s		4	5			11		10	9		3	**19**
*12	1	2				8	7				*4	5			11		10	9	6	3	**20**
	1	3				8	7	s	10	2		5			11		9		6	4	**21**
	1	3				8	7		10	2	s	5			11		9		6	4	**22**
	1	3				8	7	s	10	2		5			11		9		6	4	**23**
*12	1	3						7	*10	2	8	5			11		9		6	4	**24**
	1	3		*12		8	7			2	10	5			11		9		6	*4	**25**
7	1	3		10		8			*12	2	4	5			11		9		6		**26**
	1	3				8			10	2	7	5			11	s	9		6	4	**27**
	1	3				8			10	2	7	5			11	s	9		6	4	**28**
	1	3				8	s		10	2	7	5			11		9		6	4	**29**
	1	*3				8			10	2	7	5			11	*12	9		6	4	**30**
	1					8	4	s	10	2	7	5			11		9		6	3	**31**
	1				*12	8	*4		10	2	7	5			11		9		6	3	**32**
	1				10	8	4		s	2	7	5			11		9		6	3	**33**
*12	1	3			10	5	8			2	7				*11		9		6	4	**34**
7	1		3		10	8		11		2		5				9	s		6	4	**35**
7	1	3			10	8	*12	11		2		5				9			6	*4	**36**
7	1	3				8	4	11	10	2		5			s		9		6		**37**
	1	3				8	4	11	10	*2		5			7	*12	9		6		**38**
	1	2				8	4	11	10		s	5			7		9		6	3	**39**
	1	3				8	4	11		2		5			7		9	10	6	s	**40**
	1	3				8	4	2		5	11				7		9	10	6	s	**41**
	1	*3				8	4	2		5	11				7		9	10	6	*12	**42**
	1	3				8	4	11		2		5			s		9	10	6	7	**43**
	1	3				8	4	11		2		5			*12		9	10	*6	7	**44**
	1	3				8	4	11		2		5			*12		9	10	6	*7	**45**
	1					8	4	s		2	7	5			11		9	10	6	3	**46**
10	46	28	1	1	4	45	36	30	22	42	33	43	1	10	24	2	34	27	30	37	Apps
5				1	1		1		1				1		4	2	1			1	Subs
		1				13	2	1	3	3	3	1			1		14	8		3	Goals

Opponent 1 goal

Abbley S G	Allan J	Baddeley K S	Bailie C J	Beamish K G	Carter M	Carter R W	Emmanuel J G	Graham M A	Greenwood R T	Henry C A	Hughes B D	Lewis R	Moores J C	Peach D S	Pritchard H K	Quinn J M	Rideout P D	Rowland A A	Stroud K A	Williams G	
	1	*12				7	8	6	*10	2	4	5	11					9		3	**1/1**
	1					7	8	6		2	4	5	*11		*12		10	9		3	**1/2**
	2	0				2	2	2	1	2	2	2	2		0		1	2		2	Apps
		1													1						Subs
						1															Goals

Opponent 1 goal

Abbley S G	Allan J	Baddeley K S	Bailie C J	Beamish K G	Carter M	Carter R W	Emmanuel J G	Graham M A	Greenwood R T	Henry C A	Hughes B D	Lewis R	Moores J C	Peach D S	Pritchard H K	Quinn J M	Rideout P D	Rowland A A	Stroud K A	Williams G	
7	1					8	s	2	10	5	4			3	11			9	6		**1**
	1	2				8	7	6	s		4	5			11		10	9		3	**2**
	1	2				8	7		s	4		5			11		10	9	6	3	**3**
1	3	2				3	2	2	1	2	2	2		1	3		2	3	2	2	Apps
																					Subs
						1	1								3						Goals

ROY CARTER

SEASON 1970/71

Div.2

	Team	P	W	D	L	F	A	W	D	L	F	A	Pts	G/A	Avge. Home Gate
1	Leicester City	42	12	7	2	30	14	11	6	4	27	16	59	1.90	25,948
2	Sheffield United	42	14	6	1	49	18	7	8	6	24	21	56	1.87	25,254
3	Cardiff City	42	12	7	2	39	16	8	6	7	25	25	53	1.56	21,522
4	Carlisle United	42	16	3	2	39	13	4	10	7	26	30	53	1.51	10,657
5	Hull City	42	11	5	5	31	16	8	8	5	23	25	51	1.32	19,737
6	Luton Town	42	12	7	2	40	18	6	6	9	22	25	49	1.44	17,353
7	Middlesbrough	42	13	6	2	37	16	4	8	9	23	27	48	1.40	18,534
8	Millwall	42	13	5	3	36	12	6	4	11	23	30	47	1.40	9,861
9	Birmingham City	42	12	7	2	30	12	5	5	11	28	36	46	1.21	24,203
10	Norwich City	42	11	8	2	34	20	4	6	11	20	32	44	1.04	12,657
11	Queens Park Rangers	42	11	5	5	39	22	5	6	10	19	31	43	1.09	13,069
12	SWINDON TOWN	42	12	7	2	38	14	3	5	13	23	37	42	1.20	15,799
13	Sunderland	42	11	6	4	34	21	4	6	11	18	33	42	0.96	15,780
14	Oxford United	42	8	8	5	23	23	6	6	9	18	25	42	0.85	10,884
15	Sheffield Wednesday	42	10	7	4	32	27	2	5	14	19	42	36	0.74	15,780
16	Portsmouth	42	9	4	8	32	28	1	10	10	14	33	34	0.75	13,759
17	Orient	42	5	11	5	16	15	4	5	12	13	36	34	0.57	9,119
18	Watford	42	6	7	8	18	22	4	6	11	20	38	33	0.63	14,348
19	Bristol City	42	9	6	6	30	28	1	5	15	16	36	31	0.72	14,117
20	Charlton Athletic	42	7	6	8	28	30	1	8	12	13	35	30	0.63	10,981
21	Blackburn Rovers	42	5	8	8	20	28	1	7	13	17	41	27	0.54	8,034
22	Bolton Wanderers	42	6	5	10	22	31	1	5	15	13	43	24	0.47	8,706

SEASON 1971/72

Div.2

	Team	P	W	D	L	F	A	W	D	L	F	A	Pts	G/A	Avge. Home Gate
1	Norwich City	42	13	8	0	40	16	8	7	6	20	20	57	1.67	23,037
2	Birmingham City	42	15	6	0	46	14	4	12	5	14	17	56	1.94	32,337
3	Millwall	42	14	7	0	38	17	5	10	6	26	29	55	1.39	16,262
4	Queens Park Rangers	42	16	4	1	39	9	4	10	7	18	19	54	2.04	14,367
5	Sunderland	42	11	7	3	42	24	6	9	6	25	33	50	1.18	15,906
6	Blackpool	42	12	6	3	43	16	8	1	12	27	34	47	1.40	13,483
7	Burnley	42	13	4	4	43	22	7	2	12	27	33	46	1.27	12,893
8	Bristol City	42	14	3	4	43	22	4	7	10	18	27	46	1.24	15,225
9	Middlesbrough	42	16	4	1	31	11	3	4	14	19	37	46	1.04	17,943
10	Carlisle United	42	12	6	3	38	22	5	3	13	23	35	43	1.07	9,479
11	SWINDON TOWN	42	10	6	5	29	16	5	6	10	18	31	42	1.00	13,338
12	Hull City	42	10	6	5	33	21	4	4	13	16	32	38	0.92	13,972
13	Luton Town	42	7	8	6	25	24	3	10	8	18	24	38	0.90	11,384
14	Sheffield Wednesday	42	11	7	3	33	22	2	5	14	18	36	38	0.88	17,087
15	Oxford United	42	10	8	3	28	17	2	6	13	15	38	38	0.78	9,530
16	Portsmouth	42	9	7	5	31	26	3	6	12	28	42	37	0.87	11,918
17	Orient	42	12	4	5	32	19	2	5	14	18	42	37	0.82	10,817
18	Preston North End	42	11	4	6	32	21	1	8	12	20	37	36	0.90	15,136
19	Cardiff City	42	9	7	5	37	25	1	7	13	19	44	34	0.81	15,510
20	Fulham	42	10	7	4	29	20	2	3	16	16	48	34	0.66	11,147
21	Charlton Athletic	42	9	7	5	33	25	3	2	16	22	52	33	0.71	10,430
22	Watford	42	5	5	11	15	25	0	4	17	9	50	19	0.32	10,908

SEASON 1972/73

Div.2

	Team	P	W	D	L	F	A	W	D	L	F	A	Pts	G/A	Avge. Home Gate
1	Burnley	42	13	6	2	44	18	11	8	2	28	17	62	2.06	14,083
2	Queens Park Rangers	42	16	4	1	54	13	8	9	4	27	24	61	2.19	14,715
3	Aston Villa	42	12	5	4	27	17	6	9	6	24	30	50	1.09	27,831
4	Middlesbrough	42	12	6	3	29	15	5	7	9	17	28	47	1.07	10,418
5	Bristol City	42	10	7	4	34	18	7	5	9	29	33	46	1.24	12,892
6	Sunderland	42	12	6	3	35	17	5	6	10	24	32	46	1.20	22,603
7	Blackpool	42	12	6	3	37	17	6	4	11	19	34	46	1.10	10,782
8	Oxford United	42	14	2	5	36	18	5	5	11	16	25	45	1.21	9,197
9	Fulham	42	11	6	4	32	16	5	6	10	26	33	44	1.18	10,267
10	Sheffield Wednesday	42	14	4	3	40	20	3	6	12	19	35	44	1.07	17,076
11	Millwall	42	12	5	4	33	18	4	5	12	22	29	42	1.17	10,265
12	Luton Town	42	6	9	6	24	23	9	2	10	20	30	41	0.83	10,643
13	Hull City	42	9	7	5	39	22	5	5	11	25	37	40	1.08	9,233
14	Nottingham Forest	42	12	5	4	32	18	2	7	12	15	34	40	0.90	9,995
15	Orient	42	11	6	4	33	18	1	6	14	16	35	36	0.92	6,449
16	SWINDON TOWN	42	8	9	4	28	23	2	7	12	18	37	36	0.77	10,035
17	Portsmouth	42	7	6	8	21	22	5	5	11	21	37	35	0.71	9,477
18	Carlisle United	42	10	5	6	40	24	1	7	13	10	28	34	0.96	7,606
19	Preston North End	42	6	8	7	19	25	5	4	12	18	39	34	0.58	10,199
20	Cardiff City	42	11	4	6	32	21	0	7	14	11	37	33	0.74	11,456
21	Huddersfield Town	42	7	9	5	21	20	1	8	12	15	36	33	0.64	8,175
22	Brighton & Hove Albion	42	7	8	6	32	31	1	5	15	14	52	29	0.55	14,167

SEASON 1973/74

Div.2

	P	W	D	L	F	A	W	D	L	F	A	Pts	G/A	Avge. Home Gate
1 Middlesbrough	42	16	4	1	40	8	11	7	3	37	22	65	2.57	22,264
2 Luton Town	42	12	5	4	42	25	7	7	7	22	26	50	1.25	12,214
3 Carlisle United	42	13	5	3	40	17	7	4	10	21	31	49	1.27	8,270
4 Orient	42	9	8	4	28	17	6	10	5	27	25	48	1.31	11,793
5 Blackpool	42	11	5	5	35	17	6	8	7	22	23	47	1.43	10,120
6 Sunderland	42	11	6	4	32	15	8	3	10	26	29	47	1.32	24,409
7 Nottingham Forest	42	12	6	3	40	19	3	9	9	17	24	45	1.33	14,398
8 West Bromwich Albion	42	8	9	4	28	24	6	7	8	20	21	44	1.07	15,990
9 Hull City	42	9	9	3	25	15	4	8	9	21	32	43	0.98	8,216
10 Notts County	42	8	6	7	30	35	7	7	7	25	25	43	0.92	11,911
11 Bolton Wanderers	42	12	5	4	30	17	3	7	11	14	23	42	1.10	15,942
12 Millwall	42	10	6	5	28	16	4	8	9	23	35	42	1.00	9,516
13 Fulham	42	11	4	6	26	20	5	6	10	13	23	42	0.91	10,129
14 Aston Villa	42	8	9	4	33	21	5	6	10	15	24	41	1.07	23,413
15 Portsmouth	42	9	8	4	26	16	5	4	12	19	46	40	0.73	13,675
16 Bristol City	42	9	5	7	25	20	5	5	11	22	34	38	0.87	14,058
17 Cardiff City	42	8	7	6	27	20	2	9	10	22	42	36	0.79	10,714
18 Oxford United	42	8	8	5	27	21	2	8	11	8	25	36	0.76	8,302
19 Sheffield Wednesday	42	9	6	6	33	24	3	5	13	18	39	35	0.81	14,645
20 Crystal Palace	42	6	7	8	24	24	5	5	11	19	32	34	0.77	21,797
21 Preston North End	42	7	8	6	24	23	2	6	13	16	39	31	0.65	12,174
22 SWINDON TOWN	42	6	7	8	22	27	1	4	16	14	45	25	0.50	7,106

SEASON 1974/75

Div. 3

	P	W	D	L	F	A	W	D	L	F	A	Pts	G/A	Avge. Home Gate
1 Blackburn Rovers	46	15	7	1	40	16	7	9	7	28	29	60	1.51	12,651
2 Plymouth Argyle	46	16	5	2	38	19	8	6	9	41	39	59	1.36	14,060
3 Charlton Athletic	46	15	5	3	51	29	7	6	10	25	32	55	1.25	10,444
4 SWINDON TOWN	46	18	3	2	43	17	3	8	12	21	41	53	1.10	8,084
5 Crystal Palace	46	14	8	1	48	22	4	7	12	18	35	51	1.16	17,274
6 Port Vale	46	15	6	2	37	19	3	9	11	24	35	51	1.13	4,346
7 Peterborough United	46	10	9	4	24	17	9	3	11	23	36	50	0.89	8,446
8 Walsall	46	15	5	3	46	13	3	8	12	21	39	49	1.29	6,268
9 Preston North End	46	16	5	2	42	19	3	6	14	21	37	49	1.13	9,568
10 Gillingham	46	14	6	3	43	23	3	8	12	22	37	48	1.08	7,331
11 Colchester United	46	13	7	3	45	22	4	6	13	25	41	47	1.11	4,937
12 Hereford United	46	14	6	3	42	21	2	8	13	22	45	46	0.97	7,230
13 Wrexham	46	10	8	5	41	23	5	7	11	24	32	45	1.18	4,376
14 Bury	46	13	6	4	38	17	3	6	14	15	33	44	1.06	5,527
15 Chesterfield	46	11	7	5	37	25	5	5	13	25	41	44	0.94	4,615
16 Grimsby Town	46	12	8	3	35	19	3	5	15	20	45	43	0.86	5,962
17 Halifax Town	46	11	10	2	33	20	2	7	14	16	45	43	0.75	2,681
18 Southend United	46	11	9	3	32	17	2	7	14	14	34	42	0.90	6,655
19 Brighton & Hove Albion	46	14	7	2	38	21	2	3	18	18	43	42	0.88	11,751
20 Aldershot	46	13	5	5	40	21	1	6	16	13	42	38	0.84	4,385
21 AFC Bournemouth	46	9	6	8	27	25	4	6	13	17	33	38	0.76	5,988
22 Tranmere Rovers	46	12	4	7	39	21	2	5	16	16	36	37	0.96	2,803
23 Watford	46	9	7	7	30	31	1	10	12	22	44	37	0.69	6,460
24 Huddersfield Town	46	9	6	8	32	29	2	4	17	15	47	32	0.62	5,428

SEASON 1975/76

Div. 3

	P	W	D	L	F	A	W	D	L	F	A	Pts	G/A	Avge. Home Gate
1 Hereford United	46	14	6	3	45	24	12	5	6	41	31	63	1.56	8,273
2 Cardiff City	46	14	7	2	38	13	8	6	9	31	35	57	1.44	11,702
3 Millwall	46	16	6	1	35	14	4	10	9	19	29	56	1.26	7,689
4 Brighton & Hove Albion	46	18	3	2	58	15	4	6	13	20	38	53	1.47	15,343
5 Crystal Palace	46	7	12	4	30	20	11	5	7	31	26	53	1.33	20,124
6 Wrexham	46	13	6	4	38	21	7	6	10	28	34	52	1.20	4,159
7 Walsall	46	11	8	4	43	22	7	6	10	31	39	50	1.21	5,618
8 Preston North End	46	15	4	4	45	23	4	6	13	17	34	48	1.09	7,069
9 Shrewsbury Town	46	14	2	7	36	25	5	8	10	25	34	48	1.03	4,652
10 Peterborough United	46	12	7	4	37	23	3	11	9	26	40	48	1.00	7,607
11 Mansfield Town	46	8	11	4	31	22	8	4	11	27	30	47	1.12	7,344
12 Port Vale	46	10	10	3	33	21	5	6	12	22	33	46	1.02	4,133
13 Bury	46	11	7	5	33	16	3	9	11	18	30	44	1.11	5,936
14 Chesterfield	46	11	5	7	45	30	6	4	13	24	39	43	1.00	4,919
15 Gillingham	46	10	8	5	38	27	2	11	10	20	41	43	0.85	6,301
16 Rotherham United	46	11	6	6	35	22	4	6	13	19	43	42	0.83	5,219
17 Chester	46	13	7	3	34	19	2	5	16	9	43	42	0.69	5,116
18 Grimsby Town	46	13	7	3	39	21	2	3	18	23	53	40	0.84	5,580
19 SWINDON TOWN	46	11	4	8	42	31	5	4	14	20	44	40	0.83	7,527
20 Sheffield Wednesday	46	12	6	5	34	25	0	10	13	14	34	40	0.81	11,219
21 Aldershot	46	10	8	5	34	26	3	5	15	25	49	39	0.79	4,587
22 Colchester United	46	9	6	8	25	27	3	8	12	16	38	38	0.63	3,348
23 Southend United	46	9	7	7	40	31	3	6	14	25	44	37	0.87	5,011
24 Halifax Town	46	6	5	12	22	32	5	8	10	19	29	35	0.67	2,506

SEASON 1976/77

Div.3	P	W	D	L	F	A	W	D	L	F	A	Pts	G/D	Avge. Home Gate
1 Mansfield Town	46	17	6	0	52	13	11	2	10	26	29	64	+36	8,439
2 Brighton & Hove Albion	46	19	3	1	63	14	6	8	9	20	26	61	+43	20,197
3 Crystal Palace	46	17	5	1	46	15	6	8	9	22	25	59	+28	16,106
4 Rotherham United	46	11	9	3	30	15	11	6	6	39	29	59	+25	6,682
5 Wrexham	46	15	6	2	47	22	9	4	10	33	32	58	+26	9,328
6 Preston North End	46	15	4	4	48	21	6	8	9	16	22	54	+21	7,987
7 Bury	46	15	2	6	41	21	8	6	9	23	38	54	+5	5,299
8 Sheffield Wednesday	46	15	4	4	39	18	7	5	11	26	37	53	+10	13,688
9 Lincoln City	46	12	9	2	50	30	7	5	11	27	40	52	+7	7,145
10 Shrewsbury Town	46	13	7	3	40	21	5	4	14	25	38	47	+6	4,974
11 SWINDON TOWN	46	12	6	5	48	33	3	9	11	20	42	45	-7	7,631
12 Gillingham	46	11	8	4	31	21	5	4	14	24	43	44	-9	5,444
13 Chester	46	14	3	6	28	20	4	5	14	20	38	44	-10	4,609
14 Tranmere Rovers	46	10	7	6	31	23	3	10	10	20	30	43	-2	3,251
15 Walsall	46	8	7	8	39	32	5	8	10	18	33	41	-8	5,498
16 Peterborough United	46	11	4	8	33	28	2	11	10	22	37	41	-10	5,996
17 Oxford United	46	9	8	6	34	29	3	7	13	21	36	39	-10	5,152
18 Chesterfield	46	10	6	7	30	20	4	4	15	26	44	38	-8	5,322
19 Port Vale	46	9	7	7	29	28	2	9	12	18	43	38	-24	4,356
20 Portsmouth	46	8	9	6	28	26	3	5	15	25	44	36	-17	11,564
21 Reading	46	10	5	8	29	24	3	4	16	20	49	35	-24	6,761
22 Northampton Town	46	9	4	10	33	29	4	4	15	27	46	34	-15	5,750
23 Grimsby Town	46	10	6	7	29	22	2	3	18	16	47	33	-24	4,738
24 York City	46	7	8	8	25	34	3	4	16	25	55	32	-39	3,005

SEASON 1977/78

Div.3	P	W	D	L	F	A	W	D	L	F	A	Pts	G/D	Avge. Home Gate
1 Wrexham	46	14	8	1	48	19	9	7	7	30	26	61	+33	11,651
2 Cambridge United	46	19	3	1	49	11	4	9	10	23	40	58	+21	5,633
3 Preston North End	46	16	5	2	48	19	4	11	8	15	19	56	+25	8,799
4 Peterborough United	46	15	7	1	32	11	5	9	9	15	22	56	+14	5,974
5 Chester	46	14	8	1	41	24	2	14	7	18	32	54	+3	4,165
6 Walsall	46	12	8	3	35	17	6	9	8	26	33	53	+11	5,317
7 Gillingham	46	11	10	2	36	21	4	10	9	31	39	50	+7	7,178
8 Colchester United	46	10	11	2	36	16	5	7	11	19	28	48	+11	4,572
9 Chesterfield	46	14	6	3	40	16	3	8	12	18	33	48	+9	4,866
10 SWINDON TOWN	46	12	7	4	40	22	4	9	10	27	38	48	+7	7,162
11 Shrewsbury Town	46	11	7	5	42	23	5	8	10	21	34	47	+6	3,378
12 Tranmere Rovers	46	13	7	3	39	19	3	8	12	18	33	47	+5	3,926
13 Carlisle United	46	10	9	4	32	26	4	10	9	27	33	47	0	5,319
14 Sheffield Wednesday	46	13	7	3	28	14	2	9	12	22	38	46	-2	11,592
15 Bury	46	7	13	3	34	22	6	6	11	28	34	45	+6	4,979
16 Lincoln City	46	10	8	5	35	26	5	7	11	18	35	45	-8	4,878
17 Exeter City	46	11	8	4	30	18	4	6	13	19	41	44	-10	4,887
18 Oxford United	46	11	10	2	38	21	2	4	17	26	46	40	-3	4,972
19 Plymouth Argyle	46	7	8	8	33	28	4	9	10	28	40	39	-7	6,763
20 Rotherham United	46	11	5	7	26	19	2	8	13	25	49	39	-17	4,913
21 Port Vale	46	7	11	5	28	23	1	9	13	18	44	36	-21	3,947
22 Bradford City	46	11	6	6	40	29	1	4	18	16	57	34	-30	5,103
23 Hereford United	46	9	9	5	28	22	0	5	18	6	38	32	-26	4,900
24 Portsmouth	46	4	11	8	31	38	3	6	14	10	37	31	-34	9,678

SEASON 1978/79

Div.3	P	W	D	L	F	A	W	D	L	F	A	Pts	G/D	Avge. Home Gate
1 Shrewsbury Town	46	14	9	0	36	11	7	10	6	25	30	61	+20	6,099
2 Watford	46	15	5	3	47	22	9	7	7	36	30	60	+31	14,434
3 Swansea City	46	16	6	1	57	32	8	6	9	26	29	60	+22	13,746
4 Gillingham	46	15	7	1	39	15	6	10	7	26	27	59	+23	7,143
5 SWINDON TOWN	46	17	2	4	44	14	8	5	10	30	38	57	+22	7,760
6 Carlisle United	46	11	10	2	31	13	4	12	7	22	29	52	+11	5,204
7 Colchester United	46	13	9	1	35	19	4	8	11	25	36	51	+5	3,419
8 Hull City	46	12	9	2	36	14	7	2	14	30	47	49	+5	5,238
9 Exeter City	46	14	6	3	38	18	3	9	11	23	38	49	+5	4,408
10 Brentford	46	14	4	5	35	19	5	5	13	18	30	47	+4	7,455
11 Oxford United	46	10	8	5	27	20	4	10	9	17	30	46	-6	4,647
12 Blackpool	46	12	5	6	38	19	6	4	13	23	40	45	+2	5,647
13 Southend United	46	11	6	6	30	17	4	9	10	21	32	45	+2	6,610
14 Sheffield Wednesday	46	9	8	6	30	22	4	11	8	23	31	45	0	10,860
15 Plymouth Argyle	46	11	9	3	40	27	4	5	14	27	41	44	-1	7,526
16 Chester	46	11	9	3	42	21	3	7	13	15	40	44	-4	4,052
17 Rotherham United	46	13	3	7	30	23	4	7	12	19	32	44	-6	4,466
18 Mansfield Town	46	7	11	5	30	24	5	8	10	21	28	43	-1	5,151
19 Bury	46	6	11	6	35	32	5	9	9	24	33	42	-6	3,782
20 Chesterfield	46	10	5	8	35	34	3	9	11	16	31	40	-14	4,884
21 Peterborough United	46	8	7	8	26	24	3	7	13	18	39	36	-19	4,640
22 Walsall	46	7	6	10	34	32	3	6	14	22	39	32	-15	4,047
23 Tranmere Rovers	46	4	12	7	26	31	2	4	17	19	47	28	-33	2,179
24 Lincoln City	46	5	7	11	26	38	2	4	17	15	50	25	-47	3,168

SEASON 1980/81

Div. 3

	P	W	D	L	F - A		W	D	L	F - A		Pts	G/D	Avge. Home Gate
1 Rotherham United	46	17	6	0	43	8	7	7	9	19	24	61	+30	7,985
2 Barnsley	46	15	5	3	46	19	6	12	5	26	26	59	+27	12,800
3 Charlton Athletic	46	14	6	3	36	17	11	3	9	27	27	59	+19	7,206
4 Huddersfield Town	46	14	6	3	40	11	7	8	8	31	29	56	+31	11,548
5 Chesterfield	46	17	4	2	42	16	6	6	11	30	32	56	+24	7,331
6 Portsmouth	46	14	5	4	35	19	8	4	11	20	28	53	+8	13,514
7 Plymouth Argyle	46	14	5	4	35	18	5	9	9	21	26	52	+12	6,766
8 Burnley	46	13	5	5	37	21	5	9	9	23	27	50	+12	6,469
9 Brentford	46	7	9	7	30	25	7	10	6	22	24	47	+3	6,752
10 Reading	46	13	5	5	39	22	5	5	13	23	40	46	0	5,439
11 Exeter City	46	9	9	5	36	30	7	4	12	26	36	45	-4	4,559
12 Newport County	46	11	6	6	38	22	4	7	12	26	39	43	+3	5,683
13 Fulham	46	8	7	8	28	29	7	6	10	29	35	43	-7	5,060
14 Oxford United	46	7	8	8	20	24	6	9	8	19	23	43	-8	4,132
15 Gillingham	46	9	8	6	23	19	3	10	10	25	39	42	-10	4,676
16 Millwall	46	10	9	4	30	21	4	5	14	13	39	42	-17	4,494
17 SWINDON TOWN	46	10	6	7	35	27	3	9	11	16	29	41	-5	6,694
18 Chester	46	11	5	7	25	17	4	6	13	13	31	41	-10	2,892
19 Carlisle United	46	8	9	6	32	29	6	4	13	24	41	41	-14	4,064
20 Walsall	46	8	9	6	43	43	5	6	12	16	31	41	-15	4,265
21 Sheffield United	46	12	6	5	38	20	2	6	15	27	43	40	+2	12,772
22 Colchester United	46	12	7	4	35	22	2	4	17	10	43	39	-20	2,645
23 Blackpool	46	5	9	9	19	28	4	5	14	26	47	32	-30	5,733
24 Hull City	46	7	8	8	23	22	1	8	14	17	49	32	-31	4,319

SEASON 1981/82

Div. 3

	P	W	D	L	F - A		W	D	L	F - A		Pts	G/D	Avge. Home Gate
1 Burnley	46	13	7	3	37	20	8	10	5	29	25	80	+21	6,936
2 Carlisle United	46	17	4	2	44	21	6	7	10	21	29	80	+15	4,409
3 Fulham	46	12	9	2	44	22	9	6	8	33	29	78	+26	6,938
4 Lincoln City	46	13	7	3	40	16	8	7	8	26	24	77	+26	4,222
5 Oxford United	46	10	8	5	28	18	9	6	8	35	31	71	+14	5,851
6 Gillingham	46	14	5	4	44	26	6	6	11	20	30	71	+8	5,241
7 Southend United	46	11	7	5	35	23	7	8	8	28	28	69	+12	5,083
8 Brentford	46	8	6	9	28	22	11	5	7	28	25	68	+9	5,693
9 Millwall	46	12	4	7	36	28	6	9	8	26	34	67	0	4,626
10 Plymouth Argyle	46	12	5	6	37	24	6	6	11	27	32	65	+8	4,792
11 Chesterfield	46	12	4	7	33	27	6	6	11	24	31	64	-1	4,737
12 Reading	46	11	6	6	43	35	6	5	12	24	40	62	-8	4,026
13 Portsmouth	46	11	10	2	33	14	3	9	11	23	37	61	+5	8,544
14 Preston North End	46	10	7	6	25	22	6	6	11	25	34	61	-6	5,497
15 Bristol Rovers	46	12	4	7	35	28	6	5	12	23	37	61	-7	5,402
16 Newport County	46	9	10	4	28	21	5	6	12	26	33	58	0	4,459
17 Huddersfield Town	46	10	5	8	38	25	5	7	11	26	34	57	+5	6,746
18 Exeter City	46	14	4	5	46	33	2	5	16	25	51	57	-13	3,858
19 Doncaster Rovers	46	9	9	5	31	24	4	8	11	24	44	56	-13	5,234
20 Walsall	46	10	7	6	32	23	3	7	13	19	32	53	-4	3,744
21 Wimbledon	46	10	6	7	33	27	4	5	14	28	48	53	-14	2,596
22 SWINDON TOWN	46	9	5	9	37	36	4	8	11	18	35	52	-16	5,572
23 Bristol City	46	7	6	10	24	29	4	7	12	16	36	46	-25	6,511
24 Chester	46	2	10	11	16	30	5	1	17	20	48	32	-42	2,062

SEASON 1982/83

Div. 4

	P	W	D	L	F - A		W	D	L	F - A		Pts	G/D	Avge. Home Gate
1 Wimbledon	46	17	4	2	57	23	12	7	4	39	22	98	+51	2,347
2 Hull City	46	14	8	1	48	14	11	7	5	27	20	90	+41	6,586
3 Port Vale	46	15	4	4	37	16	11	6	6	30	18	88	+33	4,806
4 Scunthorpe United	46	13	7	3	41	17	10	7	6	30	25	83	+29	3,580
5 Bury	46	15	4	4	43	20	8	8	7	31	26	81	+28	3,097
6 Colchester United	46	17	5	1	51	19	7	4	12	24	36	81	+20	2,552
7 York City	46	18	4	1	59	19	4	9	10	29	39	79	+30	3,243
8 SWINDON TOWN	46	14	3	6	45	27	5	8	10	16	27	68	+7	4,021
9 Peterborough United	46	13	6	4	38	23	4	7	12	20	29	64	+6	2,795
10 Mansfield Town	46	11	6	6	32	26	5	7	11	29	44	61	-9	2,318
11 Halifax Town	46	9	8	6	31	23	7	4	12	28	43	60	-7	2,032
12 Torquay United	46	12	3	8	38	30	5	4	14	18	35	58	-9	2,336
13 Chester	46	8	6	9	28	24	7	5	11	27	36	56	-5	2,071
14 Bristol City	46	10	8	5	32	25	3	9	11	27	45	56	-11	4,799
15 Northampton Town	46	10	8	5	43	29	4	4	15	22	46	54	-10	2,594
16 Stockport County	46	11	8	4	41	31	3	4	16	19	48	54	-19	2,309
17 Darlington	46	8	5	10	27	30	5	8	10	34	41	52	-10	1,449
18 Aldershot	46	11	5	7	40	35	1	10	12	21	47	51	-21	1,929
19 Tranmere Rovers	46	8	8	7	30	29	5	3	15	19	42	50	-22	1,921
20 Rochdale	46	11	8	4	38	25	0	8	15	17	48	49	-18	1,688
21 Blackpool	46	10	8	5	32	23	3	4	16	23	51	49	-19	3,002
22 Hartlepool United	46	11	5	7	30	24	2	4	17	16	52	48	-30	1,368
23 Crewe Alexandra	46	9	5	9	35	32	2	3	18	18	39	41	-18	2,244
24 Hereford United	46	8	6	9	19	23	3	2	18	23	56	41	-37	2,217

SEASON 1969/70

Anglo-Italian Cup Winners Cup

				Home	Away	H-T	Goalscorers	Gate
W	Aug	27	A S Roma		L1-2	(0-1)	Noble 52	40,000
W	Sep	10	A S Roma	W4-0		(1-0)	Horsfield 5,70,89,Rogers 73	14,971

	Blick M R	Burrows F	Butler J W	Dangerfield D A	Dawson O J	Down D F	Downsborough P	Harland S C	Heath D	Horsfield A	Jones C M N	Jones R J	Kearns M	Noble P	Rogers D E	Smart R W	Smith J	Thomas R J	Trollope N J
27 Aug		5	4				1	6		*8	*12			10	11	9	7	2	3
10 Sep	5		4				1	6	s	8				10	11	9	7	2	3
Apps	1	1	2				2	2	0	2	0			2	2	2	2	2	2
Subs											1								
Goals										3				1	1				

Anglo-Italian Inter League Cup

				Home	Away	H-T	Goalscorers	Gate
S	May	2	Juventus	W4-0		(0-0)	Noble 61,Horsfield 68,85,Harland 90	12,879
S		9	S S C Napoli	L1-2		(0-0)	Smith 86	10,221
S		16	Juventus		W1-0	(1-0)	Noble 23	5,000
S		23	S S C Napoli		W1-0	(0-0)	Rogers	30,000
Th		28	S S C Napoli	(FINAL)	W3-0	(1-0)	Noble 24,47,Horsfield 63	55,000

(Abandoned in 79th minute due to crowd disturbance - result stood)

	Blick M R	Burrows F	Butler J W	Dangerfield D A	Dawson O J	Down D F	Downsborough P	Harland S C	Heath D	Horsfield A	Jones C M N	Jones R J	Kearns M	Noble P	Rogers D E	Smart R W	Smith J	Thomas R J	Trollope N J
2 May		5	4	s	s		1	6	s	9	s	s		10	11	8	7	2	3
9 May		5	4	s	s			6	s	9	s	1	s	10	11	8	7	2	3
16 May		5	4	s	s			6	s	9	*12	1	s	*10	11	8	7	2	3
23 May		5	4	s	s			6	s	9	s	1	s	10	11	8	7	2	3
28 May		5	4	s	s			6	s	9	s	1	s	10	11	8	7	2	3
Apps		5	5	0	0		1	5	0	5	0	4	0	5	5	5	5	5	5
Subs											1								
Goals								1		3				4	1		1		

SEASON 1970/71

Anglo-Italian Inter League Cup

				Home	Away	H-T	Goalscorers	Gate
W	May	26	Bologna	D2-2		(1-1)	Noble 11,Gough 60	9,542
S		29	U C Sampdoria	W4-1		(3-0)	Horsfield 11,Noble 27,Peplow 29,Rogers 82 pen.	8,805
Tu	Jun	1	Bologna		L1-3	(0-1)	Noble 70	25,000
S		5	U C Sampdoria		W2-1	(1-0)	Peplow 7,Noble 89	2,127

	Butler J W	Dawson O J	Downsborough P	Gough A M	Harland S C	Horsfield A	Jones C M N	Jones R J	Noble P	Peplow S T	Potter R C	Rogers D E	Smart R W	Thomas R J	Trollope N J
26 May	4	s	1	8	6	9	*12	s	*10	7	5	11	s	2	3
29 May	4	s	1	*16	6	9̲	1̲2̲	s	10	7	*5	11	8	2	3
1 Jun	4	s	1	6	5	9	s	s	10	7	s	11	8	2	3
5 Jun	4	s	1	6	5	*9	*12	s	10	7	s	11	8	2	3
Apps	4	0	4	3	4	4	0	0	4	4	2	4	3	4	4
Subs				1			3								
Goals				1		1			4	2		1			

Trophy won in Naples 1970

(For **1992/93** - no Italian opposition - see Page 234)

SEASON 1994/95

Substitutes :

- s denotes substitute **not** used
- * player substituted by *s
- ( ) player substituted by (s)
- _ player substituted by s̲

Anglo-Italian Cup

				Home	Away	H-T	Goalscorers	Gate
W	Aug	24	Atalanta BC	L0-2		(0-0)		5,167
Tu	Sep	6	S S C Venezia		L0-1	(0-0)		1,325
W	Oct	5	U S Lecce	W3-1		(2-0)	Mutch 32,88,Scott 44	2,375
Tu	Nov	15	Ascoli		L1-3	(0-1)	Hamon 50 pen.	750

	Beauchamp J D	Berkley A J	Bodin P J	Digby F C	Fjortoft J A	Gooden T M	Hammond N D	Hamon C A J	Horlock K	Kilcline B	Ling M	MacLaren R	Murray E J	Mutch A T	Nijholt L	O'Sullivan W StJ	Robinson M J	Scott K	Taylor S	Thomson A J
24 Aug	8		3	1	9	(s)	s		(11)	4	7			s	5	s	2	*10		6
6 Sep	8	10		(s)			1	*s	3	4	7		s̲	(9)	5	*11	2			6̲
5 Oct	8	(10)	3	1	*s		s	s	7	4	(s)			9	5		2	*11	6	s
15 Nov	8	(s)		s		s	1	*s	3	6	*10	4	s	9		(7)	2	11		5
Apps	4	2	2	2	1	0	2	0	4	4	3	1	0	3	3	2	4	3	1	3
Subs		1		1	1	1		2			1		1							
Goals								1						2				1		

*(Atalanta : *s = White S J   Venezia : s = James S E and Phillips M S)*

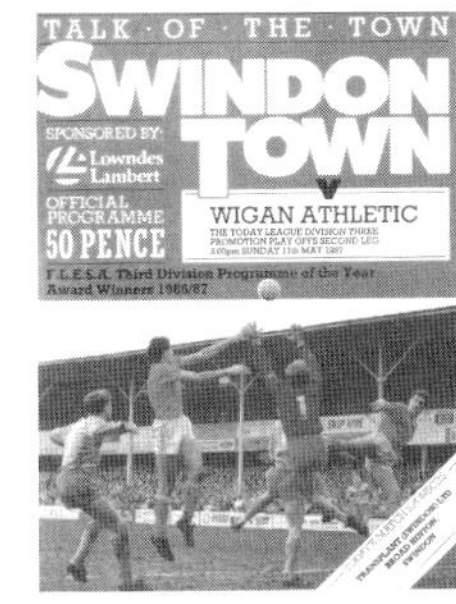

Left to right : Programme covers from 1983/84 1986/87 1990/91 and 1993/94

onwards and upwards

BASEMENT TO PREMIERSHIP

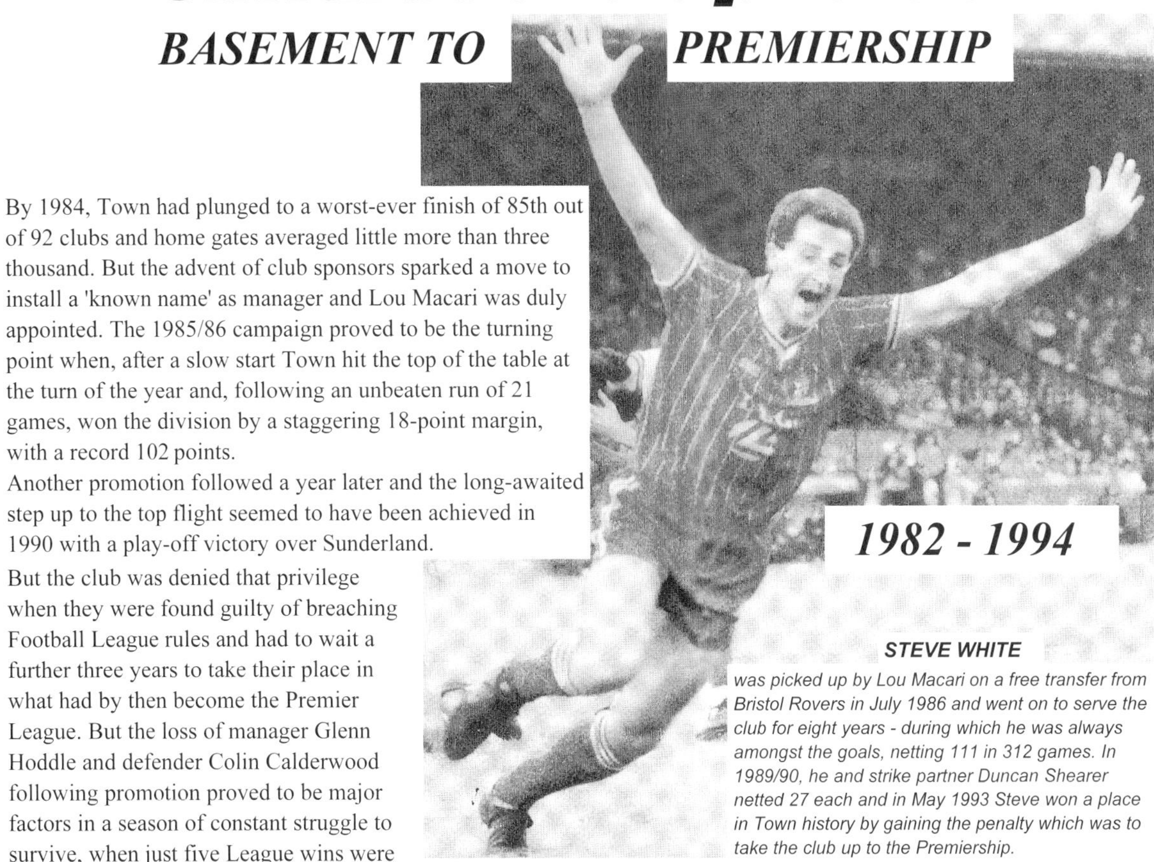

By 1984, Town had plunged to a worst-ever finish of 85th out of 92 clubs and home gates averaged little more than three thousand. But the advent of club sponsors sparked a move to install a 'known name' as manager and Lou Macari was duly appointed. The 1985/86 campaign proved to be the turning point when, after a slow start Town hit the top of the table at the turn of the year and, following an unbeaten run of 21 games, won the division by a staggering 18-point margin, with a record 102 points.

Another promotion followed a year later and the long-awaited step up to the top flight seemed to have been achieved in 1990 with a play-off victory over Sunderland.

But the club was denied that privilege when they were found guilty of breaching Football League rules and had to wait a further three years to take their place in what had by then become the Premier League. But the loss of manager Glenn Hoddle and defender Colin Calderwood following promotion proved to be major factors in a season of constant struggle to survive, when just five League wins were registered.

1982 - 1994

STEVE WHITE

was picked up by Lou Macari on a free transfer from Bristol Rovers in July 1986 and went on to serve the club for eight years - during which he was always amongst the goals, netting 111 in 312 games. In 1989/90, he and strike partner Duncan Shearer netted 27 each and in May 1993 Steve won a place in Town history by gaining the penalty which was to take the club up to the Premiership.

Left to right : Alan McLoughlin and Ossie Ardiles all smiles at Wembley 1990 : Fraser Digby (see page 282) : Glenn Hoddle (see page 232) : Andy Mutch scores at Old Trafford in the Premiership

SEASON 1982/83

Football League Fourth Division
Final League Position : 8th
Manager : John Trollope
Ken Beamish (from Apr.28)

Substitutes :
s denotes substitute **not** used
* player substituted by *12

					Home	Away	H-T	Goalscorers	Gate
1	S	Aug	28	Port Vale	W1-0		(0-0)	Rideout 64	3,604
2	S	Sep	4	Blackpool		L1-2	(1-1)	Carter 20	3,593
3	W		8	Hereford United		W2-1	(0-1)	Rowland 74,Quinn 77	2,674
4	S		11	Halifax Town	L0-1		(0-0)		3,452
5	S		18	Rochdale		D1-1	(1-1)	Emmanuel 5	1,292
6	S		25	Crewe Alexandra	W1-0		(1-0)	Rowland 34	2,968
7	Tu		28	Northampton Town		W1-0	(1-0)	Rideout 34 pen.	2,706
8	S	Oct	2	Hull City		D0-0			3,786
9	Su		10	Colchester United	W3-0		(2-0)	Rideout 32 pen.,Rowland 43,53	4,476
10	S		16	Bury		D0-0			2,497
11	W		20	Torquay United		D1-1	(0-0)	Rideout 75	2,979
12	S		23	Mansfield Town	W4-0		(2-0)	Rideout 25,Barnard 40,Rowland 57,Pritchard 74	3,920
13	S		30	Chester		W1-0	(0-0)	Rowland 77	1,544
14	Tu	Nov	2	Tranmere Rovers	W4-2		(2-1)	Rideout 27 pen.,69 pen.,Rowland 40,Barnard 64	4,408
15	S		6	Darlington		L0-1	(0-1)		1,334
16	S		13	York City	W3-2		(2-1)	Rowland 27,Rideout 31,Pritchard 72	4,081
17	F		26	Stockport County		W2-1	(1-1)	Emmanuel 13,Rowland 53	2,197
18	S	Dec	4	Peterborough United	W1-0		(0-0)	Rideout 56 pen.	3,961
19	S		18	Hartlepool United	W3-0		(1-0)	Rideout 42 pen.,Rowland 65,74	4,121
20	M		27	Aldershot		D1-1	(0-0)	Lewis 75	5,087
21	Tu		28	Wimbledon	L0-1		(0-0)		8,166
22	S	Jan	1	Bristol City		D1-1	(0-0)	Pritchard 64	9,002
23	M		3	Scunthorpe United	D2-2		(1-2)	Rowland 9,Rideout 75 pen.	6,741
24	S		15	Port Vale		L0-3	(0-1)		6,397
25	S		22	Rochdale	W4-1		(1-1)	Rideout 9,50 pen.,55,Pritchard 82	4,425
26	S	Feb	5	Crewe Alexandra		L0-3	(0-3)		2,536
27	S		12	Hereford United	W3-2		(1-0)	Pritchard 5,Rideout 65,Bray o.g.67	4,042
28	F		18	Colchester United		L0-1	(0-0)		2,386
29	S		26	Bury	D1-1		(1-1)	Pritchard 10	4,694
30	M		28	Tranmere Rovers		L0-2	(0-0)		1,521
31	S	Mar	5	Mansfield Town		L0-1	(0-0)		2,101
32	S		12	Chester	L2-3		(1-1)	Rowland 42,Rideout 75	3,239
33	Tu		15	Halifax Town		L0-1	(0-0)		1,806
34	S		19	Darlington	L1-2		(1-1)	Rowland 12	2,816
35	S		26	York City		D0-0			3,265
36	F	Apr	1	Wimbledon		D0-0			3,400
37	M		4	Aldershot	W2-0		(0-0)	Batty 66,Bailie 73	3,495
38	S		9	Peterborough United		L3-4	(1-4)	Rideout 19,Barnard 53,Rowland 69	2,522
39	S		16	Hull City	L0-1		(0-0)		3,794
40	Tu		19	Blackpool	D3-3		(2-3)	Baddeley 21,Rowland 40,Pritchard 87	2,408
41	S		23	Hartlepool United		W2-1	(1-1)	Rideout 35 pen.,73	1,126
42	Tu		26	Torquay United	W2-1		(1-0)	Pritchard 10,Rideout 67	2,509
43	S		30	Stockport County	W2-0		(0-0)	Pritchard 87,Quinn 90	2,669
44	M	May	2	Scunthorpe United		L0-2	(0-1)		3,546
45	Su		8	Northampton Town	L1-5		(1-2)	Quinn 27	3,388
46	S		14	Bristol City	W2-0		(1-0)	Barnard 39,Pritchard 71	5,103

Average Home Attendance : **4,021**
Average Away Attendance : **3,013**

Football League Cup

					Home	Away	H-T	Goalscorers	Gate
1/1	Tu	Aug	31	Bristol City	W2-1		(1-0)	Rideout 11 pen.,89	3,739
1/2	Tu	Sep	14	Bristol City		L0-2	(0-2)		3,752

F A Cup

					Home	Away	H-T	Goalscorers	Gate
1	S	Nov	20	Wealdstone	W2-0		(0-0)	Henry 47,Rideout 56	4,057
2	S	Dec	11	Brentford	D2-2		(2-0)	Lewis 38,Barnard 42	7,188
2R	Tu		14	Brentford	+	W3-1	(0-0)	Rowland 60,Pritchard 102,Batty 119	7,383
3	S	Jan	8	Aldershot	W7-0		(2-0)	Pritchard 19,21,90,Rowland 47,53,63,Batty 74	7,187
4	S		29	Burnley		L1-3	(0-2)	Pritchard 50	9,786

\+ After Extra Time

For Final League Table - see page 203

Allan J	Baddeley K S	Bailie C J	Barnard L K	Batty P W	Baverstock R	Blackler M J	Carter R W	Emmanuel J G	Graham M A	Henry C A	Hughes B D	Lewis R	Moore K J	Pritchard H K	Quinn J M	Rideout P D	Rowland A A	Stevens M A	Williams G	
1	3		11				s	4	6	2	8	5		7		9	10			1
1	*3		11		2		7	4	6		8	5		*12		9	10			2
1	3		11		2		7	*4	6		8	5			*12	9	10			3
1	3		11		2		8	*4	6		7	5			*12	9	10			4
1	3		11			s		4	6	2	8	5		7	*12	9	10			5
1	3		11	8				4	6	2		5		7		9	10		s	6
1	3		11	8				4	6	2		5		7		9	10		s	7
1	3		11	8				4	6	2		5		7		9	10		s	8
1	3		11	8				4	6	2	*12	5		*7		9	10			9
1	3		11	8				4	6	2	7	5			s	9	10			10
1	3		11	8				4	6	2	s	5		7		9	10			11
1	3		11	8				4	6	2		5		7	*12	*9	10			12
1	3		11	8				4	6	2		5		7	s	9	10			13
1	3		11	8				4	6	2		5		7	s	9	10			14
1	3		11	8	2			4	6		*7	5			*12	9	10			15
1	3		11	8				4	6	2		5		*7	*12	9	10			16
1	3		11	8				4	6	2		5		7	s	9	10			17
1	3		11	8		s		4	6	2		5		7		9	10			18
1	3	2	11	8				4	6		s	5		7		9	10			19
1	3	2	11	8		s		4	6			5		7		9	10			20
1		2	11	8	3	s		4	6			5		7	9		10			21
1		3	11	8	2	s		4	6			5		7		9	10			22
1	3	2	11	8		s		4	6			5		7		9	10			23
1		3	11	8	2	s			6		4	5		7		9	10			24
1		3	11	8	2	s			6		4	5		7		9	10			25
1		3	11	8	2			4	6			5		7	s	9	10			26
1		3	11	8	2			4	6			5		*7	*12	9	10			27
1		3	11	8	2	s		4	6		7	5			10	9				28
1		3	11	8	2			4	6		s	5		7		9	10			29
1		3	11	8	2			4	6			5		*7	*12	9	10			30
1	3		11			*12		4	6	*2	8	5			7	9	10			31
1	3		11			8		4	6	2		5		7	s	9	10			32
1	3	2	11	8		s		4	6			5		7		9	10			33
1	3	2	8	*12				4	6			5	*11	7		9	10			34
1	3	2	8	4	7	11			6			5	s			9	10			35
1	3	2	8	4	7	11			6			5	s			9	10			36
1	3	2	8	4	7	11			6			5	s			9	10			37
1	3	2	8	4	7	*11			6			5		*12		9	10			38
1	3	2	8	4		11			6		s	5		7		9	10			39
1	3	2	8	4		*11			6		*12	5		7		9	10			40
1	3	2	8	4		s			6		11	5		7		9	10			41
1	3	2	8	4		s			6		11	5		7		9	10			42
1	3	2	8	4					6		11	*5		7	*12	9	10			43
1	3	2	8	4					6	5	*11			7	*12	9	10			44
*1	3	2	8	4					6	5	11			7	*12	9	10			45
	3	2	8	4		11			6	5	s			7	9		10	1		46
45	37	26	46	38	17	8	3	32	46	19	16	43	1	35	4	44	45	1	0	Apps
				1		1					2			2	10					Subs
	1	1	4	1			1	2				1		10	3	20	16			Goals

Opponent 1 goal

Allan J	Baddeley K S	Bailie C J	Barnard L K	Batty P W	Baverstock R	Blackler M J	Carter R W	Emmanuel J G	Graham M A	Henry C A	Hughes B D	Lewis R	Moore K J	Pritchard H K	Quinn J M	Rideout P D	Rowland A A	Stevens M A	Williams G	
1	3		11				*12	4	6	2	8	5		*7		9	10			1/1
1	3		11					4	6	*2	8	5		7	*12	9	10			1/2
2	2		2				0	2	2	2	2	2		2	0	2	2			Apps
							1								1					Subs
																2				Goals

Allan J	Baddeley K S	Bailie C J	Barnard L K	Batty P W	Baverstock R	Blackler M J	Carter R W	Emmanuel J G	Graham M A	Henry C A	Hughes B D	Lewis R	Moore K J	Pritchard H K	Quinn J M	Rideout P D	Rowland A A	Stevens M A	Williams G	
1	3		11	8				4	6	2		5		7	s	9	10			1
1	3		11	8				4	6	*2		5		7	*12	9	10			2
1	3	2	*11	8				4	6		*12	5		7		9	10			2R
1		2	*11	8	3			4	6			5		7	*12	9	10			3
1		3	11	8	*2			4	6			5		7	*12	9	10			4
5	3	3	5	5	2			5	5	2	0	5		5	0	5	5			Apps
											1				3					Subs
			1	2						1		1		5		1	4			Goals

PAUL RIDEOUT

SEASON 1983/84

Football League Fourth Division
Final League Position : 17th
Manager : Ken Beamish

Substitutes :
s denotes substitute **not** used
* player substituted by *12

				Home	Away	H-T	Goalscorers	Gate
1	S	Aug	27 Chesterfield		L0-1	(0-1)		4,161
2	S	Sep	3 Chester City	W4-0		(1-0)	Nelson 29,Mayes 64,78 pen.,Rowland 84	2,894
3	Tu		6 Halifax Town	L2-3		(0-2)	Hockaday 46,Rowland 50	3,638
4	S		10 Darlington		L0-1	(0-0)		1,091
5	S		17 Blackpool	D0-0				2,867
6	F		23 Stockport County		W3-1	(1-0)	Mayes 16 pen.,87,Rowland 46	2,244
7	Tu		27 Aldershot		L1-2	(1-2)	Mayes 10	2,644
8	S	Oct	1 Rochdale	W2-1		(1-0)	Mayes 9,Quinn 82	2,631
9	S		8 Crewe Alexandra		L0-2	(0-1)		2,111
10	S		15 York City	W3-2		(2-2)	Emmanuel 2,Bailie 18,Barnard 70	2,528
11	M		17 Tranmere Rovers		L1-2	(1-1)	Mayes 10	2,543
12	S		22 Colchester United	W2-1		(0-1)	Rowland 51,Hockaday 77	3,087
13	S		29 Reading		D2-2	(2-0)	Mayes 4,Batty 26	5,918
14	Tu	Nov	1 Hereford United	W3-0		(3-0)	Gibson 17,Mayes 35 pen.,Barnard 45	3,648
15	S		5 Northampton Town		L0-2	(0-2)		2,354
16	S		12 Hartlepool United	W3-2		(1-1)	Emmanuel 24,Rowland 85,Barnard 90	3,074
17	S		26 Mansfield Town		D2-2	(1-1)	Quinn 20,77	3,327
18	S	Dec	3 Doncaster Rovers	W2-1		(1-1)	Quinn 40,Barnard 58	3,546
19	S		17 Bury	D0-0				3,554
20	M		26 Torquay United		L0-1	(0-0)		2,837
21	Tu		27 Wrexham	L0-1		(0-1)		4,305
22	S		31 Peterborough United		D1-1	(0-1)	Quinn 80	4,110
23	S	Jan	14 Chesterfield	L1-2		(1-1)	Batty 24	3,937
24	S		21 Blackpool		D1-1	(1-0)	Emmanuel 31	3,474
25	Tu		24 Bristol City	D1-1		(0-0)	Quinn 51	6,498
26	S	Feb	4 Rochdale		D3-3	(2-2)	Gibson 9,Mayes 30 pen.,59 pen.	1,297
27	W		8 Chester City		W3-0	(3-0)	Nelson 15,39,Batty 36	880
28	S		11 Stockport County	W2-1		(0-0)	Mayes 57,Rowland 90	3,022
29	W		15 Hereford United		L1-2	(1-1)	Barnard 25	2,002
30	S		18 Reading	D1-1		(0-1)	Bailie 48	4,663
31	S		25 Colchester United		D0-0			2,448
32	S	Mar	3 Tranmere Rovers	D1-1		(1-1)	Nelson 9	2,595
33	Tu		6 Northampton Town	D0-0				2,614
34	S		10 Hartlepool United		W1-0	(1-0)	Batty 21	1,274
35	Su		18 Crewe Alexandra	W1-0		(1-0)	Hockaday 25	2,954
36	S		24 York City		L0-2	(0-1)		3,341
37	F		30 Halifax Town		L1-2	(0-1)	Quinn 89	1,008
38	S	Apr	7 Aldershot	L0-2		(0-0)		2,836
39	S		14 Doncaster Rovers		L0-3	(0-1)		3,804
40	Tu		17 Darlington	W1-0		(1-0)	Barnard 45	1,681
41	F		20 Wrexham		W3-0	(2-0)	Gibson 13,Mayes 41 pen.,Emmanuel 86	1,442
42	S		21 Torquay United	L2-3		(1-1)	Mayes 6,65	2,197
43	Su		29 Mansfield Town	D1-1		(1-0)	Bailie 10	1,941
44	S	May	5 Bristol City		L0-1	(0-0)		12,786
45	M		7 Peterborough United	W2-0		(1-0)	Barnard 11,Mayes 65	1,876
46	S		12 Bury		L1-2	(0-1)	Mayes 55	1,214

Average Home Attendance : **3,156**
Average Away Attendance : **2,970**

Football League Cup

				Home	Away	H-T	Goalscorers	Gate
1/1	Tu	Aug	30 Plymouth Argyle	W1-0		(0-0)	Hockaday 55	3,346
1/2	Tu	Sep	13 Plymouth Argyle		L1-4	(0-1)	Nelson 78	3,432

F A Cup

				Home	Away	H-T	Goalscorers	Gate
1	S	Nov	19 Kettering Town		W7-0	(2-0)	Gibson 8,Quinn 45,53,Rowland 64,Henry 69,Batty 82,Barnard 86	2,834
2	S	Dec	10 Millwall		W3-2	(1-1)	Quinn 24,74,Batty 64	4,597
3	S	Jan	7 Carlisle United		D1-1	(0-1)	Rowland 68	5,778
3R	Tu		10 Carlisle United	W3-1		(1-0)	Quinn 40,Batty 72,Rowland 82	8,078
4	S		28 Blackburn Rovers	L1-2		(0-0)	Quinn 21	11,154

For Associate Members' Cup - see page 215 For Final League Table - see page 218

Allan J	Andrews I E	Baddeley K S	Bailie C J	Barnard L K	Batty P W	Emmanuel J G	Endersby S A G	Gardiner M C	Gibson S J	Graham M A	Gray N R	Henry C A	Hockaday D	Hughes M C	Mayes A K	Nelson G P	Quinn J M	Richardson P	Rowland A A	Woodruff R J	
1			3	s		4				6	5	2	7		10	11		8	9		**1**
1			3			4				6	5	2	7		10	11	s	8	9		**2**
1			3			4				6	5	*2	7		10	11	*12	8	9		**3**
1			3	s	2	4				6	5		7		10	11		8	9		**4**
1		3	2	8		4				6	5		7		*12	11	*10		9		**5**
1		3	2	8		4				6	5		7		10	11		s	9		**6**
1		3	2	8	*12	4				6	5				10	11		*7	9		**7**
*1		3	2	8	4					6	5				10	11	*12	7	9		**8**
		3	2		4	8	1			6	5	s			10	11		7	9		**9**
			3	7	4	8	1			6		2	s		10	11	9		5		**10**
			3	7	4	8	1			6		2	*12		10	*11	9		5		**11**
			3	11	4	8	1		5	6		2	7		10	s			9		**12**
			3	11	4	8	1		5	6		2	7		10	s			9		**13**
			3	11	4	8	1		5	6		2	7		10	s			9		**14**
		*12	3		4	8	1		5	6		*2	7		10	11			9		**15**
			3	11	4	8	1		5	6		*2	7		10		*12		9		**16**
			3	11	4	8	1		5	6		*2	7		*12		10		9		**17**
			3	11	4	8	1		5	6		2	7		10		9		s		**18**
			3	11	4	8	1		5	6		2	*7		10		9		*12		**19**
			3	11	4	8	1			6	s	2	7		10		9		5		**20**
			3	11	4	8	1			*6		2	7		10	*12	9		5		**21**
		3		11	4	8	1		5			2	*7		*12	10	9		6		**22**
		3		*11	4	8	1		5			2	7		*12	10	9		6		**23**
		3		11	4	8	1		5			2	7		s	10	9		6		**24**
	1	3		11	4	8			5			2	7		s	10	9		6		**25**
		3		11	4	8	1		5		2				7	10	9	s	6		**26**
		3		11	4	8	1		5		2				7	10	9	s	6		**27**
		3		*11	4	8	1		5		2		*12		7	10	9		6		**28**
		3		11	4	8	1		5		2		*12		7	10	*9		6		**29**
		3	8	11	4		1		5		2		7			10	9	s	6		**30**
		3	2	11	4		1			s	5		7		8	10	9		6		**31**
		3	2	11	4	*12	1			5			7		*8	10	9		6		**32**
		3	2	11	*4	8	1		5	6			7	*12		10			9		**33**
		3	2		4	8	1		5	6		11	7			10	s		9		**34**
		3	*12		4	8	1		5	6		*2	7		10	11			9		**35**
		3	2	*12	*4	8	1		5	6			7		10	11			9		**36**
		3	2		4	8	1		5	6			7		*10	11	*12		9		**37**
		3	2		4	8	1		5	6			7		*12	*11	10		9		**38**
			2	7	4	8	1		5	6		3	s		10	11	9				**39**
			2	7	4	8	1		5	6		3	s		10	11	9				**40**
			3	7	4	8	1		5	6		2	*12		*10	11	9				**41**
		s	3	7	4	8	1		5	6		2			10	11	9				**42**
		3	2	7	4	8	1	10		6		5		s		11	9				**43**
		5	3	7	4	8	1	s		6		2	10			11	9				**44**
		s	3	11	4		1		5	6		2	7		10		9			8	**45**
			3	11	4	8	1		5	*6		2	7		10		9			*12	**46**
8	1	24	37	35	40	41	37	1	29	36	15	29	32	0	34	35	28	7	36	1	Apps
		1	1	1	1	1							4	1	5	1	4		1	1	Subs
			3	7	4	4			3				3		17	4	7		6		Goals

Allan J	Andrews I E	Baddeley K S	Bailie C J	Barnard L K	Batty P W	Emmanuel J G	Endersby S A G	Gardiner M C	Gibson S J	Graham M A	Gray N R	Henry C A	Hockaday D	Hughes M C	Mayes A K	Nelson G P	Quinn J M	Richardson P	Rowland A A	Woodruff R J	
1			3	s		4				6	5	2	7		10	11		8	9		**1/1**
1		3	2	*12	*8	4				6		5	7			11	10		9		**1/2**
2		1	2	0	1	2				2	1	2	2		1	2	1	1	2		Apps
				1																	Subs
													1			1					Goals

Allan J	Andrews I E	Baddeley K S	Bailie C J	Barnard L K	Batty P W	Emmanuel J G	Endersby S A G	Gardiner M C	Gibson S J	Graham M A	Gray N R	Henry C A	Hockaday D	Hughes M C	Mayes A K	Nelson G P	Quinn J M	Richardson P	Rowland A A	Woodruff R J	
			3	11	4	8	1		5	6		2	7			s	10		9		**1**
			3	11	4	8	1		5	6		2	7		10		9		s		**2**
		3		11	4	8	1		5			2	7		s	10	9		6		**3**
		3		11	4	8	1		5			2	7		s	10	9		6		**3R**
		3		11	4	8	1		5			*2	7		*12	10	9		6		**4**
		3	2	5	5	5	5		5	2		5	5		1	3	5		4		Apps
															1						Subs
				1	3				1			1					6		3		Goals

JIMMY QUINN

SEASON 1984/85

Football League Fourth Division
Final League Position : 8th
Manager : Lou Macari

Substitutes :
s denotes substitute **not** used
* player substituted by *12

No	Day	Month	Date	Opponent	Home	Away	H-T	Goalscorers	Gate
1	S	Aug	25	Wrexham	W2-1		(1-1)	Macari 37,Mayes 87	3,591
2	S	Sep	1	Hartlepool United		D2-2	(0-1)	Rowland 56,Coyne 59	1,703
3	S		8	Torquay United	L1-3		(1-0)	Mayes 24 pen.	3,180
4	F		14	Tranmere Rovers		W2-0	(2-0)	Rowland 3,Nelson 28	2,051
5	Tu		18	Bury		L0-2	(0-1)		2,769
6	S		22	Hereford United	L0-3		(0-0)		3,545
7	S		29	Mansfield Town		D0-0			2,224
8	Tu	Oct	2	Blackpool	W4-1		(2-1)	Nelson 23,Mayes 34,62,67	2,511
9	Su		7	Peterborough United	D1-1		(1-1)	Mayes 20	4,017
10	S		13	Crewe Alexandra		L2-3	(1-3)	Coyne 1,Mayes 84 pen.	1,909
11	S		20	Port Vale	L0-1		(0-0)		2,861
12	W		24	Exeter City		D1-1	(0-1)	Coyne 79	2,139
13	S		27	Stockport County	W4-0		(2-0)	Batty 19,Coyne 28,Macari 59,Mayes 68	2,465
14	S	Nov	3	Rochdale		W1-0	(0-0)	Gordon 73	1,071
15	Tu		6	Scunthorpe United	D0-0				2,873
16	S		10	Northampton Town		L0-4	(0-3)		2,274
17	S		24	Aldershot	W2-1		(0-1)	Mayes 54,Macari 71	2,880
18	Su	Dec	2	Darlington		L0-1	(0-1)		6,099
19	S		15	Colchester United	W2-1		(2-1)	Coyne 19,Gordon 41	2,264
20	S		22	Halifax Town	W2-1		(1-0)	Barnard 44,Batty 65	2,414
21	W		26	Southend United		L2-3	(0-1)	O'Brien o.g.78,Gordon 89	2,942
22	Tu	Jan	1	Chesterfield	W4-0		(2-0)	Rowland 40,74,Gordon 45,56	3,583
23	S		5	Wrexham		L0-4	(0-2)		1,261
24	S		26	Tranmere Rovers	W2-1		(1-0)	Rowland 26 pen.,Coyne 56	2,679
25	W		30	Chester City		L0-2	(0-1)		1,710
26	S	Feb	2	Mansfield Town	W1-0		(0-0)	Coyne 86	2,664
27	Tu		19	Blackpool		L0-1	(0-0)		3,382
28	S		23	Rochdale	W2-1		(1-1)	Gordon 35,83	2,752
29	Tu		26	Torquay United		D0-0			1,163
30	F	Mar	1	Stockport County		L1-2	(1-1)	Hockaday 36	1,680
31	Tu		5	Exeter City	W2-0		(0-0)	Gordon 60,64	2,706
32	S		9	Port Vale		L0-2	(0-0)		3,300
33	Tu		12	Bury	W1-0		(0-0)	Coyne 49 pen.	3,153
34	S		16	Crewe Alexandra	D1-1		(0-0)	Coyne 67	2,485
35	S		23	Peterborough United		W1-0	(1-0)	Coyne 10	2,329
36	F		29	Scunthorpe United		L2-6	(1-4)	Barnard 21,Coyne 72 pen.	2,052
37	Su		31	Hartlepool United	W2-1		(0-1)	Gordon 76,Coyne 90	2,220
38	S	Apr	6	Southend United	W2-0		(1-0)	Nelson 24,Gordon 81	2,695
39	Tu		9	Chesterfield		L0-1	(0-0)		4,420
40	S		13	Northampton Town	W2-0		(1-0)	Gordon 37,Gage o.g.76	3,457
41	W		17	Hereford United		W3-0	(1-0)	Gordon 39,74,79	4,092
42	S		20	Aldershot		W1-0	(1-0)	Gordon 28	2,981
43	Su		28	Darlington	W1-0		(0-0)	Mayes 76	4,761
44	F	May	3	Colchester United		D1-1	(1-0)	Ramsey 42	1,867
45	M		6	Chester City	D4-4		(1-1)	Barnard 19,Coyne 53 pen.,Dixon o.g.74,Gordon 77	3,808
46	F		10	Halifax Town		L1-2	(0-1)	Coyne 68	2,307

Average Home Attendance : **3,025**
Average Away Attendance : **2,510**

Football League Cup

No	Day	Month	Date	Opponent	Home	Away	H-T	Goalscorers	Gate
1/1	M	Aug	27	Bristol Rovers	L1-5		(1-3)	Coyne 28	4,919
1/2	Tu	Sep	4	Bristol Rovers		W1-0	(0-0)	Mayes 53	3,862

F A Cup

No	Day	Month	Date	Opponent	Home	Away	H-T	Goalscorers	Gate
1	M	Nov	19	Dagenham		D0-0			2,951
1R	M		26	Dagenham	L1-2 +		(1-0)	Mayes 21	3,754

\+ After Extra Time

For Associate Members' Cup - see page 215 For Final League Table - see page 218

Baddeley K S	Bailie C J	Barnard L K	Batty P W	Caldwell D W	Cole D A	Coyne P D	Dempsey M J	Endersby S A G	Fulbrook G L	Gardiner M C	Gibson S J	Gordon C K	Graham M A	Gray N R	Henry C A	Hockaday D	Hughes M C	Macari L	Mayes A K	Muir I J	Nelson G P	Payne M I	Ramsey C L	Reynolds J A	Rowland A A	Sperring A	
	2	7	8			*12		1					6		*5	11		4	10		3				9		1
	6	11	7			8		1					3					4	9		10	s	2		5		2
	3	8	*7			10		1					6					4	9		11	*12	2		5		3
	*3	10	7			8		1		9			6					4	*12		11		2		5		4
	3	7	2			10		1		*8			6					4	9		11	*12			5		5
3	*2	10	7			8		1		9			6					4			11	*12			5		6
3		7	8			10		1		s			6					4	9		11		2		5		7
3		7	10			*8		1		*12			6					4	9		11		2		5		8
3	s	7	10			8		1					6					4	9		11		2		5		9
*3	*12	7	10			8		1					6					4	9		11		2		5		10
	3	7	*10			8		1			*12		6					4	9		11		2		5		11
	3	7	10			8		1			s		6	2				4	9		11				5		12
	*3	7	10			8		1			*12		6					4	9		11		2		5		13
	3	7	10			8		1				*12	6	2				*4	9		11				5		14
	3	7	4			8		1	*12			10	6	*2					9		11				5		15
	3	*12	10			8		1				7	6	2				4	9		11				5		16
	3	4	7			8		1				10	6			*2		*12	9		11				5		17
	3	s	10			8		1				9	6	2	7			4			11				5		18
	3	4	10			8		1				9		5		7		s			11		2		6		19
	3	4	10			8		1				9		5		7		s			11		2		6		20
	3		*12			8		1				9		5	*4	7		10			11		2		6		21
	3	4	10			8		1				9		5		7		s			11		2		6		22
	3	4	10			8		1				9		5		7		s			11		2		6		23
	3					8	10	1				9	7	5	s			4			11		2		6		24
						*12	10	1				9	*7	5	3			4		8	11		2		6		25
	3		*12			7	10	1				9		5				4		*8	11		2		6		26
	3		s		6	8	10	1				9		2	7			4			11				5		27
	3				6	8	10	1				9		2	7			4			11			s	5		28
	3			10	6	8		1				9	11	2	7			4			s				5		29
	3			10	6	s		1				9		2	7	11		4					8		5		30
	3			10	6	*12		1				9		5		7		*4			11		2		8		31
	3			10	6	5		1				9	s			7		4			11		2		8		32
	3		s		5	7		1				9	10		4	8					11		2		6		33
	3			10	5	7		1				9			4	8					*11		2	*12	6		34
	3				5	7		1				9	10		4	8					11		2	s	6		35
	3	11	*12		5	7		1				9	*10		4	8							2		6		36
	3	10	*12		5	7		1				9			4	*8					11		2		6		37
	3	10	4		5	*7		1				9	8						*12		11		2		6		38
	3	10	4		5	7		1				9	8		s						11		2		6		39
	3	10			5	*7		1				9			4	8			*12		11		2		6		40
	3	10			5	*7		1				9	8		2	4			*12		11				6		41
	3	10			5	7		1				9	2		4	8			s		11				6		42
	3	10			5	7		1				9	*4			8			*12		11		2		6		43
	3	10	s		5	7		1				9				8			4		11		2		6		44
	3	10	s		5	7		1				9				8			4		11		2		6		45
	3	10	s		5	7		1				9				8			4		11		2		6		46
5	41	31	24	5	20	42	5	46	0	3	0	32	29	18	16	22	0	26	18	2	43	0	32	0	46	0	Apps
	1	1	4			3			1	1	2	1						1	5			3		1			Subs
		3	2			14						17				1		3	10		3		1		5		Goals

Opponents 3 goals

Baddeley K S	Bailie C J	Barnard L K	Batty P W	Caldwell D W	Cole D A	Coyne P D	Dempsey M J	Endersby S A G	Fulbrook G L	Gardiner M C	Gibson S J	Gordon C K	Graham M A	Gray N R	Henry C A	Hockaday D	Hughes M C	Macari L	Mayes A K	Muir I J	Nelson G P	Payne M I	Ramsey C L	Reynolds J A	Rowland A A	Sperring A	
	2	10				8					5		3			*7	*12	4	9		11				6	1	1/1
3		8	7					1		10			2	6	s				9		11	4			5		1/2
1	1	2	1			1		1		1	1		2	1	0	1	0	1	2		2	1			2	1	Apps
																	1										Subs
						1													1								Goals

Baddeley K S	Bailie C J	Barnard L K	Batty P W	Caldwell D W	Cole D A	Coyne P D	Dempsey M J	Endersby S A G	Fulbrook G L	Gardiner M C	Gibson S J	Gordon C K	Graham M A	Gray N R	Henry C A	Hockaday D	Hughes M C	Macari L	Mayes A K	Muir I J	Nelson G P	Payne M I	Ramsey C L	Reynolds J A	Rowland A A	Sperring A	
	3	11	4			8		1		*12	*5		6			7			10		9				2		1
	3	7	10			8		1	2	*12			6					4	*9		11				5		1R
	2	2	2			2		2	1	0	1		2			1		1	2		2				2		Apps
										2																	Subs
																			1								Goals

SEASON 1985/86

Football League Fourth Division
Final League Position : Champions
Manager : Lou Macari

Substitutes :
s denotes substitute **not** used
* player substituted by *12

				Home	Away	H-T	Goalscorers	Gate
1	S	Aug	17 Wrexham	L0-1		(0-0)		4,159
2	S		24 Hereford United		L1-4	(0-1)	Calderwood 65	4,094
3	M		26 Torquay United	W2-1		(1-1)	Coyne 43,Henry 70	3,378
4	F		30 Southend United		D0-0			4,037
5	F	Sep	6 Northampton Town	W3-2		(2-0)	Coyne 17,31 pen.,83 pen.	3,879
6	S		14 Peterborough United		L0-3	(0-2)		2,946
7	Tu		17 Crewe Alexandra		L0-2	(0-0)		1,699
8	S		28 Hartlepool United		L0-1	(0-0)		2,727
9	Tu	Oct	1 Exeter City	W2-1		(1-1)	Gordon 31,Calderwood 89	3,118
10	S		5 Rochdale	W4-0		(3-0)	Coyne 9,Cole 16,Wade 26,Hockaday 86	3,086
11	S		12 Burnley		W2-0	(1-0)	Gordon 12,Coyne 49	2,979
12	S		19 Chester City		W1-0	(1-0)	Gordon 38	3,109
13	Tu		22 Stockport County	W1-0		(0-0)	Coyne 62	7,172
14	S		26 Port Vale		L0-3	(0-1)		5,073
15	S	Nov	2 Tranmere Rovers	W2-0		(1-0)	Barnard 10,Wade 74	4,358
16	W		6 Cambridge United	W1-0		(0-0)	Henry 64	5,489
17	S		9 Scunthorpe United		W2-0	(2-0)	Henry 12,Wade 20	1,920
18	S		23 Mansfield Town	W2-1		(1-0)	Coleman 33 pen.,Wade 47	4,784
19	S		30 Orient		L0-1	(0-1)		3,120
20	S	Dec	7 Preston North End	W4-1		(2-1)	Henry 14,30,79,Coleman 66 pen.	3,945
21	S		14 Halifax Town	W3-2		(1-1)	Coleman 38 pen.,56 pen.,Henry 62	4,516
22	Su		22 Hereford United	W1-0		(0-0)	Henry 88	7,364
23	S		28 Torquay United		W1-0	(0-0)	Gordon 55	1,710
24	W	Jan	1 Colchester United	W2-1		(2-0)	Cole 4,Wade 45	8,802
25	S		4 Tranmere Rovers		L1-3	(0-2)	Gordon 76 pen.	1,795
26	Su		12 Southend United	W2-1		(1-1)	Gordon 17 pen.,Ramsey 50	7,619
27	S		18 Wrexham		W1-0	(1-0)	Gordon 3 pen.	1,767
28	S	Feb	1 Northampton Town		W1-0	(0-0)	Henry 70	4,449
29	M		3 Stockport County		W2-0	(0-0)	Henry 80,Gordon 89	3,899
30	S		22 Preston North End		W3-0	(1-0)	Ramsey 9,Henry 62,Coyne 80	3,361
31	Tu	Mar	4 Exeter City		W3-0	(2-0)	Coyne 19,Gordon 37,Ramsey 83	2,291
32	S		8 Rochdale		W2-1	(0-0)	Gordon 78 pen.,Henry 80	1,989
33	S		15 Burnley	W3-1		(1-1)	Henry 36,Bamber 57,Gordon 85	7,212
34	Su		23 Port Vale	D0-0				10,122
35	Tu		25 Hartlepool United	W3-1		(2-1)	Wade 2,61,Smith o.g.25	6,172
36	F		28 Colchester United		D1-1	(0-0)	Bamber 62	2,997
37	M		31 Aldershot	W4-1		(3-1)	Bamber 20,54,Henry 25,Gordon 33	8,437
38	S	Apr	5 Cambridge United		D1-1	(1-1)	Gordon 42	3,128
39	Tu		8 Chester City	W4-2		(1-2)	Bamber 42,51,Wade 52,Barnard 67	12,630
40	S		12 Scunthorpe United	D1-1		(1-0)	Bamber 40	6,783
41	Tu		15 Peterborough United	W3-0		(1-0)	Collins o.g.14,Wade 79,Gordon 85	6,426
42	S		19 Mansfield Town		D1-1	(1-1)	Barnard 43	8,416
43	Tu		22 Aldershot		W4-2	(3-1)	Gordon 4,24,Henry 26,Cole 66	3,723
44	S		26 Orient	W4-1		(1-0)	Wade 13,Bamber 53,Kamara 57,Coyne 90	8,081
45	F	May	2 Halifax Town		W3-1	(1-0)	Henry 23,50,65	1,626
46	M		5 Crewe Alexandra	W1-0		(0-0)	Coyne 70	10,976

Average Home Attendance : **6,457**
Average Away Attendance : **3,168**

Football League Cup

				Home	Away	H-T	Goalscorers	Gate
1/1	Tu	Aug	20 Torquay United		W2-1	(1-1)	Hockaday 41,Moss 56	1,266
1/2	Tu	Sep	3 Torquay United	D2-2		(1-1)	Coyne 17,Pugh o.g.54	2,846
2/1	Tu		24 Sunderland		L2-3	(1-1)	Rowland 35,Coyne 74 pen.	14,207
2/2	Tu	Oct	8 Sunderland	W3-1 +		(0-1)	Rowland 58,Wade 90,99	9,111
3	Tu		29 Sheffield Wednesday	W1-0		(1-0)	Coyne 10	12,110
4	Tu	Nov	26 Ipswich Town		L1-6	(0-2)	Yallop o.g.70	12,083

\+ After Extra Time

F A Cup

				Home	Away	H-T	Goalscorers	Gate
1	Su	Nov	17 Bristol City	D0-0				10,468
1R	W		20 Bristol City		L2-4	(0-1)	Ramsey 46,Barnard 52	8,979

Allen K R	Bamber J D	Barnard L K	Calderwood C	Cole D A	Coleman N	Coyne P D	Endersby S A G	Evans A	Findlay J W	Gardiner M C	Gordon C K	Hall D R	Henry C A	Hockaday D	Kamara C	Key R M	Macari L	Moss D J	Ramsey C L	Roberts P	Rowland A A	Wade B A	
		3	6			8		4	1		9	*10		7			*12	11	2		5		1
		3	6	10				4	1		9		8	*7			*12	11	2		5		2
			6	3		8		4	1		9		7				10	11	2		5	s	3
			6	3		8		4	1		9	11	7				10	s	2		5		4
			6	5		8	1	4			9	11	3				10	s	2		7		5
			6	5		8	1	*4			9	11	3				10		2		7	*12	6
1			6	3		7		*12			9	*4	11				10	8	2		5		7
1			6	3		7		8				4	*11				10		2	9	5	*12	8
1			6	5	3	8		*12			9			*11			10		2	4	7		9
1		*12	6	5	3	8					9	*10		11					2	4		7	10
1		4	6	5	3	8					9			11					2	*12	*7	10	11
1		4	6	5	3	*8					9			11					2	*12	7	10	12
1		4	6	5	3	8		s			9			11					2	7		10	13
1		4	6	5	3	8					9			11					2	*7	*12	10	14
1		4	6	5	3	8					*9			11					2	7	*12	10	15
1		4	6	5	3	8		*7					*12	11					2		9	10	16
1		4	6	5	3	*8					9		11	7					2		*12	10	17
1	7	4	6	5	2						9		8	11					3		s	10	18
1	7	4	6	5	2						9		8	*11					3		*12	10	19
1	7	4	6	5	3						*9		8	11					2		*12	10	20
1	7	4	6	5	3						9		8	11	s				2			10	21
1	7	4	6	5							9		3	*11	*12				2	8		10	22
1	7	4	6	5							9		8	11	s				2	3		10	23
1	7	4	6	5							9		3	11	s				2	8		10	24
1	7	4	6	5							9		8	*12	*11				2	3		10	25
1	7	4	6	5		s					9		8	11					2	3		10	26
1	7	4	6	5							9		8	11	s				2	3		10	27
1		4	6	5		7					9		8	11	s				2	3		10	28
1		4	6	5		7				s	9		8	2	11					3		10	29
1		4	6	5		7				*12	9		*8	11	10				2	3			30
1		4	6			*7					9	*12	8	11	10				2	3		5	31
1		4	6	5		10					9		11	7	8				2	3		s	32
1	*7	4	6	5		10					9		8	3	11				2			*12	33
1	7	4	6	5		*10					9		8	*12	11				2	3			34
1	7	4	6	5							9		8	s	11				2	3		10	35
1	9	4	6	5							11		8	s	10				2	3		7	36
1	7	*4	6	5							9		8	*12	11				2	3		10	37
1	7	4	6	5							9		8	s	11				2	3		10	38
1	9	4	6	5		7						s	8	3	11				2			10	39
1	9	4	6	5		7					s		8	3	11				2			10	40
1	7	4	6	5		*12					*9		8	3	11					2		10	41
1	9	4	6	5		7					s		8	3	11					2		10	42
1			6	5		*7					9		8	3	11				4	2	*12	10	43
1	7	4	6	5		9					*12		*8	2	11				3			10	44
1	7	4	6	5		9					s	10	8	2	11				3				45
1	7	4	6	5		8						10	9	2	11				3		s		46
40	23	37	46	44	13	30	2	8	4	0	38	9	37	34	19	0	7	4	43	25	12	31	Apps
		1				1		2		1	1	1	1	3	1		2			2	6	3	Subs
	8	3	2	3	4	11					16		18	1	1				3			10	Goals

Opponents 2 goals

Allen K R	Bamber J D	Barnard L K	Calderwood C	Cole D A	Coleman N	Coyne P D	Endersby S A G	Evans A	Findlay J W	Gardiner M C	Gordon C K	Hall D R	Henry C A	Hockaday D	Kamara C	Key R M	Macari L	Moss D J	Ramsey C L	Roberts P	Rowland A A	Wade B A	
		3	6	s				4	1		9		8	7			10	11	2		5		1/1
			6	5		8		4	1		9	11	3				10	s	2		7		1/2
			6	5	3	8	1	*12			*9	11					10		2	4	7		2/1
		4	6	5	3	8	1				9	s		11					2		7	10	2/2
		4	6	5	3	8					9			7		1			2	s	11	10	3
	7	4	*6	5	2						9		8	11		1			3		*12	10	4
	1	4	6	5	4	4	2	2	2		6	2	3	4		2	3	1	6	1	5	3	Apps
								1													1		Subs
						3								1				1			2	2	Goals

Opponents 2 goals

Allen K R	Bamber J D	Barnard L K	Calderwood C	Cole D A	Coleman N	Coyne P D	Endersby S A G	Evans A	Findlay J W	Gardiner M C	Gordon C K	Hall D R	Henry C A	Hockaday D	Kamara C	Key R M	Macari L	Moss D J	Ramsey C L	Roberts P	Rowland A A	Wade B A	
1		4	6	5						*12	9	*8	2	11					3		7	10	1
1		4	6	5							9	*12	2	11					3	8	*7	10	1R
2		2	2	2						0	2	1	2	2					2	1	2	2	Apps
										1		1											Subs
		1																	1				Goals

KEN ALLEN

SEASON 1985/86

The Record Breakers

ALL THE FOLLOWING CLUB RECORDS WERE BROKEN

LONGEST UNBEATEN SEQUENCE IN LEAGUE GAMES : **21** (16 wins, 5 draws) - January 12 to May 5
MOST CONSECUTIVE UNBEATEN AWAY LEAGUE GAMES : **11** (8 wins, 3 draws) - January 18 to May 2
MOST LEAGUE WINS IN A SEASON : **32** (20 home, 12 away)
FEWEST LEAGUE DEFEATS IN A SEASON : **8** (1 home, 7 away)
CONSECUTIVE HOME LEAGUE WINS : **14** - August 26 to March 15
CONSECUTIVE AWAY LEAGUE WINS : **6** - January 18 to March 8
MOST HOME LEAGUE WINS IN A SEASON : **20**
MOST AWAY LEAGUE WINS IN A SEASON : **12**
LONGEST SEQUENCE WITHOUT A LEAGUE DRAW : **29** (23 wins, 6 defeats) - September 6 to March 15
LONGEST SEQUENCE WITHOUT CONCEDING A LEAGUE GOAL : **592** mins - January 12 to March 8
LONGEST SEQUENCE WITHOUT CONCEDING A LEAGUE GOAL AWAY : **516** mins - January 4 to March 8
FEWEST AWAY LEAGUE GOALS CONCEDED : **24**
MOST LEAGUE POINTS IN A SEASON : **102** (32 wins, 6 draws)
MOST HOME POINTS IN A SEASON : **62** (20 wins, 2 draws)
MOST AWAY POINTS IN A SEASON : **40** (12 wins, 4 draws)
LARGEST GOAL DIFFERENCE IN A FOOTBALL LEAGUE SEASON : **39** (82 for, 43 against)

(left to right) Andy Rowland, Nicky Coleman, Charlie Henry, Peter Coyne, Bryan Wade, Chris Ramsey, David Cole, Lou Macari, Dave Hockaday, Derek Hall, Colin Gordon and Leigh Barnard. (Inset) Colin Calderwood.

LOU MACARI
arrived in July 1984 and converted a struggling basement outfit into a record-breaking side within two years. Progress was slow at first and he was 'sacked' on Good Friday 1985, but the decision was reversed four days later. Town went almost half a season undefeated to run away with the Fourth Division title in 1986 - earning Lou the 'manager of the month' award four times. Further team changes were found necessary in mid-September, following a 6-2 home defeat, but Town recovered to finish in the inaugural season of the play-offs - and were promoted again. A season of consolidation in mid-table followed, but the play-offs were reached again in 1989 although this time Town were unsuccessful and in July Lou was appointed manager at West Ham.

COLIN CALDERWOOD
was just one of many signings by Lou Macari to earn the club a considerable profit. A transfer tribunal valued Colin at £27,500 - he was sold for £1.25 million ! Appointed captain on his arrival, in June 1985, Colin, then only 20, was 'ever-present' until February 1988 - a run of 162 games. Apart from an enforced five-month absence through injury in 1990/91, Colin was rarely missing from the Town line-up that went all the way to the Premiership in 1993. But before he could lead Town out in the top flight, Colin was signed by his former boss Ossie Ardiles at Tottenham - where he went on to play more than 150 games and gain 36 caps for Scotland.

CHARLIE HENRY
came through Town's youth ranks to sign pro forms on his 18th birthday in February 1980. He was a full-back in his early years, but gradually moved into an attacking midfield role. Having scored a maximum of three goals in a season - in 1981/82 - Charlie suddenly found himself Town's leading marksman in the Fourth Division championship year, grabbing 18 ! Brother-in-law of Paul Rideout, Charlie's son Leigh was also with Town between 2003 and 2006.

DAVE HOCKADAY
came to the County Ground on a free transfer from Blackpool in June 1983 as an orthodox winger. But, following Lou Macari's arrival a year later, Dave became a more versatile performer, slotting anywhere into a three or four-man midfield. And the transformation was complete when he moved to full-back towards the end of 1985/86. Dave remained in the side until Lou departed in 1989 and had made over 300 appearances by the time he joined Hull City in September 1990.

		P	W	D	L	F	A	W	D	L	F	A	Pts	G/D	Avge. Home Gate
1	SWINDON TOWN	46	20	2	1	52	19	12	4	7	30	24	102	+39	6,457
2	Chester City	46	15	5	3	44	16	8	10	5	39	34	84	+33	2,953
3	Mansfield Town	46	13	8	2	43	17	10	4	9	31	30	81	+27	3,764
4	Port Vale	46	13	9	1	42	11	8	7	8	25	26	79	+30	3,581
5	Orient	46	11	6	6	39	21	9	6	8	40	43	72	+15	2,629
6	Colchester United	46	12	6	5	51	22	7	7	9	37	41	70	+25	2,328
7	Hartlepool United	46	15	6	2	41	20	5	4	14	27	47	70	+1	2,593
8	Northampton Town	46	9	7	7	44	29	9	3	11	35	29	64	+21	2,385
9	Southend United	46	13	4	6	43	27	5	6	12	26	40	64	+2	2,785
10	Hereford United	46	15	6	2	55	30	3	4	16	19	43	64	+1	2,756
11	Stockport County	46	9	9	5	35	28	8	4	11	28	43	64	-8	2,667
12	Crewe Alexandra	46	10	6	7	35	26	8	3	12	19	35	63	-7	1,817
13	Wrexham	46	11	5	7	34	24	6	4	13	34	56	60	-12	1,820
14	Burnley	46	11	3	9	35	30	5	8	10	25	35	59	-5	3,204
15	Scunthorpe United	46	11	7	5	33	23	4	7	12	17	32	59	-5	1,778
16	Aldershot	46	12	5	6	45	25	5	2	16	21	49	58	-8	1,480
17	Peterborough United	46	9	11	3	31	19	4	6	13	21	45	56	-12	2,590
18	Rochdale	46	12	7	4	41	29	2	6	15	16	48	55	-20	1,790
19	Tranmere Rovers	46	9	1	13	46	41	6	8	9	28	32	54	+1	1,566
20	Halifax Town	46	10	8	5	35	27	4	4	15	25	44	54	-11	1,406
21	Exeter City	46	10	4	9	26	25	3	11	9	21	34	54	-12	1,972
22	Cambridge United	46	12	2	9	45	38	3	7	13	20	42	54	-15	2,089
23	Preston North End	46	7	4	12	32	41	4	6	13	22	48	43	-35	3,502
24	Torquay United	46	8	5	10	29	32	1	5	17	14	56	37	-45	1,240

Associate Members' Cup

					Home	Away	H-T	Goalscorers	Gate
1	Tu	Jan	21	Bristol Rovers		L1-2	(0-2)	Barnard 53	2,357
1	Tu	Mar	11	Hereford United	D1-1		(0-0)	Hockaday 90	3,692

	Allen K R	Barnard L K	Calderwood C	Cole D A	Coyne P D	Evans A	Gordon C K	Henry C A	Hockaday D	Kamara C	Moss D J	Ramsey C L	Roberts P	Rowland A A	Wade B A
1	1	4	*6	5	7	*13		8	11	9	s	2	3		10
1	1	*4	6	5	7		9	8	11	*12		2	3	13	10
Apps	2	2	2	2	2	0	1	2	2	1	0	2	2	0	2
Subs						1				1				1	
Goals		1							1						

SEASON 1995/96 *(continued from page 243)*

Football League Trophy

					Home	Away	H-T	Goalscorers	Gate
1	Tu	Oct	17	Torquay United		D1-1	(1-1)	Ling 4	1,135
2	W	Nov	8	Colchester United	W2-0		(0-0)	Thorne P 82,Finney 89	6,235
3	W		29	Hereford United	L0-1		(0-1)		6,660

	Allen P K	Allison W A	Bodin P J	Collins L	Culverhouse I B	Digby F C	Drysdale J	Finney S K	Gooden T M	Hooper D R	Horlock K	Ling M	McMahon S	Murray E J	O'Sullivan W StJ	Robinson M J	Seagraves M	Taylor S	Thorne G R	Thorne P L
1	4	10	3			1		9	11		*12	8		2	14	*7	(5)	6	(13)	
2		10				1	*3	9	4	2	11	(8)	*12		(13)	7		6	5	14
3		10		4	2	1	3	*12	11	(7)	(13)	*8				14	5	6		9
Apps	1	3	1	1	1	3	2	2	3	2	1	3	0	1	0	2	2	3	1	1
Subs								1			2		1		2	1			1	1
Goals								1				1								1

Associate Members' Cup (sponsored from 1984/85) and Football League Play-Offs

SEASON 1983/84

Rd	Day	Month	Date	Opponents	Home	Away	H-T	Goalscorers	Gate
1	W	Feb	22	Oxford United		W3-1	(0-0)	Quinn 49,67,Mayes 54	4,744
2	Tu	Mar	13	Walsall	W3-0		(2-0)	Gibson 14,Mayes 21,86 pen.	2,727
3	Tu		27	Millwall		L1-3	(0-1)	Nelson 60	2,112

	Baddeley K S	Bailie C J	Barnard L K	Batty P W	Coyne P D	Dempsey M J	Emmanuel J G	Endersby S A G	Gibson S J	Gordon C K	Graham M A	Gray N R	Henry C A	Hockaday D	Macari L	Mayes A K	Muir I J	Nelson G P	Quinn J M	Ramsey C L	Rowland A A
1	3	2	11	4				1	5		s	s		7		8		10	9		6
2	3	s		4			8	1	5		6		2	7		10		11	s		9
3	3	2	s	4			8	1	5		6			7		10		11	s		9
Apps	3	2	1	3			2	3	3		2	0	1	3		3		3	1		3
Subs																					
Goals									1							3		1	2		

SEASON 1984/85

Rd	Day	Month	Date	Opponents	Home	Away	H-T	Goalscorers	Gate
1	Tu	Jan	22	Torquay United		D1-1	(0-1)	Macari 79	1,002
1	Tu	Feb	5	Torquay United	D0-0 +				2,164

+ After Extra Time (L3-4 on penalties)

	Baddeley K S	Bailie C J	Barnard L K	Batty P W	Coyne P D	Dempsey M J	Emmanuel J G	Endersby S A G	Gibson S J	Gordon C K	Graham M A	Gray N R	Henry C A	Hockaday D	Macari L	Mayes A K	Muir I J	Nelson G P	Quinn J M	Ramsey C L	Rowland A A
1		3	4	s	8			1		9	7	5	s		10			11		2	6
1		3	*4	*12	7	10		1		9		5			13		8	11		2	6
Apps		2	2	0	2	1		2		2	1	2	0		1		1	2		2	2
Subs				1											1						
Goals															1						

SEASON 1986/87

Rd	Day	Month	Date	Opponents	Home	Away	H-T	Goalscorers	Gate
Pr	Tu	Dec	9	Orient	W3-0		(1-0)	White 42,Bamber 79,89	3,085
Pr	Tu	Jan	6	Brentford		L2-4	(2-1)	Coyne 23,White 35	1,110
1	W		28	AFC Bournemouth	D2-2 +		(0-0)	Coyne 107,119 pen.	4,522
QF	Tu	Feb	10	Hereford United	W4-2		(2-1)	Quinn 18,Coyne 33,White 56,Bamber 89	5,739
SF	Tu	Mar	10	Aldershot	L2-3		(1-0)	White 43,Quinn 48	8,450

+ After Extra Time (W4-2 on penalties)

	Bamber J D	Barnard L K	Berry S A	Calderwood C	Casserly D S	Coyne P D	Digby F C	Franklin P L	Gilligan J M	Henry C A	Hockaday D	Jones M	Kamara C	King P G	McLoughlin A F	Parkin T J	Quinn J M	Ramsey C L	Reynolds J A	Wade B A	White S J
Pr	7	11		6			1	5	s	2	3	4	8			s			10		9
Pr	7	11		6	*4	2	1				3	14 = Hughes N S				5	9	8		*12	10
1	7	11		6		4	1			9	*3		8			5	*12	2		14	10
QF	7	11		6		4	1				3		8		2	5	9		14	s	10
SF	7	3		6		4	1		s			11	8			5	9	2		s	10
Apps	5	5		5	1	4	5	1	0	2	4	2	4		1	4	3	3	1	0	5
Subs																	1		1	2	
Goals	3					4											2				4

Play-Offs

Rd	Day	Month	Date	Opponents	Home	Away	H-T	Goalscorers	Gate
SF	Th	May	14	Wigan Athletic		W3-2	(0-2)	Bamber 72,Quinn 80,Coyne 88	6,718
SF	Su		17	Wigan Athletic	D0-0				12,485
F	S		23	Gillingham		L0-1	(0-0)		16,775
F	W		27	Gillingham	W2-1		(0-1)	Coyne 61,Henry 80	14,382
Rp	F		29	Gillingham	*	W2-0	(1-0)	White 2,65	18,491

* Played at Selhurst Park

	Bamber J D	Barnard L K	Berry S A	Calderwood C	Casserly D S	Coyne P D	Digby F C	Franklin P L	Gilligan J M	Henry C A	Hockaday D	Jones M	Kamara C	King P G	McLoughlin A F	Parkin T J	Quinn J M	Ramsey C L	Reynolds J A	Wade B A	White S J
SF	7		11	6		10	1				2	4	8	3		5	9	s			
SF	10	4	11	6		7	1				2		8	3		5	9				s
F	10	4	11	6			1			*12	2	7	8	3		5	*9				
F	7	11	9	6		4	1			*12	2		*8	3		5					10
Rp	7	11	8	6		4	1			9	2	s		3		5					10
Apps	5	4	5	5		4	5			1	5	2	4	5		5	3	0			2
Subs										2											
Goals	1					2				1							1				2

SEASON 1986/87

Football League Third Division
Final League Position : 3rd
Manager : Lou Macari

Substitutes :
s denotes substitute **not** used
* player substituted by *12
_ player substituted by 14

				Home	Away	H-T	Goalscorers	Gate
1	S	Aug	23 Bolton Wanderers		W2-1	(1-0)	Coyne 35,69	5,684
2	Su		31 Notts County	L1-2		(0-1)	White 89	7,350
3	S	Sep	6 Newport County		D2-2	(1-0)	Wade 15,62	3,796
4	S		13 Chester City	D1-1		(0-0)	White 65	5,669
5	Tu		16 Blackpool	L2-6		(0-4)	Barnard 60,76	6,662
6	S		27 Rotherham United	W2-0		(0-0)	Gilligan 54,Bamber 55	4,055
7	Tu		30 Middlesbrough		L0-1	(0-1)		9,221
8	Su	Oct	5 Wigan Athletic	W3-1		(3-0)	Bamber 11,Jones 16,Kamara 28	6,450
9	S		11 Fulham		W2-0	(1-0)	Coyne 35 pen.,White 79	4,714
10	S		18 Chesterfield	W2-1		(2-0)	Bamber 11,Barnard 36	5,787
11	Tu		21 Port Vale		W4-3	(3-1)	Kamara 5,White 10,Jones 40,Gilligan 72	3,420
12	S		25 Darlington		D0-0			1,834
13	S	Nov	1 York City	W3-1		(1-1)	Jones 37,71 pen.,Gilligan 87	6,297
14	Tu		4 Bristol Rovers	L1-2		(0-2)	Gilligan 60	9,097
15	S		8 Mansfield Town		D0-0			3,911
16	S		22 Bury		W2-1	(2-0)	Gilligan 5,Wade 35	2,241
17	Tu		25 Walsall		L0-1	(0-0)		5,807
18	S		29 Carlisle United	W2-0		(0-0)	Franklin 62,Kamara 87	6,194
19	Su	Dec	14 Bristol City	L1-2		(1-0)	White 24	7,637
20	Su		21 Doncaster Rovers		D2-2	(0-1)	White 66,Henry 73	2,936
21	F		26 Brentford	W2-0		(1-0)	Jones 33 pen.,White 64	8,086
22	S		27 Gillingham		W3-1	(1-1)	Coyne 9,Jones 49 pen.,Elsey o.g.73	9,982
23	Th	Jan	1 AFC Bournemouth		L0-1	(0-0)		10,537
24	S		3 Bury	W1-0		(0-0)	Gardiner 63	6,675
25	Su		25 Newport County	W3-0		(1-0)	Quinn 18,Parkin 71,Bamber 84	6,620
26	S	Feb	7 Blackpool		D1-1	(1-1)	Bamber 15	4,839
27	S		21 Rotherham United		W2-1	(0-0)	Quinn 57,Bamber 85	3,004
28	S		28 Middlesbrough	W1-0		(0-0)	White 66	11,341
29	Tu	Mar	3 York City		W3-0	(2-0)	Quinn 6,29,Bamber 86	2,561
30	S		14 Chesterfield		W3-1	(1-0)	Quinn 8,White 64,66	2,767
31	Tu		17 Port Vale	W1-0		(1-0)	Ramsey 25	7,347
32	S		21 Fulham	W2-0		(0-0)	Quinn 59,82	7,426
33	Tu		24 Bolton Wanderers	W2-0		(1-0)	White 19,Jones 61 pen.	8,110
34	S		28 Wigan Athletic		L2-3	(1-2)	Bamber 4,Wade 47	4,424
35	W	Apr	1 Chester City		L0-2	(0-1)		2,626
36	F		3 Mansfield Town	W3-0		(1-0)	White 14,50,63	8,192
37	S		11 Bristol Rovers		* W4-3	(1-2)	White 30,Quinn 49,63,Bamber 62	8,259
38	S		18 AFC Bournemouth	D1-1		(0-1)	Hockaday 53	14,302
39	M		20 Brentford		D1-1	(0-1)	Wade 87	7,443
40	W		22 Darlington	W1-0		(0-0)	Hockaday 89	7,740
41	S		25 Doncaster Rovers	D1-1		(0-1)	Wade 75	8,218
42	Tu		28 Notts County		W3-2	(0-1)	Davis o.g.67,Calderwood 78,Wade 84	6,354
43	S	May	2 Carlisle United		W3-0	(1-0)	Parkin 45,Wade 75,Jones 88 pen.	2,086
44	M		4 Gillingham	D1-1		(0-1)	Jones 64 pen.	10,287
45	W		6 Walsall	D0-0				7,911
46	S		9 Bristol City		D1-1	(0-1)	Coyne 66	19,201

* Played at Ashton Gate

Average Home Attendance : **8,074**
Average Away Attendance : **5,550**

Football League Cup

				Home	Away	H-T	Goalscorers	Gate
1/1	Tu	Aug	26 Torquay United	W3-0		(1-0)	Bamber 31,61,Wade 55	4,749
1/2	Tu	Sep	2 Torquay United		W3-2	(2-0)	Bamber 18,52,Wade 20	1,100
2/1	Tu		23 Southampton		L0-3	(0-3)		10,826
2/2	W	Oct	8 Southampton	D0-0				9,453

F A Cup

				Home	Away	H-T	Goalscorers	Gate
1	S	Nov	15 Farnborough Town		** W4-0	(1-0)	Coyne 28,Wade 63,Gilligan 89,Baker o.g.90	5,960
2	S	Dec	6 Enfield	W3-0		(1-0)	Wade 34,Bamber 51,Jones 72	6,258
3	S	Jan	10 Fulham		W1-0	(1-0)	Bamber 38	7,077
4	Tu	Feb	3 Leeds United	L1-2		(1-1)	Bamber 12	14,031

** Played at the County Ground

For Play-Offs and Associate Members' Cup - see previous page <<   For Final League Table - see overleaf >>

Allen K R	Bamber J D	Barnard L K	Berry S A	Calderwood C	Cole D A	Coyne P D	Digby F C	Flowers T D	Franklin P L	Gardiner M C	Gilligan J M	Henry C A	Hockaday D	Jones M	Kamara C	King P G	Ling M	McLoughlin A F	Parkin T J	Quinn J M	Ramsey C L	Reynolds J A	Wade B A	White S J	
1	7	11		6	5	10						8	3		4		s				2		9		1
1	9	11		6	5	*7						8	3		4						2		10	*12	2
1	7			6	5	*10					*12	8	3		4		11	2					9		3
1	7			6	5							*8	3	11	4			10			2		9	*12	4
1		11		6	5						*12		3	7	4		*8				2		9	10	5
	10	11		6		s	1				8		3	7	4				5		2		9		6
	7	11		6		*12	1				*10		3	8	4				5		2		9		7
	10	11		6			1				8		3	7	4				5		2	s		9	8
	7	11		6		*9	1				10	5		8	4			3			2			*12	9
	7	11		6			1				*10	5	3	8	4			9			2			*12	10
	8	11		5			1				10	7	3	4	6						2		s	9	11
	8	11		5			1				*10		3	4	6			*12	7		2			9	12
	8	11		5			1				10		3	4	6				7		2		s	9	13
	8	11		5			1				*10	*12	3	4	6				7		2			9	14
	8	11		5			1				10		3	4	6				7		2		s	9	15
	9	11		5			1		8		10		3	4				7			2		6	s	16
	7	11		6		*10	1		5		*12		3	4				8			2		9		17
	9	11		5			1		8		10		3	4	7						*2	*12	6		18
	7	11		6			1		5		*10	2	3	4	8								*12	9	19
	11	3		6			1		5			2	8	4	7					10			s	9	20
	7	3		6			1			11			2	4	8				5	10			s	9	21
		3		6		7	1				*12		2	4	8			11	5	*10				9	22
		11		5		10	1			*12			3	4	7			*2	6	9				8	23
	*12	11		6		2	1			7			3	4	8				5	*9				10	24
	*12	11		6		7	1			*8			3		4				5	9	2		10		25
	*10	11		6		7	1						3	4	8	*12			5	9				2	26
	7	11		6		4	1						3		8	2			5	9			s	10	27
	7	11		6		4	1						2	s	8	3			5	9				10	28
	*7	11		6		4	1						3	*12	8	2			5	9				10	29
	7	11		6		4	1							3	8	2			5	9			s	10	30
	s	11		6		4	1							2	8	3			5	9	7			10	31
	*8	11		6		7	1							4		3			5	9	2		*12	10	32
	7	11		6				1					2	4	8	3			5	9			s	10	33
	7	11		6		5		1					*2	4	8	3					9		*12	10	34
	7	11		6		*12	1							4	8	3			5		2		9	*10	35
	*9	11		6			1							4	8	3			5	*12	2		7	10	36
	8	11		6		4	1						2	7		3			5	9			s	10	37
	7	11		6		*12	1						2	*4	8	3			5	9				10	38
	8			6		4	1						2	7	10	*3			5	9	11		*12		39
	10	11		6			1						3	7	8	2			5	9			*12	*4	40
	11			6		7	1						3	4	8	2			5	*9			*12	10	41
	*12	11		6		9	1						3	7	8	2			5				10	*4	42
	11	10		6		*7	1						3	4	8	2			5				9	*12	43
	7	11		6		10	1						2	*4	8	3			5				9	*12	44
	7	*11		6		10	1						2	4	8	3			5	*12			9		45
	7		11	6		10	1						2	4	8	3			5	*9	*12				46
5	39	41	1	46	5	25	39	2	5	3	13	9	40	39	42	20	2	8	32	20	24	0	17	29	Apps
	3					3				1	4	1		1		1		1		2	1	1	6	6	Subs
	9	3		1		5			1	1	5	1	2	9	3				2	9	1		8	15	Goals

Opponents 2 goals

Allen K R	Bamber J D	Barnard L K	Berry S A	Calderwood C	Cole D A	Coyne P D	Digby F C	Flowers T D	Franklin P L	Gardiner M C	Gilligan J M	Henry C A	Hockaday D	Jones M	Kamara C	King P G	Ling M	McLoughlin A F	Parkin T J	Quinn J M	Ramsey C L	Reynolds J A	Wade B A	White S J	
1	7			6		*10					14	8	3		4		11	*12	5		2		9		1/1
1	7			*6	4	10						8	3		4		14	11	*12		2		9		1/2
1		8		6		7					10	s	3	11	4			s	5		2		9		2/1
	10	11		6		9	1				8		3	7	4				*5		2		*12	14	2/2
3	3	2		4	1	4	1				2	2	4	2	4		1	1	3		4		3	0	Apps
											1						1	1	1				1	1	Subs
	4																						2		Goals

Allen K R	Bamber J D	Barnard L K	Berry S A	Calderwood C	Cole D A	Coyne P D	Digby F C	Flowers T D	Franklin P L	Gardiner M C	Gilligan J M	Henry C A	Hockaday D	Jones M	Kamara C	King P G	Ling M	McLoughlin A F	Parkin T J	Quinn J M	Ramsey C L	Reynolds J A	Wade B A	White S J	
		11		5		8	1			*12	10		3	4				14	7		2		*6	9	1
	7	11		6		s	1				10	5	3	4	2			8					9	s	2
	11	3		6		7	1				s		2	4				s	5	9	8			10	3
	10	*11		6		*12	1						3	7	8				5	9	2		4	14	4
	3	4		4		2	4			0	2	1	4	4	2			1	3	2	3		3	2	Apps
						1				1								1						1	Subs
	3					1					1			1									2		Goals

SEASON 1983/84

Div.4

	Team	P	W	D	L	F	A	W	D	L	F	A	Pts	G/D	Avge. Home Gate
1	York City	46	18	4	1	58	16	13	4	6	38	23	101	+57	5,008
2	Doncaster Rovers	46	15	6	2	46	22	9	7	7	36	32	85	+28	3,778
3	Reading	46	17	6	0	51	14	5	10	8	33	42	82	+28	4,471
4	Bristol City	46	18	3	2	51	17	6	7	10	19	27	82	+26	7,287
5	Aldershot	46	14	6	3	49	29	8	3	12	27	40	75	+7	2,483
6	Blackpool	46	15	4	4	47	19	6	5	12	23	33	72	+18	3,936
7	Peterborough United	46	15	5	3	52	16	3	9	11	20	32	68	+24	3,424
8	Colchester United	46	14	7	2	45	14	3	9	11	24	39	67	+16	2,220
9	Torquay United	46	13	7	3	32	18	5	6	12	27	46	67	-5	1,922
10	Tranmere Rovers	46	11	5	7	33	26	6	10	7	20	27	66	0	2,138
11	Hereford United	46	11	6	6	31	21	5	9	9	23	32	63	+1	2,984
12	Stockport County	46	12	5	6	34	25	5	6	12	26	39	62	-4	2,098
13	Chesterfield	46	10	11	2	34	24	5	4	14	25	37	60	-2	3,414
14	Darlington	46	13	4	6	31	19	4	4	15	18	31	59	-1	1,507
15	Bury	46	9	7	7	34	32	6	7	10	27	32	59	-3	2,104
16	Crewe Alexandra	46	10	8	5	35	27	6	3	14	21	40	59	-11	2,454
17	SWINDON TOWN	46	11	7	5	34	23	4	6	13	24	33	58	+2	3,156
18	Northampton Town	46	10	8	5	32	32	3	6	14	21	46	53	-25	2,343
19	Mansfield Town	46	9	7	7	44	27	4	6	13	22	43	52	-4	2,440
20	Wrexham	46	7	6	10	34	33	4	9	10	25	41	48	-15	2,083
21	Halifax Town	46	11	6	6	36	25	1	6	16	19	64	48	-34	1,412
22	Rochdale	46	8	9	6	35	31	3	4	16	17	49	46	-28	1,491
23	Hartlepool United	46	7	8	8	31	28	3	2	18	16	57	40	-38	1,505
24	Chester City	46	7	5	11	23	35	0	8	15	22	47	34	-37	1,764

SEASON 1984/85

Div.4

	Team	P	W	D	L	F	A	W	D	L	F	A	Pts	G/D	Avge. Home Gate
1	Chesterfield	46	16	6	1	40	13	10	7	6	24	22	91	+29	4,073
2	Blackpool	46	15	7	1	42	15	9	7	7	31	24	86	+34	4,907
3	Darlington	46	16	4	3	41	22	8	9	6	25	27	85	+17	3,738
4	Bury	46	15	6	2	46	20	9	6	8	30	30	84	+26	3,591
5	Hereford United	46	16	2	5	38	21	6	9	8	27	26	77	+18	3,889
6	Tranmere Rovers	46	17	1	5	50	21	7	2	14	33	45	75	+17	1,595
7	Colchester United	46	13	7	3	49	29	7	7	9	38	36	74	+22	2,081
8	SWINDON TOWN	46	16	4	3	42	21	5	5	13	20	37	72	+4	3,025
9	Scunthorpe United	46	14	6	3	61	33	5	8	10	22	29	71	+21	2,068
10	Crewe Alexandra	46	10	7	6	32	28	8	5	10	33	41	66	-4	2,271
11	Peterborough United	46	11	7	5	29	21	5	7	11	25	32	62	+1	3,157
12	Port Vale	46	11	8	4	39	24	3	10	10	22	35	60	+2	3,267
13	Aldershot	46	11	6	6	33	20	6	2	15	23	43	59	-7	2,010
14	Mansfield Town	46	10	8	5	25	15	3	10	10	16	23	57	+3	2,314
15	Wrexham	46	10	6	7	39	27	5	3	15	28	43	54	-3	1,619
16	Chester City	46	11	3	9	35	30	4	6	13	25	42	54	-12	1,940
17	Rochdale	46	8	7	8	33	30	5	7	11	22	39	53	-14	1,434
18	Exeter City	46	9	7	7	30	27	4	7	12	27	52	53	-22	2,352
19	Hartlepool United	46	10	6	7	34	29	4	4	15	20	38	52	-13	2,348
20	Southend United	46	8	8	7	30	34	5	3	15	28	49	50	-25	2,103
21	Halifax Town	46	9	3	11	26	32	6	2	15	16	37	50	-27	1,378
22	Stockport County	46	11	5	7	40	26	2	3	18	18	53	47	-21	1,895
23	Northampton Town	46	10	1	12	32	32	4	4	15	21	42	47	-21	1,824
24	Torquay United	46	5	11	7	18	24	4	3	16	20	39	41	-25	1,386

SEASON 1986/87

Div.3

	Team	P	W	D	L	F	A	W	D	L	F	A	Pts	G/D	Avge. Home Gate
1	AFC Bournemouth	46	19	3	1	44	14	10	7	6	32	26	97	+36	6,611
2	Middlesbrough	46	16	5	2	38	11	12	5	6	29	19	94	+37	10,174
3	SWINDON TOWN *	46	14	5	4	37	19	11	7	5	40	28	87	+30	7,715
4	Wigan Athletic	46	15	5	3	47	26	10	5	8	36	34	85	+23	3,398
5	Gillingham	46	16	5	2	42	14	7	4	12	23	34	78	+17	4,971
6	Bristol City	46	14	6	3	42	15	7	8	8	21	21	77	+27	9,441
7	Notts County	46	14	6	3	52	24	7	7	9	25	32	76	+21	4,729
8	Walsall	46	16	4	3	50	27	6	5	12	30	40	75	+13	5,313
9	Blackpool	46	11	7	5	35	20	5	9	9	39	39	64	+15	3,866
10	Mansfield Town	46	9	9	5	30	23	6	7	10	22	32	61	-3	3,216
11	Brentford	46	9	7	7	39	32	6	8	9	25	34	60	-2	3,918
12	Port Vale	46	8	6	9	43	36	7	6	10	33	34	57	+6	3,312
13	Doncaster Rovers	46	11	8	4	32	19	3	7	13	24	43	57	-6	2,408
14	Rotherham United	46	10	6	7	29	23	5	6	12	19	34	57	-9	2,983
15	Chester City	46	7	9	7	32	28	6	8	9	29	31	56	+2	2,732
16	Bury	46	9	7	7	30	26	5	6	12	24	34	55	-6	2,502
17	Chesterfield	46	11	5	7	36	33	2	10	11	20	36	54	-13	2,576
18	Fulham	46	8	8	7	35	41	4	9	10	24	36	53	-18	4,085
19	Bristol Rovers	46	7	8	8	26	29	6	4	13	23	46	51	-26	3,246
20	York City	46	11	8	4	34	29	1	5	17	21	50	49	-24	3,432
21	Bolton Wanderers	46	8	5	10	29	26	2	10	11	17	32	45	-12	4,851
22	Carlisle United	46	7	5	11	26	35	3	3	17	13	43	38	-39	2,644
23	Darlington	46	6	10	7	25	28	1	6	16	20	49	37	-32	2,037
24	Newport County	46	4	9	10	26	34	4	4	15	23	52	37	-37	2,063

* Promoted via Play-offs

SEASON 1987/88

Div.2

	P	W	D	L	F	A	W	D	L	F	A	Pts	G/D	Avge. Home Gate
1 Millwall	44	15	3	4	45	23	10	4	8	27	29	82	+20	8,417
2 Aston Villa	44	9	7	6	31	21	13	5	4	37	20	78	+27	18,342
3 Middlesbrough *	44	15	4	3	44	16	7	8	7	19	20	78	+27	14,509
4 Bradford City	44	14	3	5	49	26	8	8	6	25	28	77	+20	12,906
5 Blackburn Rovers	44	12	8	2	38	22	9	6	7	30	30	77	+16	9,503
6 Crystal Palace	44	16	3	3	50	21	6	6	10	36	38	75	+27	9,746
7 Leeds United	44	14	4	4	37	18	5	8	9	24	33	69	+10	20,272
8 Ipswich Town	44	14	3	5	38	17	5	6	11	23	35	66	+9	11,807
9 Manchester City	44	11	4	7	50	28	8	4	10	30	32	65	+20	19,472
10 Oldham Athletic	44	13	4	5	43	27	5	7	10	29	37	65	+8	6,907
11 Stoke City	44	12	6	4	34	22	5	5	12	16	35	62	-7	9,607
12 SWINDON TOWN	44	10	7	5	43	25	6	4	12	30	35	59	+13	9,542
13 Leicester City	44	12	5	5	35	20	4	6	12	27	41	59	+1	10,157
14 Barnsley	44	11	4	7	42	32	4	8	10	19	30	57	-1	7,683
15 Hull City	44	10	8	4	32	22	4	7	11	22	38	57	-6	8,135
16 Plymouth Argyle	44	12	4	6	44	26	4	4	14	21	41	56	-2	10,280
17 AFC Bournemouth	44	7	7	8	36	30	6	3	13	20	38	49	-12	7,873
18 Shrewsbury Town	44	7	8	7	23	22	4	8	10	19	32	49	-12	4,945
19 Birmingham City	44	7	9	6	20	24	4	6	12	21	42	48	-25	8,579
20 West Bromwich Albion	44	8	7	7	29	26	4	4	14	21	43	47	-19	10,126
21 Sheffield United	44	8	6	8	27	28	5	1	16	18	46	46	-29	10,207
22 Reading	44	5	7	10	20	25	5	5	12	24	45	42	-26	6,945
23 Huddersfield Town	44	4	6	12	20	38	2	4	16	21	62	28	-59	6,841

SEASON 1988/89

Div.2

	P	W	D	L	F	A	W	D	L	F	A	Pts	G/D	Avge. Home Gate
1 Chelsea	46	15	6	2	50	25	14	6	3	46	25	99	+46	15,731
2 Manchester City	46	12	8	3	48	28	11	5	7	29	25	82	+24	23,500
3 Crystal Palace *	46	15	6	2	42	17	8	6	9	29	32	81	+22	10,655
4 Watford	46	14	5	4	41	18	8	7	8	33	30	78	+26	12,292
5 Blackburn Rovers	46	16	4	3	50	22	6	7	10	24	37	77	+15	8,891
6 SWINDON TOWN	46	13	8	2	35	15	7	8	8	33	38	76	+15	8,670
7 Barnsley	46	12	8	3	37	21	8	6	9	29	37	74	+8	7,215
8 Ipswich Town	46	13	3	7	42	23	9	4	10	29	38	73	+10	12,666
9 West Bromwich Albion	46	13	7	3	43	18	5	11	7	22	23	72	+24	12,757
10 Leeds United	46	12	6	5	34	20	5	10	8	25	30	67	+9	21,811
11 Sunderland	46	12	8	3	40	23	4	7	12	20	37	63	0	14,878
12 AFC Bournemouth	46	13	3	7	32	20	5	5	13	21	42	62	-9	8,087
13 Stoke City	46	10	9	4	33	25	5	5	13	24	47	59	-15	9,817
14 Bradford City	46	8	11	4	29	22	5	6	12	23	37	56	-7	10,524
15 Leicester City	46	11	6	6	31	20	2	10	11	25	43	55	-7	10,694
16 Oldham Athletic	46	9	10	4	49	32	2	11	10	26	40	54	+3	7,204
17 Oxford United	46	11	6	6	40	34	3	6	14	22	36	54	-8	6,352
18 Plymouth Argyle	46	11	4	8	35	22	3	8	12	20	44	54	-11	8,628
19 Brighton & Hove Albion	46	11	5	7	36	24	3	4	16	21	42	51	-9	9,048
20 Portsmouth	46	10	6	7	33	21	3	6	14	20	41	51	-9	10,201
21 Hull City	46	7	9	7	31	25	4	5	14	21	43	47	-16	6,666
22 Shrewsbury Town	46	4	11	8	25	31	4	7	12	15	36	42	-27	4,706
23 Birmingham City	46	6	4	13	21	33	2	7	14	10	43	35	-45	6,265
24 Walsall	46	3	10	10	27	42	2	6	15	14	38	31	-39	6,108

SEASON 1989/90

Div.2

	P	W	D	L	F	A	W	D	L	F	A	Pts	G/D	Avge. Home Gate
1 Leeds United	46	16	6	1	46	18	8	7	8	33	34	85	+27	28,568
2 Sheffield United	46	14	5	4	43	27	10	8	5	35	31	85	+20	16,989
3 Newcastle United	46	17	4	2	51	26	5	10	8	29	29	80	+25	21,590
4 SWINDON TOWN	46	12	6	5	49	29	8	8	7	30	30	74	+20	9,444
5 Blackburn Rovers	46	10	9	4	43	30	9	8	6	31	29	74	+15	9,624
6 Sunderland *	46	10	8	5	41	32	10	6	7	29	32	74	+6	17,987
7 West Ham United	46	14	5	4	50	22	6	7	10	30	35	72	+23	20,311
8 Oldham Athletic	46	15	7	1	50	23	4	7	12	20	34	71	+13	9,727
9 Ipswich Town	46	13	7	3	38	22	6	5	12	29	44	69	+1	12,913
10 Wolverhampton Wanderers	46	12	5	6	37	20	6	8	9	30	40	67	+7	17,045
11 Port Vale	46	11	9	3	37	20	4	7	12	25	37	61	+5	8,978
12 Portsmouth	46	9	8	6	40	34	6	8	9	22	31	61	-3	8,959
13 Leicester City	46	10	8	5	34	29	5	6	12	33	50	59	-12	11,716
14 Hull City	46	7	8	8	27	31	7	8	8	31	34	58	-7	6,518
15 Watford	46	11	6	6	41	28	3	9	11	17	32	57	-2	10,353
16 Plymouth Argyle	46	9	8	6	30	23	5	5	13	28	40	55	-5	8,749
17 Oxford United	46	8	7	8	35	31	7	2	14	22	35	54	-9	5,820
18 Brighton & Hove Albion	46	10	6	7	28	27	5	3	15	28	45	54	-16	8,679
19 Barnsley	46	7	9	7	22	23	6	6	11	27	48	54	-22	9,033
20 West Bromwich Albion	46	6	8	9	35	37	6	7	10	32	34	51	-4	11,308
21 Middlesbrough	46	10	3	10	33	29	3	8	12	19	34	50	-11	16,971
22 AFC Bournemouth	46	8	6	9	30	31	4	6	13	27	45	48	-19	7,454
23 Bradford City	46	9	6	8	26	24	0	8	15	18	44	41	-24	8,777
24 Stoke City	46	4	11	8	20	24	2	8	13	15	39	37	-28	12,449

* Promoted via Play-offs

SEASON 1987/88

Football League Second Division
Final League Position : 12th
Manager : Lou Macari

Substitutes :
s denotes substitute **not** used
* player substituted by *12
_ player substituted by 14

No.	Day	Month	Date	Opponents	Home	Away	H-T	Goalscorers	Gate
1	S	Aug	15	Bradford City		L0-2	(0-0)		10,553
2	S		22	Sheffield United	W2-0		(2-0)	Calderwood 22,Quinn 44	8,637
3	S		29	West Bromwich Albion		W2-1	(1-1)	Kelly 42,Quinn 68	7,503
4	M		31	Hull City	D0-0				9,600
5	S	Sep	5	Middlesbrough		W3-2	(2-1)	Bamber 27,Quinn 37,Barnard 60	9,342
6	S		12	Birmingham City	L0-2		(0-0)		9,128
7	Tu		15	Barnsley		W1-0	(0-0)	Bamber 65	7,773
8	S		19	Ipswich Town		L2-3	(1-3)	Barnard 26,Quinn 62	10,460
9	S		26	Reading	W4-0		(2-0)	Parkin 23,Kamara 33,67,Quinn 85 pen.	10,073
10	Tu		29	Shrewsbury Town	D1-1		(0-0)	Quinn 68	8,261
11	S	Oct	3	Millwall		D2-2	(0-1)	Foley 71,Quinn 83 pen.	7,018
12	S		10	Oldham Athletic	W2-0		(0-0)	Bamber 76,White 78	8,160
13	Tu		20	Stoke City	W3-0		(1-0)	Quinn 1,White 60,71	9,160
14	S		24	Crystal Palace		L1-2	(1-1)	White 35	9,077
15	S		31	Manchester City	L3-4		(1-2)	Barnes 45,Bamber 52,Foley 74	11,536
16	S	Nov	7	Leicester City		L2-3	(1-0)	Barnes 9,Quinn 67	8,346
17	S		14	Plymouth Argyle	D1-1		(1-1)	Barnes 44	9,616
18	S		21	Leeds United		L2-4	(1-3)	Barnes 41,78	15,457
19	S		28	AFC Bournemouth	W4-2		(2-1)	Barnes 8,White 9,82,Quinn 54	7,934
20	Tu	Dec	1	Huddersfield Town	W4-1		(2-0)	Barnes 30,Quinn 37,Foley 73,78	6,963
21	S		5	Aston Villa		L1-2	(0-0)	Quinn 57 pen.	16,127
22	Su		20	Sheffield United		L0-1	(0-0)		7,248
23	S		26	Reading		W1-0	(0-0)	Quinn 76	8,939
24	M		28	Ipswich Town	W4-2		(2-0)	Cranson o.g.33,Quinn 43,King 76,Bamber 86	12,429
25	F	Jan	1	West Bromwich Albion	W2-0		(0-0)	White 84,89	12,155
26	S		2	Birmingham City		D1-1	(0-0)	Barnes 75	7,829
27	S	Feb	6	Middlesbrough	D1-1		(1-1)	Bamber 12	9,941
28	S		13	Huddersfield Town		W3-0	(1-0)	O'Regan 30,Bamber 55,Shearer o.g.65	5,458
29	S		20	Shrewsbury Town		L1-2	(1-2)	Bamber 10	5,649
30	S		27	Millwall	L0-1		(0-1)		9,570
31	S	Mar	12	Oldham Athletic		L3-4	(1-0)	Quinn 26,Bodin 66,Henry 90	5,193
32	Tu		15	Barnsley	W3-0		(1-0)	Quinn 33 pen.,White 61,66	7,558
33	S		19	Manchester City		D1-1	(0-0)	Bamber 75	17,022
34	Su		27	Crystal Palace	D2-2		(0-0)	White 57,Parkin 90	12,915
35	W		30	Bradford City	D2-2		(0-0)	Wegerle 49,Bamber 52	8,203
36	S	Apr	2	Leicester City	W3-2		(1-1)	Quinn 8,77,Barnes 69	9,450
37	M		4	Plymouth Argyle		L0-1	(0-1)		13,299
38	S		9	Blackburn Rovers	L1-2		(1-0)	Barnes 30	9,373
39	Tu		12	Hull City		W4-1	(2-1)	Quinn 42 pen.,71,Bamber 45,61	4,583
40	S		23	Stoke City		L0-1	(0-1)		6,293
41	M		25	Blackburn Rovers		D0-0			13,536
42	S		30	Leeds United	L1-2		(1-2)	Quinn 41	8,299
43	M	May	2	AFC Bournemouth		L0-2	(0-2)		9,212
44	S		7	Aston Villa	D0-0				10,959

Average Home Attendance : **9,542**
Average Away Attendance : **9,360**

Football League Cup

Rd	Day	Month	Date	Opponents	Home	Away	H-T	Goalscorers	Gate
1/1	Tu	Aug	18	Bristol City	W3-0		(0-0)	Quinn 65,67,85	6,807
1/2	Tu		25	Bristol City		L2-3	(1-3)	Bamber 25,Berry 54 pen.	7,013
2/1	Tu	Sep	22	Portsmouth	W3-1		(2-0)	Quinn 2,11,83 pen.	9,878
2/2	W	Oct	7	Portsmouth		W3-1	(1-1)	Bamber 43,84,White 90	8,727
3	W		28	Watford	D1-1		(1-1)	Quinn 24 pen.	13,833
3R	Tu	Nov	3	Watford		L2-4	(1-1)	Quinn 34,Foley 73	13,378

F A Cup

Rd	Day	Month	Date	Opponents	Home	Away	H-T	Goalscorers	Gate
3	S	Jan	9	Norwich City	D0-0				12,807
3R	W		13	Norwich City		W2-0	(0-0)	Bamber 67,87	12,501
4	S		30	Newcastle United		L0-5	(0-2)		28,699

For Final League Table - see page 219 For Play-Offs and Full Members' Cup - see page 226

Bamber J D	Barnard L K	Barnes D O	Berry S A	Bodin P J	Calderwood C	Casserly D S	Coyne P D	Crichton P A	Digby F C	Flowers T D	Foley S	Gittens J A	Hammond N D	Henry C A	Hockaday D	Kamara C	Kelly J	King P G	McLoughlin A F	O'Regan K M	Parkin T J	Quinn J M	Wade B A	Wegerle R C	White S J	
7	s				6		4		1			8		14	2	11	10	3			5	9				1
7	11		10		6				1		s			s		4	8	3		2	5	9				2
7	11		10		6		14		1		s				2	4	8	3			5	9				3
7	11		8		6		14		1		10			s	2	4		3			5	9				4
7	11				6				1		10			s	2	4		3		8	5	9			s	5
7	11				6		*12		1		10				2	4	14	*3		8	5	9				6
7	11				6				1		*10			14	2	4	*12	3		8	5	9				7
7	11				6				1		10				2	4	14	3		*8	5	9			s	8
7	11				6				1		10	14		*8	2	4		3			5	9			*12	9
7	11				6				1		10	14		8	2	4		3			5	9			s	10
7	11				6				1		10			9	2	4		3		8	5	14			s	11
7	11				6				1		10			s	2	4	*12	*3			5	9			8	12
7	*12	11			6				1		10			14	2	4		*3			5	9			8	13
7	10	11			6		s		1			9		14	2			3		4	5				8	14
7	4	11			6						10		1	14	2			3		*12	5	*9			8	15
7	4	11			6						10		1		2	8		3		s	5	9			s	16
7	8	11			6					1	*10				2	4		3		*12	5	9			14	17
7	8	11			6		4			1		5		*12	2			*3		10		9			s	18
8		7			6		s			1	10	5		s	2			3		4		9			11	19
7		11			6					1	10	5			2	4		3		s		9	s		8	20
8		7			6					1	*10	5			2	4		3			*12	9	14		11	21
8		7			6						10	5	1		2	4		3			s	9	14		11	22
8		7			6		s	1			10	5			2	4		3			11	9			s	23
7		11			6			1			10	5		s	2	4		3			8	9			s	24
7		11			6			1			10	8		14	2	4		3			5	*9			*12	25
*8		7			6			1			10	5			2	4		3		14	11	9			*12	26
7		14			6				1		s	8			2	4		3		11	5	9			10	27
7		10			6				1		s	8			2	4		3		11	5	9			s	28
7					6				1		10	8		s	2	4		*3		11	5	9			*12	29
7		11							1		4	6		*12	2			3		8	5	*9	s		10	30
		8		11					1			7		14	2			3	4	9	5	10	*12		*6	31
		7		11		s			1					6	2			3	8	4	5	9	s		10	32
7		*12		*11					1		8			4	2			3	s	9	5	10			6	33
8				s					1		11	6			2			3	s	4	5	9		7	10	34
8				s					1		10	6		14	2			3	11	4	5	9		7		35
7		8		s					1		10	6			2			3		4	5	9		11	s	36
7		11		s					1		8	4			2			3		9	5	10		*6	*12	37
		7		s					1		10	6			2			3	*12	*4	5	9		11	8	38
7		11		14	*12						10	8	1		2			3	4		*5	9		6		39
7		8							1		10	6			2			3	4	s	5	9		11	14	40
9		7		s	4				1		10	6			2			3	11	s	5				8	41
7		11		14	6				1		10	8			2			3	4		5	9			s	42
7		8			4				1		10	6			2			3	s	11	5	9			14	43
7		s			6				1		10	8			2			3	s	4	5	9			11	44
41	16	26	3	3	33	0	2	4	31	5	35	27	4	5	43	25	3	44	7	23	39	41	0	7	17	Apps
	1	2		2	1		3					2		10			4		1	3	1	1	3		8	Subs
12	2	10		1	1						4			1		2	1	1		1	2	21		1	11	Goals

Opponents 2 goals

Bamber J D	Barnard L K	Barnes D O	Berry S A	Bodin P J	Calderwood C	Casserly D S	Coyne P D	Crichton P A	Digby F C	Flowers T D	Foley S	Gittens J A	Hammond N D	Henry C A	Hockaday D	Kamara C	Kelly J	King P G	McLoughlin A F	O'Regan K M	Parkin T J	Quinn J M	Wade B A	Wegerle R C	White S J	
10	11				6		s		1			*8		14		4	7	3		2	5	9				1/1
10	11		8		6		*7		1		s			*12		4		3		2	5	9				1/2
7	11				6				1		10			s	2	4		3		14	5	9			8	2/1
7	11				6				1		10			14	2	4		3		8	5	*9			*12	2/2
7	11				6						10	14	1	*12	*2			3		4	5	9			8	3
7	11				6						10		1		2	8	s	3		*4	5	9			*12	3R
6	6		1		6		1		4		4	1	2	0	4	5	1	6		5	6	6			2	Apps
												1		4						1					2	Subs
3			1								1											8			1	Goals

Bamber J D	Barnard L K	Barnes D O	Berry S A	Bodin P J	Calderwood C	Casserly D S	Coyne P D	Crichton P A	Digby F C	Flowers T D	Foley S	Gittens J A	Hammond N D	Henry C A	Hockaday D	Kamara C	Kelly J	King P G	McLoughlin A F	O'Regan K M	Parkin T J	Quinn J M	Wade B A	Wegerle R C	White S J	
7					6						10	8	1		2	4		3		s	5	9	14		11	3
7		10			6							8	1		2	4		3		11	5	9	s		s	3R
7					6						11	8	1	s	2	4		3		10	5	9			s	4
3		1			3						2	3	3		3	3		3		2	3	3	0		1	Apps
																							1			Subs
2																										Goals

SEASON 1988/89

Football League Second Division
Final League Position : 6th
Manager : Lou Macari

Substitutes :
s denotes substitute **not** used
* player substituted by *12
_ player substituted by 14

No	Day	Month	Date	Opponent	Home	Away	H-T	Goalscorers	Gate
1	M	Aug	29	Barnsley		D1-1	(0-1)	White 86	6,034
2	S	Sep	3	West Bromwich Albion		L1-3	(1-3)	White 7	7,518
3	Su		11	Portsmouth	D1-1		(0-1)	Foley 86	11,443
4	S		17	Blackburn Rovers		D0-0			7,622
5	Tu		20	AFC Bournemouth	W3-1		(2-1)	Calderwood 22,MacLaren 37 pen.,Barnes 89	8,055
6	S		24	Brighton and Hove Albion	W3-0		(1-0)	Barnes 32,White 46,Calderwood 57	6,585
7	S	Oct	1	Watford		W3-2	(2-1)	Shearer 15,Barnes 37,Jones 71	11,657
8	W		5	Oxford United		D1-1	(0-0)	Parkin 75	9,387
9	Su		9	Chelsea	D1-1		(0-0)	Shearer 85	11,927
10	Su		16	Leeds United	D0-0				9,234
11	S		22	Sunderland		L0-4	(0-2)		13,520
12	W		26	Leicester City		D3-3	(3-0)	King 5,White 22,Henry 26	9,754
13	S		29	Birmingham City	W2-1		(1-0)	White 23,68	6,937
14	S	Nov	5	Hull City		L0-1	(0-1)		5,192
15	S		12	Ipswich Town	L2-3		(1-0)	Gittens 25,Henry 59	7,246
16	S		19	Stoke City		L1-2	(0-0)	Jones 65	9,339
17	S		26	Walsall	W1-0		(0-0)	Foley 59	5,328
18	S	Dec	3	Shrewsbury Town		W1-0	(1-0)	Geddis 41	3,625
19	S		10	Oldham Athletic	D2-2		(1-0)	Henry 29,Marshall o.g.84	5,540
20	S		17	Bradford City		D2-2	(2-1)	Geddis 14,Shearer 29	9,462
21	M		26	Plymouth Argyle	W1-0		(1-0)	Shearer 6	7,883
22	S		31	Manchester City	L1-2		(0-1)	White 57	10,776
23	M	Jan	2	Portsmouth		W2-0	(1-0)	Geddis 43,Shearer 67	11,681
24	S		14	Barnsley	D0-0				10,201
25	S		21	Crystal Palace		L1-2	(1-0)	Foley 39	8,109
26	Su	Feb	5	Oxford United	W3-0		(1-0)	McLoughlin 44,MacLaren 59 pen.,Calderwood 90	10,227
27	S		11	Chelsea		L2-3	(2-3)	McLaughlin o.g.13,Bodin 40	17,829
28	S		18	Sunderland	W4-1		(3-1)	Shearer 22,40,McLoughlin 39,White 54	7,432
29	S		25	Leeds United		D0-0			22,656
30	Tu		28	Leicester City	W2-1		(0-1)	Shearer 59,Jones 81 pen.	7,456
31	S	Mar	4	Ipswich Town		W2-1	(0-0)	White 72,89	12,025
32	S		11	Hull City	W1-0		(1-0)	Shearer 24	7,090
33	S		18	AFC Bournemouth		W3-2	(2-0)	Foley 28,45,Jones 59	9,752
34	S		25	West Bromwich Albion	D0-0				12,240
35	M		27	Plymouth Argyle		L1-4	(0-2)	Jones 67	8,487
36	S	Apr	1	Blackburn Rovers	D1-1		(0-0)	Foley 62	8,220
37	Tu		4	Bradford City	W1-0		(1-0)	Shearer 9	6,476
38	S		8	Manchester City		L1-2	(1-1)	Shearer 35	22,663
39	S		15	Watford	D1-1		(1-0)	White 13	9,828
40	Tu		18	Birmingham City		W2-1	(2-0)	MacLaren 25,35 pen.	4,026
41	S		22	Brighton and Hove Albion		W2-0	(0-0)	Foley 61,77	9,510
42	Tu		25	Crystal Palace	W1-0		(1-0)	White 36	11,045
43	S		29	Walsall		D2-2	(1-1)	Shearer 6,Calderwood 51	5,288
44	M	May	1	Shrewsbury Town	W1-0		(1-0)	King 19	8,698
45	S		6	Stoke City	W3-0		(0-0)	Shearer 61,88,Jones 86	9,543
46	S		13	Oldham Athletic		D2-2	(2-1)	McLoughlin 14,White 29	5,679

Average Home Attendance : **8,670**
Average Away Attendance : **10,035**

Football League Cup

Rd	Day	Month	Date	Opponent	Home	Away	H-T	Goalscorers	Gate
2/1	Tu	Sep	27	Crystal Palace	L1-2		(1-1)	Shearer 10	7,084
2/2	W	Oct	12	Crystal Palace		L0-2	(0-1)		6,015

F A Cup

Rd	Day	Month	Date	Opponent	Home	Away	H-T	Goalscorers	Gate
3	S	Jan	7	Portsmouth		D1-1	(0-1)	Foley 88	10,582
3R	Tu		10	Portsmouth	W2-0		(0-0)	Foley 81,Shearer 87	11,457
4	S		28	West Ham United	D0-0				18,677
4R	Tu	Feb	1	West Ham United		L0-1	(0-0)		24,723

For Final League Table - see page 219 For Play-Offs and Full Members' Cup - see page 226

Barnard L K	Barnes D O	Bodin P J	Calderwood C	Cornwell J A	Coyne P D	Digby F C	Foley S	Geddis D	Gittens J A	Henry C A	Hockaday D	Jones T	King P G	MacLaren R	McLoughlin A F	Parkin T J	Shearer D N	Simpson F	Viveash A L	White S J	
	11	s	8			1			6	*12	2		3	4	*7	5	9			10	**1**
	11	7	8		14	1			6	*12	2		3	4		5	*9			10	**2**
s	11	*8	5			1	7		6	*12	2		3	4			9			10	**3**
	11	s	8			1	7		6	s	2		3	4		5	9			10	**4**
	11	14	5			1	7		6	*12	2		3	4		8	9			*10	**5**
	11		8			1	7		6	s	2		3	4	s	5	9			10	**6**
	11		8			1	7		6	14	2	4	3	s		5	9			10	**7**
	11		8			1	7		6	s	2	4	3	s		5	9			10	**8**
14	11		8			1	7		6	s	2	4	3		5		9			10	**9**
	11		8			1	7		6	14	2	4	3	s		5	9			10	**10**
9	11		8			1	7		6	14	2	4	3	s		5				10	**11**
	11		8			1	7		6	9	2	4	3	s	14	5				10	**12**
	11		8			1	7	*12	6	*9	2	4	3		s	5				10	**13**
	11		8			1	7		6	9	2	4	3	s		5	14			10	**14**
	11		s			1	7		6	9	2	4	3	8		5	s			10	**15**
	11		8			1	7	s	6	9	2	4	3			5	14			10	**16**
	s		6			1	7	11		9	2	4	3	10		5	s			8	**17**
			6			1	7	11		*9	2	4	3	10		5	*12	14		8	**18**
	10		6			1	7	11		9	2	4	3	8		5	s			14	**19**
			6			1	7	11	s	9	2	4	3	10	s	5	8				**20**
			s			1	7	11	6	9	2	4	3	10		5	8			s	**21**
	s			*12		1	7		*6	9	2	4	3	10		5	11			8	**22**
			6	11		1	7	9		14	2	4	3	10		5	*8			*12	**23**
s		3	5	6		1	7	11		9		4		10	2			14		8	**24**
s		3	5	6		1	7	11	8	9		4		10	2			s			**25**
		3	5	11		1	7		6	s	2	4		10	9	s				8	**26**
		3	5	11		1	7	14	6		2	4		10	9	s				8	**27**
		3	5			1			6	*12	2	4		10	8	s	7	*11		9	**28**
		3	5			1		s	6		2	4	11	10	8	s	7			9	**29**
		3	5			1	7		6	s	2	4	14	10	9		8			11	**30**
		3	5			1	11	s			2	4	*12	10	*8	6	7			9	**31**
		3	6			1	7			s	2	4	s	10	9	5	8			11	**32**
		3	6			1	7	s			2	4	s	10	9	5	8			11	**33**
		3	6			1	7	s			2	4	*12	10	9	*5	8			11	**34**
		3	6			1	7	s	5		2	4	s	10	9		8			11	**35**
		*3	5			1	7		6	s	2	4		10	9		8	*12		11	**36**
		s	5			1	7	s	6		2	4	3	10	9		8			11	**37**
			5			1	7	s	6		2	4	3	10	9		8		s	11	**38**
			5			1	7	s			2	4	3	10	9	6	8	s		11	**39**
			5			1		s	s		2	4	3	10	9	6	8	7		11	**40**
			5			1	7		s		2	4	3	10	9	6	8	14		11	**41**
			6			1	7		s		2	4	3	10	9	5	8	s		11	**42**
			5	s		1	7		s		2	4	3	10	9	6	8			11	**43**
			6			1	7		s		2	4	3	10	9	5	8	s		11	**44**
			6			1	7		s		2	4	3	10	9	5	8	s		11	**45**
			6			1			5	s	2	4	3	10	9	s	8	7		11	**46**
1	17	15	43	5	0	46	40	8	29	13	44	40	34	37	25	32	33	3	0	41	Apps
1		1		1	1			2		9			3		1		3	4		2	Subs
	3	1	4				8	3	1	3		6	2	4	3	1	14			13	Goals

Opponents 2 goals

Barnard L K	Barnes D O	Bodin P J	Calderwood C	Cornwell J A	Coyne P D	Digby F C	Foley S	Geddis D	Gittens J A	Henry C A	Hockaday D	Jones T	King P G	MacLaren R	McLoughlin A F	Parkin T J	Shearer D N	Simpson F	Viveash A L	White S J	
	11		8			1	7		6	s	2	14	3	4		5	9			10	**2/1**
s	11		8			1	7		4	5	2	6	3		s		9			10	**2/2**
	2		2			2	2		2	1	2	1	2	1		1	2			2	Apps
												1									Subs
																	1				Goals

Barnard L K	Barnes D O	Bodin P J	Calderwood C	Cornwell J A	Coyne P D	Digby F C	Foley S	Geddis D	Gittens J A	Henry C A	Hockaday D	Jones T	King P G	MacLaren R	McLoughlin A F	Parkin T J	Shearer D N	Simpson F	Viveash A L	White S J	
			6	5		1	7	9		*11	2	4	3	10	s		8			*12	**3**
			5	8		1	7	11		*12	2	4	3	10	14		*9			6	**3R**
		3	5	8		1	7	11	6	9	14	4		10	2	s					**4**
		3	5	8		1	7	11	6	*12	*9	4		10	2	s					**4R**
		2	4	4		4	4	4	2	2	3	4	2	4	2		2			1	Apps
										2	1				1					1	Subs
							2										1				Goals

DUNCAN SHEARER

STEVE FOLEY

SEASON 1989/90

Football League Second Division
Final League Position : 4th
Manager : Ossie Ardiles

Substitutes :
s denotes substitute **not** used
* player substituted by *12
_ player substituted by 14

					Home	Away	H-T	Goalscorers	Gate
1	S	Aug	19	Sunderland	L0-2		(0-1)		10,199
2	S		26	Oldham Athletic		D2-2	(1-0)	McLoughlin 6,Shearer 49	5,531
3	Su	Sep	3	Wolverhampton Wanderers	W3-1		(2-0)	Jones 4,Shearer 26,McLoughlin 90	10,312
4	S		9	West Ham United		D1-1	(0-1)	Gittens 53	21,469
5	Tu		12	Sheffield United		L0-2	(0-0)		13,920
6	S		16	Barnsley	D0-0				6,540
7	S		23	Leeds United		L0-4	(0-2)		21,694
8	Tu		26	Plymouth Argyle	W3-0		(1-0)	Jones 37,King 77,Bodin 86	6,862
9	S		30	Bradford City		D1-1	(0-0)	White 85	8,334
10	S	Oct	7	Hull City		W3-2	(1-2)	Simpson 6,McLoughlin 59,Parkin 75	5,366
11	S		14	Ipswich Town	W3-0		(2-0)	Shearer 33,McLoughlin 41,Stockwell o.g.51	8,039
12	Tu		17	Oxford United	W3-0		(2-0)	Calderwood 28,White 45,73	10,741
13	S		21	Leicester City		L1-2	(0-0)	McLoughlin 64	8,547
14	W	Nov	1	Brighton and Hove Albion		W2-1	(1-0)	MacLaren 32,Gittens 85	8,070
15	S		4	Stoke City	W6-0		(2-0)	McLoughlin 8,Shearer 24,79,Bamber o.g.47,White 68,86	7,825
16	S		11	Middlesbrough		W2-0	(0-0)	Shearer 50,Mohan o.g.82	13,720
17	S		18	Port Vale		L0-2	(0-2)		7,393
18	Su		26	Portsmouth	D2-2		(1-0)	Shearer 30,88	10,438
19	S	Dec	2	Sunderland		D2-2	(1-0)	McLoughlin 41,Shearer 74	15,849
20	Tu		5	AFC Bournemouth	L2-3		(1-1)	Bodin 43 pen.,White 83	7,326
21	Su		10	Sheffield United	L0-2		(0-1)		10,282
22	Su		17	West Bromwich Albion		W2-1	(1-0)	Shearer 4,White 59	9,884
23	Tu		26	Blackburn Rovers	W4-3		(3-2)	Shearer 33,42,Bodin 44,Foley 77	8,426
24	S		30	Newcastle United	D1-1		(0-1)	Shearer 90	11,657
25	M	Jan	1	Watford		W2-0	(0-0)	McLoughlin 77,82	13,708
26	S		13	Oldham Athletic	W3-2		(1-0)	McLoughlin 35,White 48,84	7,785
27	S		20	Wolverhampton Wanderers		L1-2	(0-0)	White 66	17,210
28	Su	Feb	4	Leeds United	W3-2		(1-1)	McLoughlin 37,Foley 50,MacLaren 76	16,208
29	S		10	Barnsley		W1-0	(1-0)	Calderwood 36	7,179
30	Su		18	West Ham United	D2-2		(1-1)	White 43,MacLaren 67	16,105
31	S		24	Portsmouth		D1-1	(0-1)	McLoughlin 66	10,300
32	S	Mar	3	Port Vale	W3-0		(3-0)	Calderwood 11,White 26,Shearer 41	8,314
33	Tu		6	Bradford City	W3-1		(3-1)	Shearer 31,36,Foley 35	8,483
34	S		10	Plymouth Argyle		W3-0	(2-0)	White 31,57,Shearer 32	8,364
35	S		17	Hull City	L1-3		(1-2)	Shearer 30	8,123
36	Tu		20	Ipswich Town		L0-1	(0-0)		11,856
37	S		24	Oxford United		D2-2	(1-1)	White 38,Bodin 86 pen.	8,382
38	S		31	Leicester City	D1-1		(1-1)	Spearing o.g.20	8,561
39	S	Apr	7	AFC Bournemouth		W2-1	(1-1)	Simpson 7,Gittens 84	7,772
40	Tu		10	Brighton and Hove Albion	L1-2		(0-2)	White 55	8,444
41	S		14	Watford	W2-0		(0-0)	Shearer 63,White 70	8,520
42	M		16	Blackburn Rovers		L1-2	(1-1)	Gittens 44	10,689
43	S		21	West Bromwich Albion	W2-1		(0-0)	Bodin 48,White 80	8,495
44	W		25	Newcastle United		D0-0			26,568
45	S		28	Middlesbrough	D1-1		(0-1)	Foley 50	9,532
46	S	May	5	Stoke City		D1-1	(1-1)	Shearer 13	11,386

Average Home Attendance : **9,444**
Average Away Attendance : **11,878**

Football League Cup

					Home	Away	H-T	Goalscorers	Gate
2/1	Tu	Sep	19	Shrewsbury Town		W3-0	(3-0)	Shearer 12,McLoughlin 32,40	3,518
2/2	Tu	Oct	3	Shrewsbury Town	W3-1		(0-0)	White 60,75,Shearer 84	5,544
3	Tu		24	Bolton Wanderers	D3-3		(1-1)	McLoughlin 13,Shearer 73,MacLaren 79	8,318
3R	Tu	Nov	7	Bolton Wanderers	+	D1-1	(0-0)	Shearer 115	11,533
Rp	Tu		14	Bolton Wanderers	+	D1-1	(1-1)	White 42	14,129
Rp	Tu		21	Bolton Wanderers	W2-1 +		(0-0)	White 59,MacLaren 117	11,238
4	W		29	Southampton	D0-0				15,085
4R	Tu	Jan	16	Southampton		L2-4	(2-0)	McLoughlin 34,White 37	19,018

+ After Extra Time

For Final League Table - see page 219 For Play-Offs and Full Members' Cup - see overleaf >>

F A Cup

					Home	Away	H-T	Goalscorers	Gate
3	S	Jan	6	Bristol City		L1-2	(1-2)	Shearer 41	17,422

Ardiles O C	Barnard L K	Bodin P J	Calderwood C	Close S C	Cornwell J A	Dearden K C	Digby F C	Foley S	Galvin A	Gittens J A	Hockaday D	Hunt P C	Jones T	Kerslake D	King P G	MacLaren R	McLoughlin A F	Parkin T J	Shearer D N	Simpson F	Summerbee N J	White S J	
14			6		*12		1		7		2				3	10	4	*5	8	11		9	**1**
14	2		6				1		7						3	10	4	5	8	11	s	9	**2**
	*2		6		*12		1		11	5			7		3	10	4		8		14	9	**3**
	2		5	8	*12		1		*11	6		s	7		3	10	4					9	**4**
	*2		5	8	*12		1		11	6			7		3	10	4			14		9	**5**
	2	*12	6	9			1			5		14	*7		3	10	4		8	11			**6**
		9	5	s			1		14	6	2		7		3	10	4		8	11			**7**
		*12	5	9			1		14	6	2		*7		3	10	4		8	11			**8**
		9	5				1		*11	6	2		7		3	10	4		8	*12		14	**9**
		7	5	s			1				2		14		3	10	4	6	8	11		9	**10**
		11	5		14		1		s		2		7		3	10	4	6	8			9	**11**
		11	5		14		1		*12		2	*8	7		3	10	4	6				9	**12**
		11	5		s		1			s	2	8	7		3	10	4	6				9	**13**
		*12	5				1			6	2	14	7		*3	10	4		8	11		9	**14**
		3	5		s		1			6	2	s	7			10	4		8	11		9	**15**
		3	5	s	2		1		14	6			7			10	4		8	11		9	**16**
		3	5	14	*2		1	*12		6			7			10	4		8	11		9	**17**
		3	5		s		1	*12		6			7	2		*10	4		8	11		9	**18**
		3	5		*12		1	*11		6			7	2		10	4		8	14		9	**19**
		3	5		s		1	11		6			7	2		10	4		8	14		9	**20**
		3	5		*12		1	11		6		s	7	*2		10	4		8			9	**21**
		3	5		*12		1	11	14	6			7	2		10	4		8			*9	**22**
		3	5		*12		1	11		6	14		7	*2		10	4		8			9	**23**
		3	5		s		1	11		6	14		7	2		10	4		8			9	**24**
		3	5		*12		1	11		6	s		*7	2		10	4		8			9	**25**
		3	5	s	*12		1	11		6			*7	2		10	4		8			9	**26**
		3	5		s		1	11		6	14		7	2		10	4		8			9	**27**
		3	5				1	11		6	s	s	7	2		10	4		8			9	**28**
		3	5	14	*12		1	11		6			*7	2		10	4		8			9	**29**
		3	5	s			1	11		6	s		7	2		10	4		8			9	**30**
		3	5				1	11		6	s		7	2		10	4		8	14		9	**31**
		3	5				1	11		6	*12		7	2		*10	4		8	14		9	**32**
		3	5				1	11		6	*12		7	2		10	*4		8	14		9	**33**
		3	5		s		1			6	s		7	2		10	4		8	11		9	**34**
		3	5	14			1			6	s		7	2		10	4		8	11		9	**35**
		3	5	14			1			6	*12		*7	2		10	4		8	11		9	**36**
		3	5	s	*12		1			6			7	2		*10	4		8	11		9	**37**
		3	5	s			1			6	*12		7	2		10	4		8	*11		9	**38**
		3	5	*12	14	1				6			7	2		10	4		8	11		*9	**39**
		3	5	14			1			6	*12		7	2		10	4		8	*11		9	**40**
		3	5	14			1	*12		6			7	2		10	4		8	*11		9	**41**
		3	5		14		1	*11		6			7	2		10	4		8	*12		9	**42**
		3	5	s			1	*11		6	2		7			10	4		8	*12		9	**43**
		3	5		s		1	11		6			7	2		10	4		8	s		9	**44**
		3	5				1	*11		6	14		7	2		10	4		8	*12		9	**45**
		3	5		*12		1	11		6			7	2		10	4		*8	14		9	**46**
0	5	38	46	4	2	1	45	20	6	40	11	2	43	28	14	46	46	6	42	19	0	42	Apps
2		3		7	17			3	5		9	2	1							11	1	1	Subs
		5	3					4		4			2		1	3	12	1	20	2		18	Goals

Opponents 4 goals

Ardiles O C	Barnard L K	Bodin P J	Calderwood C	Close S C	Cornwell J A	Dearden K C	Digby F C	Foley S	Galvin A	Gittens J A	Hockaday D	Hunt P C	Jones T	Kerslake D	King P G	MacLaren R	McLoughlin A F	Parkin T J	Shearer D N	Simpson F	Summerbee N J	White S J	
		9	5	*12			1		14	6	2		7		3	10	4		*8	11			**2/1**
		4	5	14			1			6	2		*7		3	10	*12		8	11		9	**2/2**
		*7	5				1			6	2	*12	14		3	10	4		8	11		9	**3**
		3	5		*12		1			6	*2	14	7			10	4		8	11		9	**3R**
		3	5	*12	2		1		14	6			7			10	4		8	11		*9	**Rp**
		3	5	14	*2		1	7	*12	6						10	4		8	11		9	**Rp**
		3	5		*12		1	11		6			7	*2		10	4		8	14		9	**4**
		3	5	s	*12		1	11		6			*7	2		10	4		8			9	**4R**
		8	8	0	2		8	3	0	8	4	0	6	2	3	8	7		8	6		7	Apps
				4	3				3			2	1				1			1			Subs
																2	4		4			5	Goals

STEVE WHITE

ALAN McLOUGHLIN

Ardiles O C	Barnard L K	Bodin P J	Calderwood C	Close S C	Cornwell J A	Dearden K C	Digby F C	Foley S	Galvin A	Gittens J A	Hockaday D	Hunt P C	Jones T	Kerslake D	King P G	MacLaren R	McLoughlin A F	Parkin T J	Shearer D N	Simpson F	Summerbee N J	White S J	
		3	5		s		1	11		6	14		7	2		10	4		8			9	**3**

SEASON 1987/88

					Home	Away	H-T	Goalscorers	Gate
1	Tu	Nov	10	Blackburn Rovers		W2-1	(1-1)	Gittens 35,Parkin 82	3,638
2	W	Dec	23	Derby County	W2-1		(0-0)	Quinn 55,Hockaday 74	8,135
3	Tu	Jan	19	Chelsea	W4-0		(3-0)	Parkin 7,White 8,64,Quinn 44	12,317
QF	Tu	Feb	23	Norwich City	W2-0		(0-0)	Elliott o.g.64,Foley 72	10,491
SF	Tu	Mar	8	Luton Town	+	L1-2		O'Regan 67	10,027

+ After Extra Time

	Bamber J D	Barnard L K	Barnes D O	Bodin P J	Calderwood C	Digby F C	Foley S	Gittens J A	Hammond N D	Henry C A	Hockaday D	Jones T	Kamara C	King P G	MacLaren R	McLoughlin A F	O'Regan K M	Parkin T J	Quinn J M	Shearer D N	Wade B A	White S J
1	7	4	11		6		14	10	1	*12	2		8	3				5				*9
2	7		11		6		10	8	1		2		4	3				5	9		s	s
3	7				6			8	1	s	2		4	3			10	5	9		s	11
QF	7	s			6	1	10	8		s	2			3			4	5	9			11
SF	7		*10	11		1	4	6		s	2			3			8	5	9			*12
Apps	5	1	3	1	4	2	4	5	3	0	5		3	5			3	5	4		0	3
Subs										1												1
Goals							1	1			1						1	2	2			2

Opponents 1 goal

SEASON 1988/89

					Home	Away	H-T	Goalscorers	Gate
1	W	Nov	9	Norwich City		L1-2	(0-0)	White 74	5,014

Play-Offs

					Home	Away	H-T	Goalscorers	Gate
SF	Su	May	21	Crystal Palace	W1-0		(0-0)	Hopkins o.g.53	16,656
SF	W		24	Crystal Palace		L0-2	(0-2)		23,677

	Bamber J D	Barnard L K	Barnes D O	Bodin P J	Calderwood C	Digby F C	Foley S	Gittens J A	Hammond N D	Henry C A	Hockaday D	Jones T	Kamara C	King P G	MacLaren R	McLoughlin A F	O'Regan K M	Parkin T J	Quinn J M	Shearer D N	Wade B A	White S J
1			11	s	8	1		6		9	2	4		3		7		5		14		10
SF					6	1	7	s		s	2	4		3	10	9		5		8		11
SF					6	1	7	*12		14	2	4		3	10	9		*5		8		11
Apps					2	2	2	0		0	2	2		2	2	2		2		2		2
Subs								1		1												
Goals																						

Opponents 1 goal

SEASON 1989/90

					Home	Away	H-T	Goalscorers	Gate
2	Tu	Dec	13	Millwall	W2-1		(1-0)	White 31,Thompson o.g.47	3,223
3	W	Jan	24	Norwich City	W4-1		(1-1)	Shearer 33,Foley 44,Bodin 73,White 88	5,314
4	Tu	Feb	13	Crystal Palace		L0-1	(0-1)		6,025

	Bodin P J	Calderwood C	Close S C	Cornwell J A	Digby F C	Foley S	Gittens J A	Hockaday D	Hunt P C	Jones T	Kerslake D	MacLaren R	McLoughlin A F	Shearer D N	Simpson F	White S J
Pr.	3	5		*12	1	*11	6		s	7	2	10	4	8		9
QF	3	5	s		1	11	6	s		7	2	10	4	8		9
SF	3	5		s	1	11	6	s		7	2	10	4	8		9
Apps	3	3	0	0	3	3	3	0	0	3	3	3	3	3		3
Subs				1												
Goals	1					1								1		2

Opponents 1 goal

Play-Offs

					Home	Away	H-T	Goalscorers	Gate
SF	Su	May	13	Blackburn Rovers		W2-1	(1-0)	White 30,Foley 55	15,636
SF	W		16	Blackburn Rovers	W2-1		(2-0)	Shearer 35,White 38	12,416
F	M		28	Sunderland	*	W1-0	(0-2)	Bennett o.g.26	72,873

* Played at Wembley Stadium

	Bodin P J	Calderwood C	Close S C	Cornwell J A	Digby F C	Foley S	Gittens J A	Hockaday D	Hunt P C	Jones T	Kerslake D	MacLaren R	McLoughlin A F	Shearer D N	Simpson F	White S J
SF	3	5		s	1	11	6			7	2	10	*4	8	*12	9
F	3	5			1	11	6	s		7	2	10	*4	8	*12	9
Rp.	3	5			1	11	6	s		7	2	10	4	8	s	9
Apps	3	3		0	3	3	3	0		3	3	3	3	3	0	3
Subs															2	
Goals						1								1		2

Opponents 1 goal

PAUL BODIN

JON GITTENS

SEASON 1990/91

Div.2

	Team	P	W	D	L	F	A	W	D	L	F	A	Pts	G/D	Avge. Home Gate
1	Oldham Athletic	46	17	5	1	55	21	8	8	7	28	32	88	+30	13,247
2	West Ham United	46	15	6	2	41	18	9	9	5	19	16	87	+26	22,551
3	Sheffield Wednesday	46	12	10	1	43	23	10	6	7	37	28	82	+29	26,605
4	Notts County *	46	14	4	5	45	28	9	7	7	31	27	80	+21	8,164
5	Millwall	46	11	6	6	43	28	9	7	7	27	23	73	+19	10,846
6	Brighton & Hove Albion	46	12	4	7	37	31	9	3	11	26	38	70	-6	8,386
7	Middlesbrough	46	12	4	7	36	17	8	5	10	30	30	69	+19	17,023
8	Barnsley	46	13	7	3	39	16	6	5	12	24	32	69	+15	8,937
9	Bristol City	46	14	5	4	44	28	6	2	15	24	43	67	-3	13,495
10	Oxford United	46	10	9	4	41	29	4	10	9	28	37	61	+3	5,780
11	Newcastle United	46	8	10	5	24	22	6	7	10	25	34	59	-7	16,834
12	Wolverhampton Wanderers	46	11	6	6	45	35	2	13	8	18	28	58	0	15,837
13	Bristol Rovers	46	11	7	5	29	20	4	6	13	27	39	58	-3	5,929
14	Ipswich Town	46	9	8	6	32	28	4	10	9	28	40	57	-8	11,772
15	Port Vale	46	10	4	9	32	24	5	8	10	24	40	57	-8	8,092
16	Charlton Athletic	46	8	7	8	27	25	5	10	8	30	36	56	-4	6,548
17	Portsmouth	46	10	6	7	34	27	4	5	14	24	43	53	-12	9,689
18	Plymouth Argyle	46	10	10	3	36	20	2	7	14	18	48	53	-14	6,851
19	Blackburn Rovers	46	8	6	9	26	27	6	4	13	25	39	52	-15	8,126
20	Watford	46	5	8	10	24	32	7	7	9	21	27	51	-14	9,575
21	SWINDON TOWN	46	8	6	9	31	30	4	8	11	34	43	50	-8	9,828
22	Leicester City	46	12	4	7	41	33	2	4	17	19	50	50	-23	11,546
23	West Bromwich Albion	46	7	11	5	26	21	3	7	13	26	40	48	-9	11,993
24	Hull City	46	6	10	7	35	32	4	5	14	22	53	45	-28	6,165

SEASON 1991/92

Div.2

	Team	P	W	D	L	F	A	W	D	L	F	A	Pts	G/D	Avge. Home Gate
1	Ipswich Town	46	16	3	4	42	22	8	9	6	28	28	84	+20	14,274
2	Middlesbrough	46	15	6	2	37	13	8	5	10	21	28	80	+17	14,703
3	Derby County	46	11	4	8	35	24	12	5	6	34	27	78	+18	14,664
4	Leicester City	46	14	4	5	41	24	9	4	10	21	31	77	+7	15,202
5	Cambridge United	46	10	9	4	34	19	9	8	6	31	28	74	+18	7,078
6	Blackburn Rovers *	46	14	5	4	41	21	7	6	10	29	32	74	+17	13,251
7	Charlton Athletic	46	9	7	7	25	23	11	4	8	29	25	71	+6	6,786
8	SWINDON TOWN	46	15	3	5	38	22	3	12	8	31	33	69	+14	10,008
9	Portsmouth	46	15	6	2	41	12	4	6	13	24	39	69	+14	11,789
10	Watford	46	9	5	9	25	23	9	6	8	26	25	65	+3	8,511
11	Wolverhampton Wanderers	46	11	6	6	36	24	7	4	12	25	30	64	+7	13,743
12	Southend United	46	11	5	7	37	26	6	6	11	26	37	62	0	6,733
13	Bristol Rovers	46	11	9	3	43	29	5	5	13	17	34	62	-3	5,850
14	Tranmere Rovers	46	9	9	5	37	32	5	10	8	19	24	61	0	8,845
15	Millwall	46	10	4	9	32	32	7	6	10	32	39	61	-7	7,921
16	Barnsley	46	11	4	8	27	25	5	7	11	19	32	59	-11	7,508
17	Bristol City	46	10	8	5	30	24	3	7	13	25	47	54	-16	11,479
18	Sunderland	46	10	8	5	36	23	4	3	16	25	42	53	-4	18,390
19	Grimsby Town	46	7	5	11	25	28	7	6	10	22	34	53	-15	6,920
20	Newcastle United	46	9	8	6	38	30	4	5	14	28	54	52	-18	21,148
21	Oxford United	46	10	6	7	39	30	3	5	15	27	43	50	-7	5,671
22	Plymouth Argyle	46	11	5	7	26	26	2	4	17	16	38	48	-22	6,739
23	Brighton & Hove Albion	46	7	7	9	36	37	5	4	14	20	40	47	-21	8,002
24	Port Vale	46	7	8	8	23	25	3	7	13	19	34	45	-17	7,382

SEASON 1992/93

Div.1

	Team	P	W	D	L	F	A	W	D	L	F	A	Pts	G/D	Avge. Home Gate
1	Newcastle United	46	16	6	1	58	15	13	3	7	34	23	96	+54	29,018
2	West Ham United	46	16	5	2	50	17	10	5	8	31	24	88	+40	16,001
3	Portsmouth	46	19	2	2	48	9	7	8	8	32	37	88	+34	13,706
4	Tranmere Rovers	46	15	4	4	48	24	8	6	9	24	32	79	+16	8,071
5	SWINDON TOWN *	46	15	5	3	41	23	6	8	9	33	36	76	+15	10,576
6	Leicester City	46	14	5	4	43	24	8	5	10	28	40	76	+7	15,362
7	Millwall	46	14	6	3	46	21	4	10	9	19	32	70	+12	9,188
8	Derby County	46	11	2	10	40	33	8	7	8	28	24	66	+11	15,020
9	Grimsby Town	46	12	6	5	33	25	7	1	15	25	32	64	+1	6,088
10	Peterborough United	46	7	11	5	30	26	9	3	11	25	37	62	-8	8,064
11	Wolverhampton Wanderers	46	11	6	6	37	26	5	7	11	20	30	61	+1	13,598
12	Charlton Athletic	46	10	8	5	28	19	6	5	12	21	27	61	+3	7,029
13	Barnsley	46	12	4	7	29	19	5	5	13	27	41	60	-4	6,415
14	Oxford United	46	8	7	8	29	21	6	7	10	24	35	56	-3	6,356
15	Bristol City	46	10	7	6	29	25	4	7	12	20	42	56	-18	11,004
16	Watford	46	8	7	8	27	30	6	6	11	30	41	55	-14	8,275
17	Notts County	46	10	7	6	33	21	2	9	12	22	49	52	-15	8,151
18	Southend United	46	9	8	6	33	22	4	5	14	21	42	52	-10	5,396
19	Birmingham City	46	10	4	9	30	32	3	8	12	20	40	51	-22	12,328
20	Luton Town	46	6	13	4	26	26	4	8	11	22	36	51	-14	8,212
21	Sunderland	46	9	6	8	34	28	4	5	14	16	36	50	-14	17,258
22	Brentford	46	7	6	10	28	30	6	4	13	24	41	49	-19	8,476
23	Cambridge United	46	8	6	9	29	32	3	10	10	19	37	49	-21	5,545
24	Bristol Rovers	46	6	6	11	30	42	4	5	14	25	45	41	-32	5,745

* Promoted via Play-offs

SEASON 1990/91

Football League Second Division
Final League Position : 21st
Manager : Ossie Ardiles
Glenn Hoddle (from Apr 4)

Substitutes :
s denotes substitute **not** used
* player substituted by *12
_ player substituted by 14

					Home	Away	H-T	Goalscorers	Gate
1	S	Aug	25	Charlton Athletic		* W2-1	(2-1)	Bodin 13,Shearer 31	7,524
2	Tu		28	Ipswich Town	W1-0		(0-0)	Shearer 77	10,817
3	Su	Sep	2	Bristol City	L0-1		(0-1)		12,249
4	S		8	Hull City		D1-1	(0-0)	McLoughlin 66	5,240
5	S		15	Middlesbrough	L1-3		(1-0)	Shearer 27	9,127
6	Tu		18	Wolverhampton W	W1-0		(0-0)	Simpson 61	12,228
7	S		22	Oxford United		W4-2	(2-2)	Simpson 30,Foley 45,Shearer 69,82	7,961
8	Su		30	Millwall	D0-0				11,667
9	Tu	Oct	2	Oldham Athletic		L2-3	(1-1)	Hazard 24,Bodin 68	12,575
10	S		6	Brighton & Hove A		D3-3	(1-3)	McLoughlin 5,77,White 81	7,940
11	S		13	Bristol Rovers	L0-2		(0-1)		11,494
12	S		20	West Ham United	L0-1		(0-0)		13,658
13	W		24	Leicester City		D2-2	(1-0)	Shearer 24,White 50	9,592
14	S		27	Barnsley		L1-5	(0-1)	White 61	7,690
15	S	Nov	3	Port Vale	L1-2		(1-0)	Beckford o.g. 31	7,714
16	S		10	Portsmouth	W3-0		(2-0)	Lorenzo 29,Foley 40,Shearer 78	8,621
17	S		17	Sheffield Wednesday		L1-2	(0-1)	McLoughlin 90	22,715
18	S		24	Notts County		D0-0			6,113
19	S	Dec	1	Blackburn Rovers	D1-1		(1-0)	Shearer 34	8,091
20	S		8	Ipswich Town		D1-1	(0-0)	Shearer 70	9,358
21	S		15	Charlton Athletic	D1-1		(0-1)	Hazard 66	7,396
22	S		22	West Bromwich Albion	W2-1		(0-1)	MacLaren 72,Shearer 75	7,793
23	W		26	Newcastle United		D1-1	(1-1)	Gittens 11	17,003
24	S		29	Watford		D2-2	(2-0)	Shearer 7,Lorenzo 21	11,233
25	Tu	Jan	1	Plymouth Argyle	D1-1		(0-0)	Foley 90	9,736
26	S		12	Bristol City		W4-0	(1-0)	Hazard 38,White 62,90,Shearer 89	16,169
27	S		19	Hull City	W3-1		(2-0)	White 2,Shearer 14,74	7,297
28	S	Feb	2	Middlesbrough		L0-2	(0-2)		14,588
29	S		19	Sheffield Wednesday	W2-1		(0-0)	Simpson 75,Foley 82	8,787
30	S		23	Portsmouth		L1-2	(1-2)	White 25	8,889
31	S	Mar	2	Blackburn Rovers		L1-2	(0-1)	White 52	6,506
32	Tu		5	Oxford United	D0-0				9,570
33	Tu		12	Oldham Athletic	D2-2		(0-0)	Shearer 56,Calderwood 79	8,605
34	S		16	Millwall		L0-1	(0-0)		8,894
35	W		20	Bristol Rovers		L1-2	(1-1)	Shearer 35	6,123
36	S		23	Brighton & Hove A	L1-3		(1-1)	Shearer 37	7,342
37	S		30	Newcastle United	W3-2		(1-1)	Hazard 26 pen.,Shearer 50,Calderwood 76	9,309
38	M	Apr	1	West Bromwich Albion		L1-2	(1-1)	Rideout 31	10,415
39	S		6	Watford	L1-2		(0-1)	White 71	9,699
40	S		13	Plymouth Argyle		D3-3	(1-2)	Hazard 30,Shearer 56,64	6,712
41	Tu		16	Wolverhampton W		W2-1	(1-1)	Shearer 36,Hazard 79	9,799
42	S		20	West Ham United		L0-2	(0-1)		25,944
43	Tu		23	Notts County	L1-2		(0-1)	Shearer 62	7,853
44	S		27	Leicester City	W5-2		(3-2)	Foley 23,79,89,Hazard 29 pen.,James o.g.44	10,404
45	S	May	4	Barnsley	L1-2		(1-2)	Hazard 45 pen.	9,070
46	S		11	Port Vale		L1-3	(1-2)	Viveash 40	7,713

* Played at Selhurst Park

Average Home Attendance : **9,828**
Average Away Attendance : **10,726**

Football League Cup

					Home	Away	H-T	Goalscorers	Gate
1/1	Tu	Sep	25	Darlington		L0-3	(0-0)		4,037
1/2	Tu	Oct	9	Darlington	W4-0		(3-0)	Simpson 15,Smith o.g. 25,Close 45,McLoughlin 70	7,066
2/1	W		31	Sheffield Wednesday		D0-0			13,900
2/2	Tu	Nov	6	Sheffield Wednesday	L0-1		(0-1)		9,043

F A Cup

					Home	Away	H-T	Goalscorers	Gate
1/1	S	Jan	5	Leyton Orient		D1-1	(1-0)	Shearer 5	6,697
1/2	M		21	Leyton Orient	W1-0		(0-0)	White 90	7,395
2/2	S		26	Norwich City		L1-3	(0-0)	White 50	14,408

For Final League Table - see previous page << For Full Members' Cup - see page 234

Bennett D A	Bodin P J	Buttigieg J	Calderwood C	Close S C	Digby F C	Finnigan A	Foley S	Gittens J A	Green R E	Hammond N D	Hazard M	Hockaday D	Hunt P C	Jones T	Kerslake D	Ling M	Lorenzo N G	MacLaren R	McLoughlin A F	Murray E J	Rideout P D	Shearer D N	Simpson F	Summerbee N J	Tanner N	Trollope P J	Viveash A L	White S J	
	3		5	*9	1		11	6				*12		7	2			10	s			8	4						**1**
	3		5	9	1		11	6				s		7	2			10	14			8	4						**2**
	3		5	9	1		11	6				*12		*7	2			10	14			8	4						**3**
	3		5	9	1		*11	6				2		7				10	4			8	*12	14					**4**
	3	2	5		1		11	6						7				10	4			8	9	*12			*14		**5**
	3	2	*5		1		11	6					*12	7				10	4			8	9	s					**6**
*5	3	14			1		11	6						7	2			10	4			8	9					*12	**7**
	3				1		11	6			14			7	2			10	4			8	*9		5			*12	**8**
	3			*12	1			6			7				2			10	*4			8	9		5		s	11	**9**
	3			*12	1			6			7				2			10	4			*8	11		5		s	9	**10**
	3			*12			*11			1	7			14	2			10	4				8		5		6	9	**11**
	3			*12	1		11	6			*4			7	2			10					8		5		s	9	**12**
	3				1		11	6			s = Galvin A			7	2			10				8	4		5		s	9	**13**
	3				1		*12	6						*7	2			10	4			8	11		5		s	9	**14**
	3				1		*12	6					s	7	2			10	*4			8	11				5	9	**15**
	3			*12	1		11				14			2			6	10	4			8	7				5	9	**16**
	3				1		11		s		14			2			6	10	4			8	7				5	9	**17**
	3				1		11		s		7			2			6	10	4			8	14				5	9	**18**
	3				1		11	6						7	2		5	10	4			8	14				s	9	**19**
	3						11	6	s	1				7	2			10	4			8	*12				5	*9	**20**
	3				1		*11	6	s		4			7	2			10				8	9				5	*12	**21**
	3				1		11	6			4			7	2		5	10				8	s				s	9	**22**
	3				1		11	6			4			7	2		*5	10				8		s			*12	9	**23**
	3				1		11	6			4			7	2		5	10				8		s			s	9	**24**
	3				1		11	6			4			7	2		5	10				8		14			s	9	**25**
	3				1		11	6	s		4			7	2		5	10				8		s				9	**26**
	3				1		11	6			4			7	2		5	10				8		s			s	9	**27**
	3				1		11	6			4			7	2		5	10				8	s				s	9	**28**
	3		s	*12	1		11				4			7	2			10				8	6				5	*9	**29**
	3		14	s	1		11				4			7	2			10				8	6				5	9	**30**
	*3		6	14	1		11				4			7	2			10				8	*12				5	9	**31**
			6		1		11				4		*12	7	2			10		14		*8	3				5	9	**32**
			6		1		11	5			*4			2				10				8	7	*12		s	3	9	**33**
			6		1		11	5			4			2			14	10				8	*7	*12			3	9	**34**
			6			2	11	5		1	4			7			3	10				8	14	*12				*9	**35**
			6		1	3	*11	5			4			7	2		14	10				8	*12					9	**36**
			6		1	s	11				4			7	2		5	10			*9	8					3	*12	**37**
			6		1		11				4			7	2		5	*10			9	8	*12				3	s	**38**
			6		1	14	11				4			7	2		5				9	8	*10				3	*12	**39**
			6		1		11				4			7	2		5	10			9	8	14				3	s	**40**
			6		1		11				4			7	2		5	10			9	8	14				3	s	**41**
			6		1		11				4			7	2			10			9	8	5	s			3	14	**42**
			6	14	1		11				4			7	2		s	10				8	5				3	9	**43**
			6		1		11				4			7	2		5	10			9	*8	*12				3	14	**44**
			6	*12			11			1	4			7	2			10			9	8	*5	s			3		**45**
			6	*12			11			1	4				2	14		10			*9	8	5	7			3		**46**
1	31	2	22	4	41	2	42	28	0	5	31	1	0	42	37	0	18	45	15	0	9	44	27	1	7	0	23	28	Apps
		1	1	10		1	2				3	2	2	1		1	2		2	1			11	6			2	7	Subs
	2		2				7	1			8						2	1	4		1	22	3				1	9	Goals

Opponents 2 goals

Bennett D A	Bodin P J	Buttigieg J	Calderwood C	Close S C	Digby F C	Finnigan A	Foley S	Gittens J A	Green R E	Hammond N D	Hazard M	Hockaday D	Hunt P C	Jones T	Kerslake D	Ling M	Lorenzo N G	MacLaren R	McLoughlin A F	Murray E J	Rideout P D	Shearer D N	Simpson F	Summerbee N J	Tanner N	Trollope P J	Viveash A L	White S J	
*5	3	14			1		11	6						7	2			10	4			8	9					*12	**1/1**
	3			8			14	6		1	7		*12		2			10	*4				11				5	9	**1/2**
	3				1		11	6			s = Galvin A			7	2			10	14			8	4				5	9	**2/1**
	3				1		11	6						7	2		s	10	4			8	14				5	9	**2/2**
1	4	0		1	3		3	4		1	1		0	3	4		0	4	3				3				3	3	Apps
		1					1						1						1				1					1	Subs
				1															1				1						Goals

Opponents 1 goal

Bennett D A	Bodin P J	Buttigieg J	Calderwood C	Close S C	Digby F C	Finnigan A	Foley S	Gittens J A	Green R E	Hammond N D	Hazard M	Hockaday D	Hunt P C	Jones T	Kerslake D	Ling M	Lorenzo N G	MacLaren R	McLoughlin A F	Murray E J	Rideout P D	Shearer D N	Simpson F	Summerbee N J	Tanner N	Trollope P J	Viveash A L	White S J	
	3				1		11	6			4			7	2		5	10				8		s			s	9	**1/1**
	3				1		11	6			4			7	2		5	10				8		s			s	9	**1/2**
	3				1		11	6			4			7	2		5	10				8		14			*12	*9	**2/2**
	3				3		3	3			3			3	3		3	3				3		0			0	3	Apps
																								1			1		Subs
																						1						2	Goals

SEASON 1991/92

Football League Second Division
Final League Position : 8th
Manager : Glenn Hoddle

Substitutes :
s denotes substitute **not** used
* player substituted by *12
_ player substituted by 14

No	Day	Month	Date	Opponent	Home	Away	H-T	Goalscorers	Gate
1	S	Aug	17	Leicester City	D0-0				13,238
2	S		24	Cambridge United		L2-3	(1-1)	Shearer 43,Hazard 84 pen.	6,232
3	S		31	Barnsley	W3-1		(0-1)	White 52,Ling 70,Shearer 81	7,742
4	Tu	Sep	3	Ipswich Town		W4-1	(2-1)	White 3,Calderwood 44,Taylor 81,Hazard 88	11,002
5	S		7	Port Vale		D2-2	(0-0)	White 56,MacLaren 82	7,168
6	S		14	Sunderland	W5-3		(3-0)	White 8,Simpson 37,Hazard 39,56 pen.,Shearer 90	11,694
7	Tu		17	Bristol Rovers	W1-0		(1-0)	Jones 41	11,391
8	S		21	Wolverhampton Wanderers		L1-2	(0-1)	White 87	15,219
9	S		28	Watford	W3-1		(2-0)	Shearer 8,Simpson 45,Taylor 81	8,863
10	S	Oct	5	Plymouth Argyle		W4-0	(2-0)	Shearer 8,27,62,85	6,208
11	S		12	Derby County	L1-2		(0-1)	Hazard 63 pen.	11,883
12	S		19	Blackburn Rovers	W2-1		(0-0)	White 65,Calderwood 90	10,717
13	S		26	Brighton & Hove Albion		W2-0	(1-0)	Shearer 19,50	7,370
14	S	Nov	2	Newcastle United	W2-1		(1-0)	Calderwood 41,White 88	10,731
15	W		6	Charlton Athletic	*	D0-0			5,398
16	S		9	Southend United		L2-3	(0-1)	White 61,Shearer 81	7,709
17	S		16	Portsmouth	L2-3		(0-0)	White 58,63	10,738
18	F		22	Tranmere Rovers		D0-0			9,585
19	S		30	Grimsby Town	D1-1		(1-1)	Simpson 37	8,836
20	S	Dec	7	Middlesbrough		D2-2	(0-1)	Simpson 60,Shearer 66	13,300
21	F		20	Ipswich Town	D0-0				7,404
22	Th		26	Bristol City		D1-1	(1-0)	Shearer 10	14,636
23	S		28	Barnsley		D1-1	(1-0)	Shearer 10	8,357
24	W	Jan	1	Millwall	W3-1		(3-0)	Shearer 21,43,Ling 28	9,746
25	S		11	Cambridge United	L0-2		(0-0)		11,008
26	S		18	Leicester City		L1-3	(0-1)	Bodin 74	14,226
27	Tu		28	Oxford United	W2-1		(1-0)	Kerslake 44,Shearer 68	9,707
28	S	Feb	1	Blackburn Rovers		L1-2	(1-0)	Mitchell 41	14,887
29	Tu		4	Bristol City	W2-0		(0-0)	Jones 51,Shearer 81	9,627
30	S		8	Brighton & Hove Albion	W2-1		(0-1)	Calderwood 70,81	9,127
31	S		22	Grimsby Town		D0-0			6,817
32	S		29	Middlesbrough	L0-1		(0-0)		10,379
33	S	Mar	7	Oxford United		L3-5	(2-3)	Close 1,Mitchell 42,72	7,995
34	Tu		10	Charlton Athletic	L1-2		(0-1)	Shearer 71	7,196
35	S		14	Newcastle United		L1-3	(0-1)	Mitchell 61	23,138
36	Tu		17	Tranmere Rovers	W2-0		(1-0)	Shearer 20,48	6,780
37	S		21	Southend United	W3-1		(1-1)	Shearer 14,Bodin 57 pen.,Mitchell 63	8,628
38	S		28	Portsmouth		D1-1	(0-0)	Jones 49	16,007
39	S	Apr	4	Port Vale	W1-0		(1-0)	Jones 5	8,014
40	W		8	Millwall		D1-1	(1-1)	Gibson 37	6,722
41	Su		12	Bristol Rovers		D1-1	(0-0)	Taylor 75	6,905
42	S		18	Wolverhampton Wanderers	W1-0		(1-0)	Ling 10	10,863
43	M		20	Watford		D0-0			9,911
44	S		25	Plymouth Argyle	W1-0		(1-0)	Taylor 26	10,463
45	M		27	Sunderland		D0-0			16,716
46	S	May	2	Derby County		L1-2	(0-1)	Hazard 90	22,608

* Played at Boleyn Ground (Upton Park)

Average Home Attendance : **10,008**
Average Away Attendance : **11,222**

Football League Cup

Rd	Day	Month	Date	Opponent	Home	Away	H-T	Goalscorers	Gate
1/1	Tu	Aug	20	West Bromwich Albion	W2-0		(2-0)	Mitchell 6,Hazard 36	6,611
1/2	W		28	West Bromwich Albion		D2-2	(0-1)	Shearer 83,87	8,522
2/1	W	Sep	25	Millwall		D2-2	(2-1)	White 3,34	6,048
2/2	Tu	Oct	8	Millwall	W3-1		(0-1)	Shearer 52,77,White 55	7,137
3	Tu		29	Huddersfield Town		W4-1	(2-0)	Shearer 7,76,Summerbee 14,Taylor 83	10,088
4	Tu	Dec	17	Crystal Palace	L0-1		(0-1)		10,044

F A Cup

Rd	Day	Month	Date	Opponent	Home	Away	H-T	Goalscorers	Gate
3	S	Jan	4	Watford	W3-2		(2-1)	Shearer 4,80,Mitchell 10	9,817
4	S		25	Cambridge United		W3-0	(1-0)	Calderwood 45,Shearer 49,53	7,428
5	Su	Feb	16	Aston Villa	L1-2		(0-1)	Mitchell 76	16,402

For Final League Table - see page 227 For Full Members' Cup - see page 234

Bodin P J	Calderwood C	Close S C	Digby F C	Foley S	Gibson T B	Hammond N D	Hazard M	Hoddle G	Jones T	Kerslake D	Ling M	Lorenzo N G	MacLaren R	Mitchell D S	Moncur J F	Shearer D N	Simpson F	Summerbee N J	Taylor S	Trollope P J	Viveash A L	Waddock G P	White S J	
	5		1	*12			7	4		2			10	11		8	9	*3	6				14	1
	5		1	2			7	4	*12		14		*10	11		8	9	3	6					2
	5		1				*7	4	2		*12	14	10			8	9		6		3		11	3
	5		1				7	4	2		*12	s	10			8	9		6		3		*11	4
	5					1	*7	4	2		*12	s	10			8	9		6		3		11	5
	5					1	7	4	2		s		10			8	9	s	6		3		11	6
	5					1	7	4	2		s		10			8	9	3	6		s		11	7
	5	*12				1	*7	4	2				10			8	9	3	6		s		11	8
	5	s				1	7	4	2	14			10			8	9	3	6				11	9
	5	s	1				7	4	14	2			10			8	9	3	6				11	10
	5	*12	1	14			7		4	2			10			8	9		6		*3		11	11
	5	s		s		1	7		4	2			10			8	9	3	6				11	12
	5	s		s		1	7		4	2			10			8	9	3	6				11	13
	5	s		s		1	7		4	2			10			8	9	3	6				11	14
	5	14		*12		1	*7		4	2			10			8	9	3	6				11	15
	5			14		1	7		4	2			10			8	9	3	6		s		11	16
	5	s		s		1	7		4	2			10			8	9	3			6		11	17
	5	s		3		1	7		4	2			10			8	9	s			6		11	18
	5	s		3		1	7		4	2			10			8	9	14			6		11	19
	5			4		1	7		s	2			10	s		8	9	3			6		11	20
	5			4		1	7		3	2			10	*12		*8	9	14	6				11	21
	5					1	7		3	2	4		10	*12		8	9	14	6				*11	22
	5					1	7		3	2	4		10	*12		8	9	s	6				*11	23
	5					1	7		3	2	4		10	11		8	9	s	6				s	24
	5					1	7		3	2	4		10	11		8	*9	14	6				*12	25
3	5		1				7		s	2	4		10	11		8	9	14	6					26
3	5		1				7		*12	2	*4		10	11		8	9	s	6					27
3	5	*12	1				7		9	2	4		10	11		*8		14	6					28
3	5	s				1	7		9	2	4		10	11		8		s	6					29
3	5	s				1	7		9	2	4		10	11		8	14		6					30
3	5	s				1	7		4	2			10	11		8	9	14	6					31
3	5	*12				1	7		4	*2			10	11		8	9	14	6					32
3	5	9				1		10	4	2		*12		11		8		*7	6		s			33
3	5	9				1		10	*4	2		11				8		7	6	s	*12			34
3	5	9	1				7	10	*12	2		*4		11		8		s	6					35
3	5	s	1				7	10	4	2		s		11		8		9	6					36
3	5	s	1				7	10	4	2				11		8		s	6			9		37
3	5		1		8		7	*10	4	2	s			11				*12	6			9		38
3	5	s	1		8		7		4	2	10			11	*12				6			*9		39
3	5	s	1		8		7		4	2	10			11	9			14	6					40
3	5	s	1		8		7	10	4	2	9			11				s	6					41
3	5	s	1		8		7	10	*4	2	9			11	*12				6					42
3	5	14	1		8		7	10	4	2	9			11	s				6					43
3	5	14	1		8		7	10	*4	2	9			11					6			*12		44
3	5	14	1		8		7	10	4	2	*9			11				*12	6			4		45
3	5	8	1		14		7	10	4	2	9			11				s	6			4		46
21	46	4	21	5	8	25	44	22	37	38	17	2	32	24	1	37	29	16	42	0	9	5	21	Apps
		8		4	1				4	1	4	2		3	2		1	11			1	1	2	Subs
2	5	1			1		6		4	1	3		1	5		22	4		4				10	Goals

Bodin P J	Calderwood C	Close S C	Digby F C	Foley S	Gibson T B	Hammond N D	Hazard M	Hoddle G	Jones T	Kerslake D	Ling M	Lorenzo N G	MacLaren R	Mitchell D S	Moncur J F	Shearer D N	Simpson F	Summerbee N J	Taylor S	Trollope P J	Viveash A L	Waddock G P	White S J	
	5		1	*2			7	4	*12				10	11		8	9	3	6				14	1/1
	5		1				7	4	2		s	s	10			8	9		6		3		11	1/2
	5	s				1	7	4	2				10			8	9	3	6		14		11	2/1
	5	s	1				7		2	4			10			8	9	3	6		s		11	2/2
	5			*12		1	7		4	2			10			8	9	3	6		s		*11	3
	5	14		4		1	7		*12	2			10			8	9		6		*3		11	4
	6	0	3	2		3	6	3	4	3			6	1		6	6	4	6		2		5	Apps
		1		1					2												1		1	Subs
							1							1		6		1	1				3	Goals

Bodin P J	Calderwood C	Close S C	Digby F C	Foley S	Gibson T B	Hammond N D	Hazard M	Hoddle G	Jones T	Kerslake D	Ling M	Lorenzo N G	MacLaren R	Mitchell D S	Moncur J F	Shearer D N	Simpson F	Summerbee N J	Taylor S	Trollope P J	Viveash A L	Waddock G P	White S J	
	5					1	7		3	2	4		10	11		8	9	14	6				s	3
3	5		1				7		s	2	4		10	11		8	9	s	6					4
3	5					1	7		9	2	4		10	11		8	14	s	6					5
2	3		1			2	3		2	3	3		3	3		3	2	0	3					Apps
																	1	1						Subs
	1													2		4								Goals

SEASON 1992/93

Football League First Division
Final League Position : 5th
Manager : Glenn Hoddle

Substitutes :
s denotes substitute **not** used
* player substituted by *12
_ player substituted by 14

No	Day	Month	Date	Opponents	Home	Away	H-T	Goalscorers	Gate
1	S	Aug	15	Sunderland	W1-0		(0-0)	Hoddle 55	11,094
2	W		19	Bristol Rovers		W4-3	(3-1)	Taylor 3,Mitchell 31,47,Bodin 40 pen.	6,150
3	S		22	Wolverhampton Wanderers		D2-2	(1-1)	Maskell 15,Taylor 82	15,493
4	S		29	Cambridge United	W4-1		(2-0)	Taylor 12,Maskell 28,58,73 pen.	8,134
5	S	Sep	5	Millwall		L1-2	(1-0)	Maskell 21	8,091
6	S		12	Bristol Rovers	D2-2		(1-0)	Mitchell 23,Maskell 71	10,006
7	Su		20	Oxford United	D2-2		(1-0)	Ling 42,Taylor 67	7,717
8	S		26	Charlton Athletic	*	L0-2	(0-1)		6,742
9	Tu		29	Grimsby Town	W1-0		(1-0)	Maskell 2	5,759
10	S	Oct	3	Watford	W3-1		(0-1)	Maskell 56,83,Taylor 87	7,723
11	S		10	Portsmouth		L1-3	(0-2)	White 78	12,442
12	S		17	Notts County	W5-1		(2-0)	Ling 29,Mitchell 35,Summerbee 47,Horlock 79,Moncur 83	7,589
13	S		24	West Ham United		W1-0	(0-0)	Maskell 84	17,842
14	S		31	Barnsley	W1-0		(1-0)	Maskell 4 pen.	7,784
15	Tu	Nov	3	Brentford	L0-2		(0-2)		7,832
16	Su		8	Newcastle United		D0-0			28,091
17	S		14	Southend United	W3-2		(3-1)	Maskell 10,12,Ling 24	7,777
18	S		21	Bristol City		D2-2	(1-1)	Maskell 32,Summerbee 58	14,066
19	Su		29	Peterborough United		D3-3	(1-2)	Taylor 22,77,Maskell 58	5,976
20	S	Dec	6	Derby County	L2-4		(0-2)	Hazard 88,Maskell 90	8,924
21	S		20	Leicester City		L2-4	(0-3)	Hazard 52,Walsh o.g.82	15,088
22	S	Jan	9	Oxford United		W1-0	(1-0)	White 34	9,146
23	Tu		12	Birmingham City	D0-0				14,398
24	S		16	Charlton Athletic	D2-2		(2-2)	Summerbee 34,Calderwood 40	8,605
25	Tu		26	Grimsby Town		L1-2	(0-1)	Bodin 58	5,207
26	S		30	Wolverhampton Wanderers	W1-0		(0-0)	Bodin 69	10,812
27	S	Feb	6	Sunderland		W1-0	(0-0)	Bodin 53	17,234
28	S		13	Millwall	W3-0		(1-0)	White 45,Bodin 60,Taylor 84	10,544
29	S		20	Cambridge United		L0-1	(0-0)		5,437
30	Tu		23	Tranmere Rovers	W2-0		(1-0)	Mitchell 10,48	10,059
31	S		27	Portsmouth	W1-0		(0-0)	Bodin 88	14,077
32	S	Mar	6	Watford		W4-0	(3-0)	White 2,30,81,Mitchell 21	8,791
33	W		10	Southend United		D1-1	(0-0)	White 68	4,371
34	S		13	Newcastle United	W2-1		(0-1)	Bodin 51 pen.,Calderwood 55	17,574
35	W		17	Luton Town		D0-0			8,902
36	Su		21	Derby County		L1-2	(0-0)	Taylor 72	12,166
37	W		24	Bristol City	W2-1		(1-0)	Marwood 19,Bodin 61 pen.	13,157
38	S		27	Brentford		D0-0			10,197
39	S	Apr	3	Peterborough United	W1-0		(0-0)	Bodin 67	10,314
40	Tu		6	Tranmere Rovers		L1-3	(1-0)	Mitchell 22	8,335
41	S		10	Luton Town	W1-0		(0-0)	Bodin 83	10,934
42	M		12	Birmingham City		W6-4	(1-2)	Taylor 43,Maskell 60,78,Mitchell 65,76,90	17,903
43	S		17	Leicester City	D1-1		(0-1)	Taylor 70	15,428
44	S		24	Notts County		D1-1	(1-1)	Bodin 40 pen.	8,382
45	Su	May	2	West Ham United	L1-3		(0-1)	Hazard 61	17,004
46	S		8	Barnsley		L0-1	(0-1)		6,031

* Played at Boleyn Ground (Upton Park)

Average Home Attendance : **10,869**
Average Away Attendance : **10,960**

Football League Cup

Rd	Day	Month	Date	Opponents	Home	Away	H-T	Goalscorers	Gate
2/1	W	Sep	23	Torquay United		W6-0	(3-0)	Maskell 8,Mitchell 34,82,Ling 35,Taylor 56,White 86	3,560
2/2	Tu	Oct	6	Torquay United	W3-2		(3-0)	Hoddle 3,White 11,Mitchell 26	3,293
3	Tu		27	Oldham Athletic	L0-1		(0-0)		8,811

F A Cup

Rd	Day	Month	Date	Opponents	Home	Away	H-T	Goalscorers	Gate
3	M	Jan	4	Queens Park Rangers		L0-3	(0-3)		12,106

GLENN HODDLE
began his first managerial role in April 1991 following Ossie Ardiles' move to Newcastle while, from the role of sweeper, he sprayed passes to all corners of the County Ground. Under his guidance, Town finally made it to the Premiership - but Glenn instead decided to take up the offer of a return to Chelsea.

Berkley A J	Bodin P J	Calderwood C	Close S C	Digby F C	Gray A A	Hammond N D	Hamon C A J	Hazard M	Hoddle G	Horlock K	Hunt P C	Kerslake D	Ling M	MacLaren R	Marwood B	Maskell C D	Mitchell D S	Moncur J F	Murray E J	Phillips M S	Summerbee N J	Taylor S	Viveash A L	White S J	
	3	5	*12	1				7	4				10			*9	11	8			2	6	s		1
	3	5		1				7	4			14	10			9	*11	8			2	6		*12	2
	3	5		1				7	4			10	s			9	11	8			2	6		s	3
	3	5	s	1				7	4			2	10			9	11	8			s	6			4
	3	5		1				7	4			2	10			9	*11	8			s	6		*12	5
	3	5		1					4			2	10			9	11	8			7	6	s	s	6
	3	5	s	1				7	4			2	10			9	11	8			s	6			7
	3	5		1				*7	4			2	10			9	11	8			*12	6		14	8
	3	5				1		7	4			2	10			9	11	8			s	6		s	9
	3	5				1		7	4			2	10			9	*11			s	8	6		*12	10
	3	5				1		*7	4	14		2	10			9	11				8	6		*12	11
		5				1		7	4	3		2	10			*9	11	14			8	6		*12	12
		5				1		7	4	3		2	10			9	11	*8				6	s	*12	13
		5				1		7	4	3		2	10			9	*11				8	6	s	*12	14
		5				1		7	4	3		*2	10			9	11				8	6	s	*12	15
s		5				1		7	4	3		2	10			*9	11				8	6		*12	16
		5				1		7	4	3	14	2	10			9	11				8	6		s	17
		5				1		7	*4	3	s	2	10			9	11				8	6		*12	18
		5				1		7	4	3		2	10			9	11	s			8	6		s	19
		5				1		7	4	3		2	10			9	*11	14			8	6		*12	20
	14	5				1		7	4	3		2	10			9		*8			11	6		*12	21
	3	5		1	8			7	4	s		2	10			9	s					6		11	22
	3	5		1	8			7	4	10		2				*9	*12				s	6		11	23
	3	5		1	8			7		10		2		s		*9	*12				4	6		11	24
	3	5		1				7	4			2	*10	8		9	*12				14	6		11	25
	3	5		1				7	4			2	10	8		*9	*12				14	6		11	26
	3	5	s	1					4	s		2	10	8			9				7	6		11	27
	3	5	s	1					4	s		2	10	8			9				7	6		11	28
	3	5	*12	1					4			2	10	8		*9			s		7	6		11	29
	3	5	s	1					4		s	2	10	8			9				7	6		11	30
	3	5	s	1					4			2	10	8			9		s		7	6		11	31
	3	5	s	1					4			2	10	8			9		s		7	6		11	32
	3	5	s	1							7		10	8	s		9				2	6	4	11	33
	3	5	s	1							7		10	8	14		9				2	6	4	11	34
	3	5	s	1							7		10	8	14		9				2	6	4	11	35
	3	5	*12	1					14				10	8	*7		9				2	6	4	11	36
	3	5	*12	1					4		14		10	8	7		*9				2	6		11	37
	3	5	*12	1					4		s		10	8	*7		9				2	6		11	38
	3	5	s	1					4		s		10	8	7		9				2	6		11	39
	3	5	*12	1				14	4				10	8	*7		9				2	6		11	40
	3	5	11	1			14	*12	4				10	8	*7	9					2	6			41
	3	5	s	1				7	4				10	8	s	11	9				2	6			42
	3	5	s	1				7	4				10	8	14	11	9				2	6			43
	3	5		1				7	4				10	8	s	*11	9				2	6		*12	44
		5		1				7	4				10	8	14	*12	9				2	6	3	*11	45
		5		1			11	*7	4	3			10	8	14	9		*12			2	6			46
0	34	46	1	33	3	13	1	30	41	13	3	30	43	22	6	32	37	11	0	0	36	46	5	20	Apps
	1		6				1	2	1	1	2	1			5	1	4	3			3			14	Subs
	11	2						3	1	1			3		1	18	11	1			3	11		7	Goals

Opponents 1 goal

Berkley A J	Bodin P J	Calderwood C	Close S C	Digby F C	Gray A A	Hammond N D	Hamon C A J	Hazard M	Hoddle G	Horlock K	Hunt P C	Kerslake D	Ling M	MacLaren R	Marwood B	Maskell C D	Mitchell D S	Moncur J F	Murray E J	Phillips M S	Summerbee N J	Taylor S	Viveash A L	White S J	
	3	5		1				7	4			2	10			9	11	*8			*12	6		14	2/1
		5	*12			1		7	4	3		2	*10				11			14	8	6		9	2/2
		5				1		7	4	3		2	*10			9	11				8	6	s	*12	3
	1	3	0	1		2		3	3	2		3	3			2	3	1		0	2	3		1	Apps
			1																	1	1			2	Subs
									1				1			1	3					1		2	Goals

Berkley A J	Bodin P J	Calderwood C	Close S C	Digby F C	Gray A A	Hammond N D	Hamon C A J	Hazard M	Hoddle G	Horlock K	Hunt P C	Kerslake D	Ling M	MacLaren R	Marwood B	Maskell C D	Mitchell D S	Moncur J F	Murray E J	Phillips M S	Summerbee N J	Taylor S	Viveash A L	White S J	
	3					1		7	4	*8		2	10			9	5		14		*12	6		11	3

For Final League Table - see Page 227 For Play-Offs and Full Members' Cup - see overleaf >>

SEASON 1990/91

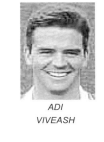

Rd	Day	Month	Date	Opponents	Home	Away	H-T	Goalscorers	Gate
2	W	Dec	12	Chelsea		L0-1	(0-0)		5,888

Bodin P J	Digby F C	Foley S	Gittens J A	Green R E	Hazard M	Jones T	Kerslake D	MacLaren R	Shearer D N	Simpson F	Viveash A L	White S J	Rd
3	1	11	6	s	4	7	2	10	8	9	5	s	2

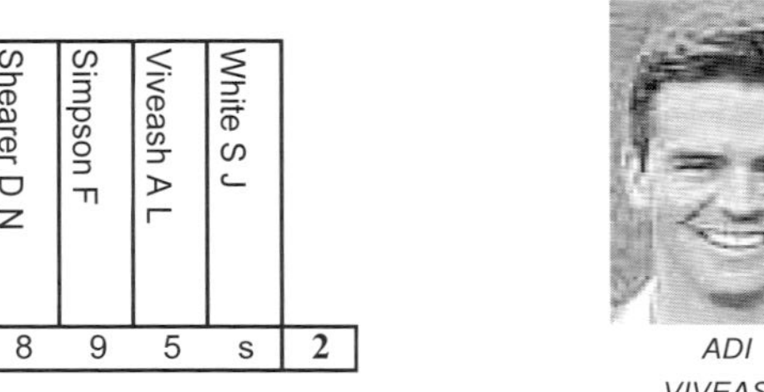
ADI VIVEASH

SEASON 1991/92

Rd	Day	Month	Date	Opponents	Home	Away	H-T	Goalscorers	Gate
1	Tu	Oct	1	Oxford United	D3-3 +		(0-0)	White 71,105,MacLaren 80	5,868
2	W		23	Chelsea		L0-1	(0-0)		5,784

+ After Extra Time (W4-3 on penalties)

Calderwood C	Close S C	Digby F C	Foley S	Hammond N D	Hazard M	Hoddle G	Jones T	Kerslake D	Ling M	MacLaren R	Shearer D N	Simpson F	Summerbee N J	Taylor S	White S J	
5	*12	1				14	2	4	*7	10	8	9	3	6	11	1
5	s		s	1	7		4	2		10	8	9	3	6	11	2
2	0	1	0	1	1	0	2	2	1	2	2	2	2	2	2	Apps
	1					1										Subs
										1					2	Goals

SHAUN TAYLOR

SEASON 1992/93

(Anglo-Italian Cup)

Rd	Day	Month	Date	Opponents	Home	Away	H-T	Goalscorers	Gate
Pr	Tu	Sep	1	Oxford United		W3-1	(2-0)	Maskell 42,Summerbee 44,Berkley 56	4,069
Pr	W		16	Brentford	L1-2		(0-1)	Mitchell 54	3,189

Play-Offs

Rd	Day	Month	Date	Opponents	Home	Away	H-T	Goalscorers	Gate
SF	Su	May	16	Tranmere Rovers	W3-1		(3-0)	Vickers o.g.2,Mitchell 3,Maskell 26	14,230
SF	W		19	Tranmere Rovers		L2-3	(1-1)	Moncur 29,Maskell 82	16,083
F	M		31	Leicester City		* W4-3	(1-0)	Hoddle 42,Maskell 47,Taylor 53,Bodin 84 pen.	73,802

* Played at Wembley Stadium

Berkley A J	Bodin P J	Calderwood C	Close S C	Digby F C	Hazard M	Hoddle G	Hunt P C	Kerslake D	Ling M	MacLaren R	Maskell C D	Mitchell D S	Moncur J F	Murray E J	O'Sullivan W St J	Summerbee N J	Taylor S	Viveash A L	White S J	
11	3	5	8	1			4		10		*9			s	2	7		6	*12	Pr
	3	5		1	7			2	10		*9	11	8			4	6	s	*12	Pr
1	2	2	1	2	1		1	1	2		2	1	1	0	1	2	1	1	0	Apps
																			2	Subs
1											1	1				1				Goals
	3	5		1	14	4			10	8	11	9	*7			2	6		*12	SF
	3	5		1	s	4			10	8	14	9	7			2	6		11	SF
	3	5		1	14	4			10	8	11	9	*7			2	6		*12	F
	3	3		3	0	3			3	3	2	3	3			3	3		1	Apps
					2						1								2	Subs
	1					1					3	1	1				1			Goals

Opponents 1 goal

SEASON 1993/94

Premier

	P	W	D	L	F	A	W	D	L	F	A	Pts	G/D	Avge. Home Gate
1 Manchester United	42	14	6	1	39	13	13	5	3	41	25	92	+42	44,244
2 Blackburn Rovers	42	14	5	2	31	11	11	4	6	32	25	84	+27	17,721
3 Newcastle United	42	14	4	3	51	14	9	4	8	31	27	77	+41	33,679
4 Arsenal	42	10	8	3	25	15	8	9	4	28	13	71	+25	30,563
5 Leeds United	42	13	6	2	37	18	5	10	6	28	21	70	+26	34,493
6 Wimbledon	42	12	5	4	35	21	6	6	9	21	32	65	+3	10,474
7 Sheffield Wednesday	42	10	7	4	48	24	6	9	6	28	30	64	+22	27,191
8 Liverpool	42	12	4	5	33	23	5	5	11	26	32	60	+4	38,493
9 Queens Park Rangers	42	8	7	6	32	29	8	5	8	30	32	60	+1	14,228
10 Aston Villa	42	8	5	8	23	18	7	7	7	23	32	57	-4	29,015
11 Coventry City	42	9	7	5	23	17	5	7	9	20	28	56	-2	13,352
12 Norwich City	42	4	9	8	26	29	8	8	5	39	32	53	+4	18,164
13 West Ham United	42	6	7	8	26	31	7	6	8	21	27	52	-11	20,572
14 Chelsea	42	11	5	5	31	20	2	7	12	18	33	51	-4	19,416
15 Tottenham Hotspur	42	4	8	9	29	33	7	4	10	25	26	45	-5	27,160
16 Manchester City	42	6	10	5	24	22	3	8	10	14	27	45	-11	26,709
17 Everton	42	8	4	9	26	30	4	4	13	16	33	44	-21	22,876
18 Southampton	42	9	2	10	30	31	3	5	13	19	35	43	-17	14,751
19 Ipswich Town	42	5	8	8	21	32	4	8	9	14	26	43	-23	16,382
20 Sheffield United	42	6	10	5	24	23	2	8	11	18	37	42	-18	19,562
21 Oldham Athletic	42	5	8	8	24	33	4	5	12	18	35	40	-26	12,563
22 SWINDON TOWN	42	4	7	10	25	45	1	8	12	22	55	30	-53	14,021

SEASON 1994/95

Div.1

	P	W	D	L	F	A	W	D	L	F	A	Pts	G/D	Avge. Home Gate
1 Middlesbrough	46	15	4	4	41	19	8	9	6	26	21	82	+27	18,702
2 Reading	46	12	7	4	34	21	11	3	9	24	23	79	+14	9,350
3 Bolton Wanderers *	46	16	6	1	43	13	5	8	10	24	32	77	+22	13,029
4 Wolverhampton Wanderers	46	15	5	3	39	18	6	8	9	38	43	76	+16	25,853
5 Tranmere Rovers	46	17	4	2	51	23	5	6	12	16	35	76	+9	8,906
6 Barnsley	46	15	6	2	42	19	5	6	12	21	33	72	+11	6,509
7 Watford	46	14	6	3	33	17	5	7	11	19	29	70	+6	8,125
8 Sheffield United	46	12	9	2	41	21	5	8	10	33	34	68	+19	14,462
9 Derby County	46	12	6	5	44	23	6	6	11	22	28	66	+15	13,589
10 Grimsby Town	46	12	7	4	36	19	5	7	11	26	37	65	+6	5,921
11 Stoke City	46	10	7	6	31	21	6	8	9	19	32	63	-3	12,910
12 Millwall	46	11	8	4	36	22	5	6	12	24	38	62	0	7,685
13 Southend United	46	13	2	8	33	25	5	6	12	21	48	62	-19	5,146
14 Oldham Athletic	46	12	7	4	34	21	4	6	13	26	39	61	0	8,444
15 Charlton Athletic	46	11	6	6	33	25	5	5	13	25	41	59	-8	10,211
16 Luton Town	46	8	6	9	35	30	7	7	9	26	34	58	-3	7,350
17 Port Vale	46	11	5	7	30	24	4	8	11	28	40	58	-6	9,174
18 Portsmouth	46	9	8	6	31	28	6	5	12	22	35	58	-10	8,269
19 West Bromwich Albion	46	13	3	7	33	24	3	7	13	18	33	58	-6	15,200
20 Sunderland	46	5	12	6	22	22	7	6	10	19	23	54	-4	15,344
21 SWINDON TOWN	46	9	6	8	28	27	3	6	14	26	46	48	-19	9,744
22 Burnley	46	8	7	8	36	33	3	6	14	13	41	46	-25	12,063
23 Bristol City	46	8	8	7	26	28	3	4	16	16	35	45	-21	8,005
24 Notts County	46	7	8	8	26	28	2	5	16	19	38	40	-21	7,195

SEASON 1995/96

Div. 2

	P	W	D	L	F	A	W	D	L	F	A	Pts	G/D	Avge. Home Gate
1 SWINDON TOWN	46	12	10	1	37	16	13	7	3	34	18	92	+37	10,602
2 Oxford United	46	17	4	2	52	14	7	7	9	24	25	83	+37	5,876
3 Blackpool	46	14	5	4	41	20	9	8	6	26	20	82	+27	5,818
4 Notts County	46	14	6	3	42	21	7	9	7	21	18	78	+24	5,130
5 Crewe Alexandra	46	13	3	7	40	24	9	4	10	37	36	73	+17	3,974
6 Bradford City *	46	15	4	4	41	25	7	3	13	30	44	73	+2	5,708
7 Chesterfield	46	14	6	3	39	21	6	6	11	17	30	72	+5	4,884
8 Wrexham	46	12	6	5	51	27	6	10	7	25	28	70	+21	3,705
9 Stockport County	46	8	9	6	30	20	11	4	8	31	27	70	+14	5,859
10 Bristol Rovers	46	12	4	7	29	28	8	6	9	28	32	70	-3	5,279
11 Walsall	46	12	7	4	38	20	7	5	11	22	25	69	+15	3,982
12 Wycombe Wanderers	46	9	8	6	36	26	6	7	10	27	33	60	+4	4,573
13 Bristol City	46	10	6	7	28	22	5	9	9	27	38	60	-5	7,017
14 AFC Bournemouth	46	12	5	6	33	25	4	5	14	18	45	58	-19	4,213
15 Brentford	46	12	6	5	24	15	3	7	13	19	34	58	-6	4,768
16 Rotherham United	46	11	7	5	31	20	3	7	13	23	42	56	-8	3,413
17 Burnley	46	9	8	6	35	28	5	5	13	21	40	55	-12	9,064
18 Shrewsbury Town	46	7	8	8	32	29	6	6	11	26	41	53	-12	3,348
19 Peterborough United	46	9	6	8	40	27	4	7	12	19	39	52	-7	4,655
20 York City	46	8	6	9	28	29	5	7	11	30	44	52	-15	3,538
21 Carlisle United	46	11	6	6	35	20	1	7	15	22	52	49	-15	5,704
22 Swansea City	46	8	8	7	27	29	3	6	14	16	50	47	-36	2,996
23 Brighton & Hove Albion	46	6	7	10	25	31	4	3	16	21	38	40	-23	5,255
24 Hull City	46	4	8	11	26	37	1	8	14	10	41	31	-42	3,803

* Promoted via Play-offs

SEASON 1993/94

F A Premier League
Final League Position : 22nd (Last)
Manager : John Gorman

Substitutes :
s denotes substitute **not** used
* player substituted by *s
_ player substituted by s

					Home	Away	H-T	Goalscorers	Gate
1	S	Aug	14	Sheffield United		L1-3	(0-1)	Moncur 47	20,904
2	W		18	Oldham Athletic	L0-1		(0-0)		11,940
3	Su		22	Liverpool	L0-5		(0-2)		17,364
4	W		25	Southampton		L1-5	(0-1)	Maskell 83 pen.	12,505
5	S		28	Norwich City		D0-0			17,614
6	W	Sep	1	Manchester City	L1-3		(0-0)	Summerbee 60	16,067
7	S		11	West Ham United		D0-0			15,777
8	S		18	Newcastle United	D2-2		(0-2)	Ling 60,Mutch 61	15,393
9	S		25	Manchester United		L2-4	(0-2)	Mutch 78,Bodin 88 pen.	44,583
10	S	Oct	2	Blackburn Rovers	L1-3		(1-1)	Taylor 32	15,847
11	S		16	Everton	D1-1		(0-1)	Taylor 89	14,437
12	S		23	Tottenham Hotspur		D1-1	(0-0)	Bodin 64 pen.	31,394
13	S		30	Aston Villa	L1-2		(1-1)	Bodin 33 pen.	16,530
14	S	Nov	6	Wimbledon		L0-3	(0-1)		7,758
15	S		20	Ipswich Town	D2-2		(1-1)	Scott 45,Bodin 83 pen.	13,860
16	W		24	Queens Park Rangers	W1-0		(1-0)	Scott 37	14,674
17	S		27	Leeds United		L0-3	(0-0)		32,630
18	S	Dec	4	Sheffield United	D0-0				12,882
19	Tu		7	Oldham Athletic		L1-2	(0-1)	Mutch 72	9,771
20	S		11	Liverpool		D2-2	(0-0)	Moncur 60,Scott 74	32,739
21	S		18	Southampton	W2-1		(1-1)	Bodin 11,Scott 65	13,565
22	M		27	Arsenal	L0-4		(0-2)		17,651
23	W		29	Sheffield Wednesday		D3-3	(2-1)	Mutch 7,Maskell 20,90	30,570
24	S	Jan	1	Chelsea	L1-3		(0-2)	Mutch 90	16,456
25	M		3	Coventry City		D1-1	(0-0)	Mutch 90	15,869
26	S		15	Everton		L2-6	(0-2)	Moncur 56,Bodin 60	20,760
27	S		22	Tottenham Hotspur	W2-1		(1-1)	Fjørtoft 38,Whitbread 80	16,563
28	S	Feb	5	Coventry City	W3-1		(2-0)	Fjørtoft 8,35 pen.,79 pen.	14,635
29	S		12	Aston Villa		L0-5	(0-1)		27,637
30	S		19	Norwich City	D3-3		(2-2)	Taylor 18,Fjørtoft 45,50	15,405
31	S		26	Manchester City		L1-2	(1-1)	Fjørtoft 8	26,360
32	S	Mar	5	West Ham United	D1-1		(0-0)	Fjørtoft 88	15,929
33	S		12	Newcastle United		L1-7	(0-2)	Moncur 78	32,219
34	S		19	Manchester United	D2-2		(1-1)	Nijholt 36,Fjørtoft 88	18,102
35	S		26	Blackburn Rovers		L1-3	(1-2)	Fjørtoft 4	20,046
36	S	Apr	2	Arsenal		D1-1	(1-1)	Bodin 30 pen.	31,635
37	M		4	Sheffield Wednesday	L0-1		(0-0)		13,927
38	S		16	Ipswich Town		D1-1	(1-0)	Fjørtoft 14	14,760
39	S		23	Wimbledon	L2-4		(0-1)	Summerbee 67,Barton o.g.80	13,727
40	W		27	Chelsea		L0-2	(0-2)		11,180
41	S		30	Queens Park Rangers		W3-1	(0-0)	Taylor 64,Fjørtoft 77,Summerbee 90	9,875
42	S	May	7	Leeds United	L0-5		(0-2)		17,539

Average Home Attendance : **14,021**
Average Away Attendance : **20,286**

Football League Cup

					Home	Away	H-T	Goalscorers	Gate
2/1	W	Sep	22	Wolverhampton Wanderers	W2-0		(1-0)	Summerbee 20,Mutch 57	8,756
2/2	Tu	Oct	5	Wolverhampton Wanderers		L1-2	(0-0)	Summerbee 60	11,756
3	Tu		26	Portsmouth		L0-2	(0-0)		12,554

F A Cup

					Home	Away	H-T	Goalscorers	Gate
3	S	Jan	8	Ipswich Town	D1-1		(1-1)	Mutch 45	12,170
3R	Tu		18	Ipswich Town		L1-2	(0-1)	Fjørtoft 75	12,796

JOHN GORMAN
had arrived at the County Ground with Glenn Hoddle in April 1991 and was offered the chance to join him when he left for Chelsea, but John was persuaded to stay and meet the challenge. Defensive lynchpin Colin Calderwood had also departed and John brought in two £500,000 signings in Adrian Whitbread and Jan-Åge Fjørtoft. But the Norwegian failed to score until January, while the young centre-back struggled to adapt to life in the big league - and Town's fate was sealed with three games to play. The 1994/95 season started brightly with just one defeat in seven, but the tide turned swiftly and by mid-November, John's reign was over. In 1996 he teamed up with Glenn Hoddle once again - in charge of the England side.

Berkley A J	Bodin P J	Digby F C	Fenwick T W	Fjørtoft JA	Gooden T M	Hammond N D	Hamon C A J	Hazard M	Heald P A	Horlock K	Kilcline B	Ling M	McAvennie F	MacLaren R	Maskell C D	Moncur J F	Mutch A T	Nijholt L	Sanchez L P	Scott K	Sheffield J	Summerbee N J	Taylor S	Thomson A J	Viveash A L	Whitbread A R	White S J	
		1		*9		s				*s		10		8	11	7		5				2	6		s	14	12	1
		1		9		s		*4		*s		10		8	11	7		5				2	6		s	14		2
		1		9		s		*s		16		10		8	s	*7	25	5				2	6			14		3
		1		9		s		*s		16		10		8	s	7	25	*5				2	6			14		4
		1		*s		s		4		16		10		8	s	7	*25	5				2	6			14		5
		1		*s		s		4		16		10		8	s	7	*25	5				2	6			14		6
		1	s	*9		s		4		16		10				7	25	5				2	6			14	*s	7
	3	1	*s	9		s		4				*10				7	25	5				2	6			14	s	8
	3	1	26	*9		s		4				10		s		7	25	5				2	6				*s	9
	3	1	26	s		s		4				10		*s		7	25	5				*2	6				12	10
	3	1	26	s		s				*s		*10		8	11	7	25	5				2	6					11
	3	1	26	9		s				*s		*10		8	s	7	25	5				2	6					12
	3	1	*26	9		s				16		s		8		7	25	5				2	6			*s		13
	3	1		*9		s				16		10		8	s	7	25					2	6			14	*s	14
	3	1	26			s				16		*s			s	7	25	5		27		*2	6			14		15
	3	1	26	s		s				16		10			s	7	25	5		27			6			14		16
	3	1	26	*s		s				*16		10		s		7	25	5		27			6			14		17
	3	1	26			s				16		*10			s	7	25	5		27		*s	6			14		18
	3	1	26			s				16		s			s	7	25	5		27		2	6			14		19
	3	1	26	s		s				16		10			*s	7	25			27		*2	6			14		20
s	3	1	26	s		s				16		10			11	7	25			27			6			14		21
	*3	1	26	s		s				16		10			11	7	25			27		*s	6			14		22
		*1	26	s		*s				16		10		s	11	7	25			27		2	6			14		23
	*s		26	s		23				16		10			*11	7	25			27		2	6			14		24
	3		26			23				16		10		s	*11	7	25			*s		2	6			14		25
	3		26	s		23				*16		10				7	25	*s		27		2	6			14		26
	*s			9		23				16	31	*10				7	25	5		s		2	6			14		27
	*s			9		23				16	31	*10			s	7		5		27	s	2	6			14		28
	*s		s	9		s				16	31	10				7		5		27	40	2	6			*14		29
	3			9		*s				16	31	s	s			7		5		27	*40	2	6			14		30
	3	1	26	*9		s				16		s	*s			7	25	5				2	6			14		31
		1		9	*s	s				16		10	*32			7	25	5		s		2	6			14		32
	*3	1	26	9	*s	s	s			16		10	32			7		5		27			6					33
		1		9		s				16	31	s	*32			7		5	33	*s		2	6			14		34
	3	1	s	9		s					31	*10				7		5	33	*s		2	6			14		35
	3			9		23			s	*s	31		s			7		5	33	*27		2	6			14		36
	3			9		23			s	*s	31		s			7		5	33	27		2	6			*14		37
	3	s	26	9		23				16	31		s			7	*s		33	27		*2	6					38
	3	s	26	9		23				16	31						*s	5	*33	27		2	6			s		39
	*3		26	9		23			s	16						7	s	5	*s	27		2	6			14		40
	3		26	9	28	23			s	16						7	s			27		2	6	s		14		41
	3			9	28	s			34	16						7	s		*s	27		2	6	*19		14		42
0	28	28	23	26	2	11	0	7	1	32	10	29	3	10	8	41	27	31	6	22	2	36	42	1	0	34	2	Apps
	4		3	10	2	2	1	2	1	6		4	4	2	6		3	1	2	5		2				1	4	Subs
	7			12								1			3	4	6	1		4		3	4			1		Goals

Matches 24,25 : s = Cook S A Matches 26,27 : s = Kerr J S

Opponents 1 goal

Berkley A J	Bodin P J	Digby F C	Fenwick T W	Fjørtoft JA	Gooden T M	Hammond N D	Hamon C A J	Hazard M	Heald P A	Horlock K	Kilcline B	Ling M	McAvennie F	MacLaren R	Maskell C D	Moncur J F	Mutch A T	Nijholt L	Sanchez L P	Scott K	Sheffield J	Summerbee N J	Taylor S	Thomson A J	Viveash A L	Whitbread A R	White S J	
	3	1	26			s		4				10		s	s	7	25	5				2	6				12	2/1
	3	s	26			23		4				s		8	*11	7	25	5				2	6				*s	2/2
	3	1	26	9		s				s		*10		8	*s	7	25	5				2	6					3
	3	2	3	1		1		2		0		2		2	1	3	3	3				3	3				1	Apps
										1					1												1	Subs
																	1					2						Goals

Berkley A J	Bodin P J	Digby F C	Fenwick T W	Fjørtoft JA	Gooden T M	Hammond N D	Hamon C A J	Hazard M	Heald P A	Horlock K	Kilcline B	Ling M	McAvennie F	MacLaren R	Maskell C D	Moncur J F	Mutch A T	Nijholt L	Sanchez L P	Scott K	Sheffield J	Summerbee N J	Taylor S	Thomson A J	Viveash A L	Whitbread A R	White S J	
	3		26	*s		23				16		10			*11	7	25	s				2	6			14		3
	3		26	*9		23				16		10		s	*s		25	5				2	6			14		3R
	2		2	1		2				2		2			1	1	2	1				2	2			2		Apps
				1											1			1										Subs
				1													1											Goals

For Final League Table - see overleaf <<

SEASON 1996/97

Div.1

		P	W	D	L	F	A	W	D	L	F	A	Pts	G/S	Avge. Home Gate
1	Bolton Wanderers	46	18	4	1	60	20	10	10	3	40	33	98	100	15,826
2	Barnsley	46	14	4	5	43	19	8	10	5	33	36	80	76	11,356
3	Wolverhampton Wanderers	46	10	5	8	31	24	12	5	6	37	27	76	68	24,763
4	Ipswich Town	46	13	7	3	44	23	7	7	9	24	27	74	68	11,953
5	Sheffield United	46	13	5	5	46	23	7	8	8	29	29	73	75	16,638
6	Crystal Palace *	46	10	7	6	39	22	9	7	7	39	26	71	78	16,085
7	Portsmouth	46	12	4	7	32	24	8	4	11	27	29	68	59	8,857
8	Port Vale	46	9	9	5	36	28	8	7	8	22	27	67	58	7,385
9	Queen's Park Rangers	46	10	5	8	33	25	8	7	8	31	35	66	64	12,554
10	Birmingham City	46	11	7	5	30	18	6	8	9	22	30	66	52	17,751
11	Tranmere Rovers	46	10	9	4	42	27	7	5	11	21	29	65	63	8,127
12	Stoke City	46	15	3	5	34	22	3	7	13	17	35	64	51	12,698
13	Norwich City	46	9	10	4	28	18	8	2	13	35	50	63	63	14,719
14	Manchester City	46	12	4	7	34	25	5	6	12	25	35	61	59	26,753
15	Charlton Athletic	46	11	8	4	36	28	5	3	15	16	38	59	52	11,081
16	West Bromwich Albion	46	7	7	9	37	33	7	8	8	31	39	57	68	15,064
17	Oxford United	46	14	3	6	44	26	2	6	15	20	42	57	64	7,608
18	Reading	46	13	7	3	37	24	2	5	16	21	43	57	58	9,160
19	SWINDON TOWN	46	11	6	6	36	27	4	3	16	16	44	54	52	9,917
20	Huddersfield Town	46	10	7	6	28	20	3	8	12	20	41	54	48	12,175
21	Bradford City	46	10	5	8	29	32	2	7	14	18	40	48	47	12,925
22	Grimsby Town	46	7	7	9	31	34	4	6	13	29	47	46	60	5,859
23	Oldham Athletic	46	6	8	9	30	30	4	5	14	21	36	43	51	7,045
24	Southend United	46	7	9	7	32	32	1	6	16	10	54	39	42	5,072

SEASON 1997/98

Div.1

		P	W	D	L	F	A	W	D	L	F	A	Pts	G/S	Avge. Home Gate
1	Nottingham Forest	46	18	2	3	52	20	10	8	5	30	22	94	82	20,584
2	Middlesbrough	46	17	4	2	51	12	10	6	7	26	29	91	77	29,994
3	Sunderland	46	14	7	2	49	22	12	5	6	37	28	90	86	33,492
4	Charlton Athletic *	46	17	5	1	48	17	9	5	9	32	32	88	80	13,275
5	Ipswich Town	46	14	5	4	47	20	9	9	5	30	23	83	77	14,973
6	Sheffield United	46	16	5	2	44	20	3	12	8	25	34	74	69	17,942
7	Birmingham City	46	10	8	5	27	15	9	9	5	33	20	74	60	18,708
8	Stockport County	46	14	6	3	46	21	5	2	16	25	48	65	71	8,322
9	Wolverhampton Wanderers	46	13	6	4	42	25	5	5	13	15	28	65	57	23,281
10	West Bromwich Albion	46	9	8	6	27	26	7	5	11	23	30	61	50	16,662
11	Crewe Alexandra	46	10	2	11	30	34	8	3	12	28	31	59	58	5,243
12	Oxford United	46	12	6	5	36	20	4	4	15	24	44	58	60	7,512
13	Bradford City	46	10	9	4	26	23	4	6	13	20	36	57	46	15,564
14	Tranmere Rovers	46	9	8	6	34	26	5	6	12	20	31	56	54	7,999
15	Norwich City	46	9	8	6	32	27	5	5	13	20	42	55	52	14,444
16	Huddersfield Town	46	9	5	9	28	28	5	6	12	22	44	53	50	12,145
17	Bury	46	7	10	6	22	22	4	9	10	20	36	52	42	6,177
18	SWINDON TOWN	46	9	6	8	28	25	5	4	14	14	48	52	42	10,298
19	Port Vale	46	7	6	10	25	24	6	4	13	31	42	49	56	8,432
= 20	Portsmouth	46	8	6	9	28	30	5	4	14	23	33	49	51	11,149
= 20	Queen's Park Rangers	46	8	9	6	28	21	2	10	11	23	42	49	51	13,083
22	Manchester City	46	6	6	11	28	26	6	6	11	28	31	48	56	28,196
23	Stoke City	46	8	5	10	30	40	3	8	12	14	34	46	44	15,025
24	Reading	46	8	4	11	27	31	3	5	15	12	47	42	39	9,676

SEASON 1998/99

Div.1

		P	W	D	L	F	A	W	D	L	F	A	Pts	G/S	Avge. Home Gate
1	Sunderland	46	19	3	1	50	10	12	9	2	41	18	105	91	38,745
2	Bradford City	46	15	4	4	48	20	11	5	7	34	27	87	82	14,299
3	Ipswich Town	46	16	1	6	37	15	10	7	6	32	17	86	69	16,920
4	Birmingham City	46	12	7	4	32	15	11	5	7	34	22	81	66	20,794
5	Watford *	46	12	8	3	30	19	9	6	8	35	37	77	65	11,822
6	Bolton Wanderers	46	13	6	4	44	25	7	10	6	34	34	76	78	18,240
7	Wolverhampton Wanderers	46	11	10	2	37	19	8	6	9	27	24	73	64	22,620
8	Sheffield United	46	12	6	5	42	29	6	7	10	29	37	67	71	16,243
9	Norwich City	46	7	12	4	34	28	8	5	10	28	33	62	62	15,761
10	Huddersfield Town	46	11	9	3	38	23	4	7	12	24	48	61	62	12,976
11	Grimsby Town	46	11	6	6	25	18	6	4	13	15	34	61	40	6,681
12	West Bromwich Albion	46	12	4	7	43	33	4	7	12	26	43	59	69	14,585
13	Barnsley	46	7	9	7	35	30	7	8	8	24	26	59	59	16,268
14	Crystal Palace	46	11	10	2	43	26	3	6	14	15	45	58	58	17,123
15	Tranmere Rovers	46	8	7	8	37	30	4	13	6	26	31	56	63	6,930
16	Stockport County	46	7	9	7	24	21	5	8	10	25	39	53	49	7,898
17	SWINDON TOWN	46	7	8	8	40	44	6	3	14	19	37	50	59	8,651
18	Crewe Alexandra	46	7	6	10	27	35	5	6	12	27	43	48	54	5,269
19	Portsmouth	46	10	5	8	34	26	1	9	13	23	47	47	57	11,973
20	Queen's Park Rangers	46	9	7	7	34	22	3	4	16	18	39	47	52	11,793
21	Port Vale	46	10	3	10	22	28	3	5	15	23	47	47	45	6,991
22	Bury	46	9	7	7	24	27	1	10	12	11	33	47	35	5,475
23	Oxford United	46	7	8	8	31	30	3	6	14	17	41	44	48	7,041
24	Bristol City	46	7	8	8	35	36	2	7	14	22	44	42	57	12,860

* Promoted via Play-offs

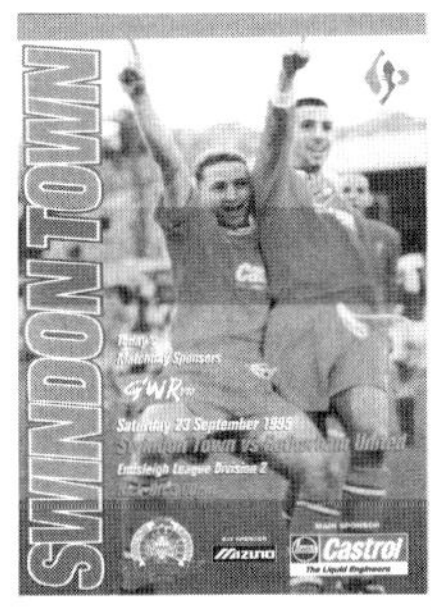
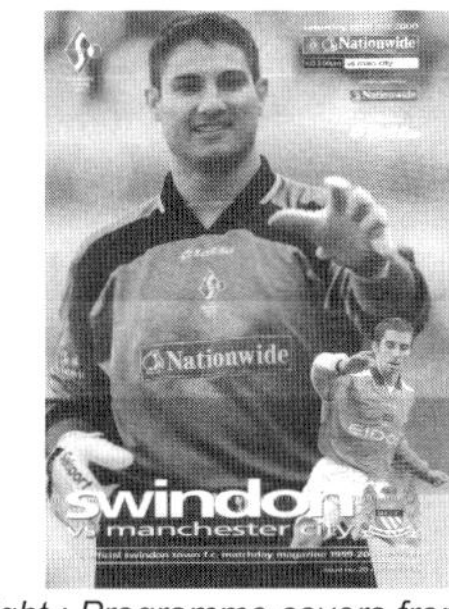

Left and right : Programme covers from seasons 1995/96 1999/2000 2003/04 and 2007/08

town in turmoil

TAKE OVERS AND TAKE AWAYS

Following John Gorman's departure from the County Ground, Steve McMahon was installed as player-manager in December 1994. But the former England midfielder was unable to arrest the slide down the table to a second successive relegation. However, with a number of players with Premiership experience still under contract, Town strode to the Second Division championship at the first attempt.

First Division status was retained until 2000 and the club looked on course to return there four years later, until plans were scuppered by a play-off defeat at Withdean.

But they sunk back to the basement division in 2006 - although Dennis Wise's brief stewardship helped guide them to automatic promotion in the following spring.

By now the club had been in financial freefall for many years. Twice plummeting into administration, in 2000 and 2002, a boardroom merry-go-round saw the media working overtime to report crisis upon crisis. Vehicles were taken away, having been repossessed and at one point there were no bona fide directors. With spiralling debts, the club teetered on the brink of extinction. And it was not until the arrival of new chairman Andrew Fitton in January 2008 that Town's future looked considerably brighter.

SAM PARKIN (see page 256)

1994 - 2009

Left to right : The new Shrivenham Road stand under construction in 1994 : Trickery from Mark Walters : Rory Fallon in celebratory mood

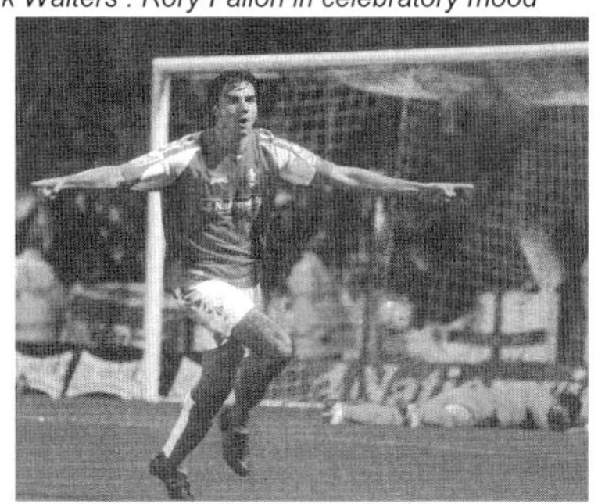

SEASON 1994/95

Football League First Division
Final League Position : 21st
Manager : John Gorman
Steve McMahon (from Nov.28)

Substitutes :
s denotes substitute **not** used
* player substituted by *12
_ player substituted by 14

					Home	Away	H-T	Goalscorers	Gate
1	S	Aug	13	Port Vale	W2-0		(1-0)	Fjørtoft 22,Scott 80	10,549
2	S		20	Tranmere Rovers		L2-3	(2-1)	Fjørtoft 9,44	8,412
3	S		27	Watford	W1-0		(1-0)	Ling 8	9,727
4	W		31	West Bromwich Albion	D0-0				10,964
5	S	Sep	3	Notts County		W1-0	(1-0)	Fjørtoft 41	6,537
6	Su		11	Derby County	D1-1		(1-1)	Fjørtoft 16	8,934
7	W		14	Reading	W1-0		(0-0)	Scott 81	11,646
8	S		17	Charlton Athletic		L0-1	(0-1)		9,420
9	S		24	Grimsby Town	W3-2		(1-1)	Bodin 18,89 pen.,Scott 90	8,758
10	S	Oct	1	Barnsley		L1-2	(0-1)	Taylor 67	3,911
11	S		8	Wolverhampton Wanderers	W3-2		(2-2)	Bodin 15,Scott 28,Beauchamp 60	14,436
12	S		15	Portsmouth		L3-4	(1-2)	Bodin 33 pen.,Fjørtoft 84,86	10,610
13	S		22	Southend United	D2-2		(1-2)	Fjørtoft 15,90	10,364
14	S		29	Middlesbrough		L1-3	(0-1)	Fjørtoft 56	17,328
15	Tu	Nov	1	Bolton Wanderers		L0-3	(0-1)		10,046
16	S		5	Millwall	L1-2		(0-0)	Bodin 76 pen.	9,046
17	Su		20	Bristol City		L2-3	(0-0)	Scott 58,90	9,086
18	W		23	Burnley	D1-1		(1-0)	Scott 17	7,658
19	S		26	Luton Town	L1-2		(1-1)	Scott 11	9,228
20	S	Dec	3	Southend United		L0-2	(0-1)		5,810
21	S		10	Tranmere Rovers	D2-2		(2-1)	Bodin 14,Fjørtoft 41	8,803
22	S		17	Port Vale		D2-2	(1-1)	Taylor 26,Fjørtoft 51	7,747
23	M		26	Stoke City		D0-0			17,633
24	Tu		27	Sheffield United	L1-3		(0-1)	Fjørtoft 54	11,013
25	S		31	Oldham Athletic		D1-1	(1-1)	Ling 25	8,917
26	Su	Jan	15	Middlesbrough	W2-1		(1-1)	Fjørtoft 23,Horlock 57	9,540
27	S	Feb	4	Burnley		W2-1	(1-0)	Thorne 43,73	10,958
28	W		15	Bristol City	L0-3		(0-1)		9,992
29	S		18	Luton Town		L0-3	(0-1)		6,595
30	S		25	Barnsley	D0-0				8,636
31	W	Mar	1	Millwall		L1-3	(0-0)	Beauchamp 68	5,950
32	S		4	Grimsby Town		D1-1	(0-1)	Taylor 90	4,934
33	S		11	Watford		L0-2	(0-0)		7,123
34	W		15	Sunderland	W1-0		(1-0)	Thorne 20	8,353
35	Su		19	West Bromwich Albion		W5-2	(0-0)	Thorne 58,85,90,Fjørtoft 74,Gooden 81	12,960
36	W		22	Derby County		L1-3	(1-1)	Viveash 20	16,839
37	S		25	Charlton Athletic	L0-1		(0-0)		9,905
38	S	Apr	1	Reading		L0-3	(0-2)		12,565
39	W		5	Bolton Wanderers	L0-1		(0-0)		8,678
40	S		8	Oldham Athletic	W3-1		(2-1)	Viveash 24,Beauchamp 27,Taylor 56	8,291
41	S		15	Sheffield United		D2-2	(1-0)	Gooden 26,Ling 53	12,217
42	M		17	Stoke City	L0-1		(0-1)		11,211
43	S		22	Sunderland		L0-1	(0-1)		16,794
44	S		29	Portsmouth	L0-2		(0-1)		10,123
45	W	May	3	Notts County	W3-0		(1-0)	Hamon 8,Thorne 58,65	8,262
46	Su		7	Wolverhampton Wanderers		D1-1	(1-1)	Thorne 38	26,254

Average Home Attendance : **9,744**
Average Away Attendance : **10,811**

Football League Cup

					Home	Away	H-T	Goalscorers	Gate
2/1	W	Sep	21	Charlton Athletic	L1-3		(0-0)	Scott 67	4,842
2/2	Tu		27	Charlton Athletic		W4-1		Fjørtoft 3,29,42,Petterson o.g.105	4,932
3	W	Oct	26	Brighton & Hove Albion		D1-1	(1-0)	Thomson 24	11,382
3R	W	Nov	9	Brighton & Hove Albion	W4-1		(2-0)	Scott 7,63,Fjørtoft 8,76	6,595
4	W		30	Derby County	W2-1		(1-1)	Fjørtoft 8,84	8,925
5	W	Jan	11	Millwall	W3-1		(2-0)	Mutch 26,61,Fjørtoft 36	11,786
SF	Su	Feb	12	Bolton Wanderers	W2-1		(1-1)	Thorne 38,76	14,450
SF	W	Mar	8	Bolton Wanderers		L1-3	(0-0)	Fjørtoft 57	19,851

F A Cup

					Home	Away	H-T	Goalscorers	Gate
3	S	Jan	7	Marlow	W2-0		(0-0)	Fjørtoft 46,Nijholt 58	7,240
4	S		28	Watford		L0-1	(0-0)		11,202

For Anglo-Italian Cup - see page 204 For Final League Table - see page 235

Beauchamp J D	Berkley A J	Bodin P J	Culverhouse I B	Digby F C	Fenwick T W	Fjørtoft JA	Gooden T M	Hammond N D	Hamon C A J	Hooper D R	Horlock K	Kilcline B	Ling M	MacLaren R	McMahon S	Murray E J	Mutch A T	Nijholt L	O'Sullivan W StJ	Pitman J R	Robinson M J	Scott K	Taylor S	Thomson A J	Thorne P L	Todd A J J	Viveash A L	Webb N J	Worrall B J	
		3		1	8	9		s			11		7				*10	5	14		2	*12	6		4 = Whitbread A R					1
14		3		1	8	9		s			11	4	7				*10	5			2	*12	6							2
8		3		1		9		s			s		7				s	5	11		2	10	6	4						3
8		3		1		9		s			*12		7				14	5	*11		2	10	6	4						4
8				1		9		s			3	s	7				*12	5	11		2	*10	6	4						5
8		3		1		9		s			11		7				*12	5	14		2	*10	6	4						6
8		3		1		9		s			*11	s	10					5	7		2	*12	6	4						7
	*12	3		1		9		s			11	14	10					5	* 7		2	8	6	4						8
8		3		1		9		s			* 7		10				14	5	*12		2	11	6	4						9
8	s	3		1		9		s			7		10				s	5			2	11	6	4						10
8		3		1		9		s			s		10				14	5			2	11	6	4				7		11
8		3		1		9		s			*12	4	10				14	5			2	11	6					*7		12
*8		3		1		9		s			*12		10				14	5			2	11	6	4				7		13
8		3		1		9		s			7		10				14	5			2	11	*6	4				*12		14
8		3		1		9		s			7	6	*12				14	*5			2	11		4				10		15
8		3		1		9		s			7	6	*12				14	5			2	11		4				*10		16
8		3		1		9		s			7	5		*4		14	10		*12		2	11				6 = Tiler C				17
8		3		1		9		s	s		*12			*4			10		7		2	11		5		6 = Tiler C				18
*12		3		1		9		s	14		8	6		*4			10		7		2	11		5						19
8		3		1		9		s			7		10		6		s	5	s		2	11		4						20
8		3	6	1		9		s			7		s		10		s	5			2	11		4						21
8		3	2	1		9		s			7		10				*12	5	s			*11	6	4						22
8		3	4	1		9		s			7		10				s	5			2	11	6	s						23
8		*3	4	1		9		s			7		10				*12	5	14		2	11	6							24
*12		3	4	s		9		1			7		11		*10	s	8	5			2		6							25
8		3	4	s		9		1			7		11			s	10	5	s		2		6							26
			4	s		9	14	1			7		11			3	s	5	8		2		6		10					27
8				s		9		1			7		11		14	3	s	5	4		2			6	10					28
8				s		9	*7	1			5		11		6	3	*12		4		2			s	10					29
8			4	s		9		1			3		s		11	s		5	7		2		6		10					30
8			*2	s		9	14	1			3		*12		11	5			7				6		10	4				31
8				1		9	7	s		14	3				11	s			2				6		10	4	5			32
*12				1		9	8	s		14	7				11			5	*2				6		10	3	4			33
8				1		9	7	s			5		s		11			s	3				6		10	2	4			34
8				1		9	*12	s			7				11			s	*2		5		6		10	3	4			35
8				1		9	7	s					*12					*5	3		11		6	s	10	2	4			36
8				1			7	s	3 = Drysdale J				* 9		11			s	*12		5		6		10	2	4			37
8				1			9		*12		3		7		11			s			*5		6		10	2	4			38
8				1			9				3		s		11			s	7		5		6		10	2	4			39
8				1			9	s	s	14			3		11			5	7		2		6		10		4			40
8				1			9	s					7		11			5	s		3		6	s	10	2	4			41
8				1			9	s					*7		11			5	*12		*3		6	14	10	2	4			42
				15			9	s	14	*12	8		11					5	* 7		2		6		10	3	4			43
8				1			9	s					11					5	7	14			6	3	10	*2	4		*12	44
8				1				s	10		3		11					5	14	*7	2		6		9		4		*12	45
11				1				s	*10		3		*12			14		5	2	7	4		6		9				8	46
38	0	25	9	39	2	36	13	7	2	0	34	6	31	3	16	4	7	35	22	2	40	21	37	20	20	13	14	5	1	Apps
4	1						3		3	4	4	1	5		1	2	13		8	1		3		1				1	2	Subs
3		6				15	2		1		1		3									8	4		9		2			Goals

Matches 38,39 : s = Hamblin C J

Match 43 : Digby wore no.15

Beauchamp J D	Berkley A J	Bodin P J	Culverhouse I B	Digby F C	Fenwick T W	Fjørtoft JA	Gooden T M	Hammond N D	Hamon C A J	Hooper D R	Horlock K	Kilcline B	Ling M	MacLaren R	McMahon S	Murray E J	Mutch A T	Nijholt L	O'Sullivan W StJ	Pitman J R	Robinson M J	Scott K	Taylor S	Thomson A J	Thorne P L	Todd A J J	Viveash A L	Webb N J	Worrall B J	
8	*12	3		1		9		s				6	10			s		*5	7		2	11		4						2/1
8		3		1		9		s			s		10				14	5	7		2	11	6	4						2/2
8		3		1		9		s			7	s	10				s	5			2	11	6	4						3
8		3		1		9		s			s	6	7			s	10	5			2	11		4						3R
14		3		1		9		s			8	*6	*12				10	5	7		2	11		4						4
8		3	4	s		9		1	s		7		11				10	5	s		2		6							5
8				s		9		1			7		11			3	s	5	4		2		6	s	10					SF
8				1		9	11	s		14	7		s			3		5	2				6		10		4			SF
7	0	6	1	6		8	1	2		0	5	3	6			2	3	8	5		7	5	5	5	2		1			Apps
1	1									1			1				1													Subs
						9											2					3		1	2					Goals

Opponents 1 goal

Beauchamp J D	Berkley A J	Bodin P J	Culverhouse I B	Digby F C	Fenwick T W	Fjørtoft JA	Gooden T M	Hammond N D	Hamon C A J	Hooper D R	Horlock K	Kilcline B	Ling M	MacLaren R	McMahon S	Murray E J	Mutch A T	Nijholt L	O'Sullivan W StJ	Pitman J R	Robinson M J	Scott K	Taylor S	Thomson A J	Thorne P L	Todd A J J	Viveash A L	Webb N J	Worrall B J	
8		3	*4	s		9		1	14		7		11				10	5	*12		2		6							3
8			4			9		1			7		11			3	*10	5	14		2		6		*12	s = Given S J				4
2		1	2			2		2	0		2		2			1	2	2	0		2		2		0					Apps
									1										2						1					Subs
						1												1												Goal

SEASON 1995/96

Football League Second Division
Final League Position : Champions
Manager : Steve McMahon

Substitutes :
s denotes substitute **not** used
* player substituted by *12
( ) player substituted by (13)
_ player substituted by 14

No	Day	Month	Date	Opponents	Home	Away	H-T	Goalscorers	Gate
1	S	Aug	12	Hull City		W1-0	(0-0)	Finney 68	6,525
2	S		19	York City	W3-0		(2-0)	Finney 2,66,Bodin 42 pen.	8,681
3	S		26	Carlisle United		W1-0	(0-0)	Murray 66	6,333
4	W		30	Oxford United	D1-1		(1-0)	Allison 40	13,556
5	S	Sep	2	Brentford		W2-0	(1-0)	O'Sullivan 39,Finney 76	7,878
6	S		9	Chesterfield	D1-1		(0-1)	Allison 46	9,067
7	W		13	Bradford City	W4-1		(2-1)	Robinson 10,Allison 18,Finney 58,Horlock 85	8,617
8	S		16	Bristol Rovers		W4-1	(1-1)	Horlock 5,63,84,Taylor 58	7,015
9	S		23	Rotherham United	W1-0		(0-0)	Gooden 64	8,922
10	S		30	Wrexham		L3-4	(2-1)	Allison 12,24,Thorne P 56	4,396
11	S	Oct	7	Bristol City	W2-0		(1-0)	O'Sullivan 11,Allison 88	12,378
12	S		14	Brighton & Hove Albion		W3-1	(3-0)	Finney 17,37,Horlock 43	7,808
13	S		21	Crewe Alexandra	W2-1		(0-0)	Allison 58,Finney 88 pen.	13,243
14	S		28	Notts County		W3-1	(2-1)	Taylor 8,79,Bodin 45	8,725
15	Tu		31	AFC Bournemouth		D0-0			6,352
16	S	Nov	4	Blackpool	D1-1		(0-0)	Finney 50	12,976
17	S		18	Stockport County		D1-1	(1-0)	Allison 45	7,196
18	S		25	Shrewsbury Town	L0-1		(0-0)		9,863
19	S	Dec	9	Rotherham United		W2-0	(0-0)	Finney 70,90	3,042
20	S		16	Wrexham	D1-1		(0-0)	O'Sullivan 76	9,891
21	S		23	Walsall		D0-0			5,624
22	Tu		26	Wycombe Wanderers	D0-0				13,355
23	W	Jan	10	Swansea City	W3-0		(1-0)	Allison 21,Thorne P 61,76	6,704
24	S		13	York City		L0-2	(0-0)		3,613
25	S		20	Hull City	W3-0		(0-0)	Thorne P 49,Grant 68,Horlock 82	8,287
26	S	Feb	3	Carlisle United	W2-1		(0-0)	Thorne P 53,Allison 71	8,367
27	S		10	Swansea City		W1-0	(1-0)	Taylor 28	4,452
28	W		21	Brentford	D2-2		(2-2)	Allison 26,Gooden 32 pen.	9,733
29	S		24	Bristol Rovers	W2-1		(0-1)	Allison 80,Taylor 81	12,054
30	S	Mar	2	Wycombe Wanderers		W2-1	(2-0)	Gooden 4,Thorne P 19	6,457
31	Tu		5	Peterborough United		W2-0	(1-0)	Allison 21,Finney 71	4,196
32	S		9	Walsall	D1-1		(0-0)	Taylor 84	10,900
33	S		16	Burnley		D0-0			9,426
34	Tu		19	Oxford United		L0-3	(0-1)		8,585
35	S		23	Peterborough United	W2-0		(2-0)	Allison 11,Thorne P 17	9,066
36	S		30	Bristol City		D0-0			11,370
37	W	Apr	3	Brighton & Hove Albion	W3-2		(1-0)	Thorne P 44,84,Allison 46	9,031
38	S		6	Notts County	W1-0		(0-0)	Horlock 89	12,311
39	M		8	Crewe Alexandra		W2-0	(1-0)	Horlock 28,Preece 48	5,162
40	S		13	AFC Bournemouth	D2-2		(1-1)	Horlock 17,73 pen.	10,862
41	W		17	Burnley	D0-0				10,915
42	S		20	Blackpool		D1-1	(1-0)	Horlock 15	9,175
43	Tu		23	Chesterfield		W3-1	(2-1)	Cowe 26,Thorne P 31,Allison 79	5,523
44	S		27	Shrewsbury Town		W2-1	(1-1)	Horlock 30,Taylor 56	4,323
45	Tu		30	Bradford City		D1-1	(0-0)	Allison 68	9,812
46	S	May	4	Stockport County	D0-0				15,062

Average Home Attendance : **10,602**
Average Away Attendance : **6,652**

Football League Cup

No	Day	Month	Date	Opponents	Home	Away	H-T	Goalscorers	Gate
1/1	Tu	Aug	15	Cambridge United		L1-2	(1-1)	Gooden 2	2,530
1/2	W		23	Cambridge United	W2-0		(0-0)	Beauchamp 78,Horlock 90	6,777
2/1	W	Sep	20	Blackburn Rovers	L2-3		(2-2)	Allison 25,Finney 26	14,941
2/2	W	Oct	4	Blackburn Rovers		L0-2	(0-1)		16,924

F A Cup

No	Day	Month	Date	Opponents	Home	Away	H-T	Goalscorers	Gate
1	S	Nov	11	Cambridge United	W4-1		(2-0)	Horlock 41,45,Finney 48,Allen 85	7,412
2	S	Dec	2	Cardiff City	W2-0		(0-0)	Allison 58,Finney 83	8,301
3	S	Jan	6	Woking	W2-0		(1-0)	Allison 17,Bodin 84	10,381
4	M	Feb	12	Oldham Athletic	W1-0		(0-0)	Ling 90	9,531
5	S		17	Southampton	D1-1		(1-0)	Horlock 32	14,591
5R	W		28	Southampton		L0-2	(0-0)		13,962

For Football League Trophy - see page 214 For Final League Table - see page 235

Allen P K	Allison W A	Beauchamp J D	Bodin P J	Collins L	Cowe S M	Culverhouse I B	Digby F C	Drysdale J	Finney S K	Given S J	Gooden T M	Grant A J	Hooper D R	Horlock K	Leitch D S	Ling M	McMahon S	Mildenhall S J	Murray E J	O'Sullivan W StJ	Pitman J R	Preece D W	Robinson M J	Seagraves M	Smith A P	Talia F	Taylor S	Thorne P L	
	10		*12			2		*3	9	1	11			s = Nijholt L			4	s		8			7	5			6		1
	10		3			2			9	1	11			*12			*4	s	s	8			7	5			6		2
		11				2	s		9	1			s	3			4		10	8	s		7	5			6		3
	10	(13)	3			2	s		9	1				11			(4)		*12	8			*7	5			6		4
	10	s	3			2	s		9	1				11			*4		*12	8			7	5			6		5
	10		(3)			2	s		9		(13)			11			4		s	8			7	5		1	6		6
	*10	(13)	3			2	s		9		*12			11			(4)			8			7	5		1	6		7
		s	3			2	s		9		*12			11			4		*10	8			7	5		1	6		8
	10		*3			2	s		(9)		*12			11			4			8			7	5		1	6	(13)	9
	10		s			2	s		*12		11			3			4			8			7	5		1	6	*9	10
	10		3			2	1		9		s		s	11			4		s	8			7	5			6		11
*12	10		3			2	1		9		s			11			*4		s	8			7	5			6		12
5	10		3			2	1		9		s			11		s	4		s	8			7				6		13
5	10		3			2	1		9		s			11		s	4		s	8			7				6		14
5	10		3			2	1		9		14			11		s	4		s	8			7				6		15
5	10		3			2	1	14	9		4			11		*12			s	*8			7				6		16
	10		3			2	1		*9		s			11		5	4			8			7			s	6	*12	17
	10					2	1	3	9		(13)			11		*5	4			(8)			7			s	6	*12	18
8	10					2	1	3	9		(13)			11			4						7	(5)		s	6	s	19
5	*10					2	1	3	(9)		8			11			4			(13)			7			s	6	*12	20
8	10					2	1	3			*12			11			*4			(13)			(7)	5		s	6	9	21
8	10					2	1	3			*12			11		s				*4			7	5		s	6	9	22
6	10		3			2	1		(13)		*12			11		(4)				8			7	5		s		9	23
8	10		3			2	1		14		*12			(11)		4			*5	6			7		(13)			9	24
(5)	10		*3			2	1		14		4	8		11		6				(13)			7		*12			9	25
	*10		3			2	1	s	*12		4	8		11		5				s			7				6	9	26
	10		3	s		2	1		s		4	8		11		5							7		s		6	9	27
5	10			s		2	1	3	*12		4			11		*8							7	s			6	9	28
(5)	10			8		2	1	3	*12		*4			11									7	(13)		s	6	9	29
	10			8		2		3	*12		4			11						s			7	5	s	1	6	*9	30
8	10			s		2	s	3	9		4			11						s			7	5		1	6		31
8	10			*12		2	s	3	9		4			*11						s			7	5		1	6		32
8	10		3	s		2			*9		4			11		*12							7	5	s	1	6		33
8	10		3			2					*12			(11)		4				14			7	*5	(13)	1	6	9	34
5	10		3		14	2								11		(13)				(8)		4	7	s		1	6	9	35
5	10		3		s	2								11	4	s				8			7	s		1	6	9	36
5	10		(3)		14	2								11	8					(13)		4	*7	*12		1	6	9	37
5	10		3		14	2								11	(8)					(13)		4	7	s		1	6	9	38
5	10		3		14	2								11	(8)							4	7	s	(13)	1	6	9	39
5	10		(3)		14	2								11	8							4	7	s	(13)	1	6	9	40
5	10		3		14	2	1							11	8							4	7	s	s		6	9	41
*5	10		3		14	2	1							11	(8)					(13)		4	7	*12			6	9	42
	10		3	s	*8	2	1							11		*12				4			7	5	s		6	9	43
	*12			14	10	2	1	(13)						(11)		4				8			7	5	3		6	*9	44
	10		s	14	9	2	1	(13)						11		4				8			7	5	(3)		6		45
*12	10		(3)		9	2	1							11		4	14			8			7	*5	(13)		6		46
25	43	1	31	2	4	46	25	11	22	5	14	3	0	44	7	12	20	0	3	27	0	7	46	25	2	16	43	22	Apps
2	1	2	1	3	7			3	8		12			1		4	1		2	7				3	6			4	Subs
	17		2		1				12		3	1		12					1	3		1	1				7	10	Goals

Allen P K	Allison W A	Beauchamp J D	Bodin P J	Collins L	Cowe S M	Culverhouse I B	Digby F C	Drysdale J	Finney S K	Given S J	Gooden T M	Grant A J	Hooper D R	Horlock K	Leitch D S	Ling M	McMahon S	Mildenhall S J	Murray E J	O'Sullivan W StJ	Pitman J R	Preece D W	Robinson M J	Seagraves M	Smith A P	Talia F	Taylor S	Thorne P L	
	10		3			2			9		11			*12			(4)	1	s	8			*7	5			6		1/1
		14	3			2			10				*12	11			4	1	7	8	s			*5			6	9	1/2
	10		3			2	1		9		14			11			4		s	8			7	5			6	s	2/1
	10		3			2	1		9		s		s	11			4		s	8			7	5			6		2/2
	3	0	4			4	2		4		1		0	3			4	2	1	4			3	4			4	1	Apps
		1									1		1	1															Subs
	1	1							1		1			1															Goals

First Round First Leg : (13) = Nijholt L

Allen P K	Allison W A	Beauchamp J D	Bodin P J	Collins L	Cowe S M	Culverhouse I B	Digby F C	Drysdale J	Finney S K	Given S J	Gooden T M	Grant A J	Hooper D R	Horlock K	Leitch D S	Ling M	McMahon S	Mildenhall S J	Murray E J	O'Sullivan W StJ	Pitman J R	Preece D W	Robinson M J	Seagraves M	Smith A P	Talia F	Taylor S	Thorne P L	
5	10		*3			2	1	*12	9		(13)			11			(4)			8			7				6	14	1
8	10					2	1	3	9		s			11			4						7	5		s	6	s	2
8	10		3			2	1		(13)					11		4	*12			s			7	5			*6	(9)	3
5	*10		3			2	1		*12		4			11		14	8						7		s		6	9	4
5	*10		(3)			2	1	(13)	*12		4			11		8							7	14			6	9	5
	10			*8		2	1	3	*12		4			11		s				s			7	5			6	9	5R
5	6		4	1		6	6	2	2		3			6		2	3			1			6	3			6	4	Apps
								2	4		1					1	1							1				1	Subs
1	2		1						2					3		1													Goals

SEASON 1996/97

Football League First Division
Final League Position : 19th
Manager : Steve McMahon

Substitutes :
s denotes substitute **not** used
* player substituted by *12
( ) player substituted by (13)
_ player substituted by 14

No.	Day	Month	Date	Opponent	Home	Away	H-T	Goalscorers	Gate
1	S	Aug	17	Norwich City		L0-2	(0-2)		15,165
2	S		24	Port Vale	D1-1		(0-1)	Robinson 63	9,384
3	W		28	Oldham Athletic	W1-0		(0-0)	Allison 59	8,024
4	S		31	Southend United		W3-1	(1-0)	Watson 13,Cowe 77,Marsh o.g.89	4,009
5	S	Sep	7	Grimsby Town		L1-2	(0-2)	Cowe 51	4,389
6	W		11	Portsmouth	L0-1		(0-0)		9,280
7	S		14	Tranmere Rovers	W2-1		(1-0)	Walters 26 pen.,Horlock 73	8,902
8	S		21	Queens Park Rangers		D1-1	(1-1)	Cowe 25	13,662
9	F		27	Wolverhampton Wanderers	L1-2		(0-1)	Horlock 66	9,285
10	W	Oct	2	Bradford City		L1-2	(1-1)	Walters 25 pen.	9,249
11	S		12	Oxford United	W1-0		(0-0)	Horlock 50	11,251
12	W		16	Huddersfield Town	W6-0		(4-0)	Walters 28,Thorne 32,47,48,Allison 34,Horlock 41	8,375
13	S		19	Crystal Palace		W2-1	(1-1)	Allison 33,Thorne 47	15,544
14	S		26	Reading		L0-2	(0-0)		11,018
15	W		30	West Bromwich Albion	L2-3		(1-0)	Allen 37,Thorne 90	9,704
16	S	Nov	2	Manchester City	W2-0		(0-0)	Allison 51,83	14,792
17	S		16	Barnsley	W3-0		(0-0)	Walters 52,Gooden 66,Finney 67	11,340
18	Tu		19	Ipswich Town		L2-3	(0-1)	Thorne 75,Allison 90	7,053
19	S		23	Birmingham City		L0-1	(0-1)		16,559
20	Tu		26	Sheffield United		L0-2	(0-1)		12,301
21	S		30	Reading	W3-1		(2-1)	Horlock 6,Allison 25,Walters 89	11,499
22	S	Dec	7	Charlton Athletic		L0-2	(0-0)		10,583
23	S		14	Stoke City		L0-2	(0-1)		10,092
24	Su		22	Bolton Wanderers	D2-2		(1-0)	Walters 33,Allison 74	9,703
25	Th		26	Portsmouth		W1-0	(0-0)	Cowe 56	10,605
26	F	Jan	10	Tranmere Rovers		L1-2	(0-1)	Horlock 64	7,763
27	S		18	Bradford City	D1-1		(0-1)	Horlock 48	8,345
28	S		25	Grimsby Town	D3-3		(0-2)	Horlock 53,Allison 65,Walters 71	10,584
29	W		29	Wolverhampton Wanderers		L0-1	(0-1)		23,003
30	S	Feb	1	Sheffield United	W2-1		(0-0)	Elkins 58,Holdsworth o.g.70	9,296
31	W		5	Queens Park Rangers	D1-1		(1-1)	Brevett o.g.38	11,671
32	S		8	West Bromwich Albion		W2-1	(1-0)	Allison 42,Smith 76	16,219
33	S		22	Manchester City		L0-3	(0-1)		27,262
34	W		26	Birmingham City	W3-1		(2-1)	Bullock 13,Broomes 39,Cowe 61	8,082
35	S	Mar	1	Charlton Athletic	W1-0		(0-0)	Allison 69	9,719
36	Tu		4	Barnsley		D1-1	(1-1)	Thorne 41	8,486
37	S		8	Bolton Wanderers		L0-7	(0-2)		13,981
38	S		15	Stoke City	W1-0		(1-0)	Thorne 27	9,352
39	S		22	Port Vale		L0-1	(0-0)		6,142
40	S		29	Norwich City	L0-3		(0-1)		11,022
41	M		31	Oldham Athletic		L1-5	(0-2)	Cowe 88	5,699
42	S	Apr	5	Southend United	D0-0				7,452
43	S		12	Ipswich Town	L0-4		(0-1)		9,410
44	S		19	Oxford United		L0-2	(0-2)		8,166
45	S		26	Crystal Palace	L0-2		(0-1)		11,621
46	Su	May	4	Huddersfield Town		D0-0			11,506

Average Home Attendance : **9,917**
Average Away Attendance : **11,672**

Football League Cup

Rd	Day	Month	Date	Opponent	Home	Away	H-T	Goalscorers	Gate
1/1	Tu	Aug	20	Wolverhampton Wanderers	W2-0		(1-0)	Allison 42,Leitch 65	7,451
1/2	W	Sep	4	Wolverhampton Wanderers		L0-1	(0-1)		10,760
2/1	W		18	Queens Park Rangers	L1-2		(0-0)	Walters 62	7,843
2/2	W		25	Queens Park Rangers		W3-1	(1-0)	O'Sullivan 43,Allison 67,Thorne 101	6,976
3	Tu	Oct	22	Manchester United		L1-2	(0-1)	Thorne 52	49,305

F A Cup

Rd	Day	Month	Date	Opponent	Home	Away	H-T	Goalscorers	Gate
3	Su	Jan	5	Everton		L0-3	(0-2)		20,411

Allen P K	Allison W A	Anthony G J	Broomes M C	Bullock D J	Collins L	Coughlan G	Cowe S M	Culverhouse I B	Darras F G A	Digby F C	Drysdale J	Elkins G	Finney S K	Gooden T M	Holcroft P I	Horlock K	Kerslake D	Leitch D S	McMahon S	O'Sullivan W StJ	Robinson M J	Seagraves M	Smith A P	Talia F	Thorne P L	Walters M E	Watson K E	
5	10		*(6) = Taylor S*						2		3		*9			11		4			7	(13)		1	*12	8	14	**1**
5	10		*6 = Taylor S*						2		3		(9)			11		4			7	s		1	(13)	8	14	**2**
s	10						9	6	2		3		s			11		4			7	5		1	s		8	**3**
*12							9	6	2		3		14			11		(4)		(13)	7	5		1	10		*8	**4**
(13)							9	6	2				14			11		4			7	5	(3)	1	10	*12	*8	**5**
	*12						9	6	2				14			11		4			3	5	s	1	10	7	*8	**6**
(8)	*12				s		9	6	2							11		4		3		5		1	*10	7	(13)	**7**
*12	10						9	6	*2			3	s			11		4		8		5		1		7	s	**8**
	10						9	6				3	14			11		4		8	*2	5		1	*12	7	s	**9**
	10						9	(6)	(13)			3				11		4		*8	2	5		1	*12	7	14	**10**
	10						*9	6	(13)			3				11		(4)		*8	2	5		1	*12	7	s	**11**
*12	(10)						(13)	6	8			3				11		4		14	*2	5		1	9	7		**12**
s	10						s	6	8			3				11		4		14	2	5		1	9	7		**13**
(5)	10						(13)	6	*8			3				11		4		14	2			1	9	7	*12	**14**
5	10						(13)	(6)	8			*3		*12		11				s	2			1	9	7	4	**15**
	10				4		5	s	8	1			9	3		6		11		7	2		s				s	**16**
	10						s		8	1		s	9	3	14	6		4		7	2	5				11		**17**
	10						*12		8	1		(13)	9	3		6		4		(7)	2	*5			14	11		**18**
	10						*12		8	1		3	14			6	2	4		s	7	*5			9	11		**19**
	10				8					1		(3)	s	(13)		6	2	4		7	5				9	11	14	**20**
	10						s			1		3	*12	14		6	2	4		7	5				*9	11	8	**21**
14	10						7			1		(3)	* 9	*12		6		4		2	5		(13)			11	8	**22**
	10				14		9	7	6	1		3					2		*12	(4)	5		(13)			*11	8	**23**
	10				s		9	7	*6	1		*12				3	2			4	5		(13)			(11)	8	**24**
	10				11		9	7		1	s	6				3	2	4	s	s	5						8	**25**
	10	*(13) = Mildenhall S J*					9	7		1	3					11	2	4	s	*12	*6	5					(8)	**26**
	10						9	7		1	3	14				11	2	4	(8)	(13)	6	*5					*12	**27**
	10		6				9		s	1	3					11	Total	4		s	2	5	s			7	8	**28**
	10		6				9	7	*3	1						11	8	4	s		2	5	(13)			*12	(8)	**29**
	10		6				9	7	2	1	3	5	s						(4)	14			8			11	(13)	**30**
	10		6				9	7	(13)	1		(3)	s					4	s		2	5	8			11		**31**
	10		6				9	7	3	1			s					4		14	2	5	8			11	s	**32**
	10		6					7	(3)	1	(13)		11		4		King P G		s	9	2	5			14		8	**33**
	10		6	8			11	7	3	1			*12					4		14	2	5			*9		s	**34**
	10		6	8			11	7	(3)	1			s					4			2	5	(13)		9	14		**35**
	10		6	8			s	7	3	1			s					4			2	5	11		9		s	**36**
	10		6	8			(13)	7		1		3	s					(4)		5	2		11		9		s	**37**
	10		6	4			8	7		1	(3)	(13)	*12								2		11		*9		5	**38**
	10		6	4			(13)	7	s	1	3		*12								*2	5	11		9		(8)	**39**
				4		*6	8	7	*12	1			10	14			3				(2)	5	11		9		(13)	**40**
		8		4		s	10	*7	6	1			*12	(13)			(3)				2	5	11		9			**41**
		7		8		5	*10		6	1			*12	11			3	4			2		s		9		s	**42**
	10			8		5	* 7		6	1	s		*12	11			3	4			2				9		14	**43**
	10	8		*12			(13)		14	1	11				(7)		3	4			2		*6		9		5	**44**
	10			8			*12		6	1	3	5		11			s			*4	2		7		9		s	**45**
	10			8			*12		6	1	3	5		11	s		s	4			2		*7		9			**46**
5	39	3	12	12	3	3	28	31	30	31	13	19	8	7	2	28	5	36	2	16	43	27	13	15	24	24	17	Apps
5	2			1	1		10		5		1	4	12	6	1				1	9		1	5		7	3	10	Subs
1	11		1	1			6					1	1	1		8					1		1		8	7	1	Goals

Match 38 : 14 = Pattimore M R

Opponents 3 goals

Allen P K	Allison W A	Anthony G J	Broomes M C	Bullock D J	Collins L	Coughlan G	Cowe S M	Culverhouse I B	Darras F G A	Digby F C	Drysdale J	Elkins G	Finney S K	Gooden T M	Holcroft P I	Horlock K	Kerslake D	Leitch D S	McMahon S	O'Sullivan W StJ	Robinson M J	Seagraves M	Smith A P	Talia F	Thorne P L	Walters M E	Watson K E	
*5	10		*6 = Taylor S*						2		3		9			11		4			7	*12		1	s	8	14	**1/1**
			**12 = Taylor S*				9	6	2		*3		s			11		4			7	5		1	10	s	8	**1/2**
8	10						9	6	2			s	s			11		4		3		5		1		7	s	**2/1**
	10		*(13) = Hulbert R J*				(9)	6				3	14			11		*4		8	2	5		1	*12	7		**2/2**
	10						(13)	6	8			3				11		4		s	2	5		1	(9)	7	s	**3**
2	4						3	4	4		2	2	1			5		5		2	4	4		5	2	4	1	Apps
							1						1									1			1		1	Subs
	2																	1		1					2	1		Goals

Allen P K	Allison W A	Anthony G J	Broomes M C	Bullock D J	Collins L	Coughlan G	Cowe S M	Culverhouse I B	Darras F G A	Digby F C	Drysdale J	Elkins G	Finney S K	Gooden T M	Holcroft P I	Horlock K	Kerslake D	Leitch D S	McMahon S	O'Sullivan W StJ	Robinson M J	Seagraves M	Smith A P	Talia F	Thorne P L	Walters M E	Watson K E	
	10				(8)		*9	7		1	14	3				6		4		(13)	2	5				11	*12	**3**

For Final League Table - see page 238

SEASON 1997/98

Football League First Division
Final League Position : 18th
Manager : Steve McMahon

Substitutes :
s denotes substitute **not** used
* player substituted by *12
( ) player substituted by (13)
_ player substituted by 14

				Opponents	Home	Away	H-T	Goalscorers	Gate
1	S	Aug	9	Crewe Alexandra	W2-0		(1-0)	Allison 43,Finney 89 pen.	9,310
2	S		16	Reading		W1-0	(1-0)	Hay 17	9,338
3	S		23	Huddersfield Town	D1-1		(1-1)	Hay 26	8,422
4	S		30	Stoke City		W2-1	(0-1)	Allison 78,Hay 81	23,859
5	Tu	Sep	2	Ipswich Town		L1-2	(1-1)	Allison 23	11,394
6	Su		7	Nottingham Forest	D0-0				14,435
7	S		13	Tranmere Rovers	W2-1		(1-1)	Walters 14,Casper 64	8,002
8	S		20	West Bromwich Albion		D0-0			16,237
9	S		27	Manchester City		L0-6	(0-2)		26,646
10	S	Oct	4	Port Vale	W4-2		(0-1)	Hay 50,81,86,Taylor 67	8,312
11	S		11	Bury	W3-1		(2-1)	Hay 4,15,Gooden 79	8,565
12	S		18	Wolverhampton Wanderers		L1-3	(1-1)	Hay 25 pen.	21,794
13	Tu		21	Sunderland		D0-0			26,893
14	S		25	Norwich City	W1-0		(0-0)	Hay 83	10,353
15	F		31	Portsmouth		W1-0	(1-0)	Hay 23	8,707
16	W	Nov	5	Queens Park Rangers	W3-1		(0-1)	Walters 66,Taylor 84,Hay 87	10,647
17	S		8	Bradford City	W1-0		(1-0)	Cowe 24	10,491
18	S		15	Stockport County		L2-4	(1-2)	Hay 20,Leitch 86	7,694
19	S		22	Middlesbrough	L1-2		(1-1)	Ndah 13	15,724
20	F		28	Charlton Athletic		L0-3	(0-2)		13,789
21	S	Dec	6	Oxford United	W4-1		(2-1)	Wilsterman o.g.28,Walters 34 pen.,Finney 56,Gooden 86	11,408
22	S		13	Sheffield United		L1-2	(1-1)	Finney 24	18,015
23	S		20	Birmingham City	D1-1		(1-1)	Finney 11	10,900
24	F		26	Nottingham Forest		L0-3	(0-3)		26,500
25	Su		28	Ipswich Town	L0-2		(0-0)		11,639
26	Su	Jan	11	Crewe Alexandra		L0-2	(0-0)		4,176
27	S		17	Reading	L0-2		(0-2)		9,986
28	S		24	Bradford City		D1-1	(0-1)	Hay 90	15,130
29	W		28	Stoke City	W1-0		(0-0)	Robinson 71	7,671
30	S		31	Huddersfield Town		D0-0			10,028
31	S	Feb	7	West Bromwich Albion	L0-2		(0-1)		10,304
32	Tu		10	Tranmere Rovers		L0-3	(0-2)		5,288
33	Tu		17	Port Vale		W1-0	(1-0)	Collins 4	5,925
34	S		21	Manchester City	L1-3		(0-1)	Cowe 71	12,987
35	S		28	Bury		L0-1	(0-1)		5,002
36	S	Mar	7	Portsmouth	L0-1		(0-0)		9,684
37	W		11	Middlesbrough		L0-6	(0-2)		29,581
38	S		14	Queens Park Rangers		W2-1	(2-1)	Walters 16 pen.,Onuora 45	13,486
39	W		18	Wolverhampton Wanderers	D0-0				8,322
40	S		21	Stockport County	D1-1		(0-0)	McDonald 74	7,707
41	S	Apr	4	Charlton Athletic	L0-1		(0-0)		8,831
42	S		11	Oxford United		L1-2	(0-2)	Ndah 64 pen.	8,066
43	M		13	Sheffield United	D1-1		(1-0)	Walters 33	7,588
44	S		18	Birmingham City		L0-3	(0-2)		17,016
45	S		25	Norwich City		L0-5	(0-2)		18,443
46	Su	May	3	Sunderland	L1-2		(0-2)	Walters 87	15,575

Average Home Attendance : **10,298**
Average Away Attendance : **14,913**

Football League Cup

				Opponents	Home	Away	H-T	Goalscorers	Gate
1/1	W	Aug	13	Watford	L0-2		(0-1)		6,271
1/2	Tu		26	Watford		D1-1	(0-1)	Leitch 58	7,712

For Final League Table - see page 238

F A Cup

				Opponents	Home	Away	H-T	Goalscorers	Gate
3	S	Jan	3	Stevenage Borough	L1-2		(1-1)	Walters 5	9,422

STEVE McMAHON
did not have the best of starts when he was red-carded at Southend on his debut. Town were 19th when he took over at the beginning of December 1994, but ended six points from safety - following the sale of 25-goal Jan-Åge Fjørtoft in March. Town won the Second Division comfortably in 1995/96, but then two poor finishes - 19th and 18th - did little to appease the fans who became increasingly disenchanted with the man in charge. He resigned in September 1998.

Allison W A	Borrows B	Bullock D J	Casper C M	Collins L	Cowe S M	Cuervo P	Culverhouse I B	Darras F G A	Davis S S	Digby F C	Drysdale J	Finney S K	Gooden T M	Hay C D	Howe S R	Leitch D S	McDonald A	Meechan A T	Mildenhall S J	Ndah G E	Robinson M J	Seagraves M	Smith A P	Taylor C	Thompson D A	Walters M E	Watson K E	
10		(13)				(8)		2		1	3	*12	11	*9		4	6				7	5				s		1
10		(13)				(8)		2		1	3	<u>*12</u>	11	*9		4	6				7	5				<u>14</u>		2
10		<u>3</u>			*12	8		2		1			11	*9		4	6					5				7	s	3
10		<u>14</u>			s	8		2		1	<u>3</u>		11	9		(4)	6					5	(13)			7		4
10		<u>14</u>			s	8		2		1	3		11	9		<u>4</u>	6					(5)	(13)			7		5
10	3	4	5			8		2		1	s		11	9			6									7	s	6
10	3	4	5					2		1	8	*12	11	*9			6						s			(7)	(13)	7
10	3	4	5	s	9			2		1	8	s	11				6					s	7					8
10	3	4	5		*9			(2)		1	(13)		11	*12		8	6						<u>7</u>			<u>14</u>		9
10	3			(13)	s			<u>14</u>		1	<u>2</u>		11	9		4	6							5		7	(8)	10
10	2		<u>14</u>	3	s					1	(13)		11	9		4	<u>6</u>							5		(7)	8	11
10	2		6	8	s		3			1			11	9		(4)		<u>14</u>						5		<u>7</u>		12
10	2	4	6	8	s		3			1			11	9										5		<u>14</u>	<u>7</u>	13
10	2	4	6		s		3			1			11	9									(13)	5		(8)	7	14
10	2	4	6		s		3						11	9					1					5		8	7	15
10	2	4	Total				(3)		(13)	1			11	9			6	s					Total	5		<u>8</u>	7	16
	2		8		10		3		s		8		11	9		<u>4</u>	6	s					2	5			7	17
	2		1		10		<u>3</u>				s	*12	11	*9		4	6				<u>14</u>		3	5		8	7	18
	2		1				s			1		9	11			4	6			<u>10</u>	3			5	7	<u>14</u>	8	19
	2	(13)			*12		<u>14</u>			1		*9	11			<u>4</u>	6			10	3			5	7		(8)	20
	2	<u>4</u>			s	<u>14</u>		5		1		9	11				6			10	3			(13)	7	(8)		21
	2	4		8	s			(5)		1		9	11				6			10	3			(13)	7	s		22
	2	4		(13)				<u>14</u>		1		*9	11	*12			6			<u>10</u>	3			5	7	(8)		23
	(2)			8						1	(13)	*9	11	*12		4	6			10	3			5	7	s		24
				(13)			2	<u>5</u>		1		*12	11	9		(4)	6			10	3			<u>14</u>	7	*8		25
	2	<u>7</u>		8		<u>14</u>	s			1		*12	11	9			*6			10	3			5			4	26
	2	<u>4</u>		*12		7	s			1		10	11	9	8		*6				3			5			<u>14</u>	27
	2			(6)	*12	*7				1		10	11	9	8	s	(13)				3			5	4			28
	2			6	s	7					<u>11</u>	10		9	8	<u>14</u>	s		1		3			5	4			29
	2			6	s	<u>14</u>					(11)	<u>10</u>		9	8	4	(13)		1		3			5	7			30
	2		Kerslake D	6	*12	(7)	<u>14</u>			1		10	<u>11</u>	*9	8	4					3		Onuora I	5			(13)	31
	2			6	*12	<u>11</u>	(7)			1		10		*9	8	4					3			5		<u>14</u>	(13)	32
	3	7		6	*12	(13)				<u>1</u>	(11)	10		*9	8	4					2			5		<u>14</u>		33
	3	7		6	*12							*10		(9)	8	4	(13)		1		2			5		<u>14</u>		34
	3	7		6	9	<u>14</u>						*10	11		<u>8</u>		4				2			5		*12		35
	3			6	10	8						9	11	s	s	4	s				2			5		7		36
	3		7	6	10					1		s	11	9	s	4	s				2			5		8		37
	3	5	2	6	s					1			11		<u>14</u>	8	4			(10)			9			<u>7</u>		38
	3	5	2	6		<u>14</u>				1			11	*12		<u>8</u>	4			*10	s		9			7		39
	3	5	2	6	s	8				1			11	10	s		4				s		9			7		40
	3	5	2			<u>14</u>				1			11	s		8	4			10	<u>6</u>		9			7	s	41
	6	5	2	9					3	1			11	*12			(4)			10	*7			(13)		<u>14</u>	<u>8</u>	42
	6	5	2	(8)	s	(13)			3	1			11	9						10	s			4		7		43
	6	5	2	<u>8</u>	*12	(13)			3	1		*10	<u>14</u>	(9)							11			4		7		44
	6	5	2		*12				3	1							s			*10	<u>11</u>		9	4		7	8	45
	6	<u>5</u>	2		10	*8			3	1				*12			4				11		9	s		7	<u>14</u>	46
16	40	26	10	22	8	14	9	12	5	38	11	17	38	30	9	25	30	0	4	14	26	5	6	28	10	25	13	Apps
		5		4	9	9	2	2	1		3	6	1	6	1	1		1			1			4		9	5	Subs
3				1	2							4	2	14		1	1			2	1		1	2		6		Goals

Additional players : see below

Opponents 1 goal

Allison W A	Borrows B	Bullock D J	Casper C M	Collins L	Cowe S M	Cuervo P	Culverhouse I B	Darras F G A	Davis S S	Digby F C	Drysdale J	Finney S K	Gooden T M	Hay C D	Howe S R	Leitch D S	McDonald A	Meechan A T	Mildenhall S J	Ndah G E	Robinson M J	Seagraves M	Smith A P	Taylor C	Thompson D A	Walters M E	Watson K E	
10					*12	8		2		1	3	*9	11			4	6				7	<u>5</u>				<u>14</u>	s	1/1
10		s			s	8		2			3		11	9		4	6					5				7		1/2
2					0	2		2		1	2	1	2	1		2	2				1	2				1		Apps
					1																					1		Subs
																1												Goals

Second Leg : 1 = Talia F   s = Elkins G

Allison W A	Borrows B	Bullock D J	Casper C M	Collins L	Cowe S M	Cuervo P	Culverhouse I B	Darras F G A	Davis S S	Digby F C	Drysdale J	Finney S K	Gooden T M	Hay C D	Howe S R	Leitch D S	McDonald A	Meechan A T	Mildenhall S J	Ndah G E	Robinson M J	Seagraves M	Smith A P	Taylor C	Thompson D A	Walters M E	Watson K E	
				4			2			1	<u>14</u>	*12	11	9			6	s	s	10	3			5		<u>8</u>	*7	3

s = Hulbert R J

Also selected :
Match 3 : <u>14</u> = McMahon S   Match 6 : s = McAreavey P   Matches 12,13,15 : (13) s s = Hulbert R J   Matches 14,15 : s = Elkins G
Matches 16,17 : <u>14</u> = Pattimore M R   Matches 17-19 : 1 1 s = Warner A R   Matches 34,38 : 11 (13) = Elliott S T
Match 35 : s = King P G   Matches 35,36 : 1 = Talia F   Match 45 : <u>14</u> = McAreavey P

SEASON 1998/99

Football League First Division
Final League Position : 17th
Manager : Steve McMahon
Jimmy Quinn (from Oct.1)

Substitutes :
s denotes substitute **not** used
* player substituted by *12
( ) player substituted by (13)
_ player substituted by _14_

				Home	Away	H-T	Goalscorers	Gate
1	S	Aug	8 Sheffield United		L1-2	(0-2)	Holdsworth o.g.60	15,977
2	S		15 Sunderland	D1-1		(1-0)	Onuora 5	10,207
3	S		22 Wolverhampton Wanderers		L0-1	(0-1)		21,537
4	S		29 Port Vale	D1-1		(0-1)	Barnett o.g.56	7,800
5	M		31 Bury		L0-3	(0-0)		4,513
6	S	Sep	5 Bristol City	W3-2		(3-0)	Walters 3 pen.,Ndah 5,Onuora 9	8,537
7	W		9 Oxford United	W4-1		(1-1)	Ndah 8,86,Onuora 72,75	8,305
8	S		12 Portsmouth		L2-5	(0-2)	Onuora 65,Ndah 76	10,105
9	S		19 Watford	L1-4		(1-2)	Ndah 29	8,781
10	F		25 Tranmere Rovers		D0-0			5,501
11	Tu		29 Bolton Wanderers		L1-2	(0-0)	Onuora 88	16,497
12	S	Oct	3 Stockport County	L2-3		(1-2)	Onuora 24,Walters 49	7,961
13	F		9 Huddersfield Town	W3-0		(3-0)	Onuora 1,Walters 14,Bullock 37	8,316
14	S		17 Ipswich Town		L0-1	(0-1)		13,212
15	Tu		20 Birmingham City		D1-1	(0-0)	Gooden 74	19,485
16	S		24 West Bromwich Albion	D2-2		(2-1)	Hall 11,Walters 38	8,567
17	S		31 Queens Park Rangers	W3-1		(1-1)	Walters 45 pen.,90,Onuora 80	8,580
18	S	Nov	7 Crewe Alexandra		W2-0	(1-0)	Onuora 19,90	4,489
19	S		14 Bradford City		L0-3	(0-0)		14,897
20	S		21 Crystal Palace	W2-0		(1-0)	Ndah 23, Walters 48 pen.	11,718
21	S		28 Grimsby Town		L0-1	(0-1)		5,657
22	S	Dec	5 Norwich City	D1-1		(1-1)	Walters 41	9,262
23	S		12 Bradford City	L1-4		(1-1)	Onuora 3	7,447
24	S		19 Barnsley		W3-1	(3-0)	Onuora 15,26,Hay 29	15,342
25	S		26 Wolverhampton Wanderers	W1-0		(0-0)	Onuora 90	11,672
26	M		28 Bristol City		L1-3	(0-1)	Ndah 46	16,257
27	S	Jan	9 Sheffield United	D2-2		(1-1)	Ndah 11,Onuora 47	7,583
28	S		16 Port Vale		W1-0	(1-0)	Ndah 9	5,405
29	S		30 Bury	D1-1		(0-0)	West o.g.87	7,797
30	S	Feb	6 Sunderland		L0-2	(0-2)		41,304
31	S		13 Oxford United		L0-2	(0-1)		8,179
32	S		20 Portsmouth	D3-3		(3-1)	Hay 31,41,Onuora 45	10,230
33	F		26 Watford		W1-0	(1-0)	Howe 45	8,692
34	W	Mar	3 Tranmere Rovers	L2-3		(1-0)	Ndah 45,Reeves 68	5,765
35	S		6 Bolton Wanderers	D3-3		(1-0)	Howe 17,Hay 48,Walters 69	8,392
36	Tu		9 Stockport County		L1-2		Walters	6,048
37	S		13 Crewe Alexandra	L1-2		(0-2)	Hay 55	7,434
38	S		20 Queens Park Rangers		L0-4	(0-0)		11,184
39	S	Apr	3 Ipswich Town	L0-6		(0-4)		10,337
40	M		5 Huddersfield Town		W2-1	(1-0)	Howe 19,Hay 67	11,719
41	S		10 Bimingham City	L0-1		(0-0)		8,896
42	Tu		13 West Bromwich Albion		D1-1	(1-1)	Ndah 32	9,601
43	S		17 Crystal Palace		W1-0	(0-0)	Onuora 51	18,660
44	S		24 Grimsby Town	W2-0		(1-0)	Onuora 3,Ndah 48	7,197
45	S	May	1 Norwich City		L1-2	(0-0)	Onuora 48 pen.	17,306
46	Su		9 Barnsley	L1-3		(1-2)	Griffin 8	8,182

Average Home Attendance : **8,651**
Average Away Attendance : **13,112**

Football League Cup

				Home	Away	H-T	Goalscorers	Gate
1/1	W	Aug	12 Wycombe Wanderers	W2-1		(1-0)	Reeves 45,Ndah 70	4,682
1/2	Tu		18 Wycombe Wanderers		L0-2	(0-1)		2,478

F A Cup

				Home	Away	H-T	Goalscorers	Gate
3	S	Jan	2 Barnsley	D0-0				8,016
3R	Tu		19 Barnsley		L1-3	(0-0)	Walters 86	10,510

For Final League Table - see page 238

Borrows B	Bullock D J	Collins L	Cowe S M	Cuervo P	Davies G M	Davis S S	Fenn N M C	Glass J R	Gooden T M	Griffin C J	Hall G D	Hay C D	Howe S R	Hulbert R J	Kerslake D	Leitch D S	Linton D M	Ndah G E	Onuora I	Reeves A	Robinson M J	Talia F	Taylor C	Walters M E	Watson K E	Williams J D	Willis A P	
6	10			s		*12			4		3	*8						11	9	5	2	1	s	7				1
6	10			14		s			11		3	s				4		8	9	5	2	1		7				2
6	10			14		4			11		3	9			2			*8	*12	5	s	1		7				3
6	10			14		s			11		3	s		4	2			8	9	5		1		7				4
6	10		s			(13)		1	11		(3)			4	2			8	9	5	s	1		7				5
6	10		s			14			11		3			*12	2	*4		8	9	5		1		7				6
6	10								11		3				2	4		8	9	5	s			7	s		s	7
6	*10		s						11		3				2	4		8	9	5	*12	1		7			s	8
6	10		(9)						11		3		(13)		*2	4		8		5		1	*12	7	s			9
6	10		14	9		4			11									8		5	2	1	s	7	s		3	10
6	10		8	*9		3			11				14						*12	5	2	1		7	s		4	11
6	s			14		3			11		s					4		10	9	5	2	1		7			8	12
6	10			s					11		3					4		8	9	5	2	1		7	s		s	13
6	(10)					14			11		3	*12				4		8	*9		2	1		7	(13)		5	14
6	10			s		4			11		3	*12						8	*9		2	1		7	(13)		5	15
6				s		s			11		3	*12				10		*8	9	5	2	1		7	4			16
6	14					4			11		3			(13)		10		*8	9	(5)	2	1		7	*12			17
6	10		14			4			11		3	8		*7					9		2	1			*12		5	18
(6)			s			4	10		11		3			*12					9			1	2	*7	8		5	19
6	(13)					4	*10		11		3							14	9		2	1	*12	7	(8)		5	20
(6)						4	10				3		*12	(13)		14		11	9		2	1		7	*8		5	21
6	14					11	*10				(3)	*12				4			9		2	1	(13)	7	8		5	22
(6)	14					11	Total				3	s		(13)		4		10	9		2	1		7	8		5	23
	14					11	4				3	*8	7	6		4		10	9		2	1	5	*12	s			24
6	10					11					3	8		4				*7	9	s	2	1	5	14	*12			25
	10		(13)			11					3	(8)		4				6	9	14	*2	1	5	7	*12			26
6						11			10		3		7	s		4		8	9		2	1	5	s	s			27
6			s			11			10		3		7	(13)		4		8	9	s	(2)	1	5					28
						11			10		3	14			2	4		8	9	6		1	5	7	s		s	29
6						*11			(13)	14	(3)	10	4		2			8	9		*12	1	5	7				30
6									11		3	14	10	(13)	(2)	4		8	9		*12	1	*5	7				31
6						11	Bradley S		14	s	3	10	*7	*12		4		8	9		2	1	5					32
6		14							11			10	7		(13)	4		8	9	3	(2)	1	5	s				33
6		2			s				11			10	7		14	4		8	9	3		1	5	s				34
*6		2			5				11	(13)	*12	10	7		s	4		(8)		3		1		9				35
6		(13)			5				11		*12	10	7		*2	(4)		8	14	3		1		9				36
*6		s = McHugh F J							11	*12	5	10	7		2			8	9	3		1	s	4				37
6								1	11	*12	5	*10	7			4	14	8	9	3			s	2				38
6						(8)	*10	1	11		5	(13)	7	14			2		9	3			4	*12				39
s					3		10		11		5	14	7	*6			2	8	9			1	4	*12				40
					3		10		11		5	14	*7				2	8	9			1	4	*12	6	s		41
					(3)		10		11		5	14	7				2	8	9			1	4	*12	*6	(13)		42
6					(3)		10		11		5	*4	7				2	8	9		(13)	1		*12	14			43
6							10		11		3	14	7				(2)	8	9		5	1		*4	*12	(13)		44
6							*12				3	*10	7				2	8	9		5	1	11		4	s		45
6		4 = McHugh F J								10	3	s	*7					8	9		5	1	11		*12	2		46
40	17	2	2	2	6	21	6	3	36	1	39	16	20	7	12	23	7	40	40	23	25	43	18	31	9	1	11	
	5	2	3	4		4	1		2	4	2	11	3	9	2	1	1	1	3	1	4		3	7	9	2		
	1								1			6						12	20					10				

Matches 18,19,46 : s (13) s = Campagna S P P   Match 45 : 14 = McAreavey P   Opponents 3 goals

Borrows B	Bullock D J	Collins L	Cowe S M	Cuervo P	Davies G M	Davis S S	Fenn N M C	Glass J R	Gooden T M	Griffin C J	Hall G D	Hay C D	Howe S R	Hulbert R J	Kerslake D	Leitch D S	Linton D M	Ndah G E	Onuora I	Reeves A	Robinson M J	Talia F	Taylor C	Walters M E	Watson K E	Williams J D	Willis A P	
6	10							1	4		*3	8			s			11	9	5	2	s	s	7	14			2/1
6	10			13				s	*11		3	*12			s			8	9	5	2	1		7	4		s	2/2
2	2			0				1	2		2	1						2	2	2	2	1		2	1			
				1								1													1			
																		1		1								

*First Leg : *12 = McHugh F J*

Borrows B	Bullock D J	Collins L	Cowe S M	Cuervo P	Davies G M	Davis S S	Fenn N M C	Glass J R	Gooden T M	Griffin C J	Hall G D	Hay C D	Howe S R	Hulbert R J	Kerslake D	Leitch D S	Linton D M	Ndah G E	Onuora I	Reeves A	Robinson M J	Talia F	Taylor C	Walters M E	Watson K E	Williams J D	Willis A P	
	10		*15					s	11		3	*8	6	4				9	16	s	2	1	5	7	s			3
6			16			*11		s	10		3		(7)	2		4		8	9	s		1	5	*12	(15)			3R
1	1		0			1			2		2	1	2	2		1		2	1		1	2	2	1	0			
			2																1					1	1			
																								1				

SEASON 1999/2000

Football League First Division
Final League Position : 24th (Last)
Manager : Jimmy Quinn
Colin Todd (from May 4)

Substitutes :
s denotes substitute **not** used
* player substituted by *s
( ) player substituted by (s)
_ player substituted by s

					Home	Away	H-T	Goalscorers	Gate
1	S	Aug	7	Walsall		D0-0			6,437
2	Su		15	Ipswich Town	L1-4		(1-1)	Grazioli 16	6,195
3	S		21	Crystal Palace		W2-1	(1-1)	Grazioli 32,Onuora 49	12,726
4	S		28	West Bromwich Albion	L1-2		(1-0)	Walters 4	6,565
5	M		30	Grimsby Town		L0-1	(0-1)		5,705
6	S	Sep	11	Nottingham Forest	D0-0				8,203
7	S		18	Crewe Alexandra		L1-2	(0-1)	Ndah 67	5,280
8	S		25	Port Vale		L0-2	(0-0)		4,629
9	Tu		28	Blackburn Rovers	W2-1		(2-0)	Dailly o.g.30,Howe 32	7,354
10	S	Oct	2	Bolton Wanderers	L0-4		(0-4)		6,711
11	S		9	Stockport County	D1-1		(1-1)	Hay 45	5,318
12	S		16	Fulham		L0-1	(0-0)		13,715
13	Tu		19	Barnsley		L0-1	(0-0)		12,026
14	S		23	Sheffield United	D2-2		(2-0)	Hay 11,22	5,504
15	Tu		26	Port Vale	W2-1		(1-1)	Musslewhite o.g.1,Grazioli 90	5,703
16	S		30	Bolton Wanderers		L0-2	(0-0)		12,486
17	S	Nov	6	Huddersfield Town		L0-4	(0-2)		11,891
18	F		12	Norwich City	D0-0				7,404
19	S		20	Wolverhampton Wanderers		D1-1	(1-0)	Onuora 27 pen.	19,917
20	Tu		23	Charlton Athletic	L1-2		(1-2)	Carrick 42	6,515
21	S		27	Birmingham City		D1-1	(0-1)	Onuora 90	22,620
22	S	Dec	4	Walsall	D1-1		(1-1)	Carrick 38	7,186
23	S		18	Manchester City		L0-3	(0-1)		31,751
24	Su		26	Portsmouth	D1-1		(1-0)	Hay 16	10,279
25	Tu		28	Tranmere Rovers		L1-3	(1-3)	Hay 12	8,068
26	M	Jan	3	Queens Park Rangers	L0-1		(0-0)		9,460
27	S		15	Ipswich Town		L0-3	(0-2)		17,326
28	F		21	Crystal Palace	L2-4		(1-1)	Reeves 21,Hall 61	5,214
29	S		29	West Bromwich Albion		D1-1	(0-0)	Hall 77	11,856
30	S	Feb	5	Grimsby Town	L0-1		(0-0)		5,784
31	S		12	Blackburn Rovers		D0-0			16,938
32	S		19	Birmingham City	L1-4		(1-3)	Hay 13	7,591
33	S		26	Crewe Alexandra	L0-1		(0-0)		5,003
34	S	Mar	4	Nottingham Forest		L1-3	(0-3)	Hay 52 pen.	19,748
35	Tu		7	Huddersfield Town	W2-0		(1-0)	Collins 11,Hay 89 pen.	4,701
36	S		11	Charlton Athletic		W1-0	(1-0)	Cowe 5	19,569
37	S		18	Wolverhampton Wanderers	L1-2		(0-0)	Williams A 82	8,748
38	W		22	Norwich City		W2-0	(0-0)	Hay 56 pen.,64	13,662
39	S		25	Portsmouth		L1-4	(0-3)	Gray 69	15,305
40	S	Apr	1	Manchester City	L0-2		(0-1)		12,397
41	S		8	Queens Park Rangers		L1-2	(1-2)	Grazioli 35	12,633
42	S		15	Tranmere Rovers	W3-1		(2-1)	Griffin 15,Grazioli 30,Gray 62	4,925
43	S		22	Fulham	W1-0		(0-0)	Grazioli 83	7,556
44	M		24	Stockport County		L0-3	(0-1)		5,362
45	S		29	Barnsley	L1-2		(0-0)	Williams J 69	6,151
46	Su	May	7	Sheffield United		D2-2	(0-1)	Grazioli 53,55	12,603

Average Home Attendance : **6,977**
Average Away Attendance : **13,576**

Football League Cup

					Home	Away	H-T	Goalscorers	Gate
1/1	Tu	Aug	10	Leyton Orient	L0-1		(0-0)		3,587
1/2	W		25	Leyton Orient		D1-1	(0-0)	Walters 57 pen.	2,750

F A Cup

					Home	Away	H-T	Goalscorers	Gate
3	S	Dec	11	Charlton Athletic		L1-2	(0-0)	Gooden 54	10,939

For Final League Table - see page 261

Campagna S P P	Carrick M	Collins L	Cowe S M	Cuervo P	Davies G M	Davis S S	Glass J R	Gooden T M	Grazioli G S L	Griffin C J	Hall G D	Hay C D	Howe S R	Hulbert R J	Leitch D S	McAreavey P	McHugh F J	Mildenhall S J	Ndah G E	Onuora I	Quinn J M	Reeves A	Robinson M J	Talia F	Thirlwell P	Walters M E	Williams A P R	Williams J D	Willis A P	
							s	11	*10	*s	3		s	22	4				8	9		s	2	1		14		32		**1**
							s		10		3	(s)	7	*22			25		8	(9)		s	2	1		*s		32	s	**2**
					5	21	s		*10		3	*s	7	s					8	9		12	2	1		14		s	s	**3**
					5	21	s			*s	3	*15	7				s		8	9		(12)	2	1		14		s	(s)	**4**
					5	21	s			(s)	3	*15	7				*s		8	(9)		12	2	1		14		s	s	**5**
					5	s	s			*s	3		7				25		8	*9		12	2	1	6		33	s	s	**6**
					5	s	s			s	3		7				25		8	9		12	*2	1	6	*s	33		s	**7**
					(5)	s	s				3		7				*25		8	*s		12	2	1	6	14	33	(s)	s	**8**
						s	13		s				7	(s)			25		8	*s		12	2		6	*14	33	32	19	**9**
							13	*s		s		s	(7)	(s)			25	s		9		12	2		6	14	33	*32	19	**10**
					*5		13	11	(s)		3	(15)	7						8	s		12	*s	s	6	14	33	s		**11**
					5		13	*11			3	s	7						8	*s		12	2	s	6	14	33	s	s	**12**
					5		13	*11	(s)		3	s	7						(8)	*s		12	2	s	6	14	33	s		**13**
					*5	21	13	11	(s)		3	15	s							9			s	s	6	(14)	33	32	*s	**14**
		s				21	13	11	(s)		*3	15	7							(9)		12	s	s	6		33	32	*s	**15**
		16	(s)			21	13	*11	10		3	15	*s				s			s		12		s	6			(32)	19	**16**
		16				21	s			s	3	15	(7)		*s		s			9		*12	2	1	6			(s)	19	**17**
	6					21					*3	15	7		(4)		s	s		9	s	12	2	1	Total		33	(s)	*s	**18**
	6	s				21	s				3	15	7	s	4					*9	*s	12	2	1	12		33	s		**19**
	6	s				21					3	15	(7)	(s)	4			s		*9	*s	12	2	1			33		s	**20**
	6	s				21	s			(s)	*3	(15)	7		4					9	*s	12	2	1			33	s		**21**
	6	s				21	Total	*s		s	3		*7	s	4			18		9	40	12	2				33		s	**22**
	6	*16			5	*s	8	11		(20)		15	(s)	s	4			s				12	2	1			33	s		**23**
		16		s	*5	21				s	3	15		(s)	(4)			s		9		12		1			33	32	*s	**24**
s		16		*s		21				s	3	15	7	(s)						9	s	12	2	1			*33	(32)		**25**
s		16				21				*s	3	15	s	(22)	4		(s)	s				12	2	1			33			**26**
s			*17				Gray W W			*s	3	15	7	22	4	s	25	s				12	(2)	1			33	(s)		**27**
24		*16	s	*s		(21)					3	15	s		4		25	s				12		1			33	(s)		**28**
s		16	s	s	5						3	15		(s)	4		(25)	*s				12	2	*1			33			**29**
s		*16	s		(5)						3	15	*s	22	4						s	12	2				33	(s)		**30**
s			(17)		5					(s)	3	15	*7	*s	4	s						12	2	s	Meaker M J		33	32		**31**
			17		5	21				*s	3	15			4	s	s					(12)	2	s			33	*32	(s)	**32**
		16	(17)	s	5	*s					*3	15	7		4						(s)	12	2	s			33		s	**33**
		16	17	(s)	5	21	9					15	*s		*4	s		s				12	2	1			(33)		s	**34**
		16	*17	s		21	(9)			(s)		15	*s		4	s		s				12	2	1			33		19	**35**
		16	17	s			(9)			(s)	*s	15			4	s		s				12	2	1			*33	32	19	**36**
		16	*17			21	9		s		s	15	(s)		(4)			s				12	2	1			*s	32	19	**37**
		16	(17)	s		*s	9		s		*3	15			4			s				12	2	1			33	(s)	19	**38**
		16	*17	(s)		s	9		*s		3				4			s				12	2	1	11		(33)	s	19	**39**
		16	*s			s	(9)		10	(s)	*3				4			s				12	2	1	11		33		19	**40**
		16	s			21	*s		10	*20					4			s				12	2	1	11		33	s	19	**41**
		16	(s)				*s		(10)	*20	3				4	s		s				12	2	1	11		33	s	19	**42**
		16	s			(s)	*s		10	*20	3				4			s				12	2	1	11		(33)	s	19	**43**
		16	s			*s	9		10	*20	3				4	s		s				(12)	2	1	11			(s)	19	**44**
		16	17			21	(s)		10	(20)	*3				4	s		18				12	2					*s	19	**45**
		16	(17)			21	s		10	(s)	3		7				s	*18				12	2					32	19	**46**
1	6	23	12	0	18	23	8	8	11	6	38	27	24	5	28	0	9	3	12	18	1	43	40	31	6	12	35	14	16	Apps
2		1	5	6		5	4	2	8	15	1	4	6	7	1		5	2		6	6		2			1	1	12	7	Subs
	2	1	1				2		7	1	2	10	1						1	3		1				1	1	1		Goals

Additional players : see below

Opponents 2 goals

		**s = Taylor C*				21			10	s	*3	s	(s)	(22)	4				8	9			2	1		14		32		**1/1**
					5	21			*10		3	*s	7				(s)		(8)	9		12	2	1		14		s	s	**1/2**
					1	2			2	0	2	0	1	1	1		0		2	2		1	2	2		2		1	0	Apps
										1		1	1				1												1	Subs
																										1				Goals

Both legs : s = Glass J R

		16			*s	21		11		s	*3	(s)		s	4		s	18		9	40		2				(33)		19	**3**

Also selected :
Matches 1,2 : s 6 = Taylor C — *Matches 9, 46 : s *s = Flanagan A* — *Matches 26,28,29 : *8 8 8 = McCammon M J*
Matches 30-33 : 31 = Griemink B J — *Matches 40,41,45 : s = Smith B J* — *Match 45 : s = Young A J* — *Match 46 : s = Mills J M*

SEASON 2000/01

Football League Second Division
Final League Position : 20th
Manager : Colin Todd
Andy King (from Oct.25)

Substitutes :
s denotes substitute **not** used
* player substituted by *s
( ) player substituted by (s)
_ player substituted by s

No.	Day	Month	Date	Opponents	Home	Away	H-T	Goalscorers	Gate
1	S	Aug	12	Colchester United	D0-0				7,296
2	S		19	Reading		L0-2	(0-1)		14,134
3	S		26	Walsall	L1-4		(1-2)	Invincibile 18	5,492
4	M		28	Port Vale		L0-3	(0-1)		3,926
5	S	Sep	9	Bristol City		W1-0	(0-0)	Reeves 81	10,110
6	Tu		12	AFC Bournemouth		L0-3	(0-2)		3,673
7	S		23	Luton Town		W3-2	(2-2)	Duke 28,Williams M 41,67	4,933
8	S		30	Wigan Athletic	D2-2		(2-1)	Alexander 21,Robinson M 22	4,895
9	S	Oct	7	Oxford United	W2-1		(1-0)	Reeves 21,Grazioli 80	7,975
10	S		14	Oldham Athletic		L0-1	(0-0)		4,009
11	Tu		17	Swansea City		D0-0			6,331
12	S		21	Bristol Rovers	L1-3		(0-3)	Robertson 90	8,097
13	Tu		24	Millwall	L0-2		(0-1)		5,030
14	S		28	Notts County		L2-3	(1-2)	Invincibile 36,53	4,502
15	Tu		31	Cambridge United	W3-1		(2-1)	Invincibile 12,35,O'Halloran 55	3,452
16	S	Nov	4	Wycombe Wanderers	D1-1		(0-1)	Reeves 90	5,226
17	Tu		7	Wrexham	D2-2		(1-1)	Invincibile 32,O'Halloran 73 pen.	4,423
18	S		11	Peterborough United		L0-4	(0-2)		5,700
19	S		25	Stoke City	L0-3		(0-2)		4,904
20	S	Dec	2	Northampton Town		W1-0	(1-0)	Alexander 23	5,816
21	S		16	Rotherham United	W2-1		(1-1)	Woan 4,Invincibile 57	4,740
22	S		23	Bury		L0-1	(0-1)		2,921
23	Tu		26	Brentford	L2-3		(1-0)	Invincibile 4,Howe 77	6,649
24	M	Jan	1	Walsall		L0-1	(0-0)		5,548
25	S		13	Port Vale	L0-1		(0-0)		5,175
26	S		27	Bury	W3-0		(2-0)	Reddy 2,O'Halloran 12 pen.,Cowe 67	4,960
27	S	Feb	3	Wrexham		D1-1	(1-0)	van der Linden 24	3,004
28	S		10	Bristol City	D1-1		(1-1)	Reddy 33	10,031
29	S		17	Cambridge United		W1-0	(0-0)	Reddy 73	4,046
30	Tu		20	AFC Bournemouth	D1-1		(0-0)	Alexander 67	5,948
31	S		24	Luton Town	L1-3		(1-1)	Alexander 38	7,160
32	S	Mar	3	Wigan Athletic		D0-0			6,563
33	Tu		6	Oldham Athletic	W3-0		(1-0)	Kelly o.g.8,McAreavey 79,Grazioli 90	4,168
34	S		10	Oxford United		W2-0	(1-0)	Robinson S 29,90	7,480
35	S		17	Swansea City	D1-1		(0-0)	O'Halloran 79 pen.	6,724
36	Tu		20	Colchester United		W1-0	(1-0)	Reddy 28	2,736
37	S		24	Bristol Rovers		D0-0			8,114
38	Tu		27	Reading	L0-1		(0-0)		9,673
39	S		31	Rotherham United		L3-4	(2-2)	Alexander 6,26,Woan 49	7,106
40	S	Apr	7	Northampton Town	D1-1		(1-1)	Woan 3	5,932
41	Tu		10	Brentford		W1-0	(0-0)	Heywood 51	4,180
42	S		14	Millwall		L0-1	(0-0)		12,266
43	M		16	Notts County	L1-2		(1-0)	Heywood 35	6,207
44	S		21	Wycombe Wanderers		D0-0			6,844
45	S		28	Peterborough United	W2-1		(1-0)	Alexander 7,Invincibile 90	8,145
46	S	May	5	Stoke City		L1-4	(0-4)	O'Halloran 54 pen.	20,591

Average Home Attendance : **6,187**
Average Away Attendance : **6,719**

Football League Cup

Rd	Day	Month	Date	Opponents	Home	Away	H-T	Goalscorers	Gate
1/1	Tu	Aug	22	Exeter City	D1-1		(1-0)	Howe 36	5,193
1/2	W	Sep	6	Exeter City		W2-1	(2-0)	Reeves 13,Invincibile 42	2,825
2/1	M		18	Tranmere Rovers		D1-1	(0-0)	Hazell o.g.54	4,289
2/2	Tu		26	Tranmere Rovers	L0-1		(0-1)		4,573

F A Cup

Rd	Day	Month	Date	Opponents	Home	Away	H-T	Goalscorers	Gate
1	S	Nov	18	Ilkeston Town	W4-1		(1-0)	Willis 44,Williams M 63,Howe 79,Young 88	4,406
2	S	Dec	9	Gateshead	W5-0		(1-0)	O'Halloran 16,51,Cowe 84,89,Howe 87	3,907
3	S	Jan	6	Coventry City	L0-2		(0-1)		14,445

For Associate Members' Cup - see page 260   For Final League Table - see page 261

Alexander G G	Cobian J M	Cowe S M	Davis S S	Dryden R A	Duke D	Grazioli G S L	Griemink B J	Griffin C J	Hewlett M P	Heywood M S	Howe S R	Invincibile D	McAreavey P	McHugh F J	Mildenhall S J	O'Halloran K J	Reddy M	Reeves A	Robertson M W	Robinson M J	Robinson S E	Tuomela M	van der Linden A	Williams A P R	Williams J D	Williams M K	Willis A P	Woan I S	Young A J	
18	s	(s)	3		*11	(10)	1	s	4		*s	17			s	7		22		2							5			1
18	s		3		*11	(10)	1	(s)	4		*s	17			s	7		22		2			s				5			2
18	12		*s		s	10	1	s	4		8	17			s	7		22					6				s			3
	s	14	3		11	*s	1	*9	4		8				s	*7		22		2			s	(s)			5			4
	s		3		11	*s	1	Total	4		8	*17			s	7		22	s	2			s			24	5			5
	s		3		11	s	1	1	(4)		8	17			s	7		22	(s)	2		*s				24	*5			6
18	(12)		3		11	s	1	1	4			s			s	7		22	*19	(s)		25				24			*s	7
18	s		3		11	s	1		4			17			s	7		22		2			s			24	5		s	8
*18	s		3		(11)	*s	1		4			17			s	7		22		2			s	(s)		24	5			9
(18)	s		3		11	(s)	1		*4			17			s	7		22		2			s	*s		24	5			10
*18			3		(11)	*s	1				8	17			s	7		22	(s)	2			s			24	5		s	11
			3		*11	10	1				8	17			s	7		(22)	s	2			(s)	*s		24	5		s	12
	s	*s	3			s	1	Hall G D			*8	17			s	7		(s)	19	(2)			6	15		24	5			13
			(3)		(s)	s	1				8	*17			s	7		22	*s	2			6	s		24	5	31		14
	s	*s			11	(s)	1					17			s	7		22	*19	2			6			(24)	5	31	s	15
	s		3		s	(s)	1				*8	17			*s	7		22	s	2			6			(24)	5	31		16
(s)			3		s	s	1				8	17			s	*7		22	*s	2			6			(24)	5	31		17
s	s		(3)		*s	(s)	1				8	17			s	7			*19	2			6			24	5	31		18
(s)			3	25	*s	s	1				8	17			s	7		22		*2			s			(24)	5	31		19
18		s	3	25	*11		1	s			8	(17)			s	7		22		2			*s			(s)		31		20
18		s	3	25	*s		1				8	(17)			s			22		2			(s)			*24		31	s	21
(18)			3	25	*s		1	s			8	17			s	*7		22		2			s			(s)		31		22
18		s	3	25	*s		1	(s)			8	17			s	7		22		(2)			s			*24		31		23
*18	(12)	s	3	25	11		1				8	17			s	7		22					*s		(s)			31		24
s		(14)	3	25	*s			30				17			23	7		22		s			6					31	(s)	25
*s		14		Total	11		s	s		19		17		20	23	7	(16)	22		s			6						(s)	26
18		14		7	11		s	s		19		(*s)			23	7	16	22		(s)			6		29		s	*31		27
		(14)	3		11	*s	s	*30	(s)	19				s	23	7	16			s			6		29		5			28
*s			*3		(11)	s	s		4	19				(s)	23	7	16	22		s	25		6		29					29
18			3		11	s	(s)		4	19		*s		s	(23)	7	16	22		s	25				*29					30
18					11	(s)	s		(4)	19		*s		s	23	7	16	22		s	25		6		*29					31
18				Bakalli A	*11	(s)	s	*s		19		17		20	23		(16)	22			25		6		29		s			32
18						10	s	*30	4	19		17	(s)	(20)	23			22		*s	25		6				s			33
18			3			*10	s	s	4	19		*s	s		23		16	22		2	25		s					31		34
18			*3			s	s		4	19		(s)	s		23	7	16	22		(2)	25		*s					31		35
18			3			*10	s	s	4	19		s			23	7	16	22		2	25		*s					s		36
18			3			*10	s	s	4	19		(s)	s		23	7		22		2	25		*s					(31)		37
18			3			(s)	s		4	19		*s	s		23	7	(16)	22		*2	25		s					31		38
(18)			3	s		s	s		4	19		*s			23	7	*16	22		2	25		(s)					31		39
*18			3			s	s	s	4	19		(s)			23	7	(16)	22		2	25		*s					31		40
18			3			s	s		4	19		17			23	*7	16	22		*s	25		s	s				31		41
18				s		(10)	s	*s		19		17	27		23		(s)	22		2	25		6	s				*31		42
18			3	s		*s	s		4	19		*17	27		23		16	22		(s)	25		s	(15)						43
18			s	s	11	*s	s		4	19		17	s		23	7	*16	22			25						5			44
18				s	11	s	s		4	19		17			23	7	(16)	22			*25		(s)				5	*s		45
(s)	s			24	11	10				19		17			23	7		*s			25		*6	(15)			5			46
30	3	5	35	1	24	10	24	3	25	21	17	32	2	3	22	40	17	42	4	29	18	1	17	3	6	17	21	21	0	Apps
6		4	1		8	18	1	4	1		2	10	1	1	1		1	2	6	5		1	16	5	1	2		1	4	Subs
7		1			1	2				2	1	9	1			5	4	3	1	1	2		1			2		3		Goals

*Match 3 : *16 = Heiselberg K* *Matches 21,22 : 16 = Whitley J* *Matches 24,32 : s = Davies G M* Opponents 1 goal

*Matches 25,26 : *9 = Lightbourne K L* *Matches 25,46 : s = Farr C J* *Match 46 : s = Mills J M*

Alexander G G	Cobian J M	Cowe S M	Davis S S	Dryden R A	Duke D	Grazioli G S L	Griemink B J	Griffin C J	Hewlett M P	Heywood M S	Howe S R	Invincibile D	McAreavey P	McHugh F J	Mildenhall S J	O'Halloran K J	Reddy M	Reeves A	Robertson M W	Robinson M J	Robinson S E	Tuomela M	van der Linden A	Williams A P R	Williams J D	Williams M K	Willis A P	Woan I S	Young A J	
18	12	(s)			*11	(10)	1		4		8				s	7		22		s			6	*s						1/1
	s	s	3		*11	(s)	1		4		8	17			s	7		22	*s	2						(24)	5			1/2
18	*12		3		11	s	1		4						s	7		22	(19)	*s		25	s	(s)		24				2/1
18	s		3		11	s	1		4			*s			s	7		22	*19	2		(25)				24	(s)			2/2
3	2	0	3		4	1	4		4		2	1				4		4	2	2		2	1	0		3	1			Apps
		1				2						1							1	1				2			1			Subs
											1	1						1												Goals

First Round First Leg : 16 = Heiselberg K s = Griffin C J Opponents 1 goal

Alexander G G	Cobian J M	Cowe S M	Davis S S	Dryden R A	Duke D	Grazioli G S L	Griemink B J	Griffin C J	Hewlett M P	Heywood M S	Howe S R	Invincibile D	McAreavey P	McHugh F J	Mildenhall S J	O'Halloran K J	Reddy M	Reeves A	Robertson M W	Robinson M J	Robinson S E	Tuomela M	van der Linden A	Williams A P R	Williams J D	Williams M K	Willis A P	Woan I S	Young A J	
s	(12)		3		(s)	s					8	*17			23	7		22					6			24	5	31	*s	1
18		*s	(3)		(s)		1				8	17			s	7		22		2			6			*24	s	31	s	2
18		14	(3)		11		1	30				17			s	*s		22					s		(s)			31	s	3
2	1	1	3		1		2	1			2	3			1	2		3		1			2		0	2	1	3	0	
1		1			2											1									1				3	
		2									2					2										1	1		1	

First Round : s = Farr C J *Third Round : *16 = Whitley J 25 = Dryden R A*

SEASON 2001/02

Football League Second Division
Final League Position : 13th
Manager : Roy Evans
Andy King (from Dec.22)

Substitutes :
s denotes substitute **not** used
* player substituted by *s
( ) player substituted by (s)
_ player substituted by s

				Home	Away	H-T	Goalscorers	Gate
1	S	Aug	11 Peterborough United	D0-0				7,934
2	S		18 Bristol City		L1-3	(0-1)	O'Halloran 77 pen.	13,818
3	S		25 Oldham Athletic	L0-2		(0-2)		5,219
4	M		27 Bury		W3-0	(0-0)	Kuffour 47,O'Halloran 71 pen.,Duke 88	3,202
5	S	Sep	1 Colchester United	W1-0		(0-0)	Ruddock 52	4,889
6	S		8 AFC Bournemouth		D0-0			3,770
7	S		15 Tranmere Rovers	D2-2		(1-1)	Grazioli 7,Gurney 86	5,922
8	Tu		18 Port Vale		W2-0	(1-0)	Invincibile 32,Hewlett 59	3,737
9	S		22 Chesterfield		L0-4	(0-0)		4,275
10	Tu		25 Brentford	W2-0		(1-0)	Invincibile 38,Grazioli 62	5,519
11	S		29 Northampton Town		D1-1	(0-0)	Grazioli 48	5,104
12	S	Oct	13 Reading		W3-1	(1-0)	Grazioli 38,Invincibile 52,Kuffour 87	14,389
13	S		20 Cardiff City	L0-3		(0-1)		8,373
14	Tu		23 Cambridge United	W2-0		(0-0)	Grazioli 84,90	4,882
15	S		27 Wycombe Wanderers		D1-1	(1-1)	Carlisle 23	7,127
16	S	Nov	3 Stoke City	L0-3		(0-1)		7,981
17	S		10 Blackpool		L0-1	(0-1)		5,018
18	Tu		20 Queens Park Rangers		L0-4	(0-3)		8,847
19	S		24 Brighton & Hove Albion	D1-1		(0-1)	Sabin 58	8,830
20	Tu		27 Wrexham	W3-1		(2-0)	Sabin 5,Invincibile 28,Heywood 60	4,127
21	S	Dec	1 Wigan Athletic		L0-1	(0-0)		5,635
22	S		22 Notts County		L1-3	(1-2)	Duke 25	4,197
23	W		26 AFC Bournemouth	D0-0				6,790
24	S		29 Bury	W3-1		(2-1)	Gurney 6,Howe 8,Carlisle 51	7,624
25	Su	Jan	13 Bristol City	L1-2		(0-1)	Foley 58	7,273
26	W		16 Oldham Athletic		L0-2	(0-1)		3,970
27	S		19 Peterborough United		D1-1	(1-0)	Sabin 19	6,598
28	W		23 Notts County	W1-0		(0-0)	Invincibile 71	3,821
29	S		26 Wrexham		D2-2	(0-1)	Grazioli 74,Reeves 90	2,879
30	W		30 Colchester United		W3-1	(0-1)	Gurney 61 pen.,74,Sabin 63	3,132
31	S	Feb	2 Northampton Town	W2-1		(1-0)	Gabbiadini o.g.5,Invincibile 64	6,585
32	Tu		5 Huddersfield Town	L0-1		(0-0)		5,094
33	S		9 Cardiff City		L0-3	(0-1)		12,045
34	Th		14 Reading	D0-0				9,264
35	F		22 Tranmere Rovers		D0-0			8,106
36	Tu		26 Chesterfield	W2-1		(1-1)	Grazioli 25,Reeves 64	4,580
37	S	Mar	2 Port Vale	W3-0		(2-0)	Gurney 43,Heywood 45,Willis 83	5,867
38	Tu		5 Brentford		L0-2	(0-1)		5,644
39	S		9 Huddersfield Town		L0-2	(0-1)		9,569
40	S		16 Wigan Athletic	D1-1		(0-0)	Sabin 64	6,226
41	S		30 Blackpool	W1-0		(0-0)	Young 46	5,085
42	M	Apr	1 Stoke City		L0-2	(0-0)		13,530
43	S		6 Queens Park Rangers	L0-1		(0-0)		6,774
44	Tu		9 Cambridge United		W2-1	(1-1)	Gurney 44,Angus o.g.83	2,406
45	S		13 Brighton & Hove Albion		D0-0			6,870
46	S		20 Wycombe Wanderers	D1-1		(0-1)	Heywood 56	7,492

Average Home Attendance : **6,354**
Average Away Attendance : **6,690**

Football League Cup

				Home	Away	H-T	Goalscorers	Gate
1	W	Aug	22 Wolverhampton Wanderers		W2-1	(0-0)	Howe 48,O'Halloran 51 pen.	7,598
2	Tu	Sep	11 West Bromwich Albion		+ L0-2	(0-0)		14,536

+ After Extra Time

F A Cup

				Home	Away	H-T	Goalscorers	Gate
1	S	Nov	17 Hartlepool United	W3-1		(2-1)	Ruddock 36 pen.,Invincibile 37,Heywood 74	4,766
2	S	Dec	8 Hereford United	W3-2		(1-2)	Invincibile 11,Edwards P 53,Howe 76	7,699
3	S	Jan	5 Manchester City		L0-2	(0-1)		21,581

For Associate Members' Cup - see page 260   For Final League Table - see page 261

Brayley A P	Carlisle W T	Davies G M	Davis S S	Duke D	Edwards N M	Edwards P	Farr C J	Foley D J	Grazioli G S L	Griemink B J	Gurney A R	Halliday K J	Herring I	Hewlett M P	Heywood M S	Howe S R	Invincibile D	Kuffour J O	McAreavey P	McKinney R	O'Halloran K J	Reeves A	Robinson M J	Robinson S E	Ruddock N	Sabin E	Willis A P	Young A J	
<u>s</u>			(s)	11					10	1	6			4	19	*8	<u>17</u>			s	7	22		*s	s	(14)			1
<u>s</u>			*s	11					(10)	1	6			4	19	(s)	*17			s	7	22		<u>25</u>	s	14			2
(s)			3	*11						1	6			4	19	(8)	17	*s		s	7	22			s	14			3
(s)			*3	11						1	6			4	19	8	*s	(9)	s	s	7	22			s	14			4
		<u>s</u>	3	*11		s				1	6			4	19	8	(s)	(9)		s	7			*s	16	<u>14</u>			5
			3	(11)		s			*s	1	6			4	19	8	(s)	9		s	*7	s		25	16				6
(s)				11		*s			(10)	1	6			4	19	8	17	*9	s	s		s		25	16				7
s				11		(20)			10	1	6			4	*s	8	17	s	(s)	s		22		25	*16				8
(s)		<u>s</u>		*11		20			(10)	1	<u>6</u>			4	19	8	17	*s	s	s		22		25					9
s		s		11		20			10	1	6			4	19	8	17	s	s	s		22		25					10
s		s		11		20			(10)	1	6			*4	19	8	17	(s)		s		22		25	*s				11
	s			11		*20			<u>10</u>	1	6			4	(s)	8	17	<u>s</u>	*s	s		22		(25)	16				12
				11	*s	20			*10	1	6			4	s	8	17	s	s	s		22		25	16				13
	*s			*11		20			10	1	6			4	s	8	17	s	s	s		22		25	16				14
	23			11	s	(20)			*10	1		s		4	19		17	*s	(s)	s				25	16		5		15
	23			(11)		20			*10	1	6			4	19	8	17	(s)		s				s	16	*s	s		16
<u>s</u>	23								*10	1	6	s		4	19	8	17		*s	s			(s)		16	<u>14</u>	(5)		17
	23			11					*s	1	6			4	19		17	*s	s	s			*2	25	16	*14	s		18
s	23			11						1	6			4	19		17	s	s	s			2	25	16	14	s		19
s	23			11						1	6			4	19	s	17		s	s			2	25	16	14	s		20
	23		<u>s</u>	11		(s)				1	6			4	19	*s	<u>17</u>		s	s			(2)	25		*14	5		21
	23		(*s)	11		*20			(s)	1					19	<u>8</u>	17		<u>s</u>	s		s		25	16	14	5		22
	*23		(s)	(11)					10	1	6				19	8	17		s	s		22	*s	25		14	s		23
	23		s	11					*10	1	6				19	8	17		*s	s		22	s	25		14	s		24
			3	11	s			24		1					19		17		(27)	s		22	s	25		*14	5	*s	25
			s	11				24		1	6				19	*8	17		27	s		22	s	25		14	s	*s	26
			<u>3</u>	(11)				*24	*s	1	6				19	<u>s</u>	17		s	s		22	2	25		14	(s)		27
			3	11				*24	*s	1	6				19	s	17			s		22	(2)	25		14	(s)	s	28
			3	(11)	s			*24	*s	1	6			(s)	19	<u>s</u>	17			s		22		<u>25</u>		14	5		29
			3	(s)	s			*s	*10	1	6			(4)	19	<u>8</u>	17		<u>s</u>	s				25		14	5		30
			3	*s	s			s	*10	1	6			4	19	8	17		s	s				25		14	5		31
				*s	<u>s</u>			s	*10	1	6			4	19	(8)	17		27	s				<u>25</u>		14	5	(s)	32
			3	<u>11</u>	s		s	*s	<u>s</u>	1	6			4	19	(s)	17		(27)					25		*14	5		33
			3	s					*10	1	6			4	19	(8)	17		(s)	s		22		25		14	*s	s	34
					*s	s	s		10	1	6			4	19	*8	17		27			22		25		(14)	s	(s)	35
			*s	s		(s)	s		10	1	6			4	19	8	17		*27			22		25		(14)	s		36
			3	*s	(s)	s	s		(10)	1	6			4	19	8	17							25			5	*26	37
			3	11		(s)	s		(10)	1	6	s		*4	19	8	17							25			5	*s	38
				11		(s)			10	1	6	s	s	4	19	(8)	*17			s				25		14	5	*s	39
s			*3	*s		(s)				1	6			4	19	8	<u>17</u>		<u>s</u>	s				25		(14)	5	26	40
s				11	s	s				1	6	s		4	19	8	17			s				25		14	5	26	41
				*s	29	*20				s	6			4	19	8	17			15		<u>22</u>		s		(14)	5	(s)	42
				11	s	s				1	6			4	19	*8	17		*s	s		(s)		25		14	5	(26)	43
				11	s	(20)				1	6			4	19	*s	(s)		27	s		s		*25		14	5	26	44
				11	s	20				1	6			4	19	8			*s	s		22		(s)		14	(5)	*26	45
				11	29	20	s			1	6		*s	4	19	s			*27			22		s		14		26	46
0	10	0	15	36	2	14	0	5	24	45	43	0	0	38	42	33	40	4	8	1	6	24	6	37	14	33	19	7	Apps
7	1	2	6	6	4	6		2	7				1	1	2	6	4	7	11			1	2	3	1	1	3	7	Subs
	2			2				1	8		6			1	3	1	6	2			2	2			1	5	1	1	Goals

Matches 3,42 : s <u>s</u> = Cobian J M | *Matches 25,45 : (s) s = Williams J D* | Opponents 2 goals

Matches 37,38 : s = Smith B J | *Match 46 : s = Thomas J O*

Brayley A P	Carlisle W T	Davies G M	Davis S S	Duke D	Edwards N M	Edwards P	Farr C J	Foley D J	Grazioli G S L	Griemink B J	Gurney A R	Halliday K J	Herring I	Hewlett M P	Heywood M S	Howe S R	Invincibile D	Kuffour J O	McAreavey P	McKinney R	O'Halloran K J	Reeves A	Robinson M J	Robinson S E	Ruddock N	Sabin E	Willis A P	Young A J	
(s)		s	3	11		s			*s	1	(6)			4	19	8	*17			s	7	22				14			1
			*3	11		<u>s</u>			*s	1	6			4	19	8	17	(9)	s	s		(s)		25	<u>16</u>				2
0			2	2		0			0	2	2			2	2	2	2	1			1	1		1	1	1			Apps
1						1			2													1							Subs
																1					1								Goals

Brayley A P	Carlisle W T	Davies G M	Davis S S	Duke D	Edwards N M	Edwards P	Farr C J	Foley D J	Grazioli G S L	Griemink B J	Gurney A R	Halliday K J	Herring I	Hewlett M P	Heywood M S	Howe S R	Invincibile D	Kuffour J O	McAreavey P	McKinney R	O'Halloran K J	Reeves A	Robinson M J	Robinson S E	Ruddock N	Sabin E	Willis A P	Young A J	
(s)				11					*10	1	6	s		4	19		17		*s	s			2	25	16	(14)	s		1
	23		s	*11		20			s	1					19	8	17		s	s			*s	25	16	14	5		2
s	23		*s	11					(s)	1	6				19	(8)	17		*27	s		22	s	25		14			3
0	2		0	3		1			1	3	2			1	3	2	3		1			1	1	3	2	3	1		Apps
1			1						1										1				1						Subs
						1									1	1	2								1				Goals

SEASON 2002/03

Football League Second Division
Final League Position : 10th
Manager : Andy King

Substitutes :
s denotes substitute **not** used
* player substituted by *s
( ) player substituted by (s)
_ player substituted by s

					Home	Away	H-T	Goalscorers	Gate
1	S	Aug	10	Barnsley	W3-1		(1-1)	Parkin 32,50,88 pen.	5,702
2	Tu		13	Chesterfield		W4-2	(3-0)	Invincibile 11,39,Sabin 42,Parkin 57	3,189
3	S		17	Blackpool		D0-0			6,404
4	S		24	Cardiff City	L0-1		(0-1)		7,564
5	M		26	Brentford		L1-3	(1-2)	Davis 17	6,299
6	S		31	Stockport County	L0-1		(0-0)		5,456
7	S	Sep	7	Port Vale	L1-2		(1-1)	Gurney 8	5,029
8	S		14	Queens Park Rangers		L0-2	(0-0)		11,619
9	Tu		17	Cheltenham Town		L0-2	(0-1)		5,761
10	S		21	Northampton Town	W2-0		(1-0)	Jackson 31,Parkin 79 pen.	4,719
11	S		28	Luton Town		L0-3	(0-1)		6,393
12	S	Oct	5	Oldham Athletic	L0-1		(0-1)		4,326
13	S		12	Colchester United	D2-2		(0-1)	Gurney 66,Sabin 69	4,152
14	S		19	Bristol City		L0-2	(0-2)		13,205
15	S		26	Mansfield Town	W2-1		(1-1)	Parkin 21,Sabin 46	4,136
16	Tu		29	Notts County		D1-1	(1-0)	Parkin 31	4,797
17	S	Nov	2	Wycombe Wanderers		W3-2	(1-1)	Davis 12,Parkin 79,90	6,021
18	S		9	Tranmere Rovers	D1-1		(1-0)	Parkin 2	5,077
19	S		23	Huddersfield Town		W3-2	(2-1)	Duke 1,Gurney 24 pen.,Parkin 90	8,334
20	S		30	Peterborough United	D1-1		(0-0)	Parkin 78 pen.	4,709
21	S	Dec	14	Plymouth Argyle		D1-1	(0-0)	Gurney 77	8,111
22	S		21	Crewe Alexandra	L1-3		(0-2)	Parkin 75 pen.	4,957
23	Th		26	Brentford	W2-0		(1-0)	Gurney 2,Parkin 66	6,045
24	S		28	Wigan Athletic		L0-2	(0-1)		6,114
25	W	Jan	1	Cardiff City		D1-1	(0-0)	Parkin 72	13,062
26	S		4	Chesterfield	W3-0		(1-0)	Parkin 33,Invincibile 52,Reeves 87	4,544
27	S		18	Stockport County		W5-2	(2-0)	Parkin 7,Robinson 11,Reeves 73,Hewlett 85,Sabin 90	4,318
28	W		22	Blackpool	D1-1		(1-0)	Miglioranzi 20	4,787
29	S		25	Wigan Athletic	W2-1		(2-0)	Invincibile 24,Gurney 35	5,238
30	S	Feb	1	Barnsley		D1-1	(1-1)	Invincibile 34	8,661
31	S		8	Tranmere Rovers		W1-0	(0-0)	Gurney 50	7,181
32	S		15	Wycombe Wanderers	L0-3		(0-1)		6,239
33	S		22	Port Vale		D1-1	(0-0)	Parkin 54	4,085
34	S	Mar	1	Queens Park Rangers	W3-1		(1-1)	Robinson 18,Parkin 64,Heywood 68	7,716
35	S		8	Northampton Town		L0-1	(0-0)		5,566
36	W		12	Cheltenham Town	L0-3		(0-2)		5,583
37	S		15	Mansfield Town		L1-2	(1-2)	Reeves 45	4,471
38	W		19	Bristol City	D1-1		(0-0)	Parkin 66	8,629
39	S		22	Notts County	W5-0		(1-0)	Parkin 43,62,89,Gurney 59,Duke 69	4,246
40	S		29	Colchester United		L0-1	(0-0)		3,787
41	S	Apr	5	Peterborough United		D1-1	(0-1)	Invincibile 71	4,310
42	S		12	Huddersfield Town	L0-1		(0-0)		4,760
43	S		19	Crewe Alexandra		W1-0	(0-0)	Miglioranzi 75	6,384
44	W		23	Plymouth Argyle	W2-0		(1-0)	Invincibile 38,Parkin 68	5,057
45	S		26	Oldham Athletic		L0-4	(0-2)		6,873
46	S	May	3	Luton Town	W2-1		(2-1)	Miglioranzi 41,Parkin 43	6,455

Average Home Attendance : **5,440**
Average Away Attendance : **6,737**

Football League Cup

					Home	Away	H-T	Goalscorers	Gate
1/1	W	Sep	11	Wycombe Wanderers	L1-2 +		(0-0)	Willis 100	2,993

+ After Extra Time

F A Cup

					Home	Away	H-T	Goalscorers	Gate
1	S	Nov	16	Huddersfield Town	W1-0		(0-0)	Gurney 85	4,212
2	Su	Dec	8	Oxford United		L0-1	(0-0)		11,645

SAM PARKIN
was almost an 'overnight success' at the County Ground - a hat-trick on his debut instantly earning him the fans 'Super Sammy Parkin' accolade. Having scored just five goals in a season-long loan at Northampton in 2001/02, Sam had doubled that by the first week of November on his way to a 26-goal haul. He followed that with 23 (when Town missed out in the 2003/04 play-offs) and 24 goal tallies - to give him an outstanding scoring rate of 51% from 142 appearances. Such a prized asset quickly attracted suitors and Sam moved to Ipswich in June 2005.

Bampton D P	Beswetherick J B	Cobian J M	Davis J R W	Duke D	Dykes D L	Edds G J	Edwards N M	Farr C J	Griemink B J	Gurney A R	Halliday K J	Herring I	Hewlett M P	Heywood M S	Ifil J C	Invincibile D	Jackson J	Lewis K J	Marney D E	Miglioranzi S	Nightingale L R	Parkin S	Reeves A	Robinson S E	Sabin E	Taylor C J	Willis A P	Young A J	
			*s	11		2	s	s	1				4	19		*17				10		9	s	25	14		5	s	1
			*s	11		2	s	s	1				*4	19		17				10		9	s	25	14		5	s	2
			8	11	s	2	*s	s	1					19		*17				10		9	s	25	14		5	s	3
				11		2	s	s	1	6				19		17				10		*s	s	*25	14		5	s	4
			8	11		2			1	6				19		*s				10		9		*25	14		5		5
		s	8	11		2	s	s	1	6				19						10		9	22	*25	14		*s	s	6
			8	11	s	2		s	1	6			s	19						10		9	*22	25	14		*s	s	7
		s		*11		*s	s	s	1	6			4	19			3			10		9	22	25	14			s	8
				11	s	2	s	s	1	6			4	19		17	3			s		9		25	14			s	9
				11		s		s	1	6			4	19		17	3			*s		9	s	*25	14		5	s	10
				11		*s	s	s	1	6			4	19		17	3					9	s	*25	14		5	s	11
s		s		11	s	*s		s	1	6			4	19		17	3			*10			22		14		5		12
		Total	8	11	s	s		s	1	6			4	19		17	3			s			22	25	14			s	13
		0	8	11		s		s	1	6			4	19		*17	s			10			22	25	14		s	*s	14
			*8	11		s		s	1	6			4	19		*s	3			10		9	22	s	14		s		15
			*s	11		s		s	1	6			4	19		*17	3			s		9	22	25	14		s		16
			8	11		s		s	1	6			4	19		*s	3			s		9	22	25	*14		s		17
			8	11		s		s	1	6			4	19		*17	3			s		9	22	25			s	*s	18
				11		s		s	1	6			4	19		17	3			10		*s	22	25	*14		s	s	19
				11		s		s	1	6			*4	19		17	3			10		9	22	*s	14		s	s	20
*s				11		s		s	1	6			4	19		17				10		9	22	*25	14		s	s	21
s				11		s		s	1	6			4	19		17				10		9	22	25	*14		s		22
				11		s			1	6			4	19		17			s	10	*16	9	22	25	*s		s		23
						s			1	6	s		4	19		17			3	10	*16	9	22	25	*s		s		24
				11		s			1	6			4	19		*17			3	10	s	9	22	25	*s		s		25
				11		s			1	6			4	19		17			3	10	s	9	22	*25	s		*s		26
				11		s		s	1	6			4	19		*17			3	10	s	9	22	25	*s		s		27
				11		s		s	1	6			4	19		*17			3	10	s	9	22	25	*s		s		28
				11		s		s	1	6			4	19		17			*3	10		9	22	25	s		*s	s	29
				11				s	1	6			4	19	*s	17				10		9	22	25	s	s	*5	s	30
				*11		s		s	1	6			4	19	*s	17			3	10		9	22	25	s	s			31
				11	s		s	s	1	6			4	19	*s	17			*3	10		9	22	25	s				32
	s			11				s	1	6			4	19	*8	17			*s	10		9	22	25	s			s	33
	*12	Draycott M R		11	s		s	s	1	6			4	19	*s					10		9	22	25	14			s	34
	*12			11	s			s	1	6			4	19	s	*s				10		9	22	25	14	s			35
	12			11	s			s	1	6			*4	19	s	17				10		9	22	25	*s	s			36
	s			11	s			s	1	6			4	19	8	17				*10		9	22	25	*s	s			37
				11	s			s	1	6			s	19	8	17		3		10		9	22	25		s		s	38
				11			s	s	1	6			*s	19	8	17		*3		10		9	22	(25)	s			(s)	39
				11	*s			s	1	6			4	19	(8)	17		3		10		9	(s)	s	*14			s	40
				*11	s		s	s	1	6			4	19		*s		3		10		9	22	25	14			s	41
					*15	*s	s		1	6		s	4	19		17		3		(10)		9		25	14			(s)	42
		s		*11				s	1		s	12	4	19		17		3		10		9	22	25		*s		s	43
*s		s		11				18	s			*12	4	19		(17)		3		10		9	22	25		s		(s)	44
		s		11				18	s	(6)		*s	4	19		17		3		10		9	22	*25		s			45
s				11				s	1	6		*s	4	19		17		3		(10)		9		25	*14	(s)			46
0	3	0	9	44	1	8	0	2	44	41	0	2	39	46	5	37	12	9	8	39	2	41	35	42	27	0	9	0	Apps
3			3		1	6	3					2	1		4	5	1		1	2	1	2	1	2	12	4	6	11	Subs
			2	2						8			1	1		7	1			3		25	3	2	4				Goals

*Match 22 : *s = Sutton J W M*

Matches 23,24 : s = Judge A G

Matches 25,26 : s = Smith S A

Matches 45, 46 : (s) s = Garrard L E

Bampton D P	Beswetherick J B	Cobian J M	Davis J R W	Duke D	Dykes D L	Edds G J	Edwards N M	Farr C J	Griemink B J	Gurney A R	Halliday K J	Herring I	Hewlett M P	Heywood M S	Ifil J C	Invincibile D	Jackson J	Lewis K J	Marney D E	Miglioranzi S	Nightingale L R	Parkin S	Reeves A	Robinson S E	Sabin E	Taylor C J	Willis A P	Young A J	
			*8	11	*s	s		s	1	6			4	19						10		9	(s)	25	14		(5)	s	1/1

Bampton D P	Beswetherick J B	Cobian J M	Davis J R W	Duke D	Dykes D L	Edds G J	Edwards N M	Farr C J	Griemink B J	Gurney A R	Halliday K J	Herring I	Hewlett M P	Heywood M S	Ifil J C	Invincibile D	Jackson J	Lewis K J	Marney D E	Miglioranzi S	Nightingale L R	Parkin S	Reeves A	Robinson S E	Sabin E	Taylor C J	Willis A P	Young A J	
				11		s		s	1	6			4	19		17	3			s		9	22	25	14		s	s	1
s				11		*2		s	1		s		4	19		17	3			10		9	22		(14)		*s	(s)	2
0				2		1			2	1			2	2		2	2			1		2	2	1	2		0	0	Apps
1																											1	1	Subs
										1																			Goals

For Associate Members' Cup - see page 260 For Final League Table - see page 270

SEASON 2003/04

Football League Second Division
Final League Position : 5th
Manager : Andy King

Substitutes :
s denotes substitute **not** used
* player substituted by *s
( ) player substituted by (s)
_ player substituted by s

No	Day	Month	Date	Opponent	Home	Away	H-T	Goalscorers	Gate
1	S	Aug	9	Sheffield Wednesday	L2-3		(1-3)	Miglioranzi 31,Igoe 57	10,573
2	F		15	Colchester United		W1-0	(0-0)	Mooney 87	3,339
3	S		23	Notts County	W4-0		(2-0)	Hewlett 8,Mooney 10,Parkin 47,Igoe 50	5,758
4	M		25	AFC Bournemouth		D2-2	(2-1)	Mooney 18,Robinson 35	6,606
5	S		30	Blackpool	D2-2		(2-2)	Mooney 7,30	6,219
6	S	Sep	6	Brighton and Hove Albion		D2-2	(1-1)	Parkin 14,67	6,534
7	S		13	Wrexham	W1-0		(0-0)	Gurney 79	8,160
8	Tu		16	Grimsby Town		W2-1	(0-1)	Gurney 53,Mooney 65	3,535
9	S		20	Barnsley		D1-1	(1-0)	Parkin 20	9,006
10	S		27	Peterborough United	W2-0		(0-0)	Parkin 84,Milner 90	6,767
11	W	Oct	1	Luton Town	D2-2		(1-0)	Milner 8,Howard 89	7,573
12	S		4	Bristol City		L1-2	(1-0)	Mooney 34	14,294
13	S		11	Stockport County	L1-2		(1-0)	Mooney 45	7,060
14	S		18	Chesterfield		L0-3	(0-2)		3,506
15	Tu		21	Tranmere Rovers		L0-1	(0-0)		6,675
16	S		25	Port Vale	D0-0				5,313
17	S	Nov	1	Wycombe Wanderers	W2-0		(1-0)	Burton 11,Miglioranzi 67	5,681
18	S		15	Oldham Athletic		W1-0	(0-0)	Parkin 61	5,282
19	S		22	Queens Park Rangers	D1-1		(1-0)	Parkin 39	10,021
20	S		29	Hartlepool United		L0-2	(0-1)		4,493
21	S	Dec	13	Plymouth Argyle	L2-3		(0-1)	Fallon 80, Parkin 90	9,374
22	S		20	Brentford		W2-0	(0-0)	Howard 66, Parkin 82	5,077
23	F		26	Rushden and Diamonds		L0-2	(0-1)		4,845
24	Su		28	Brighton and Hove Albion	W2-1		(1-0)	Parkin 45, Miglioranzi 66	9,269
25	S	Jan	3	AFC Bournemouth	W2-1		(1-1)	Mooney 15,80	7,158
26	S		10	Sheffield Wednesday		D1-1	(0-0)	Mooney 52	22,751
27	S		17	Colchester United	W2-0		(1-0)	Parkin 15,Mooney 46	6,014
28	S		24	Notts County		W2-1	(1-0)	Howard 35,Mooney 86	6,663
29	S		31	Blackpool		D2-2	(0-1)	Parkin 48,Gurney 83	6,463
30	S	Feb	7	Rushden and Diamonds	W4-2		(2-0)	Mooney 9,Gurney 17 pen.,Duke 76,Hunter o.g.90	7,023
31	S		14	Stockport County		W4-2	(3-1)	Mooney 4,90,Howard 16,Nicholas 18	4,833
32	S		21	Chesterfield	W2-0		(1-0)	O'Hanlon 33,Parkin 86	6,814
33	W	Mar	3	Tranmere Rovers	W2-0		(1-0)	Parkin 31,82	6,928
34	S		6	Brentford	W2-1		(1-1)	Gurney 14,Igoe 82	7,649
35	S		13	Plymouth Argyle		L1-2	(0-1)	Mooney 90	16,080
36	W		17	Grimsby Town	W2-0		(2-0)	Mooney 34,45	6,954
37	S		20	Wrexham		L2-3	(0-1)	Igoe 49,O'Hanlon 77	3,384
38	S		27	Barnsley	D1-1		(1-1)	Parkin 8	7,305
39	Tu		30	Port Vale		D3-3	(0-2)	Parkin 63,Hewlett 68,Fallon 83	5,702
40	S	Apr	3	Peterborough United		L2-4	(1-2)	Heywood 4,Parkin 63	4,745
41	S		10	Bristol City	D1-1		(0-1)	Fallon 74	14,540
42	M		12	Luton Town		W3-0	(3-0)	Fallon 3,21,Hewlett 44	7,008
43	S		17	Wycombe Wanderers		W3-0	(1-0)	Miglioranzi 7,Parkin 52,Gurney 75 pen.	5,769
44	S		24	Oldham Athletic	L1-2		(0-1)	Fallon 79	8,506
45	S	May	1	Queens Park Rangers		L0-1	(0-1)		18,396
46	S		8	Hartlepool United	D1-1		(1-0)	Igoe 7	11,627

Average Home Attendance : **7,925**
Average Away Attendance : **7,608**

Football League Cup

No	Day	Month	Date	Opponent	Home	Away	H-T	Goalscorers	Gate
1	Tu	Aug	12	Southend United		W3-2	(1-2)	Parkin 34,48,Mooney 73	3,385
2	W	Sep	24	Leeds United		+ D2-2	(1-0)	Gurney 44,Parkin 74	29,211

+ After Extra Time (L3-4 on penalties)

F A Cup

No	Day	Month	Date	Opponent	Home	Away	H-T	Goalscorers	Gate
1	S	Nov	8	Wycombe Wanderers		L1-4	(0-1)	Gurney 71 pen.	4,738

For Football League Trophy and Play-offs - see overleaf >> For Final League Table - see page 270

Burton D J	Duke D	Evans R K	Fallon R M	Garrard L E	Griemink B J	Gurney A R	Herring I	Hewlett M P	Heywood M S	Howard B R W	Ifil J C	Igoe S G	Lewis K J	Martin B	Miglioranzi S	Milner J P	Mooney T J	Nicholas A P	O'Hanlon S P	Parkin S	Pook M D	Reeves A	Robinson S E	Ruster S	Smith G G	Stevenson J A	Viveash A L	
	11	s			1	6		*4	19	*s		(7)			10		8			9		s	25		s	(s)	5	1
	11	s			1	6		4	19	s		7			10		8			9		s	25		s	s	5	2
	*11	s			1	6		4	19	s		7			10		(8)			9		s	25		*s	(s)	5	3
	11	s			1	6		4	19	s		7			10		8			9		s	25		s	s	5	4
	11	20			s	6		4	19	(s)		7			*10		8			9		s	(25)		*s	s	5	5
	*11	20			s	6	s	4	19	s	2				10	16	8			9		*s			s		5	6
	11	20			s	6		4	19	s	2				10	*16	8	s		9		*s				s	5	7
	11	20			s	6	s	4	19		2				10	16	8			9		s			s	s	5	8
	11	20			s	6		4	19	s	2	(s)			10	(16)	8			9		*s				s	*5	9
		20			s	6		4	19	*s	2	*7			10	16	8			9		s			s	s	5	10
	11	20			s	6		(4)	19	*s	2	*7			10	16	8					s	(s)			s	5	11
	11	20			s	6	12	4	19	17		7			*10		8					(s)		s	(*s)	s	5	12
	11	20			s	6	s	4	19	*s		(7)					8					22	25	(s)	s	*14	5	13
16	11	20			s	6		4	19	(17)				s			8	(s)				22	25	*s		s	*5	14
16	11	*20		(s)	*s	6		(4)	19	17			2				8					22	25		s	s	s	15
*16	(11)	20			s			4	19	(s)			2		10		8	15				22	25	s		*s	s	16
(16)	*11	20			s	6		4	19	s			2		10		8	15		(s)		*s	25	s				17
	11	20	*s		s	6		4	19	s	28		2		10		8	s		*9		(s)	(25)					18
	11	20	s		s	6		4	19	(17)	28				10		8	*s		9		(s)	*25		s			19
	11	20	*s		s	6		4		s	28				*10		8	15		9		22	25	s	s			20
	11	20	(s)		s	6		*4	19	s	28	(7)			10		8	*s		9		s	25					21
	(s)	20	s		s	6		s	*19	17	28	(7)			10		8	15		9		*s	25					22
	(s)	20	16		s	6		s		(17)	28	*7			10		*s	15		9		22	25	s				23
	s	20	s		s	6		4		17	28	7			10		8	15		9		22			s	s		24
	*s	20	s		s	6		4		*17	28	(7)		s	10		8	15		9		22	(s)					25
	*s	20			s	6		4	(s)	*17	28	7					8	15		9		22	(25)		s	s		26
	11	20			s			4	19	17	28	7		s			8	15		9		s	25		s	s		27
	11	20			s			4	19	(17)		7					8	15	*s	9	s	22	*25		(s)	s		28
	11	20	(s)		s	6		4	19	s		7					8	15	*s	9		(22)	*25		s			29
	11	20	*s		s	6		4	19	s		(7)			(s)		*8	15	2	9		22					s	30
	(11)	20			s	6		4	19	*17		(s)			10		8	15	2	9		s			*s	s		31
	s	20	s		s	6		4	19	17		7			10		8	15	2	9		s			s			32
	s	20	s		s	6		4	19	17		7			10		8	15	2	9		s			s			33
	*s	20	(s)		s	6		4	19	17		7			*10		8	(15)	2	9		s				s		34
	*s	20	(s)		s	6		4	19	17		7		s			8	(15)	2	9		*22			s			35
	11	20	s		s	6		4	19	17		7					8	15	2	9		s			s	s		36
	11	20	*s		s	6		4	19	*17		7					8	15	2	9	s	s			s			37
	(s)	20	*s		s			4	19	(17)		7			10		*8	15	2	9	s	22			s			38
	(11)	20	*s		s	6		4	19	(s)		*7			10		8	15	2	9	s	s						39
	11	s	*s	s	1	6			19			7			10		8	15	*2	9	s	22			s			40
	11	20	*s	s	s	6		4	19			7			10		8	*15	2	9		s			s			41
	11	20	16		s	6		4	19			7			10		*s	15	2	*9		s			s			42
	(11)	20	16		s	6		4	19	(s)		7			10		*s	15	2	*9		s					s	43
	11	20	16	s	s	6		4	19	(17)		(s)			10		8	*15	2	*s		s						44
	11	20	16		s	6		4		*s		(7)			*10		(s)	15	2	9		22			s		s	45
	11	20	16		s	6		4		17		7					s	15	2	9	s	22			s		s	46
4	35	41	6	0	5	42	1	43	39	21	16	33	4	0	34	6	41	28	17	38	0	17	20	0	0	1	14	Apps
	7		13	1	1				1	13		3			1		4	3	2	2		10	2	2	7	4	1	Subs
1	1		6			6		3	1	4		5			4	2	19	1	2	19			1					Goals

Match 42 : s = Howe E J F

Opponents 1 goal

Burton D J	Duke D	Evans R K	Fallon R M	Garrard L E	Griemink B J	Gurney A R	Herring I	Hewlett M P	Heywood M S	Howard B R W	Ifil J C	Igoe S G	Lewis K J	Martin B	Miglioranzi S	Milner J P	Mooney T J	Nicholas A P	O'Hanlon S P	Parkin S	Pook M D	Reeves A	Robinson S E	Ruster S	Smith G G	Stevenson J A	Viveash A L	
	s	20			s			4	19	(17)		7			(s)		*s	s		9		22	25		3	*14	5	1
	11	(s)			1	6	s	4	19	*s		(7)			10			s		9		22			3	*14	s	2
	1	1			1	1	0	2	2	1		2			1		0			2		2	1		2	2	1	Apps
	1	1					1			1					1		1											Subs
						1											1			3								Goals

Burton D J	Duke D	Evans R K	Fallon R M	Garrard L E	Griemink B J	Gurney A R	Herring I	Hewlett M P	Heywood M S	Howard B R W	Ifil J C	Igoe S G	Lewis K J	Martin B	Miglioranzi S	Milner J P	Mooney T J	Nicholas A P	O'Hanlon S P	Parkin S	Pook M D	Reeves A	Robinson S E	Ruster S	Smith G G	Stevenson J A	Viveash A L	
	11	20			s	6	s		19	*17					10		8	15		9		(22)	25	(s)	*s		s	1

SEASON 2000/01

Rd					Home	Away	H-T	Goalscorers	Gate
1	Tu	Jan	9	Millwall		+ D0-0			2,394
QF	Tu		30	Wycombe Wanderers	W2-1		(2-1)	Alexander 1,15	3,244
SF	Tu	Feb	13	Southend United		* L1-2	(0-0)	Reddy 72	3,337

+ After Extra Time (W3-2 on penalties)
* After Extra Time (lost on golden goal rule)

	Alexander G G	Cobian J M	Davis S S	Duke D	Grazioli G S L	Griemink B J	Hall G D	Halliday K J	Hewlett M P	Heywood M S	Invincibile D	McHugh F J	Mildenhall S J	Mills J M	O'Halloran K J	Reddy M	Reeves A	Robinson M J	Robinson S E	van der Linden A	Williams J D	Willis A P	Young A J
1	18	*s		11			30	s			17	(20)	23	(s)			22	2		6	*29		26
QF	18	s		11		1	(s)			19	*17	(20)	s		7	*s		2		6	29	5	s
SF	*s	s	3	11	s	1			(4)	19		(s)	s		7	16		2	25	6	*29		
Apps	2	0	1	3		2	1	0	1	2	2	2	1	0	2	1	1	3	1	3	3	1	1
Subs	1	2					1	1				1		1		1							
Goals	2															1							

First Round : s = Campagna S P P s = Farr C J

SEASON 2001/02

Rd					Home	Away	H-T	Goalscorers	Gate
1	Tu	Oct	16	Colchester United		L0-1	(0-0)		1,521

	Brayley A P	Duke D	Edwards N M	Edwards P	Grazioli G S L	Griemink B J	Gurney A R	Halliday K J	Heywood M S	Howe S R	Kuffour J O	McAreavey P	McKinney R	Reeves A	Ruddock N	Willis A P
1	s	11	29	20	10	1	6	s	19	8	9	27	s	22	s	s

SEASON 2002/03

Rd					Home	Away	H-T	Goalscorers	Gate
1	Tu	Oct	22	Southend United	W6-1		(3-1)	Jackson 9,Davis 25,Heywood 45,Invincibile 49 Miglioranzi 89,Parkin 90	1,747
2	Tu	Nov	12	Kidderminster Harriers		+ L2-3	(1-0)	Invincibile 39,Young 47	1,322

+ After Extra Time

	Davis J R W	Duke D	Dykes D L	Edds G J	Farr C J	Griemink B J	Gurney A R	Hewlett M P	Heywood M S	Invincibile D	Jackson J	Miglioranzi S	Parkin S	Reeves A	Robinson S E	Sabin E	Willis A P	Young A J
1	*8	11	s	2	(s)	(1)	6	s	19	17	3	10	9	s		*s	5	
2		*s	15	(2)	18	s	(s)	s	19	17	*3	10	s	22	25		5	26
Apps	1	1	1	2	1	1	1	0	2	2	2	2	1	1	1	0	2	1
Subs		1	1		1		1						1			1		
Goals	1								1	2	1	1	1					1

SEASON 2003/04

Rd					Home	Away	H-T	Goalscorers	Gate
1	W	Oct	15	Boston United		L1-2	(1-1)	Robinson 31	1,514

Play-Offs

Rd					Home	Away	H-T	Goalscorers	Gate
SF	Su	May	16	Brighton and Hove Albion	L0-1		(0-0)		14,304
SF	Th		20	Brighton and Hove Albion		+ W2-1	(0-0)	Parkin 81,Fallon 97	6,876

+ After Extra Time (L3-4 on penalties)

	Duke D	Evans R K	Fallon R M	Griemink B J	Gurney A R	Herring I	Hewlett M P	Heywood M S	Howard B R W	Igoe S G	Miglioranzi S	Mooney T J	Nicholas A P	O'Hanlon S P	Parkin S	Pook M D	Reeves A	Robinson S E	Ruster S	Smith G G	Stevenson J A	Viveash A L
1	s	s		1		12		s	17				15			*23	22	25	18	(3)	14	5

**s = Garrard L E (s) = Martin B*

	Duke D	Evans R K	Fallon R M	Griemink B J	Gurney A R	Herring I	Hewlett M P	Heywood M S	Howard B R W	Igoe S G	Miglioranzi S	Mooney T J	Nicholas A P	O'Hanlon S P	Parkin S	Pook M D	Reeves A	Robinson S E	Ruster S	Smith G G	Stevenson J A	Viveash A L
SF	*11	20	(s)	s	6		4	19	17	7		8	(15)	2	9		s			*s		s
SF		20	*s	s	6		4	19	*17	7	10	8	(s)	2	9	s	s			(3)		
Apps	1	2	0	0	2		2	2	2	2	1	2	1	2	2	0	0			1		0
Subs			2										1				1			1		
Goals			1												1							

SEASON 1999/2000

Div.1

	P	W	D	L	F	A	W	D	L	F	A	Pts	G/S	Avge. Home Gate
1 Charlton Athletic	46	15	3	5	37	18	12	7	4	42	27	91	79	19,558
2 Manchester City	46	17	2	4	48	17	9	9	5	30	23	89	78	32,088
3 Ipswich Town *	46	16	3	4	39	17	9	9	5	32	25	87	71	18,524
4 Barnsley	46	15	4	4	48	24	9	6	8	40	43	82	88	15,412
5 Birmingham City	46	15	5	3	37	16	7	6	10	28	28	77	65	21,895
6 Bolton Wanderers	46	14	5	4	43	26	7	8	8	26	24	76	69	14,244
7 Wolverhampton Wanderers	46	15	5	3	45	20	6	6	11	19	28	74	64	21,471
8 Huddersfield Town	46	14	5	4	43	21	7	6	10	19	28	74	62	14,029
9 Fulham	46	13	7	3	33	13	4	9	10	16	28	67	49	13,092
10 Queens Park Rangers	46	9	12	2	30	20	7	6	10	32	33	66	62	12,589
11 Blackburn Rovers	46	10	9	4	33	20	5	8	10	22	31	62	55	19,253
12 Norwich City	46	11	6	6	26	22	3	9	11	19	28	57	45	15,539
13 Tranmere Rovers	46	10	8	5	35	27	5	4	14	22	41	57	57	7,273
14 Nottingham Forest	46	9	10	4	29	18	5	4	14	24	37	56	53	17,196
15 Crystal Palace	46	7	11	5	33	26	6	4	13	24	41	54	57	15,662
16 Sheffield United	46	10	8	5	38	24	3	7	13	21	47	54	59	13,718
17 Stockport County	46	8	8	7	33	31	5	7	11	22	36	54	55	7,411
18 Portsmouth	46	9	6	8	36	27	4	6	13	19	39	51	55	13,906
19 Crewe Alexandra	46	9	5	9	27	31	5	4	14	19	36	51	46	6,221
20 Grimsby Town	46	10	8	5	27	25	3	4	16	14	42	51	41	6,157
21 West Bromwich Albion	46	6	11	6	25	26	4	8	11	18	34	49	43	14,584
22 Walsall	46	7	6	10	26	34	4	7	12	26	43	46	52	6,779
23 Port Vale	46	6	6	11	27	30	1	9	13	21	39	36	48	5,997
24 SWINDON TOWN	46	5	6	12	23	37	3	6	14	15	40	36	38	6,977

SEASON 2000/01

Div.2

	P	W	D	L	F	A	W	D	L	F	A	Pts	G/S	Avge. Home Gate
1 Millwall	46	17	2	4	49	11	11	7	5	40	27	93	89	11,442
2 Rotherham United	46	16	4	3	50	26	11	6	6	29	29	91	79	5,652
3 Reading	46	15	5	3	58	26	10	6	7	28	26	86	86	12,647
4 Walsall *	46	15	5	3	51	23	8	7	8	28	27	81	79	5,632
5 Stoke City	46	12	6	5	39	21	9	8	6	35	28	77	74	13,767
6 Wigan Athletic	46	12	9	2	29	18	7	9	7	24	24	75	53	6,774
7 AFC Bournemouth	46	11	6	6	37	23	9	7	7	42	32	73	79	4,403
8 Notts County	46	10	6	7	37	33	9	6	8	25	33	69	62	5,201
9 Bristol City	46	11	6	6	47	29	7	8	8	23	27	68	70	10,368
10 Wrexham	46	10	6	7	33	28	7	6	10	32	43	63	65	3,600
11 Port Vale	46	9	8	6	35	22	7	6	10	20	27	62	55	4,458
12 Peterborough United	46	12	6	5	38	27	3	8	12	23	39	59	61	6,252
13 Wycombe Wanderers	46	8	7	8	24	23	7	7	9	22	30	59	46	5,513
14 Brentford	46	9	10	4	34	30	5	7	11	22	40	59	56	4,645
15 Oldham Athletic	46	11	5	7	35	26	4	8	11	18	39	58	53	4,972
16 Bury	46	10	6	7	25	22	6	4	13	20	37	58	45	3,444
17 Colchester United	46	10	5	8	32	23	5	7	11	23	36	57	55	3,555
18 Northampton Town	46	9	6	8	26	28	6	6	11	20	31	57	46	5,654
19 Cambridge United	46	8	6	9	32	31	6	5	12	29	46	53	61	4,403
20 SWINDON TOWN	46	6	8	9	30	35	7	5	11	17	30	52	47	6,187
21 Bristol Rovers	46	6	10	7	28	26	6	5	12	25	31	51	53	7,275
22 Luton Town	46	5	6	12	24	35	4	7	12	28	45	40	52	5,754
23 Swansea City	46	5	9	9	26	24	3	4	16	21	49	37	47	4,913
24 Oxford United	46	5	4	14	23	34	2	2	19	30	66	27	53	5,148

SEASON 2001/02

Div.2

	P	W	D	L	F	A	W	D	L	F	A	Pts	G/S	Avge. Home Gate
1 Brighton & Hove Albion	46	17	5	1	42	16	8	10	5	24	26	90	66	6,598
2 Reading	46	12	7	4	36	20	11	8	4	34	23	84	70	14,115
3 Brentford	46	17	5	1	48	12	7	6	10	29	31	83	77	6,714
4 Cardiff City	46	12	8	3	39	25	11	6	6	36	25	83	75	12,523
5 Stoke City *	46	16	4	3	43	12	7	7	9	24	28	80	67	13,966
6 Huddersfield Town	46	13	7	3	35	19	8	8	7	30	28	78	65	10,881
7 Bristol City	46	13	6	4	38	21	8	4	11	30	32	73	68	11,220
8 Queens Park Rangers	46	11	10	2	35	18	8	4	11	25	31	71	60	11,749
9 Oldham Athletic	46	14	6	3	47	27	4	10	9	30	38	70	77	5,800
10 Wigan Athletic	46	9	6	8	36	23	7	10	6	30	28	64	66	5,772
11 Wycombe Wanderers	46	13	5	5	38	26	4	8	11	20	38	64	58	6,621
12 Tranmere Rovers	46	10	9	4	39	19	6	6	11	24	41	63	63	8,655
13 SWINDON TOWN	46	10	7	6	26	21	5	7	11	20	35	59	46	6,354
14 Port Vale	46	11	6	6	35	24	5	4	14	16	38	58	51	5,210
15 Colchester United	46	9	6	8	35	33	6	6	11	30	43	57	65	3,839
16 Blackpool	46	8	9	6	39	31	6	5	12	27	38	56	66	5,730
17 Peterborough United	46	11	5	7	46	26	4	5	14	18	33	55	64	5,457
18 Chesterfield	46	9	3	11	35	36	4	10	9	18	29	52	53	4,392
19 Notts County	46	8	7	8	28	29	5	4	14	31	42	50	59	5,965
20 Northampton Town	46	9	4	10	30	33	5	3	15	24	46	49	54	5,253
21 AFC Bournemouth	46	9	4	10	36	33	1	10	12	20	38	44	56	5,076
22 Bury	46	6	9	8	26	32	5	2	16	17	43	44	43	3,914
23 Wrexham	46	7	7	9	29	32	4	3	16	27	57	43	56	3,816
24 Cambridge United	46	7	7	9	29	34	0	6	17	18	59	34	47	3,507

* Promoted via Play-offs

SEASON 2004/05

Football League Championship Div.1
Final League Position : 12th
Manager : Andy King

Substitutes :
s denotes substitute **not** used
* player substituted by *s
( ) player substituted by (s)
_ player substituted by s

				Home	Away	H-T	Goalscorers	Gate
1	S	Aug	7 Wrexham		L1-2	(0-1)	Caton 90	5,099
2	W		11 Luton Town	L2-3		(1-2)	Parkin 45,Reeves 65	6,286
3	S		14 Milton Keynes Dons	W2-1		(1-1)	Parkin 23,Howard 63	5,060
4	S		21 Bristol City		W2-1	(1-1)	Henderson 23,60	13,389
5	S		28 Hartlepool United	W3-0		(3-0)	Henderson 17,Parkin 37,Nelson o.g.40	5,365
6	M		30 Walsall		L2-3	(2-2)	Howard 5,Henderson 25	5,951
7	S	Sep	4 Colchester United		W1-0	(1-0)	Parkin 7	3,868
8	S		11 Peterborough United	L0-1		(0-1)		5,777
9	S		18 Blackpool		D1-1	(0-1)	Henderson 69	5,229
10	S		25 Bradford City	W1-0		(0-0)	Igoe 87	5,189
11	S	Oct	2 Stockport County		D3-3	(2-0)	Fallon 13,66,McMaster 45	4,394
12	S		16 Oldham Athletic	W1-0		(1-0)	Roberts 14	5,522
13	Tu		19 Port Vale		L0-1	(0-0)		3,872
14	S		23 Barnsley		D2-2	(1-1)	Igoe 28,Roberts 82	8,837
15	W		27 Sheffield Wednesday	W3-2		(0-1)	Howard 78,Parkin 86,Fallon 88	6,972
16	S		30 Torquay United	D3-3		(3-1)	Parkin 27,Igoe 32,Howard 36	6,724
17	S	Nov	6 Tranmere Rovers		L1-2	(0-1)	Duke 69	8,419
18	S		20 Hull City	W4-2		(1-1)	Parkin 21,87,O'Hanlon 73,Roberts 90	6,348
19	S		27 Chesterfield		L0-1	(0-0)		4,244
20	W	Dec	8 Huddersfield Town	L1-2		(0-2)	Smith 89	4,828
21	S		11 Doncaster Rovers	D1-1		(0-1)	Parkin 72	5,452
22	S		18 AFC Bournemouth		L1-2	(0-0)	O'Hanlon 60	7,110
23	Su		26 Peterborough United		W2-0	(0-0)	Igoe 54,Parkin 85	4,212
24	Tu		28 Brentford	W3-0		(1-0)	Hewlett 42,Howard 67,Parkin 76	6,875
25	S	Jan	1 Colchester United	L0-3		(0-2)		6,468
26	M		3 Bradford City		W2-1	(0-0)	Smith 46,47	8,239
27	S		8 Sheffield Wednesday		L0-2	(0-1)		20,804
28	S		15 Blackpool	D2-2		(2-1)	Parkin 36,45	5,528
29	S		22 Brentford		L1-2	(1-1)	Smith 20	5,857
30	S		29 Stockport County	W3-0		(0-0)	Heywood 61,O'Hanlon 63,Smith 64	5,090
31	S	Feb	5 Oldham Athletic		W2-1	(0-1)	Parkin 60,Smith 69	5,810
32	S		12 Barnsley	W2-1		(1-1)	Parkin 13,76	5,511
33	S		19 Torquay United		D2-2	(1-1)	Parkin 38,58	4,190
34	W		23 Port Vale	W1-0		(1-0)	Proctor 25	4,724
35	S		26 Doncaster Rovers		D1-1	(1-1)	Holmes 5	7,696
36	S	Mar	5 AFC Bournemouth	L0-3		(0-1)		8,275
37	S		12 Luton Town		L1-3	(1-2)	Proctor 34	8,173
38	S		19 Wrexham	W4-2		(1-2)	Parkin 40,76,90 pen.,Smith 80	5,123
39	F		25 Milton Keynes Dons		D1-1	(1-1)	Smith 43	7,019
40	S	Apr	2 Hartlepool United		L0-3	(0-1)		4,936
41	S		9 Walsall	L1-2		(0-1)	Parkin 84 pen.	5,592
42	W		13 Bristol City	D0-0				6,977
43	S		16 Hull City		D0-0			23,125
44	S		23 Tranmere Rovers	W2-1		(0-1)	Smith 57,59	4,484
45	S		30 Huddersfield Town		L0-4	(0-0)		13,559
46	S	May	7 Chesterfield	D1-1		(1-1)	Parkin 13	6,044

Average Home Attendance : **5,835**
Average Away Attendance : **8,001**

Football League Cup

				Home	Away	H-T	Goalscorers	Gate
1	Tu	Aug	24 Rushden & Diamonds		W1-0	(0-0)	Hewlett 90	1,672
2	Tu	Sep	21 Leeds United		L0-1	(0-1)		18,476

F A Cup

				Home	Away	H-T	Goalscorers	Gate
1	S	Nov	13 Sheffield Wednesday	W4-1		(1-0)	Howard 43,Jenkins 47,Duke 83,Roberts 86	6,160
2	S	Dec	4 Notts County	D1-1		(1-0)	O'Hanlon 19	5,768
2R	W		15 Notts County		L0-2	(0-1)		3,770

For Final League Table - see page 270 For Football League Trophy - see page 272

Book S K	Caton A J	Duke D	Evans R K	Fallon R M	Garrard L E	Gurney A R	Henderson D A	Hewlett M P	Heywood M S	Holmes L D	Howard B R W	Ifil J C	Igoe S G	Jenkins S R	McMaster J	Miglioranzi S	Mitchell P A	Nicholas A P	O'Hanlon S P	Parkin S	Pook M D	Proctor M A	Reeves A	Roberts C J	Robinson S E	Slabber J A	Smith G G	Yeates M S	
s	s	*11	1	(8)	s	6		4			17		7			10			2	9			*s		(s)		3		1
s	*s	11	1	*8	s	6		4			17		7			10			2	9			18		s		s		2
s		11	1	*s		6		4			(17)	12	7			10			2	9			s		*16		(s)		3
s		11	1	*s		6	*21	4			(17)	12	7			10		(s)	2	9			s		s				4
s		11	1	s		*6	21	4			17	12						15	2	9			s		(s)		*s	(25)	5
s		11	1	s		6	21	4			(17)	12						15	2	9			s		(s)		*s	*25	6
s		11	1	s		Total	21	4			17	12	7			*10	6	*s	2	9					s			s	7
s		11	1	*s		6	21	4			(17)	12	7				6		2	9					s		(s)	*25	8
s		11	1	s			21	*s	s		17	12	7			(10)	6		2	9					(s)			*25	9
s		11	1	8				*s	s		17	12	7			*10	6		2	9					16		s	s	10
s	(s)	*11	1	8	s			4	*s		17	12	7		(21)		6		2						16		s		11
s		*11	1	8				4	s		17	12	7		*s		6	15	2					14	s		s		12
s		11	1	8				4	*s		17	12	*7		21		6	s	2					14	s		s		13
s		11	1	*8	s				s		17	12	7		(*s)			15	2	9				14	16		(s)		14
s		*11	1	*s	s				(s)		17	12	7					(15)	2	9			s	14	16		3		15
s		11	1	s				4	s		17	12	7	*6	Total			*s	2	9				14	(16)		(s)		16
s		*11	1	*s				4	19		17	12	7	6	2			s	2	9			s	14	s				17
s		11	1	s	s				19		17	12	7	6	2				2	9			s	14	16		s		18
s		*11	1	*s	s				19		(17)	12	7	6	1			(s)	2	9			s	14	16				19
s		(11)	1	*s	s			*4	19		17	12		6				s	2	9				14	16		(s)		20
s		*s	1	s	23			4	19		17		7	6				*15	2	9			s	14			s		21
s	s	11	1	s	23				19		17		*7					*s	2	9	(s)		18	(14)	16				22
s		11	1	s	*s			4		21		12	7	6					2	9	s		18	*14	s				23
s		11	1	*s	23			4		21	17	12	7	6				s		*9	s		18		s				24
s		11	1	s	23			4	19	21	(17)	12	7					(s)		9			s		*16	*s			25
s		11	1	(s)	23			*4	19	21	17	12	7							9			s		(*s)	s	3		26
s		11	1	*s	23				19	21	*17		7					(s)	(2)	9			18		s	s	3		27
s		(11)	1	8	23				19	21	(s)		7	*6		*s				9			18		s	s	3		28
s			1	*s	*23				19	21	s	12	(7)	6		10			2	9			s			(s)	3		29
s		11	1					4	19	21	s		(7)	6		(s)			2	9			s			*5	3		30
s		11	1	s				4	19		(s)	12	*s	6		*10			2	9			s			5	(3)		31
s		11	1	*s				4	19	21	s	s	(7)	6		(s)			2	9						*5	3		32
s		11	1	s				4	19	21	s	s	7	6		s			2	9						5	3		33
s		11	1					4	19	(21)	s	s	7	6		(s)			2	9		*26				*s	3		34
s		11	1					4	19	(21)	(s)	s	7	6		s			2	9		*26				*s	3		35
*s		11	*1			Holgate A B S		(4)	19	21	s	s	7	6	Lapham K J	(s)			2	9		26				s	3		36
s		11	1						19	(s)	s	12	7	6		(10)			2	9		*26	s	*s			3		37
20	s	(11)	s					s	19	21	*s	(s)	*7	6		10			2	9				14			3		38
s	s	11	1	s				4	19		*s	(s)	7	6		(10)			2	9				*14			3		39
s		11	1	*s				(4)	19		(s)	12	7	s		10			2	9	s			*14			3		40
s	s	*11	1	(s)				4	19			*s	7	6		10			2	9	s			(14)			3		41
s	s	*s	1	8					19		17	12	7	6		*10			2	9	s						3		42
s	s		1	*8					19		17	12	7	6		10			2	9	s			*s	s		3		43
s	(s)	11	1	8		s			19			12	7	6				*s	*2		22			(14)			3		44
s	*s	11	1	8		s			19			12	7	s	5			15			22			*14			(3)		45
s	(24)		1			(s)			19			12	*7		5	10		15		9	22			*s	s		3		46
1	1	41	45	12	8	0	6	29	28	14	28	31	42	24	2	17	7	8	40	41	3	4	6	18	11	4	23	4	Apps
1	7	2		18	1	2		2	4	1	7	4	1			5		8			2		2	3	7	5	7		Subs
	1	1		3			5	1	1	1	5		4						3	23		2	1	3			10		Goals

Match 3 : s = Opara J L   Match 8 : s = Viveash A L   Matches 42,44,45,46 : s s (s) s = Wells B   Opponents 1 goal

Book S K	Caton A J	Duke D	Evans R K	Fallon R M	Garrard L E	Gurney A R	Henderson D A	Hewlett M P	Heywood M S	Holmes L D	Howard B R W	Ifil J C	Igoe S G	Jenkins S R	McMaster J	Miglioranzi S	Mitchell P A	Nicholas A P	O'Hanlon S P	Parkin S	Pook M D	Proctor M A	Reeves A	Roberts C J	Robinson S E	Slabber J A	Smith G G	Yeates M S	
20			s	8	23			4			17	12	(s)					15	s	*s	s		18		16		(3)		1
s		11	1	*s	s			*4	(s)		17	12	7			10			2	9	s				16		(3)		2
1		1	1	1	1			2	0		2	2	1			1		1	1	1	0		1		2		2		Apps
				1					1				1						1	1	1								Subs
								1																					Goals

*First Round : *14 = Opara J L*

Book S K	Caton A J	Duke D	Evans R K	Fallon R M	Garrard L E	Gurney A R	Henderson D A	Hewlett M P	Heywood M S	Holmes L D	Howard B R W	Ifil J C	Igoe S G	Jenkins S R	McMaster J	Miglioranzi S	Mitchell P A	Nicholas A P	O'Hanlon S P	Parkin S	Pook M D	Proctor M A	Reeves A	Roberts C J	Robinson S E	Slabber J A	Smith G G	Yeates M S	
s		11	1	*s				4	19		17	12	7	6				s	2	9			s	*14			s		1
s		11	1	(8)	*s				19		17	12	*7	6				s	2	9			s		16		(s)		2
s		(11)	1	*s	23			4	19		17		7					s	2	9			*18	14	s		(s)		2R
		3	3	1	1			2	3		3	2	3	2					3	3			1	2	1		0		Apps
				2	1																				1		2		Subs
		1									1			1					1					1					Goals

SEASON 2005/06

Football League Championship Div.1
Final League Position : 23rd
Manager : Andy King
Iffy Onuora (from Sep.26)

Substitutes :
s denotes substitute **not** used
* player substituted by *s
( ) player substituted by (s)
_ player substituted by s̲

No	Day	Month	Date	Opponent	Home	Away	H-T	Goalscorers	Gate
1	S	Aug	6	Barnsley		L0-2	(0-1)		9,358
2	Tu		9	Oldham Athletic	L2-3		(0-2)	Roberts 79,Thorpe 85	5,294
3	S		13	Nottingham Forest	W2-1		(1-1)	Fallon 31,O'Hanlon 73	8,108
4	S		20	Blackpool		D0-0			4,661
5	S		27	Yeovil Town	W4-2		(1-1)	Skiverton o.g.24,Fallon 50,Heath 66,Roberts 90	6,973
6	M		29	Tranmere Rovers		L0-1	(0-0)		7,557
7	S	Sep	3	Walsall		L0-1	(0-0)		5,392
8	S		10	Southend United	L1-2		(0-1)	Fallon 90	4,785
9	S		17	AFC Bournemouth		L1-2	(1-1)	Jenkins 44	7,276
10	S		24	Bradford City	L2-3		(1-1)	Fallon 19,76	4,590
11	Tu		27	Doncaster Rovers		L0-1	(0-1)		5,282
12	S	Oct	1	Milton Keynes Dons		L1-3	(1-0)	Fallon 7	5,536
13	S		8	Port Vale	L1-2		(1-1)	Fallon 24	4,531
14	S		15	Brentford		D0-0			6,969
15	S		22	Scunthorpe United	D1-1		(0-1)	Roberts 78 pen.	4,973
16	S		29	Huddersfield Town		D1-1	(1-0)	Gurney 40 pen.	11,352
17	F	Nov	11	Bristol City	W2-1		(2-1)	McDermott 12,Fallon 31	7,572
18	S		19	Port Vale		D1-1	(0-0)	Bouazza 66	4,108
19	S		26	Barnsley	L0-3		(0-1)		5,422
20	S	Dec	3	Rotherham United		W1-0	(1-0)	Fallon 45	3,537
21	S		10	Oldham Athletic		D2-2	(1-0)	O'Hanlon 12,McDermott 48	5,354
22	S		17	Blackpool	D0-0				5,766
23	M		26	Colchester United	W1-0		(0-0)	Fallon 90	5,531
24	W		28	Chesterfield		D1-1	(0-1)	Bouazza 63 pen.	4,265
25	S		31	Swansea City	D0-0				8,985
26	M	Jan	2	Hartlepool United		D1-1	(0-1)	Fallon 78	4,169
27	S		14	Gillingham		L0-3	(0-1)		7,300
28	S		21	AFC Bournemouth	W4-2		(1-0)	Cureton 37,Miglioranzi 52,Fallon 79,Peacock 90	6,092
29	F		27	Southend United		L0-2	(0-2)		7,945
30	Tu		31	Walsall	W1-0		(1-0)	Cureton 43	4,597
31	S	Feb	4	Doncaster Rovers	W2-1		(1-0)	Shakes 29,Comyn-Platt 57	5,100
32	S		11	Bradford City		D1-1	(0-0)	O'Hanlon 90	7,283
33	Tu		14	Gillingham	W1-0		(1-0)	Cureton 27	5,530
34	S		18	Rotherham United	L2-3		(2-2)	Cureton 20,O'Hanlon 25	7,518
35	S		25	Nottingham Forest		L1-7	(0-3)	Benjamin 76	22,444
36	Tu	Mar	7	Tranmere Rovers	L1-2		(0-2)	Cureton 69	4,139
37	S		11	Yeovil Town		D0-0			7,451
38	S		18	Colchester United		L0-1	(0-1)		3,767
39	S		25	Chesterfield	W2-0		(0-0)	Cureton 53,90	5,661
40	S	Apr	8	Hartlepool United	D1-1		(0-1)	Peacock 54	5,225
41	Tu		11	Swansea City		L1-2	(0-0)	Shakes 62	12,465
42	S		15	Milton Keynes Dons	L0-1		(0-0)		7,273
43	M		17	Scunthorpe United		W2-1	(2-1)	Benjamin 26 pen.,Shakes 39	5,207
44	S		22	Brentford	L1-3		(0-2)	Brown 71	6,845
45	S		29	Bristol City		D1-1	(0-0)	Brown 49	15,632
46	S	May	6	Huddersfield Town	D0-0				6,353

Average Home Attendance : **5,951**
Average Away Attendance : **7,579**

Football League Cup

No	Day	Month	Date	Opponent	Home	Away	H-T	Goalscorers	Gate
1	Tu	Aug	23	Wycombe Wanderers	L1-3		(0-1)	Pook 58	3,976

F A Cup

No	Day	Month	Date	Opponent	Home	Away	H-T	Goalscorers	Gate
1	S	Nov	5	Boston United	D2-2		(1-2)	Gurney 32,Comyn-Platt 87	3,814
1R	W		16	Boston United		L1-4	(0-4)	Fallon 83 pen.	2,467

IFFY ONUORA
was playing for Bradford University when he was snapped up by Huddersfield in 1989. The burly front man was signed by Steve McMahon from Gillingham for £120,000 in March 1998 and made 80 appearances for Town. The club's financial plight then saw Iffy depart, returning to the Gills in January 2000. But he came back as head of youth development in October 2004 and was appointed manager at the end of September 2005. Town had mustered just seven points out of thirty by then which, ultimately, contributed to relegation back to the basement division. Iffy looked set to continue for 2006/07, but Dennis Wise was appointed - with Iffy being offered his old job back, which he declined.

Benjamin T J	Bouazza H	Brown A W	Bulman M K	Collins P P	Comyn-Platt C	Cureton J	Evans R K	Fallon R M	Gurney A R	Heath C	Heaton T D	Holgate A B S	Ifil J C	Jarrett A O	Jenkins S R	McDermott N T	Miglioranzi S	Mikolanda P	Nicholas A P	Nicolau N G	O'Hanlon S P	Peacock L A	Pook M D	Roberts C J	Shakes R U B	Smith J D	Thorpe A L	Wells B	Whalley G G	
			s	20		11	1						5		(6)				s	s	2		*19	*s	12	3	9	(s)	7	1
			s	20		11	1						5						*15	s	(2)		19	18	*s	3	9	s	7	2
			s	20		(11)	1	8					5							4	2		19	(s)	*s	3		s	7	3
				20		(11)	1	8		25	s		5		*s					4	2		19	(s)	s	3	s		*7	4
			s	20		(11)		8	*s	25	26		5				s				*2		19	(s)	12	3	s		7	5
			s	20	s	(s)		8	27		26		5				10						19	*s	(12)	3		s	7	6
			s	20		(s)		8	27	*25	26		5		s		10			s			19	*s	(12)	3			7	7
			s	20		*11		8	27		26		5		s		10			4			19	s	(s)	3	*s		(7)	8
			s	20				8	27	s	26		5		*6	*s	10						19	(s)	s	3	(9)		7	9
			s	20		s		8		(s)	26		5			*s	*10		15		2		19	s		3	(9)		7	10
			s	(20)		(s)		8		*25	26		5			23			s		2		19	*s	12	3	9	s		11
			s	20	s	(s)		8		25	26					23			15	*s	2		19		*12	3	(9)	s		12
	28		s	s				8		*25	26		5		6	23			s		2		19		*s	3		(s)	(7)	13
	28		s			s		8	27	25	26		5		*6	(s)			*s		2		19	s		(3)		Total	7	14
	28		s		*s			8	27	s	26				6	*23			15		2		19	18	(s)		s	0	(7)	15
	28		s		s				*27	(s)	26		5		6	*s	10		15		2		(19)		12		s	4		16
	28		s		s			8	27		26		5		(s)	23	10		15		2		*19	*s	s	(3)				17
	28		s		17		1	8					5		6	s	10		15		2		s	*18	*s	s			7	18
	28	(s)			17		s	8	*27		26		5		6		(10)	*s	15		2			18		s			s	19
	28	32	s	20	17		1	(8)								23	10	(s)	15				19	*s		*3		Smith P W	s	20
	28	(s)			*17		1	8			s		*s			(23)	10	s	15		2		19		12	3			s	21
	28	(s)		Total			1	8			s	s	5		s	*23	10	(31)	15		2		19		*s	3				22
	(s)	32		13			1	8			s	(30)	5		s	*23	10	s	15		2		*s		12	3				23
	(28)	32	s				1	8	27			*s	5		(s)	s		s	15		2		*19		12	3				24
	(s)	32			s		1	8	27		s	(30)	5		*s		10	s	15		2				12	*3				25
	Total	*32	s		17	(11)	1	8				s	5		6		10	(s)	15		2		s		12					26
	11	32	s		17	11	1	8				(s)	5		6		10	Total	(15)		*2		s		12			*s		27
	2	*32	s		17	(11)	1	8	27				5	*s	6		10	1	15			(s)			12	s		s		28
	2	*32	s		s	*s	1		27				5	25	6		(10)	4	15		2	9			12	s		(s)		29
s		32	s		*s	11	1		(27)			s	5				*10		15		2	9			12	3		(s)		30
	Diagouraga T	32	s	Jutkiewicz L I P	*17	11	1		*s			(s)	5				s	McPhee C S I	15		2	(9)			12	3		20		31
		32	s			*11	1		(27)				5	(s)	s		s		15		2	9		*s	12	3		20		32
		32	s			11	1		27				5	s	s		*s		15		2	9		(s)	(12)	3		*20		33
		32	s			11	1		*27				5	*s	s		10		15		2	9	s	(s)	(12)	3				34
*s		32	s			11	1		(s)				5	(25)	s		10		15		2	9		s	*12	3				35
8		32	s			11	1		27					(s)	s		(10)		15		2	9	19		*s	*3			s	36
s		32	s			11	1		27						*6		*s		15		2	9	(19)	s	(s)	3			7	37
*s		32			(s)	11	1		27						6		s		(15)		2	*9	19	s	s	3			7	38
(8)	*s	32		s	17	11	1		27				s		6			(s)			2		*19		s	3			7	39
*8	25	32			17	11	1						5		6		s	(s)	s		2	*s			s	3			(7)	40
	(25)	32		*s	17	s	1								s		(s)	23	15		2	*9	s		12	3			7	41
	25	*32		s	*s	11	1		27						s		(s)	23	15		2	s			12	3			(7)	42
8	25			26	(s)	s	1		27						*s			(23)	15		2	s	s		12	3		*20		43
8	(s)	*s		s		11	1		27						s			23	15		2	s			12	3		*20	(7)	44
s	(25)	32		26	17	s	1		*s				5		*6			23			2		(s)		s	3			7	45
s	s	32		26	17	(s)	1						5					23			*2		19		12	3			(7)	46
5	5	23	0	3	13	22	32	25	24	7	14	2	34	2	17	9	22	6	31	3	40	11	26	4	26	38	6	5	23	Apps
3	2	4		2	9	8			4	3		3	1	4	7	3	5	2	2	2		4	4	17	11		1	4	1	Subs
2		2			1	7		12	1	1					1	2	1				4	2		3	3		1			Goals

Matches 2,3 : (s) s = Reeves A *Match 3 : *23 = Summerbee N J* *Match 20 : s = Henry L C D* Opponents 1 goal

*Matches 16,26,31,46 : 29 *s s s = Stroud D A* *Match 27 : s = Lapham K J* *Match 46 : *s = Wells B*

Benjamin T J	Bouazza H	Brown A W	Bulman M K	Collins P P	Comyn-Platt C	Cureton J	Evans R K	Fallon R M	Gurney A R	Heath C	Heaton T D	Holgate A B S	Ifil J C	Jarrett A O	Jenkins S R	McDermott N T	Miglioranzi S	Mikolanda P	Nicholas A P	Nicolau N G	O'Hanlon S P	Peacock L A	Pook M D	Roberts C J	Shakes R U B	Smith J D	Thorpe A L	Wells B	Whalley G G	
					17	(s)	s	*s		25	26		5							s			19	(18)	12	3	*9		7	1

14 = Reeves A s = Lapham K J

Benjamin T J	Bouazza H	Brown A W	Bulman M K	Collins P P	Comyn-Platt C	Cureton J	Evans R K	Fallon R M	Gurney A R	Heath C	Heaton T D	Holgate A B S	Ifil J C	Jarrett A O	Jenkins S R	McDermott N T	Miglioranzi S	Mikolanda P	Nicholas A P	Nicolau N G	O'Hanlon S P	Peacock L A	Pook M D	Roberts C J	Shakes R U B	Smith J D	Thorpe A L	Wells B	Whalley G G	
			s		s				27	25	26	(s)	5		6		10		15		2		*s		12		(9)		s	1
			*s		s			8	(27)	25		s	5		6	*23			15		2		19	18	(s)	3			s	2
			0		0			1	2	2	1	0	2		2	1	1		2		2		1	1	1	1	1		0	Apps
			1		2							1											1		1					Subs
					1			1	1																					Goals

*First Round : *29 = Stroud D A*

For Final League Table - see page 271 For Football League Trophy - see page 272

SEASON 2006/07

Football League Championship Div.2
Final League Position : 3rd
Manager : Dennis Wise
Paul Sturrock (from Nov.7)

Substitutes :
s denotes substitute **not** used
* player substituted by *s
( ) player substituted by (s)
_ player substituted by s

					Home	Away	H-T	Goalscorers	Gate
1	S	Aug	5	Hartlepool United		W1-0	(1-0)	Peacock 11	4,690
2	Tu		8	Barnet	W2-1		(0-1)	Shakes 54,Brownlie 90	7,475
3	S		12	Rochdale	W1-0		(1-0)	Goodall o.g.44	6,771
4	S		19	Darlington		W2-1	(2-1)	Evans 6,Roberts 21	4,571
5	S		26	Stockport County	W2-0		(1-0)	Brown 34,Roberts 63	6,868
6	F	Sep	1	Chester City		W2-0	(0-0)	Peacock 48,74	3,382
7	S		9	Wrexham		L1-2	(1-0)	Evans 28	5,257
8	Tu		12	Milton Keynes Dons	W2-1		(1-1)	Smith J 45 pen.,Evans 56 pen.	8,304
9	S		16	Peterborough United	L0-1		(0-1)		7,329
10	S		23	Notts County		D1-1	(0-0)	Onibuje 47	6,079
11	Tu		26	Wycombe Wanderers		D1-1	(0-0)	Brownlie 51	6,090
12	S		30	Boston United	D1-1		(1-0)	Monkhouse 25	6,074
13	S	Oct	7	Accrington Stanley		D1-1	(0-1)	Peacock 67	3,083
14	S		14	Grimsby Town	W3-0		(2-0)	Pook 33,Monkhouse 44,Peacock 88	5,719
15	S		21	Shrewsbury Town		W2-1	(1-0)	Onibuje 12,Brown 81	5,218
16	S		28	Lincoln City	L0-1		(0-0)		7,685
17	S	Nov	4	Hereford United	L1-2		(1-1)	Roberts 32	6,910
18	S		18	Torquay United		W1-0	(0-0)	Roberts 62 pen.	4,029
19	S		25	Bury	W2-1		(1-1)	Roberts 34,Fitzgerald o.g.90	5,628
20	Tu	Dec	5	Mansfield Town		L0-2	(0-2)		2,274
21	S		9	Walsall		W2-0	(1-0)	Jutkiewicz 23,Roberts 69 pen.	6,812
22	S		16	Bristol Rovers	W2-1		(2-1)	Jutkiewicz 15,Weston 17	10,010
23	S		23	Macclesfield Town		L1-2	(0-1)	Peacock 64	2,377
24	Tu		26	Wycombe Wanderers	W2-1		(1-0)	Jutkiewicz 45,Peacock 53	8,878
25	S		30	Notts County	D1-1		(0-1)	Timlin 77	6,805
26	M	Jan	1	Milton Keynes Dons		W1-0	(1-0)	Peacock 31	6,797
27	S		13	Wrexham	W2-1		(1-1)	Zaaboub 9,Roberts 71 pen.	6,130
28	S		20	Boston United		W3-1	(1-1)	Roberts 10,Pook 59,Sturrock 88	2,101
29	S		27	Macclesfield Town	W2-0		(1-0)	Shakes 45,Peacock 52	6,062
30	Tu		30	Peterborough United		D1-1	(0-0)	Sturrock 88	3,516
31	S	Feb	3	Hartlepool United	L0-1		(0-0)		6,841
32	S		17	Darlington	D1-1		(1-0)	Nicholas 9	5,570
33	Tu		20	Barnet		L0-1	(0-1)		2,639
34	S		24	Chester City	W1-0		(1-0)	Smith J 9 pen.	5,462
35	S	Mar	3	Stockport County		L0-3	(0-1)		6,594
36	S		10	Accrington Stanley	W2-0		(1-0)	Smith J 45 pen.,Nicholas 48	6,197
37	S		17	Grimsby Town		L0-1	(0-0)		4,595
38	Su		25	Lincoln City		W3-2	(2-1)	Roberts 17,Corr 34,Peacock 49	5,741
39	S		31	Shrewsbury Town	W2-1		(0-1)	Corr 67,Roberts 73	7,335
40	Tu	Apr	3	Rochdale		D0-0			2,544
41	S		7	Hereford United		D0-0			4,740
42	M		9	Torquay United	W2-1		(1-0)	Sturrock 2,Jutkiewicz 83	7,389
43	S		14	Bury		W1-0	(0-0)	Jutkiewicz 85	2,401
44	S		21	Mansfield Town	W2-0		(2-0)	Corr 4,Hjelde o.g.38	10,472
45	S		28	Bristol Rovers		L0-1	(0-1)		9,902
46	S	May	5	Walsall	D1-1		(0-0)	Ifil 52	14,731

Average Home Attendance : **7,419**
Average Away Attendance : **4,584**

Football League Cup

					Home	Away	H-T	Goalscorers	Gate
1	Tu	Aug	22	Brentford	+ D2-2		(1-2)	Nicholas 38,Evans 72	5,582

+ After Extra Time (L3-4 on penalties)

F A Cup

					Home	Away	H-T	Goalscorers	Gate
1	S	Nov	11	Carlisle United	W3-1		(1-1)	Lumsden o.g.9,Roberts 70,90	4,938
2	S	Dec	2	Morecambe	W1-0		(0-0)	Roberts 89 pen.	5,942
3	S	Jan	6	Crystal Palace		L1-2	(0-1)	Ifil 85	10,238

For Final League Table - see page 271 For Football League Trophy - see page 272

Brezovan P	Brown A W	Brownlie R	Caton A J	Comyn-Platt C	Evans P	Ifil J C	Ince P E C	Jutkiewicz L I P	Monkhouse A W	Nicholas A P	Noubissie P B	Onibuje F	Peacock L A	Pook M D	Rhodes A G	Roberts C J	Shakes R U B	Smith J D	Smith P A	Stewart J H	Sturrock B D	Timlin M A	Vincent J R	Weston C J	Westwood A M	Whalley G G	Williams A	Zaaboub S	
1					*s	5		(s)	11	15		s	(10)	19		9	12	2	s				3	*23			s		1
1		s			*s	5		s	11	15		(s)	(10)	*19		9	12	2					3	23			s		2
1		(s)			18	5		s	11	s		s	10	19		(9)	*12	2					3	*s			6		3
1		s			18	5		s	*11	*s		s	10			(9)	12	2					3	23			6		4
1	*s		*28	s	(18)	5		s		15		s	10	(s)		9	12	2						23			6		5
1	8	s	(s)	17	18	5		s		15		s	10	*s		*9	12	2						(23)					6
1	*8	s	*s	17	18		(s)			15		s	10			9	12	2					s	(23)			6		7
1	s	s	28		18	5	4			15		(s)	10			(9)	*s	*2					s	23			6		8
1	*s	s	(28)		18	5	*4			15		(s)	10	s		9	12						s	23			6		9
1	*8	20			18	5		s	*s	s		(16)	10	19		(s)		2					3	s			6		10
1	s	20			(18)	5		s	11	s		16	*10	19		*s		2					3	(s)			6		11
1	(s)	20			s	5		s	(11)	s		*s	10	19		*9		2					3	23			6		12
1	s	*20			(s)	5	Total		11	s		16	10	(19)		*s	s	2					3	23			6		13
1	s	*20				5	2	s	11	s		(16)	10	19	(s)		*s	2					3	23			6		14
	*s	s				5	1		*11	s		16	(10)	19	(s)		12	2	25				3	23		s	6		15
	(8)	*s		Total						15		16	10	19	(s)		*12	2	25	s			3	23		s	6		16
	8			2	18	5				15		(s)	10	19	*s	(9)	*12	2	s				3			s	s		17
		(20)			*18	5		s	s	15			(s)	*s		9	12	2	25	s				23			6	4	18
	(8)	s				5		*s		15			*10			9	12	2	25	s		34		23		s	6	(s)	19
	(s)	*s				5		21	Total	15				s		*9	(12)	2	25	s		34		23			6	4	20
	*8					5		21	9	s				*s		(9)	(s)	2	25	s	22	34	3	23			6	4	21
	*8					5		21	1	s			*s	s		9	(s)	2	25	s		34	3	(23)			6	4	22
	8				(*s)	5		21	2	s			10	s			12		25	s	(s)	34	3	23			6	*4	23
	s					5		*21		s			(10)	19		9	*s	2	25	s	(s)	34	3				6	4	24
	(s)					5		*21		s			10	19		9	*s	2	25	s	s	34	(3)				6	4	25
	(s)					5		*s		s			10	19		*9	(12)	2	25	s	s	34	3				6	4	26
	(s)					5		*s		s			10	19		*9	12	2	25	s	s		3	23			6	(4)	27
	s					5		*s		15			10	19		*9	12	2	25	s	(s)	34		s			6	(4)	28
	s					5		s		15			10	19		9	12	2	25	s	s	34		s			6	4	29
	*s					5		(s)		*15			10	19		9	(12)	2	25	s	s	34		s			6	4	30
	s			Corr B		5	Grimes A	s	James K E A	(15)			10	19		9	*12	2	25		*s	34	s	(s)			6	4	31
	8					5		(s)		15			10	(19)		*9	12	2	25	s	*s	34	3	s				s	32
	8					5		21		*15	s			(s)		9	12	2	25	s	s	34	3	(23)				*s	33
	(s)					5		21		15	s			19		(9)		2	25	s	22	34	3	*s				*4	34
	*s					5		(s)		s	16		10	s		9	*12	2	25	s	22	34	(3)		29				35
	8							(s)		15	s		10	19		*9	(12)	2	25		*s	34	3	s	29			s	36
	8							*s		15	(s)		10	19		9	*12	2	25		s	34	(3)	s	29			s	37
				*11		5	s	21	(s)	15			10	19		(9)		2	25	s			3	*s				4	38
	*s			11		5	s	21		15			10	19		(9)		2	25		s	(s)	3					*4	39
	(s)			11		5	s	*21		15			10	19		9		2	25		s	*s	3					(4)	40
	s			11			(s)	(21)		15			10	19		9		2	25		s	*s	3		29			*4	41
	(s)			11			s	*s		15			10	19		(9)		2	25		*22	s	3		29			4	42
	s			*11		5	(s)	*s		15			10	19		9			25		(22)	s	3		29			4	43
	(s)			11		5	s	*s		15			10	19		(9)			25		*22	s	3		29			4	44
	s					5	(s)	(21)	s	15			10	19		9		s	25		*22	*s	3		29			4	45
	s			11		5		(s)	s	15			10	19		9		*2	25		(22)	s	3		*s			4	46
14	13	6	3	8	11	40	0	13	0	30	1	6	40	32	0	39	26	41	31	0	8	18	34	21	8	0	27	23	Apps
	17	8	2		4		4	20	2	5	2	8	2	6	4	3	6				12	6		6	1			4	Subs
	2	2		3	3	1		5		2		2	10	2		10	2	3			3	1		1				1	Goals

Match 4 : (s) = Holgate A B S *Match 16 : s = Henry L C D* *Match 17 : 22 = Lonergan A* Opponents 3 goals

Match 20 : s = Wells B *Match 34 : s = Hopper L* *Matches 38-44 : s = Gnakpa C*

Brezovan P	Brown A W	Brownlie R	Caton A J	Comyn-Platt C	Evans P	Ifil J C	Ince P E C	Jutkiewicz L I P	Monkhouse A W	Nicholas A P	Noubissie P B	Onibuje F	Peacock L A	Pook M D	Rhodes A G	Roberts C J	Shakes R U B	Smith J D	Smith P A	Stewart J H	Sturrock B D	Timlin M A	Vincent J R	Weston C J	Westwood A M	Whalley G G	Williams A	Zaaboub S	
	(8)	20	(s)		18	5		s		15		16		s			12	2					*3	*s					1

24 = Holgate A B S s = Wells B

Brezovan P	Brown A W	Brownlie R	Caton A J	Comyn-Platt C	Evans P	Ifil J C	Ince P E C	Jutkiewicz L I P	Monkhouse A W	Nicholas A P	Noubissie P B	Onibuje F	Peacock L A	Pook M D	Rhodes A G	Roberts C J	Shakes R U B	Smith J D	Smith P A	Stewart J H	Sturrock B D	Timlin M A	Vincent J R	Weston C J	Westwood A M	Whalley G G	Williams A	Zaaboub S	
	*8	(20)	s		18	5		(s)		15				s		9	12	2	25	s				23			6	*s	1
	(8)	s				5		s		15			10	*s		9	12	2	25	s				23		*7	6	(s)	2
	*s					5		(s)		s			10	19		(9)	12	2	25	s	s	34	3				6	*4	2R
	2	1	0		1	3		0		2			2	1		3	3	3	3	0	0	1	1	2		1	3	1	Apps
	1							3						1							1							2	Subs
						1										3													Goals

Opponents 1 goal

SEASON 2007/08

Football League Championship Div.1
Final League Position : 13th
Manager : Paul Sturrock
Maurice Malpas (from Jan.15)

Substitutes :
s denotes substitute **not** used
* player substituted by *s
( ) player substituted by (s)
_ player substituted by s

No	Day	Month	Date	Opponent	Home	Away	H-T	Goalscorers	Gate
1	S	Aug	11	Northampton Town		D1-1	(1-1)	Roberts 44 pen.	6,210
2	S		18	Luton Town	W2-1		(0-0)	Peacock 56,Easton 88	7,520
3	S		25	Cheltenham Town		D1-1	(1-0)	Sturrock 35	5,442
4	S	Sep	1	Crewe Alexandra	D1-1		(1-1)	Pook 24	6,595
5	Su		9	Yeovil Town	L0-1		(0-0)		6,944
6	S		15	Hartlepool United		D1-1	(1-0)	McGovern 31	4,943
7	S		22	AFC Bournemouth	W4-1		(1-1)	Cox 7,Paynter 48,64,85	6,668
8	S		29	Millwall		W2-1	(1-0)	Cox 8,Ifil 79	8,744
9	Tu	Oct	2	Swansea City		L1-2	(0-1)	Roberts 70	10,135
10	S		6	Gillingham	W5-0		(2-0)	McGovern 4,Cox 6,62,Paynter 52,84	6,345
11	S		20	Tranmere Rovers	W1-0		(0-0)	Corr 88	6,430
12	S		27	Port Vale		L1-2	(1-2)	Peacock 19	4,013
13	S	Nov	3	Doncaster Rovers	L1-2		(0-1)	Cox 47	6,517
14	Tu		6	Leyton Orient	D1-1		(0-0)	Aljofree 90	5,874
15	S		17	Leeds United		L1-2	(0-1)	Peacock 47	27,990
16	S		24	Bristol Rovers	W1-0		(0-0)	Roberts 67 pen.	9,342
17	Tu	Dec	4	Carlisle United		L0-3	(0-1)		5,477
18	S		8	Southend United		L1-2	(1-1)	Cox 2	7,403
19	S		15	Brighton & Hove Albion	L0-3		(0-2)		6,415
20	S		22	Hartlepool United	W2-1		(0-1)	Cox 49,Corr 73 pen.	5,875
21	W		26	Yeovil Town		W1-0	(0-0)	Corr 66	6,539
22	S		29	AFC Bournemouth		D2-2	(0-0)	Corr 49,83	6,540
23	Tu	Jan	1	Swansea City	D1-1		(0-0)	Cox 90 pen.	9,426
24	S		12	Walsall		D2-2	(0-1)	Nicholas 65,Easton 67	5,449
25	S		19	Nottingham Forest	W2-1		(1-0)	Perch o.g.35,Breckin o.g.82	9,815
26	S		26	Crewe Alexandra		D0-0			4,344
27	Tu		29	Luton Town		W1-0	(0-0)	Roberts 52	5,738
28	S	Feb	2	Northampton Town	D1-1		(0-0)	Sturrock 56	7,375
29	S		9	Huddersfield Town		L0-1	(0-1)		9,388
30	Tu		12	Cheltenham Town	W3-0		(2-0)	Cox 20,Paynter 41,Roberts 80	6,483
31	S		16	Nottingham Forest		L0-1	(0-0)		23,439
32	S		23	Walsall	L0-3		(0-1)		6,265
33	Tu		26	Oldham Athletic		D2-2	(1-0)	Peacock 29,Cox 58	3,923
34	S	Mar	1	Leeds United	L0-1		(0-1)		13,270
35	Tu		4	Huddersfield Town	W3-2		(3-1)	Paynter 4,Easton 23,31	4,840
36	Tu		11	Leyton Orient		L1-2	(1-0)	Thelwell o.g.20	3,082
37	S		15	Carlisle United	D2-2		(0-0)	Cox 61,Sturrock 80	6,004
38	S		22	Brighton & Hove Albion		L1-2	(1-1)	Easton 8	6,849
39	M		24	Southend United	L0-1		(0-1)		6,378
40	F		28	Tranmere Rovers		L1-2	(0-2)	Paynter 68	5,815
41	S	Apr	5	Oldham Athletic	W3-0		(0-0)	Peacock 49,Cox 53,70	5,384
42	F		11	Doncaster Rovers		L0-2	(0-1)		8,371
43	S		19	Port Vale	W6-0		(5-0)	Peacock 16,Easton 21,Smith J 33,McNamee 45,Timlin 45,Joyce 90	7,361
44	Tu		22	Bristol Rovers		W1-0	(0-0)	Cox 74	6,102
45	S		26	Gillingham		D1-1	(0-1)	Aljofree 88	6,334
46	S	May	3	Millwall	W2-1		(1-1)	Cox 31 pen.,McNamee 51	7,781

Average Home Attendance : **7,170**
Average Away Attendance : **7,925**

Football League Cup

No	Day	Month	Date	Opponent	Home	Away	H-T	Goalscorers	Gate
1	Tu	Aug	14	Charlton Athletic	L0-2		(0-0)		6,175

F A Cup

No	Day	Month	Date	Opponent	Home	Away	H-T	Goalscorers	Gate
1	S	Nov	10	Wycombe Wanderers		W2-1	(0-0)	Roberts 66,Paynter 72	3,332
2	S	Dec	1	Forest Green Rovers	W3-2		(1-0)	McGovern 12,Aljofree 69,Sturrock 88	7,588
3	S	Jan	5	Barnet	D1-1		(0-0)	Sturrock 60	5,944
3R	Tu		22	Barnet	+	D1-1	(1-0)	Paynter 42	2,810

+ After Extra Time (L0-2 on penalties)

For Final League Table - see overleaf >> For Football League Trophy - see page 272

Adams S M	Aljofree H	Allen C M	Arrieta I P	Blackburn C R	Brezovan P	Collins S J	Commings M	Corr B	Cox S R	Easton C	Ifil J C	Kanyuka P E	McGovern JP	McNamee A	Mohamed K	Morrison S J	Nicholas A P	Paynter W P	Peacock L A	Pook M D	Roberts C J	Smith J D	Smith P A	Sturrock B D	Timlin M A	Tozer B P A	Vincent J R	Zaaboub S	
18	16		(s)		s		*s			s	5				s				4	19	7	2	1	(21)			3	*11	1
	16		*s		s		(s)			8	5				s				4	19	7	2	1	*21		s	3	(11)	2
s	16		(s)		s		*s				5								4	19	*7	2	1	(21)		s	3	11	3
	16		(s)		s		*s			8	5				s				4	19	7	2	1	(21)		s	3	*11	4
	16		Total		s		s		*s	8	5		(s)					s	4	19	(7)	2	1	*21			3	11	5
	*16		0	*s			14		(31)	8	5		10		s			20	4	s	(s)		1	s			3	11	6
			4	17			14		31	8	5		10		s			20	4	s	*s	s	1	s			3	*11	7
				s		29	*s		31	8	5		(10)					20	4	s	*7	2	1	s			3	(s)	8
						29	*s		31	8	5		(s)		s			20	4	s	7	*2	1	s			3	(11)	9
				*s		*29	14		31	8	5		10		s			20	4	(s)	7		1	s			(3)	s	10
	16			s			14	s	31	8	5		10				15	20	(4)	(s)	*7		1	s				*s	11
s	16				12	(s)	14	s	31	8	(5)		10				*15	20	4		*s			s				11	12
s	16			s	12	Total	14	(s)	31	8	5		10				15	(20)	4		*s			s				*11	13
(18)	16			s	12	3	14	*s	31	8	5		10					*20	4	(s)	s			s				11	14
	16				12	1	14	*s	31	*8	5		(s)				s	20	4	19	(7)					s		11	15
	16	s			12		14	*s	31	8	5		10					*20		19	(7)	2		s		(s)		s	16
	16	s	Ashikodi M	s	12		14	*s	(31)	8			10				15	*20		19		2		(s)		27			17
	16	24		17	12		s		31	8			(s)		(23)		15	*s		19		2		*21					18
	16	24		17	12		s		31	8			*s		*23		15	(s)	s	19		2		(21)					19
	(16)				12		14	*9	31	8	5		10		s			*s	4	s				s			3	11	20
	*16	s			12		14	(9)	31	8	5		10		23		*s	(s)	4	s				s			3		21
		s		17	12			9	31	8	5		(10)		*s		15	s	4	s				(s)			3	*11	22
	16				12		14	9	31	(8)	5		10		s		s	*s	4	(s)				s			3	*11	23
s				s	12		14			8	5		(10)		(s)		15	20	4	s	*s			*21			3	11	24
	16		*s		12		14			8	5		10	s			s	20	4	s	s			*21			3	11	25
	16	s	(30)		12		14	(s)			5		10	*27			s	20	4	19	*s			s			3		26
	16		(30)		12		14	9				26	10	*27			s		4	s	7		s	(s)			3	*s	27
	16		30		12		14	*9			5		10	(27)			s		4	s	7		s	*s			3	(s)	28
	16		*30		12		14		31		5	s	10	s					4	*s	7		s	(s)			3	(11)	29
	16		s		12		14	(s)	31		5	s	10	*27				(20)	4	19	*s			s			3		30
	16		(s)		12		14			8	5	s	10	*27				20		19	*s		s	(21)			3	s	31
	16		(s)		s		(14)		31	8	5	s	*10	27				20	4		*s		1	s			3		32
	16	24	s		s		14		(31)	8	s	26						20	*4		7		1	(s)			3	*s	33
	16	(24)	s		s	Joyce B P	14		31	8	*s	*26	(s)	s				20	4		7		1				3		34
	16	24	(s)		s		14		*31	8	5		*s	(27)				20	4		s	2	1					s	35
	16	*24	(s)		12		14		31	8	5		10	(27)		s						2	s	21			s	*s	36
	16		*s		12		14		31	8	5		10	27		s	s					2	s	*21	18			s	37
	16				12		14	s	31	(8)	5		10	27			s	*s				2	s	*21	18			(s)	38
	16				12		14	*9	31	8	5		10	27			s	*s	(s)			2		s	(18)			s	39
	16				12		14		31	(8)	5		*10	27	*s			20	4			s	s	s	(s)		3		40
	16				12				*31	8	5		10	(27)	s		s	*s	4			2	s		18		3	(s)	41
	16				12			s	(31)	8	5		10	*27	s		(s)	*s	4			2	s		18		3		42
					12	*s	14		*31	8	5		10	27	s		s	(s)	(4)			2	s		18		3		43
	(s)				12	s	14		*31	8	5		10	27				*s	4	s		(2)	s		18		3		44
	16	s			12	s			31	8	*5		10	(27)		*s		(s)	4			2	s		18		3		45
	16	*24			12	(s)			31	8		*s	10	27		25		(20)					s		18		3		46
2	38	7	4	4	31	0	32	7	35	39	39	3	34	18	3	1	8	23	36	13	16	21	15	13	9	1	32	18	Apps
	1	1	6	3		3	8	10	1		1	1	7	1	8	1	3	13	1	9	11			8	1	1		11	Subs
	2					1		5	15	6	1		2	2			1	8	6	1	5	1		3	1				Goals

Matches 15,17,18,19 : s = Scott M(ark) J *Match 18 : s = Almeida M A deS* Opponents 3 goals

Match 20 : (s) = Williams A *Match 46 : s = Hammonds K(urt) s = Thompson N(athan) M*

Adams S M	Aljofree H	Allen C M	Arrieta I P	Blackburn C R	Brezovan P	Collins S J	Commings M	Corr B	Cox S R	Easton C	Ifil J C	Kanyuka P E	McGovern JP	McNamee A	Mohamed K	Morrison S J	Nicholas A P	Paynter W P	Peacock L A	Pook M D	Roberts C J	Smith J D	Smith P A	Sturrock B D	Timlin M A	Tozer B P A	Vincent J R	Zaaboub S	
18	16				12		*14			8	5			*s = Arrieta I P*					4	*s	(7)	2	s	21		27	s	(s)	1

Adams S M	Aljofree H	Allen C M	Arrieta I P	Blackburn C R	Brezovan P	Collins S J	Commings M	Corr B	Cox S R	Easton C	Ifil J C	Kanyuka P E	McGovern JP	McNamee A	Mohamed K	Morrison S J	Nicholas A P	Paynter W P	Peacock L A	Pook M D	Roberts C J	Smith J D	Smith P A	Sturrock B D	Timlin M A	Tozer B P A	Vincent J R	Zaaboub S	
18	16			s	12		*14	9		8			s					(s)	4	19	*s	s		(21)		27		11	1
	16	*s		s	12		14	(9)		8			10				s	20		19	*7	2		(s)		27			2
	16	s			12		14			8	5		10		(s)		s	20	4	s	*s			*21			3	(11)	3
s	16				12		14	*s			5		10				s	20	4	19	(s)		s	*21			3	(11)	3R
1	4	0			4		4	2		3	2		3		0			3	3	3	1	1		3		2	2	3	Apps
		1						1							1			1			3	1		1					Subs
	1												1					2			1			2					Goals

Second Round : s = Scott M J

SEASON 2002/03

Div.2

	P	W	D	L	F	A	W	D	L	F	A	Pts	G/D	Avge. Home Gate
1 Wigan Athletic	46	14	7	2	37	16	15	6	2	31	9	100	+43	7,288
2 Crewe Alexandra	46	11	5	7	29	19	14	6	3	47	21	86	+36	6,761
3 Bristol City	46	15	5	3	43	15	9	6	8	36	33	83	+31	11,890
4 Queens Park Rangers	46	14	4	5	38	19	10	7	6	31	26	83	+24	13,206
5 Oldham Athletic	46	11	6	6	39	18	11	10	2	29	20	82	+30	6,699
6 Cardiff City *	46	12	6	5	33	20	11	6	6	35	23	81	+25	13,050
7 Tranmere Rovers	46	14	5	4	38	23	9	6	8	28	34	80	+9	7,877
8 Plymouth Argyle	46	11	6	6	39	24	6	8	9	24	28	65	+11	8,981
9 Luton Town	46	8	8	7	32	28	9	6	8	35	34	65	+5	6,747
10 SWINDON TOWN	46	10	5	8	34	27	6	7	10	25	36	60	-4	5,440
11 Peterborough United	46	8	7	8	25	20	6	9	8	26	34	58	-3	4,955
12 Colchester United	46	8	7	8	24	24	6	9	8	28	32	58	-4	3,387
13 Blackpool	46	10	8	5	35	25	5	5	13	21	39	58	-8	6,991
14 Stockport County	46	8	8	7	39	38	7	2	14	26	32	55	-5	5,489
15 Notts County	46	10	7	6	37	32	3	9	11	25	38	55	-8	6,154
16 Brentford	46	8	8	7	28	21	6	4	13	19	35	54	-9	5,759
17 Port Vale	46	9	5	9	34	31	5	6	12	20	39	53	-16	4,436
18 Wycombe Wanderers	46	8	7	8	39	38	5	6	12	20	28	52	-7	6,002
19 Barnsley	46	7	8	8	27	31	6	5	12	24	33	52	-13	9,758
20 Chesterfield	46	11	4	8	29	28	3	4	16	14	45	50	-30	4,108
21 Cheltenham Town	46	6	9	8	26	31	4	9	10	27	37	48	-15	4,655
22 Huddersfield Town	46	7	9	7	27	24	4	3	16	12	37	45	-22	9,506
23 Mansfield Town	46	9	2	12	38	45	3	6	14	28	52	44	-31	4,887
24 Northampton Town	46	7	4	12	23	31	3	5	15	17	48	39	-39	5,211

SEASON 2003/04

Div.2

	P	W	D	L	F	A	W	D	L	F	A	Pts	G/D	Avge. Home Gate
1 Plymouth Argyle	46	17	5	1	52	13	9	7	7	33	28	90	+44	12,654
2 Queens Park Rangers	46	16	7	0	47	12	6	10	7	33	33	83	+35	14,785
3 Bristol City	46	15	6	2	34	12	8	7	8	24	25	82	+21	12,879
4 Brighton & Hove Albion *	46	17	4	2	39	11	5	7	11	25	32	77	+21	6,248
5 SWINDON TOWN	46	12	7	4	41	23	8	6	9	35	35	73	+18	7,925
6 Hartlepool United	46	10	8	5	39	24	10	5	8	37	37	73	+15	5,419
7 Port Vale	46	15	6	2	45	28	6	4	13	28	35	73	+10	5,810
8 Tranmere Rovers	46	13	7	3	36	18	4	9	10	23	38	67	+3	7,606
9 AFC Bournemouth	46	11	8	4	35	25	6	7	10	21	26	66	+5	6,913
10 Luton Town	46	14	6	3	44	27	3	9	11	25	39	66	+3	6,339
11 Colchester United	46	11	8	4	33	23	6	5	12	19	33	64	-4	3,536
12 Barnsley	46	7	12	4	25	19	8	5	10	29	39	62	-4	9,620
13 Wrexham	46	9	6	8	27	21	8	3	12	23	39	60	-10	4,440
14 Blackpool	46	9	5	9	31	28	7	6	10	27	37	59	-7	6,326
15 Oldham Athletic	46	9	8	6	37	25	3	13	7	29	35	57	+6	6,566
16 Sheffield Wednesday	46	7	9	7	25	26	6	5	12	23	38	53	-16	22,336
17 Brentford	46	9	5	9	34	38	5	6	12	18	31	53	-17	5,542
18 Peterborough United	46	5	8	10	36	33	7	8	8	22	25	52	0	5,274
19 Stockport County	46	6	8	9	31	36	5	11	7	31	34	52	-8	5,315
20 Chesterfield	46	9	7	7	34	31	3	8	12	15	40	51	-22	4,331
21 Grimsby Town	46	10	5	8	36	26	3	6	14	19	55	50	-26	4,730
22 Rushden & Diamonds	46	9	5	9	37	34	4	4	15	23	40	48	-14	4,457
23 Notts County	46	6	9	8	32	27	4	3	16	18	51	42	-28	5,940
24 Wycombe Wanderers	46	5	7	11	31	39	1	12	10	19	36	37	-25	5,291

SEASON 2004/05

Chp.D1

	P	W	D	L	F	A	W	D	L	F	A	Pts	G/D	Avge. Home Gate
1 Luton Town	46	17	4	2	46	16	12	7	4	41	32	98	+39	7,940
2 Hull City	46	16	5	2	42	17	10	3	10	38	36	86	+27	18,027
3 Tranmere Rovers	46	14	5	4	43	23	8	8	7	30	32	79	+18	9,044
4 Brentford	46	15	4	4	34	22	7	5	11	23	38	75	-3	6,082
5 Sheffield Wednesday *	46	10	6	7	34	28	9	9	5	43	31	72	+18	23,100
6 Hartlepool United	46	15	3	5	51	30	6	5	12	25	36	71	+10	5,182
7 Bristol City	46	9	8	6	42	25	9	8	6	32	32	70	+17	11,391
8 AFC Bournemouth	46	9	7	7	40	30	11	3	9	37	34	70	+13	7,123
9 Huddersfield Town	46	12	6	5	42	28	8	4	11	32	37	70	+9	11,905
10 Doncaster Rovers	46	10	11	2	35	20	6	7	10	30	40	66	+5	6,886
11 Bradford City	46	9	6	8	40	35	8	8	7	24	27	65	+2	8,839
12 SWINDON TOWN	46	12	5	6	40	30	5	7	11	26	38	63	-2	5,835
13 Barnsley	46	7	11	5	38	31	7	8	8	31	33	61	+5	9,779
14 Walsall	46	11	7	5	40	28	5	5	13	25	41	60	-4	6,085
15 Colchester United	46	8	6	9	27	23	6	11	6	33	27	59	+10	3,534
16 Blackpool	46	8	7	8	28	30	7	5	11	26	29	57	-5	6,032
17 Chesterfield	46	9	8	6	32	28	5	7	11	23	34	57	-7	4,961
18 Port Vale	46	13	2	8	33	23	4	3	16	16	36	56	-10	4,973
19 Oldham Athletic	46	10	5	8	42	34	4	5	14	18	39	52	-13	6,462
20 Milton Keynes Dons	46	8	10	5	33	28	4	5	14	21	40	51	-14	4,896
21 Torquay United	46	8	5	10	27	36	4	10	9	28	43	51	-24	3,511
22 Wrexham	46	6	8	9	26	37	7	6	10	36	43	43	-18	4,751
23 Peterborough United	46	5	6	12	27	35	4	6	13	22	38	39	-24	4,341
24 Stockport County	46	3	4	16	26	46	3	4	16	23	52	26	-49	4,999

* Promoted via Play-offs

SEASON 2005/06

Chp.D1

		P	W	D	L	F	A	W	D	L	F	A	Pts	G/D	Avge. Home Gate
1	Southend United	46	13	6	4	37	16	10	7	6	35	27	82	+29	8,053
2	Colchester United	46	15	4	4	39	21	7	9	7	19	19	79	+18	3,969
3	Brentford	46	10	8	5	35	23	10	8	5	37	29	76	+20	6,775
4	Huddersfield Town	46	13	6	4	40	25	6	10	7	32	34	73	+13	13,058
5	Barnsley *	46	11	11	1	37	19	7	7	9	25	25	72	+18	9,054
6	Swansea City	46	11	9	3	42	23	7	8	8	36	32	71	+23	14,112
7	Nottingham Forest	46	14	5	4	40	15	5	7	11	27	37	69	+15	20,257
8	Doncaster Rovers	46	11	6	6	30	19	9	3	11	25	32	69	+4	6,139
9	Bristol City	46	11	7	5	38	22	7	4	12	28	40	65	+4	11,725
10	Oldham Athletic	46	12	4	7	32	24	6	7	10	26	36	65	-2	5,797
11	Bradford City	46	8	9	6	28	25	6	10	7	23	24	61	+2	8,265
12	Scunthorpe United	46	8	8	7	36	33	7	7	9	32	40	60	-5	5,171
13	Port Vale	46	10	5	8	30	26	6	7	10	19	28	60	-5	4,657
14	Gillingham	46	13	4	6	31	21	3	8	12	19	43	60	-14	6,671
15	Yeovil Town	46	8	8	7	27	24	7	3	13	27	38	56	-8	6,668
16	Chesterfield	46	6	7	10	31	37	8	7	8	32	36	56	-10	4,772
17	AFC Bournemouth	46	7	11	5	25	20	5	8	10	24	33	55	-4	6,458
18	Tranmere Rovers	46	7	8	8	32	30	6	7	10	18	22	54	-2	7,211
19	Blackpool	46	9	8	6	33	27	3	9	11	23	37	53	-8	5,820
20	Rotherham United	46	7	9	7	31	26	5	7	11	21	36	52	-10	5,306
21	Hartlepool United	46	6	10	7	28	30	5	7	11	16	29	50	-15	4,812
22	Milton Keynes Dons	46	8	8	7	28	25	4	6	13	17	41	50	-21	5,776
23	SWINDON TOWN	46	9	5	9	31	31	2	10	11	15	34	48	-19	5,951
24	Walsall	46	7	7	9	27	34	4	7	12	20	36	47	-23	5,392

SEASON 2006/07

Chp.D2

		P	W	D	L	F	A	W	D	L	F	A	Pts	G/D	Avge. Home Gate
1	Walsall	46	16	4	3	39	13	9	10	4	27	21	89	+32	5,643
2	Hartlepool United	46	14	5	4	34	17	12	5	6	31	23	88	+25	5,096
3	SWINDON TOWN	46	15	4	4	34	17	10	6	7	24	21	85	+20	7,419
4	Milton Keynes Dons	46	14	4	5	41	26	11	5	7	35	32	84	+18	6,034
5	Lincoln City	46	12	4	7	36	28	9	7	7	34	31	74	+11	5,176
6	Bristol Rovers *	46	13	5	5	27	14	7	7	9	22	28	72	+7	5,480
7	Shrewsbury Town	46	11	7	5	38	23	7	10	6	30	23	71	+22	4,730
8	Stockport County	46	14	4	5	41	25	7	4	12	24	29	71	+11	5,514
9	Rochdale	46	9	6	8	33	20	9	6	8	37	30	66	+20	2,898
10	Peterborough United	46	10	6	7	48	36	8	5	10	22	25	65	+9	4,662
11	Darlington	46	10	6	7	28	30	7	8	8	24	26	65	-4	3,814
12	Wycombe Wanderers	46	8	11	4	23	14	8	3	12	29	33	62	+5	4,983
13	Notts County	46	8	6	9	29	25	8	8	7	26	28	62	+2	4,974
14	Barnet	46	12	5	6	35	30	4	6	13	20	40	59	-15	2,279
15	Grimsby Town	46	11	4	8	33	32	6	4	13	24	41	59	-16	4,379
16	Hereford United	46	9	7	7	23	17	5	6	12	22	36	55	-8	3,328
17	Mansfield Town	46	10	4	9	38	31	4	8	11	20	32	54	-5	3,176
18	Chester City	46	7	9	7	23	23	6	5	12	17	25	53	-8	2,473
19	Wrexham	46	8	8	7	23	21	5	4	14	20	44	51	-22	5,030
20	Accrington Stanley	46	10	6	7	42	33	3	5	15	28	48	50	-11	2,260
21	Bury	46	4	7	12	22	35	9	4	10	24	26	50	-15	2,588
22	Macclesfield Town	46	8	7	8	36	34	4	5	14	19	43	48	-22	2,863
23	Boston United	46	9	5	9	29	32	3	5	15	22	48	36	-29	2,152
24	Torquay United	46	5	8	10	19	22	2	6	15	17	41	35	-27	2,633

SEASON 2007/08

Chp.D1

		P	W	D	L	F	A	W	D	L	F	A	Pts	G/D	Avge. Home Gate
1	Swansea City	46	13	5	5	38	21	14	6	3	44	21	92	+40	13,520
2	Nottingham Forest	46	13	8	2	37	13	9	8	6	27	19	82	+32	19,964
3	Doncaster Rovers *	46	14	4	5	34	18	9	7	7	31	23	80	+24	7,978
4	Carlisle United	46	17	3	3	39	16	6	8	9	25	30	80	+18	7,835
5	Leeds United	46	15	4	4	41	18	12	6	5	31	20	76	+34	26,543
6	Southend United	46	12	6	5	35	20	10	4	9	35	35	76	+15	8,173
7	Brighton & Hove Albion	46	12	6	5	37	25	7	6	10	21	25	69	+8	5,937
8	Oldham Athletic	46	10	7	6	32	21	8	6	9	26	25	67	+12	5,326
9	Northampton Town	46	12	6	5	38	21	5	9	9	22	34	66	+5	5,409
10	Huddersfield Town	46	12	4	7	29	22	8	2	13	21	40	66	-12	9,391
11	Tranmere Rovers	46	13	4	6	32	18	5	7	11	20	29	65	+5	6,504
12	Walsall	46	7	9	7	27	26	9	7	7	25	20	64	+6	5,620
13	SWINDON TOWN	46	12	5	6	41	24	4	8	11	22	32	61	+7	7,170
14	Leyton Orient	46	9	6	8	27	29	7	6	10	22	34	60	-14	5,210
15	Hartlepool United	46	11	5	7	40	26	4	4	15	23	40	54	-3	4,507
16	Bristol Rovers	46	5	10	8	25	30	7	7	9	20	23	53	-8	6,850
17	Millwall	46	9	4	10	30	26	5	6	12	15	34	52	-15	8,691
18	Yeovil Town	46	9	4	10	19	27	5	6	12	19	32	52	-21	5,468
19	Cheltenham Town	46	10	8	5	23	21	3	4	16	19	43	51	-22	4,310
20	Crewe Alexandra	46	8	6	9	27	33	4	8	11	20	32	50	-18	4,932
21	AFC Bournemouth	46	10	4	9	31	35	7	3	13	31	37	48	-10	5,504
22	Gillingham	46	9	9	5	26	22	2	4	17	18	51	46	-29	6,077
23	Port Vale	46	5	8	10	26	35	4	3	16	21	46	38	-34	4,417
24	Luton Town	46	10	5	8	29	25	1	5	17	14	38	33	-20	6,492

* Promoted via Play-offs

Football League Trophy

SEASON 2004/05

				Home	Away	H-T	Goalscorers	Gate
2	Tu	Nov	2 Exeter City		W2-1	(1-0)	Nicholas 19,Fallon 54	1,898
QF	Tu		30 Bristol City	W1-0		(0-0)	Parkin 64	7,571
SF	Tu	Jan	25 Southend United		L0-2	(0-1)		4,270

	Book S K	Bulman M K	Caton A J	Duke D	Evans R K	Fallon R M	Garrard L E	Hewlett M P	Heywood M S	Holmes L D	Howard B R W	Ifil J C	Igoe S G	Miglioranzi S	Nicholas A P	O'Hanlon S P	Parkin S	Pook M D	Reeves A	Robinson S E	Slabber J A	Smith G G
2	20	s	*24	s		8	23	4	19			12	(s)		15	s	*s	(22)	18			3
QF	20	s				(8)	23		19		17	12	7		15	*s	9	s	*18	16		(s)
SF	s			(11)	1	8	s	4	19	*21	(s)	12		10		2	9	s			*s	3
Apps	2	0	1	1	1	3	2	2	3	1	1	3	1	1	2	1	2	1	2	1	0	2
Subs											1		1			1	1				1	1
Goals						1									1		1					

Quarter-Final : s = Wells B

SEASON 2005/06

				Home	Away	H-T	Goalscorers	Gate
1	Tu	Oct	18 Stevenage Borough	W2-0		(1-0)	Fallon 4,Bouazza 53	1,771
2	Tu	Nov	22 Peterborough United		L1-2	(0-1)	Roberts 68	959

	Bouazza H	Bulman M K	Comyn-Platt C	Cureton J	Fallon R M	Gurney A R	Heath C	Heaton T D	Holgate A B S	Ifil J C	Jenkins S R	McDermott	Nicholas A P	O'Hanlon S P	Pook M D	Roberts C J	Shakes R U B	Smith J D	Thorpe A L	Whalley G G
1	28	s	*s	(s)	8	27	s	26			(6)	23	15	2	19	18			s	*7
2	28	s	17		8		(25)	26	(s)	5	6	*s	15	2		18	s	s		*7
Apps	2	0	1	0	2	1	1	2	0	1	2	1	2	2	1	2	0	0	0	2
Subs			1	1					1			1							1	
Goals	1				1											1				

SEASON 2006/07

				Home	Away	H-T	Goalscorers	Gate
1	Tu	Oct	17 Wycombe Wanderers		L0-1	(0-1)		1,583

	Brown A W	Brownlie R	Ifil J C	Jutkiewicz L I P	Monkhouse A W	Nicholas A P	Onibuje F	Peacock L A	Pook M D	Shakes R U B	Smith J D	Smith P A	Vincent J R	Weston C J	Whalley G G	Williams A
1	8	*20	5	21	s	15	*s	s	(s)	12	2	25	3	(23)	7	s

SEASON 2007/08

				Home	Away	H-T	Goalscorers	Gate
1	Tu	Sep	4 Brentford	W4-1		(2-1)	Arrieta 26,Cox 42,Blackburn 68,81	3,118
2	Tu	Oct	9 Cheltenham Town	L1-3		(0-2)	Sturrock 56	3,765

	Adams S M	Allen C M	Almeida M A deS	Arrieta I P	Blackburn C R	Brezovan P	Comminges M	Cox S R	Easton C	Hammonds K	Joyce B P	Kennedy C E	McGovern JP	Macklin L J	Mohamed K	Pook M D	Roberts C J	Scott M J	Smith P A	Sturrock B D	Tozer B P A	Zaaboub S
1	18	24	13	*22	17	12	14	31		s	s	34	(10)	(s)	*s				s		27	
2	18	*s			17	12	14	(s)	*8			s	10		(23)	19	s	s		21	27	11
Apps	2	1	1	1	2	2	2	1	1	0	0	1	2	0	1	1	0	0	0	1	2	1
Subs		1						1						1	1		1					
Goals			1	1	2			1												1		

SEASON 2008/09

Football League Championship Div.1
Final League Position : 15th
Manager : Maurice Malpas
Danny Wilson (from Dec.24)

No	Day	Month	Date	Opponents	Home	Away	H-T	Goalscorers	Gate
1	S	Aug	9	Tranmere Rovers	W3-1		(2-0)	Paynter 5,Cox 37,McGovern 51	7,975
2	S		16	Cheltenham Town		L0-2	(0-0)		4,978
3	S		23	Colchester United	L1-3		(0-2)	Cox 67 pen.	7,031
4	S		30	Milton Keynes Dons		W2-1	(0-0)	Paynter 52,Cox 90 pen.	8,846
5	F	Sep	5	Hereford United		D1-1	(1-1)	Ifil 45	4,061
6	S		13	Leeds United	L1-3		(1-1)	Cox 45	13,001
7	S		20	Stockport County		D1-1	(0-1)	Easton 49	5,536
8	Su		28	Millwall	L1-2		(0-1)	Paynter 47	7,589
9	F	Oct	3	Hartlepool United		D3-3	(2-0)	Cox 5,39,52	4,018
10	S		11	Huddersfield Town	L1-3		(0-2)	Easton 88	7,071
11	S		18	Southend United		L1-2	(0-1)	Paynter 60	7,965
12	Tu		21	Northampton Town	W2-1		(0-0)	Paynter 48,Cox 61	6,653
13	S		25	Oldham Athletic	W2-0		(2-0)	Morrison 25,Smith J 34 pen.	6,756
14	S	Nov	1	Scunthorpe United		D3-3	(1-1)	Cox 15,52,80 pen.	4,744
15	S		15	Leicester City	D2-2		(0-0)	Cox 84,Corr 86	9,499
16	S		22	Bristol Rovers		D2-2	(1-1)	Kanyuka 39,Corr 53	8,016
17	Tu		25	Peterborough United	D2-2		(1-1)	Smith J 10,Cox 81	6,616
18	S		29	Walsall		L1-2	(0-1)	Paynter 90	3,844
19	S	Dec	6	Carlisle United	D1-1		(0-0)	Murphy o.g.50	6,787
20	S		13	Crewe Alexandra		L0-1	(0-1)		3,941
21	S		20	Yeovil Town	L2-3		(1-2)	Timlin 45,McGovern 47	7,072
22	F		26	Leyton Orient		W2-1	(1-0)	Peacock 1,Smith J 61 pen.	4,349
23	Su		28	Brighton & Hove Albion	L0-2		(0-1)		8,438
24	Tu	Jan	13	Stockport County	D1-1		(0-0)	Smith J 62	6,002
25	S		17	Huddersfield Town		L1-2	(0-0)	Cox 90	13,414
26	Tu		27	Walsall	W3-2		(2-0)	Amankwaah 8, Cox 29, Paynter 49	6,100
27	S		31	Oldham Athletic		D0-0			4,712
28	S	Feb	14	Leicester City		D1-1	(1-0)	Cox 38	19,926
29	Tu		17	Millwall		D1-1	(1-0)	Paynter 43	7,104
30	S		21	Scunthorpe United	W4-2		(0-2)	Timlin 62,Wright o.g.71,Robson-Kanu 82,Peacock 85	6,852
31	Tu		24	Hartlepool United	L0-1		(0-0)		6,010
32	S		28	Tranmere Rovers		L0-1	(0-0)		5,153
33	Tu	Mar	3	Cheltenham Town	D2-2		(1-1)	Robson-Kanu 32,Amankwaah 66	6,293
34	S		7	Milton Keynes Dons	D1-1		(1-1)	Paynter 18	7,453
35	Tu		10	Colchester United		L2-3	(1-2)	Cox 38 pen.,Robson-Kanu 64	3,827
36	S		14	Leeds United		L0-1	(0-0)		21,765
37	Tu		17	Southend United	W3-0		(2-0)	Robson-Kanu 13,Cox 19 pen.,90 pen.	6,269
38	S		21	Hereford United	W3-0		(1-0)	Cox 29,46,Paynter 76	7,129
39	Tu		24	Northampton Town		W4-3	(3-1)	Cox 18,31,79,Paynter 40	5,025
40	S		28	Yeovil Town		L0-1	(0-1)		5,476
41	S	Apr	4	Crewe Alexandra	D0-0				7,165
42	S		11	Brighton & Hove Albion		W3-2	(0-1)	Greer 47,Paynter 50,Cox 58	6,549
43	M		13	Leyton Orient	L0-1		(0-1)		7,735
44	S		18	Carlisle United		D1-1	(0-1)	Tudur-Jones 90	5,959
45	S		25	Bristol Rovers	W2-1		(1-1)	Cox 4,81	10,977
46	S	May	2	Peterborough United		D2-2	(2-1)	Cox 17,42	10,866
								Average Home Attendance :	**7,499**
								Average Away Attendance :	**7,395**

No	Aljofree H	Allen C M	Amankwaah K K O K	Brezovan P	Casal K O O	Corr B	Cox S R	Easton C	Greer G	Ifil J C	Jean-Francois L	Joyce B P	Kanyuka P E	Kennedy C E	McGovern JP	McNamee A	Macklin L J	Marshall M A	Morrison S J	Nalis L	Paynter W P	Peacock L A	Pook M D	Razak H	Robson-Kanu T H A	Smith J D	Smith P A	Sturrock B D	Timlin M A	Tudur-Jones O	Vincent J R
1	6			12	16		31	(s)		5		s		s	(10)	11				17	*20	*s				2	s		4		
2	6		s	12	16		31	s							10	11		(s)	25	17	*20	*s				2	s		(4)		
3	6		s	12			31	(s)		5			14		*10	11		*s		17	20	s				2	s		(4)		
4	6		*s	s	*16		31	8		5					s	11		s		17	(20)	(s)				2	1		4		
5	6		15	s	s		31	8		5					s	*11		*s		17	(20)	(s)				2	1		4		
6	6		15				31	(8)		5		s = Scott M J			*10	11		*s	s	17	20	s				2	1		(s)		
7	6		15	s	s	*s	(31)	8							10	s			25	17	*20	(s)				2	1		4		
8	6		15	s	s		31	8							(10)	11		*s	25	*17	20	(s)				2	1		s		
9			15	s	*s		31	8		5		s			s	s			25	17	20	32				*2	1		4		
10			15	12	s	(s)	31	8		5					s	*s			25	*17	(20)	32				2	s		4		
11	6		s	12	(16)	*s	31	s							10	(s)			25		*20	32	19			2	s		4		
12	6		s	12		(s)	31	*s							10	(11)			25	s	20	*32	19			2	s		4		
13	6		s	12		*s	31	s							10	11			25	s	*20	32	19			2	s		4		
14	6		s			(s)	31	*s			s = Scott M J				10	(11)		s	25		20	32	*19			2	1		4		
15				s		*s	31			s			14	s	s	*11			25	17	20	32	19			2	1		4		
16	(s)			s		9				s		*23	14		*s	(11)			25	17	20		19			2	1	s	4		
17	6			s			31	s		s		s	14		10	11				*s	*20	32	19			2	1		4		
18	6		s	s			31	*8		s			14		10	*s				(s)	20	32	19			2	1		(4)		
19	6		*s	s			31	s		5				*30	(10)	11		s			20	32	19			2	1	(s)			
20	6			s			31	*s		5				30	10	(11)			s		20	*32	19			2	1	(s)	s		
21	*6			s		(s)	31	8		5				30	10	(11)			*s			32	s			2	1	s	4		
22				12		s	31	8		5			14		10	s			s	17		32	*s			2	s	*21	4		
23			s	12		(s)	31	8		5			14		10	*s			s	*17		32	s			2		(21)	4		
24			(s)	12		*9	31	8		5			14		10	11				s		32	s			2	s	*s	(4)		
25			15	12			31	s		5			14		*10	*s				s	(20)	32	19			2	s	(s)	4		
26		24	15	12			31		33	5					(10)	(s)				17	20			s	7		s	s	*s		*3
27		24	15	12			31	s	33	5	s		14		10	*s					(20)			(s)	*7		s				3
28			15	12			31		33	5	s		14			s				s	20			s	7	2	s		4		3
29			15	12			31		(33)	5	(s)		14			*s					20			s	*7	2	s	s	4		3
30			(15)	12			31			5	*26		14			(s)			*s		20	s			7	2	s		4		3
31		s	*15	12			31		33	5			14			*s			s		(20)	(s)			7	2	s		4		3
32			(15)	12			31		33	5	s		*14			(s)				*s	20	s			7	2	s		4		3
33		*s	(s)	12			31		33	5	s					11		s			20	*32			7	2	s		4		(3)
34			15	12			31		33	(s)						*11		*s	(25)	17	20			s	7		s	s	4		3
35			15	12			31		33	s						11		*s	25	s	20			(s)	*7		s		4	(34)	3
36			15	s			31		33	s						*11			25	s	20			s	7	*s	1		4	34	3
37			15	s			31		33							11		*s	25	s	(20)				*7	s	1	(s)	4	34	3
38			15	s			31		33							11		s	25	(s)	20				7	*s	1	s	4	(34)	*3
39			15	s			31		33		s					*11		*s	25	(s)	20				(7)	2	1	s	4	34	
40			15	s			31		33	*s				(s)		11			*25	17	20		s	s	(7)	2	1		4		
41			15	s			31	s	33	5	s					11					20			*s	*7	(s)	1		4	34	(3)
42			15	s			31	(s)	33	5	s					11	*s				20				*7	s	1		4	(34)	3
43			15	s			31	s	33	5	s				(s)	*11	*s				20				7		1		4	34	(3)
44			(15)	s			31	8	33	5	*s		s		(s)	11					20				7	*2	1			34	s
45			15	s			31	*s	33	5	s		*14		(s)	11					20				(7)	s	1			34	3
46			*s				31	(8)		5	26				10	s		(s)		*17	20			s		s	1		4	34	3
Apps	17	2	26	21	4	2	45	14	19	28	2	1	17	3	22	30	0	0	18	18	42	17	11	0	20	34	25	2	38	11	18
Subs	1	2	5		1	9		9		2	3			1	4	13	2	12	2	6		10	3	3		4		8	3		
Goals			2			2	29	2	1	1			1		2				1		12	2			4	4			2	1	

Opponents 2 goals

Football League Cup

No	Day	Month	Date	Opponents	Home	Away	H-T	Goalscorers	Gate
1	Tu	Aug	12	Queens Park Rangers	L2-3		(2-1)	Cox 34,Paynter 41	7,230

No	Aljofree H	Allen C M	Amankwaah K K O K	Brezovan P	Casal K O O	Corr B	Cox S R	Easton C	Greer G	Ifil J C	Jean-Francois L	Joyce B P	Kanyuka P E	Kennedy C E	McGovern JP	McNamee A	Macklin L J	Marshall M A	Morrison S J	Nalis L	Paynter W P	Peacock L A	Pook M D	Razak H	Robson-Kanu T H A	Smith J D	Smith P A	Sturrock B D	Timlin M A	Tudur-Jones O	Vincent J R
1	6	s	s	12	16		31	*s				s		s	(10)	11			25	17	20	(s)				2	s		*4		

F A Cup

No	Day	Month	Date	Opponents	Home	Away	H-T	Goalscorers	Gate
1	S	Nov	8	Histon		L0-1	(0-0)		1,541

No	Aljofree H	Allen C M	Amankwaah K K O K	Brezovan P	Casal K O O	Corr B	Cox S R	Easton C	Greer G	Ifil J C	Jean-Francois L	Joyce B P	Kanyuka P E	Kennedy C E	McGovern JP	McNamee A	Macklin L J	Marshall M A	Morrison S J	Nalis L	Paynter W P	Peacock L A	Pook M D	Razak H	Robson-Kanu T H A	Smith J D	Smith P A	Sturrock B D	Timlin M A	Tudur-Jones O	Vincent J R
1	6		s	*s		s	31	s					14		10	(11)		(s)	s	s	20	32	19			2	*1		4		

Football League Trophy

No	Day	Month	Date	Opponents	Home	Away	H-T	Goalscorers	Gate
1	Tu	Sep	2	Aldershot Town	+	D2-2	(1-1)	Cox 32,Ifil 83	1,814
2	Tu	Oct	7	Hereford United		W2-1	(1-1)	Cox 45,Peacock 84	1,458
QF	W	Nov	12	Brighton & Hove Albion		L0-2	(0-1)		2,234

+ After Extra Time (W7-6 on penalties)

No	Aljofree H	Allen C M	Amankwaah K K O K	Brezovan P	Casal K O O	Corr B	Cox S R	Easton C	Greer G	Ifil J C	Jean-Francois L	Joyce B P	Kanyuka P E	Kennedy C E	McGovern JP	McNamee A	Macklin L J	Marshall M A	Morrison S J	Nalis L	Paynter W P	Peacock L A	Pook M D	Razak H	Robson-Kanu T H A	Smith J D	Smith P A	Sturrock B D	Timlin M A	Tudur-Jones O	Vincent J R
1		*s	15	s	s		31	8		5			14		(10)	11		(s)			s	32				2	1		*4		
2			15	12	s	*s	31	8		5					s	(s)			25	(17)	*20	32				2	s		4		
QF			s	s		9	31	*8					14		10	s		18	25	*s	(s)		19			(2)	1		4		
Apps		0	2	1		1	3	3		2			2		2	1		1	2	1	1	2	1			3	2		3		
Subs		1				1									1	1		1		1	2										
Goals							2			1												1									

For Final League Table - see overleaf

SEASON 2008/09

	P	W	D	L	F	A	W	D	L	F	A	Pts	G/D	Avge. Home Gate
1 Leicester City	46	13	9	1	41	16	14	6	3	43	23	96	+45	20,253
2 Peterborough United	46	14	6	3	41	22	12	5	6	37	32	89	+24	7,599
3 Milton Keynes Dons	46	12	4	7	42	25	14	5	4	41	22	87	+36	10,551
4 Leeds United	46	17	2	4	49	20	9	4	10	28	29	84	+28	23,801
5 Millwall	46	13	4	6	30	21	12	3	8	33	32	82	+10	8,940
6 Scunthorpe United *	46	13	5	5	44	24	9	5	9	38	39	76	+19	5,021
7 Tranmere Rovers	46	15	5	3	41	20	6	6	11	21	29	74	+13	5,820
8 Southend United	46	13	2	8	29	20	8	6	9	29	41	71	-3	7,850
9 Huddersfield Town	46	9	8	6	32	28	9	6	8	30	37	68	-3	13,298
10 Oldham Athletic	46	9	9	5	35	24	7	8	8	31	41	65	+1	5,636
11 Bristol Rovers	46	11	4	8	44	29	6	8	9	35	32	63	+18	7,171
12 Colchester United	46	7	4	12	21	24	11	5	7	37	34	63	+0	5,084
13 Walsall	46	10	3	10	34	36	7	7	9	27	30	61	-5	4,572
14 Leyton Orient	46	6	6	11	24	33	9	5	9	21	24	56	-12	4,692
15 SWINDON TOWN	46	8	7	8	37	34	4	10	9	31	37	53	-3	7,499
16 Brighton & Hove Albion	46	6	6	11	32	40	7	7	9	23	30	52	-15	6,092
17 Yeovil Town	46	6	10	7	26	29	6	5	12	15	37	51	-25	4,423
18 Stockport County	46	9	7	7	34	28	7	5	11	25	29	50	+2	6,130
19 Hartlepool United	46	8	7	8	45	40	5	4	14	21	39	50	-13	3,835
20 Carlisle United	46	8	7	8	36	32	4	7	12	20	37	50	-13	6,268
21 Northampton Town	46	8	8	7	38	29	4	5	14	23	36	49	-4	5,200
22 Crewe Alexandra	46	8	4	11	30	38	4	6	13	29	44	46	-23	4,537
23 Cheltenham Town	46	7	6	10	30	38	2	6	15	21	53	39	-40	3,854
24 Hereford United	46	6	4	13	23	28	3	3	17	19	51	34	-37	3,270

* Promoted via Play-offs

top targetmen - post war

	Total	League	LgeCup	FACup	Other	
Simon COX	32	29	1	0	2	2008/09
Don ROGERS	32	24	1	7	0	1966/67
Duncan SHEARER	32	22	6	4	0	1991/92
Peter EASTOE	31	26	0	5	0	1974/75
Jimmy QUINN	31	21	8	0	2	1987/88
Don ROGERS	30	22	7	1	0	1968/69
Bill STEPHENS	28	26		2	0	1946/47
Don ROGERS	28	25	1	2	0	1967/68
Andy ROWLAND	28	20	5	3	0	1979/80
Alan MAYES	28	19	6	3	0	1979/80
Arthur HORSFIELD	28	18	0	4	6	1969/70
Bob EDWARDS	27	26		1	0	1956/57
Ernie HUNT	27	24	0	3	0	1962/63
Duncan SHEARER	27	20	4	1	2	1989/90
Steve WHITE	27	18	5	0	4	1989/90
Sam PARKIN	26	25	0	0	1	2002/03
Morris JONES	25	25		0	0	1948/49
Jan-Åge FJØRTOFT	25	15	9	1	0	1994/95
Sam PARKIN	24	23	0	0	1	2004/05
Jack SMITH	24	19	3	2	0	1962/63
Keith EAST	24	19	0	5	0	1965/66
Maurice OWEN	24	18		6	0	1951/52
Duncan SHEARER	23	22	0	1	0	1990/91
Paul RIDEOUT	23	20	2	1	0	1982/83
Sam PARKIN	23	19	3	0	1	2003/04
Craig MASKELL	23	18	1	0	4	1992/93
Maurice OWEN	21	17		4	0	1952/53
Don ROGERS	21	16	4	0	1	1970/71
Dave MOSS	21	16	3	2	0	1977/78
Dave MOSS	21	14	0	7	0	1976/77
'Bronco' LAYNE	20	20		0	0	1959/60
Iffy ONUORA	20	20	0	0	0	1998/99
Tommy MOONEY	20	19	1	0	0	2003/04
Wayne ALLISON	20	17	1	2	0	1995/96
Andy ROWLAND	20	16	0	4	0	1982/83

KEITH EAST

JAN-ÅGE FJØRTOFT

SIMON COX

the nearly men

Players who failed at Swindon Town but made League appearances elsewhere….

Surname	Initials	Known As	Pos	Season(s)	Other Clubs (selected only)
Allison	N J	Neil	CD	1996/97	Hull City,Chesterfield
Allwright	C R S	Charlie	W	1920/21	Brentford,Bristol City
Balsom	C G	Cliff	FB	1964/65	Torquay United
Beswick	K	Keith	G	1961/62	Millwall,Newport County
Bratley	G W	Bill	CH	1938/39	Rotherham,Sheffied Wednesday,Barrow
Bull	G W	Gary	F	1983/84	Barnet,Nottingham Forest,Birmingham,York
Carmichael	J	Jack	FB	1980/81	Peterborough United
Collins	R L	Bob	G	1963/64	Newport County
Fleming	C	Curtis	FB	1988/89	Middlesbrough,Crystal Palace,Darlington
Gill	K	Kenny	W	1974/75	Newport County
Guest	B J	Brendan	FB	1980/81	Lincoln City
Hallworth	J G	Jon	G	1984/85	Ipswich Town,Oldham Athletic,Cardiff City
Hand	E K J C	Eoin	W	1964/65	Drumcondra,Portsmouth,Shamrock Rovers
Hague	E M	Eric	W	1926/27	Nottingham Forest,Walsall,Crewe
Head	D G	David	F	1958/59	Reading
Hellin	A	Tony	FB	1962/63,1963/64	Torquay United
Henderson	J	Joe	G	1953/54	Stenhousemuir,Accrington Stanley
Legg	H G W	Harry	FB	1929/30	Crystal Palace
Lloyd	R C	Clive	IF	1965/66	Cardiff City
Lloyd	J D	John	FB	1961/62-1964/65	Oxford United,Aldershot
Mailey	J	Jim	W	1939/40	Plymouth Argyle
Mapson	J	John	G	1934/35	Reading,Sunderland
Middleton	L J	Lee	FB	1992/93	Coventry City,Cambridge United
Morah	O H	Ollie	F	1994/95	Cambridge United
Mundee	D W J	Denny	M	1986/87	AFC Bournemouth,Brentford,Brighton
Murphy	D T	Danny	FB	2003/04	QPR,Motherwell,Cork City
Parker	W K	Billy	W	1924/25	South Shields
Plumb	R K	Dick	F	1963/64,1964/65	Bristol Rovers,Yeovil,Charlton,Exeter
Poland	G	George	W	1934/35	* Cardiff City,Wrexham,Liverpool
Richardson	D	Dave	FB	1960/61	Leicester City,Grimsby Town,Barrow
Scott	R J	Bob	HB	1961/62	Cardiff City,Newport County,Southport
Thomas	E H C	Eddie	G	1949/50	Southampton
Topping	H	Harry	FB	1934/35	Exeter City,New Brighton,Bristol Rovers
Toward	R H	Ralph	W	1920/21	Glossop,Durham City
Tyler	D H J	Dudley	W	1967/68	West Ham,Hereford United
Williams	L	Les	G	1956/57,1957/58	Sheffield Wednesday
Woodman	J A E	Jimmy	CF	1938/39	Bristol Rovers
Worrall	H	Harry	FB	1948/49	Manchester United
York	C H	Charlie	CF	1900/01	Derby County,Sunderland

(Loanees and triallists have not been included)

* also made 2 full apps for Wales - as a goalkeeper !

….and players named as substitute but who were not called into action….

* Loan players

Surname	Initials	Known As	Pos	Season(s)	Other Clubs (selected only)
Cook	S A	Shane	G	1993/94	Cheltenham Town,Gloucester City
Draycott	M R	Mark	F	2002/03	Portland Timbers,Newport Co.,Supermarine
Gnakpa	C	Claude	D	2006/07	Vaduz,Peterborough United,Luton Town
Green	R E	Richard	D	1990/91	Shrewsbury Town,Gillingham
Hamblin	C J	Chris	G	1994/95	Gloucester City,Boston Bulldogs (USA)
Henry	L C D	Leigh	D	2005/06,2006/07	Swindon Supermarine
Hopper	L	Luke	F	2006/07	Swindon Supermarine
Howe	E J F	Eddie	D	2003/04	AFC Bournemouth *
James	S E	Stuart	D	1994/95	Weymouth,Bath City,Newport County
Judge	A G	Alan	G	2002/03	Luton Town,Reading,Oxford United
Kearns	M	Mick	G	1969/70	Oxford United *
Kerr	J S R	Stewart	G	1993/94	Glasgow Celtic *
Round	D L	David	D	1980/81-1982/83	
Smith	S A	Steve	G	2002/03	
Stewart	J H	Jon	G	2006/07	Weymouth
Thomas	J O	Josh	D	2001/02	Weymouth,Salisbury City
Trollope	P J	Paul	M	1990/91,1991/92	Torquay United,Derby County,Bristol Rovers

CHARLIE ALLWRIGHT

EOIN HAND

DANNY MURPHY

DICK PLUMB

STEWART KERR

PAUL TROLLOPE

Surname	Initials	Known As	Pos	Intl	Born	Died	Previous Club	Signed	Lge Apps	Gls.	Other Apps	Gls.		Went to	When Left	Pics
Abbley	S G	Steve	W		1957		Park FC	Oct 1978	14 + 9	0	1	0		Witney Town	Jul 1982	
Abbott	H	Harry	F		1879	1970	Bolton Wanderers	May 1905	26	3				Darwen	Sep 1906	
Adams	S M	Steve	M		1980		Sheffield Wednesday	Aug 2007	2	0	3 + 1	0		Torquay United	Jan 2008	
Adey	T W	Tom	WH		1901	1986	Hull City	Aug 1925	25	0	4	0		Northampton Town	Jun 1926	
Agar	F R	Roy	IF		1936		RAPC Devizes	Dec 1955	12	0			A			
Aitken	D	Danny	WH		1882	1951	Millwall	May 1907	1	0				Released	cs 1908	
Aizlewood	S	Steve	CH		1952		Newport County	Mar 1976	111 + 1	10	26	2		Portsmouth	Jul 1979	
Alexander	G G	Gary	F		1979		West Ham United	Aug 2000	30 + 7	7	7 + 2	2		Hull City	Jun 2001	
Alford	F J	Frank	W		1901	1982	Juniors	Sep 1919	1	0				Darwen	cs 1920	
Aljofree	H	Hasney	D		1978		Plymouth Argyle	Jun 2007	55 + 2	2	8	1		Under contract for 2009/10		
Allan	J	Jimmy	G		1953		Brora Rangers	Oct 1970	371	0	65	0		Retired (injury)	Jul 1984	194
Allen	C M	Chris	M		1989		Youths	May 2007	9 + 3	0	1 + 3	0		Released	May 2009	
Allen	K R	Ken	G		1948		Torquay United	Sep 1985	45	0	4	0		Torquay United	Dec 1986	213
Allen	P K	Paul	M		1962		Southampton	Oct 1995	30 + 7	1	8	1		Bristol City	Jan 1997	
Allen	T G	Tommy	FB		1865	1911	Ealing	cs 1893	2	0	5	1	A			
Allison	W A	Wayne	F		1968		Bristol City	Jul 1995	98 + 3	31	19	5		Huddersfield Town	Nov 1997	
Almeida	M A S	Mauro	D		1982		Accrington Stanley	Aug 2007	0		1	0		Sligo Rovers	Jan 2008	
Almond	J	Jim	HB		1874	1923	Burnley	Jan 1897	42	2	3	0		Released	cs 1898	
Amankwaah	K K O K	Kevin	FB		1982		Swansea City	Jun 2008	26 + 5	2	2	0		Under contract for 2009/10		
Anderson	T	Trevor	W	NI	1951		Manchester United	Nov 1974	128 + 3	35	31	12		Peterborough United	Dec 1977	187
Andrews	A	Alf	W		1873	1951	St Marks Cambrians	Feb 1892	14	4	11	4	A	Chatham	Aug 1895	10
			Returned from				Chatham	cs 1896	14	2	2	0		Trowbridge Town	Jan 1898	
Andrews	*I E*	*Ian*	*G*		*1964*		*Leicester City*	*Jan 1984*	*1*	*0*			*L*			
Anthony	G J	Graham	M		1975		Sheffield United	Mar 1997	3	0				Plymouth Argyle	Aug 1997	
Anthony	S T	Tommy	F		1875	1957	Chorley	Nov 1897	75	11	2	0		Retired	cs 1903	
Archer	A A E	Archie	WH		1899	1982	Bristol Rovers	Oct 1920	190	4	22	0		Retired	cs 1931	
Archer	H T	Tom	FB		1882	1907	Stratton Jubilee	Dec 1903	5	0	2	0	A			
Ardiles	O C	Ossie	M	Ar	1952		Fort Lauderdale Strikers *(US)*	Jul 1989	0 + 2	0				Newcastle United (manager)	Mar 1991	205,320
Arman	B J	Bertie	FB		1894	1972	North Swindon United	cs 1915	2	0	1	0	A			
Armstrong	W	Bill	CH		1913	1995	Aston Villa	May 1934	59	0	9	0		Gillingham	May 1936	
Armstrong	T H	Tommy	IF		1906	1967	Airdrieonians	Aug 1933	64	30	6	2		Crewe Alexandra	Aug 1935	88
Arrieta	I P	Ibon	F		1977		UD Melilla *(Sp)*	Aug 2007	0 + 4	0	1 + 1	1		CS Pandurii Targu Jiu *(Ro)*	Jan 2008	
Ashikodi	*M*	*Moses*	*F*		*1987*		*Watford*	*Jan 2008*	*4 + 6*	*0*			*L*			
Atherton	F G	Gordon	WH		1934		Bury	Dec 1964	31	0	1	0		Bury	Jan 1966	
Atkins	W M	Bill	F		1939		Aston Villa	Jun 1959	75	28	4	2		Halifax Town	Aug 1965	
Atterbury	S	Sep	FB		1880	1964	Leicester Fosse	May 1903	126	1	6	3		Plymouth Argyle	May 1907	

STEVE AIZLEWOOD

WAYNE ALLISON

town roll call

1894 - 2009

For key to abbreviations used - see Page 307

ARCHIE ARCHER

SEP ATTERBURY

Surname	Initials	Known As	Pos	Intl	Born	Died	Previous Club	Signed	Lge Apps	Gls.	Other Apps	Gls.		Went to	When Left	Pics
Baddeley	K S	Kevin	FB		1962		Bristol City	Jun 1981	94 + 1	2	15 + 1	0		Wealdstone	Oct 1984	
Bailey	H	Harry	FB		1915	1994	Leeds United	May 1935	5	0	7	0		Cheltenham Town	Jul 1938	
					Returned from		*Cheltenham Town*	*Apr 1940*	*0*		*5*	*0*	*G*			
Bailey	G S J	Jerry	W		1905	1964	Swindon Butchers	Mar 1927	7	1			A			
Bailey	J S	John	F		1950		Apprentice	Aug 1968	0 + 2	0				Cheltenham Town	Jun 1971	
Bailie	C J	Colin	FB		1964		Apprentice	Apr 1982	105 + 2	4	14	0		Reading	Jun 1985	
Baillie	*D R D C*	*Doug*	*CF*		*1937*		*Airdrieonians*	*Mar 1956*	*1*	*0*			*L*			
Bain	J A	Jimmy	W		1919	2002	Chelsea	May 1947	235	40	20	3		Headington United	Jul 1954	*122*
Bakalli	A	Adrian	M		1976		Watford	Mar 2001	1	0				RWD Molenbeek *(Be)*	May 2001	
Bamber	J D	Dave	F		1959		Portsmouth	Nov 1985	103 + 3	30	31	16		Watford	Jun 1988	
Bampton	D P	Dave	M		1985		Trainee	Oct 2002	0 + 3	0	0 + 1	0		Tamworth	May 2004	
Bannister	C	Charlie	CH		1875	1947	Lincoln City	Aug 1902	60	5	8	1		Reading	May 1904	
					Returned from		Reading	May 1906	174	5	20	0		Perth YMCA *(Au)*	cs 1912	
Barnard	L K	Leigh	M		1958		Portsmouth	Jul 1982	212 + 5	22	53 + 1	4		Cardiff City	Oct 1989	
Barnes	D O	Bobby	W		1962		Aldershot	Oct 1987	43 + 2	13	7	0		AFC Bournemouth	Mar 1989	
Barraclough	A	Arthur	W		1916	2005	Chelsea	Jun 1938	21	6	1	0		Clapton Orient	Jun 1939	*106*
Barrett	C	Colin	FB		1952		Nottingham Forest	Jun 1980	3	0	2	0		Andover	Jun 1981	
Barron	J	Jim	G		1943		Nottingham Forest	Aug 1974	79	0	14	0		Connecticut Bicentennials *(US)*	Mar 1977	
Batchelor	E	Ted	HB		1930	2006	Wolverhampton Wanderers	Jul 1950	91	0	5	2		Bath City	Jul 1956	
Bates	P D	Chic	F		1949		Shrewsbury Town	Jan 1978	50 + 13	15	9 + 1	3		Bristol Rovers	Mar 1980	*191*
Batty	W	Bill	FB		1905	1974	Barnsley	May 1930	18	1				Southport	Jun 1931	
Batty	W	Billy	F		1886		Lincoln City	May 1912	110	44	9	2		Barnsley	Jun 1922	
Batty	P W	Paul	M		1964		Apprentice	Jan 1982	102 + 6	7	17 + 1	5		Chesterfield	Jul 1985	
Baverstock	R	Ray	FB		1963		Apprentice	Dec 1981	17	0	2	0		Cheltenham Town	Jul 1983	
Baynham	J	Johnnie	IF		1918	1995	Leyton Orient	Aug 1948	4	1				Guildford City	Jun 1949	
Beadsworth	A	Arthur	F		1876	1917	Manchester United	Nov 1903	54	11				Penrith	Aug 1905	
Beamish	K G	Ken	F		1947		Tranmere Rovers	Jul 1981	1 + 1	0				Contract cancelled	Jun 1984	*320*
Beards	A	Alan	W		1932		Bolton Wanderers	Mar 1954	21	4				Stockport County	Jul 1955	
Beasant	E A W	Ted	FB		1895	1969	GWR Stores FC	cs 1919	3	0			A			
Beauchamp	J D	Joey	M		1971		West Ham United	Aug 1994	39 + 6	3	13 + 2	1		Oxford United	Oct 1995	
Beaumont	W E	Billy	HB		1883	1911	Ashton Town	Feb 1906	54	0	1	0		Portsmouth	May 1907	
Becton	F	Frank	F	E	1873	1909	Preston North End	Aug 1901	45	7	4	5		Nelson	Nov 1902	
					Returned from		Nelson	Feb 1903	11	3				Ashton Town	cs 1903	
Beecham	E C	Ernie	G		1906	1985	Brighton & Hove Albion	Nov 1935	8	0				Retired	Mar 1936	
Bell	J	Jock	IF		1873	1934	Grimsby Town	May 1897	35	6	3	1		Bedminster	May 1898	
Bell	J A	John	WH		1936		Stirling Albion	Jun 1960	29	2				Released	May 1962	

COLIN BAILIE

CHARLIE BANNISTER

PAUL BATTY

FRANK BECTON

Surname	Initials	Known As	Pos	Intl	Born	Died	Previous Club	Signed	Lge Apps	Gls.	Other Apps	Gls.		Went to	When Left	Pics
Benjamin	*T J*	*Trevor*	*F*	*J*	*1979*		*Peterborough United*	*Jan 2006*	*5 + 3*	*2*			*L*			
Bennett	D A	Dave	M		1959		Sheffield Wednesday	Sep 1990	1	0	1	0		Nuneaton Borough	1992/93	
Bentley	H	Harry	FB		1885	1949	Brighton & Hove Albion	Aug 1922	11	0				Maltby Main Colliery	Sep 1926	
Berkley	A J	Austin	M		1973		Gillingham	May 1992	0 + 1	0	3 + 2	1		Shrewsbury Town	Jul 1995	
Berry	G L	Les	G		1906	1985	Bristol Rovers	Aug 1932	22	0	3	0		Nuneaton Town	Oct 1933	
Berry	S A	Steve	M		1963		Newport County	Mar 1987	4	0	6	1		Aldershot	Oct 1987	
Beswetherick	*J B*	*John*	*D*		*1978*		*Sheffield Wednesday*	*Feb 2003*	*3*	*0*			*L*			
Betteridge	R M	Mick	IF		1924	1999	West Bromwich Albion	Jul 1951	108	23	13	3		Chester	Mar 1954	
Bevan	F	Frank	F		1879	1955	Druids	Oct 1901	2	0	1	0		Aberdare Town	cs 1902	
Bew	D C	Danny	CH		1896	1951	Hull City	Jun 1923	209	5	16	0		Retired	May 1930	
Bines	H M	Mel	WH		1930	1979	(Minehead local football)	Aug 1950	6	0				Bedford Town	Jul 1954	
Bingham	W P	Peter	HB		1922	1997	Swindon Victoria	Aug 1946	20	0	2	0		Swindon Victoria	Aug 1949	
Bingley	W	Walter	FB		1930		Sheffield Wednesday	Jan 1958	101	0	2	0		York City	Aug 1960	
Birtles	T J D	Tommy	F		1886	1971	Barnsley	May 1906	38	8	1	0		Portsmouth	May 1907	*37*
Blackburn	C R	Chris	D		1982		Morecambe	Jul 2007	4 + 3	0	2	2		Aldershot Town	May 2008	
Blackler	M J	Martin	M		1963		Apprentice	Mar 1981	8 + 1	0				Witney Town	Jul 1983	
Blakemore	C	Cecil	F		1897	1963	Norwich City	Jun 1933	26	8	1	0		Brierley Hill Alliance	Jul 1934	
Blick	M R	Mick	CH		1948		Apprentice	Sep 1966	6	0	2	0		Corby Town	Jun 1971	
Bodin	P J	Paul	FB	W	1964		Newport County	Mar 1988	87 + 6	9	26	1		Crystal Palace	Mar 1991	*226*
			Returned from				Crystal Palace	Jan 1992	139 + 6	28	32	2		Reading	Jul 1996	
Boggie	A	Alec	F		1870	1923	Burton Swifts	Mar 1896	54	8	6	0		Kirkcaldy	Aug 1898	
Boland	W	Billy	F		1886	1952	Haydon Street WMC	cs 1909	1	0	1	0	A			
Bolland	W T	Tommy	W		1884	1967	The Wednesday	May 1909	168	15	32	1		Bath City	cs 1921	*55,56*
Book	S K	Steve	G		1969		Cheltenham Town	Aug 2004	1 + 1	0	3	0		Cirencester Town	Jun 2005	
Borrows	B	Brian	D		1960		Coventry City	Sep 1997	80	0	3	0		Retired	May 1999	
Bouazza	*H*	*Hameur*	*WF*	*Al*	*1985*		*Watford*	*Oct 2005*	*11 + 2*	*2*	*2*	*1*	*L*			
Boulton	F P	Frank	G		1917	1987	Derby County	Jul 1946	97	0	6	0		Crystal Palace	Oct 1950	
Boulton	T	Tom	G		1874	1958	Swindon Amateurs	cs 1898	10	0	1	0	A			
Bourne	J T	Jack	G		1901	1992	Eccles Borough	Aug 1926	41	0	2	0		Sandbach Ramblers	Aug 1929	
Bowell	O C	Oliver	W		1882	1961	Bristol East	Dec 1904	28	3				Birmingham	Aug 1906	
Bowl	T H	Harry	IF		1914	1991	Clanfield	Sep 1933	44	8	6	3		Blackpool	Jun 1936	
			Returned from				*Exeter City*	*Oct 1939*	*0*		*19*	*11*	*G*			
Bown	A J W	Archie	F		1882	1958	Swindon Casuals	Feb 1902	3	0			A			*40,56*
			Returned from				Whitehead Torpedo Works	Dec 1906	250	125	38	17		Bristol City	Nov 1919	
Bradley	J	Jack	IF		1916	2002	Huddersfield Town	Aug 1936	25	6	8	5		Chelsea	Jun 1938	

DANNY BEW

WALTER BINGLEY

BRIAN BORROWS

FRANK BOULTON

Surname	Initials	Known As	Pos	Intl	Born	Died	Previous Club	Signed	Lge Apps	Gls.	Other Apps	Gls.		Went to	When Left	Pics
Bradley	*S*	*Shayne*	*F*		*1979*		*Southampton*	*Mar 1999*	*6 + 1*	*0*			*L*			
Bradshaw	T D	Tom	F		1876	1953	New Brighton Tower	Aug 1901	12	1				Reading	Nov 1901	
Brae	W	Willie	IF		1902	1968	Ayr United	Aug 1935	6	0	2	1		Cheltenham Town	May 1936	
Braithwaite	E	Ted	WH		1900	1990	Reading	Jun 1929	142	5	5	0		Margate Town	May 1933	
Brandon	K A	Ken	W		1934	1994	Roundway Hospital FC	Dec 1952	5	0			A	Chester	Mar 1954	
Brayley	A P	Bertie	F		1981		Queens Park Rangers	Aug 2001	0 + 7	0	0 + 3	0		Canvey Island	Apr 2002	
Brennan	J	Jim	FB		1932		Birmingham City	Jun 1954	16	1	2	0		Chelmsford City	Jul 1956	
Brewer	W A	Billy	F		1893	1914	Chippenham Town	Oct 1913	1	0				Chippenham Town	Mar 1914	
Brezovan	P J	Peter	G		1979		1FC Brno *(Sv)*	Jul 2006	66	0	9 + 1	0		Released	May 2009	
Briggs	A L	Arthur	G		1900	1987	Ashton National	Feb 1933	69	0	4	0		Newport County	Jun 1935	61
Broadhead	A	Arnold	IF		1900	1973	Brighton & Hove Albion	Mar 1924	1	2				Released	cs 1924	
Brock	J G G	John	G		1915	1976	Stonehouse	Sep 1936	5	0			A			
Brooke	P	Percy	FB		1893	1971	Aberdare Athletic	Aug 1926	3	0				Accrington Stanley	Jul 1927	
Brookes	S	Syd	IF		1907	1975	Blackpool	Jun 1932	30	6	3	1		Scarborough	Aug 1933	
Broomes	*M C*	*Marlon*	*CD*		*1977*		*Blackburn Rovers*	*Jan 1997*	*12*	*1*			*L*			
Brown	A W	Aaron	M		1980		Queens Park Rangers	Nov 2005	36 + 21	4	4 + 1	0		Gillingham	May 2007	
Brown	A	Alf	WH		1898	1979	Barnsley	Aug 1926	14	1				Nelson	Sep 1927	
Brown	R E	Bob	W		1869		Bristol Rovers	Jul 1900	34	1	5	1		Released	cs 1901	
Brown	D J	Dennis	F		1944		Chelsea	Nov 1964	92	37	14	7		Northampton Town	Feb 1967	159
Brown	S	Sam	FB				Chester	Nov 1932	2	0			T			
Brownlie	R	Royce	F		1980		Queensland Roar *(Au)*	Jul 2006	6 + 8	2	3	0		Wellington Phoenix *(NZ)*	May 2007	
Bryan	W	Bill	G		1912	1944	Southend United	Jul 1937	22	0	7	0		Wrexham	Jun 1939	
Bull	M F	Mickey	W		1930		Brentford	May 1953	69	15	3	0		Hastings United	Jul 1955	129
Bullock	D J	Darren	M		1969		Huddersfield Town	Feb 1997	55 + 11	2	3	0		Bury	Feb 1999	
Bullock	A E	Teddy	F		1878	1951	Old Higher Grade FC	cs 1902	8	0	3	3	A			
Bulman	M K	Matty	G		1986		STFC Youths	Jun 2005	0		0 + 1	0		Salisbury City	Jun 2006	
Bunkell	R K	Ray	M		1949	2000	Tottenham Hotspur	Jun 1971	52 + 4	3	5	0		Colchester United	Dec 1973	
Burgess	R	Reg	W		1910	1978	Purton	Dec 1931	7	1			A			
Burkinshaw	J D L	Jack	CF		1890	1947	Rotherham County	May 1910	45	15	11	4		The Wednesday	Aug 1913	56
Burrows	F	Frank	CH		1944		Scunthorpe United	Jul 1968	293 + 4	9	53 + 1	0		Portsmouth (coach)	Jan 1978	164
Burton	*D J*	*Deon*	*F*	*J*	*1976*		*Portsmouth*	*Oct 2003*	*4*	*1*			*L*			
Burton	S	Sam	G		1926		Pinehurst YC	Jun 1945	463	0	46	0		Retired	cs 1962	130
Butcher	F	Fred	FB		1913	1996	Blackpool	May 1938	36	0	5	0		Retired	1940	
Butler	J W	Joe	M		1943		Newcastle United	Aug 1965	355 + 7	18	65 + 1	4		Aldershot	Aug 1976	164
Buttigieg	*J*	*John*	*FB*	*M*	*1963*		*Brentford*	*Sep 1990*	*2 + 1*	*0*	*0 + 1*	*0*	*L*			

TED BRAITHWAITE

PETER BREZOVAN

ARTHUR BRIGGS

DARREN BULLOCK

Surname	Initials	Known As	Pos	Intl	Born	Died	Previous Club	Signed	Lge Apps	Gls.	Other Apps	Gls.	Went to	When Left	Pics
Calderwood	C	Colin	CD	S	1965		Mansfield Town	Jun 1985	328 + 1	20	84	1	Tottenham Hotspur	Jul 1993	214
Calderwood	J	Jimmy	CF/G		1868		Kilmarnock Athletic	Dec 1895	20	1	3	0	Retired	cs 1898	
Caldwell	*D W*	*Dave*	*F*		*1960*		*Mansfield Town*	*Feb 1985*	*5*	*0*			*L*		
Cameron	D G B	Duncan	W		1936		Burnbank Athletic	Dec 1956	2	0			Bridgwater Town	Apr 1958	
Campagna	S P P	Sam	D		1980		Trainee	Jul 1999	1 + 3	0			Bromsgrove Rovers	Jun 2001	
Capes	A J	Arthur	F	E	1875	1945	Longton Hall	Nov 1905	31	11	2	1	Retired	cs 1906	
Carlisle	*W T*	*Wayne*	*M*		*1979*		*Crystal Palace*	*Oct 2001*	*10 + 1*	*2*			*L*		
Carrick	*M*	*Michael*	*M*	*E*	*1981*		*West Ham United*	*Nov 1999*	*6*	*2*			*L*		
Carter	*M*	*Mike*	*F*		*1960*		*Bolton Wanderers*	*Mar 1982*	*4 + 1*	*0*			*L*		
Carter	R W	Roy	U		1954		Hereford United	Dec 1977	193 + 7	34	34 + 2	5	Torquay United	Feb 1983	199
Casal	K O O	Yinka	FB		1987		SC Cambuur Leeuwarden *(Ho)*	Aug 2008	4 1	0	1	0	Under contract for 2009/10		
Casper	*C M*	*Chris*	*D*		*1975*		*Manchester United*	*Sep 1997*	*8 + 1*	*1*			*L*		
Casserly	D S	Dean	D		1969		Trainee	Apr 1988	0		1	0	Hungerford Town	Nov 1988	
Caton	A J	Andy	F		1987		North Leigh	Jul 2004	4 + 9	1	1 + 1	0	Witney United	Jan 2008	
Chalklin	G	Geoff	FB		1956		Apprentice	Oct 1974	3	0			Cheltenham Town	May 1977	
Chalmers	J	Jim	WF		1877	1916	Tottenham Hotspur	May 1904	74	16	4	0	Norwich City	May 1906	32
Chamberlain	P M	Peter	U		1935		Leicester City	Jun 1957	80	6	2	0	Aldershot	Oct 1962	
Chambers	J	Jimmy	CH		1918	1987	Bolton Wanderers	May 1937	4	0	3	0	Worcester City	Jun 1939	
Chambers	P	Peter	WH		1877	1951	Bristol City	May 1907	88	1	13	0	Retired	cs 1912	
Chandler	F E J	Fred	IF		1912	2005	Blackpool	May 1936	21	7	1	0	Crewe Alexandra	May 1937	
Chandler	R E J	Ray	G		1931		Bristol Rovers	Jun 1956	35	0	2	0	Cambridge United	Aug 1960	
Chapman	H	Herbert	IF		1878	1934	Grimsby Town	May 1899	3	2			Sheppey United	Nov 1899	
Chivers	W A	William	WH		1895		Newport County	Jul 1927	1	0			T Bournemouth & Boscombe Athletic	Nov 1927	
Churchill	T	Trevor	G		1923		Rochdale	May 1953	11	0			Tonbridge	Jul 1954	
Clark	F	Fred	FB		1871	1949	Birkenhead L & N W Locomen	cs 1896	6	0	1	0	Wolverton L & N W Railway	Feb 1897	
Clark	J	Jimmy	F		1895	1947	Leeds United	Jun 1925	18	7			Greenock Morton	Nov 1926	
Clarke	J	Jim	HB				Newtown Thistle	May 1897	16	0				1898	
Clarke	R C	Ray	F		1952		Tottenham Hotspur	May 1973	11 + 3	2			Mansfield Town	Aug 1974	
Clayton	L	Lew	WH		1924		Bournemouth & Boscombe Athletic	Jun 1957	35	2	1	0	Wisbech Town	Nov 1958	
Clayton	P	Percy	WH		1890		Unattached	Oct 1919	24	0	2	0	Released	cs 1920	
Close	S C	Shaun	F		1966		AFC Bournemouth	Sep 1989	13 + 31	1	2 + 7	1	Barnet	Aug 1993	
Coates	R J	Dick	WH		1886	1975	Haydon Street WMC	cs 1906	5	2			A		
Cobian	J M	Juan	D		1975		Aberdeen	Jul 2000	3 + 1	0	3 + 2	0	Deportivo Linares (*Sp*)	Jan 2003	
Cochrane	A F	Sandy	IF		1900	1967	Northampton Town	May 1935	13	1	2	0	East Stirlingshire	Aug 1936	
Cockburn	W O	Bill	CH		1899	1958	Queens Park Rangers	Jul 1930	38	1			Retired	May 1931	

ARTHUR CAPES

PETER CHAMBERLAIN

PETER CHAMBERS

BILL COCKBURN

Surname	Initials	Known As	Pos	Intl	Born	Died	Previous Club	Signed	Lge Apps	Gls.	Other Apps	Gls.	Went to	When Left	Pics
Cockerill	G	Glenn	M		1959		Lincoln City	Dec 1979	23 + 3	1	3	0	Lincoln City	Aug 1981	
Codling	R	Ralph	WH		1880	1956	Stockton St Johns	Sep 1901	21	0	2	0	Sunderland	Mar 1902	
Cole	D A	David	D		1962		Swansea City	Feb 1985	69	3	10	0	Torquay United	Nov 1986	
Colebourne	J	Joe	FB		1893	1979	Exeter City	Jun 1921	57	0	3	0	Exeter City	Aug 1923	
Coleman	*N*	*Nicky*	*FB*		*1966*		*Millwall*	*Sep 1985*	*13*	*4*	*4*	*0*	*L*		
Collins	L	Lee	M		1974		Albion Rovers	Nov 1995	52 + 11	2	5	0	Blackpool	Jul 2000	
Collins	M A	Micky	F		1953		Chelmsford City	Jul 1973	2 + 4	0	1	0	Released	May 1974	
Collins	*P P*	*Patrick*	*D*		*1985*		*Sheffield Wednesday*	*Aug 2005*	*13*	*0*			*L*		
Collins	*S J*	*Sam*	*D*		*1977*		*Hull City*	*Sep 2007*	*3 + 1*	*0*			*L*		
Colvin	R	Bob	W		1876	1940	Queens Park Rangers	Aug 1903	4	0			Maxwelltown Volunteers	Nov 1903	
Comminges	M	Miguel	M / D	Gu	1982		Stade de Reims *(Fr)*	Jul 2007	32 + 8	0	7	0	Cardiff City	Jun 2008	
Compton	R	Roy	F		1954		Millwall	Mar 1973	4	2			Released	May 1974	
Comyn-Platt	C	Charlie	D/MF		1985		Bolton Wanderers	Jul 2005	15 + 9	1	2 + 3	1	Rochdale	Jan 2007	
Cook	J	Jimmy	G		1872	1921	Garston Copper Works	Jan 1897	45	0	3	0	Bristol Eastville Rovers	May 1898	
Cooke	F R	Bob	F		1896	1976	Sunderland	May 1921	33	14	2	0	Accrington Stanley	Aug 1923	*64*
Cookson	J	Jimmy	CF		1904	1970	Plymouth Argyle	Aug 1936	50	31	3	2	Swindon Corinthians	May 1938	*94*
Cooper	R	Reggie	WH		1899	1970	Trowbridge Town	Jun 1922	92	0	8	0	Bath City	cs 1931	
Cope	H	Harry	G		1902	1980	Blackburn Rovers	May 1930	68	0	1	0	Stalybridge Celtic	Aug 1932	
Corbett	D F	Dave	W		1940		Marshfield	Jul 1958	68	3	7	0	Plymouth Argyle	Feb 1962	
Cornwell	J A	John	M		1964		Newcastle United	Dec 1988	7 + 18	0	6 + 4	0	Southend United	Aug 1990	
Corr	B	Barry	F		1985		Sheffield Wednesday	Mar 2007	17 + 19	10	3 + 3	0	Exeter City	Jul 2009	
Coughlan	*G*	*Graham*	*CD*		*1974*		*Blackburn Rovers*	*Mar 1997*	*3*	*0*			*L*		
Coupar	J	Jimmy	W		1869	1953	Luton Town	May 1898	61	12	2	1	Linfield	cs 1900	
Court	H J	Jack	IF		1919	1975	Dundee	Jun 1950	16	2			Weymouth	Jun 1951	
Cousin	D P	Doug	FB		1889	1960	Swindon Victoria	Sep 1911	1	0			A		
Cousins	H	Harry	WH		1907	1981	Chesterfield	Jul 1932	273	1	96	0	Assistant trainer	1947	*112*
Covey	A S	Sid	IF		1894	1969	Eastcott Hill FC	Jun 1914	3	1	1	0	Swindon Corinthians	cs 1922	
Cowan	D	Davie	F		1880	1939	Dumfries	Aug 1901	22	1	1	1	Fulham	Oct 1902	
Cowe	S M	Steve	F		1974		Aston Villa	Mar 1996	59 + 38	11	5 + 6	2	Newport County	Jul 2001	
Cowie	A D	Andy	WH		1913	1972	Aberdeen	Jul 1948	89	4	3	0	Chippenham United	May 1952	
Cowley	J B	Jack	WH		1877	1926	Lincoln City	Aug 1902	86	5	9	3	Retired	cs 1906	
Cox	R	Richie	F		1868	1919	Kilmarnock	Jun 1896	23	5	5	3	Kilmarnock Athletic	Sep 1898	
Cox	S R	Simon	F		1987		Reading	Aug 2007	80 + 1	44	6 + 1	4	West Bromwich Albion	Jul 2009	*274*
Coyne	P D	Peter	F		1958		Hyde United	Aug 1984	99 + 11	30	26 + 1	11	Colne Dynamoes	Oct 1989	
Crichton	*P A*	*Paul*	*G*		*1968*		*Nottingham Forest*	*Dec 1987*	*4*	*0*			*L*		

REGGIE COOPER

STEVE COWE

ANDY COWIE

JACK COWLEY

Surname	Initials	Known As	Pos	Intl	Born	Died	Previous Club	Signed	Lge Apps	Gls.	Other Apps	Gls.		Went to	When Left	Pics
Crook	G F	Geoff	G		1937	1993	RAF	May 1960	0		1	0		Released	Feb 1961	
Crook	M S	Mark	W		1903	1977	Blackpool	May 1929	1	0				Wolverhampton Wanderers	Oct 1929	
Cross	J K	Jimmy	WH		1926	1999	Everton	May 1953	154	5	9	1		Headington United	cs 1958	
Crossley	C A	Charlie	IF		1891	1965	West Ham United	Jul 1923	37	12	6	2		Ebbw Vale	Sep 1925	
Cruickshank	A	Alec	W		1900	1974	Merthyr Town	Jun 1930	26	4	1	0		St Johnstone	Aug 1931	
Cryle	G	George	WH		1928		Ayr United	Aug 1952	12	0				Dartford	Aug 1953	
Cuervo	P	Phillipe	M		1969		AS Saint-Etienne *(Fr)*	Aug 1997	16 + 19	0	2 + 1	0		US Creteil *(Fr)*	May 2000	
Culley	W N	Bill	F		1892	1955	Bristol Rovers	Aug 1928	3	1				Kilmarnock (coach)	Sep 1929	
Culverhouse	I B	Ian	D		1964		Norwich City	Dec 1994	95 + 2	0	20	0		Kingstonian	Jun 1998	
Cunningham	D	Dave	W		1953		Southend United	Jun 1977	18 + 5	3	4 + 1	0		Aston Villa	Dec 1978	
Cureton	J	Jamie	F		1975		Queens Park Rangers	Jul 2005	22 + 8	7	0 + 2	0		Colchester United	Jun 2006	
Cutts	G W	George	G		1870	1935	Mexborough Town	Sep 1899	2	0			C	Port Vale (trainer)	cs 1902	
Dangerfield	D A	Dave	W		1951		Apprentice	Aug 1969	16 + 4	0	1 + 1	0		Cheltenham Town	cs 1972	
Daniel	C H	Cyril	F		1899	1964	Swindon Victoria	Nov 1922	70	30	1	0		Bath City	Jun 1929	71
Daniels	A G	Arthur	F		1872	1958	Reading	Jan 1897	6	1			A	Trowbridge Town	cs 1897	
Darcy	A J	Arnold	W		1933		Wigan Athletic	Nov 1956	223	29	15	3		Cheltenham Town	Jul 1964	
Darras	F G A	Frederic	D		1966		SC Bastia *(Fr)*	Aug 1996	42 + 7	0	6	0		AS Red Star 93 *(Fr)*	Jan 1998	
Davenport	W	Billy	FB		1876	1908	Stoke	cs 1901	5	0				Retired (injury)	cs 1902	
Davies	A S	Bertie	W		1894	1976	Juniors	cs 1912	0		2	0		Middlesbrough	cs 1914	68
				Returned from			*Middlesbrough*	*Apr 1916*	*2*	*2*			*G*			
				Returned from			Middlesbrough	Jun 1919	258	30	20	4		Luton Town	Aug 1927	
Davies	G M	Gareth	D		1973		Reading	Mar 1999	24 + 2	0	1 + 1	0		Chippenham Town	Feb 2002	
Davies	J C	John	W				Aberaman	cs 1903	1	0				Released	Nov 1903	
Davies	J W	Jimmy	WH				West Bromwich Albion	cs 1895	11	1	3	0		Wolverton L & N W Railway	cs 1896	
Davies	T O	Tommy	W		1882	1967	Swindon Thistle	Sep 1900	93	7	14	7		Nottingham Forest	cs 1903	
Davis	*J R W*	*Jimmy*	*M*		*1982*	*2003*	*Manchester United*	*Aug 2002*	*10 + 3*	*2*	*2*	*1*	*L*			
Davis	S S	Sol	FB		1979		Trainee	May 1998	99 + 17	0	13 + 1	0		Luton Town	Aug 2002	
Dawe	E R	Eddie	WH		1899	1983	Swindon Corinthians	Jul 1921	33	2	2	0		Weymouth	cs 1924	
Dawson	O J	Owen	U		1943		Portsmouth	Jun 1962	196 + 8	4	26 + 3	0		Folkestone Town	Dec 1971	
Dawson	T	Tommy	IF		1915	1972	Brentford	May 1948	65	15	3	0		Chippenham Town	Apr 1950	119
Day	A	Alf	WH	W	1907	1997	Tranmere Rovers	Jun 1939	1	0	29	1		Retired	cs 1940	
Day	W G	Will	WH		1879	1960	Swindon Town Workmens FC	Oct 1900	14	0	1	0	A			
Dean	A	Alf	W		1877	1959	Bristol City	Jun 1905	43	13	2	0		Millwall	May 1906	
Dear	G A	Gerry	FB		1937		RAPC Devizes	Jul 1956	4	0				Gloucester City	May 1959	
Dearden	*K C*	*Kevin*	*G*		*1970*		*Tottenham Hotspur*	*Mar 1990*	*1*	*0*			*L*			
Dempsey	*M J*	*Mark*	*M*		*1964*		*Manchester United*	*Jan 1985*	*5*	*0*	*1*	*0*	*L*			

JIMMY CROSS

ARNOLD DARCY

SOL DAVIS

OWEN DAWSON

Surname	Initials	Known As	Pos	Intl	Born	Died	Previous Club	Signed	Lge Apps	Gls.	Other Apps	Gls.		Went to	When Left	Pics
Dent	F	Fred	F		1896	1983	Norwich City	May 1929	21	6				Luton Town	Jul 1930	
Denyer	A E C	Bertie	W		1893	1969	West Ham United	Apr 1914	341	51	32	8		Evesham United	cs 1930	54
Denyer	A F T	Bertie	W		1924		Garrards Athletic	Sep 1945	7	1	11	1		Cardiff City	May 1948	
Derrick	A E	Albert	F		1908	1975	Newport County	Jan 1946	1	0	17	6		Ebbw Vale	Aug 1947	
Desmeules	R L	Rod	WH		1948		Hungerford Town	Oct 1966	4	0				Northampton Town	cs 1970	
Devlin	T	Tom	IF		1903	1979	Liverpool	Jun 1928	1	0				Brooklyn Wanderers *(US)*	May 1929	
Diagouraga	*T*	*Toumani*	*M*		*1987*		*Watford*	*Mar 2006*	*5 + 3*	*0*			*L*			
Dibsdall	A G	Arthur	FB/HB		1876	1952	Swindon Baptists	cs 1894	23	0	6	0	A			
Dibsdall	G J	Goff	FB		1878	1960	Swindon Thistle	cs 1901	25	0	3	0	A	Shepherds Bush	Nov 1902	
					Returned from		Whitehead Torpedo Works	cs 1906	6	0			A			
Dickenson	W	Wally	FB		1895	1983	The Wednesday	Jun 1923	230	20	22	1		Retired	cs 1930	79
Digby	F C	Fraser	G		1967		Manchester United	Sep 1986	417	0	87 + 1	0		Crystal Palace	Jun 1998	205
Dillon	*M L*	*Mike*	*M*		*1952*		*Tottenham Hotspur*	*Mar 1975*	*7 + 2*	*0*			*L*			
Dixon	J	Jim	G				Bournville	cs 1903	4	0	2	0		Leeds City	Oct 1905	
Dixon	W E	Will	M		1950		Colchester United	Sep 1973	134 + 6	9	24 + 1	3		Aldershot	Jul 1977	
Dodd	A		CF					Dec 1894	1	0			A			
Donaldson	B L	Brian	W		1936		Chelsea	Sep 1957	1	0				Hastings United	cs 1958	
Done	C	Charlie	WH		1868	1952	Kings Own Royal Lancs Regiment	Dec 1894	6	0	1	0	A			
Dornan	P	Peter	M		1953		Linfield	Feb 1979	0 + 1	0				Linfield	Jul 1979	
Dowdall	C	Charlie	IF	EI	1898		Barnsley	May 1929	8	2				Cork Bohemians	cs 1930	
Down	D F	Dickie	F		1948		Bristol Rovers	Oct 1969	1 + 1	0				Trowbridge Town	Jun 1971	
Downie	A L B	Alec	HB		1876	1953	Bristol City	Aug 1900	85	3	5	0		Manchester United	Oct 1902	25
Downsborough	P	Peter	G		1943		Halifax Town	Aug 1965	274	0	46	0		Bradford City	Nov 1973	165
Dransfield	E	Ted	FB		1906	1986	Birmingham	May 1931	64	3	4	0		Southampton	Aug 1933	
Dryden	J G	Jackie	W		1919	2004	Hylton Colliery	May 1947	21	3	6	1		Leyton Orient	Jun 1948	
Dryden	*R A*	*Richard*	*D*		*1969*		*Southampton*	*Nov 2000*	*7*	*0*	*1*	*0*	*L*			
Drysdale	J	Jason	FB		1970		Newcastle United	Mar 1995	35 + 7	0	9 + 4	0		Northampton Town	Mar 1998	
Duckworth	T C	Tommy	FB		1908	2001	Bolton Wanderers	Jan 1934	124	0	13	0		Southport	Jun 1937	
Duke	D	David	D		1978		Sunderland	Aug 2000	181 + 23	7	26 + 5	1		Darlington	Jun 2005	
Dykes	D L	Daren	W		1981		Buckingham Town	Jul 2002	1 + 1	0	1 + 2	0		Buckingham Town	May 2003	

FRASER DIGBY

spent a month on loan at the County Ground during Town's Fourth Division championship winning season, but he was not signed on a permanent basis until December 1986, after a second loan. Fraser soon became Town's regular keeper - a position he held for the majority of his 12 years at the club. He eventually clocked up 505 appearances, second highest for a goalkeeper. Fraser saw the club rise from the Third Division to the top flight - where only injury prevented him making more than his 30 appearances. While with Town he also made five England under-21 appearances.

WILL DIXON

TED DRANSFIELD

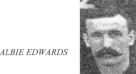

TOM DUCKWORTH

DAVID DUKE

ALBIE EDWARDS

TERRY ELWELL

Surname	Initials	Known As	Pos	Intl	Born	Died	Previous Club	Signed	Lge Apps	Gls.	Other Apps	Gls.		Went to	When Left	Pics
Earl	S J W	Stan	FB		1929		Leyton Orient	Nov 1956	23	0	2	0		Yeovil Town	Jan 1958	
East	K M G	Keith	CF		1944		Portsmouth	May 1964	43 + 2	21	5	7		Stockport County	Dec 1966	*274*
Eastoe	P R	Peter	CF		1953		Wolverhampton Wanderers	Nov 1973	91	43	17	7		Queens Park Rangers	Mar 1976	*171,183*
Easton	C	Craig	M		1979		Leyton Orient	Jun 2007	54 + 9	8	8 + 1	0		Under contract for 2009/10		
Eddleston	J	Joe	IF		1896	1959	Nelson	Aug 1926	203	64	16	2		Accrington Stanley	Jul 1932	*78*
Edds	E F	Ernie	W		1926		Plymouth Argyle	Jun 1955	3	0				Retired (injury)	May 1956	
Edds	G J	Gareth	D		1981		Nottingham Forest	Aug 2002	8 + 6	0	3 + 1	0		Bradford City	Jul 2003	
Edmonds	F H A	Fred	G		1915	2003	Swindon Rangers	cs 1935	8	0				Reading	cs 1937	
Edmunds	J T	Jim	IF			1951	Bishop Auckland	Jul 1895	1	1			T			
Edwards	A J	Albie	F		1876		Trowbridge Town	Dec 1895	13	2				Thames Ironworks	cs 1897	*above*
				Returned from			Devizes Town	cs 1900	3	0				Queens Park Rangers	Oct 1900	
				Returned from			Queens Park Rangers	cs 1901	45	10	5	2		Southall	cs 1903	
				Returned from			Southall	Sep 1905	2	0					cs 1906	
Edwards	R H	Bob	F		1931		Chelsea	Jul 1955	173	65	12	5		Norwich City	Dec 1959	*135*
Edwards	D S	Dai	IF		1916	1990	Ipswich Town	May 1946	3	1				Bath City	Jan 1948	
Edwards	J A	Jim	FB	W	1874	1939	Oswestry United	Apr 1897	1	0			T			
Edwards	N M	Nathan	M		1983		Trainee	Apr 2002	2 + 8	0	1	0		Chippenham Town	May 2003	
Edwards	P	Paul	W		1980		Altrincham	Aug 2001	14 + 6	0	2 + 1	1		Wrexham	Jun 2002	
Elkins	G	Gary	D		1966		Wimbledon	Sep 1996	19 + 4	1	3	0		AFC Wallingford	May 1998	
Elkins	E J	Ted	CH		1875	1941		cs 1896	0		1	0	A			
Elliott	*S T*	*Stuart*	*M*		*1977*		*Newcastle United*	*Feb 1998*	*1 + 1*	*0*			*L*			
Elwell	T T	Terry	FB		1926	2004	Swansea Town	Jul 1952	61	0	2	0		Lovells Athletic	Jul 1954	*above*
Emanuel	*W J*	*John*	*M*	*W*	*1948*		*Bristol City*	*Nov 1975*	*6*	*0*	*4*	*0*	*L*			
Emery	D K J	Don	U		1920	1993	Cardiff City	Jun 1937	69	3	36	9		Aberdeen	Jul 1948	
Emmanuel	J G	Gary	M		1954		Bristol Rovers	Jul 1981	109 + 2	8	20	1		Newport County	Jun 1984	
Endersby	S A G	Scott	G		1962		Tranmere Rovers	May 1983	85	0	15	0		Carlisle United	Nov 1985	
Ephgrave	G A	George	G		1918	2004	Aston Villa	Mar 1939	1	0				Southampton	Sep 1946	
Erentz	H B	Harry	FB		1874	1947	Tottenham Hotspur	Dec 1904	16	0				Retired (injury)	cs 1905	
Evans	P S	Paul	M	W	1974		Nottingham Forest	Jul 2006	11 + 4	3	2	1		Bradford City	Jul 2007	
Evans	R K	Rhys	G		1982		Chelsea	Jul 2003	118	0	9 + 1	0		Blackpool	Jul 2006	
Evans	A	Tony	M		1954		Wolverhampton Wanderers	Aug 1985	8 + 2	0	2 + 2	0		Walsall	May 1986	
Fagan	M W	Paddy	FB		1880	1962	Globe Swifts	cs 1900	27	0	2	0	A			
Fallon	R M	Rory	F		1982		Barnsley	Nov 2003	43 + 32	21	8 + 6	4		Swansea City	Jan 2006	*239*
Farr	B S	Brian	WH		1930		Swindon Victoria	Aug 1951	11	0				Bath City	Jul 1956	
Farr	C J	Craig	G		1984		Trainee	Apr 2002	2	0	1 + 1	0		Chippenham Town	Aug 2003	
Farr	I S	Ian	F		1958		Apprentice	Dec 1975	0 + 1	0				Clanfield	Jun 1976	

DON EMERY

GARY EMMANUEL

SCOTT ENDERSBY

RHYS EVANS

Surname	Initials	Known As	Pos	Intl	Born	Died	Previous Club	Signed	Lge Apps	Gls.	Other Apps	Gls.		Went to	When Left	Pics
Fellows	H A J	Haddon	FB		1892	1950	Swindon Olympic	Apr 1913	0		1	0	A			
Fenn	*N M C*	*Neale*	*F*		*1977*		*Tottenham Hotspur*	*Nov 1998*	*4*	*0*			*L*			
Fenton	F	Freddy	W		1879	1958	Bristol City	May 1907	56	10	3	0		Croydon Common	cs 1910	*11*
Fenwick	T W	Terry	D	E	1959		Tottenham Hotspur	Sep 1993	25 + 3	0	5	0		Portsmouth (Manager)	Feb 1995	
Ferguson	A S B	Alex	G		1903	1974	Bristol City	Sep 1947	7	0				Milford United	1948	*117*
Findlay	J W	Jake	G		1954		Luton Town	Jul 1985	4	0	2	0		Portsmouth	Sep 1985	
Finney	S K	Steve	F		1973		Manchester City	Jun 1995	47 + 26	17	10 + 7	4		Carlisle United	Jul 1998	
Finnigan	R P	Dick	G		1904	1979	Stockport County	Sep 1935	0		1	0	T	Winsford United	Jun 1936	
Finnigan	A	Tony	FB		1962		Hull City	Mar 1991	2 + 1	0				*(Hong Kong)*	May 1991	
Fiocca	P	Paul	M		1955		Apprentice	Jan 1973	1	0				Bath City	May 1974	
Fisher	F	Fred	F		1910	1955	Mansfield Town	May 1933	46	16	5	2		Gillingham	Jul 1935	*89*
Fjørtoft	JA	Jan-Åge	F	N	1967		SK Rapid Wien *(At)*	Jul 1993	62 + 10	27	13 + 2	11		Middlesbrough	Mar 1995	*274*
Flanagan	A	Alan	G		1980		Trainee	Mar 1999	0 + 1	0				Released	May 2000	
Flanagan	W J A	Bud	W		1908	1993	Bath City	Oct 1933	41	2	4	1		Trowbridge Town	Sep 1935	
Fleming	H J	Harold	IF	E	1887	1955	Swindon Amateurs	Oct 1907	293	183	44	23		Retired	May 1924	*11,38*
Flood	C W	Charlie	IF		1896	1978	York City	Feb 1927	8	3				Retired	cs 1928	
Flowers	*T D*	*Tim*	*G*	*E*	*1967*		*Southampton*	*Mar 1987*	*2*	*0*			*L*			
			Returned from				*Southampton*	*Nov 1987*	*5*	*0*			*L*			
Foley	*D J*	*Dominic*	*F*	*EI*	*1976*		*Watford*	*Jan 2002*	*5 + 2*	*1*			*L*			
Foley	S	Steve	M		1962		Sheffield United	Jun 1987	142 + 9	23	37 + 2	6		Stoke City	Jan 1992	*223*
Ford	A C	Andy	FB		1954		Southend United	Aug 1977	92 + 6	1	23 + 2	0		Gillingham	Jul 1980	
Fountain	J	Jack	WH		1932		Sheffield United	Jan 1957	81	2	4	0		York City	Aug 1960	
Fowler	A	Alan	F		1911	1944	Leeds United	May 1934	173	67	50	34		Killed in Action	Jul 1944	*61,90*
Fox	G R	Geoff	FB		1925	1993	Bristol Rovers	Oct 1955	48	0	5	0		Pucklechurch	Nov 1956	*132*
Foxton	J D	Jack	WH		1921		Portsmouth	Sep 1948	49	0	1	0		Barry Town	Aug 1951	
France	J	Jack	WH		1913	1995	Stalybridge Celtic	Aug 1937	1	0				Bath City	Jul 1938	
Francis	C T	Cliff	IF		1915	1961	Leeds United	Jun 1938	44	16	15	3		Retired	cs 1946	
Franklin	*P L*	*Paul*	*CD*		*1963*		*Watford*	*Nov 1986*	*5*	*1*	*1*	*0*	*L*			
Frater	D T	Dai	IF		1911	1986	Pontypridd	Jan 1934	1	0				Cardiff City	Aug 1934	
French	G E	Graham	W		1945		Shrewsbury Town	Aug 1963	5	0	2	0		Watford	Aug 1964	
French	M J	Mickey	CF		1955		Brentford	Feb 1977	5 + 5	1	1	0		Doncaster Rovers	Jul 1978	
Fulbrook	G L	Gary	FB		1966		Apprentice	Jul 1984	0 + 1	0	1	0		Bath City	May 1985	
Fulton	R W	Bob	HB		1872	1952		cs 1887	11	0	10	0	A			
Fulton	J W	Jack	FB		1876	1947	Dean Park FC	Oct 1896	3	0	2	0		Trowbridge Town	cs 1897	
			Returned from				New Brighton Tower	Dec 1899	2	0				Swindon Thistle	cs 1900	
Furniss	S	Sam	WH		1895	1977	Bristol Rovers	Jun 1924	36	1				Boston Town	Oct 1927	

ANDY FORD

JACK FOUNTAIN

CLIFF FRANCIS

Surname	Initials	Known As	Pos	Intl	Born	Died	Previous Club	Signed	Lge Apps	Gls.	Other Apps	Gls.		Went to	When Left	Pics
Gabriel	J	Jimmy	M	S	1940		AFC Bournemouth	Oct 1973	6	0			L			
Galvin	A	Tony	W	EI	1956		Sheffield Wednesday	Jul 1989	6 + 5	0	0 + 3	0		Newcastle United	Apr 1991	
Gardiner	M C	Mark	F		1966		Apprentice	Sep 1984	7 + 3	1	1 + 4	0		Torquay United	Feb 1987	
Gardner	A	Alec	F		1876		Small Heath	cs 1900	15	3	5	2		Released	Dec 1900	
Garrard	L E	Luke	M		1985		Tottenham Hotspur	Jul 2002	8 + 3	0	4 + 2	0		Bishops Stortford	Apr 2005	
Gauld	J	Jimmy	F		1931	2004	Plymouth Argyle	Aug 1959	40	14	1	0		St Johnstone	Sep 1960	
Geddis	D	David	F		1958		Shrewsbury Town	Oct 1988	8 + 2	3	4	0		Darlington	Mar 1990	
Gemmell	M	Matt	IF		1931		Portsmouth	Oct 1954	8	2	1	0		Berwick Rangers	cs 1955	
Gibbs	A M	Alan	IF		1934		Cardiff City	May 1956	16	5	1	0		Headington United	Jul 1957	
Gibson	D J	David	W		1931		Everton	Nov 1954	70	6	6	1		Headington United	Jul 1957	
Gibson	S J	Simon	CD		1964		Chelsea	Oct 1983	29 + 2	3	10	2		Preston North End	Dec 1984	
Gibson	T B	Terry	F		1962		Wimbledon	Mar 1992	8 + 1	1			L			
Gilchrist	P A	Paul	F		1951		Portsmouth	Aug 1978	10 + 7	6	5	2		Hereford United	Mar 1980	
Giles	C	Charlie	FB		1888	1953	1st Wilts Regiment	cs 1912	39	0	3	0	A			
Giles	J A	Jimmy	CH		1946		Kidlington	Mar 1965	12 + 1	0	3 + 1	0		Aldershot	Oct 1968	
Giles	S	Sid	G		1909	1938	Cowley	Aug 1931	20	0	1	0	A	Purton	Jun 1933	
Gill	C J P	Colin	G		1933		Garrards Athletic	Oct 1955	1	0				Frome Town	cs 1956	
Gill	J E	Jimmy	FB		1883		Barnsley	Jun 1905	101	0	7	0		Bury	May 1908	
Gilligan	A A	Gus	F		1959		Apprentice	Aug 1977	3 + 1	0				Trowbridge Town	Feb 1979	
Gilligan	J M	Jimmy	F		1964		Grimsby Town	Jun 1986	13 + 4	5	4 + 1	1		Lincoln City	Mar 1987	
Gilligan	J	John	M		1957		Apprentice	Oct 1975	2 + 4	0				Sligo Rovers	cs 1977	
Girvan	H McD	Hector	FB		1899	1969	Reading	May 1929	148	0	8	0		Margate	Aug 1933	83
Gittens	J A	Jon	D		1964		Southampton	Jul 1987	124 + 2	6	37 + 2	1		Southampton	Mar 1991	226
Given	S J J	Shay	G	EI	1976		Blackburn Rovers	Aug 1995	5	0			L			
Glass	J R	Jimmy	G		1973		AFC Bournemouth	Jun 1998	11	0	1	0		Cambridge United	Jan 2000	
Goddard	G W	George	W		1876	1954	Even Swindon United	Aug 1901	3	0			A			
Goddard	H J	Howard	F		1957		AFC Bournemouth	May 1976	10 + 3	0	2 + 1	1		Newport County	Aug 1977	
Godfrey	T	Tom	HB		1904	1983	Walsall	Jun 1931	49	0	1	0		Folkestone Town	Aug 1933	
Godwin	R G	Bobby	IF		1928		Old Headlandians	Aug 1945	0		6	3	A			
					Returned from		Mansfield Town	Sep 1951	2	0				Chippenham United	Jul 1952	
Gooden	T M	Ty	M		1972		Wycombe Wanderers	Dec 1993	118 + 28	9	15 + 3	1		Gillingham	Jan 2000	
Gordon	C K	Colin	CF		1963		Oldbury United	Nov 1984	70 + 2	33	11	0		Wimbledon	Jul 1986	
Gough	A M	Tony	M		1940		Bath City	Jul 1970	24 + 1	2	6 + 3	1		Hereford United	Jul 1971	175
Graham	M A	Mike	D		1959		Bolton Wanderers	Jul 1981	141	1	22	0		Mansfield Town	Jul 1985	
Grant	A J	Tony	M		1974		Everton	Jan 1996	3	1			L			

JIMMY GILL

TY GOODEN

COLIN GORDON

MIKE GRAHAM

Surname	Initials	Known As	Pos	Intl	Born	Died	Previous Club	Signed	Lge Apps	Gls.	Other Apps	Gls.	Went to	When Left	Pics
Gray	*A A*	*Andy*	*M*	*E*	*1964*		*Tottenham Hotspur*	*Dec 1992*	*3*	*0*			*L*		
Gray	G J P	George	WH		1925	1995	Grimsby Town	Jul 1951	45	0	8	0	Darlington	Jul 1953	
Gray	N R	Nigel	D		1956		Orient	Jul 1983	33	0	4	0	Enfield	May 1985	
Gray	*W W*	*Wayne*	*F*		*1980*		*Wimbledon*	*Mar 2000*	*8 + 4*	*2*			*L*		
Grazioli	G S L	Guiliano	F		1975		Peterborough United	Jul 1999	45 + 33	17	5 + 5	0	Bristol Rovers	Jun 2002	
Greaves	E	Ted	WH		1903		Swansea Town	Aug 1923	1	0			Bridgend Town	Sep 1925	
Green	A W	Arthur	CF	W	1881	1966	Ebbw Vale	Mar 1900	3	0			T Aston Villa	Aug 1900	
Green	T A	Tommy	F		1883	1967	Liverpool	cs 1903	24	2	3	2	Stockport County	Sep 1904	
Greenwell	J W	Jack	CH		1901		Norwich City	May 1931	15	1			Bath City	Oct 1932	
Greenwood	R T	Roy	F		1952		Derby County	Feb 1980	49 + 4	7	6	0	Huddersfield Town	Jul 1982	
Greer	*G*	*Gordon*	*D*		*1980*		*Doncaster Rovers*	*Jan 2009*	*19*	*1*			*L*		
Griemink	B J	Bart	G		1972		Peterborough United	Feb 2000	122 + 2	0	20	0	Southend United	May 2004	
Griffin	W E	Billy	CF		1873	1948	Swindon Wanderers	Feb 1895	1	0			A		
Griffin	C J	Charlie	F		1979		Chippenham Town	Jan 1999	8 + 20	2	0 + 2	0	Woking	Nov 2000	
Grimes	*A J*	*Ashley*	*F*		*1986*		*Manchester City*	*Mar 2007*	*0 + 4*	*0*			*L*		
Gulliver	J	Jeff	FB		1915	1999	Reading	Aug 1951	11	0	2	0	Guildford City	Nov 1952	
Gunson	J G	Gordon	W		1904	1991	Liverpool	Jun 1934	31	8	5	2	Wrexham	May 1935	
Gurney	A R	Andy	D		1974		Reading	Jul 2001	134	20	10 + 1	2	Swansea City	Sep 2004	
			Returned from				Swansea City	Aug 2005	24 + 4	1	3	1	Clevedon Town	Nov 2006	
Guthrie	C W	Chris	CF		1953		Sheffield United	Jul 1977	44 + 1	12	11	4	Fulham	Sep 1978	*189*
Guyan	G W	George	F		1901	1984	Exeter City	Jun 1930	2	0			Rochdale	Aug 1931	
Haddleton	A	Arthur	IF		1910	1971	Fulham	Jun 1933	7	0	1	0	Walsall	Jul 1934	
Haffey	F	Frank	G	S	1938		Glasgow Celtic	Oct 1964	4	0			Budapest St George *(Au)*	Jun 1965	
Hall	D R	Derek	M		1965		Torquay United	Jul 1985	9 + 1	0	3 + 1	0	Southend United	Aug 1986	
Hall	G D	Gareth	D	W	1969		Sunderland	May 1998	80 + 7	3	9 + 1	0	Havant & Waterloooville	Jul 2001	
Hall	G	George	WH		1880	1937	Swindon Thistle	Sep 1899	2	0			A		
Hallam	J	Jack	W	W	1869	1949	Small Heath	Aug 1896	14	4	2	1	Trowbridge Town	cs 1897	
			Returned from				Trowbridge Town	cs 1898	2	1			Retired	cs 1899	
Hallett	T R	Tom	HB		1939		Leeds United	Jul 1963	26	0	1	0	Bradford City	May 1966	
Halliday	K J	Kevin	D		1983		Trainee	Apr 2002	0		0 + 2	0	Worcester City	May 2003	
Hames	A	Alf	F			1940	Long Eaton Rangers	Aug 1895	5	1	3	2	Released	Dec 1895	
Hamilton	B	Bryan	M	NI	1946		Millwall	Nov 1978	19 + 5	1	1 + 2	0	Tranmere Rovers	Sep 1980	
Hamlin	C	Cliff	HB		1874	1938		1893	2	1	1	0	A		
Hamlin	S	Sid	HB		1874	1938	Swindon Villa	1894	1	0			A		
Hammond	N D	Nicky	G		1967		Arsenal	Jun 1987	65 + 2	0	26	0	Plymouth Argyle	Aug 1995	
Hammond	N	Norman	HB		1910	1975	Sunderland	May 1931	2	0			Denaby Welfare United	cs 1932	

ANDY GURNEY

GARETH HALL

NICKY HAMMOND

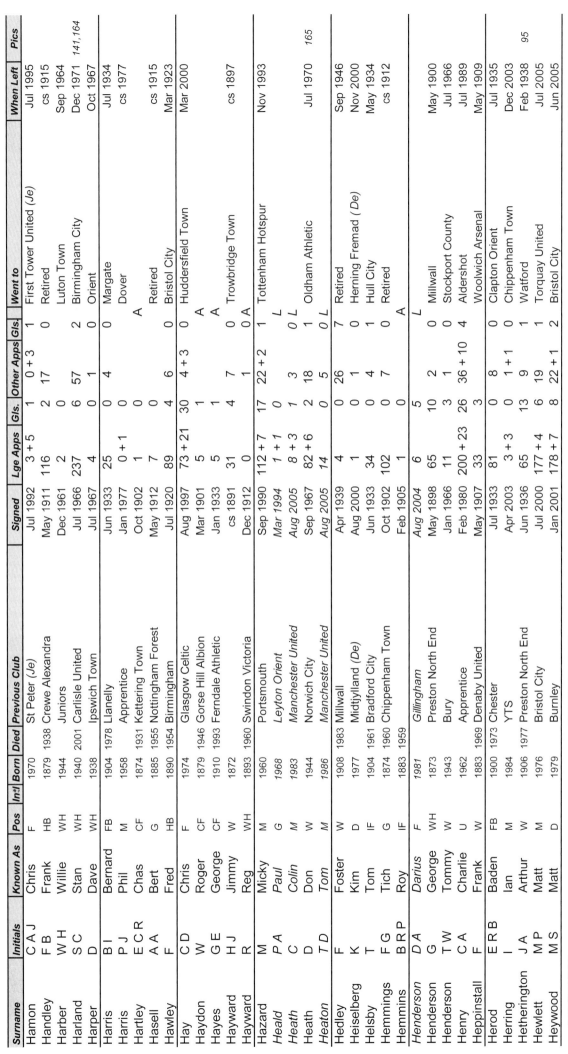

Surname	Initials	Known As	Pos	Int'l	Born	Died	Previous Club	Signed	Lge Apps	Gls.	Other Apps	Gls.	Went to	When Left	Pics
Hamon	C A J	Chris	F		1970		St Peter *(Je)*	Jul 1992	3 + 5	1	0 + 3	1	First Tower United *(Je)*	Jul 1995	
Handley	F B	Frank	HB		1879	1938	Crewe Alexandra	May 1911	116	2	17	0	Retired	cs 1915	
Harber	W H	Willie	WH		1944		Juniors	Dec 1961	2	0			Luton Town	Sep 1964	
Harland	S C	Stan	WH		1940	2001	Carlisle United	Jul 1966	237	6	57	2	Birmingham City	Dec 1971	*141,164*
Harper	D	Dave	WH		1938		Ipswich Town	Jul 1967	4	0	1	0	Orient	Oct 1967	
Harris	B I	Bernard	FB		1904	1978	Llanelly	Jun 1933	25	0	4	0	Margate	Jul 1934	
Harris	P J	Phil	M		1958		Apprentice	Jan 1977	0 + 1	0			Dover	cs 1977	
Hartley	E C R	Chas	CF		1874	1931	Kettering Town	Oct 1902	1	0			A		
Hasell	A A	Bert	G		1885	1955	Nottingham Forest	May 1912	7	0			Retired	cs 1915	
Hawley	F	Fred	HB		1890	1954	Birmingham	Jul 1920	89	4	6	0	Bristol City	Mar 1923	
Hay	C D	Chris	F		1974		Glasgow Celtic	Aug 1997	73 + 21	30	4 + 3	0	Huddersfield Town	Mar 2000	
Haydon	W	Roger	CF		1879	1946	Gorse Hill Albion	Mar 1901	5	1			A		
Hayes	G E	George	CF		1910	1993	Ferndale Athletic	Jan 1933	5	1			A		
Hayward	H J	Jimmy	W		1872			cs 1891	31	4	7	0	Trowbridge Town	cs 1897	
Hayward	R	Reg	WH		1893	1960	Swindon Victoria	Dec 1912	0		1	0	A		
Hazard	M	Micky	M		1960		Portsmouth	Sep 1990	112 + 7	17	22 + 2	1	Tottenham Hotspur	Nov 1993	
Heald	*P A*	*Paul*	*G*		*1968*		*Leyton Orient*	*Mar 1994*	*1 + 1*	*0*			*L*		
Heath	*C*	*Colin*	*M*		*1983*		*Manchester United*	*Aug 2005*	*8 + 3*	*1*	*3*	*0*	*L*		
Heath	D	Don	W		1944		Norwich City	Sep 1967	82 + 6	2	18	1	Oldham Athletic	Jul 1970	*165*
Heaton	*T D*	*Tom*	*M*		*1986*		*Manchester United*	*Aug 2005*	*14*	*0*	*5*	*0*	*L*		
Hedley	F	Foster	W		1908	1983	Millwall	Apr 1939	4	0	26	7	Retired	Sep 1946	
Heiselberg	K	Kim	D		1977		Midtjylland *(De)*	Aug 2000	1	0	1	0	Herning Fremad *(De)*	Nov 2000	
Helsby	T	Tom	IF		1904	1961	Bradford City	Jun 1933	34	0	4	1	Hull City	May 1934	
Hemmings	F G	Tich	G		1874	1960	Chippenham Town	Oct 1902	102	0	7	0	Retired	cs 1912	
Hemmins	B R P	Roy	IF		1883	1959		Feb 1905	1	0			A		
Henderson	*D A*	*Darius*	*F*		*1981*		*Gillingham*	*Aug 2004*	*6*	*5*			*L*		
Henderson	G	George	WH		1873		Preston North End	May 1898	65	10	2	0	Millwall	May 1900	
Henderson	T W	Tommy	W		1943		Bury	Jan 1966	11	3	1	0	Stockport County	Jul 1966	
Henry	C A	Charlie	U		1962		Apprentice	Feb 1980	200 + 23	26	36 + 10	4	Aldershot	Jul 1989	
Heppinstall	F	Frank	W		1883	1969	Denaby United	May 1907	33	3			Woolwich Arsenal	May 1909	
Herod	E R B	Baden	FB		1900	1973	Chester	Jul 1933	81	0	8	0	Clapton Orient	Jul 1935	
Herring	I	Ian	M		1984		YTS	Apr 2003	3 + 3	0	1 + 1	0	Chippenham Town	Dec 2003	
Hetherington	J A	Arthur	W		1906	1977	Preston North End	Jun 1936	65	13	9	1	Watford	Feb 1938	*95*
Hewlett	M P	Matt	M		1976		Bristol City	Jul 2000	177 + 4	6	19	1	Torquay United	Jul 2005	
Heywood	M S	Matt	D		1979		Burnley	Jan 2001	178 + 7	8	22 + 1	2	Bristol City	Jun 2005	

FRANK HANDLEY

MICKY HAZARD

'TICH' HEMMINGS

MATT HEYWOOD

Surname	Initials	Known As	Pos	Intl	Born	Died	Previous Club	Signed	Lge Apps	Gls.	Other Apps	Gls.		Went to	When Left	Pics
Hicks	F	Freddy	WH		1891	1955		cs 1911	5	0	2	0		Doncaster Rovers	cs 1914	
Hicks	G W	George	W		1902	1954	Bristol Rovers	Aug 1933	4	0			T	Rotherham United	Nov 1933	
Hicks	L A G	Les	FB		1908	1980	Stratton St Phillips	Mar 1927	1	0			A			
Hicks	A J	Tony	G		1945		Apprentice	Sep 1962	51	0	13	0		Dauntsey	Aug 1967	
Higgins	J W	John	FB		1930		St Mirren	May 1959	28	0	1	0		Ayr United	May 1961	
Hill	C J	Charlie	IF		1918	1998	Queens Park Rangers	Sep 1950	4	0				Barry Town	Aug 1951	
Hill	A V W P	Percy	FB		1885	1940	Airdrieonians	Dec 1911	8	0				Weymouth	cs 1912	
Hilton	P B	Peter	FB		1929	1968	West Bromwich Albion	May 1953	50	0				Chippenham Town	Jul 1956	
Hindle	W	Billy	WH		1880		Rossendale United	May 1905	37	0	2	0		Nelson	cs 1906	
Hindmarsh	J W	Billy	FB		1919	1994	Portsmouth	Jul 1951	11	0				Spennymoor United	Aug 1952	
Hinton	W F W	Freddy	G		1895	1976	Juniors	Sep 1914	39	0	2	0		Bolton Wanderers	Aug 1920	
Hobson	A T	Alf	WH		1869	1939	Wilts Regiment	Feb 1895	5	0			A			
Hockaday	D	Dave	M		1957		Blackpool	Jun 1983	227 + 18	7	61 + 2	4		Hull City	Sep 1990	
Hoddle	G	Glenn	M	E	1957		Chelsea	Apr 1991	63 + 1	1	10 + 1	2		Chelsea (player-manager)	Jun 1993	*205,232*
Hogan	C	Con	F		1878	1909	Fulham	Nov 1903	13	5				St Helens Recreation	Jul 1904	
Hogan	J	Jimmy	F		1882	1974	Fulham	Jul 1908	9	9				Bolton Wanderers	Oct 1908	
Hogg	A	Adam	FB		1934		Airdrieonians	Jun 1956	1	0				Dumbarton	Sep 1957	
Holcroft	P I	Peter	M		1976		Everton	Nov 1996	2 + 1	0				Morecambe	Oct 1998	
Holgate	A B S	Ashan	F		1986		Youths	Jul 2006	2 + 7	0	1 + 2	0		Weston-Super-Mare	Aug 2007	
Holmes	*L D*	*Lee*	*W*		*1987*		*Derby County*	*Dec 2004*	*14 + 1*	*1*	*1*	*0*	*L*			
Holmes	W	Wally	FB		1877	1966	Preston North End	cs 1902	8	0				Released	cs 1903	
Holyhead	J	Joe	WH		1879		Burslem Port Vale	May 1905	14	0				Burslem Port Vale	Nov 1905	
Hooper	D R	Dean	W		1971		Hayes	Mar 1995	0 + 4	0	2 + 2	0		Hayes	Oct 1996	
Hooper	W	Wyn	W		1952		Newport County	Dec 1976	4 + 2	0				Aldershot	Jul 1977	
Hope	A J H	Alex	W		1924		Greenock Morton	Jun 1954	11	1				Guildford City	Jul 1955	
Hopewell	R	Bob	HB		1874	1947	Doncaster Rovers	Jul 1895	31	2	6	0		Released	cs 1897	
Horlock	K	Kevin	M	NI	1972		West Ham United	Aug 1992	151 + 12	22	32 + 4	4		Manchester City	Jan 1997	
Hornby	E J	Teddy	HB		1889	1965	Swindon Amateurs	cs 1909	1	0			A			
Horrocks	S	Stan	WH		1910	1993	West Bromwich Albion	May 1934	23	1				Calne & Harris United	cs 1936	
Horsfield	A	Arthur	CF		1946		Newcastle United	May 1969	107 + 1	42	24	12		Charlton Athletic	Jun 1972	*171,177*
Hoskins	J F	John	W		1931	2006	Southampton	Jul 1959	10	3	1	0		Cambridge United	Jul 1960	
Houldsworth	F C	Freddy	G		1911	1994	Army	Jun 1933	30	0	5	0		Stoke City	Apr 1935	
Howard	B R W	Brian	M		1983		Southampton	Jul 2003	49 + 21	9	11 + 2	1		Barnsley	Jul 2005	
Howarth	J	Jack	CF		1945		Chelsea	Oct 1964	2	0				Aldershot	Jul 1965	
Howe	S R	Bobby	M		1973		Nottingham Forest	Jan 1998	103 + 19	6	12 + 1	5		Havant & Waterloooville	Jul 2002	

TONY HICKS

KEVIN HORLOCK

BOBBY HOWE

TERRY HUBBARD

Surname	Initials	Known As	Pos	Intl	Born	Died	Previous Club	Signed	Lge Apps	Gls.	Other Apps	Gls.		Went to	When Left	Pics
Howell	H A	Harry	W		1877	1961	Swindon St Johns	Oct 1899	2	0			A			
Howell	R R	Ron	M		1949		Kettering Town	Jul 1972	22 + 3	1				Brighton & Hove Albion	Jul 1973	
Hubbard	T L	Terry	M		1950		Apprentice	Nov 1968	83 + 1	2	14	0		Greek Hellenic (*SA*)	Feb 1976	*above*
Hudson	G W	Garth	CH		1923		Portsmouth	Sep 1948	401	11	26	0		Retired (injury)	Feb 1960	*113*
Hughes	B D	Brian	M		1962		Apprentice	Jul 1980	67 + 3	4	8 + 2	0		Torquay United	Aug 1983	
Hughes	M C	Mark	M		1967		Apprentice	Jul 1985	0 + 1	0				Chippenham Town	Oct 1986	
Hughes	N S	Nicky	F		1968		Apprentice	cs 1986	0		0 + 1	0		Gloucester City	cs 1987	
Hulbert	R J	Robin	M		1980		Everton	Sep 1997	12 + 17	0	3 + 1	0		Bristol City	Feb 2000	
Humphreys	B	Brinley	HB		1901	1972	Swansea Town	Jun 1927	55	2	8	0		Retired	Jun 1930	
Hunt	R P	Ernie	IF		1943		Juniors	Mar 1960	214	82	23	6		Wolverhampton Wanderers	Sep 1965	*152*
Hunt	R G A	George	FB		1922	1987	Ferndale YC	Jan 1947	304	0	24	0		Reserve Team Trainer	cs 1958	
Hunt	P C	Paul	M		1970		Apprentice	Jul 1989	5 + 6	0	1 + 3	0		SK Brann *(No)*	Jul 1993	
Hunt	R R A	Ralph	F		1933	1964	Grimsby Town	Jun 1961	21	13	4	2		Port Vale	Dec 1961	
Hunter	*R R*	*Bob*	*W*		*1931*	*2002*	*Motherwell*	*Aug 1954*	*16*	*3*	*1*	*0*	*L*			
Huxford	C J	Colin	FB		1944		Chelsea	Nov 1962	1	0				Yiewsley	Apr 1964	
Ifil	J C	Jerel	D		1982		*Watford*	*Jan 2003*	*5 + 4*	*0*			*L*			
				Returned from			*Watford*	*Sep 2003*	*6*	*0*			*L*			
				Returned from			*Watford*	*Nov 2003*	*10*	*0*			*L*			
				Returned from			Watford	Jun 2004	172 + 9	3	21	2		Under contract for 2009/10		
Igoe	S G	Sammy	M		1975		Reading	Jul 2003	75 + 4	9	9 + 2	0		Millwall	Jul 2005	
Imrie	W N	Bill	HB	S	1908	1944	Swansea Town	Jul 1939	2	0				East Fife	Nov 1939	
Ince	P E C	Paul	M	E	1967		Wolverhampton Wanderers	Aug 2006	2 + 1	0				Macclesfield Town (Manager)	Oct 2006	
Ing	A A	Jack	WH		1887	1975	Swindon Victoria	cs 1913	19	1	9	0		Retired	May 1927	
Innes	R	Bob	HB		1875	1959	Brighton & Hove Albion	Jun 1906	32	0	1	0		Swindon Victoria	cs 1914	
Invincibile	D	Danny	F		1979		Marconi Stallions *(Au)*	Aug 2000	109 + 19	22	15 + 1	5		Kilmarnock	May 2003	
Ithell	W J	Jimmy	HB		1916	1986	Bolton Wanderers	May 1946	107	1	11	0		Boston United	Apr 1950	

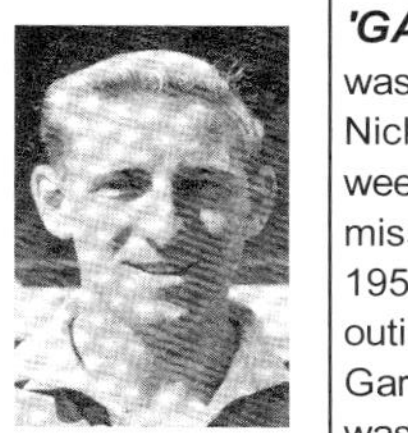

'GARTH' HUDSON

was a 'man mountain' of a centre-half at over 6'3" and weighing in at around 15 stones. Nicknamed Garth after a war-time comic strip hero, George arrived from Portsmouth a few weeks into the 1947/48 season, along with half-back colleague Jack Foxton. Garth did not miss a game for almost three years after Christmas 1949 - a run of 147 games. Early in the 1950/51 season, he deputised at centre-forward for Maurice Owen, scoring in two of his four outings there. And four goals in five games in the spring - two from the penalty spot - took Garth's total for the season to six. Injuries finally caught up with him in his 37th year and he was restricted to just five appearances in 1959/60.

GEORGE HUNT

was a winger for Ferndale Athletic before joining the Royal Artillery during the War. He signed amateur forms for Town and scored seven goals for the reserves prior to joining the professional ranks early in 1947. George made his League debut in September 1948, replacing Alec White at right-back - and all but one of his 328 appearances were in that position. George played in all nine F.A.Cup ties in 1951/52 and missed only six games in the following four seasons. He eventually lost his place to Johnny Neal in 1957, but was appointed reserve team trainer in the following summer. His first name was Reginald.

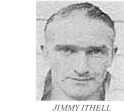

BRIAN HUGHES

JEREL IFIL

DANNY INVINCIBILE

JIMMY ITHELL

Surname	Initials	Known As	Pos	Intl	Born	Died	Previous Club	Signed	Lge Apps	Gls.	Other Apps	Gls.		Went to	When Left	Pics
Jack	R R	Rollo	IF		1902	1994	Yeovil & Petters United	Oct 1934	20	2				Yeovil & Petters United (asst.mgr)	cs 1935	
Jack	V	Vince	CH		1933	2006	Bury	Oct 1956	26	0	2	0		Accrington Stanley	Jul 1959	
Jackson	C	Cliff	F		1941		Juniors	Sep 1958	91	30	17	5		Plymouth Argyle	Jun 1963	
Jackson	*J*	*Johnnie*	*M*		*1982*		*Tottenham Hotspur*	*Sep 2002*	*12 + 1*	*1*	*4*	*1*	*L*			
Jackson	W P	Pat	WH		1924	1974	Army	Nov 1947	4	1				Tranmere Rovers	Apr 1951	
Jackson	R L	Roy	WH		1931		Pinehurst YC	Nov 1953	2	0				Trowbridge Town	cs 1957	
James	*K E A*	*Kevin*	*M*		*1980*		*Nottingham Forest*	*Mar 2007*	*0 + 2*	*0*			*L*			
Jarrett	*A O*	*Albert*	*WF*	SL	*1984*		*Brighton & Hove Albion*	*Jan 2006*	*2 + 4*	*0*			*L*			
Jeacock	A E	Ted	WH		1876	1951	Nottingham Forest	Sep 1901	1	0			A			
Jean-Francois	L	Lecs	D	H	1986		EA Guingamp *(Fr)*	Jan 2009	2 + 3	0				Under contract for 2009/10		
Jefferies	C E	Bill	IF		1906	1986	Swindon Corinthians	Mar 1927	5	4				Charlton Athletic	May 1928	
Jefferson	R W	Bob	W		1882	1966	Leeds City	May 1908	328	74	50	15		Bath City	cs 1922	*49,56*
Jenkins	S R	Steve	FB	W	1972		Peterborough United	Oct 2004	41 + 7	1	6	1		Worcester City	Jun 2006	
Jenkins	T E	Tom	WF		1947		Southampton	Nov 1972	89 + 11	4	11 + 3	1		Seattle Sounders	Mar 1976	
Jerrom	H J	Harry	WF		1871	1932	Swindon Wanderers	cs 1894	3	0			A			
Johnson	J H	Jack	IF		1897	1974	Bedminster Down Sports	Mar 1921	151	63	11	6		Queens Park Rangers	May 1927	*70*
Johnson	R	Reg	CH		1904	1984	Fulham	May 1929	11	0				Cradley Heath	Jul 1930	
Johnson	R	Roy	F		1933	2004	Chippenham United	Mar 1952	31	4	3	0		Chippenham Town	Jul 1956	
Johnson	S	Sam	WH		1901	1975	Stoke City	Jun 1926	35	1				York City	Aug 1929	
Johnston	J	Jimmy	WF		1882	1952	Third Lanark	May 1907	34	4	4	2		Third Lanark	May 1908	
Johnston	J C	Jimmy	WH		1923	2007	Reading	Mar 1953	75	0	3	0		Merthyr Tydfil	Jun 1955	*129*
Jones	A T	Albert	FB	W	1883	1963	Harborne Lynwood	Oct 1902	22	0	5	0		Nottingham Forest	Sep 1903	
Jones	A	Art	HB		1872		Bristol South End	1894	1	0			A			
Jones	G B	Benny	F		1907	1982	Hamilton Academical	May 1930	4	1				Rochdale	Aug 1931	
Jones	W J	Billy	HB	E	1876	1959	Tottenham Hotspur	May 1907	8	0				Retired (injury)	cs 1908	
Jones	R S	Bobby	W		1938		Northampton Town	Feb 1967	11	0				Bristol Rovers	Aug 1967	
Jones	C M N	Chris	F		1945		Manchester City	Jul 1968	49 + 19	18	4 + 7	2		Walsall	Feb 1972	*173*
Jones	D G	Dai	HB		1914	1988	Manchester United	Jun 1938	15	0	2	0		Cheltenham Town	cs 1945	
Jones	R L	Dick	F		1867	1951	Swindon Anchor	Feb 1885	27	7	23	16		Trowbridge Town	cs 1897	*10*
Jones	E M	Eddie	W		1914	1984	Bolton Wanderers	May 1936	126	17	62	17		Chippenham Town	Aug 1948	
Jones	A E J	Ernie	FB		1884		Wolverhampton Wanderers	May 1904	4	0	1	0		Wootton Bassett	cs 1907	
Jones	F G	Freddie	W		1938		Brighton & Hove Albion	Dec 1960	18	1				Grimsby Town	Jun 1961	
Jones	K B	Ken	FB		1937		Crystal Palace	Mar 1961	35	0	5	0		Colwyn Bay	cs 1962	
Jones	M	Mark	M		1961		Oxford United	Sep 1986	39 + 1	9	10	1		Cardiff City	Jun 1990	
Jones	M	Maurice	W				Oswestry Town	Mar 1896	9	4	3	1	A			

CLIFF JACKSON

TOM JENKINS

EDDIE JONES

MARK JONES

Surname	Initials	Known As	Pos	Intl	Born	Died	Previous Club	Signed	Lge Apps	Gls.	Other Apps	Gls.	Went to	When Left	Pics
Jones	W M	Morris	F		1919	1993	Port Vale	Nov 1947	94	48	7	4	Crystal Palace	May 1950	*118*
Jones	R W	Reg	CF		1915	2001	Wroughton	Feb 1936	1	1			A Cheltenham Town	Aug 1936	
Jones	R J	Roy	G		1942		RAF Brize Norton	Oct 1967	34	0	6	0	Johannesburg Rangers	Sep 1972	
Jones	T	Tom	M		1964		Aberdeen	Sep 1988	162 + 6	12	36 + 4	0	Reading	Jul 1992	
Joyce	B P	Ben	F		1989		Trainee	Feb 2008	1 + 3	1			Torquay United	Jul 2009	
Jutkiewicz	L I P	Lukas	F		1989		Southampton	Jul 2006	16 + 22	5	1 + 3	0	Everton	May 2007	
Kamara	C	Chris	M		1957		Portsmouth	Aug 1977	133 + 14	21	32 + 5	5	Portsmouth	Aug 1981	
				Returned from			Brentford	Aug 1985	86 + 1	6	26 + 1	0	Stoke City	Jun 1988	
Kanyuka	P E	Pat	D		1987		Queens Park Rangers	Jan 2008	20 + 1	1	3	0	*Offered terms for 2009/10*		
Kay	H	Harry	FB		1883	1954	Leeds City	May 1908	274	0	38	0	Retired	cs 1922	*47,56*
Kaye	G H	Harry	WH		1919	1992	Liverpool	May 1947	169	5	19	0	Retired (injury)	cs 1953	*120*
Keeling	H	Harry	IF		1906	1988	Torquay United	Jun 1931	24	7			Norwich City	May 1932	*85*
Kelly	J	Jimmy	CF		1933		Preston North End	Feb 1958	30	14	2	1	Walsall	Feb 1959	*142*
Kelly	J	John	M		1960		Chester City	Jun 1987	3 + 4	1	1	0	Oldham Athletic	Nov 1987	
Kemp	G C	George	IF		1876	1934	Southbroom	Mar 1895	2	1			A		
Kennedy	C E	Callum	D		1989		STFC Youths	Feb 2008	3 + 1	0	1	0	Under contract for 2009/10		
Kennedy	J J	Jim	CH		1883	1947	Tottenham Hotspur	Apr 1912	14	0	1	0	Norwich City	Jun 1913	*56*
Keogh	P J	Pat	G		1883		Reading	Nov 1901	7	0			A		
Kerslake	D	David	M/D		1966		Queens Park Rangers	Nov 1989	133 + 2	1	30	0	Leeds United	Mar 1993	
				Returned from			*Tottenham Hotspur*	*Nov 1996*	*8*	*0*			*L*		
				Returned from			Ipswich Town	Mar 1998	22 + 2	0			Canvey Island	May 1999	
Key	R M	Richard	G		1956		Brentford	Oct 1985	0		2	0	Brentford	Dec 1985	
Keyworth	K	Ken	F		1934	2000	Coventry City	Aug 1965	6	0	1	0	Retired (injury)	May 1966	
Kidd	J	Johnny	IF		1884	1927	Third Lanark	Jun 1906	44	7	2	0	Third Lanark	Jun 1908	
Kilcline	B	Brian	CH		1962		Newcastle United	Jan 1994	16 + 1	0	7	0	Mansfield Town	Dec 1995	
King	P G	Phil	FB		1967		Torquay United	Mar 1987	112 + 4	4	29	0	Sheffield Wednesday	Nov 1989	
				Returned from			Aston Villa	Mar 1997	5	0			Brighton & Hove Albion	Mar 1999	
Kirby	W	Billy	F		1882	1917	Oswaldtwistle Rovers	Aug 1902	28	6	5	5	West Ham United	cs 1903	*29*
				Returned from			West Ham United	May 1904	19	2	2	2	Portsmouth	May 1905	
Kirby	N R	Norman	W		1908	1977	Bury	Jun 1930	66	10	2	0	Distillery	Aug 1932	*82*
Kirkwood	D	Dan	F		1900	1977	Luton Town	Nov 1933	7	0	1	0	Retired	cs 1934	
Kirton	J W	Jack	W		1871	1939	Small Heath	May 1898	27	8	1	1	Sunderland	May 1899	*18*
				Returned from			Sunderland	Jul 1900	34	6	5	1	Millwall	Aug 1901	
Kuffour	*J O*	*Jo*	*F*		*1981*		*Arsenal*	*Aug 2001*	*4 + 7*	*2*	*2*	*0*	*L*		

TOM JONES

CHRIS KAMARA

DAVID KERSLAKE

PHIL KING

Surname	Initials	Known As	Pos	Intl	Born	Died	Previous Club	Signed	Lge Apps	Gls.	Other Apps	Gls.		Went to	When Left	Pics
Lamb	S	Sammy	W		1885	1960	Plymouth Argyle	May 1910	77	13	13	1		Millwall	Apr 1913	*49*
Lambert	K	Ken	IF		1928	2002	Gillingham	Jul 1953	30	5	1	0		Bradford City	Nov 1954	
Lambie	A	Alec	CH		1897	1963	Chester	Nov 1931	83	1	6	0		Belfast Distillery	cs 1934	
Langford	T S	Tommy	WH		1892	1965	Stalybridge Celtic	May 1920	43	0	4	0		Halifax Town	Jul 1922	
Langley	A E	Bert	IF		1890	1977		cs 1909	0		1	0	A			
Lapham	K J	Kyle	M		1986		Trainee	Jun 2005	2	0				Cirencester Town	Jun 2006	
Large	F	Frank	CF		1940	2003	Northampton Town	Mar 1964	17	4				Carlisle United	Sep 1964	
Lavery	J	Jack	IF		1882	1937	Leeds City	May 1908	40	16	7	1		South Shields	cs 1910	*41*
Lawless	C H J	Chris	WH		1869	1938	Eastleigh Athletic	1894	8	0	1	1	A	Eastleigh Athletic	cs 1896	
Lawley	G H	George	W		1903	1987	Sunderland	May 1931	27	4	1	0		Worcester City	Jun 1932	
Lawrence	S W	Sid	FB	W	1909	1949	Swansea Town	Jun 1939	1	0	11	1		Haverfordwest Athletic	cs 1940	
Lawton	J M	Jim	F		1942		Darlington	Sep 1965	11	3	2	1		Watford	Mar 1967	
Laycock	F W	Fred	IF		1897	1989	York City	May 1931	16	2	1	0		Derry City	Jul 1933	
Layne	D R	Bronco	CF		1939		Rotherham United	Jun 1959	41	28	5	7		Bradford City	Dec 1960	*144*
Lean	W L F	Louis	F		1879	1951	Third Lanark	cs 1903	53	11	2	2		Third Lanark	cs 1905	*31*
			Returned from				Ayr Parkhouse	Jun 1906	17	0				Ayr Parkhouse	Jun 1907	
Lee	J L	Jack	F		1889	1951	Swindon Victoria	cs 1912	4	0	5	3	A			
Lee	J	Jimmy	FB		1926	2001	Leyton Orient	Nov 1956	35	0	2	0		Hereford United	Jul 1959	
Lees	A A	Andrew	WH		1896		Aberdeen	Jul 1922	1	0				St Bernards	Feb 1923	
Legg	R D	Richard	F		1952		Chippenham Town	Mar 1971	13 + 7	3	3	2		Bath City	May 1974	
Leggett	P R	Peter	W		1943		Weymouth	May 1962	15	1	2	0		Brighton & Hove Albion	Jul 1965	
Leighfield	W J	Billy	G		1876	1944	Swindon Thistle	1895	2	0	1	0	A			
Leitch	D S	Scott	M		1969		Heart of Midlothian	Mar 1996	119 + 3	1	11	2		Motherwell	Jun 2000	
Leslie	M H	Maurice	FB		1923		H M Forces	Jan 1947	1	0			A			
Lewis	*K J*	*Junior*	*D*		*1973*		*Leicester City*	*Mar 2003*	*9*	*0*			*L*			
			Returned from				*Leicester City*	*Oct 2003*	*4*	*0*			*L*			
Lewis	R	Russell	D		1956		Bridgend Town	Oct 1976	175 + 6	7	33 + 2	2		Northampton Town	Aug 1983	
Lewis	T P	Tom	G		1878	1966	Swindon Victoria	1902	1	0	1	0	A			
Lightbourne	*K L*	*Kyle*	*F*	*B*	*1968*		*Stoke City*	*Jan 2001*	*2*	*0*			*L*			
Ling	A S	Archie	G		1881	1943	Leicester Fosse	May 1905	156	0	7	0		Brentford	cs 1909	
Ling	M	Martin	M		1966		Exeter City	Jul 1986	2	0	1 + 1	0		Southend United	Oct 1986	
			Returned from				Southend United	May 1991	132 + 18	10	33 + 3	3		Leyton Orient	Jul 1996	
Linton	*D M*	*Des*	*D*		*1971*		*Peterborough United*	*Mar 1999*	*7 + 1*	*0*			*L*			
Little	T	Tom	F		1872		Luton Town	May 1898	29	4	1	0		Barnsley	Aug 1899	

SCOTT LEITCH

RUSSELL LEWIS

ARCHIE LING

MARTIN LING

Surname	Initials	Known As	Pos	Intl	Born	Died	Previous Club	Signed	Lge Apps	Gls.	Other Apps	Gls.		Went to	When Left	Pics
Lloyd	A E	Bert	WH		1876	1951	Swindon Victoria	1900	1	0			A			
Lloyd	W L	Billy	WH		1915	1978	Milford Haven Town	Aug 1939	107	2	27	0		Barry Town	Aug 1951	
Lochhead	M	Matty	HB		1884	1964	St Mirren	Jun 1908	9	0				Manchester City	May 1909	
				Returned from			Beith Athletic	Feb 1912	50	1	5	0		Bath City	cs 1920	
Logan	N	Neil	U		1875	1949	Sheffield United	May 1898	133	5	12	0		Blackburn Rovers	Jun 1902	
				Returned from			Blackburn Rovers	cs 1903	64	1	5	0		Retired	cs 1906	
Lonergan	*A*	*Andy*	*G*		*1983*		*Preston North End*	*Nov 2006*	*1*	*0*			*L*			
Long	E J	Teddy	W		1888	1954	St Louis *(US)*	Aug 1913	2	2				Trowbridge Town	cs 1914	
Lorenzo	N G	Nestor	M	Ar	1966		AS Bari *(It)*	Nov 1990	20 + 4	2	3	0		San Lorenzo *(Ar)*	May 1992	
Lovesey	W S	Bill	HB		1922	1994	North Leaze Athletic	Jul 1945	4	0	23	0	A	Trowbridge Town	cs 1947	
Low	D	Dave	WH		1900	1971	Blackburn Rovers	Jun 1927	148	1	14	0		Crook Town	Aug 1933	
Lowe	J	Johnny	W		1888	1975	Denaby United	Apr 1909	1	0			T			
Lowe	H	Harry	FB		1907	1975	Preston North End	Jun 1939	3	0				Southport	cs 1940	
Lowes	B T	Barry	W		1939		Coventry City	Aug 1967	2	0				Released	cs 1969	
Lowry	S H	Sid	F		1912	1982	Swansea Town	Jun 1935	30	14	6	0		Newport County	Jun 1936	
Lucas	W H	Billy	IF	W	1918	1998	Wolverhampton Wanderers	May 1937	144	32	50	16		Swansea Town	Mar 1948	
Lunn	H	Harry	W		1925	1980	Portsmouth	May 1948	196	29	19	1		Bedford Town	Jul 1954	
Lyon	H H S B C	Bertie	F		1875	1927	Brighton & Hove Albion	May 1905	50	12	2	2		Carlisle United	May 1906	
				Returned from			Carlisle United	May 1907	14	1	3	0		Blackpool	May 1908	
Lyons	M C	Mike	FB		1932		Bournemouth & Boscombe Athletic	Oct 1959	2	0				Yeovil Town	Jun 1960	
Mabberley	I	Ivor	W		1889	1951	Swindon Victoria	1910	2	0	3	2		Yoker Athletic	Sep 1912	
McAlister	T G	Tom	G		1952		Blackpool	May 1980	1	0				West Ham United	May 1981	
McAreavey	P	Paul	M		1980		Trainee	Jul 1999	10 + 14	1	2 + 1	0		Portadown	Apr 2002	
McAvennie	*F*	*Frank*	*F*	*S*	*1959*		*Glasgow Celtic*	*Feb 1994*	*3 + 4*	*0*			*L*			
McCammon	*M J*	*Mark*	*F*		*1978*		*Charlton Athletic*	*Jan 2000*	*4*	*0*			*L*			
McCarthy	T T	Terry	FB		1916	1980	Queens Park Rangers	May 1935	0		1	0		Cheltenham Town	May 1936	
McCartney	J	Jimmy	W		1909	1976	Newcastle United	Jun 1929	37	4	3	0		Bath City	Aug 1931	
McClelland	W J	Johnny	IF		1930	2004	Stoke City	Jun 1954	14	1				Rochdale	Jun 1955	
McCulloch	A	Alex	F		1887	1962	Bradford Park Avenue	cs 1909	40	7	2	2		Coventry City	Oct 1912	56
McDermott	*N T*	*Neale*	*M*		*1985*		*Fulham*	*Aug 2005*	*9 + 4*	*2*	*2 + 1*	*0*	*L*			
McDonald	A	Alan	CD	NI	1963		Queens Park Rangers	May 1997	30 + 3	1	3	0		Reserve Team Manager	Jul 1999	
McDonald	G	Gordon	WH		1932	1995	Crystal Palace	Jul 1957	10	0	1	0		Headington United	cs 1958	
McDonald	R	Ronnie	FB		1912	1988	Kilmarnock	Aug 1934	0		1	0		Everton	Dec 1934	
McEleny	C	Charlie	WH		1873	1908	Aston Villa	May 1900	42	1	6	1		Brentford	Aug 1901	
McElhaney	R	Dick	F		1870	1930	Tottenham Hotspur	cs 1897	5	0				Released	Nov 1897	

NEIL LOGAN

DAVE LOW

BILLY LUCAS

HARRY LUNN

Surname	Initials	Known As	Pos	Intl	Born	Died	Previous Club	Signed	Lge Apps	Gls.	Other Apps	Gls.	Went to	When Left	Pics
McGovern	JP	Jon-Paul	M		1980		Milton Keynes Dons	Aug 2007	56 + 11	4	9 + 1	1	Under contract for 2009/10		
McGovern	M J	Mick	M		1951		Queens Park Rangers	Feb 1973	26 + 4	2	3	1	Hillingdon Borough	Aug 1975	
McHale	R	Ray	M		1950		Halifax Town	Sep 1976	171 + 2	32	43	10	Brighton & Hove Albion	May 1980	*189*
McHugh	F J	Frazer	MF		1981		Burton Joyce	Jan 1999	13 + 6	0	2 + 3	0	Bromsgrove Rovers	May 2001	
McKendrick	D	Dave	F		1879	1936	Even Swindon Thistle	1896	20	4			A		
McKinney	R	Richard	G		1979		Manchester City	Jul 2001	1	0			Colchester United	Apr 2002	
MacLaren	R	Ross	M		1962		Derby County	Jul 1988	195 + 2	9	47	3	Reserve Team Coach	Nov 1994	
McLaughlin	J	John	M/FB		1954		Colchester United	Dec 1973	199 + 3	8	36	0	Portsmouth	Jul 1979	
MacLean	H	Hugh	F		1952		West Bromwich Albion	Jul 1974	17 + 2	1	1	0	Dumbarton	Jul 1975	
McLoughlin	A F	Alan	M	EI	1967		Manchester United	Aug 1986	101 + 5	19	25 + 4	5	Southampton	Dec 1990	*205,225*
McMahon	S	Steve	M	E	1961		Manchester City	Dec 1994	38 + 4	0	7 + 2	0	Resigned as Manager	Sep 1998	*246*
McMaster	*J*	*Jamie*	*M*		*1982*		*Leeds United*	*Sep 2004*	*2 + 2*	*1*			*L*		
McNamee	A	Anthony	WF		1984		Watford	Jan 2008	48 + 14	2	3 + 1	0	Under contract for 2009/10		
McPhail	D D	Don	W		1911	1992	Nuneaton Town	Mar 1936	19	4	3	1	Dunfermline Athletic	Jul 1937	
McPhee	*C S I*	*Chris*	*F*		*1983*		*Brighton & Hove Albion*	*Mar 2006*	*6 + 2*	*0*			*L*		
McPherson	K	Ken	CF/CH		1927		New York Americans *(US)*	Aug 1961	107	3	14	3	Retired	Jul 1965	
McRobbie	A S	Allan	FB		1886	1967	Middlesbrough	Apr 1913	12	0	1	0	West Stanley	Jul 1914	
McShane	A	Tony	WH		1927		Plymouth Argyle	Jun 1955	41	0	5	0	Goole Town	Sep 1957	
Macari	L	Lou	M	S	1949		Manchester United	Jul 1984	33 + 3	3	6 + 1	1	West Ham United (Manager)	Jul 1989	*214*
Mackay	D C	Dave	D	S	1934		Derby County	May 1971	25 + 1	1	1	0	Nottingham Forest (Manager)	Nov 1972	*176*
Mackenzie	J A	John	CF		1915		Manchester United	Jul 1939	1	0			Army	1940	
Macklin	L J	Lloyd	F		1991		Youths	Feb 2008	0 + 2	0	0 + 1	0	Under contract for 2009/10		
Maconnachie	J S J	Jock	FB		1885	1956	Djurgaarden IF *(Sw)*	Aug 1920	55	3	2	0	Djurgaarden IF *(Sw)*	May 1922	*11*
			Returned from				Djurgaarden IF *(Sw)*	Dec 1922	1	0			Foleshill Great Heath	Jan 1924	
Maguire	J E	Teddy	W		1917	2000	Wolverhampton Wanderers	May 1947	28	4	3	0	Halifax Town	Sep 1948	
Major	W H	Harry	FB		1881	1957	GWR Athletic	cs 1901	22	0	4	0	A		
Mantell	W J	Will	HB		1873	1949	Cricklade Town	cs 1893	2	1	4	0	A		
Manuel	P E	Percy	WF		1909	1983	Oxford City	cs 1933	0		1	1	Stourbridge Town	cs 1934	
Marney	*D E*	*Dean*	*M*		*1984*		*Tottenham Hotspur*	*Dec 2002*	*8 + 1*	*0*			*L*		
Marshall	M A	Mark	WF		1986		Eastleigh	Aug 2008	0 + 12	0	1 + 2	0	Under contract for 2009/10		
Marshall	W	Billy	FB		1882		Denaby United	May 1908	35	0	5	0	Denaby United	May 1911	
Marshall	W F	Willie	F		1933		Bradford City	Feb 1959	30	12	1	0	Chesterfield	Jul 1961	
Martin	B D	Ben	D		1982		Aylesbury United	Aug 2003	0		0 + 1	0	St Albans City	May 2004	

ROSS MacLAREN

JOHN McLAUGHLIN

KEN McPHERSON

JOCK MACONNACHIE

Surname	Initials	Known As	Pos	Intl	Born	Died	Previous Club	Signed	Lge Apps	Gls.	Other Apps	Gls.		Went to	When Left	Pics
Marwood	B	Brian	M	E	1960		Sheffield United	Mar 1993	6 + 5	1				Barnet	Aug 1993	
Maskell	C D	Craig	F		1968		Reading	Jul 1992	40 + 7	21	9 + 3	5		Southampton	Feb 1994	
Mason	G	George	W		1896	1987	Leeds United	Jun 1923	1	0				Mexborough Town	Nov 1924	
Maunders	G C	George	IF		1892	1935	Swindon Amateurs	cs 1912	1	0			A			
May	H	Harry	FB		1928	2007	Cardiff City	Jun 1950	78	1	9	0		Barnsley	May 1952	
Mayes	A K	Alan	F		1953		Watford	Feb 1979	89	38	23	12		Chelsea	Dec 1980	194
			Returned from				Chelsea	Jul 1983	52 + 10	27	9 + 1	5		Carlisle United	Jun 1985	
Meaker	*M J*	*Michael*	*WF*		*1971*		*Bristol Rovers*	*Mar 2000*	*6*	*0*			*L*			
Medlock	O W	Owen	G		1938		Chelsea	Feb 1959	3	0	1	0		Headington United	Dec 1959	
Meechan	A T	Alex	F		1980		Norwich City	cs 1996	0 + 1	0				Bristol City	Jul 1998	
Mellars	W	Billy	FB		1872	1950	Oldham County	May 1897	29	0	3	0		Wigan County	cs 1898	
Mellor	K E	Ken	CH		1934		Mansfield Town	Jul 1959	32	4				Burton Albion	Dec 1960	
Menham	R W	Bob	G		1871	1945	Wigan County	May 1898	141	1	15	1		Retired	cs 1903	21
Merrick	C	Cliff	WH		1910	1995	Burnley	May 1933	46	0	4	0		Retired (injury)	May 1935	
Metcalf	A	Arthur	F		1889	1936	Stockport County	Jun 1920	31	7				Accrington Stanley	Jun 1922	
Micklewright	A A J	Andy	F		1931	2006	Bristol City	Sep 1955	115	31	7	3		Exeter City	Jul 1959	
Middleton	R R	Ray	IF		1933		Southend United	Nov 1958	5	0			T	Aldershot	Jul 1959	
Miglioranzi	S	Stef	M		1977		Portsmouth	Jul 2002	112 + 13	8	10 + 1	1		Los Angeles Galaxy *(US)*	Jun 2006	
Mikolanda	*P*	*Petr*	*F*		*1984*		*West Ham United*	*Nov 2005*	*1 + 4*	*0*			*L*			
Mildenhall	S J	Steve	G		1978		Trainee	Jul 1996	29 + 4	0	5	0		Notts County	Jun 2001	
Millar	W	Willie	W		1924	1995	Stirling Albion	Aug 1950	75	18	7	4		Gillingham	Jul 1953	
Miller	I	Ian	W		1955		Doncaster Rovers	Jul 1978	123 + 4	10	31 + 1	4		Blackburn Rovers	Aug 1981	194
Miller	J McS	Joe	W		1934		Hamilton Academical	Jun 1956	12	0				Yeovil Town	Feb 1957	
Milligan	A A	Alec	FB		1876	1959	Third Lanark	cs 1903	41	1	5	0		Haydon Street WMC	cs 1905	
Mills	A	Andy	FB		1876	1953	Blackburn Rovers	May 1898	29	0				Brighton United	Jun 1899	
Mills	J M	Jamie	M		1981		Trainee	Jul 1999	0 + 2	0	0 + 1	0		Bath City	Jul 2001	
Mills	A R P	Percy	WF		1872	1922		May 1893	3	0			A	Reading	Oct 1894	
Milner	*J P*	*James*	*M*		*1986*		*Leeds United*	*Sep 2003*	*6*	*2*			*L*			
Milton	A	Albert	FB		1885	1917	Sunderland	May 1914	27	0	3	0		Killed in Action	Oct 1917	
Mitchell	D S	Dave	F	Au	1962		Chelsea	Jul 1991	61 + 7	16	12	8		SK Altay Izmir *(Tu)*	Jul 1993	
Mitchell	*P A*	*Paul*	*FB*		*1981*		*Wigan Athletic*	*Sep 2004*	*7*	*0*			*L*			
Mohamed	K	Kaid	F		1984		Carmarthen Town	Aug 2007	3 + 8	0	1 + 2	0		Forest Green Rovers	Jul 2008	
Moncur	J F	John	M		1966		Tottenham Hotspur	Mar 1992	53 + 5	5	9	1		West Ham United	Jun 1994	
Monkhouse	A W	Andy	WF		1980		Rotherham United	Jun 2006	9 + 1	2	0 + 1	0		Hartlepool United	Jan 2007	
Monks	A	Albert	F		1875	1936	Nelson	May 1905	27	3				Southport Central	Nov 1906	

HARRY MAY

ANDY MICKLEWRIGHT

STEF MIGLIORANZI

WILLIE MILLAR

Surname	Initials	Known As	Pos	Intl	Born	Died	Previous Club	Signed	Lge Apps	Gls.	Other Apps	Gls.		Went to	When Left	Pics
Mooney	T J	Tommy	F		1971		Birmingham City	Jul 2003	43 + 4	19	1 + 1	1		Oxford United	Jul 2004	*below*
Moore	A	Alan	W		1927	2008	Coventry City	Jun 1957	19	3				Rochdale	Nov 1958	
Moore	I	Isaac	F		1867	1954	Burton Wanderers	Dec 1895	11	1				Retired	cs 1896	
Moore	*K J*	*Kevin*	*W*		*1956*		*Newport County*	*Mar 1983*	*1*	*0*			*L*			
Moores	J C	Craig	W		1961		Bolton Wanderers	Jul 1981	1 + 1	0	2	0		Congleton Town	Jun 1982	
Moreland	A G	Arthur	CF		1914	1996	Stafford Rangers	May 1937	0		1	1		Birmingham	May 1938	
Morgan	K	Keith	WH		1940		Westbury United	Aug 1958	325	6	40	3		Clanfield	Jul 1969	
Morrall	G R	George	CH		1905	1955	Birmingham	Jun 1936	97	5	10	0		Retired	cs 1939	
Morris	A W	Arthur	CH		1871			1901	1	0			C			
Morris	A G	Grenville	F	W	1877	1959	Aberystwyth Town	Feb 1897	45	40	3	1		Nottingham Forest	Nov 1898	*16*
Morris	D H	Harry	CF		1897	1985	Swansea Town	Jun 1926	260	215	19	14		Clapton Orient	Jul 1933	*61,74*
Morrison	J	Jack	WH		1885	1944	Hull City	Jun 1910	3	0	5	0		Sunderland	Sep 1911	
Morrison	S J	Sean	D		1991		Plymouth Argyle	Feb 2008	19 + 3	1	3	0		Under contract for 2009/10		
Morton	B W	Ben	CF		1910	1962	Torquay United	Oct 1937	71	33	10	6		Stourbridge Town	cs 1945	*61,98*
Moss	D J	Dave	W		1952		Witney Town	Jul 1969	218 + 13	60	38 + 1	21		Luton Town	May 1978	*171*
			Returned from				Luton Town	Jun 1985	4	0	1	1		Trowbridge Town	Jun 1986	
Moss	T J	Terry	W		1932		Bristol Rovers	Mar 1956	7	0			A			
Mountain	G	George	WH		1874	1936	Grimsby Town	Oct 1897	1	0			T			
Moyse	A R	Alec	IF		1935	1994	Dartford	Aug 1958	4	0			T	Millwall	Sep 1958	
Muir			CH					Oct 1905	2	0			T	Released	Nov 1905	
Muir	*I J*	*Ian*	*F*		*1963*		*Brighton & Hove Albion*	*Jan 1985*	*2*	*0*			*L*			
Munks	D	David	D		1947		Portsmouth	Dec 1973	21	0	3	0		Exeter City	Dec 1974	
Munnings	C E	Eddie	F		1906	1995	Grimsby Town	Jun 1930	14	3				Hull City	Aug 1931	*86*
			Returned from				Hull City	Jun 1932	31	10	3	1		Mansfield Town	Jul 1933	
Munro	J	Jimmy	U		1870	1899	Burton Swifts	May 1895	79	15	10	1		Deceased	Jan 1899	*15*
Murphy	J P	Jimmy	WH	W	1910	1989	West Bromwich Albion	Mar 1939	4	0				Morris Motors FC	cs 1939	
Murphy	E	Ted	W				Bury	Jun 1906	36	6	1	0		Bristol Rovers	Aug 1907	
Murray	D J	David	CH	SA			Bristol Rovers	Jun 1930	1	0				Rochdale	Aug 1931	
Murray	E J	Eddie	U		1973		Norwich City	Jul 1991	7 + 5	1	5 + 2	0		Bath City	Oct 1996	
Murray	J J	Joey	F				Everton	Jun 1896	30	5	3	1		Released	cs 1898	
Musgrave	J	Joe	IF		1908	1981	West Ham United	Jan 1937	23	3	1	0		Hartlepools United	Aug 1938	
Mutch	A T	Andy	F		1963		Wolverhampton Wanderers	Aug 1993	34 + 16	6	13 + 1	6		Stockport County	Mar 1996	*205*

TOMMY MOONEY

KEITH MORGAN

GEORGE MORRALL

ANDY MUTCH

Surname	Initials	Known As	Pos	Intl	Born	Died	Previous Club	Signed	Lge Apps	Gls.	Other Apps	Gls.		Went to	When Left	Pics
Nagy	M	Nick	IF		1929		Scunthorpe & Lindsey United	Jul 1951	3	0				Yeovil Town	Jul 1952	
Nalis	L	Lilian	M		1971		Plymouth Argyle	Jul 2008	18 + 6	0	2 + 1	0		Released	May 2009	
Nash	G	George	WH		1875	1905		1894	1	0			A			
Nash	E M	Teddy	G		1902	1985	Swindon North End	Dec 1917	235	0	18	0		Brentford	Sep 1930	66
Ndah	G E	George	F		1974		Crystal Palace	Nov 1997	66 + 1	15	7	1		Wolverhampton Wanderers	Oct 1999	
Neal	J	John	FB		1932		Kings Lynn	Jul 1957	91	2	4	0		Aston Villa	Jul 1959	
Nelson	G P	Garry	F		1961		Southend United	Aug 1983	78 + 1	7	12	2		Plymouth Argyle	Jun 1985	
Newberry	F O	Nobby	WH		1908	1984	Trowbridge Town	Aug 1934	12	1	5	0		Bath City	Jul 1936	
Neyland	M	Martin	F		1877	1947	Bolton Wanderers	cs 1902	15	2	4	3		Nelson	cs 1903	
Nicholas	A P	Andy	D		1983		Liverpool	Jul 2003	105 + 21	4	14 + 1	2		Rotherham United	May 2008	
Nickalls	J S	Jim	F		1903	1977	Chelsea	Jun 1931	13	1				Blyth Spartans	Sep 1932	
Nicolau	N G	Nicky	M		1983		Southend United	Jul 2005	3 + 2	0	0 + 1	0		Barnet	May 2006	
Nightingale	*L R*	*Luke*	*F*		*1980*		*Portsmouth*	*Dec 2002*	*2 + 1*	*0*			*L*			
Nijholt	L	Luc	M		1961		Motherwell	Jul 1993	66 + 1	1	17 + 2	1		Volendam *(Ho)*	Aug 1995	
Nixon	T	Tom	HB		1905	1966	Crystal Palace	Sep 1933	53	0	4	0		Barrow	May 1935	
Noble	P	Peter	F		1944		Newcastle United	Jan 1968	212 + 4	62	39 + 1	18		Burnley	Jun 1973	165
Noble	W A	Will	FB		1875	1920	M & S W J Railway FC	cs 1894	9	0	1	0	A			
Norton	J	Joe	W		1888	1963	Bristol Rovers	Jul 1922	26	2	1	0		Kettering Town	Jun 1923	
Noubissie	P B	Patrick	D		1983		Crewe Alexandra	Jan 2007	1 + 2	0				Hibernian	Jul 2007	
Nunn	W	Wally	HB		1920	1965	Charlton Athletic	Jun 1947	4	0				Colchester United	cs 1948	
Nurse	M T G	Mel	CH	W	1937		Middlesbrough	Aug 1965	122 + 1	10	20	3		Swansea Town	Jun 1968	
Oakden	H	Harry	WH		1877	1967	Belfast Distillery	Sep 1901	99	4	13	2		Retired (injury)	cs 1907	
Oakley	G	George	F		1880		Swindon Thistle	cs 1900	35	3	5	2		Wootton Bassett	cs 1902	
Oakley	N	Norman	G		1939		Hartlepools United	Mar 1964	21	0	1	0		Grimsby Town	Sep 1966	
O'Brien	G	Gerry	M		1949		Southampton	Mar 1976	24 + 3	0	2	0		Clydebank	Jul 1977	
O'Brien	J	Joe	FB		1875		Aberdeen	Aug 1902	29	0	5	0		Reading	cs 1903	
			Returned from				Brighton & Hove Albion	May 1905	35	0	2	0		Stalybridge Rovers	May 1906	
O'Brien	P	Paddy	IF		1873	1950	Bristol City	Nov 1902	1	0			T			
Ogden	C J	Chris	G		1953		Oldham Athletic	Aug 1978	24	0	7	0		Rotherham United	Nov 1979	
O'Halloran	K J	Keith	M		1975		St Johnstone	Jul 2000	46	7	9 + 1	3		Chippenham Town	Sep 2003	
O'Hanlon	S P	Sean	D		1983		Everton	Jan 2004	97 + 2	9	11 + 2	1		Milton Keynes Dons	Jul 2006	
O'Hara	M J	Mike	G		1944		Luton Town	Nov 1961	30	0				Bournemouth & Boscombe Athletic	Aug 1963	
Olney	J F	Jim	HB		1914	1944	Birmingham	Dec 1938	13	0				Killed in Action	Sep 1944	106
O'Mahoney	F K	Frank	CF		1935		Farnborough Town	Apr 1957	8	5				Bath City	Jan 1958	
O'Neill	H	Harry	FB		1894	1971	Bristol Rovers	Jun 1923	26	1				Runcorn	cs 1928	

JOHNNY NEAL

ANDY NICHOLAS

MEL NURSE

SEAN O'HANLON

Surname	Initials	Known As	Pos	Intl	Born	Died	Previous Club	Signed	Lge Apps	Gls.	Other Apps	Gls.		Went to	When Left	Pics
Onibuje	F	Fola	F		1984		Cambridge United	Jul 2006	6 + 8	2	1 + 1	0		Wycombe Wanderers	Jan 2007	
Onslow	L G	Les	WH		1926		South Marston	Sep 1945	4	0	8	0	A	Kidderminster Harriers	May 1951	
Onslow	R E	Roy	F		1928	2007	Sanford YC	Nov 1948	140	24	9	2		Chippenham Town	Jul 1956	123
Onuora	I	Iffy	F		1967		Gillingham	Mar 1998	64 + 9	24	6 + 1	0		Gillingham	Jan 2000	264
Opara	J L	Lloyd	F		1984		Grays Athletic	Jun 2004	0		1	0		St Albans City	Sep 2004	
O'Regan	K M	Kieran	M	EI	1963		Brighton & Hove Albion	Aug 1987	23 + 3	1	10 + 1	1		Huddersfield Town	Jul 1988	
O'Sullivan	W StJ	Wayne	M		1974		Trainee	Jul 1992	65 + 24	3	15 + 5	1		Cardiff City	Aug 1997	
Owen	M	Maurice	CF		1924	2000	Abingdon Town	Dec 1946	555	150	46	15		Club Trainer	cs 1963	113,116
Page	R M	Mick	FB		1930		Vickers Armstrong FC	Apr 1951	32	0	1	0		Chippenham United	Jul 1956	
Painter	E G	Eddie	WH		1921	2001	Marlborough Camp	Oct 1938	77	0	27	6		Bedford Town	Jul 1952	
Painter	F	Frank	W		1875	1946	Swindon Wanderers	1895	1	0			A			
Palmer	G	George	CF		1875	1940	Workington	Dec 1896	6	1	1	0		Released	cs 1897	
Parker	W	Bill	IF		1925		Reading	Feb 1953	10	0				Exeter City	Jul 1953	
Parkes	F	Freddy	WH				Swindon Wanderers	1904	1	0	1	0		Lincoln City	Mar 1906	
Parkhouse	R McD	Dick	WH		1914	1992	Calne and Harris FC	Aug 1934	29	0	28	0		Trowbridge Town	cs 1947	
Parkin	S	Sam	F		1981		Chelsea	Aug 2002	120 + 4	67	15 + 3	6		Ipswich Town	Jun 2005	239, 256
Parkin	T J	Tim	CD		1957		Bristol Rovers	Jul 1986	109 + 1	6	33 + 1	2		Port Vale	Dec 1989	
Parmley	J S	Jim	F		1908	1984	Huddersfield Town	May 1935	14	9	3	0		Darlington	May 1936	
Paterson	G L	George	IF		1916	1996	Liverpool	Oct 1946	53	7	2	1		Colts coach	Dec 1948	
Pattimore	M R	Michael	D		1979		Trainee	Jul 1997	0 + 3	0				Cwmbran Town	May 1998	
Payne	M I	Mark	M		1966		Apprentice	Sep 1984	0 + 3	0	1	0		Gloucester City	May 1986	
Paynter	W P	Billy	F		1984		Southend United	Aug 2007	65 + 13	20	6 + 3	3		Under contract for 2009/10		
Peach	D S	David	FB		1951		Southampton	Mar 1980	52 + 1	2	7	0		Orient	Mar 1982	
Peacock	L A	Lee	F		1976		Sheffield Wednesday	Jan 2006	104 + 17	20	9 + 1	1		Under contract for 2009/10		
Peapell	F D	Dennis	F		1945		Apprentice	Nov 1963	2	0				Exeter City	Jul 1965	
Peart	R C	Bobby	F		1926	1966	Pinehurst YC	Mar 1948	13	5				Yeovil Town	Jul 1952	
Peebles	R W	Dick	IF		1923	2004	St Johnstone	May 1950	12	1				Released	cs 1951	
Peers	S A	Sam	W		1881	1942	Leicester Fosse	Dec 1903	6	0				Coventry City	cs 1904	
Pembery	G D	Gordon	WH		1926		Charlton Athletic	Jun 1956	37	2	2	0		Headington United	Jul 1957	
Penman	W S T	Willie	F		1939		Newcastle United	Sep 1966	87 + 12	17	17 + 5	4		Walsall	Aug 1970	163
Penn	T	Tommy	FB		1897	1978	Gainsborough Trinity	May 1929	27	0	3	0		Yeovil & Petters United	Jan 1932	
Peplow	S T	Steve	W		1949		Liverpool	May 1970	37 + 3	11	5	2		Nottingham Forest	Jul 1973	
Peters	F	Frank	W		1910	1990	Fulham	May 1933	100	45	14	6		Bristol City	May 1936	91
Peterson	P W	Paul	FB		1949		Leeds United	Jun 1971	1	0				Stevenage Borough	May 1973	
Petrie	C	Charlie	F		1895	1972	The Wednesday	Jun 1925	32	11				Southampton	Jun 1927	

WAYNE O'SULLIVAN

EDDIE PAINTER

TIM PARKIN

LEE PEACOCK

Surname	Initials	Known As	Pos	Intl	Born	Died	Previous Club	Signed	Lge Apps	Gls.	Other Apps	Gls.		Went to	When Left	Pics
Pettican	J	Josh	F		1880	1951	Newbury Town	Feb 1901	9	1	1	0		Barry Unionists	Nov 1901	
Phillips	M S	Marcus	M		1973		Melksham Town	Jul 1992	0		0 + 1	0		Gloucester City	cs 1995	
Phillipson	T W	Tom	F		1898	1965	Newcastle United	May 1921	87	24	4	0		Wolverhampton Wanderers	Dec 1923	67
Piggin	L	Lionel	FB		1891	1973	Barrow	Sep 1914	1	0			T			
Pitman	J R	Jamie	M		1976		Trainee	Jul 1994	2 + 1	0				Hereford United	Feb 1996	
Pocock	J H	Jimmy	WH		1896	1956	Imperial Rovers	Mar 1920	12	0				Retired (injury)	cs 1922	
Pollard	W J	Jack	G		1882	1948	Newbury Town	Sep 1901	3	0			A			
Pook	M D	Michael	M		1985		Youths	May 2005	85 + 24	3	12 + 5	1		Released	May 2009	
Pope	*W E*	*Will*	*FB*		*1870*	*1948*	*Newbury Town*	*1894*	*1*	*0*			*G*			
Poppitt	J	Jimmy	F		1875	1930	Wolverhampton Wanderers	Aug 1902	28	9	5	3		Reading	May 1903	
			Returned from				Reading	May 1904	27	4	2	1		Notts County	May 1905	
Porter	C J	Chris	W		1949		Bridgwater Town	Nov 1969	33 + 3	4	2	0		Yeovil Town	cs 1974	
Potter	J W J	Jack	W		1872	1937	Wantage Town	1896	1	0			A			
Potter	J M	Jim	WH		1884		Dundee	Oct 1905	4	0				Released	Nov 1905	
Potter	R C	Ron	CD		1948		West Bromwich Albion	Nov 1970	84 + 2	0	7	0		Retired (injury)	cs 1975	
Powell	A E E	Albert	W		1908	1940	Bargoed United	Dec 1928	3	0				Coventry City	Apr 1929	
Preece	*D W*	*David*	*M*		*1963*	*2007*	*Derby County*	*Mar 1996*	*7 0*	*1*			*L*			
Preece	J C	Jack	FB		1914	2003	*Southport*	*Mar 1946*	*0*		*4*	*0*	*G*			
			Returned from				Southport	Jun 1947	7	0				Chippenham United	Aug 1948	
Price	J W	Jack	FB		1900	1984	Bristol Rovers	Jun 1924	2	0				Brentford	Nov 1925	
Price	W E	Wally	IF		1874		Old Swindon	Sep 1892	1	0	3	1	A			
Pritchard	H K	Howard	W	W	1958		Bristol City	Jul 1981	59 + 6	11	10 + 1	8		Bristol City	Aug 1983	
Proctor	*M A*	*Michael*	*F*		*1980*		*Rotherham United*	*Feb 2005*	*4*	*2*			*L*			
Prophett	C G	Colin	CD		1947		Norwich City	Aug 1974	158 + 2	10	26	2		Chesterfield	Sep 1978	
Prouton	R O	Ralph	WH		1926		Arsenal	Jul 1952	13	0	3	0		Tonbridge	cs 1953	
Pugh	J	Jimmy	F		1874	1950	Wellingborough Town	Sep 1902	56	11	10	16		Retired	cs 1905	30
Purcell	G W	George	F		1901	1968	Stockport County	Aug 1924	18	2				Exeter City	Aug 1926	
Quinn	C	Cyril	W		1910	1968	Fleetwood	Jul 1932	30	3	3	2		Ilkeston Town	Jun 1933	
Quinn	J M	Jimmy	CF	NI	1959		Oswestry Town	Dec 1981	34 + 16	10	7 + 4	8		Blackburn Rovers	Aug 1984	209,320
			Returned from				Blackburn Rovers	Dec 1986	61 + 3	30	21 + 1	13		Leicester City	Jun 1988	
			Returned from				Peterborough United	Nov 1998	1 + 6	0	1	0		Cricklade Town	May 2000	
Radford	A	Arthur	FB		1925	1981	Frickley Colliery	Aug 1952	16	0	3	0		Released	May 1953	
Ramsey	C L	Chris	FB		1962		Brighton & Hove Albion	Aug 1984	99 + 1	5	22	1		Southend United	Aug 1987	
Randall	O J H	Ossie	G		1895	1978	Brighton & Hove Albion	Aug 1922	71	0	6	0		Exeter City	Aug 1926	
Razak	H	Hamdi	F		1985		FC Igny *(Fr)*	Jan 2009	0 + 3	0				Released	May 2009	

MICHAEL POOK

RON POTTER

COLIN PROPHETT

OSSIE RANDALL

Surname	Initials	Known As	Pos	Intl	Born	Died	Previous Club	Signed	Lge Apps	Gls.	Other Apps	Gls.		Went to	When Left	Pics
Reddy	M A	Michael	F		1980		Sunderland	Jan 2001	17 + 1	4	1 + 1	1	L			
Reeves	A	Alan	CD		1967		Wimbledon	Jun 1998	190 + 18	11	26 + 3	2		Coaching Staff	Jan 2006	
Reid	E	Revd.	F			1959	Swindon Amateurs	Apr 1903	20	3	3	0	A	Exeter City	Sep 1904	
Reynolds	W	Billy	F		1879		Grimsby Town	May 1906	4	2				Croydon Common	cs 1907	
Reynolds	J A	Jamie	M		1967		Apprentice	Sep 1985	0 + 2	0	1 + 1	0		Bath City	Jul 1988	
Reynolds	R	Robbie	W		1871	1954		cs 1888	11	6	18	10	A			14
Rhodes	A G	Alex	F		1982		Brentford	Oct 2006	0 + 4	0			L			
Richards	J B	John	IF		1931	2001	RAPC Devizes	Nov 1955	104	36	5	2		Norwich City	Dec 1959	136
Richardson			F				(Cambridge area)	Apr 1906	1	0			T			
Richardson	W	Bill	WH		1908	1985	West Bromwich Albion	May 1937	9	0	3	0		Dudley Town	Jul 1938	
Richardson	W	Billy	F		1878	1950	Grimsby Town	Jan 1898	29	9				Released	cs 1899	
Richardson	B W	Brian	WH		1934		Sheffield United	Jan 1966	11	0	1	0		Rochdale	Jul 1966	
Richardson	F	Frank	CF		1897	1987	West Ham United	Jun 1924	53	33	5	10		Reading	Feb 1926	72
			Returned from				Reading	Jun 1930	38	12	1	0		Mansfield Town	Oct 1932	
Richardson	G	Georgie	U		1871		Kilmarnock	Apr 1895	141	10	13	3		Annan United	Oct 1901	25
Richardson	P	Paul	M		1949		Sheffield United	Jul 1983	7	0	1	0		Swansea City	Sep 1984	
Richardson	W	Wally	FB		1869	1911		cs 1890	32	1	18	2	A			
Ricketts	L	Len	W		1880	1939	Worcester City	cs 1903	2	0				Released	Oct 1903	
Rideout	P D	Paul	F		1964		Lymington	Jun 1980	90 + 5	38	10	3		Aston Villa	May 1983	207
			Returned from				Southampton	Mar 1991	9	1			L			
Riseborough	C	Cyril	W		1933		Silksworth Colliery Welfare	Feb 1955	26	1				Yeovil Town	Jul 1957	
Ritchie	A	Archie	FB	S	1872	1932	Bristol Rovers	May 1900	36	0	5	0		Retired	cs 1901	
Roberts	C J	Christian	F		1979		Bristol City	Oct 2004	77 + 34	21	11 + 4	6		Retired (injury)	Sep 2008	
Roberts	K J	Kevin	G		1955		Welton Rovers	Mar 1977	1	0	2	0		Weymouth	Jul 1980	
Roberts	C L	Les	IF		1901	1980	Bolton Wanderers	Jun 1927	106	34	13	1		Brentford	Jun 1930	76
Roberts	P	Paul	D		1962		(Finland)	Sep 1985	25 + 2	0	4	0		Southend United	Jul 1986	
Robertson	M W	Mark	M	Au	1977		Burnley	Aug 2000	4 + 6	1	2 + 1	0		Dundee	Mar 2001	
Robinson	M J	Mark	D		1968		Newcastle United	Jul 1994	255 + 14	4	44 + 3	0		Chippenham Town	Jul 2002	
Robinson	S E	Steve	M		1975		Birmingham City	Feb 2001	128 + 14	5	15 + 1	1		Lincoln City	May 2005	
Robson-Kanu	T H A	Hal	M		1989		Reading	Jan 2009	20	4			L			
Rogers			IF				Kings Own Lancs Regiment	1894	1	0			A			
Rogers	D	Dave	CF		1892	1975	Royal Field Artillery	Mar 1914	177	30	4	0		Gillingham	Jul 1926	52
Rogers	D E	Don	W		1945		Apprentice	Oct 1962	400	146	74	32		Crystal Palace	Oct 1972	141,165
			Returned from				Queens Park Rangers	Mar 1976	11 + 1	2	2 + 2	0		Retired (injury)	May 1977	
Rollings	A N	Andy	CD		1954		Brighton & Hove Albion	May 1980	11 + 1	1	4	1		Portsmouth	Aug 1981	

ALAN REEVES

MARK ROBINSON

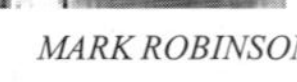
STEVE ROBINSON

GEORGE RUSHTON

Surname	Initials	Known As	Pos	Intl	Born	Died	Previous Club	Signed	Lge Apps	Gls.	Other Apps	Gls.		Went to	When Left	Pics
Roost	W C	Bill	CF		1924		Bristol Rovers	May 1957	18	3				Stonehouse	Sep 1959	
Rose	G F	George	FB		1880	1956	Swindon Thistle	Jan 1902	1	0			A			
Ross	J	Ginger	WH				Grantham Rovers	Feb 1895	7	0				Bristol South End	cs 1895	
Rowland	A A	Andy	CF		1954		Bury	Sep 1978	280 + 7	79	55 + 3	19		Reserve Team coach	cs 1986	194
Rowley	D W M	Dick	F	NI	1904	1984	Corinthian-Casuals	Apr 1926	2	2			A	Southampton	May 1926	
Ruddlesdin	A	Arthur	F		1899	1972	Barnsley	Jul 1923	30	12				Poole Town	Aug 1926	
Ruddock	N	Neil	CD	E	1968		Crystal Palace	Aug 2001	14 + 1	1	3 + 1	1		Contract cancelled	Dec 2002	
Rushton	R	Dick	WH		1902	1981	Bury	Jun 1930	7	0				Wellington Town	Aug 1931	
Rushton	G	George	F		1881	1964	Hull City	May 1907	47	13	4	0		Brentford	May 1909	above
			Returned from				Brentford	Mar 1910	14	2	7	0		Goole Town	Jul 1912	
Ruster	S	Sebastien	WF		1982		AS Cannes *(Fr)*	Oct 2003	0 + 2	0	1 + 1	0		ES Frejusienne *(Fr)*	Jan 2004	
Rutherford	J	Jack	G		1908	1966	West Ham United	May 1935	30	0	6	0		Dartford	Jul 1936	
Rutherford	J B	Jock	CF		1899	1975	Bridgend Town	May 1924	5	0				Retired (injury)	cs 1925	
Ryan	T	Tom	WH		1914	2001	Plymouth Argyle	Aug 1939	2	0	2	0		Torquay United	cs 1945	
Ryder	T R	Terry	W		1928		Portsmouth	Jul 1952	33	13	3	0		Kings Lynn (player-manager)	Jul 1953	126
Sabin	E	Eric	F		1975		ES Wasquehal *(Fr)*	Jun 2001	60 + 13	9	7 + 1	0		Queens Park Rangers	Jul 2003	
Sampson	R V	Ray	IF		1935		Juniors	May 1952	64	10	1	1		Trowbridge Town	Jul 1959	
Sanchez	L P	Lawrie	M	NI	1959		Wimbledon	Mar 1994	6 + 2	0				Sligo Rovers (player-manager)	cs 1994	
Sanderson	T	Tommy	F		1880		Chorley St George	Mar 1904	1	0	2	1		Southern United	cs 1905	
Saunders	A W	Billy	WH		1886	1954		Aug 1908	2	0				Swindon Victoria	cs 1910	
Saunders	R A	Sally	CH		1923	1999	North Leaze Athletic	Apr 1948	1	0	1	0	A	Chippenham Town	Aug 1948	
Scanlan	E	Ted	IF		1890	1939	Jarrow	May 1914	9	2	1	0		South Shields	cs 1915	
Scott	A	Alan	IF		1910	1967	Liverpool	Jun 1932	18	3				Gillingham	Jun 1933	
Scott	W H	Harry	IF		1905	1990	Bournemouth & Boscombe Athletic	Jun 1932	18	5	1	0		Doncaster Rovers	Jun 1933	
Scott	K	Keith	F		1967		Wycombe Wanderers	Nov 1993	43 + 8	12	8	4		Stoke City	Dec 1994	
Seabrook	E	Ted	HB		1909	1995	Chesterfield	Aug 1932	3	0				Chorley	Aug 1933	
Seagraves	M	Mark	D		1966		Bolton Wanderers	Jun 1995	57 + 4	0	16 + 2	0		Barrow	Jul 1998	
Selby	W R	Billy	IF		1878	1947	Swindon Victoria	cs 1900	1	0			A			
Selwood	C	Charlie	HB		1872	1962	Swindon Wanderers	1894	5	0			A			
Shakes	R U B	Ricky	W	T	1985		Bolton Wanderers	Jul 2005	52 + 17	5	7 + 1	0		Brentford	May 2007	
Shanks	R	Bob	HB		1911	1989	Leeds United	May 1935	25	1	3	0		Crystal Palace	May 1937	
			Returned from				Spennymoor United	Oct 1946	1	0				Gloucester City	Aug 1947	
Sharples	J	Jimmy	W		1872	1920	Wigan County	May 1898	64	29	2	0		Millwall	May 1900	20
Shaw	H	Harry	F		1874	1944	Swindon Wanderers	1894	6	2	1	0	A			
Shearer	D N	Duncan	F	S	1962		Huddersfield Town	Jun 1988	156 + 3	78	39 + 1	20		Blackburn Rovers	Mar 1992	223

ERIC SABIN

RAY SAMPSON

KEITH SCOTT

MARK SEAGRAVES

Surname	Initials	Known As	Pos	Intl	Born	Died	Previous Club	Signed	Lge Apps	Gls.	Other Apps	Gls.		Went to	When Left	Pics
Sheffield	*J*	*Jon*	*G*		*1969*		*Cambridge United*	*Jan 1994*	*2*	*0*			*L*			
Shergold	W F	Wilf	IF		1943		Juniors	Oct 1960	37	0	4	0		Bradford City	Jun 1966	
Shutt	H	Jack	FB		1874	1950	Bolton Wanderers	Nov 1896	107	0	3	0		Millwall	May 1900	
Silto	W A	Billy	HB		1883	1959	Barnsley	May 1909	204	5	42	0		Retired	cs 1920	56
Simms	S	Sammy	WH		1888	1952	Everton	Jun 1913	3	0	1	0		Leicester Fosse	Jun 1914	
					Returned from		Leicester Fosse	Jul 1919	46	4	2	0		Gillingham	Jun 1921	
Simner	J	Joe	IF		1923	2000	Chelsea	Jul 1949	30	12	4	1		Bedford Town	Aug 1951	
Simpson	F	Fitzroy	M	J	1970		Bristol City	Jul 1988	78 + 27	9	20 + 5	1		Manchester City	Mar 1992	
Skea	D F	David	F		1870	1939	Leicester Fosse	cs 1896	6	5				Chatham	Nov 1896	
Skeen	K A	Ken	F		1942		Trowbridge Town	Aug 1964	14	4	8	2		Oxford United	Jul 1967	
Skillen	J	John	CF		1887	1942	Ayr Parkhouse	Jul 1908	2	0				Ayr Parkhouse	May 1909	
Skiller	L F	Len	G		1885	1964	Aston Villa	Jul 1909	289	0	51	0		Truro City	cs 1922	50,56
Skull	J	Johnny	W		1932		Banbury Spencer	Sep 1957	33	10	1	0		Trowbridge Town	Jul 1960	
Slabber	*J A*	*Jamie*	*F*		*1984*		*Tottenham Hotspur*	*Dec 2004*	*4 + 5*	*0*	*0 + 1*	*0*	*L*			
Smart	R W	Roger	F		1943		Juniors	May 1960	341 + 7	43	62 + 1	16		Charlton Athletic	May 1973	165
Smith	A	Alec	WH		1873	1908	Third Lanark	May 1898	60	1	2	0		Third Lanark	Apr 1901	36
Smith	A P	Alex	M		1976		Everton	Jan 1996	17 + 14	1				Huddersfield Town	Feb 1998	
Smith	A	Andy	CF		1877		Millwall	Aug 1906	28	11	1	0		Leyton	May 1907	19
Smith	W	Billy	F		1874		Newcastle United	cs 1899	69	16	6	4		Released	cs 1901	
Smith	B J	Bryan	D		1983		Trainee	cs 1999	0 + 1	0				Swindon Supermarine	Aug 2002	
Smith	G	George	F						1	0				Retired	cs 1920	
Smith	G G	Grant	M		1980		Sheffield United	Aug 2003	23 + 14	10	8 + 5	0		Bristol City	Jul 2005	
Smith	A J	Jack	FB		1911	1975	Bristol Rovers	May 1935	114	0	15	0		Chelsea	Mar 1938	
Smith	J	Jack	CF		1936		Watford	Jun 1961	97	37	12	10		Brighton & Hove Albion	Jan 1964	151
Smith	J D	Jack	D		1983		Watford	Jul 2005	134 + 4	8	15	0		Released	May 2009	
Smith	J	John	M		1939	1988	Torquay United	Jun 1968	79 + 5	9	32	6		Walsall	Jun 1971	165
Smith	P W	Paul	M		1971		Walsall	Jan 2006	5 + 4	0				AFC Sudbury	Jun 2006	
Smith	P A	Phil	G		1979		Crawley Town	Jul 2006	71	0	8	0		Under contract for 2009/10		
Smithson	C E	Charlie	W		1877	1939		cs 1899	1	0			A			
Southall	H R	Harry	G		1862	1935	Bristol South End	cs 1894	3	0	2	0	A			
Spackman	H J	Harry	WH		1872	1935	St Marks	cs 1893	2	0	2	0	A			
Sperring	*A*	*Alistair*	*G*		*1963*		*Southampton*	*Aug 1984*	*0*		*1*	*0*	*L*			
Sperti	F	Franco	FB		1955		Apprentice	Jan 1973	1	0				Released	May 1974	
Spratley	A S	Alan	G		1949		Queens Park Rangers	Jul 1973	7	0				Guildford & Dorking United	cs 1974	
Sproates	A	Alan	WH		1944		Sunderland	Aug 1963	3	0	2	0		Darlington	Sep 1965	

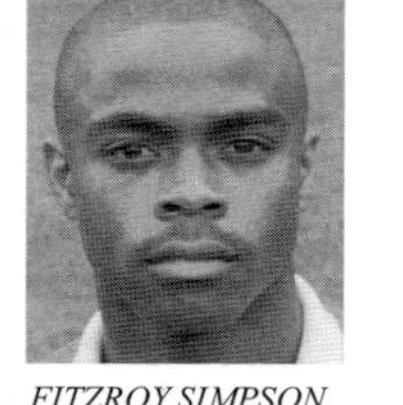

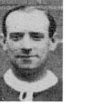

FITZROY SIMPSON

SAMMY SIMMS

JACK (A J) SMITH

JACK (J D) SMITH

Surname	Initials	Known As	Pos	Intl	Born	Died	Previous Club	Signed	Lge Apps	Gls.	Other Apps	Gls.		Went to	When Left	Pics
Stanners	J G	Jack	WH		1890	1974	Springwell	Aug 1913	1	0	1	0		South Shields	Jul 1914	
Stansfield	H F	Harold	FB		1906	1971	Bolton Wanderers	May 1930	48	1	2	0		Southport	Aug 1933	
Starsmore	J G	Jack	F		1901	1983	Kettering Town	Jun 1931	66	14	4	1		Barrow	Aug 1933	84
Stephens	A	Alf	F		1919	1993	Leeds United	Aug 1946	16	2	1	0		Dartford	cs 1948	
Stephens	J W	Bill	CF		1919	1974	Leeds United	Jul 1946	47	26	2	2		West Ham United	Dec 1947	114
Stephens	W J	Johnny	W		1935	1992	Hull City	Jun 1958	18	2				Coventry City	Jan 1960	
Stephenson	J W	Jack	FB		1874	1908	New Brighton Tower	Aug 1900	43	0	5	0		Tottenham Hotspur	Apr 1901	
Stevens	J M	John	CF		1941		RAF Kings Lynn	Jun 1962	22	10	2	0		Guildford City	May 1964	
Stevens	M A	Mark	G		1963		Bristol City	Jun 1981	1	0				Trowbridge Town	cs 1983	
Stevenson	J A	Jon	F		1982		Leicester City	Jul 2003	1 + 4	0	3	0		Cambridge City	May 2004	
Stokoe	J	Jimmy	IF		1888	1970	Jarrow	Jul 1920	18	7	1	0		Derby County	Aug 1922	
Storey	W C	Bill	IF		1912	1993	Bolton Wanderers	Feb 1936	17	2	4	0		Exeter City	May 1937	
Stringfellow	H	Harry	HB		1874	1956	Portsmouth	cs 1904	30	0	2	0		Leeds City	Jul 1905	
Stroud	D A	David	M		1986		Trainee	May 2006	1 + 1	0	1	0		Swindon Supermarine	Dec 2006	
Stroud	K A	Kenny	M/D		1953		Apprentice	Mar 1971	302 + 9	16	61 + 1	3		Newport County	Aug 1982	
Sturrock	B D	Blair	F		1981		Rochdale	Dec 2006	22 + 28	6	5 + 2	3		Released	May 2009	
Summerbee	M G	Mike	F	E	1942		Cheltenham Town	Mar 1960	218	39	26	1		Manchester City	Aug 1965	141,154
Summerbee	N J	Nicky	W		1971		Trainee	Jul 1989	89 + 23	6	18 + 4	4		Manchester City	Jun 1994	
				Returned from			Bradford City	Aug 2005	1	0				Tranmere Rovers	Aug 2005	
Sutherland	M N	Malcolm	F		1868		Leith Athletic	cs 1895	16	8	3	2		West Manchester	cs 1896	14
Sutton	J W M	John	F		1983		Tottenham Hotspur	Dec 2002	0 + 1	0				Raith Rovers	Dec 2002	
Swinden	S A	Sid	FB		1913	1987	West Bromwich Albion	May 1937	36	0	1	0		Accrington Stanley	Jun 1939	
Syrett	D K	Dave	F		1956		Apprentice	Nov 1973	110 + 12	29	10 + 3	8		Mansfield Town	Aug 1977	
Talia	F	Frank	G		1972		Blackburn Rovers	Sep 1995	107	0	11	0		Sheffield United	May 2000	
Tanner	*N*	*Nick*	*CD*		*1965*		*Liverpool*	*Sep 1990*	*7*	*0*			*L*			
Taylor	W H	Bill	WH		1898		Army	Sep 1919	3	0			T	Portsmouth	Nov 1919	
Taylor	C J	Chris	M		1985		Trainee	Jan 2003	0 + 4	0				Swindon Supermarine	Jun 2006	
Taylor	C	Craig	CD		1974		Dorchester Town	Apr 1997	47 + 8	2	3 + 1	0		Plymouth Argyle	Aug 1999	
Taylor	*G W*	*Gerry*	*FB*		*1947*		*Wolves*	*Oct 1975*	*19*	*0*	*4*	*0*	*L*			
Taylor	W H	Mac	FB		1874	1910	Swindon Wanderers	Nov 1895	7	0			A	Swindon Victoria	cs 1899	
Taylor	S	Shaun	CD		1963		Exeter City	Jul 1991	212	30	46 + 1	3		Bristol City	Sep 1996	234
Taylor	A	Tony	FB		1946		Southend United	Jul 1976	20 + 6	0	3	0		Athlone Town	Jul 1977	
Teague	W E	Mick	G		1937	1998	Gloucester City	Mar 1961	3	0				Bristol City	Aug 1962	
Templeman	J H	John	FB		1947		Exeter City	Jul 1979	20 + 1	0	7	0		Witney Town	Nov 1980	
Terry	P A	Pat	CF		1933	2007	Reading	Feb 1967	60 + 1	23	6	3		Brentford	May 1968	161

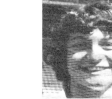

KENNY STROUD

NICKY SUMMERBEE

DAVE SYRETT

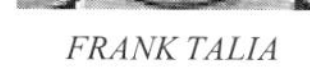
FRANK TALIA

Surname	Initials	Known As	Pos	Intl	Born	Died	Previous Club	Signed	Lge Apps	Gls.	Other Apps	Gls.		Went to	When Left	Pics
Thirlwell	P	Paul	M		1979		Sunderland	Sep 1999	12	0			L			
Thom	A	Alec	W		1894	1973	Hull City	Jun 1926	100	24	11	1		Retired	cs 1930	
Thomas	J W	Johnny	W		1926	2006	Everton	Feb 1949	17	3				Headington United	Jul 1952	
Thomas	R J	Rod	FB	W	1947		Gloucester City	Jul 1964	296	5	59	0		Derby County	Nov 1973	164
Thompson	C	Charlie	W		1903	1971	Birmingham	Jun 1923	2	0				West Ham United	Oct 1924	
Thompson	D A	David	M		1977		Liverpool	Nov 1997	10	0			L			
Thompson	F	Frank	FB		1897	1983	Manchester City	Aug 1927	7	0				Halifax Town	Aug 1928	
Thompson	F N	Freddie	WH		1937	1998	Swindon Victoria	Sep 1955	21	1				Salisbury	Feb 1962	
Thompson	J	Jimmy	F		1899		Accrington Stanley	Jun 1925	7	1	2	0		Crewe Alexandra	Jul 1926	
Thomson	A J	Andy	D		1974		Trainee	Jul 1992	21 + 1	0	8	1		Portsmouth	Dec 1995	
Thomson	M	Matt	HB		1886	1956	Woolwich Arsenal	May 1914	10	0	2	0		Released	cs 1915	
Thomson	N S	Norman	IF		1901	1984	Brentford	Aug 1932	3	0				Folkestone Town	Aug 1933	
Thorne	F L C	Frank	FB		1910	1996	Swindon Corinthians	Sep 1932	1	0			A			
Thorne	G R	Gary	D		1977		Brinkworth	Mar 1995	0		1 + 1	0		Gloucester City	Mar 1996	
Thorne	P L	Peter	F		1973		Blackburn Rovers	Jan 1995	66 + 11	27	10 + 4	5		Stoke City	Jul 1997	
Thorpe	A L	Tony	F		1974		Queens Park Rangers	Jul 2005	6 + 1	1	2 + 1	0		Colchester United	Jan 2006	
Tiler	C	Carl	CD		1970		Nottingham Forest	Nov 1994	2	0			L			
Tilley	D S	Don	CF		1930	1996	Arsenal	May 1953	0		1	0		Released	cs 1954	
Tilley	H R	Rex	WH		1929		Plymouth Argyle	Aug 1958	31	0	1	0		Trowbridge Town	Jun 1961	
Timbrell	H J	Harry	F		1912	1982	Municipal Officers FC	Feb 1932	7	3	1	1	A			
Timlin	M A	Michael	M		1985		Fulham	Nov 2006	18 + 6	1	1	0	L			
					Returned from		Fulham	Mar 2008	47 + 4	3	5	0		Under contract for 2009/10		
Todd	A J J	Andy	D		1974		Middlesbrough	Feb 1995	13	0			L			
Tonner	A E McS	Arthur	FB		1909	1983	St Mirren	Jul 1937	41	0	9	0		Swansea Town	Jun 1939	
Toombs	E R	Ernie	WF		1882	1968	Swindon Athletic	Oct 1902	10	2	1	1	A	Southern United	cs 1905	
Tout	W E B	Billy	HB		1884	1960	Bristol East	Sep 1905	391	57	45	8		Bath City	cs 1921	47
Tozer	B P A	Ben	D		1990		Plymouth Argyle	Jul 2007	1 + 1	0	5	0		Newcastle United	Jan 2008	
Travers	G E	George	F		1886	1943	Unattached	Jun 1919	34	12	2	2		Millwall	Jun 1920	58
Treacy	R C P	Ray	F	EI	1946		Charlton Athletic	Jun 1972	55	16	5 + 1	2		Preston North End	Dec 1973	179
Trim	R F	Reg	FB		1913	1997	Derby County	Jul 1946	15	0				Released	Nov 1946	
Trollope	N J	John	FB		1943		Juniors	Jul 1960	767 + 3	21	119	7		Team Manager	Nov 1980	164,179
Tucker	W J	Billy	CH		1948		Bury	Jun 1979	35	4	14 + 2	2		Cheltenham Town	Jul 1981	193
Tudur-Jones	O	Owain	M	W			Swansea City	Mar 2009	11	1			L			
Tuomela	M	Marko	D	F	1972		Tromso IL (No)	Sep 2000	1 + 1	0	2	0	L			
Turner	R F	Bob	W		1910	1978	Southport	Aug 1933	4	0			T	Carlisle United	Nov 1933	
Turner	O C	Charlie	W		1898	1968	Warminster Town	May 1921	17	1				Bridgend Town (player-manager)	Aug 1923	
Turner	C J	Chris	D		1951		New England Teamen (US)	Sep 1980	0 + 3	0				Cambridge United	Oct 1980	
Turner	M G E	Mike	G		1938		Dorchester Town	Dec 1961	75	0	12	0		Torquay United	Jun 1964	
Turner			F				Chippenham Town	Feb 1896	3	1			A			
Turner	P	Percy	IF		1880		Loughborough Town	Aug 1899	6	2				Barnsley	Jun 1900	
Uprichard	W N McC	Norman	G	NI	1928		Arsenal	Nov 1949	73	0	9	0		Portsmouth	Nov 1952	125
Uzzell	W L	Billy	FB		1871	1914	Army Service Corps	cs 1896	2	0			A			

Surname	Initials	Known As	Pos	Intl	Born	Died	Previous Club	Signed	Lge Apps	Gls.	Other Apps	Gls.		Went to	When Left	Pics
van der Linden	A	Antoine	D		1976		Sparta Rotterdam *(Ho)*	Aug 2000	17 + 16	1	6	0		BVO Emmen *(Ho)*	Jul 2001	
Vernon	C J	Charlie	FB		1876			Sep 1901	1	0			T			
Viggars	R W	Ralph	WH		1901	1971	AVTC Chiseldon	Jan 1928	15	1	1	0		Bath City	Sep 1931	
Vincent	J R	Jamie	FB		1975		Yeovil Town	Jul 2006	84	0	5	0		Released	May 2009	
Viveash	A L	Adrian	D		1969		Apprentice	Jul 1988	51 + 3	3	8 + 2	0		Walsall	Nov 1995	234
			Returned from				Reading	Jul 2003	14 + 1	0	2	0		Aldershot	Dec 2004	
Vowles	V H	Bert	FB		1875	1933	St Marks YMCA	1894	1	0			A			
Waddock	*G P*	*Gary*	*M*	*EI*	*1962*		*Queens Park Rangers*	*Mar 1992*	*5 + 1*	*0*			*L*			
Wade	B A	Bryan	F		1963		Trowbridge Town	May 1985	48 + 12	18	13 + 4	6		Swansea City	Aug 1988	
Waite	R H	Bob	HB		1904	1991	Watch Hill	Nov 1924	4	0				Bath City	Aug 1927	
Walker	B A	Bruce	W		1946		Hungerford Town	Sep 1963	26 + 3	5	10	2		Bradford City	Mar 1968	
Walker	J	Jock	FB	S	1882	1968	Cowdenbeath	Jun 1907	214	0	34	0		Middlesbrough	Apr 1913	39,56
			Returned from				*Middlesbrough*	*cs 1915*	*0*		*9*	*0*	*G*			
Walker	J	Jock	F		1902	1984	Hibernian	Jun 1927	20	4	1	0		Ebbw Vale	cs 1929	
Walker	*P G*	*Paul*	*M*		*1949*		*Wolverhampton Wanderers*	*Feb 1973*	*2 + 3*	*0*			*L*			
Wall	A	Alec	IF		1899	1978	Everton	Jun 1925	56	20	6	3		Retired (injury)	Apr 1928	
Wallace	R	Bob	FB		1909	1938	Bolton Wanderers	Jan 1935	12	0	1	0		Plymouth Argyle	May 1935	
Wallis	C J	Charlie	CF		1876	1932	Swindon Star	cs 1897	1	0			A			
Walman	H	Bert	IF		1871	1957	Swindon Wanderers	cs 1894	12	2	2	0	A			
Walsh	R	Roy	M		1955		New Jersey Americans *(US)*	Mar 1980	7	0	4	0		Linfield	cs 1981	
Walters	M E	Mark	M	E	1964		Southampton	Jul 1996	91 + 21	24	12 + 2	4		Bristol Rovers	Nov 1999	239
Warburton	F	Frank	F		1880	1948	Bury	Jun 1907	25	9	3	2		Plymouth Argyle	cs 1908	39
Ward	A	Allan	CF		1891		Parkgate	Dec 1912	0		1	0	A	Released	Feb 1913	
Wardrope	W	Billy	IF		1876		Fulham	Jun 1906	38	8	1	1		Hamilton Academical	cs 1907	
Ware	E A G	Ted	WH		1906	1976	Clapton Orient	May 1936	5	0				Crewe Alexandra	Jun 1937	
Wareing	W	Billy	HB		1887	1955	Everton	May 1920	156	8	12	2		Retired	cs 1925	63
Warman	H	Bert	FB		1878	1955	Trowbridge Town	cs 1905	2	0			A	Assistant Club Trainer	cs 1907	
Warner	*A R*	*Tony*	*G*	*T*	*1974*		*Liverpool*	*Nov 1997*	*2*	*0*			*L*			
Warren	J G	Jesse	CF		1896	1982	Highworth Town	cs 1919	3	1			A			
Watson	K E	Kevin	M		1974		Tottenham Hotspur	Jul 1996	39 + 24	1	3 + 4	0		Rotherham United	Jul 1999	
Weale	R H	Bobby	W		1903	1969	West Ham United	Jun 1927	20	7				Southampton	Dec 1928	
Weale	T J	Tommy	W		1910	1971	Folkestone Town	Nov 1929	2	1				Cardiff City	Aug 1930	
Weaver	E	Eric	W		1943		Box Rovers	Dec 1961	13	2			A	Trowbridge Town	cs 1962	
			Returned from				RAF Rudloe Manor	Aug 1965	42	4	4	1		Notts County	Aug 1967	

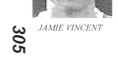

JAMIE VINCENT

BRYAN WADE

ALEC WALL

MARK WALTERS

Surname	Initials	Known As	Pos	Intl	Born	Died	Previous Club	Signed	Lge Apps	Gls.	Other Apps	Gls.		Went to	When Left	Pics
Webb	G H	Harry	CH		1875	1960	Swindon St Pauls	1893	1	0			A			
Webb	W	Billy	F		1874		Even Swindon United	1895	2	0			A			
Webb	*N J*	*Neil*	*M*	*E*	*1963*		*Nottingham Forest*	*Oct 1994*	*5 + 1*	*0*			*L*			
Webster	H	Herbie	G		1910	1970	West Bromwich Albion	May 1929	7	0	1	0		Released	cs 1931	*80*
Wegerle	*R C*	*Roy*	*F*	*US*	*1964*		*Chelsea*	*Mar 1988*	*7*	*1*			*L*			
Wells	B	Ben	M		1988		Trainee	2004	0 + 6	0				Basingstoke Town	May 2007	
Wells	T C	Tommy	W		1905	1971	Northampton Town	Jun 1935	34	7	4	0		Clapton Orient	May 1936	
Weston	C J	Curtis	M		1987		Millwall	Jul 2006	21 + 6	1	3 + 1	0		Leeds United	Jun 2007	
Weston	A M	Tober	FB		1888	1966	Calne & Harris United	Aug 1913	322	9	35	0		Retired	cs 1929	
Westwood	*A M*	*Ashley*	*D*		*1976*		*Chester City*	*Mar 2007*	*8 + 1*	*0*			*L*			
Whalley	G G	Gareth	M		1973		Wigan Athletic	Jul 2005	23 + 1	0	5	0		Altrincham	Apr 2007	
Wheatcroft	F G	Freddy	F		1882	1917	Derby County	Sep 1904	34	11	3	4	A	Fulham	Mar 1906	*43*
				Returned from			Reading	May 1909	183	77	25	6		Killed in Action	Nov 1917	
Wheeler	A J	Alf	F		1922		Blackburn Rovers	Jul 1949	23	4	2	0		Boston United	Aug 1951	
Whipp	P L	Percy	IF		1893	1962	Brentford	May 1930	9	5				Bath City	Jul 1931	
Whitbread	A R	Adrian	CD		1971		Leyton Orient	Jul 1993	35 + 1	1	2	0		West Ham United	Aug 1994	
White	A	Alex	FB		1916	1995	Chelsea	Jul 1948	35	0	3	0		Southport	Jul 1950	
White	S J	Steve	F		1959		Bristol Rovers	Jul 1986	200 + 44	83	52 + 16	28		Hereford United	Aug 1994	*205,225*
Whiteside	C W P	Charlie	IF		1927	1988	Liverpool junior foootball	Nov 1948	1	0				Bangor City	Feb 1951	
Whitley	*J*	*Jim*	*M*		*1975*		*Manchester City*	*Dec 2000*	*2*	*0*	*1*	*0*	*L*			
Whyte	F O	Frank	CH		1934	1984	Glasgow Celtic	Jun 1956	7	0				Released	Dec 1956	
Wilcockson	E S	Stan	WH		1905	1965	Leeds United	May 1935	134	5	15	0		Tunbridge Wells Rangers	May 1939	
Wildman	F R	Frank	G		1908	1994	Reading	Jul 1936	97	0	57	0		Frickley Colliery	Jul 1946	
Wilkins	L	Les	IF		1907	1979	Brentford	Aug 1932	20	8				Stockport County	Aug 1933	
Williams	A	Ady	D		1971		Coventry City	Jun 2006	27 + 1	0	3	0		Coaching Staff	cs 2008	
Williams	A P R	Andy	M		1977		Southampton	Sep 1999	38 + 6	1	1 + 2	0		Bath City	May 2001	
Williams	B	Brian	W		1955		Queens Park Rangers	Jun 1978	89 + 10	8	23	2		Bristol Rovers	Jul 1981	
Williams	C	Charlie	G			1940		cs 1893	23	0	9	0		Retired	cs 1902	*10*
Williams	G	Gary	D		1959		Blackpool	Aug 1981	37 + 1	3	4	0		Tranmere Rovers	Feb 1983	
Williams	H G	Harry	IF		1929		Bury	Jun 1954	14	7				Rhyl	Sep 1956	
Williams	J D	James	M		1982		Trainee	Dec 1998	21 + 16	1	4 + 1	0		Southport	Sep 2003	
Williams	M K	Martin	F		1973		Reading	Sep 2000	17 + 2	2	5	1		Peterborough United	Jan 2001	
Williams	G G	'Slacker'	WH		1925	1996	Pinehurst YC	Aug 1945	129	15	33	11		Retired	cs 1957	
Williamson	S H	Stewart	WH		1926		Tranmere Rovers	Jun 1953	17	0				Merthyr Tydfil	Sep 1955	
Willis	A P	Adam	D		1976		Coventry City	Apr 1998	76 + 16	1	8 + 3	2		Kidderminster Harriers	Aug 2003	

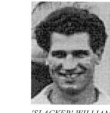

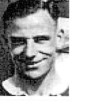

'TOBER' WESTON

STAN WILCOCKSON

FRANK WILDMAN

'SLACKER' WILLIAMS

Surname	Initials	Known As	Pos	Intl	Born	Died	Previous Club	Signed	Lge Apps	Gls.	Other Apps	Gls.		Went to	When Left	Pics
Wilson	J	Jock	FB				Small Heath	cs 1899	22	0	1	0		St Mirren	Jun 1900	
Wilson	T C	Tommy	W			1940	Oldham County	May 1897	31	6	3	1		Blackburn Rovers	May 1898	
			Returned from				Rochdale	May 1899	30	7	1	0		Millwall Athletic	May 1900	
Wise	K K	Ken	W		1914	1981	West Ham United	Jun 1936	13	1	1	0		(local football)	cs 1939	
Woan	I S	Ian	M		1967		Barnsley	Oct 2000	21 + 1	3	3	0		Columbus Crew *(US)*	May 2001	
Wolfe	G	George	HB		1878	1958	Woolwich Arsenal	cs 1903	46	0	4	0		Nottingham Forest	May 1905	
Wollen	T L	Terry	FB		1943		Juniors	Aug 1960	84	0	12	0		Trowbridge Town	Feb 1966	*141*
Woodruff	R W	Bobby	F		1940		Juniors	May 1958	180	20	24	0		Wolverhampton Wanderers	Mar 1964	*147*
Woodruff	*R J*	*Robert*	*F*		*1965*		*Newport County*	*May 1984*	*1 + 1*	*0*			*L*			
Woods	C	Cyril	CF		1915	1999	Bolton Wanderers	May 1937	4	0				Hartlepools United	Jul 1938	
Woolford	F O K	Corby	FB		1890	1913	Haydon Street WMC	cs 1909	5	0	5	0				*56*
Woolford	M E G	Mick	IF		1939		Swindon British Railways	Aug 1959	3	0				Trowbridge Town	Jun 1961	
Woolhouse	R	Ben	W		1904	1986	Walsall	Aug 1938	4	0	1	0		Released	cs 1939	
Worrall	B J	Ben	M		1975		Trainee	Jul 1994	1 + 2	0				Scarborough	Aug 1996	
Wright	R	Bob	IF				AVTC Chiseldon	Nov 1934	11	0			A			
Wright	W J	Wally	IF		1870	1945	Long Eaton Rangers	cs 1895	5	0	3	0		Released	Dec 1895	
Wylie	T	Tom	CH		1871		Burslem Port Vale	Oct 1897	1	0				Released	Dec 1897	
Wylie	T	Tommy	FB		1896	1956	Darwen	Dec 1926	82	0	8	0		Peebles Rovers	cs 1930	
Yeates	*M S A*	*Mark*	*M*		*1985*		*Tottenham Hotspur*	*Aug 2004*	*3 + 1*	*0*			*L*			
Young	A J	Alan	F		1983		Trainee	Oct 2000	7 + 22	1	2 + 4	2		Swindon Supermarine	Dec 2003	
Young	A E	Albert	FB		1917		Arsenal	Mar 1946	123	1	11	0		Chelmsford City	Aug 1950	
Young	H	Bert	W		1899	1976	Bristol Rovers	Jun 1932	14	2				Released	cs 1933	
Zaaboub	S	Sofi	M		1983		Bruxelles *(Be)*	Nov 2006	41 + 15	1	5 + 3	0		Walsall	Jul 2008	

KEY TO ABBREVIATIONS USED

Positions

CD	Central defender
CF	Centre-forward
CH	Centre-half
D	Defender
F	Forward / striker
FB	Full-back
G	Goalkeeper
HB	Half-back
IF	Inside-forward
M	Midfielder
U	Utility (any outfield)
W	Winger
WH	Wing-half
cs	Close season

* Shown in brackets ( )

Indicator following Appearances

A	Amateur
C	Coaching staff
G	*War-time Guest player*
L	*Loan player*
T	Triallist

Country of origin for prev./next Clubs *

At	Austria
Be	Belgium
De	Denmark
Fr	France
Ho	Holland
It	Italy
Je	Jersey
NZ	New Zealand
Ro	Romania
Sv	Slovakia
Sp	Spain
Sw	Sweden
Tu	Turkey

Internationals

Al	Algeria
Ar	Argentina
Au	Australia
Bm	Bermuda
E	England
Ei	Republic of Ireland
Fn	Finland
Gu	Guadeloupe
Ha	Haiti
Ja	Jamaica
M	Malta
No	Norway
NI	Northern Ireland
S	Scotland
SA	South Africa
SL	Sierra Leone
T	Trinidad & Tobago
US	United States
W	Wales

TERRY WOLLEN

TOMMY WYLIE

ALEERT YOUNG

ACCRINGTON STANLEY

Away Venue : Peel Park

Home	Season	Away	Comp.
L1-2	1958/59	D0-0	Div 3
L0-1	1959/60	L1-3	Div 3
W2-0	2006/07	D1-1c	Chp D2

c *Played at Crown Ground*

ARSENAL

Away Venue : Highbury

Home	Season	Away	Comp.
W1-0	1910/11		FAC2
D0-0	1928/29	L0-1	FAC5
	1968/69	*W3-1	FLCF
L0-2	1971/72		FAC3
W4-3	1979/80	D1-1	FLC5
L0-4	1993/94	D1-1	PL

ASTON VILLA

Away Venue : Villa Park

Home	Season	Away	Comp.
D1-1	1969/70	W2-0	Div 2
L1-3	1972/73	L1-2	Div 2
W1-0	1973/74	D1-1	Div 2
D0-0	1987/88	L1-2	Div 2
L1-2	1991/92		FAC5
L1-2	1993/94	L0-5	PL

BARNET

Away Venue : Underhill

Home	Season	Away	Comp.
W2-1	2006/07	L0-1	Chp D2
D1-1	2007/08	P1-1	FAC3

BARNSLEY

Away Venue : Oakwell

Home	Season	Away	Comp.
	1902/03	L0-4	FACIM
	1911/12	*D0-0	FACSF
		*L0-1	Rep.
D0-0	1922/23	L0-2	FAC1
D1-1	1959/60	W3-0	Div 3
W1-0	1960/61	L1-2	Div 3
D1-1	1961/62	L2-6	Div 3
W2-1	1962/63	D1-1	Div 3
W2-0	1968/69	D1-1	Div 3
L0-1	1979/80	W2-1	Div 3
W2-0	1980/81	L0-2	Div 3
W3-0	1987/88	W1-0	Div 2
D0-0	1988/89	D1-1	Div 2
D0-0	1989/90	W1-0	Div 2
L1-2	1990/91	L1-5	Div 2
W3-1	1991/92	D1-1	Div 2
W1-0	1992/93	L0-1	New D1
D0-0	1994/95	L1-2	New D1
W3-0	1996/97	D1-1	New D1
L1-3	1998/99	W3-1	New D1
D0-0		L1-3	FAC3
L1-2	1999/2000	L0-1	New D1
W3-1	2002/03	D1-1	New D2
D1-1	2003/04	D1-1	New D2
W2-1	2004/05	D2-2	Chp D1
L0-3	2005/06	L0-2	Chp D1

ALDERSHOT TOWN

Away Venue : Recreation Ground

Home	Season	Away	Comp.
	2008/09	P2-2	FLT1

BIRMINGHAM CITY

Away Venue : St Andrews

Home	Season	Away	Comp.
W2-0	1961/62	D1-1	FLC1
W4-1	1969/70	L0-2	Div 2
L1-2	1970/71	L1-2	Div 2
D1-1	1971/72	L1-4	Div 2
W2-0	1972/73		FAC3
L0-2	1987/88	D1-1	Div 2
W2-1	1988/89	W2-1	Div 2
D0-0	1992/93	W6-4	New D1
W3-1	1996/97	L0-1	New D1
D1-1	1997/98	L0-3	New D1
L0-1	1998/99	D1-1	New D1
L1-4	1999/2000	D1-1	New D1

BLACKBURN ROVERS

Away Venue : Ewood Park

Home	Season	Away	Comp.
L0-1	1921/22		FAC2
W1-0	1967/68		FAC3
W1-0	1968/69		FLC3
W1-0	1969/70	L0-2	Div 2
		W4-0	FAC3
W3-0	1970/71	L0-1	Div 2
W2-0	1974/75	L0-2	Div 3
W2-0	1979/80	L0-2	Div 3
L1-2	1983/84		FAC4
L1-2	1987/88	D0-0	Div 2
		W2-1	FMC1
D1-1	1988/89	D0-0	Div 2
W4-3	1989/90	L1-2	Div 2
W2-1		W2-1	D2 P/Off
D1-1	1990/91	L1-2	Div 2
W2-1	1991/92	L1-2	Div 2
L1-3	1993/94	L1-3	PL
L2-3	1995/96	L0-2	FLC2
W2-1	1999/2000	D0-0	New D1

BLACKPOOL

Away Venue : Bloomfield Road

Home	Season	Away	Comp.
D1-1	1969/70	L2-3	Div 2
W1-0	1971/72	L1-4	Div 2
D0-0	1972/73	L0-2	Div 2
W1-0	1973/74	L0-2	Div 2
L0-1	1978/79	L2-5	Div 3
W2-1	1979/80	W1-0	Div 3
L1-2	1980/81	D1-1	Div 3
D3-3	1982/83	L1-2	Div 4
D0-0	1983/84	D1-1	Div 4
W4-1	1984/85	L0-1	Div 4
L2-6	1986/87	D1-1	Div 3
D1-1	1995/96	D1-1	New D2
W1-0	2001/02	L0-1	New D2
D1-1	2002/03	D0-0	New D2
D2-2	2003/04	D2-2	New D2
D2-2	2004/05	D1-1	Chp D1
D0-0	2005/06	D0-0	Chp D1

AFC BOURNEMOUTH

Away Venue : Dean Court

Home	Season	Away	Comp.
W3-1	1923/24	D0-0	Div 3S
W4-0	1924/25	D0-0	Div 3S
W8-2	1925/26	L0-2	Div 3S
W2-0	1926/27	W2-1	Div 3S
L3-4		D1-1	FAC1
W3-2	1927/28	L0-2	Div 3S
D3-3	1928/29	L1-2	Div 3S
D1-1	1929/30	W3-1	Div 3S
W4-1	1930/31	L1-4	Div 3S
W3-0	1931/32	L1-2	Div 3S
W2-0	1932/33	L1-5	Div 3S
W3-2	1933/34	D1-1	Div 3S
L0-2	1934/35	D1-1	Div 3S
		L0-3	3S Cup
L2-3	1935/36	L0-1	Div 3S
W3-1	1936/37	L2-5	Div 3S
W1-0	1937/38	W2-1	Div 3S
W4-2	1938/39	L0-2	Div 3S
W2-1	1945/46	W4-2	3S(S)
D0-0		L1-6	3S Cup
L1-3	1946/47	L2-5	Div 3S
L0-1	1947/48	L0-1	Div 3S
D2-2	1948/49	L0-3	Div 3S
W3-1	1949/50	D1-1	Div 3S
W2-1	1950/51	L1-2	Div 3S
W2-0	1951/52	L1-4	Div 3S
L1-2	1952/53	D1-1	Div 3S
W2-1	1953/54	L0-4	Div 3S
L0-2	1954/55	D1-1	Div 3S
D2-2	1955/56	L0-4	Div 3S
W2-1	1956/57	L0-7	Div 3S
L0-1			FAC2
W1-0	1957/58	D1-1	Div 3S
L0-1	1958/59	D3-3	Div 3
W2-0	1959/60	L1-3	Div 3
L0-1	1960/61	L1-2	Div 3
D1-1	1961/62	D0-0	Div 3
W2-1	1962/63	D0-0	Div 3
D0-0	1965/66	L0-1	Div 3
W1-0	1966/67	W4-1	Div 3
W2-1			FLC1
W4-0	1967/68	L1-2	Div 3
W3-0	1968/69	L0-2	Div 3
W2-1	1974/75	D1-1	Div 3
W2-0	1980/81	D1-1	FLC1
D1-1	1986/87	L0-1	Div 3
D2-2			AMC1
W4-2	1987/88	L0-2	Div 2
W3-1	1988/89	W3-2	Div 2
L2-3	1989/90	W2-1	Div 2
D2-2	1995/96	D0-0	New D2
D1-1	2000/01	L0-3	New D2
D0-0	2001/02	D0-0a	New D2
W2-1	2003/04	D2-2	New D2
L0-3	2004/05	L1-2	Chp D1
W4-2	2005/06	L1-2	Chp D1
W4-1	2007/08	D2-2	Chp D1

a *Played at The Avenue,Dorchester*

BRENTFORD

Away Venue : Griffin Park

Home	Season	Away	Comp.
	1900/01	*D0-0	SL Test
D0-0	1901/02	L0-2b	SL
W3-0	1902/03	L0-1b	SL
D1-1	1903/04	L1-2b	SL
L1-3	1904/05	D1-1	SL
D1-1	1905/06	L1-3	SL
W2-0	1906/07	L2-5	SL
D0-0	1907/08	L0-2	SL
W2-1	1908/09	L0-1	SL
W4-0	1909/10	D1-1	SL
W3-0	1910/11	D1-1	SL
W2-0	1911/12	L0-2	SL
W2-0	1912/13	W3-0	SL
W3-1	1919/20	L0-2	SL
W1-0	1920/21	W1-0	Div 3
W2-1	1921/22	L0-3	Div 3S
W3-0	1922/23	L0-3	Div 3S
W2-1	1923/24	D2-2	Div 3S
W2-0	1924/25	D0-0	Div 3S
W2-1	1925/26	L1-3	Div 3S
W4-2	1926/27	D2-2	Div 3S
D1-1	1927/28	W4-1	Div 3S
W3-1	1928/29	L0-2	Div 3S
L0-2	1929/30	L2-3	Div 3S
W3-2	1930/31	L2-5	Div 3S
L1-3	1931/32	L0-2	Div 3S
D0-0	1932/33	L0-1	Div 3S
D1-1	1954/55	L2-4	Div 3S
L0-1	1955/56	W2-1	Div 3S
L1-3	1956/57	L1-4	Div 3S
W4-1	1957/58	D0-0	Div 3S
D1-1	1958/59	D2-2	Div 3
D0-0	1959/60	L1-2	Div 3
D1-1	1960/61	L1-2	Div 3
W5-2	1961/62	L0-1	Div 3
W2-1	1965/66	W1-0	Div 3
W2-1	1977/78		FAC2
W2-0	1978/79	W2-1	Div 3
W4-0	1979/80	W3-1	Div 3
W4-1			FAC1
D0-0	1980/81	D1-1	Div 3
D2-2	1982/83	W3-1	FAC2
W2-0	1986/87	D1-1	Div 3
		L2-4	AMCPr
L0-2	1992/93	D0-0	New D1
L1-2			AICPr
D2-2	1995/96	W2-0	New D2
L2-3	2000/01	W1-0	New D2
W2-0	2001/02	L0-2	New D2
W2-1	2002/03	L1-3	New D2
W2-1	2003/04	W2-0	New D2
W3-0	2004/05	L1-2	Chp D1
L1-3	2005/06	D0-0	Chp D1
P2-2	2006/07		FLC1
W4-1	2007/08		FLT1

b *Played at Boston Park*

For key to abbreviations - see Page 317

BOLTON WANDERERS

Away Venue : Burnden Park

Home	Season	Away	Comp.
	1913/14	L2-4	FAC2
L1-3	1964/65	D1-1	Div 2
W3-2	1969/70	W1-0	Div 2
W3-1	1970/71	W3-0	Div 2
D2-2	1973/74	L0-2	Div 2
W2-0	1986/87	W2-1	Div 3
D3-3	1989/90	D1-1	FLC3
W2-1		D1-1	FLC3
L0-1	1994/95	L0-3	New D1
W2-1		L1-3	FLCSF
D2-2	1996/97	L0-7	New D1
D3-3	1998/99	L1-2r	New D1
L0-4	1999/2000	L0-2r	New D1

r *Played at Burnden Way*

BRADFORD CITY

Away Venue : Valley Parade

Home	Season	Away	Comp.
D2-2	1958/59	W2-1	Div 3
W5-3	1959/60	L0-1	Div 3
W4-0	1960/61	L1-2	Div 3
W4-3	1968/69	D1-1	FLC2
L0-1	1977/78	L1-2	Div 3
D2-2	1987/88	L0-2	Div 2
W1-0	1988/89	D2-2	Div 2
W3-1	1989/90	D1-1	Div 2
W4-1	1995/96	D1-1	New D2
D1-1	1996/97	L1-2	New D1
W1-0	1997/98	D1-1	New D1
L1-4	1998/99	L0-3	New D1
W1-0	2004/05	W2-1	Chp D1
L2-3	2005/06	D1-1	Chp D1

BRIGHTON & HOVE ALBION
Away Venue : Goldstone Ground

Home	Season	Away	Comp.
D1-1	1903/04	W1-0	SL
W1-0	1904/05	L0-2	SL
W2-0	1905/06	D1-1	SL
W3-0		L0-1	UL
		L0-3	FAC1
D0-0	1906/07	L0-1	SL
W5-1	1907/08	D2-2	SL
W2-0	1908/09	L0-3	SL
W1-0	1909/10	L1-3	SL
		L1-3	SCC
W3-0	1910/11	W1-0	SL
		*D0-0	SCCF
		*W1-0	Rep.
L1-3	1911/12	L0-2	SL
W4-0	1912/13	L0-2	SL
D1-1	1913/14	L0-2	SL
W2-1	1914/15	W3-1	SL
W2-1	1919/20	L0-2	SL
W2-0	1920/21	W3-0	Div 3
W1-0	1921/22	L1-2	Div 3S
W3-0	1922/23	D1-1	Div 3S
W4-0	1923/24	D1-1	Div 3S
W3-0	1924/25	L1-3	Div 3S
W1-0	1925/26	L1-3	Div 3S
D2-2	1926/27	L3-9	Div 3S
W4-3	1927/28	L2-4	Div 3S
D2-2	1928/29	D2-2	Div 3S
L0-1	1929/30	L0-3	Div 3S
D1-1	1930/31	L0-1	Div 3S
L1-2	1931/32	L0-1	Div 3S
W5-1	1932/33	L1-5	Div 3S
D1-1	1933/34	L0-3	Div 3S
		L1-3	FAC3
D4-4	1934/35	D2-2	Div 3S
L1-2	1935/36	W2-0	Div 3S
W2-1			3S Cup
L1-2	1936/37	L0-2	Div 3S
L0-1	1937/38	L1-3	Div 3S
W3-2	1938/39	L0-4	Div 3S
W3-2	1945/46	L3-4	3S(S)
D2-2	1946/47	W4-1	Div 3S
D1-1	1947/48	L0-1	Div 3S
D0-0	1948/49	D1-1	Div 3S
W4-2	1949/50	W1-0	Div 3S
D0-0	1950/51	L0-1	Div 3S
L0-2	1951/52	L0-4	Div 3S
W3-0	1952/53	W2-1	Div 3S
L0-1	1953/54	D1-1	Div 3S
L0-2	1954/55	L1-3	Div 3S
D0-0	1955/56	L0-2	Div 3S
W3-0	1956/57	L0-2	Div 3S
D2-2	1957/58	L0-1	Div 3S
W5-1	1962/63	D1-1	Div 3
W3-2	1965/66	L0-1	Div 3
D1-1	1966/67	D2-2	Div 3
W2-1	1967/68	D0-0	Div 3
W1-0	1968/69	W3-1	Div 3
D2-2	1972/73	L1-3	Div 2
W1-0	1974/75	D1-1	Div 3
W3-2	1975/76	L0-2	Div 3
W2-1	1976/77	L0-4	Div 3
W3-0	1988/89	W2-0	Div 2
L1-2	1989/90	W2-1	Div 2
L1-3	1990/91	D3-3	Div 2
W2-1	1991/92	W2-0	Div 2
W4-1	1994/95	D1-1	FLC3
W3-2	1995/96	W3-1	New D2
D1-1	2001/02	D0-0w	New D2
W2-1	2003/04	D2-2w	New D2
L0-1		P2-1w	D2 P/Off
L0-3	2007/08	L1-2w	Chp D1
L0-2	2008/09	W3-2w	Chp D1
		L0-2w	FLTQF

w *Played at Withdean*

BRISTOL CITY
Away Venue : Ashton Gate

Home	Season	Away	Comp.
D2-2	1897/98	L1-4s	SL
W1-0		D3-3s	WL
D2-2	1898/99	L2-4s	SL
W2-1	1899/1900	L2-3s	SL
W1-0		L1-3s	WL
L0-1	1900/01	L0-2s	SL
L0-1		L0-4s	WL
L1-2	1915/16	L0-1	SWCL
L0-1	1922/23	L1-3	Div 3S
W3-0	1924/25	D0-0	Div 3S
L1-3	1925/26	L1-5	Div 3S
D2-2	1926/27	L0-2	Div 3S
L1-4	1932/33	L1-5	Div 3S
W4-2	1933/34	D2-2	Div 3S
W1-0	1934/35	L0-2	Div 3S
D1-1	1935/36	L0-5	Div 3S
L0-1	1936/37	W2-1	Div 3S
L2-3	1937/38	D1-1	Div 3S
W1-0	1938/39	D1-1	Div 3S
W7-2	1939/40	W6-2	SWRL
L1-3		L1-5	SWRL
W4-3	1945/46	L1-4	3S(S)
D1-1		L1-2	3S Cup
D1-1	1946/47	L1-3	Div 3S
D2-2	1947/48	D2-2	Div 3S
W2-1	1948/49	W3-1	Div 3S
D1-1	1949/50	L0-1	Div 3S
W1-0	1950/51	L0-2	Div 3S
D0-0	1951/52	L1-2	Div 3S
D0-0	1952/53	L2-4	Div 3S
W5-0	1953/54	L1-5	Div 3S
D2-2	1954/55	L0-3	Div 3S
W3-1	1960/61	D1-1	Div 3
L0-4	1961/62	L3-5	Div 3
W3-2	1962/63	D2-2	Div 3
D1-1	1969/70	D3-3	Div 2
W2-1	1970/71	L1-2	Div 2
L0-1	1971/72	L0-1	Div 2
W2-1	1972/73	L0-3	Div 2
L0-1	1973/74	L0-1	Div 2
D0-0	1981/82	W3-0	Div 3
W2-0	1982/83	D1-1	Div 4
W2-1		L0-2	FLC1
D1-1	1983/84	L0-1	Div 4
D0-0	1985/86	L2-4	FAC1
L1-2	1986/87	D1-1	Div 3
W3-0	1987/88	L2-3	FLC1
	1989/90	L1-2	FAC3
L0-1	1990/91	W4-0	Div 2
W2-0	1991/92	D1-1	Div 2
W2-1	1992/93	D2-2	New D1
L0-3	1994/95	L2-3	New D1
W2-0	1995/96	D0-0	New D2
W3-2	1998/99	L1-3	New D1
D1-1	2000/01	W1-0	New D2
L1-2	2001/02	L1-3	New D2
D1-1	2002/03	L0-2	New D2
D1-1	2003/04	L1-2	New D2
D0-0	2004/05	W2-1	Chp D1
W1-0			FLTQF
W2-1	2005/06	D1-1	Chp D1

s *Played at St Johns Lane*

BRISTOL ROVERS
Away Venue : Eastville

Home	Season	Away	Comp.
W3-0	1897/98	W1-0	WL
L1-3	1898/99	W2-1	WL
W1-0	1899/1900	L2-7	SL
W2-0		L1-2	WL
L0-1	1900/01	L0-1	SL
L0-1		L1-4	WL
		L1-5	FAC5Q
L0-1	1901/02	L0-1	SL
L0-2		L1-4	WL
L0-1			FAC5Q
W2-1	1902/03	W3-2	SL
L0-2	1903/04	L0-2	SL
W2-1	1904/05	L0-3	SL
L1-2	1905/06	L1-2	SL
W1-0	1906/07	L0-2	SL
W4-1	1907/08	L0-1	SL
L0-1	1908/09	W3-1	SL
W2-0	1909/10	D0-0	SL
W4-1			SCC1
D0-0	1910/11	L0-1	SL
W6-2			SCC2
W2-0	1911/12	L0-3	SL
D2-2	1912/13	W4-1	SL
W3-2			SCC1
W5-0	1913/14	L2-5	SL
W4-1	1914/15	L0-1	SL
D2-2	1915/16	D0-0	SWCL
W4-1	1919/20	L1-2	SL
W2-1	1920/21	L1-3	Div 3
L0-1	1921/22	D1-1	Div 3S
W1-0	1922/23	L0-2	Div 3S
D0-0	1923/24	W1-0	Div 3S
W3-0	1924/25	W1-0	Div 3S
W4-2	1925/26	W2-1	Div 3S
L3-5	1926/27	L1-3	Div 3S
W2-1	1927/28	L0-1	Div 3S
W2-1	1928/29	W4-1	Div 3S
D2-2	1929/30	L2-3	Div 3S
W3-1	1930/31	L1-4	Div 3S
W2-1	1931/32	W2-0	Div 3S
D1-1	1932/33	L0-1	Div 3S
W1-0	1933/34	L0-3	Div 3S
W1-0	1934/35	D2-2	Div 3S
W3-0	1935/36	L1-2	Div 3S
W4-1	1936/37	L1-2	Div 3S
L0-3			3S Cup
W2-1	1937/38	W2-1	Div 3S
W2-1	1938/39	L0-5	Div 3S
D3-3	1939/40	W4-3	SWRL
D1-1		L2-5	SWRL
L2-3	1945/46	L0-2	3S(S)
W2-1		D0-0	3S Cup
W1-0		L1-4	FAC1
W1-0	1946/47	L0-3	Div 3S
D1-1	1947/48	L1-3	Div 3S
D1-1	1948/49	D1-1	Div 3S
W1-0	1949/50	L0-2	Div 3S
W1-0			FAC1
L1-2	1950/51	L0-1	Div 3S
D0-0	1951/52	L0-1	Div 3S
L1-3	1952/53	W2-1	Div 3S
W3-0	1962/63	L0-2	Div 3
W4-3	1965/66	W1-0	Div 3
L0-1	1966/67	L0-3	Div 3
W4-1	1967/68	W2-1	Div 3
D2-2	1968/69	L1-2	Div 3
W5-2	1981/82	W4-1	Div 3
L1-5	1984/85	W1-0	FLC1
	1985/86	L1-2	AMC1
L1-2	1986/87	W4-3a	Div 3
L0-2	1990/91	L1-2t	Div 2
W1-0	1991/92	D1-1t	Div 2
D2-2	1992/93	W4-3t	New D1
W2-1	1995/96	W4-1t	New D2
L1-3	2000/01	D0-0m	New D2
W2-1	2006/07	L0-1m	Chp D2
W1-0	2007/08	W1-0m	Chp D1
W2-1	2008/09	D2-2m	Chp D1

a *Played at Ashton Gate*
t *Played at Twerton Park*
m *Played at Memorial Ground*

BURNLEY
Away Venue : Turf Moor

Home	Season	Away	Comp.
W2-0	1909/10		FAC2
D1-1	1923/24	L1-3	FAC4
W3-2	1928/29	D3-3	FAC4
L1-2	1932/33		FAC3
	1947/48	W2-0	FAC3
L1-2	1968/69	W2-1	FLCSF
		*W3-2	Rep.
L0-1	1971/72	W2-1	Div 2
L0-1	1972/73	L1-2	Div 2
L0-3	1980/81	D0-0	Div 3
L1-2	1981/82	W2-0	Div 3
	1982/83	L1-3	FAC4
W3-1	1985/86	W2-0	Div 4
D1-1	1994/95	W2-1	New D1
D0-0	1995/96	D0-0	New D2

BURY
Away Venue : Gigg Lane

Home	Season	Away	Comp.
D0-0	1958/59	D0-0	Div 3
W1-0	1959/60	W3-0	Div 3
W4-0	1960/61	L0-3	Div 3
W2-1	1963/64	L0-1	Div 2
W2-0	1964/65	L1-6	Div 2
W2-1	1966/67		FAC4
L2-3	1967/68	D1-1	Div 3
L0-2	1974/75	D0-0	Div 3
W2-1	1975/76	L0-5	Div 3
L0-1	1976/77	W1-0	Div 3
D1-1	1977/78	D0-0	Div 3
W2-1	1978/79	W1-0	Div 3
W8-0	1979/80	D0-0	Div 3
D1-1	1982/83	D0-0	Div 4
D0-0	1983/84	L1-2	Div 4
W1-0	1984/85	L0-2	Div 4
W1-0	1986/87	W2-1	Div 3
W3-1	1997/98	L0-1	New D1
D1-1	1998/99	L0-3	New D1
W3-0	2000/01	L0-1	New D2
W3-1	2001/02	W3-0	New D2
W2-1	2006/07	W1-0	New D2

For key to abbreviations - see Page 317

CARDIFF CITY
Away Venue : Ninian Park

Home	Season	Away	Comp.
L1-2	1913/14	D0-0	SL
D0-0	1914/15	L0-3	SL
L0-2	1915/16	L0-1	SWCL
D2-2	1919/20	D3-3	SL
L1-4	1931/32	L0-3	Div 3S
W6-2	1932/33	L0-3	Div 3S
W6-3	1933/34	W1-0	Div 3S
W2-1	1934/35	W3-1	Div 3S
W2-1	1935/36	L1-2	Div 3S
W4-2	1936/37	W2-1	Div 3S
		L1-2	FAC2
W2-0	1937/38	D2-2	Div 3S
W4-1	1938/39	L1-2	Div 3S
L0-1	1939/40	N/P	Div 3S
D2-2		D1-1	SWRL
D2-2		D1-1	SWRL
L1-2	1945/46	L0-3	3S(S)
W3-2		L0-2	3S Cup
W3-2	1946/47	L0-5	Div 3S
W1-0	1951/52	D1-1	FAC3
L1-2	1963/64	L0-1	Div 2
D3-3	1964/65	L0-2	Div 2
W2-1	1969/70	D2-2	Div 2
D2-2	1970/71	D1-1	Div 2
W3-1	1971/72	W1-0	Div 2
W3-0	1972/73	D1-1	Div 2
D1-1	1973/74	L1-2	Div 2
W4-0	1975/76	D0-0	Div 3
W5-1	1977/78		FLC2
W3-0	1978/79		FAC3
W2-0	1995/96		FAC2
L0-3	2001/02	L0-3	New D2
L0-1	2002/03	D1-1	New D2

CARLISLE UNITED
Away Venue : Brunton Park

Home	Season	Away	Comp.
	1949/50	L0-2	FAC2
W2-0	1962/63	D0-0	Div 3
D2-2	1969/70	D2-2	Div 2
D0-0	1970/71	L1-2	Div 2
D0-0	1971/72	D0-0	Div 2
W2-0	1972/73	L0-3	Div 2
D2-2	1973/74	L1-5	Div 2
D2-2	1977/78	D2-2	Div 3
D0-0	1978/79	L0-2	Div 3
D0-0	1979/80	L1-2	Div 3
D1-1	1980/81	L1-2	Div 3
W2-1	1981/82	D1-1	Div 3
W3-1	1983/84	D1-1	FAC3
W2-0	1986/87	W3-0	Div 3
W2-1	1995/96	W1-0	New D2
W3-1	2006/07		FAC1
D2-2	2007/08	L0-3	Chp D1
D1-1	2008/09	D1-1	Chp D1

CHELSEA
Away Venue : Stamford Bridge

Home	Season	Away	Comp.
	1910/11	L1-3	FAC4
D1-1a	1914/15	L2-5	FAC1
	1919/20	L0-4	FAC2
L0-2	1920/21		FAC2
W3-0	1963/64		FLC2
W4-0	1987/88		FMC3
D1-1	1988/89	L2-3	Div 2
	1990/91	L0-1	FMC2
	1991/92	L0-1	FMC2
L1-3	1993/94	L0-2	PL

a *Played at Stamford Bridge*

CHARLTON ATHLETIC
Away Venue : The Valley

Home	Season	Away	Comp.
D0-0	1921/22	W5-4	Div 3S
W2-1	1922/23	L1-3	Div 3S
D1-1	1923/24	L1-3c	Div 3S
D2-2	1924/25	L0-1	Div 3S
W3-0	1925/26	L0-2	Div 3S
W2-0	1926/27	D2-2	Div 3S
D2-2	1927/28	L1-3	Div 3S
D1-1	1928/29	L1-4	Div 3S
L1-3	1933/34	L0-1	Div 3S
D2-2	1934/35	L0-6	Div 3S
	1955/56	L1-2	FAC4
D2-2	1963/64	D2-2	Div 2
W2-0	1964/65	L2-3	Div 2
W5-0	1969/70	D1-1	Div 2
D1-1	1970/71	L1-2	Div 2
W2-1	1971/72	L1-3	Div 2
W2-0	1974/75	D3-3	Div 3
L0-3	1980/81	D0-0	Div 3
D1-1	1990/91	W2-1s	Div 2
L1-2	1991/92	D0-0u	Div 2
D2-2	1992/93	L0-2u	New D1
L0-1	1994/95	L0-1	New D1
L1-3		W4-1	FLC2
W1-0	1996/97	L0-2	New D1
L0-1	1997/98	L0-3	New D1
L1-2	1999/2000	W1-0	New D1
		L1-2	FAC3
L0-2	2007/08		FLC1

c *Played at Catford*
s *Played at Selhurst Park*
u *Played at Upton Park*

CHELTENHAM TOWN
Away Venue : Whaddon Road

Home	Season	Away	Comp.
L0-3	2002/03	L0-2	New D2
W3-0	2007/08	D1-1	Chp D1
L1-3			FLT2
D2-2	2008/09	L1-2	Chp D1

CHESTER CITY
Away Venue : Sealand Road

Home	Season	Away	Comp.
W4-2	1969/70		FAC4
W2-1	1975/76	L1-2	Div 3
W2-1	1976/77	L1-2	Div 3
D1-1	1977/78	L0-1	Div 3
W2-0	1978/79	L0-2	Div 3
W3-1	1979/80	L0-1	Div 3
W1-0		D1-1	FLC2
L1-2	1980/81	L0-1	Div 3
W3-0	1981/82	D0-0	Div 3
L2-3	1982/83	W1-0	Div 4
W4-0	1983/84	W3-0	Div 4
D4-4	1984/85	L0-2	Div 4
W4-2	1985/86	W1-0	Div 4
D1-1	1986/87	L0-2	Div 3
W1-0	2006/07	W2-0d	Chp D2

d *Played at Deva Stadium*

Relegated from Football League 2009

For key to abbreviations - see Page 317

CHESTERFIELD
Away Venue : Saltergate

Home	Season	Away	Comp.
W2-1	1934/35		FAC3
L1-2	1958/59	W3-1	Div 3
D1-1	1959/60	W3-1	Div 3
W2-0	1960/61	D1-1	Div 3
	1973/74	L0-1	FLC2
W1-0	1974/75	W2-0	Div 3
L0-1	1975/76	L0-4	Div 3
W3-0	1976/77	W1-0	Div 3
W2-1	1977/78	L1-3	Div 3
W1-0	1978/79	D1-1	Div 3
W2-1	1979/80	L1-2	Div 3
L0-1	1980/81	D2-2	Div 3
L1-2	1981/82	L1-2	Div 3
L1-2	1983/84	L0-1	Div 4
W4-0	1984/85	L0-1	Div 4
W2-1	1986/87	W3-1	Div 3
D1-1	1995/96	W3-1	New D2
	2001/02		New D2
	2002/03	W4-2	New D2

COLCHESTER UNITED
Away Venue : Layer Road

Home	Season	Away	Comp.
D1-1	1950/51	L1-4	Div 3S
W2-1	1951/52	L0-2	Div 3S
L0-1	1952/53	L1-3	Div 3S
W3-0	1953/54	D2-2	Div 3S
D1-1	1954/55	D0-0	Div 3S
W3-1	1955/56	L0-5	Div 3S
W4-1	1956/57	D1-1	Div 3S
W4-0	1957/58	W3-1	Div 3S
W2-0	1958/59	L0-1	Div 3
W4-3	1959/60	D0-0	Div 3
L0-2	1960/61	L1-3	Div 3
W6-1	1962/63	W2-0	Div 3
D1-1	1966/67	L1-2	Div 3
D1-1	1967/68	L1-2	Div 3
	1971/72	L1-4	FLC2
W4-1	1974/75	L0-2	Div 3
L0-1	1975/76	W2-1	Div 3
D0-0	1977/78	L0-2	Div 3
L1-2	1978/79	L2-3	Div 3
L2-3	1979/80	W3-2	Div 3
W3-0	1980/81	L0-1	Div 3
W3-0	1982/83	L0-1	Div 4
W2-1	1983/84	D0-0	Div 4
W2-1	1984/85	D1-1	Div 4
W2-1	1985/86	D1-1	Div 4
W2-0	1995/96		FLT1
D0-0	2000/01	W1-0	New D2
W1-0	2001/02	W3-1	New D2
		L0-1	FLT1
D2-2	2002/03	L0-1	New D2
W2-0	2003/04	W1-0	New D2
L0-3	2004/05	W1-0	Chp D1
W1-0	2005/06	L0-1	Chp D1
L1-3	2008/09	L2-3c	Chp D1

c *Played at Community Stadium*

CREWE ALEXANDRA
Away Venue : Gresty Road

Home	Season	Away	Comp.
W1-0	1968/69	W2-1	Div 3
W1-0	1982/83	L0-3	Div 4
W1-0	1983/84	L0-2	Div 4
D1-1	1984/85	L2-3	Div 4
W1-0	1985/86	L0-2	Div 4
W2-1	1995/96	W2-0	New D2
W2-0	1997/98	L0-2	New D1
L1-2	1998/99	W2-0	New D1
L0-1	1999/2000	L1-2	New D1
L1-3	2002/03	W1-0	New D2
D1-1	2007/08	D0-0	Chp D1
D0-0	2008/09	L0-1	Chp D1

COVENTRY CITY
Away Venue : Highfield Road

Home	Season	Away	Comp.
W2-1	1908/09	D1-1	SL
W2-1	1909/10	W2-0	SL
W3-0	1910/11	D2-2	SL
D2-2	1911/12	D1-1	SL
W1-0	1912/13	L1-2	SL
W6-1	1913/14	D1-1	SL
		L0-2	SCC1
D2-2	1926/27	W3-1	Div 3S
W6-0	1927/28	L0-4	Div 3S
L1-2	1928/29	L1-4	Div 3S
D1-1	1929/30	W2-1	Div 3S
W4-0	1930/31	L0-4	Div 3S
D2-2	1931/32	L2-3	Div 3S
L1-2	1932/33	L1-2	Div 3S
L0-1	1933/34	L1-5	Div 3S
D0-0	1934/35	L0-3	Div 3S
L1-2	1935/36	L1-2	Div 3S
L0-2		L2-3	3SCupSF
L2-3	1952/53	W2-1	Div 3S
D1-1	1953/54	D0-0	Div 3S
W3-0	1954/55	L0-1	Div 3S
D1-1	1955/56	L0-6	Div 3S
D2-2	1956/57	L0-3	Div 3S
W2-1			FAC1
W2-1	1957/58	W1-0	Div 3S
W2-0	1959/60	L1-3	Div 3
L1-2	1960/61	D1-1	Div 3
D3-3	1961/62	L1-2	Div 3
W4-1	1962/63	L0-2	Div 3
W4-1	1964/65	L2-3	Div 2
L1-2	1965/66		FAC3
W3-0	1968/69	D2-2	FLC4
W3-1	1993/94	D1-1	PL
L0-2	2000/01		FAC3

DAGENHAM & REDBRIDGE
Away Venue : Victoria Road

Home	Season	Away	Comp.
L1-2	1984/85	D0-0	FAC1

DARLINGTON
Away Venue : Feethams

Home	Season	Away	Comp.
	1910/11	W3-0	FAC3
W4-0	1962/63		FLC2
	1965/66	L1-2	FLC2
W4-0	1966/67	L1-2	Div 3
L1-2	1982/83	L0-1	Div 4
W1-0	1983/84	L0-1	Div 4
W1-0	1984/85	L0-1	Div 4
W1-0	1986/87	D0-0	Div 3
W4-0	1990/91	L0-3	FLC2
D1-1	2006/07	W2-1d	Chp D2

d *Played at Darlington Arena*

DERBY COUNTY
Away Venue : Baseball Ground

Home	Season	Away	Comp.
D0-0	1963/64	L0-3	Div 2
W4-2	1964/65	L1-4	Div 2
W1-0	1968/69	D0-0	FLC5
L0-1	1972/73		FLC2
W2-1	1987/88		FMC2
L1-2	1991/92	L1-2	Div 2
L2-4	1992/93	L1-2	New D1
D1-1	1994/95	L1-3	New D1
W2-1			FLC4

CRYSTAL PALACE

Away Venue : Selhurst Park

Home	Season	Away	Comp.
L1-6	1905/06	D1-1	UL
W2-1	1906/07	L2-3s	SL
D0-0	1907/08	L1-4s	SL
W4-0	1908/09	D1-1s	SL
W2-1	1909/10	L0-2s	SL
		W3-1s	FAC1
D0-0	1910/11	W5-2s	SL
W2-1	1911/12	D2-2s	SL
W1-0	1912/13	L0-1s	SL
L0-2	1913/14	W1-0s	SL
W5-2	1914/15	L1-3s	SL
D2-2	1919/20	W2-1n	SL
L1-3	1920/21	L0-1n	Div 3
	1923/24	W2-1n	FAC3
W3-1	1925/26	L0-1	Div 3S
W6-1	1926/27	L0-5	Div 3S
D3-3	1927/28	L0-1	Div 3S
D0-0		W2-1	FAC2
W3-2	1928/29	L1-6	Div 3S
W3-1	1929/30	L0-1	Div 3S
D4-4	1930/31	L1-3	Div 3S
W3-2	1931/32	D0-0	Div 3S
W1-0	1932/33	L3-4	Div 3S
W3-2	1933/34	D0-0	Div 3S
D1-1	1934/35	L0-7	Div 3S
L0-2	1935/36	L1-5	Div 3S
W4-0	1936/37	L0-2	Div 3S
W4-0	1937/38	W1-0	Div 3S
D2-2	1938/39	D1-1	Div 3S
L1-3	1945/46	L1-10	3S(S)
W1-0	1946/47	L1-4	Div 3S
D0-0	1947/48	D1-1	Div 3S
W1-0	1948/49	D1-1	Div 3S
W4-2	1949/50	D2-2	Div 3S
W2-0	1950/51	L0-2	Div 3S
L0-2	1951/52	W1-0	Div 3S
L3-6	1952/53	L0-3	Div 3S
D1-1	1953/54	L2-3	Div 3S
D0-0	1954/55	D0-0	Div 3S
L0-2			FAC1
D0-0	1955/56	W2-0	Div 3S
W3-1	1956/57	D0-0	Div 3S
D0-0	1957/58	L1-4	Div 3S
W5-0	1961/62	L1-3	Div 3
W1-0	1962/63	D0-0	Div 3
W2-0	1964/65	L1-3	Div 2
L0-1	1973/74	L2-4	Div 2
D1-1	1974/75	L2-6	Div 3
L1-2	1975/76	D3-3	Div 3
D1-1	1976/77	L0-5	Div 3
D2-2	1987/88	L1-2	Div 2
W1-0	1988/89	L1-2	Div 2
L1-2		L0-2	FLC2
W1-0		L0-2	D2 P/Off
	1989/90	L0-1	FMC4
L0-1	1991/92		FLC4
L0-2	1996/97	W2-1	New D1
W2-0	1998/99	W1-0	New D1
L2-4	1999/2000	W2-1	New D1
	2006/07	L1-2	FAC3

s *Played at Sydenham*
n *Played at The Nest,Selhurst*

For key to abbreviations - see Page 317

DONCASTER ROVERS

Away Venue : Belle Vue

Home	Season	Away	Comp.
D0-0	1958/59	L0-2	Div 3
L0-1	1966/67	L0-1	Div 3
W4-2		D1-1	FLC3
D2-2	1981/82	D0-0	Div 3
W2-1	1983/84	L0-3	Div 4
D1-1	1986/87	D2-2	Div 3
D1-1	2004/05	D1-1	Chp D1
W2-1	2005/06	L0-1	Chp D1
L1-2	2007/08	L0-2k	Chp D1

k *Played at Lakeside Stadium*

EXETER CITY

Away Venue : St James's Park

Home	Season	Away	Comp.
W2-1	1908/09	W4-1	SL
W3-1	1909/10	W1-0	SL
W4-0			SCC2
L0-1	1910/11	L1-2	SL
L0-1	1911/12	W4-1	SL
		L0-2	SCC1
D2-2	1912/13	W3-1	SL
		L0-2	SCC2
D1-1	1913/14	W2-0	SL
W4-0	1914/15	W1-0	SL
D1-1	1919/20	L1-3	SL
D1-1	1920/21	L0-1	Div 3
D1-1	1921/22	W4-1	Div 3S
W2-1	1922/23	L1-2	Div 3S
L0-1	1923/24	L1-3	Div 3S
W1-0	1924/25	L0-1	Div 3S
W2-1	1925/26	W2-1	Div 3S
W4-2	1926/27	L1-3	Div 3S
W3-0	1927/28	D0-0	Div 3S
W2-0	1928/29	D1-1	Div 3S
W1-0	1929/30	L1-5	Div 3S
W2-1	1930/31	L1-3	Div 3S
W2-1	1931/32	D1-1	Div 3S
D2-2	1932/33	L0-5	Div 3S
D1-1	1933/34	D2-2	Div 3S
W6-1	1934/35	D3-3	Div 3S
D1-1	1935/36	W3-0	Div 3S
W3-1	1936/37	D1-1	Div 3S
W3-0	1937/38	D0-0	Div 3S
W2-0			3S Cup
W2-1	1938/39	D0-0	Div 3S
L2-3		D1-1	3S Cup
L1-4	1945/46	D1-1	3S(S)
W2-0	1946/47	D1-1	Div 3S
W3-2	1947/48	L1-2	Div 3S
D1-1	1948/49	L1-3	Div 3S
W7-1	1949/50	L0-3	Div 3S
W1-0	1950/51	L0-1	Div 3S
		L0-3	FAC2
W3-1	1951/52	W2-1	Div 3S
W5-2	1952/53	W2-1	Div 3S
L2-4	1953/54	L1-3	Div 3S
W2-0	1954/55	L1-2	Div 3S
L0-1	1955/56	W2-1	Div 3S
L3-5	1956/57	L2-3	Div 3S
W5-1	1957/58	W1-0	Div 3S
D2-2	1965/66	D1-1	Div 3
W4-0	1977/78	D0-0	Div 3
D1-1	1978/79	W2-1	Div 3
L2-3	1979/80	L1-4	Div 3
D2-2	1980/81	W4-3	Div 3
W3-2	1981/82	W2-1	Div 3
W2-0	1984/85	D1-1	Div 4
W2-1	1985/86	W3-0	Div 4
D1-1	2000/01	W2-1	FLC1
	2004/05	W2-1	FLT2

EVERTON

Away Venue : Goodison Park

Home	Season	Away	Comp.
W2-1	1911/12		FAC4
L1-5	1962/63		FAC4
D2-2	1976/77	L1-2	FAC4
D1-1	1993/94	L2-6	PL
	1996/97	L0-3	FAC3

FULHAM

Away Venue : Craven Cottage

Home	Season	Away	Comp.
	1901/02	*W3-1	SL Test
D2-2	1903/04	W2-1	SL
W2-1	1904/05	L0-3	SL
L1-4	1905/06	D1-1	SL
D2-2	1906/07	L0-4	SL
	1919/20	W2-1	FAC1
L1-2	1924/25		FAC1
L1-2	1928/29	L0-2	Div 3S
D1-1	1929/30	L1-4	Div 3S
W4-1	1930/31	L1-6	Div 3S
D2-2	1931/32	D2-2	Div 3S
	1970/71	L0-1	FAC4
W4-0	1971/72	W4-2	Div 2
D2-2	1972/73	D0-0	Div 2
D1-1	1973/74	L1-4	Div 2
W5-0	1976/77	D3-3	FAC3
L3-4	1980/81	L0-2	Div 3
L1-4	1981/82	L0-2	Div 3
W2-0	1986/87	W2-0	Div 3
W1-0	1999/2000	L0-1	New D1

GRIMSBY TOWN

Away Venue : Blundell Park

Home	Season	Away	Comp.
D0-0	1920/21	L0-3	Div 3
W2-1	1937/38	D1-1	FAC3
W3-2	1959/60	L0-3	Div 3
W3-0	1960/61	L2-3	Div 3
D0-0	1961/62	W1-0	Div 3
W2-1	1963/64	W2-1	Div 2
D0-0	1965/66	D2-2	Div 3
W3-1	1966/67	W4-3	Div 3
W5-0	1967/68	L2-3	Div 3
W3-2	1974/75	L0-2	Div 3
W3-0	1975/76	L0-1	Div 3
W4-1	1976/77	L0-2	Div 3
W3-0	1979/80	L0-2	Div 3
D1-1	1991/92	D0-0	Div 2
W1-0	1992/93	L1-2	New D1
W3-2	1994/95	D1-1	New D1
D3-3	1996/97	L1-2	New D1
W2-0	1998/99	L0-1	New D1
L0-1	1999/2000	L0-1	New D1
W2-0	2003/04	W2-1	New D1
W3-0	2006/07	L0-1	New D2

HARTLEPOOL UNITED

Away Venue : Victoria Ground

Home	Season	Away	Comp.
D1-1	1968/69	D0-0	Div 3
W3-0	1982/83	W2-1	Div 4
W3-2	1983/84	W1-0	Div 4
W2-1	1984/85	D2-2	Div 4
W3-1	1985/86	L0-1	Div 4
W3-1	2001/02		FAC1
D1-1	2003/04	L0-2	New D1
W3-0	2004/05	L0-3	Chp D1
D1-1	2005/06	D1-1	Chp D1
L0-1	2006/07	W1-0	Chp D2
W2-1	2007/08	D1-1	Chp D1
L0-1	2008/09	D3-3	Chp D1

GILLINGHAM

Away Venue : Priestfield

Home	Season	Away	Comp.
	1894/95	*L1-5	SL Test
W4-0	1895/96	D1-1	SL
W2-1	1896/97	L1-3	SL
L0-3	1897/98	W2-1	SL
W1-0	1898/99	L1-5	SL
D1-1	1899/1900	L2-4	SL
L2-3	1900/01	L0-1	SL
D1-1	1901/02	L0-5	SL
D1-1	1902/03	L1-2	SL
W3-0	1903/04	L1-3	SL
L1-2	1904/05	D0-0	SL
W2-0	1905/06	D0-0	SL
W3-2		L0-1	UL
W2-0	1906/07	L1-2	SL
W1-0	1907/08	W1-0	SL
W6-1	1908/09	L1-3	SL
W4-1	1909/10	L2-3	SL
W5-0	1910/11	L0-1	SL
W5-0	1911/12	L1-3	SL
W2-1	1912/13	D0-0	SL
W5-1	1913/14	W3-2	SL
W5-1	1914/15	L0-4	SL
W5-2	1919/20	L1-3	SL
D1-1	1920/21	D1-1	Div 3
D0-0	1921/22	D2-2	Div 3S
L0-1	1922/23	D0-0	Div 3S
W4-1	1923/24	L0-1	Div 3S
W2-0	1924/25	D1-1	Div 3S
W1-0	1925/26	W1-0	Div 3S
W1-0	1926/27	D4-4	Div 3S
W6-1	1927/28	W1-0	Div 3S
W2-1	1928/29	D0-0	Div 3S
W3-0	1929/30	D0-0	Div 3S
W5-2	1930/31	W1-0	Div 3S
W4-0	1931/32	L1-2	Div 3S
D1-1	1932/33	L1-3	Div 3S
W3-1	1933/34	D3-3	Div 3S
W3-0	1934/35	L0-2	Div 3S
W3-0	1935/36	L1-3	Div 3S
W3-0	1936/37	L1-4	Div 3S
W3-0	1937/38	D0-0	Div 3S
		W4-3	FAC1
W2-0	1950/51	L1-2	Div 3S
W2-1	1951/52	L0-4	Div 3S
D0-0	1952/53	D0-0	Div 3S
W2-1	1953/54	L0-1	Div 3S
W2-1	1954/55	L1-2	Div 3S
L0-1	1955/56	L0-4	Div 3S
L2-3	1956/57	L0-3	Div 3S
D1-1	1957/58	L1-2	Div 3S
L0-1	1965/66	L0-1	Div 3
W2-0	1966/67	L0-1	Div 3
D2-2	1967/68	L1-3	Div 3
W1-0	1968/69	L0-2	Div 3
W1-0	1974/75	L1-3	Div 3
D2-2	1975/76	L2-3	Div 3
D2-2	1976/77	D2-2	Div 3
W3-2	1977/78	D2-2	Div 3
W3-1	1978/79	D2-2	Div 3
W3-0	1979/80	D0-0	Div 3
D0-0	1980/81	D0-0	Div 3
L0-1	1981/82	L0-1	Div 3
D1-1	1986/87	W3-1	Div 3
W2-1		L0-1	D3 P/Off
		*W2-0	Rep.
W1-0	2005/06	L0-3	Chp D1
W5-0	2007/08	D1-1	Chp D1

HEREFORD UNITED

Away Venue : Edgar Street

Home	Season	Away	Comp.
W4-0	1955/56		FAC1
W1-0	1974/75	L1-2	Div 3
L0-1	1975/76	L0-1	Div 3
W1-0	1977/78	D1-1	Div 3
W3-2	1982/83	W2-1	Div 4
W3-0	1983/84	L1-2	Div 4
L0-3	1984/85	W3-0	Div 4
W1-0	1985/86	L1-4	Div 4
D1-1			AMC1
W4-2	1986/87		AMCQF
L0-1	1995/96		FLT2
W3-2	2001/02		FAC2
L1-2	2006/07	D0-0	Chp D2
W3-0	2008/09	D1-1	Chp D1
		W2-1	FLT2

HUDDERSFIELD TOWN

Away Venue : Leeds Road

Home	Season	Away	Comp.
	1912/13	W2-1	FAC2
L1-2	1963/64	L0-2	Div 2
W4-1	1964/65	L1-2	Div 2
W2-1	1969/70	D1-1	Div 2
D1-1	1972/73	D1-1	Div 2
W4-1	1974/75	D2-2	Div 3
W1-0	1980/81	W2-0	Div 3
L1-5	1981/82	L0-3	Div 3
W4-1	1987/88	W3-0	Div 2
	1991/92	W4-1	FLC3
W6-0	1996/97	D0-0k	New D1
D1-1	1997/98	D0-0k	New D1
W3-0	1998/99	W2-1k	New D1
W2-0	1999/2000	L0-4k	New D1
L0-1	2001/02	L0-2k	New D2
L0-1	2002/03	W3-2k	New D2
W1-0			FAC1
L1-2	2004/05	L0-4k	Chp D1
D0-0	2005/06	D1-1k	Chp D1
W3-2	2007/08	L0-1k	Chp D1
L1-3	2008/09	L1-2k	Chp D1

k *Played at Kirklees Stadium*

HULL CITY

Away Venue : Boothferry Park

Home	Season	Away	Comp.
W2-0	1958/59	D0-0	Div 3
D1-1	1960/61	D0-0	Div 3
D1-1	1961/62	W1-0	Div 3
W2-0	1962/63	D1-1	Div 3
W3-1	1965/66	L0-1	Div 3
W1-0	1969/70	D1-1	Div 2
D1-1	1970/71	L0-2	Div 2
W2-1	1971/72	L0-2	Div 2
W2-1	1972/73	L2-3	Div 2
D1-1	1973/74	W1-0	Div 2
W2-0	1978/79	D1-1	Div 3
D0-0	1979/80	L0-1	Div 3
W3-1	1980/81	D0-0	Div 3
L0-1	1982/83	D0-0	Div 4
D0-0	1987/88	W4-1	Div 2
W1-0	1988/89	L0-1	Div 2
L1-3	1989/90	W3-2	Div 2
W3-1	1990/91	D1-1	Div 2
W3-0	1995/96	W1-0	New D2
W4-2	2004/05	D0-0c	Chp D1

c *Played at The Circle*

IPSWICH TOWN

Away Venue : Portman Road

Home	Season	Away	Comp.
D1-1	1938/39	L1-3	Div 3S
W2-1	1946/47	L1-3	Div 3S
L0-1	1947/48	W1-0	Div 3S
W4-2			FAC1
W4-0	1948/49	L2-4	Div 3S
L0-3	1949/50	L1-3	Div 3S
W2-0	1950/51	L1-4	Div 3S
L1-2	1951/52	W5-1	Div 3S
W2-0	1952/53	D1-1	Div 3S
L1-2	1953/54	L0-2	Div 3S
L0-1	1955/56	L2-6	Div 3S
W3-1	1956/57	L1-4	Div 3S
W3-1	1964/65	D0-0	Div 2
L1-2			FAC3
	1985/86	L1-6	FLC4
W4-2	1987/88	L2-3	Div 2
L2-3	1988/89	W2-1	Div 2
W3-0	1989/90	L0-1	Div 2
W1-0	1990/91	D1-1	Div 2
D0-0	1991/92	W4-1	Div 2
D2-2	1993/94	D1-1	PL
D1-1		L1-2	FAC3
L0-4	1996/97	L2-3	New D1
L0-2	1997/98	L1-2	New D1
L0-6	1998/99	L0-1	New D1
L1-4	1999/2000	L0-3	New D1

LEEDS UNITED

Away Venue : Elland Road

Home	Season	Away	Comp.
W2-1	1921/22		FAC1
D2-2	1963/64	D0-0	Div 2
L0-2	1969/70		FAC6
	1970/71	L0-4	FAC4
L1-2	1986/87		FAC4
L1-2	1987/88	L2-4	Div 2
D0-0	1988/89	D0-0	Div 2
W3-2	1989/90	L0-4	Div 2
L0-5	1993/94	L0-3	PL
	2003/04	P2-2	FLC2
	2004/05	L0-1	FLC2
L0-1	2007/08	L1-2	Chp D1
L1-3	2008/09	L0-1	Chp D1

LEICESTER CITY

Away Venue : Filbert Street

Home	Season	Away	Comp.
D1-1	1969/70	W2-0	Div 2
L0-1	1970/71	L1-3	Div 2
W3-2	1987/88	L2-3	Div 2
W2-1	1988/89	D3-3	Div 2
D1-1	1989/90	L1-2	Div 2
W5-2	1990/91	D2-2	Div 2
D0-0	1991/92	L1-3	Div 2
D1-1	1992/93	L2-4	New D1
		*W4-3	D1 P/Off
D2-2	2008/09	D1-1f	Chp D1

f *Played at Filbert Way*

LINCOLN CITY

Away Venue : Sincil Bank

Home	Season	Away	Comp.
W4-3	1934/35		FAC2
W4-0	1961/62	D2-2	Div 3
W2-0	1974/75		FAC3
D2-2	1976/77	D0-0	Div 3
W1-0	1977/78	L1-3	Div 3
W6-0	1978/79	W3-0	Div 3
W2-0	1980/81	D1-1	FLC2
W1-0	1981/82	L0-2	Div 3
L0-1	2006/07	W3-2	Chp D2

LEYTON ORIENT

Away Venue : Brisbane Road

Home	Season	Away	Comp.
D1-1	1905/06	L1-3	UL
W2-1	1927/28		FAC3
D0-0	1929/30	L1-2m	Div 3S
W5-1	1930/31	W3-2b	Div 3S
L2-3	1931/32	L2-4b	Div 3S
D3-3	1932/33	L1-7b	Div 3S
W3-0	1933/34	L0-1b	Div 3S
D1-1	1934/35	L0-2b	Div 3S
D2-2	1935/36	W2-1b	Div 3S
L1-3	1936/37	D1-1b	Div 3S
W1-0	1937/38	L0-1	Div 3S
W2-0	1938/39	L0-5	Div 3S
W2-0	1946/47	D0-0	Div 3S
L0-1	1947/48	W3-0	Div 3S
D1-1	1948/49	D1-1	Div 3S
L0-1	1949/50	W3-1	Div 3S
W2-0	1950/51	L1-2	Div 3S
W2-0	1951/52	L0-1	Div 3S
D1-1	1952/53	D2-2	Div 3S
W2-1	1953/54	D1-1	Div 3S
D0-0	1954/55	L0-1	Div 3S
L1-2	1955/56	L0-4	Div 3S
W5-0	1963/64	L1-2	Div 2
W1-0	1964/65	W3-0	Div 2
W5-1	1966/67	D0-0	Div 3
W4-0	1967/68	D0-0	Div 3
W1-0	1968/69	L0-1	Div 3
D1-1	1970/71	L0-1	Div 2
D2-2	1971/72	W1-0	Div 2
W3-1	1972/73	L0-1	Div 2
D2-2	1973/74	D0-0	Div 2
W4-1	1985/86	L0-1	Div 4
W3-0	1986/87		AMCPr
W1-0	1990/91	D1-1	FAC3
L0-1	1999/2000	D1-1	FLC1
D1-1	2007/08	L1-2	Chp D1
L0-1	2008/09	W2-1	Chp D1

m *Played at Millfields Road*
b *Played at Lea Bridge Road*

For key to abbreviations
- see Page 317

LIVERPOOL

Away Venue : Anfield

Home	Season	Away	Comp.
W2-0	1970/71		FLC3
	1980/81	L0-5	FLC3
L0-5	1993/94	D2-2	PL

LUTON TOWN

Away Venue : Kenilworth Road

Home	Season	Away	Comp.
	1891/92	L3-4e	FAC1Q
L0-3	1894/95	L0-2e	SL
L0-2	1895/96	L1-7e	SL
W2-1	1900/01	L1-2d	SL
L1-2	1901/02	L0-3d	SL
W2-1	1902/03	D0-0d	SL
W1-0	1903/04	L0-3d	SL
W1-0	1904/05	L1-4d	SL
D1-1	1905/06	L0-4	SL
W3-2		L2-4	UL
W4-0	1906/07	L2-6	SL
W4-0	1907/08	L0-1	SL
W4-1	1908/09	L0-1	SL
D0-0	1909/10	D1-1	SL
W4-1	1910/11	L1-2	SL
W4-2	1911/12	W3-0	SL
D2-2	1914/15	D2-2	SL
W1-0	1919/20	L1-3	SL
W9-1	1920/21	L0-2	Div 3
D1-1	1921/22	L1-2	Div 3S
D1-1	1922/23	L2-3	Div 3S
W3-2	1923/24	L2-3	Div 3S
W4-1	1924/25	D2-2	Div 3S
W2-0	1925/26	L1-4	Div 3S
W2-0	1926/27	D1-1	Div 3S
W4-2	1927/28	D1-1	Div 3S
W4-2	1928/29	L3-5	Div 3S
D1-1	1929/30	D1-1	Div 3S
D0-0	1930/31	L0-4	Div 3S
W3-2	1931/32	L0-6	Div 3S
L0-5			FAC1
D1-1	1932/33	L2-6	Div 3S
W3-1	1933/34	W3-2	Div 3S
L0-1	1934/35	L0-2	Div 3S
W3-0	1935/36	L1-2	Div 3S
W5-3			3S Cup
D2-2	1936/37	L1-5	Div 3S
	1937/38	L1-2	FAC4
	1951/52	L1-3	FAC5
	1962/63	W2-0	FAC3
W2-1	1967/68		FAC2
D0-0	1968/69	L0-2	Div 3
D0-0	1970/71	D1-1	Div 2
W2-1	1971/72	D0-0	Div 2
L0-2	1972/73	W1-0	Div 2
L0-2	1973/74	L1-2	Div 2
	1979/80	W2-0	FAC3
	1981/82	L1-2	FAC3
	1987/88	L1-2	FMCSF
W1-0	1992/93	D0-0	New D1
L1-2	1994/95	L0-3	New D1
L1-3	2000/01	W3-2	New D2
W2-1	2002/03	L0-3	New D2
D2-2	2003/04	W3-0	New D2
L2-3	2004/05	L1-3	Chp D1
W2-1	2007/08	W1-0	Chp D1

e *Played at The Excelsior*
d *Played at Dunstable Road*

Relegated from Football League 2009

MACCLESFIELD TOWN

Away Venue : Moss Rose

Home	Season	Away	Comp.
W2-0	2006/07	L1-2	Chp D2

MANCHESTER CITY
Away Venue : Maine Road

Home	Season	Away	Comp.
W2-0	1909/10		FAC4
D1-1	1929/30	L1-10	FAC4
	1952/53	L0-7	FAC3
W3-0	1963/64	D0-0	Div 2
W2-1			FAC3
L0-1	1964/65	W2-1	Div 2
L3-4	1987/88	D1-1	Div 2
L1-2	1988/89	L1-2	Div 2
L1-3	1993/94	L1-2	PL
W2-0	1996/97	L0-3	New D1
L1-3	1997/98	L0-6	New D1
L0-2	1999/2000	L0-3	New D1
	2001/02	L0-2	FAC3

MANCHESTER UNITED
Away Venue : Old Trafford

Home	Season	Away	Comp.
	1911/12	*L4-8	FAChS
W1-0	1913/14		FAC1
	1929/30	W2-0	FAC3
D2-2	1993/94	L2-4	PL
	1996/97	L1-2	FLC3

MIDDLESBROUGH
Away Venue : Ayresome Park

Home	Season	Away	Comp.
W2-0	1963/64	D1-1	Div 2
L0-1	1964/65	L1-4	Div 2
W4-1	1966/67	L0-4	Div 3
L0-3	1969/70	D0-0	Div 2
W3-0	1970/71	L0-3	Div 2
L0-1	1971/72	L0-2	Div 2
W1-0	1972/73	W2-0	Div 2
L0-1	1973/74	L1-2	Div 2
W1-0	1986/87	L0-1	Div 3
D1-1	1987/88	W3-2	Div 2
D1-1	1989/90	W2-0	Div 2
L1-3	1990/91	L0-2	Div 2
L0-1	1991/92	D2-2	Div 2
W2-1	1994/95	L1-3	New D1
L1-2	1997/98	L0-6r	New D1

r *Played at Riverside Stadium*

MILTON KEYNES DONS
Away Venue : Natl. Hockey Stadium

Home	Season	Away	Comp.
W2-1	2004/05	D1-1	Chp D1
L0-1	2005/06	L1-3	Chp D1
W2-1	2006/07	W1-0	Chp D2
D1-1	2008/09	W2-1s	Chp D1

s *Played at Stadium:mk*

MORECAMBE

Home	Season	Away	Comp.
W1-0	2006/07		FAC2

For key to abbreviations - see Page 317

MILLWALL
Away Venue : Cold Blow Lane

Home	Season	Away	Comp.
L1-5	1894/95	L0-9e	SL
D2-2	1895/96	L1-9e	SL
L2-5	1896/97	L1-2e	SL
L0-5	1897/98	L2-4e	SL
L2-4	1898/99	L1-2e	SL
W2-1	1899/1900	L1-2e	SL
D1-1	1900/01	L0-4e	SL
D1-1		L0-6e	WL
W2-1	1901/02	L0-3g	SL
D2-2		L1-3g	WL
W3-2	1902/03	W2-1g	SL
L0-4	1903/04	L1-3g	SL
W2-1	1904/05	D0-0g	SL
D0-0	1905/06	D0-0g	SL
L0-2	1906/07	L1-2g	SL
W2-0	1907/08	L0-2g	SL
W3-0	1908/09	L1-4g	SL
W4-0	1909/10	L0-1g	SL
W1-0	1910/11	L0-2	SL
W4-1	1911/12	L0-1	SL
W2-1	1912/13	W1-0	SL
W2-0	1913/14	D1-1	SL
L1-2	1914/15	W2-1	SL
W1-0	1919/20	W2-0	SL
W4-1	1920/21	L0-5	Div 3
D1-1	1921/22	D0-0	Div 3S
D0-0	1922/23	D1-1	Div 3S
W1-0	1923/24	L0-1	Div 3S
W1-0	1924/25	W2-1	Div 3S
D1-1	1925/26	L0-3	Div 3S
W3-0	1926/27	L1-4	Div 3S
W3-0	1927/28	D3-3	Div 3S
L0-1	1934/35	L0-1	Div 3S
W3-1	1935/36	L0-1	Div 3S
W3-0	1936/37	D1-1	Div 3S
L1-2	1937/38	W2-0	Div 3S
L1-2			3S Cup
W2-0	1948/49	L1-3	Div 3S
D1-1	1949/50	L0-1	Div 3S
L0-1	1950/51	L0-1	Div 3S
D2-2	1951/52	D0-0	Div 3S
L1-2	1952/53	L0-3	Div 3S
W2-1	1953/54	L1-6	Div 3S
D1-1	1954/55	L0-1	Div 3S
W1-0	1955/56	D1-1	Div 3S
W1-0	1956/57	L1-2	Div 3S
W3-0	1957/58	D1-1	Div 3S
W1-0	1962/63	W4-3	Div 3
W1-0	1965/66	L0-1	Div 3
W2-1	1969/70	L1-3	Div 2
W3-0	1970/71	D2-2	Div 2
L0-2	1971/72	D2-2	Div 2
D0-0	1972/73	D1-1	Div 2
L1-3	1973/74	L0-3	Div 2
L0-2	1975/76	D0-0	Div 3
W2-1		W1-0	FLC1
W1-0	1979/80	L2-6	Div 3
D0-0	1980/81	L1-3	Div 3
L1-2	1981/82	D0-0	Div 3
	1983/84	W3-2	FAC2
		L1-3	AMC3
L0-1	1987/88	D2-2	Div 2
W2-1	1989/90		FMC2
D0-0	1990/91	L0-1	Div 2
W3-1	1991/92	D1-1	Div 2
W3-1		D2-2	FLC2
W3-0	1992/93	L1-2	New D1
L1-2	1994/95	L1-3n	New D1
W3-1			FLC5
L0-2	2000/01	L0-1n	New D2
		P0-0n	FLT2
W2-1	2007/08	W2-1n	Chp D1
L1-2	2008/09	D1-1n	Chp D1

e *Played at East Ferry Road*
g *Played at North Greenwich*
n *Played at The New Den*

NEWCASTLE UNITED
Away Venue : St James' Park

Home	Season	Away	Comp.
	1909/10	*L0-2	FACSF
W2-0	1928/29		FAC3
D0-0	1963/64	L1-4	Div 2
L1-6	1964/65	L0-1	Div 2
	1987/88	L0-5	FAC4
D1-1	1989/90	D0-0	Div 2
W3-2	1990/91	D1-1	Div 2
W2-1	1991/92	L1-3	Div 2
W2-1	1992/93	D0-0	New D1
D2-2	1993/94	L1-7	PL

NORWICH CITY
Away Venue : Carrow Road

Home	Season	Away	Comp.
L1-3	1905/06	L0-1n	SL
W3-1	1906/07	D1-1n	SL
D1-1	1907/08	L1-3n	SL
W10-2	1908/09	D0-0n	SL
W7-1	1909/10	W3-1n	SL
W5-1	1910/11	W2-1n	SL
W5-3	1911/12	L3-4n	SL
W3-0	1912/13	W2-0n	SL
W2-0	1913/14	W2-1n	SL
W4-0	1914/15	D1-1n	SL
L0-1	1919/20	L1-4n	SL
W4-2	1920/21	L2-3n	Div 3
W6-1	1921/22	W2-1n	Div 3S
L1-2	1922/23	D0-0n	Div 3S
W4-2	1923/24	L0-2n	Div 3S
W1-0	1924/25	L0-4n	Div 3S
W3-1	1925/26	D2-2n	Div 3S
W3-2	1926/27	L1-2n	Div 3S
D1-1	1927/28	W3-1n	Div 3S
L1-2	1928/29	D1-1n	Div 3S
W2-1	1929/30	W5-1n	Div 3S
W5-2	1930/31	L0-2n	Div 3S
		L0-2n	FAC1
W2-0	1931/32	L2-4n	Div 3S
L2-4	1932/33	L2-5n	Div 3S
D0-0	1933/34	L2-3n	Div 3S
D1-1	1946/47	W5-1	Div 3S
W3-2	1947/48	D2-2	Div 3S
D3-3	1948/49	D0-0	Div 3S
D1-1	1949/50	L0-4	Div 3S
W1-0	1950/51	L0-2	Div 3S
D1-1	1951/52	L0-2	Div 3S
W2-1	1952/53	D1-1	Div 3S
D0-0	1953/54	D2-2	Div 3S
W1-0	1954/55	L1-2	Div 3S
D1-1	1955/56	L1-4	Div 3S
D1-1	1956/57	W4-2	Div 3S
L1-2	1957/58	D1-1	Div 3S
W4-3	1958/59	D1-1	Div 3
D1-1		L0-1	FAC2
L0-1	1959/60	L2-3	Div 3
D2-2	1963/64	L2-3	Div 2
L0-1	1964/65	L1-3	Div 2
W2-0	1969/70	L0-1	Div 2
W3-2	1970/71	L0-1	Div 2
L0-1	1971/72	L0-1	Div 2
D0-0	1987/88	W2-0	FAC3
W2-0			FMC4
	1988/89	L1-2	FMC1
W4-1	1989/90		FMC3
	1990/91	L1-3	FAC4
D3-3	1993/94	D0-0	PL
L0-3	1996/97	L0-2	New D1
W1-0	1997/98	L0-5	New D1
D1-1	1998/99	L1-2	New D1
D0-0	1999/2000	W2-0	New D1

n *Played at The Nest,Rosary Road*

NORTHAMPTON TOWN
Away Venue : County Ground

Home	Season	Away	Comp.
L1-3	1901/02	L0-8	SL
L0-2	1902/03	L0-1	SL
W2-0	1903/04	D1-1	SL
W3-0	1904/05	L0-5	SL
L1-2	1905/06	L0-3	SL
W5-0	1906/07	L1-2	SL
W3-1	1907/08	L0-1	SL
W1-0	1908/09	D1-1	SL
L1-4	1909/10	L0-3	SL
W2-1	1910/11	W1-0	SL
D1-1	1911/12	L0-4	SL
W2-1	1912/13	D1-1	SL
D1-1	1913/14	L0-1	SL
D2-2	1914/15	W3-2	SL
W5-2	1919/20	W3-2	SL
W2-1	1920/21	W2-1	Div 3
W4-2	1921/22	L1-2	Div 3S
W2-0	1922/23	W2-1	Div 3S
W2-0	1923/24	D1-1	Div 3S
W5-0	1924/25	D0-0	Div 3S
L1-2	1925/26	L0-2	Div 3S
W3-1	1926/27	L0-1	Div 3S
W4-0	1927/28	L0-3	Div 3S
L0-1	1928/29	D1-1	Div 3S
W2-0	1929/30	D3-3	Div 3S
W5-1	1930/31	L0-3	Div 3S
W3-0	1931/32	L1-4	Div 3S
W2-1	1932/33	L0-6	Div 3S
D1-1	1933/34	D2-2	Div 3S
W5-3	1934/35	L2-4	Div 3S
W3-1	1935/36	D0-0	Div 3S
W1-0			3S Cup
W2-0	1936/37	L0-4	Div 3S
W1-0	1937/38	L0-1	Div 3S
W1-0	1938/39	W2-0	Div 3S
N/P	1939/40	L0-1	Div 3S
L1-4	1945/46	L1-5	3S Cup
W3-1	1946/47	L1-4	Div 3S
D0-0	1947/48	D0-0	Div 3S
D2-2	1948/49	W1-0	Div 3S
W6-1	1949/50	W1-0	Div 3S
W1-0	1950/51	W2-1	Div 3S
D1-1	1951/52	L0-1	Div 3S
W3-0	1952/53	L1-3	Div 3S
W2-0			FAC2
D0-0	1953/54	L0-2	Div 3S
L0-1	1954/55	L0-1	Div 3S
L0-1	1955/56	L1-2	Div 3S
W4-0	1956/57	L0-2	Div 3S
W5-1	1957/58	L0-3	Div 3S
D2-2	1961/62	W2-1	Div 3
L2-3	1962/63	D1-1	Div 3
L2-3	1963/64	L0-4	Div 2
W4-2	1964/65	L1-2	Div 2
W4-0	1967/68	L0-2	Div 3
W1-0	1968/69	W6-2	Div 3
W5-1	1976/77	D1-1	Div 3
W3-2		L0-2	FLC1
L1-5	1982/83	W1-0	Div 4
D0-0	1983/84	L0-2	Div 4
W2-0	1984/85	L0-4	Div 4
W3-2	1985/86	W1-0	Div 4
D1-1	2000/01	W1-0s	New D2
W2-1	2001/02	D1-1s	New D2
W2-0	2002/03	L0-1s	New D2
D1-1	2007/08	D1-1s	Chp D1
W2-1	2008/09	W4-3s	Chp D1

s *Played at Sixfields*

NOTTINGHAM FOREST

Away Venue : City Ground

Home	Season	Away	Comp.
	1925/26	L0-2	FAC4
L0-5	1949/50	L1-2	Div 3S
L2-3	1950/51	L1-2	Div 3S
D1-1	1966/67	D0-0	FAC5
		*L0-3	2nd Rep
D0-0	1972/73	D2-2	Div 2
D0-0	1973/74	L0-2	Div 2
	1977/78	L1-4	FAC3
D0-0	1997/98	L0-3	New D1
D0-0	1999/2000	L1-3	New D1
W2-1	2005/06	L1-7	Chp D1
W2-1	2007/08	L0-1	Chp D1

NOTTS COUNTY

Away Venue : Meadow Lane

Home	Season	Away	Comp.
W3-1	1910/11		FAC1
W2-0	1911/12		FAC2
L1-2	1930/31	L0-2	Div 3S
W2-1	1935/36	D0-0	Div 3S
W4-3			3S Cup
D2-2	1936/37	L2-3	Div 3S
W1-0	1937/38	L0-3	Div 3S
W4-1	1938/39	L0-2	Div 3S
W4-2	1946/47	D0-0	Div 3S
		L1-2	FAC2
D1-1	1947/48	L1-2	Div 3S
W1-0			FAC4
W3-0	1948/49	W2-1	Div 3S
D1-1	1949/50	L0-3	Div 3S
W3-1	1958/59	L0-1	Div 3
W1-0	1960/61	L0-1	Div 3
W1-0	1961/62	W1-0	Div 3
W3-1	1962/63	L0-2	Div 3
		L0-5	FLC3
L1-4	1973/74	L0-2	Div 2
L1-2	1986/87	W3-2	Div 3
L1-2	1990/91	D0-0	Div 2
W5-1	1992/93	D1-1	New D1
W3-0	1994/95	W1-0	New D1
W1-0	1995/96	W3-1	New D2
L1-2	2000/01	L2-3	New D2
W1-0	2001/02	L1-3	New D2
W5-0	2002/03	D1-1	New D2
W4-0	2003/04	W2-1	New D2
D1-1	2004/05	L0-2	FAC2
D1-1	2006/07	D1-1	Chp D2

OLDHAM ATHLETIC

Away Venue : Boundary Park

Home	Season	Away	Comp.
W2-0	1923/24		FAC2
L0-1	1965/66	D1-1	Div 3
W6-3	1966/67	L0-1	Div 3
D0-0	1967/68	W2-0	Div 3
W5-1	1968/69	W3-2	Div 3
W2-0	1987/88	L3-4	Div 2
D2-2	1988/89	D2-2	Div 2
W3-2	1989/90	D2-2	Div 2
D2-2	1990/91	L2-3	Div 2
L0-1	1992/93		FLC3
L0-1	1993/94	L1-2	PL
W3-1	1994/95	D1-1	New D1
W1-0	1995/96		FAC4
W1-0	1996/97	L1-5	New D1
W3-0	2000/01	L0-1	New D2
L0-2	2001/02	L0-2	New D2
L0-1	2002/03	L0-4	New D2
L1-2	2003/04	W1-0	New D2
W1-0	2004/05	W2-1	Chp D1
L2-3	2005/06	D2-2	Chp D1
W3-0	2007/08	D2-2	Chp D1
W2-0	2008/09	D0-0	Chp D1

PETERBOROUGH UNITED

Away Venue : London Road

Home	Season	Away	Comp.
D1-1	1955/56	W2-1	FAC2
W3-2	1961/62	L2-3	Div 3
L2-3	1962/63	L1-3	Div 3
W3-0	1965/66	W3-2	Div 3
W4-1	1966/67	W2-1	Div 3
D0-0	1967/68	D1-1	Div 3
L0-1	1974/75	D0-0	Div 3
L0-3	1975/76	L1-3	Div 3
L0-4	1976/77	L0-1	Div 3
W2-0	1977/78	L0-2	Div 3
W3-1	1978/79	L1-2	Div 3
L0-2		D1-1	FLC3
W1-0	1982/83	L3-4	Div 4
W2-0	1983/84	D1-1	Div 4
D1-1	1984/85	W1-0	Div 4
W3-0	1985/86	L0-3	Div 4
W1-0	1992/93	D3-3	New D1
W2-0	1995/96	W2-0	New D2
W2-1	2000/01	L0-4	New D2
D0-0	2001/02	D1-1	New D2
D1-1	2002/03	D1-1	New D2
W2-0	2003/04	L2-4	New D2
L0-1	2004/05	W2-0	Chp D1
	2005/06	L1-2	FLT2
L0-1	2006/07	D1-1	Chp D2
D2-2	2008/09	D2-2	Chp D1

PORT VALE

Away Venue : Vale Park

Home	Season	Away	Comp.
L1-2	1906/07		FAC5Q
D1-1	1938/39	L0-2h	Div 3S
W2-1	1946/47	D1-1h	Div 3S
W1-0	1947/48	L0-1h	Div 3S
L0-2	1948/49	L0-2h	Div 3S
D0-0	1949/50	W1-0h	Div 3S
W2-1	1950/51	L1-2	Div 3S
W2-0	1951/52	D2-2	Div 3S
D0-0	1957/58	L1-3	Div 3S
L2-3	1959/60	L1-6	Div 3
W6-0	1960/61	L1-4	Div 3
W1-0	1961/62	D1-1	Div 3
L2-3	1962/63	L1-2	Div 3
W3-2	1974/75	D2-2	Div 3
W2-1	1975/76	L0-3	Div 3
W1-0	1976/77	D2-2	Div 3
D1-1	1977/78	L0-1	Div 3
W1-0	1982/83	L0-3	Div 4
L0-1	1984/85	L0-2	Div 4
D0-0	1985/86	L0-3	Div 4
W1-0	1986/87	W4-3	Div 3
W3-0	1989/90	L0-2	Div 2
L1-2	1990/91	L1-3	Div 2
W1-0	1991/92	D2-2	Div 2
W2-0	1994/95	D2-2	New D1
D1-1	1996/97	L0-1	New D1
W4-2	1997/98	W1-0	New D1
D1-1	1998/99	W1-0	New D1
W2-1	1999/2000	L0-3	New D1
L0-1	2000/01	L0-3	New D2
W3-0	2001/02	W2-0	New D2
L1-2	2002/03	D1-1	New D2
D0-0	2003/04	D3-3	New D2
W1-0	2004/05	L0-1	Chp D1
L1-2	2005/06	D1-1	Chp D1
W6-0	2007/08	L1-2	Chp D1

h *Played at Hanley*

PLYMOUTH ARGYLE

Away Venue : Home Park

Home	Season	Away	Comp.
W2-0	1903/04	D0-0	SL
		L0-2	FAC5Q
W4-0	1904/05	L0-3	SL
W2-1	1905/06	L0-3	SL
D1-1	1906/07	D2-2	SL
W1-0	1907/08	L0-2	SL
W5-0	1908/09	D1-1	SL
		L0-1	FAC1
W4-1	1909/10	D0-0	SL
W4-0	1910/11	D1-1	SL
		W2-1	SCC1
W2-0	1911/12	D1-1	SL
D2-2	1912/13	L1-3	SL
W4-1	1913/14	L1-3	SL
W3-2	1914/15	L1-3	SL
W2-1	1919/20	L0-3	SL
D1-1	1920/21	D0-0	Div 3
L1-2	1921/22	L0-1	Div 3S
W2-1	1922/23	L0-2	Div 3S
L0-1	1923/24	W3-1	Div 3S
W1-0	1924/25	L0-2	Div 3S
W2-0	1925/26	D1-1	Div 3S
L1-2	1926/27	L1-3	Div 3S
D2-2	1927/28	L0-3	Div 3S
D0-0	1928/29	L0-3	Div 3S
L1-2	1929/30	L0-5	Div 3S
W2-0	1939/40	L1-2	SWRL
D2-2		L2-4	SWRL
L1-2	1950/51	L1-5	Div 3S
D2-2	1951/52	L0-3	Div 3S
L0-3	1956/57	L0-1	Div 3S
W1-0	1957/58	D2-2	Div 3S
L3-4	1958/59	L2-3	Div 3
W2-1	1963/64	W4-2	Div 2
L2-3	1964/65	L1-2	Div 2
W3-0	1968/69	L1-2	Div 3
W2-0	1974/75	L3-4	Div 3
W3-1	1977/78	W2-0	Div 3
L1-3	1978/79	L0-2	Div 3
W2-1	1979/80	L0-2	Div 3
W3-0	1980/81	D0-0	Div 3
L0-2	1981/82	L1-2	Div 3
W1-0	1983/84	L1-4	FLC1
D1-1	1987/88	L0-1	Div 2
W1-0	1988/89	L1-4	Div 2
W3-0	1989/90	W3-0	Div 2
D1-1	1990/91	D3-3	Div 2
W1-0	1991/92	W4-0	Div 2
W2-0	2002/03	D1-1	New D2
L2-3	2003/04	L1-2	New D2

PRESTON NORTH END

Away Venue : Deepdale

Home	Season	Away	Comp.
L0-2	1934/35		FAC4
	1961/62	L1-3	FLC2
L1-4	1963/64	L0-1	Div 2
D2-2	1964/65	L1-2	Div 2
W1-0	1969/70	L1-3	Div 2
D1-1	1971/72	D2-2	Div 2
W3-2	1972/73	D1-1	Div 2
W3-1	1973/74	D1-1	Div 2
W1-0	1974/75	L0-2	Div 3
L1-3	1975/76	L2-4	Div 3
L0-1	1976/77	L0-2	Div 3
L0-2	1977/78	D1-1	Div 3
W4-0	1981/82	D0-0	Div 3
W4-1	1985/86	W3-0	Div 4

PORTSMOUTH

Away Venue : Fratton Park

Home	Season	Away	Comp.
W3-1	1899/1900	L0-1	SL
		L1-2	FAC3Q
L0-3	1900/01	L0-2	SL
L0-1		L0-1	WL
L1-2	1901/02	L0-4	SL
L0-2		L1-5	WL
W2-1	1902/03	L2-3	SL
L0-1	1903/04	L0-1	SL
W3-1	1904/05	L0-2	SL
W2-1	1905/06	W2-1	SL
D0-0	1906/07	L0-1	SL
D0-0	1907/08	L0-2	SL
W5-0	1908/09	L1-3	SL
W3-1	1909/10	L1-3	SL
W2-1	1910/11	W2-1	SL
W3-0	1912/13	W2-1	SL
W5-0	1913/14	D1-1	SL
L1-3	1914/15	D1-1	SL
L1-2	1915/16	L1-6	SWCL
L0-3	1919/20	L1-4	SL
W5-2	1920/21	D1-1	Div 3
D0-0	1921/22	W3-1	Div 3S
W3-0	1922/23	L1-4	Div 3S
D0-0	1923/24	L1-4	Div 3S
L1-3	1961/62	D2-2	Div 3
W2-0	1963/64	W4-1	Div 2
D0-0	1964/65	L0-5	Div 2
W4-1	1966/67		FLC2
W3-1	1969/70	L1-3	Div 2
W2-1	1970/71	W2-0	Div 2
W3-1	1971/72	W2-1	Div 2
D1-1	1972/73	D1-1	Div 2
L1-2	1973/74	L1-3	Div 2
L0-1		D3-3	FAC3
L0-1	1974/75		FLC1
W4-3	1976/77	L1-2	Div 3
W3-1	1977/78	W2-1	Div 3
W4-3		D1-1	FLC3
W4-2	1978/79	D0-0	FLC1
W2-0	1979/80	D1-1	FLC1
L0-2	1980/81	L0-1	Div 3
W2-0	1981/82	L0-3	Div 3
W3-1	1987/88	W3-1	FLC2
D1-1	1988/89	W2-0	Div 2
W2-0		D1-1	FAC3
D2-2	1989/90	D1-1	Div 2
W3-0	1990/91	L1-2	Div 2
L2-3	1991/92	D1-1	Div 2
W1-0	1992/93	L1-3	New D1
	1993/94	L0-2	FLC3
L0-2	1994/95	L3-4	New D1
L0-1	1996/97	W1-0	New D1
L0-1	1997/98	W1-0	New D1
D3-3	1998/99	L2-5	New D1
D1-1	1999/2000	L1-4	New D1

For key to abbreviations - see Page 317

QUEENS PARK RANGERS
Away Venue : Loftus Road

Home	Season	Away	Comp.
W4-0	1899/1900	W5-3k	SL
W4-2	1900/01	L1-7k	SL
W3-2		L1-3k	WL
L0-3	1901/02	L0-4n	SL
D1-1		L2-4n	WL
W2-0	1902/03	L0-2n	SL
D1-1	1903/04	L0-1n	SL
D0-0	1904/05	L1-4p	SL
L1-2	1905/06	L0-3p	SL
D0-0	1906/07	L1-6p	SL
W8-3	1907/08	L1-2p	SL
W2-1			FAC2
W3-1	1908/09	L1-5p	SL
W1-0	1909/10	W3-0p	SL
W2-1	1910/11	L0-1p	SL
*D1-1		*D1-1	SCCSF
*D0-0		*W3-2	SCCSF
D1-1	1911/12	W3-1p	SL
W4-1	1912/13	L0-2p	SL
W3-0	1913/14	L2-4p	SL
L1-2	1914/15	L2-4p	SL
W5-2	1919/20	L1-2	SL
L0-1	1920/21	L0-1	Div 3
W2-0	1921/22	D0-0	Div 3S
W1-0	1922/23	W2-0	Div 3S
D0-0	1923/24	D2-2	Div 3S
W5-3	1924/25	L0-1	Div 3S
W2-0	1925/26	D1-1	Div 3S
W6-2	1926/27	W1-0	Div 3S
L0-2	1927/28	W1-0	Div 3S
W2-1	1928/29	L2-4	Div 3S
D2-2	1929/30	L3-8	Div 3S
W4-1	1930/31	W2-1	Div 3S
L1-2	1931/32	W2-1w	Div 3S
D0-0	1932/33	L2-4w	Div 3S
W3-1	1933/34	L0-1	Div 3S
W3-1	1934/35	D1-1	Div 3S
D2-2	1935/36	L1-5	Div 3S
D1-1	1936/37	D1-1	Div 3S
L1-3	1937/38	L0-3	Div 3S
W2-1			FAC2
D2-2	1938/39	L1-2	Div 3S
W3-2	1946/47	L0-7	Div 3S
D0-0	1947/48	W2-0	Div 3S
L1-3	1952/53	D1-1	Div 3S
L0-1	1953/54	W2-0	Div 3S
W2-0	1954/55	L1-3	Div 3S
L0-1	1955/56	L0-1	Div 3S
W1-0	1956/57	L0-3	Div 3S
D1-1	1957/58	L1-2	Div 3S
W2-0	1958/59	L1-2	Div 3
W2-1	1959/60	L0-2	Div 3
W1-0	1960/61	L1-3	Div 3
D0-0	1961/62	L1-6	Div 3
W5-0	1962/63	D2-2w	Div 3
W2-1	1965/66	L2-3	Div 3
D1-1	1966/67	L1-3	Div 3
D0-0	1969/70	L0-2	Div 2
W1-0	1970/71	L2-4	Div 2
		W2-1	FAC3
D0-0	1971/72	L0-3	Div 2
D2-2	1972/73	L0-5	Div 2
	1992/93	L0-3	FAC3
W1-0	1993/94	W3-1	PL
D1-1	1996/97	D1-1	New D1
L1-2		W3-1	FLC2
W3-1	1997/98	W2-1	New D1
W3-1	1998/99	L0-4	New D1
L0-1	1999/2000	L1-2	New D1
L0-1	2001/02	L0-4	New D2
W3-1	2002/03	L0-2	New D2
D1-1	2003/04	L0-1	New D2
L2-3	2008/09		FLC1

k *Played at Kensal Rise*
n *Played at Notting Hill*
p *Played at Park Royal*
w *Played at White City*

READING
Away Venue : Elm Park

Home	Season	Away	Comp.
W2-1	1892/93		FAC3Q
L0-2	1893/94		FAC4Q
L3-4	1894/95	W3-0	SL
L1-2	1895/96	L1-2	SL
W4-1	1896/97	D0-0	SL
W2-1	1897/98	L0-1	SL
W5-1		L0-1	WL
W3-2		D0-0	FAC3Q
W6-1	1898/99	L0-1	SL
W2-1	1899/1900	D1-1	SL
D0-0	1900/01	L0-1	SL
D0-0		L0-1	WL
L0-4	1901/02	L0-3	SL
L0-2		L0-4	WL
D1-1	1902/03	L1-6	SL
W2-1	1903/04	D1-1	SL
L1-2	1904/05	L1-2	SL
W2-0	1905/06	D1-1	SL
W1-0	1906/07	L0-1	SL
W2-0	1907/08	W1-0	SL
W5-1	1908/09	L1-2	SL
W9-1	1909/10	W4-1	SL
W3-0	1911/12	L0-2	SL
D1-1	1912/13	W1-0	SL
W3-0	1913/14	L0-2	SL
D1-1	1914/15	D2-2	SL
		L1-3	SCC2
D0-0	1919/20	D1-1	SL
W2-0	1920/21	W3-2	Div 3
W4-0	1921/22	D1-1	Div 3S
W3-1	1922/23	L0-1	Div 3S
W1-0	1923/24	L0-1	Div 3S
W2-1	1924/25	D1-1	Div 3S
D1-1	1925/26	L0-2	Div 3S
L0-2	1931/32	L2-5	Div 3S
L0-1	1932/33	L1-7	Div 3S
W3-1	1933/34	L0-2	Div 3S
D1-1	1934/35	L1-2	Div 3S
W4-1	1935/36	L0-2	Div 3S
L1-2	1936/37	D2-2	Div 3S
D0-0	1937/38	L1-2	Div 3S
W4-2	1938/39	L0-3	Div 3S
W3-0	1945/46	W2-1	3S(S)
W3-2		L0-5	3S Cup
D2-2	1946/47	D3-3	Div 3S
D1-1	1947/48	W3-2	Div 3S
D1-1	1948/49	D0-0	Div 3S
W2-0	1949/50	L3-4	Div 3S
D1-1	1950/51	L1-3	Div 3S
W2-0	1951/52	L0-2	Div 3S
W2-0	1952/53	L1-4	Div 3S
W1-0	1953/54	L1-3	Div 3S
W2-0	1954/55	L1-2	Div 3S
D0-0	1955/56	W1-0	Div 3S
W3-2	1956/57	L0-1	Div 3S
D1-1	1957/58	W4-0	Div 3S
		L0-1	FAC1
W2-0	1958/59	L1-3	Div 3
L0-4	1959/60	L0-3	Div 3
D1-1	1960/61	D1-1	Div 3
W4-1	1961/62	D1-1	Div 3
D1-1	1962/63	W2-1	Div 3
W4-2			FAC1
W5-0	1965/66	W2-0	Div 3
L0-1	1966/67	L1-2	Div 3
W5-1	1967/68	L1-2	Div 3
D0-0	1968/69	W1-0	Div 3
W4-0	1974/75		FAC1
D2-2	1976/77	L1-4	Div 3
D0-0	1979/80	L1-2	Div 3
W3-1	1980/81	L1-4	Div 3
L0-2	1981/82	D1-1	Div 3
D1-1	1983/84	D2-2	Div 4
W4-0	1987/88	W1-0	Div 2
W1-0	1994/95	L0-3	New D1
W3-1	1996/97	L0-2	New D1
L0-2	1997/98	W1-0	New D1
L0-1	2000/01	L0-2m	New D2
D0-0	2001/02	W3-1m	New D2

m *Played at Madejski Stadium*

ROCHDALE
Away Venue : Spotland

Home	Season	Away	Comp.
	1912/13	W2-0	FAC1
W2-1	1958/59	D1-1	Div 3
W4-1	1982/83	D1-1	Div 4
W2-1	1983/84	D3-3	Div 4
W2-1	1984/85	W1-0	Div 4
W4-0	1985/86	W2-1	Div 4
W1-0	2006/07	D0-0	Chp D2

For key to abbreviations - see Page 317

ROTHERHAM UNITED
Away Venue : Millmoor

Home	Season	Away	Comp.
W3-1	1963/64	D0-0	Div 2
W3-2	1964/65	L0-1	Div 2
W1-0	1968/69	D1-1	Div 3
D1-1	1975/76	W2-0	Div 3
L2-4	1976/77	D1-1	Div 3
W2-0	1977/78	W3-1	Div 3
W1-0	1978/79	W3-1	Div 3
W6-2	1979/80	L0-3	Div 3
W2-1	1980/81	L0-1	Div 3
W2-0	1986/87	W2-1	Div 3
W1-0	1995/96	W2-0	New D2
W2-1	2000/01	L3-4	New D2
L2-3	2005/06	W1-0	Chp D1

SCUNTHORPE UNITED
Away Venue : Old Showground

Home	Season	Away	Comp.
W3-0	1963/64	L0-3	Div 2
D0-0	1965/66	L1-2	Div 3
W2-1	1966/67	W2-1	Div 3
W2-0	1967/68	L1-3	Div 3
W3-1	1969/70		FAC5
D2-2	1982/83	L0-2	Div 4
D0-0	1984/85	L2-6	Div 4
D1-1	1985/86	W2-0	Div 4
D1-1	2005/06	W2-1g	Chp D1
W4-2	2008/09	D3-3g	Chp D1

g *Played at Glanford Park*

SHEFFIELD UNITED
Away Venue : Bramall Lane

Home	Season	Away	Comp.
D0-0	1907/08	W3-2	FAC1
W1-0	1920/21		FAC1
W2-1	1969/70	W2-1	Div 2
W3-0	1970/71	L1-2	Div 2
W3-2	1979/80	L1-2	Div 3
W5-2	1980/81	L0-3	Div 3
W2-0	1987/88	L0-1	Div 2
L0-2	1989/90	L0-2	Div 2
D0-0	1993/94	L1-3	PL
L1-3	1994/95	D2-2	New D1
W2-1	1996/97	L0-2	New D1
D1-1	1997/98	L1-2	New D1
D2-2	1998/99	L1-2	New D1
D2-2	1999/2000	D2-2	New D1

SHEFFIELD WEDNESDAY
Away Venue : Hillsborough

Home	Season	Away	Comp.
L1-2	1927/28		FAC4
	1967/68	L1-2	FAC4
W3-0	1970/71	D2-2	Div 2
W1-0	1971/72	L0-1	Div 2
W1-0	1972/73	L1-2	Div 2
W3-1	1973/74	L1-2	Div 2
W2-1	1975/76	W2-0	Div 3
W5-2	1976/77	L1-3	Div 3
D2-2	1977/78	D1-1	Div 3
W3-0	1978/79	L1-2	Div 3
L1-2	1979/80	L2-4	Div 3
W1-0	1985/86		FLC3
W2-1	1990/91	L1-2	Div 2
L0-1		D0-0	FLC3
L0-1	1993/94	D3-3	PL
L2-3	2003/04	D1-1	New D2
W3-2	2004/05	L0-2	Chp D1
W4-1			FAC1

SHREWSBURY TOWN
Away Venue : Gay Meadow

Home	Season	Away	Comp.
L1-2	1951/52	W1-0	Div 3S
D2-2	1952/53	L1-2	Div 3S
W2-1	1953/54	L0-1	Div 3S
W2-1	1954/55	L0-7	Div 3S
W2-1	1955/56	D1-1	Div 3S
L1-2	1956/57	L3-7	Div 3S
W1-0	1957/58	W3-1	Div 3S
W4-2	1959/60	L0-3	Div 3
D2-2	1960/61	D1-1	Div 3
D1-1		D2-2	FLC2
L0-2			2nd Rep
L0-1			FAC1
L1-2	1961/62	W3-1	Div 3
W1-0	1962/63	W2-1	Div 3
D0-0	1965/66	D1-1	Div 3
D2-2	1966/67	L1-3	Div 3
D0-0	1967/68	W1-0	Div 3
W3-0	1968/69	D1-1	Div 3
W3-0	1975/76	L0-3	Div 3
W1-0	1976/77	D2-2	Div 3
W5-0	1977/78	W3-2	Div 3
W2-1	1978/79	D0-0	Div 3
D1-1	1987/88	L1-2	Div 2
W1-0	1988/89	W1-0	Div 2
W3-1	1989/90	W3-0	FLC2
L0-1	1995/96	W2-1	New D2
W2-1	2006/07	W2-1	Chp D2

SOUTHAMPTON

Away Venue : The Dell

Home	Season	Away	Comp.
L2-3	1894/95	L1-7a	SL
L0-2	1895/96	L2-4a	SL
L0-2	1896/97	L0-2a	SL
		L2-8a	FAC5Q
L0-2	1897/98	L1-4c	SL
L1-3			FAC4Q
D1-1	1898/99	L1-4	SL
W3-0		L2-3	WL
W2-1e	1899/1900	W1-0	SL
W2-1	1900/01	L0-1	SL
W3-1		L0-3	WL
D0-0	1901/02	L1-6	SL
L0-3		L0-4	WL
D1-1	1902/03	L0-1	SL
D1-1	1903/04	L0-2	SL
L0-2	1904/05	L3-4	SL
L0-3	1905/06	L0-2	SL
W1-0	1906/07	D1-1	SL
L0-2	1907/08	D1-1	SL
L0-2	1908/09	W6-0	SL
D1-1	1909/10	D1-1	SL
W5-1	1910/11	W4-0	SL
W2-1	1911/12	W3-1	SL
W5-0	1912/13	L0-2	SL
W3-0	1913/14	W2-1	SL
W2-0	1914/15	L1-4	SL
		W2-1	SCC1
W3-1	1915/16	L3-5	SWCL
L1-2	1919/20	L0-1	SL
W3-2	1920/21	L0-4	Div 3
L2-3	1921/22	L1-3	Div 3S
	1947/48	L0-3	FAC5
L0-1	1953/54	L1-3	Div 3S
W1-0	1954/55	D1-1	Div 3S
D1-1	1955/56	L1-2	Div 3S
D0-0	1956/57	L1-2	Div 3S
W1-0	1957/58	W3-1	Div 3S
W3-1	1958/59	D1-1	Div 3
L0-3	1959/60	L1-5	Div 3
L1-2	1963/64	L1-5	Div 2
W2-1	1964/65	L1-2	Div 2
D0-0	1986/87	L0-3	FLC2
D0-0	1989/90	L2-4	FLC4
W2-1	1993/94	L1-5	PL
D1-1	1995/96	L0-2	FAC5

a *Played at Antelope Ground*
c *Played at County Cricket Ground*
e *Played at Elm Park,Reading*

STOCKPORT COUNTY

Away Venue : Edgeley Park

Home	Season	Away	Comp.
W3-0	1958/59	L0-2	Div 3
W2-0	1967/68	L0-2	Div 3
W1-0	1968/69	L1-2	Div 3
W2-0	1982/83	W2-1	Div 4
W2-1	1983/84	W3-1	Div 4
W4-0	1984/85	L1-2	Div 4
W1-0	1985/86	W2-0	Div 4
D0-0	1995/96	D1-1	New D2
D1-1	1997/98	L2-4	New D1
L2-3	1998/99	L1-2	New D1
D1-1	1999/2000	L0-3	New D1
L0-1	2002/03	W5-2	New D2
L1-2	2003/04	W4-2	New D2
W3-0	2004/05	D3-3	Chp D1
W2-0	2006/07	L0-3	Chp D2
D1-1	2008/09	D1-1	Chp D1

SOUTHEND UNITED

Away Venue : Roots Hall

Home	Season	Away	Comp.
W4-2	1908/09	L2-6	SL
W6-1	1909/10	D1-1	SL
W4-0	1910/11	W1-0	SL
W5-0	1913/14	L0-2	SL
W4-0	1914/15	L1-2	SL
W3-2	1919/20	W1-0k	SL
W3-0	1920/21	W3-1k	Div 3
W6-1	1921/22	W2-1k	Div 3S
W3-0	1922/23	L0-2k	Div 3S
W3-0	1923/24	W2-0k	Div 3S
W3-0	1924/25	D0-0k	Div 3S
W2-0	1925/26	L0-3k	Div 3S
W5-1	1926/27	D2-2k	Div 3S
L0-1	1927/28	D2-2k	Div 3S
W3-1	1928/29	D1-1k	Div 3S
W5-1	1929/30	L1-3k	Div 3S
D1-1	1930/31	L3-5k	Div 3S
L1-2	1931/32	L0-3k	Div 3S
D2-2	1932/33	D0-0k	Div 3S
L1-4	1933/34	L1-4k	Div 3S
W5-0	1934/35	L0-2s	Div 3S
L1-3	1935/36	L0-1s	Div 3S
W4-0	1936/37	L0-2s	Div 3S
D1-1	1937/38	D0-0s	Div 3S
W2-1	1938/39	W3-2s	Div 3S
W2-1	1946/47	L0-2s	Div 3S
D0-0	1947/48	L0-1s	Div 3S
W2-1	1948/49	W4-3s	Div 3S
D2-2	1949/50	L0-2s	Div 3S
W4-1	1950/51	L2-8s	Div 3S
		W3-0s	FAC1
W1-0	1951/52	D2-2s	Div 3S
L1-3	1952/53	L0-3s	Div 3S
W3-0	1953/54	L1-3s	Div 3S
L0-1	1954/55	L1-4s	Div 3S
D1-1	1955/56	D0-0	Div 3S
W3-2	1956/57	L0-1	Div 3S
W2-1	1957/58	W3-2	Div 3S
W2-1	1958/59	W2-0	Div 3
W2-0	1959/60	W3-1	Div 3
D1-1	1960/61	W2-0	Div 3
D0-0	1961/62	W2-0	Div 3
W4-1	1962/63	D1-1	Div 3
W3-0	1963/64		FLC3
W4-0	1965/66	L2-4	Div 3
L0-2	1968/69		FAC3
W2-0	1974/75	L0-2	Div 3
D0-0	1975/76	L0-3	Div 3
W1-0	1978/79	L3-5	Div 3
W1-0	1979/80	L0-1	Div 3
D0-0	1981/82	D0-0	Div 3
W2-0	1984/85	L2-3	Div 4
W2-1	1985/86	D0-0	Div 4
W3-1	1991/92	L2-3	Div 2
W3-2	1992/93	D1-1	New D1
D2-2	1994/95	L0-2	New D1
D0-0	1996/97	W3-1	New D1
	2000/01	L1-2	FLTSF
W6-1	2002/03		FLT1
	2003/04	W3-2	FLC1
	2004/05	L0-2	FLTSF
L1-2	2005/06	L0-2	Chp D1
L0-1	2007/08	L1-2	Chp D1
W3-0	2008/09	L1-2	Chp D1

k *Played at The Kursaal*
s *Played at Southend Stadium*

STOKE CITY

Away Venue : Victoria Ground

Home	Season	Away	Comp.
W3-0	1911/12	W4-1	SL
W3-2	1912/13	D1-1	SL
L1-3	1948/49		FAC3
D1-1	1951/52	W1-0	FAC4
W2-1	1979/80	D2-2	FLC3
W3-0	1987/88	L0-1	Div 2
W3-0	1988/89	L1-2	Div 2
W6-0	1989/90	D1-1	Div 2
L0-1	1994/95	D0-0	New D1
W1-0	1996/97	L0-2	New D1
W1-0	1997/98	W2-1b	New D1
L0-3	2000/01	L1-4b	New D2
L0-3	2001/02	L0-2b	New D2

b *Played at Stanley Matthews Way*

SUNDERLAND

Away Venue : Roker Park

Home	Season	Away	Comp.
	1912/13	L2-4	FAC3
W1-0	1963/64	L0-6	Div 2
W2-0	1970/71	L2-5	Div 2
D1-1	1971/72	L0-1	Div 2
D1-1	1972/73	L2-3	Div 2
L0-2	1973/74	L1-4	Div 2
W3-1	1985/86	L2-3	FLC2
W4-1	1988/89	L0-4	Div 2
L0-2	1989/90	D2-2	Div 2
		*W1-0	D2 P/Off
W5-3	1991/92	D0-0	Div 2
W1-0	1992/93	W1-0	New D1
W1-0	1994/95	L0-1	New D1
L1-2	1997/98	D0-0s	New D1
D1-1	1998/99	L0-2s	New D1

s *Played at Stadium of Light*

SWANSEA CITY

Away Venue : Vetch Field

Home	Season	Away	Comp.
W3-1	1919/20	L0-1	SL
D0-0	1920/21	D1-1	Div 3
W1-0	1921/22	W3-1	Div 3S
W2-1	1922/23	L0-5	Div 3S
W1-0	1923/24	D1-1	Div 3S
L0-2	1924/25	L0-2	Div 3S
W4-1	1939/40	W3-1	SWRL
W4-0		L1-2	SWRL
W1-0	1947/48	L0-1	Div 3S
W1-0	1948/49	L0-4	Div 3S
W2-1	1963/64	L0-3	Div 2
W3-0	1964/65	L0-4	Div 2
		L1-3	FLC2
D2-2	1965/66	D1-1	Div 3
W4-0	1966/67	D2-2	Div 3
	1969/70	W3-1	FLC2
W2-1	1977/78	W3-1	FLC1
L0-1	1978/79	W2-1	Div 3
W3-0	1995/96	W1-0	New D2
D1-1	2000/01	D0-0	New D2
D0-0	2005/06	L1-2n	Chp D1
D1-1	2007/08	L1-2n	Chp D1

n *Played at New Stadium, Landore*

TOTTENHAM HOTSPUR

Away Venue : White Hart Lane

Home	Season	Away	Comp.
W1-0	1896/97	L1-3n	SL
W3-0	1897/98	L0-2n	SL
W4-3	1898/99	D1-1n	SL
L0-2	1899/1900	L0-3	SL
D1-1	1900/01	L0-2	SL
L0-1		L0-5	WL
L1-3	1901/02	L1-7	SL
L0-1		L0-6	WL
W2-0	1902/03	L0-2	SL
D0-0	1903/04	L0-1	SL
W2-1	1904/05	L3-6	SL
W2-0	1905/06	L1-2	SL
D0-0	1906/07	L0-3	SL
W1-0	1907/08	L0-1	SL
W3-2	1909/10		FAC3
D0-0	1979/80	L1-2	FAC4
W2-1	1993/94	D1-1	PL

n *Played at Northumberland Park*

TRANMERE ROVERS

Away Venue : Prenton Park

Home	Season	Away	Comp.
L1-2	1958/59	L1-3	Div 3
D1-1	1959/60	D2-2	Div 3
W1-0	1960/61	D2-2	Div 3
W3-1	1967/68	L2-3	Div 3
W1-0	1968/69	W5-3	Div 3
D0-0	1974/75	L0-3	Div 3
D1-1	1976/77	W1-0	Div 3
W1-0	1977/78	D1-1	Div 3
W4-1	1978/79	D1-1	Div 3
W4-2	1982/83	L0-2	Div 4
D1-1	1983/84	L1-2	Div 4
W2-1	1984/85	W2-0	Div 4
W2-1	1985/86	L1-3	Div 4
W2-0	1991/92	D0-0	Div 2
W2-0	1992/93	L1-3	New D1
W3-1		L2-3	D1 P/Off
D2-2	1994/95	L2-3	New D1
W2-1	1996/97	L1-2	New D1
W2-1	1997/98	L0-3	New D1
L2-3	1998/99	D0-0	New D1
W3-1	1999/2000	L1-3	New D1
L0-1	2000/01	D1-1	FLC2
D2-2	2001/02	D0-0	New D2
D1-1	2002/03	W1-0	New D2
W2-0	2003/04	L0-1	New D2
W2-1	2004/05	L1-2	Chp D1
L1-2	2005/06	L0-1	Chp D1
W1-0	2007/08	L1-2	Chp D1
W3-1	2008/09	L0-1	Chp D1

WEST BROMWICH ALBION

Away Venue : The Hawthorns

Home	Season	Away	Comp.
L0-2	1966/67		FLC4
	1972/73	L0-2	FAC4
W1-0	1973/74	L0-2	Div 2
W2-0	1987/88	W2-1	Div 2
D0-0	1988/89	L1-3	Div 2
W2-1	1989/90	W2-1	Div 2
W2-1	1990/91	L1-2	Div 2
W2-0	1991/92	D2-2	FLC1
D0-0	1994/95	W5-2	New D1
L2-3	1996/97	W2-1	New D1
L0-2	1997/98	D0-0	New D1
D2-2	1998/99	D1-1	New D1
L1-2	1999/2000	D1-1	New D1
	2001/02	L0-2	FLC2

WALSALL

Away Venue : Fellows Park

Home	Season	Away	Comp.
W5-0	1927/28	W2-1	Div 3S
W5-1	1928/29	D1-1	Div 3S
W3-1	1929/30	L0-4	Div 3S
W4-3	1930/31	D2-2	Div 3S
W3-0	1936/37	L2-5	Div 3S
D1-1	1937/38	W3-2	Div 3S
L1-4	1938/39	L0-5	Div 3S
W4-1	1946/47	W1-0	Div 3S
L0-3	1947/48	L0-1	Div 3S
W2-1	1948/49	W1-0	Div 3S
W4-3	1949/50	D0-0	Div 3S
D1-1	1950/51	L0-1	Div 3S
D1-1	1951/52	D0-0	Div 3S
L1-2	1952/53	W2-1	Div 3S
W3-0	1953/54	W1-0	Div 3S
D2-2	1954/55	W2-1	Div 3S
L1-2	1955/56	L0-4	Div 3S
L1-2	1956/57	W2-1	Div 3S
L2-3	1957/58	D1-1	Div 3S
L2-3	1959/60		FAC1
W1-0	1960/61	L1-2	Div 3
D0-0	1965/66	L0-5	Div 3
W3-2	1966/67	D1-1	Div 3
W3-0	1967/68	L2-3	Div 3
W1-0	1968/69	W2-0	Div 3
W3-0	1974/75	L0-2	Div 3
W5-1	1975/76	D1-1	Div 3
D2-2	1976/77	L0-2	Div 3
L2-3	1977/78	L0-2	Div 3
W4-1	1978/79	L1-4	Div 3
W3-1	1980/81	L1-2	Div 3
D2-2	1981/82	L0-5	Div 3
W3-0	1983/84		AMC2
D0-0	1986/87	L0-1	Div 3
W1-0	1988/89	D2-2	Div 2
D1-1	1995/96	D0-0b	New D2
D1-1	1999/2000	D0-0b	New D1
L1-4	2000/01	L0-1b	New D2
L1-2	2004/05	L2-3b	Chp D1
W1-0	2005/06	L0-1b	Chp D1
D1-1	2006/07	W2-0b	Chp D2
L0-3	2007/08	D2-2b	Chp D1
W3-2	2008/09	L1-2b	Chp D1

b *Played at Bescot Stadium*

WOLVERHAMPTON W.

Away Venue : Molineux Grounds

Home	Season	Away	Comp.
	1907/08	L0-2	FAC3
D2-2	1975/76	L2-3	FLC2
W2-1	1979/80	L1-3	FLCSF
W3-1	1989/90	L1-2	Div 2
W1-0	1990/91	W2-1	Div 2
W1-0	1991/92	L1-2	Div 2
W1-0	1992/93	D2-2	New D1
W2-0	1993/94	L1-2	FLC2
W3-2	1994/95	D1-1	New D1
L1-2	1996/97	L0-1	New D1
W2-0		L0-1	FLC1
D0-0	1997/98	L1-3	New D1
W1-0	1998/99	L0-1	New D1
L1-2	1999/2000	D1-1	New D1
	2001/02	W2-1	FLC1

WATFORD

Away Venue : Vicarage Road

Home	Season	Away	Comp.
	1886/87	W1-0b	FAC1
	1889/90	L3-5b	FAC1Q
D1-1	1900/01	D1-1c	SL
L1-3	1901/02	L0-3c	SL
W3-0	1902/03	L3-5c	SL
W2-0	1904/05	L0-1c	SL
D0-0	1905/06	W2-1c	SL
L1-3		D0-0c	UL
D0-0	1906/07	D0-0c	SL
W2-0	1907/08	D0-0c	SL
W4-1	1908/09	L0-1c	SL
D3-3	1909/10	W1-0c	SL
W5-1	1910/11	W3-1c	SL
W4-0	1911/12	L0-2c	SL
L1-2	1912/13	L1-3c	SL
W3-0	1913/14	W2-1c	SL
W6-0	1914/15	L0-3c	SL
L1-2	1919/20	L1-3c	SL
W2-0	1920/21	W1-0c	Div 3
L0-3	1921/22	D2-2c	Div 3S
D1-1	1922/23	W3-0	Div 3S
D0-0	1923/24	D0-0	Div 3S
L0-1	1924/25	L0-1	Div 3S
W5-3	1925/26	L2-3	Div 3S
W4-2	1926/27	D2-2	Div 3S
W4-0	1927/28	W5-2	Div 3S
W5-0	1928/29	L2-3	Div 3S
L1-3	1929/30	L1-4	Div 3S
W2-1	1930/31	L0-3	Div 3S
W4-1	1931/32	L1-4	Div 3S
L1-2	1932/33	D2-2	Div 3S
W1-0	1933/34	L0-4	Div 3S
W2-1	1934/35	L4-7	Div 3S
L1-6	1935/36	L1-2	Div 3S
D1-1	1936/37	D2-2	Div 3S
L0-2	1937/38	L0-4	Div 3S
W3-0	1938/39	L1-4	Div 3S
W5-0	1946/47	D1-1	Div 3S
W3-0	1947/48	L0-1	Div 3S
W1-0	1948/49	W3-0	Div 3S
L0-1	1949/50	W2-1	Div 3S
W3-2	1950/51	W2-1	Div 3S
L0-1	1951/52	W7-1	Div 3S
D0-0	1952/53	L1-2	Div 3S
D2-2	1953/54	L1-2	Div 3S
W6-1	1954/55	L0-3	Div 3S
D0-0	1955/56	L1-2	Div 3S
W2-0	1956/57	W4-3	Div 3S
D0-0	1957/58	D0-0	Div 3S
L1-2	1960/61	L0-1	Div 3
W3-1	1961/62	L0-2	Div 3
W3-1	1962/63	D3-3	Div 3
L0-1	1965/66	L0-2	Div 3
L1-2	1966/67	L0-2	Div 3
W2-0	1967/68	L0-2	Div 3
L0-1	1968/69	D0-0	Div 3
W1-0	1969/70	D0-0	Div 2
D1-1	1970/71	W2-1	Div 2
W4-2			FLC2
W2-0	1971/72	D0-0	Div 2
D2-2	1974/75	L0-1	Div 3
W2-0	1978/79	L0-2	Div 3
D1-1	1987/88	L2-4	FLC3
D1-1	1988/89	W3-2	Div 2
W2-0	1989/90	W2-0	Div 2
L1-2	1990/91	D2-2	Div 2
W3-1	1991/92	D0-0	Div 2
W3-2			FAC3
W3-1	1992/93	W4-0	New D1
W1-0	1994/95	L0-2	New D1
		L0-1	FAC4
L0-2	1997/98	D1-1	FLC1
L1-4	1998/99	W1-0	New D1

b *Played at Colney Butts*
c *Played at Cassio Road*

WEST HAM UNITED

Away Venue : Boleyn Ground

Home	Season	Away	Comp.
W3-1	1899/1900	L0-1c	SL
L0-1	1900/01	L1-3c	SL
L0-1	1901/02	L1-2c	SL
L0-4		L0-6c	WL
D1-1	1902/03	D1-1c	SL
W1-0	1903/04	W1-0c	SL
D3-3	1904/05	L0-2	SL
L2-3	1905/06	L0-1	SL
W2-0	1906/07	L0-2	SL
D1-1	1907/08	W2-1	SL
W3-0	1908/09	L2-4	SL
W5-0	1909/10	D2-2	SL
W4-1	1910/11	L0-1	SL
W3-1	1911/12	W2-0	SL
W4-0		D1-1	FAC3
D1-1	1912/13	L1-4	SL
W4-1	1913/14	W3-2	SL
D1-1	1914/15	D1-1	SL
D3-3	1963/64	L1-4	FLC4
L1-3			FAC5
W3-1	1966/67	D3-3	FAC3
L1-2	1974/75	D1-1	FAC4
	1978/79	W2-1	FLC2
D0-0	1988/89	L0-1	FAC4
D2-2	1989/90	D1-1	Div 2
L0-1	1990/91	L0-2	Div 2
L1-3	1992/93	W1-0	New D1
D1-1	1993/94	D0-0	PL

c *Played at Canning Town*

WIGAN ATHLETIC

Away Venue : Robin Park

Home	Season	Away	Comp.
W3-1	1986/87	L2-3s	Div 3
D0-0		W3-2s	D3 P/Off
D2-2	2000/01	D0-0	New D2
D1-1	2001/02	L0-1	New D2
W2-1	2002/03	L0-2	New D2

s *Played at Springfield Park*

WYCOMBE WANDERERS

Away Venue : Adams Park

Home	Season	Away	Comp.
D0-0	1995/96	W2-1	New D2
W2-1	1998/99	L0-2	FLC1
D1-1	2000/01	D0-0	New D2
W2-1			FLTQF
D1-1	2001/02	D1-1	New D2
L0-3	2002/03	W3-2	New D2
L1-2			FLC1
W2-0	2003/04	W3-0	New D2
		L1-4	FAC1
L1-3	2005/06		FLC1
W2-1	2006/07	D1-1	Chp D2
		L0-1	FLT1
	2007/08	W2-1	FAC1

YEOVIL TOWN

Away Venue : The Huish

Home	Season	Away	Comp.
W4-0	1901/02		FAC3Q
	1902/03	W4-0p	FAC3Q
	1962/63	W2-0	FAC1
W4-2	2005/06	D0-0	Chp D1
L0-1	2007/08	W1-0h	Chp D1
L2-3	2008/09	L0-1h	Chp D1

p *Played at Pen Mill Athletic Grd*
h *Played at Huish Park*

KEY TO ABBREVIATIONS

N/P Not played — * Played at neutral ground
P Decided by Penaly shoot-out

Competitions

AIC	Anglo-Italian Cup
AMC	Associate Members Cup +
Chp	(Football League) Championship
FAAC	F A Amateur Cup
FAC	F A Cup
FAChS	F A Charity Shield
FLC	Football League Cup +
FLT	Football League Trophy +
FMC	Full Members Cup +
PL	Premier League
SCC	Southern Charity Cup
SL	Southern League
SWCL	South Western Combination League
SWRL	South West Regional League
Test	Test Match (Relegation Play-Off)
UL	United League
WL	Western League
WLC	War League Cup
3S Cup	Third Division South Cup
3S(S)	Third Division South (Southern Section)

Rounds

F	Final	Q	Qualifying
IM	Intermediate	QF	Quarter-Final
Pr	Preliminary	Rep.	Replay
		SF	Semi-Final

+ Sponsors' names have been excluded for the sake of continuity.
New venues are similarly listed, this book hopefully being used for reference long after the current sponsors have been consigned to memory !

ABERDARE ATHLETIC
Away Venue : Ynys Field

Home	Season	Away	Comp.
D2-2	1921/22	L2-3	Div 3S
W5-4	1922/23	D3-3	Div 3S
W3-1	1923/24	D2-2	Div 3S
W2-0	1924/25	D1-1	Div 3S
W2-1	1925/26	D1-1	Div 3S
W3-2	1926/27	W4-1	Div 3S

ALDERSHOT
Away Venue : Recreation Ground

Home	Season	Away	Comp.
W3-2	1932/33	W1-0	Div 3S
W1-0	1933/34	W2-1	Div 3S
W3-2	1934/35	L0-3	Div 3S
W3-2	1935/36	W3-1	Div 3S
W5-1	1936/37	L1-2	Div 3S
W2-0	1937/38	D1-1	Div 3S
W2-1	1938/39	L0-1	Div 3S
D2-2	1939/40	N/P	Div 3S
W2-0	1945/46	D1-1	3S(S)
W4-0		W3-1	3S Cup
W7-0	1946/47	L0-2	Div 3S
W1-0	1947/48	D2-2	Div 3S
W2-0		D0-0	FAC2
W3-1	1948/49	W2-1	Div 3S
W2-1	1949/50	D0-0	Div 3S
W4-0	1950/51	W1-0	Div 3S
D1-1	1951/52	L0-4	Div 3S
W3-2	1952/53	D2-2	Div 3S
W3-1	1953/54	L0-1	Div 3S
W1-0	1954/55	D0-0	Div 3S
D1-1	1955/56	D1-1	Div 3S
L1-2	1956/57	D2-2	Div 3S
W3-0	1957/58	L1-2	Div 3S
W5-0	1958/59		FAC1
	1963/64	W2-1	FAC4
W3-2	1974/75	W1-0	Div 3
W6-3	1975/76	W1-0	Div 3
	1978/79	L1-2	FAC4
W2-0	1982/83	D1-1	Div 4
W7-0			FAC3
L0-2	1983/84	L1-2	Div 4
W2-1	1984/85	W1-0	Div 4
W4-1	1985/86	W4-2	Div 4
L2-3	1986/87		AMCSF

ASHFORD TOWN

Home	Season	Comp.
W5-0	1966/67	FAC2

BARROW
Away Venue : Holker Street

Home	Season	Away	Comp.
L0-1	1967/68	D1-1	Div 3
W2-0	1968/69	W3-0	Div 3

BATH CITY
Away Venue : Twerton Park

Home	Season	Away	Comp.
D2-2	1960/61	W6-4	FAC1

BEDFORD TOWN

Home	Season	Comp.
W2-0	1951/52	FAC1

BEDMINSTER
Away Venue : Ashton Gate

Home	Season	Away	Comp.
W4-3	1898/99	W1-0	SL
W3-1		D0-0	WL
W2-1	1899/1900	L1-2	SL
L0-1		W2-1	WL

BOREHAM WOOD
Away Venue : Meadow Park

Home	Season	Away	Comp.
W2-0	1977/78	D0-0	FAC1

BOSTON UNITED
Away Venue : York Street

Home	Season	Away	Comp.
	2003/04	L1-2	AMC1
D2-2	2005/06	L1-4	FAC1
D1-1	2006/07	W3-1	Chp D2

BRADFORD PARK AVE.
Away Venue : Park Avenue

Home	Season	Away	Comp.
W4-0	1907/08	D2-2	SL
W4-0	1923/24		FAC1
W3-2	1961/62	D2-2	Div 3
W2-1	1962/63	L0-2	Div 3

BRIGHTON UNITED
Away Venue : Withdean

Home	Season	Away	Comp.
W3-1	1898/99	L0-2	SL
W4-0	1899/1900	D2-2	SL

BRISTOL EAST

Home	Season	Away	Comp.
W5-0	1900/01	D1-1h	FAC3Q

h *Played at County Ground*

BRISTOL ST GEORGE
Away Venue : Memorial Ground

Home	Season	Away	Comp.
W4-2	1894/95		FAC1Q
W4-0	1897/98	L1-3	WL
W2-1	1898/99	W3-1	WL

BROMLEY

Home	Season	Comp.
W7-0	1976/77	FAC1

CAMBRIDGE TOWN

Home	Season	Comp.
W4-1	1946/47	FAC1

CAMBRIDGE UNITED
Away Venue : Abbey Stadium

Home	Season	Away	Comp.
D0-0	1977/78	L2-5	Div 3
W1-0	1985/86	D1-1	Div 4
L0-2	1991/92	L2-3	Div 2
		W3-0	FAC4
W4-1	1992/93	L0-1	New D1
W2-0	1995/96	L1-2	FLC1
W4-1			FAC1
W3-1	2000/01	W1-0	New D2
W2-0	2001/02	W2-1	New D2

CANTERBURY CITY

Season	Away	Comp.
1968/69	W1-0h	FAC1

h *Played at County Ground*

CHATHAM
Away Venue : Maidstone Road

Home	Season	Away	Comp.
L0-2	1894/95	L2-4	SL
L2-5	1895/96	W5-1	SL
L2-6	1896/97	L2-6	SL
L1-2	1897/98	L0-4	SL
D2-2	1898/99	L0-2	SL
W2-0	1899/1900	L0-1	SL

CHIPPENHAM TOWN

Season	Away	Comp.
1902/03	W5-0h	FAC2Q

h *Played at County Ground*

CLAPTON (not Clapton Orient)
Away Venue : Spotted Dog

Home	Season	Away	Comp.
W2-1	1894/95	L0-3	SL
D0-0	1895/96	W4-3	SL
	1925/26	W3-2b	FAC3

b *Played at Boleyn Ground*

COWES
Away Venue : Brooklyn Ground

Home	Season	Away	Comp.
	1892/93	W2-1	FAC1Q
W3-1	1899/1900	N/P	SL

CROYDON COMMON
Away Venue : The Nest, Selhurst

Home	Season	Away	Comp.
L1-2	1909/10	W3-0	SL
W7-1	1914/15	D0-0	SL

DARTFORD

Home	Season	Comp.
W1-0	1933/34	FAC2

DULWICH HAMLET

Home	Season	Comp.
W4-1	1932/33	FAC1
W6-0	1936/37	FAC1

EASTLEIGH ATHLETIC
Away Venue : Dutton Lane

Home	Season	Away	Comp.
W7-1	1897/98	L0-2	WL

ENFIELD

Home	Season	Comp.
W3-0	1978/79	FAC2
W3-0	1986/87	FAC2

FOREST GREEN ROVERS

Home	Season	Comp.
W3-2	2007/08	FAC2

FARNBOROUGH TOWN

Season	Away	Comp.
1986/87	W4-0h	FAC1

h *Played at County Ground*

FARNHAM UNITED BREWERIES
Away Venue : Red Lion Lane

Season	Away	Comp.
1925/26	W10-1	FAC1

GATESHEAD

Home	Season	Comp.
W5-0	2000/01	FAC2

GRANTHAM
Away Venue : London Road

Season	Away	Comp.
1965/66	W6-1	FAC2
1968/69	W2-0	FAC2

GRAYS UNITED
Away Venue : Recreation Ground

Home	Season	Away	Comp.
L0-1	1905/06	W1-0	UL

GRAVESEND UNITED
Away Venue : Overcliffe

Home	Season	Away	Comp.
D1-1	1896/97	L2-3	SL
L1-2	1897/98	D2-2	SL
W4-1	1898/99	L1-5	SL
W2-1	1899/1900	L1-2	SL
D0-0	1900/01	L0-2	SL

GREEN WAVES
Away Venue : South Devon Place

Season	Away	Comp.
1904/05	L1-2	FAC5Q

HALIFAX TOWN
Away Venue : The Shay

Home	Season	Away	Comp.
L0-2	1958/59	L0-1	Div 3
D1-1	1959/60	L1-3	Div 3
D1-1	1960/61	D1-1	Div 3
W6-0	1961/62	L0-2	Div 3
D1-1	1962/63	L3-4	Div 3
W3-1	1974/75	D0-0	Div 3
W3-1	1975/76	W2-0	Div 3
L0-1	1982/83	L0-1	Div 4
L2-3	1983/84	L1-2	Div 4
W2-1	1984/85	L1-2	Div 4
W3-2	1985/86	W3-1	Div 4

HASTINGS UNITED
Away Venue : Pilot Field

Season	Away	Comp.
1953/54	L1-4	FAC2

HENDON
Away Venue : Claremont Road

Season	Away	Comp.
1975/76	W1-0	FAC2

HISTON
Away Venue : Bridge Road

Season	Away	Comp.
2008/09	L0-1	FAC1

HITCHIN TOWN
Away Venue : Fishponds Road

Home	Season	Away	Comp.
W3-1	1976/77	D1-1	FAC2

HORSHAM
Away Venue : Queen Street

Season	Away	Comp.
1966/67	W3-0	FAC1

ILFORD
Away Venue : Vicarage Road

Home	Season	Away	Comp.
W7-3	1894/95	L0-1	SL
W2-0	1895/96	W10-0	SL
	1933/34	W4-2	FAC1

ILKESTON TOWN

Home	Season	Comp.
W4-1	2000/01	FAC1

KETTERING TOWN
Away Venue : Rockingham Road

Home	Season	Away	Comp.
D2-2	1900/01	D0-0	SL
L1-2	1901/02	L1-10	SL
D1-1	1902/03	L0-2	SL
D0-0	1903/04	D1-1	SL
D2-2	1961/62	L0-3	FAC1
	1983/84	W7-0	FAC1